1970 MLA International Bibliography of Books and Articles on the Modern Languages and Literatures

Volume I

General, English, American, Medieval and
Neo-Latin, Celtic Literatures; and Folklore

Compiled by

HARRISON T. MESEROLE

Bibliographer of the Association

Assisted by those whose names appear in the list of contributors.

Published by

THE MODERN LANGUAGE ASSOCIATION OF AMERICA

This is Volume I of four volumes of the *1970 MLA International Bibliography*. The four volumes are collected in a cumulative edition for libraries.

ISBN 0–87352–206–0

1970 MLA INTERNATIONAL BIBLIOGRAPHY
VOLUME I

FOLLOWING the procedure established in 1969, the *MLA International Bibliography* now appears in a multi-volume format, separate from its parent journal *PMLA*. This is Volume One of the set, and includes sections on General, English, American, Medieval and Neo-Latin, and Celtic literatures, and on Folklore. Volume Two contains sections on European, Asian, African, and Latin-American literatures, and Volume Three is devoted to linguistics. For the first time, all three volumes have been composed entirely by electronic data-processing systems.

A fourth volume, containing listings on pedagogy in foreign languages, and compiled under the auspices of the American Council on the Teaching of Foreign Languages, completes the set. All four volumes are available separately, or together in a single "Library Edition."

Like its predecessors, the Bibliography for 1970 has been compiled from a basic Master List of approximately 1,500 periodicals central to the field, and from various book sources. It is not, however, an exhaustive gathering of every comment resulting from thorough search in these sources. Selection has been made of contributions useful to scholars in the modern languages and literatures.

The master list, which precedes each volume of the bibliography, differs somewhat from that published in the June 1970 listing. Changes in it reflect recommendations from the members of the Bibliography Committee who have actually worked with the periodicals. Occasionally, however, important scholarly articles appearing in journals not central to the field have been listed with full documentation, although the journals themselves are not included in the master list. This list, then, is subject to change as occasion warrants and is broadened as publication of scholarship in the field demands. It must, nevertheless, remain compassable within the limits of resources the Association can command, and it is therefore selective.

The basic principle of the *MLA International Bibliography* is that of extended coverage published currently. Items received too late (after 15 January) any year will be entered the next, so that reasonable completeness may be achieved in two issues. Over ninety percent of the important scholarship is thus made available annually on schedule. Such a work must content itself with listing, and not with annotation unless a title requires elucidation. Other bibliographies of special areas of language, chronological periods, or literary figures exist to provide useful annotation and evaluative comment: on Shakespeare in *Shakespeare Quarterly*, English literature 1660–1800 in *Philological Quarterly*, Romanticism in *English Language Notes*, nineteenth-century English literature in *Victorian Studies*, American literature in *American Literature*, and American studies in *American Quarterly*. Attention is also called to the *International Medieval Bibliography*, and to the series edited for the Modern Humanities Research Association, *The Year's Work in Modern Language Studies* and the *Annual Bibliography of English Language and Literature*, now approaching current listings.

A committee of one hundred and fifty has been appointed to produce this bibliography. Its members have sought aid from many helpers, and have adhered to the principle of listing only those items actually seen, in no case relying merely upon publishers' announcements or entries in some other bibliography. Generally, they have listed only items published in 1970 and those published in 1969 which came in too late for inclusion last year. Exceptions are noted. The style of entry follows the *Bibliographical Style Sheet* prepared for the MLA Bibliography by Harrison T. Meserole.

Arrangement of each volume of the Bibliography for 1970 follows the three-part form introduced in preceding bibliographies. In this volume, *Festschriften* and Other Analyzed Collections are listed first. Literature entries, grouped by sections, appear next, followed by Folklore entries. Concluding the volume is an index containing the name of every author, editor, or compiler represented in the listings, together with the number of each item he has produced.

Entry format follows that introduced in the Bibliography for 1967. Arabic numbers have replaced roman to denote the volume number of a journal. Undated items are understood to have been published in 1970. When an issue number of a journal is required for a given entry, it appears in lowercase roman immediately after the arabic volume number. An arabic number preceded by F in square brackets following an entry title refers to an item listed in the *Festschriften* and Other Analyzed Collections division which begins this volume. An asterisk (*) preceding the item number of an entry in this Bibliography indicates that an abstract of that entry is stored in the MLA Abstracts System. Collections of these abstracts, arranged to correspond to the organization of materials in the volumes of the *MLA International Bibliography*, are published annually by the Association.

A fundamental principle of the bibliography is that each item be entered once only in a given volume, in the section where we believe it will be sought for by the largest group of users. Attention of others is called to it by cross-reference (these references appear as a series of item numbers at the ends of sections or subsections within this volume of the bibliography). These cross-references are intra-volume only. When the content of an item listed so demands, it will be listed in more than one volume of the bibliography. Thus, an article on a linguistic approach to the poetry of Dante and T. S. Eliot will be listed in Volume I under Eliot, in Volume II under Dante, and in Volume III under Stylistics.

Authors are invited to send offprints of articles, monographs, and notices of pertinent books for listing in the Bibliography for 1971 to Harrison T. Meserole, Bibliographer of the Association, Department of English, The Pennsylvania State University, University Park, Pennsylvania 16802.

THE MLA COMMITTEE ON BIBLIOGRAPHY
AND OTHER CONTRIBUTORS TO THE BIBLIOGRAPHY FOR 1970

VOLUME I

General Literature and Related Topics

Richard B. Gidez, Pennsylvania State University, Section Head[1]

Georg Bangen, Freie Universität (Berlin), Coordinator of *Festschriften*, Europe

Donald W. Bleznick, University of Cincinnati (Comparative Literature)

Ben Fiester, Wilkes College (General Literature)

Donna Fricke, Pennsylvania State University (General Literature)[1]

Julius Herz, Temple University (General Literature)

Jayne K. Kribbs, Pennsylvania State University (General Literature)[1]

Harrison T. Meserole, Pennsylvania State University (Bibliography)[1]

Peter Milward, S.J., Sophia University (Tokyo), (General Literature)

Phyllis Rackin, Beaver College (General Literature)

Alyce E. Sands, Queens College (General Literature)

John Sarnacki, Albion College (Comparative Literature)
Helpers:
  Robert Arner, Central Michigan University
  Linda Kitz, Cabrillo College
  Charles W. Mann, Pennsylvania State University[1]
  Helen L. Mighton, Wilmington, Delaware

English Literature

Denzell Smith, University of Maryland, Section Head[2]

John K. Crane, University of Southern California[3]

Richard J. Dunn, University of Washington

William A. Gibson, Ohio State University

Philip J. Landon, University of Maryland (Baltimore County)[4]

William E. Mahaney, Salem State College

James E. Nagel, Pennsylvania State University[1]

Margaret Ranald, Queens College
Helpers:
  Jackson C. Boswell, District of Columbia Teachers College
  Frederick Capshaw, University of Maryland[2]
  Marla Knutsen, University of Southern California[3]
  A. L. McLeod, Rider College
  Joan Roberts, University of Maryland[2]

American Literature

Jackson R. Bryer, University of Maryland, Section Head

Jean Downey, Southern Connecticut State College

Philip R. Headings, Indiana University (Fort Wayne)

Joseph V. Ridgely, Columbia University

Donald B. Stauffer, State University of New York at Albany

Peter G. Van Egmond, University of Maryland
Helpers:
  Matthew O'Brien, University of Maryland
  Donald P. Wharton, Pennsylvania State University (Altoona Campus)[1]

Medieval Latin and Neo-Latin Literature

Edmund A. Reiss, Duke University, Section Head[5]

A. Leigh DeNeef, Duke University[5]
Helpers:
  Gail M. Gibson, Duke University
  Thomas Niemann, Duke University

Celtic Literatures

Gene C. Haley, Berklee College of Music, Section Head
Helpers:
  Charles A. Bowen, Harvard University
  Elizabeth Gray, Harvard University
  Daniel F. Melia, Harvard University
  Joan Radner, Harvard University
  Harold A. Roe, Jr., Harvard University
  Edgar M. Slotkin, Harvard University

Folklore

Dan Ben-Amos, University of Pennsylvania, Section Head

Henry Glassie, Indiana University

Joseph C. Hickerson, Library of Congress (Archive of Folksong)

Barbara Krader, University of Waterloo (Ontario)
Helpers:
  Deborah Ginsburg, University of Pennsylvania
  Maxine Miska, University of Pennsylvania
  Sabra F. Petersmann, University of Pennsylvania

* * *

Carolyn James Bishop, Pennsylvania State University Serials Specialist

Jayne K. Kribbs, Pennsylvania State University Editorial Assistant, Literature

Priscilla J. Letterman, Pennsylvania State University Administrative Assistant

Gwen L. Nagel, Pennsylvania State University, Editorial Assistant, Linguistics

Karen B. Powell, Pennsylvania State University, Secretary

* * *

It is a pleasant duty to record our gratitude to The Pennsylvania State University Libraries, W. Carl Jackson, Director, for furnishing office space, equipment, and services to the Bibliography, and to the Libraries of the University of Pennsylvania, Warren Haas, Director, for their many courtesies and assistance to the editorial staff of the Bibliography.

[1] The work of Messrs. Gidez, Mann, Meserole, Nagel, and Wharton and of Mrs. Fricke and Miss Kribbs, was aided by a grant from The Pennsylvania State University.

[2] The work of Messrs. Smith and Capshaw, and of Miss Roberts was aided by a grant from the University of Maryland.

[3] The work of Mr. Crane and Mrs. Knutsen was aided by a grant from the University of Southern California.

[4] The work of Mr. Landon was aided by a grant from the University of Maryland (Baltimore County).

[5] The work of Messrs. DeNeef and Reiss was aided by a grant from the Research Council of Duke University.

TABLE OF CONTENTS
VOLUME I

AA	American Anthropologist
AAA	Archivio per l'Alto Adige
AAAH	Acta Academiae Aboensis Humaniora (Åbo, Finland)
AAASH	Acta Antiqua Academiae Scientiarum Hungaricae
AALIAM	Arcadia, Accademia Letteraria Italiana. Atti e Memorie
AAM	Atti e Memorie dell'Accademia di Scienze, Lettere, ed Arte di Modena
A&CS	Area and Culture Studies (Tokyo)
A&S	Arts and Sciences (N. Y. U.)
ÅO	Ålandsk Odling: Årsbok
AAP	Atti e Memorie della R. Accademia di Scienze, Lettere ed Arti in Padova
AAPont	Atti dell' Accademia Pontaniana
AAS	Asian and African Studies
AASF	Annales Academiae Scientiarum Fennicae
AATB	Afro-Asian Theatre Bulletin
AAW	Afro-Asian Writings
AB	Acta Baltica
Abbia (Cameroun)	
ABC	American Book Collector
ABI	Accademie e Biblioteche d'Italia
ABR	American Benedictine Review
Abruzzo	
ABS	Acta Baltico-Slavica (Białystok)
Abside	
AC	Archaeologia Classica
ACF	Annali di Ca' Foscari (Venezia)
ACist	Analecta Cisterciensis
Acme (Milano)	
ACPFM	Amitié Charles Péguy. Feuillets Mensuels
ActaA	Acta Asiatica
ActaG	Acta Germanica (Capetown)
ActaL	Acta Latgalica
ActN	L'Action Nationale
AD	American Documentation (Superseded by *JASIS*)
ADA	Arquivo do Distrito de Aveiro
Adam: International Review	
ADEB	Bull. of the Assn. of Departments of English
AdLB	Adyar Library Bulletin
ADML	Automatic Documentation and Mathematical Linguistics
ADPh	Arbeiten zur Deutschen Philologie
AdTb	Altdeutsche Textbibliothek
ADz	Akadēmiskā Dzīve (Indianapolis)
AEASH	Acta Ethnographica Academiae Scientiarum Hungaricae
Aegyptus: Revista Italiana di Egittologia et di Papirologia	
AEM	Archeion Euboïkōn Meletōn
AeP	Anima e Pensiero (Napoli)
Aevum (Milano)	
AF	Anglistische Forschungen
AFA	Archivo de Filología Aragonesa
AfB	Africana Bulletin (Warsaw)
AFH	Archivum Franciscanum Historicum (Firenze)
AFilos	Archivio di Filosofia
AFLFP	Annali della Facoltà di Lettere e Filosofia dell'Università di Perugia
AfO	Archiv für Orientforschung (Graz)
AForum	African Forum: A Quarterly Journal of Contemporary Affairs
AFP	Archivum Fratrum Praedicatorum (Roma)
AfrA	African Arts/Arts d'Afrique (Now *African Arts*)
AfrAmS	Afro-American Studies: An Interdisciplinary Journal
Africa (Rome)	
AfricaL	Africa (London)
AfricaR	Africa Report
AfrL	Africana Linguistica (Tervuren)
AfrLRev	African Language Review (Supersedes *SLLR*)
AfrLJ	Africana Library Journal: A Quarterly Bibliography and News Bulletin
AfrLS	African Language Studies
AfrN	African Notes (Ibadan)
AfrS	African Studies (Johannesburg)
AfrSch	African Scholar: Journal of Research and Analysis
AfrSR	African Studies Review (Supersedes *ASB*)
AFS	Asian Folklore Studies
AG	Anglica Germanica
AGB	Archiv für Geschichte des Buchwesens
Agenda	
AGI	Archivio Glottologico Italiano (Torino)
AGP	Archiv für Geschichte der Philosophie
AGR	American-German Review
AH	American Heritage
AHDLMA	Archives d'Histoire Doctrinale et Littéraire d[u] Moyen Âge
AI	American Imago
Aidai (Brooklyn, N. Y.)	
Aika	[Formerly *Susu* and *SuSuV*]
AINAH	Anales del Inst. Nacional de Antropología e Histori[a]
AION-SG	Annali Istituto Universitario Orientale, Napol[i,] Sezione Germanica
AION-SL	Ibid., Sezione Linguistica
AION-SO	Ibid., Sezione Orientale
AION-SR	Ibid., Sezione Romanza
AION-SS	Ibid., Sezione Slava
AIPHOS	Annuaire de l'Institut de Philologie et d'Histoir[e] Orientales et Slaves (Bruxelles)
AISD	Annali dell'Istituto di Studi Danteschi
AIV	Atti del R. Istituto Veneto di Scienze, Lettere e[d] Arti. Venezia. Classe di scienze morali e lettere
AJFS	Australian Journal of French Studies (Monash U[.,] Clayton, Victoria)
AKG	Archiv für Kulturgeschichte
AKML	Abhandlungen zur Kunst-, Musik- und Literatur[-]wissenschaft
Akzente	
AL	American Literature
ALA	L'Afrique Littéraire et Artistique (Paris)
AlaR	Alabama Review
ALASH	Acta Linguistica Academiae Scientiarum Hungari[-]cae (Budapest)
ALAŽ	ALA Žurnāls (Supersedes *KBB*)
ALB	Almanacco Letterario Bompiani
ALet	Aspetti Letterari
Alföld	Alföld: Irodalmi és Művelődési Folyóirat
ALH	Acta Linguistica Hafniensia: International Journal [of] Structural Linguistics (Copenhagen)
Alighieri	L'Alighieri
ALitASH	Acta Litteraria Academiae Scientiarum Hungarica[e] (Budapest)
AlJ	Alemannisches Jahrbuch
AllaB	Alla Bottega (Brianza)
ALM	Archives des Lettres Modernes
ALMA	Archivum Latinitatis Medii Aevi (Bull. DuCange)
Almanak	Nutid og Fortid i Ord og Billeder
ALPS	Alabama Linguistic and Philological Series
ALR	American Literary Realism, 1870–1910
ALS	Australian Literary Studies (U. of Tasmania)
ALT	African Literature Today
ALUOS	The Annual of Leeds U. Oriental Soc.
AMAT	Atti e Memorie dell'Accademia Toscana, La Colom[-]baria
AmD	American Dialog
AMDSPAM	Atti e Memorie della Deputazione di Storia Patria pe[r] le Antiche Provincie Modenesi
Américas (Pan Amer. Union)	
Amistad: Writings on Black History and Culture	
AMN	Analecta Mediaevalia Namurcensia
AMRAC	Annales du Musée Royal de l'Afrique Centrale
AMSDSP	Atti e Memorie della Società Dalmata di Storia Patri[a]
Amstel	Amstelodamum

AN Acta Neophilologica (Ljubljana)
AnaliFF Anali Filološkog Fakulteta Beogradskog Univerziteta
AN&Q American Notes and Queries (New Haven, Conn.)
Anatolica
AnBol Analecta Bollandiana
AnBret Annales de Bretagne
Andalus Al-Andalus
ANF Arkiv för Nordisk Filologi
Angelicum
Anglia
Anglica (Kansai U., Osaka)
AnL Anthropological Linguistics (Indiana U.)
AnM Annuale Mediaevale (Duquesne U.)
Année Balzacienne (Paris)
AnPraem Analecta Praemonstratensia
ANSSSR Akademija Nauk SSSR
AnST Analecta Sacra Tarraconensia
ÁNT Általános Nyelvészeti Tanulmányok
Antaios (Stuttgart)
AntC L'Antiquité Classique
Anthropologica
Anthropos
AntigR Antigonish Review
Antiquariat
Antiquity Antiquity: A Quarterly Rev. of Archaeology
Antonianum (Roma)
ANTS Anglo-Norman Text Society
ANVAO Avhandlinger Utg. av det Norske Videnskapsakademie i Oslo II, Hist. filos. klass
AOASH Acta Orientalia Academiae Scientiarum Hungaricae
AODNS Acta Orientalia (Societates Orientales Danica, Norvegica, Svecica) Copenhagen
AP Aurea Parma
AP Ars Poetica
APh Acta Philologica (Roma: Societas Academica Dacoromana)
API Annali della Pubblica Istruzione
APK Aufsätze zur Portugiesischen Kulturgeschichte
Approdo L'Approdo Letterario (Roma)
APS Acta Philologica Scandinavica
AQ American Quarterly
Aquinas
AR Antioch Review
Arabica
Arbor: Revista General de Investigación y Cultura
L'Arc: Cahiers Méditerranéens (Aix-en-Provence)
Arcadia
Archiginnasio L'Archiginnasio
Archiv Archiv für das Studium der Neueren Sprachen und Literaturen
Archīvs (Melbourne)
Archivum (Oviedo)
ArcP Archeion Pontou
Arethusa: A Journal of the Wellsprings of Western Man
ARG Archiv für Reformationsgeschichte
Argine
Argonautēs: Etēsia Hellēnoamerikanikē Ekdosis Philologias Kai Draseōs
ArH Archivo Hispalense
Ariel: A Quarterly Rev. of the Arts and Sciences in Israel
ArielE Ariel: A Review of International English Literature
Arion (U. of Texas)
ArL Archivum Linguisticum
ArlQ Arlington Quarterly
ArO Archiv Orientální
ArQ Arizona Quarterly
ARS Augustan Reprint Society
ArteP Arte e Poesia
ArtSt Arte Stampa
Arv: Journal of Scandinavian Folklore
AS American Speech
ASAW Abhandlungen der Sächsischen Akademie der Wissenschaften zu Leipzig. Philol.-hist. Klasse

ASB African Studies Bulletin (Boston U.)
ASBFC Archivio Storico per Belluno, Feltre e Cadore
ASch American Scholar
ASEA Asiatische Studien/Etudes Asiatiques
ASHFY American Swedish Historical Foundation Yearbook (Philadelphia)
ASI Archivio Storico Italiano
ASILO Adalbert Stifter Institut des Landes Oberösterreich: Vierteljahrsschrift
ASL Archivio Storico Lombardo
ASLHM American Society of Legion of Honor Magazine
AsM Asia Major
ASNSP Annali della Scuola Normale Superiore di Pisa
ASoc Arts in Society (U. of Wis.)
Asomante
Aspectos
ASR American-Scandinavian Review
AsSt Asian Student
ASt Asian Studies
AŞUI Analele Ştiinţifice ale Universităţii Iaşi
AT Africa Today
Atenea
Athēna
Athenaeum (Pavia)
Athēnaïka
Allántida: Revista del Pensamiento Actual
ATLGT Archeion tou Thrākikou Laographikou kai Glōssikou Thēsaurou
ATP Arts et Traditions Populaires
ATQ American Transcendental Quarterly
ATRJ Association of Teachers of Russian Journal
AUC Anales de la Universidad de Chile
AÜ Afrika und Übersee
AUB Analele Universitatii, Bucureşti
AuE Arheoloğija un Etnogrāfija (Formerly *AE*)
Augustiniana
Augustinianum
Augustinus
AUL Annali dell'Università di Lecce
AUMLA Journal of the Australasian Universities Language and Literature Association
AUP Annales de l'Université de Paris
Aurora: Eichendorff-Almanach
AUS Annales Universitatis Saraviensis (U. des Saarlandes)
AUS-AG&R Acta Universitatis Szegediensis. Acta Germanica et Romanica
AUS-AHLH Acta Universitatis Szegediensis de Attila József Nominatae Sectio: Acta Historiae Litterarum Hungaricarum
Ausblick: Mitteilungsblatt der Deutschen Auslandsgesellschaft (Lübeck)
AUS-E&L Acta Universitatis Szegediensis de Attila József Nominatae Sectio: Ethnographica et Linguistica
Ausonia
Aut Aut
Autores
AV Ateneo Veneto
AWR The Anglo-Welsh Review (Pembroke Dock, Wales)
BA Books Abroad
Babel: International Journal of Translation
BADL Bonner Arbeiten zur Deutschen Literatur
BAGB Bulletin de l'Association Guillaume Budé
Balcony: The Sydney Review (U. of Sydney)
BALI Bollettino dell'Atlante Linguistico Italiano
BALM Bollettino dell'Atlante Linguistico Mediterraneo
BalSt Balkan Studies
Baltistica: Baltų Kalbų Tyrinējimai (Vilnius)
BANQ Biblionews and Australian Notes and Queries
BAPEL Boletim da Academia Portuguêsa de Ex-Libros
BAR Association des Amis de Rabelais et de La Devinière. Bulletin
BaratR Barat Review
Baretti
BArn Bibliotheca Arnamagnæana

BARev	Black Academy Review: Quarterly of the Black World	*BHS*	Bulletin of Hispanic Studies
Barroco (Brazil)		*BhV*	Bharatiya Vidya
Ba Shiru (U. of Wis.)		*BI*	Books at Iowa
BASL	Bochumer Arbeiten zur Sprach- und Literaturwissenschaft	*BiafraR*	Biafra Review (M.I.T.)
BAWS	Bayerische Akademie der Wissenschaften. Phil.-hist. Klasse, Sitzungsberichte	*BIBLB*	Boletim Internacional de Bibliografia Luso-Brasileira (Lisboa)
BB	Bulletin of Bibliography	*Bibliofilia*	
BBA	Berliner Byzantinistische Arbeiten	*Bibliotheck*	The Bibliotheck (Glasgow)
BBCS	Bulletin of the Board of Celtic Studies (U. of Wales)	*BIEA*	Boletín del Instituto de Estudios Asturianos
BBK	Bibliotekininkystès ir Bibliografijos Klausimai (Lietuvos TSR Aukštųjų Mokyklų Mokslo Darbai. Vilnius.)	*BIFAN*	Bulletin de l'Institut Fondamental d'Afrique Noire: Série B—Sciences Humaines
BBL	Biblioteksbladet	*BIIRHT*	Bulletin d'Information de l'Institut de Recherche et d'Histoire des Textes
BBMP	Boletín de la Biblioteca Menéndez Pelayo	*Bikoret-u-Parshanut* (Ramat Gan, Israel)	
BBN	Berliner Beiträge zur Namenforschung	*BILAL*	Bulletin d'Information du Laboratoire d'Analyse Lexicologique
BBr	Books at Brown	*BILEUG*	Bollettino dell'Istituto de Lingue Estere (Università di Genova)
BBSIA	Bulletin Bibliographique de la Société Internationale Arthurienne		
BBSP	Botetourt Bibliographical Society Publications	*BILC*	Boletim do Istituto Luís de Camões (Macao)
BBST	Bibliothèque Bonaventurienne, Series "Textes"	*BioC*	Biologia Culturale
BC	Book Collector	*BISIMAM*	Bollettino dell'Ist. Storico Italiano per il Medioevo e Archivio Muratoriano
BCB	Boletín Cultural y Bibliográfico (Bogotá)	*BJA*	British Journal of Aesthetics (London)
BCCMP	Boletim Cultural, Câmara, Municipal do Porto	*BJRL*	Bulletin of the John Rylands Library
BCDI	Bollettino della Carta dei Dialetti Italiani	*BlackW*	Black World (Formerly *Negro Digest*)
BCH	Bulletin di Correspondance Hellénique	*BLE*	Bulletin de Littérature Ecclésiastique
BCom	Bulletin of the Comediantes	*BLI*	Beiträge zur Linguistik und Informationsverarbeitung
BCRBD	Boletim da Casa Regional da Beiro-Douro		
BCSO	Bollettino del Centro di Studi Onomastici "G. D. Serra"	*BLM*	Bonniers Litterära Magasin
		BLR	Bodleian Library Record
BDE	Boletín de Dialectología Española	BMD	Bijdragen en Mededeelingen der Dialectencommissie van de Koninklijke Akademie van Wetenschappen te Amsterdam
BdeP	Bibliothèque de la Pléiade		
BdF	Boletim de Filologia		
BDK	Beiträge zur Deutschen Klassik	*BMFEA*	Bulletin of the Museum of Far Eastern Antiquities (Stockholm)
BDLM	Bibliographien zur Deutschen Literatur des Mittelalters		
		BMFJ	Bulletin de la Maison Franco-Japonais
BDM	Bollettino del Domus Mazziniana	*BMQ*	British Museum Quarterly
BDP	Beiträge zur Deutschen Philologie	*BMSLP*	Boletim Mensal da Sociedade de Língua Portuguêsa
BDVA	Beiträge zur Deutschen Volks- und Altertumskunde (Hamburg)	BN	Beiträge zur Namenforschung (Heidelberg)
		BN&R	Botswana Notes and Records
BE	Balgarski Ezik (Sofia)	*BNJ*	Byzantinisch-Neugriechische Jahrbücher
Béaloideas		BNL	Beiträge zur Neueren Literaturgeschichte (Heidelberg)
BEFEO	Bulletin de l'Ecole Française d'Extrême-Orient		
BEG	Boletín de Estudios Germánicos (Univ. Nac. de Cuyo, Mendoza, Arg.)	*BNYPL*	Bulletin of the New York Public Library
		BO	Black Orpheus
Behaviour: An International Journal of Comparative Ethology		*BöV*	Böckernas Värld
Belfagor		*Bokvännen*	
Bellmansstudier Bellmanstudier Utg. av Bellmanssällskapet		*BollSP*	Bollettino Storico Piacentino
BEPh	Beiträge zur Englischen Philologie	*BP*	Banasthali Patrika
BEPIF	Bulletin des Etudes Portugaises et de l'Institut Français au Portugal	*BPHP*	Bulletin Philologique et Historique du Comité des Travaux Historiques et Scientifiques (Paris)
Bergomum		*BPTJ*	Biuletyn Polskiego Towarzystwa Językoznawczego
Bethléem		*BR*	Baltic Review (New York)
Bethlehem: Illustrierte Monatszeitschrift der Bethlehem-Messionane		*BRAE*	Boletín de la Real Academia Española
BEz	Balkansko Ezikoznanie	BrenS	Brenner-Studien
BF	Books from Finland	*Brigata* (Naples)	
BFC	Boletín del Instituto de Filología de la Univ. de Chíle	*BRMMLA*	Bulletin of the Rocky Mountain Mod. Lang. Assn.
BFE	Boletín de Filología Española	*Brotéria*	
BFLS	Bulletin de la Faculté des Lettres de Strasbourg	*BRP*	Beiträge zur Romanischen Philologie (Berlin)
BFM	Boletín de Filología (Montevideo)	*BRT*	Behavior Research and Therapy: International Multi-Disciplinary Journal
BFon	Biuletyn Fonograficzny (Poznań)		
BFR	Bibliothèque Française et Romane	BS	Bollingen Series
BGDSL	Beiträge zur Geschichte der Deutschen Sprache und Literatur (Tübingen)	*BSAM*	Bulletin de la Société des Amis de Montaigne
		BSci	Behavioral Science
BGDSL (Halle) Ibid. (Halle)		BSDSL	Basler Studien zur Deutschen Sprache und Literatur
BGLS	Bausteine zur Geschichte der Literatur bei den Slaven	*BSE*	Brno Studies in English
BGPTM	Beiträge zur Geschichte der Philosophie und Theologie des Mittelalters	*BSED*	Bulletin de la Société d'Etudes Dantesques du Centre Universitaire Méditerranéen
		BSEM	Boletin da Sociedade do Estudos de Moçambique
BH	Bulletin Hispanique	*BSl*	Byzantinoslavica
BHe	Baltische Hefte	*BSLP*	Bulletin de la Société de Linguistique de Paris
BHF	Bonner Historische Forschungen	BSM	Beiträge zur Schweizerdeutschen Mundartforschungen
BHR	Bibliothèque d'Humanisme et Renaissance		

BSOAS	Bulletin of the School of Oriental and African Studies
BSS	Birger Sjöberg Sällskapet
BSSL	Bibliographien zum Studium der Deutschen Sprache und Literatur
BSUF	Ball State University Forum
BTLV	Bijdragen tot de Taal-, Land- en Volkekunde
BTMG	Blätter der Thomas Mann Gesellschaft
BuR	Bucknell Review
Busara (Nairobi)	
BV	Bogens Verden (Copenhagen)
BYUS	Brigham Young University Studies
Byzantion	
BZ	Byzantinische Zeitschrift (Leipzig)
BzJA	Beihefte zum JA
BZWW	Beihefte zur Zeitschrift Wirkendes Wort
CA	Cuadernos Americanos
Cabellian	The Cabellian: A Journal of the Second American Renaissance
CACM	Communications of the Association for Computing Machinery
CACP	Cahiers de l'Amitié Charles Péguy
CadB	Cadernos Brasileiros
Caffé	
CAfr	Congo-Afrique (Kinshasa)
CAIEF	Cahiers de l'Association Internationale des Etudes Françaises
CAL	Center for Applied Linguistics (Wash., D.C.)
CALC	Cahiers Algériens de Littérature Comparée
Caliban (Toulouse)	
CalR	Calcutta Review
CalSS	California Slavic Studies
C&M	Classica et Mediaevalia
CanL	Canadian Literature
CAnth	Current Anthropology
Capitolium	
Carovana	
Carrell	The Carrell: Journal of the Friends of the U. of Miami (Fla.) Library
Carte	Carte Segrete (Supersedes EL)
CaSE	Carnegie Series in English
CAsJ	Central Asiatic Journal
CAsR	Central Asian Review (London)
CathW	Catholic World
CBAA	Current Bibliography on African Affairs
CBC	Cesare Barbieri Courier
CC	Corpus Christianorum
CCa	Civiltà Cattolica
CCanC	Cahier Canadien Claudel
CCC	College Composition and Communication
CCCist	Citeaux Commentarii Cistercienses (Abbatia, West-malle, Belgica)
CCJ	The Chung Chi Journal
CCM	Cahiers de Civilisation Médiévales (Xe–XIIe Siècles) (U. de Poitiers)
CCU	Cuadernos de la Cátedra de Unamuno
CD	Child Development
CdD	La Ciudad de Dios
CdL	Cahiers de Lexicologie
CdS	Corriere della Sera
CE	College English
CEA	CEA Critic
CEAAN	Center for Editions of American Authors Newsletter (MLA)
CEAfr	Cahiers d'Etudes Africaines
Cebela (U. do Rio Grande do Sul, Porto Alegre, Brazil)	
CEG	Cuadernos de Estudios Gallegos
CEJ	California English Journal
Célèbes	
Celi	
Celtica	
Celticum: Supplément à Ogam: Tradition Celtique	
CEMW	Columbia Essays on Modern Writers
CEn	Coleção Ensaio

Cenobio	
CentR	The Centennial Review (Mich. State U.)
Ceol (Dublin)	
CeS	Cultura e Scuola
CF	Classical Folia
CFeng	Ching Feng: Quarterly Notes on Christianity and Chinese Religion and Culture
CFMA	Classiques Français du Moyen Âge
CForum	Cultural Forum (New Delhi)
CFS	Cahiers Ferdinand de Saussure
CFSTI	Clearinghouse for Federal Scientific and Technical Information
CG	Classiques Garnier
CHA	Cuadernos Hispanoamericanos (Madrid)
ChauR	The Chaucer Review (Penn. State U.)
ChC	Chinese Culture
ChE	Chiakē Epitheōrēsis
ChinaQ	China Quarterly
ChinL	Chinese Literature
ChiR	Chicago Review
CHLSSF	Commentationes Humanarum Litterarum Societatis Scientiarum Fennica
CHR	Catholic Historical Review
ChrE	Chronique d'Egypte (Bruxelles)
CHSQ	California Historical Society Quarterly
CHum	Computers and the Humanities
CI	Cuadernos del Idioma
CIFM	Contributi dell'Istituto di Filologia Moderna. Ser. Ital. 1. Univ. Cattolica del Sacro Cuore (Milano)
CIL	Contemporary Indian Literature
CimR	Cimarron Review (Oklahoma State U.)
Cithara (St. Bonaventure U.)	
CJ	Classical Journal
CJap	Contemporary Japan
CJAS	Canadian Journal of African Studies
CJL	Canadian Journal of Linguistics
CJVŠ	Cizí Jazyky ve Škole (Prague)
CL	Comparative Literature
CLAJ	College Language Association Journal (Morgan State Coll., Baltimore)
ClareQ	Claremont Quarterly (Claremont, Calif.)
Clarté (Stockholm)	
Classic (Johannesburg)	
ClassQ	Classical Quarterly
ClassR	Classical Review
CLC	Columbia Library Columns
CLEB	Comunidad Latinoamericana de Escritores Boletín
CLing	Cercetări de Lingvistică (Cluj, Romania)
Clio (Roma)	
CLJ	Cornell Library Journal
CLLAN	Collection Langues et Littératures de l'Afrique Noire (Paris)
CLQ	Colby Library Quarterly
CLS	Comparative Literature Studies (U. of lll.)
CLTA	Cahiers de Linguistique Théorique et Appliquée
CMC	Crosscurrents/Modern Critiques
CMF	Crosscurrents/Modern Fiction
CMLR	Canadian Modern Language Review
CMRS	Cahiers du Monde Russe et Soviétique
CMTS	Clarendon Medieval and Tudor Series
CN	Cultura Neolatina (Modena)
CNat	Cahiers Naturalistes
CoA	The Coat of Arms (London)
ColF	Columbia Forum (Supersedes CUF)
CollCist	Collectanea Cisterciensa
CollFran	Collectanea Franciscana
CollG	Colloquia Germanica, Internationale Zeitschrift für Germanische Sprach- und Literaturwissenschaft
Colóquio	
ColQ	Colorado Quarterly
Comentário (Rio de Janeiro)	
Commentary	
	Commentatio: Analysen und Kommentare zur Deutschen Literatur

Commonweal

CompD — Comparative Drama

Compendia — Compendia: Computer-Generated Aids to Literary and Linguistic Research

CompJ — The Computer Journal

ComputL — Computational Linguistics

Comunità (Milan)

Conch — The Conch: A Biafran Journal of Literary and Cultural Analysis

ConL — Contemporary Literature (Supersedes *WSCL*)

ConnR — Connecticut Review

Contemp — Contemporaneo (Roma)

Contemporanul

Contrast (Cape Town)

Convivium (Barcelona)

Convivium (Bologna)

Coranto — Journal of Friends of the Libraries (U.S.C.)

CP — Concerning Poetry (West. Wash. State College)

CPe — Castrum Peregrini

CPH — Colecção Poetas de Hoje

CQ — The Cambridge Quarterly

CR — The Critical Review (Melbourne; Sydney)

CRa — Cahiers Raciniens

CRAIBL — Comptes-rendus de l'Académie des Inscriptions et Belles Lettres

CraneR — The Crane Review (Tufts U.)

Cratilo

CRB — Cahiers de la Compagnie Madeleine Renaud-Jean Louis Barrault

Credo: Kastolk Tidskrift (Uppsala)

CRevAS — Canadian Review of American Studies

Cristallo (Bolzano)

Crit — Critique: Studies in Modern Fiction

Criticism (Wayne State)

Critique (Paris)

CritQ — Critical Quarterly

CRL — College and Research Libraries

Croatica (Zagreb)

CrS — Critica Storica

CSE — Cornell Studies in English

CSEL — Corpus Scriptorum Ecclesiasticorum Latinorum

CSGLL — Canadian Studies in German Language and Literature

CSHVB — Computer Studies in the Humanities and Verbal Behavior

CSMLT — Cambridge Studies in Medieval Life and Thought

CSP — Canadian Slavonic Papers

CSS — Canadian Slavic Studies

CSt — Colecção Studium

CT — La Ciencia Tomista

CTL — Cahiers—Théâtre Louvain

CUASRLL — Catholic University of America Studies in Romance Languages and Literatures

CulEA — Cultural Events in Africa

Cultura (Milano)

Cultura (Rio de Janeiro)

Culture

CV — Città di Vita

CVS — Classiques du XXᵉ Siècle

CWCP — Contemporary Writers in Christian Perspective

CZ — Cela Zīmes

ČL — Česká Literatura

ČLid — Český Lid

ČMF — Časopis pro Moderní Filologii

ČsR — Československá Rusistika

DA — Dissertation Abstracts

Dædalus (Proc. Amer. Acad. of Arts & Sciences)

DAEM — Deutsches Archiv für die Erforschung des Mittelalters

DAI — Dissertation Abstracts International [Supersedes *DA*]

DanF — Danske Folkemaal (Copenhagen)

D&T — Drama and Theatre (Formerly *First Stage* [Purdue])

Dansk Udsyn (Askov)

Darlite (Dar es Salaam)

DASDJ — Deutsche Akademie für Sprache und Dichtung, Darmstadt. Jahrbuch

DAWB — Deutsche Akademie der Wissenschaften zu Berlin

DAWBIDSL — Deutsche Akademie der Wissenschaften zu Berlin. Institut für Deutsche Sprache und Literatur

DB — Doitsu Bungaku

DBGÜ — Deutsche Beiträge zur Geistigen Überlieferung

DdB — O Distrito de Braga

DDG — Deutsche Dialektgeographie

DDJ — Deutsches Dante Jahrbuch

DeH — De Homine

Delo (Belgrade)

Delos: A Journal on & of Translation

Delta (Amsterdam)

DHLR — The D. H. Lawrence Review (U. of Arkansas)

DHR — Duquesne Hispanic Review (Pittsburgh)

DHS — Dix-Huitième Siècle

Dialoghi

Dialogo

Dialogue (Montreal)

DialogW — Dialog (Warsaw)

DialS — Dialog: Teatertidskrift (Stockholm)

Dickensian

Diderot Studies (Genève)

Dimension: Contemporary German Arts and Letters

Dimensioni

Diogenes

Discourse (Concordia Coll.)

Discretio

DissUW — Dissertationen der Universität Wien

DJV — Deutsches Jahrbuch für Volkskunde

DM — The Dublin Magazine (formerly The Dubliner)

Dōdekanēsiaka

DownR — Downside Review

DR — Dalhousie Review

Dramaforskning (Uppsala)

Dramma (Torino)

DrB — Driemaandelijkse Bladen

DS — Danske Studier

DS — Deutsche Studien

DSA — Dickens Studies Annual [Supersedes *DiS*]

DSARDS — Dante Studies with the Annual Report of the Dante Society

DSFNS — Deutsch-Slawische Forschungen zur Namenkunde und Siedlungsgeschichte

DSN — Dickens Studies Newsletter

DSPS — Duquesne Studies, Philological Series

DSS — XVIIᵉ Siècle

DT — Divus Thomas

DTM — Deutsche Texte des Mittelalters

DU — Der Deutschunterricht

DuE — Dichtung und Erkenntnis

DUJ — Durham University Journal

Duklja (Prešov)

DuW — Dichtung und Wirklichkeit

DVLG — Deutsche Vierteljahrsschrift für Literaturwissenschaft und Geistesgeschichte

DWB — Dietsche Warande en Belfort

DzD — Dzejas Diena

EA — Etudes Anglaises

EAJ — East Africa Journal (Nairobi)

EAL — Early American Literature (Supersedes *EALN*)

EAm — Estudíos Americanos (Sevilla)

E&S — Essays and Studies by Members of the English Association

EB — The Eastern Buddhist

EBSK — Erlanger Beiträge zur Sprach- und Kunstwissenschaft

EBT — Les Etudes Balkaniques Tchécoslovaques

EC — Etudes Celtiques

ECB — Estudos de Castelo Branco

EckartJ — Eckart Jahrbuch

ECl	Etudes Classiques
ECN	Estudios de Cultura Náhuatl (Ciudad Universitaria)
ECr	L'Esprit Créateur (Lawrence, Kan.)
ECS	Eighteenth-Century Studies (U. of Calif., Davis)
EdArn	Editiones Arnamagnæanæ
Edda	
EDH	Essays by Divers Hands
EdL	Etudes de Lettres (U. de Lausanne)
EDRS	ERIC Document Reproduction Service
EdS	Les Ecrits des Saints
EDS	English Dance and Song
EE	East Europe
EEPSAPT	Epistēmonikē Epetēris Philosophikēs Scholēs Aristoteleiou Panepistēmiou Thessalonikēs
EEPSPA	Epistēmonikē Epetēris tēs Philosophikēs Scholēs tou Panepistēmiou Athēnōn
EETS	Early English Text Society
EF	Etudes Françaises
EFL	Essays in French Literature (U. of Western Australia)
EFran	Etudes Franciscaines
EG	Etudes Germaniques
EH	Eastern Horizon (Hong Kong)
EHBS	Epetēris tēs Hetaireias Byzantinōn Spoudōn
EHKM	Epetēris Hetaireias Kykladikōn Meletōn
EHR	English Historical Review
EHSM	Epetēris Hetaireias Stereoelladikōn Meletōn
EIC	Essays in Criticism (Oxford)
EIE	English Institute Essays
EigoS	Eigo Seinen [The Rising Generation] (Tokyo)
Éigse: A Journal of Irish Studies	
EIHC	Essex Institute Historical Collections
EiL	Ezik i Literatura (Sofia)
EIP	Estudos Italianos em Portugal
Éire	Ireland: A Journal of Irish Studies (St. Paul)
EIUES	English Institute of the U. of Uppsala: Essays and Studies on Eng. Lang. and Lit.
EJ	English Journal
EKEEK	Epetēris tou Kentrou Epistēmonikon Ereunōn Kyprou
EKEHL	Epetēris tou Kentrou Ereunēs tēs Hellēnikēs Laographias
ELA	Etudes de Linguistique Appliquée (Besançon)
ELCFR	English Linguistics, 1500–1800: A Collection of Facsimile Reprints
ELH	Journal of English Literary History
ELit	Etudes Littéraires
ELLS	English Literature and Language (Tokyo)
ELN	English Language Notes (U. of Colo.)
Elsinore	
ELT	English Literature in Transition (1800–1920)
ELul	Estudios Lulianos
EM	English Miscellany
EMAAA	Epetēris Mesaiōnikou Archeiou Akadēmias Athēnōn
Emerita (Madrid)	
EmSA	Emakeele Seltsi Aastaraamat
Encounter (London)	
English (London)	
EnlE	Enlightenment Essays (Chicago)
EO	Der Europäische Osten
EOMC	Estudios Orientales (Mexico City)
Ēōs	
EP	Etudes Philosophiques
ĒpH	Ēpeirōtikē Hestia
EPM	Etudes de Philosophie Médiévale
Epoca	
EPS	English Philological Studies
ER	Etudes Rabelaisiennes
Eranos: Acta Philologica Suecana	
ERBr	Etudes Romanes de Brno
ERIC	Educational Resources Information Center (CAL & MLA)
Ériu	

ES	English Studies
ESA	English Studies in Africa (Johannesburg)
EsCl	Estudios Clásicos
ESec	L'Enseignement Secondaire (Québec)
ESl	Etudes Slaves et Est-Européennes
EspA	Español Actual
Espiral (Lisbon)	
Esprit	
ESPSL	O Estado de São Paulo, Suplemento Literário
ESQ	Emerson Society Quarterly
Esquire	
ESRS	Emporia State Research Studies
Estafeta (Toronto)	
ETC.: A Review of General Semantics	
Ethnographia	A Magyar Néprajzi Társaság Folyóirata
Ethnology (Pittsburgh)	
Ethnomusicology (Bloomington, Ind.)	
ETJ	Educational Theatre Journal
Etnia (Buenos Aires)	
ÊTs	Études Tsiganes
Etudes	
EU	Estudos Universitários
EulJ	Eulenspiegel-Jahrbuch
Euphorion (Heidelberg)	
EUQ	Emory University Quarterly
EurH	Europäische Hochschulschriften
Europe	
EWN	Evelyn Waugh Newsletter
EWR	East-West Review (Doshisha U., Kyoto, Japan)
Expl	Explicator
Explorations (Dept. of English, Government Coll., Lahore)	
Expression (U. of Malawi)	
Extracta	Extracta: Resumeer af Specialeopgaver fra det Filosofiske Fakultet ved Københavns Universitet
Extrapolation	
Fabula	
FAGAAS	Frankfurter Arbeiten aus dem Gebiete der Anglistik und der Amerika-Studien
Fataburen: Nordiska Museets och Skansens Årsbok	
FB	Fontane Blätter (Potsdam)
FBG	Frankfurter Beiträge zur Germanistik
FBrab	Le Folklore Brabançon
FC	Fathers of the Church
FCR	Free China Review
FD	Filosofs'ka Dumka
FDHRS	Freies Deutsches Hochstift: Reihe der Schriften
FdL	Forum der Letteren
FDS	Fountainwell Drama Series
FDTSC	Folger Documents of Tudor and Stuart Civilization
FE	France-Eurafrique
FeL	Filologia e Letteratura
Fenarete	
FEUFJ	Far Eastern University Faculty Journal
FF	Frate Francesco
FFC	Folklore Fellows Communications
FFLR	Florida Foreign Language Reporter
FFMA	Folklore and Folk Music Archivist (Ind. U.)
FForum	Folklore Forum
FForumB	Folklore Forum Bibliographic and Special Series
FGO	Forschungen zur Geschichte Oberösterreichs
FH	Frankfurter Hefte
FHA	Fitzgerald-Hemingway Annual
FHP	Fort Hare Papers (Fort Hare U., South Africa)
FHS	French Historical Studies
FI	Forum Italicum
Filologia (Buenos Aires)	
Filologija (Zagreb)	
Filosofia	
FIMS	Folklore Institute Monograph Series [Supersedes IUFS]
FK	Filológiai Közlöny
FL	Figaro Littéraire
FLA	Foreign Language Annals

Flambeau	Le Flambeau: Revue Belge des Questions Politiques et Littéraires		*GodSU*	Godišnik na Sofijskija Universitet: Fakultet po Slavjanski Filologii
FLang	Foundations of Language (Dordrecht, Neth.)		*Goethe: Neue Folge des Jahrbuchs der Goethe-Gesellschaft* (Weimar)	
FLe	Fiera Letteraria		*Goethe-Al*	Goethe-Almanach
FM	Le Français Moderne		*GoldK*	Goldene Keyt
FMAS	Frühmittelalterliche Studien		*GorR*	The Gordon Review (Wenham, Mass.)
FMJ	Folk Music Journal (London)		*GothSE*	Gothenburg Studies in English
FMLS	Forum for Modern Language Studies (U. of St. Andrews, Scotland)		*GQ*	German Quarterly
			GR	Germanic Review
FMod	Filología Moderna (Madrid)		*Gradja*	Gradja za Povijest Književnosti Hrvatske
FMonde	Le Français dans le Monde		*Grani*	
FN	Filologičeskie Nauki		*Grial* (Vigo, Galicia)	
FoL	Folk Life (Cardiff)		*GRM*	Germanisch-romanische Monatsschrift, Neue Folge
FoLi	Folia Linguistica		*GS*	Germanistische Studien
Folklore (London)			*GSA*	German Studies in America
FolkloreC	Folklore (Calcutta)		*GSD*	Geistes- und Sozialwissenschaftliche Dissertationen
Forum (Wien)			*GSLI*	Giornale Storico della Letteratura Italíana
ForumH	Forum (Houston)		*Guardian* (Rangoon)	
ForumS	Forum: A Ukrainian Review (Scranton, Pa.)		*GuG*	Gestalt und Gedanke: Ein Jahrbuch
ForumZ	Forum (Zagreb)		*GV*	Gil Vicente (Guimarães, Port.)
FP	Filološki Pregled (Belgrade)		*GW*	Germanica Wratislaviensia (Wrocław)
FPhon	Folia Phoniatrica		*Gymnasium:*	Zeitschrift für Kultur der Antike und Humanistische Bildung
FPt	The Far Point (U. of Manitoba)			
FQ	Florida Quarterly		*HAB*	Humanities Association Bulletin (Canada)
FR	French Review		*HAHR*	Hispanic American Historical Review
FrA	France-Asie/Asia		*Harper's*	
FranS	Franciscan Studies		*HartR*	Hartwick Review
FrLM	French Literature on Microfiche		*Hasifrut: Quarterly for the Study of Literature*	
Frontiera (Rome)			*HBl*	Hofmannsthal Blätter
Fróðskaparrit (Tórshavn)			*HBSÅ*	Hjalmar Bergman Samfundet Årsbok (Stockholm)
FrSt	Franziskanische Studien		*HBV*	Hessische Blätter für Volkskunde
FS	French Studies		*HC*	The Hollins Critic (Hollins Coll., Va.)
FsD	Fonetică şi Dialectologie		*HD*	Human Development: An International Research Quarterly
FSUSP	Florida State University Slavic Papers			
FT	Finsk Tidskrift		*HDL*	Handbuch der Deutschen Literaturgeschichte
FUF	Finnisch-ugrische Forschungen: Zeitschrift für Finnisch-ugrische Sprach- und Volkskunde		*HEAS*	Harvard East Asian Series
			HeineJ	Heine Jahrbuch
FurmS	Furman Studies		*Helikon: Világirodalmi Figyelő* (Budapest)	
FVL	Forschungen zur Volks- und Landeskunde		*Hellenika*	
FW	Folktales of the World		*HellēnikaS*	Hellēnika (Salonika)
FzG	Forschungsberichte zur Germanistik (Osaka-Kobe)		*Hephaistos: A Quarterly Devoted to Computer Research in the Humanities*	
GA	Germanistische Abhandlungen		*Hermaea*	
GAf	Genève-Afrique		*Hermathena: A Dublin University Review*	
GAG	Göppinger Arbeiten zur Germanistik		*Hermes: Zeitschrift für Klassische Philologie*	
Galleria			*HF*	Heidelberger Forschungen
GaR	Georgia Review		*HGS*	Harvard Germanic Studies
GAS	German-American Studies		*Hispania* (U. of Mass.)	
GCFI	Giornale Critico della Filosofia Italiana		*Hispano*	Hispanófila (Madrid)
GdB	Giornale di Bordo: Mensile di Storia, Letteratura ed Arte		*HJAS*	Harvard Journal of Asiatic Studies
			HJb	Hebbel-Jahrbuch
GdG	Grundlagen der Germanistik		*HLB*	Harvard Library Bulletin
GdiM	Giornale di Metafisica		*HLQ*	Huntington Library Quarterly
Genre (U. of Ill. at Chicage Circle)			*HLS*	Historiska och Litteraturhistoriska Studier (Helsingfors)
GF	Grafiskt Forum			
GFF	Grillparzer Forum Forchtenstein		*HMex*	Historia Mexicana
Gids	De Gids		*HNK*	Ho Neos Koubaras
GIF	Giornale Italiano di Filologia		*Hochland*	
GJ	Gutenberg-Jahrbuch		*HoE*	Ho Eranistēs
GK	Gengo Kenkyū: Journal of the Linguistic Society of Japan		*HöJb*	Hölderlin-Jahrbuch
			Homme	L'Homme (Paris)
GKVVH	Göteborgs Kungl. Vetenskaps- och Vitterhets Samhälles Handlingar		*HorYezh* (Châteaubourg, France)	
			Horisont (Vasa)	
GL	General Linguistics		*HPEN*	Le P.E.N. Hongrois
GL&L	German Life and Letters		HPS	Hamburger Philologische Studien
GLC	Glossari di Lingua Contemporanea		*HR*	Hispanic Review
Glossa: The Journal of Linguistics			HRD	Hamburger Romanistische Dissertationen
Glotta: Zeitschrift für Griechische und Lateinische Sprache			*HS*	Humanities in the South (Ruston, La.)
Glottodidactica (Posen)			*HSan*	Helsingin Sanomat
GM	Gandhi Marg		HSCL	Harvard Studies in Comparative Literature
GN	Germanic Notes		*HSE*	Hungarian Studies in English (L. Kossuth Univ., Debrecen)
Gnomon: Kritische Zeitschrift für die Gesamte Klassische Altertumswissenschaft				
GodFFNS	Godišnjak Filozofskog Fakulteta u Novom Sadu		*HSL*	Hartford Studies in Literature

HSRL	Harvard Studies in Romance Languages
HSS	Harvard Slavic Studies
HT	Historik Tidskrift (Stockholm)
HTR	Harvard Theological Review
HudR	Hudson Review
Hufvudstadsbladet (Helsinki)	
HumB	Humanitas (Brescia)
Humboldt	
HungS	Hungarian Survey
HussR	Husson Review
HZM	Handelingen van de Zuidnederlandse Maatschappij voor Taal- en Letterkunde en Geschiedenis
IA	Insel-Almanach
IÅ	Ibsenforbundet: Årbok
IAC	Indo-Asian Culture
IAN	Izvestija Akademii Nauk S.S.S.R., Serija Literatury i Jazyka (Moscow)
IASOP	Inst. of African Studies, Occasional Pubs. (Ibadan)
IAT	Izvestija Akademija Nauk Turkmenskoj SSR Serija Obščestvennyx Nauk
Ibadan	
Ibérida	
Ibero	Ibero-romania (München)
IBLA	Institut Belles-Lettres Arabes Revue
IC	Islamic Culture
ICS	L'Italia che Scrive
ID	Italia Dialettale
IDL	Indices zur Deutschen Literatur
IER	Irish Ecclesiastical Record
IEY	Iowa English Yearbook
IF	Indogermanische Forschungen
IFr	Italia Francescana
IH	ITA Humanidades (São José dos Campos, Brazil)
IHS	Irish Historical Studies
II	Italia Intellettuale
IIBE	Izvestija na Instituta za Bəlgarski Ezik
IIBL	Izvestija na Instituta za Bəlgarska Literatura (Sofia)
IIJ	Indo-Iranian Journal
IJAL	International Journal of American Linguistics
IJAS	Indian Journal of American Studies
IJŠ	Inostrannye Jazyki v Škole
IJSLP	International Journal of Slavic Linguistics and Poetics
IK	Irodalomtörténeti Közlemények
IL	L'Information Littéraire
ILing	Initiation à la Linguistique
ILit	Iaşul Literar
Imprimatur	
IMU	Italia Medioevale e Umanistica
IncL	Incorporated Linguist (London)
IndF	Indiana Folklore
Indice (Madrid)	
IndL	Indian Literature
IndLing	Indian Linguistics
IndS	Indian Studies: Past and Present
InfC	Information and Control (M.I.T.)
Iniziative	
InozF	Inozemna Filolohija
Insula (Madrid)	
Invenção (S. Paulo)	
IPEN	Indian P.E.N.
IQ	Italian Quarterly
IqR	Iqbal Review
IR	Iliff Review (Denver)
IRAL	International Review of Applied Linguistics in Language Teaching (Heidelberg)
Iran: Journal of the British Institute of Persian Studies	
Irenikon	
IrishS	Irish Sword: The Jour. of the Military History Soc. of Ireland
IrodalF	Irodalomtörténeti Füzetek
Irodalomtörténet. History of Literature (Budapest)	
IS	Italian Studies
ISE	Ibadan Studies in English
Islam	Der Islam
ISLL	Illinois Studies in Language and Literature
ISLS	Information System Language Studies
ISS	Indiana Slavic Studies
ISSJ	International Social Science Journal (UNESCO)
ISz	Irodalmi Szemle
Italica	
IUB	Indiana University Bookman
IUFS	Indiana U. Folklore Series
IUHS	Indiana U. Humanities Series
IUPAL	Indiana U. Pubs. in Anthropology and Linguistics
IUPSEES	Indiana U. Pubs., Slavic and East Eur. Series
IUPUAS	Indiana U. Pubs., Uralic and Altaic Series
IURCAFL	Indiana U. Research Center in Anthropology, Folklore, and Linguistics
IUSHTL	Indiana U. Studies in the History and Theory of Linguistics
IWT	Indiana Writing Today
Izraz (Sarajevo)	
JA	Jahrbuch für Amerikastudien
JAAC	Journal of Aesthetics and Art Criticism
JAF	Journal of American Folklore
JAH	Journal of American History
Jahresring (Stuttgart)	
JAL	Journal of African Languages (Mich. State)
JAmS	Journal of American Studies
JanL	Janua Linguarum [All Series] (The Hague)
JAOS	Journal of the American Oriental Society
JapQ	Japan Quarterly
JARS	Journal of the Assam Research Society
JAS	Journal of the Acoustical Society
JASB	Journal of the Asiatic Society of Bombay
JAsiat	Journal Asiatique
JASIS	Journal of the American Society for Information Science [Supersedes *AD*]
JASt	Journal of Asian Studies
JATJ	Journal-Newsletter of the Association of Teachers of Japanese
JAUK	Jahrbuch der Albertus Universität zu Königsberg (Würzburg)
JBiRS	Journal of the Bihar Research Society
JBRS	Journal of the Burma Research Society
JBS	Journal of British Studies (Trinity Coll., Hartford, Conn.)
JC	Journal of Communication
JCHAS	Journal of the Cork Historical and Archaeological Society
JCL	Journal of Commonwealth Literature (U. of Leeds)
JCLTA	Journal of the Chinese Language Teachers Assn. (U. of Penn.)
JCS	Journal of Croatian Studies
JCSA	Journal of the Catch Society of America
JCunS	Journal of Cuneiform Studies
JD	Journal of Documentation
JdL	Jornal de Letras
JDSG	Jahrbuch der Deutschen Schiller-Gesellschaft
JEGP	Journal of English and Germanic Philology
JEngL	Journal of English Linguistics
JeuneA	Jeune Afrique (Paris)
Jezik (Zagreb)	
JF	Južnoslovenski Filolog
JFDH	Jahrbuch des Freien Deutschen Hochstifts (Tübingen)
JFI	Journal of the Folklore Institute (Ind. U.)
JFL	Jahrbuch für Fränkische Landesforschung
JGa	Jaunā Gaita (Hamilton, Ont.)
JGE	Journal of General Education
JGG	Jahrbuch der Grillparzer-Gesellschaft
JGJRI	Journal of the Ganganathan Jha Research Inst.
JGLS	Journal of the Gypsy Lore Society
JGWT	Jahrbuch der Gesellschaft für Wiener Theaterforschung

JHE	Journal of Higher Education
JHI	Journal of the History of Ideas
JHS	Journal of Historical Studies
JI	The Japan Interpreter
JIFMC	Journal of the International Folk Music Council (Cambridge, Eng.)
JIG	Jahrbuch für Internationale Germanistik
JIP	Journal of Indian Philosophy
JiS	Jezik in Slovstvo (Ljubljana, Yugoslavia)
JISHS	Journal of the Illinois State Historical Society
JJPG	Jahrbuch der Jean-Paul-Gesellschaft
JJQ	James Joyce Quarterly (U. of Tulsa, Okla.)
JKAHS	Journal of the Kerry Archaeological and Historical Society
JL	Journal of Linguistics (Ling. Assn. of Great Britain)
JLA	Jornal de Letras e Artes (Lisboa)
JLAEA	Journal of the Language Association of Eastern Africa
JLDS	Journal of the Lancashire Dialect Society
JMAS	Journal of Modern African Studies
JML	Journal of Modern Literature
JMM	Journal of the Manx Museum
JMSUB	Journal of the Maharaja Sayajirao U. of Baroda
JNALA	Journal of the New African Literature and the Arts
JNES	Journal of Near Eastern Studies (Chicago)
JNH	Journal of Negro History
JNMD	Journal of Nervous and Mental Diseases
JoA	Jewel of Africa: A Literary and Cultural Magazine from Zambia
JÖBG	Jahrbuch der Österreichischen Byzantinischen Gesellschaft
JoHS	Journal of Hellenic Studies
JOIB	Journal of the Oriental Institute (Baroda)
JOV	Jahrbuch für Ostdeutsche Volkskunde
JP	Journal of Philosophy
JPC	Journal of Popular Culture (Bowling Green U.)
JPNP	Journal de Psychologie Normale et Pathologique
JPol	Język Polski
JPS	Journal of the Polynesian Society (Auckland)
JQ	Journalism Quarterly
JR	Journal of Religion
JRAS	Journal of the Royal Asiatic Society
JRASM	Journal of the Royal Asiatic Society, Malayan Branch
JRG	Jahrbuch der Raabe-Gessellschaft
JRS	Journal of Russian Studies (Formerly ATRJ)
JRSAI	Journal of the Royal Soc. of Antiquaries of Ireland
JRUL	Journal of the Rutgers University Library
JSHD	Journal of Speech and Hearing Disorders
JSHR	Journal of Speech and Hearing Research
JSK	Jahrbuch der Sammlung Kippenberg (Düsseldorf)
JSO	Journal de la Société des Océanistes
JSS	Journal of Semitic Studies (Manchester)
JSSB	Journal of the Siam Society (Bangkok)
JSSR	Journal of the Scientific Study of Religion
JSUB	Jahrbuch der Schlesischen Friedrich-Wilhelm-Universität zu Breslau
JTamS	Journal of Tamil Studies
JTS	Journal of Theological Studies
Judaism	
JVLVB	Journal of Verbal Learning and Verbal Behavior
JWAL	Journal of West African Languages
JWB	Jahrbuch der Wittheit zu Bremen
JWBS	Journal of the Welsh Bibliographical Society
JWCI	Journal of the Warburg and Courtauld Institute
JWGV	Jahrbuch des Wiener Goethe-Vereins
Kadmos	Kadmos: Zeitschrift für Vor- und Frühgriechische Epigraphik
KAL	Kyushu American Literature (Fukuoka, Japan)
Kalbotyra: Lietuvos TSR Aukštųjų Mokyklų Mokslo Darbai (Vilnius)	
Kalki: Studies in James Branch Cabell	
KanoS	Kano Studies (Ahmadu Bello U., No. Nigeria)
KanQ	Kansas Quarterly (Formerly KM)

Karogs (Riga)	
KBAA	Kieler Beiträge zur Anglistik und Amerikanistik
KBB	A[merikas] L[atviešu] A[pvienības] Kultūras Biroja Biletins [Bull. of the Cultural Bureau of the Amer. Latvian Assn. in the U.S.]
KC	Krētika Chronika
KDVS	Kongelige Danske Videnskabernes Selskab. Historisk-Filosofiske Meddelelser (Copenhagen)
KeK	Keiryō Kokugogaku (Mathematical Linguistics)
KerC	Kerkyraïka Chronika
KFQ	Keystone Folklore Quarterly
KFR	Kentucky Folklore Record
KFS	Kentucky Folklore Series
KGS	Kölner Germanistische Studien
KGUAS	Kwansei Gakuin University Annual Studies
Kierunki	
KiJ	Književnost i Jezik
Kivung: Journal of the Ling. Soc. of the U. of Papua and New Guinea	
KJ	Kipling Journal
KjK	Keel ja Kirjandus (Tallinn)
KL	Kypriakos Logos
KN	Kwartalnik Neofilologiczny (Warsaw)
Knji	Književnost (Belgrade)
KnjiNov	Književne Novine (Belgrade)
KnjIst	Književna Istorija
KoJ	Korea Journal
KoK	Kirke og Kultur (Oslo)
Kolo (Zagreb)	
Komma (The Hague)	
Komos: A Quarterly of Drama and Arts of the Theatre	
Kortárs	Irodalmi és Kritikai Folyóirat
KQ	Koreana Quarterly (Seoul)
KR	Kenyon Review
KRA	Kölner Romanistische Arbeiten
Kritik (Copenhagen)	
Kritika (Budapest)	
KRQ	Kentucky Romance Quarterly (Formerly KFLQ)
KSDL	Kieler Studien zur Deutschen Literaturgeschichte
KSGT	Kleine Schriften der Gesellschaft für Theatergeschichte
KSJ	Keats-Shelley Journal
KSMB	Keats-Shelley Memorial Bulletin (Rome)
KSV	Kirjallisuudentutkijain Seuran Vuosikirja (Helsinki)
KSVK	Kalevalaseuran Vuosikirja
KuL	Kunst und Literatur
KulturaP	Kultura (Paris)
KulturaW	Kultura (Warsaw)
KV	Kirkens Verden
KVHAA	Kungl. Vitterhets Historie och Antikvitets Akademiens Handlingar. Filol. -filos. serien
KVNS	Korrespondenzblatt des Vereins für Niederdeutsche Sprachforschung
KyC	Kypriaka Chronika
KyR	The Kentucky Review (U. of Kentucky)
KyS	Kypriakai Spoudai
KŽ	Kultúrny Život (Bratislava)
LA	Linguistica Antverpiensia
LaK	Literatur als Kunst
Landfall	
L&I	Literature and Ideology (Montreal)
L&L	Linguistica et Litteraria
L&P	Literature and Psychology (U. of Hartford)
L&S	Language and Speech
Langages (Paris)	
Lang&S	Language and Style
LangQ	Language Quarterly (U. of South Fla.)
LangS	Language Sciences
Language	
LanM	Les Langues Modernes
Laographia	
LaS	Louisiana Studies
Latinitas (Gregorian U.)	
Latomus	

LATR	Latin American Theater Review
LauR	Laurel Review (West Va. Wesleyan Coll.)
Laurentianum (Rome)	
LavTP	Laval Théologique et Philosophique
LB	Leuvense Bijdragen
LBR	Luso-Brazilian Review
LC	Library Chronicle (U. of Penn.)
LCCP	Linguistic Circle of Canberra Publications
LCrit	Literary Criterion (U. of Mysore, India)
LCUT	Library Chronicle of the U. of Texas
LD	Lituanistikos Darbai: Lituanistikos Instituto Me-traštis (Chicago)
LDAA	Lexikographikon Deltion Akademiãs Athēnōn
LdP	Livros de Portugal
LE&W	Literature East and West
LeedsSE	Leeds Studies in English
Leitura (Rio de Janeiro)	
LenauA	Lenau Almanach: Hrsg. von Internationalen Lenau-Gesellschaft
LenauF	Lenau Forum
LeS	Lingua e Stile (Bologna)
Leshonenu (Tel-Aviv)	
LetN	Lettres Nouvelles
Letras	Letras: Organo de la Facultad de Letras y Ciencias Humanas de la Univ. Nacional Mayor de San Marcos
Letteratura	
Letture	
LF	Listy Filologické
LFr	Langue Française
LGF	Lunder Germanistische Forschungen
LH	Lincoln Herald
LHR	Lock Haven Review (Lock Haven State Coll., Pa.)
LI	Lettere Italiane
LiberianSJ	Liberian Studies Journal
Liberté (Montréal)	
Librarium	
Library	The Library
Libri (Copenhagen)	
Limi (Pretoria)	
LimR	Limba Română (Bucureşti)
LINCS	Language Information Network and Clearinghouse System, Center for Applied Linguistics
LingB	Linguistische Berichte
LingI	Linguistic Inquiry
LingR	Linguistic Reporter (Center for Applied Linguistics)
Lingua (Amsterdam)	
Linguistica (Ljubljana)	
Linguistics	
Linguistique (Paris)	
Literatūra: Lietuvos TSR Aukštųjų Mokyklų Mokslo Darbai (Vilnius)	
LitP	Literature in Perspective
LitR	Literary Review (Fairleigh Dickinson U.)
Lituanus: Lithuanian Quarterly (Chicago)	
LJ	Library Journal
LJb	Luther Jahrbuch
LJGG	Literaturwissenschaftliches Jahrbuch der Görres-Gesellschaft
LK	Literatūra ir Kalba (Vilnius)
LKK	Lietuvių Kalbotyros Klausimai
LL	Language Learning
LLa	Leshonenu La'am
LLBA	Language and Language Behavior Abstracts
Llên Cymru	
LM	Language Monographs
LMAD	Lietuvos TSR Mokslų Akademijos Darbai. Serija A (Vilnius)
LMi	Literaturna Misəl (Sofia)
LMLP	La Monda Lingvo-Problemo
LMS	Letopis Matice Srpske (Novi Sad)
LN	Lingua Nostra
Lochlann: A Review of Celtic Studies (Oslo)	
Looming (Tallinn)	

LP	Lingua Posnaniensis
LR	Les Lettres Romanes
LS	Le Lingue Straniere (Roma)
LSB	Linguistic Survey Bull. (Deccan Coll., Poona)
LSE	Lund Studies in English
LsL	Limbă şi Literatură
LSp	Lebende Sprachen
LSS	Leyte-Samar Studies
LSUSHS	Louisiana State U. Studies, Humanities Series
LT	Levende Talen
LTM	Leeds Texts and Monographs
LUÅ	Lunds Universitets Årsskrift
Luc	Luceafărul (Bucharest)
Lucerna	
LuK	Literatur und Kritik (Wien)
LuL	Literatur und Leben
LuM	Literatura un Māksla
LUR	Pētera Stučkas Latvijas Valsts Univ. Zinātniskie Raksti. Filoloģijas Zinātnes. A Serija (Rīga)
LuW	Literatur und Wirklichkeit
LVKJ	Latviešu Valodas Kultūras Jautājumi
LWU	Literatur in Wissenschaft und Unterricht (Kiel)
LY	Lessing Yearbook
LyC	Lenguaje y Ciencias (Univ. Nacional de Trujillo)
LyP	El Libro el Pueblo
Lyrikvännen (Stockholm)	
LZ	Literaturen Zbor
LZAV	Latvijas PSR Zinātņu Akadēmijas Vēstis (Rīga)
MA	Le Moyen Âge
M-A	Mid-America
Maatstaf (Den Haag)	
MACLCL	Memórias da Academia das Ciências de Lisboa, Classe de Letras
MÆ	Medium Ævum
MAFS	Memoirs of the American Folklore Society
MagN	Magyar Nyelvőr
MAH	Mélanges d'Archéologie et d'Histoire
Mahfil: A Quarterly of South Asian Literature (Mich. State, East Lansing)	
Maia: Rivista di Letterature Classiche	
Makedonika	
MAL	Modern Austrian Literature: Jour. of the Intl. Arthur Schnitzler Research Assn. (Supersedes *JIASRA*)
Man: Jour. of the Royal Anthropological Inst.	
Mana	
M&H	Medievalia et Humanistica (Case Western Reserve U.)
M&L	Music and Letters (London)
Mankind (Sydney)	
ManR	Manchester Review
Manuscripta	
Mapocho (Santiago)	
MAPS	Memoirs of the American Philosophical Society
Marginalien: Blätter der Pirckheimer-Gesellschaft (Berlin)	
Marianum	
MarkhamR	Markham Review
MArt	Mundus Artium (Ohio U.)
Martinella	
MASJ	Midcontinent American Studies Journal
MASO	Meijerbergs Arkiv för Svensk Ordforskning
Mattino (Napoli)	
Mawazo (Kampala)	
MB	Mare Balticum (Hamburg)
MBDL	Munstersche Beiträge zur Deutschen Literatur
MBG	Marburger Beiträge zur Germanistik
MCh	Mikrasiatiki Chronika
MCLB	Modern and Classical Language Bulletin
McNR	McNeese Review (McNeese State Coll., La.)
MD	Modern Drama
MDan	Meddelelser fra Dansklærerforeningen
Meander (Warsaw)	
Meanjin	Meanjin Quarterly (U. of Melbourne)

MelbSS	Melbourne Slavonic Studies
Menabò	Il Menabò di Letteratura (Torino)
Menckeniana	
Merkur	
Messēniaka: Etēsion Periodikon Dēmosieuma	
Metmenys (Chicago)	
Metraštis: Lietuvių Katalikų Mokslo Akademijos Metraštis (Rome)	
MFCG	Mitteilungen und Forschungsbeiträge der Cusanus-Gesellschaft
MFR	Maltese Folklore Review (Balzan)
MfS	Meddelanden från Strindbergssällskapet
MFS	Modern Fiction Studies
MGATC	Modern German Authors, Texts and Contexts
MGB	Münchener Germanistische Beiträge
MGH	Monumenta Germaniae Historica
MGSL	Minas Gerais, Suplemento Literário
MH	Museum Helveticum
MHG	Mitteilungen der E. T. A. Hoffmann-Gesellschaft
MHRADS	Modern Humanities Research Assn. Dissertation Series
MHRev	Malahat Review
MHSB	Missouri Historical Society Bulletin
MichH	Michigan History
MidM	Midwest Monographs
Midway (Chicago)	
MiltonN	Milton Newsletter (Ohio University)
MiltonQ	Milton Quarterly (Formerly *MiltonN*)
MiltonS	Milton Studies
Mind	
MinnR	Minnesota Review
Minos (Salamanca)	
MIO	Mitteilungen des Inst. für Orientforschung der Deutschen Akad. der Wissenschaften zu Berlin
MiscFr	Miscellanea Francescana
MiscMed	Miscellanea Mediaevalia
MissFR	Mississippi Folklore Register
MissQ	Mississippi Quarterly
MitJ	Mittellateinisches Jahrbuch
MJ	Makedonski Jazik
MK	Magyar Könyvszemle
MKNAL	Mededelingen der Koninklijke Nederlandse Akademie, Afdeling Letterkunde
ML	Modern Languages (London)
MLF	Modersmålslärarnas Förening: Årsskrift (Lund)
MLit	Miesięcznik Literacki (Warszawa)
MLJ	Modern Language Journal
MLN	Modern Language Notes
MLQ	Modern Language Quarterly
MLR	Modern Language Review
MLW	Mountain Life and Work
MM	Maal og Minne
MMGS	Melbourne Monographs in Germanic Studies (U. of Melbourne)
MMMSM	Millénaire Monastique du Mont Saint-Michel
MN	Monumenta Nipponica
MNCDN	Mededelingen van de Nijmeegse Centrale voor Dialect- en Naamkunde der Katholieke Universiteit te Nijmegen
Mnemosyne: Bibliotheca Classica Batava	
MNu	Mundo Nuevo (Paris)
MNy	Magyar Nyelv
MNyj	Magyar Nyelvjárások
ModA	Modern Age (Chicago)
ModSp	Moderne Sprachen: Organ des Verbandes des Österreichischen Neuphilologen für Moderne Sprachen, Litteratur, und Pädagogik
Monat	Der Monat
Monatshefte	
Mondo	
Mo'oznayim (Tel Aviv)	
Moreana (Angers)	
Mosaic: A Journal for the Comparative Study of Literature and Ideas	
Moskva	

MOstf	Marburger Ostforschungen
Mosty (Munich)	
Mov	Movoznavstvo (Kiev)
MP	Modern Philology
MPhon	Le Maître Phonétique
MQ	Midwest Quarterly (Pittsburg, Kan.)
MQR	Michigan Quarterly Review
MR	Massachusetts Review (U. of Mass.)
MRD	Memoirs of the Research Dept., Tōyō Bunko (Tokyo)
MRom	Marche Romane
MRR	Mad River Review (Dayton, Ohio)
MS	Mediaeval Studies (Toronto)
MSB	Mongolia Society Bulletin
MScan	Mediaeval Scandinavia
MSE	Massachusetts Studies in English
MSFO	Mémoires de la Société Finno-Ougrienne (Helsinki)
MSNH	Mémoires de la Société Néophilologique de Helsink
MSpr	Moderna Språk (Stockholm)
MSR	Mélanges de Science Religieuse
MSS	Manuscripts
MSt	Monastic Studies
MSzS	Münchener Studien zur Sprachwissenschaft
MT	Mechanical Translation
MTA	A Magyar Tudományos Akadémia Nyelv-és Irodalomtudományi Osztályának Közleményei
MTJ	Mark Twain Journal
MTUDLM	Münchener Texte und Untersuchungen zur Deutschen Literatur des Mittelalters
MTZ	Münchener Theologische Zeitschrift
MuK	Maske und Kothurn (Graz-Wien)
Mulino	
Muséon	Le Muséon. Revue d'Etudes Orientales (Louvain)
Muttersprache	
MVl	Monografieën over Vlaamse Letterkunde (Brussels)
MW	The Muslim World (Hartford, Conn.)
Mythlore (Maywood, Calif.)	
NA	Nuova Antologia
NAA	Narody Azii i Afriki
Nada: Rhodesia Ministry Internal Affairs Annual	
NADS	Newsletter of the American Dialect Society
NALF	Negro American Literature Forum
Names	
N&Q	Notes and Queries
NArg	Nuovi Argomenti
NAS	Norwegian-American Studies (Northfield)
NAWG	Nachrichten von der Akademie der Wissenschaften zu Göttingen. Philol.-hist. Klasse
Nazione (Firenze)	
NB	Namn och Bygd
NBB	Norsk Bibliografisk Bibliotek
NBL	Neue Beiträge zur Literaturwissenschaft
NC	Nuova Corrente
NCarF	North Carolina Folklore
NCF	Nineteenth-Century Fiction
NCHR	North Carolina Historical Review
NCl	Nossos Clássicos
NCRMM	La Nouvelle Critique, Revue du Marxisme Militant
NDH	Neue Deutsche Hefte
NDim	Nuove Dimensioni
NdL	Neudrucke Deutscher Literaturwerke
NDL	Neue Deutscher Literatur
NdM	Niederdeutsche Mitteilungen (Lund)
NDQ	North Dakota Quarterly
NdS	Niederdeutsche Studien
NDV	Notes et Documents Voltaïques
NdW	Niederdeutsches Wort: Kleine Beiträge zur Niederdeutschen Mundart- und Namenkunde
NeaH	Nea Hestia
Nef	La Nef: Cahier Trimestriel
NegroD	Negro Digest
Neo-Hellenika (Austin, Texas)	
Neophil	Neophilologus (Groningen)
NEQ	New England Quarterly

Nerthus   Nerthus: Nordisch-deutsche Beiträge
Nestor (Madison, Wis.)
Neva (Moscow; Leningrad)
NewA   New African
NFS   Nottingham French Studies
NHQ   The New Hungarian Quarterly
NigM   Nigeria Magazine
Nigrizia
NIK   Nyelv-és Irodalomtudományi Közlemények
NJ   Niederdeutsches Jahrbuch
NJe   Naš Jezik (Belgrade)
NK   Nyelvtudományi Közlemények
Nku   Naamkunde (Supersedes *MVNLA*)
NL   Nouvelles Littéraires
NLÅ   Norsk Lítterær Årbok (Oslo)
NLH   New Literary History (U. of Va.)
NLWJ   National Library of Wales Journal
NM   Neuphilologische Mitteilungen
NMQ   New Mexico Quarterly
NMS   Nottingham Medieval Studies
NMW   Notes on Mississippi Writers
NOB   New Orient Bimonthly (Prague)
NOQ   Northwest Ohio Quarterly
Nordelbingen: Beiträge zur Kunst und Kulturgeschichte
NorthernL   Northern Lights (Edmonton)
Novel: A Forum on Fiction (Brown U.)
Novi dni (Detroit)
NovM   Novyj Mir
NovŽ   Novyj Žurnal (New York)
NP   Nea Poreia
NQM   Nuovi Quaderni del Meridione (Palermo)
NRam   New Rambler (Johnson Soc., London)
NRF   Nouvelle Revue Française
NRFH   Nueva Revista de Filología Hispánica (Mexico)
NRM   Nuova Rivista Musicale Italiana (Turin)
NRs   Neue Rundschau
NRS   Nuova Rivista Storica (Roma)
NS   Die Neueren Sprachen
NSammlung   Neue Sammlung
NSAR   Nationalmusei Skriftserie, Analecta Reginensia
NSC   Names in South Carolina
NSE   Norwegian Studies in English
NsM   Neusprachliche Mitteilungen aus Wissenschaft und Praxis
NStem   De Nieuwe Stem
NStv   Narodno Stvaralaštvo. Folklor
NT   Nordisk Tidskrift
NTBB   Nordisk Tidskrift för Bok- och Biblioteksväsen
NTE   Narodna Tvorčist' ta Etnohrafija
NTemp   Nostro Tempo (Napoli)
NTg   De Nieuwe Taalgids
NTM   New Theatre Magazine (Bristol)
NTS   Norsk Tidsskrift for Sprogvidenskap
NTTS   Nordisk Tidskrift for Tale og Stemme
NUm   Narodna Umjetnost (Zagreb)
Numen (Amsterdam)
Nurt: Miesięcznik Społeczno-Kulturalny
NVT   Nieuw Vlaams Tijdschrift
NWZam   New Writing from Zambia
NY   New Yorker
NyA   Nya Argus
NYFQ   New York Folklore Quarterly
NYH   New York History
NysS   Nysvenska Studier
NZMUKS   Naukovyj Zbirnik Museju Ukrajins'koji Kul'tury v Sydnyku
NZSJ   New Zealand Slavonic Journal
OAA   Oeuvres Áfro-Asiatiques
OB   Ord och Bild
Oberon (Tokyo)
Oceania
Ocidente (Lisboa)
OcL   Oceanic Linguistics

OCNA   Ouvrages sur la Culture Nord-Africaine
Odra (Wrocław)
Odù
OE   Oriens Extremus
ÖÅ   Österbotten: Årsbok (Vasa)
ÖGL   Österreich in Geschichte und Literatur (Wien)
OEM   Oxford English Monographs
ÖstO   Österreichische Osthefte (Vienna)
OET   Oxford English Texts
ÖZV   Österreichische Zeitschrift für Volkskunde
OG   Orientalia Gandensia (Ghent)
Ogam: Tradition Celtique (Rennes)
OGK   Onsei Gakkai Kaihô (Bull. of the Phonetic Society of Japan)
OGS   Oxford German Studies
OJCH   Overijssel Jaarboek voor Cultuur en Historie
OJES   Osmania Journal of English Studies
Okt   Oktjabr' (Moscow)
Okyeame
OL   Orbis Litterarum
Onoma
Onomastica (Ukrainian Free Academy of Sciences)
Onomastica (Wrocław)
OnsE   Ons Erfdeel (Rekkem)
Ontmoetingen
OPARI   Occasional Pub. of the African and Afro-American Res. Inst., U. of Texas, Austin
OPL   Osservatore Politico Letterario
OPLLL   Occasional Papers in Language, Literature, and Linguistics (Ohio U.)
Opuscula   Opuscula aus Wissenschaft und Dichtung
Orbis (Louvain)
OrEcon   Oriental Economist
Orient
Orientalia (Roma)
Orizont: Revista a Uniunii Scriitorilor din R. S. Romania
OrP   Orientamenti Pedagogici (Torino)
Orpheus
OS   Orientalia Suecana (Uppsala)
OSP   Oxford Slavonic Papers
Osteuropa (Stuttgart)
OSUTCB   Ohio State U. Theatre Collection Bull.
OUÅ   Ortnamnssällskapets i Uppsala Årsskrift
OUR   Ohio University Review (Athens)
OUSE   Odense University Studies in English
Overland (Melbourne)
Ovyd (Chicago)
OW   Orient/West
PA   Présence Africaine
PAAS   Proceedings of the American Antiquarian Society
PADS   Publication of the American Dialect Society
PAFS   Publications of the American Folklore Society
Paideia (Genova)
PakQ   Pakistan Quarterly (Karachi)
PakR   Pakistan Review
Palaestra
Palaestra (Roma)
Palatina (Milano)
Palatino: Rivista Romana di Cultura
Palestra (Lisbon)
Palimpsest
P&R   Philosophy and Rhetoric (Penn. State U.)
Panorama (Lisboa)
PANPKHL   Polska Akademia Nauk—Oddział w Krakowie, Prace Komisji Historycznoliterackiej
PANPKS   Polska Akademia Nauk—Oddział w Krakowie, Prace Komisji Słowianoznawstwa
PAPS   Proceedings of the American Philosophical Society
Paragone
Parnasso (Helsinki)
Parnassos (Athens)
Paunch (Buffalo, N. Y.)
PBA   Proceedings of the British Academy

PBML	Prague Bulletin of Mathematical Linguistics (Charles U., Praha)
PBSA	Papers of the Bibliographical Society of America
PC	Pensiero Critico
PCP	Pacific Coast Philology
PdD	Probleme der Dichtung
PdP	Parola del Popolo
PE&W	Philosophy East and West (Honolulu)
PeC	Poesia e Critica
PEGS	Publications of the English Goethe Society
PeI	Le Parole e le Idee (Napoli)
PEL	Penguin English Library
Peloponnēsiaka (Athens)	
Pensée	La Pensée: Revue du Rationalisme Moderne
Pergalė (Vilnius)	
Person	The Personalist
Perspective (Wash. U.)	
PerspectiveK	Perspective: A Monthly Digest Published in Pakistan
PF	Pennsylvania Folklife
PFLUS	Pub. de la Fac. des Lettres de l'Univ. de Strasbourg
Philobiblon	
Phoenix (Coll. of Charleston, S. C.)	
PhoenixC	Phoenix: The Classical Assn. of Canada
PhoenixK	Phoenix (Korea U.)
Phonetica	
PhP	Philologikē Protochronia
PhQ	Philosophical Quarterly
PhR	Philosophical Review
PhS	Philosophical Studies
PhSR	Philippine Sociological Review
PHT	Personhistorisk Tidskrift
PHum	Przegląd Humanistyczny
Phylon	
PI	Pagine Istriane
PIL	Papers in Linguistics
PIMSST	Pontifical Inst. of Medieval Studies, Studies and Texts
PJ	Poradnik Językowy (Warsaw)
PJa	Papers on Japan (E. Asian Research Center, Harvard)
PJGG	Philosophisches Jahrbuch der Görres-Gesellschaft (Freiburg; München)
PJL	Philippine Journal of Linguistics
PJLT	Philippine Journal of Language Teaching
PK	Philologikē Kypros
PKy	Pneumatikē Kypros
PL	Pamiętnik Literacki
PLG	Probleme de Lingvistică Generală
PLL	Papers on Language and Literature
PLLP	Polish Literature/Littérature Polonaise
PLPLS-LHS	Proc. Leeds Philosoph. and Lit. Soc., Lit. & Hist. Sect.
PMA	Publications of the Mediaeval Academy
PMASAL	Papers of the Mich. Acad. of Science, Arts, and Letters
PMHB	Pennsylvania Magazine of History and Biography
PMHS	Proceedings of the Massachusetts Historical Society
PMLA: Publications of the Mod. Lang. Assn. of America	
PMS	Perceptual and Motor Skills
PN	Poe Newsletter (Wash. State U.)
PNJHS	Proceedings of the New Jersey Historical Society
Poetica (München)	
Poetik	
PoetryR	Poetry Review (London)
Poezja (Warszawa)	
Polityka (Warszawa)	
PolP	Polish Perspectives
PolR	Polish Review (New York)
Ponte	Il Ponte
PP	Philologica Pragensia
PPeda	Problemi di Pedagogia
PPJ	Prilozi Proučavanju Jezika
PPol	Pensiero Politico

PPR	Philosophy and Phenomenological Research
PProv	Padova e la sua Provincia
PPS	Publications of the Philological Society
PQ	Philological Quarterly (Iowa City)
PR	Partisan Review
PrA	Primer Acto (Madrid)
Prapor (Kharkiv)	
PRCAFL	Pubs. of the Research Center in Anthropology, Folklore, and Linguistics (Ind. U.)
Preuves	
PRF	Publications Romanes et Françaises
Prilozi	Prilozi za Književnost, Jezik, Istoriju i Folklor
Proc	Procellaria
Profil (Oslo)	
Proměny (New York)	
Prose (New York)	
Prospetti	
Proverbium (Helsinki)	
PrS	Prairie Schooner
PS	Pensiero e Scuola
PSA	Papeles de Son Armadans (Mallorca)
PSAS	Papers in International Studies, Africa Series. Ohio U. Center for International Studies
PSEKUT	Paar Sammukest Eesti Kirjanduse Uurimise Teed
PSJ	Philosophical Studies of Japan
PSM	Philippine Studies (Manila)
PSSEAS	Papers in International Studies, Southeast Asia Series. Ohio U. Center for International Studies
PSSHR	Philippine Social Sciences and Humanities Review
PSuQ	Philologische Studien und Quellen
PsychologR	Psychological Review
PsyR	Psychoanalytic Review
PsyRund	Psychologische Rundschau (Göttingen)
PsyS	Psychonomic Science (Austin)
PTFS	Publications of the Texas Folklore Society
PTRSC	Proceedings & Transactions Royal Soc. of Canada
PUASAL	Proceedings of the Utah Academy of Sciences, Arts, & Letters
PULC	Princeton University Library Chronicle
PuW	Poesie und Wissenschaft
PZKA	Philologus: Zeitschrift für Klassische Altertum
QCC	Quaderni di Cultura Contemporanea
QD	Quaderni Dannunziani
QeA	Questo e Altro
QFIAB	Quellen und Forschungen aus Italienischen Archiven und Bibliotheken
QFSK	Quellen und Forschungen zur Sprach- und Kulturgeschichte der Germanischen Völker, N. F.
QH	Quaker History: Bull. of the Friends Hist. Assn.
QIA	Quaderni Ibero-Americani
QJLC	Quarterly Journal of the Library of Congress
QJS	Quarterly Journal of Speech
QNL	Quarterly News Letter (Book Club of California)
QQ	Queen's Quarterly
Quadrant: An Australian Bi-monthly	
Quest (Bombay)	
Questioni	
Raam	
RABM	Revista de Archivos, Bibliotecas y Museos
RAbr	Rivista Abruzzese
RACHSP	Records of the Amer. Cath. Hist. Soc. of Phila.
Rad	Rad Jugoslavenske Akad. Znanosti i Umjetnosti
RagL	Raguaglio Librario
RAL	Research in African Literatures
RALF	Répertoire Analytique de Littérature Française (Bordeaux)
RAM	Revue d'Ascétique et de Mystique
RASIB	Atti dell'Accademia delle Scienze dell'Istituto di Bologna: Rendiconti
RB	Revue Bénédictine
RBF	Revista Brasileira de Folclore
RBPH	Revue Belge de Philologie et d'Histoire
RC	Ruperto-Carola

RCam	Revista Camoniana
RCB	Revista de Cultura Brasileña
RCCM	Rivista di Cultura Classica e Medievale
RCivB	Revista Civilização Brasileira (Rio)
RCSF	Rivista Critica della Storia della Filosofia
RCVS	Rassegna di Cultura e Vita Scolastica
RD	Rivista Dalmata
RdC	Resto del Carlino
RdE	Rivista di Estetica (U. di Padova)
RdEt	Revista de Etnografía
RdF	Rivista di Filosofia (Torino)
RdH	Revista de História
RdL	Revista do Livro
RDM	Revue des Deux Mondes
RdP	Revue de Paris
RdPac	Revista del Pacífico
RdSO	Rivista degli Studi Orientali (Roma)
RDTP	Revista de Dialectología y Tradiciones Populares
RE	La Revue d'Esthétique
REA	Revue des Etudes Augustiniennes
RealM	Realtà del Mezzogiorno
RealN	Realtà Nuova
REAnc	Revue des Etudes Anciennes
REB	Revue des Etudes Byzantines
RechA	Recherches Augustiniennes
RechSR	Recherches de Science Religieuse
RECTR	Restoration and 18th Century Theatre Research
REE	Revista de Estudios Extremeños
REF	Revista de Etnografie și Folclor
REG	Revue des Etudes Grecques
REH	Revista de Estudios Hispánicos
REI	Revue des Etudes Italiennes
REIsl	Revue des Etudes Islamiques
RELat	Revue des Etudes Latines
RELC	*RELC* Journal (Singapore)
Renascence	
RenD	Renaissance Drama (Northwestern U.)
Rendezvous: Journal of Arts and Letters (Idaho State U.)	
Rendiconti (Bologna)	
RENLO	Revue d l'Ecole Nationale des Langues Orientales
RenP	Renaissance Papers
RenQ	Renaissance Quarterly
Rep	Republika (Zagreb)
RES	Review of English Studies
RESEE	Revue des Etudes Sud-est Européennes
RESFV	Renaissance Editions, San Fernando Valley State College
RESl	Revue des Etudes Slaves
ResLit	Respublica Literaria. Studienreihe zur Europäischen Bildungstradition vom Humanismus bis zur Romantik
RET	Revista Española de Teología
RETS	Renaissance English Text Society
RevBib	Revista Bibliotecilor [Library Review]
RevER	Revue des Etudes Roumaines
RevIMA	Review of Indonesian and Malayan Affairs
RevN	La Revue Nouvelle (Paris)
RevR	Revue Romane
Revue (Intl. Organization for Ancient Languages Analysis by Computer)	
RF	Romanische Forschungen
RFE	Revista de Filología Española
RFLUL	Revista da Faculdade de Letras da U. de Lisboa
RFNS	Rivista di Filosofia Neo-Scolastica
RG	Revue Générale (Supersedes *RGB*)
RGB	Revue Générale Belge
RHA	Revue Hittite et Asianique
RHAF	Revue d'Histoire de l'Amérique Française
RHE	Revue d'Histoire Ecclésiastique
RHistM	Römische Historische Mitteilungen
RHL	Revue d'Histoire Littéraire de la France
RHLP	Revista de História Literária de Portugal
RHM	Revista Hispánica Moderna
RHSA	Rev. d'Hist. des Sciences et de Leurs Applications
RHT	Revue d'Histoire du Théâtre
RhV	Rheinische Vierteljahrsblätter
RI	Revista Iberoamericana
RIB	Revista Interamericana di Bibliografía
Ridotto	
RIE	Revista de Ideas Estéticas
RIHGSP	Revista do Inst. Hist. e Geog. de São Paulo
RIJAZUZ	Radovi Inst. Jugoslav. Akad. Znanosti i Umjetnosti u Zadru
RIL	Rendiconti dell'Ist. Lombardo di Scienze e Lettere
Rinascimento	
RIO	Revue Internationale d'Onomastique (Paris)
RIPh	Revue Internationale de Philosophie (Bruxelles)
RISULB	Revue de l'Institut de Sociologie de l'Université Libre de Bruxelles
RITL	Revista de Istorie și Theorie Literară
RJ	Romanistisches Jahrbuch
RJR	Russkij Jazyk za Rubežom
RJŠ	Russkij Jazyk v Škole
RJV	Rheinisches Jahrbuch für Volkskunde
RL	Revista de Literatura
RLA	Revista de Letras da Faculdade de Filosofia Ciências e Letras de Assis
RLC	Revue de Littérature Comparée
RLI	Rassegna della Letteratura Italiana
RLir	Realismo Lirico
RLiR	Revue de Linguistique Romane
RLit	Russkaja Literatura (Leningrad)
RLitC	Readings in Literary Criticism
RLJ	Russian Language Journal (Mich. State, East Lansing)
RLM	La Revue des Lettres Modernes
RLMC	Riv. di Letterature Moderne e Comparate (Firenze)
RLR	Revue des Langues Romanes (Montpellier)
RLS	Regional Language Studies (Newfoundland)
RLV	Revue des Langues Vivantes (Bruxelles)
RLz	Radjans'ke Literaturoznavstvo (Kiev)
RM	Rowohlts Monographien
RMI	Rivista Mensile di Israel
RMM	Revue de Métaphysique et de Morale
RMP	Rheinisches Museum für Philologie
RMS	Renaissance & Modern Studies (U. of Nottingham)
RNar	Ragioni Narrative
RNC	Revista Nacional de Cultura (Caracas)
RNI	Research Notes (Ibadan)
RNL	Review of National Literatures
RNM	Revista Nacional (Montevideo)
RO	Revista de Occidente
RocO	Rocznik Orientalistyczny (Warszawa)
RoH	Rouméliótiko Hēmerologio
RoHum	Roczniki Humanistyczne (Lublin, Poland)
RoLit	România Literară
Romania	
RomN	Romance Notes (U. of N. C.)
RomSl	Romanoslavica
RoR	Romanian Review
RORD	Research Opportunities in Renaissance Drama
RoSlaw	Rocznik Slawistyczny
RP	Revista de Portugal
RPF	Revista Portuguesa de Filologia
RPFilos	Revista Portuguesa de Filosofia
RPh	Romance Philology
RPL	Revue Philosophique de Louvain
RPLHA	Revue de Philologie de Littérature et d'Histoire Anciennes. Troisième Série
RPol	Review of Politics (Notre Dame)
RPP	Review Politique et Parlementaire
RQ	Riverside Quarterly (U. of Saskatchewan)
RQCAK	Römische Quartalschrift für Christliche Altertumskunde und Kirchengeschichte
RR	Romanic Review
RRDS	Regents Renaissance Drama Series

RRestDS — Regents Restoration Drama Series
RRL — Revue Roumaine de Linguistique (Bucharest)
RS — Research Studies (Wash. State U.)
RSBN — Rivista di Studi Bizantini e Neoellenici
RSC — Rivista di Studi Crociani
RSCl — Rivista di Studi Classici
RSH — Revue des Sciences Humaines
RSI — Rivista Storica Italiana
RSl — Ricerche Slavistiche (Roma)
RSLit — Riverside Studies in Literature
RSPT — Revue des Sciences Philosophiques et Théologiques
RSR — Rassegna Storica del Risorgimento
RSV — Revista Signos de Valparaiso
RT — Religious Theatre (Wichita State U.)
RTAM — Recherches de Théologie Ancienne et Médiévale
RThom — Revue Thomiste: Revue Doctrinale de Théologie et Philosophie
RTP — Revue de Théologie et de Philosophie (Genève)
RTSS — Revue Tunisienne de Sciences Sociales (Tunis)
RuchL — Ruch Literacki (Kraków)
RuJ — Ruský Jazyk
Rumo
RUNC — Revista de la Universidad Nacional de Córdoba
RUO — Revue de l'Université d'Ottawa
RUS — Rice University Studies
RUSE — Rutgers University Studies in English
RusR — Russian Review
RusRe — Russkaja Reč'
RUY — Revista de la Universidad de Yucatán
RVF — Revista Venezolana de Folklore
RVV — Romanistische Versuche und Vorarbeiten
RyF — Razón y Fe (Madrid)
RZSF — Radovi Zavoda za Slavensku Filologiju
SA — Studi Americani (Roma)
SAA — Schweizer Anglistische Arbeiten
SAB — South Atlantic Bulletin
SacE — Sacris Eruditi
Saga-Book (Viking Society for Northern Research)
SAH — Svenska Akademiens Handlingar
SAL — Studies in African Linguistics
SAlb — Studia Albanica (Tirana)
Salesianum (Rome)
Salmagundi (Flushing, N. Y.)
SAmL — Studies in American Literature (The Hague)
Samlaren
Samtiden
Sananjalka
S&W — South & West
SAP — Studia Anglica Posnaniensia: An Intl. Rev. of English Studies
Sapienza (Naples)
SAQ — South Atlantic Quarterly
SaS — Slovo a Slovesnost
SATF — Société des Anciens Textes Français
SatR — Saturday Review
SAV — Schweizerisches Archiv für Volkskunde
SAVL — Studien zur Allgemeinen und Vergleichenden Literaturwissenschaft
Savremenik (Belgrade)
SB — Studies in Bibliography: Papers of the Bibliographical Society of the University of Virginia
SBHT — Studies in Burke and His Time (Formerly *The Burke Newsletter*)
SBL — Studies in Black Literature
SBoc — Studi sul Boccaccio
SC — Stendhal-Club
Scan — Scandinavica
SCB — South Central Bulletin
ScEc — Science et Esprit (Formerly *Sciences Ecclésiastiques*)
SCh — Sources Chrétiennes
Schlesien
SchM — Schweizer Monatshefte
SchP — Scholarly Publishing: A Journal for Authors and Publishers

SchR — Schweizer Rundschau
ScI — Scripta Islandica
Science (Washington, D. C.)
SCN — Seventeenth-Century News
SCR — South Carolina Review
SCr — Strumenti Critici (Torino)
SCraneN — Stephen Crane Newsletter
Scriblerian — The Scriblerian: A Newsletter Devoted to Pope, Swift, and Their Circle
Scriptorium
ScS — Scottish Studies (U. of Edinburgh)
SCUL — Soundings: Collections of the Univ. Library, Univ. of California, Santa Barbara
SD — Studi Danteschi
SDAWB — Sitzungsberichte der Deutschen Akad. der Wissenschaften zu Berlin. Sprachen, Lit. und Kunst
SDG — Schriften der Droste-Gesellschaft
SdG — Studii de Gramatica
SDR — South Dakota Review
SE — Slovenski Etnograf
SeAQ — Southeast Asia Quarterly
SeC — Scuola e Cultura nel Mondo
SEEJ — Slavic and East European Journal
SEER — Slavonic and East European Review
Sefárad (Madrid; Barcelona)
Seges (U. of Fribourg)
SEL — Studies in English Literature, 1500–1900
SELit — Studies in English Literature (Eng. Literary Soc. of Japan)
Seminar: A Journal of Germanic Studies (Victoria Coll., Toronto; and Newcastle U., New South Wales)
Semiotica: Revue Publiée par l'Association Internationale de Sémiotique
SeN — Seara Nova
SEngL — Studies in English Literature (The Hague)
SeR — Studi e Ricerche
Serif — The Serif (Kent, Ohio)
Serpe
SerrC — Serraïka Chronika
SeSL — Studi e Saggi Linguistici (Supp. to *ID*)
SF&R — Scholars' Facsimiles and Reprints
SFI — Studi di Filologia Italiana
SFil — Studime Filologjike (Tirane)
SFPS — Studia z Filologii Polskiej i Słowiańskiej
SFQ — Southern Folklore Quarterly
SFr — Studi Francesi
SFran — Studi Francescani
SFrL — Studies in French Literature
SFSS — Svenska Fornskriftssällskapets Skrifter
SFUS — Sovetskoe Finno-Ugrovedenie/Soviet Fenno-Ugric Studies
SFVK — Svenska Folkskolans Vänner: Kalender (Helsingfors)
SG — Studium Generale
SGAK — Studien zur Germanistik, Anglistik und Komparatistik
SGer — Studia Germanica
SGF — Stockholmer Germanistische Forschungen
SGG — Studia Germanica Gandensia
SGh — Studia Ghisleriana (Pavia)
SGL — Studies in German Literature
SGoldoniani — Studi Goldoniani
SGor — Studi Goriziani
SGS — Scottish Gaelic Studies
SGT — Schriften der Gesellschaft für Theatergeschichte
SGym — Siculorum Gymnasium
SH — Studia Hibernica (Dublin)
ShakS — Shakespeare Studies (U. of Cincinnati)
Shavian — The Shavian
ShawR — Shaw Review
SHEH — Stanford Honors Essays in the Humanities
Shêjzat — Shêjzat/Le Pleiadi
Shenandoah
ShN — Shakespeare Newsletter

SHR	Southern Humanities Review
ShS	Shakespeare Survey
ShStud	Shakespeare Studies (Japan)
SI	Svizzera Italiana

Sigma: Revista Trimestrale di Letteratura (Turin)

SIK	Studi Italici (Kyoto)
SIL	Summer Institute of Linguistics
SIL	Studies in Linguistics

Silarus (Salerno)

SILOP	Studies in Linguistics, Occasional Papers

Sinologica: Zeitschrift für Chinesische Kultur und Wissenschaft

SINSU	Skrifter Utg. av Inst. för Nordiska Språk vid Uppsala U.

Sipario

SIR	Studies in Romanticism (Boston U.)

Sixties (Madison, Minn.)

SJ	Silliman Journal
SJA	Southwestern Journal of Anthropology
SJH	Shakespeare-Jahrbuch (Heidelberg)
SjV	Sirp ja Vasar
SJW	Shakespeare-Jahrbuch (Weimar)
SkGgD	Sammlung Kurzer Grammatiken Germanischer Dialekte

Skírnir (Reykjavik)

SL	Studia Linguistica (Lund)

Slavia

SlavR	Slavic Review (Seattle)
SLD	Studia Litteraria (U. of Debrecen)
SLF	Svenska Litteratursällskapet i Finland
SlfÅ	Svensklärarföreningens Årsskrift
SLI	Studi Linguistici Italiani
SLitI	Studies in the Literary Imagination (Ga. State Coll.)
SLJ	Southern Literary Journal
SlOr	Slavia Orientalis
SlovLit	Slovenská Literatúra (Bratislava)
SlovN	Slovenský Národopis

Slovo: Časopis Staroslavenskog Instituta u Zagrebu

SlovP	Slovenské Pohl'ady (Bratislava)
SlR	Slavistična Revija (Ljubljana, Yugoslavia)
SlReč	Slovenská Reč (Bratislava)
SLRJ	Saint Louis University Research Journal of the Graduate School of Arts and Sciences (Supersedes SLQ)
SLSÅ	Svenska Linné-sällskapets Årsskrift (Uppsala)
SLSF	Svenska Landsmål och Svenskt Folkliv (Uppsala)
SLT	Svensk Litteraturtidskrift
SLU	Svenska Litteratursällskapet i Uppsala
SM	Sammlung Metzler
SM	Speech Monographs
SMC	Studies in Medieval Culture (Western Mich. U.)
SMEA	Studi Micenei ed Egeo-Anatolici
SMed	Studi Medievali (Roma)
SML	Statistical Methods in Linguistics (Stockholm)
SMS	Studier i Modern Språkvetenskap
SMSR	Studi e Materiali di Storia della Religioni
SMus	Studia Musicologica (Budapest)
SMV	Studi Mediolatini e Volgari
SN	Studia Neophilologica
SNL	Satire Newsletter (State U. Coll., Oneonta, N. Y.)
SNNTS	Studies in the Novel (North Texas State U.)
SNSS	Skrifter Utg. av. Nämnden för Svensk Språkvård
SO	Symbolae Osloenses
SOÅ	Sydsvenska Ortnamnssällskapets Årsskrift
SocR	Social Research: An International Quarterly

Sodobnost (Ljubljana)

SÖAW	Sitzungsberichte der Österreichischen Akademie der Wissenschaften in Wien. Phil.-hist. Klasse
SoK	Sprog og Kultur (Aarhus)

Solidarity (Manila)

Sophia: Rassegna Critica di Filosofia e Storia della Filosofia

SophiaT	Sophia: Studies in Western Civilization and the Cultural Interaction of East and West (Tokyo)
SoQ	The Southern Quarterly (U. of So. Miss.)
SoR	Southern Review (Louisiana State U.)

SoRA	Southern Review: An Australian Journal of Literary Studies (U. of Adelaide)
SoS	Syn og Segn

Soundings: A Journal of Interdisciplinary Studies (Formerly ChS)

Southerly (Sydney)

SovH	Sovetish Heymland
SovL	Soviet Literature
SovR	Soviet Review

Sowjetstudien

SoWS	Southern Writers Series
SP	Studies in Philology
SpB	Språkliga Bidrag (Lund)
SPCT	Studi e Problemi di Critica Testuale

Speculum

Spf	Sprachforum: Zeitschrift für Angewandte Sprachwissenschaft
SPGL	Studien zur Poetik und Geschichte der Literatur
SPHQ	Swedish Pioneer Historical Quarterly

Spirit: A Magazine of Poetry

SpL	Spiegel der Letteren
SPol	Storia e Politica
SPR	Slavistic Printings and Reprintings

Sprache Die Sprache (Wien)

Sprachmittler	Der Sprachmittler: Informationshefte des Sprachendienstes der Bundeswehr

Sprachpflege (Leipzig)

Spsp	Sprachspiegel: Schweizerische Zeitschrift für die Deutsche Muttersprache
SQ	Shakespeare Quarterly
SR	Sewanee Review
SRAZ	Studia Romanica et Anglica Zagrabiensia
SRen	Studies in the Renaissance
SRO	Shakespearean Research Opportunities: The Report of the MLA Conference (Riverside: Dept. of Eng., U. of Calif.)
SRo	Studi Romani
SS	Scandinavian Studies
SSASH	Studia Slavica Academiae Scientiarum Hungaricae
SSAWL	Sitzungsberichte der Sächsischen Akademie der Wissenschaften zu Leipzig
SSb	Skandinavskij Sbornik (Tallinn)
SSe	Studi Secenteschi
SSEÅ	Sankt Eriks Årsbok
SSEL	Stockholm Studies in English Literature
SSF	Studies in Short Fiction (Newberry Coll., S. C.)
SSG	Schriften der Theodor-Storm-Gesellschaft
SSGS	Stanford Studies in Germanics and Slavics
SSI	Social Science Information
SSl	Scando-Slavica (Copenhagen)
SSL	Studies in Scottish Literature (U. of S. Car.)
SSLL	Stanford Studies in Language and Literature
SSLSN	Skrifter Utgivna av Svenska Litteratursällskapet. Studier i Nordisk Filologi
SSO	Studier fra Sprog- og Oldtidsforskning
ST	Studi Tassiani

Standpunte

Stasinos

StC	Studia Celtica
StCau	Studia Caucasica
StCL	Studii si Cercetări Lingvistice

Steaua

STeol	Studii Teologice
STFM	Société des Textes Français Modernes
Stgr	Studia Grammatica
StI	Studia Islandica
StIsl	Studia Islamica
StIsp	Studi Ispanici (Milano)
StJb	Stifter-Jahrbuch
StL	Studies on the Left (New York)
StM	Studia Monastica
StMed	Studia Mediewistyczne
STr	Studi Trentini di Scienze Storiche

Streven (Amsterdam)

STS	Scottish Text Society
StTh	Studia Theologica: Scandinavian Journal of Theology
Studiekamraten (Lund)	
Studies (Dublin)	
Studium	
Style (U. of Arkansas)	
Sučasnist' (Munich)	
SuD	Sprache und Dichtung
Sudetenland	
SüdoA	Südostdeutsches Archiv
SuF	Sinn und Form
SuG	Sprache und Gemeinschaft
SuL	Sprache und Literatur
Sur	
Survey	
SUS	Susquehanna University Studies (Selinsgrove, Pa.)
SUSFL	Studi Urbinati di Storia, Filosofia e Letteratura
SuSuV	Suomalainen Suomi: Kulttuuripolitttinen Aika-kauskirja/Valvoja (Beginning in 1969, *Valvoja* merged with *SuSu*)
SUVSL	Skrifter Utgivna av Vetenskaps-societeten i Lund
SV	Schweizer Volkskunde
SVEC	Studies on Voltaire and the Eighteenth Century
Svitannja	
Swahili	
SWR	Southwest Review
SWS	Southwest Writers Series
SXX	Secolul XX
Symposium	
Synthese (Dordrecht, Holland)	
Synthèses (Paris; Bruxelles)	
Syria: Revue d'Art Orientale et d'Archéologie	
SZ	Stimmen der Zeit
SzDL	Studien zur Deutschen Literatur
SzEP	Studien zur Englischen Philologie
Szinház	Szinház: Theatre, the Journal of the Institute of Theatrical Arts
SzL	Schriften zur Literatur
SzT	Schriften zur Theaterwissenschaft
TA	Theater Annual
TAI	T.A. Informations (U. of Ala.)
TamR	Tamarack Review (Toronto)
TASJ	Transactions of the Asiatic Society of Japan
TB	Tempo Brasileiro
TC	Twentieth Century
TCBS	Transactions of the Cambridge Bibliog. Soc.
TCI	Twentieth Century Interpretations
TCL	Twentieth Century Literature
TCV	Twentieth Century Views
TD	Theatre Documentation
TDR	The Drama Review [formerly Tulane Drama Review]
TE	Teología Espiritual
TEAS	Twayne's English Author Series
TelQ	Tel Quel
TeM	O Tempo e o Modo
Tenggara	
TeR	Te Reo
TeT	Taal en Tongval (Antwerpen)
Textus: Annual of the Hebrew University Bible Project	
TFSB	Tennessee Folklore Society Bulletin
TGSG	Transactions of the Gaelic Soc. of Glasgow
TGSI	Transactions of the Gaelic Soc. of Inverness
Theoria: A Journal of Studies in the Arts, Humanities and Social Sciences	
Thēsaurismata	
Thesaurus: Boletín del Instituto Caro y Cuervo	
These (N.Y.U.)	
THJCS	Tsing Hua Journal of Chinese Studies
Thoth (Dept. of English, Syracuse U.)	
Thought	
THQ	Tennessee Historical Quarterly
ThR	Theatre Research
THR	Travaux d'Humanisme et Renaissance
Thrakika	
ThS	Theatre Survey (Amer. Soc. for Theatre Research)
THSC	Transactions of the Hon. Soc. of Cymmrodorion
TICOJ	Trans. of the Internat. Conf. of Orientalists in Japan
Tiden	
Tilts	
Tirade (Antwerp)	
TITL	Tijdschrift van het Institut voor Toegepaste Linguistiek Leuven
TJQ	Thoreau Journal Quarterly
TkR	Tamkang Review
Tlalocan (Mexico)	
TLF	Textes Littéraires Français
TLL	Travaux de Linguistique et de Littérature Publiés par le Centre de Philologie et de Littératures Romanes de l'Université de Strasbourg
TLP	Travaux Linguistiques de Prague
TLS	[London] Times Literary Supplement
TM	Temps Modernes
TN	Theatre Notebook
TNTL	Tijdschr. voor Ned. Taal- en Letterkunde (Leiden)
Topic (Washington and Jefferson Coll.)	
Torre	La Torre
TP	Terzo Programma (Roma)
TPA	T'oung Pao Archives
TPJ	Tennessee Poetry Journal
TPr	Tempo Presente
TPS	Trans. of the Philological Soc. (London)
TQ	Texas Quarterly (U. of Texas)
Traditio	
Tradition: A Jour. of Orthodox Jewish Thought	
Transition	
Trimestre (Pescara)	
Tripeiro	O Tripeiro (Porto)
TriQ	Tri-Quarterly (Evanston, Ill.)
Triveni: Journal of Indian Renaissance	
Trivium (St. David's Coll., Lampeter, Cardiganshire, Wales)	
TSA	Teater SA: Quarterly for South African Theater
TSB	Thoreau Society Bulletin
TSBooklet	Thoreau Society Booklet
TSE	Tulane Studies in English
TSL	Tennessee Studies in Literature
TSLL	Texas Studies in Literature and Language
TSM	Texte des Späten Mittelalters
TSRLL	Tulane Studies in Romance Languages and Literature
TTrA	Textes et Traitement Automatique
TUD	Trudy Universiteta Družby Narodov Imeni Patrisa Lumumby
TUGAL	Texte und Untersuchungen zur Geschichte der Altchristlichen Literatur
TuK	Text und Kritik
Tulimuld (Lund)	
TUSAS	Twayne's United States Authors Series
TV	Treji Vārti
TvL	Tydskrif vir Letterkunde
TVUB	Tijdschrift van de Vrije Universiteit van Brussel
Tw	Twórczość
TWA	Trans. of the Wis. Acad. of Sciences, Arts, and Letters
TWAS	Twayne's World Authors Series
TYDS	Transactions of the Yorkshire Dialect Society
TygP	Tygodnik Powszechny
UA	United Asia
UAJ	Ural-Altaische Jahrbücher
UCDPE	U. of Calif., Davis, Pubs. in English
UCPES	U. of Calif. Pubs., English Studies
UCPFS	U. of Calif. Pubs., Folklore Studies
UCPL	U. of Calif. Pubs. in Linguistics
UCPMP	U. of Calif. Pubs. in Modern Philology
UCQ	University College Quarterly
UCR	University of Ceylon Review
UCSLL	U. of Colo. Studies in Lang. and Lit.

UCTSE   University of Cape Town Studies in English

UDL   Untersuchungen zur Deutschen Literaturgeschichte

UdLH   Universidad de La Habana

UDQ   University of Denver Quarterly

UDR   University of Dayton Review

UeL   Uomini e Libro

UES   Unisa English Studies

UF   Ulster Folklife (Belfast)

Ufahamu: Journal of the African Activist Assn.

UFMH   U. of Fla. Monographs, Humanities Series

UGM   U. of Georgia Monographs

Új Í   Új Írás: Irodalmi, Művészeti és Kritikai Folyóirat

UKPHS   U. of Kansas Pubs., Humanistic Studies

UkrM   Ukrajins'ka Mova i Literatura v Školi

UkrR   Ukrainian Review

Ulisse

ULR   University of Leeds Review

ULz   Ukrajins'ke Literaturoznavstvo

Umanesimo (U. of Md.)

UMCMP   U. of Mich. Contributions in Modern Philology

UMPAW   U. of Minn. Pamphlets on American Writers

UMPEAL   U. of Miami Pubs. in Eng. and Amer. Lit.

UMSE   U. of Mississippi Studies in English

UNCSCL   U. of N. C. Studies in Comparative Lit.

UNCSGLL   U. of N. C. Studies in Germanic Langs. and Lits.

UNCSRLL   U. of N. C. Studies in Romance Langs. and Lits.

Unilit (Secunderabad)

Unitas (Manila)

Univ   Universitas (Stuttgart)

UNNUS   Uralic News and Notes from the United States

UNS   University of Nebraska Studies

Unterrichtspraxis   Die Unterrichtspraxis

UPAL   Utrechtse Publikaties voor Algemene Literatuurwetenschap

UPB   Universidad Pontificia Bolivariana

UPMFF   University of Pennsylvania Monographs in Folklore and Folklife

UPSEELL   U. of Pa. Studies in East Eur. Langs. and Lits.

UQ   Ukrainian Quarterly: Journal of East European and Asian Affairs

UR   University Review (Kansas City, Mo.)

Urbe (Roma)

URev   University Review (Dublin)

UTDEMS   University of Tulsa Dept. of Eng. Monograph Ser.

UTFS   University of Toronto French Series

UTQ   University of Toronto Quarterly

UWPLL   U. of Wash. Pubs. in Lang. and Lit.

UWR   University of Windsor Review (Windsor, Ontario)

UZKGPI   Učenye Zapiski Kujbyševskogo Gosudarstvennogo Pedagogičeskogo Instituta im. V. V. Kujbyševa

Varaviksne

Vår Lösen: Kristen Kulturtidskrift (Uppsala)

VC   Virginia Cavalcade

VDASD   Veröffentlichungen der Deutschen Akademie für Sprache und Dichtung

VDS   Veröffentlichungen der Deutschen Schillergesellschaft

Veltro (Roma)

Ventures: Magazine of the Yale Graduate School

VeP   Vita e Pensiero

Verbum (Rio de Janeiro)

Verge (Baguio City)

Verri

Vértice (Lisboa)

VF   Voprosy Filologii

VGIEMTP   Veröffentlichungen des Grabmann Instituts zur Erforschung der Mittelalterlichen Theologie und Philosophie

VidaL   Vida Literaria

VIDSL   Veröffentlichungen d. Inst. f. Deutsche Sprache u. Lit. der Deutschen Akad. der Wissenschaften zu Berlin

VIDV   Veröffentlichungen d. Inst. für Deutsche Volkskunde der Deutschen Akad. der Wissenschaften zu Berlin

VigC   Vigiliae Christianae: A Review of Early Christian Life and Language

Vindrosen (Copenhagen)

Vinduet (Oslo)

Vir   Virittäjä: Revue de Kotikielen Seura (Société pour l'Etude de la Langue Maternelle)

ViR   Viaţa Românească (Bucharest)

VIS   Veröffentlichungen d. Inst. f. Slawistik der Deutschen Akad. zu Berlin

Vilčyzna (Kyjiv [Kiev])

Vivarium

VJa   Voprosy Jazykoznanija (Moscow)

VKR   Voprosy Kul'tury Reči

VlG   De Vlaamse Gids

VLIR   Valodas un Literatūras Institūta Raksti (Latvijas PSR Zinātņu Akadēmija, Rīga)

VLit   Voprosy Literatury

VLU   Vestnik Leningradskogo U. Ser. Istorii, Jazyka i Literatury

VMB   Vandringar Med Böcker (Lund)

VMHB   Virginia Magazine of History and Biography

VMKVA   Verslagen en Mededelingen van de Koninklijke Vlaamse Academie voor Taal- en Letterkunde

VMU   Vestnik Moskovskogo U. Ser. VII. Filologija, Žurnalistika

VN   Victorian Newsletter

VOEI   Veröffentlichungen der Abteilung für Slavische Sprachen und Literaturen des Osteuropa-Inst. (Slavisches Seminar) an der Freien Univ. Berlin

Volkskunde (Amsterdam)

VP   Victorian Poetry (W. Va. U.)

VPN   Victorian Periodicals Newsletter

VQ   Visvabharati Quarterly

VQR   Virginia Quarterly Review

VR   Vox Romanica

VS   Victorian Studies (Ind. U.)

VSL   Vetenskaps-societeten i Lund

VSLÅ   Vetenskaps-societeten i Lund Årsbok

VULT   Voprosy Uzbekskogo Jazyka i Literatury

VyV   Verdad y Vida (Milan)

WA   West Africa

WAL   Western American Literature

WALMS   West African Language Monograph Series

WascanaR   Wascana Review (Regina, Sask.)

WB   Weimarer Beiträge

WBEP   Wiener Beiträge zur Englischen Philologie

WC   Wordsworth Circle

WelshHR   Welsh History Review

Westerly (U. of W. Australia)

WF   Western Folklore

WGCR   West Georgia College Review

WHR   Western Humanities Review

WI   Die Welt des Islams

Więź (Warsaw)

WMH   Wisconsin Magazine of History

WMQ   William and Mary Quarterly

WN   A Wake Newslitter (Newcastle U. Coll., N.S.W.)

WO   Die Welt des Orients

Word

WordW   Word Watching (Formerly *WSt*)

WPL   Working Papers in Linguistics (Ohio State U.)

WPLUH   Working Papers in Linguistics, U. of Hawaii

WPQ   Western Political Quarterly (U. of Utah)

WR   Western Review: A Journal of the Humanities

WSJ   Wiener Slawistisches Jahrbuch

WSl   Die Welt der Slaven (Wiesbaden)

Wsp   Współczesność (Warsaw)

WT   Wetenschappelijke Tijdingen

WTW   Writers and Their Work

WuW   Welt und Wort

WVH   West Virginia History

WVUPP   West Virginia University Philological Papers

WW	Wirkendes Wort
WWR	Walt Whitman Review
WZPHP	Wissenschaftliche Zeitschrift der Pädagogischen Hochschule Potsdam. Gesellschafts- u. Sprach-wissenschaftliche Reihe
WZUB	Wissenschaftliche Zeitschrift der Humboldt-Universität zu Berlin. Gesellschafts- u. Sprachwissenschaftliche Reihe
WZUG	Wissenschaftliche Zeitschrift der Ernst Moritz Arndt-Universität Greifswald
WZUH	Wissenschaftliche Zeitschrift der Martin-Luther Universität Halle-Wittenberg. Gesellschafts- u. Sprachwissenschaftliche Reihe
WZUJ	Wissenschaftliche Zeitschrift der Friedrich-Schiller-Universität Jena. Gesellschafts- u. Sprachwissen-schaftliche Reihe
WZUL	Wissenschaftliche Zeitschrift der Karl-Marx-Universität Leipzig. Gesellschafts- u. Sprachwissen-schaftliche Reihe
WZUR	Wissenschaftliche Zeitschrift der U. Rostock
XH	Xerogrammata Hochschulschriften
XUS	Xavier University Studies
YCGL	Yearbook of Comparative and General Literature
YFS	Yale French Studies
YGS	Yale Germanic Studies
YIFMC	Yearbook of the International Folk Music Council
YR	Yale Review
Yr Eurgrawn	(Sir Fflint, Wales)
YS	Yidishe Shprakh
YSE	Yale Studies in English
YTELSA	Yearbook of the Estonian Learned Society in America
Y Traethodydd	(Caernarvon)
YULG	Yale University Library Gazette
YWES	Year's Work in English Studies
YWMLS	Year's Work in Modern Language Studies
ZAA	Zeitschrift für Anglistik und Amerikanistik (East Berlin)
Zambezia (Salisbury, Rhodesia)	
ZAVA	Zeitschrift für Assyriologie und Vorderasiatische Archäologie

ZB	Zeitschrift für Balkanologie
ZBDLG	Zürcher Beiträge zur Deutschen Literatur- und Geistesgeschichte
ZBDSS	Zürcher Beiträge zur Deutschen Sprach- und Stilgeschichte
ZCP	Zeitschrift für Celtische Philologie (Tübingen)
ZDA	Zeitschrift für Deutsches Altertum und Deutsch Literatur
ZDL	Zeitschrift für Dialektologie und Linguistik (Supersedes *ZMF*)
ZDMG	Zeitschrift der Deutschen Morgenländischen Gesellschaft
ZDP	Zeitschrift für Deutsche Philologie (Berlin-Bielefeld München)
ZDS	Zeitschrift für Deutsche Sprache
ZED	Zur Erkenntnis der Dichtung (München)
ZFL	Zbornik za Filologiju i Lingvistiku
ZFSL	Zeitschrift für Französische Sprache und Literatur
ZIK	Zbornik Istorije Književnosti
ZKJ	Zbornik za Književnost i Jezik
ŽLit	Życie Literackie (Kraków)
ZMF	Zeitschrift für Mundartforschung
Znak (Kraków)	
Znamja (Moscow)	
ZNTŠ	Zapysky Naukovoho Tovarystva Imeny Švečenka (Ling. Series)
ZNTŠL	Zapysky Naukovoho Tovarystva Imeny Ševčenka (Lit. Series)
ZPSK	Zeitschrift für Phonetik, Sprachwissenschaft und Kommunikationsforschung
ZR	Zadarska Revija
ZRG	Zeitschrift für Religions- und Geistesgeschichte
ZRP	Zeischrift für Romanische Philologie (Halle)
ZRTLS	Zwolse Reeks van Taal- en Letterkundige Studies
ZS	Zeitschrift für Slawistik (Berlin)
ZSP	Zeitschrift für Slavische Philologie
Zuka: A Journal of East African Creative Writing	
ZV	Zeitschrift für Volkskunde
Zvezda (Moscow; Leningrad)	
ZVS	Zeitschrift für Verlgeichende Sprachforschung
ŽA	Živa Antika

FESTSCHRIFTEN AND OTHER ANALYZED COLLECTIONS

General

1. *Annual Reports of Studies.* Vol. 20. Kyoto: Doshisha Women's College of Liberal Arts, 1969.

2. Baldner, Ralph W.,ed. *Proceedings:Pacific Northwest Conference on Foreign Languages, Twenty-First Annual Meeting, April 3–4, 1970.* Victoria, B.C.: U. of Victoria.

3. Banašević, Nikola,ed. *Actes du Vᵉ Congrès de l'Association Internationale de Littérature Comparée, Belgrade 1967.* Belgrade: U. de Belgrade; Amsterdam: Swets & Zeitlinger, 1969.

4. Boumboulidis, Phaidon K., and Maria G. Nystazopoulou, eds. *Praktika Tritou Panioniou Syndedriou, 23–29 Septembriou, 1965.* Vol. 2. En Athinais, 1969.

5. Bregenzer, Josef, and Hans Jörg Schweizer,eds. *Sodalitas Florhofiana. Festgabe für Professor Heinz Haffter zum fünfundsechzigsten Geburtstag am 1. Juni 1970.* Zürich: Juris. [Josef Bregenzer, "Bibliographie Prof. Dr. Heinz Haffter," 3–11.]

6. Bubner, Rüdiger, Konrad Cramer, and Reiner Wiehl,eds. *Hermeneutik und Dialektik:Hans Georg Gadamer zum 70. Geburtstag.* 2 vols. Tübingen: Mohr.

7. *Bull. of the Faculty of Humanities, The Seikei University* 5. Musashino City, Tokyo: Seikei U., 1969.

8. Burelbach, Frederick M.,Jr.,ed. *Proceedings:Computer Applications to Problems in the Humanities. A Conversation in the Disciplines.* April 4–5, 1969. Brockport: State U. of New York. [Frederick M. Burelbach,Jr., "Introduction," 1–4.]

9. Cameron, Angus, Roberta Frank, and John Leyerle,eds. *Computers and Old English Concordances.* Toronto: U. of Toronto P. [Proc. of a Conference.]

10. Chania, Crete. Philologikos Syllogos "Ho Chrysostomos." *Pepragmena tou B´ Diethnous Krētologikou Synedriou.* Vol. 4. En Athēnais, 1969.

11. Chiarini, Paolo,et al.,eds. *Miscellanea di studi in onore di Bonaventura Tecchi.* 2 Vols. Roma: Edizioni dell'Ateneo, 1969.

12. *The Child's Part.* YFS 43(1969). [Children's lit., mostly Fr. and Eng.]

13. Cohen, David,ed. *Mélanges Marcel Cohen:Etudes de linguistique, éthnographie et sciences connexes offertes par ses amis et ses élèves à l'occasion de son 80ème anniversaire.* (JanL, Ser. maior 27.) The Hague: Mouton. [Incl. 10 prev. uned. arts. by Marcel Cohen.]

14. *Collected Essays by the Members of the Faculty.* No. 13. Kyoritsu, Japan: Kyoritsu Women's Junior College, 1969.

15. Cormier, Raymond J., and Urban T. Holmes,eds. *Essays in Honor of Louis Francis Solano.* Chapel Hill: U. of N.C. Press.

16. Creed, Howard,ed. *Essays in Honor of Richebourg Gaillard McWilliams.* With pref. Birmingham, Ala.: Birmingham-Southern Coll. [Spec. issue of *Birmingham-Southern Coll. Bull.* 63,ii; "Check-List of Publications of Richebourg Gaillard McWilliams, 1935–1970," ix.]

17. Dube, Werner,et al.,eds. *Über Bücher, Bibliotheken und Leser:Gesammelte Beiträge zum 60. Geburtstag von Horst Kunze. Zentralblatt für Bibliothekswesen.* Beiheft 86. Leipzig: VEB Bibliog. Inst., 1969.

18. Dwivedi, R.C.,ed. *Principles of Literary Criticism in Sanskrit.* Delhi: Motilal Banarsidass, 1969.

19. Friedman, Melvin J.,ed. *The Vision Obscured:Perceptions of Some Twentieth-Century Catholic Novelists.* New York: Fordham U.P. [With introd.]

20. Friedrich, Carl-Joachim, and Benno Reifenberg,eds. *Sprache und Politik:Festgabe für Dolf Sternberger zum sechzigsten Geburtstag.* Heidelberg: Schneider, 1968. ["Auswahlbibliographie" der Schriften und Aufsätze Dolf Sternbergers, 537–45.]

21. Goetze, Albrecht, and Günther Pflaum,eds. *Vergleichen und Verändern. Festschrift für Helmut Motekat.* München: Hueber. ["Bibliographie Helmut Motekat," 397–400.]

22. Goody, Jack,ed. *Literacy in Traditional Societies.* With introd. Cambridge: Cambridge U.P., 1968.

23. Grayburn, William F.,ed. *Studies in the Humanities.* 1,ii. Indiana: Indiana U. of Pa.

24. Greimas, A.J., R. Jakobson, M.R. Mayenowa, S.K. Saumjan, W. Steinitz, and S. Żołkiewski,eds. *Sign. Language. Culture; Signe. Langage. Culture; Znak. Język. Kultura; Znak. Jazyk. Kul'tura.* (JanL, Ser. maior 1.) The Hague: Mouton.

25. Henderson, Kathryn L.,ed. *Trends in American Publishing.* (Allerton Park Inst. 14.) Papers Presented at an Inst. Conducted by the U. of Ill. Grad. School of Lib. Science, Nov. 5–8, 1967. Champaign: U. of Ill. Grad. School of Lib. Science, 1968. [Kathryn L. Henderson, "Foreword," v–ix.]

26. Hornung, Herwig H.,ed. *Disputationes ad montium vocabula aliorumque nominum significationes pertinentes.* Proceedings of the Tenth International Congress of Onomastic Sciences. 2 vols. Wien: Verlag der Wiener Medizinischen Akademie, 1969.

27. Jost, François. *Essais de littérature comparée.* II:*Europeana, première série.* Fribourg: Eds. univs.; Urbana: U. of Ill. P., 1968.

28. Kahn, Robert L.,ed. *Studies in German:In Memory of Andrew Louis. RUS* 55,iii. Houston, Texas: Rice U., 1969. [Robert L. Kahn, "In Memoriam Andrew Louis," [i]–[ii].]

29. Krauss, W.,et al.,eds. *Slawisch-deutsche Weschselbeziehungen in Sprache, Literatur und Kultur. (Hans Holm Bielfeldt zum 60. Geburtstag.)* Berlin: Akademie-Verlag, 1969. ["Verzeichnis der Veröffentlichungen von Hans Holm Bielfeldt," zusammengestellt von Heinz Pohrt, ix–xx.]

30. Kreuzer, Helmut, and Käte Hamburger,eds. *Gestaltungsgeschichte und Gesellschaftsgeschichte. Literatur-, kunst- und musikwissenschaftliche Studien. Fritz Martini zum 60. Geburtstag.* Stuttgart: Metzler, 1969.

31. Lawrenson, T.E., F.E. Sutcliffe, and G.F.A. Gadoffre,eds. *Modern Miscellany Presented to Eugène Vinaver by Pupils, Colleagues, and Friends.* Manchester: Manchester U.P.; New York: Barnes & Noble, 1969. [T.E. Lawrenson, "Foreword," v–vi; "Select Bibliography of the Works of Eugène Vinaver," ix–xiii.]

32. Lundkvist, Artur. *Utflykter med utländska författare.* Stockholm: Bonniers, [1969].

33. Mews, Siegfried,ed. *Studies in German Literature of the Nineteenth and Twentieth Centuries:Festschrift for Frederic E. Coenen.* (UNCSGLL 67.) Chapel Hill: U. of N.C. Press.

34. Porqueras Mayo, Albert, and Carlos Rojas,eds. *Filología y crítica hispánica:Homenaje al Prof. Federico Sánchez Escribano.* Madrid: Ediciones Alcalá; Atlanta, Ga.: Emory U., 1969.

35. *The Promise of English.* NCTE 1970 Distinguished Lectures. Champaign, Ill.: NCTE. [James E. Miller,Jr., "Foreword," vii.]

36. Ramseger, Georg, and Werner Schoenicke,eds. *Das Buch zwischen gestern und morgen. Zeichen und Aspekte. Georg von Holtzbrinck zum 11. Mai 1969.* Stuttgart: Deutscher Bücherbund, 1969.

37. Sammons, Jeffrey L., and Ernst Schürer,eds. *Lebendige Form:Interpretationen zur deutschen Literatur. Festschrift für Heinrich E.K. Henel.* München: Fink.

38. Scholes, Robert,ed. *The Philosopher-Critic.* (UTDEMS 10.) Tulsa, Okla.: U. of Tulsa.

39. Schou, Søren,ed. *60'ernes danske kritik:En antologi.* (Munksgaardserien 33.) Copenhagen: Munksgaard. ["Forord," 9–16.]

40. *Sociologie de la littérature:Recherches récentes et discussions. Rev. de l'Inst. de Sociologie*(U. Libre de Bruxelles) 3(1969). Spec. Issue.

41. *Studî offerti a Mirko Deanović.* (*BALM* 10–12.) Firenze: Olschki. ["Bibliografia di M. Deanović," xii–xv.]

42. Thani Nayagam, X.S., V.I. Subramoniam, L.P. Ramanathan, S. Arasaratnam, R.E. Asher, Rama Subbiah, and S. Singaravelu,eds. *Proceedings of the First International Conference Seminar of Tamil Studies.* Kuala Lumpur: Dept. of Indian Studies, U. of Malaya, 1968–69.

43. Zyla, Wolodymyr T.,ed. *Proceedings of the Comparative Literature Symposium.*Vol. III:*From Surrealism to the Absurd.* 29–30 January 1970. Lubbock: Interdept. Comm. on Comp. Lit., Texas Tech. U. [In Memoriam Dr. William Gillis. Dedicated to Samuel Beckett. Wolodymyr T. Zyla, "Preface," 1–9.]

English

44. Arinštejn, L.M.,et al.,eds. *Problemy obščego jazykoznanija i anglijskoj filologii.* (Kalinin. gos. pedag. inst., Učenye zapiski 64, vyp. 1, čast' 2.) Kalinin: Kalinin. gos. pedag. inst., 1969.

45. *Banasthali Patrika.* Special No. on Indo-English Literature [Supplement]. 5,xiii. Ed. Rameshwar Gupta. Rajasthan, India: Banasthali Vidyapith, 1969.

46. Blistein, Elmer M.,ed. *The Drama of the Renaissance: Essays for Leicester Bradner.* Providence, R.I.: Brown U.P. [Elmer M. Blistein, "Foreword," vii–xiii; "Bibliography of Leicester Bradner," 197–99.]

47. Broughton, Bradford B.,ed. *Twenty-Seven to One:A Potpourri of Humanistic Material Presented to Dr. Donald Gale Stillman on the Occasion of His Retirement from Clarkson College of Technology by Members of the Liberal Studies—Humanities Department Staff, 1949–1970.* Foreword John W. Graham,Jr. Ogdensburg, N.Y.: Ryan Press, Inc.

48. Brower, Reuben A.,ed. *Forms of Lyric:Selected Papers from the English Institute.* (EIE.) With Foreword. New York: Columbia U.P.

49. Gil'dina, Z.M., R.È. Gotxarde, and Z.P. Dorofeeva,eds. *Problemy lingvistiki i zarubežnoj literatury.* Riga: Zinatne, 1968.

50. Goodwin, K.L.,ed. *National Identity:Papers Delivered at the Commonwealth Literature Conference, University of Queensland, Brisbane, 9th–15th August, 1968.* London and Melbourne: Heinemann. [A. Norman Jeffares, "Introduction," ix–xvi.]

51. Kaul, R.K., K.N. Bakaya, and J.L. Banerji,eds. *University of Rajasthan Studies in English.* No. IV. Jaipur: U. of Rajasthan Dept. of Eng., 1969.

52. Kolb, Eduard, and Jörg Hasler,eds. *Festschrift Rudolf Stamm zu seinem sechzigsten Geburtstag.* Bern: Francke, 1969.

53. Orel, Harold, and George J. Worth,eds. *The Nineteenth-Century Writer and His Audience:Selected Problems in Theory, Form, and Content.* (UKPHS 40.) Lawrence: U. of Kan., 1969.

54. Rosier, James L.,ed. *Philological Essays:Studies in Old and Middle English Language and Literature in Honour of Herbert Dean Meritt.* (JanL, Ser. maior 37.) The Hague: Mouton.

55. Rothstein, Eric, and Richard N. Ringler,eds. *Literary Monographs* II. Madison: U. of Wis. P., 1969.

56. Watson, George,ed. *Literary English Since Shakespeare.* London: Oxford U.P.

American

57. Burrows, David J., Lewis M. Dabney, Milne Holton, and Grosvenor E. Powell. *Private Dealings:Eight Modern American Writers.* Stockholm: Almqvist & Wiksell.

58. Cadenhead, I.E.,Jr.,ed. *Literature and History.* (UTDEMS 9.) Papers Prepared on the Occasion of and in Honor of the Inauguration of J. Paschal Twyman as President of the University of Tulsa. Tulsa, Okla.: U. of Tulsa. [I.E. Cadenhead,Jr., "History and Literature:Introduction," 1–8.]

59. [Demarest, David P.,Jr., Lois S. Lamdin, and Joseph Baim,eds.] *A Modern Miscellany.* (CaSE 11.) Pittsburgh: Carnegie-Mellon U. [Dedicated to Lester Middleswarth Beattie.]

60. Friedman, Melvin J., and John B. Vickery,eds. *The Shaken Realist:Essays in Modern Literature in Honor of Frederick J. Hoffman.* Baton Rouge: La. State U.P. [John B. Vickery, "Preface," vii–xii; Melvin J. Friedman, "Introduction:The Achievement of Frederick Hoffman," xiii–xxiv; Philip R. Yannella, "A Bibliography of the Writings of Frederick J. Hoffman (1909–1967)," 327–44.]

61. *Italia e Stati Uniti nell'eta' del Risorgimento e della Guerra Civile:Atti del II Symposium di Studi Americani. Firenze, 27–29 maggio 1966.* Firenze: "La Nuova Italia," 1969.

62. Lanzinger, Klaus,ed. *Americana-Austriaca:Beiträge zur Amerikakunde.* Band 2. Vienna: W. Braumüller.

63. Madden, David,ed. *American Dreams, American Nightmares.* (CMC.) Pref. by Harry T. Moore. Carbondale and Edwardsville: So. Ill. U.P. [David Madden, "Introduction," xv–xlii; "A Selective Bibliography," 216–26.]

64. *Perspectives in American History.* Vol. IV. Cambridge: Charles Warren Center for Studies in Amer. Hist., Harvard U.

65. Robbins, J. Albert,ed. *American Literary Scholarship:An Annual:1968.* Durham, N.C.: Duke U.P.

66. Skard, Sigmund,ed. *Americana-Norvegica. Norwegian Contributions to American Studies.* Vol. II. Philadelphia: U. of Pa P., 1968. [Pubs. of the Am. Inst., U. of Oslo.]

67. Weber, Brom,ed. *Sense and Sensibility in Twentieth Century Writing:A Gathering in Memory of William Van O'Connor* (CMC.) Preface Harry T. Moore. Carbondale and Edwardsville So. Ill. U.P.; London: Feffer & Simons. [Brom Weber, "Introduction," xi–xvi; poems by Philip Larkin, Vivian de Sola Pinto Leonard Unger, Robert Penn Warren, and James Wright; chap from novel in progress by Karl Shapiro.]

Medieval Latin

68. *De doctrina Ioannis Duns Scoti (Acta Congressus Scotistic Internationalis Oxonii et Edinburghi 11–17 sept. 1966).* 4 vols Rome: Cura Commissionis Scotisticae, 1968.

69. Gericke, Horst, Manfred Lemmer, and Walter Zöllner,eds Orbis Mediaevalis:Festgabe für Anton Blaschka zum 75. Geburtstag am 7. Oktober 1967. Weimar: Böhlau.

70. Glier, Ingeborg, Gerhard Hahn,et al.,eds. *Werk—Typ —Situation:Studien zu poetologischen Bedingungen in der ältererr deutschen Literatur. Hugo Kuhn zum 60. Geburtstag.* Stuttgart: Metzler, 1969.

Folklore

71. *Africa:BBC Radio and Television.* London: British Broad casting Corp., 1967. [Transcripts of radio broadcasts.]

72. Beattie, John, and John Middleton. *Spirit Mediumship an Society in Africa.* Foreword Raymond Firth. London: Routledge & K. Paul, 1969. ["Introduction," xvii–xxx.]

73. Calame-Griaule, Geneviève. *Le thème de l'arbre dans le contes africains.* (Soc. pour l'étude des lang. africaines 16.) Paris Klincksieck, 1969.

74. Diószegi, Vilmos,ed. *Popular Beliefs and Folklore Tradition in Siberia.* (IUPUAS 57.) Eng. Tr. Rev. by Stephen P. Dunn Bloomington: Ind. U.P., 1968. [Tr. of *Glaubenswelt und Folklor der sibirischen Völker.* Budapest: Akad. Kiadó, 1963.]

75. Douglas, Mary,ed. *Witchcraft Confessions & Accusations* (A.S.A. Monographs 9.) London: Tavistock; New York: Barne & Noble.

76. Douglas, Mary, and Phyllis M. Kaberry. *Man in Africa* Foreword M.G. Smith. London: Tavistock, 1969.

77. Endo, Banri, Hiroshi Hoshi, and Shozo Masuda,eds *Proceedings, VIIIth International Congress of Anthropological and Ethnological Sciences, 1968, Tokyo and Kyoto.* 3 vols. Tokyo Science Council of Japan.

78. Fife, Austin and Alta, and Henry H. Glassie,eds. *Form Upon the Frontier:Folklife and Folk Arts in the United States* (Utah State U. Monog. Ser. 16, No. 2.) Logan: Utah State U.P. 1969. [Henry H. Glassie, "Introduction," 1–7.]

79. Foltin, Hans Friedrich,et al.,eds. *Kontakte und Grenzen Probleme der Volks-, Kultur- und Sozialforschung. Festschrift für Gerhard Heilfurth zum 60. Geburtstag.* Göttingen: Schwartz, 1969 ["Veröffentlichungen von Gerhard Heilfurth," zusammengestell von Charlotte Oberfeld, 527–44.]

80. Halpert, Herbert, and G.M. Story. *Christmas Mumming in Newfoundland:Essays in Anthropology, Folklore, and History* Toronto: U. of Toronto P. ["Introduction," 3–6; "Selecte Bibliography," 231–40; "The Newfoundland Distribution of th Mummers' Play and Christmas Disguising," 222–29.]

81. Harkort, Fritz, Karel C. Peeters, and Robert Wildhaber Volksüberlieferung:Festschrift für Kurt Ranke zur Vollendung de 60 Lebensjahres. Göttingen: Otto Schwartz, 1968.

82. Jenkins, [J.] Geraint,ed. *Studies in Folk Life:Essays i Honour of Iorwerth C. Peate.* Introd. H.J. Fleure. London Routledge & K. Paul, 1969. ["Bibliography of Books and Paper by Iorwerth C. Peate," 339–44.]

83. Leach, E[dmund] R.,ed. *Dialectic in Practical Religion* (Cambridge Papers in Soc. Anth. 5.) Cambridge: Cambridge U.P. 1968. ["Introduction," 1–6.]

84. Lüsehen, Günther. *The Cross-Cultural Analysis of Spor*

and Games. Champaign, Ill.: Stipes. [Some essays prev. pub.]

85. *Man and Culture II:Contributions of the Czechoslovak Ethnologists for the VIII International Congress of Anthropological and Ethnological Sciences in Tokyo 1968.* (Opera Ethnologica 3.) Prague: Czech. Acad. of Sciences, 1968.

86. Mayer, Philip. *Socialization:The Approach from Social Anthropology.* (A.S.A. Monographs 8.) London: Tavistock Pub.

87. Noy, Dov, and Issaehar Ben-Ami. *Folklore Research Center Studies:Volume I.* Jerusalem: Magnes P.

88. Paden, John N., and Edward W. Soja,eds. *The African Experience.* 4 vols. Evanston, Ill.: Northwestern U.P.

89. Pouillon, Jean, and Pierre Maranda. *Echanges et communications:Mélanges offerts à Claude Lévi-Strauss à l'occasion de son 60 ème anniversaire.* 2 vols. The Hague: Mouton. [J. Pouillon, "Pour un bon usage du totémisme," v–vi; P. Maranda, "An Anthropologist in Paris," vii–viii; "Bibliographie des œuvres de Claude Lévi-Strauss," xvi–xxiii.]

90. Puhvel, Jaan,ed. *Myth and Law Among the Indo-European:Studies in Indo-European Comparative Mythology.* (Pubs. of the U.C.L.A. Center for the Study of Comp. Folklore and Mythol. 1.) Berkeley and Los Angeles: U. of Calif. P. ["Preface," v–vi; "Bibliography [of Items on the Study of Indo-European Comparative Mythology]," 247–68.]

91. *VII Meždunarodnyj kongress antropologičeskix i ètnografičeskix nauk, Moskva, 3–10 avgusta 1964 g. Tom VI.* Moscow: Nauka, 1969.

92. *VII Meždunarodnyj kongress antropologičeskix i ètnografičeskix nauk, Moskva, 3–10 avgusta 1964 g. Tom VII.* Moscow: Nauka.

93. Spencer, Robert F.,ed. *Forms of Symbolic Action:Proceedings of the 1969 Annual Spring Meeting of the American Ethnological Society.* Seattle: U. of Wash. P. for the Amer. Ethnolog. Soc., 1969. [Melford E. Spiro, "Discussion," 208–14.]

94. *Studi in onore di Carmelina Naselli.* 2 vols. Catania: Univ. di Catania, Facoltà di lettere e filosofia, 1968.

95. Whitten, Norman E.,Jr., and John F. Szwed,eds. *Afro-American Anthropology:Contemporary Perspectives.* Foreword Sidney W. Mintz. New York: Free Press; London: Collier-MacMillan. ["Introduction," 23–60.]

GENERAL LITERATURE AND RELATED TOPICS†

I. AESTHETICS

96. Apresjan, G.Z. *Èstetičeskaja mysl' narodov Zakavkaz'ja:Domarksistskij period.* Moscow: Iskusstvo, 1968. [Aesthetic thought among the nations of Trans-Caucasia: the Pre-Marxist period.]

97. Averincev, S. " 'Analitičeskaja psixologija' K.-G. Junga i zakonomernosti tvorčeskoj fantazii." *VLit* 14,iii:113–43. ["Carl Gustav Jung's 'analytic psychology' and the laws of creative imagination."]

98. Bensman, Joseph, and Robert Lilienfeld. "A Phenomenological Model of the Artistic and Critical Attitudes." *PPR* 28(1968):353–67.

99. Berleant, Arnold. "Aesthetics and the Contemporary Arts." *JAAC* 24:155–68.

100. —— *The Aesthetic Field:A Phenomenology of Aesthetic Experience.* (Amer. Lect. Ser. 774.) Springfield, Ill.: Charles C Thomas.

101. Bolam, David W., and James L. Henderson. *Art and Belief.* New York: Schocken.

102. Breazu, Marcel. "A propos de la massification du Gout." *RLV* 35(1969):352–56.

103. Brown, Calvin S. "The Relations Between Music and Literature as a Field of Study." *CL* 22:97–107.

104. Brun, Jean. "Adorateurs de Dionysos et Grands Prêtres de la mort de l'homme." *RIPh* 22(1968):337–55.

105. Brunius, Teddy. "The Aesthetics of Roman Ingarden." *PPR* 30:590–95.

106. Cenkov, B. "V bor'be za leninism v èstetike." *VLit* 14,ii:141–47.

107. Chujo, Kazuo. "Hyogen ni tsuite." *EigoS* 114(1968):740–41. [On lit. expression.]

108. Clammer, John. "On Defining the Aesthetic Experience." *BJA* 10:147–51.

109. Corrigan, Robert. "This Gifted Age." *ASoc* 7:172–77.

110. Courtney, Richard. "On Langer's Dramatic Illusion." *JAAC* 29:11–20.

111. Crawford, Donald W. "Reason-Giving in Kant's Aesthetics." *JAAC* 28:505–10.

112. Davydov, Ju. "Meždu intuiciej i dolženstvovaniem (Ob èstetičeskix vozzrenijax B. Kroče)." *VLit* 13,ii(1969):90–115.

113. Dessoir, Max. *Aesthetics and Theory of Art.* Tr. into Eng. of *Ästhetik und allgemeine Kunstwissenschaft* by Stephen A. Emery. Foreword Thomas Munro. Detroit: Wayne State U.P.

114. Douglas, George H. "A Reconsideration of the Dewey-Cross Exchange." *JAAC* 28:497–504.

115. Duncan, Elmer H. "The Ideal Aesthetic Observer:A Second Look." *JAAC* 29:47–52.

116. Durgnat, Raymond. "Art and Audience." *BJA* 10:11–24.

117. Feldman, Edmund B. *Becoming Human Through Art: Aesthetic Experience in the School.* Englewood Cliffs, N.J.: Prentice-Hall.

118. Fischer, Ernst. "Reflections upon the State of the Arts." *Mosaic* 4,i:21–34. [Tr. John Regehr.]

119. Giorgini, Claudio. "Due saggi sull'arte di Carl Gustav Jung." *RdE* 14(1969):413–27.

120. Gray, Paul H. "The Romantic as Reader:S.S. Curry and Expressive Aesthetics." *QJS* 55(1969):364–71.

121. Gromow, J. "Das ästhetische Erleben und die Kunst." *KuL* 18:270–77. [Tr. Ullrich Kuhirt.]

122. Hedley, Leslie W. "The End of Esthetics." *ASoc* 7:195–98.

123. Heissenbüttel, Helmut. "Die Irrelevanz des Erfolgs in der Beziehung zwischen Literatur und Leser, Kunst und Publikum." [F 36]:233–46.

124. Hermerén, Göran. "Some Problems in the Theory of the Aesthetic Sciences." *Hasifrut* 2:483–97. [In Hebr.; Eng. sum.]

125. Hospers, John,ed. *Introductory Readings in Aesthetics.* New York: Free Press, 1969.

126. Hume, Robert D. "Kant and Coleridge on Imagination." *JAAC* 28:485–96.

127. Ivanov, V. *Dvižuščajasja èstetika:O principax literaturnoj kritiki i nekotoryx tendencijax v nej.* Moscow: Sovetskaja Rossija, 1969.

128. Jakobson, Roman. "On Realism in Art (1921)." *Hasifrut* 2:269–72. [In Hebr.; Eng. sum.]

129. Jesuitow, A. "Fragen der Ästhetik im *Kapital* von Marx." *KuL* 18:823–32. [Tr. Vera Smirnoff.]

130. Johnson, Robert V. *Aestheticism.* (Crit. Idiom 3.) London: Methuen; New York: Barnes & Noble, 1969.

131. Kagan, M. "Zur Anwendung exakter Methoden in der Ästhetik." *KuL* 17(1969):1280–97. [Tr. Gerhard Sewekow.]

132. Kähler, Hermann. "Vom Wert des Schönen:Zu einigen Fragen der ästhetischen Wertung in der Kunst des sozialistischen Realismus." *WB* 16(Heft 7):27–46.

133. Kallen, Horace M. *Art and Freedom:A Historical and Biographical Interpretation of the Relations Between the Ideas of Beauty, Use, and Freedom in Western Civilization from the Greeks to the Present Day.* New York: Greenwood, 1969. [Repr. of 1942

---

† *Festschriften* and Other Analyzed Collections are listed in the first division of this Bibliography, and have been assigned Item numbers 1–95. "F" numbers in brackets following a title refer to these items.

ed.]

134. Kaplan, Donald M. "Art and the Youth Scene." *ASoc* 7:178–80.

135. Kaplan, Max. "Art Education and the Environmental Development." *ASoc* 7:219–27.

136. Kavolis, Vytautas. "On the Crisis of Creativity in Contemporary Art." *ASoc* 7:205–07.

137. Koestler, Arthur. *The Act of Creation.* New York: Macmillan, 1969.

138. Lang, Berel. "Denotation and Aesthetic Inference." *BJA* 10:248–60.

139. Levy, Jiří. "Generative Poetics." [F 24]:548–57.

140. Lifschits, Mikhail. "On Contradictions in Contemporary Art." *SovL* 4:142–52.

141. Lifschitz, Mikhail. "Die Ästhetik Hegels." *KuL* 18: 909–17. [Tr. Carola Spiess.]

142. Lissa, Zofia. "Äesthetische Funktionen des musikalischen Zitats." [F 24]:674–89.

143. López de la Rosa, Horacio. "Significado y estética de la música en función escénica." *CHA* 247:41–54.

144. Mann, Ju. *Russkaja filosofskaja èstetika (1820—1830-e gody).* Moscow: Iskusstvo, 1969.

145. Margolis, James. "Numerical Identity and Reference in the Arts." *BJA* 10:138–46.

146. Mejlax, B. *Talent pisatelja i processy tvorčestva.* Leningrad: Sovetskij pisatel', 1969. [A writer's talent and the creative process.]

147. Mészáros, Vilma. "Lukács György:Művészet és társadalom. Válogatott esztétikai tanulmányok." *Irodalomtörténet* 2:200–08. [Rev. of L's 'Art and Society. Select Aesthetic Studies,' 1968.]

148. Mjasnikov, A.S. "Lenin i èstetičeskie problemy xx veka." *IAN* 29:108–27.

149. Myasnikov, Alexander. "Foremost Aesthetics of the 20th Century." *SovL* 3:143–50.

150. Nagy, Ferenc. "Esztétikai értékítélet, nyelv és komikum." *MagN* 94:159–65. [Aesthetic valuation, language and comicality.]

151. Nemcov, V. *Paralleli sxodjatsja (O processe tvorčestva pisatelja).* Moscow: Sovetskaja Rossija, 1969. [On the creative process.]

152. Øyslebø, Olaf. *Stilstudier.* Oslo: Universitetsforlaget.

153. Padhye, Prabhakar. "Aesthetics and Literary Criticism." *IWT* 3,iii(1969):50–60. [Rev. art. of *Aesthetics and Literary Criticism* by R.B. Patankar.]

154. Pandey, K.C. "Common Trends in Indian and Greco-Roman Aesthetics." [F 18]:129–41.

155. Panichas, George A. "A Metaphysics of Art." [F 19]:13–43.

156. Pascadi, Ion. "Il progresso dei valori estetici." *RdE* 14(1969):38–59.

157. Pleydell–Pearce, A.G. "Objectivity and Value in the Judgements of Aesthetics." *BJA* 10:25–38.

158. Praz, Mario. "The Language of Art Criticism." [F 52]:253–65.

159. Pustilnik, Jack. "Art and the Language of Action." *PPR* 28(1968):591–95.

160. Reizov, Boris. "Les origines de l'esthétique romantique L'antiquité et le romantisme." [F 3]:191–208.

161. Roditi, Edouard. "Marcus Behmer, a Master of Art Nouveau." *ASoc* 7:268–75. [In iconog., book production, etc.

162. Ruiz de Elvira, Antonio. "Mitología y estética." *RIE* 105(1969):19–51.

163. Santinello, Giovanni. "Saggezza e poetiche degli antichi." *RdE* 14(1969):275–84. [Rev. art.]

164. Schmidt, Povl. "Ontologi, digtnig og kritik." *Kritik* 12(1969):60–75.

165. Sebba, Gregor. "Baroque and Mannerism:A Retrospect." [F 34]:145–63.

166. Sis, A. "Kunst und Wirklichkeit." *KuL* 18:155–69. [Tr. Wilfried Braumann.]

167. Smith, Barbara H. "The New Imagism." *Midway* 9,iii(1969):27–44.

168. Sorell, Walter. *The Duality of Vision:Genius and Versatility in the Arts.* Indianapolis: Bobbs-Merrill.

169. Sosonkin, I.L. *Iz istorii èstetičeskoj mysli v Turkmenistane:Maxtumkuli, Kemine, Mollanepes.* Ašxabad: Ylym, 1969.

170. Steig, Michael. "Refining the Grotesque:An Attempt at a Synthesis." *JAAC* 29:253–60.

171. Stolovič, L. "Lenin i problema xudožestvenno cennosti." *VLit* 13,x(1969):11–30.

172. Svitak, Ivan. "Art in Industrial Society." *Mosaic* 3,ii:104–15. [Tr. Albert Todd; also pub. in *Vytvarna prace*(Prague 11–12(1968).]

173. Tatarkiewicz, Władysław. "Did Aesthetics Progress?" *PPR* 31:47–59.

174. ——. "L'arte è un linguaggio? Ricerca su tre termini ambigui." *RdE* 14(1969):321–36.

175. Ujfalussy, József. "Tárgyak és összefüggések." *Kritika* 8,iv:27–30. [The aesthetics of 85-year-old George Lukács.]

176. Vajanský, Svetozár Hurban. "Umenie v živote národov." *SlovP* 85,x(1969):58–65.

177. Van Haecht, Louis. "L'esthétique analytique." *RPL* 68:11–30.

178. Vivas, Eliseo. "Marcuse on Art." *ModA* 14:140–49.

179. Vosmar, Jørn. "Værkets verden, værkets holdning." *Kritik* 12(1969):76–107.

180. Walker, Jeremy. "Imagination and the Passions." *PPR* 29(1969):575–88.

181. Weiss, Auréliu. "Aesthetic Prejudices and the Perception of Ideas." *Jour. of Aesthetic Educ.* 3,i(1969):79–84.

182. Whealy, Elizabeth. "What Is Art?" *HAB* 21,i:14–26.

183. White, David A. "Revealment:A Meeting of Extremes in Aesthetics." *JAAC* 28:515–20.

184. Widmer, Kingsley. "The Electric Esthetic and the Short-Circuit Ethic of the Current Populist Culture." *ASoc* 7:163–68.

185. Zemach, Eddy M. "An Ontology of Aesthetic Objects." *Hasifrut* 2:463–82. [In Hebr.; Eng. sum.]

See also 196, 297, 322, 345, 984, 3377, 8369.

II. LITERARY CRITICISM AND LITERARY THEORY

Literary Criticism. 186. Andersson, Erik. "Vad är en metafor?" *FT* 187–88:258–67.

187. Arnaudov, M. *Psixologija literaturnogo tvorčestva.* Moscow: Progress.

188. Battilana, Marilla. "Critica letteraria e psicanalisi." *Prospetti* 5:200–10.

189. Beardsley, Monroe C. *The Possibility of Criticism.* Detroit, Mich.: Wayne State U.P.

190. Beker, Miroslav. "Marxism and the Determinants of Critical Judgment." *JAAC* 29:33–41.

191. Bhattacharya, Biswanath. "Principles of Literary Criticism of the Dhvani School:A Review." [F 18]:178–89.

* 192. Blish, Mary. "A.C. Bradley:A Summary Account." *PBSA* 62(1968):607–12.

193. Bogdanov, A.N., and L.G. Judkevič. *Metodika literaturovedčeskogo analiza.* Moscow: Prosveščenie, 1969.

194. Bohn, Oluf,ed. *Fra modernisme til ny-marxistisk kritik Litteraturkritiske holdninger.* Copenhagen: Schultz. [Torben Brostrøm, "Modernismen," 8–17; Knut Johansen, "For bemerkninger til en politisk litteraturkritikk," 18–41; interpretations of N.F.S. Grundtvig's poem "De Levendes Land" and Klaus Rifbjerg's poem "Middelaldermorgen" by Jørgen Bang 48–63, Niels Egebak, 64–81, Flemming Harrits, 82–98, and Finn Stein Larsen, 99–116; "Symposion eller åben diskussion omkring tolkningerne," 117–43.]

195. Brown, Daniel Russell. "A Look at Archetypal Criticism." *JAAC* 28:465–72.

196. Brown, Merle. "The Philosopher-Critic." [F 38]:3–12. [On the aesthetics & lit. crit. of Eliseo Vivas and Croce.]

197. Bukdahl, Jørgen K. "Hermeneutiske landvindinger

1:Kommunikation og refleksion. Inspirationen fra Hegel." *Kritik* 16:125–37.

198. Buschmin, A.S. "Die Kriterien für die Exaktheit in der Literaturwissenschaft." *KuL* 17(1969):1120–38. [Tr. Walter Schneider.]

199. Bušmin, A.S. *Metodologičeskie voprosy literaturovedčeskix issledovanij.* Leningrad: Nauka (AN SSSR, IRLI), 1969.

200. Butor, Michel. "Criticism and Invention." *Meanjin* 28(1969):461–71. [Tr. Jean Garagnon and Graeme Watson.]

201. Cameron, J.M. "Problems of Literary History." *NLH* 1(1969):7–20.

202. Carrier, Gilles. "La critique est-elle une science?" *EF* 6:221–26.

203. Cevasco, G.A. "Slings and Arrows:A Consideration of Captious Literary Criticism." *ABC* 20,vii:8–10.

204. Clecak, Peter. "Marxism, Literary Criticism, and the American Academic Scene." *Science and Society* 31(1967): 275–301.

205. Cohen, Ralph. "A Note on *New Literary History.*" *NLH* 1(1969):3–6. [On focus of *NLH.*]

206. Collinge, N.E. "Ambiguity in Literature:Some Guidelines." *Arethusa* 2(1969):13–29.

207. Davydov, Ju. "Kritika 'novyx levyx'." *VLit* 14,ii:68–99.

208. De Man, Paul. "Literary History and Literary Modernity." *Dædalus* 99:384–404.

209. Delesalle, Simone. "L'explication de textes fonctionnement et fonction." *LFr* 7(sept):87–95.

210. Dollerup, Cay. "Elementer og vurdering i læsning af noveller." *MDan* 1970:50–72.

* 211. Ducharme, Edward. "The Evasion of the Text." *Eng. Record* 20,iii:13–22.

212. Dwivedi, R.C. "Philosophical Considerations and Independence of Literary Criticism in Sanskrit." [F 18]:153–63.

213. Eaton, Marcia M. "Good and Correct Interpretations of Literature." *JAAC* 29:227–33.

214. Eichner, Hans. "Friedrich Schlegels Theorie der Literaturkritik." *ZDP* (1969, Sonderheft):2–19.

215. Ellis, Katherine. "The Function of Northrop Frye at the Present Time." *CE* 31:541–47.

216. Finch, Peter. "Concrete Poetry:A Brief Outline." *AWR* 19,xliii:207–12.

217. Fogle, Richard H. "Literary History Romanticized." *NLH* 1:237–47.

218. Forgács, László. "Műalkotás és elemzés." *Irodalomtörténet* 2:319–35. [Work of art and analysis.]

219. Fridlender, G. "Marx und Engels und Probleme des Realismus." *KuL* 18:675–97,801–22. [Tr. Irene Faix.]

220. Frye, Northrop. "Mito e logos." *SCr* 3(1969):122–43. [Cf. Bibliog. for 1969, Vol. I, Item 231.]

221. ——— "The Critical Path:An Essay on the Social Context of Literary Criticism." *Dædalus* 99:268–342.

222. Gelernt, Jules. "*The Dynamics of Literary Response.*" *L&P* 20:129–34. [Rev. art. on Bibliog. for 1968, Item 4903.]

223. Gilman, Richard. "White Standards and Negro Writing." *NALF* 3(1969):111–16. [Rev. art.]

224. Goldmann, Lucien. "Le dieu caché:La 'nouvelle critique' et le marxisme." [F 40]:559–68.

225. Gottesman, Ronald, and Scott Bennett,eds. and comps. *Art and Error:Modern Textual Editing.* Bloomington: Ind. U.P. [Reprs.]

226. Greenwood, E.B. "The Sceptical Dane:A Note on Cay Dollerup's Doubts About the Objectivity of Criticism." *EIC* 20:271–73. [See Bibliog. for 1969, Vol. I, Item 223.]

227. Günthner, Franz. "Le *new criticism.*" *LFr* 7(sept):96–101.

228. Hamm, Victor M. "From Ontology to Axiology:A Critical Problem." *CE* 32:146–54.

229. Hankiss, Elemér. "A 'struktúra'." *Kritika* 8,ix:21–30.

230. Harth, Dietrich. "Romane und ihre Leser." *GRM* 20:159–79.

231. Hartman, Geoffrey. "Toward Literary History." *Dædalus* 99:355–83.

232. Hashiguchi, Minoru. "Susan Sontag—Atarashii Jidai no Zenei." *EigoS* 115(1969):760–61. [SS—advance guard of a new age.]

233. Hellens, Franz. *Essais de critique intuitive.* Bruxelles, Paris, Amiens: Soc. Générale d'Editions, 1968.

234. Hermann, István. "Az elsüllyedt ember." *Kritika* 8,v: 16–21; vi:12–21. [Notes on structuralism.]

235. Hill, James L. "Defensive Strategies in Nineteenth- and Twentieth-Century Criticism." *JAAC* 28(1969):177–85.

236. Hirsch, E.D.,Jr. "The Paradoxes of Perspectivism." [F 37]:15–20.

237. Itterbeek, Eugène van. *Tekens van Leven.* Brussel/Den Haag: Manteau.

238. Jameson, Fredric. "The Case for George Lukács." *Salmagundi* 13:3–35.

239. Jean, Bernard. "Critique au second degré." *EA* 23:72–82.

240. Jensen, Johan Fjord. "At karakterisere." [F 39]:119–31. [Orig. pub. 1967; see Bibliog. for 1967, Item 4329.]

* 241. Jones, Howard M. "Scholarship and Relevance." *SHR* 4:1–16.

242. Joshi, Shri L. "Observations on Some Elements of Sanskrit Criticism." [F 18]:209–11.

243. Józsa, Péter. "Ami a strukturalista elemzés határain innen van." *Kritika* 8,vii:25–32.

244. Kampf, Louis. "Culture Without Criticism." *MR* 11: 624–44.

245. Keller, Joseph. "Black Writing and the White Critic." *NALF* 3(1969):103–10.

246. Kirpotin, V. "Čto trebuetsja ot istorika literatury?" *VLit* 14,viii:204–08. [What is required of a lit. historian?]

247. Kogan, Pauline. *Northrop Frye:The High Priest of Clerical Obscurantism.* (L&I Monog. 1.) Montreal: Progressive Books & Periodicals, 1969.

248. Korpan, Barbara D. "Literary Evolution as Style:The 'Intrinsic Historicity' of Northrop Frye and Juri Tynianov." *PCP* 2(1967):47–52.

249. Krieger, Murray. "The Continuing Need for Criticism." [F 67]:1–15. [Rev. version of 1968 essay.]

250. Krüger, Manfred. "Neue Wege der französischen Literaturkritik." *NS* 19:41–45. [Rev. art. of Georges Poulet, *Les chemins actuels de la critique,* 1968.]

251. Kytohonka, Arto. "Kirjallisuuskritiikin pätevyys. Näkökanta T.S. Eliotin metakritiikkiin. (Validité de la critique littéraire.)" *KSV* 24(1969):35–67.

252. Lawall, Sally N. "The Anthropology of Literature." *HSL* 2:256–62. [Rev. art. on Bibliog. for 1969, Vol. I, Item 43.]

253. Lebedev, Alexander. "The Purpose of Literary Criticism:Coercion Can't Create." *AmD* 5,ii(1958–69):13–15.

254. Lefebve, Maurice-Jean. "Critique imaginale et langage littéraire." *RLV* 35(1969):229–39.

255. Lentricchia, Frank. "The Place of Cleanth Brooks." *JAAC* 29:235–51.

256. Levin, Harry T. "Tematica e critica." *SCr* 3(1969): 98–121.

257. Maier, Rosemarie. " 'The Intentional Fallacy' and the Logic of Literary Criticism." *CE* 32:135–45.

* 258. Manning, Stephen. "Typology and the Literary Critic." *EAL* 5,i,pt.1:51–73.

259. McDonald, William E. "The Literary Criticism of Amos Wilder." *Soundings* 52(1969):99–109.

260. Menapace, John. "Some Approaches to Annotation." *SchP* 1:194–205.

261. Miner, Earl. "The Double Truth of Modern Poetic Criticism." [F 67]:16–25.

262. Moore, Arthur K. "Formalist Criticism and Literary Form." *JAAC* 29:21–31.

263. Muro, Suguru. "Basic English to Eibun no Kaishaku." *EigoS* 115(1969):160–61. [BE and interpretation of Eng. lit.]

264. Narita, Seiju. "The Function of Criticism." *EigoS* 114(1968):286–87. [In Jap.]

265. Noland, Richard W. "Literature and Theology." *HSL* 2:248–55. [Rev. art. on Nathan A. Scott, Jr., *Negative Capability* (1969).]

266. Pandey, K.C. "Seven Principles of Literary Criticism." [F 18]:8–17.

267. Panichas, George A. "G. Wilson Knight:Interpreter of Genius." *EM* 20(1969):291–312.

268. Pareyson, Luigi. "Originarietà dell'Interpretazione." [F 6],II:353–66.

269. Péczely, László. "A modern irodalomtudomány néhány kérdése." *Kortárs* 14:1933–41.

270. Potter, Hugh. "Paul Rosenfeld:Criticism and Prophecy." *AQ* 22:[82]–94.

271. Poulet, Georges. "Phenomenology of Reading." *NLH* 1(1969):53–68.

272. Poulin, A.,Jr. "Center and Circumference:Personalism in Criticism." *JML* 1:109–15. [Essay-rev.]

273. Price, Martin. "Literary History at Yale." *NLH* 1: 335–43.

274. Reiter, Robert E. "On Biblical Typology and the Interpretation of Literature." *CE* 30(1969):562–71.

275. Richards, Kent H. "Correlating Methods in the Interpretation of the Old Testament." *UDR* 7,i:121–30.

276. Ricœur, Paul. "Qu'est-ce qu'un texte?Expliquer et comprendre." [F 6],II:181–200.

277. Roberts, Jeanne A. "Literary Criticism as Dream Analysis." *CEA* 33,i:14–16.

278. Roberts, Thomas J. "The Critics' Conceptions of Literature." *CE* 31(1969):1–24.

279. Robertson, D.W.,Jr. "Some Observations on Method in Literary Studies." *NLH* 1(1969):21–33.

280. Robinson, Fred C. "Lexicography and Literary Criticism:A Caveat." [F 54]:99–110.

281. Scarpati, Claudio. "Auerbach:Il filologo insoddisfatto." *VeP* 52(1969):819–40.

* 282. Schwarz, Egon. "Hermann Hesse, the American Youth Movement, and Problems of Literary Evaluation." *PMLA* 85:977–87.

283. Scott, Nathan A.,Jr. *Negative Capability:Studies in the New Literature and the Religious Situation.* New Haven: Yale U.P., 1969. [Repr. essays plus "The Literary Imagination in a Time of Dearth."]

284. Segal, Charles. "Ancient Texts and Modern Criticism: Some Recent Trends in Classical Literary Studies." *Arethusa* 1(1968):1–25.

285. Spanos, William V. "Modern Literary Criticism and the Specialization of Time:An Existential Critique." *JAAC* 29: 87–104.

286. Spears, Monroe K. "The Newer Criticism." *Shenandoah* 21,iii:110–37.

287. Starobinski, Jean. "Consideraciones sobre el estado actual de la crítica literaria." *RO* 30:1–19.

288. Stephen, Henry. "The Principles of Criticism:As Applied to Poetry." *CalR* N.S.1:19–36.

289. Strelka, Joseph. *Vergleichende Literaturkritik:Drei Essays zur Methodologie der Literaturwissenschaft.* Bern:Francke.

290. Sullivan, J.P. "Philology and Literary Criticism at the Graduate Level." *Arethusa* 2(1969):1–12.

291. Széles, Klára. "Mütipusok és müértékelések." *Helikon* 15(1969):417–31.

292. Szili, József. "Az irodalmi mü igazsága." *Kritika* 8,v: 6–16. [Relation between lit. and reality.]

293. ——— "Uj irodalomelméleti folyóirat az Egyesült Államokban." *Helikon* 16:303–04. [On *NLH.*]

294. Thompson, J.S. "Vagabond Journalism:Literature and Criticism Underground." *L&I* 1(1969):47–72.

295. Ueda, Tamotsu. "Shochoshugi no Gendaiteki na Tenkai." *EigoS* 115(1969):690–91. [Modern devel. of symbolism.]

296. Venkatachalam, Shri V. "The Inter-relation of the Kavi and the Sahrdaya in Sanskrit Literary Criticism." [F 18]:35–46.

297. Vivas, Eliseo. "Literary Criticism and Aesthetics." [F 38]:13–39.

298. Vosmar, Jørn. "Værkets verden, værkets holdning." *Kritik* 12(1969):76–107.

299. Walter, Eric. "Critique littéraire et socialisme au tournant du siècle." *CALC* 3(1968):127–58. [Rev. art. on special no. of *Le Mouvement Social.*]

300. Weimann, Robert. "Past Significance and Present Meaning in Literary History." *NLH* 1(1969):91–109.

301. Wellek, René. *Discriminations:Further Concepts of Criticism.* New Haven: Yale U.P.

302. Wilder, Amos N. "The Uses of a Theological Criticism." *Soundings* 52(1969):84–96.

303. Xrapčenko, M. "O progresse v literature i iskusstve: Stat'ja pervaja." *VLit* 14,v:125–52.

304. Yamada, Shoichi. "Shinwa teki Sonzai toshite no Shin-hihyo." *Oberon* 30(1968):70–88. [New Crit. as mythology.]

305. Yamoto, Sadamiki. "Gendai Hihyo no Gijutsusei." *EigoS* 115(1969):12–14. [Technicality in mod. crit.]

306. ——— "Genkei Hihyo no Sekigake." *EigoS* 115(1969): 556–58,626–29. [Precursor of archetypal criticism, M. Bodkin.]

307. Zandvoort, R.W. "Blasphemy in Literary Criticism." [F 52]:249–52.

308. Zarev, P. "Ob aktual'nyx voprosax literaturovedenija i strukturalizma." *VLit* 13,xii(1969):58–72. [Structuralism in contemp. Western and Soviet lit. scholarship.]

See also 127, 153, 931, 984, 995, 1457, 1459, 1916, 2030, 3312, 3319, 3858, 5201, 5552, 5932, 7909, 8532, 9247.

Literary Theory. 309. *Aktual'nye problemy socialističeskogo realizma.* Moscow: Sovetskij pisatel', 1969.

310. Ambrosini, Riccardo. "Analisi delle strutture letterarie." *ASNSP* 38(1969):165–99.

311. Anderson, Margaret. "The Art of Prose." *Prose* 1:5–15

312. Barthes, Roland. *Litteraturens nulpunkt.* Tr. Hans-Jørgen Andersen. Copenhagen: Rhodos, 1968. [Orig. pub. in Fr., 1953; "Oversætterens forord," 7–11.]

313. Begiasvili, A. "Predely 'strukturnogo' literaturovedenija." *VLit* 14,vi:75–88.

314. Bense, Max. "Fragmentarische Angaben über das Vierfache Engagement." [F 30]:604–06.

315. Benz, Ernst. "Tonband-Literatur als geistesgeschichtliche Dokumentation," 45–65 in Kurt Töpner,ed., *Wider die Ächtung der Geschichte. Festschrift zum 60. Geburtstag von Hans-Joachim Schoeps.* München: Bechtle, 1969.

316. Berefelt, Gunnar. "On Symbol and Allegory." *JAAC* 28(1969):201–12.

317. Bhargava, P.L. "A Comparative Study of the Sanskrit and the Greek Dramatic Theory." [F 18]:18–26.

318. Bleich, David. "Emotional Origins of Literary Meaning." *CE* 31(1969):30–40.

319. Brinkmann, Richard,ed. *Begriffsbestimmung des literarischen Realismus.* Darmstadt: Wissenschaftl. Buchgesellschaft, 1969. [Erich Auerbach, "Germinie Lacerteux," 1–32; Georg Lukács, "Erzählen oder Beschreiben? Zur Diskussion über Naturalismus und Formalismus," 33–85; Winfried Hellmann, "Objektivität, Subjektivität und Erzählkunst:Zur Romantheorie Friedrich Spielhagens," 86–159; A. Iwastschenko, "Kritischer und sozialistischer Realismus," 160–92; Theodor W. Adorno, "Erpresste Versöhnung. Zu Georg Lukács:*Wider den missverstandenen Realismus*," 193–221; Richard Brinkmann, "Zum Begriff des Realismus für die erzählende Dichtung des neunzehnten Jahrhunderts," 222–35; Gerhard Kaiser, "Um eine Neubegründung des Realismusbegriffs," 236–58; Hans Mayer "Die Wirklichkeit E.T.A. Hoffmanns," 259–300; Fritz Martini "Wilhelm Raabes 'Prinzessin Fisch':Wirklichkeit und Dichtung im erzählenden Realismus des 19. Jahrhunderts," 301–36; Clemens Heselhaus, "Das Realismusproblem," 337–64; Zbigniew Folejewski, "Der sozialistische Realismus in der westlicher Literaturwissenschaft," 365–75; J.M. Ritchie, "Die Ambivalenz des 'Realismus' in der deutschen Literatur 1830–1880," 376–99. René Wellek, "Der Realismusbegriff in der Literaturwissenschaft," 400–33; E.B. Greenwood, "Überlegungen zu Welleks Realismusbegriff," 434–47; René Wellek, "Erwiderung auf E.B Greenwoods Überlegungen," 448–52; Wolfgang Preisendanz "Voraussetzungen des poetischen Realismus in der deutscher Erzählkunst des 19. Jahrhunderts," 453–79; Richard Brinkmann "Zum Stand der Diskussion," 480–96.]

320. Brooks, Harold F. "The Name of Action." *Komo.* 2(1969):37–49.

321. Brown, Richard G. "A View of Metaphor in Relation to Imagination." *BSUF* 11,iii:35–40.

322. Burnshaw, Stanley. *The Seamless Web:Language-Thinking, Creature-Knowledge, Art-Experience.* New York: Braziller

* 323. Champigny, Robert. "Implicitness in Narrative Fiction." *PMLA* 85:988–91.

324. —— "Philosophy as Literature." [F 38]:40–49.

325. Chappell, Fred. "Six Propositions about Literature and History." *NHL* 1:513–22.

326. Chatman, Seymour. *"Linguistics and Literary Theory*. By Karl D. Uitti." *IJAL* 36:302–09. [Rev. art.; see Bibliog. for 1969, Vol. III, Item 574.]

327. Clemens, Wolfgang. "Was ist literarischer Einfluss?" *NsM* 21(1968):139–47.

328. Cornez, Maurice. "Les nouveaux structuralistes." *RPL* 67(1969):582–605.

* 329. Cowden, Roy W. "The First Words a Writer Puts on Paper." *MQR* 9:7–11.

330. Crittenden, Charles. "Ontology and the Theory of Descriptions." *PPR* 31:85–96.

331. Davydov, Ju.N. *Iskusstvo kak sociologičeskij fenomen:K karakteristike èstetiko-političeskix vzgljadov Platona i Aristotelja.* Moscow: Nauka, 1968.

332. Dijk, T.A. van. "Elements of a Generative Theory of the Poetic Text." *Hasifrut* 2:447–62. [In Hebr.; orig. written in Fr.; Eng. sum.]

333. Döhl, Reinhard. "Poesie zum Ansehen, Bilder zum Lesen? Notwendiger Vorbericht und Hinweis zum Problem der Mischformen im 20. Jahrhundert." [F 30]:554–82.

334. Duducava, M. *K voprosu o suščnosti xudožestvennogo stilja.* Tbilisi: Merani (An GruzSSR, Institut istorii gruzinskoj literatury im. Š. Rustaveli), 1969.

335. Eskey, David E. "A Preface to the Study of Literary Style." *DAI* 31:376A–77A(Pittsburgh).

336. Ethier-Blais, Jean. " 'Mimésis':Réalisme et transcendance." *EF* 6:7–24.

337. Even-Zohar, Itamar. "The Nature and Functionalization of the Language of Literature under Diglossia." *Hasifrut* 2:286–302. [In Hebr.; Eng. sum.]

338. Fletcher, Angus. "Aspetti della forma trascendentale." *SCr* 3(1969):146–66.

339. Gass, W.H. "Philosophy and the Form of Fiction." [F 38]:50–66.

340. Ginzburg, Lidija. "O dokumental'noj literature i principax postroenija xaraktera." *VLit* 14,vii:62–91. [On documentary lit. and principles of character creation.]

341. Greenwood, E.B. "Literature and Philosophy." *EIC* 20:5–17.

342. Greimas, Algirdas Julien. "Grundtræk af en narrativ grammatik." *Poetik* 2,iii(1969):1–20. [Tr. Per Aage Brandt.]

343. Gueunier, Nicole. "L'information courante en stylistique." *LFr* 7(sept):102–06.

344. Guillén, Claudio. "Poetics as System." *CL* 22:193–222. The division of lit. into modes is questioned.]

345. Guljaev, N.A., A.N. Bogdanov, and L.G. Judkevič. *Teorija literatury v svjazi s problemami èstetiki.* Moscow: Vysšaja škola.

* 346. Gunn, Giles B. "Creation and Discovery:Vivas' Literary Theory." *Renascence* 22:198–206.

347. —— "Literature and Its Relation to Religion." *JR* 50:268–91.

348. Hamburger, Michael. *The Truth of Poetry.* London: Weidenfeld and Nicolson.

349. Hankiss, Elemér. *As irodalmi kifejezésformák lélektana.* Modern filológiai füzetek 7.) Budapest: Akadémiai K. [Psychology of lit. expressions.]

350. Härtling, Peter. "Das Ende der Literatur?" [F 36]:47–53.

351. Holsti, Keijo. *Motiivin käsite kirjallisuudentutkimuksessa.* Acta Universitatis Tamperensis, Ser.A,42.) Tampere: Tampereen Yliopisto. [The concept of motif in literary study.]

352. Hölzel, Miroslav. "Základy a vývoj rytmických norem." *ČL* 17(1969):453–73. [On principles and devel. of metrical norms. Sum. in Ger.]

353. Hornedo, Florentino H. "The Meaning of Tragedy." *SLRJ* 1:79–92.

354. Hultberg, Helge. *Semantisk litteraturbetragtning.* Munksgaardserien 20.) 2nd ed. Copenhagen: Munksgaard, 1969. Orig. pub. 1966.]

355. Iezuitov, A. "V.I. Lenin i problemy teorii realizma." *VLit*

14,vii:3–20.

356. Irvine, Peter L. "The 'Witness' Point of View in Fiction." *SAQ* 69:[217]–25.

357. Isoja, Takasi. "V. Ja. Propp i strukturalizm." *A&CS* 20:11–22.

358. Izevbaye, D.S. *The Relevance of Modern Literary Theory in English to Poetry and Fiction in English-speaking West Africa.* Ibadan: Ibadan U., 1968. [Diss.]

359. Jehser, Werner. "Sozialistische Parteilichkeit als zentrale ideologische Kategorie des sozialistischen Realismus und seiner Theorie." *WB* 16(Heft 3):74–90.

360. Johnson, Sabina T. "Some Tentative Strictures on Generative Rhetoric." *CE* 31(1969):155–65.

361. Jones, Evan. "Intelligence and Poetry." *Quadrant* 66:42–50.

362. Jones, Louisa. "Variations on Fantasy." *Neophil* 54:1–18.

363. Kanyó, Zoltán. "Beiträge zu einer semiotischen Literaturtheorie." *AUS-AG&R* 4(1969):27–38.

364. Kennedy, James G. "Voynich, Bennett, and Tressell: Two Alternatives for Realism in the Transition Age." *ELT* 13:254–86.

365. Kjørup, Søren. "Nelson Goodman og hans bog om kunst, sprog og kunstsprog." *Poetik* 3:96–103.

366. Klaniczay, Tibor. "A renaszánsz határai és ellentmondásai." *Kritika* 8,i:8–15. [The limits and contradiction of the Renaissance.]

367. —— "A reneszánsz válsága és a manierizmus." *IK* 74:419–50. [The crisis of the Renaissance and mannerism. Sum. in Fr.]

368. Klaus, Meredith H. "Toward a Theory of Comedy." *DAI* 30(1969):1986A(Mich.).

369. Koch, Hans. "Stichworte zum sozialistischen Realismus." *WB* 16(Heft 1):10–38.

370. Kock, Christian. "Bemærkninger til en textteori:Forsøg i retning af flere kriterier for textbeskrivelse." *Poetik* 3:178–204.

371. Krishnamoorthy, K. "Dhvani as the Meeting-Point of All Principles of Sanskrit Literary Theory." [F 18]:201–08.

372. Lefebve, Maurice-Jean. "Discours poétique et discours du récit." *NRF* 1(fév):269–78.

373. Lieberman, Marcia R. "The New Linguistics and the New Poetics." *CE* 30(1969):527–33.

374. Lipking, Lawrence. "Periods in the Arts:Sketches and Speculations." *NLH* 1:181–200.

375. Lixačev, D. "Buduščee literatury kak predmet izučenija (Zametki i razmyšlenija)." *NovM* 45,ix(1969):167–84. [On the theory of "development" in lit.]

376. Madsen, Peter. "Litteraturforskningens interesse." [F 39]:264–97.

377. Magowan, Robin. "A Note on Genre." *CE* 30(1969): 534–38.

378. Maries, Julian. "Les genres littéraires en philosophie." *RIPh* 23(1969):495–508.

379. Martinkó, András. "A stílus születése és élete." *Kritika* 8,iii:4–16. [Birth and life of a style.]

380. Meidner, Olga M. "Literature and Philosophy." *EIC* 20:385–90. [Reply to E.B. Greenwood, *EIC* 20:5–17.]

381. Meilach, B. "Wege für die komplexe Erforschung des künstlerischen Schaffens." *KuL* 17(1969):1037–58. [Tr. Gerhard Sewekow.]

382. Meschonnic, Henri. "Pour connaître une parole écriture." *NRF* 18(avril):572–83. [See also Brice Parain, "Notes sur les observations de M. Henri Meschonnic," ibid., 584–86.]

383. Michener, Richard L. "The Great Chain of Being:Three Approaches." *BSUF* 11,ii:60–71. [In Pico, Donne, Pope.]

* 384. Miller, David M. "The Location of Verbal Art." *Lang&S* 3:69–80.

385. Mink, Louis O. "History and Fiction as Modes of Comprehension." *NLH* 1:541–58.

386. Molčanov, V.V. "Avtorskij zamysel i čitatel'skoe vosprijatie (k postanovke problemy)." *IAN* 29:228–35. [Author's intent and the reader.]

387. Morawski, Stefan. "The Basic Functions of Quotation." [F 24]:690–705.

388. Naumann, Manfred. "Literatur und Leser." *WB* 16(Heft

5):92–116.

389. Nisbet, Robert. "Genealogy, Growth, and Other Metaphors." *NLH* 1:315–63.

390. Olscamp, Paul J. "How Some Metaphors May Be True or False." *JAAC* 29:77–86.

391. Parrella, Gilda C. "The Concept of Empathy:A Study in Discovery, Definition, and Design with Application to Literature and Its Performance." *DAI* 30(1969):2657A(U. of Wash.).

392. Peckham, Morse. "Is the Problem of Literary Realism a Pseudo-Problem?" *Crit* 12,ii:95–112.

393. Pedersen, Jørgen Mønster, and Per Aage Brandt. "Narratologiske noter." *Poetik* 2,iii(1969):22–37.

394. Pire, François. "Métaphores de la vie et vie des métaphores." *RIPh* 24:90–106.

395. Pittelkow, Ralf. "Strukturalisme, semiologi, produktivitet." [F 39]:299–316.

396. Plessis, P.G. du. *Die verwysing in die literatuur.* Kaapstad: Nasionale Boekhandel, 1968.

397. Podgaeckaja, I. "Poètika žanra i nacional'noe svoeobrazie." *VLit* 13,xi(1969):116–33. [The poetics of genre and distinctive national traits in lit.]

398. Pracht, Erwin. "Versuch einer Gegenstandsbestimmung der Theorie des sozialistischen Realismus:Ein Beitrag zur Diskussion." *WB* 16(Heft 6):26–47.

399. Rantavaara, Irma. "Kirjallisuudentutkimuksen strukturalistisista netodeista. (Sur les méthodes structuralistes de l'étude littéraire.)" *KSV* 24(1969):5–20.

400. Rikama, Juha. "Finalistinen selittäminen kirjallisuustieteessä. (Explication finaliste dans la science littéraire.)" *KSV* 24(1969):21–34.

401. Rosenstein, Leon. "Metaphysical Foundations of the Theories of Tragedy in Hegel and Nietzsche." *JAAC* 28:521–33.

402. Røstvig, Maren-Sofie. "Ars Aeterna:Renaissance Poetics and Theories of Divine Creation." *Mosaic* 3,ii:40–61. [On Milton, Ficino, Pico, et al.]

403. Rothenberg, Albert. "Inspiration, Insight and the Creative Process in Poetry." *CE* 32:172–83.

404. Russell, William M. "Poetics and Literary Language." *CE* 31(1969):300–08.

405. Saparow, M. "Das literarische Werk als Struktur." *KuL* 18:293–308. [Tr. Gerhard Sewekow.]

406. Sasayama, Takashi. "Saikin no Kigekiron, Higekiron." *EigoS* 115(1969):550–53. [Recent theories of comedy and tragedy: Olson, Heilman, Brereton, Calarco.]

407. Ščeglov, Jurij K. "Matrona iz èfesa." [F 24]:591–600.

408. Schädlich, Hans-Joachim. "Über Phonologie und Poetik." *JIG* 1,i(1969):44–60.

* 409. Scher, Steven P. "Notes toward a Theory of Verbal Music." *CL* 22:147–56. [Relation of lit. and music.]

410. Seidler, Herbert. *Beiträge zur methodologischen Grundlegung der Literaturwissenschaft.* (SÖAW 262,iii.) Wien: Böhlau, 1969.

411. —— "Stilistik als Wissenschaft von der Sprachkunst." *JIG* 1,i(1969):129–37.

412. Simons, Elisabeth. "Über den sozialistischen Realismus: Seine Herausbildung als allgemeine Gesetzmässigkeit in der Epoche des Übergangs vom Kapitalismus zum Sozialismus." *WB* 16(Heft 3):40–73.

413. Skwarczyńska, Stefania. "Littérature écrite et littérature orale (leurs différences comme prémisses pour une théorie postulée de l'adaption filmique d'œuvres littéraires)." [F 3]: 443–49.

414. Slochower, Harry. *Mythopoesis:Mythic Patterns in the Literary Classics.* Detroit: Wayne State U.P. [Chaps. on Dante, Cervantes, Shakespeare, Melville, Nexö, Gide, Kafka, T. Mann, *inter alia.*]

415. Sojcher, Jacques. "La métaphore généralisée." *RIPh* 23(1969):58–68.

416. Sommer, Dietrich, and Dietrich Löffler. "Soziologische Probleme der literarischen Wirkungsforschung." *WB* 16(Heft 8):51–77.

417. Sőtér, István. "A korszak és az irányzatok." *Kritika* 8,ii:1–13. [Period and trends.]

418. —— "A stílus mint tükörkép és eszmény." *Kritika* 8,vi:1–12. [Style as image and idea.]

419. —— "Az irodalomtudomány dilemmája." *Kritika* 8,viii: 5–17.

420. Sparshott, F.E. "Notes on the Articulation of Time." *NLH* 1:311–34.

421. Strauch, Edward H. "The Subjunctive-Indicative Modality (A Contribution Toward a Theory of Literature)." *DA* 30(1969):1996A–97A(Ind.).

422. Strelka, Joseph. "Esoterische Symbolik in der Literatur." *LuK* 45:278–88.

423. Széles, Klára. "Műtípusok és műértékelések." *Helikon* 15(1969):417–31. [Lit. genres and evaluations.]

424. Szili, József. "A történetiség, mint az irodalmi mű létezésmódja." *Helikon* 15(1969):360–71. [Historical orientation as existence of lit. work.]

426. —— "Az irodalomtörténeti korszakolás elmélete." *Helikon* 16:183–98. [Theory of periodization of lit. hist.]

428. Tober, Karl. *Urteile und Vorurteile über Literatur.* Stuttgart: Kohlhammer.

429. Todorov, Tzvetan. "Choderlos de Laclos et la théorie." [F 24]:601–12.

430. —— "De l'ambiguïté narrative." [F 89],II:913–18.

431. Urmeneta, Fermín de. "Sobre estética estructuralista." *RIE* 105(1969):55–58.

432. —— "Sobre estética humorística." *RIE* 106(1969): 149–52.

433. Veilleux, Jeré. "Toward a Theory of Interpretation." *QJS* 55(1969):105–15.

434. Verweyen, Theodor. *Apophthegma und Scherzrede:Die Geschichte einer einfachen Gattungsform und ihrer Entfaltung im 17. Jahrhundert.* (L&L 5.) Bad Homburg: Gehlen.

435. Vickery, John B. "Mythopoesis and Modern Literature." [F 60]:218–50.

436. Vigneault, Robert. "Jean Rousset et le baroque." *EF* 6:65–78.

437. Volkmann-Schluck, K.-H. "La doctrine de la catharsis dans la poétique d'Aristote." *CTL* 9(1968–69):24–37. [Tr. et annoté par Stéphan De Lannoy.]

438. Wald, Henri. *Relitate și limbaj.* Bucharest: Editura Academiei, 1968. [Lit. uses of lang.]

439. Walter, Achim. "Sozial bedingte Lesemotivationen." *WB* 16(Heft 11):124–44.

440. Walther, Jens. "Handlingsbeskrivelse på grundlag af den dynamiske psykologi." *Poetik* 2,iii(1969):44–55.

441. Warnke, F.J. "Baroque Once More:Notes on a Literary Period." *NLH* 1:145–62.

442. Weimann, Robert. "Gegenwart und Vergangenheit in der Literaturgeschichte:Ein ideologiegeschichtlicher und methodologischer Versuch." *WB* 16(Heft 5):31–57.

443. Weimann, Robert, et al. "Zur Tradition des Realismus und Humanismus." *WB* 16(Heft 10):31–119.

444. Weisgerber, Jean. "The Use of Quotations in Recent Literature." *CL* 22:36–45.

445. Wellek, Albert. *Witz—Lyrik—Sprache:Beiträge zur Literatur- und Sprachtheorie mit einem Anhang über den Fortschritt der Wissenschaft.* Bern: Francke.

446. Wellek, René. "The Term and Concept of Symbolism in Literary History." *NLH* 1:249–70.

447. —— "The Term and Concept of Symbolism in Literary History." [F 3]:275–92.

448. West, Paul. "Adam's Alembic or Imagination Versus mc²." *NLH* 1:523–39. [On theory of fiction.]

449. Wienold, Götz. "Probleme der linguistischen Analyse des Romans." *JIG* 1,i(1969):108–28.

* 450. Willheim, Imanuel. "Rhetoric and Musical Form: Johann Adolph Scheibe's *Schreibarten.*" *HSL* 2:238–47.

451. Wilmars, Dirk. "De magie van het woord." *HZM* 23(1969):399–419.

452. Wismann, Heinz. "Le métier de philologue." *Critique* 26:462–79,774–81.

453. Żołkiewski, S. "Deux structuralismes." [F 24]:3–12. [Influ. of Lukács (and Lévi-Strauss) on the study of lit. and culture.]

454. Żolkovskij, A.K. "Deus ex Machina." [F 24]:539–47.
See also 139, 237, 455, 894, 943, 953, 1454, 2171, 2638, 3313, 3527, 3634, 3687, 4171, 4522, 9837.

III. LITERATURE, GENERAL AND COMPARATIVE

Bibliography. 455. Bercovitch, Sacvan,et al. "Selective Check-List On Typology." *EAL* 5,i,pt.2:1–76.

456. Buchholz, Peter. *Bibliographie zur alteuropäischen Religionsgeschichte 1954–1964:Literatur zu den antiken Rand- und Nachfolgekulturen im aussermediterranen Europa unter besonderer Berücksichtigung der nichtchristlichen Religionen.* (Arbeiten zur Frühmittelalterforschung 2.) Berlin: de Gruyter, 1967.

457. [Kloss, Robert J.],et al.,comps. "Bibliography [of Articles on Literature and Psychology] for 1968." *L&P* 20,iv:143–217.

458. *Literature and Language Bibliographies from* The American Year Book, *1910–1919.* (Cumulated Bibliog. Ser. 1.) Introd. Arnold N. Rzepecki. Ann Arbor, Mich.: Pierian Press.

459. Meserole, Harrison T.,et al.,comps. *1969 MLA International Bibliography of Books and Articles on the Modern Languages and Literatures. Vol.* I:*General, English, American, Medieval and Neo-Latin, and Celtic Literatures.* New York: MLA.

460. —— *1969 MLA International Bibliography of Books and Articles on the Modern Languages and Literatures.* Vol. II:*General Romance, French, Italian, Spanish, Portuguese and Brazilian, Romanian, General Germanic, German, Netherlandic, Scandinavian, Modern Greek, Oriental, African, and East European Literatures.* New York: MLA.

461. Naaman, Antoine. *Guide bibliographique des thèses littéraires canadiennes de 1921 à 1969.* Sherbrooke, Québec: Eds. Cosmos, 1969.

462. Sammons, Jeffrey L., and Ernst Schürer. "Heinrich E.K. Henel:Bibliographie 1928–1968." [F 37]:291–96.

463. Tompkins, Margaret, and Norma Shirley,comps. *A Checklist of Serials in Psychology and Allied Fields.* Troy, N.Y.: Whitston Pub. Co.

464. Voet, Leon. *The Golden Compasses:A History and Evaluation of the Officina Plantiniana at Antwerp.* I:*Christopher Plantin and the Moretuses:Their Lives and Their World.* Amsterdam: Vangendt and Co., 1969.

465. Winniczuk, Lidia, and Zdisław Piszczek. "Antyk w Polsce:Bibliografia za rok 1965. Bibliografia za rok 1966." *Meander* 22(1967):145–96; 23(1968):215–79.

See also 737, 937.

Comparative Literature. 466. Aldridge, A.O.,ed. *Comparative Literature:Matter and Method.* With Introds. Urbana: U. of Ill. P., 1969. [17 essays repr. from *CLS.*]

467. Alekseev, M.P. "La littérature russe et sa portée européenne." [F 3]:539–46.

468. Angyal, Andreas. "Barock als internationales Literaturphänomen." [F 3]:89–99.

469. Anon. "Rapport relatif au projet d'une histoire de la littérature européenne. Antécédents." [F 3]:775–94.

470. Avni, Abraham. "The Influence of the Bible on European Literatures:A Review of Research from 1955 to 1965." *YCGL* 19:39–57.

471. Balakian, Anna. "Dada-Surrealism:Fundamental Differences." [F 43]:13–30.

472. —— "Le caractère international du symbolisme." [F 3]:293–99.

473. Barta, János. "Az összehasonlító irodalomtudomány fogalmi alapvetéséhez (Kísérlet)." *Helikon* 16:139–51. [Theoretical basis of comparative lit.]

475. Beller, Manfred. "Von der Stoffgeschichte zur Thematologie:Ein Beitrag zur komparatistischen Methodenlehre." *Arcadia* 5:1–38.

476. Bertrand de Muñoz, Maryse. "La guerre civile espagnole et la littérature." *Mosaic* 3,i(1969):62–79. [In Spanish and other lits.]

477. Betz, Louis Paul. *La littérature comparée:Essai bibliographique.* Introd. Joseph Texte. 2d ed., augm., pub. avec un index méthodique par Fernand Baldensperger. New York: AMS Press, 1969. [Repr. of Strasburg 1904 ed.]

478. Bjørnvig, Thorkild. "Beat—et dionysisk fænomen." *Kritik* 14:56–87.

479. Block, Haskell M. *Nouvelles tendances en littérature comparée.* Paris: Nizet.

480. Brahmer, Mieszysław. "Présence polonaise dans la littérature européenne." [F 3]:641–50.

* 481. Brown, Calvin S. "Musico-Literary Research in the Last Two Decades." *YCGL* 19:5–27.

482. Carandino, N. "Scrisoare către Sfînta Ioana." *SXX* 13,iv:78–88.

483. Clements, Robert J. *The Peregrine Muse:Studies in Comparative Renaissance Literature.* (UNCSRLL 82.) Chapel Hill: U. of N.C. Press, 1969.

484. Dasgupta, R.K. "Concept of World Literature:A Comparative Study of the Views of Goethe and Tagore." [F 3]:399–404.

485. Deeney, John J.,S.J. "Comparative Literature Studies in Taiwan." *TkR* 1,i:119–45.

486. Deugd, Cornelius de. "The Unity of Romanticism as an International Movement." [F 3]:173–89.

487. Dima, Al.,ed. *Probleme de literatură comparată şi sociologie literară.* Bucharest: Ed. Academiei.

488. Dimaras, C. Th. "La réceptivité locale conditionnement des courants internationaux." [F 3]:51–56.

489. Dolanski, Julius. "Zur Frage des internationalen Charakters der literarischen Strömungen." [F 3]:23–28.

490. Durišin, Dionýz. "Les courants littéraires dans le système de l'étude comparée des littératures." [F 3]:45–50.

491. Evans, Arthur R.,Jr. *On Four Modern Humanists: Hofmannsthal, Gundolf, Curtius, Kantorowicz.* (Princeton Essays in European and Comp. Lit.) Princeton: Princeton U.P.

492. Friederich, Werner P. *The Challenge of Comparative Literature, and Other Addresses.* (UNCSCL 51.) Ed. William J. DeSua. Introd. David H. Malone. Chapel Hill: U. of N.C. Press.

493. Furst, Lilian R. "Kafka and the Romantic Imagination." *Mosaic* 3,iv:81–89.

494. —— *Romanticism in Perspective:A Comparative Study of Aspects of the Romantic Movements in England, France, and Germany.* New York: Humanities.

495. Gachechiladze, Givi R. "Georgian Verse in the Comparative Aspect." [F 3]:427–28.

496. Gavrilović, Zoran. "The Theory of the Radical Movement in Literature Between Two Wars." [F 3]:379–90.

497. Gifford, Henry. *Comparative Literature.* (Concepts of Lit.) London: Routledge & K. Paul; New York: Humanities, 1969.

498. Girmounsky, Victor. "Les courants littéraires en tant que phénomènes internationaux." [F 3]:3–21.

499. Goodrich, Norma L. "Concerning Research in the Fifteenth Century." *Coranto* 6,ii:28–37.

500. Hanak, M. "The Baroque as Exaggeration and Polarization of Renaissance Exuberance:The Continental and the English View." [F 3]:111–17.

501. Hickey, Leo. "El valor de la alusión en literatura." *RO* 30:49–60.

502. Howard, Martha W. *The Influence of Plutarch in the Major European Literatures of the Eighteenth Century.* (UNCSCL 50.) Chapel Hill: U. of N.C. Press. [In Fr., Ger., Eng., and Ital. lits.]

503. Illés, László. "Die Avantgarde, als künstlerische Haltung." [F 3]:335–41.

504. Jost, François. "La littérature comparée:Une philosophie des lettres." [F 27]:312–41.

505. Kopecký, M. "K německo-česko-polské tvorbě dramatické a dialogické v 16. stoleti." [F 29]:390–98.

506. Köpeczi, Béla. "Le réalisme socialiste en tant que courant littéraire international." [F 3]:371–77.

507. Kott, Jan. "The Absurd and Greek Tragedy." [F 43]:77–93. [Tr. E.J. Czerwinski. With ref. to Kafka, Beckett, Camus, Artaud, Cocteau, Brecht, *inter alia.*]

508. Krejči, Karel. "Les tendances préromantiques dans les littératures des renaissance nationales du XVIIIe et XIXe siècles." [F 3]:165–72.

509. Kuleschow, W.I. "Die Darstellung der russischen Literaturgeschichte bei den Literaturwissenschaftlern der nichtslawischen länder." [F 3]:547–52.

510. Kurzweil, Baruch. "Al shlosha sippurei hitbagrut me-

reshit ha-me'ah ha-essrim. [Three Early 20th Century Stories Dealing with Maturing of the Personality of the Hero.]" *Bikoret u-Parshanut* 1:7–11. [On Robert Musil's *The Pupil Törless*, James Joyce's *A Portrait of the Artist as a Young Man*, and *Silvery Wind* by Franâ Sramek.]

511. Levin, Harry. "On the Dissemination of Realism." [F 3]:231–41.

512. Libera, Zdzistav. "La notion de rococo dans la littérature européenne." [F 3]:137–45.

513. Lomidse, G. "Der Nationalcharakter—kein Mythos, sondern eine Realität." *KuL* 18:1104–08. [Tr. Gerhard Sewekow.]

514. Markiewicz, Henryk. "The Concept of Literary Trend in the History of Literature." [F 3]:29–35.

515. Miner, Earl. "Formulas:Japanese and Western Evidence Compared." [F 3]:405–18.

516. Neupokojeva, I. "The Comparative Aspects of Literature in 'The History of World Literature'." [F 3]:37–43.

517. Ota, Saburo. "What Is 'Influence'?" *TkR* 1,i:109–18.

518. Pellat, Charles. "Djâhiz et la 'littérature comparée'." *CALC* 1(1966):95–108. [9th cent. Arab writer.]

* 519. Purdy, Strother B. "On the Psychology of Erotic Literature." *L&P* 20,i:23–29.

520. Rousseau, André M. "Vingt ans de littérature comparée en France (1949–1969). Bilan et perspectives." *IL* 21(1969):199–204.

521. Saul, George B. *Withdrawn in Gold:Three Commentaries on Genius.* (Studies in Gen. and Comp. Lit. 8.) The Hague: Mouton. [On J. Stephens, R. Hodgson, and K. Blixen.]

522. Smith, G. Gregory. "The Foible of Comparative Literature." *YCGL* 19:58–66.

523. Strzalko, Maria. "Le baroque littéraire est-il un phénomène européen homogene?" [F 3]:101–10.

524. Szabolsci, Miklós. "L'avant-garde littéraire et artistique comme phénomène international." [F 3]:317–34.

525. Szegedy-Maszák, Mihály. "A strukturális vizsgálat alkalmazásának lehetősége az összehasonlító irodalom-tudományban." *Helikon* 16:238–50. [Possibility of usage of structural research in comparative lit.]

527. Vajda, György Mihály. "Goethe, a világirodalom és az összehasonlító irodalomtörténet." *Helikon* 16:152–63. [Goethe, world lit. and comp. lit.]

528. Vanasco, Rocco R. *The Influence of Italian Poetics and Poetry on the Theory and Practice of French Poets, 1580–1640.* Gela: R. Trainito Pubs.

529. Vickery, Olga W. "The Inferno of the Moderns." [F 60]:147–64.

530. Wegner, Michael. "Lenins Gesellschaftstheorie und die vergleichende Literaturforschung." *WZUJ* 19:41–48.

531. Zolbrod, Leon Z. "A Comparative Approach to 'Tales of Moonlight and Rain' (*Ugetsu Monogatari*)." *HAB* 21,ii:48–56.

See also 435, 552, 633, 972, 1013, 1487, 3751, 5600, 6227, 6588, 7242, 7524.

General Literature. 532. AN SSSR, IMLI. *Istorija sovetskoj mnogonacional'noj literatury.* V 6-ti tt. T.I. Moscow: Nauka. [1st vol. of projected 6-vol. *Hist. of Soviet Multi-National Lit.*]

533. —— *Iz istorii Meždunarodnogo ob"edinenija revoljucionnyx pisatelej (MORP).* (Literaturnoe nasledstvo 81.) Moscow: Nauka, 1969.

534. —— *Poèzija socializma:Xudožestvennye otkrytija poèzii socialističeskogo realizma.* Moscow: Nauka, 1969.

535. Artemenko, E.P., and N.K. Sokolova. *O nekotoryx priemax izučenija jazyka xudožestvennyx proizvedenij.* Voronež: Izd. Voronežskogo universiteta, 1968. [On the ling. study of works of lit.]

536. Ballif, Gene. "Reading, Writing, and Reality." *Salmagundi* 12:25–42.

* 537. Barnes, Hazel E. "Literature and the Politics of the Future." *UDQ* 5,i:41–64.

538. Basler, Roy P. "A Literary Enthusiasm; or, the User Used." *Midway* 11,i:11–21.

539. Bay, Paul. *Le style coruscant. Essai, Stace, Perse, Apulée. . . .* Bruxelles: Ed. des cinquante, 1968.

* 540. Beach, Waldo. "Religion as a Humanizing Factor." *SHR* 4:197–201.

541. Beardslee, William A. *Literary Criticism of the Ne‹ Testament.* Philadelphia: Fortress P.

542. Beaufret, Jean. "La naissance de la philosophie." [. 31]:25–47.

543. Bencheneb, Saâdeddine. "Deux amants malheureu‹ Antar et Pyrrhus." *CALC* 1(1966):11–14.

544. Bersani, Leo. "Language and Politics." *PR* 37:385–40‹

545. "Bible and Literary Criticism:Remarks and Discussions. *Hasifrut* 2:580–663. [Boaz Arpali, "Caution:A Biblical Story Comments on the Story of David and Bathsheba, and on th Problems of the Biblical Narrative," 580–97; Uriel Simon, "A Ironic Approach to a Bible Story:On the Interpretation of th Story of David and Bathsheba," 598–607; Menakhem Perry an Meir Sternberg, "Caution:A Literary Text! Problems in th Poetics and the Interpretation of Biblical Narrative (A Reply t B. Arpali and to U. Simon)," 608–63. All in Hebr.; Eng. sums

546. Boase, Alan M. "The Baroque Syndrome." *EF* 6(1969):1–17.

547. Boyle, Thomas E. "The Value of Uselessness. *BRMMLA* 24:33–36. [The "Utility" of lit.]

548. Cargill, Oscar. "The Validity of Literature." *CE* 3 (1969):617–22.

549. Carleton, William G. *Technology and Humanism:Son Exploratory Essays for Our Time.* Foreword Manning J. Daue Nashville, Tenn.: Vanderbilt U.P. [Rptd. essays on hist anthropol., lit., etc., with new introds. and notes.]

550. Ceserani, Remo. "Storie letterarie e industria culturale. *Belfagor* 25:332–44.

551. Clough, Wilson O. "Measures of Tolerance." *Rendezvou 5,i:1–11.

552. Collins, R.G., and Kenneth McRobbie,eds. *The Mosa‹ Reader.* Vol. I:1967-68. With Introd. Winnipeg: U. of Manitoba [Arts., orig. ed. by R.P. Hoople and Kenneth McRobbie, co‹ from Vol. I of *Mosaic*.]

553. Davidson, Gustav. "The Named Angels in Scripture *CimR* 13:65–69.

554. "De sociale positie van de schrijver." *Raam* 61(1969 10–68. [Lambert Tegenbosch, "Het loon van de horzel," 10–1‹ Fons Sarneel, "Kunst en volk," 17–30; Eldert Willems, "D malaise van de uitgever," 31–34; Otto Dijk, "Bestormba stellingen met betrekking tot de verhouding schrijver-uitgever, 35–36; Dirk Kroon, "Wid goed is krijgt zetters," 37–39; Jef Las "De illusies van de democratisering," 40–42; P. Hagers, "D malaise van de schrijve—en uitgeverij," 43–50; Jacques Kruitho "Notities," 51–56; Corn. Verhoeven, "Afremmen in het midden, 57–65; Eldert Willems, "Gedachten over een grondrecht van d Kunst," 66–68.]

* 555. Detweiler, Robert. "Religion as a Humanizing Force ‹ Literature." *SHR* 4:201–06.

556. Dmitriev, V.G. *Skryvšie svoe imja:Iz istorii psevdonimov anonimov.* Moscow: Nauka.

557. Dockhorn, Klaus. *Macht und Wirkung der Rhetorik:Vi‹ Aufsätze zur Ideengeschichte der Vormoderne.* (ResLit 2.) Gehle‹ Bad Homburg, 1968.

558. Doroševič, A. "Mif v literature XX veka." *VL* 14,ii:122–40.

* 559. Eble, Kenneth. "Literature Is Where It's At." *BRMML 24:37–48. [Lit. in today's climate.]

560. Egri, Péter. "Társadalomábrázolás és lélekábrázolás *Helikon* 15(1969):351–59. [Representation of social conditio‹ and of characters in lit. works.]

561. Elsberg, J. "La sociologie dans l'étude bourgeois contemporaine de la littérature." [F 40]:525–37. ["Réponse," b Lucien Goldmann, 539–51.]

562. Forgács, László. *A szocialista realizmus esztétik‹ meghatározásához:Tudatosság és költőiség.* Budapest: Magvet‹ [Esthetic def. of Socialist Realism.]

563. Freccero, John. "*Blow-Up*:From the Word to th Image." *Yale/Theatre* 3,i:15–24.

564. Frenz, Horst,ed. *Nobel Lectures, Including Presentatio Speeches and Laureates' Biographies. Literature, 1901–196* Amsterdam and New York: Elsevier for the Nobel Foundatio‹ 1969.

565. Gehman, Henry S.,ed. *The New Westminster Dictiona‹

of the Bible. Philadelphia: Westminster.

566. Gianakaris, C.J. *Plutarch.* (TWAS.) New York: Twayne.

567. Goldway, David. "Appearance and Reality in Marx's *Capital.*" *Science and Society* 31(1967):428–47.

568. Gollhardt, Heinz. "Das Taschenbuch im Zeitalter der Massenkultur." [F 36]:122–32.

569. Gulyga, A. "Puti mifotvorčestva i puti iskusstva." *NovM* 45,v(1969):217–32. [The ways of mythmaking and the ways of art.]

570. Hankiss, Elemér. "Literary Movements and Structural Analysis." [F 3]:57–60.

571. Henn, T.R. *The Bible as Literature.* New York: Oxford U.P.

572. Hoggart, Richard. *Speaking to Each Other:Essays.* 1:*About Society.* II:*About Literature.* New York: Oxford U.P.; London: Chatto & Windus.

573. Hyman, Lawrence W. "Autonomy and Relevance in Literature." *CE* 30(1969):623–26.

574. Isaacson, José. *El poeta en la sociedad de masas: Elementos para una antropología literaria.* Buenos Aires: Américalee, 1969.

575. Kantorovič, Vladimir. "O nekotoryx aspektax sociologii literatury." *VLit* 13,xi(1969):43–59.

576. Kermode, Frank. "World Without End or Beginning." *MHRev* 1(1967):113–29. [Relation between lit. fictions and the 'real.']

577. Király, István,ed. *Világirodalmi lexikon, Vol. I:A-Cal.* Budapest: Akadémiai K. [*Dictionary of World Literature,* Vol. I.]

578. Köpeczi, Béla. "Művészet—tömeg—proletárforradalom. Jegyzetek a munkásmozgalom kultúra-felfogásáról." *Helikon* 15(1969):199–207. [Art—Mass—Proletarian Revolution. Notes on culture concept. of working movement. Lit. interest.]

579. Kristjánsson, Sverrir. "Þjóðfelagið og skáldið." *Tímarit* 31:66–71. [Society and the poet.]

580. Kruithof, Jacques. "De schrijver aan het werk." *Raam* 64:15–34.

581. Kurz, Paul Konrad,S.J. "De schrijvers en de christenen, 1: Bedenkingen en bezwaren van de schrijvers." *Streven* 22(1969): 635–41.

582. Lancelotti, Mario A. "Sobre lo nuevo y lo viejo." *RO* 30:200–13. [Lit. and ideas.]

583. Leary, Bernice E. "Milestones in Children's Books." *BI* 12:18–39.

584. Lebel, Maurice. "The Function of the Humanities in an Era of Technology." *PTRSC* 7(1969):17–37.

585. Leenhardt, Jacques. "Sémantique et sociologie de la littérature." *RISULB* 3(1969):99–111.

586. —— "Sémantique et sociologie de la littérature." [F 40]:427–39.

* 587. Levine, Carl. "Literature and Social Relevance." *BRMMLA* 24:25–32.

588. Lombardi del Monaco, Aurora. "Il surrealismo nella cultura contemporanea." *Annali della facoltà di lettere e filosofia dell'Università di Napoli* 11(1964–68):265–98.

589. Lukács, Borbála. "Az uj szovjet Világirodalomtörténet előkészítésének elvi kérdései." *Helikon* 16:199–206.

590. Maniu, Leonida. "Eroul literaturii contemporane—oglindă a lumii socialiste." *ILit* 20,viii(1969):54–61.

591. Mann, Yuri. "The Magnifying Glass of Grotesque." *SovL* 8:133–44.

592. McPherson, Hugo. "The Future of Literary Studies and the Media." *PTRSC* 7(1969):247–50.

593. Mertner, Edgar, and Herbert Mainusch. *Pornotopia:Das Obszöne und die Pornographie in der literarischen Landschaft.* Frankfurt: Athenäum.

594. Miklós, Pál. "A számok és az irodalomtudomány." *Helikon* 15(1969):414–16. [Numbers and lit. study.]

595. *Nasledie Lenina i nauka o literature.* Leningrad: Nauka, 1969.

596. Onimus, Jean. *La Communication littéraire.* Bruges: Desclée De Brouwer.

597. Pavlov, S. *Slovo—oružie:O naučnyx osnovax èffektivnosti pečati.* Minsk: Belarus'. [On the effectiveness of the press.]

598. Philippot-Reniers, Annie. "Traditie en actualiteit van het mythisch denken in het Westen." *TVUB* 11(1968–69):1–44.

599. Praz, Mario. *Mnemosyne:The Parallel Between Literature and the Visual Arts.* (BS 35. A.W. Mellon Lects. in Fine Arts 16.) Princeton, N.J.: Princeton U.P.

600. Preus, James S. *From Shadow to Promise:Old Testament Interpretation from Augustine to the Young Luther.* Cambridge: Belknap P. of Harvard U.P., 1969.

601. Ray, Paul C. "What Was Surrealism?" *JML* 1:133–37. [Essay-rev.]

602. Rehder, Helmut. "Planetenkinder:Some Problems of Character Portrayal in Literature." *The Graduate Jour.* 8(1968): 69–97.

603. Richards, I.A. "Tipi e campeoni." *SCr* 3(1969):187–92.

* 604. Richards, Robert F. "Literature and Politics." *ColQ* 18:97–106.

605. Richardson, Kenneth R.,ed: R. Clive Willis,assoc. ed. *Twentieth Century Writing:A Reader's Guide to Contemporary Literature.* New York: Newnes, 1969.

606. Rider, Maurice L. "Of the Titles of Many Books." [F 23]:37–41. [Titles of 20th cent. books derived from King James Version.]

607. Robinson, A.N. "O preobrazovanii tradicionnyx žanrov kak faktora vostočnoevropejskogo literaturnogo processa v perexodnoj period (XVI–XVIII vv.)." *IAN* 28(1969):408–14.

608. Ross, Werner. "Ist die christliche Literatur zu Ende?" (Studien u. Berichte der Kath. Akad. in Bayern 41.) 127–46 in Paul K. Kurz, et al., *Moderne Literature und christlicher Glaube.* Würzburg: Echter-Verl., 1968.

609. Saito, Bishu. "History and Literature (3)." *EigoS* 114(1968):26–27.

610. Scott, Nathan A.,Jr. "The 'Conscience' of the New Literature." [F 60]:251–83.

611. Shipley, Joseph T.,ed. *Dictionary of World Literary Terms, Forms, Technique, Criticism.* Rev. and Enl. Ed. Boston: The Writer.

612. Slatoff, Walter J. *With Respect to Readers:Dimensions of Literary Response.* Ithaca, N.Y.: Cornell U.P.

613. Stoehr, Taylor. "Realism and Verisimilitude." *TSLL* 11(1969):1269–88.

614. Störig, Hans Joachim. "Das Buch als Gegenstand der Wissenschaft." [F 36]:11–32.

615. Stybe, Vibeke. *Fra Askepot til Anders And:Børnebogen i kulturhistorisk perspektiv.* 2nd Rev. and Enl. Ed. Copenhagen: Munksgaard, 1969. [1st ed., 1962.]

616. Todorov, Tzvetan. "L'histoire de la littérature." *LFr* 7(sept):14–19.

617. Twining, Edward. "Politics and the Imagination." *UDQ* 5,ii:1–18.

618. Varga, Imre. "XIIIe stage international d'études humanistes. (Tours, du 2 au 13 juillet)." *Helikon* 16:304–06. [Rev. on the Conf.; in Hung.]

619. Vigolo, Giorgio. "Per una psicologia dell'antiromanticismo contemporaneo." [F 11]:723–37.

* 620. Vivas, Eliseo. "Myth:Some Philosophical Problems." *SoR* 6:89–103.

621. Waheed, A. "Children's Literature." *PakR* 18,v:25–29.

622. Watson, George. *The Literary Thesis:A Guide to Research.* London: Longman.

623. Weidhorn, Manfred. "Clothes and the Man." *ConnR* 3,ii:41–57.

624. Widmer, Eleanor, assist. by Kingsley Widmer,comps. *Freedom and Culture:Literary Censorship in the '70's.* Belmont, Calif.: Wadsworth.

625. Xrapčenko, M. "O progresse v literatur i iskusstve:Stat'ja vtoraja." *VLit* 14,vi:58–74.

626. Ziegengeist, G.,ed. *Aktuelle Probleme der vergleichenden Literaturforschung.* (VIS 49.) Berlin: Akademie-verl., 1968.

See also 309, 397, 2359, 8258.

Medieval Literature. 627. Baird, Lorrayne Y. "The Status of the Poet in the Middle Ages and the Problem of Anonymity." *DAI* 30:3422A–23A(Ky.).

628. Cartier, Normand R. "Celestial Portents and Mediaeval Chroniclers." [F 15]:15–28.

629. Dorfman, Eugene. *The Narreme in the Medieval Romance*

Epic:An Introduction to Narrative Structures. Toronto: U. of Toronto P., 1969. [Corr. of Bibliog. for 1969, Vol. I, Item 761.]

630. Grabher, Carlo. "La figura di Giuda nei moderni scrittori e una sua singolare interpretazione medievale." *AFLFP* 5(1967-68):372–85.

631. Halverson, John. "Amour and Eros in the Middle Ages." *PsyR* 57:245–58.

632. Holmes, Urban T. "The Monkey in Mediaeval Literature." [F 15]:93–100.

633. Nichols, Stephen G.,Jr. "The Spirit of Truth:Epic Modes in Medieval Literature." *NLH* 1:365–86.

* 634. Reiss, Edmund. "Number Symbolism and Medieval Literature." *M&H* N.S. 1:161–74.

635. Robinson, Fred C. "Personal Names in Medieval Narrative and the Name of Unferth in *Beowulf*." [F 16]:43–48.

636. Rouse, Richard H. *Serial Bibliographies for Medieval Studies.* (Pubs. of the Center for Mediev. and Renaissance Studies 3.) Assist. by J.H. Claxton and M.D. Metzger. Berkeley: U. of Calif. P., 1969.

637. Schlauch, Margaret. *Medieval Narrative:A Book of Translations.* New York: Gordian, 1969. [Repr. of 1928 ed.]

638. Seifarth, Wolfgang S. *Synagogue and Church in the Middle Ages:Two Symbols in Art and Literature.* Tr. from Ger. by Lee Chadeayne and Paul Gottwald. New York: Ungar.

639. Steinberg, Clarence B. "Some Medieval Traditions of Etymological Characterization." *DAI* 30(1969):2500A–01A(Pa.)

640. Szövérffy, Joseph. "The Christian Spirit of Medieval Poetry." *Thought* 44(1969):581–96.

641. Taylor, Albert B. *An Introduction to Medieval Romance.* New York: Barnes & Noble, 1969. [Repr. of 1930 ed.]

642. Voss, Bernd R. *Der Dialog in der frühchristlichen Literatur.* München: Fink.

643. Wertz, Dorothy C. "Mankind as a Type-Figure on the Popular Religious Stage." *Compar. Studies in Soc. and Hist.* 12,i:83–91.

644. Wilke, Eckhard L. *Der mitteldeutsche* Karl und Elegast. *Studien zur vergleichende Literaturwissenschaft.* (MBG 27.) Marburg: Elwert, 1969.

See also 456, 797, 1081, 1690, 1759, 1900, 8445, 8448, 8451, 8487, 8505, 8630, 8900, 9676.

IV. THEMES AND TYPES

Allegory. 645. Fleisher, Wolfgang. " 'Ascendam in Palmam': Ein Beitrag zur Überlieferung der Palmbaumallegorie im Mittelalter." *LJGG* 10(1969):1–52.

See also 316.

Arthurian. 646. Baron, Francis X. "The Alienated Hero in Arthurian Romance." *DAI* 30:2960A(Iowa).

647. Blanch, Robert J. "The History and Progress of the Tristan Legend:Drust to Malory." *RLV* 35(1969):129–35.

* 648. Carman, J. Neale. "The Conquests of the Grail Castle and Dolorous Guard." *PMLA* 85:433–43.

649. Derolez, R. "King Arthur in Flanders." [F 52]:239–47.

650. Hunt, Troy. "The Rhetorical Background to the Arthurian Prologue:Tradition and the Old French Vernacular Prologues." *FMLS* 6:1–23.

651. International Arthurian Society. "Bibliography [for 1968]." *BBSIA* 21(1969):9–105.

652. Lagorio, Valerie M. "Pan-Brittonic Hagiography and the Arthurian Grail Cycle." *Traditio* 26:29–61.

653. Laurie, Helen C.R. "The Arthurian World of *Erec et Enide.*" *BBSIA* 21(1969):111–19.

654. Roberts, Gildas. "*Arthur and Gorlagon:*A Study in Structure." *UCTSE* 1:19–24.

655. Sundel, Alfred. "Joseph Campbell's Quest for the Grail." *SR* 78:211–16. [Rev. art.]

656. Wais, Kurt,ed. *Der arthurische Roman.* Darmstadt: Wissenschaft. Buchgesellschaft. [Kurt Wais, "Einführung in die Forschungsgeschichte des arthurischen Romans," 1–18; Julius Pokorny, "Der Ursprung der Arthursage," 19–44; Jean Marx, "Die Bedeutung der britannischen Welt für die Artusepik," 45–55; Joseph Bédier, "Die Lais der Marie de France," 56–93; William A. Nitze, "Probleme des arthurischen Romans," 94–111; Roger S. Loomis, "König Arthur und die Antipoden," 112–33; Pierre le Gentil, "Die Tristansage in der Darstellung von Beroul und von Thomas:Versuch einer Interpretation," 134–64; Pentti Tilvis, "Über die unmittelbaren Vorlagen von Hartmanns *Erec* und *Iwein*, Ulrichs *Lanzelet* und Wolframs *Parzival*," 165–214; Hendricus Sparnaay, "Zu *Erec-Gereint*," 215–36; Kurt Ruh, "Lancelot," 237–55; Elaine Southward, "Die Einheit des *Lancelot* von Crestien," 256–70; Wendelin Foerster, "Besprechung von Jessie L. Weston *The Legend of Sir Gawain*," 271–81; Heinrich Zimmer, "Gawain beim Grünen Ritter," 282–300; William A. Nitze, "Was hat Robert de Boron geschrieben?" 301–09; E. Brugger, "Besprechung von Franz Rolf Schröder, *Die Parzival- frage*," 310–20; Friedrich Ranke, "Zur Symbolik des Grals bei Wolfram von Eschenbach," 321–31; Wolfgang Mohr, "Parzivals ritterliche Schuld," 332–54 + Reprs.]

657. Wilson, Simone. "The Arthurian Myth in Modern Literature." *Mythlore* 1,i(1969):30–32.

See also 1730, 4755, 5563.

Biography and Autobiography. 658. Andrews, Larry K. "The Effect of Author Biography Upon the Comprehension and Appreciation of Poetry." *DAI* 30:4395A–96A(Mo., Columbia)

659. Hart, Francis R. "Notes for an Anatomy of Modern Autobiography." *NLH* 1:485–511.

660. Hoffs, Joshua A. "Comments on Psychoanalytic Biography with Special Reference to Freud's Interest in Woodrow Wilson." *PsyR* 56(1969):402–14.

661. Kay, Ernest,comp. *Dictionary of International Biography* Seventh Ed. 2 vols. London: Melrose.

Computer-Assisted Literary Research. 662. Bailey, Richard W., and Jay L. Robinson. "Computers and Dictionaries." [F 9]:89–94.

663. Barnett, Michael P. "SNAP:A Programming Language for Humanists." *CHum* 4:225–40.

664. Bessinger, Jess B.,Jr. "Computers and Literary Studies." [F 9]:4–10.

665. Brandwood, Leonard. "Plato's *Seventh Letter*." *Revue* 4(1969):1–25. [Use of statistical methods in judging authenticity of texts.]

666. Cain, Alexander M. "Rapid Retrieval of Bibliographical Materials." [F 8]:57–70.

667. Ducretet, Pierre R. "Computers and Literary Studies Another View." [F 9]:10–21. [See art. by Bessinger, above.]

668. Gundlach, Rolf. "Maschinelle Philologie als historische Hilfswissenschaft." *FoLi* 2(1968):230–56.

* 669. Hines, Theodore C., Jessica L. Harris, and Charlotte L. Levy. "An Experimental Concordance Program." *CHum* 4 161–71.

670. Horowitz, Floyd R. "An Algorithm for Determining Iterative Formations in Natural Language Texts." *CSHVB* 1(1968):70–76.

671. Jeanneret, Marsh. "Information Retrieval and the Decision to Publish." *SchP* 1:229–43.

672. Kline, Edward A. "The Computer, Graphemics and Middle English Dialectology." *CSHVB* 2(1969):57–81.

673. Martin, W. "On Uses of the Computer in Literary Research." *TITL* 8:3–8.

674. Mau, J. "A Simple Means for Input and Output of Greek Texts on a Small IBM 1130 Outfit." *Revue* 4(1969):26–27

675. Melcher, Daniel. "The Role of Computers." [F 25] 49–59.

676. Milic, Louis T. "From Aristotle to IBM." [F 8]:71–93

677. Parrish, Stephen M. "Concordance-Making by Computer:Its Past, Future, Techniques, and Applications." [F 8]:16–33.

678. Petőfi, S. János. "On the Linear Patterning of Verbal Works of Art." *ComputL* 8(1969):37–63.

679. Raben, Joseph. "Computer Applications to Problems in the Humanities:A Keynote Address." [F 8]:5–15.

680. Richmond, Phyllis A. "An Extended Character Set for

Humanities Computer Printout." *CHum* 4:247–50.

681. Sands, Alyce E.,ed. "Annual Bibliography for 1969 [General and Language and Literature]." *CHum* 4:251–57.

682. Schanze, Helmut. "Computer-unterstützte Literaturwissenschaft." *Muttersprache* 79(1969):315–21.

683. —— "Zur Interpretation von Novalis' *Heinrich von Ofterdingen:*Theorie und Praxis eines vollständiges Wortindex." *WW* 20:19–33.

684. Sedelow, Sally. "Communicating with a Computer About Humanistic Research." [F 8]:34–56.

685. —— "The Computer in the Humanities and Fine Arts." *Computing Surveys* 2:89–110.

686. Stevens, Peter, and Robert I. Scott. "Mindlessly Mass-Producing Poetry by Computer or a Multiple-Version Poem for All Canadian Places and Seasons?" *UWR* 5,ii:27–34.

* 687. Wachal, Robert S. "The Machine in the Garden: Computers and Literary Scholarship, 1970." *CHum* 5:23–28.

688. Waite, Stephen V.F. "Computer-Supplemented Latin Instruction at Dartmouth College." *CHum* 4:313–14.

See also 864, 1106, 1157, 1346, 2016, 2040, 2264, 2642, 4966, 9151, 9605, 9635, 9637, 10850.

Drama and Theater. 689. Arnold, Lionel A. "Ambiguity and Ambivalence in Modern Drama:The Sphinx and the Playwright." *DAI* 30(1969):2188A–89A(Drew).

690. Attoun, Lucien. "Picasso et le théâtre." *Europe* 492–93: 211–13.

691. Bablet, Denis. "Conditions architecturales et scénographiques d'un théâtre à audience populaire." *CTL* 7–8(1968–69):60–64.

692. Baiwir, Albert. "Heur et malheurs du Happening." *RLV* 35(1969):341–51.

693. Band-Kuzmany, Karin R.M.,comp. *Glossary of the Theatre.* (Glossarium Interpretum 15.) In Eng., Fr., Ital., and Ger. New York: Amer. Elsevier, 1969.

694. Baumann, Gerhart. "Über das neuere Drama," 7–25 in Gerhard Neumann, Jürgen Schröder, and Manfred Karnick, *Dürrenmatt, Frisch, Weiss.* München: Fink, 1969.

695. Beckerman, Bernard. *Dynamics of Drama:Theory and Method of Analysis.* New York: Knopf.

696. Benedetti, Robert. *The Actor at Work.* Englewood Cliffs, N.J.: Prentice-Hall.

697. Berthold, Margot. *Weltgeschichte des Theaters.* Stuttgart: Kröner, 1968.

698. Bour, Pierre. *Le psychodrame et la vie.* Paris and Bruges: Desclée De Brouwer, 1968.

699. Broad, Jay. "A Look at Theatre." *CimR* 11:48–52.

700. Brustein, Robert S. *The Third Theatre.* New York: Simon & Schuster.

701. Caine, Cindy S. "Structure in the One-Act Play." *MD* 12:390–98.

702. Casty, Alan. "The New Style in Film and Drama." *MQ* 11:209–27.

703. *Chicorel Theater Index to Plays in Anthologies, Periodicals, Discs, and Tapes.* Vol. I. New York: Chicorel Lib. Pubs.

704. Cole, Toby, and Helen K. Chinoy,eds. *Actors on Acting:The Theories, Techniques, and Practices of the Great Actors of All Times as Told in Their Own Words.* With Introds. and Biog. Notes. New Rev. Ed. New York: Crown.

705. Copelin, David. "Yesterday's Festival:The First Annual American College Theatre Festival, Wash., D.C., April 28-May 12, 1969." *Yale/Theatre* 2,iii(1969):75–93.

706. Dawydow, J. "Sozialpsychologie und Theater." *KuL* 18:976–96. [Tr. Siegfried Behrsing.]

707. Desramaux, André. "Théâtre et contestation." *CTL* 6(1968–69):23–31.

708. Dickinson, Thomas H. *An Outline of Contemporary Drama.* New York: Biblo & Tannen, 1969. [Repr. of 1927 ed.]

709. "Drama and Young People." *NTM* 10,ii. [Brian Watkins, "Drama in the Classroom," 4–6; Elizabeth Jewell, "No Comment...," 7; Gordon Chambers, "Youth Drama Growing Up:A Report on the Clifton College Conference Held in 1969," 8–11; Heather Bryant, "A Report on the Conference Held at Theatre Center Ltd. December 1969," 12–13; Michael Bath, " 'Five-a-Side Drama'," 16–18; Charles Savage, "Repertory Theatre Goes to

School," 19–21; John Hodgson, "Some Thoughts on Drama Teaching in Secondary Education," 22–23.]

710. Driver, Tom F. *Romantic Quest and Modern Query:A History of the Modern Theatre.* New York: Delacorte.

711. Dubois, Pierre H. *Het binnenste buiten. Aspekten van het moderne teater.* 's-Gravenhage-Rotterdam: Nijgh & Van Ditmar, 1968.

712. Ernst, Earle. "The Influence of Japanese Theatrical Style on Western Theatre." *ETJ* 21(1969):127–38.

713. Esslin, Martin. *The Theatre of the Absurd.* Rev., Updated Ed. Garden City, N.Y.: Doubleday (Anchor), 1969.

714. Farrell, Nancy L. "A Subject Index to *Theatre Annual,* 1942–1969." *TD* 2,i–ii(1969–70):125–34.

715. Florence, Jean-Félix. "Théâtre et psychologie." *CTL* 6(1968–69):5–14.

716. Frye, Northrop. "Old and New Comedy." *ShS* 22(1969):1–5.

* 717. Girardin, Monique. "Problèmes posés par le catalogage des mises en scène écrites." *TD* 1,ii(1969):37–46.

718. Gollin, Richard M. "Film as Dramatic Literature." *CE* 30(1969):424–29.

719. Gröning, Karl, and Werner Kliess. *Friedrichs Theaterlexikon.* Hrsg. von Henning Rischbieter. Velber: Friedrich, 1969.

720. Grotowski, Jerzy. *Towards a Poor Theatre.* London: Methuen, 1969.

721. Hampton, Charles C.,Jr. "Polarity and Stasis:Drama as Reflection of a Revolution." *Yale/Theatre* 2,iii(1969):39–42.

722. Hegedüs, Géza, and Judit Kónya. *Kecskeének, az két és fél évezred drámatörténete.* Budapest: Gondolat, 1969. [Bibliog., 375–85. Tragoedia:History of 2500 years of drama.]

723. Heilman, Robert B. "Dramas of Money." *Shenandoah* 21,iv:20–33.

* 724. Hughes, Catharine. "New Ritual and New Theatre." *ASoc* 7:62–68.

725. Huneker, J.G. *Iconoclasts:A Book of Dramatists. Ibsen, Strindberg, Becque, Hauptmann, Sudermann, Hervieu, Gorky, Duse and D'Annunzio, Maeterlinck and Bernard Shaw.* Freeport, N.Y.: Books for Libs. [Repr. of 1905 ed.]

726. "Interview with Robert Brustein [14 July 1967]." *Yale/Theater* 2,iii(1969):94–103.

727. Jacobs, Roger. "De mythe in het absurde theater of een bepaalde poging tot demystificatie." *TVUB* 9(1966–67):73–85.

728. Jerome, Judson. *Plays for an Imaginary Theater.* Urbana: U. of Ill. P.

729. Johnson, Albert E. "Doctoral Projects in Progress in Theatre Arts, 1969." *ETJ* 21(1969):214–19.

730. Kerr, Walter. *Thirty Plays Hath November:Pain and Pleasure in the Contemporary Theater.* New York: Simon & Schuster.

731. Kienzle, Siegfried. *Modern World Theater:A Guide to Productions in Europe and the United States since 1945.* Tr. Alexander and Elizabeth Henderson. New York: Ungar.

732. Kott, Jan. "The Icon and the Absurd." *TDR* 14,i:17–24.

* 733. Kottwinkel, James L., Dorothy M. O'Connor, and Bonnie Jean Cogbill. "A Checklist of Current Theatre Arts Periodicals." *TD* 1,ii(1969):3–36.

734. Kreutz, Irving. "Who's Holding the Mirror?" *CompD* 4:79–88.

735. Leech, Clifford. *Tragedy.* (Crit. Idiom 1.) New York: Barnes & Noble, 1969.

736. Leeuwe, H.H.J. de. *Commedia dell'arte, dat is:Puur toneel.* Groningen: Wolters-Noordhoff, 1968.

737. Litto, Fredric M. *American Dissertations on the Drama and Theatre:A Bibliography.* Kent, Ohio: Kent State U.P., 1969.

738. Lucas, Frank. "Théâtre à scène ouverte, avec aire de jeu variable. Projet de Frank Lucas." *CTL* 7–8(1968–69):69–72.

739. Mandel, Oscar. "Reactionary Notes on the Experimental Theatre." *MR* 11:101–16.

740. —— "The Nature of the Comic." *AR* 30:73–89.

741. McHose, Janet. "The Stanford Repertory Theatre:Notes on Professional Theater and the University." *Yale/Theatre* 2,iii(1969):55–73.

742. Milhau, Denis. "Picasso, la réalité et le théâtre." *Europe* 492–93:214–28.

743. Miller, William C. and Stephanie. "All Black Showcase: The Effectiveness of a Negro Theater Production." *ETJ* 21(1969):202–04.

744. Mullin, Donald C. *The Development of the Playhouse:A Survey of Theatre Architecture from the Renaissance to the Present.* Berkeley: U. of Calif. P.

745. Nørgaard, Kjeld, and Niels Andersen,eds. *14 Forfattere: Mod et rigere Teater.* [Copenhagen]: Rhodos, [1969]. [Arts. by Joachim Israel, Bjørn Lenze-Møller, Klaus Hoffmeyer, Jakob Oschlag, Thomas Bredsdorff, Kaj Himmelstrup, Jesper Jensen, Finn Poulsen, Arne Skovhus, Jens Christian Schmidt, Ole Leonardo Petersen, Pia Dam, and Niels Andersen.]

746. Oliver, William I. "Theatre Aesthetics in Crisis." *ETJ* 21(1969):17–27.

747. Pandolfi, Vito. *Histoire du théâtre.* 5 vols. Verviers: Gérard, 1968.

748. Piscator, Erwin. *Det politiske teater.* Ny udg. ved Felix Gasbarra. Med Forord [9–16] af Sam Besekow og tillæg [257–71] af Erwin Piscator. Holstebro, Denmark: Odin Teatrets Forlag. [Tr. Ole Henrik Kock.]

749. Rogoff, Gordon. "A Natural Formation of Land: Proposal for a University's Performing Arts Center." *Yale/Theatre* 2,iii(1969):104–24. [Foll. by George Gerbner, "In Defense of 'A Natural Formation'; or, 'The Procedure'," 125–27.]

750. Roose-Evans, James. *Experimental Theatre from Stanislavsky to Today.* New York: Universe.

751. Rudin, Seymour. "Theatre Chronicle:Fall 1969." *MR* 11:117–28.

752. Saxnovskij-Pankeev, V. *Drama:Konflikt, kompozicija, sceničeskaja žizn'.* Leningrad: Iskusstvo, 1969.

753. Sharp, William L. *Language in Drama:Meanings for the Director and the Actor.* Scranton, Pa.: Chandler Pub. Co. [Sep. chaps on Chekhov, Pinter, Shakespeare, and 18th cent. Eng. comedy, *inter alia.*]

754. Simon, Alfred. "Théâtre et désastre:Qui croit encore au théâtre populaire?" *Esprit* 393:1136–56.

755. Sion, Georges. "Le théâtre à l'âge du désarroi." *Bull. de l'Acad. Royale de Lang. et de Litt. Françaises* 48:74–83.

756. Spargur, Ronn. "The New Drama:Starshine and Sunshine." *ASoc* 7:182–84.

757. Stein, Howard. "The Great Divide." *Yale/Theatre* 2,iii(1969):51–54. [Role of instructor in drama.]

758. Steinbeck, Dietrich. *Einleitung in die Theorie und Systematik der Theaterwissenschaft.* Berlin: de Gruyter.

759. Sugiyama, Makoto. "Engeki ni okeru Kako to Gendai." *EigoS* 114(1968):734–35. [Past and present in drama.]

760. Tisch, J.H. " 'Late Baroque Drama—a European Phenomenon?' " [F 3]:125–36.

761. Tiszay, Andor. "A szavalókórus kulturális és mozgalmi szerepe." *Helikon* 15(1969):295–300. [3 photos. On choral speaking.]

762. Van Laan, Thomas F. *The Idiom of Drama.* Ithaca, N.Y.: Cornell U.P.

763. Veinstein, André. "Projet de constitution d'un fonds central de documentation et de références à l'usage des professionnels des arts du spectacle." *TD* 1,ii(1969):47–50.

764. Verhoye, Bert. " 'Teatro Campesino' en 'Bread and Puppet':Theater van de revolte." *VlG* 53,vii(1969):12–14.

765. Viertel, Berthold. *Schriften zum Theater.* Hrsg. von Gert Heidenreich. München: Kösel. [Reprs.]

766. Von Sivers, Alexandre. "Stanislavski et le théâtre populaire." *CTL* 7–8(1968–69):45–49.

767. Weiss, Auréliu. "Truth and Theater." *CompD* 4:63–74. [Tr. Martin B. Friedman.]

768. Wright, Jack B. "The Living Theatre:Alive and Committed." *DAI* 30:5560A(Kan.).

769. Zajcev, N. "Lenin na sovetskoj scene." *VLit* 14,ii:13–40. [Lenin on the Soviet stage.]

770. Zamyatin, Yevgeny. "Backstage." *Midway* 9,iii(1969): 59–70. [Tr. Mirra Ginsburg.]

See also 320, 507, 643, 1462, 1514, 3840, 4937, 4938.

Emblem. 771. Hill, Elizabeth K. "What Is an Emblem?" *JAAC* 29:261–65.

772. Landwehr, John. *Emblem Books in the Low Countries*

1554–1949:A Bibliography. Rev. Ed. Utrecht: Haentjes Dekker & Gumbert.

Epic. 773. Abercrombie, Lascelles. *The Epic.* Freeport, N.Y.: Books for Libs., 1969. [Repr. of 1914 ed.]

774. Bloomfield, Morton W. "Episodic Motivation and Marvels in Epic and Romance," 97–128 in *Essays and Explorations,* ed. Morton W. Bloomfield. Cambridge: Harvard U.P.

775. Little, Edward G. "Epic Moderation:Structure, Narrative, Texture, and Purpose in Heroic Literature." *DAI* 30: 5413A(Mich. State).

776. Mueller, Martin. "Turnus and Hotspur:The Political Adversary in the *Aeneid* and *Henry IV.*" *PhoenixC* 23(1969): 278–90.

777. Rollin, Roger B. "*Beowulf* to Batman:The Epic Hero and Pop Culture." *CE* 31:431–49.

See also 633, 3165.

Essay. 778. Duhamel, Roland. "Naar een nieuw begrip: Essay." *VlG* 53,iii(1969):10–13.

779. Fischer, Andreas. *Studien zum historischen Essay und zur historischen Porträtkunst an ausgewählten Beispielen.* (QFSK 27.) Berlin: de Gruyter, 1968.

Irony. 780. Behler, Ernst. "Der Ursprung des Begriffs der tragischen Ironie." *Arcadia* 5:113–42.

781. Young, Calvin E. "A Critical Explication of Irony as a Thematic Structure." *DAI* 30:5007A–08A(Ind.).

Other Forms. 782. Anderson, Warren,tr. *Theophrastus:The Character Sketches.* With Notes and Introd. Essays. Kent, Ohio: Kent State U.P.

783. Bingham, William L. "The Journal as Literary Form." *DAI* 30(1969):1552A–53A(N.M.).

784. Catton, Bruce. *Prefaces to History.* Garden City, N.Y.: Doubleday. [See esp. Chap. 9, "History as Literature."]

785. Feibleman, James K. *In Praise of Comedy:A Study in Its Theory and Practice.* New York: Horizon.

786. Friedenthal, Richard. "Vom Nutzen und Wert der Anekdote." [F 20]:62–67.

787. Garagorri, Paulino. "Las imágenes y lo indecible." *RO* 30:214–31. [Cinema.]

788. Hyers, M. Conrad,ed. *Holy Laughter:Essays on Religion in the Comic Perspective.* New York: Seabury, 1969.

789. Katona, Anna. "Lazarillo-tól Augie Marchig:A pikareszk magatartás változásainak vizsgálata." *FK* 16:136–51.

790. Lasky, Melvin J. "The Prometheans." [F 20]:189–208. [On the imagery of fire and Revolution.]

791. Lerner, Laurence. "An Essay on Pastoral." *EIC* 20: 275–97. [Discusses works by Frost, R.S. Thomas, Sidney, Shakespeare, Marvell, Sannazaro, Shelley, Guarini.]

* 792. McGee, Michael C. "Thematic Reduplication in Christian Rhetoric." *QJS* 56:196–204.

793. Michel, Laurence. *The Thing Contained:Theory of the Tragic.* Bloomington: Ind. U.P. [Chaps. on Shakespeare, Conrad, Faulkner, and aspects of tragedy.]

794. Smith, Elizabeth N. "The Society of the Incomplete:The Psychology and Structure of Farce." *DAI* 30:3958A(Mich.).

795. Smith, Patrick J. *The Tenth Muse:A Historical Study of the Opera Libretto.* New York: Knopf.

796. Waters, Louis A.,Jr. "The Serious Pun in Modern Prose." *WR* 7,ii:30–34.

797. Whitman, F.H. "Medieval Riddling:Factors Underlying Its Development." *NM* 71:177–85.

Other Themes. 798. Alvarez, A. "The Art of Suicide." *PR* 37:339–58. [Modern writers' concerns.]

799. Bloom, Harold. "To Reason with a Later Reason: Romanticism and the Rational." *Midway* 11,i:97–112.

800. Blume, Bernhard. "The Metamorphosis of Captivity: Some Aspects of the Dialects of Freedom in Modern Literatures." *GQ* 43:357–75.

801. Borenstein, A. Farrell. "Knowing the Poor." *SAQ* 69:[96]–107.

802. Braginskij, I.S. "Obraz Lenina v literaturax vostoka." *IAN* 29:173–74. ["The Image of Lenin in the Literatures of the East."]

803. Brooks, Peter. "Toward Supreme Fictions." [F 12]:5–14. [Children's lit.]

804. Brown, Lloyd W. "The Crisis of Black Identity in the West Indian Novel." *Crit* 11,iii(1969):97–112.

805. Cebik, L.B. "Identity:An Existential Fallacy?" *GaR* 23(1969):484–500.

* 806. Cervo, Nathan A. "The Gargouille Anti-Hero-Victim of Christian Satire." *Renascence* 22:69–77. [In Chekhov, Hawthorne, G. Greene, et al.]

807. Cheney, Brainard. "Whither the Permanent Things in a Changing World?" *SR* 78:379–83. [Rev. art. on art. by Kirk, below.]

808. Deman, Paule and Albert. "Zon en maan als simbool van schepping en wederopstanding in de lente." *TVUB* 9(1966–67):14–32.

809. Dethier, H. "De ontwikkeling van het natuurbegrip en het nieuwe natuurgevoel vanaf de 13de eeuw." *TVUB* 9(1966–67):33–54.

810. Edinger, Harry G. "Episodes in the History of the Literary Bear." *Mosaic* 4,i:1–12. [Bear as lit. figure, Ovid to present.]

* 811. Engstrom, Alfred G. "The Man Who Thought Himself Made of Glass, and Certain Related Images." *SP* 67:390–405.

812. Fisch, Harold. "He'arot al ha-'dybbuk' ba-sifrut ha-hadasha. [The Theme of the Dybbuk in Modern Literature:A Comparative Study.]" *Bikoret U-Parshanut* 1:21–26. [Sum. in Eng.]

813. Gerhardt, Mia I. *Zevenslapers en andere Tijd-verliezers.* Assen: Van Gorcum, 1968. [Inaug. Lect.]

814. Glicksberg, Charles I. *The Ironic Vision in Modern Literature.* The Hague: Mouton, 1969.

815. —— "The Literature of Silence." *CentR* 14:166–76.

816. Goldin, Frederick. "The Narcissus Theme in Western European Literature (and Some Problems of Thematology)." *RPh* 23(1969):220–27.

817. Hauck, Richard B. "The Comic Christ and the Modern Reader." *CE* 31:498–506.

818. Hermsdorf, Klaus. "Weltgeschichtliches Individuum und Weltliteratur." *WB* Heft S(1969):168–82.

819. Hertel, Gerhard. *Die Allegorie von Reichtum und Armut: Ein aristophanisches Motiv und seine Abwandlungen in der abendländischen Literatur.* (EBSK 33.) Nürnberg: Carl, 1969.

820. Herting, Helga. "Zum Heldischen in der sozialistisch-realistischen Literatur." *WB* Heft S(1969):205–19.

821. Hinchliffe, Arnold P. *The Absurd.* (Crit. Idiom 5.) New York: Barnes & Noble, 1969.

822. Hinterhäuser, Hans. "Tote Städte in der Literatur des Fin de siècle." *Archiv* 206:321–44.

* 823. Hume, Kathryn. "Structure and Perspective:Romance and Hagiographic Features in the Amicus and Amelius Story." *JEGP* 69:89–107.

824. Jost, François. "Le romantisme européen:Notes bibliographiques." [F 27]:403–09.

825. —— "Romantique:La leçon d'un mot." [F 27]:181–258.

826. —— "Thomas à Beckett dans les lettres européennes: Bibliographies et documents." [F 27]:345–79.

827. —— "Un thème littéraire:Thomas à Beckett." [F 27]:9–88.

828. Kirk, Russell. *Enemies of the Permanent Things.* New Rochelle, N.Y.: Arlington House, 1969. [See art. by Cheney, above.]

829. Kliewer, Warren. "The Daughters of Lot:Legend and Fabliau." *IR* 25,i(1968):13–27.

830. Kott, Jan. "The Vertical Axis:The Ambiguities of Prometheus." *Mosaic* 3,ii:1–26. [Tr. Boleslaw Taborski.]

831. Kōzuma, Tadashi. "Existentialism and Logical Positivism:An Approach to Ethical Verities." [F 7]:48–60.

832. Kratz, Bernd. "*Pulchra ut luna.*" *Arcadia* 4(1969):300–04.

833. Krikorian, Tamara. "Le nationalisme dans la littérature écossaise contemporaine." *LanM* 63(1969):413–19. ["Traduction Bernard Gensane."]

834. Kronenberger, Louis. *The Polished Surface:Essays in the Literature of Worldliness.* New York: Knopf, 1969.

835. Littleton, C. Scott. "Lévi-Strauss and the 'Kingship in Heaven':A Structural Analysis of a Widespread Theogonic Theme." *JFI* 6(1969):70–84.

836. McClintock, Michael W. "Utopias and Dystopias." *DAI* 31:394A(Cornell).

837. McGann, Jerome J. "The Dandy." *Midway* 10,i(1969):3–18. [As Romantic phenomenon.]

838. McGrady, Donald. "Some Spanish and Italian Descendants of a Medieval Greek Tale (*The Scholar and His Imaginary Egg*)." *RPh* 23:303–05.

839. Moeller, Charles. *Man and Salvation in Literature.* Tr. Charles U. Quinn. Notre Dame, Ind.: U. of Notre Dame P.

840. Mueller, Martin. "Knowledge and Delusion in the *Iliad.*" *Mosaic* 3,ii:86–103.

* 841. Norton, David. "Toward an Epistemology of Romantic Love." *CentR* 14:421–43.

842. Obermayer, August. "Zum Toposbegriff der modernen Literaturwissenschaft." *JWGV* 73(1969):107–16.

843. Ong, Walter J.,S.J. "Worship at the End of the Age of Literacy." *Worship*(Collegeville, Minn.) 44(1969):474–87. [Effects of changes in communications media on Christian liturgy today.]

844. Owtscharenko, A. "Der Mensch des revolutionären Gedankens und der revolutionären Tat." *KuL* 18:721–25.

845. Quiñonero, J.P. "Notas breves sobre realismo fantástico." *CHA* 242:448–54.

846. Remes, Carol. "Walter Kaufman and Some Problematics in the Definition of Tragedy." *Science and Society* 33(1969):340–47. [Rev. art.]

847. Rosenberg, John D. "Varieties of Infernal Experience." *HudR* 23:54–80. [The city in lit.]

848. Santillana, Giorgio de, and Hertha von Dechend. *Hamlet's Mill:An Essay on Myth and the Frame of Time.* Boston: Gambit, 1969.

849. Shippey, Thomas A. "Listening to the Nightingale." *CL* 22:46–60. [Symbolic and historical importance of the nightingale in lit.]

* 850. Singer, Armand E. "Second Supplement to *The Don Juan Theme, Versions and Criticism:A Bibliography* (1965)." *WVUPP* 17:102–70. [See Bibliog. for 1966, Items 1705, 1706.]

851. Thomsen, Hans Hagedorn. "Androgyne problemet II." *Kritik* 15:91–118. [*Drottningens Juvelsmycke.*]

852. —— "Androgyneproblemet I." *Kritik* 14:39–55.

853. Tonkin, Humphrey. "Utopias:Notes on a Pattern of Thought." *CentR* 14:385–94.

854. Usmiani, Renate. "A New Look at the Drama of 'Job'." *MD* 13:191–200.

855. Warning, Rainer. "Ritus, Mythos und geistliches Spiel." *Poetica* 3:83–114.

856. Warnke, Frank J. "Das Spielelement in der Liebeslyrik des Barock." *Arcadia* 4(1969):225–37.

857. Whitman, Cedric H. "Existentialism and the Classic Hero," 99–115 in Konrad Gaiser,ed., *Das Altertum und jedes neue Gute:Für Wolfgang Schadewaldt zum 15. März 1970.* Stuttgart: Kohlhammer.

858. Willeford, William. *The Fool and His Scepter:A Study of Clowns, Jesters, and Their Audience.* Evanston, Ill.: Northwestern U.P., 1969.

859. Wimsatt, William K. "Imitazione come libertà." *SCr* 3(1969):208–35.

860. Woodcock, George. "The Deepening Solitude:Notes on the Rebel in Literature." *MHRev* 5(1968):45–62.

See also 414, 435, 610, 915, 929, 3306, 5286, 6430.

Parody. 861. Golopentia-Eretescu, Sanda. "Grammaire de la parodie." *CLTA* 6(1969):167–81.

862. Kiremidjian, G.D. "The Aesthetics of Parody." *JAAC* 28(1969):231–42.

Poetry. 863. Arutjunov, L. "Čerty velikogo obraza (poètičeskaja leniniana)." *VLit* 14,iii:13–39.

864. Bailey, Richard W. "Automating Poetry." *Computers and Automation* 19,iv:10–13. [See Bibliog. for 1969, Vol. I, Item 1046a.]

865. Birkinshaw, Philip. *The Thinking Voice.* Johannesburg: Witwatersrand U.P. [On the nature of poetry.]

866. Bruns, Gerald L. "Poetry as Reality:The Orpheus Myth and Its Modern Counterparts." *ELH* 37:263–86.

867. De Man, Paul. "Lyric and Modernity." [F 48]:151–76.

868. Dickinson, Patrick. "The Spoken Word." *Encounter* 34(Jan):54–62. [On reading poetry.]

* 869. Donlan, Walter. "Character Structure in Homer's *Iliad*." *JGE* 21:259–69.

870. Faber, M.D. "Metaphor and Reality." *DR* 49(1969): 497–504.

871. Gerber, Philip L., and Robert J. Gemmett,eds. "A Terrible War:A Conversation with Diane Wakoski." *FPt* 4:44–54. [On techniques of poetry.]

872. Gerus-Tarnawecky, I. "Names of Mountains in Poetry." [F 26],I:149–59.

873. Gončarov, B.P. "K probleme smyslovoj vyrazitel'nosti stixa." *IAN* 29:23–32. [On the semantic expressiveness of verse.]

874. Graff, Gerald. *Poetic Statement and Critical Dogma.* Evanston, Ill.: Northwestern U.P.

875. Gransden, K.W. "The Pastoral Alternative." *Arethusa* 3:103–21(to be cont.). [In classical Lat. poetry and its Renaissance imitations.]

876. Grushow, Ira. "The 'Experience' of Poetry." *CE* 31(1969):25–29.

877. Hamburger, Michael. *The Truth of Poetry:Tensions in Modern Poetry from Baudelaire to the 1960's.* New York: Harcourt, Brace and World. [1st Amer. ed.]

878. Hawley, Jane S. "Quantitative Semantics as an Approach to Meaning in Poetry." *JQ* 47:87–94.

879. Hertz, Peter D. "Minimal Poetry." *WHR* 24:31–40.

880. Ingram, Ilsley. "Poetry and the Evolution of Man." *PoetryR* 61:63–76.

881. Jochems, Helmut. "Englische und amerikanische Lyrik in der Schule:Kritische Anmerkungen zu einigen neueren Interpretationssammlungen." *LWU* 2(1969):268–81.

882. Kmetzo, Thomas. "Notes Toward a Prosody of Free-Verse." [F 47]:85–95.

883. Kohler, Dorothea B. "Vaudeville Act with Doppelganger." *DAI* 30:3011A–12A(Denver). [Types of modern poetic theory and practice.]

884. Kramer, Aaron. "Poetry and Interpersonal Communication," 139–48 in *Innovations in Educating Emotionally Disturbed Children and Youth.* Hawthorne, N.Y.: Assn. of New York State Educators of the Emotionally Disturbed.

* 885. LaBranche, Anthony. "Imitation:Getting in Touch." *MLQ* 31:308–29.

886. Logan, H[arry] M. "Some Applications of Linguistic Theory to Poetry." *HAB* 21,ii:40–47.

887. Mainkar, T.G. "Some Observations on the Definition of Poetry." [F 18]:114–28.

* 888. Matthews, Jack. "Poetry as the Act of Language." *OUR* 12:5–15.

889. Matthews, J.H. "Surrealism, Politics, and Poetry." *Mosaic* 3,i(1969):1–13.

890. Mayer, Peter. "Experiment in Poetry." *PoetryR* 60(1969):270–76.

* 891. Mitchell, Roger. "Toward a System of Grammatical Scansion." *Lang&S* 3:3–28.

* 892. Montgomery, Marion. "Shadows in the New Cave:The Poet and the Reduction of Myth." *SWB* 55:217–23.

893. Müller, Ulrich. "'Lügende Dichter'? (Ovid, Jaufré Rudel, Oswald von Wolkenstein)." [F 30]:32–50.

894. Nagler, Michael. "Oral Poetry and the Question of Originality in Literature." [F 3]:451–59.

895. Nemerov, Howard. "Poetry and the National Conscience." *Salmagundi* 14:34–38.

896. Nygaard, Jon and Rolf R. *Dikt og form. En innføring i diktets formlære.* Oslo: Universitetsforlaget.

897. O'Brien, Veronica. "The Language of Poetry." *Studies* 58(1969):415–26.

898. Ognev, Vladimir. "Poetry Is Radar." *AmD* 5,ii(1968–69):25–27.

899. Partee, Morriss H. "Plato's Banishment of Poetry." *JAAC* 29:209–22.

900. Perniola, Mario. "Origine della reificazione poetica nella Grecia antica." *RdE* 14(1969):361–82.

901. Pestalozzi, Karl. *Die Entstehung des lyrischen Ich:Studien zum Motiv der Erhebung in der Lyrik.* Berlin: de Gruyter.

902. Plotz, Helen,comp. *The Marvelous Light:Poets and Poetry.* New York: Crowell.

903. Rayan, Krishna. "Metaphor and Suggestion." *MHRev* 2(1967):50–64.

904. ―― "When Meaning Is Suggested." *MHRev* 7(1968): 77–89.

905. ―― "When the Green Echoes or Doesn't." *MHRev* 14:30–38. [On imagery.]

906. Rogers, Edith. "The Limitations of Quantitative Methods in the Study of Literature:The Case of Colours in Poetry." *Hasifrut* 2:303–09. [In Hebr.; Eng. sum.]

907. Rosenwald, John R. "A Theory of Prosody and Rhythm." *DAI* 30:3435A(Duke).

908. Salinger, Herman. "Time in the Lyric." [F 33]:157–73.

909. Schevill, James. "Notes on Performing Poems." *Voyages*(Wash.,D.C.) 3,i–ii:80–81. [Preceded and foll. by 3 of S's poems.]

910. Serrano Poncela, Segundo. *La metáfora.* Caracas: U. Central de Venezuela, 1968.

* 911. Smith, William J. "The Making of Poems." *QJLC* 27:91–98.

912. Spears, Monroe K. *Dionysus and the City:Modernism in Twentieth Century Poetry.* New York: Oxford U.P.

913. Thompson, Ewa M. "Sound Correlations in Verse." *LangQ* 8,i–ii(1969):39–42.

914. Tufte, Virginia J. "High Wedlock and Epithalamium." *PCP* 1(1966):32–41.

915. ――,comp. *High Wedlock Then Be Honoured:Wedding Poems from Nineteen Countries and Twenty-five Centuries.* New York: Viking.

916. Udvardi, István. "Költészet és zene." *Kortárs* 14: 1958–62.

917. Untermeyer, Jean S.,comp. & tr. *Re-creations.* Foreword Lewis Galentiere. New York: Norton. [Fr., Ger., and Hebrew poems with Eng. trs.]

918. Vogt, Alfred H. "Wird das Gedicht überleben?" *WuW* 25:267–68.

919. Wilber, Richard. "Poetry and Happiness." *Shenandoah* 20,iv(1969):3–23.

920. Zoll, Allan R. "Toward a Theory of Baroque Lyric Metaphor." *DAI* 30(1969):2050A–51A(Mich.).

921. Žovtis, A.L. "O kriterijax tipologičeskoj xarakteristiki svobodnogo stixa." *VJa* 19,ii:63–77. [On the typology of free verse.]

See also 272, 288, 322, 361, 658, 686, 1020, 1227, 1363, 1474, 1487, 1496, 3349, 7257, 9682.

Prose Fiction. 922. Anand, Mulk Raj. "Old Myths and New Myths:Recital versus Novel." [F 45]:27–36.

923. Bachtin, M. "Epos und Roman." *KuL* 18:918–42. [Tr. Rolf Göbner.]

924. Baxtin, M. "Èpos i roman (O metodologii issledovanija romana)." *VLit* 14,i:95–122.

925. Bergonzi, Bernard. *The Situation of the Novel.* London: Macmillan. [A study of contemp. Brit. and Amer. fiction.]

926. Bhattacharya, Rajlukshmee Debee. "Changing Image of Man in Fiction." *IWT* 3,i(1969):9–16.

927. *Bibliothèque universelle des romans.* Réimpr. de l'éd. de Paris, 1775–1789. Genève: Slatkine Reprs..

928. Blanco Amor, José. "Novela y sociedad." *CA* 167(1969):82–95.

929. Brace, Gerald W. "Witness:Theme in Fiction." *MR* 11:180–85.

930. Bradbury, Malcolm. *What Is a Novel?* London: E. Arnold, 1969. [The nature of the novel and its contemp. signif.]

931. Bronzwaer, W.J.M. *Tense in the Novel:An Investigation of Some Potentialities of Linguistic Criticism.* Groningen: Wolters-Noordhoff. [See Chap. 4, "*The Italian Girl*:An Explication."]

* 932. Brumm, Ursula. "Some Thoughts on History and the Novel." *CLS* 6(1969):317–30.

933. Brunner, John. "The Genesis of *Stand on Zanzibar* and Digressions." *Extrapolation* 11:34–43. [Science-fict.]

934. Bryer, Jackson R., and Nanneska N. Magee. "The Modern Catholic Novel:A Selected Checklist of Criticism." [F 19]:241–68.

935. Burns, Landon C. "A Cross-Referenced Index of Short Fiction and Author-Title Listing." *SSF* 7:1–218. [Anthols.]

936. Carneiro, André. *Introdução ao estudo da "science-fiction."* São Paulo: Conselho Estadual de Cultura, 1967.

937. Clareson, Thomas D. "An Annotated Bibliography of Critical Writings Dealing with Science Fiction." *Extrapolation* 11:56–83(to be cont.).

938. Cope, Jack,et al. "International Symposium on the Short Story." *KR* 32:78–108.

939. Dollerup, Cay. "Læseres oplevelse af forfatteren i et prosavaerk." *MDan* 1970:114–25.

940. Dyck, Martin. "Relativity in Physics and in Fiction." [F 33]:174–85.

941. Egri, Péter. "Társadalomábrázolás és lélekábrázolás." *Helikon* 15(1969):351–59.

* 942. Epstein, Seymour. "Politics and the Novelist." *UDQ* 4,iv:1–18.

943. Garrett, George. "Dreaming with Adam:Notes on Imaginary History." *NLH* 1:407–21. [On hist. fiction.]

944. Goldknopf, David. "Realism in the Novel." *YR* 60:69–84.

945. —— "What Plot Means in the Novel." *AR* 29:483–96.

946. Goodrich, Norma L. "Bachelors in Fiction, Through John Steinbeck and Jean Giono." *KRQ* 14(for 1967):367–78.

947. —— "Gothic Castles in Surrealist Fiction." [F 43]:143–62.

948. Gorp, H. van. "Recente romantheorie." *DWB* 115:57–65.

949. Gysen, René. "Romanproblemen." *Komma* 4,iii(1968):54–62.

950. Hall, James. "The New Pleasures of the Imagination." *VQR* 46:596–612.

951. Hankiss, Elemér. "A halál és a Happy Ending:A regénybefejezések értékrendszere." *Kritika* 8,xii:11–28.

952. Harris, Wilson. "Interior of the Novel:Amerindian/European/African Relations." [F 50]:138–47.

953. Johansen, Jørgen Dines. *Novelleteori efter 1945:En studie i litterær taxonomi.* Copenhagen: Munksgaard.

954. Jost, François. "L'évolution d'un genre:Le roman épistolaire dans les lettres occidentales." [F 27]:89–179.

955. —— "Un inventaire:Essai bibliographique du roman épistolaire." [F 27]:380–402.

* 956. Kellogg, Gene. "The Catholic Novel in Convergence." *Thought* 45:265–96.

957. —— *The Vital Tradition:The Catholic Novel in a Period of Convergence.* Chicago: Loyola U.P.

958. Kermode, Frank. "The Structure of Fiction." *MLN* 84(1969):891–915.

959. Klotz, Volker. *Die erzählte Stadt:Ein Sujet als Herausforderung des Romans von Lesage bis Döblin.* München: Hanser, 1969.

960. Koebner, Thomas. "Zum Wertungsproblem in der Trivialroman-Forschung." [F 21]:74–105.

961. Kraft, Quentin G. "Against Realism:Some Thoughts on Fiction, Story, and Reality." *CE* 31(1969):344–54.

962. Kuspit, Donald B. "Fiction and Phenomenology." *PPR* 29(1968):16–23.

* 963. Lange, Victor. "Fact in Fiction." *CLS* 6(1969):253–61.

964. Leiner, Friedrich. "Utopische Kurzgeschichten als Jugendlektüre." [F 21]:291–305.

965. Lester, Mark. "The Relation of Linguistics to Literature." *CE* 30(1969):366–75.

966. Levi, Elda. " 'Novel':L'affermarsi di un Genere letterario." *EM* 20(1969):101–40.

* 967. Levin, Harry. "From *Gusle* to Tape-Recorder." *CLS* 6(1969):262–73.

968. Lodge, David. "The Novelist at the Crossroads." *CritQ* 11(1969):105–32.

969. Loreis, Hector-Jan. "Wat hebben progressieve romanciers aan de techniek van de nouveau roman?" *Komma* 4, iii(1968):63–80.

970. Lundwall, Sam J. *Science fiction, från begynnelsen till våra dagar.* Stockholm: Sveriges radio, 1969.

971. Miel, Jan. "Temporal Form in the Novel." *MLN* 84(1969):916–30.

972. Morrissette, Bruce. "Le visage international du 'Nouveau roman'." [F 3]:391–97.

973. Moskowitz, Samuel,comp. *Under the Moons of Mars:A History and Anthology of the "Scientific Romance" in the Munsey Magazines, 1912–1920.* New York: Holt, Rinehart, & Winston.

974. Nabeshima, Yoshihiro. "Shosetsu no style ni tsuite." *EigoS* 114(1968):501–02. [On the style of novels.]

975. Nef, Ernst. *Der Zufall in der Erzählkunst.* Bern: Francke.

976. Nélod, Gilles. *Panorama du roman historique.* Paris: SODI, 1969.

977. Nielsen, Erik. "Jeg-novellen med stadigt hensyn til Peter Seeberg." *Poetik* 2,iii(1969):63–75.

979. Nonaka, Ryo. "Image Shosetsuron." *Oberon* 29(1968):27–34. [Image theory of novels.]

980. Pearce, Richard. *Stages of the Clown:Perspectives on Modern Fiction from Dostoyevsky to Beckett.* (CMC.) Pref. Harry T. Moore. Carbondale: So. Ill. U.P.

981. —— "The Limits of Realism." *CE* 31(1969):335–43.

* 982. Perry, Nick, and Roy Wilkie. "Homo Hydrogenesis: Notes on the Work of J.G. Ballard." *RQ* 4:98–105.

983. Peter, John. "The Self-Effacement of the Novelist." *MHRev* 8(1968):119–28. [Rev. art.]

984. Pizer, Donald. "A Primer of Fictional Aesthetics." *CE* 30(1969):572–80.

985. Plans, J.J. "Historia de la novela policíaca." *CHA* 236(1969):421–43; 237(1969):675–99; 241:127–45.

986. Rose, Lois and Stephen. *The Shattered Ring:Science Fiction and the Quest for Making.* Richmond, Va.: John Knox.

987. Rosenthal, Erwin T. *Das fragmentarische Universum: Wege und Umwege des modernen Romans.* München: Nymphenburg.

988. —— "Wirklichkeitsdarstellungen im modernen Roman." *WW* 20:126–33.

989. Said, Edward W. "Narrative:Quest for Origins and Discovery of the Mausoleum." *Salmagundi* 12:63–75.

990. Silverberg, Robert,comp. *The Mirror of Infinity:A Critics' Anthology of Science Fiction.* With Introd. New York: Harper.

991. Sloboda, Rudolf. "Dve podmienky dobrého románu." *SlovP* 85,x(1969):36–39. [Two conditions for a good romantic novel.]

992. Stanford, Raney. "The Subversive Hero and the Beginnings of Fiction." *Discourse* 13:366–78.

993. Stanton, Robert. "Outrageous Fiction:*Crime and Punishment, The Assistant,* and *Native Son.*" *PCP* 4(1969):52–58.

994. Storm, Jannick. "Om science-fiction." *Selvsyn* 11:53–59.

995. Suvin, Darko. "Significant Themes in the Criticism of Soviet Science Fiction to 1965." *Extrapolation* 11:44–52. [Incl. "A Select Bibliography of Soviet Criticism [1954–68]," 48–52.]

996. Széll, Zsuzsa. *Válság és regény.* (Modern filológiai füzetek 10.) Budapest: Akadémiai K. [Critic and novel.]

997. Taylor, Hawley C.,Jr. "The Philosophical Novel." *DAI* 30(1969):2047A(U. of Wash.).

998. Warner, Harry. *All Our Yesterdays:An Informal History of Science Fiction Fandom in the Forties.* Introd. Wilson Tucker. Chicago: Advent Pubs., 1969.

999. Watson, Harold F. *Coasts of Treasure Island.* San Antonio, Texas: Naylor, 1969. [Hist. of sea tale, 1800–1900.]

1000. Williamson, Jack. "As I Knew Hugo [Gernsback]." *Extrapolation* 11:53–55. [Ed. and pub. of science-fict.]

1001. Wilson, Angus. "Is the Novel a Doomed Art Form?" *ELLS* 6(1969):1–31.

1002. Yamoto, Sadamiki. "Shosetsu Gijitsuron no Keifu." *EigoS* 114(1968):80–81. [Hist. survey of novel technique.]

1003. Zalygin, Sergej. "Černy dokumental'nosti." *VLit* 14,ii:41–53. [Theory of the documentary novel and related genres.]
See also 339, 356, 385, 448, 804, 1004, 6430, 6734.

Satire. *1004. Fitzgerald, Gregory. "Character Typology in Satiric Short Stories." *SNL* 7:100–03.

1005. Fultz, Barbara,comp. *The Naked Emperor:An Anthology of International Political Satire.* Introd. Victor S. Navasky. New York: Pegasus.

1006. "*SNL* Bibliography:1965–1970." *SNL* 7:179–85. [Satire crit. and related matters.]

1007. Thomas, W.K. "His Highness' Dog at Kew." *CE* 30(1969):581–86.

* 1008. Thorpe, Peter. "Thinking in Octagons:Further Reflections on Norms in Satire." *SNL* 7:91–99.

1009. Walker, Willard. "The Retention of Folk Linguistic Concepts and the *ti' yčir* Caste in Contemporary Nacirean Culture." *AA* 72:102–05.

1010. Witke, Charles. "Conventions of Realism in European and Extra-European Satire." [F 3]:243–49.

See also 788, 858, 3235, 3809, 7234.

Translation. 1011. Anniah Gowda, H.H. "Cultural Values and Translation." [F 50]:90–103.

1012. Asher, R.E. "Tamil Literature in Translation." *Mahfil* 6,i:41–63.

1013. Batts, Michael. "Literature and the Art of Translation." *HAB* 21,ii:15–18.

1014. Calder, W.M. "Translating Morgenstern." *OGS* 4(1969):142–54.

1015. "Clearing House [of Translations in Progress and Titles for Which Publishers Are Seeking Translators]." *Delos* 4:242–54.

1016. Fairley, Barker. "On Translating *Faust.*" *GL&L* 23(1969):54–62.

1017. Gačečiladze, G. *Vvedenie v teoriju xudožestvennogo perevoda.* Tbilisi: Izd. Tbilisskogo universiteta. [Introd. to the theory of artistic translation.]

1018. Hennecke, Hans. "Dichterische Übertragung von Dichtung." *DASDJ 1969* :51–62.

1019. Holmes, James S. "Forms of Verse Translation and the Translation of Verse Form." *Babel* 15(1969):195–201.

1020. ——— "Poem and Metapoem:Poetry from Dutch to English." *LA* 3(1969):101–15.

1021. Huber, Thomas. *Studien zur Theorie des Übersetzens im Zeitalter der deutschen Aufklärung 1730–1770.* (DS 7.) Meisenheim: Hain, 1968.

1022. Karlinsky, Simon. "Speaking of Books:Chekhov in English." *N.Y. Times Book Rev.* 26 July:2,20.

1023. Lefevere, André. "The Translation of Literature:An Approach." *Babel* 16:75–79.

1024. Leloir, L. "Traduction latine des versions syriaques et arméniennes de l'Épitre de Jacques." *Muséon* 83:189–208.

1025. Miller, Barbara S. "Camels in the Pleasure-Garden: Notes on the Problems of Translating and Teaching Sanskrit Poetry." *Mahfil* 6,i:3–39.

1026. Ognev, Vladimir. "Vremja sinteza (Nekotorye problemy poètičeskogo perevoda)." *VLit* 14,v:185–208. [On problems of poetic tr.]

1027. Reiss, Katharina. "Textbestimmung und Übersetzungsmethode:Entwurf einer Texttypologie." *RC* 21(1969):69–75.

1028. Reynolds, Tim. "A Modern Lucretius?" *Delos* 4: 218–34. [Rev. art.]

* 1029. Rivers, J.E. "Aristophanes' Modern Translators:Translation as Criticism." *SHR* 4:115–25.

1030. Russell, Ralph. "On Translating Ghalib." *Mahfil* 5,iv(1968-69):71–87.

1031. Santarcangeli, Paolo. "Appunti sulla traduzione letteraria." *Ponte* 26:127–41.

1032. Stewart, W. McC. "Racine's Untranslatability and the Art of the Alexandrine." [F 31]:230–42.

1033. Uddin, Jasim. *Gipsy Wharf (Sojan Badiar Ghat).* (UNESCO Coll. of Rep. Works, Pakistan Ser.) Tr. from Bengali by Barbara Painter and Yann Lovelock. Illus. Hashem Kahn. Introd. Barbara Painter. London: Allen & Unwin; New York: Pegasus. [Appendix I: *Graves*, by Jasim Uddin, tr. Barbara Painter and Yann Lovelock. Appendix II: "On Translation, and on Translating Jasim Uddin," by Yann Lovelock.]

1034. Verghese, C. Paul. "Problems of the Indian Translator in English." *IndL* 12,i(1969):86–93.

1035. Whalley, George. "On Translating Aristotle's *Poetics.*" *UTQ* 39:77–106.

1036. Ziegler, Carl H.,ed. "List of Translations, 1969." *YCGL* 19:84–92.

See also 1481, 1840, 2424, 3235, 5448, 5847, 7981, 8000, 8090.

V. BIBLIOGRAPHICAL

1037. Andersen, Axel. *Håndbøgernes hvor–står det.* Copenhagen: Politiken, 1969. [Incl. sections on: "Ordbøger," 57–146; "Biografier," 320–44; "Litteraturen," 421–36; "Bibliografier," 461–71.]

1038. Austin, Gabriel. " 'From the Library of Jean Grolier'." *PULC* 31:129–34. [2 vols. in Princeton U. Lib.]

1039. Barber, Giles. *French Letterpress Printing:A List of French Printing Manuals and Other Texts in French Bearing on the Technique of Letterpress Printing 1567–1900.* (Occas. Pub. 5.) Oxford: Oxford Bibliog. Soc., 1969. [39-p. pamphlet.]

* 1040. Booth, Karen Marshall. "Two Unreported Watermarks." *PBSA* 64:338–39.

1041. Bowers, Fredson. "The New Look in Editing." *SAB* 35,i:3–10.

* 1042. Broderick, John C.,et al. "Recent Acquisitions of the Manuscript Divison." *QJLC* 27:332–75. [Incl. mss. from Spanish-America, W. Whitman, P. Roth, G. Middleton.]

* 1043. Bühler, Curt F. "Chainlines versus Imposition in Incunabula." *SB* 23:141–45.

* 1044. ——— "False Information in the Colophons of Incunabula." *PAPS* 114:398–406.

* 1045. ——— "The Date in the Colophon of Hain *12332." *PBSA* 64:323–24.

1046. Butsch, Albert F.,comp. *Handbook of Renaissance Ornament:1290 Designs from Decorated Books.* With New Introd. and Captions by Alfred Werner. New York: Dover, 1969.

1047. Carter, Harry G. *A View of Early Typography up to About 1600.* (Lyell Lectures 1968.) Oxford: Clarendon, 1969.

1048. Carter, T.E. "Comments on German Book Production in the Nineteenth Century." *GL&L* 23:112–19.

1049. Cave, Roderick, David Chambers, and Peter Hoy,eds. *Private Press Books, 1968.* Pinner, Middlesex: Private Libs. Assn., 1969. [81-p. pamphlet.]

1050. Clarke, Derek A., and Howell J. Heaney. "A Selective Check List of Bibliographical Scholarship for 1968." *SB* 23:254–73.

1051. Claus, Helmut. "Die Anfänge des Buchdrucks in Forchheim/Oberfranken." [F 17]:27–37.

1052. Daly, Simeon,O.S.B. "Lilly Manuscript Fragment —Ordo L." *Serif* 7,ii:35–36.

1053. De Vinne, Theodore L. *The Invention of Printing:A Collection of Facts and Opinions Descriptive of Early Prints and Playing Cards, the Block-Books of the Fifteenth Century, the Legend of Lourens Janszoon Gutenberg and His Associates.* Illus. with Facsims. Detroit: Gale, 1969. [Repr. of 1876 ed.]

* 1054. Dorenkamp, John H. "The Compositors of the *Cambridge Platform.*" *SB* 23:196–99.

1055. Duffy, Charles. "The Herman Muehlstein Rare Book Collection, University of Akron." *Serif* 7,ii:3–6.

1056. Dürr, Heidi. "Der Verlag auf dem Weg zum Grossunternehmen?" [F 36]:181–97.

* 1057. Ferguson, W. Craig. "Thomas Creede's Pica Roman." *SB* 23:148–53.

1058. Fern, Alan M., and Karen F. Beall. "Prints in the 'Pembroke' Album:A Revised List." *QJLC* 27:34–37.

1059. Fern, Alan M., and Karen F. Jones. "The 'Pembroke' Album of Chiaroscuro Woodcuts." *QJLC* 26(1969):[8]–20. [Illus.]

* 1060. Fredeman, William E. "The Bibliographical Significance of a Publisher's Archive:The Macmillan Papers." *SB* 23:183–91.

1061. Garvey, Eleanor M., Anne B. Smith, and Peter A. Wick,comps. *The Turn of a Century, 1885–1910:Art Nouveau-Jugendstil Books.* Cambridge: Dept. of Printing and Graphic Arts, Harvard U. [Catalogue of a Exhibition at Houghton Lib.]

* 1062. Gemmett, Robert J. "The Beckford Book Sale of 1808." *PBSA* 64:127–64.

1063. Gerritsen, Johan. "A Portable Collator Comes Cheaper." *RORD* 11(1968):29–30.

* 1064. Gerulaitis, Leonardas V. "A Fifteenth-Century Artistic Director of a Printing Firm:Bernard Maler." *PBSA* 64:324–32.

1065. Goff, Frederick R. "Early Library of Congress Bookplates." *QJLC* 26(1969):55–61. [Illus.]

* 1066. —— "Rare Books:Selected Acquisitions." *QJLC* 26(1969):149–69; 27:296–315. [Illus.]

* 1067. —— "The Preparation of the *Third Census of Incunabula in American Libraries.*" *PBSA* 64:275–81.

1068. Haebler, Konrad. *Spanische und portugiesische Bücherzeichen des XV. und XVI. Jahrhunderts.* Naarden, Holland: A.W. van Bekhoven, 1969. [Repr. of Strassburg 1898 ed.]

1069. Hellwig, Barbara, and Walter Matthey,eds. *Inkunabelkatalog des Germanischen Nationalmuseums Nürnberg.* Wiesbaden: Harrassowitz.

1070. Hetherington, John R. "An Imperfect *Book of Common Prayer* Recently Presented to the Bodleian." *BLR* 8:181–84.

1071. Hiller, Helmut. "Das Bild der Buchgemeinschaft heute." [F 36]:65–83.

1072. Hirsch, Rudolf. "Catalogue of Manuscripts in the Libraries of the University of Pennsylvania to 1800:Supplement A(2)." *LC* 36:3–36.

1073. —— "Catalogue of Manuscripts in the Libraries of the University of Pennsylvania to 1800:Supplement A(1)." *LC* 35(1969):3–32.

1074. *Hon no mondô sanbyakusen [Problems Concerning Books and Book-making].* Tokyo: Shuppan Nyûsu Sha, 1969.

1075. Horton, Carolyn. *Cleaning and Preserving Bindings and Related Materials.* Chicago: Lib. Technol. Program, Amer. Lib. Assn., 1969. [2d Ed., Rev.]

1076. Jehle, Faustin F. "Typographic Copyright, Public Domain and Unfair Competition." *SchP* 1:255–58.

* 1077. Lavin, J.A. "John Danter's Ornament Stock." *SB* 23:21–44. [Illus.]

* 1078. Leech, Clifford. "On Editing One's First Play." *SB* 23:61–70.

* 1079. Maslen, Keith I.D. " 'Press' Letters:Samuel Aris 1730-32." *SB* 23:119–26.

1080. Müller-Alfeld, Theodor. "Stetigkeit und Wandel beim Buchbonnenten." [F 36]:84–102.

1081. Narkiss, Bezalel. *Hebrew Illuminated Manuscripts.* Foreword Cecil Roth. Jerusalem: Encyclopaedia Judaica; New York: Macmillan, 1969.

* 1082. Nebenzahl, Kenneth. "Reflections on Brinley and Streeter." *PBSA* 64:165–75.

1083. Nemirovskij, E. "Var Hans Bogbinder den russiske Gutenberg?" *Bogvennen* 1968–70:217–27. [A chap. from N's *Vozniknovenie knigopečatanija v Moskve:Ivan Fedorov,* 1964; tr. and introd. by Paul Flandrup.]

1084. Norton, F.J. "Typographical Evidence as an Aid to the Identification and Dating of Unsigned Spanish Books of the Sixteenth Century." *Ibero* 2:96–103.

1085. Pacht, Otto, and J.J.G. Alexander,comps. *Illuminated Manuscripts in the Bodleian Library.* Vol. 2:*Italian.* Oxford: Clarendon. [For Vol. 1, see Bibliog. for 1967, Item 5207.]

1086. Parkes, Malcolm B. *English Cursive Book Hands, 1250–1500.* (Oxford Palaeog. Handbooks.) Oxford: Clarendon, 1969.

1087. Pearce, M.J. *A Workbook of Analytical and Descriptive Bibliography.* Hamden, Conn.: Archon.

1088. Penroes, Boies. "English Printing at Antwerp in the Fifteenth Century." *HLB* 18:21–31.

* 1089. Rhodes, Dennis E. "Variants in a Lettou Incunable." *PBSA* 64:332–34.

* 1090. Shaffer, Ellen. "The Rare Book Department, Free Library of Philadelphia." *PBSA* 64:1–11. [Incl. Dickens, Goldsmith, Pennsylvania German books, early American children's books, the common law, medieval and oriental manuscripts, and incunabula.]

1091. Skofield, Hobart O. "The Printing House of William Edwin Rudge." *SCUL* 2,i:5–16.

1092. Stillwell, Margaret B. *The Awakening Interest in Science During the First Century of Printing, 1450–1550:An Annotated Checklist of First Editions Viewed from the Angle of Their Subject Content.* New York: The Bibliog. Soc. of Amer.

1093. Sweet, Arthur. "A Layman's Guide to Book Collecting." *CLJ* 10:54–61.

* 1094. Tanselle, G. Thomas. "The Bibliographical Description of Patterns." *SB* 23:71–102. [Illus.]

* 1095. —— "The Meaning of Copy-Text:A Further Note." *SB* 23:191–96.

1096. "The Nods of Homer:Inkunabelabteilung." *Serif* 7,ii:39. [Brief bibliog. notes on Goff C-339, C-26, and C-338.]

1097. Thomson, S. Harrison. *Latin Bookhands of the Later Middle Ages, 1100–1500.* New York: Cambridge U.P.

1098. Todd, William B. *Suppressed Commentaries on the Wiseian Forgeries:Addendum to an Enquiry.* Austin: Humanities Research Center, U. of Texas, 1969.

1099. Twyman, Michael. *Lithography, 1800–1850:The Techniques of Drawing on Stone in England and France and Their Application in Works of Typography.* New York: Oxford U.P.

1100. Winter, Ursula. "Weissenauer Handscriften in der Deutschen Staatsbibliothek Berlin." [F 17]:237–42.

1101. Woodford, F. Peter. "Training Professional Editors for Scientific Journals." *SchP* 2:41–46.

1102. Wright, Louis B., and Gordon N. Ray. *The Private Collector and the Support of Scholarship.* Papers Read at a Clark Lib. Seminar April 5, 1969. Foreword Robert Vosper. Los Angeles: Wm. Andrews Clark Mem. Lib., U.C.L.A., 1969. [Robert Vosper, "Foreword," iii–vii; Louis B. Wright, "The Book Collector as Public Benefactor," 1–23; Gordon N. Ray, "The Private Collector and the Literary Scholar," 25–81 (see also "Appendix B:Advice to the Literary Scholar Approaching a Private Collector in the United Kingdom," 83–84).]

1103. Zapf, Hermann. *About Alphabets:Some Marginal Notes on Type Design.* Pref. Paul Standard. Cambridge, Mass.: M.I.T. Press. [Rev. ed. of 1960 ed.]

1104. —— *Manuale Typographicum.* Cambridge, Mass.: M.I.T. Press. [Paperback ed. of 1954 ed.]

See also 225, 260, 1027, 1197, 1200, 3213, 6122, 6128, 7448, 7856, 8546.

VI. MISCELLANEOUS

Bibliography. 1106. *A Selected Bibliography of Library & Information Science, Spring 1970.* Cleveland, Ohio: Center for Documentation and Research, School of Lib. Science, Case Western Reserve U. [16-p. pamphlet.]

1107. Beaurline, L.A. "Library Cooperation and Faculty Opinion." *SAB* 35,ii:46–59.

1108. Hart, James D., and Ward Ritchie. *Influences on California Printing:Papers Read at a Clark Library Seminar, April 11, 1970.* Introd. Andrew H. Horn. Bibliog. of The Primavera Press by J.M. Edelstein. Los Angeles: Wm. Andrews Clark Mem. Lib., U.C.L.A. [Andrew H. Horn, "Introduction," 1–6; James D. Hart, "The Book Club of California:Its Impress on Fine Printing," 7–35; Ward Ritchie, "The Primavera Press," 37–64; J.M. Edelstein, "The Primavera Press:A Bibliography," 65–80 (rev. rpt.).]

1109. James, Rowena G. "Et alia." *SchP* 2:59–65. [Ed. probs. in multiauthor work.]

1110. Liebert, Herman W. "The Beinecke Library Accessions 1969." *YULG* 44:165–203.

1111. Yasumoto, Yoshinari. "Suri Bunkengaku no Hatten." *EigoS* 115(1969):164–65. [Devel. of statistical bibliog.]

See also 666.

Other Miscellaneous Items. 1112. Altenhein, Hans. "Die Zukunft des Lesens." [F 36]:219–32.

1113. Anhava, Tuomas. "Kirjailijoiden kouluttamisesta." *Parnasso* 20:351–57. [On contemporary high-school education as a means of producing writers.]

1114. Anon. "Love and Death and the Satiric Way of Life." *SNL* 7:162–63. [On "mistiled" scholarly arts.]

1115. Barzun, Jacques, and Henry F. Graff. *The Modern Researcher.* Rev. Ed. New York: Harcourt, Brace, and World.

1116. Bell, J.G. "The Proper Domain of Scholarly

Publishing." *SchP* 2:12–18.

1117. Benge, Ronald C. *Libraries and Cultural Change.* Hamden, Conn.: Archon.

1118. Blackburn, Robert H. "Photocopying in a University Library." *SchP* 2:49–58.

1119. Blackwell, Richard. "Bookselling in the Seventies." *TLS* 6 Nov:1307–08. [See also Frederick T. Bell, *TLS* 20 Nov:1358; David Burnett, *TLS* 20 Nov:1358.]

1120. Boardman, Fon W.,Jr. "Of Selling Many Books." *SchP* 1:171–77.

1121. Brown, John. "University Press Publishing." *SchP* 1:133–42.

1122. Chadbourne, Richard M. "The Humanities:A Foreign Language." *ColQ* 18:255–67.

1123. Chase, Bill. "Sacred or Secular:The Context of Culture." *LJ* 95:3871–76. [Cultural value of libraries.]

1124. Collier, Arlen. "Censorship of Ideas and I.B.M., or Swift's 'Moderns' are Winning Again." *WR* 7,ii:57–63.

* 1125. Colvert, James B. "The Function of the Academic Critical Quarterly." *MissQ* 23:95–101.

1126. *Copyright Law Symposium Number Eighteen.* Nathan Burkan Memorial Competition Sponsored by the American Society of Composers, Authors, and Publishers. Foreword by Herman Finkelstein. New York: Columbia U.P. [Thomas A. Reed, "The Role of the Register of Copyrights in the Registration Process:A Critical Appraisal of Certain Exclusionary Regulations," 1–49; Paul Sherman, "Incorporation of the *Droit de suite* into United States Copyright Law," 50–91; John Iskrant, "The Impact of the Multiple Forms of Computer Programs on Their Adequate Protection by Copyright," 92–134; Andrew O. Shapiro, "The Standard Author Contract:A Survey of Current Draftsmanship," 135–73; Peter F. Nolan, "Copyright Protection for Motion Pictures:Limited or Perpetual?" 174–205; "Papers Appearing in Copyright Law Symposia Numbers One Through Seventeen," 210–17; "Law Schools Contributing Papers to Previous Copyright Law Symposia," 218–25; plus statutes and cases, list of works cited, and index.]

* 1127. Crews, Frederick. "Do Literary Studies Have an Ideology?" *PMLA* 85:423–28.

1128. Crosby, Muriel. "Discovering the Art of the Language Arts." [F 35]:27–54.

1129. Eastman, Richard M. "Literary Specialization and Manpower Needs:A Model Letter, a Pilot Study, a Call to the Profession." *ADEB* 24:29–34.

1130. Epstein, Louis. "Bookstores:A Main Distribution Agency for Books." [F 25]:89–94.

1131. Findlater, Richard. "The Future of the Book: Publishing in the Seventies." *TLS* 16 Oct:1185–86.

1132. Finkelstein, Sidney. "What Society Expects of Its Writers." *AmD* 5,ii(1968–69):22–24.

1133. Follett, Robert J.R. "Current Trends in Educational Publishing—A Personal View." [F 25]:60–74.

1134. Frank, Joseph. "English Departments and the Social Revolution." *ADEB* 24:3–9.

1135. Frase, Robert W. "The Economics of Publishing." [F 25]:29–38.

* 1136. Fraser, John. "Violence and Thought in Art." *SoR* 6:651–73.

1137. Goldman, Abe A. "The Prospective New Copyright Law." [F 25]:39–48.

1138. Goody, Jack, and Ian Watt. "The Consequences of Literacy." [F 22]:27–68.

1139. Haacke, Wilmont. "Geistesgeschichte der politischen Zeitschrift." *ZRG* 21(1969):115–51.

1140. Halpenny, Frances G. "Of Time and the Editor." *SchP* 1:159–69.

* 1141. Hare, William F. "The Roles of Teacher and Critic." *JGE* 22:41–49.

1142. Harman, Eleanor. "On Seeking Permission." *SchP* 1:188–92.

1143. Harvey, William B. "Orphans of the Storm." *SchP* 1:299–305. [The "out-of-print" problem.]

1144. Heumann, Rainer. "Der literarische Agent." [F 36]: 168–80.

1145. Houle, Sister Sheila. "The English Department and the Liberal Arts College." *ADEB* 24:24–28.

1146. Johnson, Elmer D. *A History of Libraries in the Western World.* 2d Ed. Metuchen, N.J.: Scarecrow.

1147. King, Robert T. "The Bivalent Economics of the University Press." *SchP* 1:261–73.

1148. Kinsley, William. "Further Thoughts on Scholarly Publication." *SNL* 7:157–62. [A "modest proposal."]

1149. Klemin, Diana. *The Illustrated Book:Its Art and Craft.* New York: Clarkson N. Potter, Inc.

1150. Langley, John H. "Starting a New Journal?" *SchP* 2:75–86.

1151. Levi, Albert W. *The Humanities Today.* Bloomington: Ind. U.P. [5 lects. deliv. at U. of Notre Dame, 1968.]

1152. Lyle, Guy R. *The Librarian Speaking:Interviews with University Librarians.* Athens: U. of Ga. P.

1153. Marissal, Günther. "Buchhandel und junge Generation." [F 36]:147–67.

1154. Marsh, John L., and Jack E. Tohtz. "The Student Literary Magazine:A Barometer." *UCQ* 15,ii:12–18.

1155. Mayer, Hans-Otto. "Früher waren die Kunden anders." [F 36]:133–46.

1156. McCrimmon, James M. "Writing as a Way of Knowing." [F 35]:115–30.

1157. Meetham, Roger. *Information Retrieval:The Essential Technology.* Garden City, N.Y.: Doubleday.

1158. Meier-Ewert, Charity, and Adrian Gibbs. "An Adansonian Classification of Various Texts." *AUMLA* 33:39–47.

1159. Mesrobian, Arpena. "Banditry, Charity, or Equity?" *SchP* 1:179–87.

1160. Mitchell, David. "Les humanités reprendront-elles leur essor?" *HAB* 21,ii:5–6.

1161. Morot-Sir, Edouard. "Les humanités à l'épreuve." *FR* 44:271–80.

1162. *Mostly for Authors:A Handbook.* Cambridge: Harvard U.P. [36-p. pamphlet.]

1163. Mumford, L. Quincy. *Annual Report of the Librarian of Congress for the Fiscal Year Ending June 30, 1969.* Wash., D.C.: Lib. of Congress. [Avail. from Supt. of Documents, U.S. Govt. Printing Office, Wash., D.C. 20402.]

1164. *National Faculty Directory, 1970:An Alphabetical List, with Addresses, of 320,000 Faculty Members at Junior Colleges, Colleges, and Universities in the United States.* Detroit: Gale.

1165. Orr, David. "The Job Market in English and Foreign Languages." *PMLA* 85:1185–98.

* 1166. Osborn, Scott C. "Academic Challenge and the Humanities." *SHR* 4:293–98.

1167. Perelman, Charles. "Analogie et métaphore en science, poésie et philosophie." *RIPh* 23(1969):3–15.

1168. Pomfret, John E. *The Henry E. Huntington Library and Art Gallery, from Its Beginnings to 1969.* San Marino, Calif.: Huntington Lib., 1969.

1169. Rakowski, Franz. "Die Öffentlichen Büchereien und ihre Leser." [F 36]:103–21.

* 1170. Reck, Rima D. "The Politics of Literature." *PMLA* 85:429–32.

1171. Rice, Warner G. "Higher Education in the 1970's." [F 35]:55–72.

1172. Richards, Lewis A. "Modern Readers of Rhetoric:The Purposelessness of Purpose." *WR* 5,ii(1968):15–20.

1173. Rudowski, Victor A. "Minding One's P's and Q's:A Dilemma for Authors and Editors." *MLJ* 54:247–49.

1174. Samuel, Irene. "Milton Speaks to Academe." *MiltonQ* 4:2–4.

1175. Samuel, Richard. "XI. Internationaler F.I.L.L.M.-Kongress in Islamabad, Pakistan." *JIG* 1,ii(1969):99–106.

1176. Sandberg, Karl. "Teaching Language and Literature in a Changing and Technological Society." *BRMMLA* 24:90–95.

1177. Sarkowski, Heinz. "Vom Kolportagebuchhandel zur Buchgemeinschaft." [F 36]:33–64.

1178. "Scholarly Publishing Lives! (Sort of)." *Publishers' Weekly* 27 July:34–48. [AAUP Meeting, U. of Wis., 14–17 June.]

1179. Sharp, Roy C. "Licensing the Photocopier." *SchP* 1:245–53.

* 1180. Smith, Henry N. "Something Is Happening But You Don't Know What It is, Do You, Mr. Jones?" *PMLA* 85:417–22.

1181. Steiner, George. "The Future of the Book:Classic Culture and Post-culture." *TLS* 2 Oct:1121–23. [See also Jack Lindsay, *TLS* 9 Oct:1164; Ken Baynes, *TLS* 9 Oct:1164.]

1182. Stith, Mary E. "Some Observations on Regional Scholarly Publishing." *SchP* 1:151–57.

1183. Suppan, Adolph A. "The Creative Temper in a Computerized Society." *TWA* 58:1–7. [Influ. of computers on creative arts.]

1184. Texas Joint English Committee for School and College. *Selected Workshop Papers.* Vol. II. San Marcos: San Marcos Record P., 1968. [Papers by Meade Harwell, E.D. Smith, Louise Cowan, Maxine Inteso, Ozella Dew, J. Haywood, et al. on problems of composition, instruct. media, etc.]

1185. *The MLA Style Sheet.* Second Ed. New York: MLA.

[Revision begun by William R. Parker and completed by John H. Fisher, Harrison T. Meserole, et al.]

1186. Wessling, Joseph H. "Pressures on the Black Intellectual." *NALF* 3(1969):117–18.

1187. Williamson, Hugh. "The Book of the Future." *TLS* 23 Oct:1215–16.

1188. Wilson, Clyde. "The Liberty and Responsibility of the Press." *Intercollegiate Rev.*(Bryn Mawr, Pa.) 6,iii:113–21.

1189. Wilson, Francis G. "On Judging Idols of the Mind." *ModA* 14:279–92.

1190. Wilson, William E. "The Throes of Academe." *ColQ* 18:231–40.

1191. Zahn, Carl. "Book Design Competitions:Pro and Con." *SchP* 1:307–13.

See also 7163.

ENGLISH LITERATURE†

I. GENERAL

Bibliography. 1192. Emben, A.B. *Donors of Books to S. Augustine's Abbey, Canterbury.* (Occas. Pub. 4.) Oxford: Oxford Bibliog. Soc., 1969. [Pamphlet.]

1193. Frey, John R.,ed. "Anglo-German Literary Bibliography for 1969." *JEGP* 69:470–75.

1194. Garrett, Kathleen I.,ed. *Thomas James Wise and Guildhall Library.* London: Corporation of London. [Contains list of books in the Lib. associated with TJW.]

1195. Harlow, Geoffrey, and James Redmond. *The Year's Work in English Studies.* Vol. 48, 1967. London: John Murray for the English Assn., 1969.

1196. Hasler, Jörg. "Bibliographie der wissenschaftlichen Veröffentlichungen von Rudolf Stamm." [F 52]:285–91.

1197. Kendall, Lyle H.,Jr.,comp. *A Descriptive Catalogue of the W.L. Lewis Collection, Part One:Manuscripts, Inscriptions, Art.* Fort Worth: Texas Christian U.P.

1198. Korshin, Paul J. "New B.M. MSS." *TLS* 9 July:750. [See also 14 Aug:903; 18 Sept:1039.]

1199. Myers, Robin. *A Dictionary of Literature in the English Language from Chaucer to 1940.* 2 vols. London: Pergamon.

1200. Sommerblad, M.J. *Scottish "Wheel" and "Herring-Bone" Bindings in the Bodleian Library.* (Occas. Pub. 1.) Oxford: Oxford Bibliog. Soc., 1967. [Pamphlet.]

* 1201. Williams, Franklin B.,Jr. "Photo-Facsimiles of *STC* Books:A Sequel." *SB* 23:252–53. [See Bibliog. for 1968, Item 5692.]

See also 459.

General and Miscellaneous. 1203. Chwalewik, Witold. *Z literatury angielskiej:Studia i wrażenia.* Warsaw: PIW, 1969. [Essays on Shakespeare, Conrad, Wells, Kipling, Eliot, Sterne, Fielding, and Chaucer.]

1204. Fernando, Lloyd. *English, Literature, and Technology in South East Asia.* An Inaug. Lect. Deliv. at the U. of Malaya on 29 Dec 1969. Kuala Lumpur: U. of Malaya. [32 pp.]

1206. Gillis, William. "From Classicism to the Absurd or Waiting for Freneau." [F 43]:135–41. [The evolution of Depts. of Eng.]

1207. Habicht, Werner,ed. *English and American Studies in German:Summaries of Theses and Monographs.* A Supp. to *Anglia,* 1969. Tübingen: Niemeyer. [Covers West Ger. and Austrian studies dated 1969, incl. a few from 1968 and 1970.]

1208. Hammond, Dorothy, and Alta Jablow. *The Africa That Never Was:Four Centuries of British Writing About Africa.* Foreword Charles R. Lawrence. New York:Twayne.

1209. Inglis, Fred. "The English Intellectual at the Present

Time." *UDQ* 5,i:1–40.

1210. Johnson, Lemuel A. "The Negro as Metaphor:A Study of Esthetic and Ethical Negativism in English, Spanish and French Literatures." *DAI* 30:3908A–09A(Mich.).

1211. Ker, Neil. "A.S. Napier, 1853–1916." [F 54]:152–81.

1212. Kröger, Franz. "Das Deutschlandbild der Engländer und Amerikaner in der Vergangenheit." *NS* 19:91–102.

1213. Mair, G.H. *English Literature, 1450–1900.* 3rd Ed. London: Oxford U.P., 1969.

1214. O'Dowd, M.C. "Writing and Injustice." *Contrast* 23:48–61. [On social commitment in lit.; examines Chaucer, Shakespeare, Jane Austen, Emily Brontë, T.S. Eliot.]

1215. Ormond, Richard and Leonee. *Great Poets.* London: H.M.S.O., 1969. [Portraits, etc. of two dozen major poets from Chaucer to T.S. Eliot, with biog. notes and physiognomic descriptions by contemporaries.]

1216. *Pelican Book of English Prose.From the Beginning to 1780,* ed. Roger Sharrock; *From 1780 to the Present Day,* ed. Raymond Williams. 2 vols. Harmondsworth: Penguin.

1217. Perry, Bernard. "British University Presses:An American View." *SchP* 1:144–49.

1218. Rosenblatt, Louise M. "Literature and the Invisible Reader." [F 35]:1–26.

1219. Schofield, R.S. "The Measurement of Literacy in Pre-Industrial England." [F 22]:311–25.

1220. Strang, Barbara M.H. *A History of English.* London: Methuen.

1221. Thomas, Donald. *A Long Time Burning:A History of Literary Censorship in England.* New York: Praeger, 1969.

1222. Tucker, Martin,gen. ed. *The Critical Temper:A Survey of Modern Criticism on English and American Literature from the Beginnings to the Twentieth Century.* 3 Vols. New York: Ungar, 1969. [Vol. 1: Old Eng. to Shakespeare; Vol. 2: Milton to Romantics; Vol. 3: Victorian and American Lit.]

1223. Turner, Darwin T. "Is College English Relevant?" *WGCR* 2,ii(1969):3–15.

1224. University of Leeds. *Publications and Titles of Theses, 1967–68.* Leeds: U. of Leeds. [18th annual issue, 1954-present.]

1225. Wardroper, John,ed. *Jest upon Jest:A Selection from the Jestbooks and Collections of Merry Tales Published from the Reign of Richard III to George III.* London: Routledge & K. Paul.

1226. Watson, George,comp. *Literary English Since Shakespeare.* London and New York: Oxford U.P.

1227. Wilson, Colin. *Poetry and Mysticism.* London: Hutchinson.

1228. Zandvoort, R.W. *Collected Papers II:Articles in English Published Between 1955 and 1970.* (Groningen Studies in Eng. 10.) Groningen: Wolters-Noordhoff.

See also 572, 622, 1060, 1086, 6037, 6041.

---

† *Festschriften* and Other Analyzed Collections are listed in the first division of this Bibliography, and have been assigned Item numbers 1–95. "F" numbers in brackets following a title refer to these items.

II. AUSTRALIA, CANADA, ETC.

Bibliography. 1229. "Annual Bibliography of Commonwealth Literature, 1968." *JCL* 8(1969):1–106.

General and Miscellaneous. 1230. Anon. "Literary Magazines and Commonwealth Literature." [F 50]:214–18.

1231. Fernando, Lloyd. "Literary English in the South-East Asian Tradition." [F 50]:57–65.

1232. Jones, Joseph. "The Outer Spaces of English." *Meanjin* 28(1969):558–64. [On Commonwealth Lit.]

1233. Kachru, Braj B. "Some Style Features of South Asian English." [F 50]:122–35.

1234. McAuley, James. "Is a Sociology of Commonwealth Literatures Possible?" [F 50]:33–37.

1235. Srinivasa Iyengar, K.R. "Commonwealth Literature: Themes and Their Variations." [F 50]:18–32.

1236. Walsh, William. *A Manifold Voice:Studies in Commonwealth Literature.* New York: Barnes & Noble. [R.K. Narayan, Nirad C. Chaudhuri, Olive Schreiner, Chinua Achebe, V.S. Naipaul, Patrick White, A.D. Hope, Katherine Mansfield, Morley Callaghan.]

See also 1199.

Australia. 1237. Allison, Jack. " 'Futurity':Norman Lindsay's Creative Stimulus." *Meanjin* 29:346–55.

1238. Anderson, Hugh. "A Checklist of the Poems of Robert D. FitzGerald, 1917–1965." *ALS* 4:280–86.

1239. —— *Bernard O'Dowd.* Melbourne: Hill of Content.

1240. Arnold, Rollo. "Henry Lawson:'The Sliprails and the Spur' at Pahiatua?" *ALS* 4:286–92.

1241. Austin, Lloyd. "Alan Rowland Chisholm:An 81st Birthday Tribute." *Meanjin* 28(1969):531–37.

1242. Banfield, Edmund J. *The Confessions of a Beachcomber.* London: Angus and Robertson.

1243. Barnard, Marjorie. "How *Tomorrow and Tomorrow* Came to be Written." *Meanjin* 29:328–30.

1244. —— *Miles Franklin.* Melbourne: Hill of Content.

1245. Barnes, John. "Henry Handel Richardson." *BANQ* 3,iii(1969):23–25.

1246. Barnes, Richard J.,ed. *The Writer in Australia:A Collection of Literary Documents, 1856–1964.* Melbourne and New York: Oxford U.P., 1969.

1247. Bayliss, John F. "Slave and Convict Narratives:A Discussion of American and Australian Writing." *JCL* 8(1969):142–49.

1248. Brady, Charles A. *"Bring Larks and Heroes,* by Thomas Keneally." *Éire* 3,iii(1968):169–72. [Rev. art.]

1249. Brissenden, R.F. "A.D. Hope's *New Poems.*" *Southerly* 30:83–96.

1250. Buckley, Vincent. "The Poetry of Francis Webb." *Quadrant* 64:11–15.

1251. Burns, Robert. "Flux and Fixity:M. Barnard Eldershaw's *Tomorrow and Tomorrow.*" *Meanjin* 29:320–27.

1252. —— "The Underdog-Outsider:The Achievement of [Peter] Mathers' *Trap.*" *Meanjin* 29:95–105.

1253. Burrows, J.F. "Stan Parker's *Tree of Man.*" *Southerly* 29(1969):257–79.

1254. Cantrell, K.M. "Some Elusive Passages in 'Essay on Memory':A Reading Based on a Discussion with R.D. FitzGerald." *Southerly* 30:44–52.

1255. Chisholm, A.R. "Christopher Brennan, Poet and Scholar:A Centenary Assessment." *Meanjin* 29:277–80.

1256. Clutton-Brock, M.A. "The Melancholy Optimist:An Account of Walter Lindsay Richardson and His Family." *Meanjin* 29:192–208.

1257. Conron, Brandon. "Voyager from Eden." *ArielE* 1,iv:96–102. [On Randolph Stow's *A Counterfeit Silence.*]

1258. Davis, Diana. "A Checklist of Kenneth Mackenzie's Works, Including Manuscript Material." *ALS* 4:398–404.

1259. Day, A. Grove. *Louis Becke.* Melbourne: Hill of Content.

1260. Douglas, Dennis, and Margery M. Morgan. "Gregan McMahon and the Australian Theatre." *Komos* 2(1969):50–62.

1261. Dunlop, Ronald. "Recent Australian Poetry." *Poetry Australia* 32:50–57.

1262. Earnshaw, John. *"Love and Horror:*A Question Mark in Colonial Literature." *BANQ* 3,iii(1969):15–16. [Suggests Horatio Wells as author.]

1263. Foster, I.M. "Richard Mahony's Trilogy." *ALS* 4:279–80.

1264. Geering, R.G. *Christina Stead.* (TWAS 95.) New York: Twayne, 1969.

1265. —— "Elizabeth Harrower's Novels:A Survey." *Southerly* 30:131–47.

1266. Green, Dorothy. *"The Young Cosima.*" *ALS* 4:215–26.

1267. —— "Walter Lindsay Richardson:The Man, the Portrait and the Artist." *Meanjin* 29:5–20.

1268. Hadgraft, Cecil. "Frederick T. Macartney's Autobiography." *Meanjin* 28(1969):552–57.

1269. Hall, Rodney. "Attitudes to Tradition in Contemporary Australian Poetry." *Poetry Australia* 32:44–45.

1270. Harrison-Ford, Carl. "Poetics Before Politics:A Note on Kris Hemensley's 'New Australian Poetry'." *Meanjin* 29:226–31.

1271. Hemensley, Kris. "First Look at 'the New Australian Poetry'." *Meanjin* 29:118–21.

1272. Herbert, Xavier. "The Writing of *Capricornia.*" *ALS* 4:207–14.

1273. Hergenhan, L.T. "The Corruption of Rufus Dawes." *Southerly* 29(1969):211–21.

1274. Heseltine, H.P. "C. Hartley Grattan in Australia:Some Correspondence, 1937–38." *Meanjin* 29:356–64.

1275. —— "Towards an 'Inside Narrative':John Barnes' *The Writer in Australia.*" *Meanjin* 28(1969):541–49.

1276. Hewett, Dorothy. "Excess of Love:The Irreconcilable in Katharine Susannah Porter." *Overland* 43(1969–70):27–31.

1277. Holroyd, John. "Early Victorian Booksellers and Publishers, 1835–1886." *BANQ* 4,i:5–19.

* 1278. Hope, A.D. "The Frontiers of Literature." *QJLC* 27:99–103.

1279. Keesing, Nancy. "Norman Lindsay." *Quadrant* 62(1969):13–15.

1280. Kiernan, Brian. "The Fortunes of Richard Mahony." *Southerly* 29(1969):199–209.

1281. —— "Xavier Herbert:*Capricornia.*" *ALS* 4:360–70.

1282. Kirby-Smith, Virginia. "The Development of Australian Theatre and Drama:1788–1964." *DAI* 30:4989A(Duke).

1283. Kirsop, Wallace. " 'The Greatest Renewal, the Greatest Revelation':Brennan's Commentary on Mallarmé." *Meanjin* 29:303–11.

1284. Knight, Nina. "Furphy and Romance:*Such Is Life* Reconsidered." *Southerly* 29(1969):243–55.

1285. Laird, J.T. "Australian Poetry of the First World War:A Survey." *ALS* 4:241–50.

1286. Lebedeva, I.A. "Iz istorii avstralijskogo rasskaza." [F 49]:167–80. [Sum. in Eng. About Australian short story.]

1287. Lindsay, Daryl. "Memories of Walter Murdoch." *Overland* 45:34–35.

1288. Lindsay, Jack. "A Triumph over Adversity:Comments on Alan Marshall's Writing." *Meanjin* 28(1969):437–45.

1289. —— "Norman Lindsay:Problems of His Life and Work." *Meanjin* 29:39–48.

1290. Lord, Mary. "A Contribution to the Bibliography of Hal Porter." *ALS* 4:405–09.

1291. —— "Hal Porter's Comic Mode." *ALS* 4:371–82.

1292. Lundkvist, Artur. "Patrick White, Australien." [F 32]:189–95.

1293. Mann, Leonard. "A Double Life." *Southerly* 29(1969):163–74. [Reminis.]

1294. Mather, Rodney. "Patrick White and Lawrence:A Contrast." *CR* 13:34–50.

1295. Matthews, Brian. " 'The Nurse and Tutor of Eccentric Minds':Some Developments in Lawson's Treatment of Madness." *ALS* 4:251–57.

1296. McAuley, James. *The Personal Element in Australian Poetry.* Sydney: Angus and Robertson.

1297. McInnes, Graham. " 'Thirk':Further Comment."

Meanjin 29:115–17.

1298. Mendelsohn, Oscar. " 'Waltzing Matilda' Again." *Meanjin* 29:377–79.

1299. Muir, Marcie. *A Bibliography of Australian Children's Books.* London: André Deutsch.

1300. Nesbitt, Bruce. " 'J.H.G.':J.H. Greene and 'Over the Coals'." *ALS* 4:404–05.

1301. Oliver, Harold J. *Shaw Neilson.* New York: Oxford U.P., 1969.

1302. Pennington, Richard. *Christopher Brennan.* Sydney: Angus and Robertson.

1303. Phillips, A.A. "Confessions of an Escaped Censor." *Meanjin* 28(1969):508–15. [Austral. lit. censorship.]

1304. —— "Growing Pains of a Culture." *Spirit* 36,iv:52–56.

1305. Phillips, Arthur. "Frank Dalby Davison, M.B.E.: 1893–1970." *Meanjin* 29:251–52.

1306. Poole, Joan E. "Maurice Frere's Wife:Marcus Clarke's Revision of *His Natural Life.*" *ALS* 4:383–94.

1307. Richards, Max. "Australian Poetry:New Readers Start Here." *Spirit* 36,iv:48–51.

1308. Rodda, Linda,comp. *E.M.M.:A Handlist of the Published Works and Manuscripts of Edmund Morris Miller, 1881–1964.* Hobart: Morris Miller Lib., U. of Tasmania. [L.A. Triebel, "Edmund Morris Miller:A Tribute," 1–3.]

1309. Roderick, Colin,ed. *Henry Lawson Letters, 1890–1922.* Sydney: Angus and Robertson.

1310. Roe, Michael. "Thirk:A Tragic Australian:1891–1959." *Meanjin* 28(1969):522–29. [Angela Thirkell's husband.]

1311. Roland, Betty. "Requiem for K.S.P." *Overland* 44: 29–31. [Katharine Susannah Porter.]

1312. Routh, S.J., and L.M. Burns,comps. "Annual Bibliography of Studies in Australian Literature, 1969." *ALS* 4:258–78.

1313. Scott, S.J. "A.R. Chisholm:Creative Translation." *Meanjin* 28(1969):538–40.

1314. Semmler, Clement. "Australian Poetry of the 1960s: Some Personal Impressions." *Poetry Australia* 35:44–52.

1315. Shapcott, Tom. "Hold on to Your Crystal Balls Or:Cocksure in the 70s." *Poetry Australia* 32:46–47.

1316. Sinclair, K.V. "R.A. Crouch (1868–1949):Politician, Soldier, Man of Letters, Bibliophile and Public Benefactor." *BANQ* 3,iii(1969):5–14. [Biog. of noted collector.]

1317. —— "R.A. Crouch (1868–1949)." *BANQ* 4,i:20–27.

1318. Steele, Peter. "Contemporary Australian Poetry." *Spirit* 36,iv:44–47.

1319. —— "To Move in Light:The Poetry of Chris Wallace-Crabbe." *Meanjin* 29:149–55.

1320. Stewart, Annette. "Christopher Brennan:The Disunity of *Poems 1913.*" *Meanjin* 29:281–302.

1321. Stewart, Douglas. "A Send-Off for Norman Lindsay." *Southerly* 30:53–54. [Eulogy.]

1322. Stewart, Kenneth. "The Prototype of Richard Mahony." *ALS* 4:227–40.

1323. Stoller, Alan, and R.H. Emmerson. "The Fortunes of Walter Lindesay Richardson." *Meanjin* 29:21–33.

1324. Sturm, T.L. "R.D. FitzGerald's Poetry and A.N. Whitehead." *Southerly* 29(1969):288–304.

1325. Tulip, James. "The Australian-American Connexion." *Poetry Australia* 32:48–49.

1326. —— "The Poetry of Francis Webb." *Southerly* 29(1969):184–91.

1327. Vintner, Maurice. "Rediscovery—I:Leonard Mann's *A Murder in Sydney.*" *Overland* 44:39–40.

1328. Watters, R.E. "English Social Patterns in Early Australian and Canadian Fiction." [F 50]:66–75.

1329. Webster, Owen. "Frank Dalby Davison." *Overland* 44:35–37.

1330. —— "The Literary Life of Australia." *Overland* 45: 27–32.

1331. Wilkes, G.A. *Australian Literature:A Conspectus.* London: Angus and Robertson.

1332. Wilkes, G.A.,ed. *Ten Essays on Patrick White, Selected from* Southerly *(1964–67).* Sydney: Angus and Robertson.

See also 7933, 10231.

Canada. 1333. Atwood, Margaret, "MacEwen's Muse." *CanL* 45:24–32.

1334. Barbour, Douglas. "The Young Poets and the Little Presses, 1969." *DR* 50:112–26. [Rev. art.]

* 1335. Beasley, David. "Tempestuous Major:The Canadian Don Quixote." *BNYPL* 74:95–106.

* 1336. Bessai, Frank. "The Ambivalence of Love in the Poetry of Isabella Valancy Crawford." *QQ* 77:404–18.

1337. Birbalsingh, Frank. "Grove and Existentialism." *CanL* 43:67–76.

1338. Bowering, George. "Purdy:Man and Poet." *CanL* 43:24–35.

1339. Brewster, Elizabeth. "Chronology of Summer." *HAB* 21,i:34–39. [On her *Passage of Summer.*]

1340. Cameron, Donald. "Thomas Raddall:The Art of Historical Fiction." *DR* 49(1969):540–48.

1341. Carson, Neil. "George Ryga and the Lost Country." *CanL* 45:33–40.

1342. Clark, J. Wilson. "The Line of National Subjugation in Canadian Literature." *L&I* 7:81–88.

1343. Cox, John D. "Norman Levine." *CanL* 45:61–67. [Interview.]

1344. Daniells, Roy. "National Identity in English-Canadian Writing." [F 50]:76–88.

1345. Davey, Frank. "E.J. Pratt:Apostle of Corporate Man." *CanL* 43:54–66.

1346. Djwa, Sandra A. "Metaphor, World View and the Continuity of Canadian Poetry:A Study of the Major English Canadian Poets with a Computer Concordance to Metaphor." *DAI* 30(1969):1132A(British Columbia).

1347. Dudek, Louis. "Poetry in English." *CanL* 41(1969): 111–20. [Symposium:The Writing of the Decade.]

1348. "Ernest Buckler:A Conversation with an Irritated Oyster." *Mysterious East*(New Brunswick, Canada) Jan:21–24.

1349. Fischer, G.K. "A.M. Klein's Forgotten Play." *CanL* 43:42–53. [*Hershel of Ostropol.*]

* 1350. Fraser, Keath. "Futility at the Pump:The Short Stories of Sinclair Ross." *QQ* 77:72–80.

1351. —— "Notes on Alden Nowlan." *CanL* 45:41–51.

1352. Gibbs, Jean. "Dorothy Livesay and the Transcendentalist Tradition." *HAB* 21,ii:24–39.

1353. Gutteridge, Don. "Riel:Historical Man or Literary Symbol?" *HAB* 21,iii:3–15. [Author's reply to a rev.]

* 1354. Harrison, Dick. "The American Adam and the Canadian Christ." *TCL* 16:161–67.

1355. Hayne, David M.,ed. "Letters in Canada 1969." *UTQ* 39:324–453. [Michael Hornyanky, "Poetry," 324–37; Gordon Roper, "Fiction," 338–45; "Literary Studies," 345–81; Tony Emery, "Art," 381–84; John M. Robson, "Light Prose," 384–86; Donald V. Wade, "Religion," 386–94; Robin S. Harris, "Education," 394–402; Jean-Charles Bonenfant, "Les études sociales," 402–22; Jean-Louis Major, "Poésie," 422–33; Rejean Robidoux, "Romans, récits, nouvelles, contes," 433–41; Rejean Robidoux, "Theatre," 441–44; C.H. Andrusyshen, "Publications in Other Languages," 444–53.]

1356. "Irving Layton:Worksheets." *MHRev* 2(1967):121–23.

1357. Jackel, Susan. "The House on the Prairies." *CanL* 42(1969):46–55. [Prairie Novels.]

1358. Jones, D.G. *Butterfly on Rock:A Study of Themes and Images in Canadian Literature.* Toronto: U. of Toronto P.

1359. Jones, Joseph and Johanna. *Authors and Areas of Canada.* (People and Places in World-English Lit. 1.) Austin, Texas: Steck-Vaughn.

1360. Kostelanetz, Richard. "Il pensiero di Marshall McLuhan." *Nuova presenza* 11(1968):13–33.

1361. Laurence, Margaret. "Dave Godfrey:Ancestral Voices Prophesying . . ." *Mysterious East*(New Brunswick) Dec Book Supp.:6–10. [In Fr. in *Ellipse*, Autumn 1970.]

1362. Legris, Maurice. "The Modern French-Canadian Novel." *TCL* 16:169–74.

1363. Livesay, Dorothy "Song and Dance." *CanL* 41(1969): 40–48. [Poetry.]

1364. Macklem, Michael. "A Book a Mile." *TamR* 55:58–67. [On the Canadian book trade.]

* 1365. Mandel, Eli. "Modern Canadian Poetry." *TCL* 16: 175–84.

1366. Mathews, Robin. "The Imperial Butterfly." *Mysterious East*(New Brunswick) Dec Book Supp.:11–13. [Rev. of D.G. Jones' *Butterfly on Rock*.]

1367. McBrine, R.W. "Archibald MacMechan, Canadian Essayist." *DR* 50:23–33.

1368. Morriss, Margaret. "The Elements Transcended." *CanL* 42(1969):56–71. [Sheila Watson's *The Double Hook*.]

1369. Muise, D.A. "Some Nova Scotian Poets of Confederation." *DR* 50:71–82.

1370. New, W.H. "The Novel in English." *CanL* 41(1969): 121–25. [Symposium:The Writing of the Decade.]

* 1371. ——— "The Mind's (I's) (Ice):The Poetry of Margaret Avison." *TCL* 16:185–202.

* 1372. Newton-De Molina, David. "McLuhan:Ice-Cold." *CritQ* 12:78–88.

1373. Noel-Bentley, Peter C. "Our Garrison Mentality." *Mosaic* 4,i:127–33. [Rev. art. on Jones's *Butterfly on Rock*.]

1374. Ó Broin, Pádraig. "After Strange Gods." *AntigR* 1,i:70–80. [On Canad. poetry.]

1375. Ower, John. "Black and Secret Poet:Notes on Eli Mandel." *CanL* 42(1969):14–25.

* 1376. Page, Malcolm. "Three New Canadian Plays." *TCL* 16:203–06.

* 1377. Parker, George L. "A Brief Annotated Bibliography of Available Titles in Canadian Fiction, Poetry, and Related Background Material." *TCL* 16:217–24.

1378. Reaney, James. "Ten Years at Play." *CanL* 41(1969): 53–61.

1379. Ringrose, Christopher X. "Patrick Anderson and the Critics." *CanL* 43:10–23.

1380. Robertson, George,ed. "Alan Crawley and Contemporary Verse." *CanL* 41(1969):87–96. [Symposium:The Writing of the Decade.]

1381. Saeki, Shoichi. "Canada Bungaku Kaigan." *EigoS* 114(1968):720–21; 115(1969):14–16. [Discovery of Can. lit.]

1382. Saunders, Doris, and Robin Hoople,eds. "Manitoba in Literature:An Issue on Literary Environment." *Mosaic* 3,iii: 1–225. [W.L. Morton, "Seeing an Unliterary Landscape," 1–10; Charles Gordon, "Ralph Connor and the New Generation," 11–18; Douglas Spettigue, "Frederick Philip Grove in Manitoba," 19–33; Chester Duncan, "The University of Manitoba as a Literary Environment," 34–38; Watson Kirkconnell, "Ukrainian Literature in Manitoba," 39–47; W.J. Lindal, "The Contribution of Icelanders to Manitoba's Poetry," 48–57; Paul Hiebert, "The Comic Spirit at Forty Below Zero," 58–68; Gabrielle Roy, "Mon Héritage du Manitoba," 69–79; Margaret Lawrence, "Sources," 80–84 (i.e. for her own writing); Dorothy Livesay, "A Prairie Sampler," 84–92; Sinclair Ross, "On Looking Back," 93–94; James Reaney, "Manitoba as a Writer's Environment," 95–97; Adele Wiseman, "A Brief Anatomy of an Honest Attempt at a Pithy Statement About the Impact of Manitoba Environment on My Development as an Artist," 98–106; Jack Ludwig, "You Always Go Home Again," 107–11; Jackson Beardy,comp., "Two Cree Legends," 112–17. Plus anthol. of poetry and prose selections.]

1383. Scobie, Stephen. "Magic, Not Magicians:*Beautiful Losers* and *Story of O.*" *CanL* 45:56–60.

1384. Smith, A.F.M. "Canadian Literature:The First Ten Years." *CanL* 41(1969):93–103.

1385. Stephens, Donald. "The Short Story in English." *CanL* 41(1969):126–30. [Symposium:The Writing of the Decade.]

1386. Stevens, Peter. "Criticism." *CanL* 41(1969):131–38. [Symposium:The Writing of the Decade.]

* 1387. ——— "The Development of Canadian Poetry Between the Wars and Its Reflection of Social Awareness." *DAI* 30:3959A(Saskatchewan).

1388. Sutherland, Ronald. "The Fourth Separatism." *CanL* 45:7–23. [Socially conscious fiction.]

1389. Thompson, Laurel. "Canadian Poetry." *UWR* 6,i: 86–90. [Rev. art on colls. of poems by Raymond Fraser, Glen Siebrasse, R.G. Everson, and Dorothy Farmiloe.]

1390. Waddington, Miriam. "All Nature into Motion." *CanL*

41(1969):73–85.

1391. ——— "Canadian Tradition and Canadian Literature." *JCL* 8(1969):125–41.

1392. Walsh, William. "Streets of Life:Novels of Morley Callaghan." *ArielE* 1,i:31–42.

1393. Waterston, Elizabeth. "The Politics of Conquest in Canadian Historical Fiction." *Mosaic* 3,i(1969):116–24.

1394. Watson, Wilfred. "Education in the Tribal/Global Village." *TCL* 16:207–16. [On McLuhan.]

See also 686, 1328, 6086.

Ceylon. 1395. Goonewardene, James. "Ceylonese Writing in English and British Literary Traditions." [F 50]:148–52.

India. 1396. Ashraf, S.A. "Bengali and English Literatures: Impacts, Correspondences, and Conflicts." [F 50]:115–21.

1397. Davies, M. Bryn. "British and Indian Images of India." *ArielE* 1,iv:48–55. [Rev. art. on Allen J. Greenberger's *The British Image of India* and Mulk Raj Anand's *Private Life of an Indian Prince*.]

1398. Gowda, H.H. Anniah. "The English Plays of Bharati Sarabhai:With a Brief Note on Indian Stage." [F 45]:44–52.

1399. Gupta, G.S.B. "Anand's *Big Heart*:A Study." [F 45]:37–43.

1400. Harrex, S.C. "R.K. Narayan's *The Printer of Malgudi*." *LE&W* 13(1969):68–82.

1401. Karnani, Chetan. "Renaissance in Indo-Anglian Literature." [F 45]:110–12.

1402. Kumar, Shiv K. "Tradition and Change in the Novels of Kamala Markandaya." *Osmania Jour. of Eng. Studies* 7, i(1969):1–9. [Repr. from *BA* 43(1969). See Bibliog. for 1969, Vol. II, Item 10818.]

1403. Lago, Mary M. "English Literature and Modern Bengali Short Fiction:A Study in Influences." *DAI* 30:3465A(Mo., Columbia).

1404. Malhotra, Tara. "Old Places, Old Faces, Old Tunes:A Critical Study of R.K. Narayan's Latest Fiction." [F 45]:53–59.

1405. McDowell, Robert E., Marlene Fisher, and Paul C. Chaffee,eds. "A Bibliography of Twentieth Century Indo-English Fiction." *World Lit. Written in Eng. Newsl.* 17 Supp.:1–22.

1406. Mishra, A.L. "The Problems Indo-Anglian Literature Is Faced With." [F 51]:63–66.

1407. Mukerji, N. "Some Aspects of the Literary Development of R.K. Narayan." [F 45]:76–87.

1408. Mukherjee, Sujit. "The Indo-Anglian Novelist as Best Seller." *LE&W* 13(1969):83–93.

1409. Murthy, V. Rama. "Nirad C. Chaudhuri and the Indian Psyche." [F 45]:102–09.

1410. Narasimhaiah, C.D. "National Identity in Literature and Language:Its Range and Depth in the Novels of Raja Rao." [F 50]:153–69.

1411. Pal, Satyabrata. "Workpoints for a Study of Pritish Nandy's *In Transit, Mind Seeks*." [F 45]:88–101.

1412. Parameswaran, Uma. "An Indo-English Minstrel:A Study of Manjeri Isvaran's Fiction." *LE&W* 13(1969):43–67.

1413. Sastry, L.S.R. Krishna. "Two Poems of Sri Aurobindo." [F 45]:18–26.

1414. Shahane, V.A. "Theme and Symbol in Khushwant Singh's *I Shall Not Hear the Nightingale*." *Osmania Jour. of Eng. Studies* 7,i(1969):11–36.

1415. Siddiqui, M. Naimuddin. "Nirad Chaudhuri:A Study in Alienation." *Osmania Jour. of Eng. Studies* 7,i(1969):37–49.

1416. Singh, Ram Sewak. "Bhabani Bhattacharya:A Novelist of Dreamy Wisdom." [F 45]:60–75.

1417. Singh, Satyanarain. "Ramanujan and Ezekiel." *Osmania Jour. of Eng. Studies* 7,i(1969):67–75.

1418. Venkatachari, K. "R.K. Narayan's Novels:Acceptance of Life." *Osmania Jour. of Eng. Studies* 7,i(1969):51–65.

* 1419. Williams, H. Moore. "English Writing in Free India." *TCL* 16:3–15.

Malta. 1420. Aquilina, J. "Malta's Current Contribution to Commonwealth Literature." [F 50]:104–14.

New Zealand. 1421. Beveridge, Michael. "Conversation with Frank Sargeson." *Landfall* 24:4–27,142–60.

1422. Curnow, Allen. "Distraction and Definition:Centripetal Directions in New Zealand Poetry." [F 50]:170–86.

1423. Graham, John. "A Reminiscence." *Landfall* 23(1969): 391–94. [On Karl Wolfskehl.]

1424. Hoffman, Paul. "Karl Wolfskehl, 1869–1948:A German Poet in New Zealand." *Landfall* 23(1969):381–91.

1425. "James K. Baxter:Worksheets." *MHRev* 5(1968):114–17.

1426. McNaughton, Howard. "In the Sargeson World." *Landfall* 24:39–43.

1427. O'Sullivan, Vincent. " 'Brief Permitted Morning':Notes on the Poetry of Charles Brasch." *Landfall* 23(1969):338–53.

1428. Pearson, Bill. "The Maori and Literature, 1938–65," 217–56 in *The Maori People in the Nineteen Sixties:A Symposium.* Eric Schwimmer, ed. London: C. Hurst; New York: Academic Press, 1968. [See also Bibliog., 373–84.]
See also 938.

West Indies. 1429. Birbalsingh, F.M. "The Novels of Ralph DeBoissière." *JCL* 9:104–08.

1430. Brathwaite, Edward. "*The Islands in Between*:Reflections on West Indian Literature." *SoRA* 3(1969):264–71.

1431. Brown, Lloyd W. "The West Indian Novel in North America:A Study of Austin Clarke." *JCL* 9:89–103.

1432. Drayton, Arthur D. "The European Factor in West Indian Literature." *Lit. Half-Yearly*(Mysore) 11,i:71–95.

1433. —— "West Indian Consciousness in West Indian Verse:A Historical Perspective." *JCL* 9:66–88.

1434. Gowda, H.H. Anniah. "Wilson Harris's *Tumatumari*." *Lit. Half-Yearly*(Mysore) 11,i:31–38.

* 1435. Grant, Damian. "Emerging Image:The Poetry of Edward Brathwaite." *CritQ* 12:186–92.

1436. Howard, W.J. "Wilson Harris's *Guiana Quartet*:From Personal Myth to National Identity." *ArielE* 1,i:46–60.

1437. Jones, Joseph and Johanna. *Authors and Areas of the West Indies.* (People and Places in World-English Lit. 2.) Austin, Texas: Steck-Vaughn.

1438. Kent, George E. "The Soulful Way of Claude McKay." *BlackW* 20,i:37–51.

1439. Lacovia, R.M. "Roger Mais and the Problem of Freedom." *BARev* 1,iii:45–54.

1440. Lamming, George. *In the Castle of My Skin.* Introd. Richard Wright. New York: Collier. [Repr.]

1441. McDowell, Robert E. "Mothers and Sons:A View of Black Literature from South Africa, the West Indies, and America." *PrS* 43:356–58.

1442. Moore, Gerald. *The Chosen Tongue:English Writing in the Tropical World.* London: Longmans, 1969.

1443. Nazareth, Peter. "*The Mimic Men* as a Study of Corruption." *EAJ* 7,vii:18–22. [V.S. Naipaul.]

1444. Ramchand, Kenneth. *The West Indian Novel and Its Background.* New York: Barnes & Noble; London: Faber.

1445. Singh, H.B. "V.S. Naipaul:A Spokesman for New-Colonialism." *L&I* 2(1969):71–85.

III. THEMES, TYPES, AND SPECIAL TOPICS

Ballads. 1446. Cox, J. Stevens,ed. *Two Dorset Ballads, c. 1700.* St. Peter Port, Guernsey: Toucan Press, 1969. ["The Unnatural Father" and "The Dorsetshire Garland, or, The Beggar's Wedding."]

1447. Matchett, William H. "The Integrity of 'Sir Patrick Spence'." *MP* 68:25–31.

Bible. 1448. Duschnes, Philip C. "Bruce Rogers' Oxford Lectern Bible." *Serif* 7,i:31–32.

1449. Henn, T.R. "On Trying to Write About the Bible." *ArielE* 1,i:9–19. [Influ. of Bible on Eng. Lit.]
See also 2712.

Bibliography. 1450. Goetsch, Paul. "Anglistische Zeitschriften." *NS* 19:201–06,527–32.

Biography and Autobiography. 1451. Piper, David. "The Development of the British Literary Portrait up to Samuel Johnson." *PBA* 54(1968):51–72.

1452. Plourde, Ferdinand J.,Jr. "Time Present and Time Past:Autobiography as a Narrative of Duration." *DAI* 30(1969): 334A–35A(Minn.).

Comedy. 1453. Kaul, A.N. *The Action of English Comedy: Studies in the Encounter of Abstraction and Experience from Shakespeare to Shaw.* New Haven and London: Yale U.P.

Criticism. 1454. Butler, Christopher. *Number Symbolism.* London: Routledge & K. Paul. [A hist. of numerological allegory with particular emphasis on Eng. poetry.]

1455. Daiches, David. *New Literary Values.* Freeport, N.Y.: Books for Libraries, 1968.

1456. Kato, Ryutaro. "Keimo no Igirisu Hihyo no Kadai." *EigoS* 114(1968):288–89. [Task of Eng. crit. in age of enlightenment.]

1457. Nassar, Eugene P. *The Rape of Cinderella:Essays in Literary Continuity.* Bloomington: Ind. U.P. [Essays on Milton, Hopkins, Keats, W. Stevens, Joyce, Fielding, Sterne, Shakespeare, Hart Crane, and on the act of crit.]

1458. Okerlund, Arlene N. "Literature and Its Audience:The Reader in Action in Selected Works of Spenser, Dryden, Thackeray, and T.S. Eliot." *DAI* 30(1969):1991A(Calif., San Diego).

1459. Paulson, Ronald. "English Literary History at The Johns Hopkins University." *NLH* 1:559–64.

1460. Yamakawa, Kozo. *Two Critical Traditions in Modern English Literature.* (Memoirs of the Faculty of Letters, Osaka U. 15.) Osaka: Osaka U., 1969. [In Jap.; Eng. sum. Chaps. on Coleridge, Pater, Read, Arnold, and T.S. Eliot.]

Drama and Theater. 1461. Jacob, Giles. *The Poetical Register:Or, The Lives and Characters of the English Dramatic Poets.* New York: Garland Pub. [Facsim.]

1462. Olson, Elder. *The Theory of Comedy.* Bloomington: Ind. U.P., 1969.

1462a. Smith, Elizabeth N. "The Society of the Incomplete:The Psychology and Structure of the Farce." *DAI* 30: 3958A(Mich.).
See also 1980, 4421.

Folk Songs. 1463. Lloyd, A.L. *Folk Song in England.* London: Granada (Panther) for the Workers' Music Assn., 1969. [Orig. pub. 1967.]

Folklore. 1464. Briggs, Katharine M. *A Dictionary of Folk Tales in the English Language, Incorporating the F.J. Norton Collection.* 4 vols. *Part A:Folk Narratives.* London: Routledge & K. Paul; Bloomington: Ind. U.P.

Newspapers. 1465. Wilkerson, Marjorie. *News and the Newspapers.* London: Batesford. [Hist. of the newspaper, 1702 to present.]

Poetry. 1466. Berry, Edmund. "The Poet of Love and Wine." *Mosaic* 3,ii:132–43. [Anacreon's popularity in England.]

1467. Bold, Alan,ed. *The Penguin Book of Socialist Verse.* Harmondsworth: Penguin.

1467a. Bunn, James H.,III. "The Palace of Art:A Study of Form in Retrospective Poems about the Creative Process." *DAI* 30:4400A(Emory).

1468. Chalker, John. *The English Georgic:A Study in the Development of a Form.* London: Routledge & K. Paul.

1469. Combs, Bruce E. "A Linguistic Analysis of Rime with Studies in Chaucer, Donne, and Pope." *DAI* 30:4963A(Ore.).

1470. Drake, J.T. "Statistical Trivia Relating to the First Ten Years of the Aldrich Catch Club." *JCSA* 2:55–60.

1471. Engsberg, Richard C. "Two by Two:Analogues of Form in Poetry and Music." *DAI* 30(1969):278A(N.Y.U.).

1472. Ern, Lothar. *Freivers und Metrik:Zur Problematik der englischen Verwissenschaft.* Darmstadt: Blaeschke. [Diss., Freiburg, 1968.]

1473. Göller, Karl H. *Die englische Lyrik:Von der Renaissance bis zur Gegenwart.* 2 vols. Düsseldorf: Bagel, 1968. [Analyses of representative poems.]

1474. Heath-Stubbs, John F. *The Pastoral.* London: Oxford U.P., 1969. [86-p. pamphlet.]

1475. Hendricks, William O. "Geoffrey N. Leech, *A Linguistic Guide to English Poetry*." *Lingua* 25:165–77. [Rev. art.]

1476. Leech, Geoffrey N. *A Linguistic Guide to English Poetry.* Harlow: Longmans, 1969. [Emphasizes stylistic relationship between poetic and other uses of lang.]

1477. Malof, Joseph. *A Manual of English Meters.* Bloomington: Ind. U.P.

1478. Meyers, Gerald W. "Modern Theories of Meter:A Critical Review." *DAI* 30:3912A(Mich.).

1479. Nelson, Malcolm A.,ed. "Canons and Catches:Epitaphs and Elegies." *JCSA* 2:23–44. [17th–20th cents.]

1480. Racin, John. "Research Opportunities and the Catches." *JCSA* 2:3–15. [16th, 17th, & 18th cents.]

1481. Ramos Orea, Tomás. *Antología de poemas inglesas románticos en español.* Con dos advertencias, una nota y un ensayo preliminar. Kingston, Ontario: Queen's U. [Poets from Burns to Dylan Thomas.]

1482. Reeves, James, and Martin Seymour-Smith. *A New Canon of English Poetry.* New York: Harper, 1969.

1483. Robinson, B.W. "An Account of the Aldrich Catch Club, London." *JCSA* 2:47–54.

1484. Stevenson, Charles L. "The Rhythm of English Verse." *JAAC* 28:327–44.

1485. Strzetelski, Jerzy. *The English Sonnet:Syntax and Style.* Cracow: Jagiell. Univ.

1486. Truchlar, Leo. *Zum Symbol des Schiffes in der englisch-sprachigen Lyrik.* (*ModSp* Schriftenreihe 12.) Wien: Verband der Österreichischen Neuphilologen, 1968.

1487. Tufte, Virginia. *The Poetry of Marriage:The Epithalamium in Europe and Its Development in England.* (U. of So. Calif. Studies in Comp. Lit. 2.) Los Angeles: Tinnon-Brown. *See also* 1454, 1505, 3930.

Prose Fiction. 1488. Day, Robert A. *Told in Letters:Epistolary Fiction Before Richardson.* Ann Arbor: U. of Mich. P., 1966.

1489. Edwards, Lee R. "Forces Against Structure:Some Problems of Form in the Development of the English Novel." *DAI* 30(1969):2019A(Calif., San Diego).

1490. Fietz, Lothar. "Fiktionsbewusstsein und Roman-struktur in der Geschichte des englischen und amerikanischen Romans." [F 30]:115–31.

1491. Zall, P.M. "English Prose Jestbooks in the Huntington Library:A Chronological Checklist (1535?–1799)." *SRO* 4(1968–69):78–91.
See also 938.

Romances. 1492. Beer, Gillian. *The Romance.* London: Methuen.

Satire. 1493. Fischer, Hermann,ed. *English Satirical Poetry from Joseph Hall to Percy B. Shelley.* Tübingen: Niemeyer.

Special Topics. 1494. Eidson, Donald R. "The Sun as Symbol and Type of Christ in English Non-Dramatic Poetry from the Anglo-Saxon Period Through the Victorian Period." *DAI* 30:4407A–08A(Mo., Columbia).

1495. Fields, Albert W. "*Nosce Teipsum*:The Study of a Common-Place in English Literature, 1500–1900." *DAI* 30(1969):1979A–80A(Ky.).

1496. Fowler, Alastair,ed. *Silent Poetry:Essays in Numero-logical Analysis.* New York: Barnes & Noble; London: Routledge & K. Paul.

1497. Fox, Vivian C. "Deviance in English Utopias in the 16th, 17th, and 18th Centuries." *DAI* 30(1969):1955A(Boston).

1498. Jones, Eldred D. "Washing the Ethiop White:The African in English Poetry 16th–18th Century." *ISE* 1(1969):26–35.

1499. Mercier, Vivian. *The Irish Comic Tradition.* New York: Oxford U. P., 1969.

1500. Merrill, Elizabeth. *The Dialogue in English Literature.* Hamden, Conn.: Archon, 1969.

1501. Philmus, Robert M. *Into the Unknown:The Evolution of Science Fiction from Francis Goodwin to H.G. Wells.* Berkeley: U. of Calif. P.

1502. Ruthven, K.K. *The Conceit.* London: Methuen, 1969.

Stylistics. 1503. Crystal, David, and Derek Davy. *Investigating English Style.* (IUSHTL.) Bloomington: Ind. U.P.

1504. Dahlberg, Edward. "The Sacred Logoi." *Prose* 1:63–67. [Excerpt from forthcoming *Confessions.*]

1505. Kroeber, Karl, and Alfred L. and Theodora K. Kroeber. "Life Against Death in English Poetry:A Method of Stylistic Definition." *TWA* 57(1969):29–40.

Themes. 1506. Poenicke, Klaus. "Der Drachentöter und das Menschenbild des Naturalismus." *JA* 15:88–100.

1507. Rowland, Beryl. "The Mill in Popular Metaphor from Chaucer to the Present Day." *SFQ* 33(1969):69–79.

Translation. 1508. Birse, A.H. "The Anonymous Men in Between." *TLS* 18 Sept:1047–48.

1509. Burgess, Anthony. "Bless Thee, Bottom." *TLS* 18 Sept:1024–25. [Problems in tr.]

1510. Callois, Roger. "Culture to Culture." *TLS* 25 Sept:1071–73.

1511. Ivanov, Vyacheslav V. "Translation and the Linguist." *TLS* 25 Sept:1079–80.

1512. Manheim, Ralph. "In the Translator's Kitchen." *TLS* 18 Sept:1041–42.

1513. Paz, Octavio. "The Literal and the Literary." *TLS* 18 Sept:1019–21.

IV. OLD ENGLISH

General and Miscellaneous. 1516. Baker, D.C. " 'Therefor to wepe, cum Lerne off me':A *Planctus* Fragment in MS Corpus Christi College, Oxford, F. 261." *MÆ* 38(1969):291–94.

1517. Brown, Alan K. "The Epinal Glossary Edited with Critical Commentary of the Vocabulary. (Volumes I and II)." *DAI* 30:5428A(Stanford).

1518. Campbell, Alistair. "Verse Influences in Old English Prose." [F 54]:93–98.

1519. Clemnoes, Peter. *Rhythm and Cosmic Order in Old English Christian Literature.* London: Cambridge U.P.

1520. Economou, Georges D. "The Goddess Natura in Medieval Literature." *DAI* 31:1224A–25A(Columbia).

1521. Gerritsen, Johan. "A Note on the Vespasian Psalter Gloss." *ES* 51:228–30.

1522. Grohskopf, Bernice. *The Treasure of Sutton Hoo:Ship-Burial for an Anglo-Saxon King.* New York: Atheneum. [Freq. ref. to *Beowulf.*]

1523. Hallander, Lars-G. "Two Old English Confessional Prayers." *SMS* 3:87–110.

1524. Heimann, Adelheid. "Three Illustrations from the Bury St. Edmunds Psalter and Their Prototypes:Notes on the Iconography of Some Anglo-Saxon Drawings." *JWCI* 29(1966):39–59.

1525. Keith, George H. "An English Version of a French Moral Treatise (*Voie de Paradis*)." *RPh* 23(1969):55–56.

1526. Lawrence, R.F. "Formula and Rhythm in *The Wars of Alexander.*" *ES* 51:97–112.

1527. Most, Sheila M. "Intensive and Restrictive Modification in a Select Corpus of Old English Poetry and Prose." *DAI* 30:2992A–93A(Northwestern).

1528. Page, Ray. "Old English *cyningstan.*" *LeedsSE* N.S. 3(1969):1–5.

1529. Pilch, Herbert. "Syntactic Prerequisites for the Study of Old English Poetry." *Lang&S* 3:51–61.

1530. Pillsbury, Paul W. "A Concordance to *The West Saxon Gospels.*" [F 9]:48–56.

1531. Thundyil, Father Zacharias P. "A Study of the Anglo-Saxon Concept of Covenant and Its Sources with Special Reference to Anglo-Saxon Laws and the Old English Poems:*The Battle of Maldon* and *Guthlac.*" *DAI* 30(1969):1997A–98A(Notre Dame).

1532. Venezky, Richard L. "Computer Processing of Old English Texts." [F 9]:65–75.

1533. —— "Concordances to the Rushworth Matthew and the Vercelli Homilies." [F 9]:43–46.

1534. Weber, Gerd W. *Wyrd:Studien zum Schicksalsbegriff der altenglischen und altnordischen Literatur.* (FBG 8.) Bad Homburg: Gehlen, 1969.
See also 280, 9029.

Poetry. 1535. Calder, Daniel G. "Symbolic Settings in Old English Poetry." *DAI* 30:2999A(Ind.).

1536. Capek, Michael J. "A Note on Formula Development in Old Saxon." *MP* 67:357–63.

1537. Coffey, Jerome E. "The Evolution of an Oral-Formulaic Tradition in Old and Middle English Alliterative Verse." *DAI* 30(1969):2477A–78A(S.U.N.Y., Buffalo).

* 1538. Fakundiny, Lydia. "The Art of Old English Verse Composition." *RES* 21:129–42,257–66.

1539. Gardner, Thomas [J.] "The Old English Kenning:A Characteristic Feature of Germanic Poetic Diction?" *MP* 67(1969):109–17.

1540. Hamer, Richard F.S.,ed. *A Choice of Anglo-Saxon Verse.* London: Faber. [Tr. by ed. with orig. text and notes.]

1541. Jabbour, Alan A. "The Memorial Transmission of Old English Poetry:A Study of the Extant Parallel Texts." *DAI* 30(1969):282A–83A(Duke).

1542. Keenan, Hugh T. "The Apocalyptic Vision in Old English Poetry." *DAI* 30(1969):1138A–39A(Tenn.).

1543. Keyser, Samuel Jay. "Old English Prosody." *CE* 30(1969):331–56.

1544. Metcalf, Allan A. "On the Authorship and Originality of the *Meters of Boethius.*" *NM* 71:185–87.

1545. O'Brien, Michael. "Poetic Diction in Old English Poetry." *ELLS* 6(1969):32–41.

1546. Opland, Jeffrey. "The Oral Origins of Early English Poetry." *UCTSE* 1:40–54.

1547. Pender, Robert L. "A Structural Study of the Old English Metrical Charms." *DAI* 30:4952A–53A(Ind.).

1548. Reynolds, Elizabeth R. "The Concept of Fate in Old English Poetry." *DAI* 30(1969):2497A–98A(S.C.).

1549. Rollinson, Philip. "Some Kinds of Meaning in Old English Poetry." *AnM* 11:5–21.

1550. Smith, Albert H.,ed. *Three Northumbrian Poems: Caedmon's Hymn, Bede's Death Song, the Leiden Riddle.* New York: Appleton-Century-Crofts, 1969.

1551. Spolsky, Ellen S. "Old English Lyric Poetry." *DAI* 30(1969):697A–98A(Ind.).

1552. Starr, David. "Metrical Changes:From Old to Middle English." *MP* 68:1–9. [Uses as examples *The Battle of Maldon* and *The Owl and the Nightingale.*]

1553. Watts, Ann C. *The Lyre and the Harp:A Comparative Reconsideration of Oral Tradition in Homer and Old English Epic Poetry.* New Haven: Yale U.P., 1969.

See also 1710, 9322.

Riddles. 1554. Crossley-Holland, Kevin,ed. *Storm, and Other Old English Riddles.* London: Macmillan. [36 riddles tr. from the *Exeter Book* by C-H.]

1555. Garvin, Katharine. "Nemnað hy sylfe:A Note on Riddle 57, Exeter Book." *C&M* 27(1966):294–95. [Corr. of Bibliog. for 1969, Vol. ɪ, Item 1863.]

Aelfric. 1558. Hurt, James R. "A Note on Aelfric's *Lives of Saints*, No. xvɪ." *ES* 51:231–34.

* 1559. Lipp, Frances R. "Aelfric's Old English Prose Style." *SP* 66(1969):689–718.

1560. Taylor, Arnold. "*Hauksbók* and Aelfric's *De Falsis Diis.*" *LeedsSE* N.S. 3(1969):101–09.

Alfred. 1561. Bak, Walter. "A Concordance to MS Hatton 20." [F 9]:61–65.

1562. Brown, William H.,Jr. *A Syntax of King Alfred's Pastoral Care.* The Hague and Paris: Mouton.

Andreas. 1563. Grosz, Oliver J.H. "The Island of Exiles:A Note on *Andreas* 15." *ELN* 7:241–42.

See also 1584.

Anglo-Saxon Chronicle. 1564. Clark, Cecily. " 'France' and 'French' in the *Anglo-Saxon Chronicle.*" *LeedsSE* N.S. 3(1969): 35–45.

1565. Waterhouse, Ruth. "The Theme and Structure of 755 *Anglo-Saxon Chronicle.*" *NM* 70(1969):630–40.

Athelwold. 1566. Whitelock, Dorothy. "The Authorship of the Account of King Edgar's Establishment of Monasteries." [F 54]:125–36.

Battle of Maldon. 1567. Anderson, Earl R. "*Flyting* in The *Battle of Maldon.*" *NM* 71:197–202.

1568. Macrae-Gibson, O.D. "*Maldon:*The Literary Structure of the Later Part." *NM* 71:192–96.

* 1569. Metcalf, Allan A. " 'West' in *Maldon.*" *PLL* 6:314–16. *See also* 1531, 1552.

Bede. *See* 8720, 8721, 8722, 8723, 8725.

Beowulf. 1570. Baird, Joseph L. "The Rhetorical Strategies of the *Beowulf* Poet." *DAI* 30(1969):1976A(Ky.).

1571. Barnes, Daniel R. "Folktale Morphology and the Structure of *Beowulf.*" *Speculum* 45:416–34.

1572. Bessinger, Jess B.,Jr. "A Concordance to *Beowulf.*" [F 9]:35–39.

1573. Bloomfield, Morton W. "Beowulf, Byrhtnoth, and the Judgement of God:Trial by Combat in Anglo-Saxon England." *Speculum* 44(1969):545–59.

1574. Cable, Thomas M. "Old English Meter:Problems, Principles, and Abstract Form in *Beowulf.*" *DAI* 30:5401A–02A(Texas, Austin).

* 1575. ——— "Rules for Syntax and Metrics in *Beowulf.*" *JEGP* 69:81–88.

1576. Crane, John K. "To Thwack or Be Thwacked:An Analysis of Available Translations and Editions of *Beowulf.*" *CE* 32:321–40.

1577. Dow, Janet. "Beowulf and the 'Walkers in Darkness'." *ConnR* 4,i:42–48.

1578. Einersen, Dorrit. "De vigtigste træk af ordstillingen i *Beowulf, Krøniken* indtil 930 og de 30 første sider af *Wulfstans* prædikener." *Extracta* 2(1969):80–87. [Abst.]

1579. Fry, Donald K. "The Location of Finnsburh:*Beowulf* 1125–29a." *ELN* 8:1–3.

1580. ——— 'Wið Earm Gesæt' and Beowulf's Hammerlock." *MP* 67:364–66.

* 1581. Gardner, John. "Fulgentius's *Exposito Vergiliana Continentia* and the Plan of *Beowulf:*Another Approach to the Poem's Style and Structure." *PLL* 6:227–62.

1582. Goldsmith, Margaret E. *The Mode and Meaning of Beowulf.* London: Athlone Press.

1583. Halverson, John. "The World of *Beowulf.*" *ELH* 36(1969):593–608.

1584. Hart, Francis A. "Paradoxical Ideals in *Beowulf* and *Andreas.*" *DAI* 30(1969):1982A–83A(Utah).

* 1585. Hart, Thomas E. "*Ellen:*Some Tectonic Relationships in *Beowulf* and Their Formal Resemblance to Anglo-Saxon Art." *PLL* 6:263–90.

1586. Kühlwein, Wolfgang. "Andreascrux 1241 und Beowulfcrux 849." *BGDSL* 91(1969):77–81.

1587. Lee, Alvin A. "Heorot and the 'Guest-Hall' of Eden." *MScan* 2:78–91.

1588. Milosh, Joseph. "A Supplement for Teaching *Beowulf.*" *EJ* 59:646–54.

1589. Murray, Alexander C. "The Lending of Hrunting and the Anglo-Saxon Laws." *N&Q* 17:83–84.

1590. Osborn, Marijane L. "Foreign Studies of *Beowulf:*A Critical Study of *Beowulf* Scholarship Outside English-Speaking Countries and Germany, with Bibliographies." *DAI* 30(1969): 1146A(Stanford).

1591. Pope, John C. "Beowulf's Old Age." [F 54]:55–64.

1592. Puhvel, Martin. "The Melting of the Giant-Wrought Sword in *Beowulf.*" *ELN* 7(1969):81–84. [Parallels in Icelandic and Irish folklore.]

1593. Rosenberg, Bruce A. "The Necessity of Unferth." *JFI* 6(1969):50–60.

1594. Smithers, G.V. "Destiny and the Heroic Warrior in *Beowulf.*" [F 54]:65–81.

1595. Travis, James. "Hiberno-Saxon Christianity and the Survival of *Beowulf.*" *Lochlann* 4(1969):226–34.

See also 635, 1522, 5843, 5854, 6289.

Blickling Homilies. 1596. Collins, Rowland L. "Six Words in the *Blickling Homilies.*" [F 54]:137–41.

1597. Dalbey, Marcia A. "Hortatory Tone in the Blickling Homilies:Two Adaptations of Caesarius." *NM* 70(1969):641–58.

1598. ——— "Structure and Style in The Blickling Homilies for the Temporale." *DAI* 30(1969):275A(Ill.).

Byhrtferth. 1599. Murphy, James J. "The Rhetorical Lore of the Boceras in Byhrtferth's *Manual.*" [F 54]:111–24.

Caedmon. 1600. Fritz, Donald W. "Caedmon:A Traditional Christian Poet." *MS* 31(1969):334–37.

1601. Golden, John. "An Onomastic Allusion in Cædmon's *Hymn*?" *NM* 70(1969):627-29.

See also 1595.

Christ and Satan. 1602. Finnegan, Robert E. "MS Junius XI *Christ and Satan* and the Latin and Vernacular Prose Homiletic Traditions." *DAI* 30(1969):684A(Notre Dame).

* 1603. Hill, Thomas D. "Apocryphal Cosmography and the 'Stream Uton Sæ':A Note on *Christ and Satan*, Lines 4–12." *PQ* 48(1969):550–54.

1604. —— " 'Byrht Word' and 'Hælendes Heafod':Cristological Allusion in the Old English *Christ and Satan*." *ELN* 8:6–9.

Christ III. 1605. Hill, Thomas D. "Notes on the Eschatology of the Old English *Christ III*." *NM* 70(1969):672–79.

Cynewulf. 1606. Bleeth, K.A. "*Juliana*." *MÆ* 38(1969): 119–22.

1607. Gardner, John. "Cynewulf's *Elene*:Sources and Structure." *Neophil* 54:65–76.

Dream of the Rood. *1608. Edwards, Robert R. "Narrative Technique and Distance in the *Dream of the Rood*." *PLL* 6:291–301.

1609. Macrae-Gibson, O.D. "Christ the Victor-Vanquished in *The Dream of the Rood*." *NM* 70(1969):667–72.

1610. Wolf, Carol Jean. "Christ as Hero in *The Dream of the Rood*." *NM* 71:202–10.

Durham. 1611. Brown, T. Julian, Francis Wormald, A.S.C. Ross, and E.G. Stanley,eds. *The Durham Ritual*. (Early Eng. Manuscripts 16.) Copenhagen: Rosenkilde & Bagger, 1969.

Exeter Book. 1612. Conlee, John W. "Artistry in the Riddles of *The Exeter Book*." *DAI* 30(1969):274A–75A(Ill.).

1613. Reisner, Thomas A. "Riddle 75 (Exeter Book)." *Expl* 28:Item 78.

1614. Trahern, Joseph B.,Jr. "The *Ioca Monachorum* and the Old English *Pharaoh*." *ELN* 7:165–68.

See also 1554.

Exodus. *1615. Farrell, Robert T. "A Reading of OE. *Exodus*." *RES* 20(1969):401–17.

1616. Lieberman, Leo. "Old English *Exodus* and *Sefer Shemoth*:A Comparative Study." *DAI* 30(1969):1531A(Fordham).

1617. Lucas, Peter J. "The Cloud in the Interpretation of the Old English *Exodus*." *ES* 51:297–311.

1618. McLoughlin, Eleanor. "OE *Exodus* and the *Antiphonary of Bangor*." *NM* 70(1969):658–67.

Finnsburh. *See* 1579.

Genesis. *1619. Cherniss, Michael D. "Heroic Ideals and the Moral Climate of *Genesis B*." *MLQ* 30(1969):479–97.

1620. Faiss, Klaus. " 'Gnade' und seine Kontexte in der altenglischen *Genesis*:Ein Beitrag zum Problem der altenglischen Dichtersprache." *Linguistics* 56:5–30.

1621. Lucas, Peter J. "*Genesis B* 623–5:Part of the Speech to Eve?" *N&Q* 17:243–44.

1622. Rosier, James. "*Hrincg* in *Genesis A*." *Anglia* 88:334–36.

1623. Vickrey, John F. "A Note on *Genesis* Lines 242–244." *NM* 71:191–92.

Guthlac B. 1624. Rosier, James L. "Death and Transfiguration:*Guthlac B*." [F 54]:82–92.

Guthlac. *See* 1531.

Judgment Day II. 1625. Geoghegan, Patrick M. "*Judgment Day II*, An Edition." *DAI* 30(1969):280A(Ill.).

Judith. 1626. Heinemann, Fredrik J. "*Judith* 236–291a:A Mock Heroic Approach-to-Battle Type Scene." *NM* 71:83–96.

1627. Rose, Nancy G. "The Old English *Judith*:The Problem of Leadership." *DAI* 30(1969):1180A(Calif., Berkeley).

Leiden Riddle. 1628. Gerritsen, Johan. "The Text of the Leiden Riddle." *ES* 50(1969):529–44.

Orosius. 1629. Liggins, Elizabeth M. "The Authorship of the Old English *Orosius*." *Anglia* 88:289–322.

Phoenix. 1630. Thormann, Janet. "Variations on the Theme of 'The Hero on the Beach' in *The Phoenix*." *NM* 71:187–90.

Riming Poem. *1631. Lehmann, Ruth P.M. "The Old English *Riming Poem*:Interpretation, Text, and Translation." *JEGP* 69:437–49.

Soul's Address. *1632. Ferguson, Mary H. "The Structure of the *Soul's Address to the Body* in Old English." *JEGP* 69:72–80.

Stowe Psalter. 1633. Kimmens, Andrew C. "An Edition of British Museum MS. Stowe 2:The Stowe Psalter." *DAI* 30(1969):1139A(Princeton).

Vainglory. 1634. Regan, Catharine A. "Patristic Psychology in the Old English *Vainglory*." *Traditio* 26:324–35.

Vercelli Book. 1635. Halsall, Maureen. "More About C. Maier's Transcript of the *Vercelli Book*." *ELN* 8:3–6.

Vercelli Homilies. 1636. Szarmach, Paul E. "Caesarius of Arles and the Vercelli Homilies." *Traditio* 26:315–23.

Wanderer. 1636a. Bolton, W.F. "The Dimensions of *The Wanderer*." *LeedsSE* N.S. 3(1969):7–34. [On struct., lexical clusters, and rhetor. features.]

1637. Dunning, T.P., and A.J. Bliss,eds. *The Wanderer*. London: Methuen, 1969; New York: Appleton, 1969. [With introd., notes, glossary.]

1638. Malmberg, Lars. "*The Wanderer*:'WaÞema Gebind'." *NM* 71:96–99.

Wife's Lament. 1639. Patrick, Michael D. " 'The Wife's Lament,' 24–41." *Expl* 28:Item 50.

Worcester Chronicle. 1640. Woodell, Thomas M.,II. "Selected Syntactical Aspects of the *Worcester Chronicle* from 1054 through 1079." *DAI* 30(1969):309A(Fla.).

Wulfstan. *See* 1578.

V. MIDDLE ENGLISH

Bibliography. 1641. Ker, Neil R. *Medieval Manuscripts in British Libraries*. London: Oxford U.P., 1969.

1642. Pollard, Graham. "The Names of Some English Fifteenth-Century Binders." *Library* 25:193–218. [Incl. 7 plates.]

1643. Scattergood, V.J. "Correspondence." *RES* 21:337–38. [On 2 unlisted ME poems in BM MS. Harley 1735.]

1644. Severs, J. Burke,ed. *A Manual of the Writings in Middle English 1050–1500*. Vol. II. Pub. by the Conn. Acad. of Arts and Sciences. [Marie P. Hamilton, "The *Pearl* Poet"; Ernest W. Talbert and S. Harrison Thomson, "Wyclyf and His Followers"; Laurence Muir, "Translations and Paraphrases of the Bible, and Commentaries"; Charlotte D'Evelyn and Frances A. Foster, "Saints' Legends"; Charlotte D'Evelyn, "Instructions for Religious."]

General and Miscellaneous. 1645. Altschul, Michael. *Anglo-Norman England, 1066–1154*. London: Cambridge U.P. for the Conf. on British Studies, 1969.

1646. Baltzell, Jane. "Rhetorical 'Amplification' and 'Abbreviation' and the Structure of Medieval Narrative." *PCP* 2(1967):32–39.

1647. Bazire, Joan,ed. *The Metrical Life of St. Robert of Knaresborough:Together with the Other Middle English Pieces in the British Museum*. New York: Oxford U.P.

1648. Blaicher, Günther. "Über das Lachen im englischen Mittelalter." *DVLG* 44:508–29.

1649. Blake, N.F. "The Fifteenth Century Reconsidered." *NM* 71:146–57.

1650. Bonfield, June P. "The Penitence of the Medieval Magdalen:A Study in the Meanings of Her Appellation 'Penitent' as Reflected in Vernacular Literature of the British Isles c. 1250–c. 1500." *DAI* 30:5400A(Texas, Austin).

1651. Bowers, R.H. "A Twelfth Century Battle of the Books." *AnM* 11:65–73.

1652. Braekman, Willy L., and Peter S. Macaulay. "The Story of the Cat and the Candle in Middle English Literature." *NM* 70(1969):690–702.

1653. Caluwé-Dor, Juliette de. "Les études anglaises médiévales à Liège." *RLV* 35(1969):452–60.

1654. Davis, Norman. "Two Unprinted Dialogues in Late Middle English, and Their Language." *RLV* 35(1969):461–72.

1655. Downing, Janay Y. "A Critical Edition of Cambridge University MS FF.5.48." *DAI* 30(1969):2480A(U. of Wash.).

1656. Fink, Hanno. *Die sieben Todsünden in der mittelenglischen erbaulichen Literatur.* (Britannica et Americana 17.) Hamburg: Cram, de Gruyter, 1969. [Diss., Hamburg.]

1657. Hakutani, Yoshinobu. "The Doctrine of Courtesy in Certain Medieval Writings." *Discourse* 13:259–74.

1658. Hargreaves, Henry. "Additional Information for the Brown-Robbins 'Index'." *N&Q* 16(1969):446–47.

1659. Heyworth, P.L. "Notes on Two Uncollected Middle English Proverbs." *N&Q* 17:86–88.

1660. Jacobs, Nicolas. "Old French 'Degare' and Middle English 'Degarre' and 'Deswarre'." *N&Q* 17:164–65.

1661. Jones, Charles. "The Computer in Middle English Studies:A Note." *CJL* 14(1968):58–62. [See Bibliog. for 1968, Item 234.]

1662. Paull, Michael R. "The Figure of Mahomet in Middle English Literature." *DAI* 30:3915A(N.C.).

1663. Pichaske, David R. "The Reynardian Tradition in Medieval and Renaissance English Literature." *DAI* 30:3953A(Ohio).

1664. Pickering, Frederick. *Literature and Art in the Middle Ages.* Coral Gables, Fla.: U. of Miami P.; London: Macmillan.

* 1665. Robbins, Rossell H. "A Note on the Singer Survey of Medical Manuscripts in the British Isles." *ChauR* 4:66–70.

1666. —— "Medical Manuscripts in Middle English." *Speculum* 45:393–415.

1667. —— "The English Fabliau:Before and After Chaucer." *MSpr* 64:231–44.

1668. Steinberg, Clarence B. "Some Medieval Traditions of Etymological Characterization." *DAI* 30(1969):2500A–01A(Pa.).

1669. Vladimirovas, L[evas]. "Lietuvis—pirmasis Londono spaustuvininkas." *Pergalė* 10:153–59. [On John Lettou, the first printer in London.]

1670. Weiss, Judith. "The Auchinleck Ms. and the Edwardes Mss." *N&Q* 16(1969):444–46.

1671. Wimsatt, James I. *Allegory and Mirror:Tradition and Structure in Middle English Literature.* New York: Pegasus.

1672. Zacher, Christian K. "*Curiositas* and the Impulses for Pilgrimage in Fourteenth-Century English Literature." *DAI* 30:4429A(Calif., Riverside).

See also 855, 1965, 8456.

Drama and Theater. 1673. Clopper, Lawrence M.,Jr. "The Structure of the Chester Cycle:Text, Theme and Theatre." *DAI* 30:4403A(Ohio State).

1674. Collier, Richard J. "A Re-evaluation of the Poetry of the York Corpus Christi Plays, with Special Reference to Plays I (Creation); XLI (Purification); XXI (Baptism); XXXVI (Mortificatio Cristi); XLIII (Ascension)." *DAI* 30:5402A(Wash. U.).

1675. Collins, Sister Mary E.,O.S.F. "The Allegorical Motifs in the Early English Moral Plays." *DAI* 30(1969):682A(Yale).

1676. Eccles, Mark,ed. *The Macro Plays.* (EETS 262.) London and New York: Oxford U.P., 1969.

1677. Griffin, John R. "The Hegge Pilate:A Tragic Hero?" *ES* 51:234–44.

1678. Helterman, Jeffrey A. "Symbolic Action in the Plays of the Wakefield Master." *DAI* 30:3430A(Rochester).

* 1679. Hieatt, Constance B. "A Case for *Duk Moraud* as a Play of the Miracles of the Virgin." *MS* 32:345–51.

1680. Horall, Sally. "The Secularization of the Middle English Morality Plays." *RUO* 40:149–62.

1681. Jambeck, Thomas J. "The Elements of Grotesque Humor in the Passion Sequences of the English Medieval Cycle Drama." *DAI* 30:4415A(Colo.).

1682. Kaplan, Joel H., and George Shand. "The *Poculi Ludique Societas*:Medieval Drama at the University of Toronto." *RORD* 11(1968):141–61.

1683. Leigh, David J. "The Doomsday Mystery Play:An Eschatological Morality." *MP* 67:211–23. [Incl. as appendix to art. "The General Judgment in Medieval Theology."]

1684. Malvern, Marjorie M. "The Magdalen:An Exploration of the Shaping of Myths Around the Mary Magdalene of the New Testament Canonical Gospels and an Examination of the Effects of the Myths on the Literary Figure, Particularly on the Heroine of the Fifteenth-Century Digby Play *Mary Magdalene*." *DAI* 30(1969):1532A(Mich. State).

1685. McCracken, Natalie J. "Medieval Mysteries for Modern Production." *DAI* 30(1969):1264A–65A(Wis.).

1686. Meyers, Walter E. *A Figure Given:Typology in the Wakefield Plays.* Pittsburgh: Duquesne U.P.

1687. Mill, Anna J. "Medieval Stage Directions:That Apple Tree Again." *TN* 24:122–24.

1688. —— "The Edinburgh Hammermen's Corpus Christi Herod Pageant." *Innes Rev.* 21,i:77–80.

1689. —— "The Perth Hammermen's Play:A Scottish Garden of Eden." *Scottish Hist. Rev.* 49:146–53.

1690. Mills, David. "Approaches to Medieval Drama." *LeedsSE* N.S. 3(1969):47–61.

1691. Nelson, Alan H. "Early Pictorial Analogues of Medieval Theatre-in-the-Round." *RORD* 12(1969):93–106.

1692. —— "Principles of Processional Staging:York Cycle." *MP* 67:303–20.

1693. Poteet, Daniel P.,II. "The *Hegge Plays*:An Approach to the Aesthetics of Medieval Drama." *DAI* 30:3020A–21A(Ill.).

1694. Schmitt, Natalie C. "Was There A Medieval Theatre in the Round? Part II." *TN* 24(1969):18–25. [For Part I see *TN* 23(1969):130–42.]

1695. Steinberg, Clarence B. "*Kemp Towne* in the Townley *Herod* Play:A Local Wakefield Allusion?" *NM* 71:253–60.

1696. Stevens, Martin. "The Staging of the Wakefield Plays." *RORD* 11(1968):115–28.

1697. Wall, Carolyn. "The Apocryphal and Historical Background of *The Appearance of Our Lady to Thomas* (Play XLVI of the York Cycle)." *MS* 32:172–92.

See also 643, 8487.

Poetry. 1698. Amassian, Margaret. "A Verse Life of John of Bridlington." *NM* 71:136–45.

1699. Baird, Lorrayne Y. "The Status of the Poet in the Middle Ages and the Problem of Anonymity." *DAI* 30:3422A(Ky.).

1700. Besserman, Lawrence L., Gail Gilman, and Victor Weinblatt. "Three Unpublished Middle English Poems from the Commonplace-Book of John Colyns (B.M. MS Harley 2252)." *NM* 71:212–38.

1701. Blake, N.F. "Rhythmical Alliteration." *MP* 67(1969):118–24.

1702. Curry, Jane L. "Image and Ænigma:The Middle English Religious Lyric in the Thirteenth and Fourteenth Centuries." *DAI* 30(1969):1131A–32A(Stanford).

1703. Danielsson, Bror. "The Percy Poem on Falconry." *SMS* 3:5–60.

1704. Edwards, A.S.G. "A Fifteenth Century Didactic Poem in British Museum Add. Ms. 29729." *NM* 70(1969):702–06.

1705. —— "Stanzas on Troy." *ELN* 7:246–48. [Hitherto unpub. stanzas from MS. McLean 182 in Fitzwilliam Museum, Cambridge.]

1706. Gardner, John,ed. *The Complete Works of the Gawain-Poet.* Illus. Fritz Kredel. Carbondale: So. Ill. U.P. ["Pearl," "Purity," "Patience," "Sir Gawain and the Green Knight," "St. Erkenwald"; Mod. Eng. versions.]

1707. Geddes, Sharon S. "The Middle English Poem of *Floriz and Blauncheflur* and the *Arabian Nights* Tale of 'Ni'amah and Naomi,' a Study in Parallels." *ESRS* 19,i:14–21,23–24.

1708. Hanna, Ralph. "A Note on a Harley Lyric." *ELN* 7:243–46. ["Middelerd for mon wes mad."]

1709. Harris, Patricia J. "The Anonymous Middle English Religious Lyrics:A Handbook." *DAI* 30:5430A(Mo., Columbia).

1710. Hascall, Dudley L. "Some Contributions to the Halle-Keyser Theory of Prosody." *CE* 30(1969):357–65.

1711. Hirsh, John C. "A Fifteenth-Century Commentary on 'Ihesu for Thy Holy Name'." *N&Q* 17:44–45.

1712. Jeffrey, David L. "Franciscan Spirituality and Popular Middle English Poetry." *DAI* 30(1969):1138A(Princeton).

1713. Keller, Henning. "Die me. Rezepte des Ms. Harley 2253." *Archiv* 207:94–100.

1714. Lampe, David E. "Middle English Debate Poems:A

Genre Study." *DAI* 30:3910A–11A(Neb.).

1715. Magnuson, Karl, and Frank G. Ryder. "The Study of English Prosody:An Alternative Proposal." *CE* 31:789–820.

1716. Muraoka, Yu. *"The Maiden Makeless." EigoS* 115(1969):346–48. [In Jap.]

1717. Noll, Dolores L. "The Love Universe in Late-Medieval English and Scottish Allegorical Love Poetry." *DAI* 30(1969): 2493A(Ky.).

1718. Oliver, Raymond. *Poems Without Names:The English Lyric, 1200–1500.* Berkeley: U. of Calif. P.

1719. Reiss, Edmund. "Religious Commonplaces and Poetic Artistry in the Middle English Lyric." *Style* 4:97–106.

1720. ── "The Art of the Middle English Lyric:Two Poems on Winter." *AnM* 11:22–34.

1721. Robbins, Rossell H. "Signs of Death in Middle English." *MS* 32:282–98.

1722. Ross, Alan S.C. "Some Alliterative Phrases in the 'Bodley Homilies'." *N&Q* 17:46–48.

1723. Scattergood, V.J. " 'The Debate Between Nurture and Kynd'—An Unpublished Middle English Poem." *N&Q* 17: 244–46.

1724. Stemmler, Theo,ed. *Medieval English Love-Lyrics.* Tübingen: Niemeyer.

1725. Tydeman, William,ed. *English Poetry, 1400–1580.* New York: Barnes & Noble; London: Heinemann.

See also 1537, 1552, 1643.

Romances. 1727. Gates, Robert J.,ed. *The Awntyrs of Arthure at the Terne Wathelyne.* Philadelphia: U. of Pa. P., 1969.

1728. Green, D.H. "Irony and the Medieval Romance." *FMLS* 6:49–64.

1730. Stephany, William A. "A Study of Four Middle English Arthurian Romances." *DAI* 30(1969):1537A(Del.). [*Golagros and Gawain, The Avowing of King Arthur, The Awntyrs of Arthur, Sir Gawain and the Green Knight.*]

See also 823.

Ancrene Riwle. 1731. Zettersten, Arne. "French Loan-Words in the *Ancren Riwle* and Their Frequency," (Etudes Romanes de Lund 18.) 227–50 in *Mélanges de philologie offerts à Alf Lombard à l'occasion de son soixante-cinquième anniversaire par ses collègues et ses amis.* Lund: Gleerup, 1969.

Arthour and Merlin. 1732. Sklar, Elizabeth S. "England's Arthur:A Study of the Middle English Poem *Arthour and Merlin.*" *DAI* 30:5004A(Pa.).

Awntyrs off Arthure. *1733. Hanna, Ralph III. *"The Awntyrs off Arthure:*An Interpretation." *MLQ* 31:275–97.

See also 1730.

Barbour. 1734. Coldwell, David F. "The Literary Background of Barbour's *Bruce.*" *DAI* 30(1969):682A(Yale).

1735. Kliman, Bernice W. "John Barbour, The First of the Makars:A Study of the Poet as Craftsman." *DAI* 30(1969): 1986A–87A(C.U.N.Y.).

Becket. 1736. Murray, Patrick. "Thomas Becket of Canterbury:Eight Hundred Years On." *Studies* 59:68–80.

Bird with Four Feathers. *1737. Hieatt, A. Kent and Constance. " 'The Bird with Four Feathers':Numerical Analysis of a Fourteenth-Century Poem." *PLL* 6:18–38.

Caxton. 1738. Blake, N.F. *Caxton and His World.* London: London House & Maxwell, 1969.

1739. Gaines, Barry. "A Forgotten Artist:John Harris and the Rylands Copy of Caxton's Edition of Malory." *BJRL* 52(1969): 115–28.

1740. Stelboum, Judith P. "William Caxton's Romance of *Blanchardyn and Eglantine.*" *DAI* 30(1969):294A–95A(N.Y.U.).

Chaucer. 1741. Alderson, William L., and Arnold C. Henderson. *Chaucer and Augustan Scholarship.* (UCPES 35.) Berkeley: U. of Calif. P.

1742. Allen, Judson B., and Patrick Gallacher. "Alisoun Through the Looking Glass:Or Every Man His Own Midas." *ChauR* 4:99–105.

1743. Ando, Shinsuke. "The Language of *The Romaunt of the Rose* (Fragment A), with Particular Reference to Chaucer's Relationship to Middle English Provincial Poetry." *SELit* Eng. No.:63–74.

* 1744. apRoberts, Robert P. "The Boethian God and the Audience of the *Troilus.*" *JEGP* 69:425–36.

1745. Badendyck, J. Lawrence. "Chaucer's Portrait Technique and the Dream Vision Tradition." *Eng. Record* 21,i:113–25.

1746. Baird, Joseph L. "Jason and His 'Sekte'." *AN&Q* 8:151–52.

1747. ── "Law and the *Reeve's Tale.*" *NM* 70(1969):679–83.

1748. Bauer, Gero. *Studien zum System und Gebrauch der 'Tempora' in der Sprache Chaucers und Gowers.* (WBEP 73.) Wien: Braumüller.

1749. Bisson, Lillian M. "Chaucer's Use of the Student-Teacher Relationship as an Artistic Technique in His Early Poems." *DAI* 30:5400A(Fla. State).

1750. Blanch, Robert J.,ed. *Geoffrey Chaucer:*Merchant's Tale. (Merrill Casebooks.) With Introd. and Notes. Columbus, Ohio: Charles E. Merrill. [Text and rptd. crit.]

1751. Bloomfield, Morton W. "Il racconto dell'*Uomo di legge*:La tragedia di una vittima e la commedia cristiana." *SCr* 3(1969):195–207.

1752. Broughton, Bradford B. "Chaucer's *Book of the Duchess*:Did John [of Gaunt] Love Blanche [of Lancaster]?" [F 47]:71–84.

* 1753. Brown, Emerson,Jr. "*Hortus Inconclusus*:The Significance of Priapus and Pyramus and Thisbe in the *Merchant's Tale.*" *ChauR* 4:31–40.

1754. Brown, James N. "Narrative Focus and Function in *The Book of the Duchess.*" *MSE* 2:71–79.

1755. Burrow, John A.,ed. *Geoffrey Chaucer:A Critical Anthology.* Harmondsworth: Penguin.

1756. Chamberlain, David S. "The Nun's Priest's Tale and Boethius's *De Musica.*" *MP* 68:188–91.

1757. Colmer, Dorothy. "*The Franklin's Tale*:A Palimpsest Reading." *EIC* 20:375–80. [Reply to A. M. Kearney; see Bibliog. for 1969, Vol. I, Item 2111.]

1758. Combs, Bruce E. "A Linguistic Analysis of Rime with Studies in Chaucer, Donne, and Pope." *DAI* 30:4963A(Ore.).

* 1759. Cook, Richard G. "Chaucer's Pandarus and the Medieval Ideal of Friendship." *JEGP* 69:407–24.

1760. Copland, R.A. "A Line from Chaucer's *Prologue to the Canterbury Tales.*" *N&Q* 17:45–46.

* 1761. Corsa, Helen S. "Dreams in *Troilus and Criseyde.*" *AI* 27:52–65.

1762. Daley, A. Stuart. "Chaucer's 'Droghte of March' in Medieval Farm Lore." *ChauR* 4:171–79.

1763. Dean, Christopher. "Imagery in the *Knight's Tale* and the *Miller's Tale.*" *MS* 31(1969):149–63.

* 1764. Delasanta, Rodney. "The Theme of Judgment in *The Canterbury Tales.*" *MLQ* 31:298–307.

1765. ── "Uncommon Commonplaces in *The Knight's Tale.*" *NM* 70(1969):683–90.

* 1766. DiPasquale, Pasquale,Jr. " 'Sikernesse' and Fortune in *Troilus and Criseyde.*" *PQ* 49:152–63.

1767. Donaldson, E. Talbot. *Speaking of Chaucer.* London: Athlone Press. [12 essays, 4 published for the first time.]

1768. Elbow, Peter H. "Complex Irony in Chaucer." *DAI* 30(1969):2480A–81A(Brandeis).

1769. Eldredge, Laurence. "Chaucer's *Hous of Fame* and the *Via Moderna.*" *NM* 71:105–19.

1770. ── "Poetry and Philosophy in the *Parlement of Foules.*" *RUO* 40:441–59.

1771. Farrell, Robert T. "Chaucer's Use of the Theme of the Help of God in the *Man of Law's Tale.*" *NM* 71:239–43.

1772. Field, P.J.C. "Chaucer's Merchant and the Sin Against Nature." *N&Q* 17:84–86.

* 1773. Friend, Albert C. "The Tale of the Captive Bird and the Traveler:Nequam, Berechiah, and Chaucer's *Squire's Tale.*" *M&H* N.S. 1:57–65.

1774. Garbáty, Thomas. "Chaucer's Weaving Wife." *JAF* 81(1968):342–46.

1775. Geissman, Erwin W. "The Style and Technique of Chaucer's Translations from French." *DAI* 30(1969):320A(Yale).

* 1776. Golden, Samuel A. "Chaucer in Minsheu's *Guide into the Tongues.*" *ChauR* 4:49–54.

1777. Gordon, Ida L. *The Double Sorrow of Troilus.* London: Oxford U.P.

1778. Halverson, John. "Chaucer's Pardoner and the Progress f Criticism." *ChauR* 4:184–202.

1779. Herzman, Ronald B. "A Study of Chaucer's Use of ime in *Troilus and Criseyde*." *DAI* 30:2969A(Del.).

1780. Hieatt, Constance B.,ed. *The Miller's Tale*. New York:)dyssey.

1781. Hodgson, Phyllis,ed. *General Prologue to the Canterbury ales*. London: Athlone P., 1969.

1782. Hoy, Michael, and Michael Stevens. *Chaucer's Major ales*. London: Norton Bailey. [Crit. essays.]

1783. Kauffman, Corinne E. "Dame Pertelote's Parlous arle." *ChauR* 4:41–48.

1784. Kirby, Thomas A. "Chaucer Research, 1969:Report Jo. 30." *ChauR* 4:211–27.

1785. Kivimaa, Kirsti. *Clauses in Chaucer Introduced by Conjunction with Appended 'that'*. (CHLSSF 43:1.) Helsinki: Leskuskirjapaino, 1969.

1786. Knight, Stephen. "Rhetoric and Poetry in the *Franklin's ale*." *ChauR* 4:14–30.

1787. Knoepflmacher, U.C. "Irony Through Scriptural Al-usion:A Note on Chaucer's Prioresse." *ChauR* 4:180–83.

1788. Labriola, Albert C. "The Doctrine of Charity and the Jse of Homiletic 'Figures' in the *Man of Law's Tale*." *TSLL* 2:5–14.

1789. Lawlor, John. *Chaucer*. New York: Harper, 1969.

1790. Lenaghan, R.T. "Chaucer's *General Prologue* as History nd Literature." *Compar. Studies in Soc. and Hist.* 12,i:73–82.

1791. Levy, Bernard S. "The Wife of Bath's *Queynte Fantasye*." *ChauR* 4:106–22.

1792. Lewis, Robert E. "Alisoun's *Coler*:Chaucer's *Miller's ale* ll. 3239, 3242, 3265." *MS* 32:337–39.

1793. Loomis, Dorothy Bethurum. "The Venus of Alanus de nsulis and the Venus of Chaucer." [F 54]:182–95.

1794. Lorrah, Jean. "The 'Present Eternite' of Chaucer's Troilus and Criseyde." *DAI* 30(1969):688A(Fla. State).

1795. Macey, Samuel L. "Dramatic Elements in Chaucer's Troilus." *TSLL* 12:301–23.

1796. Markland, Murray F. "*Troilus and Criseyde*:The nviolability of Ending." *MLQ* 31:147–59.

1797. Masi, Michael. "Troilus:A Medieval Psychoanalysis." *AnM* 11:81–88.

1798. Mathews, Johnye E. "A Study of *The Book of the Duchess*:Problems in Chaucer's Relationship with His Audience." *DAI* 30:2974A–75A(Ark.).

1799. McCabe, John D. "The Comic in the Poetry of Chaucer:Congruence of 'Sentence' and 'Solaas'." *DAI* 30(1969):?85A(Minn.).

1800. Meech, Sanford B. *Design in Chaucer's Troilus*. New York: Greenwood, 1969. [Repr. of 1959 ed.]

1801. Meier, T.K. "Chaucer's Knight as 'Persona':Narration ls Control." *EM* 20(1969):11–21.

1802. Meredith, Peter. "Chauntecleer and the Mermaids." *Neophil* 54:81–83.

1803. Milosh, Joseph. "Chaucer's Too-Well Told *Franklin's Tale*:A Problem of Characterization." *Wisconsin Studies in Lit.* 5:1–11.

1804. Mogan, Joseph J.,Jr. "Chaucer and the *Bona Matrimonii*." *ChauR* 4:123–41.

1805. Nist, John. "Chaucer's Apostrophic Mode in *The Canterbury Tales*." *TSL* 15:85–98.

1806. North, J.D. "Kalenderes Enlumyned Ben They, Part II." *RES* 20(1969):418–44. [See Bibliog. for 1969, Vol. I, Item 2130.]

1807. Olson, Glending R. "The Cultural Context of Chaucer's Fabliaux." *DAI* 30(1969):1145A–46A(Stanford).

1808. Ono, Shigeru. "Gengo, Buntai, Shahon—Chaucer no ?aai." *EigoS* 114(1968):456–57. [Language, Style, MSS—the case of C.]

1809. Overbeck, M. Patricia T. "The Lyf So Short—Studies in Chaucer's Dream Visions." *DAI* 30:2977A(Cincinnati).

1810. Owen, Charles A.,Jr. "Mimetic Form in the Central Love Scene of *Troilus and Criseyde*." *MP* 67(1969):125–32.

1811. Page, Barbara. "Concerning the Host." *ChauR* 4:1–13.

1812. Parker, David. "Can We Trust the Wife of Bath?"

ChauR 4:90–98.

1813. Pearcy, Roy J. "The Marriage Costs of Chaucer's Friar." *N&Q* 17:124–25.

1814. Peters, F.J.J. "*Bo D*:Line 47." *AN&Q* 8:135.

1815. Reid, David S. "Crocodilian Humor:A Discussion of Chaucer's Wife of Bath." *ChauR* 4:73–89.

1816. Reiss, Edmund. "Daun Gerveys in the *Miller's Tale*." *PLL* 6:115–24.

1817. ——— "The Pilgrimage Narrative and the *Canterbury Tales*." *SP* 67:295–305.

1818. Richardson, Cynthia C. "The Function of the Host in the *Canterbury Tales*." *TSLL* 12:325–44.

1819. Richardson, Janette. *Blameth Nat Me:A Study of Imagery in Chaucer's Fabliaux*. (SEngL 58.) The Hague: Mouton.

1820. Sadler, Lynn V. "Chaucer's *The Book of the Duchess* and the 'Law of Kinde'." *AnM* 11:51–64.

1821. Schlauch, Margaret. "The Doctrine of 'Vera Nobilitas' as Developed After Chaucer." *KN* 17:119–27.

1822. Schroeder, Mary C. "Fantasy in *The Merchant's Tale*." *Criticism* 12:167–79.

1823. Shores, David L. "*The Merchant's Tale*:Some Lay Observations." *NM* 71:119–33.

1824. Silvia, D.S. "Chaucer's *Canterbury Tales*, D. 44a-f." *Expl* 28:Item 44.

1825. Smyser, Hamilton M. "A View of Chaucer's Astronomy." *Speculum* 45:359–73.

1826. Snipes, Katherine. "Intellectual Villains in Dostoyevsky, Chaucer and Albert Camus." *Discourse* 13:240–50.

1827. Spencer, William. "Are Chaucer's Pilgrims Keyed to the Zodiac?" *ChauR* 4:147–70.

1828. Sullivan, Sheila,ed. *Critics on Chaucer*. London: Allen and Unwin; Coral Gables, Fla.: U. of Miami P. [Crit. essays.]

1829. Taylor, Estelle W. "Chaucer's 'Monk's Tale':An Apology." *CLAJ* 13(1969):172–82.

1830. Taylor, Willene P. "Chaucer's Technique in Handling Anti-Feminist Material in 'The Merchant's Tale':An Ironic Portrayal of the *Senex-Amans* and Jealous Husband." *CLAJ* 13(1969):153–62.

1831. ——— "Supposed Antifeminism in Chaucer's *Troilus and Crysede* and Its Retraction in *The Legend of Good Women*." *XUS* 9,ii:1–18.

1832. Tisdale, Charles P. "The Medieval Pilgrimage and Its Use in *The Canterbury Tales*." *DAI* 30:4958A(Princeton).

1833. Topliff, Delores E. "Analysis of Singular Weak Adjective Inflection in Chaucer's Works." *JEngL* 4:78–79.

1834. Tripp, Raymond P.,Jr. "Chaucer's Psychologizing of Virgil's Dido." *BRMMLA* 24:51–59.

1835. Ussery, Huling E. "Fourteenth-Century English Logicians:Possible Models for Chaucer's Clerk." *TSE* 18:1–15.

1836. Von Kreisler, Nicolai. "A Recurrent Expression of Devotion in Chaucer's *Book of the Duchess*, *Parliament of Fowls*, and *Knight's Tale*." *MP* 68:62–64.

1837. Wimsatt, W.K. "The Rule and the Norm:Halle and Keyser on Chaucer's Meter." *CE* 31:774–88.

1838. Witlieb, Bernard L. "Chaucer and the *Ovide Moralisé*." *N&Q* 17:202–07.

1839. ——— "Chaucer and the *Ovide moralisé*." *DAI* 31: 1245A(N.Y.U.).

See also 1469, 1507, 1646, 1710, 2899, 3314, 4075, 8017, 8614, 8787, 9062, 9900.

Chestre. 1840. Williams, Elizabeth. "*Lanval* and *Sir Landevale*:A Medieval Translator and His Methods." *LeedsSE* N.S. 3(1969):85–99.

Cronica. *1841. Robbins, Rossell H. "Victory at Whitby, A.D. 1451." *SP* 67:495–504. [Rpts. text.]

Dame Siriþ. 1842. Martin, Lawrence H. "A *Dame Siriþ* Compendium." *DAI* 30(1969):1989A(Mass.).

Davy. 1843. Scattergood, V.J. "Adam Davy's *Dreams* and Edward II." *Archiv* 206:253–60.

Dunbar. 1844. Brookhouse, Christopher. "Deschamps and Dunbar:Two Elegies." *SSL* 7:123.

1845. Hay, Bryan S. "William Dunbar's Vision of Disorder." *DAI* 30:3429A–30A(Rochester).

Everyman. 1846. Degroote, Gilbert. "*Everyman* en *Murder in* *the Cathedral." HZM* 23(1969):42–46.

Flower and the Leaf. 1847. Harrington, David V. "The Function of Allegory in the *Flower and the Leaf." NM* 71:244–53.

Genesis and Exodus. 1848. Buehler, Philip G. "A Glossary to the Middle English *Genesis and Exodus." DAI* 30(1969):1157A–58A(Pa.).

1849. Morris, Richard,ed. *The Story of* Genesis and Exodus: *An Early English Song, About A.D. 1250.* (EETS.) New York: Greenwood, 1969.

Gower. *1850. Byrd, David G. "Gower's *Confessio Amantis,* III,585." *Expl* 29:Item 2.

1851. Economou, George D. "The Character Genius in Alain de Lille, Jean de Meun, and John Gower." *ChauR* 4:203–10.

1852. Grellner, Sister Mary A. "John Gower's *Confessio Amantis:*A Critical Assessment of Themes and Structure." *DAI* 30(1969):2483A–84A(Wis.).

1853. Hoben, Sister Marian W.,I.H.M. "John Gower's *Confessio Amantis:*An Analysis of the Criticism and a Critical Analysis." *DAI* 30(1969):1136A–37A(Pa.).

1854. Regan, Charles L. "John Gower and the Fall of Babylon:*Confessio Amantis,* Prol. *11.* 670–686." *ELN* 7(1969): 85–92.

See also 1748.

Hardyng. *See* 1878.

Henryson. 1855. Roerecke, Howard H. "The Integrity and Symmetry of Robert Henryson's *Moral Fables." DAI* 30: 4999A–5000A(Penn. State).

1856. Stephens, John. "Devotion and Wit in Henryson's 'The Annunciation'." *ES* 51:323–31.

Holland. 1857. McDiarmid, Matthew P. "Richard Holland's *Buke of the Howlat:*An Interpretation." *MÆ* 38(1969):277–90.

Joseph of Arimathea. 1858. Skeat, Walter W.,ed. *Joseph of Arimathie.* (EETS 44.) New York: Greenwood, 1969. [Rpt. of 1871 ed.]

Julian of Norwich. *See* 1859.

Kempe. 1859. Stone, Robert K. *Middle English Prose Style: Margery Kempe and Julian of Norwich.* (SEngL 36.) The Hague: Mouton.

King Horn. 1860. Hurt, James R. "The Texts of *King Horn." JFI* 7:47–59.

King of Tars. 1861. Shores, Doris. "*The King of Tars:*A New Edition." *DAI* 30:3437A(N.Y.U.).

Langland. 1862. Schmidt, A.V.C. "Langland and Scholastic Philosophy." *MÆ* 38(1969):134–56.

Layamon. *See* 1701.

Lydgate. 1863. Edwards, A.S.G. "Lydgate's *Siege of Thebes:*A New Fragment." *NM* 71:133–36.

1864. Gathercole, Patricia M. "Lydgate's *Fall of Princes* and the French Version of Boccaccio's *De Casibus,*" 165–78 in *Miscellanea de studi e ricerche sul Quattrocento francese.* Torino: Giappichelli, 1967.

* 1865. Hascall, Dudley L. "The Prosody of John Lydgate." *Lang&S* 3:122–46.

1866. Jones, Harold G.,III. "An Unedited Manuscript of John Lydgate's *Life of Our Lady:*Book v, Verses 344–364 and 372–392." *ELN* 7(1969):93–96. [Incl. texts of examined passages.]

1867. Lovell, Robert E. "John Lydgate's *Siege of Thebes* and *Churl and Bird,* Edited from the Cardigan-Brudenell Manuscript." *DAI* 30:2974A(Texas, Austin).

1868. Miller, James I.,Jr. "Literature to History:Exploring a Medieval Saint's Legend and Its Context." [F 58]:59–72. [On St. Edmund, its relation to the Offa Saga, etc.]

1869. Pearsall, Derek A. *John Lydgate.* Charlottesville: U.P. of Va.; London: Routledge & K. Paul.

1870. Studer, John. "History as Moral Instruction:John Lydgate's Record of *Troie Toun." ESRS* 19,i:5–13,22.

Malory. 1871. Ackerman, Robert. " 'The Tale of Gareth' and the Unity of *Le Morte Darthur.*" [F 54]:196–203.

1872. Brewer, D.S. "The Present Study of Malory." *FMLS* 6:83–97.

1873. Kelly, Robert L. "The Pattern of Triumph:Parallels Between Arthur and Galahad in Malory's *Morte Darthur." DAI* 30:4948A–49A(Ore.).

1874. Kennedy, Edward D. "Arthur's Rescue in Malory and

the Spanish *Tristán." N&Q* 17:6–10.

* 1875. ——— "Malory and the Marriage of Edward IV." *TSLL* 12:155–62.

1876. Vinaver, Eugene,ed. *King Arthur and His Knights: Selected Tales.* Boston: Houghton, 1968.

1877. Vonalt, Joyce O. "The Thematic Design of Malory's *Morte Darthur." DAI* 30(1969):296A(Fla.).

1878. Wilson, Robert H. "More Borrowings by Malory from Hardyng's *Chronicle." N&Q* 17:208–10.

See also 1739, 1917, 4628, 4755.

Mandeville. 1879. Moseley, Charles. "Sir John Mandeville's Visit to the Pope:The Implications of an Interpolation." *Neophil* 54:77–80.

1880. Moseley, C.W.R.D. "The Lost Play of Mandeville." *Library* 25:46–49. [Comments on the possible existence of a sensational play of the *Travels.*]

Morte Arthure. 1880a. Brewer, Derek S.,ed. *The Morte Darthur:Parts Seven and Eight.* (York Medieval Texts.) With Introd. Evanston, Ill.: Northwestern U.P., 1968.

1881. Finlayson, John,ed. *Morte Arthure.* (York Medieval Texts.) Evanston, Ill.: Northwestern U.P., 1968.

1881a. Hissiger, Paul F. "An Edition of *Le Morte Arthur." DAI* 30(1969):2528A(Pa.).

1882. Johnson, James D. "Formulaic Diction and Thematic Composition in the Alliterative *Morte Arthure." DAI* 30: 3462A(Ill.).

Nassyngton. 1883. Gunn, Sister Agnes D. "Accidia and Prowess in the Vernon Version of Nassyngton's *Speculum Vitae:*An Edition of the Text and a Study of the Ideas." *DAI* 30:4945A(Pa.).

Owl and the Nightingale. 1884. De Vries, F.C. "A Note on *The Owl and the Nightingale* 951, 1297." *N&Q* 16(1969):442–44.

See also 1552.

Patience. 1885. Anderson, J.J.,ed. *Patience.* Manchester: Manchester U.P.; New York: Barnes & Noble, 1969.

1886. Vantuono, William. "*Patience:*An Edition." *DAI* 30(1969):2502A(N.Y.U.).

1887. Williams, David. "The Point of *Patience." MP* 68: 127–36.

See also 1907.

Pearl. 1888. Conley, John,comp. *The Middle English* Pearl: *Critical Essays.* Notre Dame, Ind.: U. of Notre Dame P.

1889. Emert, Joyce R. "*Pearl* and the Incarnate Word:A Study in the Sacramental Nature of Symbolism." *DAI* 30: 4940A–41A(N.M.).

1890. Fritz, Donald W. "The Arbor of Wisdom:An Essay on the *Pearl." DAI* 30(1969):1523A–24A(Stanford).

1891. Williams, Sister Margaret,R.S.C.J. "Oriental Backgrounds and the *Pearl*-Poet." *TkR* 1,i:93–107.

See also 1900.

Peterborough Chronicle. 1892. Ohba, Keizo. "The Underlying Elements in *The Peterborough Chronicle.*" [F 1]:328–47. [In Jap.]

1893. Shores, David L. ."The Subject–Noun Object–Verb Pattern in the Peterborough Chronicle." *NM* 70(1969):623–26.

1894. Way, Annette. "Old English Prenominal Modifiers in Noun-Headed Objects of Prepositions in the First and Second Continuations of the *Peterborough Chronicle* (1122–54)." *JEngL* 4:90–94.

Piers Plowman. 1895. Ames, Ruth M. *The Fulfillment of the Scriptures:Abraham, Moses, and Piers.* Evanston, Ill.: Northwestern U.P.

1896. Brian, Beverly D. "Satire in *Piers Plowman." DAI* 30:4936A(Duke).

1897. Orsten, Elizabeth M. "Patientia in the B-Text of *Piers Plowman." MS* 31(1969):317–33.

1898. Polak, Lucie. "A Note on the Pilgrim in *Piers Plowman." N&Q* 17:282–85.

1899. Prince, Helen M. "Long Will:The First-Person Narrator in *Piers Plowman." DAI* 30:4423A–24A(Northwestern).

1900. Salter, Elizabeth. "Medieval Poetry and the Figural View of Reality." *PBA* 54(for 1968):73–92.

* 1901. Schroeder, Mary C. "*Piers Plowman:*The Tearing of the Pardon." *PQ* 49:8–18.

* 1902. ——— "The Character of Conscience in *Piers Plowman.*"

SP 67:13–30.

1903. Skeat, Walter W.,tr. and ed. *Pierce the Ploughmans Crede.* (EETS 30.) New York: Greenwood, 1969. [Rpt. of 1867 ed.]

1904. St.-Jacques, Raymond C. "Conscience's Final Pilgrimage in *Piers Plowman* and the Cyclical Structure of the Liturgy." *RUO* 40:210–23.

1905. Trower, Katherine B. "The Plowman as Preacher:The Allegorical and Structural Significance of Piers the Plowman in *Piers Plowman.*" *DAI* 30(1969):712A(Ill.).

1906. Wittig, Joseph S. "*Piers Plowman* B, Passus IX–XII: Elements in the Design of the Inward Journey." *DAI* 30: 5425A(Cornell).

Purity. 1907. Grant, William M. "*Purity* and *Patience*:A History of Scholarship and a Critical Analysis." *DAI* 30(1969): 280A(Brown).

Richard Coer de Lyon. 1908. Davis, Norman. "Another Fragment of *Richard Coer de Lyon.*" *N&Q* 16(1969):447–52.

Richard of Devizes. See 6833.

Rolle. 1909. Dolan, James C. "The *Tractatus Super Psalmum Vicesimum* of Richard Rolle of Hampole." *DAI* 30(1969): 277A(Ill.).

See also 1883.

Sayings of St. Bernard. 1910. Monda, Joseph B. "*The Sayings of Saint Bernard* from Ms. Bodleian Additional E6." *MS* 32:299–307.

Second Shepherds' Play. 1911. Cutts, John P. "The Shepherds' Gifts in *The Second Shepherds' Play* and Bosch's 'Adoration of the Magi'." *CompD* 4:120–24.

Sir Gawain and the Green Knight. 1912. Barton, Robert J. "A Figural Reading of *Sir Gawain and the Green Knight.*" *DAI* 30:3423A(Stanford).

1913. Como, Frank T. "*Sir Gawain and the Green Knight*:A Normalized and Glossed Text." *DAI* 30(1969):2512A(Ariz. State).

1914. Davis, Norman. "*Sir Gawain and the Green Knight* 2073." *N&Q* 17:163–64.

1915. Gallant, Gerald. "The Three Beasts:Symbols of Temptation in *Sir Gawain and the Green Knight.*" *AnM* 11:35–50.

1916. Halverson, John. "Template Criticism:*Sir Gawain and the Green Knight.*" *MP* 67(1969):113–39.

1917. Jensen, Elisabeth N. "Uoverensstemmelserne i Gawains karakter belyst ud fra *Sir Gawain and the Green Knight* og Sir Thomas Malory's *Morte d'Arthur.*" *Extracta* 2(1969):196–201. [Abst.]

1918. Jones, Edward T. "The Sound of Laughter in *Sir Gawain and the Green Knight.*" *MS* 31(1969):343–45.

1919. Peyton, Henry H.,III. "An Edition of Ten Poems from the Gawain Cycle." *DAI* 30(1969):334A(Brown).

1920. Skinner, Veronica L. "The Concept of 'Trawᵽe' in *Sir Gawain and the Green Knight.*" *MSE* 2(1969):49–58.

1921. Steele, Peter. "*Sir Gawain and the Green Knight*:The Fairy Kind of Writing." *SoRA* 3(1969):358–65.

1922. Waldron, R.A.,ed. *Sir Gawain and the Green Knight.*

London: E. Arnold.

Sir Launfal. 1923. Knight, S.T. "The Oral Transmission of *Sir Launfal.*" *MÆ* 38(1969):164–70.

Sir Orfeo. 1924. Bristol, Michael D. "The Structure of the Middle English *Sir Orfeo.*" *PLL* 6:339–47.

Song of Roland. 1925. Russ, Jon R. "For the *MED* and *OED* from the 'Song of Roland'." *AN&Q* 8(1969):37–38.

1926. —— "The Middle English *Song of Roland*:A Critical Edition." *DAI* 30(1969):291A–92A(Wis.).

St. Erkenwald. *1927. McAlindon, T. "Hagiography into Art:A Study of *St. Erkenwald.*" *SP* 67:472–94.

Sutton. 1928. Schmaus, Michael, and Maria González-Haba, eds. *Thomas von Sutton*:Quodlibeta. München: Verl. Bayr. Akad. d. Wiss., 1969.

Tale of Beryn. 1929. Tamanini, Mary E. "*The Tale of Beryn* (an Edition with Introduction, Notes, and Glossary)." *DAI* 30:3437A–38A(N.Y.U.).

The Vox and the Wolf. 1930. Von Kreisler, Nicolai. "Satire in *The Vox and the Wolf.*" *JEGP* 69:650–58.

Thomas of Erceldoune. See 1937.

Three Kings' Sons. 1931. Grinberg, Henry. "The *Three Kings' Sons*:Notes and Critical Commentary." *DAI* 30(1969):280A–81A(N.Y.U.).

Tiptoft. See 1821.

Towneley Cycle. *1932. Brawer, Robert A. "The Dramatic Function of the Ministry Group in the Towneley Cycle." *CompD* 4:166–76.

1933. Collins, Suzanne R. "Conventional Speeches in the Towneley Mystery Plays." *DAI* 30:2962A(Iowa).

1934. Hill, Francis A. "The Marian Pageants in the Towneley Cycle:A Critical Edition." *DAI* 30:5410A(So. Miss.).

1935. Munson, William F. "Typology and the Towneley Isaac." *RORD* 11(1968):129–39.

1936. Stevens, Martin. "The Missing Parts of the Towneley Cycle." *Speculum* 45:254–65.

Turk and Gawain. 1937. Lyle, E.B. "*The Turk and Gawain* as a Source of *Thomas of Erceldoune.*" *FMLS* 6:98–102.

Usk. 1938. Schlauch, Margaret. "The Two Styles of Thomas Usk." *BSE* 8(1969):167–72.

William of Palerne. 1939. Simms, Norman T. "*William of Palerne*:A New Edition." *DAI* 30:3437A(Wash. U.).

William of Vere. 1940. Bethell, Denis. "The Lives of St. Osyth of Essex and St. Osyth of Aylesbury." *AnBol* 88:75–127.

Wyclif. 1941. Fristedt, Sven L. "New Light on John Wycliffe and the First Full English Bible." *SMS* 3:61–86.

1942. Sankey, Robert W. "A Rhetorical Study of Selected English Sermons of John Wycliff." *DAI* 30:5098A–99A(Northwestern).

See also 9202, 9203, 9204.

Wynkyn de Worde. 1943. Blake, N.F. "Wynkyn de Worde and the *Quatrefoil of Love.*" *Archiv* 206(1969):189–200.

Ywain and Gawain. *1944. Harrington, Norman T. "The Problem of Lacunae in *Ywain and Gawain.*" *JEGP* 69:659–65.

VI. RENAISSANCE AND ELIZABETHAN

Bibliography

1946. Elton, William R. "Shakespeare and Renaissance Intellectual Contexts:A Selective, Annotated List, 1967–1968." *SRO* 4(1968–69):122–202.

See also 1966.

Literature (Excluding Shakespeare)

General and Miscellaneous. 1947. Bawcutt, N.W. "Some Elizabethan Allusions to Machiavelli." *EM* 20(1969):53–74.

1948. Bennett, H.S. *English Books and Readers II:1558–1603.* London: Cambridge U.P.

1949. Bland, D.S. "Arthur Broke, Gerard Legh and the Inner Temple." *N&Q* 16(1969):453–55.

1950. Coogan, Robert,C.F.C. "Petrarch's *Trionfi* and the English Renaissance." *SP* 67:306–27.

1951. Dawson, Giles E. "Opportunities Offered by Collec-

tions of Correspondence." *SRO* 4(1968/69):16–17.

* 1952. Dent, R[obert] W. "Marlowe, Spenser, Donne, Shakespeare—and Joseph Wybarne." *RenQ* 22(1969):360–62.

1952a. Dorsten, J.A. van. "Mr. Secretary Cecil, Patron of Letters." *ES* 50(1969):545–53.

1953. Fike, Claude E. "A Character Study of Henry VIII." *SoQ* 8(1969):57–74.

1954. Frantz, David O. "Concepts of Concupiscence in English Renaissance Literature." *DAI* 30(1969):1133A(Pa.).

1955. Greenlee, Elizabeth T. "Origins of English Antiquarianism." *DAI* 30:3943A(Case Western Reserve).

* 1956. Haugaard, William P. "Katherine Parr:The Religious Convictions of a Renaissance Queen." *RenQ* 22(1969):346–59.

1957. Jones, Whitney R.D. *The Tudor Commonwealth, 1529–1559.* London: Athlone Press. [A study, through contemporary sources, of the Tudor philosophy.]

1958. Kelly, Henry A. *Divine Providence in the England of*

Shakespeare's Histories. Cambridge: Harvard U.P.

1959. Levine, Gerald M. "Violence and Sensationalism in Elizabethan England." *DAI* 30:5413A(N.Y.U.).

1960. MacDonald, William W. "The Evolution of Henry VIII." *HussR* 3(1969):5–10.

* 1961. Miner, Earl. "Patterns of Stoicism in Thought and Prose Styles, 1530–1700." *PMLA* 85:1023–34.

1961a. O'Connor, John J. *Amadis de Gaule and Its Influence on Elizabethan Literature.* New Brunswick, N.J.: Rutgers U.P.

1962. Ostrowski, Witold. *Romans i dramat:Angielsko-polskie studia renesansowe.* Warsaw: Inst. Wydawniczy "Pax.".

1963. Partridge, Astley C. *Tudor to Augustan English.* London: André Deutsch, 1969.

1964. Patterson, Annabel M. *Hermogenes and the Renaissance:Seven Ideas of Style.* Princeton: Princeton U.P.

* 1965. Pratt, Samuel M. "Jane Shore and the Elizabethans: Some Facts and Speculations." *TSLL* 11:1293–1306. [Discusses More, Churchyard, Shakespeare, Deloney, Chute, Drayton, Heywood.]

* 1966. Schoeck, R. J. "Recent Studies in the English Renaissance." *SEL* 10:215–50. [Rev. art., with list of bibliogs., ref. works, and colls. appended.]

1967. Williams, Clyde V. "Taverners, Tapsters, and Topers:A Study of Drinking and Drunkenness in the Literature of the English Renaissance (Volumes I and II)." *DAI* 30(1969):1539A(La. State).

See also 771, 1077, 1663, 1970, 2441, 2743, 2969, 3091, 3202.

Bible. 1968. Berry, Lloyd E.,introd. *The Geneva Bible:A Facsimile of the 1560 Edition.* Madison: U. of Wis. P., 1969.

Drama and Theater. 1969. Anon. "English Renaissance Plays in the University of London Library." *RORD* 11(1968):65–72.

* 1970. Bergeron, David M. "The Elizabethan Lord Mayor's Show." *SEL* 10:269–85.

1971. —— "Venetian State Papers and English Civic Pageantry, 1558–1642." *RenQ* 23:37–47.

1972. Bland, D.S. "A Checklist of Drama at the Inns of Court:Supplementary Entries." *RORD* 12(1969):57–59. [See Bibliog. for 1966, Item 4293.]

1973. Bluestone, Max, and Norman Rabkin,eds. *Shakespeare's Contemporaries:Modern Studies in English Renaissance Drama.* 2d ed. Englewood Cliffs, N.J.: Prentice-Hall. [Prev. pub. essays. Selected bibliogs.]

1974. Boas, Frederick S.,ed. *Five Pre-Shakespearian Comedies.* London: Oxford U.P. [Repr. of 1934 ed.]

1975. Boyer, Norman P. "A Critical Edition of *Mucedorus.*" *DAI* 30:4977A(Denver).

1976. Brownstein, Oscar. "The Popularity of Baiting in England Before 1600:A Study in Social and Theatrical History." *ETJ* 21(1969):237–50.

1977. Cannon, Charles D. "*A Warning For Fair Women* and the Puritan Controversy." *UMSE* 9(1968):85–99.

1978. Cleary, James J. "Seneca, Suicide, and English Renaissance Tragedy." *DAI* 30(1969):1521A–22A(Temple).

* 1979. Cole, Douglas. "Recent Studies in Elizabethan and Jacobean Drama." *SEL* 10:425–38.

1980. Dodd, Kenneth M. "Another Elizabethan Theater in the Round." *SQ* 21:125–56.

1981. Elliott, John R.,Jr. "The History Play as Drama." *RORD* 11(1968):21–28.

1982. Galloway, David,ed. *The Elizabethan Theatre:Papers Given at the International Conference on Elizabethan Theatre Held at the University of Waterloo, Ontario, in July, 1968.* With an Introd. Toronto: Macmillan, 1969. [T.J.B. Spencer, "Shakespeare:The Elizabethan Theatre-Poet," 1–20; Glynne Wickham, "The Privy Council Order of 1597 for the Destruction of All London's Theatres," 21–44; Herbert Berry, "The Playhouse in the Boar's Head Inn, Whitechapel," 45–73; Richard Hosley, "A Reconstruction of the Second Blackfriars," 74–88; D.F. Rowan, "The Cockpit-in-Court," 89–102; Clifford Leech, "The Function of Locality in the Plays of Shakespeare and His Contemporaries," 103–16; Terence Hawkes, "Postscript:Theatre Against Shakespeare?" 117–26.]

1983. Gamble, Giles Y. "Institutional Drama:Elizabethan Tragedies of the Inns of Court." *DAI* 30:3428A–29A(Stanford).

1984. Gentili, Vanna. *Le figure della pazzia nel teatro elisabettiano.* (Studi e testi 11.) Lecce: Ediz. Milella, 1969

1985. Goldberg, Larry A. "The Role of the Female in the Drama of Lyly, Greene, Kyd, and Marlowe." *DA* 30:4410A(Northwestern).

1986. Golden, Bruce. "Elizabethan Revenge and Spanish Honor:Analogues of Action in the Popular Drama of the Renaissance." *DAI* 30(1969):1526A(Columbia).

1987. Goodstein, Peter. "New Light on an Old Proclamation." *N&Q* 17:212. [Restrictions on dramatic performances 1544–45.]

1988. Greenfield, Thelma N. *The Induction in Elizabethan Drama.* Eugene: U. of Ore. Books, 1969.

1989. Herndl, George C. *The High Design:English Renaissance Tragedy and the Natural Law.* Lexington: U. of Ky. P

1990. Horn, Frederick D. "*The Raigne of King Edward the Third*:A Critical Edition." *DAI* 30:2969A–70A(Del.).

1991. Ingram, William. "The Playhouse at Newington Butts: A New Proposal." *SQ* 21:385–98.

1992. Johnson, Jean E. "The Persecuted Heroine in English Renaissance Tragicomedy." *DAI* 30(1969):1984A(Columbia).

1993. Johnson, Robert C. "Audience Involvement in the Tudor Interlude." *TN* 24:101–11.

1994. Krogh-Poulsen, Ursula C. "Sækulariseringen af moraliteterne i første halvdel af det 16. århundrede." *Extracta* 2(1969):240–48. [Abst.]

1995. Lake, James H. "The Influence of the Old Testament Upon the Early Drama of the English Renaissance." *DA* 30(1969):1530A–31A(Del.).

1996. Levin, Harry. "The End of Elizabethan Drama." *CompD* 3(1969-70):275–81.

1997. McMillin, Scott. "*The Book of Sir Thomas More*:A Theatrical View." *MP* 68:10–24.

1998. Omans, Stuart. "Newberry Library:English Renaissance Drama from the Silver Collection." *RORD* 11(1968):59–63

1999. Patton, Jon F. "Essays in the Elizabethan She Tragedies or Female-Complaints." *DAI* 30(1969):1534A(Ohio U.).

2000. Pinciss, G.M. "Thomas Creede and the Repertory of the Queen's Men, 1583–1592." *MP* 67:321–30.

2001. Poggi, Valentina. *L'uomo e le corti nel teatro elisabettiano.* (Studi e Ricerche 24.) Bologna: Zanichelli, 1968

2002. Rhome, Frances D. "Variations of Festive Revel in Four English Comedies, 1595–1605." *DAI* 30:5418A(Ind.).

2003. Robertson, Roderick. "Oxford Theatre in Tudor Times." *ETJ* 21(1969):41–50.

2004. Sabol, Andrew J. "Recent Studies in Music and English Renaissance Drama." *SRO* 4(1968/69):1–15.

2005. Schuman, Samuel. "Emblems and the English Renaissance Drama:A Checklist." *RORD* 12(1969):43–56.

2006. Shapiro, Michael. "Three Notes on the Theatre at Paul's, c. 1569–c. 1607." *TN* 24:147–54. [Location; interior design; admission prices and audience.]

2007. Sjögren, Gunnar. *Shakespeares samtida och deras dramatik.* Stockholm: Wahlström & Widstrand, 1969.

2008. —— "Thomas Bull and Other 'English Instrumentalists' in Denmark in the 1580's." *ShS* 22(1969):119–24.

2009. Slover, George W. "The Elizabethan Playhouse and the Tradition of Liturgical Stage Structure." *DAI* 30(1969):435A–36A(Ind.).

2010. Sturgess, Keith,ed. *Three Elizabethan Domestic Tragedies.* Baltimore: Penguin, 1969. [*Arden of Faversham, A Yorkshire Tragedy, A Woman Killed with Kindness.*]

2011. West, Herbert F.,Jr. "Unifying Devices in Four Globe Plays." *DAI* 30:5424A(Ga.). [*The Faire Maide of Bristow, Thomas Lord Cromwell, The Revenger's Tragedy, The Malcontent.*]

2012. Woodman, David R. "White Magic in English Renaissance Drama." *DAI* 30(1969):699A–700A(Columbia).

2013. Woodson, William C. "Elizabethan Villains and the Seared Conscience:The Application of a Theological Concept to Suggest the Credibility of Barabas, Aaron, Richard III, and Iago." *DAI* 30(1969):1154A–55A(Pa.).

2014. Yamada, Akihiro. "A Checklist of English Printed Drama Before 1641 at the Library of the University of Illinois.

CORD 11(1968):31–53.

2015. Yamaguchi, Seiji. "Daigaku saijin ni tsuite." *ELLS* (1968):70–79. [On the university wits.]
See also 2056, 2441, 3042, 3833.

Poetry. 2016. Donow, Herbert S. *A Concordance to the Sonnet Sequences of Daniel, Drayton, Shakespeare, Sidney, and Spenser.* Carbondale and Edwardsville: So. Ill. U.P.; London: Feffer & Simons, 1969.

2017. Fraser, Russell. *The War Against Poetry.* Princeton: Princeton U.P.

2018. Grabes, Herbert,ed. *Elizabethan Sonnet Sequences.* Tübingen: Niemeyer.

2019. Gransden, K.W.,ed. *Tudor Verse Satire.* London: Athlone Press.

2020. Grundy, Joan. *The Spenserian Poets:A Study in Elizabethan and Jacobean Poetry.* London: E. Arnold, 1969. [Incl. Spenser, Drayton, Wither, W. Browne, G. and P. Fletcher.]

2021. Henderson, Katherine U. "A Study of the Dramatic Mode in the English Renaissance Love Lyric:Sidney's *Astrophil and Stella* and Donne's *Songs and Sonnets*." *DAI* 30:4413A–14A(Columbia).

2022. Hunter, G.K. "Drab and Golden Lyrics of the Renaissance." [F 48]:1–18.

2023. Inglis, Fred. *The Elizabethan Poets.* (LitP.) London: Evans, 1969.

2024. Jayne, Sears. "Hallett Smith's Analysis of the Historical Assumptions Behind His *Elizabethan Poetry*." *NLH* 1(1969): 45–51. [See art. by Smith, below.]

2025. Johnson, Paula C. "Form and Transformation in Serial Art, with Reference to English Poetry and Music, 1570–1620." *DAI* 30:4948A(Yale).

2026. Long, John H. "The Ballard Medley and the Fool." *SP* 7:505–16.

2027. Rhinehart, Raymond P. "The Elizabethan Ovidian Epyllion:A Definition and Re-Evaluation." *DAI* 30(1969): 3040A(Princeton).

2028. Richmond, Hugh M. "Ronsard and the English Renaissance." *CLS* 7:141–60.

2029. Shire, Helena M. *Song, Dance and Poetry of the Court of Scotland under King James VI.* London: Cambridge U.P., 1969.

2030. Smith, Hallett. "An Apologie for *Elizabethan Poetry*." *NLH* 1(1969):35–43. [S comments on genesis and method of his 1952 book. See art. by Jayne, above.]
See also 885, 914, 1725, 2159, 2763.

Prose Fiction. 2031. Lanham, Richard. "Opaque Style in Elizabethan Fiction." *PCP* 1(1966):25–31.

2032. Weiss, Adrian. "The Rhetorical Concept of *Narratio* and Narrative Structure in Elizabethan Prose Fiction." *DAI* 30(1969):2503A–04A(Ohio).
See also 1491.

Satire. 2033. McGrath, Lynette F. "Studies in the Norms and Techniques of Sixteenth-Century English Satire from Skelton to Donne." *DAI* 30(1969):285A–86A(Ill.).

2034. Weiss, Robert H. "Primitivism and the Satiric Mode in English Renaissance Verse and Prose (to Spenser's *Prosopopoia*): The Shaping of a Tradition." *DAI* 30(1969):2504A(Temple).

Achelley. 2035. Freeman, Arthur. "The Writings of Thomas Achelley." *Library* 25:40–42.

Ascham. 2036. Greene, Thomas M. "Roger Ascham:The Perfect End of Shooting." *ELH* 36(1969):609–25.

Ayton. *See* 2029.

Barclay. 2037. Lyall, R.J. "Alexander Barclay and the Edwardian Reformation 1548–52." *RES* 20(1969):455–61.

Book of Common Prayer. *2038. Devereux, James A.,S.J. "The Collects of the First *Book of Common Prayer* as Works of Translation." *SP* 66(1969):719–38.

Bourchier. 2039. Taylor, Anne R. "*Grant Translateur*:The Life and Translations of John Bourchier, Second Baron Berners." *DAI* 30(1969):343A(Brown).

Chettle. 2040. Austin, Warren B. *A Computer-Aided Technique for Stylistic Discrimination:The Authorship of* Greene's Groatsworth of Wit. (Proj. 7-G-036, Grant No. OEG-1-7-070036-4593, U.S. Dept. of Health, Educ., & Welfare.) Wash., D.C.: U.S. Office of Educ., 1969. [Avail. from EDRS as ED 030 322.]

2041. —— "Technique of the Chettle-Greene Forgery: Supplementary Material on the Authorship of the *Groatsworth of Wit*." *ShN* 20:43.

2042. Marder, Louis. "Chettle's Forgery of the *Groatsworth of Wit* and the 'Shake-scene' Passage." *ShN* 20:42.
See also 2058.

Churchyard. 2043. Brown, Barbara. "Thomas Churchyard and the Worthiness of Wales." *AWR* 18,xlii:131–39.

Constable. *2044. Sledd, Hassell B. "The '1584' Publication of Henry Constable's *Diana Augmented*." *SB* 23:146–48.

Cranmer. *See* 2038.

Daniel. 2045. Boni, John M. "Two Epics of English History: Samuel Daniel's *Civile Wars* and Michael Drayton's *Barons Warres*." *DAI* 30:4398A(Denver).

2046. Clark, Ira. "Samuel Daniel's 'Complaint of Rosamond'." *RenQ* 23:152–62.

2047. Freeman, Arthur. "An Epistle for Two." *Library* 25:226–36. [Comments on the Hatton Manuscript; illus.]

2048. Kau, Joseph. "Samuel Daniel and the Renaissance *Impresa*-makers:Sources for the First English Collection of *Imprese*." *HLB* 18:183–204.

* 2049. Rice, Julian C. "The Allegorical Dolabella." *CLAJ* 13:402–07.
See also 2016.

Davies. *See* 2989.

Day. *See* 2090.

Devereux. 2050. Bird, George L. "The Earl of Essex, Patron of Letters." *DAI* 30:3935A(Utah).

Douglas. *2051. Blyth, Charles R. "Gavin Douglas' Prologues of Natural Description." *PQ* 49:164–77.

Drayton. *2052. Hiller, Geoffrey G. "Drayton's *Muses Elizium*:'A New Way Over Parnassus'." *RES* 21:1–13. [Cites Robert White's "Cupid's Banishment" as a source.]
See also 2016, 2045, 2205, 2452.

Fowler, W. 2053. Jack, R.D.S. "William Fowler and Italian Literature." *MLR* 65:481–92.

Gager. 2054. Baytop, Adrianne. "William Gager's Momus Criticism." *LangQ* 8,i–ii(1969):23–26,42.

2055. Binns, J.W. "William Gager's Additions to Seneca's *Hippolytus*." *SRen* 17:153–91.

2056. Schramm, Harold B. "William Gager and the Dido Tradition in English Drama of the Renaissance." *DAI* 30: 3919A(Del.).
See also 9279.

Gascoigne. *See* 2031, 2501.

Greene. 2057. Anderson, Thelma M. "A Critical Old-Spelling Edition of Robert Greene's *Morando:The Tritameron of Loue*." *DAI* 30:4932A(Kent State).

2058. Austin, Warren B. "The Authorship of Certain Renaissance English Pamphlets:An Informal Account of Work in Progress." [F 8]:93–99. [On *Greene's Groatsworth of Wit*.]

2059. Fitzwater, Eva A. "Robert Greene's Plays:A Study in Structure." *DAI* 30:2965A–66A(Neb.).

2060. Lavin, J.A.,ed. *Friar Bacon and Friar Bungay.* (The New Mermaids.) With Introd. and Notes. London: Benn, 1969.

2061. Oba, Kenji. "Robert Greene no *James IV*." *EigoS* 115(1969):622–23. [G's *James IV*.]

2062. Sanders, Norman,ed. *The Scottish History of James the Fourth.* (Revels Play Ser.) London: Methuen.
See also 1985, 2040, 2041, 2042, 2083, 2084, 2501.

Greville. *2063. Farmer, Norman,Jr. "Fulke Greville and Sir John Coke:An Exchange of Letters on a History Lecture and Certain Latin Verses on Sir Philip Sidney." *HLQ* 33:217–36.

Harington, J. *2064. Nelson, T.G.A. "Sir John Harington as a Critic of Sir Philip Sidney." *SP* 67:41–56.

2065. —— "Harington and Dante." *N&Q* 16(1969):456–57.

2066. —— "Sir John Harington—A Mistaken Attribution." *N&Q* 16(1969):457.

Hariot. 2067. Quinn, David B. "Thomas Hariot and the Virginia Voyages of 1602." *WMQ* 27:268–81.

Harvey. 2068. Biller, Janet E. "Gabriel Harvey's *Foure Letters* (1592):A Critical Edition." *DAI* 30:3901A(Columbia).

2069. Harlow, C.G. "Did Gabriel Harvey Read Nashe's 'Christ's Tears'?" *N&Q* 16(1969):459–61.

* 2070. Snare, Gerald. "Satire, Logic, and Rhetoric in Harvey's Earthquake Letter to Spenser." *TSE* 18:17–33.

Haughton. See 2090.

Heywood. 2071. Johnson, Robert C. "A Textual Problem in *Johan Johan*." *N&Q* 17:210–11. [Eng. version of the *Farce nouvelle du pasté*.]

2072. —— John Heywood. (TEAS 92.) New York: Twayne. See also 2624.

Hooker. 2073. Hill, W. Speed. "Hooker's 'Preface,' Chapters VIII and IX." *N&Q* 16(1969):457–59.

* 2074. —— "The Authority of Hooker's Style." *SP* 67:328–38.

Howard, C. 2075. Kenny, R.W. "Notes on the 'Catholicism' of Charles Earl of Nottingham." *N&Q* 16(1969):461–64.

Kyd. 2076. Burrows, Ken C. "The Dramatic and Structural Significance of the Portuguese Sub-plot in *The Spanish Tragedy*." *RenP* 1969:25–35.

2077. Edwards, Philip,ed. *The Spanish Tragedy*. (Revels Plays.) London: Methuen, 1969.

2078. Kohler, Richard C. "The Dramatic Artistry of Thomas Kyd's *Spanish Tragedy*:A Study in Context, Meaning, and Effect." *DAI* 30:4950A(U.C.L.A.).

2079. Mulryne, J.R.,ed. *The Spanish Tragedy*. London: Benn.

2080. Murray, Peter B. *Thomas Kyd*. (TEAS 88.) New York: Twayne.

2081. Wyler, Siegfried. "'Death' in Thomas Kyd's *Spanish Tragedy*:A Study of a Semantic Field." [F 52]:163–87. See also 1985.

Lindsay. 2082. Harward, Vernon. "*Ane Satyre of the Thrie Estaitis* Again." *SSL* 7:139–46.

Lodge. 2083. Hayashi, Tetsumaro. "*A Looking Glasse for London and England*:Collaboration Between Thomas Lodge and Robert Greene." *CalR* N.S.1:441–45.

2084. —— *A Textual Study of* A Looking Glasse for London and England *by Thomas Lodge and Robert Greene*. (Ball State Mono. 17, Pubs. in Eng. 11.) Muncie, Ind.: Ball State U., 1969.

2085. Pollack, Claudette H. "Studies of the Novels of Thomas Lodge." *DAI* 30:3435A(Yale).

Lyly. 2086. Begor, Anne,ed. *Gallathea and Midas*. (RRDS.) Lincoln: U. of Neb. P., 1969.

* 2087. Smith, John H. "Sempronia, John Lyly, and John Foxe's Comedy of *Titus and Gesippus*." *PQ* 48(1969):554–61. See also 1985, 2031, 2390, 2565.

Marlowe. 2088. Ahrends, Günter. "Die Bildersprache in Marlowes *Edward II*." *GRM* 19(1969):353–79.

2089. Annis, Leroy E. "Christopher Marlowe's Multiple Perspective:The Source of Dramatic Ambivalence." *DAI* 30(1969):1975A(U. of Wash.).

2090. Ayres, Philip J. "The Revision of 'Lust's Dominion'." *N&Q* 17:212–13. [Disputed authorship and revisions.]

2091. Barnet, Sylvan,ed. *Doctor Faustus*. New York: New Amer. Lib., 1969.

2092. Benaquist, Lawrence M. "The Ethical Structure of *Tamburlaine*, Part I." *Thoth* 10,ii(1969):3–19.

2093. Bobin, Donna. "Marlowe's Humor." *MSE* 2(1969):29–40.

2094. Collins, S. Ann. "Sundrie Shapes, Committing Headdie Ryots, Incest, Rapes:Functions of Myth in Determining Narrative and Tone in Marlowe's *Hero and Leander*." *Mosaic* 4,i:107–22.

2095. French, A.L. "The Philosophy of *Dr. Faustus*." *EIC* 20:123–42.

2096. French, William W. "Double View in *Doctor Faustus*." *WVUPP* 17:3–15.

* 2097. Goldfarb, Russell and Clare. "The Seven Deadly Sins in *Doctor Faustus*." *CLAJ* 13:350–63.

2098. Jensen, Ejner J. "Marlowe Our Contemporary?Some Questions of Relevance." *CE* 30(1969):627–32.

2099. Jump, John D.,ed. *Doctor Faustus*. (Revels Play Ser.) London: Methuen, 1968.

2100. Kurokawa, Takashi. "*De Casibus* Theme and Machiavellism—In Connection with the Theme of *Edward II*." *ShStud* 7(1968–69):61–80.

2101. Morris, Brian,ed. *Christopher Marlowe*. New York: Hill and Wang, 1969.

2102. Nagarajan, S. "The Philosophy of Dr. Faustus." *EIC* 20:485–87. [Reply to A.L. French, *EIC* 20:123–42.]

2103. Nelson, T.G.A. "Marlowe and His Audience:A Study of *Tamburlaine*." *SoRA* 3(1969):249–63.

2104. O'Brien, Margaret A. "Christian Belief in *Doctor Faustus*." *ELH* 37:1–11.

2105. O'Neill, Judith,ed. *Critics on Marlowe*. Coral Gables, Fla.: U. of Miami P.

2106. Perret, Marion D. "Theme and Structure in the Plays of Christopher Marlowe." *DAI* 30(1969):288A–89A(Yale).

2107. Ribner, Irving,ed. *Edward II:Text and Major Criticism*. New York: Odyssey.

2108. —— The Jew of Malta:*Text and Major Criticism*. New York: Odyssey.

2109. Seyler, Dorothy U. "The Critical Reputation of Christopher Marlowe, 1800–1899." *DAI* 30:3435A–36A (S.U.N.Y., Albany).

* 2110. Sheidley, William E. "The Seduction of the Reader in Marlowe's *Hero and Leander*." *CP* 3,i:50–56.

* 2111. Smith, Warren D. "The Substance of Meaning in *Tamburlaine Part I*." *SP* 67:156–66.

* 2112. Sternfeld, Frederick, W., and Mary J. Chan. " 'Come Live with Me and Be My Love'." *CL* 22:173–87. [On M's lyric.]

2113. Vota, Lorenzo. "Marlowe, poeta asociale." *Cenobio* 19:229–30.

2114. Walsh, Maureen P. "Demigod, Devil, or Man:A Reconsideration of the Character of Faustus." *Nassau Rev.*(Nassau [N.Y.] Comm. Coll.) 2,i:54–65.

* 2115. Weisstein, Ulrich. "The First Version of Brecht/Feuchtwanger's *Leben Eduards des Zweiten von England* and Its Relation to the Standard Text." *JEGP* 69:193–210.

* 2116. Woods, Susanne. " 'The Passionate Shepherd' and 'The Nimphs Reply':A Study of Transmission." *HLQ* 34:25–33. See also 1962, 1985, 2013, 2673, 3128.

Marprelate Tracts. *2117. Anselment, Raymond A. "Rhetoric and the Dramatic Satire of Martin Marprelate." *SEL* 10:103–19.

Martin. 2118. Parks, George B.,ed. *Roma Sancta* (1581). Rome: Ediz. de Storia e Letteratura, 1969. [A description in Eng. of post-Tridentine Rome.]

Melbancke. 2119. Colby, Arthur L. "Brian Melbancke's *Philotimus* (1583):A Critical Edition." *DAI* 30:3426A(N.C.).

Montgomerie. See 2029.

More, J. 2120. Blackburn, Elizabeth B. "*The Legacy of* 'Prester John,' by Damião à Goes and John More." *Moreana* 14(1967):37–98. [Facsim., 44–98.]

More, T. 2122. Ainger, Canon Alfred. "Sir Thomas More's *Utopia*." *Moreana* 23(1969):71–76.

2123. Davis, J.C. "More, Morton, and the Politics of Accommodation." *JBS* 9,ii:27–49.

2124. Derrett, J. Duncan M. "St. Thomas More and the Would-Be Suicide." *DownR* 88:372–77.

2125. Graff, Bob de. "More's *Choriambicum de Vita Suavi* as a Fill-up in a Sixteenth-Century Strasburg Schoolbook." *Moreana* 23(1969):53–55.

* 2126. Graziani, René. "Non-Utopian Euthanasia:An Italian Report, c. 1554." *RenQ* 22(1969):329–33.

2127. Herbrüggen, H. Schulte. "A Prayer-Book of Sir Thomas More." *TLS* 15 Jan:64.

2128. —— "More's Genealogy." *TLS* 18 June:662.

2129. Khanna, Lee C. "More's *Utopia*:A Literary Perspective on Social Reform." *DAI* 30(1969):1530A(Columbia).

2130. Marc'hadour, G. "Thomas More and René Choppin." *Moreana* 26:55–58. [See Bibliog. for 1969, Vol. I, Item 2455 Davis.]

2131. —— "Thomas More et la Bible:Mise au point." *Moreana* 25:57–65.

2132. —— "Une Utopie chrétienne au dix-neuvième siècle." *Moreana* 26:49–54.

2133. Mareš, F. "Die glagolitische Schrift als Vorbild für das 'Utopiensium alphabetum' des Thomas Morus?" [F 29]:120–25.

2134. Martz, Louis L., and Richard S. Sylvester,eds. *Thomas More's Prayer Book:A Facsimile Reproduction of the Annotated Pages*. Transcribed, Tr., with Introd. New Haven: Yale U.P., 1969.

2135. Meulon, Henri. "Un poème inédit de Thomas More?" *Moreana* 23(1969):66–68.

2136. Meulon, Robert,ed. "Un sermon prêché devant More: *L'oraison de la paix* de Robert Ceneau." *Moreana* 25:31–40. [See *Moreana* 15, 16, 17.]

2137. Miller, Clarence H. "A Vatican Manuscript Containing Three Brief Works by St. Thomas More [Barb. Lat. 2567.]." *Moreana* 26:41–44.

2138. More, Thomas. "Thomas More on Matrimony." *Moreana* 26:18–31. [Postscript by G. Marc'hadour, 32.]

2139. Ossinovsky, Igor. "Rare Editions of Thomas More's Works in Libraries of USSR." *Moreana* 25:67–76.

2140. Reiter, Robert E. "On the Genre of Thomas More's *Richard III*." *Moreana* 25:5–16.

2141. Reynolds, E.E. "The Mores and Hatfield." *Moreana* 23(1969):31–32.

2142. Schoeck, R.J. "Thomas More's *Dialogue of Comfort* and the Problem of the Real Grand Turk." *EM* 20(1969):23–35. [Appendix:*Thomas More and the Turks, 1528–1534*, 35–37]

2143. Sowards, J.K. "Thomas More, Erasmus, and Julius II:A Case of Advocacy." *Moreana* 24(1969):81–99.

2144. Thompson, Craig R. "Erasmus, More, and the Conjuration of Spirits:A Possible Source of a Practical Joke." *Moreana* 24(1969):45–50.

2145. Wheeler, Thomas. "An Italian Account of Thomas More's Trial and Execution." *Moreana* 26:33–39.

See also 1997, 2158, 2246, 2869, 3049, 5029.

Munday. *See* 1997.

Nashe. *2146. Robinson, Fred C. " 'Strength Stoops unto the Grave':Nashe's 'Adieu, Farewell Earth's Bliss,' l. 22." *PLL* 6:89–92.

2147. Weimann, Robert. "*Jest-book* und Ich-Erzählung in *The Unfortunate Traveller*. Zum Problem des *point of view* in der Renaissance-Prosa." *ZAA* 18:11–29.

See also 2031, 2069.

Painter. 2148. Buchert, Jean R. "Cinthio in the *Palace of Pleasure*:William Painter's Translations from *Gli Hecatommithi*." *RenP* 1969 :1–8.

Peele. 2149. Ball, Bona W. "Rhetoric in the Plays of George Peele." *DAI* 30(1969):2011A–12A(Ky.).

2150. Benbow, Robert M. "A Critical Edition of the *Araygnement of Paris* by George Peele." *DAI* 30:4396A–97A(Yale). [1950.]

2151. Prouty, Charles T.,ed. *The Life and Works of George Peele*, III:*The Dramatic Works of George Peele. The Araygnement of Paris*, ed. R. Mark Benbow; *David and Bethsabe*, ed. Elmer Blistein; *The Old Wives Tale*, ed. Frank S. Hook. New Haven and London: Yale U.P.

2152. Rockey, Laurilyn J. "*The Old Wives Tale* as Dramatic Satire." *ETJ* 22:268–75.

See also 1970.

Raleigh. 2154. Adamson, J.H., and H.F. Folland. *The Shepherd of the Ocean:An Account of Sir Walter Raleigh and His Times*. Boston: Gambit, 1969.

2155. Duncan-Jones, Katherine. "The Date of Raleigh's '21th:And Last Booke of the Ocean to Scinthia'." *RES* 21:143–58.

2156. Lockwood, William J. "The Thought and Lyrics of Sir Walter Ralegh." *DAI* 30:5414A(Pa.).

Rich. 2157. Vesci, Ornella. "A Looking Glass for Ireland, di Barnaby Rich." *AION-SG* 12(1969):297–319.

Roper, W. 2158. Maguire, John. "William Roper's *Life of More*:The Working Methods of a Tudor Biographer." *Moreana* 23(1969):59–65.

Rowley. *See* 2624.

Sackville. *See* 2653.

Sadler. *See* 4692.

Scott. 2159. MacQueen, John. "Alexander Scott and Scottish Court Poetry of the Middle Sixteenth Century." *PBA* 54(for 1968):93–116.

See also 2029.

Sidney. 2160. Buxton, John. "Sir Philip Sidney's First Passport Rediscovered." *Library* 25:42–46.

2161. Cohen, E.Z. "The *Old Arcadia*:A Treatise on Moderation." *RBPH* 46(1968):749–70.

* 2162. Cotter, James F. "The *Baiser* Group in Sidney's *Astrophil and Stella*." *TSLL* 12:381–403.

* 2163. —— "The Songs in *Astrophil and Stella*." *SP* 67:178–200.

* 2164. Davidson, Clifford. "Nature and Judgement in the *Old Arcadia*." *PLL* 6:348–65.

* 2165. Dipple, Elizabeth. " 'Unjust Justice' in the *Old Arcadia*." *SEL* 10:83–101.

2166. Elia, R.L. "Platonic Irony in Sidney's *An Apology for Poetrie*." *RLV* 36:401–05.

2167. Evans, Frank B. "The Concept of the Fall in Sidney's *Apologie*." *RenP* 1969:9–14.

* 2168. Fabry, Frank J. "Sidney's Verse Adaptations to Two Sixteenth-Century Italian Art Songs." *RenQ* 23:237–55.

2169. Georgas, Marilyn D. "Sir Philip Sidney and the Victorians." *DAI* 30:2966A–67A(Texas, Austin).

* 2170. Gregory, E.R.,Jr. "Du Bartas, Sidney, and Spenser." *CLS* 7:437–49.

* 2171. Hyman, Virginia R. "Sidney's Definition of Poetry." *SEL* 10:49–62.

2172. Isler, Alan D. "The Moral Philosophy of Sidney's Two *Arcadias*:A Study of Some Principal Themes." *DAI* 30(1969):1567A(Columbia).

2173. Kimbrough, Robert,ed. *Sir Philip Sidney:Selected Prose and Poetry*. New York: Holt, 1969.

2174. Knowlton, Edgar C. "Sir Philip Sidney on Italian Rhymes." *N&Q* 16(1969):455–56.

2175. Levy, Charles S. "A Supplementary Inventory of Sir Philip Sidney's Correspondence." *MP* 67(1969):177–81.

2176. Mahl, Mary R.,ed. *The Norwich Sidney Manuscript [of] The Apology for Poetry By Sir Philip Sidney*. (RESFV 1.) Northridge, Calif.: San Fernando Valley State Coll., 1969.

2177. Murphy, Philip M. "A Critical Edition of Sir Philip Sidney's *The Lady of May*." *DAI* 30:5432A(Wis.).

2178. Osborn, James M. "New Light on Sir Philip Sidney." *TLS* 30 Apr:487–88.

2179. Robinson, Forrest G.,ed. *Sir Philip Sidney:An Apology for Poetry*. With Introd. and Notes. Indianapolis: Bobbs-Merrill.

2180. Taylor, A.B. "A Note on Ovid in *Arcadia*." *N&Q* 16(1969):455.

2181. Taylor, Arvilla K. "The Manège of Love and Authority:Studies in Sidney and Shakespeare." *DAI* 30:3025A–26A(Texas, Austin).

2182. Thomas, W.K. "Sidney's 'Leave Me, O Love, Which Reachest but to Dust'." *Expl* 28:Item 45.

2183. Tufte, Virginia. "England's First Epithalamium and the 'Vespar Adest' Tradition." *EM* 20(1969):39–51.

* 2184. Turner, Myron. "The Heroic Ideal in Sidney's Revised *Arcadia*." *SEL* 10:63–82.

2185. Washington, Mary A. "A Bibliography of Criticism of Sir Philip Sidney, 1940–1965." *DAI* 30:5007A(Mo., Columbia).

See also 2016, 2021, 2063, 2064, 2352.

Skelton. *2186. Carpenter, Nan C. "Skelton's Hand in William Cornish's Musical Parable." *CL* 22:157–72.

2187. Kinsman, Robert S.,ed. *Poems of John Skelton*. (CMTS.) Oxford: Clarendon, 1969.

2188. McGrath, Lynette F. " 'Speke, Parrot' and Plautus." *N&Q* 16(1969):452–53.

2189. Tucker, Melvin J. "Setting in Skelton's *Bowge of Courte*:A Speculation." *ELN* 7:168–75. [Suggests c. 1480 as date of composition.]

* 2190. Tucker, M.J. "The Ladies in Skelton's 'Garland of Laurel'." *RenQ* 22(1969):333–45.

2191. Winser, Leigh. "Skeleton's *Magnyfycence*." *RenQ* 23:14–25.

2192. —— "Skelton's *Magnyfycence* and the Morality Tradition." *DAI* 30(1969):1154A(Columbia).

See also 2033, 3835.

Smith, H. 2193. Dewar, Mary,ed. *Discourse of the Commonweal of This Realm of England*. (FDTSC.) Charlottesville: For the Folger Shakespeare Lib. by the U.P. of Va., 1969.

Southwell. 2194. Gappa, Richard J. "Robert Southwell's *Marie Magdelens Fvneral Teares*:An Edition." *DAI* 30(1969):1524A(St. Louis).

2195. Scallon, Joseph D.,S.J. "The Poetry of Robert Southwell, S.J." *DAI* 30(1969):1181A–82A(Kan.).

2196. Schten, Carolyn A. "Southwell's 'Christs Bloody Sweat':A Meditation on the Mass." *EM* 20(1969):75–80.

Spenser. 2197. Alpers, Paul J.,ed. *Edmund Spenser:A Critical Anthology.* Harmondsworth: Penguin.

* 2198. Anderson, Judith H. " 'Nor Man It Is':The Knight of Justice in Book v of Spenser's *Faerie Queene.*" *PMLA* 85:65–77.

* 2199. —— "The July Eclogue and the House of Holiness: Perspective in Spenser." *SEL* 10:17–32.

* 2200. —— "The Knight and the Palmer in *The Faerie Queene,* Book II." *MLQ* 31:160–78.

2201. Aziz, Paul D. "The Poet's Poetry:Edmund Spenser's Uses of the Pastoral." *DAI* 30(1969):271A–72A(Brown).

2202. Belson, Joel J. "Escaped Faults in the Spenser Concordance." *AN&Q* 8:69–72.

2203. Berger, Harry,Jr. "Mode and Diction in *The Shepheardes Calender.*" *MP* 67(1969):140–49.

2204. Blitch, Alice F. "The Mutability Cantos 'In Meet Order Ranged'." *ELN* 7:179–86.

* 2205. Bristol, Michael D. "Structural Patterns in Two Elizabethan Pastorals." *SEL* 10:33–48. [*The Shepheardes Calender* and Drayton's *The Shepheards Garland.*]

* 2206. Court, Franklin E. "The Theme and Structure of Spenser's *Muiopotmos.*" *SEL* 10:1–15.

* 2207. Cummings, Peter M. "Spenser's *Amoretti* as an Allegory of Love." *TSLL* 12:163–79.

2208. Cummings, R.M. "A Note on the Arithmological Stanza:*The Faerie Queene,* II.ix.22." *JWCI* 30(1967):410–14.

2209. Dhesi, Nirmal S. "The Paynims and Saracens of Spenser's *The Faerie Queene.*" *DAI* 30(1969):317A(Mich. State).

2210. Dorn, Alfred. "The Mutability Theme in the Poetry of Edmund Spenser and John Donne." *DAI* 30:4407A(N.Y.U.).

2211. Edwards, Calvin R. "Spenser and the Ovidian Tradition." *DAI* 30(1969):1155A(Yale). [1958.]

2212. Freeman, Rosemary. The Faerie Queene:*A Companion for Readers.* Berkeley and Los Angeles: U. of Calif. P.; London: Chatto & Windus.

2213. Fujii, Haruhiko. "Spenser no Graces." *EigoS* 114(1968):442–43. [The Graces in *Faerie Queene.*]

2214. —— "Spenser no Shinko." *EigoS* 115(1969):697–99. [S's religious faith.]

2215. Geller, Lila G. "The Three Graces in Spenser's *Faerie Queene:*Image and Structure in Books III and VI." *DAI* 30:4985A(U.C.L.A.).

2216. Gransden, K.W. *A Critical Commentary on Spenser's* The Faerie Queene. (Macmillan Crit. Commentaries.) London: Macmillan, 1969.

2217. —— "Allegory and Personality in Spenser's Heroes." *EIC* 20:298–310. [Emphasis on Guyon and Artegall.]

2218. Greco, Francis G. "Torquato Tasso's Theory of the Epic and Its Influence on Edmund Spenser's *The Faerie Queene.*" *DAI* 30:2967A–68A(Duquesne).

2219. Heninger, S.K.,Jr.,ed. *Selections From the Poetical Works of Edmund Spenser.* Boston: Houghton.

2220. Herron, Dale S. "The 'Trial of True Curtesie':Book VI of *The Faerie Queene.*" *DAI* 30:2968A–69A(Northwestern).

2221. Hieatt, A. Kent and Constance,eds. *Selected Poetry.* (Crofts Classics.) New York: Appleton.

2222. Hill, John M. "Braggadoccio and Spenser's Golden World Concept:The Function of Unregenerative Comedy." *ELH* 37:315–24.

2223. Hill, R.F. "Spenser's Allegorical 'Houses'." *MLR* 65:721–33.

2224. Johnson, William C. " 'Vowd to Eternity':A Study of Spenser's *Amoretti.*" *DAI* 30:3909A(Iowa).

2225. —— "Rhyme and Repetition in Spenser's *Amoretti.*" *XUS* 9,ii:15–25.

2226. —— "Spenser's Sonnet Diction." *NM* 71:157–67.

2227. Jortin, John. *Remarks on Spenser's Poems.* New York: Garland. [Facsim.; Remarks on Milton, pp. 171–86.]

2228. Kennedy, William J. "Modes of Allegory in Ariosto, Tasso and Spenser." *DAI* 30:3431A–32A(Yale).

* 2229. Knight, W. Nicholas. "The Narrative Unity of Book v of *The Faerie Queene:*'That Part of Justice Which Is Equity'." *RES* 21:267–94.

2230. Lopach, John A. "Educative Allegory:Poet and Reader in *The Faerie Queene,* v." *DAI* 30:4951A(Notre Dame).

2231. Lord, John B. "Apposite Grammatical Patterns in Spenser's *Epithalamion.*" *PCP* 3(1968):73–77.

2232. Louthan, Vincent A. "Spenser's Double:The Dark Conceit of Reality in *The Faerie Queene.*" *DAI* 30(1969): 688A–89A(Conn.).

2233. MacIntyre, Jean. "*The Faerie Queene,* Book I:Toward Making It More Teachable." *CE* 31:473–82.

* 2234. Magill, A.J. "Spenser's Guyon and the Mediocrity of the Elizabethan Settlement." *SP* 67:167–77.

2235. McMurtry, Josephine S. "Spenser's Narrative Imagery:The Visual Structure of *The Faerie Queene.*" *DAI* 30(1969): 1989A–90A(Rice).

2236. Nagle, John D. "From Personification to Personality: Characterization in *The Faerie Queene.*" *DAI* 30(1969):1533A–34A(Fordham).

* 2237. Phillips, James E. "Renaissance Concepts of Justice and the Structure of *The Faerie Queene,* Book v." *HLQ* 33:103–20.

2238. Preston, Michael J. "The Folk Play:An Influence on the *Faerie Queene.*" *AN&Q* 8(1969):38–39.

2239. Renwick, W.L.,ed. *A View of the Present State of Ireland.* London: Oxford U.P.

2240. Røstvig, Maren-Sofie. " 'The Shepheardes Calender':A Structural Analysis." *RMS* 13(1969):49–75.

2241. Salmon, Phillips C. "Spenser's Representation of Queen Elizabeth I." *DAI* 30(1969):2498A–99A(Columbia).

2242. Shaheen, Naseeb. "Spenser's Use of Scripture in *The Faerie Queene.*" *DAI* 30(1969):1535A–36A(U.C.L.A.).

2243. Sowton, Ian C.,ed. *Edmund Spenser:A Selection of His Works.* New York: Odyssey.

2244. Spurgeon, Patrick O. "Spenser's Muses." *RenP* 1969: 15–23.

2245. Wright, Carol von Pressentin. "The Lunatic, the Lover and the Poet:Themes of Love and Illusion in Three Renaissance Epics." *DAI* 30:3962A(Mich.). [Ariosto, Tasso, Spenser]

See also 1458, 2016, 2031, 2034, 2070, 2170, 3121, 3151, 3613, 5842, 6166.

Stapleton. 2246. Crawford, Charles. "Thomas Stapleton and More's *Letter to Bugenhagen.*(Cont.)." *Moreana* 26:5–13. [Postscript by G. Marc'hadour, 14–15. See also Bibliog. for 1969, Vol I, Item 2947; Vol. II, Item 6802.]

Stubbs. 2247. Berry, Lloyd E.,ed. *Gaping Gulf, with Letters and Other Relevant Documents.* (FDTSC.) Charlottesville: U.P. of Va., 1968.

Surrey. 2248. Jentoft, Clyde W. "Rhetoric and Structure in the Poetry of Henry Howard, Earl of Surrey." *DAI* 30: 4415A–16A(Ohio State).

2249. Pratt, Samuel M. "Surrey and the Fair Geraldine:A Review and a Discovery." *CLJ* 10:36–39.

See also 2254, 2259.

Taverner. 2250. Yost, John K. "Taverner's Use of Erasmus and the Protestantization of English Humanism." *RenQ* 23: 266–76.

Tilney. 2251. Moncada, Ernest J. "The Spanish Source of Edmund Tilney's *Flower of Friendshippe.*" *MLR* 65:241–47.

Turberville. *2252. Sheidley, William E. "George Turberville and the Problem of Passion." *JEGP* 69:631–49.

Wilkins. *See* 2624.

Willobie. 2253. De Luna, Barbara N. *The Queen Declined:An Interpretation of* Willobie His Avisa *with the Text of the Original Edition.* Oxford: Clarendon.

Wotton. *See* 2183.

Wyatt. 2254. Cermak, Mary M. "Terminal Structures in the Sonnets of Wyatt and Surrey." *DAI* 30(1969):2522A–23A(Catholic U.).

2255. Fiero, John W. "The Bright Transparent Glass:A Critical Study of the Poetry of Sir Thomas Wyatt." *DAI* 30(1969):683A–84A(Fla. State).

2256. Hashiguchi, Minoru. "Sir Thomas Wyatt—Kyuteif Renai to Humanism." *Oberon* 29(1968):13–26. [Sir Thomas

Wyatt—Courtly love and humanism.]

2257. —— "Wyatt Kenkyu no Mondaiten." *EigoS* 114(1968): 222–23,306–07. [Problems in study of W.]

2258. Muir, Kenneth, and Patricia Thomson,eds. *Collected Poems of Sir Thomas Wyatt.* Liverpool: Liverpool U.P., 1969.

2259. Ostriker, Alicia. "Thomas Wyatt and Henry Surrey: Dissonance and Harmony in Lyric Form." *NLH* 1:387–405.

* 2260. Twombly, Robert G. "Thomas Wyatt's Paraphrase of the Penitential Psalms of David." *TSLL* 12:345–80.

Shakespeare

Bibliography. 2261. Genzel, Peter. "Shakespeare-Bibliographie für 1967." *SJW* 105(1969):269–354.

2262. —— "Shakespeare-Bibliographie für 1968." *SJW* 106: 277–370.

2263. Habenicht, Rudolph E., and Bruce Nesbitt,eds. "Shakespeare:An Annotated World Bibliography for 1969." *SQ* 21: 255–381.

2264. Howard-Hill, T.H. "Shakespeare Sought Out by Computation." *SRO* 4(1968–69):103–16. [Rev. art of vols. I and II of Marvin Spevack's *Concordance of the Works of Shakespeare.*] *See also* 1946.

General and Miscellaneous. 2265. Adling, Wilfried. "Gorki und Shakespeare:Zur Shakespeare-Rezeption im dramatischen Spätwerk Maxim Gorkis." *SJW* 105(1969):89–103.

* 2266. *AI* 27,iii. Spec. Shakespeare No. [M.D. Faber, "Falstaff Behind the Arras," 197–225; Stephen Reid, "In Defense of Goneril and Regan," 226–44; Stephen Reid, "Desdemona's Guilt," 245–62; Stephen Reid, *"The Winter's Tale,"* 263–78; Robert Dickes, "Desdemona:An Innocent Victim?" 279–97.]

2267. Anzai, Tetsuo. "Shakespeare to Montaigne." *ELLS* 5(1968):80–98. [S and M; in Jap.]

2268. —— "Yoshikishi toshite no Engekishi no tame no Oboegaki." *ELLS* 6(1969):81–107. [Notes on dramatic hist. as hist. of ideas.]

2269. Aronson, Alex. "Shakespeare and the Ocular Proof." *SQ* 21:411–29.

2270. Bandel, Betty. "Ellen Terry's Foul Papers." *ThS* 10(1969):43–52. [Shakespeare critic.]

2271. —— "The Champlain Shakespeare Festival." *SQ* 20(1969):469–72.

2272. Batley, E.M. "Rational and Irrational Elements in Lessing's Shakespeare Criticism." *GR* 45:5–25.

2273. Bircher, Martin. "Shakespeare im Zürich des 18. Jahrhunderts," 59–102 in Martin Bircher, Franz Hafner, and Richard Zürcher, *Geist und Schönheit im Zürich des 18. Jahrhunderts.* Zürich: Füssli, 1968.

2274. Bloch, Peter A. "Schillers Shakespeare-Verständnis." [F 52]:81–101.

2275. Borinski, Ludwig. "Konstante Stilformen in Shakespeares Prosa." *SJH* (1969):81–102.

2276. Bradbrook, Muriel C. *Shakespeare the Craftsman.* London: Chatto & Windus, 1969.

* 2277. Braun, Theodore E.D. "A French Classicist's View of Shakespeare." *RomN* 11:569–73.

2278. Brown, Ivor. *Shakespeare and the Actors.* London: Bodley Head.

2279. Burgess, Anthony. *Shakespeare.* London: Jonathan Cape.

2280. —— "Shakespeare's Marriage." *Prose* 1:45–62.

2281. Calderwood, James L., and Harold E. Toliver,eds. *Essays in Shakespearean Criticism.* Englewood Cliffs, N.J.: Prentice-Hall. [Rptd. essays plus Arthur Mizener, "The Structure of Figurative Language in Shakespeare's Sonnets," 85–100(rev. version); Harold E. Toliver, "Shakespeare's Kingship:Institution and Dramatic Form," 58–82.]

2282. Carey, Robin. "The Oregon Shakespeare Festival —1970." *SQ* 21:461–64.

* 2283. Cohen, Eileen Z. "The Visible Solemnity:Ceremony and Order in Shakespeare and Hooker." *TSLL* 12:181–95.

2284. Coursen, Herbert R.,Jr. "Shakespeare in Maine: Summer, 1970." *SQ* 21:487–90.

2285. Crawford, John W. "Romantic Criticism of Shake-

spearian Drama." *DAI* 30(1969):1130A–31A(Okla. State).

2286. Crouch, J.H. "The Colorado Shakespeare Festival —1969." *SQ* 20(1969):455–58.

2287. —— "The Colorado Shakespeare Festival—1970." *SQ* 21:465–67.

2288. Cunningham, J.V.,ed. *In Shakespeare's Day.* Greenwich, Conn.: Fawcett.

2289. Cusack, Bridget. "Shakespeare and the Tune of the Time." *ShS* 23:1–12. [Ling. changes within works of S.]

2290. Danson, Lawrence N. "The Tragic Alphabet:Language, Ritual, and Action in Shakespeare's Tragedies." *DAI* 30: 3427A(Yale).

2291. Der, Don W. "Imitation and Imagery in Shakespeare: Factors of Originality in *Romeo and Juliet, As You Like It,* and *Twelfth Night.*" *DAI* 30(1969):1978A(Fla.).

2292. DeVillier, Mary Anne G. "Much Ado:The Moral and Religious Approach to Shakespeare Criticism." *WGCR* 2,i(1969): 26–31.

2293. Dollarhide, Louis E. "The Logic of Villainy:Shakespeare's Use of the Fallacies." *UMSE* 10(1969):49–57. [Discusses Richard III, Iago, Edmund, Brutus, Othello, Leontes, Don John.]

2294. Draper, John W. "Closing Lines of Shakespeare's Plays." *NM* 70(1969):706–14.

2295. Dunn, Catherine M. "The Function of Music in Shakespeare's Romances." *SQ* 20(1969):391–405.

2296. Eaves, Morris. "The Real Thing:A Plan for Producing Shakespeare in the Classroom." *CE* 31:463–72.

2297. Ebihara, Hajime. "Shakespeare ni okeru Chitsujo no Mondai." *EigoS* 114(1968):588–89. [Problem of order in S.]

2298. Edelman, Edward. "Shakespeare's Tragedy of Definition." *DAI* 30(1969):1979A(Columbia).

2299. Edinborough, Arnold. "A Gallic Romp Through Shakespeare:An Account of the 1970 Season at Ontario's Stratford Festival." *SQ* 21:457–59.

2300. —— "The Director's Role at Canada's Stratford." *SQ* 20(1969):443–46.

2301. Enright, Dennis J. *Shakespeare and the Students.* London: Chatto & Windus.

2302. Evans, Gareth L. "Interpretation or Experience? Shakespeare at Stratford." *ShS* 23:131–35. [The 1969 season.]

2303. —— *Shakespeare 1564–1592, 1587–1598.* (Writers and Critics Ser.) 2 vols. Edinburgh: Oliver and Boyd, 1969.

2304. —— "The Reason Why:The Royal Shakespeare Season 1968 Reviewed." *ShS* 22(1969):135–44.

2305. Evans, Hugh C. "Comic Constables—Fictional and Historical." *SQ* 20(1969):427–33.

2306. Faber, Melvin D.,comp. *The Design Within:Psychoanalytic Approaches to Shakespeare.* New York: Science House.

2307. Figueiredo, Fidelino. *Shakespeare e Garrett.* São Paulo: Conselho estadual de Cultura.

2308. Fitch, Robert E. *Shakespeare:The Perspective of Value.* Philadelphia: Westminster, 1969.

2309. Freehafer, John. "Leonard Digges, Ben Jonson, and the Beginning of Shakespeare Idolatry." *SQ* 21:63–75.

2310. Fuhara, Yoshiaki. "Shakespeare Geki no Keitai." *EigoS* 115(1969):492–93. [Form of S's Plays—Johnson's theory.]

2311. Fujita, Minoru. "The Concept of the Royal in Shakespeare." *ShStud* 7(1968–69):1–32.

2312. Gardner, C.O. "Themes of Manhood in Five Shakespeare Tragedies:Some Notes on *Othello, King Lear, Macbeth, Antony and Cleopatra* and *Coriolanus.*" *Theoria* 29(1967):1–24; 30(1968):19–43.

2313. Gilbert, Miriam A. "The Shrew and the Disguised Girl in Shakespeare's Comedy." *DAI* 30:2967A(Ind.).

2314. Green, Richard L. "The Shakespearean Acting of Edwin Forrest." *DAI* 30(1969):1266A(Ill.).

2315. Grivelet, Michel. "Shakespeare, Molière, and the Comedy of Ambiguity." *ShS* 22(1969):15–26.

* 2316. Guthke, Karl S. "Hallers Shakespeare-Bild." *Seminar* 6:91–110.

2317. Habicht, Walter, and Hans W. Gabler. "Shakespeare Studies in German:1959–68." *ShS* 23:113–23.

2318. Halio, Jay L. "Rhetorical Ambiguity as a Stylistic Device in Shakespeare's Problem Comedies [with] Volume

II:Appendix." *DAI* 30(1969):1135A(Yale). [1956.]

2319. Hamer, Douglas. "Was William Shakespeare William Shakeshafte?" *RES* 21:41–48. [Evidence for rejecting the ident.]

2320. Harbage, Alfred,ed. *Shakespeare's Songs.* Philadelphia: Macrae Smith. [Illus. with the orig. musical settings.]

2321. Harder, Harry R. "A Critical Study of Shakespeare's Last Plays." *DAI* 30(1969):2485A(Bowling Green).

2322. Harrison, George B. *Shakespeare's Tragedies.* New York: Oxford U.P., 1969.

2323. Hartsock, Mildred E. "Major Scenes in Minor Key." *SQ* 21:55–62. [Examination of "mirror" scenes.]

2324. Hibbard, G.R. "Words, Action, and Artistic Economy." *ShS* 23:49–58.

2325. Hibbard, G.R., Leah Scragg, and Richard Proudfoot. "The Year's Contributions to Shakespearian Study." *ShS* 22(1969):145–83; 23:137–86.

2326. Hirai, Masao. "Shakespeare ni okeru kami no mondai (3)." *EigoS* 114(1968):14–15. [Problem of God in S.]

2327. Hirsch, Foster. "The New York Shakespeare Festival —1970." *SQ* 21:477–80.

2328. Horobetz, Lynn K. "Shakespeare at the Old Globe, 1970." *SQ* 21:469–71.

2329. Howarth, Herbert. *The Tiger's Heart:Eight Essays on Shakespeare.* New York: Oxford U.P.; London: Chatto & Windus.

2330. Hudson, Kenneth. "Shakespeare's Use of Colloquial Language." *ShS* 23:39–48.

2331. Huesmann, Heinrich. *Shakespeare-Inszenierungen unter Goethe in Weimar.* (SÖAW 258,ii.) Wien: Böhlau, 1968.

2332. Humphreys, A.R. "Shakespeare's Histories and 'The Emotion of Multitude'." *PBA* 54(for 1968):265–87.

2333. Irvin, Eric. "Shakespeare in the Early Sydney Theatre." *ShS* 22(1969):125–33.

2334. Iwasaki, Soji. "Shakespeare Kenkyu no Hoho—Imagery to Rekishi." *EigoS* 114(1968):574–75. [Approaches to S:imagery and hist.]

2335. Jackson, B.A.W.,ed. *Manner and Meaning in Shakespeare.* (Stratford Papers, 1965–67.) Dublin: Irish U.P. [Lectures delivered at Stratford, Ontario.]

2336. —— *Stratford Papers, 1965–67.* Hamilton, Ont.: McMaster U. Lib. P.; Shannon: Irish U.P., 1969. [L.C. Knights, "The Teaching of Shakespeare," 1–20; Arthur C. Sprague, "Manner and Meaning in Shakespeare's Plays," 21–28; Bamber Gascoigne, "Will They Ridicule Our Shakespeare?" 29–50; John Russell Brown, "Shakespeare Study Today," 51–64; John Russell Brown, "Shakespeare Production Today," 65–81; Herbert Whittaker, "Second Century Shakespeare," 82–95; F.H. Mares, "Viola and Other Transvestist Heroines in Shakespeare's Comedies," 96–109; Charles T. Prouty, "*Twelfth Night*," 110–28; Arnold Edinborough, "*Julius Caesar*," 129–44; John Pettigrew, "The Mood of *Henry IV,* Part 2," 145–67; Muriel C. Bradbrook, "*King Henry IV*," 168–85; G.P.V. Akrigg, "*Henry V:*The Epic Hero as Dramatic Protagonist," 186–207; Michael Burn, "Why No *Henry VII*? (with a Postscript on Malvolio's Revenge)," 208–31.]

2337. Jensen, Ejner J. "A New Allusion to the Sign of the Globe Theater." *SQ* 21:95–97.

2338. Judelevičius, Dovydas. "Jausmui ar protui? Mintys iš šekspyrinių spektaklių." *Muzika ir Teatras*(Vilnius) 5(1969): 32–50. [On plays staged recently in Lithuania.]

2339. Kaieda, Susumu. "Koya Tozawa and Hyokyo Asano: Early Shakespeare Translators in Japan, II." *A&CS* 20:63–72. [In Jap.; sum. in Eng. See Bibliog. for 1969, Vol.II, Item 11150.]

2340. Kantak, V.Y. "An Approach to Shakespearian Comedy." *ShS* 22(1969):7–13.

2341. Kernan, Alvin B.,ed. *Modern Shakespearean Criticism: Essays on Style, Dramaturgy, and the Major Plays.* New York: Harcourt, Brace & World. [Prev. pub. essays.]

2342. Kéry, László. "Einige Bemerkungen zu der Komplexität der komischen Gestalten bei Shakespeare." *SJW* 106:76–84.

2343. Kittredge, George L.,ed. *The Minor Poems.* Rev. Irving Ribner. Waltham, Mass.: Blaisdell, 1969.

2344. Kohl, Norbert. "Die Shakespeare-Kritik zum Wortspiel:Ein Beitrag zur historischen Wertung eines Sprach-

phänomens." *DVLG* 44:530–43.

2345. Koppenfels, Werner von. "Plutarch, Shakespeare, Quevedo und das Drama der Ermordung Caesars." *GRM* 20:1–23.

2346. Kott, Jan. *Shakespeare, contemporanul nostru.* Bucharest: Editura pentru literatură universală, 1969.

2347. Kuckhoff, Armin-Gerd. "Erbe—Gegenwart—Prognose." *SJW* 106:29–62. [See art. by Rohmer, below.]

2348. —— "Zufall und Notwendigkeit im Drama William Shakespeares." *SJW* 105(1969):121–39.

2349. Kuner, Mildred C. "The New York Shakespeare Festival, 1969." *SQ* 20(1969):451–54.

* 2350. Lasser, Michael L. "Shakespeare:Finding and Teaching the Comic Vision." *Eng. Record* 20,ii(1969):4–17.

2351. Lee, Virgil J.,Jr. "The Face in Shakespeare:A Study of Facial Gesture and Attitude as Aspects of Dramatic *Energeia.*" *DAI* 30:4416A(Columbia).

2352. Leimberg, Inge. "Shakespeares Komödien und Sidneys 'Goldene Welt'." *SJH* 105(1969):174–97.

* 2353. Lewis, Allan. "But It's Not Shakespeare." *ASoc* 7:78–84.

2354. Lord, Gisela. "Die Figur des Pedanten bei Shakespeare." *SJH* (1969):213–44.

2355. Maharajan, S. "Some Problems of Shakespeare-Translation Into Tamil." [F 42],II:847–57.

2356. Mansinha, Mayadhar. *Kalidasa and Shakespeare.* New Delhi: Motilal Banarsidass, 1969; Mystic, Conn.: Verry.

2357. Marder, Louis. "Prologue to a New Critical Life of Shakespeare." *ShN* 20:34–35.

2358. McCluskey, Donald. "The Rise of Historical Criticism of Shakespeare:The Plays and Their Sources." *DAI* 30:4951A (Yale). [1941.]

* 2359. McDonald, Daniel. "'Anyone Can Teach Shakespeare'." *JGE* 22:187–92.

2360. McGovern, Ann,comp. *Shakespearean Sallies, Sullies, and Slanders:Insults for All Occasions.* Illus. James and Ruth McCrea. New York: Crowell, 1969.

2361. McKay, Margaret R. "Shakespeare's Use of the Apostrophe, Popular Rhetorical Device of the Renaissance." *DAI* 30:4459A–60A(Colo.).

2362. McManaway, James G. *Studies in Shakespeare, Bibliography, and Theater.* New York: Shakespeare Assoc. of Amer. 1969. [Rpt. essays 1934–67; "A List of the Published Writings of James G. McManaway," 385–400.]

2363. McMullen, Glenys. "The Fool as Entertainer and Satirist, on Stage and in the World." *DR* 50:10–22.

2364. Mercier, Joseph R. "Shakespeare and the Function of Irony." *DAI* 30:2975A(Conn.).

2365. Milosevich, Vincent M. "Propriety as an Esthetic Principle in Dryden, Shakespeare and Wagner." *HAB* 21,i:3–13

2366. Milward, Peter. "Prolegomena to a Study of Shakespeare's Religious Background." *EigoS* 114(1968):673–76.

2367. —— "Shakespeare in the Modern World." *EigoS* 115(1969):772–74.

2368. —— "Shakespeare wa Warera no Dojidaijin." *Sophia* 18(1969):219–35. [Sh our contemporary.]

2369. —— "What's in a Name?A Study in Shakespearian Nomenclature." *ELLS* 5(1968):1–11.

2370. Mociornița, Maria. "Contribuția lui George Călinescu la receptarea operei lui Shakespeare în țara noastră." *RITL* 19:423–30.

2371. Muir, Kenneth. "Shakespeare's Poets." *ShS* 23:91–100 [Poets and refs. to poetry in S's plays.]

2372. Murphy, Garry N. "Aspects of Shakespeare's Development in the Art of Opening Exposition." *DAI* 30(1969) 691A(U. of Wash.).

2373. Murray, Patrick. *The Shakespearian Scene:Some Twentieth-Century Perspectives.* New York: Barnes & Noble, 1969

2374. Nedden, Otto C.A. zur. *Europäische Akzente Ansprachen und Essays.* Wuppertal: Staats-Verl., 1968. [See esp. "Shakespeare und das abendländische Theater," 129–46, and "Die Bereitschaft sein ist alles," 147–51 (on *Hamlet*).]

2375. Neely, Carol T. "Speaking True:Shakespeare's Use of the Elements of Pastoral Romance." *DAI* 30:3433A(Yale).

2376. Ogawa, Kazuo. "Shakespeare on Imagination." *EigoS* 14(1968):156–58,224–26,302–05. [In Jap.]

2377. Ornstein, Robert. "Shakespearian and Jonsonian Comedy." *ShS* 22(1969):43–46.

2378. —— "The Great Lakes Shakespeare Festival." *SQ* 20(1969):459–61; 21:473–75.

2379. Oyama, Toshikazu. "Shakespeare to Akumagaku." *EigoS* 114(1968):437–38. [S and demonology.]

2380. Oyama, Toshiko. "Dento to Giko to Shi—Shakespeare to Elizabethan Rhetoric." *EigoS* 115(1969):220–21. [Convention, Technique, Poetry—S and Elisabethan rhetoric.]

2381. Payne, Michael D. "Irony in Shakespeare's Roman Plays." *DAI* 30:4952A(Ore.).

2382. Pearson, D'Orsay W. "Shakespeare and the Doctrines of Witchcraft." *DAI* 30:4422A–23A(Kent State).

2383. Petronella, Vincent F. "The Drama of the Soul in Shakespeare's Second Tetralogy:An Historical and Critical Study." *DAI* 30(1969):1991A–92A(Mass.).

2384. Pichois, Claude. "Michelet et Shakespeare." [F 52]:103–16.

2385. Picoff, Ghita. "The Champlain Shakespeare Festival, an Overview." *SQ* 21:483–85.

2386. Piemme, Michèle. "Shakespeare et Césaire:D'une tempête à l'autre." *Revue Nouvelle*(Brussels) 52:295–302.

2387. Prange, Klaus. "Shakespeare in Unterricht." *LWU* 3:109–19.

2388. Ray, P.C. "The Shakespearean Puzzle—Endeavours After Its Solution." *CalR* N.S. 1:381–400.

2389. Ribner, Irving. *Patterns in Shakespearian Tragedy.* London: Methuen, 1969. [Paperback.]

2390. Robbins, Martin L. "Shakespeare's Sweet Music:A Glossary of Musical Terms in the Work of Shakespeare (with Additional Examples from the Plays of Lyly, Marston, and Jonson)." *DAI* 30(1969):1534A–35A(Brandeis).

2391. Roberts, Jeanne A. "The Washington Shakespeare Summer Festival, 1970." *SQ* 21:481–82.

2392. Rohmer, Rolf,et al. "Beiträge zum Kolloquium über das Thema 'Erbe—Gegenwart—Prognose'." *SJW* 106:63–75. [See art. by Kuckhoff, above.]

2393. Ross, Lawrence J. "Wingless Victory:Michelangelo, Shakespeare, and the 'Old Man'." [F 55]:3–56. [Plus 20 pp. of illus.; notes, 197–212.]

2394. Rubinstein, Annette T. "Shakespeare Taken Seriously." *Science and Society* 32(1968):413–21. [Rev. art.]

2395. Rudolph, Johanna. "Karl Marx und Shakespeare." *SJW* 105(1969):25–53.

2396. Rüegg, August. "Englische und spanische Soldateska im Zeitalter Shakespeares." [F 52]:151–54.

2397. Salmon, Vivian. "Some Functions of Shakespearian Word-Formation." *ShS* 23:13–26.

2398. Santilli, Tommaso. "Giuseppe Baretti innanzi a Shakespeare e Voltaire, il verso sciolto e la questione della lingua." *PS* 5,iv(1969):31–57.

2399. Saslaw, Naomi R. "Shakespearian Humanism." *DAI* 30:3919A(Case Western Reserve).

2400. Schäfer, Jürgen. "The Orthography of Proper Names in Modern-Spelling Editions of Shakespeare." *SB* 23:1–19.

2401. Schanzer, Ernest. "Plot-Echoes in Shakespeare's Plays." *SJH* (1969):103–21.

2402. Schlösser, Anselm. "Zur Bedeutung der Anachronism bei Shakespeare." *SJW* 105(1969):7–24.

2403. Schmoller, Hans. "The Complete Pelican Shakespeare." *Philobiblon* 14:91–102.

2404. Schoenbaum, S. "Shakespeare the Ignoramus." [F 46]:154–64.

2405. Schotta, Sarita G. "A Linguistic Analysis of the Marginal Stage Directions of Shakespeare's *First Folio.*" *PIL* 2:152–69.

2406. Sedlak, Werner. "Typen des Blankverses bei Shakespeare." *SJH* (1969):122–42.

2407. Shaaber, M.A. "The Comic View of Life in Shakespeare's Comedies." [F 46]:165–78.

2408. *Shakespeare Series II:*Hamlet, *ed. Marion B. Smith;* The Tempest, *ed. David Galloway;* Henry the Fourth Part One, *ed.*

John F. Sullivan. With Introds. New York: Odyssey, 1969.

2409. Shakespeare, William. *Verzameld Werk III.* Antwerpen: De Nederlandsche Boekhandel.

2410. Shapiro, Susan C. "Paradox, Analogy, and the Imitation of an Action in Shakespearean Tragedy." *DAI* 30:5420A (Bryn Mawr).

2411. Shattuck, Charles H. "The Shakespeare Promptbooks: First Supplement." *TN* 24(1969):5–17. [Supplements Shattuck's *The Shakespeare Promptbooks:A Descriptive Catalogue* (Urbana: U. of Ill. P., 1965).]

2412. Sheriff, William E. "The Comic Elements in Shakespeare's Early English History Plays." *DAI* 30:2980A(Ind.).

2413. *ShN* 20,i–ii–iii. [Louis Marder, "Shakespeare in the Theatre of Theatrical Discontinuity," 2; Elizabeth N. Smith, "On Directing a Collage of Shakespeare's *Macbeth*," 2–3; Louis Marder, "A Hairy *Measure for Measure*," 4; Louis Marder, "A Cry of Players:Shakespeare's Biography Dramatized," 5; Louis Marder, "New Shakespeare Concordance," 8–10; Bernard Beckerman, "The Itinerant Scholar:Henslowe's Role in Theatrical Productions Between 1585 and 1616," 13; John J. McAleer, "James Henry Hackett:Shakespeare's Learned Falstaff," 14–15; Louis Marder, "On Punctuating Shakespeare Concordances and Line References," 16; Vincent F. Petronella, "The Itinerant Scholar:Design for Shakespeare," 17.]

2414. *ShN* 20,iv. [Louis Marder, "Halliwell-Phillips' Controversy with Stratford," 26–27; Robert F. Willson,Jr., "The Audience Reaction to *Cymbeline*," 27; Peter Lindenbaum, "The Itinerant Scholar:The Uses of Pastoral in *The Winter's Tale*," 28; Robert F. Willson,Jr.,ed., "Landmarks of Criticism:*Timon of Athens*," 28; Barbara Mowat, "The Beckoning Ghost:Stage-Gesture in Shakespeare," 29.]

2415. Smith, Peter. "The 1970 Season at Stratford, Connecticut." *SQ* 21:451–55.

2416. —— "The 1969 Season at Stratford, Connecticut." *SQ* 20(1969):447–50.

2417. Smithers, G.V. "Guide-Lines for Interpreting the Uses of the Suffix *-ed* in Shakespeare's English." *ShS* 23:27–37.

2418. Speaight, Robert. "Shakespeare in Britain." *SQ* 21: 439–49. [Rev. of 1970 season.]

2419. —— "Shakespeare in Britain." *SQ* 20(1969):435–41. [The 1969 season.]

2420. Sprague, Arthur C. "Shakespeare's Characters as Parts for Players." [F 52]:125–33.

2421. Stack, V.E. "Shakespeare in Translation." *English* 18(1969):53–56.

2422. Steck, Paul. "Shakespeare-Motive im Drama Schillers." *NS* 19:271–83.

2423. Streiter, Aaron. "Against Discord:The Evolution of the Idea of Order in Certain Shakespearean Plays." *DAI* 30(1969): 295A(Brown).

2424. Suerbaum, Ulrich. "Der deutsche Shakespeare: Übersetzungsgeschichte und Übersetzungstheorie." [F 52]:61–80.

2425. Suga, Yasuo. "Shakespeare to Kindaigeki." *EigoS* 114(1968):146–49. [S and modern drama.]

2426. Swander, Homer D. "Shakespeare at the 'Old Globe' San Diego." *SQ* 20(1969):463–67.

2427. Taylor, Estelle W. "Shakespeare's Use of *S/TH* Endings of Certain Verbs." *DAI* 30(1969):2046A(Catholic U.).

2428. Torbarina, Josip. "Ivanjska noć u djelu Držića i Shakespearea." *ForumZ* 20:5–20.

2429. Toyama, Shigehiko. "Shakespeare no Sekai." *EigoS* 114(1968):74–77. [The World of S.]

2430. Trafton, Dain A. "Ideology and Politics in the Second Tetralogy of Shakespeare's History Plays." *DAI* 30(1969): 295A–96A(Calif., Berkeley).

2431. Tschumi, Raymond. "Shakespeare in His Time and in Ours." [F 52]:141–50.

2432. Velie, Alan R. "Shakespeare's Repentance Plays:The Search for an Adequate Form." *DAI* 30:5422A–23A(Stanford).

2433. Viswanatham, K. "The Imitative and Iterative Shakespeare." *Triveni* 39,i:20–33(to be cont.).

2434. Viswanathan, S. " 'Illeism With a Difference' in Certain Middle Plays of Shakespeare." *SQ* 20(1969):407–15. [*Hamlet, Julius Caesar, Othello, Troilus and Cressida.*]

2435. Voitl, Herbert. "Shakespeares Komposita:Ein Beitrag zur Stilistik seiner Wortneuprägungen." *SJH* (1969):152–73.

2436. Vroonland, Jewell K. "Mannerism and Shakespeare's 'Problem Plays': An Argument for Revaluation." *DAI* 30(1969): 2502A–03A(Kan. State).

2437. Weil, Herbert S.,Jr. "Comic Structure and Tonal Manipulation in Shakespeare and Some Modern Plays." *ShS* 22(1969):27–33.

2438. Weller, Philip J. "Politics in Shakespeare's Later Drama." *DAI* 30:5423A–24A(Kent State).

2439. Widmann, R.L. "Morgann's Copy of Theobald." *N&Q* 17:125.

2440. Wilson, Edward M. "Shakespeare and Christian Doctrine:Some Qualifications." *ShS* 23:79–89.

2441. Wilson, Frank P. *Shakespearian and Other Studies.* Ed. Helen Gardner. Oxford: Clarendon, 1969.

2442. Wright, Louis B., and Virginia A. LaMar,eds. *Shakespeare's Poems.* New York: Wash. Sq. P., 1969.

2443. Wright, Louis B., and Virginia A. LaMar. *The Folger Guide to Shakespeare.* New York: Wash. Square Press, 1969.

See also 793, 1453, 1457, 1958, 1962, 1979, 1982, 1989, 2181, 2711, 2936, 3022, 3128, 3151, 3632, 4147, 4310, 4526, 4567, 4931, 5052, 5747, 5748, 5757, 5762, 5957, 6544, 6718.

All's Well That Ends Well. 2445. Howard-Hill, T.H.,ed. All's Well That Ends Well:*A Concordance to the Text of the First Folio.* (Oxford Shakespeare Concordances.) Oxford: Clarendon.

2446. Huston, J. Dennis. " 'Some Stain of Soldier':The Functions of Parolles in *All's Well That Ends Well.*" *SQ* 21:431–48.

2447. Warren, Roger. " 'A Lover's Complaint,' *All's Well,* and the Sonnets." *N&Q* 17:130–32.

2448. ——. "Why Does It End Well? Helena, Bertram, and the Sonnets." *ShS* 22(1969):79–92.

See also 2681.

Antony and Cleopatra. 2449. Altmann, Ruth. "Shakespeare's Craftsmanship:A Study of His Use of Plutarch in *Antony and Cleopatra.*" *DAI* 30(1969):2474A(U. of Wash.).

2450. Aoyama, Seika. "Magnificence and Folly:A Study of Value in *Antony and Cleopatra.*" [F 14]:12–25.

2451. Fisch, Harold. "*Antony and Cleopatra*:The Limits of Mythology." *ShS* 23:59–67.

2452. Friedman, Stanley. "*Antony and Cleopatra* and Drayton's *Mortimeriados.*" *SQ* 20(1969):481–84.

2453. Gianakaris, C.J. *Antony and Cleopatra.* (Blackfriars Shakespeare Ser.) Dubuque, Iowa: Wm. Brown, 1969.

2454. Lyons, Charles R. "The Serpent, the Sun and 'Nilus Slime':A Focal Point for the Ambiguity of Shakespeare's *Antony and Cleopatra.*" *RLMC* 21(1968):13–34.

2455. Moore, John Rees. "Enemies of Love:The Example of Antony and Cleopatra." *KR* 31(1969):646–74.

2456. Rose, Paul L. "The Politics of *Antony and Cleopatra.*" *SQ* 20(1969):379–89.

2457. Traci, Philip J. *The Love Play of* Antony and Cleopatra:*A Critical Study of Shakespeare's Play.* (SEngL 64.) The Hague: Mouton.

2458. Wertime, Richard A. "Excellent Falsehood:Theme and Characterization in *Antony and Cleopatra.*" *DAI* 30:2983A(Pa.).

2459. Williamson, Marilyn. "The Political Context in *Antony and Cleopatra.*" *SQ* 21:241–51.

See also 2049, 2311.

As You Like It. 2460. Faber, M.D. "On Jaques:Psychoanalytic Remarks." *UR* 36(1969-70):89–96, 179–82.

2461. Giffin, David A. "Deus Ex Machina in *As You Like It.*" *AN&Q* 9:23–24.

2462. Howard-Hill, T.H.,ed. As You Like It:*A Concordance to the Text of the First Folio.* (Oxford Shakespeare Concordances.) London: Oxford U.P.

2463. Knowles, Richard. "Rough Notes on Editions Collated for *As You Like It.*" *SRO* 4(1968/69):66–72.

2464. Mattern, Sister Evelyn J. "A Survey of the Criticism of Shakespeare's *As You Like It.*" *DAI* 30(1969):2539A(Pa.).

2465. Østergaard, V.,tr. *Helligtrekongersaften, eller Hvad I vil.* Copenhagen: J.H. Schultz, 1969. ["Kommentar," 117–26; "Noter," 127–36.]

* 2466. Palmer, D.J. "Art and Nature in *As You Like It.*" *PQ* 49:30–40.

2467. Puchner, Judith A. "*As You Like It, Much Ado About Nothing,* and *Twelfth Night*:A Study in the Structure of Shakespeare's Romantic Comedy." *DAI* 30:3918A(Cornell).

2468. Trautvetter, Christine, and Ernst Leisi. "Some New Readings in *As You Like It.*" *SJH* (1969):143–51.

2469. Yagi, Takeshi. "Jaques—sono Seikaku to Yakuwari." *Oberon* 29(1968):44–55. [J—his character and role.]

See also 791.

Coriolanus. 2470. Langman, F.A. " 'Atmosphere' and Repeated Action in *Coriolanus.*" *SoRA* 3(1969):324–33.

2471. Phillips, James E.,ed. *Twentieth Century Interpretations of* Coriolanus:*A Collection of Critical Essays.* (TCI.) Englewood Cliffs, N.J.: Prentice-Hall.

* 2472. Stockholder, Katherine. "The Other Coriolanus." *PMLA* 85:228–36.

Cymbeline. 2473. Middleton, David L. "Shakespeare's *Cymbeline* and British Mythical History." *DAI* 30:5415A–16A(Wis.).

2474. Stoltzenberg, Gisela von. "Christliche Lehre in *Cymbeline* und *The Winter's Tale.*" *LWU* 3:87–97.

See also 5315.

Hamlet. *2475. Baker, James V. "Anguish and Certain Existential Anticipations in *Hamlet.*" *ForumH* 8,ii:33–37.

2476. Barroll, J. Leeds,ed. *Hamlet.* (Blackfriars Shakespeare Ser.) Dubuque, Iowa: Wm. Brown.

2477. Battenhouse, Roy. "The Significance of Hamlet's Advice to the Players." [F 46]:3–26.

2478. Bonjour, Adrien. "About the Heart of Hamlet." [F 52]:51–60.

2479. Budanova, N.F. "Roman *Nov'* v svete turgenevsko koncepcii Gamleta i Don-Kixota." *RLit* 12,ii(1969):180–90.

2480. Coursen, Herbert R.,Jr. "The Rarer Action:Hamlet' Mousetrap." [F 55]:59–97. [Notes, 213–17.]

2481. Davidson, Clifford. "The Triumph of Time." *DI* 50:170–81.

2482. Demadre, A. "Linguistique et littérature:Le système verbal dans le grand monologue de *Hamlet.*" *LanM* 64:273–78.

2483. Dent, R.W. "*Hamlet,* i.v.162:'Well Said Old Mole'." *N&Q* 17:128–29.

2484. Faber, M.D. "Hamlet's 'Canon' Revisited." *SQ* 21 97–99.

* 2485. Gellert, Bridget. "The Iconography of Melancholy in the Graveyard Scene of *Hamlet.*" *SP* 67:57–66.

2486. Georgi, Renate. "*Hamlet* in filmischer Poesie." *SJW* 106:176–201.

2487. Gross, Lorraine H. "The Influence of Thrust and Proscenium Stage Forms on Audience Response to a Production of *Hamlet.*" *DAI* 30(1969):435A(Mich. State).

2488. Hutton, Virgil. "Hamlet's Fear of Death." *UR* 37 11–19.

2489. Lee, Robin. "Their Scourge and Minister:A Study o *Hamlet.*" *Standpunte* 87:26–35.

2490. McKenzie, James J. "Exit Ophelia." *N&Q* 17:129–30

2491. McManaway, James G. "Ophelia and Jephtha' Daughter." *SQ* 21:198–200.

* 2492. Morris, Harry. "*Hamlet* as a *memento mori* Poem." *PMLA* 85:1035–40.

2493. Mueller, Dennis M. "Wieland's *Hamlet* Translation and Wilhelm Meister." *SJH* 105(1969):198–212.

2494. Okubo, Junichiro. "*Hamlet* to *Kusamakura.*" *Eigo* 115(1969):548–49. [*H* and *K,* by N. Soseki.]

2495. Østergaard, V.,tr. *Hamlet, Prins af Danmark* Copenhagen: J.H. Schultz, 1969. ["Kommentar," 159–85 "Noter," 186–204.]

2496. Otis, John F. "The Barrymore *Hamlet,* 1922–1925." *DAI* 30(1969):431A(Ill.).

2497. Pitts, Rebecca E. "This Fell Sergeant, Death." *SQ* 20(1969):486–91.

2498. Puhalo, Dušan. "Prevodi Laze Kostić:*Hamlet* i *Ca Lir.*" *ZIK* 6(1968):79–154. [Sum. in Eng.]

2499. Ram, Alur J. "Hamlet's Heroic Identity and Submission to Providence:A Comparative Approach." [F 51]:67–8C

2500. Reis, Ilse H. "Gerhart Hauptmann's Roman *Im Wirbel er Berufung* als Selbstbekenntnis im Sinne von *Neue Leidenschaft* nd *Siri* und als *Hamlet*-Interpretation in der Nachfolge oethes." *DAI* 30:4953A–54A(N.Y.U.).

2501. Replogle, Carol. "Not Parody, Not Burlesque:The Play ithin the Play in *Hamlet*." *MP* 67(1969):150–59.

2502. Seaman, John E. "The 'Rose of May' in the 'Unweeded arden'." *EA* 22(1969):337–45.

2503. Skulsky, Harold. "Revenge, Honor, and Conscience in *amlet*." *PMLA* 85:78–87.

2504. Takahashi, Yasunari. "Kyoki to Engi—*Hamlet* kara endai e." *EigoS* 115(1969):540–42,610–11,640. [Madness and ethod—from H to today.]

2505. Taylor, Michael. "A Note on the 'Pyrrhus Episode' in *amlet*." *SQ* 21:99–103.

2506. Upton, Albert. "That Monster Custom," (JanL, Ser. aior 41.) 295–302 in Johnnye Akin et al.,eds., *Language ehavior:A Book of Readings in Communication.* The Hague: Iouton.

2507. Wimsatt, James I. "The Player King on Friendship." *lLR* 65:1–6.

2508. Zitner, S.P. "Hamlet, Duelist." *UTQ* 39(1969):1–18. *See also* 2374, 2678, 3329, 5988, 7439.

Henry IV. 2509. Bowers, Fredson. "Theme and Structure in *ing Henry IV*, Part I." [F 46]:42–68.

2510. Fackler, Herbert V. "Shakespeare's 'Irregular and Wild' ilendower:The Dramatic Use of Source Materials." *Discourse* 3:306–14.

2511. Hunter, George K.,ed. *Shakespeare:Henry IV, Parts I nd II:A Casebook.* (Macmillan Casebook Series.) London: Iacmillan.

2512. Østergaard, V.,tr. *Første Del af Henrik IV.* Copenhagen: H. Schultz, 1969. ["Kommentar," 125–33; "Noter," 134–41.]

2513. Rubinstein, E. "*I Henry IV*:The Metaphor of Liabil- y." *SEL* 10:287–95.

2514. Yamada, Akihiro. "An Early Eighteenth-Century Stage daptation of *The First Part of Henry IV*." *SELit* Eng. Io.:75–80.

2515. —— "An Eighteenth-Century Stage Adaptation of the alstaff Part in *The First Part of Henry IV*." *SQ* 21:103–04. *See also* 776.

Henry V. 2516. Coursen, Herbert R.,Jr. "Henry V and the Jature of Kingship." *Discourse* 13:279–305.

2517. Lawless, Donald S. "Shakespeare's Indebtedness to Homily xvii'?" *ShN* 20:13.

2518. Leisi, Ernst. "'Now entertain conjecture of a time': prachliche Probleme in *Henry V*, Chorus 4." [F 52]:117–24.

2519. Spanabel, Robert R. "A Stage History of *Henry the ifth*:1583–1859." *DAI* 30:3133A–34A(Ohio State).

Henry VI. 2520. Addison, Michael C. "The Dramatic and heatrical Form of Military Combat in William Shakespeare's Ienry VI Trilogy." *DAI* 30(1969):1227A(Stanford).

2521. Billings, Wayne L. "Heroical Irony:A Reconsideration f *Henry VI*." *DAI* 30(1969):1519A–20A(Stanford).

2522. Müller, Heiner. "Die Gestaltung des Volkes in Shake- peares Historiendramen, untersucht am Beispiel *Heinrichs VI*." JW 106:127–75.

II Henry IV. 2523. Gardner, Helen. "Scilence and Scilens." LS 2 Oct:1137.

2524. Schell, Edgar T. "Prince Hal's Second 'Reformation'." Q 21:11–16.

2525. Taylor, Neil. "Variants in the Quarto of 2 *Henry IV*." ibrary 25:249–50. *See also* 2511.

Julius Caesar. *2526. Bellringer, A.W. "*Julius Caesar*:Room nough." *CritQ* 12:31–48.

2527. Chang, Joseph S.M.J. "*Julius Caesar* in the Light of Renaissance Historiography." *JEGP* 60:63–71. [Discusses Iachiavelli, Montaigne, Jean Bodin, and Daniel.]

2528. Del Re, Gabriele. "Il Bruto di Shakespeare e il Brutto di Plutarco." *Cristallo* 12,i:73–86.

2529. Habenicht, Rudolph E.,ed. *Julius Caesar.* (Blackfriars hakespeare Ser.) Dubuque, Iowa: Wm. Brown.

2530. Henze, Richard. "Power and Spirit in *Julius Caesar*." UR 36:307–14.

2531. Herbert, Edward T. "Myth and Archetype in *Julius Caesar*." *PsyR* 57:303–08.

2532. Kaufmann, R.J., and Clifford J. Ronan. "Shakespeare's *Julius Caesar*:An Apollonian and Comparative Reading." *CompD* 4:18–51.

2533. Maxwell, J.C. "Brutus's Philosophy." *N&Q* 17:128.

2534. Palmer, D.J. "Tragic Error in *Julius Caesar*." *SQ* 21:399–409.

2535. Spakowski, R.E. "Deification and Myth-Making in the Play *Julius Caesar*." *UR* 36(1969):135–40.

2536. Velz, John W. "Clemency, Will, and Just Cause in *Julius Caesar*." *ShS* 22(1969):109–18.

* 2537. —— "'Pirate Hills' and the Quartos of *Julius Caesar*." *PBSA* 63(1969):177–93.

2538. Yamamoto, Tadao. "Brutus no Kuno." *EigoS* 114(1968):362–63. [B's suffering.]

King John. 2539. Lewis, Alan. "Shakespeare and the Morality of Money." *SocR* 36(1969):373–88.

* 2540. Ortego, Philip D. "Shakespeare and the Doctrine of Monarchy in *King John*." *CLAJ* 13:392–401.

2541. Price, Jonathan R. "*King John* and Problematic Art." *SQ* 21:25–28.

King Lear. 2542. Barron, Frank, and Marvin Rosenberg. "King Lear and His Fool:A Study of the Conception and Enactment of Dramatic Role in Relation to Self-Conception." *ETJ* 22:276–83.

2543. Brady, William E. "King Lear's Definition of 'The Good Years'." *SQ* 21:495–97.

2544. Bullough, Geoffrey. "*King Lear* and the Annesley Case:A Reconsideration." [F 52]:43–49.

2545. Burke, Kenneth. "*King Lear*:Its Form and Psychosis." *Shenandoah* 21,i(1969):3–18.

2546. Clemen, Wolfgang,et al. "*König Lear*:Der theatralische Vorwurf Shakespeares und seine Verwirklichung auf der Bühne. Das Bochumer Podiumsgespräch vom 20. April 1968." *SJH* (1969):10–80.

2547. D'Amico, Masolino. "Una nuova lettura del *Lear*." *Paragone* 21,ccxliv:57–82.

2548. Eddy, Darlene M. *The Worlds of* King Lear. (Ball State Monogs.) Muncie, Ind.: Ball State U.P.

2549. Hargeaves, H.A. "Visual Contradiction in *King Lear*." *SQ* 21:491–95.

2550. Jones, James H. "*Leir* and *Lear*:Matthew 5:33–37, the Turning Point, and Rescue Theme." *CompD* 4:125–31.

2551. La Belle, Maurice-M. "Le *paradeigma* dans *Oedipe roi* et le *Roi Lear*." *BAGB* (1969):345–47.

2552. Leider, Emily W. "Plainness of Style in *King Lear*." *SQ* 21:45–53.

2553. Lesser, Simon O. "Act One, Scene One, of *Lear*." *CE* 32:155–71.

2554. Oppel, Horst. "*King Lear* in der Bildkunst." [F 52]:31–41.

2555. Østergaard, V.,tr. *Kong Lear.* Copenhagen: J.H. Schultz, 1969. ["Kommentar," 137–49; "Noter," 150–54.]

2556. Püschel, Ursula. "Gesichtspunkte für die Wahl der Herwegh-Übersetzung bei der Inszenierung von *König Lear* in Dresden." *SJW* 105(1969):70–88.

2557. Quinn, Edward G.,ed. *King Lear.* New York: Crowell. [Incl. selections from sources and crit.]

2558. Rackin, Phyllis. "Delusion as Resolution in *King Lear*." *SQ* 12:29–34.

2559. Sløk, Johannes,tr. *Kong Lear.* Copenhagen: Berlingske Forlag. ["Noter," 117–52; "Kommentarer," 155–88.]

2560. Stetner, S.C.V., and Oscar B. Goodman. "Regan's Profession." *ES* 51:331–36.

2561. Winterton, J.B. "*King Lear*, iv.vii:An Improved Stage- Direction." *N&Q* 17:133–34. *See also* 2498, 5780.

Love's Labour's Lost. 2562. Berry, Ralph. "The Words of Mercury." *ShS* 22(1969):69–77.

* 2563. Coursen, Herbert R.,Jr. "*Love's Labour's Lost* and the Comic Truth." *PLL* 6:316–22.

2564. Crawley, Thomas I. "*Love's Labour's Lost* and the

Pageant of the Nine Worthies:A Thematic and Structural Analysis." *DAI* 30(1969):1522A(Neb.).

2565. Thorne, Barry. " *'Love's Labour's Lost*:The Lyly Gilded'." *HAB* 21,iii:32–37.

See also 2501.

Macbeth. 2566. Davidson, Clifford. *The Primrose Way:A Study of Shakespeare's* Macbeth. Conesville, Iowa: J. Westburg and Associates.

2567. Fergusson, Sir James. *The Man Behind Macbeth and Other Studies.* London: Faber, 1969.

2568. Griot [pseud.]. "Afro-Shakespeare." *WA* 20(Dec 1969): 1539. [Senegalese adaptation of *Macbeth* in Paris.]

2569. Iwasaki, Soji. "*Macbeth* ni okeru Door-Image." *EigoS* 114(1968):722–24. [Door image in *Macbeth.*]

2570. Law, Richard A. "The Tragic Vision of Life in *Macbeth.*" [F 23]:1–12.

2571. Lüthi, Max. "*Macbeth*, Tragödie der Selbstspaltung und Selbstentfremdung." [F 52]:23–30.

2572. Lyle, E.B. "The Speech-Heading 'I' in Act IV, Scene I, of the Folio Text of *Macbeth.*" *Library* 25:150–51.

2573. Marenco, Franco. "Attualità del *Macbeth.*" *Comunità* 24(1969-70):160–63.

2574. Niki, Hisae. "Kurosawa's *Kumonosujó*:A Japanese *Macbeth.*" *ShStud* 7(1968–69):33–60.

2575. Odajima, Yushi. "*Macbeth—Shujinko no Joken.*" *EigoS* 114(1968):78–79. [*Macbeth—Condition of a hero.*]

2576. Parker, Barbara L. "*Macbeth*:The Great Illusion." *SR* 78:476–87.

2577. Rissanen, Matti. " 'Nature's Copy,' 'Great Bond,' and 'Lease of Nature' in *Macbeth.*" *NM* 70(1969):714–23.

2578. Roaten, Darnell H. "Baroque Configurations in the Language of *Macbeth.*" [F 34]:259–66.

2579. Standop, Ewald. "Stilistisches zu *Macbeth*, erster Akt." *LWU* 3:209–20.

2580. Swaminathan, S.R. "The Image of Pity in *Macbeth.*" *N&Q* 17:132.

See also 2678.

Measure for Measure. 2581. Brashear, Lucy M. "Character and Prosody in Shakespeare's *Measure for Measure.*" *DAI* 30:3424A–25A(N.C.).

2582. Geckle, George L.,ed. *Twentieth Century Interpretations of* Measure for Measure:*A Collection of Critical Essays.* (TCI.) Englewood Cliffs, N.J.: Prentice-Hall.

2583. Hamburger, Michael P. "Besonderheiten der Herzogsfigur in *Measure for Measure.*" *SJW* 105(1969):158–67.

2584. Leech, Clifford. " 'More Than Our Brother is Our Chastity'." *CritQ* 12:73–74.

2585. Schlösser, Anselm. "Implizierte Satire in *Mass für Mass.*" *SJW* 106:100–26.

2586. Urnov, Dmitrij M. "Puschkin und Shakespeares *Mass für Mass.*" *SJW* 105(1969):140–57.

2587. Wasson, John. "*Measure for Measure*:A Text for Court Performance?" *SQ* 21:17–24.

* 2588. Weil, Herbert,Jr. "Form and Contexts in *Measure for Measure.*" *CritQ* 12:55–72.

See also 2685.

Merchant of Venice. 2589. Cooper, John R. "Shylock's Humanity." *SQ* 21:117–24.

2590. Cutts, John P.,ed. *The Merchant of Venice.* (Blackfriars Shakespeare Ser.) Dubuque, Iowa: Wm. Brown, 1969.

2591. Howard-Hill, T.H.,ed. The Merchant of Venice:*A Concordance to the Text of the First Folio.* (Oxford Shakespeare Concordances.) Oxford: Clarendon.

2592. Hyman, Lawrence W. "The Rival Lovers in *The Merchant of Venice.*" *SQ* 21:109–16.

2593. Leeuwe, Hans de. "Shakespeares Shylock:Europäische Darsteller einer berühmten Rolle." *KSGT* 23(1969):3–22.

2594. Milward, Peter. "The Religious Implications of *The Merchant of Venice.*" *ELLS* 6(1969):62–80.

2595. Nathan, Norman. " 'Abram,' Not 'Abraham,' in *The Merchant of Venice.*" *N&Q* 17:127–28.

2596. Østergaard, V.,tr. *Købmanden i Venezia.* Copenhagen: J.H. Schultz, 1969. ["Kommentar," 107–23; "Noter," 124–36.]

* 2597. Siemon, James E. "*The Merchant of Venice*:Act V as

Ritual Reiteration." *SP* 67:201–09.

Midsummer Night's Dream. 2598. Bennewitz, Fritz. "Ei Sommernachstraum am Deutschen Nationaltheater Weimar. *SJW* 106:11–28.

2599. Blount, Dale M. "Shakespeare's Use of the Folklore c Fairies and Magic in *A Midsummer Night's Dream* and *Th Tempest.*" *DAI* 30(1969):679A–80A(Ind.).

2600. Brooks, Harold F. "A Notorious Shakespearian Crux *Midsummer Night's Dream*, v,i.208." *N&Q* 17:125–27.

2601. Henning, Standish. "The Fairies of *A Midsumme Night's Dream.*" *SQ* 20(1969):484–86.

2602. Jochums, Milford C. "Artificial Motivation in *Midsummer Night's Dream.*" *Ill. State U. Jour.* 32,v:16–21.

2602a. Lewis, Allan. "*A Midsummer Night's Dream*—Fair Fantasy or Erotic Nightmare?" *ETJ* 21(1969):251–58.

2603. Østergaard, V.,tr. *En Skærsommernatsdrøm.* Copen hagen: J.H. Schultz, 1969. ["Kommentar," 89–99; "Noter, 100–06.]

2604. Scanlan, David,ed. *A Midsummer Night's Drean* Boston: Houghton Mifflin, 1969.

See also 2501.

Much Ado About Nothing. 2605. Draffan, Robert A. "Abou Much Ado." *EIC* 20:488–92. [Reply to Steven Rose, *EI 20*:143–50.]

2606. Lewalski, Barbara K. "Hero's Name—and Namesal —in *Much Ado About Nothing.*" *ELN* 7:175–79. [Chapman's tr. c Musaeus' *Hero and Leander.*]

2607. Lewalski, Barbara K.,ed. *Much Ado About Nothin* (Blackfriars Shakespeare Ser.) Dubuque, Iowa: Wm. Brow 1969.

2608. Rose, Steven. "Love and Self-Love in *Much Ado Abo Nothing.*" *EIC* 20:143–50.

See also 2467.

Othello. 2609. Baker, Stewart A. "Othello's 'Cause':A Ne Reading." *ELN* 7(1969):96–98.

2610. Dollarhide, Louis E. "Othello's Descent from Reason *UMSE* 9(1968):37–45.

2611. Doran, Madeleine. "Iago's 'if':An Essay on the Synta of *Othello.*" [F 46]:69–99.

2612. Faber, M.D. "The Summoning of Desdemona:*Othell* v,ii,1–82." *AN&Q* 9:35–37.

2613. Fleissner, Robert F. "The Magnetic Moor:An Ant Racist View." *Jour. of Human Relations* 17(1969):546–66.

2614. Hyman, Stanley E. "Iago Psychoanalytically Mot vated." *CentR* 14:369–84.

2615. —— "Portraits of the Artist:Iago and Prospero *Shenandoah* 21,ii:18–42.

2616. Loeffler, Peter. "Gordon Craig und Alfred Reucke Zwei Zürcher *Othello*-Aufführungen vom Jahre 1914 im Spieg der Kritik." [F 52]:135–40.

2617. Low, Anthony. "Othello and Cassio:'Unfortunately i the Infirmity'." *Archiv* 206:428–33.

2618. Matteo, Gino J. "Shakespeare's *Othello*:The Study an the Stage, 1604–1904." *DAI* 30(1969):689A–90A(Toronto).

2619. O'Dea, Richard J. "Desdemona:Tragic Heroine *Coranto* 6,i(1969):19–21.

2620. Østergaard, V.,tr. *Othello, Moren fra Venezia.* Cope hagen: J.H. Schultz, 1969. ["Kommentar," 145–62; "Noter 163–66.]

* 2621. Schwartz, Elias. "Stylistic 'Impurity' and the Meanir of *Othello.*" *SEL* 10:297–313.

* 2622. Zacha, Richard B. "Iago and the *Commedia dell'arte* *ArlQ* 2,ii(1969):98–116.

See also 2013.

Pericles. 2623. Barber, C.L. " 'Thou That Beget'st Him Th. Did Thee Beget':Transformation in *Pericles* and *The Winter Tale.*" *ShS* 22(1969):59–67.

2624. Lake, D.J. "The 'Pericles' Candidates—Heywoo Rowley, Wilkins." *N&Q* 17:135–41.

Phoenix and the Turtle. 2625. Campbell, K.T.S. "*The Phoen and the Turtle* as a Signpost of Shakespeare's Development." *B.* 10:169–79.

Richard II. 2626. Harris, Kathryn M. "Sun and Wate Imagery in *Richard II*:Its Dramatic Function." *SQ* 21:157–6

2627. Okubo, Junichiro. "*King Richard II* to Seiji." *EigoS* 15(1969):96–98. [*R2* and politics.]

2628. Trousdale, Marion. "Reality and Illusion in the Theatre." *CritQ* 11(1969):347–59.
See also 2643.

Richard III. 2629. Faure, François. "Langage religieux et langage pétrarquiste dans *Richard III* de Shakespeare." *EA* 23:23–37.

2630. Iwasaki, Soji. "*Richard III* ni okeru Sword-Image." *EigoS* 114(1968):676–78. [Sword-image in *Rich. III*.]

2631. Østergaard, V.,tr. *Richard III*. Copenhagen: J.H. Schultz, 1969. ["Noter," 157–62; "Kommentar," 163–71.]
See also 2013.

Romeo and Juliet. 2632. Berman, Ronald. "The Two Orders of *Romeo and Juliet*." *MSpr* 64:244–52.

2633. Burkhart, Robert E. "The Evidence for a Provincial Performance of Q1 *Romeo and Juliet*." *ELN* 7:9–13.

2634. Cole, Douglas,ed. *Twentieth Century Interpretations of Romeo and Juliet:A Collection of Critical Essays.* (TCI.) Englewood Cliffs, N.J.: Prentice-Hall. [Prev. pub. essays.]

2635. Gaines, Barry J. "The 'Grey-eyed Morne' Passage in *Romeo and Juliet*." *SQ* 21:196–98.

2636. Johnson, Robert C. "Four Young Men." *UR* 36(1969): 41–47.

2637. Østergaard, V.,tr. *Romeo og Julie*. Copenhagen: J.H. Schultz, 1969. ["Kommentar," 127–38; "Noter," 139–44.]

2638. Snyder, Susan. "*Romeo and Juliet*:Comedy into Tragedy." *EIC* 20:391–402.

2639. Spevack, Marvin,ed. *Romeo and Juliet.* (Blackfriars Shakespeare Ser.) Dubuque, Iowa: Wm. Brown.

2640. Versteeg, Robert. "A Multi-Media Production of *Romeo and Juliet*." *ETJ* 21(1969):259–74.

Sonnets. 2641. Campbell, S.C. "Only Begotten Sonnets." *TLS* 4 Sept:976.

2642. Donow, Herbert S. "Linear Word Count as a Function of Rhythm:An Analysis of Shakespeare's Sonnets." *Hephaistos* 1,i:1–27.

2643. Grivelet, Michel. "Shakespeare's 'War with Time':The Sonnets and *Richard II*." *ShS* 23:69–78.

2644. Haefner, Gerhard. "William Shakespeare Sonnet 130: Skizzen zu einer Interpretation." *NsM* 23:48–49.

2645. Helgerson, Richard. "Shakespeare's Sonnet CXXXVIII." *Expl* 28:Item 48.

2646. Ingram, W.G., and Theodore Redpath,eds. *Sonnets.* New York: Barnes & Noble, 1968.

2647. Jakobson, Roman, and Lawrence G. Jones. *Shakespeare's Verbal Art in "Th' Expense of Spirit."* (De Proprietatibus Litterarum, Ser. pract. 35.) The Hague: Mouton.

2648. Kogan, Pauline. "A Materialist Analysis of Shakespeare's Sonnets." *L&I* 1(1969):8–21.

2649. Koskimies, Rafael. "The Question of Platonism in Shakespeare's Sonnets." *NM* 71:260–70.

2650. Masui, Michio. "Shakespeare no *Sonnets* no Eigo." *EigoS* 114(1968):366–67. [English of S's sonnets.]

2651. Parker, David. "A Misprint in the New Cambridge Sonnets." *ShN* 20:46.

2652. Richards, I.A. "Jakobson's Shakespeare:The Subliminal Structures of a Sonnet." *TLS* 28 May:589–90.

2653. Rundle, James U. "The 'Source' of Shakespeare's Sonnet 30." *N&Q* 17:132–33.

2654. Smith, Barbara H.,ed. *Sonnets*. With Introd. New York: Avon, 1969.

2655. Steiner, George. "Commentary [on Sonnet 87 in Trs. by Stefan George and Karl Kraus]." *Delos* 4:175–84.
See also 2016, 2447, 2448, 2708.

Taming of the Shrew. *2656. Henze, Richard. "Role Playing in *The Taming of the Shrew*." *SHR* 4:231–40.

2657. Howard-Hill, T.H.,ed. The Taming of the Shrew:A Concordance to the Text of the First Folio. (Oxford Shakespeare Concordances.) Oxford: Clarendon.

Tempest. 2658. Barber, Lester E. "*The Tempest* and New Comedy." *SQ* 21:207–11.

2659. Boughner, Daniel C. "Jonsonian Structure in *The Tempest*." *SQ* 21:3–10.

2660. Dutu, Alexandru. "Le réveil de Prospero." *EA* 22(1969):225–30.

2661. Fehrenbach, Robert J. "Performance Dates of *The Tempest* in the 1677–78 Theatrical Season." *N&Q* 17:217–18.

2662. Levin, Harry. "Two Magian Comedies:*The Tempest* and *The Alchemist*." *ShS* 22(1969):47–58.

2663. Meyers, Jeffrey. "Savagery and Civilization in *The Tempest*, *Robinson Crusoe*, and *Heart of Darkness*." *Conradiana* 2:171–79.

2664. Østergaard, V.,tr. *Stormen*. Copenhagen: J.H. Schultz, 1969. ["Kommentar," 91–111; "Noter," 112–14.]

* 2665. Seiden, Melvin. "Utopianism in *The Tempest*." *MLQ* 31:3–21.

2666. Smith, Irwin. "Ariel and the Masque in *The Tempest*." *SQ* 21:213–22.

2667. Thomas, Paruvananit. "Dramatic Form and the Use of Verse in *The Tempest* and *Sakuntalam*." *DAI* 30:5005A(N.Y.U.).

* 2668. Uphaus, Robert W. "Virtue in Vengeance:Prospero's Rarer Action." *BuR* 18,ii:34–51.
See also 2599, 2615, 2909, 4137.

The Merry Wives of Windsor. 2669. Baudemont, Mme. "Shakespeare's Prose in *The Merry Wives of Windsor*." *LanM* 63(1969):61–65.

2670. Glenn, George D. "*The Merry Wives of Windsor* on the Nineteenth-Century Stage." *DAI* 30(1969):1264A(Ill.).

2671. Østergaard, V.,tr. *De muntre Koner i Windsor*. Copenhagen: J.H. Schultz, 1969. ["Kommentar," 137–44; "Noter," 145–53.]

Timon of Athens. *2672. Bergeron, David M. "Alchemy and *Timon of Athens*." *CLAJ* 13:364–73.

2673. Lancashire, Anne. "*Timon of Athens*:Shakespeare's *Dr. Faustus*." *SQ* 21:35–44.

2674. Nojima, Hidekatsu. "Timon to Apemantus." *EigoS* 114(1968):433–34. [T and A; in Jap.]

2675. Pauls, Peter. "Shakespeare's *Timon of Athens*:An Examination of the Misanthrope Tradition and Shakespeare's Handling of Sources." *DAI* 30(1969):1146A–47A(Wis.).

2676. Reid, Stephen A. " 'I am Misanthropos'—A Psychoanalytic Reading of Shakespeare's *Timon of Athens*." *PsyR* 56(1969):442–52.

Titus Andronicus. 2677. Ettin, Andrew V. "Shakespeare's First Roman Tragedy." *ELH* 37:325–41.

2678. Jorgensen, Paul A. "Shakespeare's Dark Vocabulary." [F 46]:108–22. [In *Titus Andronicus*, *Hamlet*, and *Macbeth*.]

2679. Reese, Jack E. "The Formalization of Horror in *Titus Andronicus*." *SQ* 21:77–84.

2680. Shadoian, Jack. "Titus Andronicus." *Discourse* 13: 152–75.
See also 2013.

Troilus and Cressida. 2681. Cary, Cecile E. "*Troilus and Cressida* and *All's Well That Ends Well*:Shakespeare's Two Ironic Plays." *DAI* 30:2961A(Wash. U.).

2682. Kawaji, Yoshiko. "A Study of Shakespeare's *Troilus and Cressida*." [F 14]:26–40.

2683. Okamoto, Yasumasa. "*Troilus and Cressida*—Owari no nai Owari." *EigoS* 115(1969):228–29. [*T&C*—end without end.]

2684. Ramsey, Jarold W. "The Provenance of *Troilus and Cressida*." *SQ* 21:223–40.

2685. Reid, Stephen A. "A Psychoanalytic Reading of *Troilus and Cressida* and *Measure for Measure*." *PsyR* 57:263–82.

2686. Rowland, Beryl. "A Cake-Making Image in *Troilus and Cressida*." *SQ* 21:191–94.

* 2687. Sacharoff, Mark. "Tragic vs. Satiric:Hector's Conduct in II, ii of Shakespeare's *Troilus and Cressida*." *SP* 67:517–31.

2688. Sampietro, Luigi. "Su *Troilo e Cressida*." *AllaB* 8,ii: 26–29.

2689. Stockholder, Katherine. "Power and Pleasure in *Troilus and Cressida*:Or, Rhetoric and Structure of the Anti-Tragic." *CE* 30(1969):539–54.

2690. Zulandt, George K. "Shakespeare's *Troilus and Cressida* in Relation to English Drama of 1597 to 1604." *DAI* 30(1969): 347A–48A(Ohio State).

Twelfth Night. 2691. Calkins, Roger. "The Renaissance Idea of 'Imitation' and Shakespeare's *Twelfth Night*." [F 47]:52–66.

2692. Howard-Hill, T.H.,ed. *Twelfth Night.* (Blackfriars Shakespeare Ser.) Dubuque, Iowa: Wm. Brown, 1969.

2693. Musgrove, S. "Feste's Dishonesty:An Interpretation of *Twelfth Night* I.v.1–30." *SQ* 21:194–96.

2694. Musgrove, S.,ed. *Twelfth Night:Or, What You Will.* (Fountainwell Drama Texts 12.) London: Oliver and Boyd; Berkeley: U. of Calif. P., 1969.

2695. Preston, Dennis R. "The Minor Characters in *Twelfth Night.*" *SQ* 21:167–76.

* 2696. Schuchter, J.D. "Shakespeare's *Twelfth Night,* I,iii,42." *Expl* 29:Item 3.

2697. Twelfth Night:*A Concordance to the Text of the First Folio.* (Oxford Shakespeare Concordances.) Oxford: Clarendon, 1969.

See also 2467.

Two Gentlemen of Verona. 2698. Howard-Hill, T.H.,ed. Two Gentlemen of Verona:*A Concordance to the Text of the First Folio.* (Oxford Shakespeare Concordances.) London: Oxford U.P., 1969.

2700. Weimann, Robert. "Das 'Lachen mit dem Publikum': *Die beiden Veroneser* und die volkstümliche Komödientradition." *SJW* 106:85–99.

2701. —— "Laughing with the Audience:*The Two Gentlemen of Verona* and the Popular Tradition of Comedy." *ShS* 22(1969): 35–42.

Winter's Tale. 2702. Hartwig, Joan. "The Tragicomic Perspective of *The Winter's Tale.*" *ELH* 37:12–36.

2703. Holland, Joanne F. "The Gods of *The Winter's Tale.*" *PCP* 5:34–38.

2704. Howard-Hill, T.H.,ed. The Winter's Tale:*A Concordance to the Text of the First Folio.* (Oxford Shakespeare Concordances.) Oxford: Clarendon.

2705. Matchett, William H. "Some Dramatic Techniques in *The Winter's Tale.*" *ShS* 22(1969):93–107.

2706. Ortego, Philip D. "The *Winter's Tale* as a Pastoral Tragicomic Romance." *Rendezvous* 5,i:31–34.

2707. Rittenhouse, David. "A Victorian *Winter's Tale.*" *QQ* 77:41–55.

2708. Warren, Roger. " 'Gust' and Poisoned Cups in The *Winter's Tale* and Sonnet 114." *N&Q* 17:134–35.

2709. Wickham, Glynne. "Shakespeare's Investiture Play:The Occasion and Subject of *The Winter's Tale.*" *TLS* 18 Dec(1969): 1456. [See also 8 Jan:34; 22 Jan:84.]

See also 2474, 2623.

VII. SEVENTEENTH CENTURY

Bibliography. 2710. Guffey, George R.,comp. *Elizabethan Bibliographies Supplements XI:Traherne and the Seventeenth-Century English Platonists 1900–1966.* London: Nether P., 1969. [On Cudworth, Culverwel, H. More, Norris, Rust, J. Smith, Sterry, Whichcote, Worthington.]

2711. Stensgaard, Richard. "Shakespeare, Paracelsus, and the Plague of 1603:An Annotated List." *SRO* 4(1968–69):73–77. *See also* 1966.

General and Miscellaneous. 2712. Barber, Giles. "Bindings from Oxford Libraries III:The Vice-Chancellor's Official *New Testament,* Oxford, 1721." *BLR* 8:191–95.

2713. Bekkers, J.A.,ed. *Correspondence of John Morris with Johannes de Laet (1634–1649).* Assen: Van Gorcum.

2714. Bennett, H.S. *English Books and Readers III:1603–1640.* London: Cambridge U.P.

2715. Breslow, M.A. *A Mirror of England:English Puritan Views of Foreign Nations, 1616–1640.* (Harvard Hist. Studies 84.) Cambridge: Harvard U.P.

2716. Chaussy, Dom Yves. "New Evidence on the English Benedictines:I. John Barnes (1581?–1661), II. William Gifford, Archbishop of Rheims." *DownR* 88:36–56.

2717. Cope, Jackson I. "Modes of Modernity in Seventeenth-Century Prose." *MLQ* 31:92–111.

2718. Fietz, Lothar. "Fragestellung und Tendenzen der anglistischen Barock-Forschung." *DVLG* 43(1969):752–63.

2719. Geduld, Harry N. *Prince of Publishers.* (IUHS 66.) Bloomington: Ind. U.P. [Works and career of Jacob Tonson.]

2720. Hoare, P.A. "An Early Serial Publication:*A General View of the World, or the Marrow of History.*" *Library* 25:53–57.

2721. Illo, John P. "The Decline of Belief in the Miraculous in English Thought and Letters." *DAI* 30(1969):1983A (Columbia).

2722. Macfarlane, Alan. *The Family Life of Ralph Josselin, a Seventeenth-Century Clergyman:An Essay in Historical Anthropology.* New York: Cambridge U.P. [Lit. interest.]

2723. MacGillivray, Royce. "Edmund Borlase, Historian of the Irish Rebellion." *SH* 9(1969):86–92.

2724. Peel, Edgar, and Pat Southern. *The Trials of the Lancashire Witches:A Study of Seventeenth Century Witchcraft.* New York: Taplinger, 1969.

2725. Rauchbauer, Otto. "Zur Definition und Konzeption des englischen Essays im 17. Jahrhundert." *GRM* 20:146–59.

2726. Sprott, S.E. "Sir Edmund Baynham." *Recusant Hist.* 10,ii(1969; pub. 1970):96–110. [B=captain of the "Damned Crew"; see Bibliog. for 1969, Vol. I, Item 2974.]

* 2727. Steiner, Thomas R. "Precursors to Dryden:English and French Theories of Translation in the Seventeenth Century." *CLS* 7:50–81.

* 2728. Waingrow, Marshall. "Recent Studies in the Restoration and Eighteenth Century." *SEL* 10:605–36. [Rev. art.]

2729. Wedgwood, C.V. *Seventeenth-Century English Literature.* London: Oxford U.P. [2d ed.]

2730. Weidhorn, Manfred. *Dreams in Seventeenth-Century Literature.* (SEngL 57.) The Hague: Mouton.

2731. Wrenn, C.L. "The Earliest English Students of Russian." *BSE* 8(1969):197–203. [G. Fletcher, J. Horsey, M. Ridley, R. James, *inter alia.*]

2732. Zacharasiewicz, Waldemar. *Die "Cosmic Voyage" und die "Excursion" in der englischen Dichtung des 17. und 18. Jahrhunderts.* Wien: Notring, 1968. [Diss., Graz.]

2733. Zall, P.M.,ed. A Nest of Ninnies *and Other English Jestbooks of the Seventeenth Century.* Lincoln: U. of Neb. P. *See also* 1054, 1961, 1963, 1964, 2441, 2951, 3091, 3202, 3227, 3282.

Biography and Autobiography. 2734. Singleton, Robert R. "English Criminal Biography, 1651–1722." *HLB* 19:63–83.

Drama and Theater. 2735. Allen, Richard O. "Jacobean Drama and the Literature of Decay:A Study of Conservative Reaction in Literature." *DAI* 30:3899A–900A(Mich.).

2736. Cameron, Kenneth M. "Jo Haynes, *Infamis.*" *TN* 24:56–57.

2737. Crandall, Coryl,ed. Swetnam the Woman-Hater:*The Controversy and the Play.* Lafayette, Ind.: Purdue U. Studies, 1969.

2738. Davison, Dennis,ed. *Restoration Comedies.* London: Oxford U.P. [Anthol.]

2739. Dewey, Nicholas. "The Academic Drama of the Early Stuart Period (1603–1642):A Checklist of Secondary Sources." *RORD* 12(1969):33–42.

2740. Donaldson, Ian. *The World Upside-Down:Comedy from Jonson to Fielding.* London: Oxford U.P.

2741. Huneycutt, Melicent. "The Changing Concept of the Ideal Statesman as Reflected in English Verse Drama During the Reign of Charles II:1660–1685." *DAI* 30(1969):685A–86A(N.C., Chapel Hill).

2742. James, E. Nelson. " 'Drums and Trumpets' (Part I)." *RECTR* 9,ii:46–55. [On battle scenes in heroic drama.]

* 2743. Jones, Robert C. "Italian Settings and the 'World' of Elizabethan Tragedy." *SEL* 10:251–68. [Emphasis on Marston, Tourneur, and Webster.]

2744. Koonce, Howard L. "Comic Values and Comic Form:The Restoration Comedy of Manners in Its Tradition." *DAI* 30:4990A(Pa.).

2745. Love, Harold. "Bear's Case Laid Open:Or, a Timely Warning to Literary Sociologists." *Komos* 2(1969):72–80. [Reply to Bibliog. for 1969, Vol. I, Item 2982a.]

3229. Ochester, Edwin F. "A Source for Shirley's *The Contention of Ajax and Ulysses.*" *N&Q* 17:217.

See also 2748.

Sibbes. 3230. Affleck, Bert. "The Theology of Richard Sibbes, 1577–1635." *DAI* 30(1969):2120A(Drew).

Southerne. *See* 2927.

Suckling. *3232. Beaurline, L.A., and Thomas Clayton. "Notes on Early Editions of *Fragmenta Aurea.*" *SB* 23:165–70.

3233. Madoc-Jones, Enid. "Mary Bulkeley:The Aglaura of the Poet Suckling." *AWR* 18,xlii:196–203.

Temple. 3234. Steensma, Robert C. *Sir William Temple.* (TEAS 109.) New York: Twayne.

Tofte. *3235. Hardin, Richard F. "Robert Tofte's Translation of Ariosto's Satires." *SNL* 7:104–08.

Tourneur. 3236. Kaufmann, R.J. "Theodicy, Tragedy and the Psalmist:Tourneur's *Atheist's Tragedy.*" *CompD* 3(1969-70): 241–62.

3237. Maxwell, J.C. "*The Atheist's Tragedy* 1792 and 1794." *N&Q* 17:214–15.

3238. Stagg, Louis C. *An Index to the Figurative Language of Cyril Tourneur's Tragedies.* Charlottesville: Bibliog. Soc. of the U. of Va.

* 3239. Sternlicht, Sanford. "Tourneur's Imagery and *The Revenger's Tragedy.*" *PLL* 6:192–97.

See also 2011.

Traherne. 3240. Clements, A.L. *The Mystical Poetry of Thomas Traherne.* Cambridge: Harvard U.P., 1969.

3241. —— "Thomas Traherne:A Chronological Bibliography." *LC* 35(1969):36–51.

3243. Stewart, Stanley N. *The Expanded Voice:The Art of Thomas Traherne.* San Marion, Calif.: Huntington Lib.

Ussher. 3244. Coe, Michael D. "The Fall of the House of Ussher." *Midway* 8,iv(1968):81–89.

Vanbrugh. 3245. Berkowitz, Gerald M. "The Plays of Sir John Vanbrugh and the Comedy of the Late Seventeenth Century." *DAI* 30:2997A(Ind.).

3246. Mayo, Marianne K. "John Vanbrugh's *The Relapse*:A Study of Its Meaning." *DAI* 30(1969):331A–32A(Fla.).

3247. Van Niel, Pieter Jan. "*The Relapse*—Into Death and Damnation." *ETJ* 21(1969):318–32.

3248. Zimansky, Curt A.,ed. *The Provoked Wife.* (RRestDS.) Lincoln: U. of Neb. P., 1969.

Vaughan, H. 3249. Dale, James. "Biblical Allusion in Vaughan's 'The World'." *ES* 51:336–39.

3250. Daniels, Edgar F. "Vaughan's 'Regeneration':An Emendation." *AN&Q* 9:19–20.

3251. Oleyar, Rita B. "The Biblical Wilderness in Vaughan, Herbert and Milton." *DAI* 30(1969):287A–88A(Calif., Irvine).

3252. Wilson, Gayle E. "A Characteristic of Vaughan's Style and Two Meditative Poems:'Corruption' and 'Day of Judgement'." *Style* 4:119–31.

See also 2874, 2893.

Vaughan, T. 3253. Crawshaw, Eluned. "Thomas Vaughan and 'That Slidynge Science,' Alchemy." *AWR* 18,xlii:146–55.

3254. —— "Thomas Vaughan, Magician." *AntigR* 1,i:93–97.

Waller. *3255. Wikelund, Philip R. "Edmund Waller's Fitt of Versifying:Deductions from a Holograph Fragment, Folger MS. x.d. 309." *PQ* 49:68–91.

See also 2931.

Walton. *See* 5304.

Webster. 3256. Ansari, K.H. *John Webster:Image Patterns and Canon.* Delhi: Sterling Pubs.; Mystic, Conn.: Verry, 1969.

3257. Brown, John R.,ed. *The Duchess of Malfi.* (Revels Play Ser.) London: Methuen, 1969.

3258. Carey, Robin B. "A Critical Edition of John Webster's *The Duchess of Malfi.*" *DAI* 30:4937A–38A(U. of Wash.).

3259. Davison, Richard A. "John Webster's Moral View Re-examined." *MSpr* 63(1969):213–23.

3260. Gentry, Thomas B. "The Dramatic Functions of Rhetorical Devices in the Plays of John Webster." *DAI* 30(1969):1980A–81A(Ky.).

3261. Giannetti, Louis D. "A Contemporary View of *The Duchess of Malfi.*" *CompD* 3(1969-70):297–307.

3262. Gunby, D.C. "Webster:Another Borrowing from Jonson's *Sejanus.*" *N&Q* 17:214.

3263. Hunter, G.K. and S.K.,eds. *John Webster:A Critical Anthology.* With Introd. Baltimore: Penguin, 1969. [Selected crit. 17th–20th c.]

3264. Knight, G. Wilson. "*The Duchess of Malfi.*" *MHRev* 4(1967):88–113.

3265. Loftis, John. "*The Duchess of Malfi* on the Spanish and English Stages." *RORD* 12(1969):25–31.

3266. Mulryne, J.R.,ed. *The White Devil.* Lincoln: U. of Neb. P.

3267. Murray, Peter B. *A Study of John Webster.* (SEngL 50.) The Hague: Mouton, 1969.

3268. Ono, Kyoichi. "Malfi Koshaku Fujin no Higeki." *EigoS* 114(1968):584–85. [Tragedy of *The Duchess of Malfi.*]

* 3269. Pratt, Samuel M. "Webster's *The White Devil*, v,iv,115." *Expl* 29:Item 11.

3270. Schuman, Samuel. "The Theater of Fine Devices: Emblems and the Emblematic in the Plays of John Webster." *DAI* 30:4425A(Northwestern).

Whitlock. *See* 2808.

Wither. 3271. Hensley, Charles S. *The Later Career of George Wither.* (SEngL 43.) The Hague and Paris: Mouton, 1969.

Wycherley. 3272. Lagarde, Fernand. "L'art de Wycherley créateur de personnages dans *The Country Wife.*" *Caliban* 7:3–21.

3273. Malekin, Peter. "Wycherley's Dramatic Skills and the Interpretation of *The Country Wife.*" *DUJ* 31(1969):32–40.

3274. Richardson, William M. "Wycherley and the Shock of Disillusionment." *DAI* 30(1969):1992A–93A(Texas Christian).

3275. Rump, Eric S. "The Drama of William Wycherley." *DAI* 30:4425A(Toronto).

See also 2744, 3512.

VIII. EIGHTEENTH CENTURY

Bibliography. 3276. [Anon.] "The Osborn Collection at Yale." *Scriblerian* 3,i:33–34. [Incl. text of anon. "Eulogium of A. Pope."]

3277. Brack, O M,Jr.,et al. "English Literature, 1660–1800:A Current Bibliography." *PQ* 49:289–399.

3278. Cordasco, Francesco. *Eighteenth Century Bibliographies.* Handlists of Critical Studies Relating to Smollett, Richardson, Sterne, Fielding, Dibdin, 18th Cent. Medicine, the 18th Cent. Novel, Godwin, Gibbon, Young, and Blake. To Which Is Added John P. Anderson's Bibliography of Smollett. Metuchen, N.J.: Scarecrow. [Repr. in 1 vol. of *18th Century Bibliography Pamphlets,* Nos. 1–12. With new Introd.]

3279. Hartog, Curt H. "The George Sherburn Collection at the University of Illinois." *Scriblerian* 2:68–70.

3280. Montgomerie, William. "A Bibliography of the Scottish Ballad Manuscripts 1730–1825." *SSL* 7:60–75.

See also 1079, 3357, 3484.

General and Miscellaneous. 3281. Bauter, Herbert. *Die Sprachauffassung der englischen Vorromantik in ihrer Bedeutung für die Literaturkritik und die Dictungstheorie der Zeit.* (Frankfurter Beiträge zur Anglistik und Amerikanistik.) Bad Homburg: Gehlen.

3282. Binni, Francesco. "Inizi della critica di sensibilità." *EM* 20(1969):163–82.

3283. Braudy, Leo. *Narrative Form in History and Fiction.* Princeton, N.J.: Princeton U.P. [Hume, Fielding, Gibbon.]

3284. Burke, Joseph. "Hogarth, Handel and Roubiliac:A Note on the Interrelationships of the Arts in England, c. 1730 to 1760." *ECS* 3(1969):157–74.

3285. Cuthbertson, Gilbert. "Commentaries on Constitutional Innovations in the Eighteenth Century." *SBHT* 11: 1452–62.

* 3286. Dickinson, Harry. "The October Club." *HLQ* 33: 155–73.

3287. Downey, James. *The Eighteenth Century Pulpit:A Study of The Sermons of Butler, Berkeley, Secker, Sterne, Whitefield and Wesley.* Oxford: Clarendon, 1969.

3288. Duffy, Eamon. "Doctor Douglass and Mister Berington—An Eighteenth-Century Retraction." *DownR* 88: 246–69. [On Roman Catholic thought in England.]

3289. Gilmore, Thomas B.,Jr. *The Eighteenth-Century Controversy Over Ridicule as a Test of Truth:A Reconsideration.* (Research Paper 25.) Atlanta: Ga. State U.

3290. Greenway, George L. "Some Predecessors of Sir Joshua Reynolds in the Criticism of the Fine Arts." *DAI* 30:3905A–06A(Yale).

3291. Hamilton-Edwards, Gerald. "Varied Information in Scotland's Register of Deeds." *N&Q* 17:96–98.

3292. Hytier, Adrienne. "An Eighteenth-Century Experiment in Historical Realism:The Marquis d'Argenson and Bonnie Prince Charlie." *ECS* 3(1969):200–41.

3293. Kahn, Robert L. "Seume and the English." [F 28]: 47–68. [On travel lit. esp.]

3294. Kaufman, Paul. *Libraries and Their Users:Collected Papers in Library History.* London: The Library Assn., 1969. ["Coffee Houses as Reading Centres," 115–27.]

3295. —— "The Eighteenth-Century London and Westminster Library Societies:A Sequel." *Library* 25:237–47.

3296. —— "Two Eighteenth-Century Guides to the Choice of Books." *Lib. Hist.* 1(1969):146–52.

3297. King, E.H. "A Scottish 'Philosophical' Club in the Eighteenth Century." *DR* 50:201–14.

3298. Lipking, Lawrence. *The Ordering of the Arts in Eighteenth-Century England.* Princeton: Princeton U.P.

* 3299. Malek, James. "Art as Mind Shaped by Medium:The Significance of James Harris' 'A Discourse on Music, Painting and Poetry' in Eighteenth-Century Aesthetics." *TSLL* 12:231–39.

3300. McElroy, Davis D. *Scotland's Age of Improvement:A Survey of Eighteenth-Century Literary Clubs and Societies.* Pullman: Wash. State U.P., 1969.

3301. Pagliaro, Harold E.,comp. *Major English Writers of the Eighteenth Century.* New York: Free Press, 1969.

3302. Paulson, Ronald. "Zoffany and Wright of Derby: Contexts of English Art in the Late Eighteenth Century." *ECS* 3(1969):278–95. [Rev. art.]

3303. Perry, Norma. "Jean-Jacques Rousseau and the West Country." *FS* 24:14–22.

* 3304. Preston, Thomas R. "Historiography as Art in Eighteenth-Century England." *TSLL* 11(1969):1209–21.

3305. Quintana, Ricardo. "Augustan Politics and Men of Letters:Some Problems, Some Approaches." *EA* 22(1969):386–92.

* 3306. Rawson, C[laude] J. "Nature's Dance of Death, Part I:Urbanity and Strain in Fielding, Swift and Pope." *ECS* 3:307–38.

3307. Reid, B.L. *The Long Boy and Others:Eighteenth-Century Studies.* Athens: U. of Ga. P.

3308. Shaw, David. "The First English Editions of Horace, Juvenal, and Persius." *Library* 25:219–25.

3309. Spacks, Patricia M.,ed. *Late Augustan Prose.* Englewood Cliffs, N.J.: Prentice-Hall.

3310. Stewart, Mary M. "The Account Books of John Caryll." *N&Q* 17:288–93. [Incl. refs. to Pope.]

3311. Tillotson, Geoffrey, Paul Fussell,Jr., and Marshall Waingrow,eds. *Eighteenth-Century English Literature.* New York: Harcourt, Brace & World, 1969. [Anthol.]

3312. Traugott, John L. "The Professor as Nibelung." *ECS* 3:532–43. [Critique of some trends and problems in 18th c. crit. and scholarship, using Swift as primary ex.]

3313. Trickett, Rachel. "The Difficulties of Defining and Categorizing in the Augustan Period." *NLH* 1:163–79.

3314. White, Robert B.,Jr. "An Eighteenth Century Allusion to Chaucer's *Cook's Tale.*" *ELN* 7:190–92.

See also 502, 1741, 1963, 2721, 2728, 2732, 3351, 3467, 3663, 3741, 3792, 3892.

Biography and Autobiography. 3315. Hankins, John R. "The Eighteenth-Century English Biographer and His Sources." *DAI* 30:3906A(Case Western Reserve).

See also 2734.

Criticism. 3316. Eberwein, Robert T. "The Imagination and

Didactic Theory in Eighteenth-Century English Criticism." *DAI* 30(1969):1132A–33A(Wayne State).

3317. Kallich, Martin. *The Association of Ideas and Critical Theory in Eighteenth-Century England:A History of Psychological Method in English Criticism.* (SEngL 55.) The Hague: Mouton.

3318. Keig, Judith. "Theories of Cultural History in Eighteenth-Century English Literary Criticism." *DAI* 30:4416A (Columbia).

3319. Rands, Alma Clare. "Thomas Brown's Theories of Association and Perception as They Relate to His Theories of Poetry." *JAAC* 28:473–83.

See also 3467, 3634.

Drama and Theater. 3320. Bevis, Richard W.,ed. *Eighteenth Century Drama:Afterpieces.* With Introd. New York and London: Oxford U.P.

3321. Burgess, C.F. "Thomas Davies and the Authorship of *A Genuine Narrative...*, The Life of John Henderson." *RECTR* 9,i:24–34. [Evidence for attrib. *A Genuine Narrative* to D.]

3322. Kaufman, Paul. "The Reading of Plays in the Eighteenth Century." *BNYPL* 73(1969):562–80.

3323. Keenan, Joseph J.,Jr. "The Poetic of High Georgian Comedy:A Study of the Comic Theory and Practice of Murphy, Colman, and Cumberland." *DAI* 30:5412A–13A(Wis.).

3324. Largmann, Malcolm G. "Stage References as Satiric Weapon:Sir Robert Walpole as Victim." *RECTR* 9,i:35–43.

3325. Lawhon, Minnie L. " 'Angel of Dulness':The Career of John Rich." *DAI* 30(1969):1140A–41A(Cornell).

3326. Milburn, Douglas,Jr. "The Popular Reaction to German Drama in England at the End of the Eighteenth Century." [F 28]:149–62.

3327. Mitchell, Louis D. "Command Performances During the Reign of Queen Anne." *TN* 24:111–19.

3328. Nalbach, Daniel F. "History of the King's Opera House 1704–1867." *DAI* 30(1969):2188A(Pittsburgh).

3329. Pearlman, E. "The Hamlet of Robert Wilks." *TN* 24:125–33.

3330. Sawyer, Paul. "The Popularity of Various Types of Entertainment at Lincoln's Inn Fields and Covent Garden Theatres, 1720–1733." *TN* 24:154–63.

3332. Tasch, Peter A. "Bickerstaff, Colman and the Bourgeois Audience." *RECTR* 9,i:44–50. [An attempt to account for the success of Bickerstaffe's *Love in the City* and the failure of Colman's *The English Merchant.*]

3333. Taylor, William D.,ed. *Eighteenth Century Comedy.* Introd. and notes by Simon Trussler. London: Oxford U.P. [New ed. of anthol. which incl. *The Beaux Stratagem, The Conscious Lovers, The Beggar's Opera, The Tragedy of Tragedies,* and *She Stoops to Conquer.*]

3334. Thomson, Margaret H. "The Theatrical Value of the English Eighteenth Century Satirical Print." *DAI* 30(1969): 859A(Yale).

* 3335. Tobin, Terence. "A List of Plays and Entertainments by Scottish Dramatists, 1660–1800." *SB* 23:103–17.

3336. —— "A List of Anonymous Pieces Presented at the Theatre Royal, Edinburgh, 1767–1800." *SSL* 7:29–34.

3337. Trussler, Simon,ed. *Burlesque Plays of the Eighteenth Century.* London: Oxford U.P., 1969. [Anthol.]

3338. Wagner, Charlotte A. "Theatrical Narrative Dance in England:1747–1776." *DAI* 30(1969):699A(N.Y.U.).

3339. Whitty, John C. "The Half-Price Riots of 1763." *TN* 24(1969):25–32.

See also 2740, 2746, 2747, 2752, 2754, 2755, 3465, 3680, 3910.

Periodicals. *See* 3551, 3922.

Poetry. 3340. Budick, Sanford. "The Demythological Mode in Augustan Verse." *ELH* 37:389–414.

* 3341. Foster, John W. "A Redefinition of Topographical Poetry." *JEGP* 69:394–406. [Incl. discussions of Jonson, Denham, Waller, Pope, Dyer, Jago, Bowles, Woodhouse, Wordsworth.]

3342. Lowth, Robert. *Lectures on the Sacred Poetry of the Hebrews (1787).* (Anglistica & Americana 43.) Introd. Vincent Freimark. Hildesheim: Olms, 1969.

3343. Maresca, Thomas E. "Language and Body in Augustan Poetic." *ELH* 37:374–88.

3344. Morris, David B. "The Religious Sublime:Judeo-

Christian Tradition in Eighteenth-Century English Poetry and Criticism." *DAI* 30(1969):287A(Minn.).

* 3345. Sambrook, A.J. "Additions to Bond's Register of Burlesque Poems." *SB* 23:176–79.

3346. —— "An Essay on Eighteenth-Century Pastoral, Pope to Wordsworth (I)." *Trivium* 5:21–35.

3347. Sambrook, James. "Some Heirs of Goldsmith:Poets of the Poor in the Late Eighteenth Century." *SBHT* 11(1969): 1348–61.

3348. Stratmann, Gerd,ed. *Augustan Poetry.* Tübingen: Niemeyer.

3349. Wimsatt, W.K. "Imitation as Freedom—1717–1798." *NLH* 1:215–36.

3350. —— "Imitation of Freedom:1717–1798." [F 48]:47–74. *See also* 2765, 2766, 3319, 3927.

Prose Fiction. *3351. Donaldson, Ian. "The Clockwork Novel:Three Notes on an Eighteenth-Century Analogy." *RES* 21:14–22. [Uses of analogy by Hobbes, Locke, Descartes, Leibniz, Fielding, Johnson, Sterne, Richardson.]

* 3352. Evans, James E. "Fiction Rather Than Fact:A New Look at *The King and the Beggar*." *LC* 36:110–14.

3353. Greenberg, Linda D. "The Clerical Hero in the Fiction of the Later Eighteenth Century." *DAI* 30:5408A–09A(Wis.).

3354. Grieder, Josephine. "The Prose Fiction of Baculard d'Arnaud in Late Eighteenth-Century England." *FS* 24:113–26.

3355. Kuhn, Albert J.,ed. *Three Sentimental Novels.* New York: Holt, Rinehart and Winston, 1969. [*A Sentimental Journey Through France and Italy*, Sterne; *The Man of Feeling*, Mackenzie; *The History of Sandford and Merton* (abridged), Day.]

3356. Lovett, Robert W. "The Use of America for Setting and as Image in Eighteenth-Century Fiction from the Restoration to the American Revolution." *DAI* 30(1969):2030A(Emory).

3357. Meeker, Richard K. "Bank Note, Corkscrew, Flea and Sedan:A Checklist of Eighteenth-Century Fiction." *LC* 35(1969): 52–57. [Restricted to "works of fiction written from a non-human point of view."]

3358. Mews, Hazel. *Frail Vessels:Women's Role in Women's Novels from Fanny Burney to George Eliot.* London: Athlone Press, 1969.

3359. Poenicke, Klaus. " 'Schönheit im Schosse des Schreckens':Raumgefüge und Menschenbild im englischen Schauerroman." *Archiv* 207:1–19. [Radcliffe, Reeve, and Walpole.]

* 3360. Sacks, Sheldon. "Golden Birds and Dying Generations." *CLS* 6(1969):274–91. [18th and 19th c. Eng. Novelists.]

3361. Topf, Melvyn A. "An Inquiry into Some Relations Between the Epistemology of the Novel and Its Origins." *DAI* 30:5006A(Penn. State). [On Defoe, Fielding, Richardson, and Sterne.]

3362. Williams, Ioan M. *Novel and Romance, 1700–1800:A Documentary Record.* London: Routledge & K. Paul. [A coll. of essays on the novel and romance by 18ᵗʰ cent. novelists and writers.]

See also 966, 1488, 1491, 2775.

Satire. *3363. Carnochan, W.B. "Satire, Sublimity, and Sentiment:Theory and Practice in Post-Augustan Satire." *PMLA* 85:260–67.

3364. Lockwood, Thomas. "The Augustan Author-Audience Relationship:Satiric vs. Comic Forms." *ELH* 36(1969):648–58.

3365. Macey, Samuel L.,ed. Anon. *A Learned Dissertation on Dumpling* (1726) and *Pudding and Dumpling Burnt to Pot. Or, a Compleat Key to the Dissertation on Dumpling* (1727). (ARS Pub. 140.) With Introd. Los Angeles: Wm. Andrews Clark Mem. Lib., U.C.L.A.

See also 2777, 4135.

Translation. 3366. Bussy, Carvel de. "A Study of William Kenrick's English Translation of Rousseau's *Julie, ou la nouvelle Héloise*." *DAI* 30(1969):2524A–25A(Catholic U.).

Addison. 3367. Abernethy, Cecil. "Addison and Swift:A Note on Style and Manners." [F 16]:1–8.

3368. Campbell, Hilbert H. "The Intellectual Position of Joseph Addison in Philosophy, Religion, and Science." *DAI* 30(1969):2015A(Ky.).

3369. Carter, Charlotte A. "Personae and Characters in the Essays of Addison, Steele, Fielding, Johnson, Goldsmith." *DAI* 30:4938A(Denver).

3370. Rau, Fritz. "Zum Gehalt des *Tatler* und *Spectator*: Forschungsbericht." *Anglia* 88:42–93.

See also 3116, 3723.

Akenside. *3371. Norton, John. "Akenside's *The Pleasures of Imagination*:An Exercise in Poetics." *ECS* 3:366–83.

Anstey. *See* 3363.

Arbuthnot. 3372. Freehafer, John. "Arbuthnot and the Dublin Pirates." *Scriblerian* 2:65–67.

3374. Weidenborner, Stephen S. "The Influence of John Arbuthnot on the Scientific Attitudes Expressed by Pope, Swift, and the Scriblerus Club." *DAI* 30:3440A(N.Y.U.).

Atterbury. 3375. Hill, Patricia K. "The Jacobite Bishop of Rochester." *DAI* 30:3400A(Ga.).

Barbauld. 3376. Moore, Catherine E. "The Literary Career of Anna Laetitia Barbauld." *DAI* 30:3912A(N.C.).

Beattie. 3377. Malek, James S. "The Influence of Empirical Psychology on Aesthetic Discourse:Two Eighteenth Century Theories of Art." *EnlE* 1,i:1–16. [B's and Sir Wm. Jones's.]

See also 4870.

Beckford. 3378. Carnero, Guillermo. "William Beckford (1760–1844) o el erotismo de fina estampa." *Insula* 24(Oct–Nov 1969):18–19.

Bickerstaffe. *See* 3332.

Blake. 3379. Adams, Hazard,ed. *Jerusalem. Selected Poems, and Prose.* New York: Holt, Rinehart and Winston.

3381. Bacon, M.E. "Blake's Imitation of Pope:'A Compliment to the Ladies and a Pretty Epigram for That Entertainment of Those Who Paid Great Sums in the Venetian and Flemish Ooze'." *Expl* 28:Item 79.

* 3382. Baine, Rodney. "Some Recent Blake Books." *GaR* 24:38–45. [Rev. art.]

3383. Beer, John B. *Blake's Visionary Universe.* Manchester: Manchester U.P.

3384. Bentley, Gerald E.,Jr. *Blake Records.* London: Oxford U.P.

3385. *Blake Newsl.* 4,ii. [David Bindman, "An Unpublished Blake Pencil Drawing of the Lambeth Period," 39–40(Illus.); Michael Phillips, "Blake's Corrections in *Poetical Sketches*," 40–47; W.H. Stevenson, " 'Death's Door'," 49; Ruthven Todd, "Blake's Copy of Dante," 49–50; Laura Gorham, "A Checklist of Blake Scholarship:June 1969—September 1970," 51–59.]

3386. *Blake Studies.* 2,ii. [William S. Doxey, "William Blake and William Herschel:The Poet, the Astronomer, and 'The Tyger'," 5–13; Roland A. Duerksen, "The Life-in-Death Theme in *The Book of Thel*," 15–22; Christopher Keane, "Blake and O'Neill:A Prophecy," 23–34; G.E. Bentley,Jr., "William Blake, Samuel Palmer, and George Richmond," 43–50; Joseph A. Wittreich,Jr., "Blake in the Kitto Bible," 51–54; Marcia Allentuck, "William Blake and William Bell Scott:Unpublished References to Blake's Late Nineteenth-Century Reputation," 55–56.]

3387. *Blake Studies* 2,i(1969). [Warren Stevenson, " 'The Tyger' as Artifact," 5–19; Susan C. Fox, "The Structure of a Moment:Parallelism in the Two Books of Blake's *Milton*," 21–35; Eve Teitelbaum, "Form as Meaning in Blake's *Milton*," 37–64; Stuart Curran, "Detecting the Existential Blake," 67–76; Michael J. Tolley, "Blake's Blind Man," 77–84 (See Bibliog. for 1969, Vol. I, Item 3579); Jean H. Hagstrum, "Rebuttal"(To Tolley) 84–86 and "Reply"(by Tolley) 86–88.]

3388. *Blake Studies* 1,ii(1969). [John Adlard, "A 'Triumphing Joyfulness':Blake, Boehme, and the Tradition," 109–22; Raymond Lister, "W.B. Yeats as an Editor of Blake," 123–38; Karl Kiralis, "William Blake as an Intellectual and Spiritual Guide to Chaucer's *Canterbury* Pilgrims," 139–90; John E. Grant, "You Can't Write About Blake's Pictures Like That," 193–202; Eugene DeGruson, "Bentley and Nurmi Addendum:Haldeman-Julius' Blake," 203–05.]

3389. *Blake Studies* 3,i. [Karl Kroeber, "Graphic-Poetic Structuring in Blake's *Book of Urizen*," 7–18; John Howard, "An Audience for *The Marriage of Heaven and Hell*," 19–52; Eli Pfefferkorn, "The Question of the Leviathan and the Tiger," 53–60; Thomas E. Connolly, "A Blakean Maze," 61–68; Morris

Eaves, "A List of the Entries in Damon's *Blake Dictionary*," 69–85.]

3390. Bloom, Harold. *Blake's Apocalypse:A Study in Poetic Argument.* Ithaca, N.Y.: Cornell U.P.

3391. Bogen, Nancy. "William Blake, the Pars Brothers, and James Basire." *N&Q* 17:313–14.

* 3392. —— "A New Look at Blake's *Tiriel*." *BNYPL* 74:153–65.

3393. Bronowski, Jacob. *William Blake and the Age of Revolution.* New York: Harper, 1969.

3394. Callahan, Patrick J. "Historical and Critical Problems in William Blake's *America*." *DAI* 30(1969):717A(U. of Wash.).

3395. Corrigan, Matthew. "Metaphor in William Blake:A Negative View." *JAAC* 28(1969):187–99.

3396. Cruttwell, Patrick. "Blake, Tradition, and Miss Raine." *HudR* 23:133–42. [Rev. art.]

3397. De Groot, H.B. "The Ouroboros and the Romantic Poets:A Renaissance Emblem in Blake, Coleridge, and Shelley." *ES* 50(1969):553–64. [Incl. 8 plates.]

* 3398. DeLuca, Vincent A. "Ariston's Immortal Palace:Icon and Allegory in Blake's Prophecies." *Criticism* 12:1–19.

3399. Downing, Richard. "Blake and Augustine." *TLS* 18 June:662. [See also 2 July:726–27.]

3400. Durrant, G.H. "Blake's 'My Pretty Rose-Tree'." *Theoria* 30(1968):1–5.

3401. Erdman, David V., and John E. Grant,eds. *Blake's Visionary Forms Dramatic.* Princeton: Princeton U.P.

3402. Essick, Robert N. "The Art of William Blake's Early Illuminated Books." *DAI* 30(1969):2020A–21A(Calif., San Diego).

3403. Frosch, Thomas R. "The Awakening of Albion:The Renovation of the Body in William Blake's *Jerusalem*." *DAI* 30(1969):1561A(Yale).

3404. Hagstrum, Jean H. "Kathleen Raine's Blake." *MP* 68:76–82. [Rev. art.; see Bibliog. for 1969, Vol. I, Item 3606.]

* 3405. Hall, Mary S. "Blake's *Tiriel*:A Visionary Form Pedantic." *BNYPL* 74:166–76.

3406. Harding, Eugene J. "Jacob Boehme and Blake's *The Book of Urizen*." *UES* 8,ii:3–11.

3407. Haya, Kenichi. "Honto no Kami no Sugata—Blake no Imi." *Oberon* 32:15–19. [Figure of the true God—Blake's meaning.]

* 3408. Helms, Randel. "Orc:The Id in Blake and Tolkien." *L&P* 20,i:31–35.

* 3409. Helmstadter, Thomas H. "Blake's *Night Thoughts*: Interpretations of Edward Young." *TSLL* 12:27–54.

3410. Hume, Robert D. "The Development of Blake's Psychology:The Quest for an Understanding of Man's Position in the World." *RLV* 35(1969):240–58.

3411. Humma, John B. "From Transcendental to Descendental:The Romantic Thought of Blake, Nietzsche, Lawrence." *DAI* 30:4454A(So. Ill.).

3412. Jackson, Mary V. "A Study of the Use of Poetic Myth in the Work of William Blake from 1783 to 1794." *DAI* 30:5410A–11A(Wash U.).

3413. Jakobson, Roman. "On the Verbal Art of William Blake and Other Poet-Painters." *LingI* 1:3–23. [Others are Henri Rousseau and Paul Klee.]

* 3414. Johnson, Mary L. "Beulah, 'Mne Seraphim,' and Blake's *Thel*." *JEGP* 69:258–77.

3415. Jones, Myrddin. "Blake's 'To Spring':A Formative Source?" *N&Q* 17:314–15.

3416. Keynes, Geoffrey. "Blake's *Little Tom The Sailor*." *BC* 17(1968):421–27.

3417. Kolker, Robert P. "The Altering Eye:William Blake's Use of Eighteenth-Century Poetics." *DAI* 30(1969):1987A (Columbia).

3418. Kostelanetz, Anne T. "The Human Form Divine in the Poetry and Art of William Blake." *DAI* 30(1969):1987A–88A(Columbia).

3419. Lesnick, Henry G. "Blake's Antithetical Vision:A Study of the Structure of *Jerusalem*." *DAI* 30(1969):2533A–34A(S.U.N.Y., Buffalo).

3420. Olivier, T. "The Voice of the Bard in Blake's 'Songs of Experience'." *Theoria* 33(1969):71–76.

3421. Paley, Morton D. *Energy and the Imagination:A Study of the Development of Blake's Thought.* Oxford: Clarendon.

3422. Raine, Kathleen. "*Blake and Tradition*." *TLS* 8 Jan:34. [See also 22 Jan:85.]

3423. Raine, Kathleen,ed. *A Choice of Blake's Verse.* London: Faber.

* 3424. Rose, Edward J. "Blake's Fourfold Art." *PQ* 49:400–23.

* 3425. —— "Blake's Illustrations for *Paradise Lost*, 'L'Allegro,' and 'Il Penseroso':A Thematic Reading." *HSL* 2:40–67.

3426. Stein, Kenneth. "Blake's Apocalyptic Poetry:A Study of the Genre of Blake's Prophetic Books." *DAI* 30(1969): 2500A(Brandeis).

3427. Taylor, Peter A. "A Reading of Blake's *Milton*." *DAI* 30(1969):737A–38A(Conn.).

3428. Watson, Alan M. "William Blake's Illustrated Writings:The Early Period." *DAI* 30(1969):1538A(N.M.).

3429. Weathers, Winston,ed. *The Tyger.* Columbus, Ohio: Charles E. Merrill, 1969.

3430. Witke, Joanne. "*Jerusalem*:A Synoptic Poem." *CL* 22:265–79. [A poetic interpretation.]

3431. Woodworth, Mary K. "Blake's Illustrations for Gray's Poems." *N&Q* 17:312–13.

See also 1471, 3126, 3133, 4088.

Bolingbroke. 3432. [Anon.] "Bolingbroke on Swift's *History*." *Scriblerian* 3,i:1–3. [Incl. reprod. and transcrip. of letter by B.]

3433. Burkett, Tommy R. "Bolingbroke and the Poets of the New Opposition." *DAI* 30(1969):2476A–77A(Kan.).

* 3434. Fletcher, Dennis J. "Le Législateur and the Patriot King:A Case of Intellectual Kinship." *CLS* 6(1969):410–18. *See also* 3544, 3797.

Boswell. 3435. Benjamin, Curtis G. "An Author's Progress." *SchP* 2:25–31.

3436. Clifford, James L.,ed. *Twentieth Century Interpretations of Boswell's* Life of Johnson. Englewood Cliffs, N.J.: Prentice-Hall. [Prev. pub. essays.]

3438. Cole, Richard C. "James Boswell and the Irish Press, 1767–1795." *BNYPL* 73(1969):581–98.

3439. —— "James Boswell's Irish Cousins." *Genealogists' Mag.*(London) 16,iii(1969):81–87.

3440. Waingrow, Marshall,ed. *The Correspondence and Other Papers of James Boswell Relating to the Making of the* Life of Johnson. London: Heinemann; New York: McGraw-Hill, 1969.

Burke. 3441. O'Gorman, Frank. "Edmund Burke and the Idea of Party." *SBHT* 11:1428–41.

3442. Reitan, E.A. "Burke, Trevelyan, and Ashley:The Meaning of the Glorious Revolution of 1688–89." *SBHT* 11:1463–70.

3443. Smith, Robert A.,ed. *Edmund Burke on Revolution.* New York: Harper, 1968.

3444. Wilkins, Burleigh T. "Burke on Words." *SBHT* 11(1969):1305–09.

3445. Willis, Richard E. "Some Further Reflections on Burke's *Discontents*." *SBHT* 11:1417–27.

3446. Zoll, Donald A. "Burke and the Vitalistic Tradition." *ModA* 14:150–57.

See also 3542, 3544, 3565.

Burnes, A. *See* 3992.

Burney. 3447. Bloom, Edward A.,ed. *Evelina.* London: Oxford U.P.

3448. Mulliken, Elizabeth Y. "The Influence of the Drama on Fanny Burney's Novels." *DAI* 30:3913A(Wis.).

Burns. 3449. Di Monaco, Bartolomeo. "Robert Burns." *Silarus* 5(1969):72–77.

3450. Fitzhugh, Robert T. *Robert Burns:The Man and the Poet.* Boston: Houghton Mifflin.

3451. Kinsley, James,ed. *Burns:Poems and Songs.* London: Oxford U.P., 1969.

3452. Kuosaitė, Elena. "Robertas Bernsas ir škotų liaudies daina." *Literatūra* 11,iii(1969):47–68. [B. and the Scottish folksong. Sums. in Eng. and Rus.]

3453. Lindsay, Maurice. *Robert Burns.* New York: Hillary House, 1969.

3454. MacKenzie, Fraser. "Burns and Ramuz." *Adam* 319–

21(1967):51–52.

3455. Nibbelink, Herman. "Society at Poosie-Nansie's." *SSL* 7:124–27.

* 3456. Robotham, John S. "The Reading of Robert Burns." *BNYPL* 74:561–76.

3457. Thornton, Robert D. "Burns Letters and the Currie Notebook." *SSL* 7:35–39.

* 3458. Weston, John C. "Robert Burns' Use of the Scots Verse-Epistle Form." *PQ* 49:188–210.

See also 8148.

Carey, H. 3459. Oldfield, Edward L. "The Achievement of Henry Carey (1687–1743)." *DAI* 30(1969):1145A(U. of Wash.).

Chatterton. 3460. Lamoine, Georges. "Chatterton:Un poète tombé du ciel." *NL* 27 août:11.

Chesterfield. *3461. Kelly, Richard M. "Chesterfield's *Letters to His Sons*:The Victorian Judgment." *TSL* 15:109–23.

See also 3589.

Chudleigh. 3462. Coleman, Antony. " 'The Provok'd Wife' and 'The Ladies Defence'." *N&Q* 17:88–91.

Churchill. 3463. Barron, Joseph M. "Stylistic Development in the Poetry of Charles Churchill." *DAI* 30:3900A–01A(Case Western Reserve).

See also 3363.

Cibber, C. 3464. Fone, B.R.S. "*Love's Last Shift* and Sentimental Comedy." *RECTR* 9,i:11–23.

3465. Koon, Helene W. "The Kind Impostor:Colley Cibber's Dramatic Technique." *DAI* 30:4950A(U.C.L.A.).

See also 3512.

Clive. 3466. Frushell, Richard C. "The Textual Relationship and Biographical Significance of Two Petite Pièces by Mrs. Catherine (Kitty) Clive." *RECTR* 9,i:51–58. [*The Sketch of a Fine Lady's Return from a Rout* and *The Faithful Irish Woman*.]

Collins, A. 3467. Bloom, Edward A. and Lillian D.,eds. *Anthony Collins, A Discourse Concerning Ridicule and Irony in Writing (1729).* (ARS Pub. 142.) With an Introd. Los Angeles: Wm. Andrews Clark Mem. Lib., U.C.L.A.

Collins, W. *3468. Stewart, Mary M. "Further Notes on William Collins." *SEL* 10:569–78. [Primarily biographical.]

See also 3835.

Colman. *See* 3323, 3332, 3531.

Coventry. 3470. Olshin, Toby A. "*Pompey the Little*:A Study in Fielding's Influence." *RLV* 36:117–24.

Cowper. 3471. Blom, Thomas E. "The Structure and Meaning of *The Task*." *PCP* 5:12–18.

* 3472. Mandel, Barrett J. "Artistry and Psychology in William Cowper's *Memoir*." *TSLL* 12:431–42.

3473. Neve, John. *A Concordance to the Poetical Works of William Cowper.* New York: Haskell House, 1969. [Repr. of 1887 ed.]

See also 3579.

Cumberland. 3474. Detisch, Robert J. "The Synthesis of Laughing and Sentimental Comedy in *The West Indian*." *ETJ* 22:291–300.

* 3475. Dircks, Richard J. "Richard Cumberland's Political Associations." *SBHT* 11:1555–70.

3476. Olsen, Olaf S. "*The Choleric Man*:A Laughing Comedy by Richard Cumberland." *DAI* 30(1969):288A(N.Y.U.).

See also 3323.

Curll. *See* 3663.

Darwin, E. 3477. Hassler, Donald M. "Comment on the Relation of Erasmus Darwin to the Wordsworth Circle." *WC* 1:73.

Day, T. *See* 3355.

Defoe. 3478. Anon. "Daniel Defoe Desiderata." *YULG* 45:25–31.

3479. Blewett, David. "*Roxana* and the Masquerades." *MLR* 65:499–502.

3480. Brooks, Douglas. "*Moll Flanders* Again." *EIC* 20:115–18. [Reply to Arthur Sherbo; see Bibliog. for 1969, Vol. I, Item 3678.]

3481. Conti, Paola Colaiacomo. "*Captain Singleton* fra *Robinson Crusoe* e *Moll Flanders*." *EM* 20(1969):141–61.

3482. Defoe, D. *Moll Flanders.* Introd. Elizabeth Tate. New York: Airmont, 1969.

3483. Elliott, Robert C. *Twentieth Century Interpretations of Moll Flanders:A Collection of Critical Essays.* (TCI.) Englewood Cliffs, N.J.: Prentice-Hall.

3484. Heidenreich, Helmut,ed. *The Libraries of Daniel Defoe and Phillips Farewell:Olive Payne's Sales Catalogue (1731).* Berlin: Selbstverl. [Berlin 45, Curtiusstrasse 67.]

3485. Hocks, Richard. "Defoe and the Problem of Structure: Formal 'Ropes' and Equivalent Technique." *LWU* 3:221–35.

* 3486. Hume, Robert D. "The Conclusion of Defoe's *Roxana*: Fiasco or Tour de Force?" *ECS* 3:475–90.

3487. Hunter, J. Paul,ed. *Moll Flanders.* New York: Crowell.

3488. Jenkins, Ralph E. "The Structure of *Roxana*." *SNNTS* 2:145–58.

* 3489. Kennedy, Joyce D. "Defoe's *An Essay upon Projects*: The Order of Issues." *SB* 23:170–75.

3490. Kumar, Shiv K.,ed. *The Life, Adventures, and Pyracies of the Famous Captain Singleton.* London: Oxford U.P., 1969.

3491. Landa, Louis,ed. *A Journal of the Plague Year. . . .* New York: Oxford U.P., 1969.

3492. McMaster, Juliet. "The Equation of Love and Money in *Moll Flanders*." *SNNTS* 2:131–44.

3493. McVeagh, John. " 'The Blasted Race of Old *Cham*': Daniel Defoe and the African." *ISE* 1(1969):85–109.

3494. Needham, J.D. "Moll's 'Honest Gentleman'." *SoRA* 3(1969):366–74.

3495. Novak, Maximillian E. "A Whiff of Scandal in the Life of Daniel Defoe." *HLQ* 34:35–42.

* 3496. —— "Defoe's 'Indifferent Monitor':The Complexity of *Moll Flanders*." *ECS* 3:351–65.

3497. Singleton, Robert R. "Defoe and Criminal Biography." *DAI* 30(1969):2550A(N.Y.U.).

* 3498. Snyder, Henry L. "Daniel Defoe, Arthur Maynwaring, Robert Walpole, and Abel Boyer:Some Considerations of Authorship." *HLQ* 33:133–54.

3499. Woodcock, George. "*Colonel Jack* and *Tom Jones*: Aspects of a Changing Century." *WascanaR* 5:67–73.

See also 959, 2663, 3116, 3158, 3500, 3686, 3830.

Dennis. *See* 3223.

Dunton. 3500. Merritt, Henry C. "The Life, Travels, and Adventures of John Dunton, Late of London Author, Bookseller, and Publisher." *DAI* 30:5415A(Syracuse).

Edgeworth. 3501. Colvin, Christina E. "Maria Edgeworth's Literary Manuscripts in the Bodleian Library." *BLR* 8:196–201.

3502. Hurst, Michael. *Maria Edgeworth and the Public Scene.* London: Macmillan, 1969.

3503. Jeffares, A. Norman. "Maria Edgeworth's *Ormond*." *English* 18(1969):85–90.

Faulkner, G. 3504. Ward, Robert E. "The Literary World of George Faulkner:Dublin and London, 1726–1775." *DAI* 30:3922A(Iowa).

Fergusson. 3505. Lindstrand, Gordon. "Fairley's Checklist of Robert Fergusson:Corrections and a Problem in Analytical Bibliography." *SSL* 7:159–68.

Fielding, H. 3506. Bennett, Robert C. "Fielding and the Satiric Dance." *DAI* 30:4397A(Pa.).

3507. Coley, William B.,II. "Fielding's Comic:A Study of the Relation Between Wit and Seriousness in a Comic Augustan." *DAI* 30:4403A(Yale).

3508. —— "Hogarth, Fielding, and the Dating of the *March to Finchley*." *JWCI* 30(1967):317–26.

3509. Cooper, Frank B. "The Structure of the Novels of Henry Fielding." *DAI* 30:5404A(Claremont).

* 3510. Goldgar, Bertrand A. "The Politics of Fielding's *Coffee-House Politician*." *PQ* 49:424–29.

3511. Jobe, Alice. "Fielding's Novels:Selected Criticism (1940–1969)." *SNNTS* 2:246–59.

3512. Johnson, Jeffrey L. "The Good-Natured Young Man and Virtuous Young Woman in the Comedies of Henry Fielding." *DAI* 30:5411A–12A(Fla. State).

3513. Krause, Lothar P. "The Conflict Between Social Communities and Individuals in the Novels of Henry Fielding." *DAI* 30:4991A(Pittsburgh).

3514. Morrissey, L.J.,ed. *Tom Thumb:And, the Tragedy of Tragedies.* Edinburgh: Oliver and Boyd. [Old Spelling ed.]

3515. Park, William. "What Was New about the 'New Species of Writing'?" *SNNTS* 2:112–30.

3516. Paulson, Ronald, and Thomas Lockwood,eds. *Henry Fielding:The Critical Heritage.* London: Routledge & K. Paul; New York: Barnes & Noble, 1969.

* 3517. Rogers, Pat. "Fielding's Parody of Oldmixon." *PQ* 49:262–66.

3518. Rosenblood, Bryan N. "Some Aspects of Henry Fielding's Heroes." *DAI* 30(1969):695A(Pittsburgh).

3519. Roy, G. Ross. "French Stage Adaptations of *Tom Jones.*" *RLC* 44:82–94.

3520. Rundus, Raymond J. "The History of *Tom Jones* in Adaptation." *DAI* 30(1969):1535A(Neb.).

3521. Sellery, J'nan. "Language and Moral Intelligence in the Enlightenment:Fielding's Plays and Pope's *Dunciad*. Part I." *EnlE* 1,i:17–26.

3522. Sherbo, Arthur. "Fielding's Dogs." *N&Q* 17:302–03.

3523. Shesgreen, Sean. "The Moral Function of Thwackum, Square, and Allworthy." *SNNTS* 2:159–67.

3524. Solomon, Stanley J. "Fielding's Presentational Mode in *Tom Jones.*" *CEA* 31,iii(1969):12–13.

3525. Stitzel, Judith G. "Blifil and Henry Fielding's Conception of Evil." *WVUPP* 17:16–24.

* 3526. Weinbrot, Howard D. "Chastity and Interpolation:Two Aspects of *Joseph Andrews.*" *JEGP* 69:14–31.

3527. Wess, Robert V. "The Probable and the Marvellous in *Tom Jones.*" *MP* 68:32–45.

3528. Williams, Ioan M.,ed. *The Criticism of Henry Fielding.* London: Routledge & K. Paul.

3529. Wood, David C. "The Dramatic Tradition of Henry Fielding's Regular Comedies." *DAI* 30:4428A(Bowling Green).
See also 1453, 1457, 2740, 3279, 3283, 3306, 3333, 3369, 3470, 3499, 3693, 3695.

Garrick. 3530. *Garrick's London:[An Exhibition] as Drawn from the Philbrick Library of English & American Drama & Theatre.* Stanford, Calif.: Stanford U. Libs., 1969. [Norman Philbrick, "Of Books and the Theatre," 5–10; John Loftis, "Garrick & the Rise of Theatrical Scholarship," 13–19.]

* 3531. Walch, Peter. "David Garrick in Italy." *ECS* 3:523–31.
See also 2909, 3351.

Garth. 3532. Dwyer, Warren F. "Profit, Poetry, and Politics in Augustan Translation:A Study of the Tonson-Garth *Metamorphoses* of 1717." *DAI* 30:3004A–05A(Ill.).

3533. Phillips, Steven R. "Sir Samuel Garth, *The Dispensary* (1699):An Old Spelling Edition, with Introduction and Historical Notes." *DAI* 30:3916A(Rochester).

Gay. *3534. Sherbo, Arthur. "Virgil, Dryden, Gay, and Matters Trivial." *PMLA* 85:1063–71.

3535. Sherman, Dorothy L. "Ambivalence in the Theater Plays of John Gay." *DAI* 30:3575A(Stanford).

* 3536. Weisstein, Ulrich. "Brecht's Victorian Version of Gay:Imitation and Originality in the *Dreigroschenoper.*" *CLS* 7:314–35.
See also 3333, 3579.

Gibbon. *3537. Mandel, Barrett J. "The Problem of Narration in Edward Gibbon's *Autobiography.*" *SP* 67:550–64.

3538. Smith, Beverley E. "Gibbon and Mohammedanism." *UMSE* 9(1968):11–22.

3539. Wildi, Max. "Gibbons Memoiren." [F 52]:203–15.
See also 3283.

Gifford. *See* 3363.

Godwin. 3540. Davies, H. Neville. "Bishop Godwin's *Lunatique Language.*" *JWCI* 30(1967):296–316.

3541. Krnacik, John,Jr. "The Hero of Feeling in William Godwin's Fiction." *DAI* 30(1969):284A(Mich.).

* 3542. McCracken, David. "Godwin's *Caleb Williams*:A Fictional Rebuttal of Burke." *SBHT* 11:1442–52.

* 3543. —— "Godwin's Literary Theory:The Alliance Between Fiction and Political Philosophy." *PQ* 49:113–33.

3544. —— "Godwin's Reading in Burke." *ELN* 7:264–70.

3545. Myers, Mitzi. "Aspects of William Godwin's Reputation in the 1790's." *DAI* 30(1969):2034A–35A(Rice).

3546. Pollin, Burton R. "Godwin's Account of Shelley's Return in September, 1814:A Letter to John Taylor." *KSMB*

21:21–31.
See also 4645, 4830, 4864.

Goldsmith. 3547. Cole, Richard C. "Oliver Goldsmith's Reputation in Ireland, 1762–74." *MP* 68:65–70.

* 3548. Storm, Leo F. "Literary Convention in Goldsmith's *Deserted Village.*" *HLQ* 33:243–56.
See also 3333, 3369, 3699, 5602, 6199, 6395.

Gray. 3549. Watson-Smyth, Peter. "The Origins of the Elegy." *ArielE* 1,iv:39–47. [On "Elegy Written in a Country Churchyard."]
See also 3431.

Gwynn. 3550. Gibson, William A.,ed. [John Gwynn]. *The Art of Architecture:A Poem in Imitation of Horace's Art of Poetry (1742).* (ARS Pub. 144.) With an Introd. Los Angeles: Wm. Andrews Clark Mem. Lib., U.C.L.A.

Hartley. *See* 4863.

Hawkesworth. *3551. Abbott, John L. "John Hawkesworth: Friend of Samuel Johnson and Editor of Captain Cook's *Voyages* and of the *Gentleman's Magazine.*" *ECS* 3:339–50.

Hayley. 3552. Williamson, Sister M. Celeste,S.S.J.,ed. *An Essay on Epic Poetry (1782).* With Introd. Gainesville, Fla.: SF&R, 1968.

Haywood. *3553. Kent, John P. "Crébillon fils, Mrs. Eliza Haywood and *Les heureux orphelins*:A Problem of Authorship." *RomN* 11(1969):326–32.

Headley. *See* 4875.

Hill, Aaron. 3554. Chouillet, Jacques. "Une source anglaise du *Paradoxe sur le comédien.*" *DHS* 2:209–26.

Hogarth. *See* 3284, 3531.

Holcroft. 3555. Faulkner, Peter,ed. *Anna St. Ives.* London and New York: Oxford U.P.

Hughes, J. 3556. Shea, Nancy M. "John Hughes, Augustan:A Critical Study of His Works." *DAI* 30:3957A(U.C.L.A.).

Hume. 3557. Bourke, John. "David Hume's Influence on Kant and Its Limits." [F 21]:350.

3558. Frazer, Catherine S. "Pattern and Predictability in Hume's *History.*" *EnlE* 1,i:27–32.

3559. Glidden, Jocelyn C. "Hume on Superstition." *DAI* 30(1969):2569A(Colo.).

3560. Hilson, J.C. "More Unpublished Letters of David Hume." *FMLS* 6:315–26.

* 3561. Popkin, Richard H. "Hume and Isaac de Pinto." *TSLL* 12:417–30.

3562. Ring, Benjamin A. "David Hume:Historian or Tory Hack?" *NDQ* 36,i(1968):50–59.

3563. Vercruysse, Jérôme. "Lettre et corrections inédites de David Hume." *DHS* 2:33–37.
See also 3283.

Huntington, W. *See* 4155.

Idler. 3564. Rawson, C.J. "Frozen Words:A Note to *Idler*, No. 46." *N&Q* 17:300.

Johnson, S. 3565. Barnouw, Jeffrey. " 'Action' for Johnson, Burke and Schiller:An Approach to the Unity of Romanticism." *DAI* 30:3446A(Yale).

3566. Bate, W.J., and Albrecht B. Strauss,eds. *The Rambler.* (Yale Ed. of Works of Samuel Johnson, Vols. III, IV, V.) New Haven: Yale U.P., 1969.

3567. Bate, W.J.,ed. *Essays from the* Rambler, Adventurer, and Idler. New Haven: Yale U.P., 1968.

* 3568. Battersby, James L. "John Nichols on a Johnson Letter." *SB* 23:179–83.

* 3569. Bloom, Edward A. and Lilian D. "Johnson's *London* and Its Juvenalian Texts." *HLQ* 34:1–23.

* 3570. Braudy, Leo. "Lexicography and Biography in the *Preface* to Johnson's *Dictionary.*" *SEL* 10:551–56.

3571. Campbell, J.L. "Dr. Johnson and the Laird of Lochbuie." *TLS* 2 Oct:1137. [See also 16 Oct:1195; 23 Oct:1225; 27 Nov:1391.]

3572. Capossela, Toni-Lee C. "Samuel Johnson and Religious Tradition." *DAI* 30(1969):2015A–16A(Brandeis).

* 3573. Carnochan, W.B. "Johnsonian Metaphor and the 'Adamant of Shakespeare'." *SEL* 10:541–49.

3574. Clifford, James L., and Donald J. Greene. *Samuel Johnson:A Survey and Bibliography of Critical Studies.* Minneapolis: U. of Minn. P.

3575. Cruttwell, Patrick,ed. *Selected Writings.* Harmondsworth: Penguin, 1968.

3576. Damrosch, Leopold,Jr. "Samuel Johnson and Tragedy." *DAI* 30(1969):275A–76A(Princeton).

* 3577. Dankert, Clyde E. "Samuel Johnson's Economic Ideas." *PLL* 6:58–76.

3578. Eade, J.C. "Johnson and Dryden's Answer to Rymer." *N&Q* 17:302.

3579. Easson, Angus. "Dr. Johnson and the Cucumber:The Question of Value." *N&Q* 17:300–02.

3580. Edinger, William C. "Classical and Neoclassical Background to Samuel Johnson's Criticism of Poetic Style." *DAI* 30:5406A–07A(Wis.).

3581. Fleissner, Robert F. "*Aroint* and Doctor Samuel Johnson." *WordW* 45,iii:1–3.

3582. Greene, Donald J. *Samuel Johnson.* (TEAS.) New York: Twayne.

3583. Hart, Francis R. "Johnson as Philosophic Traveler:The Perfecting of an Idea." *ELH* 36(1969):679–95.

3584. Hayashi, Tetsumaro. "Dr. Johnson as a Shakespeare Critic." *Lumina*(Okayama U., Japan) Spec. *Festschrift* 1(1968): 17–32.

3585. Jenkins, Ralph E. "Some Sources of Samuel Johnson's Literary Criticism." *DAI* 30(1969):1528A(Texas, Austin).

3586. Jones, Beverley F. "The Foundations of Dr. Johnson's Political Thought." *DAI* 30(1969):2026A–27A(Mich.).

3587. Kempter, Matthias. "Samuel Johnsons 'London' und Juvenals dritte Satire." [F 5]:150–57.

* 3588. Korshin, Paul J. "Johnson and Swift:A Study in the Genesis of Literary Opinion." *PQ* 48(1969):464–78.

* 3589. —— "The Johnson-Chesterfield Relationship:A New Hypothesis." *PMLA* 85:247–59.

3590. Lascelles, Mary. "*Rasselas*:A Rejoinder." *RES* 21: 49–56. [To such critics as W.P. Ker, Gwin J. Kolb, Alvin Whitley, Frederick W. Hilles, Emrys Jones, and J.P. Hardy.]

3591. Lindberg, Stanley W. "Johnsonian Irony:The Theory and Practice of Irony in the Prose Writings of Samuel Johnson." *DAI* 30(1969):2534A(Pa.).

3592. Linscott, Everett W. "Dr. Johnson's Debt to Seventeenth-Century Anglicanism." *DAI* 30(1969):687A–88A(U. of Wash.).

3593. Mudrick, Marvin "The Ogre at the Feast of Life." *HudR* 23:278–92. [Rev. art.]

3594. O'Flaherty, Patrick. "Dr. Johnson:Timid Giant." *DR* 49(1969):474–86.

* 3595. —— "Dr. Johnson as Equivocator:The Meaning of *Rasselas*." *MLQ* 31:195–208.

* 3596. —— "Johnson as Rhetorician:The Political Pamphlets of the 1770's." *SBHT* 11:1571–85. [With "Comment" by Donald J. Greene, 1585–88, and "Reply" by O'Flaherty, 1588–91.]

3597. —— "Johnson's *Idler*:The Equipment of a Satirist." *ELH* 37:211–25.

3598. Peters, Michael. "Doctor Johnson and the Epitaph Catch." *JCSA* 2:16–21.

3599. Rewa, Michael. "Johnson, Anna Seward, and Tacitus." *AN&Q* 7(1969):134–35.

* 3600. Rewa, Michael P. "Aspects of Rhetoric in Johnson's 'Professedly Serious' *Rambler* Essays." *QJS* 56:75–84.

3601. Reynolds, Richard R. "Samuel Johnson's Early Lives." *DAI* 30:5417A–18A(Notre Dame).

3602. Richman, Jordan P. "Samuel Johnson's Part in the Swiftian Tradition:A Study of Johnson as Swift's Biographer, Critic, and Associate Moralist." *DAI* 30(1969):290A–91A(N.M.).

* 3603. Riely, John C. "Johnson to Baretti:New Evidence for the Text of 21 December 1762." *LC* 36:115–17.

* 3604. —— "The Pattern of Imagery in Johnson's Periodical Essays." *ECS* 3:384–97.

3605. Schwartz, Richard B. "Dr. Johnson and the Satiric Reaction to Science." *SBHT* 11(1969):1336–47.

* 3606. —— "Johnson's *Journey*." *JEGP* 69:292–303.

3607. Selden, R. "Dr. Johnson and Juvenal:A Problem in Critical Method." *CL* 22:289–302.

3608. Sharma, Vinod C. "Johnson's Criticism of Milton's

Scheme of Education." [F 51]:32–43.

3609. Stecher, Carl A. "Samuel Johnson's Political Pamphlets." *DAI* 30(1969):698A(Conn.).

3610. Stockwell, Joseph E. "Samuel Johnson's Reputation as a Critic." *DAI* 30:3024A(La. State).

3611. Sullivan, Victoria D. "The Biographies of Samuel Johnson:A Study of the Relationship of the Biographer to His Subject." *DAI* 30:4427A–28A(Columbia).

3612. Thackrey, Donald E. "The Uses of Argument in the Prose of Samuel Johnson." *DAI* 30:3921A(Mich.).

* 3613. Turnage, Maxine. "Samuel Johnson's Criticism of the Works of Edmund Spenser." *SEL* 10:557–67.

3614. Vesterman, William. "Johnson and *The Life of Savage*." *ELH* 36(1969):659–78.

* 3615. Weinbrot, Howard D. "Samuel Johnson's 'Short Song of Congratulation' and the Accompanying Letter to Mrs. Thrale:The Huntington Library Manuscripts." *HLQ* 34:79–80.

3616. Woodman, T.M. "An Echo of Parnell in Johnson's 'London'." *N&Q* 17:300.

See also 3340, 3369, 3435, 3550, 3551, 3793, 3829.

Jones. See 3377.

Junius. 3617. Cordasco, Francesco. "The Dove Edition of Junius." *N&Q* 17:308.

3618. —— "The 'Vicarius' Junius." *N&Q* 17:307–08.

3619. —— "W. Fraser Rae and the Political Poems of Junius." *N&Q* 17:308.

Kames. 3620. McGuinness, Arthur E. *Henry Home, Lord Kames.* (TEAS 82.) New York: Twayne.

Lennox, C. 3621. Small, Miriam R. *Charlotte Ramsey Lennox:An Eighteenth-Century Lady of Letters.* Hamden, Conn: Archon, 1969.

See also 4002.

Lillo. 3622. Burgess, C.F. " 'Fatal Curiosity' in Berkshire." *N&Q* 17:92–93.

See also 3623.

Mackenzie. *3623. Barker, Gerard A. "Henry Mackenzie's Adaptation of Lillo's *Fatal Curiosity*." *BNYPL* 74:532–48.

3624. Punzo, Franca Ruggieri. "Henry Mackenzie:Lettere degli ultimi anni del *Man of Feeling* a Sir Walter Scott." *EM* 20(1969):183–89. ["Testi Inediti," 190–227.]

See also 3355.

Macpherson. 3625. Cristea, S.N. "Ossian vs. Homer, An Eighteenth-century Controversy.Melchior Cesarotti and the Struggle for Literary Freedom." *IS* 24(1969):93–111.

* 3626. Montiel, Isidoro. "Notas sobre Ossián en la *Vita* de Alfieri." *RomN* 11(1969):305–08.

3627. —— "Ossian en *Il bardo della selva nera*." *FI* 4:203–07.

3628. —— "Ossian en la obra de Leopardi." *Italica* 46(1969): 390–401.

3629. Tanskanen, Taimi. "Edda ja Ossian. (Edda et Ossian.)" *KSV* 24(1969):109–19.

3630. —— *Ossian Suomen kirjallisuudessa Aleksis Kiven vuosikymmenellä.* (Acta Universitatis Tamperensis, Ser.A,35.) Tampere: Tampereen Yliopisto. [Eng. sum.]

3631. Tyson, Gerald P. " 'Feast of Shells':The Context of James Macpherson's Ossianic Poetry." *DAI* 30(1969):2501A (Brandeis).

See also 4144.

Mason. 3632. Low, Donald A. "William Mason's Notes on Shakespeare." *N&Q* 17:309–12.

Morgann. See 2439.

Murphy. See 3323, 3698.

Museum. 3633. Tierney, James E. "A Study of *The Museum*: Or, Literary and Historical Register." *DAI* 30:3438A(N.Y.U.).

Ogilvie. 3634. Jackson, Wallace,ed. *John Ogilvie, An Essay on the Lyric Poetry of the Ancients (1762).* (ARS Pub. 139.) With an Introd. Los Angeles: Wm. Andrews Clark Mem. Lib., U.C.L.A.

O'Hara, K. 3635. Dircks, P.T. "The Dublin Manuscripts of Kane O'Hara." *N&Q* 17:99–100.

3636. —— "Two Burlettas of Kane O'Hara, *Midas* and *The Golden Pippin*:An Edition with Commentary." *DAI* 30:4405A–06A(N.Y.U.).

Oldmixon. *3637. Rogers, J.P.W. "A Lost Poem by Oldmixon." *PBSA* 63(1969):291–94.

* 3638. —— "Congreve's First Biographer:The Identity of 'Charles Wilson'." *MLQ* 31:330–44.

3639. Rogers, Pat. "Two Notes on John Oldmixon and His Family." *N&Q* 17:293–300.

See also 3663.

Parnell. *See* 3616, 3622.

Pennant. 3640. Rees, Eiluned, and G. Walters. "The Library of Thomas Pennant." *Library* 25:136–49.

Percy. *See* 1447.

Peterborough. *See* 3648.

Pope. *3641. Aden, John M. "Pope's 'Affected Fool/At Court'." *SNL* 7:114–15.

3642. Anon. "Pope's Nymphs in Manuscript." *Scriblerian* 2:37–39. [Incl. photo. reprod. of MS. poem by P.]

3643. Brownell, Morris R. "Pope and the Painters." *TLS* 18 Dec(1969):1451.

3644. Butt, John. *Pope, Dickens, and Others:Essays and Addresses.* Edinburgh: Edinburgh U.P., 1969.

3645. Crewe, J.V. "Sporus:A Reconsideration." *Theoria* 34:51–56.

3646. DeSole, Gloria M. " 'What Friends Two Wits Could Be':A Consideration of Alexander Pope's Friendship and Correspondence with Jonathan Swift." *DAI* 30:3427A–28A (S.U.N.Y., Albany).

3647. Dixon, Peter. "Pope and James Miller." *N&Q* 17:91–92.

3648. Grundy, Isobel. "Pope, Peterborough, and the Characters of Women." *RES* 20(1969):461–68.

3649. Guerinot, J.V. *Pamphlet Attacks on Alexander Pope 1711–1744:A Descriptive Bibliography.* London: Methuen, 1969.

* 3650. Hart, John A. "Pope as Scholar-Editor." *SB* 23:45–59.

3651. Hunter, G.K. "Pope's Sporus and Guilpin's 'Skialetheia'." *N&Q* 17:288.

3652. Johnson, Alice. "An American Publication Date for Alexander Pope's Translation of the 'Hymn of St. Francis Xavier'." *ELN* 7:262–64. [Jan. 1790.]

3653. Jones, Emrys. "Pope and Dulness." *PBA* 54(for 1968):231–63.

3654. Kaul, R.K. "The *Theodicy* of Leibniz." [F 51]:45–55. [L, Pope, Shaftesbury, and Voltaire.]

3655. Keyser, Lester J. "Alexander Pope's 'Living Examples'." *XUS* 8,iii(1969):19–27.

3656. Leranbaum, Miriam. "Alexander Pope's *Magnum Opus*, 1729–1744." *DAI* 30:4456A–57A(Calif., Berkeley).

3657. Lonsdale, Roger. "A New Text for a Letter of Pope." *N&Q* 17:288.

3658. Madaan, R.K. "Pope on Satire." [F 51]:85–95.

* 3659. Marks, Emerson R. "Pope on Poetry and the Poet." *Criticism* 12:271–80.

3660. Means, James A. " 'A Pope Anecdote'." *AN&Q* 9:55–56.

* 3661. Piper, William B. "The Conversational Poetry of Pope." *SEL* 10:505–24.

3662. Rogers, J.P.W. "Pope and the Syntax of Satire." [F 56]:236–65.

3663. Rogers, Pat. "The Conduct of the Earl of Nottingham: Curll, Oldmixon and the Finch Family." *RES* 21:175–81.

3664. Sherbo, Arthur. "No Single Scholiast:Pope's *The Dunciad*." *MLR* 65:503–16.

3665. Simon, Irène. "Traduttore Traditore." *RLV* 35(1969): 490–97. [*Essay on Man*.]

* 3666. Spacks, Patricia M. "Imagery and Method in *An Essay on Criticism*." *PMLA* 85:97–106.

3667. Stumpf, Thomas A. "Pope's *To Cobham, To a Lady* and the Traditions of Inconstancy." *SP* 67:339–58.

3668. Vonalt, Larry P. "Pope's *Epistles to Several Persons*." *DAI* 30(1969):297A(Fla.).

3669. White, Douglas H. *Pope and the Context of Controversy: The Manipulation of Ideas in* An Essay on Man. Chicago: U. of Chicago P.

3670. Williams, Aubrey,ed. *Poetry and Prose of Alexander Pope.* Boston: Houghton Mifflin, 1969.

See also 383, 1007, 1469, 1471, 1758, 2853, 3019, 3071, 3276, 3279, 3284, 3306, 3310, 3340, 3374, 3381, 3521, 3717, 3769, 3793, 3849.

Prior. 3671. Held, Leonard E.,Jr. "Prior's 'To the Honourable Charles Montague, Esq'." *Expl* 28:Item 75.

Radcliffe, A. 3672. Wright, Eugene P. "A Divine Analysis of *The Romance of the Forest*." *Discourse* 13:379–87.

Radcliffe, W. 3673. Arnaud, Pierre. "William Radcliffe journaliste." *EA* 22(1969):231–49.

Reynolds. *3674. Bevilacqua, Vincent M. "*Ut Rhetorica Pictura*:Sir Joshua Reynolds' Rhetorical Conception of Art." *HLQ* 34:59–78.

Richardson, S. 3675. Abraham, David. "Clarissa and Tess: Two Meanings of Death." *MSE* 1(1968):96–99.

* 3676. Barker, Gerard A. "Clarissa's 'Command of her Passions':Self-Censorship in the Third Edition." *SEL* 10:525–39.

* 3677. Bell, Michael D. "Pamela's Wedding and the Marriage of the Lamb." *PQ* 49:100–12.

* 3678. Benoist, Howard. "An Unpublished Letter of Samuel Richardson." *LC* 36:63–66.

3679. Cohen, Richard. *Literary References and Their Effect Upon Characterization in the Novels of Samuel Richardson.* (Husson Coll. Mono.) Bangor, Me.: Husson Coll. P. [46-p. pamphlet.]

3680. Coleman, Viralene J. "The English Dramatic Adaptations of Richardson's *Pamela* in the 1740's." *DAI* 30:3002A (Ark.).

* 3681. Costa, Richard H. "The Epistolary Monitor in *Pamela*." *MLQ* 31:38–47.

3682. Dalziel, Margaret. "Richardson and Romance." *AUMLA* 33:5–25.

3683. Downs, Brian W. *Richardson.* London: Cass, 1969. [Rpt. of 1928 ed.]

* 3684. Dussinger, John A. "What Pamela Knew:An Interpretation." *JEGP* 69:377–93.

3685. Enomoto, Futoshi. "Richardson no Atarashisa." *EigoS* 114(1968):586–87. [Newness of R.]

3686. Goldknopf, David. "Studies in the Novel's Search for Form." *DAI* 30:3458A–59A(Syracuse).

3687. Gopnik, Irwin. *A Theory of Style and Richardson's Clarissa.* (De Proprietatibus Litterarum, Ser. pract. 10.) The Hague: Mouton.

* 3688. Knight, Charles A. "The Function of Wills in Richardson's *Clarissa*." *TSLL* 11(1969):1183–90.

* 3689. Levin, Gerald. "Lovelace's Dream." *L&P* 20:121–27.

3690. Manheim, Leonard H. "The Absurd Miss Pamela and the Tragic Miss Clarissa:A Brief Study of Samuel Richardson as a Developing Artist." *Nassau Rev.*(Nassau [N.Y.] Comm. Coll.) 2,i:1–10.

3691. Moynihan, Robert D. "Richardson and Esthetic Compromise in *Clarissa*." *DAI* 30(1969):1990A–91A(Ariz.).

3692. Needham, Gwendolyn B. "Richardson's Characterization of Mr. B. and the Double Purpose in *Pamela*." *ECS* 3:433–74.

3693. Pons, Christian. *Samuel Richardson:Pamela.* Paris: Colin. [Bound with Jean Dulck, *Henry Fielding:Joseph Andrews*.]

3694. Schmitz, Robert M. "Death and Colonel Morden in *Clarissa*." *SAQ* 69:[346]–53.

3695. Sherwood, Irma Z. "The Influence of Digressive Didacticism on the Structure of the Novels of Richardson and Fielding." *DAI* 30:3436A(Yale).

3696. Suzuki, Yoshizo. "Juhachi Seiki Eikoku Shosetsu Kenkyu." *EigoS* 115(1969):298–99. [Study of the 18th cent. Eng. novel; focus on R.]

See also 1488.

Scriblerians. *See* 3779.

Shaftesbury. *3697. Hayman, John G. "Shaftesbury and the Search for a Persona." *SEL* 10:491–504.

Sheridan, R.B. *3698. Bloch, Tuvia. "The Antecedents of Sheridan's Faulkland." *PQ* 49:266–68. [Arthur Murphy's *All in the Wrong* (1761).]

3699. Macey, Samuel L. "Sheridan:The Last of the Great Theatrical Satirists." *RECTR* 9,ii:35–45.

3700. Price, C.J.L.,ed. *The Rivals.* With Introd. and Notes. London: Oxford U.P., 1968.

3701. Taylor, Garland F. "Richard Brinsley Sheridan's *The Duenna*." *DAI* 30(1969):1537A–38A(Yale).

See also 1453.

Sheridan, T. 3702. Benzie, William. "Thomas Sheridan and Eighteenth-Century Rhetoric and Belles-Lettres." *LeedsSE* N.S. 3(1969):63–84.

Smart. 3703. Agnew, Jocelyn E. "The Relationship of Painting and Music to the Aesthetic of Christopher Smart." *DAI* 30(1969):270A(Mich.).

* 3704. Christensen, Allan C. "Liturgical Order in Smart's *Jubilate Agno*:A Study of Fragment C." *PLL* 6:366–73.

3705. Davie, Donald. "Christopher Smart:Some Neglected Poems." *ECS* 3(1969):242–64.

3706. Dearnley, Moira. "Christopher Smart:Seed of the Welch Woman." *AWR* 18,xlii:171–77.

3707. Guidacci, Margherita. "Su Christopher Smarte e il suo *Jubilate agno*." *Approdo* 47(1969):47–60.

* 3708. Parkin, Rebecca P. "Christopher Smart's Sacramental Cat." *TSLL* 11(1969):1191–96.

3709. Saltz, Robert D. "Reason in Madness:Christopher Smart's Poetic Development." *SHR* 4:57–68.

Smith, Adam. 3710. Stewart, Mary M. "Adam Smith and the Comtesse de Boufflers." *SSL* 7:184–87.

Smollett. 3711. Bloch, Tuvia. "A Source for Smollett's Sir Mungo Barebones." *N&Q* 17:95–96.

* 3712. Brack, O M,Jr. *"The History and Adventures of an Atom,* 1769." *PBSA* 64:336–38.

* 3713. Brack, O M,Jr., and James B. Davis. "Smollett's Revisions of *Roderick Random*." *PBSA* 64:295–311.

3714. Eickelberg, Frederick C. "Sensibility in the Novels of Tobias Smollett." *DAI* 30(1969):1166A(Kan. State).

3715. Helmcke, E.T. "Voltaire and *Humphry Clinker*," 59–64 in Theodore Besterman,ed., *Studies on Voltaire and the Eighteenth Century*. Vol. 67. Genève: Inst. et Musée Voltaire, 1969.

3716. Korte, Donald M. *An Annotated Bibliography of Smollett Scholarship:1946–1968*. Toronto: U. of Toronto P., 1969.

3717. —— "Verse Satire and Smollett's *Humphry Clinker*." *SSL* 7:188–92.

3718. Lightner, Claude M. "Calvinism and Characterization in the Novels of Tobias Smollett." *DAI* 30(1969):329A–30A(Ill.).

3719. Norwood, Luella F. "A Descriptive Bibliography with Notes, Bibliographical and Biographical of the Creative Works of Tobias Smollett, M.D., 1746–1771, with the Posthumous Ode to Independence, 1773." *DAI* 30:3914A(Yale).

3720. Rice, Scott B. "The Significance of Smollett's Weather Register." *N&Q* 17:94–95.

* 3721. Underwood, Gary N. "Linguistic Realism in *Roderick Random*." *JEGP* 69:32–40.

* 3722. West, William A. "Matt Bramble's Journey to Health." *TSLL* 11(1969):1197–1208.

See also 6505.

Spectator. 3723. Bond, Donald F.,ed. *Critical Essays from The Spectator*. London: Oxford U.P. [Essays on ancient and modern lit.]

3724. Ito, Hiroyuki. "The Uses of Word[s] in *The Spectator* with Special Reference to Semantic Deviation." *ERA*(Bull. of Eng. Res. Assn. of Hiroshima) 6(Oct 1969):2–35.

Sprat. 3725. Cluett, Robert. "These Seeming Mysteries:The Mind and Style of Thomas Sprat (1635–1713)." *DAI* 30: 4939A(Columbia).

Steele. 3726. Rogers, Pat. "A New Letter by Steele:The Earl of Nottingham and *The Conscious Lovers*." *ELN* 7(1969):105–07. [Text of letter incl.]

3727. Winton, Calhoun. *Sir Richard Steele, M.P.:The Later Career*. Baltimore: Johns Hopkins.

See also 3333, 3369, 3370, 3723.

Sterne. 3728. Beck, Ronald. "The Date of Walter Shandy's Arrival." *AN&Q* 8:152–53.

3729. Day, W.G. "A Note on Sterne:'Des Eaux'." *N&Q* 17:303.

3730. —— "Sterne, Josephus and Donne." *N&Q* 17:94.

* 3731. Faurot, Ruth M. "Mrs. Shandy Observed." *SEL* 10:579–89.

3732. Goutkin, Elaine P. "Laurence Sterne as a Dramatic Novelist:A Study of *Tristram Shandy*." *DAI* 30(1969):2482A–83A(N.Y.U.).

3733. Haas, Rudolf. "Laurence Sterne." *NsM* 21(1968): 102–05.

* 3734. Hartley, Lodwick. " 'Tis a Picture of Myself':The Author in *Tristram Shandy*." *SHR* 4:301–13.

* 3735. —— "The Dying Soldier and the Love-Lorn Virgin: Notes on Sterne's Early Reception in America." *SHR* 4:69–80.

3736. Holtz, William V. *Image and Immortality:A Study of Tristram Shandy*. Providence, R.I.: Brown U.P.

3737. Koppel, Gene. "Fulfillment Through Frustration:Some Aspects of Sterne's Art of the Incomplete in *A Sentimental Journey*." *SNNTS* 2:168–72.

3738. Maskell, Duke. "The Authenticity of Sterne's First Recorded Letter." *N&Q* 17:303–07.

3739. Monkman, Kenneth. "The Bibliography of the Early Editions of *Tristram Shandy*." *Library* 25:11–39. [Incl. 4 plates and illus.]

3740. Moran, Charles,III. "An Analysis of Sterne's Intention:*Tristram Shandy* and *A Sentimental Journey*." *DAI* 30(1969): 286A–87A(Brown).

* 3741. New, Melvyn. "Laurence Sterne and Henry Baker's *The Microscope Made Easy*." *SEL* 10:591–604. [Sees B's work as a source for S's use of "psychological duration."]

3742. —— *Laurence Sterne as Satirist:A Reading of* Tristram Shandy. Gainesville: U. of Fla. P.

* 3743. Parish, Charles. "The Shandy Bull Vindicated." *MLQ* 31:48–52.

3744. Petrakis, Byron. "Laurence Sterne and the Tradition of Christian Folly." *DAI* 30(1969):289A(Fla.).

3745. Petrie, Graham. "A Rhetorical Topic in *Tristram Shandy*." *MLR* 65:261–66.

* 3746. —— "Rhetoric as Fictional Technique in *Tristram Shandy*." *PQ* 48(1969):479–94.

* 3747. Roth, Martin. "Laurence Sterne in America." *BNYPL* 74:428–36.

3748. Ruff, Lawrence A. "The True Line of Beauty:Style in *Tristram Shandy*." *DAI* 30(1969):337A(Ohio State).

3749. Sena, John F. "Sterne's *A Sentimental Journey*." *Expl* 28:Item 46.

3750. Stewart, Jack F. "Some Critical Metaphors for Shandean Style." *CLAJ* 13(1969):183–87.

3751. —— "Sterne's Absurd Comedy." *UWR* 5,ii:81–95.

3752. Stonys, Juozas. "Psichologinė analizė Lorenso Sterno prozoje." *Literatūra* 12,iii(1969):51–69. [Sums. in Eng. and Rus.]

3753. Thomson, J.E.P. "Contrasting Scenes and Their Part in the Structure of *A Sentimental Journey*." *AUMLA* 32(1969): 206–13.

See also 1457, 3355, 3500, 3759, 3772, 4305, 5399.

Swift. 3754. Clark, John R. *Form and Frenzy in Swift's "Tale of a Tub*." Ithaca, N.Y.: Cornell U.P.

* 3755. —— "Swift's Knaves and Fools in the Tradition: Rhetoric Versus Poetic in *A Tale of a Tub*, Section ix." *SP* 66(1969):777–96.

3756. Crewe, J.V. "Further Travels with Gulliver." *Theoria* 29(1967):51–66.

3757. Crider, J.R. "Swift's *A Tale of a Tub*, Section X." *Expl* 28:Item 62.

3758. Daw, Carl P.,Jr. "Swift and *The Whole Duty of Man*." *AN&Q* 8:86–87.

* 3759. DePorte, Michael V. "Digressions and Madness in *A Tale of a Tub* and *Tristram Shandy*." *HLQ* 34:43–57.

3760. Donoghue, Denis. *Jonathan Swift:A Critical Introduction*. London: Cambridge U.P., 1969.

* 3761. Dooley, D.J. "Image and Point of View in Swift." *PLL* 6:125–35.

3762. Dubašinskij, I.A. Putešestvie Gullivera *Džonatana Svifta*. Moscow: Vysšaja škola, 1969.

3763. —— "Žanr 'putešestvij gullivera'." *FN* 13,ii:44–56. [*Gulliver's Travels* as a genre.]

3764. Ehrenpreis, Irvin. "Jonathan Swift." *PBA* 54(for 1968):149–64. [On S's quality of mind.]

3765. Fischer, John I. "The Echoic Poetry of Jonathan Swift:Studies in Its Meaning." *DAI* 30(1969):278A(Fla.).

3766. Freeman, James A. "Sources of 'Tile, Stone, Brook' in *Gulliver's Travels* ii.7." *Scriblerian* 2:67–68.

* 3767. Gill, James E. "Beast Over Man:Theriophilic Paradox in Gulliver's 'Voyage to the Country of the Houyhnhnms'." *SP* 67:532–49.

3768. Graham, Edward. "Swift and Systems." *DAI* 30(1969): 1526A(Columbia).

3769. Greenberg, Robert A.,ed. Gulliver's Travels:*An Authoritative Text, the Correspondence of Swift, Pope's Verses on Gulliver's Travels, Critical Essays.* New York: Norton.

* 3770. Harris, Kathryn M. " 'Occasions so few':Satire as a Strategy of Praise in Swift's Early Odes." *MLQ* 31:22–37.

3771. Holzknecht, G.K. "Swift and Mr. Rawson." *EIC* 20:496–97. [Reply to C.J. Rawson, *EIC* 20:24–56.]

3772. Houston, Beverle A. "*A Tale of a Tub* and *Tristram Shandy*:Continuity and Change in Persona, Structure, and Style." *DAI* 30:4946A(U.C.L.A.).

3773. Jacobson, Richard. "A Biblical Allusion in *Gulliver's Travels*." *N&Q* 17:286–87.

3774. Johnston, Denis. "Swift of Dublin." *Éire* 3,iii(1968): 38–50.

3775. Jones, Gareth. "Swift's *Cadenus and Vanessa*:A Question of 'Positives'." *EIC* 20:424–40.

3776. Kallich, Martin. *The Other End of the Egg:Religious Satire in* Gulliver's Travels. New York: N.Y.U. Press.

3777. Kallich, Martin,ed. Anon. *A Letter From a Clergyman to His Friend, With an Account of The Travels of Captain Lemuel Gulliver (1726).* (ARS Pub. 143.) With Introd. Los Angeles: Wm. Andrews Clark Mem. Lib., U.C.L.A.

* 3778. Kinahan, Frank. "The Melancholy of Anatomy:Voice and Theme in *A Tale of a Tub*." *JEGP* 69:278–91.

3779. Koon, Helene. "A Lilliputian Poem." *ELN* 7(1969): 107–10. [Text of poem incl.]

3780. Köster, Patricia. "Words and Numbers:A Quantitative Approach to Swift and Some Understrappers." *CHum* 4:289–304. [Comment by Louis T. Milic, 304–06.]

3781. Lacasce, Steward. "The Fall of Gulliver's Master." *EIC* 20:327–33.

3782. Lenfest, David S. "Gessner's Illustration for the Fourth Part of *Gulliver's Travels*." *Scriblerian* 3,i:34–35. [Incl. reprod. of illus.]

3783. Lindstrom, James D. "Metaphoric Structure in the Verse Fables and Horatian Imitations of Jonathan Swift:An Introduction to His Poetic Style." *DAI* 30(1969):2489A–90A (U.C.L.A.).

3784. MacAndrew, M. Elizabeth. "A Splacknuck and a Dung-Beetle:Realism and Probability in Swift and Kafka." *CE* 31(1969):376–91.

3785. McElrath, Joseph R.,Jr. "Swift's Friend:Dr. Patrick Delany." *Éire* 5,iii:53–62.

3786. Milham, Mary E. "The *Art of Cookery*." *TLS* 2 July:726. [Dr. Wm. King and S. See also 21 Aug:928.]

3787. Murray, Patrick. "Swift:The Sceptical Conformist." *Studies* 58(1969):357–67.

* 3788. Parkin, Rebecca P. "Swift's *Baucis and Philemon*:A Sermon in the Burlesque Mode." *SNL* 7:109–14.

3789. Perez, Hertha. "Jonathan Swift:Viziune și stil." *AȘUI* 14,i(1968):103–09.

3790. Pinkus, Philip,ed. *Jonathan Swift:A Selection of His Works.* New York: Odyssey.

3791. Prahl-Lauersen, Vagn. "Jonathan Swift, mennesket bag satirikeren." *Extracta* 2(1969):281–87. [Abst.]

* 3792. Quinlan, Maurice J. "Treason in Lilliput and in England." *TSLL* 11:1317–32.

3793. Rawson, Claude [J]. "Order and Cruelty:A Reading of Swift (with Some Comments on Pope and Johnson)." *EIC* 20:24–56.

* 3794. Roberts, Philip. "Swift, Queen Anne, and *The Windsor Prophecy*." *PQ* 49:254–58.

3795. —— "The Original of a Swift Letter." *N&Q* 17:287–88. [To George Lyttelton.]

3796. Rogers, Pat. "Anthony Henley and Swift." *AN&Q* 8:99–101,116–20.

3797. —— "Swift and Bolingbroke on Faction." *JBS* 9,ii: 71–101.

3798. Rousseau, G.S., and David Woolley. "A New Letter of Swift to Marcus Antonius Morgan, 23 July [1735]." *HLB* 18:94–97.

3799. Sarfatt, Roberta F. "Jonathan Swift and the Quarrel of the Ancients and Moderns." *DAI* 30(1969):2042A(Calif., San Diego).

3800. Schakel, Peter J. "Method and Meaning in the Poems of Swift." *DAI* 30(1969):1182A(Wis.).

3801. —— "Swift's 'Verses Wrote in a Lady's Ivory Table-Book'." *Expl* 28:Item 83.

3802. Seijas, Joaquín Rojo. "Swift y la revolución de 1688–89." *FMod* 38:113–30.

3803. Skau, Michael W. "Flimnap, Lilliput's Acrobatic Treasurer." *AN&Q* 8:134–35.

3804. —— "Glumdalclitch, Gulliver's 'Little Nurse'." *AN&Q* 8:116.

3805. Söderlund, Johannes. "Swift and Linguistics." *ES* 51:137–43.

3806. Speck, Gerald E. *Swift.* (LitP.) London: Evans, 1969.

3807. Sterne, Noel D. "Jonathan Swift's Imitations of Horace." *DAI* 30:4426A–27A(Columbia).

3808. Stout, Gardner D.,Jr. "Speaker and Satiric Vision in Swift's *A Tale of a Tub*." *ECS* 3(1969):175–99.

* 3809. Tilton, John W. "Swift Among the Cannibals." *SNL* 7:153–57. [I.e., in Johnstown, Pa., 1965.]

* 3810. Timpe, Eugene F. "Swift as Railleur." *JEGP* 69:41–49.

3811. Uphaus, Robert W. " 'The Narrow Path of Sense':A Study of Jonathan Swift's Poetry." *DAI* 30(1969):2502A(U. of Wash.).

3812. —— "Swift's Stella and Fidelity to Experience." *DM* 8,iii:31–42.

3813. —— "Swift's Stella Poems and Fidelity to Experience." *Éire* 5,iii:40–53.

3814. Vickers, Brian,ed. *The World of Jonathan Swift:Essays for the Tercentary.* Cambridge: Harvard U.P., 1968.

3815. Washington, Eugene H. "A Chief Design of *Gulliver's Travels*." *DAI* 30:4428A(Mo., Columbia).

* 3816. Weygant, Peter S. "Three Kinds of Reply to *A Tale of a Tub*." *LC* 36:47–62. [18th c. comments and responses.]

3817. Williams, Kathleen,ed. *Swift:The Critical Heritage.* London: Routledge & K. Paul; New York: Barnes & Noble.

3818. Wilson, T.G. "Pooley's Portrait of Swift." *DM* 8, i–ii(1969):47–50.

See also 3276, 3306, 3312, 3343, 3367, 3374, 3432, 3500, 3588, 3602, 3646, 3697, 4120, 4430, 5354, 9378.

Tate. *3819. Lippincott, Henry F.,Jr. "Tate's *Lear* in the Nineteenth Century:The Edwin Forrest Promptbooks." *LC* 36:67–75.

Tatler. *3820. Köster, Patricia. " 'Monoculus' and Party Satire." *PQ* 49:259–62.

See also 3564.

Theobald. *See* 2439.

Thomson, J. 3821. Campbell, Hilbert H. " 'A Defence of the New Sophonisba'." *N&Q* 17:300.

3822. —— "Thomson and the Countess of Hertford Yet Again." *MP* 67:367–69. [Incl. text of MS. poem by T.]

* 3823. Cohen, Ralph. "*Spring*:The Love Story of James Thomson." *TSLL* 11(1969):1108–82.

3824. —— *The Unfolding of* The Seasons. Baltimore: Johns Hopkins U.P.; London: Routledge & K. Paul.

3825. Hamilton, Horace E. "Travel and Science in Thomson's *Seasons*." *DAI* 30:4945A–46A(Yale). [1941].

3826. Maxwell, J.C. " 'Wildly Devious':James Thomson and Christopher Wordsworth." *N&Q* 17:169.

3827. Napolitano, Maria. "La Contesa fra Operosità e Contemplazione nel *Castle of Indolence* di James Thomson." *AION-SG* 12(1969):403–27.

3828. Rogers, Pat. "James Thomson:An Unnoticed Contribution." *AN&Q* 9:3–6.

Thrale, H. 3829. Spacks, Patricia M. "Scrapbook of a Self:Mrs. Piozzi's Late Journals." *HLB* 18:221–47.

Trosse. *3830. Brink, Andrew. "A Possible Predecessor of Robinson Crusoe:*The Life of the Reverend Mr. George Trosse*." *PQ* 48(1969):433–51.

Walpole. 3831. Binford, Joseph N. "The Politics of Horace

Walpole." *DAI* 30(1969):1936A(Ky.).

3832. Rogers, Donnita M. "Horace Walpole, Amateur Architect and Art Historian." *DAI* 30(1969):291A(Minn.).

Warburton, J. *3833. Freehafer, John. "John Warburton's Lost Plays." *SB* 23:154–64.

Ward. *See* 3314.

Warton, J. 3834. Powers, James G.,S.J. "A Fact About Warton's 'Ode to Fancy'." *N&Q* 17:93.

Warton, T. 3835. Baine, Rodney M. "Warton, Collins, and Skelton's *Necromancer*." *PQ* 49:245–48.

See also 3834.

Wesley, C. 3836. Morris, Gilbert L. "Imagery in the Hymns of Charles Wesley." *DAI* 30:3018A(Ark.).

Wesley, J. 3837. Boraine, Alexander L. "The Nature of Evangelism in the Theology and Practice of John Wesley." *DAI* 30(1969):2121A–22A(Drew).

3838. Fox, Harold G. "John Wesley and Natural Philosophy." *UDR* 7,i:31–39.

3839. Scanlon, Rev. Michael J. "The Christian Anthropology of John Wesley." *DAI* 30(1969):2611A(Catholic U.).

Whately. *3840. Freeman, William G. "Whately and Stanislavski:Complementary Paradigms of Naturalness." *QJS* 56:61–66.

Wolcot. *See* 3363.

Young, E. *3841. Hall, Mary S. "On Light in Young's *Night Thoughts*." *PQ* 48(1969):452–63.

3842. Webb, Ewing J. "Edward Young's *Conjectures on Original Composition* (1759):A Critical Edition." *DAI* 30:3960A–61A(Northwestern).

See also 3409.

Young, W. 3843. Berry-Hart, Alice. "Sir William Young's Manuscript Book." *N&Q* 16(1969):407–09.

IX. NINETEENTH CENTURY

Bibliography. 3844. Erdman, David V.,ed. "The Romantic Movement:A Selective and Critical Bibliography for 1969." *ELN* 8,Sup. to i:1–158.

* 3845. Miller, J. Hillis. "Recent Studies in the Nineteenth Century." *SEL* 9(1969):737–53; 10:183–214. [Rev. art.]

3846. Minerof, Arthur F. "Recent Publications:A Selected List." *VN* 38:28–31.

3847. —— "Recent Publications:A Selected List—September 1969–January 1970." *VN* 37:29–32.

3848. Tobias, R.C. "The Year's Work in Victorian Poetry:1969." *VP* 8:219–60.

3849. Weinglass, David H. "The Publishing History of William Roscoe's Edition of the *Works of Alexander Pope,Esq.* (1824)." *DAI* 30(1969):1153A(Kan. State).

See also 3280.

General and Miscellaneous. 3850. Altick, Richard D. "Victorian Readers and the Sense of the Present." *Midway* 10,iv:95–119. [Illus.]

3851. Bayley, John. *The Romantic Survival:A Study in Poetic Evolution.* London: Chatto & Windus, 1969.

3852. Beaty, Jerome. "All Victoria's Horses and All Victoria's Men." *NLH* 1:271–92.

* 3853. Beckson, Karl. "New Dates for the Rhymers' Club." *ELT* 13:37–38.

3854. Betjeman, Sir John. *Victorian and Edwardian London.* London: Batsford, 1969. [Photos. with introd. and comment., illus. var. aspects of London life.]

3855. Beyette, Thomas K. "Symbolism and Victorian Literature." *DAI* 30:5440A(Texas, Austin).

3856. Bloom, Harold. "First and Last Romantics." *SIR* 9:225–32.

3857. —— "Recent Studies in the Nineteenth Century." *SEL* 10:817–29. [Rev. art.]

3858. Buckley, Jerome H. "*The Victorian Temper* Revisited." *NLH* 1(1969):69–73. [B comments on genesis and method of his book.]

* 3859. Conway, Jill. "Stereotypes of Femininity in a Theory of Sexual Evolution." *VS* 14:47–62.

3860. Dobell, Robert J. "Bertram Dobell and T.J. Wise." *BC* 19:348–55.

3861. Downs, B.W. "Anglo-Swedish Relations 1867–1900:The Fortunes of English Literature in Sweden." *MLR* 65:829–52.

3862. Fleissner, Robert F. " 'Pot Luck':Drugs and Romanticism." *Eng. Assn. of Ohio Bull.* 11,iv:9–11.

3863. Forsyth, R.A. " 'Europe,' 'Africa' and Problem of Spiritual Authority." *SoRA* 3(1969):294–321.

3864. Fulford, Roger,ed. *Dearest Mama:Letters Between Queen Victoria and the Crown Princess of Prussia.* New York: Holt, 1969.

3865. Goldfarb, Russell M. *Sexual Repression and Victorian Literature.* Lewisburg, Pa.: Bucknell U. P.

* 3866. Hartman, Geoffrey. "Reflections on Romanticism in France." *SIR* 9:233–48.

3867. Hayden, John O. *The Romantic Reviewers.* London:

Routledge & K. Paul, 1969.

3868. Hosmon, Robert S. "Adventure in Bohemia:A Study of the Little Magazines of the Aesthetic Movement." *DAI* 30:3907A(Ariz.).

3869. Hutchins, Patricia. "Elkin Mathews, Poets' Publisher." *ArielE* 1,iv:77–95.

* 3870. Kroeber, Karl. "The Relevance and Irrelevance of Romanticism." *SIR* 9:297–306.

3871. Kumar, Shiv K.,ed. *British Victorian Literature:Recent Revaluations.* New York: N.Y.U. Press, 1969.

3872. Langbaum, Robert. *The Modern Spirit:Essays on the Continuity of Nineteenth- and Twentieth-Century Literature.* New York: Oxford U.P.

3873. Maurice, Frederick D. *Sketches of Contemporary Authors, 1828.* Ed. A.J. Hartley. With Pref. and Introd. Hamden, Conn.: Archon Books. [Chaps. on Southey, Cobbett, Wordsworth, Moore, Shelley, Scott, et al.]

* 3874. McClary, Ben H.,ed. "Murrayana:Thirty-Four Atrocious Anecdotes Concerning Publisher John Murray II." *TSL* 15:125–41.

* 3875. McCullen, J.T.,Jr. "Tobacco and Victorian Literature." *ForumH* 8,ii:20–26.

3876. Micklewright, F.H. Amphlett. "The Bishop of Clogher's Case." *N&Q* 16(1969):421–30.

3877. —— "The Dean of Arches and the Central Criminal Court." *N&Q* 17:179–81.

3878. Mitchell, William R. "Theological Origins of the Christ-Image in Victorian Literature with Special Reference to *In Memoriam*." *DAI* 30(1969):1990A(Okla.).

3879. Miyoshi, Masao. *The Divided Self:A Perspective on the Literature of the Victorians.* New York: N.Y.U. Press, 1969.

3880. Monod, Sylvère. *Histoire de la littérature anglaise:De Victoria à Elisabeth II.* Paris: Colin.

3881. Monsman, Gerald C. "Old Mortality at Oxford." *SP* 67:359–89. [Hist. of Old Mortality Soc.]

3882. O'Connell, Marvin R. *The Oxford Conspirators:A History of the Oxford Movement, 1833–45.* New York: Macmillan, 1969.

3883. Pappas, John J. "Victorian Literature of the Divided Mind:A Study of the Self in Relation to Nature." *DAI* 30(1969):693A–94A(Columbia).

3884. Parry, Graham. "The Purpose and Tendency of Early Pre-Raphaelite Art, 1848–1857." *DAI* 30(1969):734A(Columbia).

3885. Peckham, Morse. "On Romanticism:Introduction." *SIR* 9:217–24.

3886. —— *Victorian Revolutionaries:Speculations on Some Heroes of a Cultural Crisis.* New York: Braziller.

* 3887. Peterson, M. Jeanne. "The Victorian Governess:Status Incongruence in Family and Society." *VS* 14:7–26.

3888. Pike, E. Royston. *Human Documents of the Age of the Forsytes.* London: Allen & Unwin. [Coll. of documents from the 1880's and 1890's which illus. life style of the propertied and other classes.]

3889. Quennell, Peter. *Romantic England.* London:

Weidenfeld and Nicolson.

3890. Rapson, Richard L. "The British Traveler in America, 1860–1935." *DAI* 30(1969):1117A(Columbia).

* 3891. Reed, John R. "Emblems in Victorian Literature." *HSL* 2:9–39.

3892. Rosen, Marvin S. "Authors and Publishers:1750–1830." *Science and Society* 32(1968):218–32.

3893. Schmidt, Arno. *Der Triton mit dem Sonnenschirm: Grossbritannische Gemütsergetzungen.* Karlsruhe: Stahlberg Verl., 1969. [Essays on the Brontës, Bulwer-Lytton, Dickens, Wilkie Collins, et al.]

3894. Schneewind, J.B. *Backgrounds of English Victorian Literature.* New York: Random House.

* 3895. Shea, F.X.,S.J. "Religion and the Romantic Movement." *SIR* 9:285–96.

* 3896. Showalter, Elaine and English. "Victorian Women and Menstruation." *VS* 14:83–89.

3897. Soper, Dom Laurence. "An English Liberal." *DownR* 88:27–35. [On Thomas Hill Green.]

3898. Trewin, J.C. "The Romantic Poets in the Theatre." *KSMB* 20(1969):21–30.

3899. Tyrrell, Alexander. "Class Consciousness in Early Victorian Britain:Samuel Smiles, Leeds Politics, and the Self-Help Creed." *JBS* 9,ii:102–25.

3900. Wiegner, Kathleen. "French Symbolism in England: 1890–1900." *Wisconsin Studies in Lit.* 6(1969):50–57.

See also 494, 799, 847, 1060, 2169, 3209, 3960, 4079, 4307, 4380, 4916, 5930, 8390.

Biography and Autobiography. 3901. Gracie, William J.,Jr. "Father-Son Conflict in Selected Victorian Autobiographies and Autobiographical Novels." *DAI* 30:4411A(Northwestern). [J.S. Mill, E. Gosse, Carlyle, Ruskin, J.A. Froude, S. Butler.]

3902. Gwiasda, Karl E. "The Boswell Biographers:A Study of 'Life and Letters' Writing in the Victorian Period." *DAI* 30:4412A–13A(Northwestern).

Criticism. 3903. Park, Roy. " 'Ut Pictura Poesis':The Nineteenth-Century Aftermath." *JAAC* 28(1969):155–64.

Drama and Theater. 3904. Barker, B. Ashley. "The Lyric Theatre, Hammersmith." *TN* 24:119–22.

3905. Baum, Joan M. "The Theatrical Compositions of the Major English Romantic Poets." *DAI* 30(1969):1976A (Columbia).

3906. Davidson, Pamela. "Theatre in Hampstead in the Early Nineteenth Century." *N&Q* 17:168–69.

3907. Donohue, Joseph W.,Jr. *Dramatic Character in the English Romantic Age.* Princeton: Princeton U.P.

3908. Evans, T.F. "A Note on Hankin." *Shavian* 4:52–53. [The dramatist St. John Hankin.]

3909. Herring, Paul D. "Nineteenth-Century Drama." *MP* 68:83–90. [Rev. art., new anthols.]

3910. Lorenzen, Richard L. "Managers of the Old Prince of Wales's Theatre." *TN* 24(1969):32–36.

3911. Melchiori, Barbara. "Fanny Kemble in Rome, with Some Unpublished Letters." *EM* 20(1969):269–89.

3912. Miller, Tice L. "John Ranken Towse:Last of the Victorian Critics." *ETJ* 22:161–78.

3913. Olshen, B.N, "Early Nineteenth-Century Revisions of *Love for Love.*" *TN* 24:164–75.

3914. *Problemy anglo-amerikanskoj dramaturgii konca XIX i pervoj poloviny XX veka:Sbornik statej.* (Učenye zapiski 88.) Sverdlovsk: Izd. Sverdlovsk. pedag. inst., 1969.

See also 2670, 2707, 4567.

Periodicals. 3915. Bell, A.S. "An Unpublished Letter on the *Edinburgh Review.*" *TLS* 9 Apr:388. [S. Smith to J. Mackintosh.]

3916. Casey, Ellen M. "Novels in Teaspoonfuls:Serial Novels in *All The Year Round*, 1859–1895." *DAI* 30(1969):1521A(Wis.).

3917. Deguchi, Yasuo. "19 Seiki Shoki no Eikoku Bungei Zasshi to sono Haikei." *EigoS* 114(1968):310–11. [Eng. lit. magazines in 19th cent. and their background.]

3918. Hollis, Patrica. *The Pauper Press:A Study in Working-Class Radicalism of the 1830's.* London: Oxford U.P.

3919. Jones, Calvin P. "Spanish-America in Selected British Periodicals, 1800–1830." *DAI* 30(1969):1941A(Ky.).

3920. *VPN* 7. [Peter F. Morgan, "Problems in Examining Periodical Criticism," 9–11; Henry and Sheila Rosenberg, "Bibliography of Writings on Nineteenth-Century Periodicals," 11–13; James O'Neill, "Victorian Periodicals and Newspapers in Microform:A Preliminary List, and Proposals," 14–28; Dorothy Deering, "Computer Programming for the Victorian Periodicals Project," 29–44.]

3921. *VPN* 8. [Douglas H. Shepard, "Some Early Lists of Victorian Periodicals," 9–11; Scott Bennett, "The Bentley and Constable Records," 12–15; Wayne Somers, "Aids to the Use of *Poole's Index*," 15–22; H.B. de Groot, "Lord Brougham and the Founding of the *British and Foreign Review,*" 22–32; Philip Collins, "W.H. Wills' Plan for *Household Words,*" 33–46.]

3922. *VPN* 9. [Helene E. Roberts, "British Art Periodicals of the Eighteenth and Nineteenth Centuries," 2–56.]

See also 4139, 5802.

Poetry. 3923. Arinštejn, L.M. "Ob èstetičeskom svoeobrazii revoljucionnoj rabočej poèzii (Na materiale revoljucionnoj poèzii anglijskogo socialističeskogo dviženija 80-x godov XIX v.)." [F 44]:103–48.

3924. Bewley, Marius,comp. *The English Romantic Poets:An Anthology with Commentaries.* New York: Mod. Lib.

3925. Bloom, Harold,ed. *Romanticism and Consciousness: Essays in Criticism.* New York: Norton. [Blake, Wordsworth, Coleridge, Keats, Byron, Shelley.]

3926. Bright, Michael H. "The Nineteenth-Century English Pastoral Elegy." *DAI* 30:4443A(Tulane).

3927. Bunn, James H. "The Palace of Art:A Study of Form in Retrospective Poems About the Creative Process." *DAI* 30: 4400A(Emory). [Pope, Thomson, Keats, Yeats, Stevens.]

3928. Colander, Raymond E. "The Victorian Verse-Novel." *DAI* 30:3001A(Northwestern).

3929. Colville, Derek. *Victorian Poetry and the Romantic Religion.* Albany: State U. of New York P.

3930. Faas, K.E. "Notes Towards a History of the Dramatic Monologue." *Anglia* 88:222–32.

3931. Gingerich, Solomon F. *Essays in the Romantic Poets.* New York: Octagon, 1969. [Coleridge, Wordsworth, Shelley, Byron.]

3932. Grierson, Sir Herbert J. *Lyrical Poems of the Nineteenth Century.* New York: AMS Press. [Repr.]

3933. Isoda, Koichi. "Sozoryoku no Gyakusetsu." *EigoS* 114(1968):736–37. [Paradox of imagination in Romantic poets.]

3934. Langbaum, Robert. "Victorians Reconsidered." *EIC* 20:451–65. [Rev. art. on *The Major Victorian Poets: Reconsiderations*; see Bibliog. for 1969, Vol. I, Item 4060.]

3935. Ray, Ann A. "Romanticism:A Collection of Essays on Poetic Style." *DAI* 30:2977A(Texas, Austin).

3936. Rose, Alan. "The Impersonal Premise in Wordsworth, Keats, Yeats, and Eliot." *DAI* 30(1969):2547A–48A(Brandeis).

* 3937. Rutenberg, Daniel. "A New Date for the Rhymers' Club." *ELT* 13(1969):155–57.

3938. Subrahmanian, Krishnaswami. "The Theory of 'Suggestion' in Sanskrit Poetics, English Romanticism and French Symbolism." *DAI* 30:4957A(Ind.).

3939. Vicinus, Martha J. "The Lowly Harp:A Study of Nineteenth Century Working Class Poetry." *DAI* 30(1969): 1152A–53A(Wis.).

3940. Wiley, Paul L., and Harold Orel,eds. *British Poetry, 1880–1920:Edwardian Voices.* New York: Appleton, 1969.

See also 1467, 3346, 3903, 4887, 8390.

Prose. 3941. Smith, Julia A. "Narrative Art in Victorian Nonfiction:Theory and Practice in Carlyle, Newman, and Pater." *DAI* 30:5421A(Texas, Austin).

Prose Fiction. 3942. Bennett, Joseph T. "The Critical Reception of the English Novel:1830–1880." *DAI* 30(1969):272A (N.Y.U.).

3943. Bergner, Heinz,ed. *English Short Stories of the Nineteenth Century.* With Introd. Hildesheim: Georg Olms, 1969.

3944. Biddison, Larry T. "The *Femme Fatale* as Symbol of the Creative Imagination in Late Victorian Fiction." *DAI* 30: 4976A(La. State).

3945. Bleich, David. "Utopia:The Psychology of a Cultural Fantasy." *DAI* 30:4935A–36A(N.Y.U)

3946. Breuninger, Margarete. *Funktion und Wertung des*

Romans im frühviktorianischen Roman. Tübingen: Niemeyer.

3947. Brightfield, Myron F. *Victorian England in Its Novels (1840–1870).* 4 Vols. Los Angeles: U. of Calif. P. [Extr. from novels linked by comm.]

3948. Curzon, Gordon A. "Paradise Sought:A Study of the Religious Motivation in Representative British and American Literary Utopias, 1850–1950." *DAI* 30:4405A(Calif., Riverside).

3949. Ewbank, David R. "The Role of Woman in Victorian Society:A Controversy Explored in Six Utopias, 1871–1895." *DAI* 30(1969):318A(Ill.).

3950. Fellman, Anita C. "The Fearsome Necessity: Nineteenth-Century British and American Strike Novels." *DAI* 30:4369A(Northwestern).

3951. Gingrich, Patricia C. "The Writer as Hero:A Changing Ideal in the British Novel from 1832 to 1914." *DAI* 30: 3941A–42A(Wayne State).

3952. Goewey, Herbert J. "The Apology for Death and the Rejection of Extended Life in Nineteenth- and Twentieth-Century British Visionary Fiction." *DAI* 30:3942A(Wayne State).

3953. Goldknopf, David. "Coincidence in the Victorian Novel:The Trajectory of a Narrative-Device." *CE* 31(1969): 41–50.

3954. Griest, Guinevere L. *Mudie's Circulating Library and the Victorian Novel.* Bloomington and London: Ind. U.P.

3955. Jeffares, A. Norman. "Some Academic Novels." *WascanaR* 5:5–27.

3956. Kawamoto, Shizuko. "Bildungsroman no Pattern." *EigoS* 114(1968):725–26. [Bildungsroman in novels from Dickens to Joyce.]

3957. —— "Bildungsroman no Tojo." *Oberon* 30(1968):42–52. [Emergence of Bildungsroman in the 1840's.]

3958. Levine, George. "Realism, or, in Praise of Lying:Some Nineteenth Century Novels." *CE* 31(1969):355–65.

3959. Sabiston, Elizabeth J. "The Provincial Heroine in Prose Fiction:A Study in Isolation and Creativity." *DAI* 30(1969): 1150A(Cornell).

* 3960. Smith, Sheila M. "Blue Books and Victorian Novelists." *RES* 21:23–40. [Treatment of govt. reports on soc. problems by Dickens, Eliot, Hardy, Kingsley, Disraeli.]

3961. Stambaugh, Sara E. "Towards the Short Story:British Short Fiction of the Eighteen-Nineties." *DAI* 30(1969):1536A–37A(Minn.).

3962. Stanford, Derek,comp. *Short Stories of the Nineties:A Biographical Anthology.* New York: Roy, 1969.

* 3963. Stoll, John E. "Psychological Dissociation in the Victorian Novel." *L&P* 20:63–73.

3964. Swanson, Roger M. "Guilt in Selected Victorian Novels." *DAI* 30(1969):342A(Ill.).

3965. Walch, Günter. "Roman und Wirklichkeit:1880 bis zum ersten Weltkrieg. Anglistische Forschungsergebnisse und -probleme." *ZAA* 18:88–110.

3966. Wenh-In Ng., Greer A. "The Figure of the Child in Victorian Novels of Protest." *DAI* 30:4419A(Columbia).

3967. Wilcox, James M. "East End Novelists:The Working Class in English Fiction, 1880–1900." *DAI* 30(1969):1579A–80A(Wayne State).

3968. Williams, Raymond. *The English Novel from Dickens to Lawrence.* New York: Oxford U.P.

See also 3358, 3360, 3901, 3916, 3971, 4360.

Satire. 3969. Sutton, Max K. "The Affront to Victorian Dignity in the Satire of the Eighteen-Seventies." [F 53]:93–117.

Ainsworth. 3970. Ligocki, Llewellyn. "William Harrison Ainsworth's Use of History:*The Tower of London* and Other Tudor Novels." *DAI* 30(1969):330A(Kan.).

3971. Worth, George J. "Early Victorian Criticism of the Novel and Its Limitations:*Jack Sheppard*, a Test Case." [F 53]:51–60.

Allan, W. See 4461.

Allingham. 3972. McMahon, Seán. "The Boy from His Bedroom Window." *Éire* 5,ii:142–53. [Biog. and crit.]

Arnold, M. 3973. Corner, Martin. "Steadily and Whole: Arnold's Early Understanding of Poetry, 1845-9." *ISE* 1(1969): 7–25.

* 3974. Farrell, John P. "Matthew Arnold's Tragic Vision."
PMLA 85:107–17.

* 3975. Godshalk, William L. "Autograph Fragments of Two Arnold Poems." *PMLA* 85:118–19. ["The Buried Life" and "Stanzas in Memory of the Late Quillinan, Esq."]

3977. Going, William T. "Matthew Arnold's Sonnets." *PLL* 6:387–406.

3978. Mahan, Charles. "Matthew Arnold's Concept of History." [F 23]:19–30.

3979. Meyers, Daniel E. "Anarchy and Authority:The Dialectical Unity of Matthew Arnold's Prose." *DAI* 30(1969): 2540A(N.Y.U.).

3980. Moyer, Charles R. "The Idea of History in Thomas and Matthew Arnold." *MP* 67(1969):160–67.

3981. Noland, Richard W. "Matthew Arnold's Religion of the Future." *DAI* 30:4420A–21A(Columbia).

3982. —— "The Uses of Imaginative Reason." *HSL* 2:75–84. [Rev. art. on 6 recent books on A.]

3983. Peterson, William S. "G.W.E. Russell and the Editing of Matthew Arnold's Letters." *VN* 37:27–29.

3984. Racin, John. " 'Dover Beach' and the Structure of Meditation." *VP* 8:49–54.

* 3985. Ray, Linda L. "Callicles on Etna:The Other Mask." *VP* 7(1969):309–20.

3986. Reed, John R. "Matthew Arnold and the Soul's Horizons." *VP* 8:15–24.

3987. Roper, Alan. *Arnold's Poetic Landscapes.* Baltimore: Johns Hopkins U.P., 1969.

3988. Sharples, Edward. "The Holistic Principle in Arnold." *English* 19:49–53.

3989. Starzyk, Lawrence J. "Arnold and Carlyle." *Criticism* 4:281–300.

3990. Super, Robert H. *The Time-Spirit of Matthew Arnold.* Ann Arbor: U. of Mich. P.

3991. Walcott, Fred G. *The Origins of Culture and Anarchy: Matthew Arnold and Popular Education in England.* Toronto: U. of Toronto P.

3992. Walker, Warren S. "Burns' Influence on *Sohrab and Rustum*:A Closer Look." *VP* 8:151–58.

* 3993. Waller, John O. "Doctor Arnold's Sermons and Matthew Arnold's 'Rugby Chapel'." *SEL* 9(1969):633–46.

See also 3883, 4731.

Arnold, T. See 3980, 3993.

Austen. 3994. Beattie, Thomas C. "From *Pride and Prejudice* to *Emma*:A Study of Jane Austen as Moralist." *DAI* 30(1969): 311A–12A(Mich.).

3995. Bellot-Antony, Michèle. "*Pride and Prejudice*:Comédie des erreurs?" *LanM* 64:67–74.

3996. Craik, Wendy A. *Jane Austen in Her Time.* London: Nelson, 1969; New York: N.Y.U. Press, 1969.

* 3997. Emmett, Victor J.,Jr. "Jane Austen's Plots." *MQ* 11:393–409.

3998. Gould, Gerald L. "The Gate Scene at Sotherton in *Mansfield Park*." *L&P* 20:75–78.

3999. Green, Maria. "Snobbery as a Pursuit and Disease in Proust and Jane Austen." [F 2]:255–62.

4000. Hayter, Alethea. "Xanadu at Lyme Regis." *ArielE* 1,i:61–64. [Influ. of "Kubla Khan" on *Persuasion*.]

4001. Holly, Marcia V. "Jane Austen and the Uniqueness of *Emma*." *DAI* 30(1969):1137A(Wash. State).

4002. Kauvar, Elaine M. "Jane Austen and *The Female Quixote*." *SNNTS* 2:211–21.

4003. Kissane, James D. "Comparison's Blessed Felicity: Character Arrangement in *Emma*." *SNNTS* 2:173–84.

4004. Knight, Charles A. "Irony and Mr. Knightley." *SNNTS* 2:185–93. [*Emma*.]

4005. Lauber, John. "Minds Bewildered and Astray:The Crawfords in *Mansfield Park*." *SNNTS* 2:194–210.

4006. Marshall, Sarah L. "Rationality and Delusion in Jane Austen's *Emma*." *UMSE* 9(1968):57–67.

* 4007. McMaster, Juliet. "The Continuity of Jane Austen's Novels." *SEL* 10:723–39.

* 4008. Moore, E. Margaret. "Emma and Miss Bates:Early Experiences of Separation and the Theme of Dependency in Jane Austen's Novels." *SEL* 9(1969):573–85.

4009. O'Neill, Judith,ed. *Critics on Jane Austen.* (RLitC 5.) London: Allen and Unwin.

4010. Rohmann, Gerd. "Jane Austen:*Pride and Prejudice*: Auktorialer Kommentar und Perspektivtechnik." *NS* 19:455–61.

4011. Rubinstein, E. "Jane Austen's Novels:The Metaphor of Rank." [F 55]:101–93. [Notes, 218–25.]

4012. Ryals, Clyde de L. "Being and Doing in *Mansfield Park*." *Archiv* 206:345–60.

4013. Soye, Brigitte de. "Bath dans *Northanger Abbey*." *EA* 23:83–86.

* 4014. Stone, Donald D. "Sense and Semantics in Jane Austen." *NCF* 25:31–50.

4015. Tanner, Tony,ed. *Sense and Sensibility.* Baltimore: Penguin, 1969.

4016. Watson, J.R. "Mr. Perry's Patients:A View of *Emma*." *EIC* 20:334–43.

4017. Welty, Eudora. "A Note on Jane Austen." *Shenandoah* 20,iii(1969):3–17.

See also 1453, 2567, 3527, 3959, 6310, 6936.

Bailey. 4018. Hudnall, Clayton E. "An Unpublished Memoir of Keats' Friend, Benjamin Bailey." *N&Q* 17:175–77.

Baillie. 4019. Lambertson, C.L.,ed. "Speaking of Byron." *MHRev* 12(1969):18–42; 13:24–46. [Letters from Joanna Baillie to Sir Walter Scott, 1814–19.]

Baker. 4020. Childs, James B. "*Mémoires d'un voyageur qui se repose*:A Bibliographical Interlude on an Elusive Foreign Service Officer's Impressions of the United States, 1811–32." *PBSA* 64:193–204. [Anthony St. John Baker.]

Beardsley. 4021. Brophy, Brigid. *Black and White:A Portrait of Aubrey Beardsley.* New York: Stein and Day, 1969.

4022. Reade, Brian. "The Beardsley Foreground." *AntigR* 1,i:3–26.

Bentham. 4023. Mack, Mary P.,ed. *A Bentham Reader.* New York: Pegasus, 1969.

4024. Scott, Joseph W. "Bentham's Poem on George II." *TLS* 2 Oct:1137.

Bradley, F.H. 4025. Assad-Mikhail, Fauzia. "Bradley et Heidegger." *RMM* 75:151–88.

Brontë, C. 4026. Burnett, T.A.,ed. *The Search After Hapiness/*sic*]:A Tale.* Illus. Carolyn Dinan. New York: Simon & Schuster, 1969.

4027. Chambers, L.R. "*The Search after Happiness*." *TLS* 22 Jan:85. [Bibliog. note; see also 5 Feb:135.]

4028. Gerin, Winifred. *Charlotte Brontë:The Evolution of Genius.* New York and London: Oxford U.P. [Paperback.]

4029. Jack, Jane, and Margaret Smith,eds. *Jane Eyre.* (Clarendon Ed. of the Novels of the Brontës.) Oxford: Clarendon, 1969.

4030. Passel, Anne. "Charlotte Brontë:A Bibliography of the Criticism of Her Novels." *BB* 26(1969):118–20(to be cont.).

4031. ——— "Charlotte Brontë." *BB* 27:13–20. [Pt. 2.]

4032. Stevens, Joan. "Charlotte Brontë's Mistake." *N&Q* 17:19.

4033. Winnifrith, T.J. "Charlotte Brontë and Calvinism." *N&Q* 17:17–18.

See also 3942, 3964.

Brontë, E. 4034. Allott, Miriam. *Emily Brontë.* London: Macmillan.

4035. Flahiff, Frederick R.,ed. *Wuthering Heights.* New York: Odyssey.

4036. Hewish, John. *Emily Brontë:A Critical and Biographical Study.* London: Macmillan, 1969.

4036a. Van de Laar, Elisabeth Th. M. *The Inner Structure of Wuthering Heights:A Study of an Imaginative Field.* The Hague: Mouton, 1969.

4037. Vančura, Zdeněk. "The Stones of *Wuthering Heights*." *PP* 13:1–15.

4038. *Wuthering Heights, and Selected Poems.* (Bestsellers of Lit. Ser.) Introd. Elizabeth Jennings and Notes by Phyllis Bentley. London: Pan, 1967.

Brontës. 4039. Bellour, Raymond and Hélène. "Le jeu des Jeunes Hommes:Introduction à l'analyse comparée des écrits de jeunesse de Charlotte et Branwell Brontë." *RE* 22:337–62.

4040. Gregor, Ian,ed. *The Brontës:A Collection of Critical Essays.* Englewood Cliffs, N.J.: Prentice-Hall. [Prev. pub. essays.]

4041. Maurat, Charlotte. *The Brontës' Secret.* Tr. Margaret Meldrum. New York: Barnes & Noble.

4042. Morrison, Nancy B. *Haworth Harvest:The Lives of the Brontës.* London: Dent, 1969.

4043. Sherry, Norman. *Charlotte and Emily Brontë.* (LitP.) London: Evans, 1969.

4044. Stephens, Fran C. "Hartley Coleridge and the Brontës." *TLS* 14 May:544.

Brown, G.D. 4045. Smith, Iain C. "*The House with the Green Shutters*." *SSL* 7:3–10.

Browning, E.B. 4046. Taplin, Gardner B. *The Life of Elizabeth Barrett Browning.* Hamden, Conn.: Archon.

See also 3928, 4529.

Browning, R. *4047. Bieman, Elizabeth. "An Eros Manqué": Browning's 'Andrea del Sarto'." *SEL* 10:651–68.

4048. Bloom, Harold. "Browning's Childe Roland:All Things Deformed and Broken." *Prose* 1:29–44.

4049. *Browning Newsletter.* 4. [Thomas J. Collins, "Robert Browning:A Review of the Year's Research," 3–17; Jack W. Herring, "The Meynell Collection of the Armstrong Browning Library," 18–19; Michael Hancher and Jerrold Moore, " 'The Sound of a Voice that is Still':Browning's Edison Cylinder," 21–33; Lionel Stevenson and Thomas J. Collins, "The Source for 'Clive'," 40–41; Michael Hancer, "A Note on the Prose Life of Strafford," 42–45; Nathaniel I. Hart, "A Second Supplement to 'A Calendar of Letters'," 46–56; Sharon Tucker, "A Hitherto Unpublished Letter from Robert Browning to James Thomas Fields," 57–58; Robert F. Fleissner, "*Pauline*:Another Merely 'Random Relation of Browning to Shakespeare'?" 59; Helen M. Barthelme, "A Checklist of Publications (July 1969-December 1969)," 66–69.]

* 4050. Chambers, Leland H. "Gide, Santayana, Chesterton, and Browning." *CLS* 7:216–28.

4051. Chell, Samuel L. "Browning and Bergson:A Time-Centered Approach to *Childe Roland*." *Wisconsin Studies in Lit.* 6(1969):1–13.

4052. Crowder, Bland. "Browning's 'L.D.I.E.' " *AN&Q* 8(1969):52.

4053. Drew, Philip. *The Poetry of Browning:A Critical Introduction.* London: Methuen.

4054. Eggenschwiler, David. "Psychological Complexity in 'Porphyria's Lover'." *VP* 8:39–48.

4055. Fleck, Richard. "Browning's 'Up at a Villa—Down in the City' as Satire." *VP* 7(1969):345–49.

4056. Fleissner, Robert F. " 'My Last Duchess'." *TLS* 4 Dec(1969):1405.

4057. Gridley, Roy E. "Browning and His Reader, 1855–1969." [F 53]:75–92.

4058. Guidi, Augusto. "Robert Browning e il Veneto." *FeL* 16:77–86.

4059. Isaacs, Neil D., and Richard M. Kelly. "Dramatic Tension and Irony in Browning's 'The Glove'." *VP* 8:157–59.

* 4060. Johnson, Alan P. "*Sordello*:Apollo, Bacchus, and the Pattern of Italian History." *VP* 7(1969):321–38.

4061. Kelley, Philip, and Ronald Hudson. "A Note on Browning's Variants." *N&Q* 17:22–23.

4062. Litzinger, Boyd, and Donald Smalley,eds. *Browning: The Critical Heritage.* New York: Barnes & Noble; London: Routledge & K. Paul.

4063. Low, Donald A. "Browning's Rhetoric:A Reappraisal of *The Ring and the Book*." *FMLS* 6:195–99. [Rev. art.]

4064. MacEachen, Dougald B. "Browning's Use of His Sources in 'Andrea del Sarto'." *VP* 8:61–64.

* 4065. Monteiro, George. "The Apostasy and Death of St. Praxed's Bishop." *VP* 8:209–18.

4066. Perrine, Laurence. "Browning's 'Too Late':A Re-Interpretation." *VP* 7(1969):339–45.

4067. Phipps, Charles T.,S.J. "Browning's Canon Giuseppe Caponsacchi:Warrior-Priest, Dantean Lover, Critic of Society." *ELH* 36(1969):696–718.

* 4068. ——— "The Bishop as Bishop:Clerical Motif and Meaning in 'The Bishop Orders His Tomb at St. Praxed's Church'." *VP* 8:199–208.

4069. Shields, Ellen F. "Bishop and Blougram and the Cardinals." *VN* 37:21–24.

4070. Steffey, Mary L. "Browning's Metaphors of Transformation." *DAI* 30:4956A(Baylor).

4071. Stuart, Floyd R. "Browning's Attitude Toward Miracles." *UMSE* 9(1968):1–10.

4072. Sutton, Max Keith. "Language as Defense in 'Porphyria's Lover'." *CE* 31(1969):280–89.

4073. Takiyama, Tokuzo. "The Shaping of *The Ring and the Book*, Book VII Pompilia." [F 1]:370–96. [In Jap.]

* 4074. Thompson, Gordon W. "Authorial Detachment and Imagery in *The Ring and the Book*." *SEL* 10:669–86.

4075. Toole, William B.,III. "Wit and Symbol:The Prior's Niece and the Structure of 'Fra Lippo Lippi'." *SAB* 35,ii:3–8.

4076. Viswanathan, S. " 'Ay, Note that Potter's Wheel': Browning and 'That Metaphor'." *VP* 7(1969):349–52.

4077. Ward, Maisie. *Robert Browning and His World*. Vol. III:*Two Robert Brownings?* London: Cassell, 1969.
See also 1471, 3886, 4102, 4122, 4329, 4529, 4549, 4738, 5985.

Brownings. 4078. Ricks, Christopher B.,comp. *The Brownings:Letters and Poetry*. Illus. Barnett I. Plotkin. Garden City, N.Y.: Doubleday.

Buchanan. *4079. Forsyth, R.A. "Robert Buchanan and the Dilemma of the Brave New Victorian World." *SEL* 9(1969): 647–57.

Bulwer-Lytton. 4080. Eigner, Edwin M. "Raphael in Oxford Street:Bulwer's Accommodation to the Realists." [F 53]:61–74.
See also 3942, 4238.

Butler. 4081. Aldaz, Anna-Marie D. "Valery Larbaud as Translator of Samuel Butler." *DAI* 31:1256A(Ore.).

4082. Čekalov, I.I. "Antiklerikal'naja satira Samuèlja Batlera ('Muzykal'nye banki' v *Edgine*)." *IAN* 29:217–27. [On *Erewhon*.]

* 4083. Daniels, R. Balfour. "Names in the Fiction of Samuel Butler (1835–1902)." *SCB* 29(1969):129–32.

4084. Hoyenga, Betty R. "Samuel Butler's *Erewhon*:A Critical and Annotated Edition." *DAI* 30:2970A(Neb.).
See also 4377, 5387.

Byron. 4085. Ashton, Thomas L. "Naming Byron's Aurora Raby." *ELN* 7(1969):114–20.

4086. Beer, Gavin de. "Byron's French Passport." *KSMB* 20(1969):31–36.

4087. —— "Maillons du filet byronien en Suisse." *EdL* 3:110–29.

* 4088. Bentley, G.E.,Jr. "Byron, Shelley, Wordsworth, Blake, and *The Seaman's Recorder*." *SIR* 9:21–36.

4089. Brennecke, Detlef. "Die vier Übersetzungen Gottlieb Mohnikes aus dem Englischen des Lord Byron." *LWU* 3:15–27.

4090. Cunningham, John M.,Jr. "Byron's Poetics in *Don Juan*." *DAI* 30:4979A(Duke).

4091. Diakonova, Nina. "Byron and the English Romantics." *ZAA* 18:144–67.

* 4092. Elledge, W. Paul. "Byron's Hungry Sinner:The Quest Motif in *Don Juan*." *JEGP* 69:1–13.

4093. Giddey, Ernest. "Les trahisons du Byronisme." *EdL* 3:89–109.

4094. Henley, V.W. "The Trouble with Byron." *FHP* 4,iv: 25–46.

4095. Kahn, Arthur D. "Byron's Single Difference with Homer and Virgil:The Redefinition of the Epic in *Don Juan*." *Arcadia* 5:143–62.

4096. Klein, H.M. " 'Sangrado'—Byron Before Scott." *N&Q* 17:174.

4097. Manning, Peter J. "Byron and the Stage." *DAI* 30(1969):689A(Yale).

4098. Marshall, William H. *Selected Poems and Letters*. (Riverside Eds.) With Introd. Boston: Houghton, 1968.

4099. McConnell, Frank D. "Byron's Reductions:'Much Too Poetical'." *ELH* 37:415–32.

4100. Mosier, John F. "Byron's *Don Juan*:History as Epic." *DAI* 30(1969):2492A(Tulane).

4101. Ogawa, Kazuo. "Byron:*Don Juan*, Canto II." *Oberon* 29(1968):64–76; 30(1968):53–69. [The Jap. tr.]

4102. Orel, Harold. "The Relationships Between Three Poet-Dramatists and Their Public:Lord Byron, Thomas Talfourd, and Robert Browning." [F 53]:31–49.

4103. Paananen, Victor N. "Byron and the Caves of Ellora." *N&Q* 16(1969):414–16.

4104. Pratt, John M. "Byron and the Stream of Wit:Studies in the Development, Survival and Culmination of the Colloquial Mode in English Poetry." *DAI* 30(1969):2495A(Pa.).

* 4105. Robinson, Charles E. "The Devil as Doppelanger in *The Deformed Transformed*:The Sources and Meaning of Byron's Unfinished Drama." *BNYPL* 74:177–202.

4106. Rutherford, Andrew,comp. *Byron:The Critical Heritage*. New York: Barnes & Noble; London: Routledge & K. Paul.

4107. Steffan, Truman G. "Byron and Old Clothes:An Unpublished Letter." *N&Q* 16(1969):416–20.

4108. —— *Lord Byron's* Cain:*Twelve Essays and a Text with Variants and Annotations*. Austin: U. of Texas P., 1969.

4109. Stringham, Scott. "*I due Foscari*:From Byron's Play to Verdi's Opera." *WVUPP* 17:31–40.

* 4110. Sundell, Michael G. "The Development of *The Giaour*." *SEL* 9(1969):587–99.

4111. Trease, Geoffrey. *Byron:A Poet Dangerous to Know*. New York: Holt, Rinehart and Winston, 1969. [Biog.]

4112. Wallis, Bruce E. "Lord Byron's Critical Opinions." *DAI* 30(1969):1186A(Princeton).

4113. Witt, Robert W. " 'So We'll Go No More A Roving'." *UMSE* 9(1968):69–84. [B's affair with Teresa Guiccioli and its influ. on his poetry.]
See also 999, 3116, 3931, 4259, 4756, 5718.

Callanan, J.J. 4114. Lee, B.S. "Callanan's 'The Outlaw of Loch Lene'." *ArielE* 1,iii:89–100.

Carleton, W. 4115. Ibarra, Eileen. "William Carleton:An Introduction." *Éire* 5,i:81–86.

Carlyle. 4116. Arecchi, Paolo. "Mazzini critico di Machiavelli, Carlyle, Renan." *Proc* 16,iv(1969):200–03.

4117. Brée, Germaine. "Rencontre avec Carlyle." *RHL* 70,ii:286–95.

4118. Campbell, Ian. "James Barrett and Carlyle's *Journal*." *N&Q* 17:19–21.

4119. Carter, Geoffrey. "Carlyle's Use of Metaphor in His Essays." *DAI* 30(1969):2521A(Pa.).

* 4120. Coulling, Sidney M.B. "Carlyle and Swift." *SEL* 10:741–58.

4121. Fiumara, Francesco. *Mazzini e la legge del progresso negli scritti su Machiavelli, Carlyle, Renan*. Napoli: Centro napoletano di studi mazziniani, 1969.

4122. Gadziola, David S. "The Prophet and the Poet:The Relationship of Thomas Carlyle with Robert Browning, Alfred Tennyson and Arthur Hugh Clough." *DAI* 30(1969):1562A(Md.).

4123. Reed, Walter L. "Meditations on the Hero:Narrative Form in Carlyle, Kierkegaard, and Melville." *DAI* 31:1288A (Yale).

4124. Spivey, Herbert E. "Carlyle and Mill on the Individual in Society." *DAI* 30:3478A(Duke).

4125. Sussman, Herbert,ed. *Thomas Carlyle*:Sartor Resartus *and Selected Prose*. New York: Holt, Rinehart and Winston.

4126. Tarr, Rodger L. " 'A Sentimental Journey':Carlyle's Final Visit to the Grange." *N&Q* 17:21–22.

4127. Wolfsohl, Clarence J. "Thomas Carlyle:Comedy and the Comic Vision." *DAI* 30:5459A–60A(N.M.).
See also 3884, 3886, 3941, 3989, 4152, 4265, 4317, 4545, 4565, 4605, 6677.

Cholmondeley. 4128. Colby, Vineta. " 'Devoted Amateur': Mary Cholmondeley and *Red Pottage*." *EIC* 20:213–28.

Clare. 4129. Robinson, Eric, and Geoffrey Summerfield. "Unpublished Poems by John Clare." *MHRev* 2(1967):106–20.

4130. Storey, Mark. "Clare's 'Love and Beauty'." *Expl* 28:Item 60.

Clough. 4131. Allott, Kenneth. "The Image of the Rising Tide in Clough's 'Say Not the Struggle Nought Availeth'." *N&Q* 17:23.

4132. Clough, Blanche S.,ed. *The Poems and Prose Remains of Arthur Hugh Clough*. 2 Vols. St. Clair Shores, Mich.: Scholarly Press, 1969.

4133. Greenberger, Evelyn B. "Clough's 'The Judgement of Brutus':A Newly Found Poem." *VP* 8:129–50.

4134. Torikai, Hisayoshi. "Yume to Bi to Genjitsu to."

Oberon 32:48–58. [Dream, beauty, reality—poems of C.]
   See also 3883, 3928, 4122, 4766.
   Cobbett. *4135. Duff, Gerald. "William Cobbett and the Prose of Revelation." *TSLL* 11:1349–65.
   Coleridge, H. 4136. Kreutz, Christian. "Hartley Coleridges Prometheusbild." *Anglia* 88:197–221.
   See also 4044.
   Coleridge, S. *See* 1040.
   Coleridge, S.T. *4137. D'Avanzo, Mario L. "Coleridge's 'This Lime-tree Bower my Prison' and *The Tempest*." *WC* 1:66–68.
   4138. Delson, Abe. "A Search for Meaning:A Critical History of the Thematic Interpretations of 'The Rime of the Ancient Mariner,' 1798–1965." *DAI* 30:4447A–48A(N.Y.U.).
   4139. D'Itri, Patricia A. "A Study of Samuel Taylor Coleridge's Critical Reception in Five Major Nineteenth Century Periodicals." *DAI* 30(1969):2479A–80A(Mich. State).
   4140. Doughty, Oswald. "Coleridge as Statesman." *EM* 20(1969):241–55.
   4141. Duff, Gerald. "Speech as Theme in 'The Rime of the Ancient Mariner'." *HAB* 21,iii:26–31.
   4142. Duffy, John J. "From Hanover to Burlington:James Marsh's Search for Unity." *Vt. Hist.* 38:27–48. [The 1st Amer. ed. of Coleridge.]
   4143. —— "Problems in Publishing Coleridge:James Marsh's First American Edition of *Aids to Reflection*." *NEQ* 43:193–208.
   4144. Dunn, John J. "Coleridge's Debt to Macpherson's *Ossian*." *SSL* 7:76–89.
   4145. Emslie, MacDonald, and Paul Edwards. "The Limitations of Langdale:A Reading of *Christabel*." *EIC* 20:57–70.
   4146. Enrico, Harold. "Shipwreck in Infinity:Leopardi, Coleridge, and Wordsworth on the Imagination." [F 2]:93–101.
   4147. Foakes, R.A. "The Text of Coleridge's 1811–12 Shakespeare Lectures." *ShS* 23:101–11.
   * 4148. Fulmer, O. Bryan. "The Ancient Mariner and the Wandering Jew." *SP* 66(1969):797–815.
   4149. Gaskins, Avery F. "Real and Imaginary Time in 'The Rime of the Ancient Mariner'." *NDQ* 37,iv(1969):43–47.
   4150. Gibbons, Edward E. "The Conversation Poems of Samuel Taylor Coleridge:Coleridgean Art and Coleridgean Theory." *DAI* 30:3429A(Pa.).
   4151. Hall, Roland. "Words from Coleridge's *Biographia Literaria*." *N&Q* 17:171–74.
   4152. Harris, Wendell V. "The Shape of Coleridge's 'Public' System." *MP* 68:46–61.
   4153. Jackson, James R. de J.,ed. *Coleridge:The Critical Heritage.* London: Routledge & K. Paul.
   4154. —— *Method and Imagination in Coleridge's Criticism.* Cambridge: Harvard U.P., 1969.
   4155. Jacobus, Mary. "William Huntington's 'Spiritual Sea-Voyage':Another Source for *The Ancient Mariner*." *N&Q* 16(1969):409–12.
   4156. Kennedy, Wilma L. *The English Heritage of Coleridge of Bristol, 1798:The Basis in Eighteenth-Century English Thought for His Distinction Between Imagination and Fancy.* (YSE 104.) Hamden, Conn.: Archon, 1969. [Rpr.]
   4157. Lawrence, Berta. *Coleridge and Wordsworth in Somerset.* Newton Abbot, Devonshire: David and Charles.
   4158. Leitz, Robert C.,III. "Fletcher Christian and the Ancient Mariner:A Refutation." *DR* 50:62–70. [See Bibliog. for 1966, Item 6026.]
   4159. Lupton, Mary J. "A Psychoanalytic Study of the Poetry of Samuel Taylor Coleridge." *DAI* 30(1969):1530A–31A(Temple).
   * 4160. —— "'The Rime of the Ancient Mariner':The Agony of Thirst." *AI* 27:240–59.
   4161. Mackenzie, Norman. " 'Kubla Khan':A Poem of Creative Agony and Loss." *EM* 20(1969):229–40.
   4162. Magnuson, Paul A. "The Problems of Personal Identity and Guilt in Coleridge's Poetry." *DAI* 30:3466A–67A(Minn.).
   4163. Okamoto, Akio. "Coleridge to Marco Polo." *EigoS* 114(1968):580–81. [C and Marco Polo; in Jap.]
   4164. Orsini, G.N.G. *Coleridge and German Idealism:A Study in the History of Philosophy with Unpublished Materials from Coleridge's Manuscripts.* Carbondale: So. Ill. U.P., 1969.
   4165. Pachori, Satya S. "The Transcendentalism of Samuel Taylor Coleridge." *DAI* 30:4421A–22A(Mo., Columbia).
   4166. Parker, A. Reeve. "Wordsworth's Whelming Tide: Coleridge and the Art of Analogy." [F 48]:75–102.
   4167. Patton, Lewis, and Peter Mann,eds. *The Collected Works of Samuel Taylor Coleridge. Volume I:Lectures 1795, On Politics and Religion.* Princeton: Princeton U.P.
   4168. Patton, Lewis,ed. *The Collected Works of Samuel Taylor Coleridge, II:The Watchman.* London: Routledge & K. Paul; Princeton, N.J.: Bollingen.
   * 4169. Pollin, Burton R., assist. by Redmond Burke. "John Thelwall's Marginalia in a Copy of Coleridge's *Biographia Literaria*." *BNYPL* 74:71–94.
   4170. Prickett, Stephen. *Coleridge and Wordsworth:The Poetry of Growth.* London: Cambridge U.P.
   * 4171. Rahme, Mary. "Coleridge's Concept of Symbolism." *SEL* 9(1969):619–32.
   4172. Rooke, Barbara E. *The Collected Works of Samuel Taylor Coleridge. Volume IV:The Friend.* Princeton: Princeton U.P.
   * 4173. Schwartz, Lewis M. "A New Review of Coleridge's *Christabel*." *SIR* 9:114–24. [Rev. attrib. to Lamb.]
   4174. Shaffer, Elinor S. "Coleridge's Revolution in the Standard of Taste." *JAAC* 28(1969):213–21.
   * 4175. —— "The 'Postulates in Philosophy' in the *Biographia Literaria*." *CLS* 7:297–313.
   * 4176. Stephens, Fran. "The Coleridge Collection:A Sample." *LCUT* N.S. 1:33–38.
   4177. Visweswariah, H.S. "Motive-Finding in 'The Rime of the Ancient Mariner'." *LCrit* 8,iv(1969):27–38.
   4178. Warner, Oliver. "Coleridge's 'Naval Poetry' and Southey's *Life of Nelson*." *N&Q* 17:169–70.
   4179. Werkmeister, Lucyle, and P.M. Zall. "Coleridge's 'The Complaint of Ninathoma'." *N&Q* 16(1969):412–14.
   4180. Whalley, George. "Coleridge's Marginalia Lost." *BC* 17(1968):428–42.
   4181. Wojcik, Manfred. "Coleridge and the Problem of Transcendentalism." *ZAA* 18:30–58.
   4182. —— "The Mimetic Orientation of Coleridge's Aesthetic Thought." *ZAA* 17(1969):344–91.
   4183. Yura, Kimiyoshi. "Coleridge's Terror Corporeus Sive Materialism." *EigoS* 114(1968):505–07. [In Jap.]
   See also 126, 3397, 3862, 3931, 4000, 4135, 4718, 4846, 4855, 4857, 4891, 5852.
   Collins, W. 4184. Marshall, William H. *Wilkie Collins.* (TEAS 94.) New York: Twayne.
   See also 4309.
   Combe. 4185. Hamilton, Harlan W. *Doctor Syntax:A Silhouette of William Combe,Esq.* Kent, Ohio: Kent State U.P.; London: Chatto & Windus, 1969.
   Corelli. *4186. Kowalczyk, Richard L. "New Evidence on Maria Corelli and Arthur Severn:Some Unpublished Letters." *ELT* 13:27–36.
   Crabbe. 4187. Diffey, Carole T. "Journey to Experience: Crabbe's 'Silford Hall'." *DUJ* 30(1969):129–34.
   4188. Hsia, C.T. "Crabbe's Poetry:Its Limitations." *TkR* 1,i:61–77.
   Crackanthorpe. 4189. Peden, William. "Hubert Crackanthorpe:Forgotten Pioneer." *SSF* 7:539–48.
   Darwin, C. 4190. Appleman, Philip,ed. *Darwin:Texts, Background, Contemporary Opinion, Critical Essays.* New York: Norton.
   4191. Grove, Richard S. "A Re-examination of Darwin's Argument in *On the Origin of Species*." *DAI* 30:4411A–12A(Mo., Columbia).
   Davis. 4192. McMahon, Seán. "Eagle of the Empty Eyrie." *Éire* 4,i(1969):138–51. [On Thomas Osborne Davis (1814-45).]
   De Quincey. *See* 4613.
   Dickens. 4193. Adamowski, Thomas H. "The Dickens World and Yoknapatawpha County:A Study of Character and Society in Dickens and Faulkner." *DAI* 30:2995A–96A(Ind.).
   4194. Allombert, Guy. "Dickens au cinéma." *Europe* 488(1969):42–50.
   4195. —— "Essai de filmographie de Dickens." *Europe* 488(1969):51–54.

4196. Anikst, Alexander. "Dickens in Russia." *TLS* 4 un:617.

4197. Beaulieu, Jacqueline. "Dickens à la télévision:Une nterview de Claude Santelli." *Europe* 488(1969):55–61.

4198. Bennett, Joseph T. "A Note on Lord Acton's View of Charles Dickens." *ELN* 7:282–85.

4199. Bizám, Lenke. *Kritikai allegóriák Dickensröl és Kafkáról.* Budapest: Akadémiai K.

4200. Bogolepova, T.G. "Izobraženie gorodskoj žizni v Očerkax Boza'." *VLU* 24,iv(1969):100–09. [On city life as presented in *Sketches by Boz*.]

4201. Bony, Alain. "Réalité et l'imaginaire dans *Hard Times*." *EA* 23:168–82.

4202. Bouvier-Ajam, Maurice. "L'Angleterre au temps de Dickens." *Europe* 488(1969):3–12.

4203. Bracher, Peter. "The Lea & Blanchard Edition of Dickens' *American Notes*, 1842." *PBSA* 63(1969):296–300.

4204. Brice, Alec W.C. " 'A Truly British Judge':Another Article by Dickens." *Dickensian* 66:30–35.

4205. Briggs, Katharine M. "The Folklore of Charles Dickens." *JFI* 7:3–20.

4206. Brook, George L. *The Language of Dickens.* London: André Deutsch.

4207. Brown, Ivor. *Charles Dickens, 1812–1870.* London: Jackdaw.

4208. —— *Dickens and His World.* London: Lutterworth.

4209. Brown, James W. "Charles Dickens and Norwegian Belles-Lettres in the Nineteenth Century." *Edda* 70:65–84.

4210. —— "Charles Dickens in Norway:1839–1912." *DAI* 30(1969):273A(Mich.).

4211. Burke, Alan R. "The Strategy and Theme of Urban Observation in *Bleak House*." *SEL* 9(1969):659–76.

4212. Carlton, W.J. "A Friend of Dickens's Boyhood." *Dickensian* 66:8–15. [Louis d'Elboux.]

4213. Churchill, R.C. "Dickensian Criticism." *TLS* 23 July: 314. [See also 7 Aug:878; 21 Aug:927.]

4214. Clément, Marilène. "Le grillon du foyer." *Europe* 488(1969):83–87.

4215. Cohn, Alan M. "The Dickens Checklist." *DSN* 1,iii: 26–29.

4216. Collins, Philip. " 'Carol Philosophy, Cheerful Views'." *EA* 23:158–67.

4217. —— " 'To Lose No Drop of That Immortal Man'." *Dickensian* 66:42–49. [Rev. art. on Harry Stone,ed., *Charles Dickens:Uncollected Writings from* Household Words, *1850–1859* 1968).]

4218. —— "1940–1960:Enter the Professionals." *Dickensian* 66:143–61. [Dickens crit.]

4219. —— "Dickens Editions." *TLS* 16 Apr:430. [See also 30 Apr:480; 14 May:539.]

4220. —— "Dickens in 1870." *TLS* 4 June:605–06.

4221. —— "The Texts of Dickens' Readings." *BNYPL* 74:360–80.

4222. Coudert, Marie-Louise. "Le brouillard et le réel." *Europe* 488(1969):37–42.

4223. Cowden, Roy W. "Dickens at Work." *MQR* 9:125–32.

4224. Cox, C.B. "Realism and Fantasy in *David Copperfield*." *BJRL* 52:267–83.

4225. Curran, Stuart. "The Lost Paradises of *Martin Chuzzlewit*." *NCF* 25:51–67.

4226. Daleski, H.M. "*Oliver Twist*:Home, Street, and Virtue." *Hasifrut* 2:333–46. [In Hebr.; Eng. sum.]

4227. Dennis, Carl. "Dickens' Moral Vision." *TSLL* 11(1969):1237–46.

4228. Devienne, Sylvette. "Le syndrome pickwickien." *Europe* 488(1969):80–83.

4229. DeVries, Duane. "The *Bleak House* Page-Proofs:More Shavings from Dickens's Workshop." *Dickensian* 66:3–7.

4230. Dickens, C. *Bleak House.* Introd. and Notes by Albert J. Guérard. New York: Holt, Rinehart and Winston.

4231. Donoghue, Denis. "The English Dickens and *Dombey and Son*." *NCF* 24:383–403.

4232. Dontchev, Nicolaï. "Dickens in Bulgaria." *Europe* 488(1969):130–35.

4233. *DSN* 1,ii. [Stanley Friedman, "A Loose Thread in *Our Mutual Friend*," 18–20.]

4234. *DSN* 1,i. [Robert Patten, "The Unpropitious Muse: Pickwick's 'Interpolated' Tales," 7–10 (dating evidence).]

4235. Dyson, Anthony E. "*Edwin Drood*:A Horrible Wonder Apart." *CritQ* 11(1969):138–57.

4236. —— *The Inimitable Dickens:A Reading of the Novels.* London: Macmillan.

4237. Easson, Angus. "Dickens's Marchioness Again." *MLR* 65:517–18.

* 4238. Eigner, Edwin M. "Bulwer-Lytton and the Changed Ending of *Great Expectations*." *NCF* 25:104–08.

4239. Fens, K. "Dickens en Multatuli." *Streven* 24:54–59.

4240. Field, J.C. "Fantasy and Flaw in *The Old Curiosity Shop*." *RLV* 35(1969):609–22.

4241. Fielding, K.J. "1870–1900:Forster and Reaction." *Dickensian* 66:85–100. [Dickens crit.]

4242. Fielding, K.J., and Anne Smith. "*Hard Times* and the Factory Controversy." *NCF* 24:404–27.

4243. Flamm, Dudley. "The Prosecutor Within:Dickens's Final Explanation." *Dickensian* 66:16–23.

4244. Fletcher, Geoffrey S. *The London Dickens Knew.* London: Hutchinson. [Chiefly illustrations.]

4245. Fluchère, Henri. "Lecture et relecture de *Great Expectations*." *Europe* 488(1969):62–77.

4246. Ford, George H. "Dickens and the Voices of Time." *NCF* 24:428–48.

4247. —— "Dickens in the 1960's." *Dickensian* 66:163–82. [Dickens crit.]

4248. Fujimori, Yoshiko. "Dickens no Sashie no kenkyu ni tsuite." *Oberon* 32:41–47. [The study of D illus.]

4249. Gál, István. "Dickens és folyóirata Kossuthról és Széchenyiröl." *FK* 16:199–214.

4250. Gattegno, Jean. "D'un procès à l'autre, ou de *Pickwick* à *Alice*." *EA* 23:208–09.

4251. Gouirand, Jacqueline. "Charles Dickens et l'Amérique." *Europe* 488(1969):136–46.

* 4252. Green, Robert. "*Hard Times*:The Style of a Sermon." *TSLL* 11:1375–96.

4253. Greenberg, Robert A. "On Ending *Great Expectations*." *PLL* 6:152–62.

4255. Haines, Charles. *Charles Dickens.* New York: Watts, 1969.

4256. Hall, William F. "Caricature in Dickens and James." *UTQ* 39:242–57.

4257. Hardwick, Michael and Molly. *Dickens' England.* London: Hardwick.

4258. Hardy, Barbara. "Dickens and the Passions." *NCF* 24:449–66.

* 4259. Harvey, William R. "Charles Dickens and the Byronic Hero." *NCF* 24(1969):305–16.

4260. Heamen, Robert J. "Love, Adversity, and Achievement of Identity:A Study of the Young Men in the Novels of Charles Dickens." *DAI* 30(1969):2024A(Mich.).

4261. Herring, Paul D. "The Number Plans for *Dombey and Son*:Some Further Observations." *MP* 68:151–87.

4262. Hurley, Edward. "Dickens' Portrait of the Artist." *VN* 38:1–5.

4263. Kaplan, Fred. "Pickwick's 'Magnanimous Revenge': Reason and Responsibility in the *Pickwick Papers*." *VN* 37:18–21.

4264. Karbanova, I. Ju. "Tema rabočego klassa v proiz-vedenijax Dikkensa." [F 49]:127–34. [Theme of the working class in Dickens.]

4265. Kenney, Blair G. "Carlyle and *Bleak House*." *Dickensian* 66:36–41.

* 4266. Kincaid, James R. "The Education of Mr. Pickwick." *NCF* 24(1969):127–41.

4267. Klieneberger, H.R. "Charles Dickens and Wilhelm Raabe." *OGS* 4(1969):90–117.

4268. Kogztur, Gizella. "Dickens en Hongrie." *Europe* 488(1969):124–30.

4269. Kotzin, Michael C. "Dickens and the Fairy Tale." *DAI* 30(1969):328A(Minn.).

4270. Lane, Margaret. "Prologue:The Last Months."

Dickensian 66:83–84.

4271. Larson, George S. "Religion in the Novels of Charles Dickens." *DAI* 30(1969):328A–29A(Mass.).

4272. Lauran, Annie. "Dickens dans ma nuit." *Europe* 488(1969):23–26.

4273. Leavis, F.R. and Q.D. *Dickens:The Novelist.* London: Chatto & Windus.

4274. Lelchuk, Alan. "Self, Family, and Society in *Great Expectations.*" *SR* 78:407–26.

4275. Linfield, Nicholas G. "The Languages of Charles Dickens." *DAI* 30:5449A–50A(Texas, Austin).

* 4276. Lougy, Robert E. "Pickwick and 'The Parish Clerk'." *NCF* 25:100–04.

4277. Luedtke, Luther S. "System and Sympathy:The Structural Dialectic of Dickens' *Bleak House.*" *LWU* 3:1–14.

4278. Madaule, Jacques. "Un univers fantastique et vrai." *Europe* 488(1969):26–37.

4279. McLean, Robert S. "Tory Noodles in Sydney Smith and Charles Dickens:An Unnoticed Parallel." *VN* 38:24–25.

4280. McMaster, R.D. " 'Society (Whatever That Was)': Dickens and Society as an Abstraction." *EA* 23:125–35.

4281. McMaster, R.D.,ed. *Great Expectations.* Toronto, New York: Odyssey.

4282. —— *Little Dorrit.* New York: Odyssey.

* 4283. Middlebro', Tom. "Esther Summerson:A Plea for Justice." *QQ* 77:252–59.

4284. Miller, J. Hillis. "The Source of Dickens's Comic Art." *NCF* 24:467–76.

4285. Mills, Nicolaus C. "Social and Moral Vision in *Great Expectations* and *Huckleberry Finn.*" *JAmS* 4:61–72.

4286. Milner, Ian. "The Dickens Drama:Mr. Dombey." *NCF* 24:477–87.

4287. Monod, Sylvère. "1900–1920:The Age of Chesterton." *Dickensian* 66:101–20. [Dickens crit.]

4288. —— "Bilan et perspectives d'une recherche Dickensienne française." *EA* 23:197–207.

4289. —— "Charles Dickens, ou la genèse d'un art moderne." *Europe* 488(1969):12–23.

4290. —— "Dickens's Attitude in *A Tale of Two Cities.*" *NCF* 24:488–505.

4291. Nowell-Smith, Simon. "Editing Dickens:For Which Reader? From Which Text?" *TLS* 4 June:615–16. [See also 11 June:638.]

* 4292. Olshin, Toby A. " 'The Yellow Dwarf' and *The Old Curiosity Shop.*" *NCF* 25:96–99.

4293. Page, Norman. "Convention and Consistency in Dickens' Cockney Dialect." *ES* 51:339–44.

4294. Palmer, William J. "The Involved Self:Affirmation in Dickens' Novels." *DAI* 30:5454A(Notre Dame).

4295. Paraf, Pierre. "Charles Dickens et Hans Christian Andersen." *Europe* 488(1969):105–09.

4296. Parker, Sandra A. "Dickens and the Art of Characterization." *DAI* 30:3915A(Case Western Reserve).

4297. Partlow, Robert B.,Jr.,ed. *Dickens Studies Annual.* Vol. I. Carbondale: So. Ill. U.P.; London: Feffer & Simons. [Harry Stone, "The Unknown Dickens:With a Sampling of Uncollected Writings," 1–22; Margaret Ganz, "The Vulnerable Ego:Dickens' Humor in Decline," 23–40; John R. Reed, "Confinement and Character in Dickens' Novels," 41–54; Duane DeVries, "Two Glimpses of Dickens' Early Development as a Writer of Fiction," 55–64; Louis James, "Pickwick in America!" 65–80; Jane R. Cohen, "Strained Relations:Charles Dickens and George Cattermole," 81–92; Angus Easson, "*The Old Curiosity Shop*: From Manuscript to Print," 93–128; Jerome Meckier, "The Faint Image of Eden:The Many Worlds of *Nicholas Nickleby*," 129–46; Henri Talon, "*Dombey and Son*:A Closer Look at the Text," 147–60; Michael Steig, "Iconography of Sexual Conflict in *Dombey and Son*," 161–67; J. Miriam Benn, "A Landscape with Figures:Characterization and Expression in *Hard Times*," 168–82; Trevor Blount, "Dickens and Mr. Krook's Spontaneous Combustion," 183–211; Lance Schachterle, "*Bleak House* as a Serial Novel," 212–24; Leonard Manheim, "A Tale of Two Characters:A Study in Multiple Projection," 225–37; Robert Barnard, "Imagery and Theme in *Great Expectations*," 238–51;

Annabel M. Patterson, "*Our Mutual Friend*:Dickens as the Compleat Angler," 252–64; Paul Gottschalk, "Time in *Edwin Drood*," 265–72.]

4298. —— *Dickens the Craftsman:Strategies of Presentation.* Carbondale: So. Ill. U.P.

4299. Patten, Robert L. "Portraits of Pott:Lord Brougham and *The Pickwick Papers.*" *Dickensian* 66:205–24.

4300. Piscopo, Ugo. "Dickens en Italie." *Europe* 488(1969): 116–24. [Tr. Camille Sinaï.]

4301. Pook, John. "*Bleak House* and *Little Dorrit*:A Comparison." *AWR* 19,xliii:154–59.

4302. Pothet, Lucien. "Sur quelques images d'intimité chez Dickens." *EA* 23:136–57.

4303. Powell, Dilys. "Postscript:Dickens on Film." *Dickensian* 66:183–85.

4304. Reinhold, Heinz,ed. *Charles Dickens:Sein Werk im Lichte neuer deutscher Forschung.* Heidelberg: Winter, 1969. [Some reprs.]

4305. Robison, Roselee. "Dickens and the Sentimental Tradition:Mr. Pickwick and My Uncle Toby." *UTQ* 39:258–73.

4306. —— "Innocence in the Novels of Charles Dickens." *DAI* 30:4424A–25A(Toronto).

4307. Rooke, Patrick J. *The Age of Dickens.* London: Wayland.

4308. Roudy, Pierre. "Dickens en Angleterre." *Europe* 488(1969):110–16.

4309. Ruer, Jean. "Charles Dickens, Wilkie Collins et *The Frozen Deep.*" *EA* 23:183–89.

4310. Ryan, Sister M. Rosario. "Dickens and Shakespeare: Probable Sources of *Barnaby Rudge.*" *English* 19:43–48.

4311. Saijo, Takao. "Unity and *The Pickwick Papers.*" *Hiroshima Studies in Eng. Lang. and Lit.* 16,i–ii(1969):30–40.

4312. Sampson, Edward. "The Problem of Communication in *Bleak House.*" [F 47]:121–24.

4313. Saywood, B.C. "Dr. Syntax:A Pickwickian Prototype?" *Dickensian* 66:24–29.

4314. Schilling, Bernard N. "Balzac, Dickens and 'This Harsh World'." *Adam* 331–33(1969):109–22.

4315. —— "Realism in 19th Century Fiction:Balzac, Dickens and the Bildungsroman." [F 3]:251–59.

4316. Slater, Michael. "1920–1940:'Superior Folk' and Scandalmongers." *Dickensian* 66:121–42. [Dickens crit.]

4317. —— "Carlyle and Jerrold into Dickens:A Study of *The Chimes.*" *NCF* 24:506–26.

4318. —— "*The Bastille Prisoner*:A Reading Dickens Never Gave." *EA* 23:190–96.

4319. —— "The Year's Work in Dickens Studies, 1969." *Dickensian* 66:225–30.

4321. —— *Dickens 1970:Centenary Essays.* London: Chapman and Hall.

4322. Smith, Mary D. " 'All Her Perfections Tarnished':The Thematic Function of Esther Summerson." *VN* 38:10–14.

4323. Steig, Michael. "*Dombey and Son*:Chapter XXXI, Plate 20." *ELN* 7(1969):124–27.

4324. —— "Structure and the Grotesque in Dickens:*Dombey and Son*; *Bleak House.*" *CentR* 14:313–30.

* 4325. —— "The Iconography of *David Copperfield.*" *HSL* 2:1–18.

4326. Stéphane, Nelly. "Chronologie de Dickens." *Europe* 488(1969):147–56.

4327. —— "Double Dickens:*Les contes de Noël.*" *Europe* 488(1969):88–104.

4328. Stokes, E. "*Bleak House* and *The Scarlet Letter.*" *AUMLA* 32(1969):177–89.

4329. Stone, Harry. "Dickens, Browning, and the Mysterious Letter." *PCP* 1(1966):42–47. [Concerning *A Blot in the 'Scutcheon.*]

4330. —— "Dickens Rediscovered:Some Lost Writings Retrieved." *NCF* 24:527–48.

4331. Stone, Harry,ed. *Charles Dickens' Uncollected Writings from Household Words, 1850–1859.* 2 vols. Bloomington: Ind. U.P., 1968. [Pub. in England as *The Uncollected Writings of Charles Dickens*: Household Words, *1850–1859.* London: Penguin, 1969.]

* 4332. Sucksmith, Harvey P. "Dickens and Mayhew:A Further Note." *NCF* 24(1969):345–49.

4333. —— *The Narrative Art of Charles Dickens:The Rhetoric of Sympathy and Irony in His Novels.* Oxford: Clarendon.

4334. Sullivan, Mary R. "Black and White Characters in *Hard Times*." *VN* 38:5–10.

4335. Theimer, Robert H. "Fairy Tale and the Triumph of the Ideal in Three Novels by Charles Dickens." *DAI* 30(1969): 1185A(Stanford).

* 4336. Tick, Stanley. "The Memorializing of Mr. Dick." *NCF* 24(1969):142–53.

4337. Tolstoï, Catherine. "Le rendez-vous de Gad's Hill: Dickens cent ans après." *NL* 16 juil:3.

4338. Tomlin, Eric W.F.,ed. *Charles Dickens, 1812–1870:A Centenary Volume.* London: Weidenfeld and Nicolson, 1969. [Crit. essays by Nicholas Bently, Ivor Brown, Christopher Hibbert, Edgar Johnson, J.B. Priestly, Harry Stone, Emlyn Williams, and E.W.F. Tomlin.]

4339. Tomlin, E.W.F. "The Englishness of Dickens." *EA* 23:113–24.

4340. Wagner, Karl H. "Charles Dickens oder die humane Qualität des Humors." *NsM* 23:102–03.

4341. Wilkie, Katharine E. *Charles Dickens:The Inimitable Boz.* London and New York: Abelard. [Biog.]

4342. Wilson, Angus. *The World of Charles Dickens.* Illus. New York: Viking.

4343. Wing, George. "Some Recent Dickens Criticism and Scholarship." *ArielE* 1,iv:56–66. [Rev. art.]

4344. Ziegler, Gilette. "Dickens et l'enfance malheureuse." *Europe* 488(1969):77–80.

See also 959, 1452, 3644, 3916, 3942, 3964, 4403, 4776, 5664, 5665, 5678, 6246, 6778, 7843.

Disraeli, B. 4345. Blake, Robert. *Disraeli and Gladstone.* London: Cambridge U.P. [The 1969 Leslie Stephen Lecture.]

4346. Rooke, Patrick J. *Gladstone and Disraeli.* London: Wayland.

D'Israeli, I. 4347. Ogden, James. *Isaac D'Israeli.* (OEM.) Oxford: Clarendon, 1969.

See also 6561.

Dixon, R.W. 4348. Summerfield, H. "The Lyric Poetry of R.W. Dixon (1833–1900)." *Trivium* 5:57–71.

Dodgson. 4349. Davies, Ivor. "Looking-Glass Chess." *AWR* 19,xliii:189–91.

4350. Flescher, Jacqueline. "The Language of Nonsense in *Alice*." [F 12]:128–44.

4351. Holquist, Michael. "What is a Boojum? Nonsense and Modernism." [F 12]:145–64.

4352. Hudson, Derek. "Lewis Carroll and G.M. Hopkins: Clergyman on a Victorian See-Saw." *DR* 50:83–87.

* 4353. Matthews, Charles. "Satire in the *Alice* Books." *Criticism* 12:105–19.

4354. Rollins, Ronald G. "Carroll and Osborne:Alice and Alison in Wild Wonderlands." *ForumH* 7,iii(1969):16–20.

4355. Sutherland, Robert D. *Language and Lewis Carroll.* (JanL, Ser. maior 26.) The Hague: Mouton.

See also 7983.

Doughty. 4356. Safady, Issam. "Attempt and Attainment:A Study of Some Literary Aspects of Doughty's *Arabia Deserta* as the Culmination of Late-Victorian Anglo-American Travel Books to the Levant." *DAI* 30(1969):2548A(Ky.).

Doyle. *4357. De Waal, Ronald B. "A Bibliography of Sherlockian Bibliographies and Periodicals." *PBSA* 64:339–54.

4358. Egan, Joseph J. "Conan Doyle's *The Adventure of the Creeping Man* as Stevensonian Analogue." *SSL* 7:180–83.

4359. Galichet, François. " 'Epistémologie' de Sherlock Holmes." *Critique* 26:115–23.

4360. Greene, Sir Hugh. *The Rivals of Sherlock Holmes:Early Detective Stories.* London: Bodley Head.

4361. Hall, Trevor H. *Sherlock Holmes:Ten Literary Studies.* London: Duckworth, 1969.

4362. Rose, Phyllis. "Huxley, Holmes, and the Scientist as Aesthete." *VN* 38:22–24.

See also 7425.

Du Maurier. 4363. Ormond, Leonée. *George Du Maurier.*

Pittsburgh: U. of Pittsburgh P., 1969.

Eliot. 4364. Adam, Ian. *George Eliot.* (Profiles in Lit. Ser.) New York: Humanities, 1969.

4365. Arnold, Mary A. "The Unity of *Middlemarch*." *HussR* 1(1968):137–41.

4366. Cartwright, Jerome D. "Authorial Commentary in the Novels of George Eliot as Primarily Exemplified in *Adam Bede*, *The Mill on the Floss*, and *Middlemarch*." *DAI* 30:5402A(Wis.).

4367. Clark, Robert N. "The Idealist, the Missionary, and the Overreacher in the Novels of George Eliot." *DAI* 30:3903A(Fla. State).

4368. Creeger, George R.,ed. *George Eliot:A Collection of Critical Essays.* (TCV.) Englewood Cliffs, N.J.: Prentice-Hall.

4369. Geibel, James W. "An Annotated Bibliography of British Criticism of George Eliot, 1858–1900." *DAI* 30:4450A (Ohio State).

4370. Goldfarb, Russell M. "Warren's Tollivers and Eliot's Tullivers II." *UR* 36:275–79.

4371. Greene, Mildred S. "Isolation and Integrity:Madame da LaFayette's Princesse de Clèves and George Eliot's Dorothea Brooke." *RLC* 44:145–54.

4372. Hardy, Barbara,ed. *Critical Essays on George Eliot.* London: Routledge & K. Paul.

4373. Higdon, David L. "The Sovereign Fragments:A Study of George Eliot's Epigraphs." *DAI* 30(1969):725A–26A(Kan.).

* 4374. Hurley, Edward T. "Death and Immortality:George Eliot's Solution." *NCF* 24(1969):222–27.

4375. Kenyon, F.W. *The Consuming Flame:The Story of George Eliot.* New York: Dodd, Mead.

4376. Kilcullen, Elizabeth A. "George Eliot's Treatment of Marriage." *DAI* 30:5447A–48A(Toronto).

4377. Knoepflmacher, U.C. *Religious Humanism and the Victorian Novel:George Eliot, Walter Pater, and Samuel Butler.* Princeton: Princeton U.P.

* 4378. Levenson, Shirley F. "The Use of Music in *Daniel Deronda*." *NCF* 24(1969):317–34.

4379. Lund, Mary G. "George Eliot and the Jewish Question." *Discourse* 13:390–97.

4380. McCarthy, Patrick J. "Lydgate, 'The New, Young Surgeon' of *Middlemarch*." *SEL* 10:805–16.

4381. Miyazaki, Koichi. "*Daniel Deronda* no Ketsumatsu ni tsuite." *EigoS* 115(1969):86–87. [On the ending of *DD*.]

* 4382. Moldstad, David. "*The Mill on the Floss* and *Antigone*." *PMLA* 85:527–31.

4383. Paris, Bernard J. "The Otherness of George Eliot." *JML* 1:272–77. [Rev. art.]

4384. Perry, Jill. " 'Esse Videtur' in *Romola*." *N&Q* 17:19.

4385. Secor, Cynthia A. "The Poems of George Eliot:A Critical Edition with Introduction and Notes." *DAI* 30:5457A–58A(Cornell).

4386. Sedgley, Anne. "*Daniel Deronda*." *CR* 13:3–19.

4387. Siff, David H. "The Choir Invisible:The Relation of George Eliot's Poetry and Fiction." *DAI* 30(1969):293A–94A(N.Y.U.).

4388. Sudrann, Jean. "*Daniel Deronda* and the Landscape of Exile." *ELH* 37:433–55.

4389. Supp, Dorothea. *Tragik bei George Eliot.* (AF 97.) Heidelberg: Winter, 1969.

4390. Wiesenfarth, Joseph. "Demythologizing *Silas Marner*." *ELH* 37:226–44.

See also 1452, 3942, 3959, 3964, 4435, 4719, 4806, 6876, 8301.

FitzGerald. 4391. Hammat, A. " 'Orientalism' in Edward Fitzgerald Seen Through His Adaptation of Omar Khayyam's Quatrains." *CALC* 1(1966):22–42.

Galt. 4392. Costain, Keith M. "The Rhetoric of Realism:Art and Ideas in the Fiction of John Galt." *DAI* 30:2963A(Wash. U.).

Gaskell. 4393. McVeagh, John. *Elizabeth Gaskell.* New York: Humanities.

4394. —— "The Making of *Sylvia's Lovers*." *MLR* 65:272–81.

4395. Smith, Frank G.,ed. *Wives and Daughters.* Introd. Laurence Lerner. Baltimore: Penguin, 1969.

Gilbert. 4396. Ellis, James. "The Unsung W.S. Gilbert." *HLB* 18:109–40.

* 4397. Stedman, Jane W. "From Dame to Woman:W.S.

Gilbert and Theatrical Transvestism." *VS* 14:27–46.

* 4398. —— "Three New Gilbert Lyrics." *BNYPL* 74:629–33.

Gissing, G. 4399. Adams, Elsie B. "Gissing's Allegorical 'House of Cobwebs'." *SSF* 7:324–26.

4400. *Born in Exile.* Introd. Walter Allen. London: Gollancz.

4401. Collins, P. "Gissing in Russia." *TLS* 2 July:726. [See also 4 Sept:974.]

4402. Coustillas, Pierre,ed. *Essays and Fiction.* Baltimore: Johns Hopkins U.P.

4403. —— *Gissing's Writings on Dickens.* London: Enitharman.

4404. —— *Isabel Clarendon.* 2 Vols. Brighton: Harvester Press, 1969.

* 4405. Keech, James M. "Gissing's *New Grub Street* and the 'Triple-Headed Monster'." *Serif* 7,i:20–24.

* 4406. Selig, Robert L. "A Sad Heart at the Late-Victorian Culture Market:George Gissing's *In the Year of Jubilee*." *SEL* 9(1969):703–20.

See also 5665.

Gordon, Mary. *4407. Wilson, F.A.C. "Swinburne in Love: Some Novels by Mary Gordon." *TSLL* 11:1415–26.

Gosse. *See* 5062.

Griffin. 4408. Cronin, John. "Gerald Griffin:A Forgotten Novel." *Éire* 5,iii:32–39.

4409. —— "Gerald Griffin, Dedalus *Manqué*." *Studies* 58(1969):267–78.

4410. —— "Gerald Griffin's Commonplace Book A." *Éire* 4,iii(1969):22–37.

Grossmith. *4411. MacGillivray, Royce, and Paul Beam. "Acceptance in Holloway:*The Diary of a Nobody*." *QQ* 77:600–13.

Guest, C. *See* 4757.

Hardy, T. 4412. Bachman, Charles R. "Communion and Conflict in Hardy and Hauptmann:A Contrast in Artistic Temperaments." *RLV* 35(1969):283–93.

4413. Bailey, James O. *The Poetry of Thomas Hardy:A Handbook and Commentary.* Chapel Hill: U. of N. C. Press.

4414. Benvenuto, Richard. "Modes of Perception:The Will to Live in *Jude the Obscure*." *SNNTS* 2,i:31–41.

4415. Buckler, William E. "Thomas Hardy in New Perspective," (JanL, Ser. maior 44.) 13–17 in R.C. Lugton and Milton Saltzer,eds., *Studies in Honor of J. Alexander Kerns.* The Hague: Mouton.

4416. Bull, Philip. "Thomas Hardy and Social Change." *SoRA* 3(1969):199–213.

4417. Campbell, Michael L. "Animals in the Works of Thomas Hardy." *DAI* 30:3451A(N.C.).

4418. Clarke, Robert W. "Hardy's Farmer Boldwood:Shadow of a Magnitude." *WVUPP* 17:45–56.

4419. Coulthard, Arthur R. "The Love Poetry of Thomas Hardy." *DAI* 30(1969):1557A(Fla. State).

4420. Cox, J. Stevens, and Gregory Stevens-Cox,eds. *The Thomas Hardy Yearbook.* Guernsey: Toucan Press.

4421. Cox, James S. *Mumming and the Mummers'* Play of St. George. Guernsey: Toucan Press. [Three versions, incl. that of Hardy.]

4422. Cox, Reginald G.,ed. *Thomas Hardy:The Critical Heritage.* London: Routledge & K. Paul; New York: Barnes & Noble.

4423. Dillon, Robert W. "Thomas Hardy's Aesthetic of Nature:An Organic Study of Three Representative Novels:*Far from the Madding Crowd, The Return of the Native*, and *Tess of the D'Urbervilles*." *DAI* 30:3904A(Ohio).

4424. Dobrée, Bonamy. "The Poems of Thomas Hardy:Lyric or Elegiac?" *MHRev* 3(1967):77–92.

* 4425. Edwards, Duane. "Chance in Hardy's Fiction." *MQ* 11:427–41.

* 4426. Egan, Joseph J. "The Fatal Suitor:Early Foreshadowings in *Tess of the d'Urbervilles*." *TSL* 15:161–64.

4427. Hardy, Evelyn. *Thomas Hardy:A Critical Biography.* New York: Russell.

4428. Hardy, T. *The Return of the Native.* Introd. Albert J. Guérard. New York: Holt, Rinehart and Winston.

4429. Hartwell, Patrick M. "The Prose Style of Thomas

Hardy's Fiction." *DAI* 30:4986A–87A(U.C.L.A.).

* 4430. Heilman, Robert B. "*Gulliver* and Hardy's *Tess*: Houyhnhnms, Yahoos, and Ambiguities." *SoR* 6:277–301.

4431. Herbert, Lucille. "Hardy's Views in *Tess of the D'Urbervilles*." *ELH* 37:77–94.

4432. Howarth, Herbert. "The Poor Man and *The Dynasts*." *Mosaic* 3,i(1969):102–15.

4433. Hyde, William J. "Hardy's Spider Webs." *VP* 8:265–68.

4434. Hyman, Virginia R. "The Illuminations of Time:A Study of the Influence of Ethical Evolution on the Novels of Thomas Hardy." *DAI* 30:4947A(Columbia).

4435. Ingham, Patricia. "Dialect in the Novels of Hardy and George Eliot." [F 56]:347–63.

4436. Kano, Hideo. "Shi to Genso—Hardy no baai." *Oberon* 31(1969):2–11. [Poetry and fantasy in H.]

* 4437. May, Charles E. "Thomas Hardy and the Poetry of the Absurd." *TSLL* 12:63–73.

4438. Miller, J. Hillis. " 'I'd have my Life unbe':La ricerca dell'obblio nell'opera di Thomas Hardy." *SCr* 3(1969):263–85.

4439. Morgan, William W., Jr. "Thomas Hardy's Reputation as a Poet." *DAI* 30:4996A(Tenn.).

4440. Morimatsu, Kensuke. "Hardy no Koki San-shosetsu." *EigoS* 114(1968):794–96. [Three later novels of H.]

4441. Morrison, Donald J.,ed. *Stories and Poems.* Introd. J.I.M. Stewart. London: Dent.

4442. Mourol, Mary F. de. "Thomas Hardy's Novels of the 1870's." *DAI* 30(1969):2018A(N.M.).

4443. Mullwee, Deloris R. "The Ballad Tradition in Hardy's Major Novels." *DAI* 30:5416A(S.C.).

4444. Noonan, John F. "An Analysis of Time in the Poetry of Thomas Hardy." *DAI* 30:4421A(Bowling Green).

4445. Ownbey, E.S. "A Reading of Thomas Hardy's 'The Darkling Thrush'." [F 16]:29–32.

4446. Pinion, F.B. "The Composition of *The Return of the Native*." *TLS* 21 Aug:931.

* 4447. Schwartz, Barry N. "*Jude the Obscure* in the Age of Anxiety." *SEL* 10:793–804.

4448. Springer, Marlene A. "Allusion in Thomas Hardy's Early Novels:A Stylistic Study." *DAI* 30:3023A–24A(Ind.).

* 4449. Steig, Michael. "The Problem of Literary Value in Two Early Hardy Novels." *TSLL* 12:55–62. [*A Pair of Blue Eyes* and *Far From the Madding Crowd*.]

4450. Steinberg, M.W.,ed. *Tess of the d'Urbervilles.* New York: Odyssey.

4451. Takiyama, Sueno. "Recent Critical Tendencies Concerning *The Dynasts*." [F 1]:397–423. [In Jap.]

4452. Thatcher, David S. "Another Look at Hardy's 'Afterwards'." *VN* 38:14–18.

4453. Weatherby, H.L. "Atheological Symbolism in Modern Fiction:An Interpretation of Hardy's *Tess of the D'Urbervilles*." *SHR* 4:81–91.

See also 3675, 3964, 6540, 7599.

Haydon. *See* 4529.

Hazlitt. 4454. Albrecht, W.P. "Hazlitt, Keats, and the Sublime Pleasures of Tragedy." [F 53]:1–30.

4455. Blythe, Ronald,ed. *Selected Writings.* Baltimore: Penguin.

4456. Connolly, Paul H. "William Hazlitt:The Validity of Critical Impressionism." *DAI* 30:3938A(Va.).

4457. Hazlitt, William. *Men and Manners:Sketches and Essays.* London: Ward Lock. [Facsim. of 1st ed., 1852.]

4458. Jones, Stanley. "Howe's Edition of Hazlitt's Works: Two Notes." *N&Q* 17:174–75.

4459. Nabholtz, John R.,ed. *Selected Essays.* New York: Appleton.

4460. Park, Roy. "The Painter as Critic:Hazlitt's Theory of Abstraction." *PMLA* 85:1072–81.

* 4461. Story, Patrick L. "A Contemporary Continuation of Hazlitt's *Spirit of the Age*." *WC* 1:59–65.

4462. Stouck, David. "The Modernity of Hazlitt's Familiar Essays." *HAB* 21,ii:10–14.

See also 3116, 4135, 4526.

Henley. 4463. Flora, Joseph M. *William Ernest Henley.* (TEAS 107.) New York: Twayne.

Hogg. 4464. Carey, John,ed. *The Private Memoirs and Confessions of a Justified Sinner, Written by Himself.* Oxford: Oxford U.P., 1969.

Hood. 4465. Clubbe, John,ed. *Selected Poems of Thomas Hood.* Cambridge: Harvard U.P.

Hopkins. 4466. Abbick, John F. " 'The Wreck of the Deutschland,' Stanza 28:The Dragon's Domain." *Wisconsin Studies in Lit.* 6(1969):39–49.

4467. Bender, Todd K. "Gerard Manley Hopkins:Greek Art and the Barbarians." *Wisconsin Studies in Lit.* 6(1969):14–26.

4468. Bremer, R. "Hopkins' Use of the Word 'Combs' in 'To R.B.'." *ES* 51:144–48.

4469. Dilligan, Robert J., and Todd K. Bender. *A Concordance to the English Poetry of Gerard Manley Hopkins.* Madison: U. of Wis. P.

4470. Ellis, Virginia R. " 'Authentic Cadence':The Sacramental Method of Gerard Manley Hopkins." *DAI* 30(1969): 2481A(Brandeis).

4471. Gardner, W.H. "Gerard Manley Hopkins and the Poetry of Inscape." *Theoria* 33(1969):1–16.

4472. Haydock, James. "What 'The Windhover' Says." *Wisconsin Studies in Lit.* 6(1969):27–38.

4473. Holloway, Sr. Marcella. "The Nun's Cry in *The Wreck of the 'Deutschland'.*" *DownR* 88:288–94.

4474. Jayantha, R.A. " 'Patience Exquisite' in 'Peace':A Poem by Gerard Manley Hopkins." *LCrit* 8,iv(1969):70–72.

4475. Jordan, Frank,Jr. "Hopkins' 'The Caged Skylark'." *Expl* 28:Item 80.

4476. Mackenzie, Norman H. "Gerard Manley Hopkins:The Dragon's Treasure Horde Unlocked." *MLQ* 31:236–44.

4477. Mariani, Paul L. *A Commentary on the Complete Poems of Gerard Manley Hopkins.* Ithaca: Cornell U.P.

4478. Mellown, Elgin W. "Hopkins and the *Odyssey*." *VP* 8:263–65.

4479. Page, Barbara J. "Gerard Manley Hopkins:Ideas of Order and the Singular Poet." *DAI* 30:5454A(Cornell).

4480. Pick, John,comp. *Gerard Manley Hopkins:"The Windhover."* (Merrill Casebooks.) Columbus, Ohio: Charles E. Merrill, 1969.

4481. Revol, E.L. "El sacerdote como poeta:Gerard Manley Hopkins." *CHA* 244:207–17.

4482. Scheve, Charles J. "The Prosodic Practice of Gerard Manley Hopkins in 'The Wreck of the *Deutschland*'." *DAI* 30(1969):1150A–51A(Catholic U.).

4483. Seelhammer, Ruth. *Hopkins Collected at Gonzaga.* Chicago: Loyola U.P. [Lists 3301 items avail. in Hopkins Collection at Crosby Library, Gonzaga U.]

4484. Thomas, Alfred,S.J. *Hopkins the Jesuit:The Years of Training.* New York: Oxford U.P., 1969.

4485. Troddyn, P.M.,S.J. "Gerard Manley Hopkins:Two Unpublished Letters on Anglo-Irish Relations." *Studies* 59:19–25.

4486. White, Norman. "A Date for G.M. Hopkins's 'What Being in Rank-Old Time . . .'." *RES* 20:319–20.

4487. Yasuda, Shoichiro. "*Deutschland-go no Nanpa no Kaishaku wo megutte.*" *EigoS* 115(1969):226–27. [On the interpretation of *The Wreck of the D.*]

See also 1457, 4352, 4517.

Hudson. 4488. Hitchcock, Kay W. "Rima's Nature." *PCP* 1(1966):48–55.

Hunt. 4489. Duff, Gerald. "Leigh Hunt's Criticism of the Novel." *CLAJ* 13(1969):109–18.

* 4490. Hudnall, Clayton E. "Leigh Hunt on Keats:Two New Poems." *SHR* 4:358–62.

4491. Nowell-Smith, Simon. "Leigh Hunt as Bellman." *TLS* 2 Apr:367. [See also 16 Apr:430.]

Huxley, T.H. 4492. Ashforth, Albert. *Thomas Henry Huxley.* (TEAS 84.) New York: Twayne, 1969.

4493. Randel, William P. "Huxley in America." *PAPS* 14:73–99.

See also 4362.

Jefferies. 4494. Perry, P.J. "An Agricultural Journalist in the 'Great Depression':Richard Jefferies." *JBS* 9,ii:126–40.

Jeffrey. 4495. Hatch, Ronald B. " 'This Will Never Do'." *RES* 21:57–62. [On J's alterations to the texts of his *Contributions* to *The Edinburgh Review* (1844).]

Jerrold, D. *See* 4317.

Joynes. 4496. Arinshtein, Leonid M. "Die revolutionär-romantische Lyrik von James Joynes:Aus der Geschichte der revolutionären Dichtung Englands." *ZAA* 18:131–43.

Keats. 4497. Allott, Miriam,ed. *The Poems of John Keats.* (Longman Annotated English Poets.) London: Longmans.

4498. Anderson, James B. "Ambiguity and Paradox in the Poetry of Keats." *DAI* 30(1969):2474A–75A(Tulane).

4499. Andrews, C.T. "Keats and Mercury." *KSMB* 20(1969): 37–43.

4500. Bagchi, Krishna. "Keats' Sensuousness Re-Defined." [F 51]:103–10.

* 4501. Cohn, Robert G. "Keats and Mallarmé." *CLS* 7: 195–203.

4502. Deguchi, Yasuo. "Keats to Catholicism." *EigoS* 115(1969):362–63. [K and Catholicism; in Jap.]

4503. Dickie, James. "The Grecian Urn:An Archaeological Approach." *BJRL* 52(1969):96–114.

4504. Fogle, Richard H. *The Imagery of Keats and Shelley:A Comparative Study.* Chapel Hill: U. of N.C. Press, 1969.

4505. Frascato, Gerald. "John Keats 'In Thrall'." *MHRev* 11(1969):113–19.

4506. Fujihira, Takeaki. " 'Ode on a Grecian Urn' no Taiwa Kosei." *EigoS* 114(1968):373–75. [Dialogue structure of "Ode."]

4507. Gittings, Robert,ed. *Letters of John Keats.* London: Oxford U.P.. [Selection.]

4508. —— *The Odes of Keats and Their Earliest Known Manuscripts.* Kent, Ohio: Kent State U.P.

4509. Harwell, Thomas M. "Keats and the Critics, 1848–1900." *DA* 26(1966):4628A–29A(Columbia).

* 4510. Haworth, Helen E. "Keats's Copy of Lamb's *Specimens of English Dramatic Poets*." *BNYPL* 74:419–27.

* 4511. —— "The Titans, Apollo, and the Fortunate Fall in Keats's Poetry." *SEL* 10:637–49.

4512. Hudnall, Clayton E. "New Lines by Keats." *ELN* 7(1969):111–14. [A stanza of "Isabella."]

4513. Jabbar, Abdul. "Keats's View of Poetry." *DAI* 30: 3907A–08A(Case Western Reserve).

4514. Jarvis, William A.W. "The Jennings Family." *KSMB* 20(1969):44–46.

4515. Johnson, Richard E. "Settings of Innocence and Experience in the Poetry of Keats." *DAI* 30(1969):2487A (Tulane).

4516. Jones, Henry J. *John Keats's Dream of Truth.* New York: Barnes & Noble, 1969.

4517. Jones, James L. "Keats and the Last Romantics: Hopkins and Yeats." *DAI* 30(1969):2530A(Tulane).

4518. Jones, John. "John Keats's Dream of Truth." *TLS* 1 Jan:12. [See also 22 Jan:85.]

4519. —— *John Keats's Dream of Truth.* London: Chatto & Windus, 1969.

4520. Kamijima, Kenkichi. "Kaette Kita Visionary." *EigoS* 114(1968):514–15. [A Visionary's return; reconsideration of *La Belle Dame Sans Merci*.]

4521. Kissane, James. "Light and Shade:An English Life of Keats." *SR* 78:203–11. [Rev. art.]

4522. Lindenberger, Herbert. "Keats's 'To Autumn' and Our Knowledge of a Poem." *CE* 32:123–34.

4523. Little, Judy R. "Large-Limbed Visions:Structure in the Long Poems of John Keats." *DAI* 30:2973A–74A(Neb.).

* 4524. Lott, James. "Keats's *To Autumn*:The Poetic Consciousness and the Awareness of Process." *SIR* 9:71–81.

* 4525. Luke, David. "*The Eve of Saint Mark*:Keats's 'ghostly Queen of Spades' and the Textual Superstition." *SIR* 9:161–75.

* 4526. Margolis, John D. "Keats's 'Men of Genius' and 'Men of Power'." *TSLL* 11:1333–47. [K's attitudes toward Haydon, Bailey, Hazlitt, Wordsworth, Shakespeare.]

4527. Mincoff, Marco. "Beauty Is Truth—Once More." *MLR* 65:267–71.

4528. Oikonomou, Merope. *Ho John Keats kai he Hellada. Melete.* Athinai: Ekdotikos Oikos I. Sideri, 1969.

4529. Origo, Iris. "Additions to the Keats Collection." *TLS* 23 Apr:457–58. [Important literary memorabilia from the Dallas

Pratt coll. now in the Keats-Shelley Memorial House in Rome; see also 14 May:539; 28 May:586.]

4530. Paciosi, Filelfo. "Classicismo e romanticismo in Keats." *Dialoghi* 16(1968):94–122.

4531. Patterson, Charles I.,Jr. *The Daemonic in the Poetry of John Keats.* Urbana: U. of Ill. P.

4532. Pereira, E. "Aspects of English Romanticism with Special Reference to Keats." *UES* 8,ii:35–40.

4533. Rees, Joan. *Bright Star:The Story of John Keats and Fanny Brawne.* London and Toronto: Harrap, 1968.

4534. Robertson, Margaret Y. "The Consistency of Keats's 'Ode on Indolence'." *Style* 4:133–43.

4535. Sakata, Katsuzo. "Keats no Dilemma." *EigoS* 114(1968):82–83. [K's dilemma; in Jap.]

4536. Schwartz, Lewis M. "Keats's Reception by His English Contemporaries:A Collection of Reviews and Notices of the Poet for the Years 1816–1821." *DAI* 30(1969):339A(N.Y.U.).

* 4537. Sperry, Stuart M.,Jr. "Keats and the Chemistry of Poetic Creation." *PMLA* 85:268–77.

4538. Straumann, Heinrich. "Keats und die gläserne Wand: Bemerkungen zu 'The Eve of St. Agnes'." [F 52]:217–24.

4539. Swaminathan, S.R. "Keats's 'The Fall of Hyperion'." *KSMB* 20(1969):11–12.

4540. Whalley, George. "Keats and the Painters." *MHRev* 7(1968):123–29. [Rev. art.]

4541. Yasunaga, Yoshio. "On Keats's *Lamia*:Dream and Reality." *Hiroshima Studies in Eng. Lang. and Lit.* 16,i–ii(1969): 18–29. [In Jap.]

See also 1457, 3126, 3936, 4018, 4454, 4490, 4872, 6382, 7687.

Kemble, F. 4542. Rushmore, Robert. *Fanny Kemble.* New York: Crowell.

Kinglake. 4543. Pritchett, V.S. "Kinglake's *Eothen*:A Nineteenth-Century Travel Classic." *PrS* 44:11–18.

Kingsley, C. *4544. Baker, William J. "Charles Kingsley on the Crimean War:A Study in Chauvinism." *SHR* 4:247–56.

4545. Campbell, Robert A. "Victorian Pegasus in Harness:A Study of Charles Kingsley's Debt to Thomas Carlyle and F.D. Maurice." *DAI* 30:3902A(Wis.).

4546. Daumas, Ph. "Charles Kingsley's style in *Alton Locke*." *LanM* 63(1969):169–75.

Kingsley, H. 4547. Baxter, Rosilyn. "Henry Kingsley and the Australian Landscape." *ALS* 4:395–98.

4548. Scheuerle, William H. "Henry Kingsley and the Governor Eyre Controversy." *VN* 37:24–27.

Kipling. 4549. Carrington, C[harles] E. "Browning and Kipling." *KJ* 175:6–14.

4550. Corrit, J. " 'Just So' and 'Jungle' Stories:A Note on Origins." *KJ* 172(1969):5–7.

4551. Daintith, T.L.A. "Kipling as Prophet." *KJ* 175:16–20. [On K's futuristic fiction.]

4552. Drachmann, A.G. *Hævnmotivet i Kiplings fortællinger.* (SSO 272.) Copenhagen: G.E.C. Gad, 1969.

4553. Fraser, Robert S., and Paula Morgan. "Addenda to Stewart:Kipling's Musical Settings." *KJ* 172(1969):12–13. [Addenda to Stewart and Yeats, *Rudyard Kipling. A Bibliographical Catalogue* (Toronto, 1959).]

4554. Garst, Tom. "Beyond Realism:Short Fiction of Kipling, Conrad, and James in the 1890's." *DAI* 30(1969):1167A(Wash. U.).

4555. Gilbert, Elliot L. "Kipling's 'The Gardener':Craft into Art." *SSF* 7:308–19.

4556. Green, Roger L.,ed. *Stories and Poems.* London: Dent.

4557. Hanson, R.M. " 'British Columbia Regrets'." *KJ* 172(1969):16–18. [On K's property in Vancouver.]

4558. Islam, Shamsul. "The Islamic Tradition in Kipling's Work." *KJ* 174:10–14.

* 4559. Meyers, Jeffrey. "The Quest for Identity in *Kim*." *TSLL* 12:101–10.

4560. ——— "Thoughts on 'Without Benefit of Clergy'." *KJ* 172(1969):8–11.

4561. Page, Malcolm. "The Nationality of the Airman in 'Mary Postgate'." *KJ* 174:14–15. [Argues airman may be Fr. rather than Ger.]

4562. Peterson, William S. "Kipling's First Visit to Chicago."

JISHS 53:290–301.

4563. R.L.G., R.E.H., and P.W.I. "Reader's Guide to 'The Village That Voted The Earth Was Flat'." *KJ* 175:20–23.

4564. Sethi, Lalit K. "Kipling's Attitude Toward India:A Thematic Study of His Indian Tales." *DAI* 30(1969):292A–93A(N.M.).

4565. Sparrow, W. Keats. "The Work Theme in Kipling's Novels." *KJ* 173:10–19.

4566. Witt, Robert W. "Kipling as Representative of the Counter-Aesthetes." *KJ* 174:6–9.

See also 4916, 4987, 7093, 7855.

Lamb. *4567. Ades, John I. "Charles Lamb, Shakespeare, and Early Nineteenth-Century Theater." *PMLA* 85:514–26.

4568. Frank, Robert J. "The Balanced Art of Charles Lamb:A Study of the *Essays of Elia*." *DAI* 30:3905A(Minn.).

4569. Fukuda, Takashi. "*The Old Familiar Faces* no naka no Mondai." *EigoS* 114(1968):160–62. [Problem in this essay.]

4570. Garton, Charles. "Lamb's Paternal Forebears." *N&Q* 16(1969):420–21.

4571. Randel, Fred V. "Eating and Drinking in Lamb's Elia Essays." *ELH* 37:57–76.

See also 4173, 4510.

Le Fanu. 4572. Cooley, Leo P. "Joseph Sheridan Le Fanu: The Struggle of an Irish Imagination." *DAI* 30:3453A–54A (N.Y.U.).

Lear. 4573. Richardson, Joanna. "Edward Lear:Man of Letters." *ArielE* 1,iv:18–28.

Leverson, A. *See* 4813.

Lewes. 4574. Jones, Helen E. "George Henry Lewes's Use in His Literary Criticism of Ideas from His Empirical Metaphysics." *DAI* 30(1969):2530A(Colo.).

Lytton, R. *See* 3928.

Macaulay. 4575. Allen, Peter R. "Lord Macaulay's Gift to Harriet Beecher Stowe:The Solution to a Riddle in Trevelyan's *Life*." *N&Q* 17:23–24.

* 4576. Millgate, Jane. "Father and Son:Macaulay's *Edinburgh* Debut." *RES* 21:159–67.

See also 779.

MacDonald. 4577. Sadler, Glenn E. "At the Back of the North Wind:George MacDonald, a Centennial Appreciation." *Orcrist* 3(1969):20–22.

Magazine of Art. 4578. Rumbaugh, Liela M. "*The Magazine of Art*." *DAI* 30:2979A(Northwestern).

Maturin. 4579. Harris, John B. "Charles Robert Maturin:A Study." *DAI* 30(1969):282A(Wayne State).

4580. Kennedy, Veronica M.S. "Myth and the Gothic Dream:C.R. Maturin's *Melmoth the Wanderer*." *PCP* 4(1969): 41–47.

4581. Mayoux, Jean-Jacques. "La grande création satanique du Révérend Maturin." *EA* 22(1969):393–96. [Rev. art.]

Mayhew. *See* 4332.

McGonagall. *See* 4769.

Meredith. 4582. Arinstein, L. "Two Letters Concerning the Early Russian Translation of *The Egoist*." *N&Q* 17:34–36.

4583. Bilder, J. Raban. "Meredith's Experiments with Ideas." *VN* 38:18–21.

4584. Bogner, Delmar. "The Sexual Side of Meredith's Poetry." *VP* 8:107–25.

4585. Cline, C.L.,ed. *The Letters of George Meredith.* London: Oxford U.P.

4586. Foster, David E. "The Narrative Voice in Three Novels of George Meredith." *DAI* 30:5407A–08A(Wis.).

4587. Fowler, Henry R. "George Meredith:A Study of the Comic." *DAI* 30(1969):2021A–22A(Mich.).

* 4588. Hergenhan, L.T. "Meredith Achieves Recognition:The Reception of *Beauchamp's Career* and *The Egoist*." *TSLL* 11(1969):1247–68.

4589. Hergenhan, L.T.,ed. *The Adventures of Harry Richmond.* Lincoln: U. of Neb. P.

4590. Johnson, Diane L. "A Closer Reading of Earth:Sexual Mysticism in the Poetry of George Meredith." *DAI* 30(1969): 1529A(U.C.L.A.).

4591. McCullen, Maurice L. "A Matter of 'Principle': Treatment of the Poor in George Meredith's Fiction 1879–1895."

ELN 7:203–09.

4592. Meredith, G. *The Shaving of Shagpat.* Introd. Lin Carter. New York: Ballantine.

4593. Olsen, George C. "George Meredith's Late Concept of Nature." *DAI* 30(1969):2494A(Ky.).

4594. Perkus, Gerald H. "Meredith's Unhappy Love Life: Worthy of the Muse." *Cithara* 9,ii:32–46.

4595. —— "Toward Disengagement:A Neglected Early Meredith Manuscript Poem." *VP* 8:268–72.

4596. Plunkett, P.M.,S.J. "Meredith's *Modern Love*, I." *Expl* 28:Item 42.

4597. Pritchett, Victor S. *George Meredith and English Comedy.* New York: Random House; London: Chatto & Windus. [Clark Lectures for 1969.]

4598. Reader, Willie D. "Stanza Form in Meredith's *Modern Love*." *VN* 38:26–27.

4599. Simpson, Arthur L.,Jr. "Meredith's Pessimistic Humanism:A New Reading of *Modern Love*." *MP* 67:341–56.

4600. Spanberg, Sven-Johan. "George Meredith and the Techniques of Literary Appropriation:A Study of *The Ordeal of Richard Feverel* in Relation to the Traditions and Conventions of the Novel." *DAI* 30(1969):1576A(Princeton).

* 4601. Sundell, Michael G. "The Functions of Flitch in *The Egoist*." *NCF* 24(1969):227–35.

4602. Williams, Bernice A. "The Self-Education of George Meredith, Philosopher and Poet." *DAI* 30(1969):1999A (C.U.N.Y.).

See also 3692, 7093.

Meynell. 4603. Colliard, Laure Aimé. *Paul Claudel et Alice Meynell poètes-traducteurs.Etude enrichie de plusieurs lettres inédites.* Verona: Lib. ed. universitaria, 1968.

Mill. 4604. Alexander, Edward. "John Stuart Mill on Dogmatism, *Liberticide*, and Revolution." *VN* 37:12–18.

4605. —— "Mill's Marginal Notes on Carlyle's 'Hudson's Statue'." *ELN* 7(1969):120–23.

4606. Baker, William J. "Gradgrindery and the Education of John Stuart Mill:A Clarification." *WHR* 24:49–56.

4607. Cowling, Maurice,ed. *Selected Writings.* New York: New Amer. Lib., 1968.

4608. Foulk, Gary J. "Kendall's Criticisms of J.S. Mill." *Person* 51:314–23.

4609. Hall, Roland. "Further Addenda to 'The Diction of John Stuart Mill'." *N&Q* 17:10–11.

4610. Harris, Wendell V. "The Warp of Mill's 'Fabric' of Thought." *VN* 37:1–7.

4611. Kelly, Charles J. "The Presuppositions of John Stuart Mill's Theory of Names and Propositions." *DAI* 30(1969): 763A–64A(Notre Dame).

4612. Land, Berel, and Gary Stahl. "Mill's 'Howlers' and the Logic of Naturalism." *PPR* 29(1969):562–74.

4613. Murray, James G. "Mill on De Quincey:*Esprit Critique* Revoked." *VN* 37:7–12.

4614. Rossi, Alice S. "Sentiment and Intellect:The Story of John Stuart Mill and Harriet Taylor Mill." *Midway* 10,iv:29–51.

4615. Ryan, Alan. *John Stuart Mill.* New York: Pantheon.

4616. —— *The Philosophy of John Stuart Mill.* London: Macmillan.

4617. Stillinger, Jack,ed. *Autobiography, and Other Writings.* With Introd. Boston: Houghton Mifflin, 1969.

See also 4124, 4675.

Monthly Magazine. *See* 6337.

Morier. *4618. Grabar, Terry H. "Fact and Fiction:Morier's *Hajji Baba*." *TSLL* 11(1969):1223–36.

4619. Weitzman, Arthur J. "Who Was Hajji Baba?" *N&Q* 17:177–79.

Morley. 4620. Constantine, John. " 'The Flying Burgomaster' or the Animated Prosthesis." *HussR* 2(1968):28–41. [Text with brief introd.]

Morris. 4621. Blench, J.W. "William Morris's *Sigurd the Volsung*:A Re-appraisal." *DUJ* 30(1969):1–17.

4622. Chen, Karl C. "A Study of the Sources and Influences Upon William Morris's *The Defense of Guenevere and Other Poems*." *DAI* 30(1969):1977A(Yale).

4623. Hawkins, Mark F. "The Late Prose Romances of William Morris:A Biographical Interpretation." *DAI* 30:4451A–52A(Calif., Berkeley).

4624. Hollow, John. "William Morris' 'The Haystack in the Floods'." *VP* 7(1969):353–55.

4625. —— "Singer of an Empty Day:William Morris and the Desire for Immortality." *DAI* 30:3461A(Rochester).

* 4626. Lougy, Robert E. "William Morris' *News From Nowhere*:The Novel as Psychology of Art." *ELT* 13:1–8.

4627. Polis, T.V. "Ėstetičeskie vzgljady Uil'jama Morrisa - socialista." [F 49]:145–66. [Aesthetic views of W.M.]

* 4628. Silver, Carole G. " 'The Defence of Guenevere':A Further Interpretation." *SEL* 9(1969):695–702.

4629. Talbot, Norman. "Women and Goddesses in the Romances of William Morris." *SoRA* 3(1969):339–57.

4630. Tompkins, J.M.S. "The Work of William Morris:A Cord of Triple Strand." *DR* 50:97–111.

See also 3945, 5164.

Newman, J.H. 4632. Anthony, Sister Geraldine. "Newman's Definition of Faith from the *Oxford University Sermons* to the *Grammar of Assent*." *Cithara* 9,ii:47–63.

4633. Blehl, Vincent F. "Newman, the Fathers, and Education." *Thought* 45:196–212.

4634. Bryden-Brook, Simon. "The Arms of Cardinal Newman." *CoA* 10(1968):134–40.

4634a. Capps, Donald. "John Henry Newman:A Study of Vocational Identity." *JSSR* 9:33–51.

4635. DeSantis, Edward. "Newman's Concept of the Church in the World in His *Parochial and Plain Sermons*." *ABR* 21:203–17.

4636. Dessain, C.S.,ed. *Letters and Diaries of John Henry Newman, XIX:Consulting the Laity, January 1859 to June 1861.* London: Nelson, 1969.

4637. Mulcahey, Donald C. "The Prophetic Role of the Laity According to John Henry Cardinal Newman." *DAI* 30(1969): 2609A(Catholic U.).

4638. Ryan, John D. "Newman's Theory of Conscience." *UDR* 7,i:7–19.

4639. White, W.D. "John Henry Newman's Critique of Popular Preaching." *SAQ* 69:[108]–17.

See also 3941, 4069, 4252, 4817.

Ouida. *See* 3116.

Pater. 4640. Court, Franklin E. "Symmetry and Semantics: An Analysis of Walter Pater's Historical and Fictional Portraits." *DAI* 30:4404A(Kent State).

4641. Evans, Lawrence,ed. *The Letters of Walter Pater.* Oxford: Clarendon.

* 4642. Goff, Penrith. "Hugo von Hofmannsthal and Walter Pater." *CLS* 7:1–11.

4643. Tirumalai, Candadai K. "Continuity and Development in the Thought of Walter Pater." *DAI* 30:3027A(Pa.).

4644. Ward, Hayden W. "The Religious Aesthetic of Walter Pater." *DAI* 30(1969):2503A(Columbia).

See also 3941, 4377, 4738.

Patmore. *See* 5075.

Peacock. 4645. Colmer, John. "Godwin's *Mandeville* and Peacock's *Nightmare Abbey*." *RES* 21:331–36.

4646. Dawson, Carl. *His Fine Wit:A Study of Thomas Love Peacock.* Berkeley: U. of Calif. P.

4647. Fain, John T. "Peacock's Essay on Steam Navigation." *SAB* 35,iii:11–15.

4648. Hawkins, Peter A. "Correspondence." *RES* 21:338. [Reply to D.N. Gallon; see Bibliog. for 1969, Vol. I, Item 4676.]

4649. Hewitt, Douglas. "Entertaining Ideas:A Critique of *Crotchet Castle*." *EIC* 20:200–12.

4650. Wright, Raymond,ed. *Nightmare Abbey and Crotchet Castle.* Harmondsworth: Penguin, 1969.

Rae. *See* 3619.

Reynolds. 4651. Gittings, Robert. "The Poetry of John Hamilton Reynolds." *ArielE* 1,iv:7–17.

Rolfe. 4652. Glucker, John. "Metrical Pattern in Rolfe." *AntigR* 1,i:46–51.

4653. Weeks, Donald. "More Light on *Hadrian the Seventh*." *AntigR* 1,i:54–69.

Rossetti, C. 4654. Festa, Conrad D. "Studies in Christina

Rossetti's *'Goblin Market' and Other Poems.*" *DAI* 30:5407A (S.C.).

4655. Jennings, Elizabeth,comp. and introd. *A Choice of Christina Rossetti's Verse.* London: Faber.

4656. Kohl, James A. "Sparks of Fire:Christina Rossetti's Artistic Life." *DAI* 30:2972A(Del.).

4657. Owen, Marion. "Christina Rossetti:'Affairs of the Heart'." *HAB* 21,iii:16–25.

4658. Uffelman, Larry K. "Christina Rossetti's *A Pageant and Other Poems*:An Annotated Critical Edition." *DAI* 30:5422A (Kan. State).

4659. Waller, John O. "Christ's Second Coming:Christina Rossetti and the Premillennialist William Dodsworth." *BNYPL* 73(1969):465–82.

4660. Zaturenska, Marya,ed. *Selected Poems of Christina Rossetti.* New York: Macmillan.

Rossetti, D.G. 4661. Baker, Houston A.,Jr. "The Poet's Progress:Rossetti's *The House of Life.*" *VP* 8:1–14.

4662. Fredeman, William E. "Rossetti's Letters." *MHRev* 1(1967):134–41; 6(1968):115–26. [Rev. art.]

* 4663. Harris, Wendell V. "A Reading of Rossetti's Lyrics." *VP* 7(1969):299–308.

* 4664. Ryals, Clyde de L. "The Narrative Unity of *The House of Life.*" *JEGP* 69:241–57.

* 4665. Seigel, Jules P. "*Jenny*:The Divided Sensibility of a Young and Thoughtful Man of the World." *SEL* 9(1969):677–93.

* 4666. Stein, Richard L. "Dante Gabriel Rossetti:Painting and the Problem of Poetic Form." *SEL* 10:775–92.

See also 4525.

Rossetti, W. *See* 4525.

Ruskin. 4667. Bose, Amalendu. "Ghandi and Ruskin:Ideological Affinities." *CalR* N.S.1:423–40.

4668. Burd, Van Akin. *The Winnington Letters:John Ruskin's Correspondence with Margaret Alexis Bell.* London: Allen and Unwin.

4669. Claiborne, Jay W. "Two Secretaries:The Letters of John Ruskin to Charles Augustus Howell and the Rev. Richard St. John Tyrwhitt." *DAI* 30:3000A(Texas, Austin).

4670. Dearden, James S.,ed. *I Teriad:Or, Three Weeks Among the Lakes.* Newcastle upon Tyne: Graham.

4671. Fontana, Ernest L. "Ruskin and Three Venetian Painters." *DAI* 30(1969):1980A(Notre Dame).

4672. Halladay, Jean. "Ruskin's Reputation as Seen in Various British Literary Periodicals, 1837–1855." *DAI* 30(1969):1982A(Ky.).

4673. Joseph, Robert J. "John Ruskin:Radical and Psychotic Genius." *PsyR* 56(1969):425–41.

4674. Landow, George P. "J.D. Harding and John Ruskin on Nature's Infinite Variety." *JAAC* 28:369–80.

4675. Millett, Kate. "The Debate Over Women:Ruskin Versus Mill." *VS* 14:63–82.

See also 3884, 5540.

Scott. 4676. Calder, Angus and Jenni. *Scott.* (LitP.) London: Evans, 1969.

4677. Clark, Arthur M. *Sir Walter Scott:The Formative Years.* London: Blackwood, 1969.

4678. Cockshut, Anthony O.J. *The Achievement of Walter Scott.* London: Collins, 1969.

4679. Cusac, Marian H. *Narrative Structure in the Novels of Sir Walter Scott.* The Hague: Mouton, 1969.

4680. Hayden, John O.,ed. *Scott:The Critical Heritage.* London: Routledge & K. Paul.

4681. Jeffares, A. Norman,ed. *Scott's Mind and Art.* (Essays Old and New 6.) Edinburgh: Oliver and Boyd.

4682. Johnson, Edgar. *Sir Walter Scott:The Great Unknown.* London: Hamish Hamilton; New York: Macmillan.

4683. MacNalty, Sir Arthur S. *Sir Walter Scott:The Wounded Falcon.* (Medical Viewpoint Series.) London: Johnson. [Based on and incl. pts. of M's *The Great Unknown:A Short Life of Sir Walter Scott.*]

4684. McLoren, Moray. *Sir Walter Scott:The Man and Patriot.* London: Heinemann.

4685. Morgan, Peter F. "Scott as Critic." *SSL* 7:90–101.

4686. Rubenstein, Jill. "Scott's Historical Poetry." *DAI*

30(1969):2497A–98A(Johns Hopkins).

4687. Shafer, Michael R. "Distance in Scott's Fiction:The 'Tales of My Landlord'." *DAI* 30(1969):1994A–95A(Calif., San Diego).

4688. Shimamura, Akira. "Scott no Shosetsu." *Oberon* 31(1969):12–26. [S's novels—on *Old Mortality.*]

4689. —— "Scott no Shosetsu—*Redgauntlet* ni tsuite." *Oberon* 30(1968):2–9. [S's novels—*Redgauntlet* esp.]

4690. Spink, Gerald W. "Walter Scott's Musical Acquaintances." *M&L* 51:61–65.

4691. Valkama, Leevi. "Kuusi ja seitsemän veljestä. [Six and Seven Brothers.]" *Sananjalka* 12:133–47. [Relationship between Kivi's *The Seven Brothers* and Scott's *Rob Roy.*]

4692. Wood, G.A.M. "Sir Walter Scott and Sir Ralph Sadler:A Chapter in Literary History." *SSL* 7:11–20,147–58.

See also 3624, 4019, 4096, 6604.

Shairp. 4693. Bishop, Allan R. "John Campbell Shairp:A Study of His Early Life, with Annotated List of His Correspondence and Primary Bibliography." *DAI* 30:4397A–98A(Northwestern).

Sharp. 4694. Hopkins, Konrad. "Wilfion and the Green Life:A Study of William Sharp and Fiona Macleod." [F 47]:26–44.

Shelley, M. 4695. George, Margaret. *One Woman's "Situation":A Study of Mary Wollstonecraft.* Urbana: U. of Ill. P.

4696. Joseph, M.K.,ed. *Frankenstein, or the Modern Prometheus.* With Introd. New York: Oxford U.P., 1969.

Shelley, P.B. *4697. Antippas, Andy P. "The Structure of Shelley's *St. Irvyne*:Parallelism and the Gothic Mode of Evil." *TSE* 18:59–71.

4698. Curran, Stuart. *Shelley's* Cenci:*Scorpions Ringed with Fire.* Princeton: Princeton U.P.

4699. —— "Shelley's Emendations to the *Hymn to Intellectual Beauty.*" *ELN* 7:270–73.

4700. Duerkson, Roland A.,ed. *The Cenci.* Indianapolis: Bobbs-Merrill.

* 4701. Elledge, W. Paul. "Good, Evil, and the Function of Art:A Note on Shelley." *TSL* 14(1969):87–92.

4702. Faure, Georges. *Les éléments du rythme poétique en anglais moderne:Esquisse d'une nouvelle analyse et Essai d'application au* Prometheus Unbound *de Shelley.* (SEngL 53.) The Hague: Mouton.

* 4703. Flagg, John S. "Shelley and Aristotle:Elements of the *Poetics* in Shelley's Theory of Poetry." *SIR* 9:44–67.

* 4704. French, Roberts W. "Shelley's 'Adonais,' 36." *Expl* 29:Item 16.

4705. Hall, James M. "The Spider and the Silkworm:Shelley's 'Letter to Maria Gisborne'." *KSMB* 20(1969):1–10.

* 4706. Hughes, Daniel. "Shelley, Leonardo, and the Monsters of Thought." *Criticism* 12:195–212. [S on Da Vinci.]

* 4707. Maddox, Donald L. "Shelley's *Alastor* and the Legacy of Rousseau." *SIR* 9:82–98.

4708. McNiece, Gerald. *Shelley and the Revolutionary Idea.* Cambridge: Harvard U.P., 1969.

4709. Miller, Sara M. "Irony in Shelley's *The Cenci.*" *UMSE* 9(1968):23–35.

4710. Murphy, John V. "Gothic Elements in Shelley's Canon." *DAI* 30:3913A–14A(Mich.).

4711. Richards, George D. "Shelley's *Queen Mab*:A Critical Edition." *DAI* 30:2977A–78A(Duke).

4712. Scales, Luther L.,Jr. "Miltonic Elements and the Humanization of Power in Shelley's Poetry, Culminating in Demogorgon's Song." *DAI* 30(1969):2043A(Drew).

* 4713. Steffan, Truman G. "Seven Accounts of the Cenci and Shelley's Drama." *SEL* 9(1969):601–18.

4714. Stock, A.G. "Shelley's Universe." [F 51]:1–5.

* 4715. Webb, Timothy. "Shelley's 'Hymn to Venus':A New Text." *RES* 21:315–24. [Text of poem incl.]

4716. Williams, Duncan. "Shelley's Demogorgon." *WVUPP* 17:25–30.

See also 866, 3126, 3397, 3546, 3931, 4088, 4504, 4846, 4872, 5934, 5953, 6449, 7817.

Smiles. *See* 3899.

Smith, S. *See* 4279, 6249.

Southcott. 4717. Wright, Eugene P. "A Descriptive Catalogue of the Joanna Southcott Collection at the University of Texas." *DAI* 30:2984A(Texas, Austin).

Southey. 4718. Gittings, Robert. *Omniana:Or, Horae Otiosiores.* Slough, Buckinghamshire: Centaur. [Contains the S portion plus Coleridge's contributions, incl. the additions of 1836 and 1884 to the 1812 vol. plus several censored portions.] *See also* 4178.

Stephen. 4719. Singh, Brijraj. "The Changing Concepts of 'Charm' in Leslie Stephen's Criticism of George Eliot." [F 51]:7–12.

Stevenson. 4720. Booth, Bradford A.,ed. *Selected Poetry and Prose of Robert Louis Stevenson.* Boston: Houghton, 1968.

4721. Cooper, Lettice. *Robert Louis Stevenson.* London: Burns and Oates. [Pictorial biog.]

4722. Egan, Joseph J. "Dark in the Poet's Corner:Stevenson's 'A Lodging for the Night'." *SSF* 7:402–08.

* 4723. —— "Grave Sites and Moral Death:A Reexamination of Stevenson's 'The Body-Snatcher'." *ELT* 13:9–15.

4724. Greene, Graham. "The Wrong Box." *TLS* 30 Oct:1276. [See also 6 Nov:1300; 13 Nov:1328.]

4725. Neider, Charles,ed. *The Complete Short Stories of Robert Louis Stevenson.* New York: Doubleday, 1969.

4726. Van Thal, Herbert,ed. *New Arabian Nights.* Introd. David Holloway. London: Cassell, 1968. [*The Suicide Club, The Rajah's Diamond, The Pavilion on the Links, A Lodging for the Night, The Sire de Malatroit's Door, Providence and the Guitar.*]

4727. Walt, James. "Stevenson's 'Will O' the Mill' and James's 'The Beast in the Jungle'." *UES* 8,ii:19–25.

* 4728. Warner, Fred B.,Jr. "Stevenson's First Scottish Story." *NCF* 24(1969):335–44.

4729. Watson, Harold F. *Coasts of Treasure Island:A Study of the Backgrounds and Sources for Robert Louis Stevenson's Romance of the Sea.* San Antonio, Texas: Naylor, 1969. *See also* 4358, 5315, 8249.

Surtees. 4730. Hamilton, Alex,ed. *Jorrocks' Jaunts and Jollities.* (First Novel Library 16.) London: Cassell, 1969. *See also* 3116.

Swinburne. *4731. Coulling, Sidney M.B. "Swinburne and Arnold." *PQ* 49:211–33.

4732. Hyder, Clyde K.,ed. *Swinburne:The Critical Heritage.* London: Routledge & K. Paul.

4733. Peckham, Morse,ed. *Swinburne:Poems and Ballads and Atlanta in Calydon.* With Introd., Chronol., and Bibliog. Indianapolis: Bobbs-Merrill.

4734. Wilson, F.A.C. "Swinburne's Sicilian Blade:Three Biographical Studies." *NDQ* 36,iv(1968):5–18. *See also* 3886, 4407, 4745.

Symonds. 4735. Going, William T. "John Addington Symonds and the Victorian Sonnet Sequence." *VP* 8:25–38.

4736. Maxwell, J.C., Caroline Ryan, and James Bertram. "The Letters of John Addington Symonds." *N&Q* 17:24–33. [Rev. art.]

4737. Weber, B.C. "An Unpublished Letter of John Addington Symonds." *N&Q* 17:33–34. *See also* 7115, 7116.

Symons. *4738. Beckson, Karl, and John M. Munro. "Symons, Browning, and the Development of Modern Aesthetic." *SEL* 10:687–99.

4739. Goodman, John F. "Arthur Symons and French Symbolism:The Critical Theory." *DAI* 30:5408A(Wis.).

4740. Munro, John M. "The Poet and the Nightingale:Some Unpublished Letters from Sarojini Naidu to Arthur Symons." *CalR* N.S.1:135–46. *See also* 5930.

Talfourd. *See* 4102.

Tennyson, A. 4741. Adey, Lionel. "Tennyson's Sorrow and Her Lying Lip." *VP* 8:261–63.

* 4742. Adler, Thomas P. "The Uses of Knowledge in Tennyson's *Merlin and Vivien*." *TSLL* 11:1397–1403. [Stresses parallel with *Paradise Lost*.]

* 4743. Assad, Thomas J. "Tennyson's 'Courage, Poor Heart of Stone'." *TSE* 18:73–80.

4744. Elliott, Philip L. "Tennyson's *In Memoriam*, XLI,9–12."

Expl 28:Item 66.

4745. Enzensberger, Christian. *Viktorianische Lyrik:Tennyson und Swinburne in der Geschichte der Entfremdung.* (LaK.) München: Hanser, 1969.

4746. Fricke, Donna G. "Tennyson's *The Hesperides*:East of Eden and Variations on the Theme." *Tennyson Res. Bull.* 1:99–103.

4747. Gray, J.M. "A Feature Characterizing Lancelot in Tennyson's 'Lancelot and Elaine'." *N&Q* 17:15.

4748. —— "Two Transcendental Ladies of Tennyson's *Idylls*:The Lady of the Lake and Vivien." *Tennyson Res. Bull.* 1:104–05.

4749. Hirsch, Gordon D. "Tennyson's *Commedia*." *VP* 8:93–106.

* 4750. Hunt, John D. "The Symbolist Vision of *In Memoriam*." *VP* 8:187–98.

4751. Hunt, John D.,ed. *In Memoriam:A Casebook.* (Macmillan Casebook Ser.) London: Macmillan.

* 4752. Kaplan, Fred. "Woven Paces and Waving Hands: Tennyson's Merlin as Fallen Artist." *VP* 7(1969):285–98.

4753. Kissane, James D. *Alfred Tennyson.* (TEAS 110.) New York: Twayne.

4754. Lavabre, Simone. "Une lecture de *Maud*." *Caliban* 7:25–34.

4755. Lee, B.S. "Two Arthurian Tales:What Tennyson Did to Malory." *UCTSE* 1:1–18.

* 4756. Leggett, B.J. "Dante, Byron, and Tennyson's Ulysses." *TSL* 15:143–59.

4757. Meinhold, George D. "The *Idylls of the King* and the *Mabinogion*." *Tennyson Res. Bull.* 1(1969):61–63.

4758. Motter, T.H. Vail. "Tennyson's Lines to Adelaide Kemble." *TLS* 16 July:780.

4759. Niermeier, Stuart F. "The Poetic Structure of *In Memoriam*." *DAI* 30:4419A–20A(Toronto).

4760. Nishimae, Yoshimi. "The Tennyson Manuscripts at Trinity College, Cambridge." *Hiroshima Studies in Eng. Lang. and Lit.* 16,i–ii(1969):48–54.

4761. Nodelman, Perry M. "Art Palace to Evolution: Tennyson's Metaphors of Organization." *DAI* 30(1969):1570A–71A(Yale).

4762. Petrie, Neil H. "Psychic Disintegration in the Early Poetry of Tennyson." *DAI* 30:4423A(Kent State).

4763. Ricks, Christopher. "Tennyson as a Love-Poet." *MHRev* 12(1969):73–88.

4764. —— "Tennyson's 'To E. FitzGerald'." *Library* 25:156.

4765. Ricks, Christopher,ed. *The Poems of Tennyson.* London: Longmans, 1969.

4766. Scott, P.G. "Tennyson and Clough." *Tennyson Res. Bull.* 1(1969):64–70.

4767. —— *Tennyson's* Enoch Arden:A Victorian Best-Seller. Lincoln, Eng.: Tennyson Res. Centre. [38-p. pamphlet, illus.; avail. from Tennyson Res. Centre, Free School Lane, Lincoln.]

4768. Simmons, William K. "*The Passing of Arthur* by Alfred, Lord Tennyson:An Edition with Variants, Annotated." *DAI* 30:3958A(Ohio).

4769. Smith, James L. "William McGonagall and the Poet Laureate." *SSL* 7:21–28.

4770. Sonstroem, David. " 'Crossing the Bar' as Last Word." *VP* 8:55–60.

4771. Wheeler, Edd. "Tennyson's *In Memoriam* as a Gauge of Victorian Aesthetics." [F 23]:31–36. *See also* 3878, 3883, 3886, 4122, 5218.

Tennyson, L. 4772. Tennyson, Sir Charles. "A Poet's Child: The Early Days of Lionel Tennyson." *Tennyson Res. Bull.* 1:91–98.

Thackeray. 4773. Bergner, Heinz. *Die Kurzerzählungen W.M. Thackerays.* Inaug. Diss. der Philosophischen Fakultät der Friedrich-Alexander-Univ. zu Erlangen—Nürnberg. Berlin: The Author.

4774. Hollahan, Eugene. "Thackeray's *Barry Lyndon*:A Study of Genre, Structure, Background, and Meaning." *DAI* 30: 3460A(N.C.).

4775. Maxwell, J.C. "Thackeray and Die *Wahlverwandt-schaften*." *N&Q* 17:16–17.

* 4776. Patten, Robert L. "The Fight at the Top of the Tree:*Vanity Fair* versus *Dombey and Son*." *SEL* 10:759–73.

4777. Priestly, F.E.,ed. Vanity Fair:*A Novel Without a Hero.* New York: Odyssey.

* 4778. Rogers, Katherine M. "A Defense of Thackeray's Amelia." *TSLL* 11:1367–74.

4779. Schroeder, Gertrude S. "Thackeray, a Study of His Methods of Characterization." *DAI* 30:4955A(Cincinnati).

4780. Segel, Elizabeth J. "'The Same Michael Angelo Still....':Thackeray as Journalist-Novelist." *DAI* 30(1969): 2499A(Brandeis).

4781. Stewart, J.I.M.,ed. *Vanity Fair.* With Introd. Harmondsworth: Penguin, 1968.

4782. Sundell, Michael G.,ed. *Twentieth Century Interpretations of* Vanity Fair:*A Collection of Critical Essays.* (TCI.) Englewood Cliffs, N.J.: Prentice-Hall, 1969.

4783. Sutherland, John. "Thackeray as Victorian Racialist." *EIC* 20:441–45.

See also 1458, 3116, 3964.

Thomas. 4784. Cooke, William. *Edward Thomas.* London: Faber.

Thompson. 4785. Atkinson, F.G. "Q and Francis Thompson." *TLS* 5 Feb:140. [Prev. unpub. letter from T found in papers of Sir Arthur Quiller-Couch.]

Trevelyan. 4786. Collins, J.A. "R.C. Trevelyan and His Edwardian Sisyphus." *MD* 12:346–56.

Trollope, A. 4787. Brown, Beatrice C. *Anthony Trollope.* 2nd Ed. London: Barker, 1969.

4788. Condray, Martha J. "Woman's One Career:Trollope's View of the Character and Proper Rôle of Woman." *DAI* 30:5403A(Texas, Austin).

4789. Edwards, Peter D. *Anthony Trollope.* (Profiles in Lit. Ser.) London: Routledge & K. Paul, 1969.

4790. Gulliver, Antony F. "The Political Novels of Trollope and Snow." *DAI* 30(1969):684A(Conn.).

4791. Hart, Charles W. "Courtship and Marriage in the Novels of Anthony Trollope." *DAI* 30(1969):685A(Columbia).

4792. Kenney, Mrs. David J. "Anthony Trollope's Theology." *AN&Q* 9:51–54.

* 4793. Kleis, John C. "Passion vs. Prudence:Theme and Technique in Trollope's Palliser Novels." *TSLL* 11:1405–14.

4794. Laine, Michael. "The Concept of Power in the Novels of Anthony Trollope." *DAI* 30:4455A(Toronto).

4795. Spina, Brother Michael,O.S.F. "Trollope's Parliamentary Novels:A Study in Transition." *DAI* 30(1969):1151A–52A(St. John's).

4796. Stevens, Joan. "An Unrecorded Trollope Letter." *N&Q* 17:17.

Trollope, F. 4797. Bigland, Eileen. *The Indomitable Mrs. Trollope.* London: Barrie and Jenkins.

4798. Del Litto, Victor. "Sur les marges des *Domestic Manners of the Americans* de Mrs. Trollope:Deuxième édition revue et corrigée des marginalia de Stendhal." *SC* 12(1969):11–24.

* 4799. Heineman, Helen. "Frances Trollope in the New World." *AQ* 21(1969):544–59.

See also 6579.

Tyndall. *4800. Haugrud, Raychel A. "Tyndall's Interest in Emerson." *AL* 41:[507]–17.

Ward. *4801. Peterson, William S. "Mrs. Humphry Ward on *Robert Elsmere*:Six New Letters." *BNYPL* 74:587–97.

4802. Williams, Kenneth E. "Faith, Intention, and Fulfillment:The Religious Novels of Mrs. Humphry Ward." *DAI* 30(1969):2553A–54A(Temple).

Warren. *4803. Steig, Michael. "Subversive Grotesque in Samuel Warren's *Ten Thousand a-Year*." *NCF* 24(1969):154–68.

White. 4804. Nowell-Smith, Simon. "The Case of Arthur Craven." *MHRev* 13:47–54.

4805. Willey, Basil,ed. *Autobiography; and, Deliverance.* Leicester: Leicester U.P. [1888; 2nd rev. and corr. ed. of Mark Rutherford's autobiog.]

White, W.H. 4806. Kapoor, S.D. "An Ideal Come True:Hale White's Search for an Ideal Woman Character in His Novels." *CalR* N.S.1:411–18.

4807. Rayson, R.J. "Is *The Revolution in Tanner's Lane*

Broken-Backed?" *EIC* 20:71–80.

Wilde. 4808. Bader, Earl D. "The Self-Reflexive Language: Uses of Paradox in Wilde, Shaw, and Chesterton." *DAI* 30:4934A(Ind.).

* 4809. Baker, Houston A.,Jr. "A Tragedy of the Artist:*The Picture of Dorian Gray*." *NCF* 24(1969):349–55.

4810. Breugelmans, R. "The Reconciliation of Opposites in the Mythopoesis of Wilde, George, and Hofmannsthal." [F 2]:248–54.

4811. Brontë, Diana. "The Influence of Oscar Wilde in the Life and Works of André Gide." *DAI* 30:3425A–26A(N.C., Chapel Hill).

* 4812. Brooks, Michael. "Oscar Wilde, Charles Ricketts, and the Art of the Book." *Criticism* 12:301–15.

4813. Burkhart, Charles. "Ada Leverson and Oscar Wilde." *ELT* 13:193–200.

4814. Clive, H.P. "Oscar Wilde's First Meeting with Mallarmé." *FS* 24:145–49.

4815. Ellman, Richard,ed. *The Artist as Critic.* London: W.H. Allen. [Selections from W's critical writings.]

4816. Fraser, Russell,ed. *Selected Writings of Oscar Wilde.* Boston: Houghton Mifflin, 1969.

* 4817. Gordon, Jan B. "Wilde and Newman:The Confessional Mode." *Renascence* 22:183–91.

4818. Jordan, Robert J. "Satire and Fantasy in Wilde's *The Importance of Being Earnest*." *ArielE* 1,iii:101–09.

4819. Jullian, Philippe. *Oscar Wilde.* Tr. Violet Wyndham. New York: Viking, 1969.

4820. Mikhail, E.H. "The Four-Act Version of *The Importance of Being Earnest*." *MD* 11(1968):263–66.

4821. Poteet, Lewis J. "Romantic Aesthetics in Oscar Wilde's 'Mr. W.H.'" *SSF* 7:458–64.

4822. Recoulley, Alfred L.,III. "Oscar Wilde, the Dandy-Artist:A Study of Dandyism in the Life and Works of Oscar Wilde, With Particular Attention Given to the Intellectual Bases of Wilde's Dandyism." *DAI* 30(1969):290A(N.C., Chapel Hill).

4823. Rossi, Dominick. "Parallels in Wilde's *The Picture of Dorian Gray* and Goethe's *Faust*." *CLAJ* 13(1969):188–91.

4824. Shafer, Elizabeth. "The Wild, Wild West of Oscar Wilde." *Montana Mag. of Western Hist.* 20,ii:86–89.

* 4825. Ware, James M. "Algernon's Appetite:Oscar Wilde's Hero as Restoration Dandy." *ELT* 13:17–26.

4826. Yogi, L.L. "Oscar Wilde:A Poet." [F 51]:27–36.

See also 4529, 5947.

Wordsworth, C. See 3826.

Wordsworth, D. 4828. Woof, Robert. "Dorothy Wordsworth —A Profile." *TLS* 26 Mar:343. [Newly ident. silhouette.]

Wordsworth, W. 4828a. Applewhite, James W.,Jr. "Wordsworth's Imaginative Use of Place." *DAI* 30:4974A(Duke).

4829. Austin, Frances O. "Time, Experience and Syntax in Wordsworth's Poetry." *NM* 70(1969):724–38.

4830. Banerji, Jibon. "The Role of Godwinian Ideas in *The Borderers*." *CalR* N.S.1:419–32.

4831. Bates, Merete. "Toward the Premier of 'The Borderers,' Grasmere Production." *WC* 1:57–58.

4832. Bell, Arthur H. "Wordsworth and the Stabilizing 'Frame'." *XUS* 9,ii:9–14.

* 4833. Betz, Paul F. "An Unpublished Wordsworth Letter." *WC* 1:53–54.

4834. Camp, Dennis D. "Wordsworth and Frost:A Study in Poetic Tone." *DAI* 30(1969):1129A–30A(Wis.).

4835. Clark, Bruce B. "Thoughts on William Wordsworth:A Commemorative Essay." *BYUS* 10:201–17.

4836. *CLJ* 11:*Wordsworth Bicentenary Issue.* [Jonathan Wordsworth, "The Growth of a Poet's Mind," 3–24; Carl H. Ketcham, "The Death of Wordsworth's Brother John:Manuscript Materials in the Cornell-Dove Cottage Collection," 25–43; Jared R. Curtis, "From the Language of Men to the Language of Vision:Two Versions of 'Resolution and Independence'," 45–75; Robert Frost, "A Tribute to Wordsworth," 77–99 (20 Apr. 1950 address).]

4837. Curtis, Jared R. "The Best Philosopher:New Variants for Wordsworth's 'Immortality Ode'." *YULG* 44:139–47.

4838. Davis, Charles G. "The Structure of Wordsworth's

Sonnet 'Composed Upon Westminster Bridge'." *English* 19:18–21.

4839. de Selincourt, Ernest,ed. *Wordsworth:*The Prelude or Growth of a Poet's Mind *(Text of 1805).* New ed. corr. by Stephen Gill. London: Oxford U.P.

4840. Durrant, Geoffrey. *William Wordsworth.* London: Cambridge U.P., 1969.

4841. —— *Wordsworth and the Great System:A Study of Wordsworth's Poetic Universe.* London: Cambridge U.P.

4842. Edwards, Paul. "The Narrator's Voice in 'Goody Blake and Harry Gill'." *English* 19:13–17.

4843. Elmessiri, Abdelwahab M. "The Critical Writings of Wordsworth and Whitman:A Study of the Historical and Anti-Historical Imaginations." *DAI* 30:3904A–05A(Rutgers).

4844. Furst, Lilian R. "A Comparison of Romanticism as Seen in Three Poems." [F 3]:209–14.

4845. George, Andrew J.,ed. *The Complete Poetical Works of Wordsworth.* Boston: Houghton, n.d.

4846. Glimm, James Y. "Five Essays on Mystical Experience in the Works of Wordsworth, Coleridge, and Shelley." *DAI* 30(1969):1525A(Texas, Austin).

4847. Gotimer, Sister Mary E. "Wordsworth's Attitude Toward His Critics with Particular Reference to the Poems of 1807." *DAI* 30(1969):1981A(C.U.N.Y.).

4848. Grandine, Jonathan R. *The Problem of Shape in* The Prelude:*The Conflict of Private and Public Speech.* Cambridge: Harvard U.P., 1968. [47-p. prize essay.]

4849. Haefner, Gerhard. "Zum 200. Geburtstag von William Wordsworth (1770–1850)." *NsM* 23:46–47.

4850. Halliday, Frank E. *Wordsworth and His World.* New York: Viking.

4851. Hara, Ichiro. "Wordsworth no fatatsu no Shukyo." *EigoS* 115(1969):620–21. [W's two religions.]

* 4852. Haswell, Richard H. "A Narrative Point of View in Wordsworth's *Lyrical Ballads.*" *PLL* 6:197–202.

4853. Hedetoft, Ulf. "De ensomme personers betydning og funktion i Wordsworth's digtning til og med *The Excursion.*" *Extracta* 2(1969):163–67. [Abst.]

* 4854. Hunt, Bishop C.,Jr. "Wordsworth and Charlotte Smith." *WC* 1:85–103.

4855. Immaculate, Sister Margaret,C.S.J. "Odes of Wordsworth and Coleridge." *Horizontes*(Puerto Rico) 24(Abril 1969):63–67.

4856. Jaye, Michael C. "The Growth of a Poem:The Early Manuscripts of William Wordsworth's *The Prelude.*" *DAI* 30(1969):2486A(N.Y.U.).

4857. Jones, Alun R. "The Compassionate World:Some Observations on Wordsworth's *Lyrical Ballads* of 1798." *English* 19:7–12.

4858. Maxwell, J.C. "Wordsworth and the Subjugation of Switzerland." *MLR* 65:16–18.

4859. Moorman, Mary. "The Ruined Cottage." *ArielE* 1,ii:39–41. [Rev. art.]

4860. Nesbitt, George L. *Wordsworth:The Biographical Background of His Poetry.* New York: Pegasus.

4861. Noyes, Russell. "More on Wordsworth in Japan." *WC* 1:65.

* 4862. Noyes, Russell, Kenkichi Kamijima, Mine Okachi, and Koicki Senbokuya. "Wordsworth in Japan." *WC* 1:5–13.

* 4863. Pearsall, Robert B. "Wordsworth Reworks His Hartley." *BRMMLA* 24:75–83.

* 4864. Pollin, Burton R. " 'The World Is Too Much with Us':Two More Sources—Dryden and Godwin." *WC* 1:50–52.

* 4865. —— "Wordsworth's 'Miserrimus' Sonnet:Several Errors Corrected." *WC* 1:22–24.

4866. Rawnsley, Hardwicke D. *Reminiscences of Wordsworth*

Among the Peasantry of Westmoreland. Introd. Geoffrey Tillotson. London: Dillon, 1969.

4867. Rice, H.A.L. "Wordsworth in Easedale." *ArielE* 1,ii: 31–38.

4868. Rogers, David. "God and Pre-existence in Wordsworth's *Immortality Ode.*" *DUJ* 30(1969):143–46.

4869. Ross, Robert N. "The Ecstatic Eye:Wordsworth and Eighteenth-Century Modes of Seeing." *DAI* 30:5419A(Cornell).

4870. Rountree, Thomas J. "Wordsworth and Beattie's *Minstrel.*" *SAQ* 69:[257]–63.

* 4871. Sabin, Margery. "Imagination in Rousseau and Wordsworth." *CL* 22:328–45.

4872. Saito, Yuso. "Basho, Buson and Wordsworth, Shelley, Keats." [F 3]:419–25.

* 4873. Sanderson, David R. "Wordsworth's World, 1809:A Stylistic Study of the Cintra Pamphlet." *WC* 1:104–13.

4874. Sharrock, Roger. "*The Prelude:*The Poet's Journey to the Interior." *English* 19:1–6.

4875. Shawcross, John T. "Wordsworth's 'The World Is Too Much With Us':A Source?" *ELN* 7:192–94. [Henry Headley's "An Invocation to Melancholy" (1785).]

4876. Sheats, Paul D. "Excursion and Return in *The Prelude.*" *WC* 1:123–30.

4877. Silz, Walter. "Hölderlin and Wordsworth:Bicentenary Reflections." *GR* 45:259–72.

* 4878. Sperry, Stuart M.,Jr. "From 'Tintern Abbey' to the 'Intimations Ode':Wordsworth and the Function of Memory." *WC* 1:40–49.

4879. Stephenson, William C. "The Meditative Poetry of Wordsworth and Wallace Stevens." *DAI* 30(1968):2552A(Minn.).

4880. Stoll, John E. "Wordsworth for Modern Students." *BSUF* 11,iii:50–56.

* 4881. Storch, R.F. "Wordsworth and the City:'Social Reason's Inner Sense'." *WC* 1:114–22.

* 4882. Teich, Nathaniel. "Correcting the Reference to the *Monthly Magazine* in the Fenwick Note to Wordsworth's 'We Are Seven'." *WC* 1:55–56.

4883. *The Indiana Wordsworth Collection:A Brief Account of the Collection Together with a Catalogue of the Exhibit Held in the Lilly Library on the Occasion of the Bicentenary of Wordsworth's Birth.* Bloomington: Ind. U., Lilly Lib.

4884. Thomson, A.W. "Wordsworth's Spots of Time." *ArielE* 1,ii:23–30.

4885. Walsh, T. "A Country School at the End of the Eighteenth Century:Wordsworth at Hawkshead." *ManR* 11: 299–301.

4886. Warren, Leland E. "Wordsworth's Conception of Man:A Study in Apocalyptic Vision." *SHR* 4:155–62.

4887. Wesling, Donald. "The Inevitable Ear:Freedom and Necessity in Lyric Form, Wordsworth and After." [F 48]:103–26.

4888. —— *Wordsworth and the Adequacy of Landscape.* New York: Barnes & Noble; London: Routledge & K. Paul.

4889. Wlecke, Albert O. "Wordsworth and the Sublime:An Essay on Wordsworth's Imagination." *DAI* 30(1969):1539A (Mich. State).

4890. Woodring, Carl. *Wordsworth.* Cambridge: Harvard U.P., 1968.

4891. Woof, R.S. "John Stoddart, 'Michael' and *Lyrical Ballads.*" *ArielE* 1,ii:7–22.

See also 557, 1471, 3341, 3931, 3935, 3936, 4088, 4146, 4157, 4166, 4170, 4526, 5189, 8234.

Zangwill. 4892. Adams, Elsie B. "Israel Zangwill:An Annotated Bibliography of Writings About Him." *ELT* 13:209–44.

4893. —— "Israel Zangwill:Ghetto Realist and Romancer." *ELT* 13:203–09.

X. TWENTIETH CENTURY

Bibliography. 4894. Millett, Fred B.,ed. *Contemporary British Literature:A Critical Survey and 232 Author-Bibliographies.* New York: Johnson Rpt., 1969. [Rpt. of 3d rev. ed., 1935.]

4895. Morgan, A. Mary,ed. *British Government Publications: An Index to Chairmen and Authors, 1941–1966.* London: Sta-

tionery Office, 1969; Detroit: Gale.

General and Miscellaneous. 4896. Annan, Noël. "The University and the Intellect:The Miasma and the Menace." *TLS* 30 Apr:465–68.

4897. Báti, László, and István K. Nagy,eds. *Az angol irodalom a huszadik században.* 2 vols. Budapest: Gondolat. [Eng. lit. in the 20th c.]

4898. Bleich, David. "Utopia:The Psychology of a Cultural Fantasy." *DAI* 30:4935A–36A(N.Y.U.). [Early 20th c. utopias in England and Amer.]

4899. Bosonnet, Felix R. "Angloamerikanische Literaturkritik im 20. Jahrhundert:Ein Überblick," (Editionen Materialen 1.) 35–73 in Felix P. Ingold,ed., *Literaturwissenschaft und Literaturkritik im 20. Jahrhundert.* Bern: Kandelaber Verl. [Mit "Bibliographie," 74–84.]

4900. Cecil, Robert. *Life in Edwardian England.* London: Batsford; New York: Putnam, 1969.

4901. Comyn, Andrew F. "Censorship in Ireland." *Studies* 58(1969):42–50.

4902. Curzon, Gordon A. "Paradise Sought:A Study of the Religious Motivation in Representative British and American Literary Utopias, 1850–1950." *DAI* 30:4405A(Calif., Riverside).

4903. Daiches, David. *The Present Age in British Literature.* Bloomington: Ind. U.P., 1969.

4904. Drew, Fraser. "Next Parish to Boston:The Blasket Islands and Their Literature." *Éire* 3,i(1968):6–22.

4905. Dugan, Michael. "Britain's Small Poetry Presses." *Overland* 45:35–37.

4906. Eagleton, Terence. *Exiles and Emigrés:Studies in Modern Literature.* London: Chatto & Windus. [On Auden, Conrad, T.S. Eliot, G. Greene, D.H. Lawrence, Orwell, and E. Waugh.]

4907. Farr, D. Paul. "The Edwardian Golden Age and Nostalgic Truth." *DR* 50:378–93.

4908. Fricker, Robert. "Das Kathedralenmotiv in der modernen englischen Dichtung." [F 52]:225–38.

4909. Hampshire, Stuart. *Modern Writers, and Other Essays.* London: Chatto & Windus. [Essays on Auden, Joyce, Forster, V. Woolf, James, and Proust.]

4910. Hynes, Samuel. *The Edwardian Turn of Mind.* Princeton: Princeton U.P.; London: Oxford U.P., 1968.

4911. Ivaševa, V.V. "Sovremennaja anglijskaja literatura v svete učenija V.I. Lenina o dvux kul'turax v každoj nacional'noj kul'ture." *FN* 13,ii:3–13. [Contemp. Eng. lit. in the light of Lenin's two-culture theory.]

4912. Leavis, F.R. " 'Literarism' versus 'Scientism':The Misconception and the Menace." *TLS* 23 Apr:441–44. [See Snow art., below. See also 14 Aug:902–03.]

4913. —— *English Literature in Our Time and the University.* London: Chatto & Windus.

4914. Levidova, I. "Ukroščenie absurda (Zametki ob anglijskom komičeskom romane)." *VLit* 14,viii:121–40.

4915. Matthews, James H. "History to Literature:Alternatives to History in Modern Irish Literature." [F 58]:73–87.

4916. Maurois, André. *Points of View from Kipling to Greene.* Foreword Walter Allen. Tr. Hamish Miles. London: Muller. [Essays on var. British writers.]

4917. Potter, Simeon. *Changing English.* London: André Deutsch, 1969.

4918. Robson, W.W. *Modern English Literature.* London: Oxford U.P.

4919. Snow, Charles P. "The Case of Leavis and the Serious Case." *TLS* 9 July:736–40. [See Leavis art., above; see also 16 July:774; 23 July:814–15; 31 July:854.]

4920. Speaight, Robert. "Literary London in the Thirties." *MHRev* 10(1969):5–15.

See also 608, 3854, 3872, 5640, 6945, 9414.

Criticism. 4921. Aihara, Koichi. "Itanteki Koga to Seito Shiko." *EigoS* 115(1969):420–21. [Heretical ego and search for orthodoxy—in Hulme, Eliot, Read.]

4922. —— "Koga no Mondai wo meguru Sannin no Hihyoka." *EigoS* 115(1969):278–79. [Three critics on problem of Ego: Hulme, Eliot, Read.]

4923. —— "Tagenteki Jokyo to Sannin no Hihyoka." *EigoS* 115(1969):350–51. [Pluralistic society and 3 critics: Hulme, Eliot, Read.]

4924. Brinton, George A. "The Fly in the Bottle:Literary Theory and the Philosophy of Ludwig Wittgenstein." *DAI* 30(1969):2476A(U. of Wash.).

4925. Cary, Norman R. " 'Christian Criticism' in the Twentieth Century:A Survey of Theological Approaches to Literature." *DAI* 30(1969):1130A(Wayne State).

4926. Pattinson, John P. "A Study of British Poetic Criticism Between 1930 and 1965 as Exemplified in the Critics of Yeats, Pound, and Eliot." *DAI* 30:4460A–61A(N.Y.U.).

4927. Winter, Helmut. "Von F.R. Leavis bis Donald Davie: Notizen zur modernen englischen Literaturkritik." *NRs* 81: 170–79.

4928. Yamakawa, Kozo. "Eikoku Kindai Hikyo no Hoho." *EigoS* 115(1969):142–43. [Methods of mod. Eng. crit.]

See also 4738.

Drama and Theater. 4929. Amette, Jacques-Pierre. "Osborne, Pinter, Saunders & Cie." *NRF* 18(janv):95–99.

4930. Arnold, Lionel A. "Ambiguity and Ambivalence in Modern Drama:The Sphinx and the Playwright." *DAI* 30(1969): 2188A–89A(Drew).

4931. Barker, Clive. "Contemporary Shakespearean Parody in British Theatre." *SJW* 105(1969):104–20.

4932. Esslin, Martin. "Contemporary English Drama and the Mass Media." *English* 18(1969):5–11.

4933. Flockton, Avril. "Edward Gordon Craig and 'The New Stagecraft'." *DR* 50:88–96.

4934. Flory, Claude R. "A Rare Theatrical Journal:*The Arthurian Theatre Magazine.*" *MD* 13:129–32.

4935. French, Frances-Jane. *The Abbey Theatre Series of Plays:A Bibliography.* Dublin: Dolmen P., 1969.

4936. Gelber, Sholome M. "The Image of the Jew in the Productions of the London Stage from 1919 to 1965." *DAI* 30(1969):1563A–64A(N.Y.U.).

4937. Holmes, Jerry D. "An Ancient Structure:A Study of the Influence of Medieval Drama on Selected Contemporary English and American Plays." *DAI* 30(1969):2529A(Miss.).

4938. Jurak, Mirko. "The Group Theatre:Its Development and Significance for the Modern English Theatre." *AN* 2(1969): 3–43.

4939. Kosok, Heinz. "Das moderne englische Kurzdrama." *NsM* 23:131–41.

4940. McCormick, Jane L. "Drive That Man Away:The Theme of the Artist in Society in Celtic Drama, 1890–1950." *SUS* 8(1969):213–29.

4941. O'Mahony, T.P. "Theatre in Ireland." *Éire* 4,ii(1969): 93–100.

4942. Richards, Stanley,ed. *Modern Short Comedies from Broadway and London.* New York: Random House. [*Black Comedy*, by P. Shaffer; *Visitor from Mamaroneck*, by N. Simon; *Losers*, by B. Friel; *Trevor*, by J. Bowen; *The Shock of Recognition*, by R. Anderson; *Shadows of the Evening*, by N. Coward; *The Sponge Room*, by K. Waterhouse and W. Hall; *The Diary of Adam and Eve*, by S. Harnick and J. Bock; *George's Room*, by A. Owen; *Noon*, by T. McNally; *Bea, Frank, Richie and Joan*, by R. Taylor and J. Bologna; *Madly in Love*, by P. Ableman.]

4943. Rushe, Desmond. "When the Wind Blows . . ." *Éire* 5,iv:84–87. [Abbey Theatre productions 1969–70.]

4944. Sanders, Walter E. "The English-Speaking Game-Drama." *DAI* 30:5001A–02A(Northwestern).

4945. Schrey, Helmut. "Das moderne englische Drama im Unterricht." *NsM* 23:141–47.

4946. Splendore, Paola. "Il Teatro Politico in Inghilterra, 1930–1940." *AION–SG* 12(1969):429–49.

4947. Swander, Homer D. "Shields at the Abbey:A Friend of Cathleen." *Éire* 5,ii:25–41.

4948. Van Heyningen, Christina. "The Contemporary Theatre." *Theoria* 32(1969):25–37. [In England.]

4949. Weise, Wolf-Dietrich. *Die "neuen englischen Dramatiker" in ihrem Verhältnis zu Brecht.* (Frankfurter Beiträge zur Anglistik und Amerikanistik 3.) Bad Homburg: Gehlen, 1969.

See also 3914, 5459.

Periodicals. 4950. Martin, Peter A. "British Magazines and the Literary Temper of the 1930's." *DAI* 30:5450A(Wis.).

4951. Sullivan, Daniel J.,C.M. "Standish James O'Grady's *All Ireland Review.*" *SH* 9(1969):125–36.

Poetry. 4952. Arinštejn, L.M. "Anglijskaja poèzija meždu 1955 i 1965 godom." [F 44]:149–59.

4953. Bhalla, M.M. "Modern Poetry." *Quest* 63(1969):78–88. [Eliot, Auden, D. Thomas, et al.]

4954. Blackburn, Thomas. "Poetry Today." *English* 18(1969):12–17.

4955. Dodsworth, Martin,ed. *The Survival of Poetry:A Contemporary Survey, by Donald Davie [and Others].* London: Faber. [Crit. Essays.]

4956. Donoghue, Denis. "The Holy Language of Modernism." [F 56]:386–407.

4957. Fauchereau, Serge. "Tradition et révolution dans la poésie irlandaise." *Critique* 26:438–56.

4958. Fraser, G.S. "Proper Names in Poetry." *TLS* 11 June:638–39.

4959. Fuller, Roy. "The Filthy Aunt and the Anonymous Seabird." *TLS* 21 May:561–63.

4960. Funato, Hideo. "Gendai Eishi to Shukyo." *EigoS* 115(1969):694–95. [Mod. Eng. poetry and religion.]

4961. Guest, Harry. "The Language of Modern Poetry." *EigoS* 114(1968):370–73.

4962. Kobayashi, Manji. "Gendaishi to Dento." *EigoS* 114(1968):439–40. [Modern poetry and tradition.]

4963. Kuna, F.M. "A New Myth-Consciousness in Contemporary English Poetry." *ES* 51:214–28.

4964. Lucie-Smith, Edward. *British Poetry Since 1945.* Harmondsworth: Penguin. [Anthol.]

* 4965. Martin, Wallace. "The Sources of the Imagist Aesthetic." *PMLA* 85:196–204.

4966. Masterman, Margaret, and Robin McK. Wood. "The Poet and the Computer." *TLS* 18 June:667–68.

4967. Rosenthal, M.L. "Dynamics of Form and Motive in Some Representative Twentieth-Century Lyric Poems." *ELH* 37:136–51.

4968. —— "Poetry of the Main Chance." *TLS* 29 Jan:113. [Anglo-Amer. poetic relations.]

4969. Seehase, Georg. " '*The Sense of Movement*.'Über den Aktionsraum des lyrischen Helden in einigen Werken englischer Gegenwartsdichtung." *ZAA* 18:71–87.

4970. Sen, Mihir K. *Inter-War English Poetry:With Special Reference to Eliot's 'Objective Correlative' Theory.* Burdwan, India: U. of Burdwan, 1967.

4971. Spender, Stephen. "Form and Pressure in Poetry." *TLS* 23 Oct:1226–28. [From the text of S's Inaug. Lect. at Univ. College London. See also 30 Oct:1276.]

* 4972. White, William. "Little Leather Library's *Fifty Best Poems of England.*" *PBSA* 64:209.

See also 912, 1467, 3927, 3936, 3940, 7261.

Prose Fiction. 4973. Allen, Walter. "Recent Trends in the English Novel." *English* 18(1969):2–5.

4974. Ausmus, Martin R. "Some Forms of the Sequence Novel in British Fiction." *DAI* 30(1969):1975A(Okla.).

4975. Bergonzi, Bernard. *Situation of the Novel.* London: Macmillan.

4976. Brooke-Rose, Christine. "Le roman expérimental en Angleterre." *LanM* 63(1969):158–68.

4977. Cunningham, Lawrence S. "The Image of the Priest in Contemporary Anglo-American Fiction." *DAI* 30:4446A(Fla. State).

* 4978. Davis, Robert M. "Market Depressed and Unstable: Surveys of the Recent English Novel." *PLL* 6:211–23.

4979. Kahrmann, Bernd. *Die idyllische Szene im zeitgenössischen englischen Roman.* (L&L 8.) Bad Homburg v.d.H.: Gehlen, 1969.

4980. Marković, Vida E. *The Changing Face:Disintegration of Personality in the Twentieth-Century British Novel, 1900–1950.* Pref. Harry T. Moore. Carbondale: So. Ill. U.P.; London: Feffer & Simons.

4981. Meyers, Carolyn H. "Psychotechnology in Fiction about Imaginary Societies, 1923–1962." *DAI* 30(1969):2490A–91A(Ky.).

4982. Pérez Minik, Domingo. *Introducción a la novela inglesa actual.* Madrid: Guadarrama, 1968.

4983. Quiñonez, Sister Lora A. "The Concept of Man in Representative Dystopian Novels." *DAI* 30(1969):2038A–39A (Mich.).

4984. Rabinovitz, Rubin. "The Reaction Against Experiment:A Study of the English Novel, 1950–1960." *DAI* 30(1969): 1177A(Columbia). [1966.]

4985. Rubin, Donald S. "The Recusant Myth in Modern Fiction." *DAI* 30:4462A(Toronto). [On English Catholic lit.]

4986. Summers, Marcia P. "The Use of Subordinate Characters as Dramatized Narrators in Twentieth-Century Novels." *DAI* 30:3024A–25A(Ill.).

4987. Wagner, Geoffrey. "The Novel of Empire." *EIC* 20:229–42. [Incl. discussion of Kipling, Conrad, Forster, Orwell.]

See also 925, 930, 950, 987, 3948, 3952, 3955, 3956, 3965, 3968, 5024, 6726, 7293, 7297.

Aldington. 4988. Kershaw, Alister,ed. *Richard Aldington: Selected Critical Writings, 1928–1960.* Pref. Harry T. Moore. Carbondale and Edwardsville: So. Ill. U.P.; London and Amsterdam: Feffer & Simons.

4989. Rosenthal, Sidney. "Richard Aldington and the Excitement of Reason." [F 47]:133–43.

4990. Thatcher, David S.,ed. and introd. "Richard Aldington's Letters to Herbert Read." *MHRev* 15:5–44.

Amis. 4991. "Kingsley Amis:Worksheets." *MHRev* 12(1969): 105–16.

4992. Vann, J. Donn, and James T.F. Tanner. "Kingsley Amis:A Checklist of Recent Criticism." *BB* 26(1969):105, 111,115–17.

Arden. 4993. Blindheim, Joan T. "John Arden's Use of the Stage." *MD* 11(1968):306–16.

4994. Epstein, Arthur D. "John Arden's Fun House." *UR* 36:243–51. [On *The Happy Haven*.]

4995. Jordan, Robert J. "Serjeant Musgrave's Problem." *MD* 13:54–62.

Auden. 4996. Bahlke, George. *The Later Auden:From "New Year Letter" to "About the House."* New Brunswick, N.J.: Rutgers U.P.

4997. Bloom, Robert. "Poetry's Auden." *JML* 1:119–22. [Rev. art.]

4998. Brophy, James D. *W.H. Auden.* (CEMW 54.) New York and London: Columbia U.P.

4999. Callan, Edward. "W.H. Auden:Annotated Checklist II (1958–1969)." *TCL* 16:27–56.

5000. Clark, Vera F. "The Rhetoric of W.H. Auden's Verse Plays." *DAI* 30(1969):2651A(U. of Wash.).

5001. Cozarinsky, Edgardo. "Desencantar, desintoxicar:Nota sobre W.H. Auden y W.A. Mozart." *PSA* 55(1969):307–17.

5002. Fuller, John. *A Reader's Guide to W.H. Auden.* London: Thames and Hudson.

5003. Grant, Damian. "Tones of Voice." *CritQ* 11(1969): 195,197–98.

5004. Hashiguchi, Minoru. "W.H. Auden Saisetsu." *Oberon* 31(1969):71–76. [Reconsideration of A.]

* 5005. Hazard, Forrest E. "*The Ascent of F 6*:A New Interpretation." *TSL* 15:165–75.

5006. Jäger, Dietrich. "Das Haus als Raum des lyrischen Geschehens und als Gegenstand der lyrischen Meditation:Das Thema der nächsten Umwelt des Menschen in Audens *About the House* und bei deutschen und angelsächsischen Zeitgenossen." *LWU* 2(1969):238–57.

5007. Masutani, Toyotsugu. "Auden no Shi no Kozo." *Oberon* 31(1969):55–66. [Struct. of A's poetry.]

* 5008. Morse, Donald E. "Meaning of Time in Auden's *For the Time Being*." *Renascence* 22:162–68.

5009. —— "Two Major Revisions in W.H. Auden's 'For the Time Being'." *ELN* 7:294–97.

* 5010. Natterstad, J.H. "Auden's 'It's No Use Raising a Shout':A New Perspective." *CP* 3,i:17–20.

5011. Robertson, Duncan. "Auden's 'The Wanderer'." *Expl* 28:Item 70.

5012. Stiehl, Harry C.,Jr. "Auden's Artists:Portraits of the Artist in the Poetry of W.H. Auden." *DAI* 30(1969):1576A–77A(Texas, Austin).

* 5013. Weisstein, Ulrich. "Reflections on a Golden Style:W.H. Auden's Theory of Opera." *CL* 22:108–24.

See also 4909, 5049, 5594, 5947, 8165.

Barrie. 5014. Lamacchia, Grace A. "Textual Variations for

Act IV of *The Admirable Crichton.*" *MD* 12:408–18.

Bates. 5015. Sharfman, William L. "Ralph Bates:The Self-Consuming Fires." *DAI* 30:5458A(Columbia).

Beerbohm. 5016. Cecil, Lord David,ed. *The Bodley Head Max Beerbohm.* London: Bodley Head. [Anthol.]

5017. Hart-Davis, Rupert,ed. *More Theatres 1898–1903.* London: Granada. [Selections from B's reviews in the *Saturday Review*, 1898–1903.]

Behan. 5018. Boyle, Ted E. *Brendan Behan.* (TEAS 91.) New York: Twayne, 1969.

5019. McMahon, Seán. "*The Quare Fellow.*" *Éire* 4,iv(1969): 143–57.

5020. O'Connor, Ulick. *Brendan Behan.* London: Hamilton.

Belloc. 5021. Jebb, Dom Philip. "Hilaire Belloc as a Grandfather." *DownR* 88:339–43. [A personal reminiscence.]

5022. Thody, Philip. "The Cosmic Pessimism [sic!] of Hilaire Belloc." *ULR* 13:73–88.

5023. Van Thal, Herbert,ed. *Belloc:A Biographical Anthology.* New York: Knopf. [1st Amer. ed.]

Bennett. 5024. Goldfarb, Richard L. "Arnold Bennett and James Joyce on the Art of Fiction:Realism and Symbolism in Modern English Theories of the Novel." *DAI* 30:3008A(Northwestern).

5025. Hepburn, James,ed. *Letters of Arnold Bennett, III: 1916–1931.* London: Oxford U.P.

See also 4974, 5769.

Betjeman. 5027. "John Betjeman:Worksheets." *MHRev* 1(1967):130–34.

Blunt. 5028. Ljubarskaja, A.M. *Vil'frid Skouèn Blant (1840–1922):Žizn', tvorčestvo, bor'ba.* Moscow: Nauka, 1969.

Bolt. 5029. Reynolds, E.E. "The Significance of *A Man for All Seasons.*" *Moreana* 23(1969):34–39.

5030. Wiszniowska, Marta. "Characters in Robert Bolt's Dramas (A Study in Internal Relations)." *KN* 17:147–57.

Bond, E. 5031. Mori, Yasuaki. "Edward Bond Tojo." *EigoS* 115(1969):614–15. [Enter EB.]

Bowen. *5032. Sellery, J'nan. "Elizabeth Bowen:A Check List." *BNYPL* 74:219–74.

Boyle, P. 5033. Matthews, Jack. "An Interview with Patrick Boyle." *MHRev* 16:85–90.

Brooke. 5034. Hughes, Mark H. "The Paternal Ancestry of Rupert Brooke." *N&Q* 17:49.

5035. Rogers, Timothy. "Rupert Brooke:Man and Monument." *English* 17(1968):79–84.

Bunting. 5036. Suter, Anthony. "Un 'Raleigh' moderne: Introduction à la vie et à l'oeuvre poétique de Basil Bunting." *Caliban* 7:121–32.

Burgess. 5037. Aggeler, Geoffrey. "Mr. Enderby and Mr. Burgess." *MHRev* 10(1969):104–10.

5038. Hoffmann, Charles G. and A.C. "Mr. Kell and Mr. Burgess:Inside and Outside Mr. Enderby." [F 60]:300–10.

Campbell, J. 5039. Clark, David R. "Joseph Campbell's 'The Dancer'." *Éire* 4,iii(1969):82–86.

Campbell, R. *5040. Smith, Rowland. "Roy Campbell and His French Sources." *CL* 22:1–19.

Cary. 5041. Fisher, Barbara. "Joyce Cary's Published Writings." *BLR* 8:213–28.

5042. Mitchell, Giles. "Joyce Cary's *Except the Lord.*" *ArlQ* 2,ii(1969):71–82.

* 5043. Reed, Peter J. "Getting Stuck:Joyce Cary's Gulley Jimson." *TCL* 16:241–52.

5044. Wolkenfeld, Jack S. "Joyce Cary:The Developing Style." *DAI* 30:1187A(Columbia).

See also 4974.

Caudwell. 5045. Caudwell, C. *Romance and Realism:A Study in English Bourgeois Literature.* Ed. with Introd. by Samuel Hynes. Princeton: Princeton U.P.

5046. Margolies, David N. *The Function of Literature:A Study of Christopher Caudwell's Aesthetics.* London: Lawrence and Wishart.

5047. Maxwell, D.E.S. "The *Poems* of Christopher Caudwell." *ArielE* 1,i:73–82.

Chesterton. 5048. Auden, W.H. "G.K. Chesterton's Non-Fictional Prose." *Prose* 1:17–28.

5049. Auden, W.H.,ed. *G.K. Chesterton:Selection from His Non-Fictional Prose.* London: Faber.

5050. Collins, Dorothy,ed. *A Miscellany of Men.* Philadelphia: Dufour, 1969.

5051. Hollis, Christopher. *The Mind of Chesterton.* London: Hollis and Carter.

5052. Milward, Peter. "Chesterton no Shakespeare-kan." *Oberon* 29(1968):56–63. [C's view of Shakespeare.]

5053. Nakano, Kii. "Chesterton no Juyoshi." *SophiaT* 18(1969):38–59. [Reception of C in Japan.]

5054. ——— "G.K. Chesterton no Bungei Hyoden." *ELLS* 5(1968):99–128. [C's lit. biogs.]

See also 4050, 4287, 4808, 5746.

Christie, A. 5055. Bernstein, Marcelle. "Cu Agatha Christie la 80 de ani şi 80 de romane." *Contemporanul* 25 Sept:9.

Churchill. 5056. Hull, Keith N. "The Literary Art of Winston Churchill's *The Second World War.*" *DAI* 30:4987A–88A(U. of Wash.).

Clarke, A. 5057. Weber, Richard. "Austin Clarke:The Arch Poet of Dublin." *MR* 11:295–308.

Colum. 5058. Bowen, Zack. *Padraic Colum:A Biographical-Critical Introduction.* Carbondale and Edwardsville: So. Ill. U.P.; London and Amsterdam: Feffer & Simons.

5059. ——— "Padraic Colum and Irish Drama." *Éire* 5,iv: 71–82.

Compton-Burnett. 5060. Nevius, Blake. *Ivy Compton-Burnett.* (CEMW 47.) New York and London: Columbia U.P.

5061. Pittock, Malcolm. "Ivy Compton-Burnett's Use of Dialogue." *ES* 51:43–46.

Conrad. 5062. Barringer, George M. "Joseph Conrad and *Nostromo:*Two New Letters." *Thoth* 10,ii(1969):20–24. [Incl. texts of the letters to Mrs. Dummett and Gosse.]

* 5063. Bojarski, Edmund A., and Harold R. Stevens. "Joseph Conrad and the *Falconhurst.*" *JML* 1:192–208.

5064. Bojarski, Edmund A. and Henry T. "Joseph Conrad:A Bibliography of Masters Theses and Doctoral Dissertations, 1917–1963." *BB* 26(1969):61–66,79–82.

5065. Carson, Herbert L. "The Second Self in *The Secret Sharer.*" *Cresset*(Valparaiso U.) 34,i:11–13.

5066. Cheney, Lynne. "Joseph Conrad's *The Secret Agent* and Graham Greene's *It's a Battlefield:*A Study in Structural Meaning." *MFS* 16:117–31.

5067. Chiampi, Rubens. "*Heart of Darkness.*" *IH* 5(1969): 52–68. [Crit.]

5068. Conrad, Borys. *My Father:Joseph Conrad.* London: Calder and Boyar.

5069. *Conradiana* 2,i. [Edgar Wright, "Joseph Conrad and Bertrand Russell," 7–16; Dale B.J. Randall, "Conrad Interviews, No. 1:Perriton Maxwell," 17–22; Gordon Lindstrand, "A Bibliographical Survey of the Literary Manuscripts of Joseph Conrad," 23–32; Derick R.C. Marsh, "A Note on the *Otago,*" 33–35; David H. Karrfalt, "Accepting Lord Jim on His Own Terms:A Structural Approach," 37–47; Kenneth Bernard, "Conrad's Fools of Innocence in *The Nigger of the 'Narcissus'*," 49–57; Cheris Kramer, "Parallel Motives in *Lord Jim,*" 58; Patricia A. Morley, "Conrad's Vision of the Absurd," 59–68; Kenneth R. Lincoln, "Glass Beads:The American Edition of *Lord Jim,*" 69–72; Edwin P. Conquest,Jr., "Conrad's Evening at the Polish-American Arts Association," 73–74; Kazimierz Wyka, "An Island in the Polish Gulf," 75–83(tr. Jadwiga Zwolska Sell and S. Dwight Stevens,III); Gordon Lindstrand, "Conrad's Literary Manuscripts:John Quinn and the New York Public Library," 85–88; Patsy C. Howard, "Borys Conrad Reminiscences." 89–93; Patricia Ault, "Conradiana on Display," 94; Bruce E. Teets, "Conrad and Guides to Art as Psychagogia," 127–31; H. Ray Stevens, "Conrad Bibliography:A Continuing Checklist," 135–46.]

5070. *Conradiana* 2,ii. [J. Walt, "Mencken and Conrad," 9–21; Harold E. Davis, "Shifting Rents in a Thick Fog:Point of View in the Novels of Joseph Conrad," 23–38; William Bysshe Stein, "*The Heart of Darkness:*A Bodhisattva Scenario," 39–52; William E. Messenger, "Conrad and Melville Again," 53–64; Albert C. Yoder, "Oral Artistry in Conrad's *Heart of Darkness:*A Study of Oral Aggression," 65–78; Bill Kaler Addison, "Marlow,

Aschenback, and We," 79–81; Dale B. J. Randall, "Conrad Interviews, No. 2: James Walter Smith," 83–93; Carroll Sibley, "Mrs. Joseph Conrad," 95–96; Cyril Clemens, "A Chat with Joseph Conrad," 97–103; Gordon Lindstrand, "A Bibliographical Survey of the Literary Manuscripts of Joseph Conrad, Part II," 105–14; Joseph D. Stamey, "Conrad's 'Dearest Russell' (1872–1970)," (sic) 115–17; Henry J. Laskowsky, "Joseph Conrad's Letters to R.B. Cunninghame Graham," 125–27; Ugo Mursia, "Joseph Conrad's Works:An Italian Bibliography," 135–51; H. Ray Stevens, "Conrad Bibliography:A Continuing Checklist," 153–63.]

5071. Cooper, Christopher. *Conrad and the Human Dilemma.* New York: Barnes & Noble; London: Chatto & Windus.

5072. Cummings, David E. "A World of Secret Agents: Subversion and Survival in the Fiction of Joseph Conrad." *DAI* 30(1969):1558A(Neb.).

5073. Deurbergue, Jean. "Homo duplex quelques ouvrages récents sur Joseph Conrad." *EA* 22(1969):397–412.

5074. Dowden, Wilfred S. *Joseph Conrad:The Imaged Style.* Nashville: Vanderbilt U.P.

5075. Duncan-Jones, E.E. "Some Sources of *Chance.*" *RES* 20(1969):468–71. [Coventry Patmore.]

5076. Emmett, V.J.,Jr. " 'Youth':Its Place in Conrad's *Oeuvre.*" *ConnR* 4,i:49–58.

5077. Faulkner, Peter. "Vision and Normality:Conrad's *Heart of Darkness.*" *ISE* 1(1969):36–47.

5078. Gale, Bell. "Conrad and the Romantic Hero." *DAI* 30(1969):719A–20A(Yale).

5079. Gillon, Adam. "Polish and Russian Literary Elements in Joseph Conrad." [F 3]:685–94.

5080. Greenstein, David M. "Conrad and the Congo." *DAI* 30(1969):723A(Columbia).

5081. Hervouet, Yves. "Conrad and Anatole France." *ArielE* 1,i:84–99.

* 5082. Howarth, Herbert. "The Meaning of Conrad's *The Rover.*" *SoR* 6:682–97.

5083. Inniss, Kenneth. "Conrad's Native Girl:Some Social Questions." *PCP* 5:39–45.

5084. Johnston, John H. "*The Secret Agent* and *Under Western Eyes*:Conrad's Two Political Novels." *WVUPP* 17:57–71.

5085. Karl, Frederick R. "Conrad, Ford, and the Novel." *Midway* 10,ii(1969):17–34.

5086. —— "Conrad—Galsworthy:A Record of Their Friendship in Letters." *Midway* 9,ii(1968):87–106.

5087. —— "Joseph Conrad's Letters to the Sandersons." *YULG* 45:1–11.

5088. —— "Three Conrad Letters in the Edith Wharton Papers." *YULG* 44:148–51.

5089. Kronsky, Betty J. "*Joseph Conrad:A Psychoanalytic Biography.*" *L&P* 20,i:37–41. [Rev. art.]

5090. Lafferty, William L. "Moral Problems in the Short Fiction of Joseph Conrad." *DAI* 30:3910A(Wis.).

5091. Lee, Robert F. *Conrad's Colonialism.* (SEngL 54.) The Hague and Paris: Mouton, 1969.

5092. Liljegren, S. Bodvar. *Joseph Conrad as a "Prober of Feminine Hearts."Notes on the Novel* The Rescue. (Essays and Studies on Eng. Lang. and Lit. 27.) Uppsala: Lundequistska bokh., 1968.

5093. Lincoln, Kenneth R. "Joseph Conrad:The Comedy of Perception." *DAI* 30:3014A(Ind.).

5094. Marble, James E. "Joseph Conrad:A Structural Reading." *DAI* 30(1969):2538A–39A(U. of Wash.).

5095. Matthaei, Renate. "Reise in den Abgrund:Zum Werk Joseph Conrads." *Merkur* 24:437–45.

5096. Maxwell, J.C. "Mr. Stephens on 'Heart of Darkness'." *EIC* 20:118–19. [Reply to R.C. Stephens; see Bibliog. for 1969, Vol. I, Item 5094.]

5097. —— "*Victory.*" *TLS* 4 Dec(1969):1405. [Textual corruption noted.]

5098. McDowell, Frederick P.W. "Joseph Conrad:Current Criticism and the 'Achievement and Decline' Question." *JML* 1:261–72. [Rev. art.]

5099. Messenger, William E. "Conrad's Early Sea Fiction:A Study in Reputation, Convention, and Artistic Achievement." *DAI* 30(1969):1175A(Calif., Berkeley).

5100. Mueller, William R. "Man and Nature in Conrad's *Nostromo.*" *Thought* 45:559–76.

5101. Najder, Zdzisław,ed. "Joseph Conrad:A Selection of Unknown Letters." *PolP* 13,ii:31–45. [Texts of C's unpub. letters to Quiller-Couch, Galsworthy, Wells, et al.]

* 5102. Newell, Kenneth B. "The Destructive Element and Related 'Dream' Passages in the *Lord Jim* Manuscript." *JML* 1:31–44.

5103. Nowak, Jadwiga,comp. *The Joseph Conrad Collection in the Polish Library in London:Catalogue (Nos. 1–399).* London: Biblioteka Polska. [59 pp.]

5104. O'Connor, Peter D. "The Developing Pattern:Imagery in Five of the Novels of Joseph Conrad." *DAI* 30:3472A(Lehigh).

5105. Ordonez, Elmer. "Notes on the 'Falk' Manuscript." [F 47]:45–51.

5106. Palmer, John A.,ed. *Twentieth Century Interpretations of* The Nigger of the "Narcissus":*A Collection of Critical Essays.* Englewood Cliffs, N.J.: Prentice-Hall, 1969. [Prev. pub. essays.]

5107. Pavlov, Grigor. "Two Studies in Bourgeois Individualism by Joseph Conrad." *ZAA* 17(1969):229–38.

5108. Pulc, I.P. "Two Portrayals of a Storm:Some Notes on Conrad's Descriptive Style in *The Nigger of the 'Narcissus'* and 'Typhoon'." *Style* 4:49–57.

5109. Randall, Dale B. *Joseph Conrad and Warrington Dawson:The Record of a Friendship.* Durham, N.C.: Duke U.P.

5110. Rosa, Alfred F. "The Counterforce of Technology on the Pastoral Ideal in *Nostromo.*" *MSE* 1(1968):88–93.

5111. Ryf, Robert S. *Joseph Conrad.* (CEMW 49.) New York: Columbia U.P.

5112. Sadoff, Ira. "Sartre and Conrad:Lord Jim as Existentialist Hero." *DR* 49(1969):518–25.

* 5113. Saveson, John E. "Conrad's View of Primitive Peoples in *Lord Jim* and *Heart of Darkness.*" *MFS* 16:163–83.

5114. —— "Contemporary Psychology in *The Nigger of the 'Narcissus'.*" *SSF* 7:219–31.

* 5115. —— "Marlow's Psychological Vocabulary in *Lord Jim.*" *TSLL* 12:457–70.

5116. Schwartz, Daniel R. "The Function of the Narrator in Conrad's Shorter Fiction." *DAI* 30(1969):338A–39A(Brown).

5117. Sherry, Norman. "A Conrad Manuscript." *TLS* 25 June:691. [New ms. from 1898.]

5118. Solomon, Barbara H. "Conrad's First-Person Narrators:A Study in Point of View." *DAI* 30(1969):341A(Pittsburgh).

5119. Solomon, Petre. "Conrad și Gide." *SXX* 13,i:71–74.

5120. Tarnawski, Wit. "Conrad ma własną bazę." *KulturaP* 271:138–41. [On E. Bojarski and *Conradiana.*]

5121. Thomas, Edward. " 'Truer than History'." *ArielE* 1,i:65–72. [Conrad's intentions.]

5122. Ursell, Geoffrey. "Conrad:Two Misdated Letters." *N&Q* 17:36–37. [Letters to Stephen Crane and David Meldrum.]

5123. Van Domelen, John E. "Conrad and Journalism." *JQ* 47:153–56.

5124. Verschoor, Edith E. "Joseph Conrad's World." *UES* 8,ii:12–18.

5125. Watts, Cedric T.,ed. *Joseph Conrad's Letters to R.B. Cunninghame Graham.* London: Cambridge U.P., 1969.

5126. Yajima, Goichi. "*Lord Jim.*" *Oberon* 31(1969):27–54. [In Jap.]

5127. —— "Himitsu no Kyoyusha." *Oberon* 32:31–40. [*Secret Sharer.*]

5128. Zabel, Morton D.,ed. "*The Shadow-line,*" *and Two Other Tales:*"Typhoon," "The Secret Sharer." Garden City, N.Y.: Doubleday.

5129. Zgorzelski, Andrzej. "Funkcjonalność struktur w *Lagunie* Conrada." *KN* 16(1969):401–09. [On functionality of structure in *Lagoon.*]

See also 793, 2663, 3883, 4554, 4986, 6550, 6825.

Coward. See 7319.

Cross. 5130. McMahon, Seán. "Tailor-Made." *Éire* 5,iii:134–42. [*The Tailor and Ansty.*]

Davie. 5131. Böker, Uwe. "Lyrik und Poetik Donald Davies." *Akzente* 17:81–95.

See also 4927.

De la Mare. 5132. Press, John. "The Poetry of Walter de la Mare." *ArielE* 1,iv:29–38.

Douglas. 5133. Flory, Evelyn A. "Norman Douglas:The Role of Nature." *DAI* 30:3456A(N.Y.U.).

Durrell. 5134. Creed, Walter G. "Contemporary Scientific Concepts and the Structure of Lawrence Durrell's *Alexandria Quartet*." *DAI* 30(1969):1165A(Pa.).

5135. Fraser, George S. *Lawrence Durrell*. London: Longmans.

5136. Friedman, Alan W. *Lawrence Durrell, and the* Alexandria Quartet:*Art for Love's Sake*. Norman: U. of Okla. P.

5137. Lebas, Gérard. "The Mechanisms of Space-Time in *The Alexandria Quartet*." *Caliban* 7:80–97.

5138. Misiego, Micaela. "Lawrence Durrell y su *Alexandria Quartet*." *FMod* 37(1969):59–71.

5139. Russo, John Paul. "Love in Lawrence Durrell." *PrS* 43:396–407.

Eliot. 5140. Adell, Alberto. "Releyendo a Eliot." *Insula* 24(Dec 1969):12.

5141. Ashraf, A.S.,ed. *T.S. Eliot Through Pakistani Eyes*. Karachi: Dept. of Eng., U. of Karachi, 1968.

5142. Bantock, G.H. *T.S. Eliot and Education*. London: Faber.

5143. Bergonzi, Bernard. "Allusion in *The Waste Land*, II." *EIC* 20:382–85. [Reply to John Lucas and William Myers; see Bibliog. for 1969, Vol. I, Item 5147.]

5144. Bergonzi, Bernard,ed. *T.S. Eliot,* Four Quartets:*A Casebook*. London: Macmillan, 1969.

5145. Berry, Francis. "Allusion in *The Waste Land*, I." *EIC* 20:380–82. [Reply to William Myers, *EIC* 20:120–22.]

5146. Blamires, Harry. *Word Unheard:A Guide Through Eliot's* Four Quartets. London: Methuen, 1969.

* 5147. Bollier, E.P. "La Poésie Pure:The Ghostly Dialogue Between T.S. Eliot and Paul Valéry." *ForumH* 8,i:54–59.

* 5148. Brandabur, Edward. "Eliot and the Myth of Mute Speech." *Renascence* 22:141–50.

5149. Burch, Francis F. *Tristan Corbière:L'originalité des Amours jaunes et leur influence sur T.S. Eliot*. Paris: Nizet.

* 5150. Cameron, Elspeth. "T.S. Eliot's 'Marina':An Exploration." *QQ* 77:180–89.

5151. Caretti, Laura. "Eliot come Pécuchet." *SA* 14(1968):247–64.

5152. Coleman, Antony. "T.S. Eliot and Keith Douglas." *TLS* 2 July:731. [See also 16 July:775; 31 July:854; 21 Aug:928.]

* 5153. Cook, Robert G. "Emerson's 'Self-Reliance', Sweeney, and Prufrock." *AL* 42:[221]–26.

5154. Counihan, Sister Bernadette. "*Four Quartets:*An Ascent to Mount Carmel?" *Wisconsin Studies in Lit.* 6(1969):58–71.

5155. Dalton, Jack P. "A Letter from T.S. Eliot." *JJQ* 6(1968):79–81. [On *Finnegans Wake*.]

5156. El-Azma, Nazeer. "The Tammūzī Movement and the Influence of T.S. Eliot on Badr Shākir al-Sayyāb." *JOAS* 88(1968):671–78.

* 5157. Farrell, William J. "*The Waste Land* as Rhetoric." *Renascence* 22:127–40.

5158. Farrelly, James. " 'Gerontion':Time's Eunuch." *UDR* 6,ii(1969):27–34.

5159. Fink, Ernst O. "Zur *Waste Land*—Übertragung von Ernst Robert Curtius." *NS* 19:507–13.

5160. Fleissner, Robert F. "Reacting to *The Reactionaries*: Libertarian Views." *Jour. of Human Relations* 17(1969):138–45. [Rev. art.]

5161. French, A.L. "Death by Allusion?" *EIC* 20:269–71. [Reply to Juliet McLauchlan; see Bibliog. for 1969, Vol. I, Item 5149.]

5162. Gallup, Donald. *T.S. Eliot:A Bibliography*. London: Faber, 1969. [2nd rev. ed.]

5163. —— "T.S. Eliot & Ezra Pound:Collaborators in Letters." *Poetry Australia* 32:58–80.

5164. Gent, Margaret. "The Drowned Phoenician Sailor:T.S. Eliot and William Morris." *N&Q* 17:50–51.

5165. George, Arapura G. *T.S. Eliot:His Mind and Art*. New York: Asia Pub. House, 1969. [2nd rev. ed.]

5166. Gil, Kim Jong. "T. S. Eliot's Influence on Modern Korean Poetry." *LE&W* 13(1969):359–76.

5167. Gunter, Bradley. *The Merrill Guide to T.S. Eliot*. Columbus, Ohio: Charles E. Merrill.

5168. —— "T.S. Eliot and Anglicanism:The Man of Letters as Religious and Social Critic." *DAI* 30:4450A(Va.).

5169. Hager, Philip E. "T.S. Eliot's 'A Game of Chess': Another 'Source' of the Dressing Room Scene." *AntigR* 1,ii:91–93.

5170. Hewitt, Elizabeth K. "Structural Unity in *The Waste Land*." *DAI* 30(1969):2513A(S.U.N.Y., Buffalo).

5171. Hobsbaum, Philip. "Eliot, Whitman, and American Tradition." *JAmS* 3(1969):239–64.

5172. Hobson, Harold. "Enduring Drama of T.S. Eliot." *EigoS* 115(1969):306–07.

5173. Hollahan, Eugene. "A Structural Dantean Parallel in Eliot's 'The Love Song of J. Alfred Prufrock'." *AL* 42:91–93.

* 5174. Holland, Joyce M. "Human Relations in Eliot's Drama." *Renascence* 22:151–61.

5175. Hošek, Chaviva, and Viiu Menning. *An Index to References in T.S. Eliot's* Selected Essays. Montreal: Priv. ptd., 196[8]. [20 pp., mimeo. Avail. from C. Hošek, 6225 Wilderton, Apt. 101, Montreal 26, Quebec.]

5176. Krieger, Murray. "*Murder in the Cathedral:*The Limits of Drama and the Freedom of Vision." [F 60]:72–99.

5177. Kudo, Yoshimi. "Strether to Prufrock." *EigoS* 114(1968):790–91. [James's influ. on E; in Jap.]

5178. Kumar, Jitendra. "Consciousness and Its Correlates: Eliot and Husserl." *PPR* 28(1968):332–52.

5179. —— "La coscienza e i suoi correlati:Eliot e Husserl." *Verri* 31(1969):37–59.

5180. —— "Poesia e percezione:Eliot e Merleau-Ponti." *Verri* 31(1969):60–82.

5181. Little, Roger. "T.S. Eliot and Saint-John Perse." *ArlQ* 2,ii(1969):5–17.

5182. Lucas, John. "The Waste Land Today." *EIC* 20:497–500. [Reply to Bernard Bergonzi, *EIC* 20:282–85.]

5183. Maccoby, H.Z. "A Commentary on 'Burnt Norton,' II." *N&Q* 17:53–59.

5184. Margolis, John D. "Towards a New Beginning:The Development of T.S. Eliot's Thought, 1922–1939." *DAI* 30(1969):1173A–74A(Princeton).

5185. Martin, Graham,ed. *Eliot in Perspective:A Symposium*. London: Macmillan; New York: Humanities.

5186. Maxfield, Malinda R. "A Comparative Analysis of T.S. Eliot's *Murder in the Cathedral* and Jean Anouilh's *Becket* in the Light of Medieval and Contemporary Religious Drama in England and France." *DAI* 30:4458A(Vanderbilt).

5187. Maxwell, D.E.S. "After *The Waste Land*." *ISE* 1(1969):73–84.

5188. Mineo, Adinolfa. "I tre misteri dell'arcivescovo." *AION–SG* 12(1969):331–49. [Dramas by Anouilh, Fry, and Eliot about Becket.]

5189. Montgomery, Marion. "Emotion Recollected in Tranquility:Wordsworth's Legacy to Eliot, Joyce, and Hemingway." *SoR* 6:710–21.

5190. —— *T.S. Eliot:An Essay on the American Magus*. Athens: U. of Ga. P., 1969.

5191. Moreh, Shmuel. "The Influence of Western Poetry and Particularly T.S. Eliot on Modern Arabic Poetry." *AAS* 5(1969):1–50.

5192. Myers, William. "Allusion in *The Waste Land*:A Reply." *EIC* 20:120–22. [Reply to Juliet McLauchlan; see Bibliog. for 1969, Vol. I, Item 5149.]

5193. O'Connor, Daniel. *T.S. Eliot,* Four Quartets:*A Commentary*. New Delhi: Aarti Bk. Ctr.; Mystic, Conn.: Verry, 1969.

5194. Ohashi, Isamu. "*Arechi* no Kaishaku ni tsuite." *EigoS* 115(1969):687–89,776–78. [On interpretation of *Waste Land*.]

5195. —— "Hiru to Yoru to Tasogare to." *EigoS* 115(1969):354–56. [Daylight—darkness—twilight.]

5196. —— "Jikan no Genzonsei to Ishiki—*Yotsu no Shijuso* boto ni tsuite." *EigoS* 115(1969):222–24. [Presence of time and consciousness—on *Four Quartets*.]

5197. —— "Jikan no Seishiten." *EigoS* 115(1969):296–98.

[Still point of time.]

5198. —— "T.S. Eliot no Shiron." *EigoS* 115(1969):413–15. [E's poetic theory.]

5199. Olshin, Toby A. "A Consideration of *The Rock*." *UTQ* 39:310–23.

5200. Panaro, Cleonice. "Il problema della communicazione nella poesia di T.S.Eliot." *SA* 14(1968):193–245.

5201. Praz, Mario. "What is a Classic?" [F 31]:195–202.

5202. Püschel, Brita. "T.S. Eliot:*Murder in the Cathedral*." *NsM* 21(1968):23–32.

5203. Ramsey, Jarold. "*The Waste Land* and Shackleton on South Georgia." *ELN* 8:42–45. [The Antarctic explorer.]

5204. Rauber, D.F. "The Notes on *The Waste Land*." *ELN* 7:287–94.

5205. Ray, Mohit K. "T.S. Eliot and Irving Babbitt:A Question of Critical Influence." [F 51]:97–102.

* 5206. Rees, Thomas R. "T.S. Eliot's Early Poetry as an Extension of the Symbolist Technique of Jules Laforgue." *ForumH* 8,i:46–52.

5207. Revol, Enrique L. "Permanencia de T.S. Eliot." *Torre* 65(1969):43–52.

5208. Rhoads, Kenneth W. "The Musical Elements of T.S. Eliot's *Four Quartets*." *DAI* 30:5454A–55A(Mich. State).

* 5209. Rodgers, Audrey T. "T.S. Eliot's 'Purgatorio':The Structure of *Ash Wednesday*." *CLS* 7:97–112.

* 5210. San Juan, E[pifanio],Jr. "Form and Meaning in 'Gerontion'." *Renascence* 22:115–26.

* 5211. Semaan, Khalil I.H. "T.S. Eliot's Influence on Arabic Poetry and Theater." *CLS* 6(1969):472–89.

5212. Sheehan, Donald G. "The Poetics of Influence:A Study of T.S. Eliot's Uses of Dante." *DAI* 30(1969):2043A–44A(Wis.).

* 5213. Spanos, William V. " 'Wanna Go Home, Baby?': *Sweeney Agonistes* as Drama of the Absurd." *PMLA* 85:8–20.

5214. Stanley, John M. "Church and World:A Critical Evaluation of the Corpus Christianum Approach in the Thought of John Baillie, V.A. Demant, and T.S. Eliot." *DAI* 30(1969):1628A(Columbia).

5215. Takayanagi, Shunichi. "Search after the Whole:F.H. Bradley and T.S. Eliot." *ELLS* 5(1968):12–69.

5216. Turner, A.J. "A Note on *Murder in the Cathedral*." *N&Q* 17:51–53.

5217. Ward, David E. "Il culto dell'impersonalità:Eliot, Sant'Agostino e Flaubert." *Verri* 31(1969):83–95.

5218. Weinstock, Donald J. "Tennysonian Echoes in 'The Love Song of J. Alfred Prufrock'." *ELN* 7:213–14.

5219. Williams, Philip. "The Resurrection Lyric of *Four Quartets*." *EigoS* 114(1968):590–92.

* 5220. Wright, Nathalia. "A Source for T.S. Eliot's 'Objective Correlative'." *AL* 41:589–91.

5221. Yamada, Yoichi. "T.S. Eliot no *Ninshiki to Keiken* no Shuppan." *Oberon* 29(1968):2–12. [Pub. of E's *Knowledge and Experience*.]

5222. Yasuda, Shoichiro. " 'Naraba' to 'Totemo'." *EigoS* 115(1969):496–97. [If and even if—on *Burnt Norton*.]

See also 251, 1458, 1846, 3936, 4926, 4970, 5573, 5947, 7901, 8073, 8093.

Firbank. 5223. Benkovitz, Miriam J. *Ronald Firbank*. London: Weidenfeld and Nicolson.

5224. Davis, Robert Murray. "Ronald Firbank:A Selected Bibliography of Criticism." *BB* 26(1969):108–11.

5225. Merritt, James D. *Ronald Firbank*. (TEAS 93.) New York: Twayne, 1969.

5226. Potoker, Edward M. *Ronald Firbank*. (CEMW 43.) New York and London: Columbia U.P., 1969.

5227. Tyler, Parker. "The Prince Zoubaroff:Praise of Ronald Firbank. Part One." *Prose* 1:135–52.

Fitzmaurice. 5228. Slaughter, Howard K. "Fitzmaurice and the Abbey." *ETJ* 22:146–54.

Ford. 5229. Braybrooke, Neville. "Ford Maddox Ford:A Reappraisal." *DM* 8,i–ii(1969):67–77.

5230. Cohen, Mary B. "Ford Madox Ford:Two Passions, Writing and Provence." *DAI* 30(1969):315A(Ill.).

5231. Jones, Lawrence W. "The Quality of Sadness in Ford's *The Good Soldier*." *ELT* 13:296–302.

5232. Kennedy, Alan. "Tietjens' Travels:*Parade's End* as Comedy." *TCL* 16:85–95.

* 5233. Levin, Gerald. "Character and Myth in Ford's *Parade's End*." *JML* 1:183–96.

5234. Mizener, Arthur. "The Good Soldier." *SoR* 6:589–602.

5235. —— "The Historical Romance and Twentieth-Century Sensibility:Ford's 'Fifth Queen'." *SR* 78:563–77.

* 5236. Stang, Sondra J. "A Reading of Ford's *The Good Soldier*." *MLQ* 30(1969):545–63.

See also 4986, 5085.

Forster. 5237. Blaise, Bharati M. "The Use of Indian Mythology in E.M. Forster's *A Passage to India* and Hermann Hesse's *Siddhartha*." *DAI* 30:3901A(Iowa).

5238. Bradbury, Malcolm,ed. A Passage to India:*A Casebook*. (Macmillan Casebook Series.) London: Macmillan.

5239. Brierre, Annie. "Hommage à Edward Morgan Forster." *RDM* 8:414–18.

5240. Cahill, Daniel J. "E.M. Forster's *The Longest Journey* and Its Critics." *IEY* 15:39–49.

5241. Davis, Edward. "E.M. Forster (died July 1970)." *Standpunte* 91:24–25.

5242. Grandsen, Karl W. *E.M. Forster*. (Writers and Critics Ser.) Edinburgh: Oliver and Boyd. [Rev. ed.]

5243. Laurent, C. "E.M. Forster et D.H. Lawrence." *LanM* 64:281–88.

* 5244. Levine, June P. "An Analysis of the Manuscripts of *A Passage to India*." *PMLA* 85:284–94.

5245. McDowell, Frederick P. *E.M. Forster*. (TEAS 89.) New York: Twayne, 1969.

* 5246. —— "E.M. Forster:An Annotated Secondary Bibliography." *ELT* 13:93–173. [Prec. by McDowell, "Some Preliminary Observations," 89–92.]

5247. Meyers, Jeffrey. " 'Vacant Heart and Hand and Eye':The Homosexual Theme in *A Room with a View*." *ELT* 13:181–92.

5248. —— "E.M. Forster and T.E. Lawrence:A Friendship." *SAQ* 69:205–16.

5249. Missey, James. "The Connected and the Unconnected in *Howards End*." *Wisconsin Studies in Lit.* 6(1969):72–89.

5250. Morley, Patricia A. "E.M. Forster's 'Temple':Eclectic or Visionary." *UTQ* 39:229–41.

5251. Onodera, Ken. "E.M. Forster to Jidai." *EigoS* 115(1969):80–83. [F and the Age.]

5252. Ramsaran, J.A. "An Indian Reading of E.M. Forster's Classic." *ISE* 1(1969):48–55. [*A Passage to India*.]

5253. Rutherford, Andrew. *Twentieth Century Interpretations of* A Passage to India:*A Collection of Critical Essays*. Englewood Cliffs, N.J.: Prentice-Hall. [Prev. pub. essays.]

5254. Stallybrass, Oliver,ed. *Aspects of E.M. Forster:Essays and Recollections Written for His Ninetieth Birthday 1st January, 1969*. London: E. Arnold, 1969. [Elizabeth Bowen, "A Passage to E.M. Forster," 1–12; Patrick Wilkinson, "Forster and King's," 13–28; David Garnett, "Forster and Bloomsbury," 29–35; K. Natwar-Singh, "Only Connect...:Forster and India," 37–50; Alec Randall, "Forster in Rumania," 51–60; William Roerick, "Forster and America," 61–72; W.J.H. Sprott, "Forster as a Humanist," 73–80; Benjamin Britten, "Some Notes on Forster and Music," 81–86; John Arlott, "Forster and Broadcasting," 87–92; B.W. Fagan, "Forster and His Publishers," 93–98; William Plomer, "Forster as a Friend," 99–105; Wilfred Stone, "Forster on Love and Money," 107–21: Malcolm Bradbury, "Two Passages to India:Forster as Victorian and Modern," 123–42; Oliver Stallybrass, "Forster's 'wobblings':The Manuscripts of *A Passage to India*," 143–54; George H. Thomson, "A Forster Miscellany:Thoughts on the Uncollected Writings," 155–75; "Bibliography," 177–78.]

* 5255. Wagner, C. Roland. "The Excremental and the Spiritual in *A Passage to India*." *MLQ* 31:359–71.

5256. Watson, Ian. "E.M. Forster:Whimsy and Beyond." *EigoS* 115(1969):282–85.

5257. Yoneda, Kazuhiko. "Forster to Orwell." *EigoS* 115(1969):348–50. [F and O.; in Jap.]

See also 4241, 4909, 6950.

Foster. 5258. Londreville, Richard. "Jeanne Robert Foster."

Éire 5,i:38–44. [Lit. collector, confidante of J.B. Yeats, F.M. Ford, A.E., et al.]

Fowles. 5259. Allen, Walter. "The Achievement of John Fowles." *Encounter* 35(Aug):64–67.

5260. Bradbury, Malcolm. "John Fowles's *The Magus*." [F 67]:26–38.

5261. Ditsky, John. "The Watch and Chain of Henry James." *UWR* 6,i:91–101. [Rev. art. on novels by John Fowles and Saul Bellow.]

Fry. 5262. Sherry, Ruth G. " 'A Certain Apparent Irrelevance':Genre, Theme, and Technique in the Drama of Christopher Fry." *DAI* 30(1969):293A(Brown).

5263. Stanford, Derek. "In Retrospect:Christopher Fry." *TC* 1043:54–56.

5264. Varshney, R.L. "The Mystical Element in the Plays of Christopher Fry." [F 51]:13–26.

See also 5188.

Galsworthy. 5265. Dooley, D.J. "Character and Credibility in *The Forsyte Saga*." *DR* 50:373–77.

5266. Hawkes, Carol A. "Galsworthy:The Paradox of Realism." *ELT* 13:288–95.

5267. Marchant, Peter. "*The Forsyte Saga* Reconsidered:The Case of the Common Reader Versus Literary Criticism." *WHR* 24:221–29.

5268. Smith, Philip E.,II. "John Galsworthy's Plays:The Theory and Practice of Dramatic Realism." *DAI* 30:4465A–66A(Northwestern).

5269. Thody, Philip. "The Politics of the Family Novel:Is Conservatism Inevitable?" *Mosaic* 3,i(1969):87–101. [On Zola, Galsworthy, Duhamel, T. Mann, et al.]

See also 3888, 4974, 5086.

Garner, A. *See* 5868.

Golding. 5270. Adriaens, Mark. "Style in W. Golding's *The Inheritors*." *ES* 51:16–30.

5271. Ali, Masood Amjad. "*The Inheritors*:An Experiment in Technique." *Venture*(U. of Karachi) 5(1969):123–31.

5272. Antonini, Maria. "*Free Fall* di William Golding." *Convivium*(Bologna) 37(1969):486–93.

5273. Babb, Howard S. *The Novels of William Golding*. Columbus: Ohio State U.P.

5274. Baker, James R. "The Decline of *Lord of the Flies*." *SAQ* 69:[446]–60.

5275. Davies, Cecil W. "The Novels Foreshadowed:Some Recurring Themes in Early Poems by William Golding." *English* 17(1969):86–89.

5276. Delbaere-Garant, Jeanne. "The Evil Plant in William Golding's *The Spire*." *RLV* 35(1969):623–31.

5277. Diemer, Kirsten. "William Golding's *The Spire*:En analyse af idé og struktur set i sammenhæng med de øvrige romaner." *Extracta* 2(1969):67–70. [Abst.]

* 5278. Fackler, Herbert V. "Paleontology and Paradise Lost:A Study of Golding's Modifications of Fact in *The Inheritors*." *BSUF* 10,iii(1969):64–66.

5279. Hollahan, Eugene. "Running in Circles:A Major Motif in *Lord of the Flies*." *SNNTS* 2,i:22–30.

5280. Pérez Minik, Domingo. "William Golding de *La pirámide* a *Martín el náufrago*." *Insula* 25(June):5.

5281. Rocco-Bergera, Niny. "William Golding." *RLMC* 22(1969):204–29.

5282. Spitz, David. "Power and Authority:An Interpretation of Golding's *Lord of the Flies*." *AR* 30:21–33.

5283. Wicht, Wolfgang. " '*Oh, the continent of a man!*':Das Menschenbild in William Goldings Romanen *Free Fall*, *The Spire* und *The Pyramid*." *ZAA* 18:59–70.

See also 5300.

Graves. 5284. Buckman, Peter, and William Fifield. "Conversación con Robert Graves:Sobre el arte poético." *RO* 31:1–25.

5285. Burns, Albert W. "Robert Graves and Laura Riding:A Literary Partnership." *DAI* 30(1969):2014A–15A(Boston).

5286. Leiber, Fritz. "Utopia for Poets and Witches." *RQ* 4:194–205. [On speculative fiction.]

See also 5961.

Greene, G. 5287. Astier, Colette. "La tentation du roman

policier dans *Un crime* de Georges Bernanos et *Le Rocher de Brighton* de Graham Greene." *RLC* 44:224–43.

* 5288. Braybrooke, Neville. "Graham Greene—The Double Man:An Approach to His Novel, *The End of the Affair*." *QQ* 77:29–39.

5289. Céleste, Sister Marie,S.C. "Bernanos and Graham Greene on the Role of the Priest." *Culture* 30(1969):287–98.

5290. Coroneou, Marianthi. "Suffering as Part of the Human Condition in the Fiction of Graham Greene, Albert Camus, and Nikos Kazantzakis." *DAI* 30:3454A(Ky.).

5291. Cunningham, Lawrence. "The Alter Ego of Greene's 'Whiskey Priest'." *ELN* 8:50–52.

5292. Davidson, Arnold C. "Graham Greene's Spiritual Lepers." *IEY* 15:50–55.

* 5293. Kort, Wesley. "The Obsession of Graham Greene." *Thought* 45:20–44. [The religious dilemma of G's characters.]

5294. MacSween, R.J. "Exiled from the Garden:Graham Greene." *AntigR* 1,ii:41–48.

5295. Manly, Jane B. "Graham Greene:The Insanity of Innocence." *DAI* 30:3016A(Conn.).

5296. Poole, Roger. " 'Those Sad Arguments':Two Novels of Graham Greene." *RMS* 13(1969):148–60.

5297. Sonnenfeld, Albert. "Children's Faces:Graham Greene." [F 19]:109–28.

5298. "Special:Graham Greene." *Renascence* 23,i. [Sister Sheila Houle,B.V.M., "The Subjective Theological Vision of Graham Greene," 3–13; Gerald Levin, "The Rhetoric of Greene's *The Heart of the Matter*," 14–20; Gerard H. Cox,III, "Graham Greene's Mystical Rose in Brighton," 21–30; David L. Kubal, "Graham Greene's *Brighton Rock*:The Political Theme," 46–54.]

5299. Stenberg, Carl E. "The Quest for Justice in the Fiction of Graham Greene." *DAI* 30:3024A(Conn.).

5300. Sternlicht, Sanford. "Two Views of the Builder in Graham Greene's *A Burnt-Out Case* and William Golding's *The Spire*." *CalR* N.S.1:401–04.

5301. *The Collected Edition, I:Brighton Rock*. London: Heinemann and Bodley Head.

5302. *The Collected Edition, III:England Made Me*. London: Heinemann and Bodley Head.

5303. *The Collected Edition, IV:Our Man in Havana*. London: Heinemann and Bodley Head.

5304. Thomas, D.P. "Mr. Tench and Secondary Allegory in *The Power and the Glory*." *ELN* 7(1969):129–33.

5305. Torres M., Manuel. "*El socio* y *Our Man in Havana*, novelas paralelas." *Mapocho* 17(1968):61–67.

5306. Vann, J. Don. *Grahame Greene:A Checklist of Criticism*. (Serif Bibliogs. and Checklists Ser. 14.) Kent, Ohio: Kent State U.P.

See also 806, 4916, 5066.

Gregory. 5307. *Cuchulain of Muirthemne*. The Story of the Men of the Red Branch of Ulster Arranged and Put into English. Pref. Daniel Murphy. New York: Oxford U.P. [New ed.]

5308. *Gods and Fighting Men*. The Story of the Tuatha de Danaan and the Fianna of Ireland. Introd. Daniel Murphy. Pref. W.B. Yeats. New York: Oxford U.P. [New ed.]

5309. Mikhail, Edward Halim. "The Theatre of Lady Gregory." *BB* 27:9–10.

5310. Saddlemyer, Ann,ed. "Lady Gregory, *The Shoelace*." *MHRev* 16:20–30. [Text with brief introd.]

Gwenallt. 5311. Page, Alun. "Valiant for Truth:Some Comments on Part of the Elegy, 'John Edward Daniel,' by Gwenallt." *AWR* 19,xliii:32–43.

Hamilton. 5312. Nichols, Reuben B. "Ian Hamilton:A Study in Military Biography and the Literature of War, 1870–1914." *DAI* 30:4997A(Baylor).

Hartley. 5313. Mulkeen, Anne M. "The Symbolic Novels of L.P. Hartley." *DAI* 30:5452A(Wis.).

Hewitt. 5314. Sealy, Douglas. "An Individual Flavour:The Collected Poems of John Hewitt." *DM* 8,i–ii(1969):19–24.

Hodgson. *See* 521.

Housman, A.E. 5315. Gray, Allan. "A Shakespearian Allusion in Housman, *Last Poems* XXIX." *ELN* 8:36–39. [To *Cymbeline*.]

5316. Otis, Brooks. "Housman and Horace." *PCP* 2(1967): 5–23.

Hughes. 5317. Tamura, Einosuke. "Ted Hughes." *Oberon* 2:69–84. [In Jap.]

Hulme. 5318. Heaton, David M. "Two French Philosophical Sources of T.E. Hulme's Imagism." *DAI* 31:759A(Mich.).
See also 5715.

Huxley, A. 5319. Bentley, Joseph. "The Later Novels of Huxley." *YR* 59:507–19.

5320. Bergonzi, Bernard,ed. *Great Short Works of Aldous Huxley.* With Introd. New York: Harper.

5321. Doi, Kochi. "Chikaku no Tobira:Tengoku to Jigoku." *EigoS* 114(1968):214–15. [Doors of perception; heaven and hell.]

5322. Elliott, Robert C. "L'estetica dell'utopia." *SCr* 3(1969): 301–20.

5323. Fietz, Lothar. *Menschenbild und Romanstruktur in Aldous Huxleys Ideenromanen.* (SzEP 13.) Tübingen: Niemeyer, 1969.

5324. Firchow, Peter E. "The Brave New World of Huxley Studies." *JML* 1:278–83. [Rev. art.]

5325. Friedman, Martin B.,ed. *Brave New World.* (Classiques Etrangers.) With Introd. and Notes. Paris: Bordas.

5326. Holmes, Charles M. *Aldous Huxley and the Way to Reality.* Bloomington and London: Ind. U.P.

5327. Macdermott, Doireann. "The Zoologist of Fiction: Aldous Huxley." *FMod* 37(1969):27–45.

* 5328. Marovitz, Sanford E. "Aldous Huxley's Intellectual Zoo." *PQ* 48(1969):495–507.

5329. Scurani, Alessandro. "Il sincretismo di Aldous Huxley." *Lettere* 25:263–82.

5330. Smith, Grover,ed. *Letters of Aldous Huxley.* London: Chatto & Windus, 1969.

5331. Watt, Donald J. "Aldous Huxley's Stereoscopic Vision." *HSL* 2:263–69. [Rev. art. on Bibliog. for 1969, Vol. I, Item 5250.]

5332. —— "The Absurdity of the Hedonist in Huxley's 'The Gioconda Smile'." *SSF* 7:328–30.

5333. —— "The Criminal-Victim Pattern in Huxley's *Point Counter Point.*" *SNNTS* 2,i:42–51.

5334. Witschel, Günter. *Rausch und Rauschgift bei Baudelaire, Huxley, Benn und Burroughs.* Bonn: Bouvier, 1968.

5335. [Wolden-Ræthinge, Anne.] *Ninka & Bendix:33 portrætter.* Illus. Hans Bendix. Copenhagen: Rhodos, 1969. [Interviews. See "Aldous Huxley," 163–67.]
See also 8159.

Isherwood. 5336. Graffin, Walter R. "The Novels of Christopher Isherwood." *DAI* 30(1969):1168A(Wis.).

5337. Heilbrun, Carolyn G. *Christopher Isherwood.* (CEMW 53.) New York and London: Columbia U.P.
See also 5005, 5777.

Johnston. 5338. Jugaku, Bunsho. "Edward Johnston." *EigoS* 114(1968):570–71. [In Jap.]

Jones, D. 5339. Rees, Samuel. "The Achievement of David Jones, Anglo-Welsh Poet." *DAI* 30(1969):2546A(U. of Wash.).

Jones, J. 5340. Jones, Glyn. "Jack Jones:1884–1970." *AWR* 19,xliii:17–21.

Joyce. 5341. Ando, Ichiro. "Joyce Kenkyu no Fukko." *EigoS* 114(1968):792–93. [Renaissance in Joyce studies.]

5342. Baker, James R., and Thomas F. Staley,eds. *James Joyce's Dubliners:A Critical Handbook.* Belmont, Calif.: Wadsworth, 1969.

5343. Beck, Warren. *Joyce's Dubliners:Substance, Vision, and Art.* Durham, N.C.: Duke U.P., 1969.

5344. Beckson, Karl. "Stephen Dedalus and the Emblematic Cosmos." *JJQ* 6(1968):95–96.

5345. Begnal, Michael H. "Mourners at the *Wake:*The Family and Friends of HCE." *WHR* 24:383–93.

5346. —— "The Narrator of *Finnegans Wake.*" *Éire* 4, iii(1969):38–49.

5347. Benstock, Bernard. "*Exiles:*'Paradox Lust' and 'Lost Paladays'." *ELH* 36(1969):739–56.

* 5348. —— "*Exiles,* Ibsen, and the Play's Function in the Joyce Canon." *BSUF* 11,ii:26–37.

5349. —— "Redhoising JJ:USSR/11." *JJQ* 6(1968):177–80. [Russ. censorship of J.]

5350. Berger, Alfred P. "Wakeful Ad-Venture." *JJQ* 7(1969):

52–60. [Use of advertisements in *Uly* and *FW.]*

5351. Bollettieri, Rosa M.B. "The Importance of Trieste in Joyce's Work, with Reference to His Knowledge of Psycho-Analysis." *JJQ* 7:177–85.

5352. Bowen, Zack. "Hungarian Politics in 'After the Race'." *JJQ* 7:138–39.

5353. —— "Lizzie Twigg:Gone but not Forgotten." *JJQ* 6(1969):368–70.

5354. Boyle, Robert,S.J. "Swiftian Allegory and Dantean Parody in Joyce's 'Grace'." *JJQ* 7(1969):11–21.

5355. Bredin, Hugh. "Joyce e L'Aquinate." *Verri* 31(1969): 96–112.

5356. —— "Applied Aquinas:James Joyce's Aesthetics." *Éire* 3,i(1968):61–78.

5357. Brivic, Sheldon R. "Structure and Meaning in Joyce's *Exiles.*" *JJQ* 6(1968):29–52.

5358. —— "Time, Sexuality and Identity in Joyce's *Ulysses.*" *JJQ* 7(1969):30–51.

5359. Budgen, Frank. *Myselves When Young.* New York: Oxford U.P. ["Mr. Joyce," pp. 181–212.]

5360. Bulhof, Francis. "Agendath Again." *JJQ* 7:326–32.

5361. Butor, Michel. "Crossing the Joycean Threshold." *JJQ* 7:160–76. [Tr. Jerry A. Stewart.]

5362. Campbell, Joseph. "Contransmagnificaandjewbangtantiality." *SLitI* 3,ii:3–18.

5363. Card, James. "The Misleading Mr. McAlmon and Joyce's Typescript." *JJQ* 7:143–47.

5364. Clark, Earl J. "James Joyce's *Exiles.*" *JJQ* 6(1968): 69–78.

5365. Cohn, Alan M. "Supplemental JJ Checklist, 1967." *JJQ* 6(1969):242–61.

5366. —— "Supplemental JJ Checklist, 1968." *JJQ* 7:229–50. [Supplements 1968 *MLA* Bibliog.]

5367. Collins, Ben L. "Joyce's Use of Yeats and of Irish History:A Reading of 'A Mother'." *Éire* 5,i:45–66.

5368. Cope, Jackson I. "An Epigraph for *Dubliners.*" *JJQ* 7:362–64.

5369. —— "*Ulysses:*Joyce's Kabbalah." *JJQ* 7:93–113.

5370. Crise, Stelio. "Ahab, Pizdrool, Quark." *JJQ* 7(1969): 65–69.

5371. Crosman, Robert. " 'Who Was M'Intosh?' " *JJQ* 6(1968):128–36.

5372. Cunningham, Frank R. "Joyce's *Exiles:*A Problem of Dramatic Stasis." *MD* 12:399–407.

5373. —— "Joyce's 'Grace':Gracelessness in a Lost Paradise." *JJQ* 6(1969):219–23.

5374. Curran, Stuart. " 'Bous Stephanoumenos':Joyce's Sacred Cow." *JJQ* 6(1968):163–70. [On *Portrait.]*

5375. Dahl, Liisa. *Linguistic Features of the Stream-of-Consciousness Techniques of James Joyce, Virginia Woolf and Eugene O'Neill.* (Turun Yliopiston julkaisuja, ser.B,116.) Turku: Turun Yliopisto.

5376. —— "The Linguistic Presentation of the Interior Monologue in James Joyce's *Ulysses.*" *JJQ* 7:114–19.

5377. Dalton, Jack P. "The *Finnegans Wake* Concordance:A Further Note." *JJQ* 6(1969):275.

5378. Davis, Joseph K. "The City as Radical Order:James Joyce's *Dubliners.*" *SLitI* 3,ii:79–96.

5379. Davis, Roderick. "The Fourfold Moses in *Ulysses.*" *JJQ* 7:120–31.

5380. Deane, Paul. "Motion Picture Techniques in James Joyce's 'The Dead'." *JJQ* 6(1969):231–36.

5381. Deming, Robert H. *James Joyce:The Critical Heritage.* London: Routledge & K. Paul; New York: Barnes & Noble.

5382. Doxey, William S. " 'Ithaca's' Westward-turning Earth:A New Portal of Discovery in *Ulysses.*" *JJQ* 7:371–74.

5383. Duytschaever, Joris. "Magistrale vertaling voor loopjongensloon:James Joyce in het Nederlands." *VlG* 54,iv: 20–25.

5384. Dyrkøb, Jan Ulrik. "En analyse af James Joyces *A Portrait of the Artist as a Young Man* med særligt henblik på forholdet mellem fortæller og hovedpersonen." *Extracta* 2(1969): 71–79. [Abst.]

5385. Easson, Angus. "Parody as Comment in James Joyce's

'Clay'." *JJQ* 7:75–81.

5386. Epstein, E.L. "Hidden Imagery in James Joyce's 'Two Gallants'." *JJQ* 7:369–70.

5387. —— "James Joyce and *The Way of All Flesh*." *JJQ* 7(1969):22–29.

5388. —— "Tom and Tim." *JJQ* 6(1968):158–62.

5389. Evans, William A. "Wordagglutinations in Joyce's *Ulysses*." *SLitI* 3,ii:27–36.

5390. Ferris, William R.,Jr. "Rebellion Matured:Joyce's *Exiles*." *Éire* 4,iv(1969):73–81.

5391. Fiedler, Leslie. "Bloom on Joyce; or, Jokey for Jacob." *JML* 1:19–29.

5392. Finas, Lucette. "Le critique exilé." *Critique* 25(1969): 992–99.

5393. Freimarck, John. " 'Araby':A Quest for Meaning." *JJQ* 7:366–68.

5394. Geckle, George L. "Stephen Dedalus as Lapwing:A Symbolic Center of *Ulysses*." *JJQ* 6(1968):104–14.

5395. Goldman, Arnold. "Stephen Dedalus's Dream of Parnell." *JJQ* 6(1969):262–64.

5396. Gysling, Fritz. "A Doctor's Look at a Neglected Poem." *JJQ* 7:251–52. ["Bahnhofstrasse."]

5397. Hardy, Anne. "A Fugal Analysis of the Siren Episode in Joyce's *Ulysses*." *MSE* 2:59–67.

5398. Hart, Clive,ed. *James Joyce's* Dubliners:*Critical Essays*. New York: Viking, 1969.

5399. Hartley, Lodwick. " 'Swiftly-Sterneward':The Question of Sterne's Influence on Joyce." *SLitI* 3,ii:37–47.

5400. Hayman, David. Ulysses:*The Mechanics of Meaning*. Englewood Cliffs, N.J.: Prentice-Hall.

5401. Henrietta, Sister M.,I.H.M. "James Joyce's 'Clay'." *Horizontes*(Puerto Rico) 24(Abril 1969):59–62.

5402. Henseler, Donna L. " 'Harpsdichord,' the Formal Principle of HCE, ALP, and the Cad." *JJQ* 6(1968):53–68.

5403. Herman, William. " 'Within His Handiwork':Self-Conscious Artistry in the Fiction of James Joyce." *DAI* 30:5445A–46A(Fordham).

5404. Hunter, Robert. "Joyce's 'The Dead'." *JJQ* 7:365.

5405. Jacobson, Howard. "Joyce and the *Iliad*:A Suggestion." *JJQ* 7:141–42.

* 5406. Jameson, F.R. "Seriality in Modern Literature." *BuR* 18,i:63–80.

5407. Jenkins, William D. "From a Hugglebeddy Fann." *JJQ* 6(1968):89–91. [On *Finnegans Wake*.]

5408. Kain, Richard M. "A Possible Source for the Galway Bay Accident in *Ulysses*." *JJQ* 6(1969):82–83.

5409. —— "James Joyce and the Game of Language." *SLitI* 3,ii:19–25.

5410. Kennedy, Sister Eileen. "Another Root for Blooms-day?" *JJQ* 6(1969):271–72.

5411. Kenner, Hugh. "Homer's Sticks and Stones." *JJQ* 6(1969):285–98.

5412. Keogh, J.G. "*Ulysses'* 'Parable of the Plums' as Parable and Periplum." *JJQ* 7:377–78.

5413. Knuth, Leo. "Dutch in *Finnegans Wake* Holograph Workbooks VI.B.22 and VI.B.26." *JJQ* 7:218–28.

5414. —— "How Stately Was Plump Buck Mulligan?" *JJQ* 7:204–09.

5415. Kreutzer, Eberhard. *Sprache und Spiel im* Ulysses *von James Joyce*. Bonn: Bouvier, 1969. [Diss., Bonn.]

5416. Lachtman, Howard. "The Magic-Lantern Business: James Joyce's Ecclesiastical Satire in *Dubliners*." *JJQ* 7:82–92.

5417. Lameyer, Gordon A. "The Automystic and the Cultic Twalette:Spiritual and Spiritualistic Concerns in the Works of James Joyce." *DAI* 30:4455A–56A(Columbia).

5418. Lee, L.L. "The Mormons at The Wake." *JJQ* 6(1968): 87–88.

5419. Lidderdale, Jane, and Mary Nicholson. "Mr. Joyce's Dreadful Eye Attack." *JJQ* 7:186–90.

5420. Link, Viktor. "*Ulysses* and the 'Eighth and Ninth Book of Moses'." *JJQ* 7:199–203.

5421. Malings, Ron. "Cricketers at the Wake." *JJQ* 7:333–49.

5422. Marcus, Philip L. "Three Irish Allusions in *Ulysses*." *JJQ* 6(1969):299–305.

5423. Mathews, F.X. "Festy King in *Finnegans Wake*." *JJQ* 6(1968):154–57.

5424. McCarroll, David L. "Stephen's Dream—and Bloom's." *JJQ* 6(1968):174–76.

5425. McCarthy, Patrick A. "Further Notes on the Mass in *Ulysses*." *JJQ* 7:132–37.

5426. McMichael, Charles T., and Ted R. Spivey. " 'Chaos —hurray!—is come again':Heroism in James Joyce and Conrad Aiken." *SLitI* 3,ii:65–68.

5427. Montgomery, Judith. "The Artist as Silent Dubliner." *JJQ* 6(1969):306–20.

5428. Moore, John Rees. "Artifices for Eternity:Joyce and Yeats." *Éire* 3,iv(1968):66–73.

5429. Morley, Patricia A. "Fish Symbolism in Chapter Seven of *Finnegans Wake*:The Hidden Defence of Shem the Penman." *JJQ* 6(1969):267–70.

5430. Moseley, Virginia. "The 'Coincidence' of 'Contraries' in 'Grace'." *JJQ* 6(1968):3–21.

5431. Murillo, J.A. *The Cyclical Night:Irony in James Joyce and Jorge Luis Borges*. Cambridge: Harvard U.P., 1968.

5432. Parish, Charles. "Agenbite of Agendath Netaim." *JJQ* 6(1969):237–41.

5433. Peden, William. "Joyce Among the Latins." *JJQ* 7:287–96.

5434. Phul, Ruth von. " 'Not a Leetle Beetle' (*FW* 417.3–4)." *JJQ* 6(1969):265–66.

5435. Pinguentini, Gianni. "James Joyce a Trieste nella casa di Via Bramante." *Porta Orientale* 6:75–80.

5436. Pomeraz, Victory. "Leonardo of Pisa." *JJQ* 7:148–50.

5437. Reddick, Bryan. "The Importance of Tone in the Structural Rhythm of Joyce's *Portrait*." *JJQ* 6(1969):201–18.

* 5438. Robinson, Eleanor M. "Gabriel Conroy's Cooked Goose." *BSUF* 11,ii:25. [In "The Dead."]

5439. Ruff, Lillian M. "James Joyce and Arnold Dolmetsch." *JJQ* 6(1969):224–30.

5440. San Juan, E.,Jr. "Form and Meaning in Joyce's 'Ivy Day in the Committee *Archiv* 207:185–91.

5441. San Juan, E[pifanio],Jr. " 'Eveline':Joyce's Affirmation of Ireland." *Éire* 4,i(1969):46–52.

5442. Schutte, William M. "Allusions in 'Scylla and Cha-rybdis':A Supplement to Weldon Thornton's List." *JJQ* 7:315–25.

5443. Senn, Fritz. "Buybibles." *JJQ* 7:257–58. [Bibles in *FW*.]

5444. —— "Chaste Delights." *JJQ* 7:253–54. [*Conjugal* or *conjugial* in *Uly*.]

5445. —— "In That Earopean End." *JJQ* 6(1968):91–95.

5446. —— "No Trace of Hell." *JJQ* 7:225–56. [Source of remarks about Prof. Pokorny in *Uly*.]

5447. —— "Quoint a quincidence." *JJQ* 7:210–17. [*FW* 299.8.]

5448. —— "Zeven tegen *Ulysses*." *Raam* 63:6–35. [Tr. B. Wijffels-Smulders.]

5449. Shawcross, John T. " 'Tilly' and Dante." *JJQ* 7(1969): 61–64.

5450. Silverstein, Norman. "Toward a Corrected Text of *Ulysses*." *JJQ* 6(1969):348–56.

5451. Smidt, Kristian. "Joyce and Ibsen:A Study in Literary Influence." *Edda* 70:85–103. [Incl. reply by Bjørn J. Tysdal, 98 ff.]

5452. Spivey, Ted R. "Editor's Comment [on Special Joyce No., *SLitI*(Oct 1970).]" *SLitI* 3,ii:1–2.

5453. —— "The Reintegration of Modern Man:An Essay on James Joyce and Hermann Hesse." *SLitI* 3,ii:49–64.

5454. Staley, Harry C. "Joyce's Catechisms." *JJQ* 6(1968): 137–53.

5455. Steinberg, Erwin R. " ' . . . the steady monologue of the interiors;the pardonable confusion. . .'." *JJQ* 6(1969):185–200.

5456. —— "Rogue's Rum Lingo:The Language of Stephen, Bloom, and Molly." *F* 59]:21–30.

* 5457. Stoll, John E. "Common Womb Imagery in Joyce and Lawrence." *BSUF* 11,ii:10–24.

5458. Suter, August. "Some Reminiscences of James Joyce." *JJQ* 7:191–98.

5459. Swinson, Henry W. "Joyce and the Theater." *DAI* 30(1969):1184A–85A(Ill.).

5460. Torchiana, Donald T. "Joyce's 'Eveline' and the

Blessed Margaret Mary Alacoque." *JJQ* 6(1968):22–28.

5461. —— "Joyce's 'Two Gallants':A Walk Through the Ascendancy." *JJQ* 6(1968):115–27.

5462. Toth, Alexander S.,Jr. "Joyce–Bergson Correspondences in the Theory and Time Structure of *Dubliners*, *A Portrait*, and *Ulysses*." *DAI* 30(1969):738A–39A(So. Calif.).

5463. Turaj, Frank. " 'Araby' and *Portrait*:Stages of Pagan Conversion." *ELN* 7:209–13.

5464. Wagner, Richard. "Danish at the Wake." *JJQ* 6(1968):171–73. [Glossary of Danish expressions.]

5465. Walsh, Ruth M. "In the Name of the Father and of the Son . . .:Joyce's Use of the Mass in *Ulysses*." *JJQ* 6(1969):321–47.

5466. Ware, Thomas C. "A Miltonic Allusion in Joyce's 'The Dead'." *JJQ* 6(1969):273–74.

5467. West, Michael. "Old Cotter and The Enigma of Joyce's 'The Sisters'." *MP* 67:370–72.

5468. Wigginton, B. Eliot. "*Dubliners* in Order." *JJQ* 7:297–314.

5469. Wilson, Don A. "Joyce's *A Portrait of the Artist as a Young Man*." *Expl* 28:Item 84.

5470. *WN* 7,i. [William D. Jenkins, "From Solation to Solution," 3–11; Michael Schuldiner, "Napoleon-Aristotle-Lipoleum," 11; William Menary, "The Speckled Church Once More," 12; Helmut Bonheim, "Humpty Dumpty and the Earwig," 13; Philip B. Sullivan, "W.B. Murphy, A.B.S.," 14–15.]

5471. *WN* 7,ii. [James Blish, "Formal Music at the Wake, Part I," 19–27; Roland McHugh, "The Pelagian Heresy," 28–29; E.L. Epstein, "Yet Another Book at the Wake," 29–30; Rosa M. Bosinelli, "Erminia's Capecloaked Hoodooman," 30.]

5472. *WN* 7,iii. [James Blish, "Formal Music at the Wake, Part II," 35–43; Nathan Halper, "A Kidscad," 44–46.]

5473. Woodbery, Potter. "The Blueribboned Hat:A Possible Reference to Emma Clery in *Ulysses*." *JJQ* 7:151–52.

5474. —— "The Irrelevance of Stephen Dedalus:Some Reflections on Joyce and the Student Activist Movement." *SLitI* 3,ii:69–78.

See also 510, 944, 4409, 5024, 5155, 5189, 5621, 5931, 5947, 7766, 8093, 9345.

Kavanagh. 5475. Freyer, Grattan. "Patrick Kavanagh." *Éire* 3,iv(1968):17–23. [Biog. and crit.]

5476. Kennelly, Brendan. "Patrick Kavanagh." *ArielE* 1,iii:7–28.

5477. McMahon, Seán. "The Parish and the Universe:A Consideration of *Tarry Flynn*." *Éire* 3,iii(1968):157–69.

5478. Warner, Alan. "The Poetry of Patrick Kavanagh (1904–1967)." *English* 18(1969):98–103.

Kiely. 5479. Eckley, Grace. "The Fiction of Benedict Kiely." *Éire* 3,iv(1968):55–65.

Kingsmill. 5480. Holroyd, Michael,ed. *The Best of Hugh Kingsmill*. London: Gollancz.

Kinsella. 5481. Skelton, Robin. "The Poetry of Thomas Kinsella." *Éire* 4,i(1969):86–108.

5482. "Thomas Kinsella:Worksheets." *MHRev* 3(1967):109–20.

Lavin. 5483. Caswell, Robert W. "Irish Political Reality and Mary Lavin's *Tales from Bective Bridge*." *Éire* 3,i(1968):48–60.

* 5484. Doyle, Paul A. "Mary Lavin:A Checklist." *PBSA* 63(1969):317–21.

Lawrence, D.H. 5485. Balbert, Peter H. "D.H. Lawrence and the Psychology of Rhythm:The Meaning of Form in *The Rainbow*." *DAI* 30:3934A(Cornell).

5486. Barber, David S. "Can a Radical Interpretation of *Women in Love* Be Adequate?" *DHLR* 3:168–74. [See also arts. by Briscoe & Vicinus, below.]

5487. Baron, Carl E. "Two Hitherto Unknown Pieces by D.H. Lawrence." *Encounter* 33(Aug 1969):3–6.

5488. Barrière, Françoise. "*Women in Love* ou le roman de l'antagonisme." *LanM* 63(1969):293–303.

5489. Beards, Richard D., assisted by Barbara Willens. "D.H. Lawrence:Criticism; September 1968–December 1969; a Checklist." *DHLR* 3:70–86.

5490. Boulton, James T. "D.H. Lawrence's *Odour of Chrysanthemums*:An Early Version." *RMS* 13(1969):5–48. [Rpts. text.]

5491. Briscoe, Mary L., and Martha Vicinus. "Lawrence Among the Radicals:MMLA, 1969:An Exchange." *DHLR* 3:63–69. [See also art. by Barber, above.]

5492. Burke, Herbert. "One Man's Lawrence." *Mysterious East*(New Brunswick) Dec Book Supp.:16–19. [Rev. art.]

5493. Burwell, Rose Marie. "A Catalogue of D.H. Lawrence's Reading from Early Childhood." *DHLR* 3:193–330.

5494. —— "A Chronological Catalogue of D.H. Lawrence's Reading from Early Childhood." *DAI* 30:3937A(Iowa).

5495. Clark, L.D. "The Apocalypse of Lorenzo." *DHLR* 3:141–60.

5496. Comerford, Anthony. "*Women in Love*." *TLS* 11 Dec(1969):1426. [See also 1 Jan:12; 12 Feb:169.]

5497. Consolo, Dominick P.,ed. *The Rocking-Horse Winner*. (Merrill Casebooks.) Columbus, Ohio: Charles E. Merrill, 1969.

5498. Cowan, James C. *D.H. Lawrence's American Journey:A Study in Literature and Myth*. Cleveland: Case Western Reserve U.P.

5499. Draper, R.P.,ed. *D.H. Lawrence:The Critical Heritage*. New York: Barnes & Noble; London: Routledge & K. Paul.

5500. Edwards, Luch I.,comp. *D.H. Lawrence:A Finding List*. Nottingham: Nottinghamshire County Council, 1968. [Lists Lawrence material, primary and secondary, in the City, County and Univ. Libs. of Nottingham, with cross-refs. to Warren Roberts's Soho Bibliog. of Lawrence.]

5501. Eichrodt, John M. "Doctrine and Dogma in *Sons and Lovers*." *ConnR* 4,i:18–32.

5502. Farmer, David. "An Unpublished Version of D.H. Lawrence's Introduction to *Pansies*." *RES* 21:181–84. [Incl. text of Introd.]

5503. Farr, Judith,ed. *Twentieth Century Interpretations of Sons and Lovers:A Collection of Critical Essays*. Englewood Cliffs, N.J.: Prentice-Hall.

5504. Friedman, Alan. "The Other Lawrence." *PR* 37:239–53.

5505. Fu, Shaw-shien. "Death in Lawrence's Last Poems:A Study of Theme in Relation to Imagery." *TkR* 1,i:79–91.

5506. Gajdusek, Robert E. "A Reading of 'A Poem of Friendship':A Chapter in Lawrence's *The White Peacock*." *DHLR* 3:47–62.

5507. Garcia, Reloy. "Adam in Nottingham:Literary Archetypes in the Novels of D.H. Lawrence." *DAI* 30(1969):720A(Kent State).

5508. —— "The Quest for Paradise in the Novels of D.H. Lawrence." *DHLR* 3:93–114.

5509. Gilbert, Sandra M. " 'Acts of Attention':The Major Poems of D.H. Lawrence." *DAI* 30(1969):721A–22A(Columbia).

5510. Goldberg, Michael. "Lawrence's 'The Rocking-Horse Winner':A Dickensian Fable." *MFS* 15(1969):525–36.

5511. Heuzenroeder, John. "D.H. Lawrence's Australia." *ALS* 4:319–33.

5512. Hinz, Evelyn J. "Juno and *The White Peacock*:Lawrence's English Epic." *DHLR* 3:115–35.

5513. Hojman, Baruj. *Another Ego:The Changing View of Self and Society in the Work of D.H. Lawrence*. Columbia: U. of S.C. Press.

5514. Hyde, G.M. "D.H. Lawrence as Translator." *Delos* 4:146–74.

5515. Johnson, Dale S. "The Development of the Non-Formalistic Modern English Novel and Its Relation to D.H. Lawrence's *Sons and Lovers*." *DAI* 30(1969):726A(Mich.).

5516. Kain, Richard M. "*Lady Chatterley's Lover*." *TLS* 8 Jan:34. [A variant piracy noted.]

5517. Kettle, Arnold. "D.H. Lawrence—Some New Letters." *Mosaic* 4,i:123–26. [Rev. art.]

5518. Kleinbard, David J. "The Invisible Man Made Visible, Representation of the Unconscious in the Writings of D.H. Lawrence." *DAI* 30(1969):727A–28A(Yale).

5519. Kuramochi, Saburo. "Shosetsu wa ika ni Owaru ka? D.H. Lawrence no Shosetsu to *Kaishin*." *EigoS* 115(1969):224–26. [How to end a novel? L's novels and "conversion."]

5520. Lainoff, Seymour. "The Wartime Setting of Lawrence's 'Tickets, Please'." *SSF* 7:649–51.

5521. Leavis, F.R. *D.H. Lawrence, Novelist*. New York: Simon & Schuster. [Paperback.]

5522. Littlewood, J.C.F. "Son and Lover." *CQ* 4(1969):

323–61.

5523. Melchiori, Barbara. " 'Objects in the powerful light of emotion'." *ArielE* 1,i:21–30. [Visual symbols in *Sons and Lovers.*]

5524. Meyers, Jeffrey. " 'The Voice of Water':*The Virgin and the Gipsy.*" *EM* 21:199–207.

5525. Miko, Stephen J.,ed. *Twentieth Century Interpretations of* Women in Love:*A Collection of Critical Essays.* Englewood Cliffs, N.J.: Prentice-Hall, 1969. [Prev. pub. essays plus David J. Gordon, *"Women in Love* and the Lawrencean Aesthetic," 50–60.]

5526. Miles, Kathleen M. *The Hellish Meaning:The Demonic Motif in the Works of D.H. Lawrence.* (So. Ill. U. Monographs, Hum. Series 2.) Carbondale: So. Ill. U.P., 1969.

5527. Millett, Robert. "Great Expectations:D.H. Lawrence's 'The Trespasser'." [F 47]:125–32.

5528. Nishimura, Koji. "Nigenron no Yukue." *EigoS* 115(1969):624–26. [Outcome of dualism in D.H. Lawrence.]

5529. Panichas, George A. "The End of the Lamplight." *ModA* 14:65–74.

5530. Richardson, John Adkins, and John I. Ades. "D.H. Lawrence on Cézanne:A Study in the Psychology of Critical Intuition." *JAAC* 28:441–53.

5531. Rossman, Charles. "Lawrence on the Critics' Couch: Pervert or Prophet?" *DHLR* 3:175–85.

5532. —— "The Gospel According to D.H. Lawrence: Religion in *Sons and Lovers.*" *DHLR* 3:31–41.

5533. Sagar, Keith. " 'Little Living Myths':A Note on Lawrence's 'Tortoises'." *DHLR* 3:161–67.

5534. Samuels, Marilyn S. "Water, Ships, and the Sea: Unifying Symbols in Lawrence's *Kangaroo.*" *UR* 37:46–57.

5535. San Juan, Epifanio,Jr. "Theme Versus Imitation:D.H. Lawrence's 'The Rocking-Horse Winner'." *DHLR* 3:136–40.

* 5536. Singh, Vishnudat. "Lawrence's Use of 'Pecker'." *PBSA* 64:355.

5537. Smailes, T.A. "D.H. Lawrence:Poet." *Standpunte* 85(1969):24–36.

5538. Smailes, T.A.,ed. "D.H. Lawrence:Seven Hitherto Unpublished Poems." *DHLR* 3:42–46.

* 5539. Squires, Michael. "Lawrence's *The White Peacock*:A Mutation of Pastoral." *TSLL* 12:263–83.

* 5540. Stroupe, John H. "Ruskin, Lawrence, and Gothic Naturalism." *BSUF* 11,ii:3–9.

5541. Suckow, Ruth. "Modern Figures of Destiny:D.H. Lawrence and Frieda Lawrence." *DHLR* 3:1–30.

5542. Trail, George Y. "A Prolegomena to the Poetry of D.H. Lawrence." *DAI* 30:3479A(Mo., Columbia).

5543. Truchlar, Leo. "Zur Spätlyrik von D.H. Lawrence." *NS* 18(1969):600–06.

5544. Wilding, Michael. " 'A New Show':The Politics of *Kangaroo.*" *Southerly* 30:20–40.

5545. —— "*Kangaroo* and the Form of the Political Novel." *ALS* 4:334–48.

5546. Williams, Raymond,ed. *Three Plays.* Harmondsworth: Penguin, 1969. [*A Collier's Friday Night*; *The Daughter-In-Law*; *The Widowing of Mrs. Holroyd.*]

5547. Zytaruk, George J.,ed. "D.H. Lawrence:Letters to Koteliansky." *MHRev* 1(1967):17–40. [Introd. & texts of 20 letters, annotated.]

5548. —— *The Quest for Rananim:D.H. Lawrence's Letters to S.S. Koteliansky, 1914–1930.* Montreal: McGill-Queen's U.P. See also 944, 1294, 1352, 3411, 5160, 5243, 5457, 5574, 7065.

Lawrence, T.E. 5549. Knightley, Phillip, and Colin Simpson. *The Secret Lives of Lawrence of Arabia.* New York: McGraw.

5550. Meyers, Jeffrey. "Nietzsche and T.E. Lawrence." *Midway* 11,i:77–85.

5551. —— "*The Secret Lives of Lawrence of Arabia.*" *Commonweal* 93:100–04. [Rev. art.]
See also 5005, 5248.

Leavis. 5552. Gribble, James. "Logical and Psychological Considerations in the Criticism of F.R. Leavis." *BJA* 10:39–57.

5553. Leavis, Frank R. *Lectures in America.* New York: Pantheon, 1969.
See also 4927.

Leitch, Maurice. 5554. McMahon, Seán. "May the Lord in His Mercy." *Éire* 4,ii(1969):128–40. [On L's *The Liberty Lad* and

Poor Lazarus.]
See also 5613.

Lewis, A. 5555. Davies, John. "The Poetry of Darkness:Alun Lewis's Indian Experience." *AWR* 19,xliii:176–83.

Lewis, C. Day. 5556. Bouyssou, Roland. "L'angoisse existentielle de C. Day Lewis." *Caliban* 7:59–65.

5557. Narita, Seiju. "Cecil Day Lewis no Shi." *EigoS* 114(1968):218–19. [CDL's poems.]

Lewis, C.S. 5558. Anon. "Hard, Polemical, Black-or-White, Them-or-Us." *TLS* 31 July:853–54. [Rev. art. See also 14 Aug:903; 28 Aug:951.]

5559. Carnell, Corbin S. "C.S. Lewis:An Appraisal." *Mythlore* 1,iv(1969):18–20,

5560. Christopher, Joe R. "The Romances of Clive Staples Lewis." *DAI* 30:3937A–38A(Okla.).

5561. —— "An Introduction to Narnia. Part I:The Chronology of the Chronicles." *Mythlore* 2,ii:23–25.

5562. Futch, Ken. "The Syntax of C.S. Lewis's Style:A Statistical Look at Some Syntactic Features." *DAI* 30(1969): 2002A(So. Calif.).

5563. Hannay, Margaret. "Arthurian and Cosmic Myth in *That Hideous Strength.*" *Mythlore* 2,ii:7–9.

5564. —— "C.S. Lewis' Theory of Mythology." *Mythlore* 1,i(1969):14–24.

5565. —— "The Mythology of *Out of the Silent Planet.*" *Mythlore* 1,iv(1969):11–14.

5566. —— "The Mythology of *Perelandra.*" *Mythlore* 2,i: 14–16.

5567. Hooper, Walter,ed. *Narrative Poems.* London: Geoffrey Bles, 1969.

5568. Kranz, Gisbert. "Amor und Psyche:Metamorphose eines Mythos bei C.S. Lewis." *Arcadia* 4(1969):285–99.

5569. Milward, Peter. "C.S. Lewis on Allegory." *EigoS* 114(1968):227–32.

5570. *Narnia Conference Proceedings.* Maywood, Calif.: Mythopoeic Soc. [Doris Robin, "An Introduction to Middle Earth and Narnia," 2–3; Laura A. Ruskin, "What Is Narnia?" 4–7; Bruce McMenomy, "Arthurian Themes in the Narnia Books," 8–10; Gracia F. Ellwood, " 'Which Way I Flie is Hell'," 11–14; Glen GoodKnight, "Lilith in Narnia," 15–19; David Hulan, "Narnia and the Seven Deadly Sins," 21–23; Nancy Lou Patterson, "Lord of the Beasts:Animal Archetypes in C.S. Lewis," 24–32; Peter Kreeft, "Narnia as Myth," 35–39.]

* 5571. Norwood, W.D.,Jr. "C.S. Lewis' Portrait of Aphrodite." *SoQ* 8:237–72.

5572. Puttkamer, Annemarie von. "Clive Staples Lewis," 227–39 in Otto Mann,ed., *Christliche Dichter im 20 Jahrhundert: Beiträge zur europäischen Literatur.* Bern: Francke, 1968.

5573. Weatherby, H.L. "Two Medievalists:Lewis and Eliot on Christianity and Literature." *SR* 78:330–47.
See also 5841, 5849, 5865, 5869, 5898, 5901.

Lewis, W. 5574. *Agenda* 7,iii–8,i (combined issue):Spec. Wyndham Lewis No. [Martin Seymour-Smith, "Wyndham Lewis as Imaginative Writer," 9–15; I.A. Richards, "A Talk on 'The Childermass'," 16–21 (rpt.); Penelope Palmer, " 'The Human Age'," 22–30; Peter Dale, " 'Self Condemned'," 31–36; Julian Symons, "The Thirties Novels," 37–48; Ezra Pound, "Augment of the Novel," 49–56 (rpt.); Timothy Materer, "The Great English Vortex," 57–65; Rebecca West, " 'Tarr'," 67–69 (rpt.); Peter Dale, " 'The Revenge for Love'," 71–77; Walter Michel, "Wyndham Lewis the Painter," 78–84; Ezra Pound, "The War Paintings of Wyndham Lewis," 85–87 (rpt.); Edmund Gray, "Wyndham Lewis and the Modern Crisis of Painting," 88–92; Hugh G. Porteus, "Random Samples," 93–96 (rev. art.); E.W.F. Tomlin, "Reflections on 'Time and Western Man'," 97–108; C.H. Sisson, "The Politics of Wyndham Lewis," 109–16; W.K. Rose, "Pound and Lewis:The Crucial Years," 117–33 (rpt.); Kenneth Cox, "Dualism and Les Autres," 134–39; William H. Pritchard, "Lawrence and Lewis," 140–47; Alan Bold, " 'One-Way Song'," 148–55; Annamaria Sala, "Some Notes on Vorticism and Futurism," 156–62; D.G. Bridson, "The Making of 'The Human Age'," 163–71; Hugh G. Porteus, "A Man Apart:A Few Recollections of Wyndham Lewis," 172–79; Hugh Kenner, "Excerpts from 'The Man of the World'," 181–83; Wyndham

Lewis, "Further Note," 184–86, "from *Hoodopip*," 187–96; Hugh Kenner, "Note on 'Joint'," 197; Wyndham Lewis, "From *Joint*," 198–208, "from *The Infernal Fair*," 209–15, "The Do-Nothing Mode:An Autobiographical Fragment," 216–21; "A List of Books, with Approximate Dates," 223–24.]

5575. Materer, Timothy. "The Short Stories of Wyndham Lewis." *SSF* 7:615–24.

See also 5160.

Lowbury. *5576. Press, John. "Edward Lowbury." *SoR* 6:302–16.

Lowry, M. 5577. Benham, David. "Lowry's Purgatory: Versions of 'Lunar Caustic'." *CanL* 44:28–37.

5578. Corrigan, Matthew. "Malcolm Lowry, New York Publishing, & the 'New Illiteracy'." *Encounter* 35(July):82–93.

5579. Costa, Richard H. "A Quest for Eridanus:The Evolving Art of Malcolm Lowry's *Under the Volcano*." *DAI* 30(1969): 1556A–57A(Purdue).

5580. —— "Malcolm Lowry and the Addictions of an Era." *UWR* 5,ii:1–10.

5581. Dodson, Daniel B. *Malcolm Lowry*. (CEMW 51.) New York and London: Columbia U.P.

5582. Durrant, Geoffrey. "Death in Life:Neo-Platonic Elements in 'Through the Panorama'." *CanL* 44:13–27.

5583. Epstein, Perle. "Swinging the Maelstrom:Malcolm Lowry and Jazz." *CanL* 44:57–66.

5584. —— *The Private Labyrinth of Malcolm Lowry:Under the Volcano, and* The Cabbala. New York: Holt, 1969.

5585. Lowry, Malcolm. "Two Letters." *CanL* 44:50–56. [To Albert Erskine and David Markson.]

5586. New, W.H. "Lowry's Reading:An Introductory Essay." *CanL* 44:5–12.

5587. Tiessen, Paul G. "Malcolm Lowry and the Cinema." *CanL* 44:38–49.

5588. Wright, Terence. "*Under the Volcano*:The Static Art of Malcolm Lowry." *ArielE* 1,iv:67–76.

Macaulay. 5589. Bensen, Alice R. *Rose Macaulay*. (TEAS 85.) New York: Twayne, 1969.

MacDiarmid. 5590. Lundkvist, Artur. "Rebell och utopist: Hugh MacDiarmid." [F 32]:141–54.

5591. Smith, Iain C. "Hugh MacDiarmid:*Sangschaw* and *A Drunk Man Looks at the Thistle*." *SSL* 7:169–79.

MacManus. 5592. McMahon, Seán. "Francis MacManus's Novels of Modern Ireland." *Éire* 5,i:116–30.

MacNeice. *5593. Dorrill, James F. "MacNeice's 'The Riddle'." *Expl* 29:Item 7.

* 5594. Irwin, John T. "MacNeice, Auden, and the Art Ballad." *ConL* 11:58–79.

5595. Kano, Hideo. "Gendaishi no Mondai—Louis MacNeice no baai." *EigoS* 114(1968):364–65. [Problems of modern poetry:the case of LM.]

5596. McKinnon, William T. "The Cad with the Golden Tongue." *EIC* 20:109–15.

5597. Smith, Elton E. *Louis MacNeice*. (TEAS 99.) New York: Twayne.

Manning. 5598. Hergenhan, L.T. "Novelist at War:Frederic Manning's *Her Private We*." *Quadrant* 66:19–29.

Mansfield. 5599. Baldeshwiler, Eileen. "Katherine Mansfield's Theory of Fiction." *SSF* 7:421–32.

5600. Busch, Frieder. "Katherine Mansfield and Literary Impressionism in France and Germany." *Arcadia* 5:58–76.

5601. Gennari, Geneviève. "La littérature au féminin." *NL* 16 avril:1,7.

5602. Prasad, Sarla. "Cultural Difficulties in the Appreciation of English Literature for an Average Indian Student." [F 51]:57–62. [With ref. to M's "Her First Ball" and Goldsmith's "The Man in Black."]

Masefield. 5603. Drew, Fraser. "The Irish Allegiances of an English Laureate:John Masefield and Ireland." *Éire* 3,iv(1968): 24–34.

Maugham. 5604. Showalter, Craig V.,comp. *Seventeen Lost Stories*. With Introd. Garden City, N.Y.: Doubleday, 1969.

McGahern. 5605. Cronin, John. " 'The Dark' Is Not Light Enough:The Fiction of John McGahern." *Studies* 58(1969): 427–32.

McLaverty. *See* 5613.

Metcalfe. 5606. Gawsworth, John. "In Memoriam:John Metcalfe." *AntigR* 1,ii:72–75. [Foll. by 2 of M's brief prose pieces, 76–78.]

Mew. *5607. Boll, Theophilus E.M. "The Mystery of Charlotte Mew and May Sinclair:An Inquiry." *BNYPL* 74: 445–53.

Milne. 5608. Ogawa, Kazuo. "Kuma no Pu San." *Oberon* 31(1969):67–70. [Winnie the Pooh.]

* 5609. Payne, John R. "Four Children's Books by A.A. Milne." *SB* 23:127–39.

Monro. 5610. Anon. "Harold Monro as Shopkeeper and Poet." *TLS* 11 Sept: 985–86. [Rev. art. See also 18 Sept:1039.]

5611. Monro, Alida,ed. *Collected Poems*. London: Duckworth.

Moore, B. 5612. Brady, Charles A. "*I Am Mary Dunne*, by Brian Moore." *Éire* 3,iv(1968):136–40. [Rev. art.]

5613. Cronin, John. "Ulster's Alarming Novels." *Éire* 4, iv(1969):27–34. [On novels by Michael McLaverty, Brian Moore, Forrest Reid, and Maurice Leitch.]

5614. Foster, John W. "Crisis and Ritual in Brian Moore's Belfast Novels." *Éire* 3,iii(1968):66–74.

Moore, G. 5615. Cassagnau, M. "G. Moore traducteur de lui-même." *RLC* 44:120–24.

5616. Cox, H.H. "Warnock on Moore." *Mind* 79:265–69.

5617. Egleson, Janet F. "The Aesthetic Development of George Moore:Changes in Structure, Style, and Technique of Moore's Novels, 1883–1917." *DAI* 30:4982A(N.Y.U.).

5618. Gilcher, Edwin,ed. *A Bibliography of George Moore*. Delkalb: No. Ill. U.P.

* 5619. Jernigan, E. Jay. "The Bibliographical and Textual Complexities of George Moore's *A Mummer's Wife*." *BNYPL* 74:396–410.

5620. Kennedy, Sister Eileen. "Circling Back:The Influence of Ireland on George Moore." *DAI* 30(1969):727A(Columbia).

5621. —— "Moore's *Untilled Field* and Joyce's *Dubliners*." *Éire* 5,iii:81–89.

5622. Ware, Thomas C. "George Moore's Theory and Practice of the Novel." *DAI* 30:3439A–40A(N.C.).

5623. Weaver, Jack W. "An Exile Returned:Moore and Yeats in Ireland." *Éire* 3,i(1968):40–47.

See also 5941.

Moore, G.E. 5624. Ambrose, Alice, and Morris Lazerowitz, eds. *G.E. Moore:Essays in Retrospect*. London: Allen & Unwin; New York: Humanities.

5625. Rosenbaum, S.P. "G.E. Moore's *The Elements of Ethics*." *UTQ* 38(1969):214–32. [Corr. of Bibliog. for 1969, Vol. I, Item 5424.]

5626. Watt, Donald J. "G.E. Moore and the Bloomsbury Group." *ELT* 12(1969):119–34. [Corr. of Bibliog. for 1969, Vol. I, Item 5428.]

Morgan, C. 5627. Giffard, Hugh. "The Writer and the Naturalist." *EA* 23:3–5.

5628. Painting, David E. "Charles Morgan:A Revaluation." *AWR* 18,xliii:90–94.

5629. Pugh-puis, Claude. "Visite à ballater." *EA* 23:6–18.

5630. Wieder, Robert. "Les lettres de Morgan." *EA* 23:19–22. [Rev. art.]

Muir, E. 5631. Boyer, Dale K. "A Descriptive and Comparative Study of the Poetry of Edwin Muir." *DAI* 30:4443A(Mo., Columbia).

5632. Hixson, Allie C. "Light Dust of Fame:A Critical Study of the Life and Thought of Edwin Muir." *DAI* 30:3010A (Louisville).

5633. Hoy, Peter. "Edwin Muir Addenda:Checklist of Secondary References." *Serif* 7,i:11–19.

5634. Huberman, Elizabeth L. "The Field of Good and Evil:A Study of the Poetry of Edwin Muir." *DAI* 30(1969): 2529A(N.Y.U.).

5635. Ogoshi, Hinzo. "Edwin Muir no Caliban." *EigoS* 114(1968):435–36. [M's Caliban; in Jap.]

See also 5961.

Munro. 5636. Gillen, Charles H. *H.H. Munro (Saki)*. (TEAS 102.) New York: Twayne, 1969.

5637. Otto, Don H. "The Development of Method and Meaning in the Fiction of 'Saki' (H.H.Munro)." *DAI* 30(1969): 2035A–36A(So. Calif.).

Murdoch. 5638. Baldanza, Frank. "The Murdoch Manuscripts at the University of Iowa:An Addendum." *MFS* 16: 201–02. [See Bibliog. for 1969, Vol. I, Item 5435.]

5639. Emerson, Donald. "Violence and Survival in the Novels of Iris Murdoch." *TWA* 57(1969):21–28.

5640. Ivaševa, V. "Ot Sartra k Platonu." *VLit* 13,xi(1969): 134–55. [Existentialism in recent Eng. lit., esp. in M.]

5641. Kogan, Pauline. "Beyond Solipsism to Irrationalism:A Study of Iris Murdoch's Novels." *L&I* 2(1969):47–69.

5642. Narita, Seiju. "Tokyo no Iris Murdoch." *EigoS* 115(1969):218–19. [M's visit to Tokyo.]

5643. Thomson, P.W. "Iris Murdoch's Honest Puppetry —The Characters of *Bruno's Dream*." *CritQ* 11(1969):277–83. *See also* 931.

Murry. 5644. Rees, Richard,ed. *Poets, Critics, Mystics:A Selection of Criticisms Written Between 1919 and 1955 by John Middleton Murry.* Carbondale and Edwardsville: So. Ill. U.P.; London and Amsterdam: Feffer & Simons.

Newby. 5645. Mathews, F.X. "Witness to Violence:The War Novels of P.H. Newby." *TSLL* 12:121–35.

5646. Poss, Stanley. "Manners and Myths in the Novels of P.H. Newby." *Crit* 12,i:5–19.

O'Brien, F. 5647. Benstock, Bernard. "The Three Faces of Brian Nolan." *Éire* 3,iii(1968):51–65. [Brian Nolan = Brien O'Nolan = Myles na Gopaleen = Flann O'Brien.]

5648. Janik, Del Ivan. "Flann O'Brien:The Novelist as Critic." *Éire* 4, iv(1969):64–72.

5649. Lee, L.L. "The Dublin Cowboys of Flann O'Brien." *WAL* 4(1969):219–25.

O'Casey. 5650. Atkinson, Justin B.,ed. *The Sean O'Casey Reader:Plays, Autobiographies, Opinions.* With Introd. New York: St. Martin's; London: Macmillan, 1968.

* 5651. Benstock, Bernard. "The Mother-Madonna-Matriarch in Sean O'Casey." *SoR* 6:603–23.

5652. Daniel, Walter C. "The False Paradise Pattern in Sean O'Casey's *Cock-a-Doodle Dandy*." *CLAJ* 13(1969):137–43.

5653. Darin, Doris d. "Influences on the Dramas of Sean O'Casey:'Past Experiences—The Molds in Which Myself Was Made'." *DAI* 30(1969):2523A–24A(N.Y.U.).

5654. Habart, Michael. "Introducción a Sean O'Casey." *PrA* 114(1969):12–24.

5655. Kosok, Heinz. "Sean O'Caseys *Hall of Healing*." *NS* 19:168–79.

5656. Krause, David. "O'Casey and Yeats and the Druid." *MD* 11(1968):252–62.

5657. McLaughlin, John J. "Political Allegory in O'Casey's *Purple Dust*." *MD* 13:47–53.

5658. Pixley, Edward E. "A Structural Analysis of Eight of Sean O'Casey's Plays." *DAI* 30:4053A(Iowa).

* 5659. Rollins, Ronald G. "O'Casey's *Within the Gates*." *Expl* 29:Item 8.

5660. Schrank, Bernice S. "Reflections of Reality:A Study in the Uses of Language and Time in the Plays of Sean O'Casey." *DAI* 30:3022A–23A(Wis.).

O'Connor. 5661. Kramer, C.R. "Experimentation in Technique:Frank O'Connor's 'Judas'." *DM* 8,i–ii(1969):31–38.

5662. McHugh, Roger. "Frank O'Connor and the Irish Theatre." *Éire* 4,ii(1969):52–63.

O'Flaherty. 5663. Doyle, Paul A. "O'Flaherty's Real View of *The Informer*." *DM* 8,iii:67–70.

Orwell. 5664. Beadle, Gordon. "George Orwell and Charles Dickens:Moral Critics of Society." *JHS* 2(1969–70):245–55.

5665. Chialant, Maria Teresa. "Dickens, Gissing e Orwell." *AION-SG* 12(1969):373–94.

5666. Fiderer, Gerald. "Masochism as Literary Strategy: Orwell's Psychological Novels." *L&P* 20,i:3–21.

5667. Hobbs, Albert H. "Welfarism and Orwell's Reversal." *Intercollegiate Rev.*(Bryn Mawr, Pa.) 6,iii:105–12.

5668. Koike, Shigeru. "*Bokushi no Musume* ga unda mono." *EigoS* 114(1968):503–04. [Outcome of *A Clergyman's Daughter*.]

5669. Kubal, David L. "*Down and Out in Paris and London*:

The Conflict of Art and Politics." *MQ* 12:199–209.

5670. ——. "George Orwell and the Aspidistra." *UR* 37:61–67.

5671. Lief, Ruth A. *Homage to Oceania:The Prophetic Vision of George Orwell.* Columbus: Ohio State U.P., 1969.

5672. Mellichamp, Leslie R. "A Study of George Orwell:The Man, His Import, and His Outlook." *DAI* 30(1969):729A–30A(Emory).

5673. Meyers, Jeffrey. "Review Article:George Orwell, the Honorary Proletarian." *PQ* 48(1969):526–49. [See Bibliog. for 1969, Vol. I, Item 5459.]

5674. ——. "The Ethics of Responsibility:Orwell's *Burmese Days*." *UR* 25(1968):83–87.

5675. O'Flinn, J.P. "Orwell on Literature and Society." *CE* 31:603–12.

5676. Thody, Philip. "The Curiosity of George Orwell." *ULR* 12(1969):69–80.

5677. Voorhees, Richard J. "Justice to George Orwell." *JML* 1:127–33. [Rev. art.]

5678. Warncke, Wayne. "George Orwell's Dickens." *SAQ* 69:[373]–81. *See also* 4079, 5257.

Osborne. 5679. Budd, Dirk R. "The Vicissitudes of the Osborne Protest from 1956 to 1964." *DAI* 30(1969):1163A(Pa.).

5680. Faber, M.D. "The Character of Jimmy Porter:An Approach to *Look Back in Anger*." *MD* 13:67–77.

5681. Karrafalt, David H. "The Social Theme in Osborne's Plays." *MD* 13:78–82.

5682. Kato, Kyohei. "An Essay on John Osborne." [F 14]:103–19. [In Jap.] *See also* 4354.

Owen. 5683. White, William. "Wilfred Owen:Bibliographical Notes and Addenda." *Serif* 7,i:25–27. *See also* 5987.

Paget. *5684. *CLQ* 9,iii. Spec. Paget No. [Leonee Ormond, "Vernon Lee as a Critic of Aestheticism in *Miss Brown*," 131–54; Richard Ormond, "John Singer Sargent and Vernon Lee," 154–78; Richard Cary, "Vernon Lee's Vignettes of Literary Acquaintances," 179–200.]

Pinero. 5685. Miner, Brother Sylvester E. "The Individual and Society:The Plays of Arthur Pinero." *DAI* 30(1969): 731A–32A(Notre Dame).

5686. Wearing, J.P. "Pinero's Letters in the Brotherton Collection of the University of Leeds." *TN* 24:74–79. *See also* 5768.

Pinter. 5687. Burkman, Katherine H. "Pinter's *A Slight Ache* as Ritual." *MD* 11(1968):326–35.

5688. Esslin, Martin. *The Peopled Wound:The Work of Harold Pinter.* Garden City, N.Y.: Doubleday.

5689. Ganz, Arthur. "A Clue to the Pinter Puzzle:The Triple Self in *The Homecoming*." *ETJ* 21(1969):180–87.

* 5690. Gillen, Francis. " '. . . Apart from the Known and the Unknown':The Unreconciled Worlds of Harold Pinter's Characters." *ArQ* 26:17–24.

5691. Heilman, Robert B. "Demonic Strategies:*The Birthday Party* and *The Firebugs*." [F 67]:57–74.

5692. Hollis, James R. *Harold Pinter:The Poetics of Silence.* Pref. Harry T. Moore. Carbondale: So. Ill. U.P.; London: Feffer & Simons.

5693. Morrison, Kristin. "Pinter and the New Irony." *QJS* 55(1969):388–93.

5694. Odajima, Yushi. "Pinter Notes." *EigoS* 115(1969): 416–17. [In Jap.]

* 5695. Palmer, David S. "A Harold Pinter Checklist." *TCL* 16:287–96.

5696. Pierce, Roger N. "Three Play Analyses." *DAI* 30(1969):2660A(Iowa).

5697. States, Bert O. "Pinter's *Homecoming*:The Shock of Nonrecognition." *HudR* 21(1968):474–86.

* 5698. Warner, John M. "The Epistemological Quest in Pinter's *The Homecoming*." *ConL* 11:340–53. *See also* 4944.

Porter, P. 5699. Douglas, Dennis. "Conversation with Peter Porter." *Overland* 44:33–34.

Potter, B. 5700. Sandman-Lilius, Irmelin. "Beatrix Potter:

Böcker som besvärjelser." *FT* 187–88:30–40.

Powell, A. 5701. Gutierrez, Donald K. "A Critical Study of Anthony Powell's *A Dance to the Music of Time*." *DAI* 30(1969):724A(U.C.L.A.).

5702. McLeod, Dan D. "The Art of Anthony Powell." *DAI* 30(1969):1174A(Claremont).

Powys, J.C. 5703. Brebner, John A. "Owen Glendower:The Pursuit of the Fourth Dimension." *AWR* 18,xlii:207–16.

5704. *Powys Newsl.*(Colgate U.) 1. [Isobel Powys Marks, "The Powys Family Magazine"; Heraclitus(T.F. Powys), "The Child Queen"; Clayton Hoaglund, " 'I Am a Born Orator' "; Clifford Tolchard, "John Cowper Powys:A Memoir"; "American Libraries Holding Powys Manuscripts, ı ." Issue unpaged.]

Powys, L. See 5704.

Powys, T.F. 5705. Buning, M. "Folly Down Revisited:Some New Light on T.F. Powys." *ES* 50(1969):588–97.

5706. Pouillard, M. "T.F. Powys conférencier à Eastbourne 1902-03." *EA* 22(1969):346–50.

See also 5704.

Prince. 5707. Hedley, Jane. "Imprisoning and Expressing Him:The Dramatic Monologues of F.T. Prince." *MHRev* 7(1968):92–105.

Read. 5708. Aihara, Koichi. "Read no Kyoikuron." *EigoS* 114(1968):656–57. [R's theory of educ.]

5709. Arakawa, Tatsuhiko. "Read no Chusho-Bijutsuron." *EigoS* 114(1968):658–59. [R's theory of abstract art.]

5710. Eto, Takashi. "Read-kyo no Nihon Homon." *EigoS* 114(1968):666–67. [R's visit to Japan.]

5711. Fukai, Tatsuo. "Herbert Read no Ningen to Shiso." *EigoS* 114(1968):664–66. [R on man and his thought.]

5712. Fukuhara, Rintaro. "Herbert Read no Wakai Koro." *EigoS* 114(1968):638–39. [R in 1930.]

5713. Kano, Hideo. "Herbert Read no Shiron." *EigoS* 114(1968):648–49. [R's theory of poetry.]

5714. Kishimoto, Hirokichi. "Herbert Read no Shogai." *EigoS* 114(1968):640–41. [Life of R.]

5715. Maekawa, Yuichi. "H. Read to T.E. Hulme." *EigoS* 114(1968):660–61. [R and H; in Jap.]

5716. Masuno, Masae. "Anarchist—Read." *EigoS* 114(1968):654–55. [In Jap.]

5717. Narita, Seiju. "Gendai Hihyo ni okeru Herbert Read no Ichi." *EigoS* 114(1968):642–43. [R's position in mod. crit.]

5718. Skelton, Robin,ed. "Sir Herbert Read (1893–1968):A Memorial Symposium." *MHRev* 9(1969):Spec. Issue. [Denise Levertov, "Herbert Read:A Memoir," 10–13; Michael Hamburger, "Herbert Read:Instead of an Elegy," 14–26; Walter Gropius, "On Herbert Read," 27–30; Henry Moore, "A Tribute," 31–36 (incl. drawings); Herbert Read, "The Limits of Permissiveness in Art," 37–50; Ben Nicholson, "A Tribute," 51–56 (incl. drawings); Sam Black, "Herbert Read:His Contribution to Art Education and to Education Through Art," 57–65; Stephen Spender, "Four Sketches for Herbert Read," 66–67 (poems); George Woodcock, "The Philosopher of Freedom," 68–87; Barbara Hepworth, "Four Drawings," 88–92; Reginald C. Terry,ed., "Edward Dahlberg and Herbert Read:An Exchange of Letters," 95–126; G. Wilson Knight, "Herbert Read and Byron," 130–34; Kathleen Raine, "Herbert Read as a Literary Critic," 135–57; Robin Skelton, "The Poetry of Herbert Read," 161–74; Bonamy Dobrée and Herbert Read, "Beauty—or the Beast:A Conversation in a Tavern," 178–86; Roland Penrose, "Herbert Read," 187–91; Howard Gerwing, with the assist. of Michael W. Pidgeon, "A Checklist of the Herbert Read Archive in the McPherson Library at the University of Victoria," 192–258; plus poems by George Barker, Norman Nicholson, Denise Levertov, Thomas Kinsella, John Holloway, Donald Davie, Anthony Kerrigan, Robin Skelton, and Roy Fuller.]

5719. Tanaka, Yukio. "Read no Hihyo to Seishin-Bunsekigaku." *EigoS* 114(1968):650–51. [R's crit. and psychoanal.]

5720. Toyama, Shigehiko. "Read no Buntairon." *EigoS* 114(1968):652–53. [R on Style.]

5721. Ueda, Tamotsu. "Shijin Read." *EigoS* 114(1968):661–62. [R as poet.]

5722. Wada, Tetsuzo. "Read to Senso." *EigoS* 114(1968):

663–64. [R and war.]

5723. Yamakawa, Teizo. "Read no Bungei Hihyo ni okeru Shuchishugi." *EigoS* 114(1968):644–45. [Intellectualism in R's lit. crit.]

5724. Yura, Kimiyoshi. "Read to Romanshugi." *EigoS* 114(1968):646–47. [R and Romanticism.]

See also 4990.

Reid. See 5613.

Renault. 5725. Wolfe, Peter. *Mary Renault.* (TEAS 98.) New York: Twayne, 1969.

Richards. 5726. Anon. "Of Poetry and Meaning:Looking Back at the Critical Achievement of I.A. Richards." *TLS* 26 Feb:213–14. [Rev. art.; see also 19 Mar:311.]

Richardson, D. *5727. Rose, Shirley. "Dorothy Richardson's Theory of Literature:The Writer as Pilgrim." *Criticism* 12:20–37.

Richardson, H.H. 5728. Nichols, James R. "Theme and Technique in Henry Handel Richardson:A Discussion of the Relationship Between Theme and Technique in the Major Novels of Henry Handel Richardson." *DAI* 30:3952A(N.C.).

Riding. See 5285.

Ross. 5729. Bogle, Edra C. "The Life and Literary and Artistic Activities of Robert Baldwin Ross, 1869–1918." *DAI* 30(1969):1553A(So. Calif.).

Rowse, A.L. 5730. Wilson, Colin. "The Poetry of A.L. Rowse." *PoetryR* 61:140–60.

Russell, B. 5731. Vásquez, Francisco. "Bertrand Russell en la cultura contemporánea." *Arbor* 290:17–24.

Russell, G. 5732. Summerfield, Henry. "A Mystic in the Modern World." *IR* 26,iii(1969):13–21.

5733. Summerfield, H[enry],ed. "Unpublished Letters from AE to John Eglinton." *MHRev* 14:84–107.

Ryan, F. 5734. Kelly, John. "A Lost Abbey Play:Frederick Ryan's *The Laying of the Foundations.*" *ArielE* 1,iii:29–48.

Sassoon. See 4974.

Scrutiny. 5735. Grosman, Meta. "*Scrutiny's* Reviews of I.A. Richards' Works." *AN* 2(1969):45–51.

Shaw, G.B. 5736. Arnold, Armin. "Georg Kaiser und G.B. Shaw:Eine Interpretation der *Jüdischen Witwe.*" *GL&L* 23(1969):85–92.

* 5737. Barnett, Gene A. "Don Juan's Hell." *BSUF* 11,ii:47–52.

5738. Boxill, Roger. "Shaw and the Doctors." *DAI* 30(1969):1553A(Columbia). [1966.]

5739. Carpenter, Charles A. "Notes on Some Obscurities in 'The Revolutionist's Handbook'." *ShawR* 13:59–64.

5740. Cirillo, Nancy R. "The Poet Armed:Wagner, D'Annunzio, Shaw." *DAI* 30(1969):155A(N.Y.U.).

5741. Couchman, Gordon W. "The First Playbill of 'Caesar': Shaw's List of Authorities." *ShawR* 13:79–82.

5742. Dietrich, R.F. *Portrait of the Artist as a Young Superman:A Study of Shaw's Novels.* Gainesville: U. of Fla. P., 1969.

5743. Evans, T.F. "On Richmond Hill." *Shavian* 4:93–97.

5744. —— "Shaw and Education." *Shavian* 4(1969):16–21.

5745. Frank, Joseph. "Take It Off! Take It Off!" *ShawR* 13:10–12. [S's dramatic legerdemain.]

5746. Furlong, William B. *GBS/GKC:Shaw and Chesterton, the Metaphysical Jesters.* University Park: Penn. State U.P.

5747. Haywood, Charles. "George Bernard Shaw on Incidental Music in the Shakespearean Theater." *SJW* 105(1969):168–82.

5748. —— "George Bernard Shaw on Shakespearian Music and the Actor." *SQ* 20(1969):417–26.

5749. Hibbs, Christopher. "*Bernard Shaw:A Reassessment.*" *TLS* 18 Dec(1969):1450.

5750. Huggett, Richard. *The First Night of* Pygmalion. London: Faber.

5751. Hugo, Leon H.,ed. "[J.B. Fagan's] 'Shakespear v. Shaw'." *ShawR* 13:105–31.

* 5752. Jordan, Robert J. "Theme and Character in *Major Barbara.*" *TSLL* 12:471–80.

5753. Kaufman, Michael V. "The Dissonance of Dialectic: Shaw's *Heartbreak House.*" *ShawR* 13:2–9.

5754. Keough, Lawrence C. "Shaw's Introduction to New York:The Mansfield Productions 1894–1900." *Shavian* 4(1969):

6–10. [On Amer. critics' response to G.B.S.]

5755. Keunen, J. "Napoleon in Shaviaanse stijl." *DWB* 115:35–45.

* 5756. Leary, Daniel J. "A Deleted Passage from Shaw's *John Bull's Other Island*," *BNYPL* 74:598–606.

5757. Mason, Ronald. "Shaw on Shakespeare." *Shavian* 4:46–51.

5758. Matthews, John F. *George Bernard Shaw.* (CEMW 45.) New York and London: Columbia U.P., 1969.

5759. Mendelsohn, Michael J. "Bernard Shaw's Soldiers." *ShawR* 13:29–34.

5760. Mills, Carl H. "Shaw's Superman:A Re-Examination." *ShawR* 13:48–58.

5761. Mills, John A. "Acting Is Being:Bernard Shaw on the Art of the Actor." *ShawR* 13:65–78.

5762. Muir, Kenneth. "Shaw and Shakespeare." [F 52]:13–22.

5763. Munteanu, George. "Liviu Rebreanu și G.B. Shaw." *Teatrul*(Bucharest) 4,ix:62–64.

5764. Nelson, Raymond S. "Blanco Posnet—Adversary of God." *MD* 13:1–9.

5765. —— "Shaw's Keegan." *ShawR* 13:92–95.

5766. —— "The Church, the Stage, and Shaw." *MQ* 11:293–308.

* 5767. —— "*The Simpleton of the Unexpected Isles*:Shaw's 'Last Judgment'." *QQ* 76(1969):692–709.

5768. Nethercot, Arthur C. "*Mrs. Warren's Profession* and *The Second Mrs. Tanqueray*." *ShawR* 13:26–28.

5769. Roby, Kinley. "Arnold Bennett:Shaw's Ten O'clock Scholar." *ShawR* 13:96–104.

5770. Rodenbeck, John. "A Continuing Checklist of Shaviana." *ShawR* 13:43–45,89–91.

5771. Rogers, Richard E. "Didacticism, Plot, and Comedy: Ways in Which George Bernard Shaw Uses Plot to Keep Comic His Didactic Purpose." *DAI* 30:5000A(Ind.).

* 5772. Roy, Emil. "Pygmalion Revisited." *BSUF* 11,ii:38–46.

5773. Schöler-Beinhauer, Monica. "George Bernard Shaw und das Wunder." *LWU* 2(1969):149–58.

5774. Schuchter, J.D. "Shaw's *Major Barbara*." *Expl* 28:Item 74.

5775. Sidnell, M.J. "*John Bull's Other Island*:Yeats and Shaw." *MD* 11(1968):245–51.

5776. Turco, Alfred. "Sir Colenso's White Lie." *ShawR* 13:14–25. [*The Doctor's Dilemma*.]

5777. Ware, James M. "Shaw's 'New' Play:*The Black Girl*." *Shavian* 4(1969):11–15.

5778. Watson, Barbara B. "Sainthood for Millionaires:*Major Barbara*." *MD* 11(1968):227–44.

5779. Weintraub, Stanley. "Recent Shavian Criticism." *Éire* 4,iv(1969):82–89.

5780. —— "Shaw's *Lear*." *ArielE* 1,iii:59–68. [On *Heartbreak House*.]

5781. —— "The Making of an Irish Patriot:Bernard Shaw 1914–1916." *Éire* 5,iv:9–27.

5782. Weintraub, Stanley,ed. *Shaw:An Autobiography, 1856–1898, Selected from His Writings.* New York: Weybright & Talley, 1969; London: Rinehardt.

5783. Wilson, Colin. "Bernard Shaw." *TLS* 18 Dec(1969):1450.

5784. Zimbardo, Rose A.,ed. *Twentieth Century Interpretations of* Major Barbara:*A Collection of Critical Essays.* (TCI.) Englewood Cliffs, N.J.: Prentice-Hall.

See also 1453, 4808.

Shaw, R. 5785. Neumeyer, Peter F. "Arcadia Revisited: Arthur Goldman and Nicolas Poussin." *UR* 36:263–67. [On *The Man in the Glass Booth*.]

Sheehan. 5786. Coleman, Antony. "Priest as Artist:The Dilemma of Canon Sheehan." *Studies* 58(1969):30–41.

Shute. 5787. Pira, Gisela. "Nevil Shute:*On the Beach* (Versuch einer Interpretation)." *NS* 19:53–59.

Sillitoe. 5788. Penner, Allen R. "*The General*:Exceptional Proof of a Critical Rule." *SHR* 4:135–43.

Sinclair. *5789. Boll, Theophilus E.M. "May Sinclair:A Check List." *BNYPL* 74:454–67.

5790. Taylor, Corrine Y. "A Study of May Sinclair—Woman and Writer, 1863–1946—with an Annotated Bibliography." *DAI* 30:3026A(Wash. State).

See also 5607.

Sitwell, E. 5791. Bennett, Gordon W. "The Form and Sensibility of Edith Sitwell's Devotional Poems:A Study of Baroque Tradition." *DAI* 30(1969):2520A(Kan.).

* 5792. Ower, John. "Edith Sitwell's Metaphysical Medium and Metaphysical Message." *TCL* 16:253–67.

Smith, S.G. 5793. Crawford, Thomas. "The Poetry of Sydney Goodsir Smith." *SSL* 7:40–59.

Snow. See 4790.

Somerville and Ross. 5794. Fehlmann, Guy. *Somerville et Ross:Témoins de l'irlande d'hier.* Caen: Assoc. des Pubs. de la Faculté des Lettres et Sciences Humaines de l'Univ. de Caen.

5795. Lyons, F.S.L. "The Twilight of the Big House." *ArielE* 1,iii:110–22. [Rev. art. on Maurice Collis' *Somerville and Ross*.]

5796. McMahon, Seán. "John Bull's Other Ireland:A Consideration of *The Real Charlotte* by Somerville and Ross." *Éire* 3,iv(1968):119–35.

5797. Powell, Lady Violet. *The Books and Background of Somerville and Ross.* London: Heinemann.

Spark. 5798. Dobie, Ann B. "Muriel Spark's Definition of Reality." *Crit* 12,i:20–27.

5799. Malin, Irving. "The Deceptions of Muriel Spark." [F 19]:95–107.

5800. Quinn, Joseph A. "A Study of the Satiric Element in the Novels of Muriel Spark." *DAI* 30:3954A(Purdue).

Spender. 5801. Cowan, S.A. "Spender's 'He Will Watch the Hawk with an Indifferent Eye'." *Expl* 28:Item 67.

Stephen. 5802. Tindall, Samuel J.,Jr. "Leslie Stephen as Editor of the *Cornhill Magazine*." *DAI* 30:5422A(S.C.).

Stephens, J. *5803. Finneran, Richard J. "Three Unpublished Letters from James Stephens." *PLL* 6:77–88.

5804. McFate, Patricia Ann. "James Stephens's *Deirdre* and Its Legendary Sources." *Éire* 4,iii(1969):87–93. [Sources are *Longes mac n'Uislenn, Oidheadh Chloinne hUisneach,* and other tales.]

See also 521.

Stewart. 5805. Shaw, Wayne E. "God's Herald:A Rhetorical Analysis of the Preaching of James S. Stewart." *DAI* 30:5099A(Ind.).

Stoppard. 5806. Gardner, C.O. "Correspondence:*Rosencrantz and Guildenstern are Dead*." *Theoria* 34:83–84. [Reply to R.H. Lee art., below.]

5807. Lee, R.H. "The Circle and Its Tangent." *Theoria* 33(1969):37–43. [On Stoppard's *Rosencrantz and Guildenstern Are Dead*.]

Strachey, L. 5808. Merle, Gabriel. "Une biographie monumentale:*Lytton Strachey* de Michael Holroyd." *EA* 22(1969):293–301. [Rev. art.]

5809. Strachey, L. *Biographical Essays.* New York: Harcourt, Brace and World, 1969.

See also 7093.

Sturm. 5810. Taylor, Richard,ed. *Frank Pearce Sturm:His Life, Letters, and Collected Work.* With Introd. Urbana: U. of Ill. P., 1969.

Summers. 5811. Sewell, Brocard. "The Manuscripts of Montague Summers." *AntigR* 1,ii:30–36. [Foll. by "The Gothic Romance," text of unpub. holograph ms. by Summers, 37–40.]

Synge. 5812. Flood, Jeanne. "The Pre-Aran Writings of J.M. Synge." *Éire* 5,iii:63–80.

5813. Levitt, Paul M. "The Structural Craftsmanship of J.M. Synge's *Riders to the Sea*." *Éire* 4,i(1969):53–61.

5814. McMahon, Seán. "Clay and Worms." *Éire* 5,iv:116–34.

5815. Mikhail, Edward Halim. "Sixty Years of Synge Criticism, 1907–1967:A Selective Bibliography." *BB* 27:11–13(to be cont.)

5816. Price, Alan. "Synge's Prose Writings:A First View of the Whole." *MD* 11(1968):221–26.

5817. Saddlemyer, Ann. *J.M. Synge and Modern Comedy.* Dublin: Dolmen P., 1968.

5818. Salmon, Eric. "J.M. Synge's *Playboy*:A Necessary Reassessment." *MD* 13:111–28.

5819. Skelton, Robin. "J.M. Synge and *The Shadow of the*

Glen." *English* 18(1969):91–97.

5820. Smith, Harry W. "Synge's *Playboy* and the Proximity of Violence." *QJS* 55(1969):381–87.

5821. Sullivan, Mary R. "Synge, Sophocles, and the Unmaking of Myth." *MD* 12:242–53.

5822. Yamamoto, Shuji. "Synge no Mihappyo Gikyoku." *EigoS* 115(1969):138–39. [Unpub. play: *When the Moon Has Set*.]

Thomas, D. 5823. FitzGibbon, Constantine. "Dylan Thomas:A Letter." *DM* 8,iii:56–58.

5824. Jenkins, David C. "Shrine of the Boily Boy:The Dylan Thomas Notebooks at Buffalo." *AWR* 19,xliii:114–29.

5825. Kannel, Gregory J. "Word, Structure, and Meaning in the Poetry of Dylan Thomas." *DAI* 30:5412A(Kent State).

5826. Kohak, Frances M. "Concepts of Time in the Poetry of Dylan Thomas." *DAI* 30(1969):2028A(Boston).

5827. Maud, Ralph. "Dylan Thomas in Welsh Periodicals." *NLWJ* 15(1968):265–89. [Pt. 3.]

5828. Maud, Ralph, and Albert Glover. *Dylan Thomas in Print:A Bibliographical History*. Pittsburgh: U. of Pittsburgh P.

5829. McCormick, Jane. " 'Sorry, Old Christian'." *AWR* 18,xliii:78–82. [Thomas and V. Watkins.]

5830. Murphy, Michael W. "Thomas' 'Do Not Go Gentle Into That Good Night'." *Expl* 28:Item 55.

5831. Murty, G. Sri Rama. "Dylan Thomas's 'The Hunchback in the Park'." *Triveni* 38,iv:22–32.

5832. Neill, Michael. "Dylan Thomas's 'Tailor Age'." *N&Q* 17:59–63.

5833. Pratt, Annis. *Dylan Thomas' Early Prose:A Study in Creative Mythology*. Pittsburgh: U. of Pittsburgh P.

5834. Thompson, Thomas N. "Patterns of Imagery in the Poetry of Dylan Thomas." *DAI* 30:3026A(Pa.).

Thomas, E. 5835. Cooke, William. *Edward Thomas:A Critical Bibliography*. London: Faber.

5836. Hooker, Jeremy. "The Writings of Edward Thomas:II. The Sad Passion." *AWR* 19,xliii:63–78. [See Bibliog. for 1969, Vol. I, Item 5571.]

Thomas, R.S. 5837. Castay, Marie-Thérèse. "Les images dans la poésie de R.S. Thomas." *Caliban* 7:115–20.

5838. Thomas, R. George. "Humanus Sum:A Second Look at R.S. Thomas." *AWR* 18,xlii:55–62.

Tolkien. 5839. Ballif, Sandra. "A Sindarin-Quenya Dictionary, More or Less, Listing All Elvish Words Found in *The Lord of the Rings*, *The Hobbit*, and *The Road Goes Ever On* by J.R.R. Tolkien." *Mythlore* 1,i(1969):41–44; ii(1969):33–36; iv(1969):23–26.

5840. Boswell, George W. "Proverbs and Phraseology in Tolkien's *Lord of the Ring* Complex." *UMSE* 10(1969):59–65.

5841. Braude, Nan. "Sion and Parnassus:Three Approaches to Myth." *Mythlore* 1,i(1969):6–8. [In Tolkien, C. Williams, and C.S. Lewis.]

5842. —— "Tolkien and Spenser." *Mythlore* 1,iii(1969):8–13.

5843. Christensen, Bonniejean M. "*Beowulf* and *The Hobbit*:Elegy into Fantasy in J.R.R. Tolkien's Creative Technique." *DAI* 30:4401A–02A(So. Calif.).

5844. —— "Report from the West:Exploitation of *The Hobbit*." *Orcrist* 4(1969):15–16.

5845. Duriez, Colin. "Leonardo, Tolkien, and Mr. Baggins." *Mythlore* 1,iii(1969):18–28.

5846. Ellwood, Gracia F. *Good News from Tolkien's Middle Earth:Two Essays on the "Applicability" of the* Lord of the Rings. Grand Rapids, Mich.: Eerdmans.

5847. Ellwood, Robert. "The Japanese *Hobbit*." *Mythlore* 1,iii(1969):14–17.

* 5848. Epstein, E.L. "The Novels of J.R.R. Tolkien and the Ethnology of Medieval Christendom." *PQ* 48(1969):517–25.

5849. GoodKnight, Glen. "A Comparison of Cosmological Geography in the Works of J.R.R. Tolkien, C.S. Lewis, and Charles Williams." *Mythlore* 1,iii(1969):18–22.

5850. Green, William H. "*The Hobbit* and Other Fiction by J.R.R. Tolkien:Their Roots in Medieval Heroic Literature and Language." *DAI* 30:4944A(La. State).

5851. Juhren, Marcella. "The Ecology of Middle Earth." *Mythlore* 2,i:4–6,9.

5852. Kilby, Clyde S. "Tolkien and Coleridge." *Orcrist*

3(1969):16–19.

5853. Kuhl, Rand. "Arrows from a Twisted Bow:Misunderstanding Tolkien." *Mythlore* 1,iv(1969):45–49. [Rev. art. on Ready's *Understanding Tolkien . . .*]

5854. —— "Lore of Logres." *Mythlore* 1,iii(1969):34–37. [On T's "*Beowulf*:The Monsters and the Critics."]

5855. Levitin, Alexis. "Power in *The Lord of the Rings*." *Orcrist* 4(1969):11–14.

5856. —— "The Genre of *The Lord of the Rings*." *Orcrist* 3(1969):4–8,23.

5857. Mesibov, Bob. "Tolkien and Spiders." *Orcrist* 4(1969):3–5.

5858. Miller, David M. "Hobbits:Common Lens for Heroic Experience." *Orcrist* 3(1969):11–15.

5859. Monsman, Gerald. "The Imaginative World of J.R.R. Tolkien." *SAQ* 69:[264]–78.

5860. Ready, William. *Understanding Tolkien and* The Lord of the Rings. New York: Paperback Lib., 1969.

5861. Robinson, James. "The Wizard and History:Saruman's Vision of a New Order." *Orcrist* 1(1966–67):13–17.

5862. St. Clair, Gloria A. "Studies in the Sources of J.R.R. Tolkien's *The Lord of the Rings*." *DAI* 30:5001A(Okla.).

5863. Webster, Deborah C.,Jr. "Good Guys, Bad Buys:A Clarification on Tolkien." *Orcrist* 2(1967–68):18–23.

5864. West, Richard C. "An Annotated Bibliography of Tolkien Criticism." *Orcrist* 1(1966–67):32–55; 2(1967–68):40–54; 3(1969):22–23.

5865. —— "Contemporary Medieval Authors." *Orcrist* 3(1969):9–10,15.

5866. —— "Progress Report on the Variorum Tolkien." *Orcrist* 4(1969):6–7.

5867. —— "The Interlace and Professor Tolkien:Medieval Narrative Technique in *The Lord of the Rings*." *Orcrist* 1(1966–67):19–31.

5868. —— "The Tolkinians:Some Introductory Reflections on Alan Garner, Carol Kendall, and Lloyd Alexander." *Orcrist* 2(1967–68):4–15.

5869. —— "Tolkien in the Letters of C.S. Lewis." *Orcrist* 1(1966–67):3–13.

5870. Winter, Karen C. "Grendel, Gollum, and the Un-Man." *Orcrist* 2(1967–68):28–37.

See also 3408, 5898, 5901, 7408, 10066.

Tynan. 5871. Weightman, John. "Flashing the Old Job." *Encounter* 35(Oct):38–40. [*Oh! Calcutta!*]

Watt, I. 5872. Hirsch, David H. "The Reality of Ian Watt." *CritQ* 11(1969):164–79.

Waugh, E. 5873. Davis, Robert M. "Guy Crouchback's Children—A Reply." *ELN* 7(1969):127–29. [Reply to Joseph F. Mattingly; see Bibliog. for 1969, Vol. I, Item 5597.]

* 5874. —— "*Harper's Bazaar* and *A Handful of Dust*." *PQ* 48(1969):508–16.

5875. Dooley, D.J. "The Council's First Victim." *Triumph* 5,vi:33–35.

* 5876. *EWN* 4,i. [Calvin W. Lane, "Waugh's Book Reviews for *Night and Day*," 1–3; James F. Carens, "The Year's Work in Waugh Studies," 3–6; Heinz Kosok, "Evelyn Waugh:A Supplementary Checklist of Criticism," 6–8; Charles E. Linck,Jr., "A Waugh Letter Postmarked Chicago," 8; Yvon Tosser, "Bibliography of Waugh Criticism (French Area)," Part I, 8–9.]

* 5877. *EWN* 4,ii. [Heinz Kosok, "The Film World of *Vile Bodies*," 1–2; Roger T. Burbridge, "The Function of Gossip, Rumor, and Public Opinion in Evelyn Waugh's *A Handful of Dust*," 3–5; Robert Murray Davis, "Evelyn Waugh and Brian Howard," 5–6; Winnifred M. Bogaards, "The Conclusion of Waugh's Trilogy: Three Variants," 6–7; Marston LaFrance, "Charles E. Linck's Bibliography of Waugh's Early Work, 1910–1930:Some Additions and Corrections," 8–9.]

* 5879. *EWN* 4,iii. [Alfred Borrello, "Evelyn Waugh and Erle Stanley Gardner," 1–3; Gene D. Phillips, "Waugh's *Sword of Honour* on BBC-TV," 3–4; Paul A. Doyle, "Evelyn's Letters at Boston University," 5–6; Robert M. Davis, "Some Unidentified Works by Evelyn Waugh," 6–7; Paul A. Doyle, Winnifred Bogaards and Robert M. Davis, "Words of Waugh, 1940–66:A Supplementary Bibliography, Part I," 7–10.]

5880. Farr, D. Paul. "Evelyn Waugh:A Supplemental Bibliography." *BB* 26(1969):67–68,87.

5881. Lowe, Keith D. "Evelyn Waugh:Man Against History." *DAI* 30(1969):1142A(Stanford).

5882. Newnham, Anthony. "Evelyn Waugh's Library." *LCUT* N.S. 1:25–29.

5883. Paul, Martin T. "The Comic-Romantic Hero in Eight Novels of Evelyn Waugh." *DAI* 30(1969):288A(Wis.).

5884. Ulanov, Barry. "The Ordeal of Evelyn Waugh." [F 19]:79–93.

See also 4907.

Welch. 5885. Phillips, Robert. "*Brave and Cruel*:The Short Stories of Denton Welch." *SSF* 7:357–76.

Wells. 5886. Parrinder, Patrick. *H.G. Wells.* (Writers and Critics Ser.) Edinburgh: Oliver and Boyd.

5887. —— "Wells on Hardy." *TLS* 23 Apr:455. [W. as anon. critic for the *Saturday Review*; see also 28 May:586.]

5888. Potts, Willard C. "H.G. Wells on the Novel." *DAI* 30(1969):2544A(U. of Wash.).

5889. Vernier, J.P. "*The New Machiavelli*, roman de la confusion." *EA* 23:62–71.

5890. Williamson, Jack. "Wells and the Great Debate." *RQ* 4(1969):24–33.

5891. Zamyatin, Yevgeny. "H.G. Wells." *Midway* 10,i(1969):97–126. [Tr. Mirra Ginsburg.]

See also 3945.

Wesker. 5892. Breitback, Joseph. "Unakademische Betrachtungen zu einem gut gemachten Stück." *DASDJ* 1969 :99–105.

5893. Gustavsson, Torgny. "Mannen mot strömmen:Ett samtal med Arnold Wesker." *Horisont* 17,ii:57–64.

5894. Kleinberg, Robert. "Seriocomedy in *The Wesker Trilogy*." *ETJ* 21(1969):36–40.

5895. Page, Malcolm. "Whatever Happened to Arnold Wesker? His Recent Plays." *MD* 11(1968):317–25.

5896. Peinert, Dietrich. "*Chicken Soup with Barley*:Untersuchungen zur Dramentechnik Arnold Weskers." *LWU* 3:169–86.

White, T.H. *See* 5304, 5865.

Whiting. 5897. Lyons, Charles R. "The Futile Encounter in the Plays of John Whiting." *MD* 11(1968):283–98.

Williams, C. 5898. GoodKnight, Glen. "The Social History of the Inklings, J.R.R. Tolkien, C.S. Lewis, and Charles Williams." *Mythlore* 2,i:7–9.

5899. Peoples, Galen. "The Agnostic in the Whirlwind:The Seven Novels of Charles Williams." *Mythlore* 2,ii:10–15.

5900. Sadler, Glenn E.,introd. "*The Noises That Weren't There* by Charles Williams." *Mythlore* 2,ii:17–21. [Fragment of unpub. novel; to be cont.]

5901. Weinig, Sister Mary Anthony. "Images of Affirmation: Perspectives of the Fiction of Charles Williams, C.S. Lewis, J.R.R. Tolkien." *U. of Portland Rev.* 20,i(1968):43–46.

5902. Zylstra, Sape A. "Charles Williams:An Analysis and Appraisal of His Major Work." *DAI* 30:4468A(Emory).

See also 5841, 5849.

Williams, D.J. 5903. Evans, Gwynfor, and Saunders Lewis. "Two Tributes to D.J. Williams." *AWR* 19,xliii:25–31.

Wilson, A. 5904. Biles, Jack I. "A *Studies in the Novel* Interview:An Interview in London with Angus Wilson." *SNNTS* 2,i:76–87.

5905. Lindberg, Margaret. "Angus Wilson:*The Old Men at the Zoo* as Allegory." *IEY* 14(1969):44–48.

5906. Narita, Seiju. "A Reformer, not a Revolutionary." *EigoS* 115(1969):752–59. [Interview with A. Wilson on novels.]

* 5907. Shaw, Valerie A. "*The Middle Age of Mrs. Eliot* and *Late Call*:Angus Wilson's Traditionalism." *CritQ* 12:9–27.

Wilson, C. 5908. Wilson, Colin. *Voyage to a Beginning:An Intellectual Autobiography.* New York: Crown, 1969.

Woolf, V. 5909. Bazin, Nancy G. "The Aesthetics of Virginia Woolf." *DAI* 30(1969):1551A(Stanford).

5910. Brewer, Wanda M. "Virginia Woolf and the Painter's Vision." *DAI* 30(1969):716A–17A(Colo. State).

5911. Fleishman, Avrom. "Woolf and McTaggart." *ELH* 36(1969):719–38.

5912. Gorsky, Susan R. " 'The Central Shadow':Dualism in Form and Meaning in *The Waves*." *DAI* 30:3943A(Case Western Reserve).

5913. Graham, J.W. "Point of View in *The Waves*:Some Services of the Style." *UTQ* 39:193–211.

5914. Henig, Suzanne. "The Literary Criticism of Virginia Woolf." *DAI* 30(1969):323A–24A(N.Y.U.).

5915. Leaska, Mitchell A. *Virginia Woolf's* Lighthouse:*A Study in Critical Method.* London: Hogarth Press.

5916. Love, Jean O. *Worlds in Consciousness:Mythopoetic Thought in the Novels of Virginia Woolf.* Berkeley: U. of Calif. P.

* 5917. Majumdar, R. "Virginia Woolf and Thoreau." *TSB* 109(1969):4–5.

5918. Miller, J. Hillis. "Virginia Woolf's All Souls' Day:The Omniscient Narrator in *Mrs. Dalloway*." [F 60]:100–27.

5919. Noel, Roger. "Nathalie Sarraute's Criticism of Virginia Woolf." *RLV* 36:266–71.

5920. Richardson, Robert O. "Virginia Woolf's *The Waves*:A Reading." *DAI* 30:3955A(Cornell).

5921. Richter, Harvena. *Virginia Woolf:The Inward Voyage.* Princeton: Princeton U.P.

5922. Sagiyama, Yoko. "A Study of *To the Lighthouse*." *KGUAS* 17(1968):21–37.

5923. Steinmann, Theo. "Virginia Woolf:*To the Lighthouse*. Die doppelte Funktion der Malerin." *NS* 19:537–47.

* 5924. Szladits, Lola L. " 'The Life, Character and Opinions of Flush the Spaniel'." *BNYPL* 74:211–18.

5925. Wilson, Janice L. " 'A House that Fits Us All':Search for Form in *Jacob's Room, Orlando,* and *The Waves*." *DAI* 30:4467A(Calif.,Berkeley).

See also 4171, 4909, 5375, 5601, 6950.

Yeats, J.B. 5926. Rose, Marilyn G. "Solitary Companions in Beckett and Jack B. Yeats." *Éire* 4,ii(1969):66–80.

See also 5983.

Yeats, W.B. 5929. Adams, Hazard. "Criticism, Politics and History:The Matter of Yeats." *GaR* 24:158–82.

5930. Adlard, John. *Stenbock, Yeats and the Nineties:With an Hitherto Unpublished Essay by Arthur Symons and a Bibliography by Timothy Smith.* London: Cecil and Amelia Woolf, 1969.

5931. Anghinetti, Paul W. "Alienation, Rebellion, and Myth:A Study of the Works of Nietzsche, Jung, Yeats, Camus, and Joyce." *DAI* 30(1969):1974A–75A(Fla. State).

5932. Archibald, Douglas N. "Yeats's Encounters:Observations on Literary Influence and Literary History." *NLH* 1:439–69.

5933. Barton, Ruth P. " 'The Natural Words in the Natural Order':A Study of W.B. Yeats's Verse Syntax." *DAI* 30: 5438A(Wis.).

5934. Bornstein, George. *Yeats and Shelley.* Chicago: U. of Chicago P.

5935. Brilli, Attilio. "Dionisio, Cristo e il 'fascio degli anni' in Yeats." *SUSFL* 42(1969):269–76.

5936. Broder, Peggy F. "Positive Folly:The Role of the Fool in the Works of W.B. Yeats." *DAI* 30:3902A(Case Western Reserve).

5937. Buckley, Vincent. "Yeats:The Great Comedian." *MHRev* 5(1968):77–89.

5938. Bushrui, Suheil Badi,tr. and introd. *Shai'un min Yeats:Shi'r, Nathr, Masrah [On Yeats:Poetry, Prose, Drama].* Lebanon: U. of Beirut, Dept. of Eng., 1969. [Trs. into Arabic, with introds. & a bibliog.]

5939. Byrd, Thomas L.,Jr., and Carolyn G. Kahn. "The Stone as a Symbol in the Lyric Poetry of W.B. Yeats." *XUS* 8,iii(1969):28–35.

5940. Carden, Mary. "The Few and the Many:An Examination of W.B. Yeats's Politics." *Studies* 58(1969):51–62.

5941. Cary, Meredith. "Yeats and Moore—An Autobiographical Conflict." *Éire* 4,iii(1969):94–109.

5942. Caswell, Robert W. "Yeats's Odd Swan at Coole." *Éire* 4,ii(1969):81–86.

5943. Comprone, Joseph J. "Unity of Being and W.B. Yeats' 'Under Ben Bulben'." *BSUF* 11,iii:41–49.

5944. Cowell, Raymond. *W.B. Yeats.* (LitP.) London: Evans, 1969.

* 5945. Denham, Robert D. "Yeats' 'A Bronze Head'." *Expl* 29:Item 14.

5946. Egleson, Janet F. "Christ and Cuchulain:Interrelated Archetypes of Divinity and Heroism in Yeats." *Éire* 4,i(1969): 76–85.

5947. Ellmann, Richard. *Eminent Domain:Yeats Among Wilde, Joyce, Pound, Eliot and Auden.* London and New York: Oxford U.P.

* 5948. Farrelly, James P. "Cuchulain:Yeats' 'Mental Traveller'." *HussR* 4:32–41.

5949. Finneran, Richard J. "A Critical Edition of William Butler Yeats's *John Sherman and Dhoya.*" *DAI* 30(1969): 318A(N.C., Chapel Hill).

5950. Fraser, G.S. "Yeats and the Ballad Style." *Shenandoah* 21,iii:177–94.

5951. Frayne, John P. "The Early Critical Prose of W.B. Yeats:Forty-One Reviews, Edited, with an Introduction and Notes." *DAI* 30:4449A–50A(Columbia).

5952. Frayne, John P.,ed. *Uncollected Prose by W.B. Yeats Vol. I:First Reviews and Articles, 1886–1896.* New York: Columbia U.P.

* 5953. Friedman, Barton R. "Under a Leprous Moon:Action and Image in *The King's Threshold.*" *ArQ* 26:39–53.

5954. Fullwood, Daphne. "The Influence on W.B. Yeats of Some French Poets (Mallarmé, Verlaine, Claudel)." *SoR* 6: 356–79.

* 5955. Gallagher, Michael P. "Yeats, Syntax, and the Self." *ArQ* 26:5–16.

5956. Garab, Arra M. "The Legacy of Yeats." *JML* 1:137–40. [Rev. art.]

5957. Gibbs, A.M. "The 'Rough Beasts' of Yeats and Shakespeare." *N&Q* 17:48–49.

5957a. Green, J.T. "Symbolism in Yeats's Poetry." *FHP* 4,iii(1969):11–23.

5958. Harris, Daniel A. "The Spreading Laurel Tree:Yeats and the Aristocratic Tradition." *DAI* 30(1969):1982A(Yale).

5959. Heller, Erich. "Als der Dichter Yeats zum ersten Mal Nietzsche las." [F 20]:116–31.

5960. —— "Yeats and Nietzsche:Reflections on a Poet's Marginal Notes." *Encounter* 33(Dec 1969):64–72.

5961. Hoffman, Daniel. *Barbarous Knowledge:Myth in the Poetry of Yeats, Graves, and Muir.* London: Oxford U.P.

5962. Hume, Martha H. "Yeats:Aphorist and Epigrammatist, a Study of *The Collected Poems.*" *DAI* 30:4454A(Colo.).

* 5963. Jain, Sushil K. "Indian Elements in the Poetry of W.B. Yeats with Special Reference to Yeats' Relationship with Chatterji and Tagore." *CLS* 7:82–96.

5964. John, Brian. "Yeats's 'Crazy Jane Reproved'." *Éire* 4,iv(1969):52–55.

5965. Johnson, Josephine. "Yeats:What Methods? An Approach to the Performance of the Plays." *Carrell* 10,ii(1969): 19–32.

5966. Kim, Myung Whan. "Mythopoetic Elements in the Later Plays of W.B. Yeats and the Noh." *DAI* 30:4949A(Ind.).

5967. —— "The Vision of the Spiritual World in Yeats's Plays and the Noh." *PhoenixK* 14:39–79.

5968. Levine, Bernard. *The Dissolving Image:The Spiritual-Esthetic Development of W.B. Yeats.* Detroit: Wayne State U.P.

5969. MacNeice, Louis. *The Poetry of W.B. Yeats.* Foreword by Richard Ellmann. New York and London: Oxford U.P., 1969.

5970. McHugh, Roger,ed. *Ah, Sweet Dancer:W.B.Yeats, Margot Ruddock:A Correspondence.* London: Macmillan.

5971. Melone, Thomas. "Architecture du Monde:Chinua Achebe et W.B. Yeats." *Conch* 2,i:44–52.

5972. Miller, Liam. "W.B. Yeats and Stage Design at the Abbey Theatre." *MHRev* 16:50–64. [Foll. by 20 pp. of illus.]

5973. Munro, John H. " 'Byzantium' or The Imperial Palace? — Ultimate Vision or Variable Compromise?" *Venture*(U. of Karachi) 5(1969):93–109.

5974. Oates, Joyce Carol. "Tragic Rites in Yeats' *A Full Moon in March.*" *AR* 29:547–60.

5975. O'Brien, James H. "Self vs. Soul in Yeats's *The Winding Stair.*" *Éire* 3,i(1968):23–39.

5976. O'Mahony, C.C.S. "High Days at the Abbey Theatre." *TLS* 11 Sept:999.

5977. Pacey, Desmond. "Children in the Poetry of Yeats." *DR* 50:233–48.

5978. Parkin, Andrew. " 'scraps of an ancient voice in me not mine . . .':Similarities in the Plays of Yeats and Beckett." *ArielE* 1,iii:49–58.

* 5979. Perloff, Marjorie. " 'Another Emblem There':Theme and Convention in Yeats's 'Coole Park and Ballyee, 1931'." *JEGP* 69:223–40.

5980. —— *Rhyme and Meaning in the Poetry of Yeats.* (De Proprietatibus Litterarum, Ser. pract. 5.) The Hague: Mouton.

5981. Pinciss, G.M. "A Dancer for Mr. Yeats." *ETJ* 21(1969):386–91. [Ninette de Valois.]

5982. Quivey, James R. "Yeats and the Epigram:A Study of Technique in the Four-Line Poems." *Discourse* 13:58–72.

5983. Rose, Marilyn G. "The Kindred Vistas of W.B. and Jack B. Yeats." *Éire* 5,i:67–79.

5984. Sena, Vinod. "W.B. Yeats and the Storm-Beaten Threshold." *DM* 8,iv–v:56–75.

* 5985. Shmiefsky, Marvel. "Yeats and Browning:The Shock of Recognition." *SEL* 10:701–21.

5986. Snoddy, Oliver. "Yeats and Irish in the Theatre." *Éire* 4,i(1969):39–45.

5987. Stallworthy, Jon. "W.B. Yeats and Wilfred Owen." *CritQ* 11(1969):199–214.

* 5988. Unger, Leonard. "Yeats and *Hamlet.*" *SoR* 6:698–709.

5989. Verhulst, Margaret M. "Myth and Symbol in the Plays of William Butler Yeats." *DAI* 30:3028A(Texas, Austin).

5989a. Vordtriede, Werner. "William Butler Yeats:Urbild und Gegenwart." *NDH* 124(1969):61–80.

5990. Watanabe, Junko. "The Symbolism of W.B. Yeats:A Study of His Later Poems." [F 14]:41–66.

See also 1471, 3936, 4517, 4926, 5160, 5367, 5428, 5623, 5656, 5775.

AMERICAN LITERATURE†

I. GENERAL

Bibliography. *See* 1193.
General and Miscellaneous. *5991. Adams, Thomas R. "*Bibliotheca Americana*:A Merry Maze of Changing Concepts." *PBSA* 63(1969):247–60.

5992. Asselineau, Roger. "Ishmael—or the Theme of Solitude in American Literature," 107–19 in *USA in Focus:Recent Re-Interpretations.* (Pubs. of the Nordic Assn. for Amer. Studies 2.) Ed. Sigmund Skard. Oslo/Bergen/Tromsø: Universitets-

† *Festschriften* and Other Analyzed Collections are listed in the first division of this Bibliography, and have been assigned Item numbers 1–95. "F" numbers in brackets following a title refer to these items.

forlaget, 1966.

5993. Beers, Paul B.,comp. *The Pennsylvania Sampler:A Biography of the Keystone State and Its People.* Harrisburg, Pa.: Stackpole. [Rptd. and new essays on Conrad Richter, Dreiser, O'Hara, Pa. in fiction, et al.]

5994. Bell, Bernard. "Cashing in on Blackness." *MR* 11: 187–92.

5995. Berry, Thomas E.,ed. *Readings in American Criticism.* With Introd. New York: Odyssey. [Prev. pub. essays.]

* 5996. Bier, Jesse. "The Romantic Coordinates of American Literature." *BuR* 18,ii:16–33.

5997. Brumm, Ursula. *American Thought and Religious Typology.* Tr. by John Hooglund of *Die religiöse Typologie im amerikanischen Denken.* New Brunswick, N.J.: Rutgers U.P.

5998. Brüning, Eberhard. "Probleme der Rezeption amerikanischer Literatur in der DDR." *WB* 16(Heft 4):175–86.

5999. Cairns, William B. *A History of American Literature.* Introd. James A. Sappenfield. New York: Johnson Repr., 1969.

6000. Cargill, Oscar. "Gift to the World." [F 63]:204–13. [That is, from America.]

6001. Castagna, Edwin. "A Librarian Looks at American Publishing." [F 25]:75–88.

6002. Cawelti, John G. "Prolegomena to the Western." *WAL* 4:259–71.

6003. Clements, Clyde C.,Jr. "Black Studies for White Students." *NALF* 4:9–11.

6004. Cowley, Malcolm. *A Many-Windowed House:Collected Essays on American Writers and American Writing.* Ed. and Introd. by Henry D. Piper. Carbondale: So. Ill. U.P. [Rptd. crit.]

6005. Fiedler, Leslie A. "The Dream of the New." [F 63]:19–27.

6006. Filler, Louis. "Machiavelli for the Millions:Some Notes on Power Structures." [F 63]:28–44. [With ref. to the "American Dream."]

6007. Finestone, Harry. "Themes, Topics, and Criticism." [F 65]:300–12.

6008. Flak, Micheline. "Léon Bazalgette, découvreur de la littérature américaine." *Europe* 483–84(1969):180–87.

6009. Foner, Philip S. "Marx's *Capital* in the United States." *Science and Society* 31(1967):461–66.

6010. Frank, Mortimer H. "Music in American Literary History:A Survey of the Significance of Music in the Writings of Eight American Literary Figures." *DAI* 30:4943A–44A(N.Y.U.). [Poe, Whitman, Lanier, Clemens, Huneker, Mencken, Pound, E. Wilson.]

6011. Gayle, Addison,Jr. "Cultural Hegemony:The Southern Writer and American Letters." *Amistad* 1:3–24.

6012. Geismar, Maxwell. "The Shifting Illusion:Dream and Fact." [F 63]:45–57. [The "American Dream."]

6013. Green, Claud B. "American Studies in the South Pacific." *GaR* 24:54–63. [Rev. art.]

6014. Greene, Theodore P. *America's Heroes:The Changing Models of Success in American Magazines.* New York: Oxford U.P.

6015. Hakac, John. "Southwestern Regional Material in a Literature Class." *WR* 7,i:12–18.

6016. Heilman, Robert B. "The Dream Metaphor:Some Ramifications." [F 63]:1–18. [In the "American Dream."]

6017. Inge, M. Thomas. "Miguel de Unamuno's *Canciones* on American Literature:Translated with Commentary." *ArlQ* 2, ii(1969):83–97.

6018. Inge, M. Thomas,ed. *Agrarianism in American Literature.* New York: Odyssey, 1969. [Anthol. of lit. and hist. documents, with comment.]

6019. James, Stuart B. "Western American Space and the Human Imagination." *WHR* 24:147–55.

6020. Jody, Marilyn. "Alaska in the American Literary Imagination:A Literary History of Frontier Alaska with a Bibliographical Guide to the Study of Alaskan Literature." *DAI* 30:5411A(Ind.).

6021. Johnson, Ellwood G. "Some Versions of Individualism in American Literature and Thought." *DAI* 30(1969):2486A–87A(U. of Wash.). [Edwards, Hawthorne, Emerson, Twain, Dos Passos, W. James, Faulkner.]

6022. Kaufmann, Walter. "The Reception of Existentialism in the United States." *Salmagundi* 10–11(1969-70):69–96.

6023. Kimball, W. J. "Naturalism in Some Representative American Novelists." *Venture*(U. of Karachi) 5(1969):81–92.

6024. Krishnamurthi, M.G.,ed. "Point Counterpoint:An Exchange on American Studies in India." *IJAS* 1,i(1969):73–89. [Comments by William Mulder, Richard Tyner, et al.]

6025. Kwiat, Joseph J., and Gerhard Weiss. "Responses of German Men of Letters to American Literature, 1945-1955." [F 62]:30–44.

6026. Lacy, Dan. "Major Trends in American Book Publishing." [F 25]:1–15.

6027. Leverenz, Lanqmuir D. "A Psychoanalysis of American

Literature." *DAI* 31:763A(Calif., Berkeley).

6028. Lewis, Hanna B. "Hofmannsthal and America." [F 28]:131–41.

6029. Lieber, Todd M. "The Continuing Encounter:Studies of the American Romantic Hero." *DAI* 30:3911A(Case Western Reserve).

6030. Lubbers, Klaus. *Einführung in das Studium der Amerikanistik.* Tübingen: Niemeyer.

6031. MacDougall, Mary A., Francelia Butler, and Wesley McClure. "The Reaction of Polish Students to American Literature." *PolR* 15,ii:81–94. [Results of a survey.]

6032. Madison, Charles. "Current Trends in American Publishing." [F 25]:16–28.

6033. Marovitz, Stanford E. "The Literature Survey:Its Definition and Purpose." *UCQ* 15,iv:18–26. [Amer. lit.]

6034. Marx, Leo. "American Studies:A Defense of an Unscientific Method." *NLH* 1(1969):75–90.

6035. Matthews, F.H. "The Revolt Against Americanism: Cultural Pluralism and Cultural Relativism as an Ideology of Liberation." *CRevAS* 1:4–31.

6036. Miller, James E.,Jr. "The 'Classic' American Writers and Radicalized Curriculum." *CE* 31:565–70.

6037. Morley, Felix. "Not a Great Divide." *ModA* 14:57–64.

6038. Morsberger, Robert E. "Segregated Surveys:American Literature." *NALF* 4:3–8.

6039. North, Joseph. "Why a USA–USSR Cultural Exchange? It's Dialogue or Disaster." *AmD* 5,ii(1968–69):3–5.

6040. Oras, Ants. "New York:The Be-All and the End-All?" *SR* 78:156–63. [Rev. art. on Janssens, *The American Literary Review* (1968).]

6041. Pavese, Cesare. *American Literature:Essays and Opinions.* Tr. and with Introd. by Edwin Fussell. Berkeley: U. of Calif. P. [Rptd. essays and revs.; incl. sec. on Eng. authors.]

6042. Pearce, Roy H. "La critica americana e la cultura americana." *SCr* 3(1969):167–86.

6043. Perosa, Sergio. "Romanzieri americani a Venezia." [F 61]:379–401. [Cooper, Hawthorne, Howells, H. James, T.S. Fay, *inter alia.*]

6044. Pilkington, William T.,Jr. "My Blood's Country:Studies in Southwestern Literature." *DAI* 30:4998A–99A(Texas Christian).

6045. Reynolds, Albert E.,II. "The California Gold Rush as a Basis for Literature." [F 62]:61–80.

6046. Rossi, Joseph. "Il mito americano nel pensiero politico del Risorgimento." [F 61]:241–60.

6047. Rubel, Warren. "The American Dream:Antique at Noon." *Cresset*(Valparaiso U.) 33,v:11–15.

6048. Rubin, Louis D.,Jr. "Southern Literature:A Piedmont Art." *MissQ* 23:1–16.

6049. Salomone, A. William. "Il Risorgimento nella storiografia americana." [F 61]:69–117.

6050. Sayre, Robert F. "American Myths of Utopia." *CE* 31:613–23.

6051. Schossberger, Emily. "The American University Press." [F 25]:95–105.

6052. Skillin, Glenn B. *The Achievement of William Van O'Connor:A Checklist of Publications and an Appreciation.* With Introd. Syracuse, N.Y.: George Arents Research Lib., Syracuse U., 1969.

6053. Smith, Chard P. "Plain Humor:New England Style." *NEQ* 43:465–72.

6054. Tebbel, John. *The American Magazine:A Compact History.* New York: Hawthorn, 1969.

6055. *The American Writer in England:An Exhibition Arranged in Honor of the Sesquicentennial of the University of Virginia.* With a Foreword by Gordon N. Ray and an Introd. by C. Waller Barrett. Charlottesville: U.P. of Va., 1969. [Illus.]

6056. Weber, Brom,ed. *The Art of American Humor:An Anthology.* Foreword Lewis Leary. With Notes. New York: Apollo. [Orig. pub. 1962 under title *An Anthology of American Humor.*]

6057. Whitehill, Walter M. "Local History in the United States." *TLS* 13 Nov:1331–33.

6058. Wolfe, Don M. *The Image of Man in America.* 2d ed.

New York: Crowell. [Essays on intellect. hist. and lit. from Jefferson to present.]

See also 204, 572, 622, 1082, 1207, 1222, 1247.

Serial Bibliographies Current. 6060. "1968 Bibliography of Mississippi Writers." *NMW* 2:115–25.

6061. Bullen, John S.,et al. "Annual Bibliography of Studies in Western American Literature." *WAL* 4:321–30.

6062. King, Kimball,et al. "Articles on American Literature Appearing in Current Periodicals." *AL* 41:[631]–39; 42:[132]–38, [280]–87,[439]–56.

6063. King, Kimball,et al.,comps. "Research in Progress." *AL* 41:[630]; 42:[131],[278]–79,[435]–38.

6064. Koster, Donald N.,et al.,comps. "Articles in American Studies, 1969." *AQ* 22:[328]–98. [Sel. bibliog. incl. folklore, lang., lit., psychiatry and psychol.]

6065. Lyon, Thomas J.,ed. "Research in Western American Literature." *WAL* 4:331–34.

6065a. Reeves, Paschal,ed. "A Checklist of Scholarship on Southern Literature for 1969." *MissQ* 23:181–217.

6066. Vander Ven, Tom, and John H. Wrenn,comps. "American Studies Dissertations, 1969–70." *AQ* 22: [399]–411.

Special Bibliographies, Check Lists, and Dictionaries. 6067. "American Studies in India:Selected Articles Appearing in Indian Periodicals During 1966–1967." *IJAS* 1,i(1969):143–52.

* 6068. Belknap, George N. "Addenda to Belknap, Oregon Imprints." *PBSA* 64:213–34.

6069. Bristol, Roger P. *Supplement to Charles Evans'* American Bibliography. Charlottesville: U.P. of Va.

6070. Corrigan, Robert. "Bibliography of Afro-American Fiction:1853–1970." *SBL* 1,ii:51–86.

6071. DeGruson, Gene,comp. *Kansas Authors of Best Sellers: A Bibliography of the Works of Martin and Osa Johnson, Margaret Hill Carpenter, Charles M. Sheldon, and Harold Bell Wright.* Pittsburg: Kan. State College, Porter Lib.

6072. "Doctoral Dissertations [Completed and in Progress] on American Subjects by Indian Scholars." *IJAS* 1,i(1969):123–30.

6073. "Doctoral Dissertations in American Studies Completed in the U.S. in 1966 (Compiled from *Dissertation Abstracts*)." *IJAS* 1,i(1969):131–41.

6074. Howard University Library. *Dictionary Catalog of the Arthur B. Spingarn Collection of Negro Authors.* 2 vols. Boston: G.K. Hall. [Photo repr. of catalog card index.]

6075. Johnson, Richard C. "Addendum to Harrisse:Jakob Stoppel." *PBSA* 64:334–36.

6076. Johnson, Robert O. *An Index to Literature in* The New Yorker, *Volumes I-XV, 1925–1940.* Metuchen, N.J.: Scarecrow, 1969.

6077. —— *An Index to Literature in* The New Yorker, *Volumes XVI-XXX, 1940–1955.* Metuchen, N.J.: Scarecrow.

6078. Jones, Lawrence W. "Canadian Graduate Studies in American Literature:A Bibliography of Theses and Dissertations, 1921–1968." *CRevAS* 1:116–29.

6079. Lada-Mocarski, Valerian. *A Bibliography of Books on Alaska Published Before 1868.* New Haven: Yale U.P., 1969.

6080. Leary, Lewis, assisted by Carolyn Bartholet, and Catharine Roth,eds. *Articles on American Literature 1950–1969.* Durham, N.C.: Duke U.P.

6081. Meaney, N.K.,ed. and introd. *A Survey of Publications in American Studies by Australian and New Zealand Scholars.* Australia: Australian and New Zealand Amer. Studies Assn.

6082. Powell, Donald M.,comp. "Current Arizona Bibliography." *ArQ* 26:76–81,265–68.

6083. Stratman, Carl J.,C.S.V. *American Theatrical Periodicals, 1798–1967:A Bibliographical Guide.* Durham, N.C.: Duke U.P.

See also 459, 737, 1199.

Afro-American. 6084. Bayliss, John F.,ed. *Black Slave Narratives.* New York: Collier.

6085. Black, Michael. "Black Literature:Three Critical Works." *GaR* 24:46–53. [On Edward Margolies' *Native Sons*, Robert Bone's *The Negro Novel in America*, and David Littlejohn's *Black on White*.]

6086. Brown, Lloyd W. "Beneath the North Star:The Canadian Image in Black Literature." *DR* 50:317–29.

6087. Chapman, Abraham. "The Black American Contribution to Literature," 361–97 in J.S. Roucek and T. Kiernan,eds., *The Negro Impact on Western Civilization.* New York: Philosophical Lib. [Rev. version of AC's Introd. to *Black Voices* (New York, 1968).]

6088. Davis, Charles T., and Daniel Walden,eds. *On Being Black:Writings by Afro-Americans from Frederick Douglass to the Present.* Greenwich, Conn.: Fawcett. [Introd., 13–39.]

* 6089. Farrison, W. Edward. "What American Negro Literature Exists and Who Should Teach It?" *CLAJ* 13:374–81.

* 6090. Gross, Seymour L. "Literature and the Cultural History of the Negro." *SLJ* 2,ii:148–55.

6091. Hemenway, Robert,ed. *The Black Novelist.* (Merrill Literary Texts.) Columbus, Ohio: Charles E. Merrill. [On C. Chesnutt, R. Wright, J. Baldwin, J. Toomer, et al.]

* 6092. Jones, Harry L. "Black Humor and the American Way of Life." *SNL* 7(1969):1–4.

* 6093. Liebman, Arthur. "Patterns and Themes in Afro-American Literature." *Eng. Record* 20,iii:2–12.

* 6094. Mabbutt, Fred R. "The Bitter Years of Slavery:A Response to the Arguments of John Hope Franklin." *ForumH* 8,iii:13–18.

6095. Sellin, Eric. "Neo-African and Afro-American Literatures." *JML* 1:249–53. [Rev. art.]

6096. Turner, Darwin T. "The Teaching of Afro-American Literature." *CE* 31:666–70.

6097. —— "The Teaching of Literature by Afro-American Writers." [F 35]:73–98.

Drama and Theater. 6098. Meserve, Walter J. "Drama." [F 65]:260–72.

Folklore. 6099. Cheney, Thomas E.,ed. *Mormon Songs From the Rocky Mountains:A Compilation of Mormon Folksong.* Austin: U. of Texas P., 1968.

6100. Flanagan, John T. "Folklore." [F 65]:273–99.

6101. Fowke, Edith. *Lumbering Songs From the Northern Woods.* Tunes Transcribed by Norman Cazden. Austin: U. of Texas P.

Poetry. 6102. Berbrich, Joan D.,ed. *Sounds and Sweet Airs:The Poetry of Long Island.* With Introd. Port Washington, N.Y.: Kennikat. [Anthol.]

6103. Donahue, Jane P. " 'Neglected Muse':Neoclassical Forms and Attitudes in American Poetry From the Connecticut Wits to James Russell Lowell." *DAI* 31:354A(Brown).

6104. Griffith, John W. "Studies in American Narrative Historical Poetry." *DAI* 30:3459A(Ore.).

6105. Haslam, Gerald. "American Indians:Poets of the Cosmos." *WAL* 5:15–29.

6106. Robinson, William H.,ed. *Early Black American Poets.* Dubuque, Iowa: Wm. C. Brown, 1969. [29 poets, 1746–1900.]

See also 1486, 10186.

Prose Fiction. 6107. Barsness, John. "Creativity Through Hatred—and a Few Thoughts on the Western Novel." *WR* 6,ii(1969):12–17.

6108. Bowen, James K., and Richard Van Der Beets,eds. *American Short Fiction:Readings and Criticism.* With Introd. Foreword Lewis Leary. Indianapolis: Bobbs-Merrill. [Anthol.]

6109. Bush, Lewis M. "The Genesis of the American Psychological Novel." *DAI* 31:352A(Md.).

6110. Garaty, John A. "A Century of American Realism." *AH* 21(June):[12]–15,86–90. [Interview of Alfred Kazin.]

6111. Knox, George. "In Search of the Great American Novel." *WR* 5,i(1968):64–77.

6112. Malin, Irving. "The Compulsive Design." [F 63]:58–75. [An "American Nightmare" in fiction from Irving to Hemingway.]

6113. Nicolaisen, Peter. "Neuere Literatur sum amerikanischen Roman." *LWU* 2(1969):47–63.

6114. Perkins, George,ed. *The Theory of the American Novel.* With Introd. New York: Holt, Rinehart and Winston. [Anthol. of novelists' views on art of novel.]

6115. Phy, Allene S. "The Representation of Christ in Popular American Fiction." *DAI* 30:4953A(Geo. Peabody Coll. for Teachers).

6116. Popescu, Petru. "Picaresc şi aventură în ficţiunea

americană." *ViR* 23,vi:95–99.

6117. Sears, Donald A., and Margaret Bourland. "Journalism Makes the Style." *JQ* 47:504–09.

6118. Smith, F. Lannom. "Man and Minister in Recent American Fiction." *DAI* 30(1969):1151A(Pa.).

6119. Steensma, Robert C. " 'Stay Right There and Toughy It Out':The American Homesteader as Autobiographer." *WR*

6,i(1969):10–18.

6120. Stineback, David C. "Social Change and Nostalgia in Ten American Novels." *DAI* 31:1242A–43A(Yale). [*The Pioneers, The House of Seven Gables, Democracy, The Bostonians, The House of Mirth, The Professor's House, The Sheltered Life, The Fathers, The Hamlet, These Thousand Hills.*]

See also 938, 1490, 6070.

II. SEVENTEENTH AND EIGHTEENTH CENTURIES

Bibliography. 6121. Gidez, Richard B., assisted by A. Barry Cameron. "Seventeenth-Century Americana." *SCN* 27(1969): 71–75.

6122. Hildeburn, Charles R. *Sketches of Printers and Printing in Colonial New York.* Illus. Detroit: Gale. [Repr. of 1895 ed.]

6123. Mann, Charles. "A Hitherto Unseen Virginia Imprint: An Explanatory Note." *Serif* 7,i:32–33. [Evans 22632.]

6124. Neiman, Fraser,introd. *The Henley-Horrocks Inventory.* (BBSP 1.) With Introd. Williamsburg, Va.: The Botetourt Bibliog. Soc. and the Earl Gregg Swem Lib., 1968. [18th cent. Va. lib.; 12-p. pamphlet.]

6125. Rink, Evald. *Printing in Delaware, 1761–1800.* Wilmington: Eleutherian Mills Hist. Lib., 1969.

6126. Shipton, Clifford K., and James E. Mooney. *The National Index of American Imprints Through 1800–The Short-Title Evans.* 2 vols. Barre, Mass.: Barre Pub. Co..

See also 455, 6069.

General and Miscellaneous. *6127. Benton, Robert M. "An Annotated Check List of Puritan Sermons Published in America before 1700." *BNYPL* 74:286–337.

6128. Dallett, Francis J. "A Colonial Binding and Engraving Discovery:The College [of New Jersey] Ledger of 1769." *PULC* 31:122–28. [Illus.]

6129. Davis, Richard B. "Literature to 1800." [F 65]:121–41.

* 6130. —— "The Intellectual Golden Age in the Colonial Chesapeake Bay Country." *VMHB* 78:[131]–43.

* 6131. Davis, Thomas M. "The Exegetical Traditions of Puritan Typology." *EAL* 5,i,pt.1:11–50.

6132. Demos, John. *A Little Commonwealth:Family Life in Plymouth Colony.* New York: Oxford U.P.

6133. —— "Underlying Themes in the Witchcraft of Seventeenth-Century New England." *Amer. Hist. Rev.* 75: 1311–26.

6134. Dorenkamp, John H. "The New England Puritans and the Name of God." *PAAS* 80:67–70.

6135. Edwards, Owen D. "The American Image of Ireland:A Study of Its Early Phases." [F 64]:199–282. [Incl. discussion of Franklin, Jefferson,et al.]

6136. Garrison, Joseph M.,Jr. "Teaching Early American Literature:Some Suggestions." *CE* 31:487–97.

6137. Haugh, Georgia C. "Rivington's *Songs, Naval and Military.*" *Serif* 7,ii:30–33.

6138. Jennings, John M. *The Library of The College of William and Mary in Virginia, 1693–1793.* Charlottesville: U.P. of Va., 1968.

6139. Kolodny, Annette. "The Pastoral Impulse in American Writing, 1590–1850:A Psychological Approach." *DAI* 31:731A (Calif., Berkeley).

6140. Mastellone, Salvo. "La Costituzione degli Stati Uniti d'America e gli uomini del Risorgimento." [F 61]:261–94.

6141. May, Henry F. "The Problem of the American Enlightenment." *NLH* 1:201–14.

6142. Modlin, Charles E. "Political Satire in America, 1789–1801." *DAI* 30:3470A(Tenn.).

6143. Parker, Peter J. "Asbury Dickens, Bookseller, 1789–1801, or, The Brief Career of a Careless Youth." *PMHB* 94:464–83.

6144. Parrington, Vernon L.,ed. *The Connecticut Wits.* With Introd. Foreword Kenneth Silverman. New York: Crowell, 1969. [Anthol.]

6145. Pope, Robert G. *The Half-Way Covenant:Church Membership in Puritan New England.* Princeton, N.J.: Princeton U.P., 1969.

6146. Roddey, Gloria J. "The Metaphor of Counsel:A Shift From Objective Realism to Psychological Subjectivism in the Conceptual Cosmology of Puritanism." *DAI* 31:367A–68A(Ky.).

6147. Rosenmeier, Jesper. "New England's Perfection:The Image of Adam and the Image of Christ in the Antinomian Crisis 1634 to 1638." *WMQ* 27:435–59.

6148. Rutman, Darrett B. *American Puritanism:Faith and Practice.* Philadelphia: J.B. Lippincott.

6149. Seaver, Paul S. *The Puritan Lectureships:The Politics of Religious Dissent, 1560–1662.* Stanford, Calif.: Stanford U.P.

6150. Strohecker, Edwin C. "American Juvenile Literary Periodicals, 1789–1826." *DAI* 30:3964A(Mich.).

6151. Tresp, Lothar L. "Early Negro Baptisms in Colonial Georgia by the Salzburgers at Ebenezer." [F 62]:159–70. [Incl. entries from the *Diary* of Johann Martin Bolzius.]

See also 1054, 2067, 2811, 3652, 3747, 6247, 7160.

Criticism. *See* 3735.

Drama and Theater. 6152. Curtis, Julia. "John Joseph Stephen Leger Sollee and the Charleston Theatre." *ETJ* 21(1969):285–98.

See also 6263.

Poetry. 6153. Lemay, J.A. Leo. "A Calendar of American Poetry in the Colonial Newspapers and Magazines and in the Major English Magazines Through 1765:Part Two:1740 Through 1759." *PAAS* 80:71–222.

6154. —— "A Calendar of American Poetry in the Colonial Newspapers and Magazines and in the Major English Magazines Through 1765. Part One:Through 1739." *PAAS* 79(1969): 291–392. [Repr. as sep. monograph by the Amer. Antiq. Soc., Worcester, Mass., 1970.]

6155. Nagy, N. Christoph de. "Tendenzen in der frühen amerikanischen Lyrik." [F 52]:267–76.

Prose Fiction. *6156. Kable, William S. "Addenda to Wright:Mancur, Pise, Tuthill, Weld." *PBSA* 63(1969):294.

6157. Pridgeon, Charles T.,Jr. "Insanity in American Fiction from Charles Brockden Brown to Oliver Wendell Holmes." *DAI* 31:1766A–67A(Duke).

Allen, E. 6158. Ditsky, John. "The Yankee Insolence of Ethan Allen." *CRevAS* 1:32–38. [In the *Narrative.*]

Barlow. *6159. Ball, Kenneth R. "American Nationalism and Esthetics in Joel Barlow's Unpublished 'Diary—1788'." *TSL* 15:49–60.

Bartram, W. 6160. Sullivan, William J. "Towards Romanticism:A Study of William Bartram." *DAI* 30:3959A(Utah).

Belknap, J. 6161. Belknap, J. *The Foresters, An American Tale (1792).* Introd. Lewis A. Turlish. Gainesville, Fla.: SF&R, 1969.

Brackenridge. 6162. Kennedy, W. Benjamin. "Hugh Henry Brackenridge:Thoughts and Acts of a Modern Democrat." *WGCR* 2,ii(1969):26–38.

Bradford. *6163. Major, Minor W. "William Bradford Versus Thomas Morton." *EAL* 5,ii:1–13.

Bradstreet. 6164. Contenti, Alessandra. "Anne Bradstreet, il Petrarchismo e il 'Plain Style'." *SA* 14(1968):7–27.

6165. Hutchinson, Robert,ed. *Poems of Anne Bradstreet.* With Introd. New York: Dover, 1969.

6166. Kehler, Dorothea. "Anne Bradstreet and Spenser." *AN&Q* 8:135.

* 6167. Laughlin, Rosemary M. "Anne Bradstreet:Poet in Search of Form." *AL* 42:[1]–17.

6168. Rosenfeld, Alvin H. "Anne Bradstreet's 'Contemplations':Patterns of Form and Meaning." *NEQ* 43:79–96.

Branagan. *6169. Johnson, Richard C. "Addendum to Sabin, Shaw-Shoemaker, and Wegelin:Thomas Branagan." *PBSA* 64: 205–06.

Brown, C.B. *6170. Brancaccio, Patrick. "Studied Ambiguities:*Arthur Mervyn* and the Problem of the Unreliable Narrator." *L* 42:[18]–27.

6171. Greiner, Donald J. "Brown's Use of the Narrator in *Vieland*:An Indirect Plea for the Acceptance of Fiction." *CLAJ* 3(1969):131–36.

6172. Justus, James H. "Arthur Mervyn, American." *AL* 2:[304]–24.

6173. Schulz, Max F. "Brockden Brown:An Early Casualty of the American Experience." [F 62]:81–90.
See also 6447.

Brown, W.H. 6174. Kable, William S.,ed. *The Power of Sympathy*. With Introd. Columbus: Ohio State U.P., 1969.

Byrd. *6175. Marambaud, Pierre. "William Byrd of Westover:Cavalier, Diarist, and Chronicler." *VMHB* 78:[144]–83.

Cooke. *6176. Cohen, Edward H. "The 'Second Edition' of *The Sot-Weed Factor*." *AL* 42:[289]–303.

Crèvecoeur. 6177. Babuscio, Jack. "Crèvecoeur in Charles Town:The Negro in the Cage." *JHS* 2(1969-70):283–86.

6178. Mohr, James C. "Calculated Disillusionment: Crèvecoeur's *Letters* Reconsidered." *SAQ* 69:[354]–63.

6179. Philbrick, Thomas. *St. John de Crèvecoeur*. (TUSAS 54.) New York: Twayne. [Crit.]

6180. Rapping, Elayne A. "Harmonic Patchwork:The Art of Hector St. John de Crèvecoeur." *DAI* 31:1768A(Pittsburgh). *See also* 6192.

Dwight. *6181. Volkomer, Walter E. "Timothy Dwight and New England Federalism." *ConnR* 3,ii:72–82.

6182. Whitford, Kathryn and Philip. "Timothy Dwight's Place in Eighteenth-Century American Science." *PAPS* 114: 60–71.

Edwards. *6183. Buckingham, Willis J. "Stylistic Artistry in the Sermons of Jonathan Edwards." *PLL* 6:136–51.

6184. Bushman, Richard L. "Jonathan Edwards as Great Man:Identity, Conversion, and Leadership in the Great Awakening." *Soundings* 52(1969):15–46.

* 6185. Cowan, James C. "Jonathan Edwards' Sermon Style: The Future Punishment of the Wicked Unavoidable and Intolerable'." *SCB* 29(1969):119–22.

6186. Grabo, Norman S. "Jonathan Edwards' *Personal Narrative*:Dynamic Stasis." *LWU* 2(1969):141–48.

6187. Laskowsky, Henry J. "Jonathan Edwards:A Puritan Philosopher of Science." *ConnR* 4,i:33–41.

* 6188. Lowance, Mason I.,Jr. "Images or Shadows of Divine Things:The Typology of Jonathan Edwards." *EAL* 5,i,pt.1: 41–81.

6189. Nagy, Paul J. "Jonathan Edwards and the Metaphysics of Consent." *Person* 51:434–46.

6190. Opie, John,ed. *Jonathan Edwards and the Enlightenment*. With Introd. Boston: D.C. Heath, 1969. [Rptd. essays by and about E.]

6191. Richmond, Arthur A.,III. "Jonathan Edwards,Jr., and Union College." *Union Coll.* (N.Y.) *Symposium* 8,iv:20–29. [JE's son becomes president of Union Coll., 1799. Illus.]

Franklin. 6192. Agee, William H. "Franklin and Crèvecoeur: Individualism and the American Dream in the Eighteenth Century." *DAI* 31:380A(Minn.).

6193. Currey, Cecil B. *Road to Revolution:Benjamin Franklin in England:1765–1775*. Garden City, N.Y.:Doubleday (Anchor), 1968.

6194. Kushen, Betty S. "Benjamin Franklin and His Biographers:A Critical Study." *DAI* 30:3946A–47A(N.Y.U.).

6195. Labaree, Leonard W.,ed. *The Papers of Benjamin Franklin*. Vol. xiv:*1 Jan. 1767–31 Dec. 1767*. New Haven: Yale U.P.

* 6196. Miller, C. William. "Benjamin Franklin's Way to Wealth." *PBSA* 63(1969):231–46.

6197. Sappenfield, James A. "*The Autobiography of Benjamin Franklin*:The Structure of Success." *Wisconsin Studies in Lit.* 5(1969):90–99.

6198. Wright, Esmond,ed. *Benjamin Franklin:A Profile*. New York: Hill and Wang. [Rptd. essays.]
See also 7903.

Freneau. *6199. Andrews, William L. "Goldsmith and Freneau in 'The American Village'." *EAL* 5,ii:14–23.

6200. Eckert, Edward K. "Philip Freneau:New Jersey's Poet as Propagandist." *New Jersey Hist.* 88:25–42.

6201. Marsh, Philip. *Freneau's Published Prose:A Bibliography*. Metuchen, N.J.: Scarecrow.

Hammon. 6202. Ransom, Stanley A.,Jr.,ed. *America's First Negro Poet:The Complete Works of Jupiter Hammon of Long Island*. (Empire State Hist. Pubs. Ser. 82.) Biog. Sketch of Jupiter Hammon by Oscar Wegelin. Crit. Anal. of the Works of Jupiter Hammon by Vernon Loggins. Port Washington, N.Y.: Kennikat. [Biog. sketch & crit. anal. are reprs.]

Higginson. 6203. Gildrie, Richard P. "Francis Higginson's New World Vision." *EIHC* 106:182–89.

Hooker, T. 6204. Allen, Ward. "Hooker and the Utopians." *ES* 51:37–39.

Logan. *6205. Lokken, Roy N. "The Social Thought of James Logan." *WMQ* 27:68–69.

Low. *6206. Leary, Lewis. "Samuel Low:New York's First Poet." *BNYPL* 74:468–80.

Mather, C. *6207. Andrews, William D. "The Printed Funeral Sermons of Cotton Mather." *EAL* 5,ii:24–44.

6208. Bercovitch, Sacvan. " 'Delightful Examples of Surprising Prosperity':Cotton Mather and the American Success Story." *ES* 51:40–43.

6209. Isani, Mukhtar A. "Cotton Mather and the Orient." *NEQ* 43:46–58.

6210. Weeks, Louis,III. "Cotton Mather and the Quakers." *QH* 59,i:24–33.

Mather, I. 6211. Nelsen, Anne Kusener. "King Philip's War and the Hubbard-Mather Rivalry." *WMQ* 27:615–29.

Mather, R. 6212. Burg, B. Richard. "The Record of an Early Seventeenth Century Atlantic Crossing." *HussR* 4:72–77. [Richard Mather's *Journal* (1635).]

Paine, R.T. 6213. Leary, Lewis. "The First Published Poem of Thomas Paine of Boston:A Note on the Generation Gap in 1786." *NEQ* 43:130–34.

Paine, T. *See* 7108.

Sewall, S. 6214. Arner, Robert D. "Plum Island Revisited: One Version of the Pastoral." *SCN* 27(1969):58–61.

Taylor, E. 6215. Akiyama, Ken. "Edward Taylor no shi to Topology." *EigoS* 114(1968):507-09. [T's poems and typology.]

6216. Alexis, Gerhard T. "A Keen Nose for Taylor's Syntax." *EAL* 4,iii:97–101.

6217. Allen, Judson B. "Edward Taylor's Catholic Wasp: Exegetical Convention in 'Upon a Spider Catching a Fly'." *ELN* 7:257–60.

* 6218. Bales, Kent, and William J. Aull. "Touching Taylor Overly:A Note on 'Meditation Six'." *EAL* 5,ii:57–58.

* 6219. Combellack, C.R.B. "Taylor's 'Upon Wedlock, and Death of Children'." *Expl* 29:Item 12.

6220 *EAL* 4,iii. Spec. Taylor No. [Karl Keller, "The Example of Edward Taylor," 5–26; Thomas M. Davis, "Edward Taylor and the Traditions of Puritan Typology," 27–47; Sargent Bush,Jr., "Paradox, Puritanism, and Taylor's *God's Determinations*," 48–66; Donald Junkins, "Edward Taylor's Creative Process," 67–78; Kenneth R. Ball, "Rhetoric in Edward Taylor's *Preparatory Meditations*," 79–88; James T. Callow, "Edward Taylor Obeys Saint Paul," 89–96; Gerhard T. Alexis, "A Keen Nose for Taylor's Syntax," 97–101; Kathy Siebel and Thomas M. Davis, "Edward Taylor and the Cleansing of *Aqua Vitae*," 102–09; Charles W. Mignon, "A Principle of Order in Edward Taylor's *Preparatory Meditations*," 110–16; Kenneth A. Requa and Karl Keller, "Additions to the Edward Taylor Checklist," 117–19.]

6221. Grabo, Norman S. "*God's Determinations*:Touching Taylor's Critics." *SCN* 28:22–24.

6222. Keller, Karl. "The Rev. Mr. Edward Taylor's Bawdry." *NEQ* 43:382–406.

* 6223. ——— " 'The World Slickt Up In Types':Edward Taylor As a Version of Emerson." *EAL* 5,i,pt.1:124–40.

* 6224. Reiter, Robert. "Poetry and Typology:Edward Taylor's *Preparatory Mediations*, Second Series, Numbers 1–30." *EAL* 5,i,pt.1:111–23.

* 6225. Scheick, William J. "A Viper's Nest, the Featherbed of Faith:Edward Taylor on the Will." *EAL* 5,ii:45–56.

6226. —— "The Will and the Word:The Experience of Conversion in the Poetry of Edward Taylor." *DAI* 30:2979A–80A(Ill.).

6227. Sharma, Mohan Lal. "Of Spinning, Weaving, and Mystical Poetry:The Fine Yarn of Taylor, Indian Yogis, and Persian Sufis." *Mahfil* 6,ii–iii:51–61.

6228. Smith, Roy H. "A Study of the Platonic Heritage of Love in the Poetry of Edward Taylor." *DAI* 30:4466A(Bowling Green).

Tenney. 6229. Cabibbo, Paola. "Il negro come personaggio." *SA* 14(1968):29–39. [Esp. in *Female Quixotism*.]

Tyler. 6230. Dell, Robert M., and Charles A. Huguenin. "Vermont's Royall Tyler in New York's John Street:A Theatrical Hoax Exploded." *Vt. Hist.* 38:103–12.

Wheatley. 6231. Kuncio, Robert C. "Some Unpublished Poems of Phillis Wheatley." *NEQ* 43:287–97.

Wigglesworth. 6232. Brack, O M,Jr. "Michael Wigglesworth and the Attribution of 'I Walk'd and Did a Little Molehill View'." *SCN* 28:41–44.

Williams, R. 6233. Chupack, Henry. *Roger Williams.* (TUSAS 157.) New York: Twayne, 1969.

6234. Garrett, John. *Roger Williams, Witness Beyond Christendom, 1603–1683.* New York: Macmillan.

6235. Hines, Donald M. "Odd Customs and Strange Ways The American Indian c.1640." *WR* 7,ii:20–29. [Major ref. to W': *Key into the Language of America.*]

* 6236. Reinitz, Richard. "The Typological Argument fo Religious Toleration:The Separatist Tradition and Roge Williams." *EAL* 5,i,pt.1:74–110.

Williams, W. 6237. Dickason, David H. *William Williams* (IUHS 67.) Bloomington: Ind. U.P.

III. NINETEENTH CENTURY, 1800–1870

Bibliography. 6238. Bennett, Josiah. "Editorial Progress Report—Sail on, Sail on . . . ." *Serif* 7,ii:37–38. [Adds data to D.P. Welch art. below.]

6239. Welch, Darrell P. "How Did the *New American Practical Navigator* Navigate?" *Serif* 7,i:33–34.

See also 6069.

General and Miscellaneous. *6240. Adams, Richard P. "Permutations of American Romanticism." *SIR* 9:249–68.

* 6241. Calhoun, Richard J. "The Ante-Bellum Literary Twilight:*Russell's Magazine*." *SLJ* 3,i:89–110.

6242. Cameron, Kenneth Walter. "Literary News in American Renaissance Newspapers (3)." *ESQ* 59:10–11,40.

6243. Childs, James B. "*Mémoires d'un Voyageur qui se repose*:A Bibliographical Interlude on an Elusive Foreign Service Officer's Impressions of the United States, 1811–32." *PBSA* 64:193–204.

* 6244. Dean, Dennis. "Hitchock's Dinosaur Tracks." *AQ* 21(1969):639–44. [Incl. refs. to Melville, Thoreau, Longfellow, Dickinson, Twain, et al.]

6245. Doherty, Joseph F.,Jr. "The 'Desolation of Solitude': Studies in American Solipsistic Loneliness During the First Half of the Nineteenth Century." *DAI* 30:4406A(Minn.).

* 6246. Hauck, Richard. "The Dickens Controversy in the *Spirit of the Times*." *PMLA* 85:278–83.

6247. Hill, Douglas B.,Jr. "Studies in the Development of First-Person Narrative in American Literature to 1850." *DAI* 30:4414A(Columbia).

6248. Krickel, Edward. "The Study of the Expatriates." *SAB* 35,iii:29–39.

6249. Lanzinger, Klaus. "The Prejudice of Sidney Smith and the Early Reviews." [F 62]:45–52.

6250. Marraro, Howard R. "Miscellaneous Notes on Italian Literature in America in the Nineteenth Century." *MLJ* 54:324–28.

* 6251. McHaney, Thomas L. "An Early 19th Century Literary Agent:James Lawson of New York." *PBSA* 64:177–92.

6252. Meriwether, James B. "House-Styling, Vintage 1856." *CEAAN* 3:11–12.

6253. Nirenberg, Morton I. "The Reception of American Literature in German Periodicals, 1820–1850." *DAI* 31:1284A (Johns Hopkins).

6254. Stubbs, John C. "The Ideal in the Literature and Art of the American Renaissance." *ESQ* 55(1969):55–63.

6255. Walker, Franklin. *San Francisco's Literary Frontier.* Seattle: U. of Wash. P., 1969. [New ed. incl. new Introd. by author.]

6256. Wohl, R. Richard. "The 'Country Boy' Myth and Its Place in American Urban Culture:The Nineteenth-Century Contribution." *Perspectives in Amer. Hist.*(Harvard) 3(1969): 77–156. [Ed. by Moses Rischin.]

See also 6139, 6142, 6143, 6150, 6460, 6712.

Criticism. 6257. Calhoun, Richard J. "Literary Criticism in Southern Periodicals During the American Renaissance." *ESQ* 55(1969):76–82.

See also 3735.

Drama and Theater. 6258. Behrmann, Alfred. "Kotzebue on the American Stage." *Arcadia* 4(1969):274–84.

6259. Green, Alan W.C. " 'Jim Crow,' 'Zip Coon':The Northern Origins of Negro Minstrelsy." *MR* 11:385–97.

* 6260. Smither, Nelle. " 'A New Lady-Actor of Gentlemen' Charlotte Cushman's Second New York Engagement." *BNYPI* 74:391–95.

* 6261. Srnka, Alfred H. "An Index to:*Personal Recollections o the Stage* by William Burke Wood." *TD* 1,ii(1969):51–73.

* 6262. Wilmeth, Don B. "An Index to:*The Life of Georg Frederick Cooke* by William Dunlap." *TD* 2,i-ii(1969–70):109–20

6263. —— "The Posthumous Career of George Frederick Cooke." *TN* 24:68–74.

See also 3819.

Newspapers. 6264. Cameron, Kenneth Walter. "Literary News in American Renaissance Newspapers." *ATQ* 2(1969) 29–36.

Periodicals. *See* 6372, 6607.

Poetry. 6265. Anderson, David D. "Ohio's Pioneer Poets." *NOQ* 42(1969):9–18.

* 6266. Bridges, William. "Warm Hearth, Cold World:Socia Perspectives on the Household Poets." *AQ* 21(1969):764–79

6267. Celli, Aldo. "Il Risorgimento nella poesia americana." [F 61]:19–39. [Whittier, Bryant, Holmes, Lowell,et al.]

6268. Raïzis, M. Byron. "Epeirotikoi agones kai Amerikano poiites." *ÈpH* 19:224–32. [On Amer. poets inspired by Gree Revolution of 1821.]

See also 6155, 6610.

Prose Fiction. 6269. Grade, Arnold. *Guide to Early Juvenil Literature.* (Merrill Guides.) Columbus, Ohio: Charles E. Merrill

* 6270. Lawton, James N. "The Authorship of Item 165 in Lyl Wright's *American Fiction 1851–1875*." *PBSA* 64:83.

6271. Levy, David W. "Racial Stereotypes in Antislavery Fiction." *Phylon* 31:265–79.

6272. Marler, Robert F.,Jr. "The American Tale and Shor Story, 1850–1861." *DAI* 31:1764A(Geo. Wash.).

6273. Ridgely, Joseph V. "Nineteenth-Century Fiction." [I 65]:142–57.

6274. Trensky, Anne T. "The Cult of the Child in Mino American Fiction of the Nineteenth Century." *DAI* 30(1969) 2048A–49A(C.U.N.Y.).

6275. Tuttleton, James W. "Romance and Novel:The Dis integration of a Form." *ESQ* 55(1969):110–21.

6276. Yellin, Jean F. "The Negro in Pre-Civil War Litera ture." *DAI* 30(1969):1187A–88A(Ill.).

See also 999, 6157, 6458, 6473, 6720, 6723, 6725, 7278

Adams. *6277. Harbert, Earl N. "John Quincy Adams and His Diary." *TSE* 18:81–93.

6278. Kaiser, Leo M. "John Quincy Adams and His Trans lation of Juvenal 13." *PAPS* 114:272–93. [With text.]

* 6279. Wasser, Henry. "John Quincy Adams on the Opening Lines of Milton's *Paradise Lost*." *AL* 42: [373]–75.

Alcott, B. 6281. Herrnstadt, Richard L.,ed. *The Letters of A*

Bronson Alcott. With Introd. Ames: Iowa State U.P., 1969.

6282. Strickland, Charles. "A Transcendentalist Father:The Child-Rearing Practices of Bronson Alcott." *Perspectives in Amer. Hist.*(Harvard) 3(1969):5–73.

See also 6646.

Alcott, L.M. *6283. Hamblen, Abigail Ann. "Louisa May Alcott and the 'Revolution' in Education." *JGE* 22:81–92.

American Quarterly Review. *6284. Woodall, Guy R. "More on the Contributors to the *American Quarterly Review* (1827–1837)." *SB* 23:199–207.

Barker, J.N. 6285. Sata, Masanori. "*Superstition* (1824) to *Winterset* (1935):Romeo-Juliet theme kara no kosatsu." *ELLS* 6(1969):131–46.

Bartlett. 6286. Fobes, Charles S. "Robert Bartlett:A Forgotten Transcendentalist." *ATQ* 1(1969):130–34. [Rptd. from *New England Magazine* 23,ii(Oct 1900):211–19.]

Boker. 6287. Kincaid, Arthur Noel. "Italian and English Sources of Boker's *Francesca da Rimini* (1853)." *ATQ* 1(1969): 91–100.

Book of Mormon. 6288. Jessee, Dean C. "The Original Book of Mormon Manuscript." *BYUS* 10:259–78.

6289. Nichols, Robert E.,Jr. "Beowulf and Nephi:A Literary View of the *Book of Mormon*." *Dialogue:A Jour. of Mormon Thought* 4,iii(1969):40–47.

6290. Welch, John W. "Chiasmus in the Book of Mormon." *BYUS* 10(1969):69–84.

Boucicault. *6291. Harrison, A. Cleveland. "Boucicault on Dramatic Action:His Confirmation of the Poetics." *QJS* 56: 45–53.

6292. —— "Boucicault's Formula:Illusion Equals Pleasure." *ETJ* 21(1969):299–309.

6293. Hogan, Robert. *Dion Boucicault.* (TUSAS 163.) New York: Twayne, 1969. [Crit.]

Briggs. 6294. Briggs, C.F. *The Adventures of Harry Franco.* Introd. Bette S. Weidman. New York: Garrett.

6295. —— *Working a Passage.* Introd. Bette S. Weidman. New York: Garrett.

Brown, W.W. 6296. Farrison, William E. *William Wells Brown:Author & Reformer.* Chicago: U. of Chicago P., 1969.

Bryant. 6297. Woodward, Robert H. " 'The Wings of Morning' in 'Thanatopsis'." *ESQ* 58:153.

See also 6305.

Caruthers. 6298. Caruthers, W.A. *The Knights of the Golden Horse-Shoe.* (Southern Lit. Classics.) Introd. Curtis C. Davis. Chapel Hill: U. of N.C. Press.

Channing, E. 6299. Hudspeth, Robert N. "Ellery Channing's Paradoxical Muse." *ESQ* 57(1969):34–40.

Child. 6300. Child, L.M. *Hobomok.* Introd. Edward H. Foster. New York: Garrett.

See also 6366.

Christian Examiner. 6301. "Index to the *Christian Examiner*." *ATQ* 4(1969):3–82.

Cobb. 6302. Rogers, Tommy W. "The Folk Humor of Joseph B. Cobb." *NMW* 3:13–35.

Cooper. *6303. Baym, Max I., and Percy Matenko. "The Odyssey of *The Water-Witch* and a Susan Fenimore Cooper Letter." *NYH* 51:33–41.

* 6304. Bender, Thomas. "James Fenimore Cooper and the City." *NYH* 51:287–305. [Illus.]

6305. Berbrich, Joan D. *Three Voices from Paumanok:The Influence of Long Island on James Fenimore Cooper, William Cullen Bryant, and Walt Whitman.* (Empire State Hist. Pubs. Ser. 81.) Port Washington, N.Y.: Ira J. Friedman, Inc., 1969.

6306. Irving, Donald C. "James Fenimore Cooper's Alternatives to the Leatherstocking Hero in the Frontier Romances." *DAI* 30:4947A–48A(Ind.).

* 6307. Kesterson, David B. "Milton's Satan and Cooper's Demonic Chieftains." *SCB* 29(1969):138–42.

* 6308. Kligerman, Jack. "Notes on Cooper's Debt to John Jay." *AL* 41(1969):415–19.

6309. Lindroth, James R. "The Comic Perspective of James Fenimore Cooper." *DAI* 31:1234A(N.Y.U.).

6310. Martien, Norman G. "I. An Essay and Materials Toward an Edition of Fenimore Cooper; II. *Mansfield Park* and

Jane Austen's Heroine; III. A Reading of Marvell's 'Upon Appleton House'." *DAI* 30:3468A(Rutgers).

* 6311. McWilliams, John P.,Jr. "Cooper and the Conservative Democrat." *AQ* 22:665–77.

6312. Overland, Orm H. "James Fenimore Cooper's *The Prairie*:The Making and Meaning of an American Classic." *DAI* 31:1285A(Yale).

6313. Philbrick, Thomas L. "Language and Meaning in Cooper's *The Water-Witch*." *ESQ* 60:10–16.

6314. Pickering, James H. "Fenimore Cooper in Our Time." *NYH* 51:545–55.

6315. Reiss, John P.,Jr. "Problems of the Family Novel: Cooper, Hawthorne, and Melville." *DAI* 30(1969):1178A–79A (Wis.).

* 6316. Ringe, Donald A. "James Fenimore Cooper:An American Democrat." *PLL* 6:420–31.

6317. Rose, Marilyn G. "Time Discrepancy in *Last of the Mohicans*." *AN&Q* 8:72–73.

6318. Sandy, Alan F.,Jr. "The Voices of Cooper's *The Deerslayer*." *ESQ* 60:5–9.

6319. Smith, Aleck L. "The Indian and Black in Cooper:A Study in Racist Stereotypes." [F 1]:424–38.

6320. Staggs, Kenneth W. "Cooper's *Gleanings in Europe. England*:A Problem in Copy-Text." *CEAAN* 3:14–15.

Cranch. 6321. Williams, Paul O. "The Persistence of Cranch's 'Enosis'." *ESQ* 57(1969):41–46.

Crockett. 6322. Arpad, Joseph J. "David Crockett, an Original Legendary Eccentricity and Early American Character." *DAI* 30:3422A(Duke).

Cummins. 6323. Cummins, M. *The Lamplighter.* Introd. Edward H. Foster. New York: Garrett.

Douglass. 6324. Douglass, F. *My Bondage and My Freedom.* Introd. Philip S. Foner. New York: Dover, 1969.

Dunlap. 6325. Canary, Robert H. *William Dunlap.* (TUSAS 164.) New York: Twayne, 1969. [Crit.]

6326. Dunlap, W. *A History of the Rise and Progress of the Arts of Design in the United States.* 3 vols. Ed. Rita Weiss. Introd. James T. Flexner. New York: Dover, 1969.

See also 6262.

Duyckinck, E. 6327. Mize, George E. "Evert Duyckinck: Critic to His Times." *ESQ* 55(1969):89–95.

Emerson. 6328. Adams, Richard P. "The Basic Contradiction in Emerson." *ESQ* 55(1969):106–10.

6329. Bettarini, Mariella. "Il pensiero di Ralph W. Emerson." *CV* 23(1968):172–77.

6330. Binney, James. "Emerson Revisited." *MQ* 12:109–22.

6331. Broderick, John C. "Emerson, Thoreau, and Transcendentalism." [F 65]:3–18.

6332. Burke, Phyllis B. "Emerson's Prose Style:His Created World." *DAI* 30:4937A(U. of Wash.).

6333. Cameron, Kenneth Walter. "A Note on Lidian Emerson and Anti-Slavery." *ATQ* 2(1969):38–39.

6334. —— "Current Bibliography on Ralph Waldo Emerson." *ATQ* 2(1969):46–50.

6335. —— "Theodore Clapp on Emerson's Williamstown Address." *ATQ* 2(1969):37–38.

6336. Clarkson, John W.,Jr. "Emerson at Seventy." *ATQ* 1(1969):119.

6337. Cummins, Roger William. "The *Monthly Magazine* and Emerson (1841)." *ATQ* 1(1969):64–75.

6338. D'Avanzo, Mario L. "Emerson's 'Days' and *Proverbs*." *ATQ* 1(1969):83–85.

6339. Dennis, Carl. "Emerson's Poetry of Mind and Nature." *ESQ* 58:139–53.

6340. Ferguson, Alfred R. *Checklist of Ralph Waldo Emerson.* (Merrill Checklists.) Columbus, Ohio: Charles E. Merrill.

6341. Gilman, William H. "*The Journals and Miscellaneous Notebooks of Ralph Waldo Emerson*." *CEAAN* 3:26–27.

6342. Glick, Wendell. "The Moral and Ethical Dimensions of Emerson's Aesthetics." *ESQ* 55(1969):11–18.

6343. Hansen, Arlen J. "Emerson's Poetry of Thought." *DAI* 30:3944A(Iowa).

6344. Hart, John E. "Man Thinking as Hero:Emerson's 'Scholar' Revisited." *ESQ* 55(1969):102–06.

6345. Helmick, E.T. "Emerson's 'Uriel' as Poetic Theory." *ATQ* 1(1969):35–38.

6346. Herndon, Jerry A. "St. Paul and Emerson's 'Self-Reliance'." *ATQ* 1(1969):90.

6347. Johnson, Ellwood. "Emerson's Psychology of Power." *Rendezvous* 5,i:13–25.

6348. Kyle, Carol A. "Emerson's 'Uriel' as a Source for Frost." *ESQ* 58:111.

6349. LaRosa, Ralph C. "Emerson's Proverbial Rhetoric: 1818–1838." *DAI* 30(1969):1140A(Wis.).

6350. —— "Emerson's Sententiae in *Nature* (1836)." *ESQ* 58:153–59.

6351. Lindner, Carl M. "Ralph Waldo Emerson: The Conceptualization of Experience." *DAI* 31:1233A–34A(Wis.).

6352. Matle, John H. "Emerson and Brook Farm." *ESQ* 58:84–88.

6353. Mead, C. David, ed. *"The American Scholar" Today: Emerson's Essay and Some Critical Views.* With Pref. New York: Dodd, Mead. [Incl. text of essay plus rptd. crit.]

6354. Mulqueen, James E. "The Poetics of Emerson and Poe." *ESQ* 55(1969):5–11.

6355. Newfeldt, Leonard. "The Severity of the Ideal: Emerson's 'Thoreau'." *ESQ* 58:77–84.

6356. Noda, Hisashi. "The Concepts of Symbolism in Traditional Japanese Literary Criticism and the Poetics of Emerson." *KAL* 12:45–53. [In Jap.]

6357. Obuchowski, Peter A.,Jr. "The Relationship of Emerson's Interest in Science to His Thought." *DAI* 30: 3914A–15A(Mich.).

6358. Pulos, C.E. "*Walden* and Emerson's 'The Sphinx'." *ATQ* 1(1969):7–11.

6359. Reid, Alfred S. "Emerson's Prose Style: An Edge to Goodness." *ESQ* 60:37–42.

6360. Richard, Blakeney J. "Emerson and Berkeleian Idealism." *ESQ* 58:90–97.

6361. Schamberger, John E. "Emerson's Concept of the 'Moral Sense': A Study of Its Sources and Its Importance to His Intellectual Development." *DAI* 31:1292A(Pa.).

* 6362. Sealts, Merton M.,Jr. "Emerson on the Scholar, 1833–1837." *PMLA* 85:185–95.

6363. Shepard, Douglas H. "Ungathered Commentary on Emerson." *ATQ* 1(1969):47–50,52–62.

6364. Strauch, Carl F. "Emerson's Use of the Organic Method." *ESQ* 55(1969):18–24.

6365. —— "The Mind's Voice: Emerson's Poetic Styles." *ESQ* 60:43–59.

6366. Tarr, Rodger L. "Emerson's Transcendentalism in L.M. Child's Letter to Carlyle." *ESQ* 58:112–15.

6367. Terry, R. Franklin. "Emerson, Cox, and God." *IR* 25,iii(1968):27–30. [Ref. is to Harvey Cox, *The Secular City* (1965).]

6368. Tuerk, Richard. "Emerson's *Nature*: Miniature Universe." *ATQ* 1(1969):110–13.

6369. Whitford, Kathryn. "Water, Wind, and Light Imagery in Emerson's Essay 'The Oversoul'." *Wisconsin Studies in Lit.* 6(1969):100–05.

See also 4800, 5153, 6372, 6373, 6402, 6596, 6670, 6677, 6855, 7690, 8147.

Fay. 6370. Fay, T.S. *Norman Leslie.* Introd. Edward H. Foster. New York: Garrett.

Fuller, M. 6371. Hopkins, Vivian C. "Margaret Fuller: American Nationalist Critic." *ESQ* 55(1969):24–41.

6372. Rosenthal, Bernard. "*The Dial*, Transcendentalism, and Margaret Fuller." *ELN* 8:28–36.

Furness, W.H. 6373. Van Egmond, Peter. "Harned on Emerson's Friend William Henry Furness." *ATQ* 1(1969):15–18.

Harris, G.W. *6374. Howell, Elmo. "Timon in Tennessee: The Moral Fervor of George Washington Harris." *GaR* 24:311–19.

6375. Plater, Ormonde. "Narrative Folklore in the Works of George Washington Harris." *DAI* 30:4461A(Tulane).

Hart. 6376. Hart, J.C. *Miriam Coffin.* Introd. Edward H. Foster. New York: Garrett.

Hawthorne. 6377. Abel, Darrel. " 'A More Imaginative Pleasure': Hawthorne on the Play of Imagination." *ESQ*

55(1969):63–71.

* 6378. —— " 'A Vast Deal of Human Sympathy': Idea and Device in Hawthorne's 'The Snow Image'." *Criticism* 4:316–32.

* 6379. Baym, Nina. "Hawthorne's Holgrave: The Failure of the Artist-Hero." *JEGP* 69:584–98.

6380. —— "Passion and Authority in *The Scarlet Letter*." *NEQ* 43:209–30.

6381. Borges, Jorge Luis. "Nathaniel Hawthorne." *LetN* (sept-oct):69–90.

6382. Bowen, James K. "More on Hawthorne and Keats." *ATQ* 2(1969):12.

* 6383. Burns, Rex S. "Hawthorne's Romance of Traditional Success." *TSLL* 12:443–54.

6384. Canaday, Nicholas,Jr. "Hawthorne's *The Scarlet Letter*." *Expl* 28:Item 39.

* 6385. Carnochan, W.B. " 'The Minister's Black Veil': Symbol, Meaning, and the Context of Hawthorne's Art." *NCF* 24(1969): 182–92.

6386. Charvat, William,et al.,eds. *Our Old Home: A Series of English Sketches.* Introd. Claude M. Simpson. Textual Introd. Fredson Bowers. *The Centenary Edition of the Works of Nathaniel Hawthorne*, v. Columbus: Ohio State U.P.

6387. Chisholm, Richard M. "The Use of Gothic Materials in Hawthorne's Mature Romances." *DAI* 31:382A(Columbia).

6388. Cifelli, Edward. "Hawthorne and the Italian." *SA* 14(1968):87–96.

6389. Clark, C.E. Frazer,Jr. *Checklist of Nathaniel Hawthorne.* (Merrill Checklists.) Columbus, Ohio: Charles E. Merrill.

6390. —— "Hawthorne's First Appearance in England." *CEAAN* 3:10–11.

6391. Cook, Larry W. "Narrators in the Works of Nathaniel Hawthorne." *DAI* 30(1969):2478A(Duke).

6392. Cook, Reginald. "The Forest of Goodman Brown's Night: A Reading of Hawthorne's 'Young Goodman Brown'." *NEQ* 43:473–81.

6393. Curran, Ronald T. "Hawthorne as Gothicist." *DAI* 30:4404A–05A(Pa.).

6394. Dunne, Michael F. "Order and Excess in Hawthorne's Fiction." *DAI* 30:3003A–04A(La. State).

6395. Durham, Frank. "Hawthorne and Goldsmith: A Note." *JAmS* 4:103–05.

6396. Ensor, Allison. " 'Whispers of the Bad Angel': A *Scarlet Letter* Passage as a Commentary on Hawthorne's 'Young Goodman Brown'." *SSF* 7:467–69.

6397. Estrin, Mark W. "Dramatizations of American Fiction: Hawthorne and Melville on Stage and Screen." *DAI* 30:3428A(N.Y.U.).

6398. Fogle, Richard H. "Hawthorne's Pictorial Unity." *ESQ* 55(1969):71–76.

6399. Foley, Marie L. " 'The Key of Holy Sympathy': Hawthorne's Social Ideal." *DAI* 30:4409A(Tulane).

6400. Franklin, Benjamin,V. "Hawthorne's Non-Fiction: His Attitude Toward America." *DAI* 31:1226A–27A(Ohio).

6401. Gallagher, Edward J. "Sir Kenelm Digby in Hawthorne's 'The Man of Adamant'." *N&Q* 17:15–16.

6402. Goldfarb, Clare R. "*The Marble Faun* and Emersonian Self-Reliance." *ATQ* 1(1969):19–23.

6403. Gupta, R.K. "Hawthorne's Ideal Reader." *IJAS* 1,i(1969):97–99.

* 6404. Hall, Spencer. "Beatrice Cenci: Symbol and Vision in *The Marble Faun*." *NCF* 25:85–95.

6405. Hawthorne, N. *Selected Tales and Sketches.* 3d ed. Introd. Hyatt H. Waggoner. New York: Holt, Rinehart and Winston.

6406. —— *The Life of Franklin Pierce.* Foreword Richard C. Robey. New York: Garrett.

6407. Horne, Lewis B. "The Heart, the Hand, and 'The Birthmark'." *ATQ* 1(1969):38–41.

6408. Janssen, James G. "Dimmesdale's 'Lurid Playfulness'." *ATQ* 1(1969):30–34.

6409. Kamogawa, Takahiro. "On the Family Name 'Pyncheon' in *The House of the Seven Gables*." *Hiroshima Studies in Eng. Lang. and Lit.* 16,i–ii(1969):41–47. [In Jap.]

6410. Karita, Motoshi. "Shosetsu to Denki no Shudai-sentaku

o Imi." *SophiaT* 17(1968):29–45. [Matter and meaning in fiction and biog. in Hawthorne and H. James.]

6411. Kelly, Richard. "Hawthorne's 'Ethan Brand'." *Expl* 28:Item 47.

6412. Klinkowitz, Jerome F. "The Significance of the Ending o *The House of the Seven Gables*." *DAI* 31:392A(Wis.).

6413. Laverty, Carroll D. "Some Touchstones of Hawthorne's Style." *ESQ* 60:30–36.

6414. Lease, Benjamin. "Hawthorne and 'A Certain Venerable Personage':New Light on 'The Custom-House'." *JA* 15:201–07.

* 6415. Levy, Leo B. "*The Marble Faun*:Hawthorne's Landscape of the Fall." *AL* 42:[139]–56.

6416. Liebman, Sheldon W. "Ambiguity in 'Lady Eleanore's Mantle'." *ESQ* 58:97–101.

6417. Lohmann, Christoph K. "Nathaniel Hawthorne:The American Janus." *DAI* 30(1969):1172A(Pa.).

6418. Male, Roy R. "Hawthorne." [F 65]:19–29.

6419. —— "Hawthorne's *The Blithedale Romance*." *Expl* 28:Item 56.

6420. Marks, Alfred H. "Ironic Inversion in *The Blithedale Romance*." *ESQ* 55(1969):95–102.

6421. McCarthy, Harold T. "Hawthorne's Dialogue with Rome:*The Marble Faun*." *SA* 14(1968):97–112.

6422. Meixsell, Anne B. "Symbolism in *The Marble Faun*." *DAI* 30(1969):1174A(Penn. State).

* 6423. Monteiro, George. "A Nonliterary Source for Hawthorne's 'Egotism; or the Bosom Serpent'." *AL* 41:575–77.

6424. —— "Hawthorne Letters in Old Catalogues." *ATQ* 1(1969):122.

6425. Nirenberg, Morton. "Hawthorne's Reception in Germany." *JA* 15:141–61.

6426. Normand, Jean. *Nathaniel Hawthorne:An Approach to an Analysis of Artistic Creation*. Tr. Derek Coltman. Foreword Henri Peyre. Cleveland: Press of Case Western Reserve U.

6427. Okamoto, Katsumi. "Hawthorne—Hatashi naki Kikyu." *EigoS* 114(1968):801–02. [H—infinite longings.]

* 6428. Paulits, Walter J. "Ambivalence in 'Young Goodman Brown'." *AL* 41:577–84.

6429. Pikuleff, Michael J. "The Role of Community in the Major Writings of Nathaniel Hawthorne." *DAI* 31:1809A–10A(Wis.).

* 6430. Plank, Robert. "Heart Transplant Fiction." *HSL* 2:102–12. [Focuses on Hauff's *Das kalte Herz* and Hawthorne's *Ethan Brand*.]

6431. Prater, William G. "Nathaniel Hawthorne:A Self-Characterization in the Novels." *DAI* 30(1969):2494A–95A (Ohio).

6432. Richard, Claude. "Poe et Hawthorne." *EA* 22(1969): 351–61.

6433. Rose, Marilyn Gaddis. "Miles Coverdale as Hawthorne's Persona." *ATQ* 1(1969):90–91.

6434. Ross, Donald,Jr. "Hawthorne and Thoreau on 'Cottage Architecture'." *ATQ* 1(1969):100–01.

6435. Santangelo, G.A. "The Absurdity of *The Minister's Black Veil*." *PCP* 5:61–66.

* 6436. Schneiderman, Lee. "Hawthorne and the Refuge of the Heart." *ConnR* 3,ii:83–101.

6437. Sharma, T.R.S. "Diabolic World and Naive Hero in 'My Kinsman, Major Molineux'." *IJAS* 1,i(1969):35–43.

6438. Smith, Julian. "A Hawthorne Source for *The House of the Seven Gables*." *ATQ* 1(1969):18–19.

6439. Spigel, Helen T. "The Sacred Image and the New Truth:A Study in Hawthorne's Women." *DAI* 30:2981A(Wash. U.).

6440. Spinucci, Pietro. "Hawthorne tra presente e passato: *Our Old Home*." *SA* 14(1968):113–63.

6441. Stephens, Rosemary. " 'A' is for 'Art' in *The Scarlet Letter*." *ATQ* 1(1969):23–27.

6442. Strout, Cushing. "Hawthorne's International Novel." *NCF* 24(1969):169–81.

6443. Stubbs, John C. *The Pursuit of Form:A Study of Hawthorne and the Romance*. Urbana: U. of Ill. P.

6444. Travis, Mildred K. "Past vs. Present in *The House of the Seven Gables*." *ESQ* 58:109–11.

6445. Tremblay, William A. "A Reading of Nathaniel Hawthorne's 'The Gentle Boy'." *MSE* 2:80–87.

6446. Turner, Arlin,ed. *Studies in* The Scarlet Letter. (Merrill Studies.) Columbus, Ohio: Charles E. Merrill. [Rptd. crit.]

6447. Van Der Beets, Richard, and Paul Witherington. "My Kinsman, Brockden Brown:Robin Molineux and Arthur Mervyn." *ATQ* 1(1969):13–15.

6448. Van Winkle, Edward S. "Aminadab, the Unwitting 'Bad Anima'." *AN&Q* 8:131–33. [On "The Birthmark."]

6449. White, Robert L. " 'Rappaccini's Daughter,' *The Cenci*, and the Cenci Legend." *SA* 14(1968):63–86.

See also 806, 4328, 6315, 6676, 6723, 6900, 6969, 7633, 7937, 9821.

Hayne. 6450. Moore, Rayburn S. "Hayne the Poet:A New Look." *SCR* 2,i:4–13.

Hentz. 6451. Hentz, C.L. *The Planter's Northern Bride*. Introd. Rhoda C. Ellison. Chapel Hill: U. of N.C. Press. [Novel orig. pub. in 1854.]

Hildreth. 6452. Hildreth, R. *The Slave; or, Memoirs of Archy Moore*. Introd. Douglas B. Hill,Jr. New York: Garrett.

Hooper. 6453. Smith, Winston. "*Simon Suggs* and the Satiric Tradition." [F 16]:49–56.

Ingraham. 6454. Ingraham, J.H. *Lafitte:The Pirate of the Gulf*. Introd. J.V. Ridgely. New York: Garrett.

Irving, W. 6455. Aderman, Ralph M. "The Editors' Intentions in the Washington Irving Letters." *CEAAN* 3:23–24.

6456. Cracroft, Richard H. "The American West of Washington Irving:The Quest for a National Tradition." *DAI* 31:1221A(Wis.).

* 6457. Durant, David. "Aeolism in *Knickerbocker's A History of New York*." *AL* 41:[493]–506.

6458. Jenney, Adele G. "The Irvingesque Story in the United States:1820–1860." *DAI* 31:1760A–61A(Geo. Wash.).

6459. Kime, Wayne R. "Alfred Seton's Journal:A Source for Irving's *Tonquin* Disaster Account." *Ore. Hist. Quart.* 71,iv: 309–24.

6460. McClary, Ben H. "A Bracebridge-Hall Christmas for Van Buren:An Unpublished Irving Letter." *ELN* 8:18–22. [Text of letter incl.]

6461. Noble, Donald R. "Washington Irving's 'Peter' Pun." *AN&Q* 8:103–04.

6462. Pochmann, Henry A. "An Example of Progressive Plate Deterioration." *CEAAN* 3:16. [In 1857 ed. of *Mahomet*.]

6463. Reed, Kenneth T. " 'Oh These Women! These Women!':Irving's Shrews and Coquettes." *AN&Q* 8:147–50.

6464. —— "Washington Irving and the Negro." *NALF* 4:43–44.

* 6465. Weatherspoon, M.A. "1815–1819:Prelude to Irving's *Sketch Book*." *AL* 41:[566]–71.

Kennedy, T. 6466. Mehlman, Robert. "The Poems of Thomas Kennedy of Maryland." *JRUL* 33:9–19.

Kirkland. 6467. Kirkland, C.M. *A New Home—Who'll Follow?* Introd. Douglas B. Hill,Jr. New York: Garrett.

Lincoln. 6468. Anderson, David D. *Abraham Lincoln*. (TUSAS 153.) New York: Twayne. [Crit.]

6469. Angle, Paul M.,ed., assisted by Richard G. Case. *A Portrait of Abraham Lincoln in Letters by His Oldest Son*. Chicago: Chicago Hist. Soc., 1968.

* 6470. Dibos, William G. "Concerning a Quotation Commonly Attributed to Abraham Lincoln." *RomN* 11:579–80.

6471. Tagliacozzo, Enzo. "Lincoln e il Risorgimento." [F 61]:313–38.

Lippard. 6472. De Grazia, Emilio. "The Life and Works of George Lippard." *DAI* 31:741A(Ohio State).

6473. Fiedler, Leslie. "The Male Novel." *PR* 37:74–89.

6474. Fiedler, Leslie,ed. *[The Quaker City, or] The Monks of Monk Hall*. By George Lippard. With Introd. New York: Odyssey.

6475. Seecamp, Carsten E. "The Chapter of Perfection:A Neglected Influence on George Lippard." *PMHB* 94:192–212. [Influ. of Kelpius' Christian-socialist community on L's novels.]

Longfellow. 6476. Allaback, Steven. "Mrs. Clemm and Henry Wadsworth Longfellow." *HLB* 18:32–42.

6477. Bellavance, Thomas E. "The Periodical Prose of Henry Wadsworth Longfellow (Volumes I and II)." *DAI* 31:1260A(Mich. State).

* 6478. Burwick, Frederick. "Longfellow and German Romanticism." *CLS* 7:12–42.

6479. Cohn, Jack R. "A Note on Longfellow's Letter 416." *ESQ* 58:129–31.

6480. Mathews, J. Chesley,ed. "Longfellow Symposium." *ESQ* 58:3–75. [Steven Allaback, "Voices of Longfellow:*Kavanagh* as Autobiography," 3–14; Phyllis Franklin, "The Importance of Time in Longfellow's Works," 14–22; Richard A.S. Arnell and Robert L. Volz, "Longfellow and Music," 32–38; Evelyn T. Helmick, "Longfellow's Lyric Poetry," 38–40; Carl L. Johnson, "Longfellow's Studies in France," 40–48; Ernest J. Moyne, "Longfellow and Kah-ge-ga-gah-bowh," 48–52; Edward Wagenknecht, "Longfellow and Howells," 52–57; Robert S. Ward, "The Influence of Vico upon Longfellow," 57–62; Richard Harwell, "Librarian Longfellow," 63–69.]

6481. Shaw, W. David. "A Note on Longfellow's Auroral References." *ATQ* 2(1969):13–15. [Incl. 2 plates.]

6482. Stanovnik, Janez. "Potovanje Longfellowa skozi Slovenijo leta 1828." *SE* 18–19(1965–1966):123–28. [On L's trip through Slovenia in summer of 1828.]

See also 6583.

Longstreet. 6483. Longstreet, A.B. *"Georgia Scenes:*'A Night in the Cars'." *MissQ* 23:169–74. [Repr. from *South. Miscellany* (1842).]

Lowell, J.R. 6484. Smith, Herbert F.,ed. *Literary Criticism of James Russell Lowell.* With Introd. Lincoln: U. of Neb. P., 1969.

Mathews. 6485. Mathews, C. *Behemoth.* Introd. Donald J. Yanella,Jr. New York: Garrett.

6486. —— *Big Abel and the Little Manhattan.* Introd. Donald J. Yanella,Jr. New York: Garrett.

6487. —— *The Career of Puffer Hopkins.* Introd. Donald J. Yanella,Jr. New York: Garrett.

6488. Stein, Allen F. "The Presentation and Criticism of the American Scene in the Works of Cornelius Mathews." *DAI* 30(1969):2551A(Duke).

Melville. *6489. Andersen, Marilyn. "Melville's Jackets: *Redburn* and *White-Jacket*." *ArQ* 26:173–81.

6490. Anderson, Charles R. "Melville's South Sea Romance." *EigoS* 115(1969):478–82.

6491. Baim, Joseph. "The Confidence-Man as 'Trickster'." *ATQ* 1(1969):81–83.

6492. Bezanson, Walter E. "Herman Melville's *Clarel*." *DAI* 30(1969):2520A(Yale).

6493. Bickley, Robert B.,Jr. "Literary Influences and Technique in Melville's Short Fiction:1853–1856." *DAI* 30:4935A (Duke).

* 6494. Bigelow, Gordon E. "The Problem of Symbolist Form in Melville's 'Bartleby the Scrivener'." *MLQ* 31:345–58.

6495. Bray, Richard T. "Melville's *Mardi*:An Approach Through Imagery." *DAI* 30:5401A(Wis.).

6496. Bredahl, Axel C.,Jr. "Melville's Angles of Vision:The Function of Shifting Perspective in the Novels of Herman Melville." *DAI* 31:1263A(Pittsburgh).

6497. Brophy, Robert J. "Benito Cereno, Oakum, and Hatchets." *ATQ* 1(1969):89–90.

6498. Burns, Graham. "The Unshored World of *Moby Dick*." *CR* 13:68–83.

6499. Cameron, Kenneth Walter. "Scattered Melville Manuscripts." *ATQ* 1(1969):63–64.

* 6500. Caraber, Andrew J.,Jr. "Melville's *The Confidence-Man*." *Expl* 29:Item 9.

6501. Carothers, Robert L. "Herman Melville and the Search for the Father:An Interpretation of the Novels." *DAI* 30: 4445A(Kent State).

6502. Carter, Angela. *"Redburn:His First Voyage* by Herman Melville." *AntigR* 1,i:103–05.

6503. Daiker, Donald A. "The Motif of the Quest in the Writings of Herman Melville." *DAI* 30:4979A–80A(Ind.).

6504. Deane, Paul. "Herman Melville:The Quality of Balance." *Serif* 7,ii:12–17.

* 6505. Dillingham, William B. "Melville's Long Ghost and Smollett's Count Fathom." *AL* 42:232–35. [*Omoo* and *The Adventures of Ferdinand Count Fathom.*]

* 6506. Donaldson, Scott. "The Dark Truth of *The Piazza Tales*." *PMLA* 85:1082–86.

* 6507. Ellis, Theodore. "Another Broadside into *Mardi*." *AL* 41(1969):419–22.

6508. Fisher, Marvin. " 'The Lightning-Rod Man':Melville's Testament of Rejection." *SSF* 7:433–38.

6509. ——— "Focus on Herman Melville's 'The Two Temples' The Denigration of the American Dream." [F 63]:76–86.

6510. Franks, Jesse G. "Air and Brass:Faith, Philosophy, and Events in the First Six Novels of Herman Melville." *DAI* 30(1969):2482A(Ball State).

* 6511. Frederick, John T. "Melville's Last Long Novel *Clarel*." *ArQ* 26:151–57.

6512. Friedman, Maurice. *Problematic Rebel:Melville, Dostoievsky, Kafka, Camus.* Rev. Ed. Chicago: U. of Chicago P.

* 6513. Fulwiler, Toby. "The Death of the Handsome Sailor:A Study of *Billy Budd* and *The Red Badge of Courage*." *ArQ* 26:101–12.

6514. Giorcelli, Cristina. "Le poesie 'italiane' di Herman Melville." *SA* 14(1968):165–91.

6515. Hashiguchi, Minoru. "Melville no Shi." *EigoS* 115(1969):485–86. [M's poetry.]

6516. Hayford, Harrison, Hershel Parker, and G. Thomas Tanselle,eds. *Redburn:His First Voyage.* Historical Note by Hershel Parker. Evanston, Ill.: Northwestern U.P., 1969.

6517. Hays, Peter. "Slavery and *Benito Cereno*:An Aristotelian View." *EA* 23:38–46.

6518. Henchey, Richard F. "Herman Melville's *Israel Potter*: A Study in Survival." *DAI* 31:1758A–59A(Mass.).

6519. Herbert, Thomas W.,Jr. "Spiritual Exploration in *Moby-Dick*:A Study of Theological Background." *DAI* 31: 1278A(Princeton).

6520. Holder, Alan. "Style and Tone in Melville's *Pierre*." *ESQ* 60:76–86.

* 6521. Jaster, Frank. "Melville's Cosmopolitan:The Experience of Life in *The Confidence-Man:His Masquerade*." *SoQ* 8:201–10.

6522. Johnson, Richard C. "An Attempt at a Union List of Editions of Melville, 1846–91." *BC* 19:333–47.

6523. Kauvar, Gerald B. "Chapter 54 of *Moby Dick*." *ArlQ* 2,iii:133–41.

6524. Kearns, Edward A. "Omniscient Ambiguity:The Narrators of *Moby-Dick* and *Billy Budd*." *ESQ* 58:117–20.

6525. Ketterer, David. "Some Co-ordinates in *Billy Budd*." *JAmS* 3(1969):221–37.

6526. Keyssar, Alexander. *Melville's* Israel Potter:*Reflections on the American Dream.* (LeBaron Russell Briggs Prize Honors Essays in English.) Cambridge: Harvard U.P., 1969.

6527. Kimura, Harumi. "Tensai yue no Shippai." *EigoS* 115(1969):483–84. [Failure because of genius:M's *Pierre*.]

* 6528. Kinnamon, Jon M. *"Billy Budd*:Political Philosophies in a Sea of Thought." *ArQ* 26:164–72.

6529. Kirkham, E. Bruce. "The Iron Crown of Lombardy in *Moby Dick*." *ESQ* 58:127–29.

6530. Kirkland, James W. "Animal Imagery in the Fiction of Herman Melville." *DAI* 31:1803A–04A(Tenn.).

* 6531. Knight, Karl F. "Melville's Variations of the Theme of Failure in 'Bartleby' and *Billy Budd*." *ArlQ* 2,ii(1969):44–58.

6532. Lannon, Diedre. "A Note on Melville's 'Benito Cereno'." *MSE* 2:68–70.

6533. Lebowitz, Alan. *Progress into Silence:A Study of Melville's Heroes.* Bloomington: Ind. U.P.

* 6534. Lowance, Mason I.,Jr. "Veils and Illusion in *Benito Cereno*." *ArQ* 26:113–26.

6535. Lynde, Richard D. "Melville's Success in 'The Happy Failure:A Story of the River Hudson'." *CLAJ* 13(1969):119–30.

6536. Mandel, Ruth B. "Herman Melville and the Gothic Outlook." *DAI* 30:3015A–16A(Conn.).

6537. McCarthy, Harold T. *"Israel R. Potter* as a Source for *Redburn*." *ESQ* 59:8–9.

6538. Metzger, Charles R. "Melville's Saints:Allusion in *Benito Cereno*." *ESQ* 58:88–90.

6539. Middleton, John A. "Shark-Talk:The Uses of Dialogue in *Moby-Dick*." *DAI* 30:4995A(Ind.).

* 6540. Mills, Nicolaus C. "The Discovery of Nil in *Pierre* and *Jude the Obscure*." *TSLL* 12:249–62.

6541. Ortego, Philip D. "The Existential Roots of *Billy Budd*." *ConnR* 4,i:80–87.

* 6542. Parker, Hershel. "A Reexamination of *Melville's Reviewers*." *AL* 42:226–32.

* 6543. —— "Three Melville Reviews in the London *Weekly Chronicle*." *AL* 41:584–89.

* 6544. Rice, Julian C. "*Moby-Dick* and Shakespearean Tragedy." *CentR* 14:444–68.

6545. Saeki, Shoichi. "Shosetsuka Melville to Shin-hihyo." *EigoS* 115(1969):472–73. [M the novelist and new crit.]

6546. Sander, Lucille A. "Melville's Symbolism of the Pipe." *ESQ* 59:4–7.

6547. Schultz, Donald D. "Herman Melville and the Tradition of the Anatomy:A Study in Genre." *DAI* 30:4463A (Vanderbilt).

6548. Sealts, Merton M.,Jr. "Melville." [F 65]:30–49.

6549. Seelye, John. *Melville:The Ironic Diagram*. Evanston, Ill.: Northwestern U.P. [Crit.]

6550. Seltzer, Leon F. *The Vision of Melville and Conrad:A Comparative Study*. Athens: Ohio U.P.

6551. Shimada, Taro. "*Moby Dick* ni tsuite." *EigoS* 115(1969):476–78. [A study of *Moby Dick*.]

6552. Shimura, Masami. " 'The Tartarus of Maids' no Sekai." *EigoS* 115(1969):487–88. [World of "Tartarus of Maids."]

6553. Shurr, William H. "The Symbolic Structure of Herman Melville's *Clarel*." *DAI* 30:3477A(N.C., Chapel Hill).

6554. Springer, Haskell,ed. *Studies in Billy Budd*. (Merrill Studies.) With Introd. Columbus, Ohio: Charles E. Merrill. [Rptd. crit.]

6555. Stencel, Michelle M. "Knowledge in the Novels of Herman Melville." *DAI* 30:4956A–57A(S.C.).

* 6556. Stout, Janis. "Melville's Use of the Book of Job." *NCF* 25:69–83.

6557. Takamura, Katsuji. "Melville no Shosetsu-gun." *EigoS* 115(1969):474–75. [Novels of M.]

6558. Tanimoto, Taiji. "Melville ni okeru Sukui." *EigoS* 115(1969):489–90. [Salvation in M.]

* 6559. Tanselle, G. Thomas. "*Typee* and DeVoto:A Footnote." *PBSA* 64:207–09.

6560. Thakur, D. "The Tales of Melville." *LCrit* 8,iv(1969): 39–53.

6561. Tuerk, Richard. "Melville's 'Bartleby' and Isaac D'Israeli's *Curiosities of Literature, Second Series*." *SSF* 7:647–49.

6562. Turlish, Lewis A. "A Study of Teleological Concepts in the Novels of Herman Melville." *DAI* 30:3922A(Mich.).

6563. Vernon, John. "Melville's 'The Bell-Tower'." *SSF* 7:264–76.

6564. Watson, Charles N.,Jr. "Characters and Characterization in the Works of Herman Melville." *DAI* 31:372A(Duke).

6565. Werge, Thomas. "*Moby-Dick*:Scriptural Source of 'Blackness and Darkness'." *AN&Q* 9:6.

* 6566. Witherington, Paul. "The Art of Melville's *Typee*." *ArQ* 26:136–50.

6567. Wolfrum, Max D. "Responsible Failure in Melville." *DAI* 31:1821A(Wash. U.).

* 6568. Wright, Nathalia. "Melville and 'Old Burton' with 'Bartleby' as an Anatomy of Melancholy." *TSL* 15:1–13.

6569. —— *Melville's Use of the Bible*. New York: Octagon, 1969. [New ed. incl. "Appendix:Moby Dick:Jonah's or Job's Whale," 189–94.]

* 6570. Yeager, Henry J. "Melville's Literary Debut in France." *MQ* 11:413–26.

* 6571. Yellin, Jean F. "Black Masks:Melville's 'Benito Cereno'." *AQ* 22:[678]–89.

6572. Yoder, B.A. "Poetry and Science:'Two Distinct Branches of Knowledge' in *Billy Budd*." *SoRA* 3(1969):223–39.

6573. Zolla, Elémire. "Melville dinanzi al Risorgimento ed alla Guerra di Secessione." [F 61]:7–18.

See also 4123, 5370, 6315, 6397, 6798.

Morse. 6574. Gorlier, Claudio. "L'Italia (e l'America) di Samuel F.B. Morse." [F 61]:353–78.

New Jerusalem Magazine. 6575. "Index to the *New Jerusalem Magazine*." *ATQ* 4(1969):161–297.

Newcomb. 6576. Francis, Richard L. "Charles King Newcomb:Transcendental Hamlet." *ESQ* 57(1969):46–52.

North American Review. 6577. "Index to the *North American Review*." *ATQ* 4(1969):83–160.

Paulding. *6578. Gerber, Gerald E. "James Kirke Paulding and the Image of the Machine." *AQ* 22:[736]–41.

* 6579. Mason, Melvin R. "*The Lion of the West*:Satire on Davy Crockett and Frances Trollope." *SCB* 29(1969):143–45.

Payne. 6580. Saxon, A.H. "John Howard Payne, Playwright with a System." *TN* 24:79–84.

Poe. 6581. Barzun, Jacques. "A Note on the Inadequacy of Poe as a Proofreader and of His Editors as French Scholars." *RR* 61:23–26.

6582. Benton, Richard P. " 'The Masque of the Red Death':The Primary Source." *ATQ* 1(1969):12–13.

6583. Benton, Richard P.,ed. "Poe Symposium." *ESQ* 60, Supp. [Sidney P. Moss, "Poe as Probabilist in Forgues' Critique of the *Tales*," 4–13; Joseph M. Garrison,Jr., "The Irony of 'Ligeia'," 13–17; James W. Gargano, "Art and Irony in 'William Wilson'," 18–22; J. Lasley Dameron, "Symbolism in the Poetry of Poe and Stephen Crane," 22–28; David M. Rein, "The Appeal of Poe Today," 29–33; Alice M. Claudel, "Poe as Voyager in 'To Helen'," 33–37; G.R. Thompson, "Poe's 'Flawed' Gothic: Absurdist Techniques in 'Metzengerstein' and the *Courier* Satires," 38–58; Harriet R. Holman, "Longfellow in 'The Rue Morgue'," 58–60; Burton R. Pollin, "Poe's 'Some Words with a Mummy' Reconsidered," 60–67; H. Allen Greer, "Poe's 'Hans Pfaall' and the Political Scene," 67–73; Alice Chandler, " 'The Visionary Race':Poe's Attitude Toward His Dreamers," 73–81; David M. LaGuardia, "Poe, *Pym*, and Initiation," 82–84; L. Lynn Hogue, "Eroticism in Poe's 'For Annie'," 85–87; Gerald E. Gerber, "The Coleridgean Context of Poe's *Blackwood* Satires," 87–91.]

6584. Canario, John W. "The Dream in 'The Tell-Tale Heart'." *ELN* 7:194–97.

6585. Dameron, J. Lasley. "Poe and *Blackwood's* Alexander Smith on Truth and Poetry." *MissQ* 22(1969):355–59.

* 6586. Davis, Richard B. "Poe Criticism:Some Advances Toward Maturity." *MissQ* 23:67–76. [Rev. art.]

6587. Delaney, Joan. "Edgar Allan Poe and I.S. Turgenev." *SSASH* 15(1969):349–54.

* 6588. —— "Poe's 'The Gold Bug' in Russia:A Note on First Impressions." *AL* 42:375–79.

6589. Doxey, William S. "Concerning Fortunato's 'Courtesy'." *SSF* 4(1966):266.

6590. Forclaz, Roger. "Edgar Poe et la psychanalyse I; II." *RLV* 36:272–88; 36:375–89.

6591. Friedl, Herwig. "Poe und Lanier." *JA* 15:123–40.

* 6592. Halms, Randel. "Another Source for Poe's *Arthur Gordon Pym*." *AL* 41:572–75.

6593. Henninger, Francis J. "The Bouquet of Poe's 'Amontillado'." *SAB* 35,ii:35–40.

* 6594. Hess, Jeffrey A. "Sources and Aesthetics of Poe's Landscape Fiction." *AQ* 22:[177]–89.

* 6595. Hirsch, David H. "Another Source for 'The Pit and the Pendulum'." *MissQ* 23:35–43. ["Singular Recovery From Death," *Blackwood's*, Dec. 1821.]

6596. Hughes, James M. "The Dialectic of Death in Poe, Dickinson, Emerson and Whitman." *DAI* 31:1280A(Pa.).

6597. Kilburn, Patrick E. "Poe's 'Evening Star'." *Expl* 28:Item 76.

* 6598. Lees, Daniel E. "An Early Model for Poe's 'The Raven'." *PLL* 6:92–95.

6599. Lerner, Arthur. *Psychoanalytically Oriented Criticism of Three American Poets:Poe, Whitman, and Aiken*. Rutherford, N.J.: Fairleigh Dickinson U.P.

6600. Liebman, Sheldon W. "Poe's Tales and His Theory of the Poetic Experience." *SSF* 7:582–96.

* 6601. Lord, John B. "Two Phonological Analyses of Poe's 'To Helen'." *Lang&S* 3:147–58.

6602. Meister, John G.H. "The Descent of the Irrelative

One:The Metaphysics and Cosmology of Edgar Allan Poe's *Eureka*." *DAI* 30(1969):2490A(Pa.).

6603. Mulqueen, James E. "The Meaning of Poe's 'Ulalume'." *ATQ* 1(1969):27–30.

6604. Newlin, Paul A. "Scott's Influence on Poe's Grotesque and Arabesque Tales." *ATQ* 2(1969):9–12.

* 6605 *PN* 3,i. [George P. Clark, "Two Unnoticed Recollections of Poe's Funeral," 1–2; William H. Gravely,Jr., "A Note on the Composition of Poe's 'Hans Pfaal'," 2–5; J.V. Ridgely, "The Continuing Puzzle of *Arthur Gordon Pym*:Some Notes and Queries," 5–6; J.M. Pemberton, "Poe's 'To Helen':Functional Wordplay and a Possible Source," 6–7; Burton R. Pollin, "Figs, Bells, Poe, and Horace Smith," 8–10; Richard P. Benton, "Edgar Allan Poe:Current Bibliography," 11–16; Judy Osowski, "Fugitive Poe References:A Bibliography," 16–19; Ralph M. Aderman, "Poe in Rumania:A Bibliography," 19–20; David K. Jackson, "A Typographical Error in the B Version of Poe's 'Sonnet—To Science'," 21; June and Jack L. Davis, "An Error in Some Recent Printings of 'Ligeia'," 21; Joel Salzberg, "Preposition and Meaning in Poe's 'The Spectacles'," 21; Roger O'Connor, "Letters, Signatures, and 'Juws' in Poe's 'Autography'," 21–22; Richard Schuster, "More on the 'Fig-Pedler'," 22; W.T. Bandy, "More on 'The Angel of the Odd'," 22; Joseph H. Harkey, "A Note on Fortunato's Coughing," 22.]

6606. Pollin, Burton R. *Discoveries in Poe.* Notre Dame, Ind.: U. of Notre Dame P.

6607. —— "Poe and the *Boston Notion*." *ELN* 8:23–28.

* 6608. —— "Poe's Dr. Ollapod." *AL* 42:[80]–82. [In "A Predicament."]

6609. —— "Poe's Pen of Iron." *ATQ* 2(1969):16–18. [On "Usher."]

6610. Quinn, Patrick F. "Poe and Nineteenth-Century Poetry." [F 65]:158–76.

* 6611. Reece, James B. "A Reexamination of a Poe Date:Mrs. Ellet's Letters." *AL* 42:[157]–64.

6612. Reilly, John E. "The Lesser Death-Watch and 'The Tell-Tale Heart'." *ATQ* 2(1969):3–9.

6613. Richard, Claude,ed. "Configuration critique d' Edgar Allan Poe." *RLM* 193–98(1969). [Claude Richard, "Avertissement," 9–13; Edmund Wilson, "Poe critique littéraire (1942; révisé en 1955)," 15–21(tr. Annette Richard); Richard Wilbur, "Les poèmes d'Edgar Allan Poe:Introduction (1959)," 23–56 (tr. Gabriel Calori); Eric W. Carlson, " 'Ulalume':Symbolisme et signification (1963)," 57–77 (tr. Claude Richard); Claude Richard, "Les contes du Folio Club et la vocation humoristique d'Edgar Allan Poe (1968)," 79–96; Roy P. Basler, "L'interprétation de 'Ligeia' (1948)," 97–112 (tr. Alain Blayac); Darrel Abel, "La clef de la maison Usher (1949)," 113–29 (tr. Claude Richard); Richard Wilbur, "Le cas mystérieux d'Edgar Allan Poe (1967)," 131–45 (tr. Claude Richard); Patrick Quinn, "Le voyage imaginaire de Poe (1957)," 147–89 (tr. Yvette Camée); Allen Tate, "L'imagination angélique, ou De la divinité de Poe (1952;fevisé en 1959)," 191–213 (tr. Didier Coupaye); Claude Richard, "Edgar Allan Poe:Sélection bibliographique (1968)," 215–51.]

6614. Shulman, Robert. "Poe and the Powers of the Mind." *ELH* 37:245–62.

6615. Smuda, Manfred. "Variation und Innovation:Modelle literarischer Möglichkeiten der Prosa in der Nachfolge Edgar Allan Poes." *Poetica* 3:165–87.

6616. Stauffer, Donald B. "Poe's Views on the Nature and Function of Style." *ESQ* 60:23–30.

* 6617. Thompson, G.R. "Unity, Death, and Nothingness: Poe's 'Romantic Skepticism'." *PMLA* 85:297–300.

6618. Uchida, Ichigoro. "A Review of Psychological Studies on Edgar Allan Poe 1860–1967." [F 14]:120–39. [Text in Jap.; checklist (85 items) in Eng.]

* 6619. Vitt-Maucher, Gisela. "E.T.A. Hoffmanns 'Ritter Gluck' and E.A. Poes 'The Man of the Crowd':Eine Gegenüberstellung." *GQ* 43:35–46.

6620. Yagi, Toshio. "Poe to America Shosetsu no Dento." *EigoS* 115(1969):8–9. [P and tradit. of Amer. novel.]

6621. Zeydel, Edwin H. "Edgar Allan Poe's Contacts with German as Seen in His Relations with Ludwig Tieck." [F 33]:47–54.

6622. Zimmerman, Melvin. "Baudelaire's Early Conception of Poe's Fate." *RLC* 44:117–20.

See also 866, 6354, 6432, 7043.

Prescott. 6623. Gardiner, C. Harvey. *William Hickling Prescott:A Biography.* Introd. Allan Nevins. Austin: U. of Texas P., 1969.

Putnam's. 6624. Kotzin, Miriam N. "*Putnam's Monthly* and Its Place in American Literature." *DAI* 31:1232A–33A(N.Y.U.).

6625. Tew, Arnold G. "*Putnam's Magazine*:Its Men and Their Literary and Social Policies." *DAI* 30:3921A(Case Western Reserve).

Ray. *6626. Kable, William S. "Addenda to Wright:William Ray's *Sophia*." *PBSA* 64:206. [Cf. Bibliog. for 1969, Vol. I, Item 6317.]

Sanborn, F.B. 6627. Swennes, Robert H. "Note on Sanborn's 'To John Brown'." *ATQ* 1(1969):43–44.

See also 6631.

Sedgwick. *6628. Bell, Michael D. "History and Romance Convention in Catharine Sedgwick's *Hope Leslie*." *AQ* 22:[213]–21.

6629. Sedgwick, C.M. *Hope Leslie.* Introd. Edward H. Foster. New York: Garrett.

6630. —— *Redwood.* Introd. Edward H. Foster. New York: Garrett.

Sill. 6631. Ferguson, Alfred R. "Sill's Poems Wrongly Ascribed to Sanborn." *ESQ* 58:131.

Simms. 6632. Doxey, William S. "Dogs and Dates in Simms' *The Yemassee*." *ATQ* 1(1969):41–43.

6633. Guilds, John C. "The Literary Criticism of William Gilmore Simms." *SCR* 2,i:49–56.

6634. Howell, Elmo. "The Concept of Character in Simms' Border Romances." *MissQ* 22(1969):303–12.

6635. Lease, Benjamin. "William Gilmore Simms, a New Simms Letter." *Ga. Hist. Quart.* 54:427–30.

6636. Ridgely, Joseph V. "Simms's Concept of Style in the Historical Romance." *ESQ* 60:16–23.

* 6637. Wimsatt, Mary Ann. "Leonard Voltmeier's 'Invictus': Vol. One of the *Centennial Simms*." *SLJ* 2,ii:135–47.

Smith, S. 6638. Miller, Alan R. "America's First Political Satirist:Seba Smith of Maine." *JQ* 47:488–92.

Stowe. *6639. Grimsted, David A. "*Uncle Tom* from Page to Stage:Limitations of Nineteenth-Century Drama." *QJS* 56: 235–44.

6640. Woodress, James. "*La capanna dello zio Tom* in Italia." [F 61]:295–312.

See also 4575.

Taylor. 6641. Doughty, Nanelia S. "Bayard Taylor:First California Booster." *WR* 7,i:22–27.

Thompson. 6642. Ellison, George R. "William Tappan Thompson and the *Southern Miscellany* 1842–1844." *MissQ* 23:155–68.

Thoreau. 6643. Becker, Isadore H. "Thoreau's Princely Leisure." *HussR* 3:161–67.

6644. Cameron, Kenneth Walter. "Damning National Publicity for Thoreau in 1849." *ATQ* 2(1969):18–27. [Illus.]

6645. —— "Thoreau and His Harvard Classmates:Henry Williams' *Memorials of the Class of 1837* with a Commentary and an Index." *ATQ* 3(1969):5–132.

6646. —— "Thoreau's *Walden* and Alcott's Vegetarianism." *ATQ* 2(1969):27–28.

* 6647. Davidson, Frank. "Thoreau and David Starr Jordan." *TSB* 109(1969):5–6.

6648. DeMott, Robert J. " 'The Eccentric Orbit':Dimensions of the Artistic Process in Henry David Thoreau's Major Writings." *DAI* 30:5405A–06A(Kent State).

6649. Dennis, Carl. "Correspondence in Thoreau's Nature Poetry." *ESQ* 58:101–09.

6650. Ford, Arthur L. "The Poetry of Henry David Thoreau." *ESQ* 61:1–26.

6651. Galligan, Edward L. "The Comedian at Walden Pond." *SAQ* 69: [20]–37.

6652. Gurney, Richard C. "The Worst of Thoreau." *ConnR* 3,ii:68–71.

6653. Hanley, Katherine,C.S.J. "*Walden*:Forest Sonata."

ATQ 1(1969):108–10.

* 6654. Harding, Walter. "Elizabeth Oakes Smith on Thoreau." *TSB* 110:2–3.

6655. —— "George Sturt and Thoreau." *TSB* 111:3–5.

6656. Hoch, David G. "Annals and Perennials:A Study of Cosmogonic Imagery in Thoreau." *DAI* 30:5446A(Kent State).

* 6657. —— "Concord's Coat of Arms." *TSB* 110:1.

6658. Homan, John,Jr. "Thoreau, the Emblem, and the *Week*." *ATQ* 1(1969):104–08.

6659. King, Bruce. "Emerson's Pupil." *Venture*(U. of Karachi) 5(1969):112–22.

6660. Kleinfeld, Leonard F. "Thoreau Chronology." *ATQ* 1(1969):113–17.

6661. Kurtz, Kenneth. "Style in *Walden*." *ESQ* 60:59–67.

6662. Lambert, L. Gary. "Rousseau and Thoreau:Their Concept of Nature." *DAI* 30(1969):1988A(Rice).

* 6663. Lane, Lauriat,Jr. " 'Civil Disobedience':A Bibliographical Note." *PBSA* 63(1969):295–96.

6664. —— "Finding a Voice:Thoreau's Pentameters." *ESQ* 60:67–72.

* 6665. —— "Thoreau's Two Walks:Structure and Meaning." *TSB* 109(1969):1–3.

6666. Lombardo, Agostino. "Thoreau nella cultura italiana." *SA* 14(1968):41–62.

6667. Mattfield, Mary S. "Thoreau's Poem #189:An Emended Reading." *CEA* 33,i:10–11.

* 6668. Michaelson, L.W. "The Man Who Burned the Woods." *Eng. Record* 20,iii:72–75.

6669. Millichap, Joseph R. "Plato's Allegory of the Cave and the Vision of *Walden*." *ELN* 7:274–82.

6670. Moyne, Ernest J. "Thoreau and Emerson:Their Interest in Finland." *NM* 70(1969):738–50.

* 6671. Noverr, Douglas A. "Thoreau's July 16, 1860 Letter to Charles Sumner:An Additional Note." *TSB* 110:2. [See Bibliog. for 1969, Vol. I, Item 6372.]

6672. Parsons, Vesta M. "Thoreau's *The Maine Woods*:An Essay in Appreciation." *HussR* 1(1967-68):17–27.

6673. Phillips, Emmett L. "A Study of Aesthetic Distance in Thoreau's Walden." *DAI* 30:3953A(Okla.).

6674. Reaver, J. Russell. "Thoreau's Ways with Proverbs." *ATQ* 1(1969):2–7.

6675. Reger, William. "Beyond Metaphor." *Criticism* 4:333–44.

6676. Ribbens, Dennis N. "The Reading Interests of Thoreau, Hawthorne, and Lanier." *DAI* 31:777A(Wis.).

6677. Ross, Donald,Jr. "Composition as a Stylistic Feature." *Style* 4:1–10.

6678. Salminen, Johannes. "Våga börja leva." *Horisont* 17,iv:11–16. [T's carpe diem.]

* 6679. Seaburg, Alan. "A Thoreau Document." *TSB* 109(1969):5.

6680. Shanley, J. Lyndon. "Rationale of the Intention of the Editors of Thoreau's Journal." *CEAAN* 3:24–25.

6681. Sherwin, J. Stephen, and Richard C. Reynolds. *A Word Index to* Walden *with Textual Notes:A Corrected Edition.* *ESQ* 57(1969)Supp. [Orig. pub. 1960.]

* 6682. Stein, William B. "The Hindu Matrix of *Walden*:The King's Son." *CL* 22:303–18.

6683. —— "The Yoga of *Walden*:Chapter I(Economy)." *LE&W* 13(1969):1–26.

6684. Stibitz, E. Earle. "Thoreau's Humanism and Ideas on Literature." *ESQ* 55(1969):110–16.

6685. Stowell, Robert F. *A Thoreau Gazetteer.* Ed. William L. Howarth. Princeton, N.J.: Princeton U.P.

6686. —— "Poetry About Thoreau:19th Century." *TSB* 112:1–3.

6687. Thomas, Robert K. "The Tree and the Stone:Time and Space in the Works of Henry David Thoreau." *DAI* 31:1776A(Columbia).

6688. Thoreau, H.D. *Walden and Other Writings.* Introd. Nat Hentoff. Garden City, N.Y.: Internat. Collectors Lib.

6689. Timpe, Eugene F. "Thoreau's Developing Style." *ESQ* 58:120–24.

6690. Treat, Robert and Betty. "Thoreau and Institutional Christianity." *ATQ* 1(1969):44–47.

6691. Volkman, Arthur G. "Thoreau as a Seer." *TSB* 111:2–3.

6692. Whishnant, David E. "The Sacred and the Profane in *Walden*." *CentR* 14:267–83.

6693. Whitaker, Rosemary. "*A Week on the Concord and Merrimack Rivers*:An Experiment in the Communication of Transcendental Experience." *DAI* 31:737A(Okla.).

* 6694. Woodson, Thomas. "Thoreau on Poverty and Magnanimity." *PMLA* 85:21–34.

See also 1352, 5917, 6331, 6355, 6358, 6434.

Timrod. 6695. Green, Claud B. "Henry Timrod and the South." *SCR* 2,ii:27–33.

Transcendentalism. 6696. Bier, Jesse. "Weberism, Franklin, and the Transcendental Style." *NEQ* 43:179–92.

6697. Mueller, Roger C. "Transcendental Periodicals and the Orient." *ESQ* 57(1969):52–57.

See also 6331, 6372, 6715.

Tucker, G. 6698. Tucker, G. *The Valley of Shenandoah or Memoirs of the Graysons.* (Southern Lit. Classics.) Introd. Donald R. Noble,Jr. Chapel Hill: U. of N.C. Press.

Tucker, N.B. *6699. Wrobel, Arthur. " 'Romantic Realism': Nathaniel Beverly Tucker." *AL* 42:[325]–35.

Tuckerman, H.T. 6700. Anzilotti, Rolando. "L'Italia e il Risorgimento nell'opera di Henry Theodore Tuckerman." [F 61]:41–67.

6701. Lombard, C.M. "A Neglected Critic—Henry T. Tuckerman." *EA* 22(1969):362–69.

Very. 6702. Dennis, Carl. "Correspondence in Very's Nature Poetry." *NEQ* 43:250–73.

Walsh. *6703. Woodall, Guy R. "Robert Walsh's War with the New York Literati:1827–1836." *TSL* 15:25–47.

Webster. *6704. Bromberger, Bonnie. "Noah Webster's Notes on His Early Political Essays in the *Connecticut Courant*." *BNYPL* 74:338–42.

Whipple, E.P. 6705. Smith, Frederick A. "E.P. Whipple, Nineteenth Century American Literary Critic." *DAI* 30:2980A (Ill.).

Whittier. 6706. Cameron, Kenneth Walter. "Ungathered Whittier Poem?" *ATQ* 1(1969):102. ["Unity."]

6707. Cary, Richard. "More Whittier Letters to Jewett." *ESQ* 58:132–39.

6708. Kime, Wayne R. "Whittier's 'Ichabod'." *Expl* 28:Item 59.

6709. Poger, Sidney. " 'Snow-Bound' and Social Responsibility." *ATQ* 1(1969):85–87.

6710. *Whittier Newsl.* 7. ["Whittier Bibliography for 1969," 1–2; "Research in Progress and Work Completed," 2; "Whittier Library Collections and Whittier Clubs," 2–3; "Notes and Queries," 3; Scott Donaldson, "Winfield Townley Scott and Whittier," 4.]

Wirt. 6711. Wirt, W. *The Letters of the British Spy.* Introd. Richard B. Davis. Chapel Hill: U. of N.C. Press. [Orig. pub. in 1803.]

IV. NINETEENTH CENTURY, 1870–1900

General and Miscellaneous. 6712. Contoski, Victor J. "The Southern Aristocratic Lover:Symbol of National Unity 1865–1885." *DAI* 30:3903A–04A(Wis.).

6713. Doxey, William S.,Jr. "American Literary Response to the Philippine Problem:1899–1906." *WGCR* 2,i(1969):10–19.

6714. Hardin, Nancy S. "French Student Taste in American Literature:A Study in Attitudes and Conceptions." *DAI* 30:5409A(Wis.).

* 6715. Jackson, Carl T. "The Orient in Post-Bellum American Thought:Three Pioneer Popularizers." *AQ* 22:[67]–81. [J.F. Clarke, S. Johnson, and M. Conway; deals also with transcendentalist writers.]

6716. Jones, Howard M. "The Genteel Tradition." *HLB* 18:5–20.

6717. Karlson, Robert E. "American Short Story Criticism, 1885–1919." *DAI* 31:1803A(Geo. Wash.).

See also 1108, 3890, 6240, 6244, 6248, 6250, 6255, 6256.

Drama and Theater. 6718. Oggel, Lynwood T. "Edwin Booth and America's Concept of Shakespearean Tragedy." *DAI* 31:364A(Wis.).

See also 3914, 5754, 6259.

Poetry. *See* 6267, 6610, 7244.

Prose Fiction. 6719. Fine, David M. "The Immigrant Ghetto in American Fiction, 1885–1917." *DAI* 31:755A(U.C.L.A.).

6720. Gittlen, Arthur J. "Political and Social Thought Contained in the Jewish-American Novel (1867–1927)." *DAI* 30(1969):2527A–28A(Mich. State).

6721. Griffith, Kelley E.,Jr. "The Genteel Romance in American Fiction, 1880–1910." *DAI* 30(1969):1134A–35A(Pa.).

6722. Kolb, Harold H.,Jr. *The Illusion of Life:American Realism as a Literary Form.* Charlottesville: U.P. of Va., 1969. [Emphasis on H. James, Twain, and Howells.]

6723. Lycette, Ronald L. "Diminishing Circumferences: Feminine Responses in Fiction to New England Decline." *DAI* 31:1764A(Purdue).

6724. Marks, Barry A. "Retrospective Narrative in Nineteenth Century American Literature." *CE* 31(1969):366–75.

6725. Miller, Theodore C. "Some Representative Figures of the Southern Gentleman in American Fiction, 1865–1915." *DAI* 30(1969):2541A–42A(N.Y.U.).

6726. Mills, Nicolaus C. "The Machine in the Anglo-American Garden." *CentR* 14:201–12.

6727. Settle, William A.,Jr. "Literature as History:The Dime Novel as an Historian's Tool." [F 58]:9–20.

See also 999, 3948, 3950, 6269, 6273, 6274, 6717, 7273, 7278, 7294.

Adams. 6728. Conder, John J. *A Formula of His Own:Henry Adams's Literary Experiment.* Chicago: U. of Chicago P.

6729. Friedlaender, Marc. "Henry Hobson Richardson, Henry Adams, and John Hay." *PMHS* 81:137–66. [Also in *Jour. of the Soc. of Architectural Historians*, Oct. 1970; illus.]

6730. Lyon, Melvin. *Symbol and Idea in Henry Adams.* Lincoln: U. of Neb. P.

* 6731. Martin, John S. "Henry Adams on War:The Transformation of History into Metaphor." *ArQ* 24(1968):325–41.

* 6732. Scheik, William J. "Symbolism in *The Education of Henry Adams*." *ArQ* 24(1968):350–60.

6733. Scheyer, Ernst. *The Circle of Henry Adams:Art & Artist.* Detroit: Wayne State U.P. [On A and the visual arts.]

6734. Strout, Cushing. "Personality and Cultural History in the Novel:Two American Examples." *NLH* 1:423–37. [On H. Adams' *Esther* and Abraham Cahan's *The Rise of David Levinsky* (1917).]

* 6735. Vandersee, Charles. "The Four Menageries of Henry Adams." *ArQ* 24(1968):293–308.

Ade. 6736. Hasley, Louis. "George Ade, Realist, Fabulist." *Four Quarters* 19,iii:25–32.

Aldrich, T.B. *See* 4529.

Barr. *See* 6837.

Barrett. 6737. McAleer, John J. "Lawrence Barrett:'The Scholar of the American Theater'." *ShN* 20:44–45.

Bellamy. *See* 3945.

Bierce. *6738. Highsmith, James M. "The Forms of Burlesque in *The Devil's Dictionary*." *SNL* 7:115–27.

Burroughs. 6739. Westbrook, Perry. "John Burroughs and the Transcendentalists." *ESQ* 55(1969):47–55.

Channing, E. 6740. Joyce, Davis D. "History as Literature: Edward Channing's *History of the United States* as Literature." [F 58]:21–30.

Chesnutt. 6741. Chesnutt, C.W. *The House Behind the Cedars.* Introd. Darwin Turner. New York: Collier, 1969.

Chopin. 6742. Arner, Robert D. "Kate Chopin's Realism:'At the Cadian Ball' and 'The Storm'." *MarkhamR* 2,ii:[1]–[4].

* 6743. Leary, Lewis. "Kate Chopin, Liberationist?" *SLJ* 3:138–44.

6744. Leary, Lewis,ed. *The Awakening and Other Stories.* With

Introd. New York: Holt, Rinehart and Winston.

* 6745. May, John R. "Local Color in *The Awakening*." *SoR* 6:1031–40.

6746. Potter, Richard H. "Kate Chopin and Her Critics:An Annotated Checklist." *MHSB* 26:306–17.

6747. Seyersted, Per. "Kate Chopin (1851–1904)." *ALR* 3:153–59. [Bibliog.]

6748. Seyersted, Per,ed. *The Complete Works of Kate Chopin.* 2 vols. With Introd. Foreword Edmund Wilson. Baton Rouge: La. State U.P., 1969.

Clemens. 6749. Andersen, Kenneth. "Mark Twain, W.D. Howells, and Henry James:Three Agnostics in Search of Salvation." *MTJ* 15,i:13–16.

6750. Babcock, C. Merton. "Mark Twain as 'A Majority of One'." *UCQ* 15,iv:3–7.

6751. —— "Mark Twain's Chuck-Wagon Specialties." *WAL* 5:147–51.

6752. Bader, Judith F. "The Dominant Character in Mark Twain's Major Fiction." *DAI* 30:4934A(Ind.).

6753. Baetzhold, Howard G. *Mark Twain and John Bull:The British Connection.* Bloomington: Ind. U.P.

* 6754. Belson, Joel J. "The Nature and Consequences of the Loneliness of Huckleberry Finn." *ArQ* 26:243–48.

6755. Bickley, R. Bruce,Jr. "Humorous Portraiture in Twain's News Writing." *ALR* 3:395–98.

6756. Blair, Walter,ed. *Mark Twain's Hannibal, Huck & Tom.* With Introd. Berkeley: U. of Calif. P., 1969.

6757. Blues, Thomas. *Mark Twain & the Community.* Lexington: U. of Ky. P. [Crit.]

6758. Boland, Sally. "The Seven Dialects in *Huckleberry Finn*." *NDQ* 36,iii(1968):30–40.

6759. Bowen, James K., and Richard Van Der Beets,eds. *Adventures of Huckleberry Finn.* Glenview, Ill.: Scott, Foresman. [Incl. Edgar M. Branch, "Mark Twain Scholarship:Two Decades," 344–49.]

6760. Branch, Edgar M. "Samuel Clemens and the Copperheads of 1864." *MRR* 2,i(1967):3–20.

6762. Budd, Louis J. "Baxter's Hog:The Right Mascot for an Editor (with CEAA Standards) of Mark Twain's Political and Social Writings." *CEAAN* 3:3–10.

6763. Burrison, John A. *"The Golden Arm":The Folk Tale and Its Literary Use by Mark Twain and Joel C. Harris.* (Research Paper 19.) Atlanta: Ga. State U., 1968.

* 6764. Chambliss, Amy. "The Frendship of Helen Keller and the Mark Twain." *GaR* 24:305–10.

6765. Clemens, S.L. *Your Personal Mark Twain:In Which the Great American Ventures an Opinion on Ladies, Language, Liberty, Literature, Liquor, Love and Other Controversial Subjects.* Introd. Phoebe Standart. New York: Internat. Pubs., 1969.

6766. Clemens, S.L., and C.D. Warner. *The Gilded Age:A Tale of Today.* Introd. Marvin Felheim. New York: New Amer. Lib., 1969.

6767. Coburn, Mark D. "The Progress of Twain's Pilgrims." *DAI* 30(1969):1164A–65A(Stanford).

* 6768. —— " 'Training Is Everything':Communal Opinion and the Individual in *Pudd'nhead Wilson*." *MLQ* 31:209–19.

6769. Coplin, Keith. "John and Sam Clemens:A Father's Influence." *MTJ* 15,i:1–6.

6770. Dickinson, Leon T. "[Review of] Dewey Ganzel, *Mark Twain Abroad:The Cruise of the "Quaker City"* (Chicago: Univ. of Chicago Press, 1968.)" *MP* 68:117–19. [Incl. text of hitherto unpub. letter by Mark Twain.]

6771. Doyle, Paul A. "Henry Harper's Telling of a Mark Twain Anecdote." *MTJ* 15,ii:13.

6772. Durham, John M.,Jr. "Mark Twain Comments on Religious Hypocrisy." *RLA* 10(1967):60–75.

6773. Elsbree, Langdon. "Huck Finn on the Nile." *SAQ* 69:[504]–10.

* 6774. Ensor, Allison. "The Birthplace of Samuel Clemens:A New Mark Twain Letter." *TSL* 14(1969):31–34.

6775. —— "The 'Opposition Line' to the King and the Duke in *Huckleberry Finn*." *MTJ* 14,iii(1968–69):6–7.

* 6776. —— "The 'Tennessee Land' of *The Gilded Age*:Fiction and Reality." *TSL* 15:15–23.

6778. Gardner, Joseph H. "Dickens in America:Mark Twain, Howells, James, and Norris." *DAI* 30:4409A–10A(Calif., Berkeley).

6779. Geismar, Maxwell. *Mark Twain:An American Prophet.* Boston: Houghton Mifflin. [Crit.]

6780. Gerber, John C. "Mark Twain." [F 65]:66–83.

6781. Gervais, Ronald J. "Mark Twain and the Fall into the Moral Sense." *DAI* 30:4985A–86A(Ore.).

6782. —— "*The Mysterious Stranger*:The Fall as Salvation." *PCP* 5:24–33.

6783. Goto, Akio. "Seijuku no Kyozetsu—M. Twain no Americateki Seikaku." *EigoS* 115(1969):286–87. [Rejection of maturity—T's American character.]

6784. Hakac, John. "*Huckleberry Finn*:A Copy Inscribed in 1903." *ABC* 20,i:7–9.

6785. Harkey, Joseph H. "When Huck Finn Smouched That Spoon." *MTJ* 15,ii:14.

6786. Howell, Elmo. "In Defense of Tom Sawyer." *MTJ* 15,i:17–19.

6787. Johnson, Ellwood. "Mark Twain's Dream Self in the Nightmare of History." *MTJ* 15,i:6–12.

6788. Kolin, Philip C. "Mark Twain, Aristotle, and Pudd'nhead Wilson." *MTJ* 15,ii:1–4.

6789. Leary, Lewis. "Mark Twain Among the Malefactors." [F 67]:109–17. [Rev. version of Item 10285, Bibliog. for 1968.]

* 6790. —— "More Letters from the *Quaker City*." *AL* 42:[197]–202.

6791. Leary, Lewis,ed. *Mark Twain's Correspondence with Henry Huttleston Rogers:1893–1909.* With Introd. Berkeley: U. of Calif. P., 1969.

6792. Lewis, Stuart A. "Pudd'nhead Wilson's Election." *MTJ* 15,i:21.

6793. Lowrey, Robert E. "The Grangerford-Shepherdson Episode:Another of Mark Twain's Indictments of the Damned Human Race." *MTJ* 15,i:19–20.

6794. "Mark Twain to Chatto & Windus:Two Unpublished Letters." *CEAAN* 3:1–2.

* 6795. McCarthy, Harold T. "Mark Twain's Pilgrim's Progress:*The Innocents Abroad*." *ArQ* 26:249–58.

6796. McCullough, Joseph B.,Jr. "A Complete Edition of the Contributions of Hy Slocum and Carl Byng to the Buffalo *Express*, 1868–1871, with a Discussion of Samuel L. Clemens' Authorship." *DAI* 30:3949A(Ohio).

6797. McKee, John D. "*Roughing It* as Retrospective Reporting." *WAL* 5:113–19.

6798. Miller, Ruth. "But Laugh or Die:A Comparison of *The Mysterious Stranger* and *Billy Budd*." *Lit. Half-Yearly*(Mysore) 11,i:25–29.

6799. Molter, Leticia S.R. "A Study of the Social Criticism in the Essays of Mark Twain." *DAI* 31(1969):2491A–92A(Pittsburgh).

6800. Reed, Kenneth T. "Mirth and Misquotation:Mark Twain in Petoskey, Michigan." *MTJ* 15,ii:19–20.

6801. Rees, Robert A. "*Captain Stormfield's Visit to Heaven* and *The Gates Ajar*." *ELN* 7:197–202.

6802. Rodnon, Stewart. "*The Adventures of Huckleberry Finn* and *Invisible Man*:Thematic and Structural Comparisons." *NALF* 4:45–51.

6803. Rubin, Louis D.,Jr. "Three Installments of Mark Twain." *SR* 78:678–84. [Rev. art. on 3 vols. of Twain papers.]

6804. Serrano Plaja, Arturo. *"Magic" Realism in Cervantes: Don Quixote as Seen Through Tom Sawyer and The Idiot.* Tr. Robert S. Rudder. Berkeley: U. of Calif. P.

6805. Shults, Donald. "On *The Gilded Age*." *KAL* 12:1–13.

6806. Simonson, Harold P. "*Huckleberry Finn* as Tragedy." *YR* 59:532–48.

* 6807. Spangler, George M. "*Pudd'nhead Wilson*:A Parable of Property." *AL* 42:[28]–37.

6808. Spofford, William K. "Mark Twain's Connecticut Yankee:An Ignoramus Nevertheless." *MTJ* 15,ii:15–18.

6809. Trachtenberg, Alan. "The Form of Freedom in *Adventures of Huckleberry Finn*." *SoR* 6:954–71.

* 6810. Tuckey, John S. "Hannibal, Weggis, and Mark Twain's Eseldorf." *AL* 42:235–40.

* 6811. —— "Mark Twain's Later Dialogue:The 'Me' and the Machine." *AL* 41:[532]–42.

6812. Tyler, Ronald T. "Mark Twain's Mythic Vision:An Affirmation of Man's Possibilities." *DAI* 31:1777A(Nev.).

6813. Wagenknecht, Edward. "*The Mark Twain Papers* and *Henry James:The Treacherous Years*." *SNNTS* 2,i:88–98. [Rev. art.]

6814. Werge, Thomas. "Mark Twain and the Fall of Adam." *MTJ* 15,ii:5–13.

6815. Wheelock, C. Webster. "The Point of Pudd'nhead's Half-A-Dog Joke." *AN&Q* 8:150–51.

6816. Yoshida, Hiroshige. "Huckleberry Finn ko." *EigoS* 114(1968):84–86. [On *Huckleberry Finn*.]

See also 4285, 6722, 7513, 7561.

Crane. 6817. Brown, Ellen A.R. "The Uneasy Balance:A Study of Polarity in the Work of Stephen Crane." *DAI* 31:1220A(Mich. State).

6818. Crane, S. *Maggie:A Girl of the Streets (A Story of New York).* Introd. Philip J. Jordan. Lexington: U.P. of Ky.

6819. Davison, Richard A. "Crane's 'Blue Hotel' Revisited: The Illusion of Fate." *MFS* 15(1969):537–39.

6820. Dusenbery, Robert. "The Homeric Mood in the *Red Badge of Courage*." *PCP* 3(1968):31–37.

6821. Edelstein, Arthur,introd. *Three Great Novels by Stephen Crane:Maggie, George's Mother, The Red Badge of Courage.* New York: Fawcett.

6822. Ewing, James M.,Jr. "Figurative Language in the Prose Fiction of Stephen Crane." *DAI* 30:4941A–42A(So. Miss.).

* 6823. Ford, Philip H. "Illusion and Reality in Crane's *Maggie*." *ArQ* 25(1969):293–303.

6824. Forster, Imogen,ed. "The *Thoth* Annual Bibliography of Stephen Crane Scholarship." *Thoth* 10,ii(1969):25–27.

6825. Fox, Austin M. "Stephen Crane and Joseph Conrad." *Serif* 6,iv(1969):16–20.

6826. Frohock, W.M. "*The Red Badge* and the Limits of Parody." *SoR* 6:137–48.

6827. Gilkes, Lillian. "Stephen Crane's Burial Place:Some Inconsequential Ghost Laying." *Serif* 7,ii:7–11.

6828. —— "Stephen Crane and the Harold Frederics." *Serif* 6,iv(1969):21–48.

6829. Giorgio, Benjamin D. "Stephen Crane:American Impressionist." *DAI* 30(1969):1167A–68A(Wis.).

6830. Itabashi, Yoshie. "Stephen Crane ni okeru Shizenshugi no Henyo." *EigoS* 115(1969):352–53. [Transformation of naturalism in C.]

* 6831. Jackson, Agnes M. "Stephen Crane's Imagery of Conflict in *George's Mother*." *ArQ* 25(1969):313–18.

* 6832. Knapp, Daniel. "Son of Thunder:Stephen Crane and the Fourth Evangelist." *NCF* 24(1969):253–91.

6833. LaFrance, Marston. "Crane, Zola, and the Hot Ploughshares." *ELN* 7:285–87.

6834. Monteiro, George. "*The Illustrated American* and Stephen Crane's Contemporary Reputation." *Serif* 6,iv(1969): 49–54.

6835. —— "With Proper Words (or Without Them) the Soldier Dies:Stephen Crane's 'Making an Orator'." *Cithara* 9,ii:64–72.

6836. Noel, Edgar E. "Stephen Crane:A Realist Who Painted with Words." *KAL* 12:20–31.

6837. O'Donnell, Bernard. *An Analysis of Prose Style to Determine Authorship:The O'Ruddy, a Novel by Stephen Crane and Robert Barr.* (Studies in Gen. and Comp. Lit. 4.) The Hague: Mouton.

6838. Pizer, Donald,ed. *Maggie:A Girl of the Streets.* Facsim of 1893 Ed. With Introd. San Francisco: Chandler, 1968.

* 6839. Rogers, Rodney O. "Stephen Crane and Impressionism." *NCF* 24(1969):292–304.

6840. *SCraneN* 4,ii. [Elizabeth W. Cady, "Stephen Crane to Miss Daisy D. Hill:The Letter Recovered," 1–4; G.L. Williams, "Henry Fleming and the 'Cheery Voiced' Stranger," 4–7; George Monteiro, "Brazilian Translations of Stephen Crane's Fiction," 7–8; Joseph Katz, "The Reception of *Wounds in the Rain*," 9–10].

6841. *SCraneN* 4,iii. [Joseph Katz, "Crane's Chapter Headings for *The O'Ruddy*," 1; Richard M. Weatherford, "Stephen Crane in *The Lotus* and *Chips*," 2–3; Joseph Katz, "Stephen Crane in *The Fly Leaf*," 3–4; Joseph Katz, "*The Red Badge of Courage*:A Preliminary History of the Appleton Printings," 5–7; George Monteiro, "Cora Crane to John Hay:A Last Communication," 8; Matthew J. Bruccoli, "Robert Barr's Proofs of *The O'Ruddy*," 8; Joseph Katz, "Elbert Hubbard's Watermark," 8–10; Joseph Katz, "The Lanthorn Book:A Census (Part I), 10–12.]

6842. *SCraneN* 2,ii(1967). [Stanley Wertheim, "Franklin Garland's *Maggie*," 1–4; Joseph Katz, "DeWitt Miller's *Maggie*:A Correction," 4–6; Joseph Katz, "Stephen Crane to an Unknown Recipient:A New Letter," 4–5; Joseph Katz, "Stephen Crane to *Youth's Companion*:A New Letter," 5; Joseph Katz, "Joline's *Meditations*, Crane, and Spelling," 5; Joseph Katz, "*Maggie:A Girl of the Streets* (1893):A Census (Part I)," 7–9; Joseph Katz, "Stephen Crane to the *Chap-Book*:Two New Letters," 9–10.]

6843. *SCraneN* 4,i. [Matthew J. Bruccoli, " 'The Wonders of Ponce':Crane's First Puerto Rico Dispatch," 1–3; Joseph Katz, "Stephen Crane to the Atlanta *Journal*: A New Letter," 3; Joseph Katz, "Stephen Crane's Passport Applications:Part IV," 4–5; Joseph Katz, "John William De Forest on Stephen Crane," 6; Joseph Katz, "Stephen Crane to the American Press Association: A New Letter," 6–7.]

6844. Shima, Hideo. "Nature, Love, and Solitude in Stephen Crane's Poems." [F 14]:82–102. [In Jap.]

6845. Slote, Bernice. "Stephen Crane and Willa Cather." *Serif* 6,iv(1969):3–15.

6846. White, John W.,Jr. "Stephen Crane's Fascination with Man:A Study of Christian Themes in His Fiction." *DAI* 30(1969):1153A–54A(Geo. Peabody Coll. for Teachers).
See also 529, 1041, 6513, 6583.

Crawford. *See* 6721.

Davis, R.H. 6847. Solensten, John M. "Richard Harding Davis (1864–1916)." *ALR* 3:160–66. [Bibliog.]
See also 6721.

De Forest. 6848. De Forest, J.W. *Miss Ravenel's Conversion from Secession to Loyalty.* (Merrill Editions.) Introd. Arlin Turner. Columbus, Ohio: Charles E. Merrill, 1969.

6849. Hagemann, E.R. "A John William De Forest Supplement, 1970." *ALR* 3:148–52. [Bibliog.]

Dickinson. *6850. Bowman, Elizabeth. "Dickinson's 'The Soul Selects Her Own Society'." *Expl* 29:Item 13.

6851. Buckingham, Willis J.,ed. *Emily Dickinson:An Annotated Bibliography:Writings, Scholarship, Criticism, and Ana: 1850–1968.* Bloomington: Ind. U.P.

6852. Chaliff, Cynthia. "Emily Dickinson as the Deprived Child." *Emily Dickinson Bull.* 13:34–43.

6853. —— "The Psychology of Economics in Emily Dickinson." *L&P* 18(1968):93–100.

* 6854. Cody, John. "Metamorphosis of a Malady:Summary of a Psychoanalytic Study of Emily Dickinson." *HSL* 2:113–32.

6855. D'Avanzo, Mario L. "Emily Dickinson's and Emerson's 'Presentiment'." *ESQ* 58:157–59.

6856. Donoghue, Denis. *Emily Dickinson.* (UMPAW 81.) Minneapolis: U. of Minn. P., 1969.

6857. Fagundo Guerra, Ana M. "The Influence of Emily Dickinson on Juan Ramón Jiménez' Poetry." *DA* 29(1968): 258A(U. of Wash.).

6858. Fisher, C.J. "Emily Dickinson as a Latter-Day Metaphysical Poet." *ATQ* 1(1969):77–81.

6859. Galinsky, Hans. *Wegbereiter moderner amerikanischer Lyrik:Interpretations- und Rezeptionsstudien zu Emily Dickinson und William Carlos Williams.* Heidelberg: Winter, 1968.

6860. Goudie, Andrea K. " 'The Earth Has Many Keys':A Study of Emily Dickinson's Responses to Nature." *DAI* 30(1969):1134A(Ind.).

6861. Greene, Elsa P. "The Splintered Crown:A Study of Eve and Emily Dickinson." *DAI* 31:387A–88A(Minn.).

* 6862. Gross, John J. "Tell All the Truth but—." *BSUF* 10,i(1969):71–77. [D's indirect style.]

* 6863. Jumper, Will C. "Dickinson's 'The Soul Selects Her Own Society'." *Expl* 29:Item 5.

6864. Kahn, Salamatullah. *Emily Dickinson's Poetry:The Flood Subjects.* New Delhi: Aarti Book Centre; Mystic, Conn.:

Verry, 1969.

* 6865. Lowrey, Robert E. " 'Boanerges':An Encomium for Edward Dickinson." *ArQ* 26:54–58. [ED's father.]

6866. Lucas, Dolores D. *Emily Dickinson and Riddle.* DeKalb: No. Ill. U.P., 1969. [Crit.]

6867. Patterson, Rebecca. "Emily Dickinson's Geography: Latin America." *PLL* 5(1969):441–57.

6868. Pollak, Vivian R. "Emily Dickinson's Early Poems and Letters." *DAI* 31:366A(Brandeis).

6869. Porter, David. "Emily Dickinson:The Poetics of Doubt." *ESQ* 60:86–93.

6870. Sprague, Rosemary. *Imaginary Gardens:A Study of Five American Poets.* Philadelphia: Chilton, 1969. [D, Amy Lowell, Sara Teasdale, Edna St. Vincent Millay, Marianne Moore.]

6871. Suško, Mario. "Unutarnja gravitacija Emily Dickinson." *Kolo* 15:143–70. [On D's "internal gravitation."]

6872. White, William. "Emily Dickinsoniana:An Annotated Checklist of Books About the Poet." *BB* 26(1969):100–04.

6873. —— "The Tyranny of Book Collecting:Emily Dickinson." *ABC* 21,i:9.
See also 6596, 7052, 7965.

Eddy. 6874. Parker, Gail. "Mary Baker Eddy and Sentimental Womanhood." *NEQ* 43:3–18.

Eggleston. 6875. Eggleston, E. *The Circuit Rider:A Tale of the Heroic Age.* Introd. Holman Hamilton. Lexington: U.P. of Ky.
* 6876. Wilson, Jack H. "Eggleston's Indebtedness to George Eliot in *Roxy*." *AL* 42:[38]–49.

Frederic. 6877. Garmon, Gerald M. "Naturalism and *The Damnation of Theron Ware*." *WGCR* 2,ii(1969):44–51.

6878. Garner, Stanton. *Harold Frederic.* (UMPAW 83.) Minneapolis: U. of Minn. P., 1969.

6879. Sage, Howard. "Harold Frederic's Narrative Essays:A Realistic-Journalistic Genre." *ALR* 3:388–92.

6880. Williams, David. "The Nature of the Damnation of Theron Ware." *MSE* 2(1969):41–48.

6881. Wilson, Edmund. "Two Neglected American Novelists:II—Harold Frederic, the Expanding Upstater." *NY* 46(6 June):112–34.

6882. Woodward, Robert H. "Harold Frederic:Supplemental Critical Bibliography of Secondary Comment." *ALR* 3:95–147.
See also 6828, 6884, 6930.

Fuller, H.B. 6883. Abel, Darrel. "Expatriation and Realism in American Fiction in the 1880's:Henry Blake Fuller." *ALR* 3:245–57. [Incl. first pub. of essay by F, "The American School of Fiction" (ca. 1886).]

6884. Cheshire, David, and Malcolm Bradbury. "American Realism and the Romance of Europe:[H.B.] Fuller, Frederic, Harland." [F 64]:285–310.

6885. Pilkington, John. "Aftermath of a Novelist." *UMSE* 10(1968):1–23.

6886. Wilson, Edmund. "Two Neglected American Novelists:I—Henry B. Fuller:The Art of Making It Flat." *NY* 46(23 May):112–39.

Garland. 6887. Bryer, Jackson R., and Eugene Harding. "Hamlin Garland (1860–1940):A Bibliography of Secondary Comment." *ALR* 3:290–387.

6888. Earley, Jane F. "An Edition of Hamlin Garland's 'Miller of Boscobel'." *DAI* 30:2964A(Northwestern).

6889. French, Warren. "What Shall We Do About Hamlin Garland?" *ALR* 3:283–89.

6890. Garland, H. *Main-Travelled Roads.* (Merrill Editions.) Introd. Donald Pizer. Columbus, Ohio: Charles E. Merrill.

6891. —— *Rose of Dutcher's Coolly.* Ed. Donald Pizer. With Introd. Lincoln: U. of Neb. P., 1969.
See also 6842, 6885.

George. 6894. Rose, Edward J. "Henry George:America's Apostle to the Irish." *Éire* 3,iv(1968):7–16.

Hale, E.E. 6895. James, Nancy E. "Realism in Romance:A Critical Study of the Short Stories of Edward Everett Hale." *DAI* 31:1802A(Penn. State).

Harland. *See* 6884.

Harper's. 6896. Dowgray, John G.,Jr. "Literature and History:*Harper's Monthly*—The Magazine and the Popularization of Knowledge." [F 58]:88–101.

Harris, J.C. 6897. Glazier, Lyle. "The Uncle Remus Stories: Two Portraits of American Negroes." *JGE* 22:71–79. [Rev. art.]
See also 6763.

Harte. 6898. Morrow, Patrick. "Bret Harte (1836–1902)." *ALR* 3:167–77. [Bibliog.]

6899. —— "The Literary Criticism of Bret Harte:A Critical, Annotated Edition." *DAI* 30:4996A–97A(U. of Wash.).

Hawthorne, J. 6900. Bassan, Maurice. *Hawthorne's Son:The Life and Literary Career of Julian Hawthorne.* Columbus: Ohio State U.P.

6901. Monteiro, George. "Further Additions to the Bibliography of Julian Hawthorne." *BB* 27:6–7.

Hay. 6902. Sloane, David E.E. "John Hay (1838–1905)." *ALR* 3:178–88. [Bibliog.]
See also 6729.

Hearn. 6903. Coyne, Robert F. "Lafcadio Hearn's Criticism of English Literature." *DAI* 30:4940A(Fla. State).

6904. Kunst, Arthur E. *Lafcadio Hearn.* (TUSAS 158.) New York: Twayne, 1969. [Crit.]

Howe, E. 6905. Pickett, Calder M. "Edgar Watson Howe and the Kansas Scene." *KanQ* 2,ii:39–45.

Howells. 6906. Arms, George. "The William Dean Howells Correspondence." *CEAAN* 3:26.

6907. Baldwin, Marilyn. "The Transcendental Phase of William Dean Howells." *ESQ* 57(1969):57–61.

* 6908. Berces, Francis A. "Mimesis, Morality and *The Rise of Silas Lapham.*" *AQ* 22:[190]–202.

6909. Boardman, Arthur. "Howellsian Sex." *SNNTS* 2,i:52–60.

6910. Dean, James L. *Howells' Travels Toward Art.* Albuquerque: U. of N.M. Press. [On H's travel writing.]

* 6911. Fischer, William C.,Jr. "William Dean Howells:Reverie and the Nonsymbolic Aesthetic." *NCF* 25:1–30.

6912. Howells, W.D. *The Shadow of a Dream* and *An Imperative Duty.* With Introd. and Notes by Martha Banta. Text Estab. by Martha Banta, Ronald Gottesman, and David J. Nordloh. Bloomington: Ind. U.P.

6913. —— *The Son of Royal Langbrith.* With Introd. and Notes by David Burrows. Text Estab. by David Burrows, Ronald Gottesman, and David J. Nordloh. Bloomington: Ind. U.P., 1969.

6914. Johns, Berit Spilhaug. "William Dean Howells and Bjørnstjerne Bjørnson:A Literary Relationship." [F 66]:94–117.

6915. Kirk, Rudolf and Clara M. "Kirk-Howells Collection." *LC* 35(1969):67–74.

6916. Lynn, Kenneth S. "Howells in the Nineties." [F 64]:27–82.

* 6917 *MFS* 16,iii. William Dean Howells Spec. No. [James W. Tuttleton, "Howells and the Manners of the Good Heart," 271–87; Charles L. Campbell, "Realism and the Romance of Real Life:Multiple Fictional Worlds in Howells' Novels," 289–302; Jerome Klinkowitz, "Ethic and Aesthetic:The Basil and Isabel March Stories of William Dean Howells," 303–22; Joseph H. Gardner, "Howells: The 'Realist' as Dickensian," 323–43; Sanford E. Marovitz, "Howells and the Ghetto:The Mystery of Misery," 345–62; Marion W. Cumpiano, "Howells' Bridge:A Study of the Artistry of *Indian Summer*," 363–82; Tom H. Towers, " 'The Only Life We've Got':Myth and Morality in *The Kentons,*" 383–94; Maurice Beebe, "Criticism of William Dean Howells:A Selected Checklist," 395–419.]

6918. Nordloh, David J. "A Critical Edition of W.D. Howells' *Years of My Youth.*" *DAI* 30:4997A(Ind.).

6919. —— "Eating Off the Same Plates:First Editions of W.D. Howells in Great Britain." *Serif* 7,i:28–30.

6920. —— "Substantives and Accidentals vs. New Evidence: Another Strike in the Game of Distinctions." *CEAAN* 3:12–13. [In *The Son of Royal Langbrith.*]

6921. Payne, Alma J. "Howells' American Families—An Economic Mosaic." *HussR* 3(1969):20–34.

6922. Potter, Hugh. "Howells and the Shakers." *Shaker Quart.* 9(Spring 1969):3–13.

6923. Sessler, Harvey M. "Concept and Craft:Sources of Ambiguity in Howells' Novels." *DAI* 30:3476A(N.Y.U.).

* 6924. Sweeney, Gerard M. "The *Medea* Howells Saw." *AL* 42:83–89. [*A Modern Instance* and Grillparzer's *Medea.*]

6925. Taylor, James W. "The Swedenborgianism of W.D. Howells." *DAI* 31:735A–36A(Ill.).

6926. Vanderbilt, Kermit. "The Conscious Realism of Howells' *April Hopes.*" *ALR* 3:53–66.

6927. Watanabe, Toshio. "W.D. Howells to *O.E.D.*" *EigoS* 114(1968):241–43. [WDH and *O.E.D.*; in Jap.]

6928. Woodress, James. "An Interview with Howells." *ALR* 3:71–75. [Rpts. text from New York *Sun,* 6 Feb 1898.]

6929. Woodress, James, and Stanley P. Anderson. "A Bibliography of Writing About William Dean Howells." *ALR* Spec. No.(1969):1–139.

6930. Woodward, Robert H. "*Punch* on Howells and James." *ALR* 3:76–77.
See also 6480, 6722, 6749, 6778, 6995.

James, H. 6931. Ballorain, Rolande. "*The Turn of the Screw*:L'adulte et l'enfant ou les deux regards." *EA* 22(1969):250–58.

6932. Bass, Eben. "Henry James and the English Country House." *MarkhamR* 2,ii:[4]–[10].

6933. Beck, Ronald. "James' *The Beast in the Jungle*:Theme and Metaphor." *MarkhamR* 2,ii:[17]–[20].

6934. Bellringer, Alan W. "*The Tragic Muse*:The Objective Centre." *JAmS* 4:73–89.

* 6935. Bercovitch, Sacvan. "The Revision of Rowland Mallet." *NCF* 24(1969):210–21.

6936. Bonincontro, Marilia. "Le ascendenze austeniane del *Portrait of a Lady* di Henry James." *PS* 4,ii(1968):31–39.

* 6937. Bontly, Thomas J. "Henry James's 'General Vision of Evil' in *The Turn of the Screw.*" *SEL* 9(1969):721–35.

6938. —— "The Moral Perspective of *The Ambassadors.*" *Wisconsin Studies in Lit.* 6(1969):106–17.

6939. Brennan, Joseph G. "Three Novels of *Dépaysement.*" *CL* 22:223–36.

6940. Buitenhuis, Peter. *The Grasping Imagination:The American Writings of Henry James.* Toronto: U. of Toronto P.

6941. Burde, Edgar J. "The Double Vision of Henry James:An Essay on the Three Late Novels." *DAI* 31:1753A (Claremont).

6942. Burgess, Charles E. "Henry James's 'Big' Impression:St. Louis, 1905." *MHSB* 27:30–63.

* 6943. *CLQ* 9,i. Spec. James No. [Harold A. Larrabee, "The Fourth William James," 1–34; J. Seelye Bixler, "James Family Letters in Colby College Library," 35–47; Blair G. Kenney, "Henry James's Businessmen," 48–58; Richard Cary, "Henry James Juvenilia:A Poem and a Letter," 58–62.]

6944. Conn, Peter J. "Seeing and Blindness in 'The Beast in the Jungle'." *SSF* 7:472–75.

6945. Cranfill, Thomas M., and Robert L. Clark,Jr. "The Provocativeness of *The Turn of the Screw.*" *TSLL* 12:93–100.

6946. Dietrichson, Jan W. "Henry James and Emile Zola." [F 66]:118–34.

* 6947. Edelstein, Arnold. " 'The Tangle of Life':Levels of Meaning in *The Spoils of Poynton.*" *HSL* 2:133–50.

6948. Emerson, Donald. "The Relation of Henry James's Art Criticism to His Literary Standards." *TWA* 57(1969):9–19.

6949. Garis, Robert. "Anti-Literary Biography." *HudR* 23:143–53. [Rev. art.]

6950. Gillen, Francis X. "The Relationship of Rhetorical Control to Meaning in the Novels of Henry James, Virginia Woolf, and E.M. Forster." *DAI* 30(1969):1525A(Fordham).

6951. Grewal, Om P. "Henry James and the Idealogy of Culture:A Critical Study of *The Bostonians, The Princess Casamassima* and *The Tragic Muse.*" *DAI* 30:5444A–45A (Rochester).

6952. Gurko, Leo. "The Missing Word in Henry James's 'Four Meetings'." *SSF* 7:298–307.

* 6953. Habegger, Alfred. "The Disunity of *The Bostonians.*" *NCF* 24(1969):193–209.

6954. Hagemann, E.R. " 'Unexpected light in shady places': Henry James and *Life,* 1883–1916." *WHR* 24:241–50.

6955. Hamblen, Abigail A. "*Confidence*:The Surprising Shadow of Genius." *UR* 36(1969):151–54.

6956. Han, Pierre. "Organic Unity in 'Europe'." *SAB* 35,iii:40–41.

6957. Hartsock, Mildred E. "Biography:The Treacherous Art." *JML* 1:116–19. [Rev. art.]

* 6958. Horrell, Joyce T. "A 'Shade of Special Sense':Henry James and the Art of Naming." *AL* 42:[203]–20.

6959. James, H. *Partial Portraits*. Introd. Leon Edel. Ann Arbor: U. of Mich. P.

6960. —— *The Wings of the Dove*. (Merrill Editions.) Introd. Reynolds Price. Columbus, Ohio: Charles E. Merrill.

6961. Jones, Granville H. "The Jamesian Psychology of Experience:Innocence, Responsibility, and Renunciation in the Fiction of Henry James." *DAI* 30:5447A:(Pittsburgh).

6962. Kenney, William. "Doctor Sloper's Double in *Washington Square*." *UR* 36:301–06.

* 6963. Kimmey, John L. "*The Tragic Muse* and Its Forerunners." *AL* 41:[518]–31.

6964. Kraft, James L. "A Perspective on 'The Beast in the Jungle'." *LWU* 2(1969):20–26.

6965. Labrie, Ross. "Sirens of Life and Art in Henry James." *Lakehead U. Rev.*(Port Arthur, Ont.) 2(1969):150–69.

* 6966. Liebman, Sheldon W. "The Light and the Dark: Character Design in *The Portrait of a Lady*." *PLL* 6:163–79.

6967. Lind, Sidney E. " 'The Turn of the Screw':The Torment of Critics." *CentR* 14:225–40.

6968. MacNaughton, William R. "The First-Person Fiction of Henry James." *DAI* 31:1805A–06A(Wis.).

* 6969. Marovitz, Sanford E. "*Roderick Hudson*:James's *Marble Faun*." *TSLL* 11:1427–43. [On J's debt to Hawthorne.]

6970. Maves, Carl E. "Sensuous Pessimism:Italy in the Work of Henry James." *DAI* 30:5450A–51A(Stanford).

6971. Menikoff, Barry. "Punctuation and Point of View in the Late Style of Henry James." *Style* 4:29–47.

* 6972. Monteiro, George. "Henry James and His Reviewers: Some Identifications." *PBSA* 63(1969):300–04.

* 6973. Morgan, Alice. "Henry James:Money and Morality." *TSLL* 12:75–92.

6974. Namekata, Akio. "Some Notes on *The Spoils of Poynton*." *SELit* Eng. No.:19–35.

* 6975. Nettels, Elsa. "*The Ambassadors* and the Sense of the Past." *MLQ* 31:220–35.

6976. Nicoloff, Philip L. "At the Bottom of All Things in Henry James's 'Louisa Pallant'." *SSF* 7:409–20.

* 6977. Nowell-Smith, Simon. "Texts of *The Portrait of a Lady* 1881–1882:The Bibliographical Evidence." *PBSA* 63(1969): 304–10.

6978. Pearce, Brian. "Perpetuated Misprints." *TLS* 4 June: 613. [Textual errors in *Washington Square*.]

6979. Powers, Lyall H. *Henry James:An Introduction and Interpretation*. New York: Holt, Rinehart and Winston.

6980. Powers, Lyall H.,ed. *Studies in* The Portrait of a Lady. (Merrill Studies.) Columbus, Ohio: Charles E. Merrill. [Rptd. crit.]

6981. Purdy, Strother B. "Henry James and the *Mot Juste*." *Wisconsin Studies in Lit.* 6(1969):118–25.

6982. Recchia, Edward J. "Form and the Creative Process: Lesson and Example in Eleven of Henry James's Artist Tales." *DAI* 30(1969):2495A–96A(Ohio State).

6983. Saul, Frank J. "Autobiographical Surrogates in Henry James:The Aesthetics of Detachment." *DAI* 30(1969):2549A–50A(Johns Hopkins).

6984. Schuhmann, Kuno. "Ethik und Ästhetik im Spätwerk von Henry James." *JA* 15:77–87.

6985. Segal, Ora. *The Lucid Reflector:The Observer in Henry James' Fiction*. New Haven: Yale U.P.

6986. Stafford, William T. "Henry James." [F 65]:84–99.

6987. Stoehr, Taylor. "Words and Deeds in *The Princess Casamassima*." *ELH* 37:95–135.

6988. Thomas, Glen R. "The Freudian Approach to James's 'The Turn of the Screw':Psychoanalysis and Literary Criticism." *DAI* 31:770A(Emory).

6989. Thorberg, Raymond. "*Germaine*, James's *Notebooks*, and *The Wings of the Dove*." *CL* 22:254–64.

* 6990. Tompkins, Jane P. " 'The Beast in the Jungle':An Analysis of James's Late Style." *MFS* 16:185–91.

6991. Tournadre, C. "Propositions pour une psychologie

sociale de *The Turn of the Screw*." *EA* 22(1969):259–69.

6992. Veeder, William R. "*Watch and Ward*:The Mixed Beginning." *DAI* 31:772A(Calif., Berkeley).

6993. Weithaus, Sister Barbara M.,O.S.F. "Represented Discourse in Selected Novels of Henry James." *DAI* 31: 407A–08A(Catholic U.).

6994. Winner, Viola H. *Henry James and the Visual Arts*. Charlottesville: U.P. of Va.

6995. Woodard, James E.,Jr. "Pragmatism and Pragmaticism in James and Howells." *DAI* 31:408A(N.M.).

6996. Zimmerman, Everett. "Literary Tradition and 'The Turn of the Screw'." *SSF* 7:634–37.

See also 1453, 3945, 3959, 4256, 4554, 4727, 4909, 5177, 5261, 6410, 6722, 6749, 6778, 6813, 6930, 8078.

James, W. 6997. Roth, John K.,ed. *The Moral Philosophy of William James*. With Introd. New York: Thomas Y. Crowell, 1969. [Anthol.]

6998. Smith, John E. "William James as Philosophical Psychologist." *Midway* 8,iii(1968):3–19.

See also 6943, 8307.

Jewett. *See* 6707.

Lanier. 6999. Havens, Elmer A. "Lanier's Critical Theory." *ESQ* 55(1969):83–89.

7000. Lanier, S. *Poems and Letters*. Introd. and Notes by Charles R. Anderson. Baltimore: Johns Hopkins P., 1969.

7001. Lease, Benjamin,ed. "Sidney Lanier and *Blackwood's Magazine*:An Unpublished Letter." *Ga. Hist. Quart.* 53(1969): 521–23.

* 7002. Reamer, Owen J. "Lanier's 'The Marshes of Glynn' Revisited." *MissQ* 23:57–63.

See also 6591, 6676.

Locke. 7003. Harrison, John M. *The Man Who Made Nasby:David Ross Locke*. Chapel Hill: U. of N.C. Press, 1969.

Lowell, P. 7004. Ellwood, Robert S. "Percival Lowell's Journey to the East." *SR* 78:285–309.

Markham. 7005. [Slade, Joseph W.] "Recent Additions to the Markham Archives." *MarkhamR* 2,ii:[14]–[17].

7006. Stern, Madeleine B. "The Head of a Poet:A Phrenograph of Edwin Markham." *Coranto* 6,i(1969):6–12.

Mitchell, S.W. 7007. Armstrong, Jean M. "The Novels of S. Weir Mitchell." *DAI* 30:4975A(N.Y.U.).

See also 6721.

Muir, J. 7008. Pool, John P. "John Muir:The Last of the Puc-Puggies." [F 16]:33–42.

Murfree. 7009. Loyd, Dennis. "Tennessee's Mystery Woman Novelist." *THQ* 29:272–77.

7010. Murfree, M.N. *In the Tennessee Mountains*. Introd. Nathalia Wright. Knoxville: U. of Tenn. P.

* 7011. Warfel, Harry R. "Local Color and Literary Artistry: Mary Noailles Murfree's *In the Tennessee Mountains*." *SLJ* 3:154–63.

Norris. 7012. Hill, John S. *Checklist of Frank Norris*. (Merrill Checklists.) Columbus, Ohio: Charles E. Merrill.

* 7013. —— "The Influence of Cesare Lombroso on Frank Norris's Early Fiction." *AL* 42:89–91.

7014. Norris, F. *The Pit*. (Merrill Editions.) Introd. James D. Hart. Columbus, Ohio: Charles E. Merrill.

* 7015. Stronks, James B. "John Kendrick Bangs Criticizes Norris's Borrowings in *Blix*." *AL* 42:380–86.

See also 6778, 7534, 7855.

O'Reilly. 7016. Shanley, Kevin T.,O.Carm. "John Boyle O'Reilly and Civil Rights." *Éire* 4,iii(1969):55–81.

Page. *7017. Holman, Harriet R. "Attempt and Failure: Thomas Nelson Page as Playwright." *SLJ* 3,i:72–82.

7018. —— "The Kentucky Journal of Thomas Nelson Page." *Register of the Ky. Hist. Soc.* 68,i:1–16.

See also 8056.

Phelps. *See* 6801.

Riley. 7019. Revell, Peter. *James Whitcomb Riley*. (TUSAS 159.) New York: Twayne. [Crit.]

Stickney. 7020. Lopez, Manuel D. "Joseph Trumbull Stickney (1870–1904)." *BB* 26(1969):83–85.

Tourgée. 7021. Tourgée, A.W. *Bricks Without Straw*. Introd. Otto H. Olsen. Baton Rouge: La. State U.P., 1969.

Ward. 7022. Garrow, Scott. "The Drama in Ward's Tower of London." *AN&Q* 9:22–23.

Warner, C.D. *See* 6766.

Whitman. 7023. Aspiz, Harold. " 'Children of Adam' and Horace Greeley." *WWR* 15(1969):49–51.

7024. Beardshear, William M. "Charge to a Walt." *Palimpsest* 51:349–52.

7025. Beck, Ronald. "The Structure of 'Song of Myself' and the Critics." *WWR* 15(1969):32–38.

7026. Bennett, Frances H. " 'Starting from Paumanok' as Functional Poetry." *WWR* 15(1969):117–20.

7027. Bennett, Josiah Q. "Whitman Loses His Ego; or, 'Not I, said the fly':*Leaves of Grass*, 1855." *Serif* 7,i:35–36.

7028. Bergman, Herbert. "The Influence of Whitman's Journalism on *Leaves of Grass*." *ALR* 3:399–404.

* 7029. ——. "Walt Whitman:Self Advertiser." *BNYPL* 74:634–39. [Illus.]

7030. Bergman, Herbert, and William White. "Walt Whitman's Lost 'Sun-Down Papers,' Nos. 1–3." *ABC* 20,i:17–20.

* 7031. Black, Stephen A. "Whitman and Psychoanalytic Criticism:A Response to Arthur Golden." *L&P* 20:79–81. [Foll. by Arthur Golden, "A Reply," 83–92.]

7032. ——. "Whitman and the Failure of Mysticism:Identity and Identifications in 'Song of Myself'." *WWR* 15(1969):223–30.

7033. Bordier, Roger. "Whitman et Lorca." *Europe* 483–84(1969):188–91.

7034. Bowering, George. "The Solitary Everything." *WWR* 15(1969):13–26.

7035. Brasher, Thomas L. *Whitman as Editor of* The Brooklyn Daily Eagle. Detroit: Wayne State U.P.

* 7036. Broderick, John C. "The Greatest Whitman Collector and the Greatest Whitman Collection." *QJLC* 27:109–28. [Illus.]

7037. Brumleve, Sister Barbara A.,S.S.N.D. "Whitman and Stevens:From an Organic to a Process Metaphor." *DAI* 30:3450A–51A(St. Louis).

7038. Claudel, Alice M. "Poems as Laurels for Walt Whitman." *WWR* 16:81–86.

7039. Coffeen, Robert G. "Naming Techniques in Whitman's *Leaves of Grass*:A Study in Problems of Power." *DAI* 30:3903A(N.C., Chapel Hill).

7040. Cosentino, Vincent. "Walt Whitman's Influence on Thomas Mann, the 'Non-Political' Writer." [F 21]:224–42.

7041. Cronin, Frank C. "Modern Sensibility in Stanza 2 of 'Crossing Brooklyn Ferry'." *WWR* 15(1969):56–57.

7042. Das, Manoj. "The Good Gray Poet and the Last Great Rishi." *IndL* 12,iii(1969):87–91. [Sri Aurobindo.]

* 7043. DeFalco, Joseph M. "Whitman's Changes in 'Out of the Cradle' and Poe's 'Raven'." *WWR* 16:22–27.

7044. Domina, Lyle. "Whitman's 'Lilacs':Process of Self-Realization." *ESQ* 58:124–27.

7045. Doyle, Charles C. "Poetry and Pastoral:A Dimension of Whitman's 'Lilacs'." *WWR* 15(1969):242–45.

7046. Doyle, Glenn E. "A Note on Thomson's Biography of Whitman." *WWR* 15(1969):122–24.

7047. *EigoS* (1969). *Whitman Special No.* [Bunsho Jugaku, "Whitman to Toyo," 2–5 (W and East); Junichiro Okubo, "Soseki no Whitman," 6–8 (Soseki's W); Koichi Kodama, "Arishima Takero ni okeru Whitman," 9–12 (W in TA); Tatsumaro Tezuka, "Doshisha de Kiita Arishima Takero no Whitman Kogi," 13 (Lecture on W by TA at Doshisha University); Shogo Shiratori, "Hyakunen sai igo," 14–15 (After the 100th anniversary); Masao Yaku, "Whitman to no Deai," 22–25 (Meeting with W); Saburo Ota, "Whitman to Minshu Shiha," 26–28 (W and democratic poetry group); Shunsuke Kamei, "Whitman in Japan," 29–36; Shunichi Shinkura, "Mirai no Shijin—Whitman to America Gendaishi," 92–95 (Poet of the future—W and modern American poetry); Shiro Tsunata, "Whitman Hyoka no Nagare," 96–99 (Survey of W evaluation); Yoshihiro Nabeshima, "Whitman no Buntai," 100–02 (W's style); William L. Moore, "On the Difficulty in Reading *Leaves of Grass*," 103–08; Masayuki Sakamoto, "Whitman no okeru Shiso," 109–11 (Thoughts in W); Yozo Tokunaga, "Randall Jarrell no Whitman-ron," 112–14 (RJ's view of W).]

7048. Fein, Richard J. "Lamentations and 'When Lilacs Last'." *WWR* 15(1969):115–17.

* 7049. Freedman, Florence B. "A Whitman Letter to Josiah Child." *WWR* 16:55–57.

7050. Golden, Samuel A. "Whitman to Mrs. Vine Coburn: Three Letters." *WWR* 15(1969):59–60.

* 7051. Goodson, Lester. "Whitman and the Problem of Evil." *WWR* 16:45–50.

7052. Grier, Edward F. "Whitman and Dickinson." [F 65]:50–65.

* 7053. Hanson, R. Galen. "Whitman as Social Theorist: Worker in Poetics and Politics." *WWR* 16:41–45.

7054. Harrison, Stanley R. "Sacrilege of Preference in Whitman and Sartre." *WWR* 15(1969):51–54.

7055. Hench, Atcheson L. "Walt Whitman and Folger McKinsey." *AN&Q* 8(1969):53.

7056. Henseler, Donna L. "The Voice of the Grass-Poem 'I':Whitman's 'Song of Myself'." *WWR* 15(1969):26–32.

7057. Holloway, Emory. *Whitman:An Interpretation in Narrative.* New York: Biblo and Tannen, 1969. [New ed. incl. new, second pref.]

* 7058. Hoople, Robin P. " 'Chants Democratic and Native American':A Neglected Sequence in the Growth of *Leaves of Grass*." *AL* 42:[181]–96.

7059. Hughes, Charles. "Impact of Evil on the Poetry of Walt Whitman." *WWR* 15(1969):237–42.

7060. Jaén, D.T. "Walt Whitman:Tema literario." *Torre* 60(1968):77–100.

7061. Jaffe, Harold. "Bucke's *Walt Whitman*:A Collaboration." *WWR* 15(1969):190–94.

7062. ——. "Richard Maurice Bucke's Walt Whitman." *Serif* 7,i:3–10.

7063. Kahn, Sholom J. "Whitman's 'New Wood'." *WWR* 15(1969):201–14.

7064. Kallen, Horace M. "Of Love, Death and Walt Whitman." *WWR* 15(1969):171–80.

7065. Kamei, Shunsuke. "Whitman to Lawrence." *EigoS* 114(1968):430–32. [W and L; in Jap.]

7066. Keller, Dean H. "Walt Whitman in England:A Footnote." *WWR* 15(1969):54–55.

7067. Kornblatt, Joyce. "Whitman's Vision of the Past in 'The Sleepers'." *WWR* 16:86–89.

7068. Lara, J.G.M. de. "Walt Whitman, poeta de la libertad." *CHA* 243:572–87.

7069. Livingston, James L. "With Whitman and Hegel Around the Campfire." *WWR* 15(1969):120–22.

7070. Magee, John D. " 'Crossing Brooklyn Ferry':A Hundred Years Hence." *WWR* 15(1969):38–43.

7071. Magowan, Robin. "The Horse of the Gods:Possession in 'Song of Myself'." *WWR* 15(1969):67–76.

7072. Male, Roy R. "Whitman's Radical Utterance." *ESQ* 60:73–75.

7073. Maria, Sister Flavia,C.S.J. " 'Song of Myself':A Presage of Modern Teilhardian Paleontology." *WWR* 15(1969):43–49.

7074. Marinacci, Barbara. *O Wondrous Singer! An Introduction to Walt Whitman.* New York: Dodd, Mead.

7075. Mary, Sister Eva,O.S.F. "Shades of Darkness in 'The Sleeper'." *WWR* 15(1969):187–90.

7076. Mathew, V. John. "Self in 'Song of Myself':A Defense of Whitman's Egoism." *WWR* 15(1969):102–07.

7077. McGhee, Richard D. "Concepts of Time in Whitman's Poetry." *WWR* 15(1969):76–85.

7078. ——. "*Leaves of Grass* and Cultural Development." *WWR* 16:3–14.

7079. McKeithan, Daniel M. *Whitman's "Song of Myself" 34 and Its Background.* (Essays and Studies on Amer. Lang. and Lit. 18.) Uppsala: Lundequistska bokh., 1969.

7080. Mendel'son, M. " 'He Dreamed of the Brotherhood of People':On the 150th Anniversary of the Birth Date of Walt Whitman." *WWR* 16:57–59. [Tr. Frank J. Corliss,Jr.]

7081. Metzger, Charles R. "Walt Whitman's Philosophical Epic." *WWR* 15(1969):91–96.

7082. Miller, Edwin H.,ed. *A Century of Whitman Criticism.* With Introd. Bloomington: Ind. U.P., 1969. [Rptd. crit.]

7083. Mills, Barriss. "Whitman's Poetic Theory." *ESQ*

55(1969):42–47.

7084. Mulqueen, James E. "Organic Growth of *Leaves of Grass*." *WWR* 15(1969):85–91.

7085. Murphy, Francis,ed. *Walt Whitman:A Critical Anthology*. With Introds. Baltimore: Penguin. [Rptd. crit.]

7086. Nagle, John M. "Toward a Theory of Structure in 'Song of Myself'." *WWR* 15(1969):162–71.

7087. Nilsen, Helge N. "The Mystic Message:Whitman's 'Song of Myself'." *Edda* 69(1969):400–09.

7088. Pearce, Howard D. " 'I Lean and Loafe':Whitman's Romantic Posture." *WWR* 15(1969):3–12.

7089. Peattie, R.W. "Postscript to Charles Kent on Whitman." *WWR* 15(1969):107–11.

7090. Petersen, William J. "The Walt Whitman Club." *Palimpsest* 51:323–48.

7091. Petterson, Dale E. "Mayakovsky and Whitman:The Icon and the Mosaic." *SlavR* 28:416–25.

* 7092. Phillips, Elizabeth. " 'Song of Myself':The Numbers of the Poem in Relation to Its Form." *WWR* 16:67–81.

7093. Reisiger, Hans. *Literarische Porträts*. (VDASD 42.) Hrsg. von Ulrick K. Dreikandt. Heidelberg: Schneider, 1969.

7094. Rose, Alan H. "Destructive Vision in the First and Last Versions of 'Song of Myself'." *WWR* 15(1969):215–22.

7095. Rule, Henry B. "Walt Whitman and George Caleb Bingham." *WWR* 15(1969):248–53.

7096. Runden, John P. "Whitman's 'The Sleepers' and the 'Indiana' Section of Crane's *The Bridge*." *WWR* 15(1969):245–48.

7097. Sachithanandan, V. "Whitman and Bharati as Vedantists." [F 42],II:247–59.

7098. —— "Whitman and the Serpent Power." *WWR* 16:50–55.

7099. Sastry, C.N. "Walt Whitman and Rabindranath Tagore:A Study in Comparison and Contrast." *Triveni* 38, i(1969):22–31.

7100. Sharma, Mohan Lal. "Whitman, Tagore, Iqbal: Whitmanated, Under-Whitmanated, and Over-Whitmanated Singers of Self." *WWR* 15(1969):230–37.

7101. Sharma, Om Prakash. "Walt Whitman and the Doctrine of Karman." *PE&W* 20:169–74.

7102. Singh, Raman K. "Whitman:*Avatar* of Shri Krishna?" *WWR* 15(1969):97–102.

7103. Slattery, Sister Margaret Patrice. "Patterns of Imagery in Whitman's 'There Was a Child Went Forth'." *WWR* 15(1969):112–14.

* 7104. Sugg, Richard P. "Whitman's Symbolic Circle and a 'Broadway Pageant'." *WWR* 16:35–40.

7105. Sutton, Larry. "Structural Music in Whitman's 'Out of the Cradle'." *WWR* 15(1969):57–59.

* 7106. Templin, Lawrence. "The Quaker Influence on Walt Whitman." *AL* 42:[165]–80.

7107. Thompson, Bert A. "Edward Wilkins:Male Nurse to Walt Whitman." *WWR* 15(1969):194–96.

* 7108. Vandehaar, Margaret M. "Whitman, Paine, and the Religion of Democracy." *WWR* 16:14–22.

7109. "Walt Whitman--The Man and the Poet." *QJLC* 27:[170]–76.

7110. "Walt Whitman, 1819–1969." *AmD* 5,iii(1969). [" 'I Am the Hounded Slave . . .'," 4; Walter Lowenfels, "The Eternal Meanings," 5–7; Langston Hughes, "The Ceaseless Rings of Walt Whitman," 8–9; Harold Blodgett, "Who Listens to Him Today?" 10–12,36–38; Abe Capek, "Whitman:A Re-evaluation," 13–15; Roger Asselineau, " 'Camerado, This Is no Book; Who Touches This Touches a Bomb'," 16–17; Lenore Marshall, "Whitman' Modernism," 17; Sidney Finkelstein, "Whitman's Mannahatta," 18–23(Illus.); Kornei I. Chukovsky, "What Walt Whitman Means to Me," 24–26; François Hugot, "Poets to Come," 27–28(Tr. Nan Braymer); Robert Mezey, "Happy Birthday, Old Man," 28; Kirby Congdon, "Whitman's Vision," 34–35; Clarence Major, "Close to the Ground," 35.]

7111. *Walt Whitman in Our Time. WWR* 16. Supp. [William White, "Introduction," 3–4; Roy P. Basler, "Walt Whitman in Perspective," 5–8; William Meredith, "Whitman to the Poet," 9–13 (Illus.); Edwin H. Miller, "And Gladly Edit," 13–16; James E. Miller,Jr., "Whitman:Dead or Alive?" 17–20.]

7112. Wells, Elizabeth. "The Structure of Whitman's 1860 *Leaves of Grass*." *WWR* 15(1969):131–61.

7113. White, William. "Four Recent Whitman Editions." *WWR* 16:27–28.

7114. —— "Mrs. Walter Whitman, Sr. Writes to Her Son." *WWR* 16:63.

7115. —— "My 'Six Children':Whitman to Symonds." *WWR* 16:31.

7116. —— "On the Whitman—Symonds Correspondence." *WWR* 15(1969):125–26.

7117. —— "Some New Whitman Items." *PrS* 44:47–55 [Poem and 4 letters.]

7118. —— "Tasistro and the *Daybook*." *WWR* 16:89–90.

7119. —— "Whitman:A Current Bibliography." *WWR* 15(1969):126–27,196–97,253–55; 16:29–30,61–63,94–95.

* 7120. —— "Whitman on Himself:An Unrecorded Piece." *PLL* 6:202–05.

7121. —— "Whitman or Whitmaniana?" *ATQ* 1(1969): 120–21.

7122. Whitman, W. *Leaves of Grass:Selections*. Ed. Edwin H. Miller. With Introd. New York: Appleton-Century-Crofts.

See also 4529, 4843, 5171, 6305, 6596, 6599.

Williams, E. 7123. Talbot, Frances G. "Rediscovered—Espy W.H. Williams, Louisiana Playwright:A Checklist." *LaS* 105–17.

Woolson. 7124. Helmick, Evelyn T. "Constance Fenimore Woolson:First Novelist of Florida." *Carrell* 10,ii(1969):8–18.

7125. Simms, L. Moody,Jr. "Constance Fenimore Woolson on Southern Literary Taste." *MissQ* 22(1969):362–66.

V. TWENTIETH CENTURY

Bibliography. 7127. Cappon, Alexander P. "Early Volume Numbers of *The University Review*:A Bibliographical Curiosity." *UR* 36:238–39.

7128. Goode, Stephen H.,comp. *Index to American Little Magazines 1920–1939*. Troy, N.Y.: Whitston Pubs., 1969.

7129. Kaiser, Ernest. "Recent Literature on Black Liberation Struggles and the Ghetto Crisis:A Bibliographical Survey." *Science and Society* 33(1969):168–96.

General and Miscellaneous. 7130. Aaron, Daniel, and Robert Bendiner,eds. *The Strenuous Decade:A Social and Intellectual Record of the Nineteen-Thirties*. With Pref. Garden City, N.Y.: Doubleday (Anchor).

7131. Berry, Wendell. "The Regional Motive." *SoR* 6:972–77.

7132. Boitano, Piero. "L'intellettuale americano tra la nuova scienza e l'arte." *SA* 14(1968):431–50.

7133. Bush-Brown, Albert. "Art in America, 1970–1985 (Six Dour Predictions and One Hopeful One)." *ASoc* 7:189–92.

7134. Carlson, Julie A. "A Comparison of the Treatment of the Negro in Children's Literature in the Periods 1929–1938 and 1959–1968." *DAI* 30:3452A(Conn.).

7135. Cawelti, John G. "Beatles, Batman, and the New Aesthetic." *Midway* 9,ii(1968):49–70.

7136. Davis, David B. "American Ideals and Contemporary Domestic Problems." *IJAS* 1,i(1969):1–10.

7137. Della Terza, Dante. "Tendenze attuali della critica americana." *SCr* 3(1969):81–97.

7138. Erno, Richard B. "The New Realism in Southwestern Literature." *WR* 7,i:50–54.

7139. Fava, Luigi. "Letteratura e poesia 'Beat' negli Stati Uniti." *AllaB* 7,ii(1969):1–23.

7140. Fetscher, Iring. "Bertolt Brecht and America." *Salmagundi* 10–11(1969–70):246–72.

7141. Fitch, Noel R. "An American Bookshop in Paris:The Influence of Sylvia Beach's Shakespeare and Company on American Literature." *DAI* 30:3005A–06A(Wash. State).

7142. Fox, Hugh. "Some Notes on the Underground." *UWR*

5,i:18–24.

7143. Genthe, Charles V. *American War Narratives, 1917–1918:A Study and Bibliography.* New York: David Lewis, 1969.

7144. Gottesman, Leslie, Hilton Obenzinger, and Alan Senauke,eds. *A Cinch:Amazing Works From the* Columbia Review. With Introd. New York: Columbia U.P., 1969. [Anthol.]

7145. Grundy, Ernest B. "The Lost Generation in the Perspective of Historical Criticism, 1930–1960." *DAI* 31:1277A (Denver).

* 7146. Guenther, Paul, and Nicholas Joost. "Little Magazines and the Cosmopolitan Tradition." *PLL* 6:100–10.

7147. Halperin, Irving. "Books and Bodies at San Francisco State." *MR* 11:367–72.

* 7148. Haslam, Gerald W. "The Subtle Thread:Asian-American Literature." *ArQ* 25(1969):197–208.

7149. Hatfield, Henry. "Thomas Mann and America." *Salmagundi* 10–11(1969–70):174–85.

7150. Havard, William C. "Southwest Humor:Contemporary Style." *SoR* 6:1185–90.

7151. Herrscher, Walter J. "Some Ideas in Modern American Nature Writing." *DAI* 30(1969):2025A(Wis.). [Rachel Carson, August Derleth, Joseph Wood Krutch, Aldo Leopold, E.B. White.]

7152. Howell, Elmo. "The Greenville Writers and the Mississippi Country People." *LaS* 8(1968):348–60.

* 7153. Hubbell, Jay B. "1922:A Turning Point in American Literary History." *TSLL* 12:481–92.

* 7154. Johnson, Richard C., and G. Thomas Tanselle. "The Haldeman-Julius 'Little Blue Books' as a Bibliographical Problem." *PBSA* 64:29–78.

7155. Kariel, Henry S. "Making Scenes in a Liberal Society." *MR* 11:223–55.

7156. Karpf, Stephen L. "The Gangster Film:Emergence, Variation and Decay of a Genre, 1930–1940." *DAI* 30:4587A (Northwestern).

7157. Klaw, Barbara. "The New Nostalgia . . . Many Happy Returns." *AH* 21(June):34–38. [Current nostalgic reprs.]

7158. Klotman, Phyllis R. "The Running Man as Metaphor in Contemporary Negro Literature." *DAI* 30:3946A(Case Western Reserve).

7159. Kovács, József. "Kísérletek a tömegkultúra megteremtésére az amerikai szocialista irodalomban." *Helikon* 15(1969):259–62. [Attempts of Amer. Socialist lit. to create mass culture.]

* 7160. McGiffert, Michael. "American Puritan Studies in the 1960's." *WMQ* 27:36–67.

7161. Mendel'son, M.O., A.N. Nikoljukin, and R.M. Samarin,eds. *Sovremennoe literaturovedenie SŠA:Spory ob amerikanskoj literature.* Moscow: Nauka, 1969. [Lit. scholarship in the U.S.]

7162. Merriam, H.G.,ed. *Way Out West:Recollections and Tales.* Norman: U. of Okla. P., 1969. [Anthol. of writings from *Frontier* and *Frontier and Midland*, regional magazines pub. at U. of Montana.]

7163. Miles, Mildred L. *Index to* Playboy:*Belles-Lettres, Articles and Humor, December 1953–December 1969.* Metuchen, N.J.: Scarecrow.

7164. Milton, John R.,ed. *The American Indian Speaks.* With Introd. Vermillion: U. of So. Dak. P., 1969. [Anthol.]

7165. Mintz, Lawrence E. "Brother Jonathan's City Cousin: The Urban Wise Fool in Twentieth Century American Social and Political Satire." *DAI* 31:1234A–35A(Mich. State).

7166. Montgomery, Marion. "Richard Weaver Against the Establishment." *GaR* 23(1969):433–59. [Rev. art. on W's *The Southern Tradition at Bay*.]

* 7167. Moore, Rayburn S. " 'A Distinctively Southern Magazine':The *Southern Bivouac.*" *SLJ* 2,ii:51–65.

7168. Nemoianu, Virgil. "Polarizări și dezorientări." *SXX* 13,vi:185–89.

7169. Newman, Charles, and William A. Henkin,Jr.,eds. *Under 30:Fiction, Poetry and Criticism of the New American Writers.* Bloomington: Ind. U.P., 1969. [Anthol.]

7170. Nichols, Charles H. " 'Beat':The Religion of the Disinherited." *NsM* 21(1968):148–55.

7171. Norris, Carolyn B. "The Image of the Physician in Modern American Literature." *DAI* 31:765A(Md.).

7172. Pryce-Jones, Alan. "Translation and the Americans." *TLS* 25 Sept:1109–10.

7173. Richwine, Keith N. "The Liberal Club:Bohemia and the Resurgence in Greenwich Village, 1912–1918." *DAI* 30(1969):1179A(Pa.).

* 7174. Rubin, Louis D.,Jr. "Southern Literature:A Piedmont Art." *MissQ* 23:1–16.

* 7175. —— "Southern Local Color and the Black Man." *SoR* 6:1011–30.

7176. Schatt, Stanley. "The Faceless Face of Hatred:The Negro and Jew in Recent American Literature." *WR* 7,ii:49–55.

7177. Stewart, David H. "The Decline of WASP Literature in America." *CE* 30(1969):403–17.

7178. Straumann, Heinrich. "Bestseller und Zeitgeschehen in den USA der sechziger Jahre." *JA* 15:25–37.

* 7179. Sullivan, Walter. "Southern Writers in the Modern World:Death by Melancholy." *SoR* 6:907–19.

7180. Tingley, Donald F. "The 'Robin's Egg Renaissance': Chicago and the Arts, 1910–1920." *JISHS* 63:35–54.

7181. Tripp, Wendell. "Fifty Years of New York History." *NYH* 50(1969):355–96. [Illus.]

7182. Wickes, George. *Americans in Paris.* Garden City, N.Y.: Doubleday, 1969. [Chaps. on Stein, Cummings, Dos Passos, Hemingway, Miller.]

7183. Wirzberger, Karl-Heinz. *Probleme der Bürgerrechts-bewegung in der amerikanischen Prosaliteratur der Gegenwart.* (SDAWB 2[1967].) Berlin: Akad.-Verl., 1967. [36–p. pamphlet.]

7184. Young, William H. "Images of Order:American Comic Strips During the Depression, 1929–1938." *DAI* 30(1969): 2049A–50A(Emory).

See also 608, 1108, 1438, 3890, 4898, 4899, 4902, 4914, 6240, 6248, 6714, 6717, 6945.

Afro-American. 7185. Anon. "The Institute of the Black World:Martin Luther King, Jr. Memorial Center, Atlanta Georgia. Statement of Purpose and Program, Fall 1969." *MR* 10(1969):713–17.

7186. Berceanu, Vera. "The Harlem Renaissance." *Contemporanul* 10 July:9.

7187. Berry, Faith. "Voice for the Jazz Age, Great Migration or Black Bourgeoisie." *BlackW* 20,i:10–16. [Harlem Ren.]

7188. Bontemps, Arna. "The Black Renaissance of the Twenties." *BlackW* 20,i:5–9.

7189. Brown, Lloyd W. "Black Entitles:Names as Symbols in Afro-American Literature." *SBL* 1,i:16–44.

7190. Chametzky, Jules, and Sidney Kaplan,eds. *Black & White in American Culture:An Anthology from* The Massachusetts Review. Amherst: U. of Mass. P., 1969.

7191. Chapman, Abraham,ed. *Black Voices:An Anthology of Afro-American Literature.* With Introd. New York: New Amer. Lib., 1968. [Anthol.]

7192. Clarke, John H. "The Neglected Dimensions of the Harlem Renaissance." *BlackW* 20,i:118–29.

7193. Collier, Eugenia W. "Heritage from Harlem." *BlackW* 20,i:52–59. [Harlem Ren.]

* 7194. Davis, Arthur P. "The New Poetry of Black Hate." *CLAJ* 13:382–91.

7195. Dent, Thomas C., Richard Schechner, and Gilbert Moses,eds. *The Free Southern Theater by the Free Southern Theater:A Documentary of the South's Radical Black Theater, with Journals, Letters, Poetry, Essays and a Play Written by Those Who Built It.* Indianapolis: Bobbs-Merrill, 1969.

7196. Fontaine, William T. "The Negro Continuum from Dominant Wish to Collective Act." *AForum* 3,iv/4,i(1968):63–96. [Dunbar, DuBois, Hughes, Wright, Ellison.]

7197. Hare, Nathan. "Questions and Answers about Black Studies." *MR* 10(1969):727–36.

7198. Jordan, June,ed. *Soulscript:Afro-American Poetry.* With Introd. Garden City, N.Y.: Zenith. [Anthol.]

7199. Kieser, Rolf. "The Black American Dream:Das Dilemma des farbigen Amerikaners, dargestellt in *The Autobiography of Malcolm X*." *LWU* 2(1969):89–97.

7200. Killens, John O. "Another Time When Black Was

Beautiful." *BlackW* 20,i:20–36. [Harlem Ren.]

7201. —— "Run Like Hell and Holler Fire." *AmD* 5, ii(1968–69):10–12. [The task of the Black writer.]

7202. Kilson, Martin. "Anatomy of the Black Studies Movement." *MR* 10(1969):718–25.

7203. Lee, Don L. "Black Critics." *BlackW* 19,xi:24–30.

7204. Lowenfels, Walter. "Black Renaissance." *AmD* 5, i(1968):30–31. [On contemp. Black poets.]

7205. Margolies, Edward,ed. *A Native Sons Reader.* With Introd. Philadelphia: J.B. Lippincott. [Anthol.]

7206. Mitchell, Loften. "Harlem My Harlem." *BlackW* 20,i:91–97. [Harlem Ren.]

7207. Molette, Carlton W.,II. "The First Afro-American Theater." *NegroD* 19,vi:4–9.

7208. Portelli, Alessandro. "Cultura poetica afro-americana." *SA* 14(1968):401–29.

7209. Riche, James. "Anarchism and Reaction in Contemporary Afro-American Literature." *L&I* 1(1969):22-38.

7210. Rodgers, Carolyn M. "Breakforth. In Deed." *BlackW* 19,xi:13–22. [Black Am. lit. scene.]

7211. Stuckey, Sterling. "Contours of Black Studies:The Dimension of African and Afro-American Relationships." *MR* 10(1969):747–56.

7212. Thelwell, Mike. "Black Studies:A Political Perspective." *MR* 10(1969):703–12.

7213. Turner, Darwin T. "Afro-American Literary Critics." *BlackW* 19,ix:54–67.

7214. Williams, John A. "The Harlem Renaissance:Its Artists, Its Impact, Its Meaning." *BlackW* 20,i:17–18.

7215. Wilson, William J. "The Quest for Meaningful Black Experience on White Campuses." *MR* 10(1969):737–46.

See also 1441, 6086, 6091, 10341.

Criticism. *7216. Douglas, George H. "Croce's Early Aesthetic and American Critical Theory." *CLS* 7:204–15.

7217. Houghton, Donald E. "Vernon Louis Parrington's Unacknowledged Debt to Moses Coit Tyler." *NEQ* 43:124–30.

7218. Peck, David R. " 'The Orgy of Apology':The Recent Reevaluation of Literature of the Thirties." *Science and Society* 32(1968):371–82.

7219. Pérez Minik, Domingo. "Susan Sontag nos cuenta una ordalía histórica." *Insula* 24(Oct-Nov 1969):21.

* 7220. Thompson, Ewa M. "The Russian Formalists and the New Critics:Two Types of the Close Reading of the Text." *SHR* 4:145–54.

Drama and Theater. 7221. Bailey, Peter, et al. "Black Theater in America:A Report." *NegroD* 19,vi:25–37,42,85,98.

7222. Douglas, James S. "The Small Town in American Drama, 1900–1940." *DAI* 31:1223A(Wash. State).

7223. Downer, Alan S. "More Strange than True:Notes on the New York Theatre, 1968–1969." *QJS* 55(1969):225–36.

7224. Fratti, Mario. "Interview with Ellen Stewart." *D&T* 8:87–89.

7225. Goldman, William. *The Season:A Candid Look at Broadway.* New York: Harcourt, Brace & World, 1969.

7226. Gottfried, Martin. *A Theater Divided:The Postwar American Stage.* Boston: Little, Brown, 1969. [Paperback ed.; incl. new Introd.]

7227. Johnson, Helen A. "Playwrights, Audiences, and Critics:Black Theater." *NegroD* 19,vi:17–24.

7228. King, Woodie,Jr. "The Dilemma of Black Theater." *NegroD* 19,vi:10–15,86–87.

7229. Kurahashi, Ken. "Saikin no America Engeki." *EigoS* 114(1968):444–45. [Recent Amer. drama.]

7230. Lawson, John H. "Our Film and Theirs:*Grapes of Wrath* and *Bonnie and Clyde.*" *AmD* 5,ii(1968–69):30–33.

7231. Moore, Thomas G. *The Economics of the American Theater.* Durham, N.C.: Duke U.P., 1968.

7232. Myers, Norman. "Early Recognition of Gordon Craig in American Periodicals." *ETJ* 22:78–86.

7233. Narumi, Hiroshi. "Kankyo-engeki to Kankyaku-sanka." *EigoS* 115(1969):618–19. [Environmental theatre and audience participation; Off-off Broadway new theater.]

* 7234. Peavy, Charles D. "Satire and Contemporary Black Drama." *SNL* 7(1969):40–49.

7235. Piemme, Jean-Marie. "Le théâtre sans texte, ou la parole convertie." *MRom* 19(1969):91–99.

* 7236. Riach, William A.D. " 'Telling It Like It Is':An Examination of Black Theatre as Rhetoric." *QJS* 56:177–86.

7237. Sadkin, David. "Emblem of an Era:A Critical History of the Group Theatre in Its Times." *DAI* 30:5456A(Kan. State).

7238. Smith, Michael. *Theatre Journal:Winter 1967.* Introd. Warren French. Columbia: U. of Mo. P., 1968. [Revs. of Off-Broadway season.]

7239. Verhoye, Bert. "De fascistische geest van het Living Theatre." *VIG* 53,viii–ix(1969):30–31.

7240. Wills, Arthur. "Where the 'Green-Whiskered Irishman' Went." [F 23]:13–18. [On vaudeville.]

See also 764, 2437, 3914, 4937, 4942, 5777, 7710.

Poetry. 7241. Berry, Wendell. "A Secular Pilgrimage." *HudR* 23:401–24. [Nature poetry.]

7242. Block, Haskell M. "The Impact of French Symbolism on Modern American Poetry." [F 60]:165–217.

7243. Bly, Robert. "Poetry—What Is It Saying and to Whom?" *AmD* 5,ii(1968–69):28.

7244. Christensen, J.A. "Poetry in Its Western Setting." *WR* 7,ii:10–19.

7245. Dorbin, Sanford. "Charles Bukowski and the Little Mag/Small Press Movement." *SCUL* 2,i:17–32.

7246. Hewitt, Geof,ed. *Quickly Aging Here:Some Poets of the 1970's.* With Introd. Garden City, N.Y.: Doubleday (Anchor), 1969. [Anthol.]

7247. Howard, Richard. "Reflections on a Strange Solitude." *Prose* 1:81–91. [On H's *Alone with America.*]

7248. Hughes, Daniel. "American Poetry 1969:From B to Z." *MR* 11:650–86.

7249. Kanazeki, Yoshio. "Haiku to America Gendaishi." *EigoS* 114(1968):358–61. [Haiku and mod. Amer. poetry.]

7250. Kostelanetz, Richard. "La poesia americana del secondo dopoguerra." *Nuova presenza* 12,xxxiv–xxxv(1969):1–25.

7251. Munson, Gorham, and Ann Stanford. "Poetry:1900 to the 1930's." [F 65]:228–44.

7252. Nagata, Masao. "American Poetry, 1912." [F 7]:i–xii. [In Jap.]

* 7253. Naremore, James. "The Imagists and the French 'Generation of 1900'." *ConL* 11:354–74.

* 7254. Novak, Estelle G. "The *Dynamo* School of Poets." *ConL* 11:526–39.

7255. Padgett, Ron, and David Shapiro,eds. *An Anthology of New York Poets.* With Pref. New York: Random House.

7256. Poulin, A.,Jr. "Center and Circumference:Personalism in Criticism." *JML* 1:109–15. [Rev. art.]

7257. Reid, Alfred S. "A Look at the Living Poem:Rock, Protest and Wit." *Furman Mag.* (Spring):6–11,35. [On Shapiro, Bly, A. Dugan, R. Lowell, *inter alia.*]

7258. Ricks, Christopher. "Recent American Poetry." *MR* 11:313–39. [Rev. art.]

7259. Schneidau, Herbert N. "The Age of Interpretation and the Moment of Immediacy:Contemporary Art vs. History." *ELH* 37:287–313.

7260. Shapiro, Karl. "The Poetry Wreck." *LJ* 95:632–35. [Degeneration of Amer. poetry in last decade.]

7261. Templeman, William D. "On the Modern Element in American and English Poetry." *WR* 5,i(1968):52–63.

* 7262. Tolley, A.T. "Rhetoric and the Moderns." *SoR* 6:380–97.

7263. Weatherhead, A. Kingsley. "Poetry:The 1930's to the Present." [F 65]:245–59.

7264. Zhuravlev, Igor. "The Relationships Between Socialist Poetry in the U.S.A. at the Beginning of the Twentieth Century and the Graphic Arts of the Socialist Press." *ZAA* 18:168–82.

See also 912, 1325, 4955, 4967, 4968, 7194, 7702.

Prose Fiction. 7265. Berry, Thomas E. *The Newspaper in the American Novel 1900–1969.* Metuchen, N.J.: Scarecrow.

7266. Bus, Heiner. "Die Figur des 'Helden' im modernen amerikanischen Roman:Ein Forschungsbericht." *JA* 15:208–20.

7267. Cioffari, Philip E. "Major Themes in Southern Fiction Since World War II." *DAI* 30:4402A(N.Y.U.).

7268. Coulombe, Michael J. "The Trilogy as Form in Modern

American Fiction." *DAI* 31:1792A(Purdue). [Dreiser, Dos Passos, W.C. Williams, Richter, Stribling, Faulkner.]

* 7269. Durham, Frank. "The Reputed Demises of Uncle Tom; or, the Treatment of the Negro in Fiction by White Southern Authors in the 1920's." *SLJ* 2,ii:26–50.

7270. Emerson, O.B.,ed. *Alabama Prize Stories:1970.* With Introd. Huntsville, Ala.: Strode. [Anthol.]

7271. Ezor, Edwin L. "The Image of the Teacher in the American Academic Novel, 1900–1960." *DAI* 31:1271A(N.Y.U.).

7272. French, Warren. "Fiction:1900 to the 1930's." [F 65]:177–200.

7273. Gartner, Carol B. "A New Mirror for America:The Fiction of the Immigrant of the Ghetto, 1890–1930." *DAI* 31:1797A–98A(N.Y.U.).

7274. Geismar, Maxwell. "Some Reflections on Contemporary Fiction." *AmD* 5,i(1968):13–16; 5,ii(1968–69):40–44.

7275. Greenberg, Alvin. "Choice:Ironic Alternatives in the World of the Contemporary American Novel." [F 63]:175–87.

7276. Grella, George. "Murder and the Mean Streets:The Hard-Boiled Detective Novel." *Contempora*(Atlanta, Ga.) 1,i: 6–15.

7277. —— "Thrillers, Chillers, and Killers." *Rochester Rev.*(U. of Rochester) 32,iii:11–15. [On "thriller" novels.]

7278. Guthmann, Herbert J. "The Characterization of the Psychiatrist in American Fiction, 1859–1965." *DAI* 30:4451A(So. Calif.).

7279. Hicks, Granville, assisted by Jack Alan Robbins. *Literary Horizons:A Quarter Century of American Fiction.* New York: N.Y.U. Press. [Rptd. revs. of fiction by contemp. Amer. novelists.]

7280. Justus, James H. "Fiction:The 1930's to the Present." [F 65]:201–27.

7281. Katona, Anna. "Picaresque Satires in Modern American Fiction." *ALitASH* 12:105–20.

* 7282. Knox, George. "The Great American Novel:Final Chapter." *AQ* 21(1969):[667]–82.

7283. Lundkvist, Artur. "Fem amerikanska romaner." [F 32]:170–88.

7284. May, John R.,S.J. "Images of Apocalypse in the Black Novel." *Renascence* 23:31–45. [Esp. in *Native Son, Invisible Man, Go Tell It on the Mountain,* and *The System of Dante's Hell.*]

7285. Mengeling, Marvin E. "The State of Contemporary American Fiction:Some Opinions and Prejudices." [F 47]:13–16.

7286. Moore, Edward M. "Some Recent Southern Things." *SR* 78:366–78. [Rev. art.]

7287. Olderman, Raymond M. "Beyond the Waste Land:A Study of the American Novel in the Nineteen-Sixties." *DAI* 30:4998A(Ind.). [Kesey, Barth, Heller, Pynchon, Hawkes, Vonnegut, Beagle.]

7288. Papapanos, Kostas. "To Amerikaniko mythistorima sta teleutaia peninta chronia." *NeaH* 87:607–20.

7289. Powers, Richard G. "Towards a New Literature: Novelistic Experimentation in America During the First Decades of the Twentieth Century." *DAI* 31:399A–400A(Brown).

7290. Rank, Hugh D. "The Image of the Priest in American Catholic Fiction, 1945–1965." *DAI* 30(1969):2039A(Notre Dame).

7291. Riche, James. "Revisionism and the Radical Literature of the 1930's in the U.S.A." *L&I* 7:1–14.

7292. Rupp, Richard H. *Celebration in Postwar American Fiction, 1945–1967.* Coral Gables, Fla.: U. of Miami P. [Chaps. on Cheever, Updike, Welty, F. O'Connor, Agee, Salinger, Baldwin, Ellison, Malamud, and Bellow.]

7293. Samuelson, David N. "Studies in the Contemporary American and British Science Fiction Novel." *DAI* 30(1969): 1181A(So. Calif.).

7294. Shames, Priscilla. "The Long Hope:A Study of American Indian Stereotypes in American Popular Fiction, 1890–1950." *DAI* 30:5003A(U.C.L.A.).

7295. Shuman, R. Baird. "Clarence Darrow's Contribution to Literary Naturalism:*An Eye for an Eye.*" *RLV* 36:390–400.

7296. Sniderman, Stephen L. "The 'Composite' in Twentieth Century American Literature." *DAI* 31:403A(Wis.).

7297. Sullivan, Walter. " 'Where Have All the Flowers Gone?' Part II:The Novel in the Gnostic Twilight." *SR* 78:654–64. [Rev. art. on recent Eng. & Amer. novels by Malamud, G. Greene, E. Bowen, Bellow, *inter alia.*]

7298. —— " 'Where Have All the Flowers Gone?' The Short Story in Search of Itself." *SR* 78:531–42. [Rev. art.]

7299. Vorlat, Emma. *Mens en maatschappij in de naoorlogse Amerikaanse roman 1944–1968.* Antwerpen: De Nederlandsche Boekhandel.

7300. Waldmeir, Joseph J. "Only an Occasional Rutabaga: American Fiction since 1945." *MFS* 15(1969):467–81.

7300a. Weinberg, Helen. *The New Novel in America:The Kafkan Mode in Contemporary Fiction.* Ithaca, N.Y.: Cornell U.P. [Incl. chaps. on Bellow, Salinger, Mailer.]

7301. Wisse, Ruth R. "The Schlemihl as Hero in Yiddish and American Fiction." *DAI* 30:2983A(McGill).

See also 925, 930, 950, 987, 3948, 4975, 4977, 6717, 6719, 6720, 6721, 6723, 6725, 6726.

Abbey. 7302. Wylder, Delbert E. "Edward Abbey and the 'Power Elite'." *WR* 6,ii(1969):18–22.

Agee. 7303. Barson, Alfred T. "James Agee:A Study of Artistic Consciousness." *DAI* 30:5438A(Mass.).

* 7304. Broughton, George and Panthea R. "Agee and Autonomy." *SHR* 4:101–11.

7305. Concannon, Jeanne M. "The Poetry and Fiction of James Agee:A Critical Analysis." *DAI* 30:2962A–63A(Minn.).

* 7306. Curry, Kenneth. "Notes on the Text of James Agee's *A Death in the Family.*" *PBSA* 64:84–99.

7307. Kramer, Victor A. "Agee:A Study of the Poetry, Prose, and Unpublished Manuscript." *DAI* 30(1969):2533A(Texas, Austin).

7308. Mayo, Charles W. "James Agee:His Literary Life and Work." *DAI* 30:4993A(Geo. Peabody Coll. for Teachers).

7309. Shepherd, Allen. " 'A Sort of Monstrous Grinding Beauty':Reflections on Character and Theme in James Agee's *A Death in the Family.*" *IEY* 14(1969):17–24.

7310. Snyder, John J. "James Agee:A Study of His Film Criticism." *DAI* 30:3477A–78A(St. John's).

See also 7659.

Aiken. 7311. Ruffini, Rosalia,ed. "Due lettera di Conrad Aiken." *SA* 14(1968):451–54.

See also 5426, 6599.

Albee. 7312. Bigsby, C.W.E. *Albee.* Edinburgh: Oliver and Boyd, 1969. [Crit.]

7313. Campbell, Mary Elizabeth. "The Tempters in Albee's *Tiny Alice.*" *MD* 13:22–33.

7314. Capellán Gonzalo, Angel. "Albee:Una década." *PrA* 116:67–74.

* 7315. Falk, Eugene H. "*No Exit* and *Who's Afraid of Virginia Woolf*:A Thematic Comparison." *SP* 67:406–17.

7316. Force, William M. "The *What* Story? or, Who's Who at the Zoo?" [F 23]:47–53.

7317. Haas, Rudolf. "Wer hat Angst vor Edward Albee?Gedanken zum modernen amerikanischen Drama." *Univ* 25:347–62.

7318. Jánský, Ann L.L. "Albee's First Decade:An Evaluation." *DAI* 31:3462A(St. Louis U.).

7319. Kishi, Tetsuo. "Coward to Albee." *EigoS* 114(1968): 308–09. [C and A; in Jap.]

7320. Lee, A. Robert. "Illusion and Betrayal:Edward Albee's Theatre." *Studies* 59:53–67.

7321. Narumi, Hiroshi. "Edward Albee no Mondaiten." *EigoS* 114(1968):220–21. [Problems in Albee.]

7322. Post, Robert M. "Fear Itself:Edward Albee's *A Delicate Balance.*" *CLAJ* 13(1969):163–71.

* 7323. Szeliski, John J. von. "Albee:A Rare *Balance.*" *TCL* 16:123–30.

* 7324. White, James E. "An Early Play by Edward Albee." *AL* 42:98–99. [*Schism.*]

* 7325. Witherington, Paul. "Albee's Gothic:The Resonances of Cliché." *CompD* 4:151–65.

See also 4944, 7368.

Alexander, L. *See* 5868.

Ammons. *See* 7241.

Anderson, M. 7326. Anderson, Maxwell. "Love Letter to a University." *NDQ* 38,i:89–90.

7327. Avery, Laurence G. "Maxwell Anderson and *Both Your Houses.*" *NDQ* 38,i:5–24.

7328. Buchanan, Randall J. "A Playwright's Progress." *NDQ* 38,i:60–73.

7329. Gilbert, Robert L. "Mio Romagna:A New View of Maxwell Anderson's *Winterset.*" *NDQ* 38,i:33–43.

7330. Hagan, John P. "Frederick H. Koch and North Dakota:Theatre in the Wilderness." *NDQ* 38,i:75–87.

7331. Hershbell, Jackson K. "The Socrates and Plato of Maxwell Anderson." *NDQ* 38,i:45–59.

7332. Tees, Arthur T. "Legal and Poetic Justice in Maxwell Anderson's Plays." *NDQ* 38,i:25–32.

7333. Wilkins, Robert P.,ed. *Maxwell Anderson Issue. NDQ* 38,i. [Arts. listed separately above and below.]
See also 6285.

Anderson, P. *7334. Miesel, Sandra. "Challenge and Response:Poul Anderson's View of Man." *RQ* 4:80–95.

Anderson, S. 7335. Binni, Francesco. "Il 'personaggio' di Sherwood Anderson." *SA* 14(1968):265–87.

7336. Bort, Barry D. *"Winesburg, Ohio:*The Escape from Isolation." *MQ* 11:443–56.

7337. Frohock, W.M. "Sherwood Anderson e l'elegia americana." *SCr* 3(1969):286–99.

7338. Landor, M. "Die Schule Sherwood Andersons." *KuL* 18:841–55,961–75. [Tr. Wilfried Braumann.]

7339. —— "Škola Šervuda Andersona." *VLit* 13,xii(1969):141–72.

7340. Miller, William V. "The Technique of Sherwood Anderson's Short Stories." *DAI* 30(1969):1175A–76A(Ill.).

7341. Monigle, Martha. "Sherwood Anderson in Boulder." *MQR* 9:55–56.

7342. Nemanic, Gerald C. *"Talbot Whittingham:*An Annotated Edition of the Text Together with a Descriptive and Critical Essay." *DAI* 30(1969):2035A(Ariz.).

Arensburg. 7343. Fields, Kenneth. "Past Masters:Walter Conrad Arensburg and Donald Evans." *SoR* 6:317–39.

Atkins. *See* 7801.

Austin. 7344. Ford, Thomas W. *"The American Rhythm:*Mary Austin's Poetic Principle." *WAL* 5:3–14.

Babbitt. *See* 5205.

Baldwin. 7345. Fabre, Michel. "Pères et fils dans *Go Tell It on the Mountain,* de James Baldwin." *EA* 23:47–61.

7346. Farès, Nabile. "James Baldwin:Une interview exclusive." *JeuneA* 1 sept:20–24.

7347. Hernton, Calvin C. "Blood of the Lamb and a Fiery Baptism:The Ordeal of James Baldwin." *Amistad* 1:183–225.

7348. Reilly, John M. " 'Sonny's Blues':James Baldwin's Image of Black Community." *NALF* 4:56–60.

* 7349. Standley, Fred L. "James Baldwin:The Artist as Incorrigible Disturber of the Peace." *SHR* 4:18–30.
See also 993, 8408.

Barry. 7350. Meserve, Walter J. "Philip Barry:A Dramatist's Search." *MD* 13:93–99.

Barth. 7351. Kennard, Jean E. "John Barth:Imitations of Imitations." *Mosaic* 3,iii:116–31.

* 7352. Majdiak, Daniel. "Barth and the Representation of Life." *Criticism* 13:51–67.

7353. Sommavilla, Guido. "Il cinismo cosmico di John Barth." *Letture* 24(1969):98–110.

7354. Sugiura, Ginsaku. "Imitations-of-Novels—John Barth no Shosetsu." *EigoS* 115(1969):612–13. [Novels of JB.]

* 7355. Tilton, John W. *"Giles Goat-Boy:*An Interpretation." *BuR* 18,i:93–119.

Barthelme. 7356. Longleigh, Peter J.,Jr. "Donald Barthelme's *Snow White.*" *Crit* 11,iii(1969):30–34.

Belitt. 7357. Hutton, Joan. "Antipodal Man:An Interview with Ben Belitt." *Midway* 10,iii:19–47. [Incl. 4 new poems by B.]

Bellow. 7358. Baim, Joseph. "Escape From Intellection:Saul Bellow's *Dangling Man.*" *UR* 37:28–34.

7359. Baim, Joseph, and David P. Demarest,Jr. *"Henderson the Rain King:*A Major Theme and a Technical Problem." [F 59]:53–63.

7360. Cohen, Sarah B. "The Comic Elements in the Novels of Saul Bellow." *DAI* 30:3000A–01A(Northwestern).

7361. Cordesse, Gérard. "L'unité de *Herzog.*" *Caliban* 7:99–113.

7362. Davis, William V. "Bellow's *Herzog.*" *Orion* 118(1969):73.

7363. Fossum, Robert H. "Inflationary Trends in the Criticism of Fiction:Four Studies of Saul Bellow." *SNNTS* 2,i:99–104. [Rev. art.]

7364. Howard, Jane. "Mr. Bellow Considers His Planet." *Life* 3 Apr:57–60.

7365. Michael, Bessie. "What's the Best Way to Live? A Study of the Novels of Saul Bellow." *DAI* 30:5451A–52A (Lehigh).

7366. Moss, Judith P. "The Body as Symbol in Saul Bellow's *Henderson the Rain King.*" *L&P* 20:51–61.

7367. Nadon, Robert J. "Urban Values in Recent American Fiction:A Study of the City in the Fiction of Saul Bellow, John Updike, Philip Roth, Bernard Malamud, and Norman Mailer." *DAI* 30(1969):2543A(Minn.).

7368. Normand, J. "L'homme mystifié:Les héros de Bellow, Albee, Styron et Mailer." *EA* 22(1969):370–85.

7369. Porter, Marvin G. "The Novels of Saul Bellow:A Formalist Reading." *DAI* 31:1287A(Ore.).

7370. Scheer-Schäzler, Brigitte. *A Taste for Metaphors:Die Bildersprache als Interpretationsgrundlage des modernen Romans, dargestellt au Saul Bellows* Herzog. *(ModSp* Schriftenreihe 2.) Wien: Verband der Österreichischen Neuphilologen, 1968.

7371. Wieting, Molly S. "A Quest for Order:The Novels of Saul Bellow." *DAI* 30:3030A–31A(Texas, Austin).
See also 5261, 7301, 8099.

Benchley. 7372. Hasley, Louis. "Robert Benchley:Humorist's Humorist." *ConnR* 4,i:65–72.

7373. Rosmond, Babette. *Robert Benchley:His Life and Good Times.* Garden City, N.Y.: Doubleday. [Biog.]

Berger. 7374. Dippie, Brian W. "Jack Crabb and the Sole Survivors of Custer's Last Stand." *WAL* 4(1969):189–202.

Berry. 7375. Payne, Warren E. "Wendell Berry and the Natural." *Resonance*(Louisville, Ky.) 1,ii(1969):5–16.

Berryman. 7376. Kostelanetz, Richard. "Conversation with Berryman." *MR* 11:340–47.

7377. Martz, William J. *John Berryman.* (UMPAW 85.) Minneapolis: U. of Minn. P., 1969.

7378. Oberg, Arthur. "John Berryman:*The Dream Songs* and the Horror of Unlove." *UWR* 6,i:1–11.

7379. Tokunaga, Yozo. "Yume no Henkyo wo yuko John Berryman." *EigoS* 115(1969):616–18. [JB in the borderland of dreams.]

Bly. 7380. Janssens, G.A.M. "The Present State of American Poetry:Robert Bly and James Wright." *ES* 51:112–37.

7381. Piccione, Anthony. "Robert Bly and the Deep Image." *DAI* 31:1286A(Ohio).

Bourjaily. 7382. Muste, John M. "The Second Major Subwar:Four Novels by Vance Bourjaily." [F 60]:311–26.

Bourne. *See* 8332.

Bowles. 7383. Kraft, James. "Jane Bowles as Serious Lady." *Novel* 1(1968):273–77. [Rev. art.]

Bradbury. 7384. Xmel'nickaja, T. "Ot naučnoj fantastiki k detskoj skazke." *Zvezda* 9:195–204.

Bromfield. 7385. Anderson, David D. " 'Shane's Castle':Myth and Reality in Louis Bromfield's Fiction." *NOQ* 42:38–46.

Brooks, G. 7386. Stavros, George. "An Interview with Gwendolyn Brooks." *ConL* 11:1–20.

Brooks, V.W. 7387. Vitelli, James R. *Van Wyck Brooks.* (TUSAS 134.) New York: Twayne, 1969. [Crit.]

Broom. 7388. Loeb, Harold. *"Broom:*Beginning and Revival." *ConnR* 4,i:5–12.

Brown, S. 7389. Henderson, Stephen A. "A Strong Man Called Sterling Brown." *BlackW* 19,xi:5–12.

Burke. 7390. Fillion, Bryant P. "Rhetoric as Symbolic Action:An Explication of Kenneth Burke's Theory of Rhetoric and Its Implications for the Teaching of Rhetoric in Secondary Schools." *DAI* 30:4942A(Fla. State).

7391. Frank, Armin P. *Kenneth Burke.* (TUSAS 160.) New

York: Twayne, 1969. [Crit.]

7392. Rueckert, William H. "Kenneth Burke and Structuralism." *Shenandoah* 21,i(1969):19–28.

Burroughs, E.R. 7393. El Goulli, S. "Tarzan, un mythe africain reconté par un blanc américain." *ALA* 13(oct):11–15.

* 7394. Kyle, Richard. "Out of Time's Abyss:The Martian Stories of Edgar Rice Burroughs." *RQ* 4:110–22.

* 7395. Mullen, Richard D. "Edgar Rice Burroughs and the Fate Worse than Death." *RQ* 4:186–91.

Burroughs. *See* 5334.

Cabell. 7396. Anderson, Poul. "Something about the Gods." *Kalki* 3,i(1969):20–21.

7397. Austin, Bliss. "Dartmoor Revisited." *Kalki* 3,iv(1969):131–34.

7398. Blish, James. "At the Altar of Sesphra:An Approach to the Allegory." *Kalki* 2,i–ii(1968):6–7,17.

7399. —— "Cabell as Kabbalist." *Kalki* 3,i(1969):11–12.

7400. —— "Cabell as Voluntarist." *Kalki* 3,iv(1969):120–22.

7401. —— "Cabellian Economics:The Uses of the Short Stories." *Kalki* 2,iv(1969):101–02.

7402. —— "From the Third Window." *Kalki* 2,iv(1968):71,106–07.

7403. —— "Source Notes:Ninzian Gets One Right." *Kalki* 2,i–ii(1968):2.

7404. —— "The Mirror and Pigeons Resolved." *Kalki* 2,iv(1968):97.

7405. Blish, James, and James N. Hall. "Cabell as Historical Actor." *Kalki* 3,ii(1969):43–45.

7406. Boardman, John. "The Escape from Escape Literature." *Kalki* 2,iv(1968):84–86,96.

7407. —— "The Two Cabells." *Kalki* 3,iii(1969):83–85.

7408. Carter, Lin. "Horvendile:A Link Between Cabell and Tolkien." *Kalki* 3,iii(1969):85–87.

7409. —— "More on Cabell in Paperback." *Kalki* 3,iii(1969):100–03.

7410. Chancellor, Ann. "Messire Jurgen." *Kalki* 3,i(1969):3–8.

7411. Cover, James P. "Notes on *Jurgen*." *Kalki* 3,i(1969):13–15; ii:70–72; iii:92–97,104–07; iv:136–42.

7412. Cranwell, John P., and James P. Cover. "Notes on *Figures of Earth*." *Kalki* 3,i(1969):22–33.

7413. —— "Notes on *Figures of Earth*." *Kalki* 2,iv(1968):91–95(to be cont.).

* 7414. Duke, Maurice. "James Branch Cabell's Personal Library." *SB* 23:207–16.

7415. Godshalk, William L. "James Branch Cabell at William and Mary:The Education of a Novelist." *Kalki* 2,iv(1968):77–83,96.

7416. Hall, James N. "Cabell Deluxe:A Bibliographic Postscript." *Kalki* 3,ii(1969):76–77.

7417. —— "In Charteris' Library." *Kalki* 2,iv(1968):97–98.

7418. —— "The Biography of Manuel:A Brief Bibliography." *Kalki* 2,i–ii(1968):3–5.

7419. —— "The Re-evolution of a Vestryman:A Study in Cabellian Theology." *Kalki* 2,iv(1968):72–76.

7420. —— "Trifles Found by Moonlight." *Kalki* 3,ii(1969):62,72.

7421. Hartman, Harry. " 'The Comstock Lewd':*Jurgen* and the Law—Updated." *Kalki* 3,i(1969):16–19.

7422. Herrick, Thomas C. "Ch. 51:Of Compromises with Time." *Kalki* 3,iv(1969):128–29.

7423. Jenkins, William D. "A Time for Airy Persiflage." *Kalki* 3,ii(1969):50–52.

7424. —— "Another Way of Elusion." *Kalki* 3,ii(1969):63–69.

7425. —— "Elementary, My Dear Cabell." *Kalki* 3,iv(1969):134–35.

7426. —— "The Shirt of Nessus." *Kalki* 3,i(1969):9–10.

7427. Johannsen, Kris. "Color in *Jurgen*." *Kalki* 3,iv(1969):129–30.

7428. Keller, David H. "The Sigil of Scoteia." *Kalki* 2,i–ii(1968):27–28.

* 7429. MacDonald, Edgar E. "Cabell's Richmond Trial." *SLJ* 3,i:47–71.

7430. Page, Jerry. " 'The Man at Storisende':A Biographical Note." *Kalki* 2,i–ii(1968):8–12.

7431. Peter, Emmett,Jr. "Another Mirror for Pigeons." *Kalki* 3,iii(1969):88–91.

7432. Schilmeister, Deborah. "Revelations of a Sunrise." *Kalki* 3,iv(1969):124–27.

7433. Smith, Nelson J.,III. "Cabell:Realist or Romantic?" *Kalki* 3,ii(1969):53–56,77.

7434. Spencer, Paul. " 'After the Style of Maurice Hewlett'." *Kalki* 3,iv(1969):143–45.

7435. —— "A Life Beyond Life." *Kalki* 2,i–ii(1968):23–26.

7436. —— "A Manual of Non-Manuels." *Kalki* 2,i–ii(1968):29–31.

7437. Tarrant, Desmond. "James Branch Cabell." *Menckeniana* 33:4–9.

7438. *The Cabellian* 2,ii. [Betty F. Carson, "Richmond Renascence:The Virginia Writers' Club of the 1920's and *The Reviewer*," 39–47; Emmons Welch, "*Beyond Life* and *Jurgen*:The Demiurge," 48–53; Warren A. McNeill, "*Cabellian Harmonics*:Why and How?" 55–58; Maurice Duke, "Virginiana at the Cabell Library," 59–60.]

7439. *The Cabellian* 3,i. [Edgar E. MacDonald, "The Influence of Provençal Poetry on James Branch Cabell," 1–6; Joseph M. Flora, "Vardis Fisher and James Branch Cabell:A Postscript," 7–9; Desmond Tarrant, "Cabell's *Hamlet Had an Uncle* and Shakespeare's *Hamlet*," 10–11; G.N. Gabbard, "Deems Taylor's Musical Version of *Jurgen*," 12–15; Gerard P. Meyer, "Young *Jurgen*:A Comedy of Derision," 16–21; Penn Dameron, "Inside Book Two of James Branch Cabell's *The Silver Stallion*," 22–23; Opal Fisher, "Vardis Fisher Memorial," 25–26; Betty Adler, "The Mencken Room," 28–30; Julius Rothman, "James Branch Cabell Library:Phase One," 32–33; Julius Rothman, "Cabell's Books at This Time & Other Matters," 34; Julius Rothman, "The Cabell Society:A Report," 35–36.]

7440. Zirkle, Conway. "Cabell and [Woodrow] Wilson." *Kalki* 3,ii(1969):46–49.

Cahan, A. 7441. Chametzky, Jules. "Focus on Abraham Cahan's *The Rise of David Levinsky*:Boats Against the Current." [F 63]:87–93.

7442. Marovitz, Sanford E., and Lewis Fried. "Abraham Cahan (1860–1951):An Annotated Bibliography." *ALR* 3:197–243.

See also 6734.

Capote. 7443. Keith, Don Lee. "An Interview with Truman Capote." *Contempora*(Atlanta, Ga.) 1,iv:36–40.

7444. Pini, Richard. "Fiction et réalité chez Truman Capote." *LanM* 63(1969):176–85.

* 7445. Trimmier, Dianne B. "The Critical Reception of Capote's *Other Voices, Other Rooms*." *WVUPP* 17:94–101.

Capp. 7446. Berger, Arthur A. L'il Abner:*A Study in American Satire*. New York: Twayne.

Cather. *7447. Bush, Sargent,Jr. "*Shadows on the Rock* and Willa Cather's View of the Past." *QQ* 76(1969):269–85.

7448. Crane, Joan St. C. "Rare or Seldom-Seen Dust Jackets of American First Editions:I." *Serif* 7,ii:27–30. [All Cather titles; all in Alderman Lib., U. of Va.]

7449. Ferguson, J.M.,Jr. " 'Vague Outlines':Willa Cather's Enchanted Bluffs." *WR* 7,i:61–64.

* 7450. Schneider, Sister Lucy,C.S.J. "Cather's 'Land-Philosophy' in *Death Comes for the Archbishop*." *Renascence* 22:78–86.

7451. Slote, Bernice. "Willa Cather as a Regional Writer." *KanQ* 2,ii:7–15.

* 7452. Stouck, David. "Perspective as Structure and Theme in *My Ántonia*." *TSLL* 12:285–94.

7453. Throne, Marilyn E. "The Two Selves:Duality in Willa Cather's Protagonists and Themes." *DAI* 30:3026A–27A(Ohio State).

See also 6845, 7911, 8114.

Chandler. *7454. Jameson, Fredric. "On Raymond Chandler." *SoR* 6:624–50.

* 7455. Miller, Robert H. "The Publication of Raymond Chandler's *The Long Goodbye*." *PBSA* 63(1969):279–90.

See also 7719.

Chase, J.S. 7456. Dillon, Richard H. "Prose Poet of the Trail:J. Smeaton Chase." *QNL* 35:27–36.

Churchill. See 6721.

Ciardi. 7457. Perrine, Laurence. "Ciardi's 'Tenzone'." *Expl* 28:Item 82.

Clark, W.V. 7458. Andersen, Kenneth. "Character Portrayal in *The Ox-Bow Incident*." *WAL* 4:287–98.

7459. —— "Form in Walter Van Tilburg Clark's *The Ox-Bow Incident*." *WR* 6,i(1969):19–25.

7460. Cohen, Edward H. "Clark's 'The Portable Phonograph'." *Expl* 28:Item 69.

7461. Westbrook, Max. *Walter Van Tilburg Clark*. (TUSAS 155.) New York: Twayne, 1969. [Crit.]

Cleaver. 7462. Nower, Joyce. "Cleaver's Vision of America and the New White Radical:A Legacy of Malcolm X." *NALF* 4:12–21.

Connelly. 7463. Phillips, John L. "Before the Colors Fade: *Green Pastures* Recalled." *AH* 21(Feb):28–29,74–76.

Coover. 7464. Hertzel, Leo J. "An Interview with Robert Coover." *Crit* 11,iii(1969):25–29.

7465. —— "What's Wrong with the Christians." *Crit* 11, iii(1969):11–24. [Incl. "A Coover Checklist."]

Cozzens. 7466. Keefe, Joseph C. "Social Behaviorism in the Novels of James Gould Cozzens." *DAI* 30:3463A(Syracuse).

* 7467. Krickel, Edward. "Cozzens and Saroyan:A Look at Two Reputations." *GaR* 24:281–96.

Crane, H. 7468. Bryant, J.A.,Jr. "Hart Crane, Poet of the Sixties." *JML* 1:283–88. [Rev. art.]

7469. Butterfield, R.W. *The Broken Arc:A Study of Hart Crane*. Edinburgh: Oliver & Boyd, 1969.

7470. Cowley, Malcolm. "Hart Crane:The Evidence in the Case." *SR* 78:176–84. [Rev. art.]

7471. Hashiguchi, Minoru. "America no Homerostachi." *Oberon* 30(1968):10–41. [The Homers of America: H. Crane's *Bridge* and W.C. Williams' *Paterson*.]

7472. Houston, Robert W. "Hart Crane and Arthur Rimbaud:A Comparison." [F16]:13–19.

7473. Huberman, Elizabeth. "Hart Crane's Use of 'Symphonic Form'." [F 62]:15–29.

7474. Hutson, Richard. "Hart Crane's 'Black Tambourine'." *LWU* 3:31–36.

7475. Ickstadt, Heinrich. *Dichterische Erfahrung und Metaphernstruktur:Eine Untersuchung der Bildersprache Hart Cranes*. Heidelberg: Winter.

* 7476. Kahn, Sy. "Hart Crane and Harry Crosby:A Transit of Poets." *JML* 1:45–56.

* 7477. Keller, Dean H. "*CALM* Addenda No. 2:Hart Crane." *PBSA* 64:98–99.

* 7478. Kessler, Edward. "Crane's 'Black Tambourine'." *Expl* 29:Item 4.

7479. Leibowitz, Herbert A. "A Stylistic Analysis of Hart Crane's Poetry." *DAI* 30(1969):2029A–30A(Columbia). [Cf. Bibliog. for 1968, Item 10791.]

7480. Lewis, Thomas S.W. "Hart Crane and His Mother:A Correspondence." *Salmagundi* 9(1969):61–87.

7481. Nilsen, Helge N. *Hart Crane's "The Bridge."* A Study in Sources and Interpretation. Bergen, 1969. [Diss.]

7482. Pacernick, Gary B. "Logic of Metaphor:An Aesthetic Approach to the Poetry and the Poetics of Hart Crane." *DAI* 30(1969):2544A(Ariz. State).

7483. Simon, Marc. "Samuel Greenberg and Hart Crane:A Study of the Lost Manuscripts." *DAI* 30:4464A–65A(N.Y.U.).

7484. Uroff, M[argaret] D. "Hart Crane's 'Voyages VI,' Stanza 6." *ELN* 8:46–48.

* 7485. —— "Hart Crane's 'Recitative'." *CP* 3,i:22–27.

7486. Weber, Brom. *Hart Crane:A Biographical and Critical Study*. New York: Russell & Russell. [Repr. of 1948 ed. with new Preface and corrections.]

7487. Wheat, Linda R. "A Comparative Study of Jules Laforgue and Hart Crane." *DAI* 31:1245A(Vanderbilt).

See also 1457, 7096.

Crosby. See 7476.

Cullen. See 7916.

Cummings. 7488. Attaway, Kenneth R. *E.E. Cummings' Aloofness:An Underlying Theme in His Poetry*. (Research Paper 24.) Atlanta: Ga. State U., 1969.

7489. Davis, William V. "Cummings' 'next to of course god america i'." *CP* 3,i:14–15.

7490. Donahue, Jane. "Cummings' Last Poem:An Explication." *LWU* 3:106–08.

7491. Eckley, Wilton. *Checklist of e.e. cummings*. (Merrill Checklists.) Columbus, Ohio: Charles E. Merrill.

7492. —— *Guide to e.e. cummings*. (Merrill Guides.) Columbus, Ohio: Charles E. Merrill.

7493. Lord, John B. "Para-Grammatical Structure in a Poem of E.E. Cummings." *PCP* 1(1966):66–73. ["Anyone lived in a pretty how town."]

* 7494. Metcalf, Allan A. "Dante and E.E. Cummings." *CLS* 7:374–86.

7495. Powers, Richard G. "Cummings' 'I Will Be'." *Expl* 28:Item 54.

7496. Schleiner, Winfried. "Drei Gedichte von E.E. Cummings." *LWU* 2(1969):27–37.

7497. Triem, Eve. *E.E. Cummings*. (UMPAW 87.) Minneapolis: U. of Minn. P., 1969.

Dahlberg. 7498. Dahlberg, Edward. "A Letter to *Prose*." *Prose* 1:69–80.

7499. Moramarco, Fred S. "Edward Dahlberg:A Critical Introduction." *DAI* 30(1969):2033A–34A(Utah).

7500. Stringher, Bonalda. "Edward Dahlberg e la ricerca del mito." *SA* 14(1968):309–38.

See also 1504, 5718.

Davidson. 7501. Allen, Ward. "Donald Davidson." *SR* 78:390–404.

7502. Buffington, Robert. "Mr. Davidson in the Formal Garden." *GaR* 24:121–31.

Davis, H.L. 7503. Etulain, Richard W. "H.L. Davis:A Bibliographical Addendum." *WAL* 5:129–35.

Dell. 7504. Smith, John T. "Feminism in the Novels of Floyd Dell." *DAI* 31:1814A(Texas, Austin).

DeVoto. See 6559.

Dewlen. 7505. Merren, John. "Character and Theme in the Amarillo Novels of Al Dewlen." *WR* 6,i(1969):3–9.

Dickens. 7506. Hamblen, Abigail A. "Another Dickens Come to Judgment." *Cresset*(Valparaiso U.) 33,iii:12–15. [On Monica Dickens (Charles Dickens' great granddaughter) as a novelist.]

Dickey. 7507. Calhoun, Richard J. "Whatever Happened to the Poet-Critic?" *SLJ* 1,i(1968):75–88. [Rev. art. on James Dickey, *Bable to Byzantium:Poets and Poetry Now*.]

7508. Fukuda, Rikutaro. "James Dickey no Shi to Shiron." *EigoS* 114(1968):576–77. [Poems and poetics of D.]

7509. "James Dickey:Worksheets." *MHRev* 7(1968):113–17.

7510. Marin, Daniel B. "James Dickey's *Deliverance*:Darkness Visible." *SCR* 3,i:49–59.

7511. Skelton, Robin. "The Verge of Greatness." *MHRev* 4(1967):119–24. [Rev. art.]

Dobie. 7512. Richards, Lewis A. "Frank Dobie's Use of Folklore:The Lost Adams Digging Story." *WR* 7,i:38–48. [Illus.]

7513. Turner, Martha Anne. "Was Frank Dobie a Throwback to Mark Twain?" *WR* 5,ii(1968):3–12.

Donleavy. 7514. Vintner, Maurice. "The Novelist as Clown: The Fiction of J.P. Donleavy." *Meanjin* 29:108–14.

Dos Passos. 7515. Brierre, Annie. "Littérature américaine: Hommage à John Roderigo Dos Passos." *RDM* 12:688–93.

7516. England, Donald G. "The Newsreels of John Dos Passos' *The 42nd Parallel*:Sources and Techniques." *DAI* 31: 1794A–95A(Texas, Austin).

7517. Gado, Frank,ed. "An Interview with John Dos Passos." *Idol*(Union College, Schenectady, N.Y.) 45(1969):5–25.

7518. Goldman, Arnold. "Dos Passos and His *U.S.A.*" *NLH* 1:471–83.

7519. Ludington, Charles T.,Jr. "An Individual's Focus on Existence:The Novels of John Dos Passos." *DAI* 31:393A(Duke).

* 7520. —— "The Neglected Satires of John Dos Passos." *SNL* 7:127–36.

7521. Pires, Alves. "O cinema na literatura:John dos Passos." *Brotéria* 87(1968):74–87.

7522. Winner, Anthony. "The Characters of John Dos Passos." *LWU* 2(1969):1–19.

See also 529, 959.

Dreiser. 7523. Blacksin, Ida. "Law and Literature:Dreiser and the Courts." *DAI* 31:1261A(Mich. State).

7524. Block, Haskell M. *Naturalistic Tryptych:The Fictive and the Real in Zola, Mann, and Dreiser.* New York: Random House.

7525. Davis, Nancy H. "The Women in Theodore Dreiser's Novels." *DAI* 30:3003A(Northwestern).

7526. Dowell, Richard W.,ed. " 'You Will Not Like Me, I'm Sure':Dreiser to Miss Emma Rector:November 28, 1893, to April 4, 1894." *ALR* 3:259–70. [Incl. texts of 5 letters.]

7527. *Dreiser Newsl.*(Ind. State U., Terre Haute) 1,i. [W.A. Swanberg, "Airmail Interview," 2–6; Philip L. Gerber, "Two Dreisers Plus One," 6–10 (Rev. art.); Donald Pizer, "Dreiser Studies:Work to Be Done," 10–13; Richard W. Dowell, "Dreiser Holdings at the Lilly Library," 13–15.]

7528. Heuston, Dustin H. "Theodore Dreiser's Search for Control:A Critical Study of His Novels." *DAI* 30:4453A(N.Y.U.).

7529. Hoppe, Ralph H. "The Theme of Alienation in the Novels of Theodore Dreiser." *DAI* 31:389A–90A(Denver).

* 7530. Hovey, Richard B., and Ruth S. Ralph. "Dreiser's The 'Genius':Motivation and Structure." *HSL* 2:169–83.

7531. Kennell, Ruth E. *Dreiser and the Soviet Union (1927–1945):A First-Hand Chronicle.* New York: Internat. Pubs., 1969. [Biog.]

7532. Moers, Ellen. *Two Dreisers.* New York: Viking, 1969. [Crit.]

7533. Mookerjee, R.N. "An Embarrassment of Riches: Dreiser Research. Materials and Problems." *IJAS* 1,i(1969): 91–96.

* 7534. Pizer, Donald. "The Problem of Philosophy in the Novel." *BuR* 18,i:53–62.

7535. Pizer, Donald,ed. *Sister Carrie.* (Norton Crit. Ed.) With Notes and an Introd. New York: Norton.

7536. Salzman, Jack,ed. *Sister Carrie.* With Introd. Indianapolis: Bobbs-Merrill.

7537. Schneider, Ralph T. "Theodore Dreiser and the American Dream of Success:The Early Years." *DAI* 30: 5456A–57A(Kan. State).

Eastlake. See 8310.

Edmonds. *7538. Wyld, Lionel D. "At Boyd House:Walter Edmonds' York State." *Eng. Record* 20,ii(1969):89–92.

Ellison. *7539. *CLAJ* 13,iii:Ralph Ellison Spec. No. [Archie D. Sanders, "Odysseus in Black:An Analysis of the Structure of *Invisible Man*," 217–28; Lawrence J. Clipper, "Folkloric and Mythic Elements in *Invisible Man*," 229–41; Eleanor R. Wilner, "The Invisible Black Thread:Identity and Nonentity in *Invisible Man*," 242–57; Darwin Turner, "Sight in *Invisible Man*," 258–64; George E. Kent, "Ralph Ellison and Afro-American Folk and Cultural Tradition," 265–76; Phyllis R. Klotman, "The Running Man as Metaphor in Ellison's *Invisible Man*," 277–88; Lloyd W. Brown, "Ralph Ellison's Exhorters:The Role of Rhetoric in *Invisible Man*," 289–303; Floyd R. Horowitz, "An Experimental Confession from a Reader of *Invisible Man*," 304–14; Thomas LeClair, "The Blind Leading the Blind:Wright's *Native Son* and a Brief Reference to Ellison's *Invisible Man*," 315–20.]

7540. Clarke, John H. "The Visible Dimensions of *Invisible Man.*" *BlackW* 20,ii:27–30.

7541. Collier, Eugenia W. "The Nightmare Truth of an Invisible Man." *BlackW* 20,ii:12–19.

7542. Corry, John. "Profile of an American Novelist:A White View of Ralph Ellison." *BlackW* 20,ii:116–25.

7543. Ducornet, Guy. "Ralph Ellison:Homme invisible, pour qui chantes-tu? Grasset, 1969, traduction de Robert Merle." *LanM* 63(1969):394–401.

7544. Ford, Nick A. "The Ambivalence of Ralph Ellison." *BlackW* 20,ii:5–9.

7545. Greene, Maxine. "Against Invisibility." *CE* 30(1969): 430–36.

7546. Guttmann, Allen. "Focus on Ralph Ellison's *Invisible Man*:American Nightmare." [F 63]:188–96.

7547. Hays, Peter L. "The Incest Theme in *Invisible Man.*" *WHR* 23(1969):335–39.

7548. Kaiser, Ernest. "A Critical Look at Ellison's Fiction and at Social and Literary Criticism by and about the Author." *BlackW* 20,ii:53–59,81–97.

7549. Kostelanetz, Richard. "Ralph Ellison:Novelist as Brown Skinned Aristocrat." *Shenandoah* 20,iv(1969):56–77.

7550. Lee, A. Robert. "Sight and Mask:Ralph Ellison's *Invisible Man.*" *NALF* 4:22–33.

* 7551. Ludington, Charles T.,Jr. "Protest and Anti-Protest: Ralph Ellison." *SHR* 4:31–39.

7552. Mason, Clifford. "Ralph Ellison and the Underground Man." *BlackW* 20,ii:20–26.

7553. Moorer, Frank E., and Lugene Baily. "A Selected Check List of Materials by and about Ralph Ellison." *BlackW* 20,ii:126–30.

7554. Neal, Larry. "Ellison's Zoot Suit." *BlackW* 20,ii:31–52.

7555. Nichols, William W. "Ralph Ellison's Black American Scholar." *Phylon* 31:70–75.

7556. Plessner, Monika. "Bildnis des Künstlers als Volksaufwiegler." *Merkur* 24:629–43.

7557. Powell, Grosvenor E. "Role and Identity in Ralph Ellison's *Invisible Man.*" [F 57]:95–105.

7558. Reilly, John M.,ed. *Twentieth Century Interpretations of Invisible Man:A Collection of Critical Essays.* (TCI.) With Introd. Englewood Cliffs, N.J.: Prentice-Hall. [Rptd. crit.]

* 7559. Schafer, William J. "Irony from Underground—Satiric Elements in *Invisible Man.*" *SNL* 7(1969):22–29.

7560. Williams, John A. "Ralph Ellison and *Invisible Man*: Their Place in American Letters." *BlackW* 20,ii:10-11.

See also 6802, 8406, 8411.

Empey. See 8332.

Eustis. 7561. Burns, Stuart L. "St. Petersburg Re-Visited: Helen Eustis and Mark Twain." *WAL* 5:99–112.

Evans, D. See 7343.

Evans, M. See 7656.

Falkner. 7562. Anderson, Hilton. "Colonel Falkner's Preface to *The Siege of Monterey.*" *NMW* 3:36–40.

7563. Faulkner, J. *Cabin Road.* Introd. Redding S. Sugg,Jr. Baton Rouge: La. State U.P., 1969.

* 7564. White, Helen, and Redding S. Sugg,Jr. "John Faulkner:An Annotated Check List of His Published Works and of His Papers." *SB* 23:217–29.

Farrell. 7565. Fried, Lewis F. "The Naturalism of James Farrell:A Study of His Major Novels." *DAI* 30:4985A(Mass.).

Faulkner. 7566. Adams, Richard P. "Focus on William Faulkner's 'The Bear':Moses and the Wilderness." [F 63]:129–35.

7567. Angell, Leslie E. "The Umbilical Cord Symbol as Unifying Theme and Pattern in *Absalom, Absalom!*" *MSE* 1(1968):106–10.

7568. Barbour, Brian M. "Faulkner's Decline." *DAI* 30: 5436A–37A(Kent State).

7569. Bedell, George C. "Kierkegaard and Faulkner: Modalities of Existence." *DAI* 30:5056A–57A(Duke).

* 7570. Blanchard, Margaret. "The Rhetoric of Communion: Voice in *The Sound and the Fury.*" *AL* 41:[555]–65.

7571. Boswell, George W. "Picturesque Faulknerisms." *UMSE* 9(1968):47–56.

* 7572. Bradford, M.E. "Addie Bundren and the Design of *As I Lay Dying.*" *SoR* 6:1093–99.

7573. ——— "Brother, Son, and Heir:The Structural Focus of Faulkner's *Absalom, Absalom!*" *SR* 78:76–98.

7574. Brooks, Cleanth. "Faulkner's First Novel." *SoR* 6: 1056–74.

7575. ——— "The Poetry of Miss Rosa Canfield." *Shenandoah* 20,iii:199–206.

7576. Brown, Calvin. "A Dim View of Faulkner's Country." *GaR* 23(1969):501–11. [Rev. art on Elizabeth Kerr's *Yoknapatawpha:Faulkner's "Little Postage Stamp of Native Soil."*]

7577. ——— "Faulkner's Use of the Oral Tradition." [F 3]:519–26.

* 7578. Campbell, Harry M. "Faulkner's Philosophy Again:A Reply to Michel Gresset." *MissQ* 23:64–66.

* 7579. Cecil, L. Moffitt. "A Rhetoric for Benjy." *SLJ* 3,i:32–46.

7580. Collins, R.G. "The Game of Names:Characterization Device in *Light in August.*" *Eng. Record* 21,i:82–87.

* 7581. Cooley, Thomas W.,Jr. "Faulkner Draws the Long Bow." *TCL* 16:268–77.

7582. Dennis, Stephen N. "The Making of *Sartoris*:A Description and Discussion of the Manuscript and Composite Typescript of William Faulkner's Third Novel." *DAI* 31:384A(Cornell).

* 7583. Ditsky, John. "Faulkner's Carousel:Point of View in *As I Lay Dying*." *LauR* 10,i:74–85.

7584. Ewell, Barbara N. "To Move In Time:A Study of the Structure of Faulkner's *As I Lay Dying, Light in August,* and *Absalom, Absalom!*" *DAI* 30:3940A(Fla. State).

7585. Fusini, Nadia. "La caccia all'orso di Faulkner." *SA* 14(1968):289–308.

7586. Gidley, M. "Some Notes on Faulkner's Reading." *JAmS* 4:91–102.

7587. Gregg, Alvin L. "Style and Dialect in *Light in August* and Other Works of William Faulkner." *DAI* 30:3009A(Texas, Austin).

7588. Hafner, John H. "William Faulkner's Narrators." *DAI* 30:5445A(Wis.).

* 7589. Harter, Carol C. "The Winter of Isaac McCaslin: Revisions and Irony in Faulkner's 'Delta Autumn'." *JML* 1:209–25.

* 7590. Hemenway, Robert. "Enigmas of Being in *As I Lay Dying*." *MFS* 16:133–46.

7591. Hermann, John. "Faulkner's Heart's Darling in 'That Evening Sun'." *SSF* 7:320–23.

7592. Hodges, Elizabeth L. "The Bible as Novel:A Comparative Study of Two Modernized Versions of Biblical Stories, Zola's *La faute de l'abbé Mouret* and Faulkner's *A Fable*." *DAI* 30:5447A(Ga.).

* 7593. Houghton, Donald E. "Whores and Horses in Faulkner's 'Spotted Horses'." *MQ* 11:361–69.

* 7594. Howell, Elmo. "Faulkner's Elegy:An Approach to 'The Bear'." *ArlQ* 2,iii:122–32.

* 7595. —— "William Faulkner's Chickasaw Legacy:A Note on 'Red Leaves'." *ArQ* 26:293–303.

7596. —— "William Faulkner's General Forrest and the Uses of History." *THQ* 29:287–94.

7597. —— "William Faulkner's Mule:A Symbol of the Post-War South." *KFR* 15(1969):81–86.

7598. Inge, M. Thomas,ed. *William Faulkner:*A Rose for Emily. (Merrill Casebooks.) With Introd. Columbus, Ohio: Charles E. Merrill. [Text of story plus rptd. crit.]

* 7599. Irvine, Peter L. "Faulkner and Hardy." *ArQ* 26:357–65.

7600. Ivănescu, Mircea. "Dostoievski și Faulkner." *SXX* 12,iv(1969):209–12.

7601. Jarrett-Kerr, Fr. Martin. *William Faulkner.* (CWCP.) Grand Rapids, Mich.: William B. Eerdmans. [Crit.]

* 7602. Kinney, Arthur F. "Faulkner and the Possibilities for Heroism." *SoR* 6:1110–25.

* 7603. Levins, Lynn G. "The Four Narrative Perspectives in *Absalom, Absalom!*" *PMLA* 85:35–47.

7604. Lhamon, W.T.,Jr. "*Pylon*:The Ylimaf and New Valois." *WHR* 24:274–78.

7605. Lillqvist, Holger. "Det förflutnas närvaro och fantasins styrka." *NyA* 63:55–57. [*Absalom, Absalom!*]

7606. Logan, John. "Nota sobre el personaje balbuciente como héroe." *Sur* 322–23:148–54.

7607. Loghin, Georgeta. "W. Faulkner și problema populației de culoare." *AȘUI* 13,ii(1967):245–48.

7608. Madeya, Ulrike. "Interpretationen zu William Faulkners 'The Bear':Das Bild des Helden und die Konstellation der Charaktere." *LWU* 3:45–60.

7609. Massey, Tom M. "Faulkner's Females:The Thematic Function of Women in the Yoknapatawpha Cycle." *DAI* 30:3468A(Nev.).

7610. McCants, Maxine. "From Humanity to Abstraction: Negro Characterization in *Intruder in the Dust*." *NMW* 2:91–104.

7611. McHaney, Thomas L. "William Faulkner's *The Wild Palms*:A Textual and Critical Study." *DAI* 30(1969):2540A–41A(S.C.).

7612. McWilliams, David D. "The Influence of William Faulkner on Michel Butor." *DAI* 31:1282A–83A(Ore.).

7613. Mellard, James M. "*The Sound and the Fury*:Quentin Compson and Faulkner's 'Tragedy of Passion'." *SNNTS* 2,i: 61–75.

7614. Meriwether, James B. *Checklist of William Faulkner.* (Merrill Checklists.) Columbus, Ohio: Charles E. Merrill.

* 7615. —— "The Novel Faulkner Never Wrote:His *Golden Book* or *Doomsday Book*." *AL* 42:93–96.

7616. Meriwether, James B.,ed. *Studies in* The Sound and the Fury. (Merrill Studies.) Columbus, Ohio: Charles E. Merrill. [Rptd. crit. plus Eileen Gregory, "Caddy Compson's World," 89–101.]

7617. Minter, David L.,ed. *Twentieth Century Interpretations of* Light in August. (TCI.) With Introd. Englewood Cliffs, N.J.: Prentice-Hall, 1969. [Rptd. crit.]

* 7618 *MissQ* 23,iii:William Faulkner Spec. Issue. [Mary M. Dunlap, "William Faulkner's 'Knight's Gambit' and Gavin Stevens," 223–39; Raleigh W. Smith,Jr., "Faulkner's 'Victory': The Plain People of Clydebank," 241–49; Carl Ficken, "The Christ Story in *A Fable*," 251–64; François L. Pitavy, "The Landscape in *Light in August*," 265–72; Gorman Beauchamp, "*The Unvanquished*: Faulkner's *Oresteia*," 273–77; Rosemary Stephens, "Ike's Gun and Too Many Novembers," 279–87; Margaret Yonce, "Faulkner's 'Atthis' and 'Attis':Some Sources of Myth," 289–98; M. Gidley, "One Continuous Force:Notes on Faulkner's Extra-Literary Reading," 299–314; Thomas L. McHaney, "A Deer Hunt in the Faulkner Country," 315–20; James E. Kibler,Jr., "A Possible Source in Ariosto for Drusilla," 321–22.]

7619. Muehl, Lois. "Word Choice and Choice Words in Faulkner's *Sartoris*." *LC* 35(1969):58–63.

7620. Myres, William V. "Faulkner's Parable of Poetic Justice." *LaS* 8(1969):224–30.

* 7621. Nebeker, Helen E. "Emily's Rose of Love:Thematic Implications of Point of View in Faulkner's 'A Rose for Emily'." *BRMMLA* 24:3–13.

7622. Ochi, Michio. "Kuhaku wo toshite minaoshita Faulkner." *EigoS* 115(1969):558–60. [F as seen through the void.]

7623. Pastore, Philip E. "The Structure and Meaning of William Faulkner's *A Fable*." *DAI* 31:397A–98A(Fla.).

7624. Pate, Frances W. "Names of Characters in Faulkner's Mississippi." *DAI* 30(1969):2036A–37A(Emory).

7625. Pate, Willard. "Pilgrimage to Yoknapatawpha." *Furman Mag.* (Winter 1969):6–13.

* 7626. Peavy, Charles D. "Jason Compson's Paranoid Pseudo-community." *HSL* 2:151–56.

7627. Pochmann, Henry A., and Joel A. Hunt. "Faulkner and His Sources." *ConL* 11:310–12.

7628. Powell, Irma A. "Man in His Struggle:Structure, Technique, and Theme in Faulkner's Snopes Trilogy." *DAI* 31:1287A–88A(Fla. State).

7629. Presley, Delma E. "Is Reverend Whitefield a Hypocrite?" *RS* 36(1968):57–61.

* 7630. Rea, J. "Faulkner's 'Spotted Horses'." *HSL* 2:157–64.

7631. Rinaldi, Nicholas M. "Game Imagery in Faulkner's *Absalom, Absalom!*" *ConnR* 4,i:73–79.

7632. Riskin, Myra J. "Faulkner's South:Myth and History in the Novel." *DAI* 30(1969):1148A–49A(Calif., Berkeley).

7633. Rodnon, Stewart. "*The House of the Seven Gables* and *Absalom, Absalom!* Time, Tradition, and Guilt." [F 23]:42–46.

7634. Rosenberg, Bruce A. "The Oral Quality of Rev. Shegog's Sermon in William Faulkner's *The Sound and the Fury*." *LWU* 2(1969):73–88.

7635. Rossky, William. "The Pattern of Nightmare in *Sanctuary*:Or, Miss Reba's Dogs." *MFS* 15(1969):503–15.

* 7636. Samway, Patrick,S.J. "War:A Faulknerian Commentary." *ColQ* 18:370–78. [*A Fable*.]

* 7637. Spilka, Mark. "Quentin Compson's Universal Grief." *ConL* 11:451–69.

7638. Sternberg, Meir. "The Compositional Principles of Faulkner's *Light in August* and the Poetics of the Modern Novel." *Hasifrut* 2:498–537. [In Hebr.; Eng. sum.]

7639. Swink, Helen M. "The Oral Tradition in Yoknapatawpha County." *DAI* 30:3920A(Va.).

* 7640. Taylor, Walter. "Faulkner:Social Commitment and the Artistic Temperament." *SoR* 6:1075–92.

* 7641. VandeKieft, Ruth M. "Faulkner's Defeat of Time in

Absalom, Absalom!" *SoR* 6:1100–09.

7642. Vickery, Olga W. "Faulkner." [F 65]:100–06.

7643. Vizioli, Paulo. "Guimarães Rosa e William Faulkner." *ESPSL* 11 Apr:1.

* 7644. Waggoner, Hyatt H. "The Historical Novel and the Southern Past:The Case of *Absalom, Absalom!"* *SLJ* 2,ii:69–85.

* 7645. Wall, Carey. "*The Sound and the Fury*:The Emotional Center." *MQ* 11:371–87.

7646. Watson, James G. *The Snopes Dilemma:Faulkner's Trilogy.* Coral Gables, Fla.: U. of Miami P.

7647. Weber, Robert W. *Die Aussage der Form:Zur Textur und Struktur des Bewusstseinsromans. Dargestellt an William Faulkners* The Sound and the Fury. Heidelberg: Winter, 1969.

7648. Weisgerber, Jean. "Faulkner's Monomaniacs:Their Indebtedness to Raskolnikov." [F 3]:625. [Brief summary.]

7649. Williams, Ora G. "The Theme of Endurance in *As I Lay Dying.*" *LaS* 9:100–04.

See also 793, 4193, 4986.

Faust, F. 7650. Easton, Robert. *Max Brand:The Big 'Westerner.'* Norman: U. of Okla. P. [Biog.]

Fergusson. *7651. Leonard, Bob F. "Francis Fergusson, Critic and Poet:A Checklist of His Works." *TD* 2,i-ii(1969–70): 3–17.

Ferril. 7652. Richards, Robert F. "Thomas Hornsby Ferril and the Problems of the Poet in the West." *KanQ* 2,ii:110–16.

Fisher, D.C. 7653. McCallister, Lois. "Dorothy Canfield Fisher:A Critical Study." *DAI* 30:3948A–49A(Case Western Reserve).

Fisher, V. 7654. Grover, Dorys N.C. "A Study of the Poetry of Vardis Fisher." *DAI* 30:3009A(Wash. State).

7655. Kellogg, George. "Vardis Fisher:A Bibliography." *WAL* 5:45–64.

7656. Milton, John R.,ed. *Three West:Conversations with Vardis Fisher, Max Evans, Michael Straight.* With Introd. Vermillion: U. of So. Dak. Press.

See also 7439, 8184.

Fitzgerald. 7657. Bonincontro, Marilia. "L'assolo di F.S. Fitzgerald (*Tender Is the Night*)." *PS* 5,i(1969):18–23.

7658. Bruccoli, Matthew J. *Checklist of F. Scott Fitzgerald.* (Merrill Checklists.) Columbus, Ohio: Charles E. Merrill.

7659. Bruccoli, Matthew J., and C.E. Frazer Clark,Jr.,eds. *Fitzgerald/Hemingway Annual 1970.* Wash., D.C.: NCR/Microcard Eds. [Philip Young and Charles W. Mann, "Fitzgerald's *Sun Also Rises*:Notes and Comment," 1–9; F. Scott Fitzgerald, "Letter to Ernest Hemingway," 10–13; M(atthew) J. B(ruccoli), "'Sleep of a University':An Unrecorded Fitzgerald Poem," 14–15; Elizabeth Beckwith Mackie, "My Friend Scott Fitzgerald," 16–27; Jennifer E. Atkinson, "Fitzgerald's Marked Copy of *The Great Gatsby*," 28–33; R.L. Samsell, "Won't You Come Home, Dick Diver?" 34–42; R.W. Lid, "The Passion of F. Scott Fitzgerald," 43–59; Paul Wagner, "'I Just Can't See Daylight . . .'," 60–68; Colin S. Cass, "Fitzgerald's Second Thoughts about 'May Day':A Collation and Study," 69–95; Susan H. Smith, "Some Biographical Aspects of *This Side of Paradise*," 96–101; F.S.F., "Six Letters to the Menkens," 102–04; Alan Margolies, "F. Scott Fitzgerald and *The Wedding Night*," 224–25; James L.W. West,III, "James Agee's Early Tribute to *Tender Is the Night*," 226–27; M(atthew) J. B(ruccoli), "Fitzgerald's List of Neglected Books," 229–30(from Malcolm Cowley's essay in *New Republic*[1934]); James L.W. West,III, "The Wrong Duel in *Tender Is the Night*," 231; M(atthew) J. B(ruccoli), "A Note on Jordan Baker," 232–33; Bryant Mangum, "The Reception of *Dearly Beloved*," 241–44; M(atthew) J. B(ruccoli), "Editorial," 265(on the text of *The Great Gatsby*); Burke Wilkinson, "Andrew Turnbull, 1921–1970," 266–67; "Checklist:F. Scott Fitzgerald," 272–73. For Hemingway material, see American V Hemingway, s.v. Bruccoli.]

7660. Bufkin, E.C. "A Pattern of Parallel and Double:The Function of Myrtle in *The Great Gatsby*." *MFS* 15(1969):517–24.

7661. Cohen, Richard. "The Inessential Houses of *The Great Gatsby*." *HussR* 2(1968):48–57.

7662. Coleman, Tom C.,III. "The Rise of Dr. Diver." *Discourse* 13:226–38.

7663. Elmore, A.E. "Color and Cosmos in *The Great Gatsby*." *SR* 78:427–43.

7664. Foster, Richard. "The Way to Read *Gatsby*." [F 67]:94–108.

7665. Goodwin, Donald W. "The Alcoholism of F. Scott Fitzgerald." *Jour. of the Amer. Med. Assn.* 212:86–90.

7666. Gross, Barry. " 'Our Gatsby, Our Nick'." *CentR* 14:331–40.

* 7667. —— "Scott Fitzgerald's *The Last Tycoon*:The Great American Novel?" *ArQ* 26:197–216.

7668. Higgins, John A. "F. Scott Fitzgerald as a Writer of the Short Story:A Critical Study of His Basic Motifs and Techniques." *DAI* 30(1969):1169A–70A(St. John's).

7669. Hohki, Tsutomu. "Fitzgerald and His Romantic World." [F 14]:67–81. [In Jap.]

7670. Johnson, Richard. "The Eyes of Dr. T.J. Eckleburg Re-Examined." *AN&Q* 9:20–21.

7671. Kinahan, Frank. "Focus on F. Scott Fitzgerald's *Tender Is the Night*." [F 63]:115–28.

7672. Kruse, Horst H. " 'Gatsby' and 'Gadsby'." *MFS* 15(1969):539–41.

7673. Lehan, Richard. "Focus on F. Scott Fitzgerald's *The Great Gatsby*:The Nowhere Hero." [F 63]:106–14.

7674. Margolies, Alan. "The Impact of Theatre and Film on F. Scott Fitzgerald." *DAI* 30:3467A(N.Y.U.).

7675. Prigozy, Ruth M. "The Stories and Essays of F. Scott Fitzgerald." *DAI* 30(1969):2544A–45A(C.U.N.Y.).

7676. Rao, E. Nageswara. "The Structure of *Tender Is the Night*." *LCrit* 8,iv(1969):54–62.

7677. Schitter, Hans G. *Die drei letzten Romane F. Scott Fitzgeralds:Untersuchungen zur Spiegelung von zeitgeschichtlichem und mythischem Bewusstsein im literarischen Kunstwerk.* Bonn: Bouvier, 1968.

7678. Stafford, William T. "Fitzgerald's *The Great Gatsby*, Chapter II, Paragraph 1." *Expl* 28:Item 57.

7679. Stern, Milton R. *The Golden Moment:The Novels of F. Scott Fitzgerald.* Urbana: U. of Ill. P.

7680. Winter, Keith. "Artistic Tensions:The Enigma of F. Scott Fitzgerald." *RS* 37(1969):285–97.

See also 4986, 7682, 7790, 7838.

Fitzgerald, Z. 7681. Going, William T. "Two Alabama Writers:Zelda Sayre Fitzgerald and Sara Haardt Mencken." *AlaR* 23:3–29.

7682. Milford, Nancy. *Zelda:A Biography.* New York: Harper & Row.

Foote. 7683. Carr, John. "It's Worth a Grown Man's Time:An Interview with Shelby Foote." *Contempora*(Atlanta, Ga.) 1,iii:2–16.

Francis, H.E. 7684. McKee, Mel,ed. "H.E. Francis Issue." *DeKalb Lit. Arts Jour.*(Clarkston, Ga.) 4,ii. [Robert L. Welker, "Something of H.E. Francis, of Happening, of Becoming," 26–39; Mary Hollingsworth, "The Setting for the Novel *Death in Argentina*," 40–47 (incl. 6 photos.); Antonio di Benedetto, "Francis Migratorio," 48–50; H.E. Francis, "Letters to Molly," 52–65; Lydia Tubino de Toso, "Notes on H.E. Francis in Argentina," 78–79; "H.E. Francis:Biography," 80–82; "H.E. Francis:Bibliography," 83–87.]

Francis, R. 7685. "Robert Francis:Worksheets." *MHRev* 4(1967):114–18.

Friedman. See 8271.

Frost. *7686. Bosmajian, Hamida. "Robert Frost's 'The Gift Outright':Wish and Reality in History and Poetry." *AQ* 22: [95]–105.

* 7687. *BSUF* 11,i:Robert Frost No. [Lesley F. Ballantine, "Somewhat Atavistic," 3–6; Dorothy J. Hall, "Painterly Qualities in Frost's Lyric Poetry," 9–13; Thomas R. Thornburg, "Mother's Private Ghost:A Note on Frost's 'The Witch of Coos'," 16–20; Elmer F. Suderman, "The Frozen Lake in Frost's 'Stopping by Woods on a Snowy Evening'," 22; Keith Cox, "A Syntactic Comparison of Robert Frost's '. . . Snowy Evening' and 'Desert Places'," 25–28; William B. Bache, "Rationalization in Two Frost Poems," 33–35; Robert F. Fleissner, "Frost's Response to Keats' Risibility," 40–43; Sister Catherine Theresa, "New Testament Interpretations of Robert Frost's Poems," 50–54; William A. Sutton, "A Frost-Sandburg Rivalry?" 59–61; R. Glenn Martin, "Two Versions of a Poem by Robert Frost," 65–68.]

7688. Carpenter, Thomas P. "Robert Frost and Katherine Blunt:A Confrontation." *AN&Q* 8(1969):35–37. [Biog.]

7689. Chamberlain, William. "The Emersonianism of Robert Frost." *ESQ* 57(1969):61–66.

7690. —— "Robert Frost, Pragmatic Emersonian." *DAI* 30:5440A–41A(Ind.).

7691. Cohen, Edward H. "Robert Frost in England:An Unpublished Letter." *NEQ* 43:285–87.

7692. Dabney, Lewis M. "Mortality and Nature:A Cycle of Frost's Lyrics." [*F* 57]:11–31.

* 7693. Dendinger, Lloyd N. "Robert Frost:The Popular and the Central Poetic Images." *AQ* 21(1969):[792]–804.

7694. Haynes, Donald T. "The Evolution of Form in the Early Poetry of Robert Frost:The Emergence of a Poetic Self." *DAI* 30:4453A(Notre Dame).

7695. Herndon, Jerry A. "Frost's 'The Oven Bird'." *Expl* 28:Item 64.

7696. Hiatt, David. "Frost's 'In White' and 'Design'." *Expl* 28:Item 41.

7697. Kern, Alexander. "Frost's 'The Wood-Pile'." *Expl* 28:Item 49.

7698. Kjørven, Johannes. "Two Studies in Robert Frost." [*F* 66]:191–218.

7699. Mersch, Arnold R.G.,F.S.C. "Themes of Loneliness and Isolation in the Poetry of Robert Frost." *DAI* 30:3470A(St. Louis U.).

7700. Nilakantan, Mangalam. " 'Something Beyond Conflict':A Study of the Dual Vision of Robert Frost." *IJAS* 1,i(1969):25–34.

* 7701. Parsons, D.S.J. "Night of Dark Intent." *PLL* 6:205–10.

7702. Pritchard, William H. "Wildness of Logic in Modern Lyric." [*F* 48]:127–50.

7703. Rao, C. Vimala. "The 'Other Mood':A Note on the Prose Works of Robert Frost." *LCrit* 8,iv(1969):63–69.

7704. Rubinstein, Annette T. "A Stay Against Confusion." *Science and Society* 33(1969):25–41.

7705. Stone, Virginia S. "Robert Frost:The Breathless Swing Between Content and Form." *DAI* 30(1969):2501A(E. Texas State).

* 7706. Swennes, Robert H. "Man and Wife:The Dialogue of Contraries in Robert Frost's Poetry." *AL* 42:[363]–72.

7707. Vinson, Robert S. "The Roads of Robert Frost." *ConnR* 3,ii:102–07.

See also 791, 886, 4834, 6348.

Gale. 7708. Monteiro, George. "Zona Gale and Ridgely Torrence." *ALR* 3:77–79.

Gallico. 7709. Gallico, Paul. "One Writer's Working Methods." *CLC* 20,i:19–23.

Gerould, D. 7710. Gerould, Daniel. "*Candaules* and the Uses of Myth." *MD* 12:270–78.

Ginsberg. 7711. Charters, Ann. "Allen Ginsberg and Jack Kerouac, Columbia Undergraduates." *CLC* 20,i:10–17.

7712. Merrill, Thomas F. *Allen Ginsberg.* (TUSAS 161.) New York: Twayne, 1969. [Crit.]

Glasgow. 7713. Murphy, Denis M. "Vein of Ambivalence: Structural, Stylistic, and Personal Dualisms in Ellen Glasgow's Major Novels." *DAI* 31:1283A(Princeton).

Gordon, C. *7714. Rocks, James E. "The Short Fiction of Caroline Gordon." *TSE* 18:115–35.

Greenberg. *See* 7483.

Grey. 7715. Gruber, Frank. *Zane Grey.* New York: World. [Biog.]

7716. Scott, Kenneth W. "*The Heritage of the Desert*:Zane Grey Discovers the West." *MarkhamR* 2,ii:[10]–[14].

Hailey, A. 7717. Lutz, Paul V. "Arthur Hailey—Novelist at Work." *MSS* 22,i:12–17.

Hall, J.N. 7718. Johnson, Robert L. *The American Heritage of James Norman Hall, The Woodshed Poet of Iowa and Co-Author of Mutiny on the Bounty.* Philadelphia: Dorrance, 1969. [Biog.]

Hammett. 7719. De Vecchi Rocca, Luisa. "Apoteosi e decadenza del romanzo poliziesco d'azione." *NA* 506(1969): 532–40. [On Hammett and Chandler.]

Harris, F. 7720. Muggeridge, Malcolm. "Frank Harris:Vita e menzogna." *Caffè* 17:112–17.

Hathaway. 7721. Brun, Christian. "The Papers of Charles M. Hathaway:A Diplomat's Experience in Ireland and Germany." *SCUL* 2,ii:17–29. [Illus.]

Havighurst. 7722. Jones, Joel M. "To Feel the Heartland's Pulse:The Writing of Walter Havighurst." *KanQ* 2,ii:88–96.

Hawkes. 7723. Frost, Helen L.P. "A Legacy of Violence:John Hawkes' Vision of Culture." *DAI* 30:3941A(Rochester).

* 7724. Greiner, Donald J. "The Thematic Use of Color in John Hawkes' *Second Skin*." *ConL* 11:389–400.

7725. Johnson, Joseph J. "The Novels of John Hawkes and Julien Gracq:A Comparison." *DAI* 31:1280A(Vanderbilt).

See also 529.

Haydn. 7726. "A Celebration of Hiram Haydn." *Voyages* (Wash., D.C.) 3,i–ii:7–55. [Brief comments, crit., and biog. by a dozen of H's contemporaries.]

7727. Chappell, Fred. "Hiram Haydn's Other World." *Voyages*(Wash., D.C.) 3,i–ii:22–29.

7728. Nin, Anais. "Anais Nin on Hiram Haydn's *Report from the Red Windmill*." *Voyages*(Wash., D.C.) 3,i–ii:29–30.

Heller. 7729. Castelli, Jim. "*Catch-22* and the New Hero." *CathW* 211:199–202.

* 7730. Gaukroger, Doug. "Time Structure in *Catch-22*." *Crit* 12,ii:70–85.

7731. Milne, Victor J. "Heller's 'Bologniad':A Theological Perspective on *Catch-22*." *Crit* 12,ii:50–69.

See also 8257.

Hellman. 7732. Ackley, Meredith E. "The Plays of Lillian Hellman." *DAI* 30:4441A(Pa.).

Hemingway. 7733. Alderman, Taylor. "Ernest Hemingway: Four Studies in the Competitive Motif." *DAI* 31:380A(N.M.).

7734. Anderson, Paul V. "Nick's Story in Hemingway's 'Big Two-Hearted River'." *SSF* 7:564–72.

* 7735. Barba, Harry. "The Three Levels of 'The End of Something'." *WVUPP* 17:76–80.

* 7736. Bennett, Warren. "Character, Irony, and Resolution in 'A Clean, Well-Lighted Place'." *AL* 42:[70]–79.

7737. Benson, Jackson J. "Literary Allusion and the Private Irony of Hemingway." *PCP* 4(1969):24–29.

7738. Bonet, Laureano. "Los dos rostros de Ernest Hemingway." *RO* 30:176–99.

7739. Bresard, Suzanne. *Empreintes:L'Analyse des écritures de Colette, Hemingway, Balzac, Musset.* Paris: Delachaux et Niestlé, 1968.

7740. Brøgger, Fredrik Chr. "Hemingway—der kjærlighet og religion møtes." *KoK* 74(1969):224–31.

7741. Bruccoli, Matthew J., and C.E. Frazer Clark,Jr.,eds. *Fitzgerald/Hemingway Annual 1970.* Wash., D.C.: NCR/Microcard Eds. [Ernest M. Hemingway, "Will You Let These Kiddies Miss Santa Claus?" 105–07(H's contrib. to The Co-Operative Commonwealth, II[Dec 1920]); Fraser Drew, "April 8, 1955 with Hemingway:Unedited Notes on a Visit to Finca Vigia," 108–16; Lawrence D. Stewart, "Hemingway and the Autobiographies of Alice B. Toklas," 117–23; William B. Smith, "A Wedding up in Michigan," 124–26(on E's and Hadley's wedding); Bertram D. Sarason, "Pauline Hemingway:In Tranquillity," 127–35; William Goldhurst, "The Hyphenated Ham Sandwich of Ernest Hemingway and J.D. Salinger:A Study in Literary Continuity," 136–50; Col. C.E. Frazer Clark, "This Is the Way It Was on the *Chicago* and at the Front: 1917 War Letters," 153–68(illus.); Winifred Healey, "When Ernest Hemingway's Mother Came to Call," 170–72; Robert P. Mai, "Ernest Hemingway and Men Without Women," 173–86; C.E. Frazer Clark,Jr., "The Beginnings of Dealer Interest in Hemingway," 191–94; Audre Hanneman, "Hanneman Addenda," 195–218; Thomas J. Jackson, "The 'Macomber' Typescript," 219–22(illus.); M(atthew) J. B(ruccoli), "Francis Macomber and Francis Fitzgerald," 223; "Another Lost Hemingway Review," 228(i.e., to be found); David M. McClellan, "Hemingway's Colonel Appropriately Quotes Jackson," 234; Constance Drake, " 'A Lake Superior Salmon Fisherman'," 235; M(atthew) J. B(ruccoli), " 'Oh, Give Them Irony and Give Them Pity'," 236; J.M. Linebarger, "Eggs as Huevos in *The Sun Also Rises*," 237–39; Caresse Crosby, "The Last Time I Saw Hemingway," 240(excerpt from letter). For Fitzgerald material see American v Fitzgerald, s.v. Bruccoli.]

7742. Bruccoli, Matthew J.,ed. *Ernest Hemingway, Cub Reporter*:Kansas City Star *Stories.* With Pref. Pittsburgh: U. of Pittsburgh P. [Rpts. 12 H stories from *Star*, plus Theodore Brumback, "With Hemingway Before *A Farewell to Arms*," also from *Star*.]

* 7743. Bunnell, W.A. "Who Wrote the Paris Idyll?The Place and Function of *A Moveable Feast* in the Writing of Ernest Hemingway." *ArQ* 26:334–46.

7744. Byrd, Lemuel B. "Characterization in Ernest Hemingway's Fiction:1925–1952, with a Dictionary of the Characters." *DAI* 30:4444A(Colo.).

7745. Charters, James. "Pat and Duff:Some Memories." *ConnR* 3,ii:24–27. [On Pat Guthrie and Duff Twysden, models for Mike Campbell and Lady Brett Ashley in *The Sun Also Rises*.]

7746. Davies, Phillips G. and Rosemary R. " 'A Killer Who Would Shoot You for the Fun of It':A Possible Source for Hemingway's 'The Killers'." *IEY* 15:36–38.

7747. Dunbar, John R. "Hemingway's 'Moment of Truth'." [*F* 62]:3–14.

7748. *Ernest Xeminguèj:Bio-bibliografičeskij ukazatel'.* Moscow: Kniga.

7749. Fisher, Marvin. "More Snow on Kilimanjaro." [*F* 56]:343–53.

7750. Frigeri, Pier R. "Ernest Hemingway dieci anni dopo." *Cenobio* 19:219–26.

7751. Gebhardt, Richard C. "Denial and Affirmation of Values in the Fiction of Ernest Hemingway." *DAI* 31:1274A–75A(Mich. State).

7752. Gellens, Jay,ed. *Twentieth Century Interpretations of* A Farewell to Arms. (TCI.) With Introd. Englewood Cliffs, N.J.: Prentice-Hall. [Rptd. crit.]

7753. Gotxarde, R.È. "Hemingway's New Epic Genre in His Spanish Novel." [*F* 49]:205–22.

7754. Griffin, Gerald R. "Hemingway's Fictive Use of the Negro:'The Curious Quality of Incompleteness'." *HussR* 1(1968):104–11.

7755. Hamada, Seijiro. "Kilimanjaro e no Hisho." *EigoS* 115(1969):699–701. [Flight to K.]

7756. Hassan, Ihab. "The Silence of Ernest Hemingway." [*F* 50]:5–20.

7757. Hayashi, Tetsumaro. "*A Farewell to Arms*:The Contest of Experience." *KAL* 12:14–19.

7758. Heaton, C.P. "Style in *The Old Man and the Sea*." *Style* 4:11–27.

7759. Hily, Geneviève. "Langage et communication:Un aspect inédit de la pensée de Hemingway." *EA* 22(1969):279–92.

* 7760. Johnston, Kenneth G. "The Star in Hemingway's *The Old Man and the Sea*." *AL* 42:388–91.

7761. Jones, Edward T. "Hemingway and Cézanne:A Speculative Affinity." *UES* 8,ii:26–28.

7762. Joost, Nicholas. "Ernest Hemingway." *ConL* 11: 293–302.

7763. Kann, Hans-Joachim. "Ernest Hemingway's Knowledge of German." *JA* 15:221–32.

7764. Kawasaki, Toshihiko. "Hemingway to futatsu no Bunseki Hihyo." *EigoS* 114(1968):498–500. [H and 2 crit. analyses.]

* 7765. Kobler, J.F. "Hemingway's 'The Sea Change':A Sympathetic View of Homosexuality." *ArQ* 26:318–24.

7766. Kruse, Horst. "Hemingway's 'Cat in the Rain' and Joyce's *Ulysses*." *LWU* 3:28–30.

7767. Kvam, Wayne E. "The Critical Reaction to Hemingway in Germany, 1945–1965." *DAI* 30(1969):1139A–40A(Wis.).

7768. Lewis, Robert W.,Jr., and Max Westbrook. " 'The Snows of Kilimanjaro' Collated and Annotated." *TQ* 13,ii: 67–143.

* 7769. Longmire, Samuel E. "Hemingway's Praise of Dick Sisler in *The Old Man and the Sea*." *AL* 42:96–98.

7770. Martine, James J. "A Little Light on Hemingway's 'The Light of the World'." *SSF* 7:465–67.

7771. Morrison, Robert W. "The Short Stories of Ernest Hemingway:A Search for Love and Identity." *DAI* 30:3018A–19A(Wash. State).

7772. Nelson, Jon E. "Religious Experience in the Fiction of Ernest Hemingway." *DAI* 31:396A(N.C., Chapel Hill).

7773. Peterson, Richard K. *Hemingway, Direct and Oblique.* (SAmL 14.) The Hague: Mouton, 1969.

7774. Raeburn, John H. "Ernest Hemingway:The Writer as Object of Public Attention." *DAI* 30:4462A(Pa.).

7775. Rodgers, Paul C.,Jr. "Levels of Irony in Hemingway's 'The Gambler, the Nun, and the Radio'." *SSF* 7:439–49.

* 7776. Rogers, Jean M., and Gordon Stein. "Bibliographical Notes on Hemingway's *Men Without Women*." *PBSA* 64:210–13.

7777. Rosen, Kenneth M. "Ernest Hemingway:The Function of Violence." *DAI* 30:5456A(N.M.).

7778. Serravalli, Luigi. "Ernest Hemingway inviato speciale." *Cristallo* 10,i(1968):142–64.

7779. Smith, Julian. "Hemingway and the Things Left Out." *JML* 1:169–82.

7780. —— "More Products of the Hemingway Industry." *SSF* 7:638–46.

7781. *Special Hemingway Issue. Rendezvous* 5,ii. [Philip Young, "Locked in the Vault with Hemingway," 1–5 (rev. version of report in *N.Y. Times Book Rev.*, 29 Sept 1968); L.M. Dougherty, "Father L.M. Dougherty Talks About Ernest Hemingway," 7–17; Robert W. Lewis,Jr., "Hemingway's Concept of Sport and 'Soldier's Home'," 19–27; D.E. Wylder, "Hemingway's Satiric Vision—The High School Years," 29–35; Jackson J. Benson, "Patterns of Connection and Their Development in Hemingway's *In Our Time*," 37–52; Richard Etulian, "Ernest Hemingway and His Interpreters of the 1960's," 53–70.]

7782. St. John, Donald. "Leicester Hemingway, Chief of State." *ConnR* 3,ii:5–19.

7783. Takamura, Katsuji. "Hemingway no Rojin to Shonen." *EigoS* 114(1968):300–01. [H's old men and small boys.]

7784. Takigawa, Motoo. "*The Short Happy Life of Francis Macomber* no Shusei." *EigoS* 115(1969):98–100. [Revisions in the story.]

7785. Tanaka, Keisuke. "The Bipolar Construction in the Works of Ernest Hemingway." *KAL* 12:32–44.

7786. Thomaneck, Jurgen K.A. "Hemingway's Riddle of Kilimanjaro Once More." *SSF* 7:326–27.

7787. Vargas, Germán. "Un libro de crónicas de Hemingway." *BCB* 11,xii(1968):55–56.

* 7788. Vorpahl, Ben M. "Ernest Hemingway and Owen Wister:Finding the Lost Generation." *LC* 36:126–37.

7789. White, William. *Checklist of Ernest Hemingway.* (Merrill Checklists.) Columbus, Ohio: Charles E. Merrill.

7790. —— "Hemingway and Fitzgerald." [*F* 65]:107–17. *See also* 5189.

Herrick. 7791. Franklin, Phyllis. "Robert Herrick as Novelist and Journalist." *ALR* 3:393–95.

7792. —— "Time and Place in the Work of Robert Herrick." *DAI* 30:3457A(U. of Miami).

Heyward. 7793. Durham, Frank. "*Porgy* Comes Home—at Last!" *SCR* 2,ii:5–13.

Himes, C. 7794. Margolies, Edward. "The Thrillers of Chester Himes." *SBL* 1,ii:1–11.

7795. Williams, John A. "My Man Himes:An Interview with Chester Himes." *Amistad* 1:25–93.

Hoffman, D. 7796. Sylvester, William. "Daniel Hoffman's Poetry of Affection." *Voyages*(Wash., D.C.) 3,i–ii:110–19. [Incl. "A Daniel Hoffman Checklist," 119.]

Hoffman, F.J. 7797. Tanksley, William R. "Frederick J. Hoffman as Literary Scholar and Critic." *DAI* 31:769A(Ill.).

Hollander. 7798. Gerber, Philip L., and Robert J. Gemmett. "The Poem as Silhouette." *MQR* 9:253–60. [Interview.]

Holmes, J. 7799. Holmes, Doris. "Holmes' 'Herself'." *Expl* 28:Item 77.

Hughes, L. 7800. Anon. "Langston Hughes and the Example of Simple." *BlackW* 19,viii:35–38.

7801. Finger, Hans. "Zwei Beispiele moderner amerikanischer Negerlyrik:Langston Hughes, 'Mother to Son' und Russell Atkins, 'Poem'." *LWU* 2(1969):38–46.

7802. Hughes, L. *Not Without Laughter.* Introd. Arna Bontemps. New York: Collier, 1969.

7803. —— "The Negro Artist and the Racial Mountain." *Amistad* 1:301–05. [Repr. of 1926 *Nation* art.]

* 7804. Mintz, Lawrence E. "Langston Hughes's Jesse B. Simple:The Urban Negro as Wise Fool." *SNL* 7(1969):11–21.

7804a. Presley, James. "Langston Hughes:A Personal Farewell." *SWR* 54(1969):79–84.

See also 9954.

Hyman, M. 7805. Blackburn, William,ed. *Love, Boy:The Letters of Mac Hyman.* Introd. Max Steele. Baton Rouge: La. State U.P., 1969.

Inge. 7806. Hamblet, Edwin J. "The North American Outlook of Marcel Dubé and William Inge." *QQ* 77:374–87.

7807. Miller, Jordan Y. "William Inge:Last of the Realists?" *KanQ* 2,ii:17–26.

Ives. *7808. Davidson, Audrey. "Transcendental Unity in the Works of Charles Ives." *AQ* 22:35–44.

Jaffe. *See* 8002.

Jarrell. 7809. Donahue, Jane. " 'Trading Another's Sorrows for Our Own':The Poetry of Randall Jarrell." *LWU* 2(1969): 258–67.

7810. Fisher, Nancy M. "Fantasy and Reality in the Poetry of Randall Jarrell." *DAI* 31:755A–76A(Tenn.).

7811. Hoffman, Frederick J.,ed. *The Achievement of Randall Jarrell:A Comprehensive Selection of His Poems with a Critical Introduction.* With Introd. Glenview, Ill.: Scott, Foresman.

7812. Mazzaro, Jerome. "Arnoldian Echoes in the Poetry of Randall Jarrell." *WHR* 23(1969):314–18.

7813. Quinn, Sister M. Bernetta. "Randall Jarrell:Landscapes of Life and *Life*." *Shenandoah* 20,ii(1969):49–78.

7814. Schwarz, John M. "An Introduction to the Poems of Randall Jarrell." *DAI* 30:5002A(U.C.L.A.).

7815. Wilson, Emily. "Jarrell and Reid Celebrate a Woman:A Comparative Explication." *SCR* 3,i:45–48.

Jeffers. 7816. Barschi, Jack. "The Sexual Imagery in Robinson Jeffers' Narrative Poetry." *DAI* 30(1969):2519A (N.Y.U.).

* 7817. Brophy, Robert J. " 'Tamar,' 'The Cenci,' and Incest." *AL* 42:241–44.

* 7818. Keller, Karl. "California, Yankees, and the Death of God:The Allegory in Jeffers' *Roan Stallion*." *TSLL* 12:111–20.

7819. Nolte, William H. *Guide to Robinson Jeffers.* (Merrill Guides.) Columbus, Ohio: Charles E. Merrill.

7820. *Robinson Jeffers Newsl.* 27(Nov). ["News and Notes," 1–5; Richard Eberhart, "A Tribute and Appreciation," 6–7; Kamil Bednar, "Jeffers in Czechoslovakia," 8–9.]

7821. *Robinson Jeffers Newsl.* 26(July). ["News and Notes," 1–8; Andrew K. Mauthe, "Jeffers' Inhumanism and Its Poetic Significance," 8–10.]

7822. *Robinson Jeffers Newsl.* 25(Feb). ["News and Notes," 1–3; William White and Robert Brophy, "*Not Man Apart*," 3–4 (Rev. art.); "Jeffers Research:Masters' Theses, Occidental College Library," 4–8; Andrew K. Mauthe, "The Significance of Point Lobos in *Tamar*," 8–10.]

Johnson, J.W. 7823. Jackson, Miles,Jr. "James Weldon Johnson." *BlackW* 19,viii:32–34.

Jones, LeRoi. *7824. Brecht, Stefan. "LeRoi Jones' *Slave Ship*." *TDR* 14,ii:212–19.

7825. Brown, Cecil M. "Black Literature and LeRoi Jones." *BlackW* 19,viii:24–31.

7826. Lewis, Ida. "Leroi Jones:Une interview exclusive." *JeuneA* 1 sept:24–27.

* 7827. Otten, Charlotte. "LeRoi Jones:Napalm Poet." *CP* 3,i:5–11.

7828. Peavy, Charles D. "Myth, Magic, and Manhood in LeRoi Jones' *Madheart*." *SBL* 1,ii:12–20.

7829. Reck, Tom S. "Archetypes in LeRoi Jones' *Dutchman*." *SBL* 1,i:66–68.

7830. Reed, Daphne S. "LeRoi Jones:High Priest of the Black Arts Movement." *ETJ* 22:53–59.

7831. "The LeRoi Jones Case:Letter about a Wolf-Pack." *AmD* 5,i(1968):17.

See also 529.

Kelley, W.M. 7832. Kelley, W.M. *dem.* Introd. Willie E. Abraham. New York: Collier, 1969.

Kendall, C. *See* 5868.

Kerouac. *See* 7711.

Kesey. 7833. Maxwell, Richard. "The Abdication of Masculinity in *One Flew Over The Cuckoo's Nest*." [F 47]:203–11.

7834. Witke, Charles. "Pastoral Convention in Virgil and Kesey." *PCP* 1(1966):20–24.

See also 529.

Knowles. 7835. Mengeling, Marvin E. "*A Separate Peace*: Meaning and Myth." *EJ* 58(1969):1323–29.

7836. Wolfe, Peter. "The Impact of Knowles's *A Separate Peace*." *UR* 36:189–98.

Lardner. *7837. Hasley, Louis. "Ring Lardner:The Ashes of Idealism." *ArQ* 26:219–32.

7838. Lease, Benjamin. "An Evening at the Scott Fitzgeralds':An Unpublished Letter of Ring Lardner." *ELN* 8:40–42. [Text of letter incl.]

Laughlin. 7839. Perrine, Laurence. "Laughlin's 'Go West Young Man'." *Expl* 28:Item 61.

Levertov. 7840. Goldoni, Annalisa. "La Poesia di Denise Levertov." *SA* 14(1968):377–99.

See also 7241.

Lewis, S. 7841. Austin, James C. "Sinclair Lewis and Western Humor." [F 63]:94–105.

* 7842. Conroy, Stephen S. "Sinclair Lewis's Sociological Imagination." *AL* 42:[348]–62.

* 7843. Fleissner, Robert F. " 'Something Out of Dickens' in Sinclair Lewis." *BNYPL* 74:607–16.

7844. Hill, John S. "Sinclair Lewis, *Dodsworth*, and the Nobel Prize." *HussR* 3:105–11.

7845. Lundquist, James. *Checklist of Sinclair Lewis.* (Merrill Checklists.) Columbus, Ohio: Charles E. Merrill.

7846. —— *Guide to Sinclair Lewis.* (Merrill Guides.) Columbus, Ohio: Charles E. Merrill.

Lindsay. 7847. Ames, Van Meter. "Vachel Lindsay—or, *My Heart Is a Kicking Horse*." *Midway* 8,iv(1968):63–70.

7848. Bradbury, David L. "Vachel Lindsay and His Heroes." *Ill. State U. Jour.* 32,v:22–57.

7849. Lindsay, V. *Springfield Town Is Butterfly Town and Other Poems for Children.* Pref. Louis Untermeyer; Introd. Pierre Dussert. Kent, Ohio: Kent State U.P., 1969.

7850. Massa, Ann. *Vachel Lindsay:Fieldworker for the American Dream.* Bloomington: Ind. U.P. [Crit.]

Locke, A. 7851. Long, Richard A. "Alain Locke:Cultural and Social Mentor." *BlackW* 20,i:87–90.

London. 7852. Čeremin, T.S. "Majakovskij i roman Džeka Londona *Martin Iden*." *RLit* 13,i:121–35.

7853. Chapman, Arnold. "Between Fire and Ice:A Theme in Jack London and Horacio Quiroga." *Symposium* 24:17–26.

7854. Diesbach, Ghislain de. "Jack London." *RDM* 4:29–35.

7855. Giles, James R. "Some Notes on the Red-Blooded Reading of Kipling by Jack London and Frank Norris." *Jack London Newsl.* 3:56–62.

7856. Goldstein, Jack J. "Learning the Hard Way?" *Seri* 7,ii:36–37. [Odd ed. of *Call of the Wild*.]

7857. *Jack London Newsl.* 3,iii. [Sakae Fujiwara, "Jack London's Socialism:A Summary of One Chapter from *Jack London in Connection with the American Dream*," 73–81; Edwin B. Erbentraut, "The Symbolic Triad in London's *The Little Lady of the Big House*," 82–89; Earle Labor, " 'To the Man on Trail':Jack London's Christmas Carol," 90–94; Arthur Sherko, "An Analogue for *Lost Face*," 95–98; James A. Hamby, "Note on Jack London:A View in Oil," 102–03; Russ Kingman, "London's Yukon Cabin Now at Jack London Square in Oakland, California," 104–07; Sylvia Gibbs, "Jesse Stuart's Cyclic Vision," 120–29; Kenneth Clarke, "Kentucky Heritage in Jesse Stuart's Writing," 130–31; Hensley C. Woodbridge, "Jesse and Jane Stuart:A Bibliography—Supplement 4," 132–34; Laird McNeel, "More on *The Son of the Wolf*," 135–36.]

* 7858. McClintock, James I. "Jack London's Use of Carl Jung's *Psychology of the Unconscious*." *AL* 42:[336]–47.

7859. Nichol, John. "The Role of 'Local Color' in Jack London's Alaskan Wilderness Tales." *WR* 6,ii:51–56.

7860. Wilcox, Earl. "*Le Milieu, Le Moment, La Race*:Literary Naturalism in Jack London's *White Fang*." *Jack London Newsl.* 3:42–55.

See also 8056.

Lovecraft. 7861. Lévy, Maurice. "Fascisme et fantastique ou le cas Lovecraft." *Caliban* 7:67–78.

Lowell, A. 7862. Flint, F. Cudworth. *Amy Lowell.* (UMPAW 82.) Minneapolis: U. of Minn. P., 1969.

7863. Healey, Claire. "Some Imagist Essays:Amy Lowell." *NEQ* 43:134–38.

7864. Ruihley, Glenn R. "Amy Lowell:Symbolic Impressionist." *DAI* 31:401A(Wis.).

7865. Watanabe, Shoichi. "Imagist and Haiku—with Special Reference to Amy Lowell." *ELLS* 6(1969):108–30.

See also 6870.

Lowell, R. 7866. Boyers, Robert. "On Robert Lowell." *Salmagundi* 13:36–44.

7867. Buckley, Vincent. "Trial and Error:The Poetry of Robert Lowell." *Quadrant* 63:20–31.

7868. Freimarck, Vincent. "Another Holmes in Robert Lowell's 'Hawthorne'." *ELN* 8:48–49. [Oliver Wendell Holmes, Jr.]

7869. Holton, Milne. "Unlikeness:The Poetry of Robert Lowell." [F 57]:115–45.

7870. Lunz, Elisabeth. "The True and Insignificant:A Study of Robert Lowell's Nature Imagery." *DAI* 30(1969):2537A (Tulane).

7871. McKain, David W. "Poetic Diction, Nonsense and Robert Lowell." *DAI* 30:4993A–94A(Conn.).

* 7872. Perloff, Marjorie G. "Realism and the Confessional Mode of Robert Lowell." *ConL* 11:470–87.

7873. Vogler, Thomas A. "Robert Lowell and the Classical Tradition." *PCP* 4(1969):59–64.

7874. Weales, Gerald. "Robert Lowell as Dramatist." *Shenandoah* 20,i(1968):3–28.

7875. Winters, Anne,ed. "Poèmes par Robert Lowell." *Esprit* 397:711–22. [Tr. Claire Larrière, Jean-Marie Amertin, and Robert Marteau.]

7876. Yenser, Stephen I. "Circle to Circle:Structures in the Poetry of Robert Lowell." *DAI* 31:773A(Wis.).

Lyon. 7877. Eichelberger, Clayton L., and Zoë Lyon. "A Partial Listing of the Published Work of Harris Merton Lyon." *ALR* 3:41–52.

7878. Lyon, Zoë. "Harris Merton Lyon:An Author to be Reappraised." *MHSB* 26:318–20.

7879. —— "Harris Merton Lyon (1883–1916)." *ALR* 3:36–40. [Bibliog.]

MacKaye. *7880. Mendelsohn, Michael J. "Percy MacKaye's Dramatic Theories." *BRMMLA* 24:85–89.

MacLeish. 7881. McKulik, Benjamin M. "Archibald MacLeish and the French Symbolist Tradition." *DAI* 30:3950A(S.C.).

* 7882. Stroupe, John H. "The Masks of MacLeish's *J.B.*" *TSL* 15:75–83.

7883. White, W.D. "MacLeish's *J.B.*—Is It a Modern Job?" *Mosaic* 4,i:13–20.

Mailer. 7884. Flaherty, Joe. *Managing Mailer.* New York: Coward-McCann. [Personal reminis.]

7885. Hassan, Ihab. "Focus on Norman Mailer's *Why Are We in Vietnam?*" [F 63]:197–203.

7886. Iwamoto, Iwao. "Gendai wo Ikiru Messiah." *EigoS* 115(1969):554–55. [Messiah of the Modern Age: Mailer.]

7887. Lawler, Robert W. "Norman Mailer:The Connection of New Circuits." *DAI* 31:1804A–05A(Claremont).

7888. Lundkvist, Artur. "Ordspruta och gentlemann-agangster:Norman Mailer." [F 32]:155–69.

7889. Sokoloff, B.A. *A Comprehensive Bibliography of Norman Mailer.* Folcroft, Pa.: Folcroft P.

7890. Stark, John O. "Norman Mailer's Work From 1963 to 1968." *DAI* 31:403A(Wis.).

* 7891. Tanner, Tony. "On the Parapet:A Study of the Novels of Norman Mailer." *CritQ* 12:153–76.

7892. Witt, Grace. "The Bad Man as Hipster:Norman Mailer's Use of Frontier Metaphor." *WAL* 4(1969):203–17.

See also 7367, 7368, 7894, 8099.

Mainwaring. *See* 8214.

Malamud. 7893. Burrows, David. "The American Past in Malamud's *A New Life.*" [F 57]:86–94.

7894. Flint, Joyce M. "In Search of Meaning:Bernard Malamud, Norman Mailer, John Updike." *DAI* 30:3006A(Wash. State).

7895. Goodman, Oscar B. "There Are Jews Everywhere." *Judaism* 19:283–94.

7896. Hill, John S. "Malamud's 'The Lady of the Lake':A Lesson in Rejection." *UR* 36(1969):149–50.

7897. Hoag, Gerald. "Malamud's Trial:*The Fixer* and the Critics." *WHR* 24:1–12.

7898. Lamdin, Lois S. "Malamud's Schlemiels." [F 59]:31–42.

* 7899. Lefcowitz, Barbara F. "The *Hybris* of Neurosis: Malamud's *Pictures of Fidelman.*" *L&P* 20:115–20.

7900. May, Charles E. "The Bread of Tears:Malamud's 'The Loan'." *SSF* 7:652–54.

7901. Schulz, Max F. "Malamud's *A New Life*:The New Wasteland of the Fifties." *WR* 6,i(1969):37–44.

7902. Stamerra, Silvana. "Il protagonista nelle narrativa di Bernard Malamud." *Zagaglia* 10(1968):333–43.

See also 993, 7301, 7367.

Malcolm X. *7903. Ohmann, Carol. "*The Autobiography of Malcolm X*:A Revolutionary Use of the Franklin Tradition." *AQ* 22:[131]–49.

See also 7199.

Manfred. 7904. Manfred, F. *The Golden Bowl.* Introd. John R. Milton. Vermillion: U. of So. Dak. P., 1969.

Marquand. 7905. Walker, Dorothea R. "Failure to Protest: The Tragedy of J.P. Marquand's Apley, Pulham, and Wayde." *Nassau Rev.*(Nassau [N.Y.] Comm. Coll.) 2,i:15–22.

Masters. *7906. Hahn, Henry. "Evolution in the Graveyard." *MQ* 10(1969):275–90.

7907. Robinson, Frank K. "The Edgar Lee Masters Collection at the University of Texas at Austin:A Critical, Bibliographical, and Textual Study." *DAI* 30:5455A–56A(Texas, Austin).

7908. Tetlow, Joseph A.,Jr. "The Intellectual and Spiritual Odyssey of Edgar Lee Masters, 1868–1950." *DAI* 31:405A–06A(Brown).

Matthiessen. *7909. Gunn, Giles B. "Criticism as Repossession and Responsibility:F.O. Matthiessen and the Ideal Critic." *AQ* 22:[629]–48.

7910. Stern, Frederick C. "The Lost Cause:F.O. Matthiessen, Christian Socialist as Critic." *DAI* 31:1816A(Purdue).

Mayer. *See* 7917.

McAlmon. *See* 5363.

McClure. *7911. Stinson, Robert. "S.S. McClure's *My Autobiography*:The Progressive as Self-Made Man." *AQ* 22:[203]–12.

McCullers. 7912. Gozzi, Francesco. "La narrativa di Carson McCullers." *SA* 14(1968):339–76.

7913. Graver, Lawrence. *Carson McCullers.* (UMPAW 84.) Minneapolis: U. of Minn. P., 1969.

7914. Hamilton, Alice. "Loneliness and Alienation:The Life and Work of Carson McCullers." *DR* 50:215–29.

McKay. 7915. Kaye, Jacqueline. "Claude McKay's 'Banjo'." *PA* 73:165–69.

7916. Larson, Charles R. "Three Harlem Novels of the Jazz Age." *Crit* 11,iii(1969):66–78. [Claude McKay's *Home to Harlem*, Carl Van Vechten's *Nigger Heaven*, Countée Cullen's *One Way to Heaven.*]

See also 1438.

McMurtry. *7917. Davis, Kenneth W. "The Themes of Initiation in the Works of Larry McMurtry and Tom Mayer." *ArlQ* 2,iii:29–43.

7918. Peavy, Charles D. "Coming of Age in Texas:The Novels of Larry McMurtry." *WAL* 4(1969):171–88.

Mencken, S. *See* 7681.

Mencken. 7919. Barrick, Nancy D., and Ernest B. Brown. "Mencken, the Negro, and Civil Rights." *Menckeniana* 35:4–7.

7920. Clark, Ellery H.,Jr. "HLM and the Naval Academy." *Menckeniana* 32(1969):6–9.

7921. Dunlap, Richard L. "The Sage at Dusk." *Menckeniana* 35:7–11.

7922. Durham, Frank. "Mencken as Midwife." *Menckeniana* 32(1969):2–6.

* 7923. LaBelle, Maurice M. "H.L. Mencken's Comprehension

of Friedrich Nietzsche." *CLS* 7:43–49.

7924. Leighton, Clare. "Cynical Fantasy." *Menckeniana* 35:1–4. [Reminis.]

7925. Lora, Ronald G. "The Politics of a Conservative Libertarian." *Menckeniana* 34:4–11.

7926. Nolte, William H. *Checklist of H.L. Mencken.* (Merrill Checklists.) Columbus, Ohio: Charles E. Merrill, 1969.

7927. Vandercook, Sharon,ed. "The Mencken-Hench Correspondence." *Menckeniana* 34:1–4.

* 7928. Wycherley, H. Alan. "H.L. Mencken vs the Eastern Shore:December 1931." *BNYPL* 74:381–90.

See also 7439, 7659.

Merton. 7929. Rice, Edward. *The Man in the Sycamore Tree:The Good Times and Hard Life of Thomas Merton.* Garden City, N.Y.: Doubleday. [Biog.]

7930. Zeik, Michael. "Le voyage du Pèlerin:La vie de Thomas Merton." *Esprit* 395:451–60.

Merwin. *7931. Andersen, Kenneth. "The Poetry of W.S. Merwin." *TCL* 16:278–86.

7932. MacShane, Frank. "A Portrait of W.S. Merwin." *Shenandoah* 21,ii:3–14.

See also 8180.

Michener. 7933. Leib, Amos P. "History and Setting in Michener's Story of Norfolk Island:'Mutiny'." *ALS* 4:349–59.

Millay. 7934. Brittin, Norman A. "Millay Bibliography: Additions and Corrections." *AN&Q* 8(1969):52.

See also 6870.

Millen. *7935. Robinson, Clayton. "Gilmore Millen's *Sweet Man*:Neglected Classic of the Van Vechten Vogue." *ForumH* 8,iii:32–35.

Miller, A. 7936. "Arthur Miller and the Meaning of Tragedy." *MD* 13:34–39. [Interview by Robert A. Martin.]

7937. Bergman, Herbert. " 'The Interior of a Heart':*The Crucible* and *The Scarlet Letter*." *UCQ* 15,iv:27–32.

* 7938. Bigsby, C.W.E. "What Price Arthur Miller? An Analysis of *The Price*." *TCL* 16:16–25.

7939. Bronson, David. "*An Enemy of the People*:A Key to Arthur Miller's Art and Ethics." *CompD* 2(1968–69):229–47.

7940. Eisinger, Chester E. "Focus on Arthur Miller's *Death of a Salesman*:The Wrong Dreams." [F 63]:165–74.

7941. Epstein, Arthur D. "Arthur Miller's Major Plays:A Critical Study." *DAI* 30:4983A(Ind.).

7942. Flanagan, James K. "Arthur Miller:A Study in Sources and Themes." *DAI* 30:4984A(Notre Dame).

7943. Hombitzer, Eleonore. "Die Selbstentfremdung des modernen Menschen im dramatischen Werk Arthur Millers." *NS* 19:409–16.

7944. Martin, Robert A. "The Creative Experience of Arthur Miller:An Interview." *ETJ* 21(1969):310–17.

7945. Schraepen, Edmond. "Arthur Miller's Constancy:A Note on Miller as a Short Story Writer." *RLV* 36:62–71.

7946. Ungar, Harriet. "The Writings of and about Arthur Miller:A Check List 1936–1967." *BNYPL* 74:107–34.

7947. White, Sidney H. *Guide to Arthur Miller.* (Merrill Guides.) Columbus, Ohio: Charles E. Merrill.

7948. Willis, Robert J. "Arthur Miller's *The Crucible*: Relevant for All Times." *Faculty Jour.*(East Stroudsburg [Pa.] State Coll.) 1,i:5–14.

Miller, H. 7949. Hoffman, Michael J. "Yesterday's Rebel." *WHR* 24:271–74.

7950. Jackson, Paul R. "The Balconies of Henry Miller." *UR* 36(1969):155–60; 36:221–25.

7951. Katz, Al. "The *Tropic of Cancer* Trials:The Problem of Relevant Moral and Artistic Controversy." *Midway* 9,iv(1969):99–125.

7952. Nascimento, Esdras,ed. *O mundo de Henry Miller.* Rio: Record. [Coll. of arts. on M.]

7953. Nelson, Jane A. *Form and Image in the Fiction of Henry Miller.* Detroit: Wayne State U.P.

7954. Rios, José Arthur. "O outro lado de Henry Miller." *Comentário* 10(1968):299–304.

7955. Trachtenberg, Alan. " 'History on the Side':Henry Miller's American Dream." [F 63]:136–48.

Miller, V. *7956. Owen, Guy. "Vassar Miller:A Southern

Metaphysical." *SLJ* 3,i:83–88.

Milner, R. 7957. Evans, Donald. "*Who's Got His Own* at Cheyney." *NegroD* 19,vi:43–48,97–98. [Perf. of M's play at Cheyney State Coll.]

Mitchell, M. *7958. Draper, John W. "A Letter from Margaret Mitchell." *WVUPP* 17:81–83. [Incl. text of letter.]

* 7959. Watkins, Floyd C. "*Gone with the Wind* as Vulgar Literature." *SLJ* 2,ii:86–103.

Montgomery. 7960. Colvert, James B. "An Interview with Marion Montgomery." *SoR* 6:1041–53.

Moore. 7961. Hall, Donald. *Marianne Moore:The Cage and the Animal.* New York: Pegasus.

7962. Hayes, Ann L. "Marianne Moore." [F 59]:1–19.

7963. Jaskoski, Helen M. " 'A Method of Conclusions':A Critical Study of the Poetry of Marianne Moore." *DAI* 30(1969):1137A–38A(Stanford).

7964. Nitchie, George W. *Marianne Moore:An Introduction to the Poetry.* New York: Columbia U.P., 1969.

7965. Tomlinson, Charles,ed. *Marianne Moore:A Collection of Critical Essays.* (TCV.) With Introd. Englewood Cliffs, N.J.: Prentice-Hall, 1969. [Rptd. crit. plus Henry Gifford, "Two Philologists," 172–78; Richard A. Macksey, "Marianne (Craig) Moore:A Brief Chronology," 179–81.]

7966. Vonalt, Larry P. "Marianne Moore's Medicines." *SR* 78:669–78. [Rev. art.]

See also 6870.

More. 7967. Tanner, Stephen L. "Paul Elmer More:The Continuity of His Literary Criticism." *DAI* 31:405A(Wis.).

Morris, W. 7968. Crump, Gail B. "Wright Morris and the Immediate Present." *DAI* 31:1267A(Ark.).

7969. Morris, W. *Wright Morris:A Reader.* Introd. Granville Hicks. New York: Harper & Row. [Anthol.]

7970. Waldeland, Lynne M. "Wright Morris:His Theory and Practice of the Craft of Fiction." *DAI* 31:1819A(Purdue).

Morris, Willie. 7971. Mitchell, Paul. "*North Toward Home*: The Quest for an Intellectual Home." *NMW* 2:105–09.

Nabokov. 7972. Alter, Robert. "*Invitation to a Beheading*: Nabokov and the Art of Politics." *TriQ*

7973. Appel, Alfred,Jr. "*Ada* Described." *TriQ* 17:160–86.

7974. —— "Backgrounds of *Lolita*." *TriQ* 17:17–40.

7975. Appel, Alfred,Jr.,ed. *The Annotated Lolita.* With Introd., Bibliog., and Notes. New York: McGraw-Hill.

7976. Berberova, Nina. "Nabokov in the Thirties." *TriQ* 17:220–33.

7977. —— "The Mechanics of *Pale Fire*." *TriQ* 17:147–59.

7978. Bishop, Morris. "Nabokov at Cornell." *TriQ* 17:234–39.

7979. Bitsilli, P.M. "The Revival of Allegory." *TriQ* 17:102–18.

7980. Elkin, Stanley. "Three Meetings." *TriQ* 17:261–65.

7981. Hughes, Robert P. "Notes on the Translation of *Invitation to a Beheading*." *TriQ* 17:284–92.

7982. Hyman, Stanley Edgar. "The Handle:*Invitation to a Beheading* and *Bend Sinister*." *TriQ* 17:60–71.

7983. Karlinsky, Simon. "Anya in Wonderland:Nabokov's Russified Lewis Carroll." *TriQ* 17:310–15.

7984. —— "Nabokov and Chekhov:The Lesser Russian Tradition." *TriQ* 17:7–16.

7985. Khodasevich, Vladislav. "On Sirin." *TriQ* 17:96–101.

7986. Leonard, Jeffrey. "In Place of Lost Time:*Ada*." *TriQ* 17:136–46.

7987. Lewald, H.E. "Antecedentes y claves para *El fuego pálido* de Nabokov." *Sur* 322–23:199–207.

7988. Lubin, Peter. "Kickshaws and Motley." *TriQ* 17:187–208.

7989. Monter, Barbara Heldt. " 'Spring in Fialta':The Choice That Mimics Chance." *TriQ* 17:128–35.

7990. Moynahan, Julian. "*Lolita* and Related Memories." *TriQ* 17:247–52.

7991. Nilsson, Nils Åke. "A Hall of Mirrors:Nabokov and Olesha." *SSl* 15(1969):5–12.

7992. Noel, Lucie Léon. "Playback." *TriQ* 17:209–19.

7993. Parker, Stephen J. "Vladimir Nabokov—Sirin as Teacher:The Russian Novels." *DAI* 30:3952A–53A(Cornell).

7994. Pifer, Ellen I. "Nabokov's *Invitation to a Beheading*:The

Parody of a Tradition." *PCP* 5:46–53.

7995. Proffer, Carl R. "A New Deck for Nabokov's Knaves." *TriQ* 17:293–309.

7996. Proffer, Ellendea. "Nabokov's Russian Readers." *TriQ* 17:253–60.

7997. Scott, W.B. "The Cypress Veil." *TriQ* 17:316–31.

7998. Steiner, George. "Extraterritorial." *TriQ* 17:119–27.

7999. Stuart, Dabney. "*Laughter in the Dark*:Dimensions of Parody." *TriQ* 17:72–95.

8000. Weil, Irwin. "Odyssey of a Translator." *TriQ* 17: 266–83.

8001. Wetzsteon, Ross. "Nabokov as Teacher." *TriQ* 17: 240–46.

Neihardt. 8002. Rothwell, Kenneth S. "In Search of a Western Epic:Neihardt, Sandburg, and Jaffe as Regionalists and 'Astoriadists'." *KanQ* 2,ii:53–63.

New Yorker. 8003. Johnson, Robert O. *An Index to Literature in The New Yorker:Volumes I–XV, 1925–1940.* Metuchen, N.J.: Scarecrow, 1969.

Nin. 8004. Durand, Régis. "Anaïs Nin et le 'langage des nerfs'." *LanM* 64:289–96.

8005. McEvilly, Wayne. "Dos rostros de la muerte en *Seducción del minotauro*, de Anaïs Nin." *Sur* 322–23:233–47.

Norton. *8006. McGhan, Barry R. "Andre Norton:Why Has She Been Neglected?" *RQ* 4:128–31.

O'Connor, E. 8007. Rank, Hugh. "O'Connor's Image of the Priest." *NEQ* 41(1968):3–29. [Corr. of Bibliog. for 1968, Item 11217.]

See also 7290.

O'Connor, Flannery. *8008. Abbot, Louise H. "Remembering Flannery O'Connor." *SLJ* 2,ii:3–25.

* 8009. Asals, Frederick. "Flannery O'Connor's 'The Lame Shall Enter First'." *MissQ* 23:103–20.

8010. Bleikasten, André. "Théologie et dérision chez Flannery O'Connor." *LanM* 64:124–38.

* 8011. Burns, Stuart L. "The Evolution of *Wise Blood*." *MFS* 16:147–62.

8012. Casper, Leonard. "The Unspeakable Peacock:Apocalypse in Flannery O'Connor." [F 60]:287–99.

8013. Davis, Jack and June. "Tarwater and Jonah:Two Reluctant Prophets." *XUS* 9,i:19–27.

8014. Feeley, Sister Mary K.,SSND "Splendor of Reality:The Fiction of Flannery O'Connor." *DAI* 31:1272A(Rutgers).

8015. Friedman, Melvin J. "By and About Flannery O'Connor." *JML* 1:288–92. [Rev. art.]

8016. —— "Flannery O'Connor's Sacred Objects." [F 19]: 67–77.

8017. Gafford, Charlotte K. "Chaucer's Pardoner and Haze Motes of Georgia." [F 16]:9–12.

8018. Hendin, Josephine. *The World of Flannery O'Connor.* Bloomington: Ind. U.P. [Crit.]

8019. —— "In Search of Flannery O'Connor." *ColF* 13,i:38–41.

* 8020. Littlefield, Daniel F.,Jr. "Flannery O'Connor's *Wise Blood*:'Unparalleled Prosperity' and Spiritual Chaos." *MissQ* 23:121–33.

8021. Maida, Patricia D. " 'Convergence' in Flannery O'Connor's 'Everything That Rises Must Converge'." *SSF* 7:549–55.

8022. Male, Roy R. "The Two Versions of 'The Displaced Person'." *SSF* 7:450–57.

* 8023. May, John R.,S.J. "The Pruning Word:Flannery O'Connor's Judgment of Intellectuals." *SHR* 4:325–38.

8024. Montgomery, Marion. "A Note on Flannery O'Connor's Terrible and Violent Prophecy of Mercy." *ForumH* 7,iii(1969):4–7.

8025. —— "Flannery O'Connor's Territorial Center." *Crit* 11,iii(1969):5–10.

8026. Nance, William L. "Flannery O'Connor:The Trouble with Being a Prophet." *UR* 36(1969):101–08.

8027. Orvell, Miles D. "Flannery O'Connor." *SR* 78:184–92. [Rev. art. on recent books of crit.]

8028. Short, Donald A. "The Concrete Is Her Medium:The Fiction of Flannery O'Connor." *DAI* 30:3476A–77A(Pittsburgh).

* 8029. Smith, Francis J.,S.J. "O'Connor's Religious Viewpoint in *The Violent Bear It Away*." *Renascence* 22:108–12.

Odets. 8030. Shuman, R. Baird. "Thematic Consistency in Odets' Early Plays." *RLV* 35(1969):415–20.

8031. Willett, Ralph. "Clifford Odets and Popular Culture." *SAQ* 69:[68]–78.

O'Hara. 8032. McCormick, Bernard. "A John O'Hara Geography." *JML* 1:151–68.

Olson. 8033. Combs, Maxine. "Charles Olson's 'The Kingfishers':A Consideration of Meaning and Method." *FPt* 4:66–76.

O'Neill. 8034. Asselineau, Roger. "*Desire Under the Elms*:A Phase of Eugene O'Neill's Philosophy." [F 52]:277–83.

8035. Bakó, Endre. "Hosszú út az éjszakába:O'Neill —bemutató Csokonai Színházban." *Alföld* 21,ii:89–90. [O'Neill première in Debrecen, Hungary.]

8036. Carpenter, Frederic I. "Focus on Eugene O'Neill's *The Iceman Cometh*:The Iceman Hath Come." [F 63]:158–64.

8037. Das, P.N. "The Alienated Ape." *Lit. Half-Yearly* (Mysore) 11,i:53–69.

8038. Frazer, Winifred L. "Chris and Poseidon:Man Versus God in *Anna Christie*." *MD* 12:279–85.

8039. Gey, Guy. "Dynamo de Eugene O'Neill:'La Maladie Contemporaine' et l'exploitation d'un mythe moderne." *Caliban* 7:35–41.

8040. Halfmann, Ulrich. *Unreal Realism:O'Neills dramatisches Werk im Spiegel seiner szenischen Kunst.* München: Franke, 1969.

8041. Hoffmann, Gerhard. "Lachen und Weinen als Gestaltungsmittel der dramatischen Grenzsituation:Zum Verhältnis von direkten und indirekten Ausdrucksformen im Drama O'Neills." *JA* 15:101–22.

* 8042. Holtan, Orley I. "Eugene O'Neill and the Death of the 'Covenant'." *QJS* 56:256–63.

* 8043. Presley, Delma E. "O'Neill's Iceman:Another Meaning." *AL* 42:387–88.

8044. Real, Jere. "The Brothel in O'Neill's *Mansions*." *MD* 12:383–89.

8045. Roy, Emil. "The Archetypal Unity of Eugene O'Neill's Drama." *CompD* 3(1969–70):263–74.

8046. Stroupe, John H. "O'Neill's *Marco Millions*:A Road to Xanadu." *MD* 12:377–82.

8047. Tinsley, Mary A. "Two Biographical Plays by Eugene O'Neill:The Drafts and the Final Versions." *DAI* 31:1297A (Cornell).

8048. Törnqvist, Egil. *A Drama of Souls:Studies in O'Neill's Supernaturalistic Technique.* Stockholm: Almqvist & Wiksell, 1968.

* 8049. —— "O'Neill's Lazarus:Dionysus and Christ." *AL* 41:[543]–54.

8050. —— "Personal Addresses in the Plays of O'Neill." *QJS* 55(1969):126–30.

8051. Winchester, Otis W. "History in Literature:Eugene O'Neill's *Strange Interlude* as a Transcript of America in the 1920's." [F 58]:43–58.

See also 5375.

Parker. 8052. Keats, John. *You Might as Well Live:The Life and Times of Dorothy Parker.* New York: Simon and Schuster. [Biog.]

Patchen. 8053. Nelson, Raymond J. "An American Mysticism:The Example of Kenneth Patchen." *DAI* 30:5453A–54A(Stanford).

Percy. *8054. Lawson, Lewis A. "Walker Percy's Southern Stoic." *SLJ* 3,i:5–31.

8055. Van Cleave, Jim. "Versions of Percy." *SoR* 6:990–1010.

Phillips. 8056. Sloane, David E.E. "David Graham Phillips, Jack London, and Others on Contemporary Reviewers and Critics, 1903–1904." *ALR* 3:67–71.

8057. Stallings, Frank L.,Jr. "David Graham Phillips (1867–1911):A Critical Bibliography of Secondary Comment." *ALR* 3:1–35.

Plath. 8058. Newman, Charles,ed. *The Art of Sylvia Plath:A Symposium.* With Introd. London: Faber. [Rptd. crit. plus Charles Newman, "Candor Is the Only Wile:The Art of Sylvia Plath,"

21–55; Richard Howard, "Sylvia Plath:'And I Have No Face, I Have Wanted to Efface Myself...'," 77–88; Edward Lucie-Smith, "Sea-Imagery in the Work of Sylvia Plath," 91–99; Annette Lavers, "The World as Icon:On Sylvia Plath's Themes," 100–35; John F. Nims, "The Poetry of Sylvia Plath:A Technical Analysis," 136–52; Wendy Campbell, "Remembering Sylvia," 182–86; Mary Ellmann, "*The Bell Jar*:An American Girlhood," 221–26; Mary Kinzie, "An Informal Check List of Criticism," 283–304; Mary Kinzie, Daniel L. Conrad, and Suzanne D. Kurman, "Bibliography," 305–19.]

* 8059. Perloff, Marjorie. "*Angst* and Animism in the Poetry of Sylvia Plath." *JML* 1:57–74.

* 8060. Salamon, Lynda B. " 'Double, Double':Perception in the Poetry of Sylvia Plath." *Spirit* 37,ii:34–39.

8061. Zollman, Sol. "Sylvia Plath and Imperialist Culture." *L&I* 2(1969):11–22.

Porter, B. *8062. *CLQ* 9,ii. *Spec. Bern Porter No.* [Richard Cary, "Bern Porter Chronology," 65–67; James Schevill, "Bern Porter:Further Notes on *The Roaring Market and the Silent Tomb*," 68–81; Dick Higgins, "Thinking About Bern Porter," 82–84; Harriet S. Blake, "The Leaves Fall in the Bay Area: Regarding Bern Porter and Four Little Magazines," 85–104; Renee B. Simon, "Bern Porter:A Bibliographical Sampling," 105–13; Richard Cary, "Bern Porter's Friends in Books," 114–29(esp. H. Miller, Algren, Shapiro, and Ginsberg).]

Porter, K.A. 8063. Baker, Howard. "The Upward Path:Notes on the Work of Katherine Anne Porter." [F 67]:75–93. [Rev. version of Item 11259, Bibliog. for 1968.]

8064. Liberman, M.M. "Circe." *SR* 78:689–93. [Rev. art. on P's *Collected Essays and Occasional Writings*.]

8065. Madden, David. "The Charged Image in Katherine Anne Porter's 'Flowering Judas'." *SSF* 7:277–89.

* 8066. Nance, William L. "Katherine Anne Porter and Mexico." *SWR* 55:143–53.

8067. Partridge, Colin. " 'My Familiar Country':An Image of Mexico in the Work of Katherine Anne Porter." *SSF* 7:597–614.

8068. Pinkerton, Jan. "Katherine Anne Porter's Portrayal of Black Resentment." *UR* 36:315–17.

8069. Porter, K. *The Collected Essays and Occasional Writings of Katherine Anne Porter.* New York: Delacorte.

* 8070. Sullivan, Walter. "Katherine Anne Porter:The Glories and Errors of Her Ways." *SLJ* 3,i:111–21.

Porter, W.S. 8071. Gallegly, Joseph. *From Alamo Plaza to Jack Harris's Saloon:O'Henry and the Southwest He Knew.* (SAmL 27.) The Hague: Mouton.

Pound. 8072. Awiszus, Sabine. "Kung in Venedig:Die Erscheinung Ezra Pounds." [F 21]:385–93.

8073. Barilli, Renato. *Poetica e retorica.* Milano: Mursia, 1969. [Fracastoro, Castelvetro, Patrizi, Vico, Leopardi, Pound, Eliot.]

8074. Baumann, Walter. *The Rose in the Steel Dust:An Examination of the Cantos of Ezra Pound.* Coral Gables, Fla.: U. of Miami P.

8075. Bayes, Ronald H. "Who Sprung Ezra? Continued Speculation." *U. of Portland Rev.* 20,i(1968):47–48.

8076. Călinescu, Matei. "Conceptul modern de poezie—modernism şi tradiţie:Ezra Pound şi 'imagismul'." *SXX* 13,v:8–28.

* 8077. Chace, William M. "Ezra Pound and the Marxist Temptation." *AQ* 22:[714]–25.

8078. Donoghue, Denis. "James's *The Awkward Age* and Pound's 'Mauberley'." *N&Q* 17:49–50.

* 8079. Fussell, Edwin. "Dante and Pound's *Cantos*." *JML* 1:75–87.

8080. Graham, D.B. "From Chinese to English:Ezra Pound's 'Separation on the River Kiang'." *LE&W* 13(1969):182–95.

8081. Hénault, Marie P. *Guide to Ezra Pound.* (Merrill Guides.) Columbus, Ohio: Charles E. Merrill.

8082. Hlawatsch, Wolfhard. "Ezra Pounds Weg zum Licht: Eine Interpretation von *Canto XV*." *NS* 18(1969):551–57.

8083. Hutchins, Patricia. "Ezra Pound's 'Approach to Paris'." *SoR* 6:340–55.

8084. Kodama, Jitsuei. "Pound no Naso to Fenollosa MSS no Hakken." *EigoS* 115(1969):234–37. [P's riddle and discovery of the F MSS.]

8085. Kodama, Sanehide. "The Chinese Subject in Ezra Pound's Poetry." *SELit* Eng. No.:37–62.

8086. Montgomery, Marion. *Ezra Pound.* (CWCP.) Grand Rapids, Mich.: William B. Eerdmans. [Crit.]

8087. Schwartz, Joseph. "[Review Essay on Four Recent Books on Pound]." *Spirit* 37,ii:42–46.

8088. "Special Pound Issue." *St. Andrews Rev.* 1,i. [Lewis Leary, "Pound-Wise, Penny Foolish:Correspondence on Getting Together a Volume of Criticism," 5–9; Forrest Read, " '76:The Cantos of Ezra Pound," 11–16; James Laughlin, "Pound the Teacher:The Ezuversity," 17–18; Guy Davenport, "Il Vecchio," 19–20; Harry Meacham, "I Remember Ezra," 21–24; Akiko Miyake, "Pound and Confucianism," 45; Hugh Kenner, "Scatter—From the Pound Era," 51–55.]

8089. Sutton, Walter. "*The Pisan Cantos*:The Form of Survival." [F 67]:118–29.

8090. Taylor, James,ed. *Ezra Pound Birthday Issue, October 30, 1970. Sou'wester*(So. Ill. U.) [Eustace Mullins, "Ezra and America," 3–5; Hugh Kenner, "Douglas" (Clifford Hugh Douglas and Pound), 6–20; R.P. Dickey, "Introduction to the Esthetic and Philosophy of the *Cantos*," 21–35; Henry F. Lippincott,Jr., "Pound, Richmond Lattimore and *Odyssey IX*," 36–45; Marion Montgomery, "Ezra Pound's Arrogance," 46–54 (repr. of chap. from *Ezra Pound:A Critical Essay*); Marcella Span, "Ezra Pound:*Drafts and Fragments of Cantos CX-CXVII*," 55–58; Nicholas Joost, "Ezra Pound and *The Dial*—And a Few Translations," 59–71; William J. Meyer, "The Imagist and the Translator:Ezra Pound's 'Separation on the River Kiang'," 72–80; Randolph Splitter, "Pound's Dream of the Gods:A Baker's Half-Dozen of the *Cantos*," 81–99; Douglas L. Cooney, "Ezra Pound:A Study of His Prosody," 100–17; James Taylor, "The Typical Critic of Pound," 118–23; poems by Eugene Warren, R.P. Dickey, D.F. Drummond, Thomas McAfee, James Taylor, Victoria McCabe, John Ciardi, and "A Statement" by John E. Matthias.]

8091. Vasse, William W.,Jr. "Traveler in a Landscape:The Structure of History in Ezra Pound's *Cantos*." *DAI* 31:772A (Calif., Berkeley).

8092. Wagner, Linda W. "The Poetry of Ezra Pound." *JML* 1:293–98. [Rev. art.]

8093. Wain, John. "The Prophet Ezra v. 'The Egotistical Sublime'." *Encounter* 33(Aug 1969):63–70.

8094. Wigginton, Waller B. "The Pounds at Hailey." *Rendezvous* 4,i(1969):31–68.

8095. Wigginton, Waller B.,ed. "A Homer Pound Letter." *Rendezvous* 4,ii(1969):27–29.

8096. Zverev, A. "Ézra Paund—literaturnaja teorija, poèzija, sud'ba." *VLit* 14,vi:123–47.

See also 4926, 4965, 5160, 5163, 5574, 5947, 8375.

Powers, J.F. 8097. Stewart, D.H. "J.F. Powers' *Morte D'Urban* as Western." *WAL* 5:31–44.

8098. Vickery, John B. "J.F. Powers' *Morte D'Urban*: Secularity and Grace." [F 19]:45–65.

See also 7290.

Purdy. *8100. Baldanza, Frank. "Playing House for Keeps with James Purdy." *ConL* 11:488–510.

8101. Rosen, Gerald. "James Purdy's World of Black Humor." *DAI* 31:1290A–91A(Pa.).

8102. Schwarzschild, Bettina. *The Not-Right House:Essays on James Purdy.* (Mo. Literary Frontiers Ser. 5.) Columbia: U. of Mo. P., 1968.

Pynchon. *See* 950.

Ramparts. 8103. Blanchard, Carlene M.B. "*Ramparts* Magazine:Social Change in the 'Sixties'." *DAI* 31:726A–27A(Mich.).

Rand. 8104. Deane, Paul. "Ayn Rand's Neurotic Personalities of Our Times." *RLV* 36:125–29.

Randall, Julia. 8105. Sanders, Frederick K. "The Poet and the Taxi-Cab-Driver Test." *SR* 78:358–65. [Rev. art.]

Ransom. 8106. Meyers, Walter E. "A Commentary on 'John Crowe Ransom's Poetic Revisions'." *PMLA* 85:532–33. [Comment on Bibliog. for 1968, Item 11305; foll. by reply.]

Rawlings. 8107. Bellman, Samuel I. "Marjorie Kinnan Rawlings:A Solitary Sojourner in the Florida Backwoods." *KanQ* 2,ii:78–87.

Reed. 8108. Starcev, A. "V arxive Džona Rida." *VLit* 14,i:151–57.

Reese. 8109. Milne, W. Gordon. "Lizette Reese Revisited." *SUS* 8(1969):207–12.

Rhodes. 8110. Rhodes, E.M. *Stepsons of Light.* Introd. W.H. Hutchinson. Norman: U. of Okla. P., 1969.

8111. Skillman, Richard, and Jerry C. Hoke. "The Portrait of the New Mexican in the Fiction of Eugene Rhodes." *WR* 6,i(1969):26–36.

Rich, A. *See* 8180.

Richardson, J. 8112. Debusscher, Gilbert. "Modern Masks of the Orestes:*The Flies* and *The Prodigal.*" *MD* 12:308–18.

Richter. 8113. Edwards, Clifford D. *Conrad Richter's Ohio Trilogy:Its Ideas, Themes, and Relationship to Literary Tradition.* (SAmL 18.) The Hague: Mouton.

8114. La Hood, Marvin J. "Conrad Richter and Willa Cather:Some Similarities." *XUS* 9,i:33–46.

Robinson. 8115. Barnard, Ellsworth,ed. *Edwin Arlington Robinson:Centenary Essays.* Athens: U. of Ga. P. ["Edwin Arlington Robinson:A Chronology," viii–ix; "Robinson's Major Publications," x; "Bibliography," xi–xvii; Ellsworth Barnard, " 'Of This or That Estate':Robinson's Literary Reputation," 1–14; William J. Free, "The Strategy of 'Flammonde'," 15–30; David H. Hirsch, " 'The Man Against the Sky' and the Problem of Faith," 31–42; Scott Donaldson, "The Book of Scattered Lives," 43–53; Robert D. Stevick, "The Metrical Style of E.A. Robinson," 54–67; Wallace L. Anderson, "The Young Robinson as Critic and Self-Critic," 68–87; Charles T. Davis, "Robinson's Road to Camelot," 88–105; Nathan C. Starr, "The Transformation of Merlin," 106–19; Christopher Brookhouse, "Imagery and Theme in *Lancelot*," 120–29; Jay Martin, "A Crisis of Achievement:Robinson's Late Narratives," 130–56; J.C. Levenson, "Robinson's Modernity," 157–74; Radcliffe Squires, "Tilbury Town Today," 175–83.]

8116. Bierk, John C. "Edwin Arlington Robinson as Social Critic and Moral Guide." *DAI* 30:2997A–98A(Northwestern).

8117. Burton, David H. "E.A. Robinson and Christianity." *Spirit* 37,i:30–35.

8118. —— "The Intellectualism of Edwin Arlington Robinson." *Thought* 44(1969):565–80.

8119. Crawford, John. "Success and Failure in the Poetry of Edwin Arlington Robinson." *Rendezvous* 5,i:27–29.

8120. Crowley, John W. "E.A. Robinson and Henry Cabot Lodge." *NEQ* 43:115–24.

8121. Lucas, John. "The Poetry of Edwin Arlington Robinson." *RMS* 13(1969):132–47.

8122. Murphy, Francis,ed. *Edwin Arlington Robinson:A Collection of Critical Essays.* (TCV.) With Introd. Englewood Cliffs, N.J.: Prentice-Hall. [Prev. pub. essays, plus Josephine Miles, "Robinson's Inner Fire," 110–16.]

8123. Satterfield, Leon J. "Major Categories of Irony in the Poetry of Edwin Arlington Robinson." *DAI* 30:3022A(Neb.).

8124. Thompson, W.R. "Broceliande:E.A. Robinson's Palace of Art." *NEQ* 43:231–49.

8125. Turner, Steven. "Robinson's 'Richard Cory'." *Expl* 28:Item 73.

Roethke. 8126. Bullis, Jerald. "Theodore Roethke." *MR* 11:209–12.

8127. Gangewere, R.J. "Theodore Roethke:The Future of a Reputation." [F 59]:65–73.

8128. Gloege, Randall G. "Suspension of Belief in the Poetry of Theodore Roethke." *DAI* 31:757A(Bowling Green).

8129. LaBelle, Jenijoy. "Theodore Roethke and Tradition: 'The Pure Sense of Memory in One Man'." *DAI* 30(1969): 2029A(Calif., San Diego).

8130. McDade, Gerard F. "The Primitive Vision of Theodore Roethke:A Study of Aboriginal Elements in His Poetry." *DAI* 31:1806A(Temple).

* 8131. Schumacher, Paul J. "The Unity of Being:A Study of Theodore Roethke's Poetry." *OUR* 12:20–40.

8132. Skelton, Robin. "The Poetry of Theodore Roethke." *MHRev* 1(1967):141–44. [Rev. art.]

Rogers. 8133. Eitner, Walter H. "Will Rogers:Another Look at His Act." *KanQ* 2,ii:46–52.

Roth, P. *8134. Donaldson, Scott. "Philip Roth:The Meanings of *Letting Go.*" *ConL* 11:21–35.

8135. Iwamoto, Iwao. "Philip Roth—Judayasei e no Hangyaku." *EigoS* 115(1969):762–63. [PR—opposition to Judaism.]

8136. Petillon, Pierre-Yves. "Philip Roth n'est pas mort." *Critique* 26:821–38.

8137. Roskolenko, Harry. "Portrait of the Artist as a Young Schmuck." *Quadrant* 64:25–30. [*Portnoy's Complaint.*]

8138. Shrubb, Peter. "Portnography." *Quadrant* 64:16–24. *See also* 7367.

Russell. 8139. Brunvand, Jan H. "From Western Folklore to Fiction in the Stories of Charles M. Russell." *WR* 5,i(1968):41–49.

Sackler. 8140. Trousdale, Marion. "Ritual Theatre:*The Great White Hope.*" *WHR* 23(1969):295–303.

Salinger. 8141. Amur, G.S. "Theme, Structure, and Symbol in *The Catcher in the Rye.*" *IJAS* 1,i(1969):11–24.

8142. Burrows, David. "Allie and Phoebe:Death and Love in J.D. Salinger's *The Catcher in the Rye.*" [F 57]:106–14.

8143. Goldstein, Bernice and Sanford. " 'Seymour:An Introduction'—Writing as Discovery." *SSF* 7:248–56.

8144. —— "Bunnies and Cobras:Zen Enlightenment in Salinger." *Discourse* 13:98–106.

* 8145. —— "Zen and *Nine Stories.*" *Renascence* 22:171–82.

8146. Hamada, Seijiro. " 'The Laughing Man' ni tsuite." *EigoS* 114(1968):578–79. [On "The Laughing Man."]

8147. Karlstetter, Karl. "J.D. Salinger, R.W. Emerson and the Perennial Philosophy." *MSpr* 63(1969):224–36.

* 8148. Luedtke, Luther S. "J.D. Salinger and Robert Burns: *The Catcher in the Rye.*" *MFS* 16:198–201.

8149. Méral, Jean. "The Ambiguous Mr. Antolini in Salinger's *Catcher in the Rye.*" *Caliban* 7:55–58.

8150. Pickering, John K. "J.D. Salinger:Portraits of Alienation." *DAI* 30:3954A(Case Western Reserve).

8151. Sakamoto, Masayuki. "Salinger ni okeru 'Sezuku' to 'Chozoku'." *EigoS* 115(1969):692–93. [Profane and sacred in S.]

8152. Sethom, Mohamed. "La société dans l'œuvre de J.D. Salinger." *EA* 22(1969):270–78.

8153. Takenaka, Toyoko. "On Seymour's Suicide." *KAL* 12:54–61. [In Jap.]

See also 7741, 8099.

Sandburg. 8154. Basler, Roy P. "Your Friend the Poet:Carl Sandburg." *Midway* 10,ii(1969):3–15.

8155. Callahan, North. *Carl Sandburg:Lincoln of Our Literature.* New York: N.Y.U. Press. [Biog.]

8156. Mearns, David C. " 'Ever and Ever, Carl'." *MSS* 21(1969):169–73.

8157. Quigley, Michael J. "A Study of Carl Sandburg:A Major Writer for the Secondary School of Today." *DAI* 31:1767A(Ohio State).

See also 7687, 8002.

Santayana. 8158. Ballowe, James. "The Intellectual Traveller:An Essay on George Santayana." *DR* 50:157–69.

8159. Cecil, David. "Santayana." *TLS* 15 Jan:58. [Aldous Huxley on S.]

8160. Holzberger, William G. "The Published Poems of George Santayana:A Critical Edition." *DAI* 30:3010A–11A(Northwestern).

See also 4050.

Saroyan. *See* 7467.

Schevill. 8161. Robbins, Martin. "James Schevill:Poet with Music, and Playwright with a Message." *Voyages*(Wash., D.C.) 3,i–ii:85–87.

See also 909.

Schwartz. 8162. Knapp, James F. "Delmore Schwartz:Poet of the Orphic Journey." *SR* 78:506–16.

Selby. 8163. Peavy, Charles D. "The Sin of Pride and Selby's *Last Exit to Brooklyn.*" *Crit* 11,iii(1969):35–42.

Sexton. 8164. "Anne Sexton:Worksheets." *MHRev* 6(1968): 105–14.

Shapiro. 8165. Thornburg, Thomas R. "The Man with the Hatchet:Shapiro on Auden." *BSUF* 11,iii:25–34.

Sherwood. 8166. Meserve, Walter J. *Robert E. Sherwood: Reluctant Moralist.* New York: Pegasus.

Sinclair, U. 8167. Soderbergh, Peter A. "Upton Sinclair and Hollywood." *MQ* 11:173–91.

8168. Turner, Justin G. "Conversation with Upton Sinclair." *ABC* 20,viii:7–10.

8169. Zanger, Martin. "Politics of Confrontation:Upton Sinclair and the Launching of the ACLU in Southern California." *Pacific Hist. Rev.* 38(1969):383–406.

Singer. 8170. Salamon, George. "In a Glass Darkly:The Morality of the Mirror in E.T.A. Hoffmann and I.B. Singer." *SSF* 7:625–33.

8171. Siegel, Ben. *Isaac Bashevis Singer.* (UMPAW 86.) Minneapolis: U. of Minn. P., 1969.

8172. Singer, Isaac. "Un ami de Kafka." *NL* 20 août:1,6. [Unpub. text tr. by Marc-Pierre Castelnau.]
See also 7301.

Smith, L.E. 8173. Thornburn, Neil. "*Strange Fruit* and Southern Tradition." *MQ* 12:157–71.

Smith, W.J. *8174. Burgess, C.F. "William Jay Smith's 'American Primitive':Toward a Reading." *ArQ* 26:71–75.

8175. [Ritchie, Elisavietta]. "An Interview with William Jay Smith." *Voyages*(Wash., D.C.) 3,i–ii:89–103.

Snodgrass. 8176. Gerber, Philip L., and Robert J. Gemmett, eds. " 'No Voices Talk to Me':A Conversation with W.D. Snodgrass." *WHR* 24:61–71.

Snyder. 8177. Altieri, Charles. " 'Gary Snyder's Lyric Poetry:Dialectic as Ecology'." *FPt* 4:55–65.

8178. Lyon, Thomas J. "The Ecological Vision of Gary Snyder." *KanQ* 2,ii:117–24.

8179. Shinkura, Shunichi. "Gary Snyder:Shinwa to Honbun." *EigoS* 115(1969):82–83. [GS: Myth and text.]
See also 7241.

Stafford. 8180. Ahmad, Aijaz. "Ghalib:'The Dew Drop on the Red Poppy...'." *Mahfil* 5,iv(1968-69):59–69. [Incl. poetic versions by William Stafford, Adrienne Rich, and W.S. Merwin.]

8181. Hugo, Richard. "Problems with Landscapes in Early Stafford Poems." *KanQ* 2,ii:33–38.

8182. Kelley, Patrick. "Legend and Ritual." *KanQ* 2,ii:28–31.

Steele. 8183. Wyman, Willard G. "Wilbur Daniel Steele:The Man and His Work." *DAI* 30:5460A(Stanford).

Stegner. 8184. Flora, Joseph M. "Vardis Fisher and Wallace Stegner:Teacher and Student." *WAL* 5:121–28.

Stein. 8185. Brinnin, John M.,ed. *Selected Operas and Plays of Gertrude Stein.* With Introd. Pittsburgh: U. of Pittsburgh P. [Incl. also Donald Gallup, "The Published Works of Gertrude Stein," 323–25.]

* 8186. Purdy, Strother B. "Gertrude Stein at Marienbad." *PMLA* 85:1096–1105.

8187. Weinstein, Norman. *Gertrude Stein and the Literature of the Modern Consciousness.* New York: Ungar. [Crit.]

Steinbeck. 8188. Astro, Richard. "Into the Cornucopia: Steinbeck's Vision of Nature and the Ideal Man." *DAI* 30(1969): 2517A–18A(U. of Wash.).

* 8189. —— "Steinbeck's Post-War Trilogy:A Return to Nature and the Natural Man." *TCL* 16:109–22.

8190. Bleeker, Gary W. "Setting and Animal Tropes in the Fiction of John Steinbeck." *DAI* 30:2998A(Neb.).

* 8191. Clarke, Mary W. "Bridging the Generation Gap:The Ending of Steinbeck's *Grapes of Wrath.*" *ForumH* 8,ii:16–17.

8192. DeLisle, Harold F. "Style and Idea in Steinbeck's 'The Turtle'." *Style* 4:145–54. [Discusses chap. 3 of *The Grapes of Wrath.*]

8193. Gadda Conti, Giuseppe. "Ricordo di John Steinbeck." *OPL* 15,ii(1969):29–38.

8194. Hamby, James A. "Steinbeck's *The Pearl:*Tradition and Innovation." *WR* 7,ii:65–66.

8195. Hayashi, Tetsumaro. "John Steinbeck:A Checklist of Movie Reviews." *Serif* 7,ii:18–22.

8196. Inazawa, Hideo. "Steinbeck no Bunmeiron." *EigoS* 115(1969):216–19. [S's theory of civilization.]

8197. —— *Sutainbekku Ron [Essays on Steinbeck].* Tokyo: Shicho-sha, 1967. [In Jap.]

8198. Inoue, Kenji. "Aku wo Egakikirenakatta Sakka." *EigoS* 115(1969):206–08. [Author unable to portray the depths of evil.]

8199. Iseri, Ryusei. "*Eden no Higashi.*" *EigoS* 115(1969):

209–10. [*East of Eden.*]

8200. Justus, James H. "The Transient World of *Tortilla Flat.*" *WR* 7,i:55–60.

* 8201. Levant, Howard. "*Tortilla Flat:*The Shape of John Steinbeck's Career." *PMLA* 85:1087–95.

8202. Machidori, Matayoshi. "*Warera ga Fuman no Fuyu.*" *EigoS* 115(1969):214–15. [*The Winter of Our Discontent.*]

8203. Magnusson, Bo. "Komisk rationalisering hos Steinbeck." *Studiekamraten* 52:29–30.

8204. Marks, Lester J. *Thematic Design in the Novels of John Steinbeck.* (SAmL 11.) The Hague: Mouton, 1969.

8205. Marussig, Antonio. "Violência e realismo na ficção americana:John Steinbeck." *IH* 5(1969):139–42.

8206. Morsberger, Robert E. "In Defense of 'Westering'." *WAL* 5:143–46.

* 8207. Nimitz, Jack. "Ecology in *The Grapes of Wrath.*" *HSL* 2:165–68.

8208. Noonan, Gerald. "A Note on 'The Chrysanthemums'." *MFS* 15(1969):542.

8209. O'Connor, Richard. *John Steinbeck.* New York: McGraw-Hill. [Biog.]

8210. Ohashi, Kichinosuke. "*Nagai Tani.*" *EigoS* 115(1969): 211–12. [*The Long Valley.*]

8211. Steinbeck, J. *Journal of a Novel:The* East of Eden *Letters.* New York: Viking, 1969.

8212. *Steinbeck Quart.* 3,iii. [Sanford E. Marovitz, "John Steinbeck and Adlai Stevenson:The Shattered Image of America," 51–62; Andreas K. Poulakidas, "Steinbeck, Kazantzakis and Socialism," 62–72.]

8213. *Steinbeck Quart.* 3,ii. [Lawrence W. Jones, "Random Thoughts from Paris:Steinbeck's *Un Américain à New York et à Paris,*" 27–30; Lawrence W. Jones, "An Uncited Post-War Steinbeck Story:'The Short Story of Mankind'," 30–31; Robert DeMott, "A Miscellany of Bibliographical Notes," 41–43; Lee R. Hayman, "Report from Salinas," 43–44.]

8214. *Steinbeck Quart.* 3,i. [Richard Astro, "Steinbeck and Mainwaring:Two Californians for the Earth," 3–11; Lawrence W. Jones, "The Real Authorship of Steinbeck's 'Verse'," 11–12.]

8215. Tatsunokuchi, Naotaro. "Steinbeck Country." *EigoS* 115(1969):213. [In Jap.]

8216. West, Philip J. "Steinbeck's 'The Leader of the People':A Crisis in Style." *WAL* 5:137–41.
See also 946, 7230.

Stevens, W. *8217. Adams, Richard P. " 'The Comedian as the Letter C':A Somewhat Literal Reading." *TSE* 18:95–114.

8218. Baym, Nina. "The Transcendentalism of Wallace Stevens." *ESQ* 57(1969):66–72.

8219. Bevis, William W. "The Arrangement of *Harmonium.*" *ELH* 37:456–73.

8220. Blessing, Richard A. *Wallace Stevens' "Whole Harmonium."* Syracuse, N.Y.: Syracuse U.P. [Crit.]

8221. Brezianu, Andrei. "Pe marginea motivului solar în poezia lui Wallace Stevens." *SXX* 12,ix(1969):156–63.

8222. Brown, Merle E. "A Critical Performance of 'Asides on the Oboe'." *JAAC* 29:121–28.

8223. Buhr, Marjorie C. "The Essential Poem:A Study of Wallace Stevens' Ontology." *DAI* 30:3451A(U. of Miami).

8224. Dietrichson, Jan W. "Wallace Stevens' 'Sunday Morning'." *Edda* 70:105–16.

8225. Eder, Doris L. "The Meaning of Wallace Stevens' Two Themes." *CritQ* 11(1969):181–90.

8226. —— "Wallace Stevens:Heritage and Influences." *Mosaic* 4,i:49–61.

8227. Fuller, Roy. "Both Pie and Custard." *Shenandoah* 21,iii:61–76. [Biog.]

8228. Girlinghouse, Mary J. "The New Romantic of Wallace Stevens." *DAI* 31:387A(Catholic U.).

8229. Guereschi, Edward F. "The Inventive Imagination: Wallace Stevens' Dialectic of Secular Grace." *DAI* 31:1229A–30A(Syracuse).

* 8230. Hafner, John H. "One Way of Looking at 'Thirteen Ways of Looking at a Blackbird'." *CP* 3,i:61–65.

8231. Hashiguchi, Minoru. "Wallace Stevens Oboegaki." *EigoS* 115(1969):146–48. [Notes on WS.]

8232. Hines, Thomas J. "'The Outlines of Being and Its Expressings':Husserl, Heidegger, and the Later Poetry of Wallace Stevens." *DAI* 31:1278A–79A(Ore.).

8233. Huguelet, Theodore L. *Checklist of Wallace Stevens.* (Merrill Checklists.) Columbus, Ohio: Charles E. Merrill.

8234. Huston, J. Dennis. "*Credences of Summer*:An Analysis." *MP* 67:263–72.

8235. McGrory, Kathleen. "Wallace Stevens as Romantic Rebel." *ConnR* 4,i:59–64.

8236. Morse, Samuel F. *Wallace Stevens:Poetry as Life.* New York: Pegasus.

8237. Mulqueen, James E. "A Reading of Wallace Stevens' *The Comedian as the Letter C*'." *CimR* 13:35–42.

* 8238. —— "Wallace Stevens:Radical Transcendentalist." *MQ* 11:329–40.

8239. Nilsen, Helge Normann. "The Quest for Reality:A Study in the Poetry of Wallace Stevens." [F 66]:219–98.

8240. Powell, Grosvenor E. "Wallace Stevens and the Pressures of Reality." [F 57]:32–49.

8241. Ransom, James C. "The Anecdotal Imagination:A Study of Wallace Stevens' *Harmonium*." *DAI* 31:1288A(Yale).

8242. Schleiner, Louise. "The Angel and the Necessary Angel:Formalist Readings of Rilke and Stevens." *LWU* 2(1969):215–37.

8243. Stoenescu, Ştefan. "Wallace Stevens şi reactivarea poetică a umanului." *SXX* 12,ix(1969):149–55.

8244. *Wallace Stevens Newsl.* 1,ii. [Marjorie Buhr, "When Half-Gods Go:Stevens' Spiritual Odyssey," 9–11; Edwin Honig, "Meeting Wallace Stevens," 11–12.]

8245. Whitaker, Thomas R. "On Speaking Humanly." [F 38]:67–88. [The meaning for S of the act of speech.]

8246. Yeargers, Marilyn M. "Poesis:The Theme of Poetry-Making in the Poetry of Wallace Stevens and Paul Valéry." *DAI* 31:1298A(Mich. State).

See also 866, 1457, 3927, 4879, 7037.

Still. 8247. Wing, Fred E. "James Still:An Inquiry Into the Intrinsic Value of the Works of a Regional Writer." *DAI* 30:4467A–68A(Colo. State).

Stone. 8248. Moore, L. Hugh. "The Undersea World of Robert Stone." *Crit* 11,iii(1969):43–56.

Straight. *See* 7656.

Strong. 8249. Liebmann, William B. "Austin Strong—Playwright, Artist, Seaman." *CLC* 19,ii:13–24.

Stuart, J. 8250. Foster, Ruel E. "Jesse Stuart's W-Hollow:Microcosm of the Appalachians." *KanQ* 2,ii:66–72.

8251. LeMaster, J.R. "Jesse Stuart:The Man and His Poetry." *ABC* 20,viii:13–19.

8252. Woodbridge, Hensley C. "Jesse and Jane Stuart:A Bibliography—Supplement 3." *Jack London Newsl.* 3:65–69.

8253. —— "Jesse Stuart:A Bibliographical Note." *LauR* 10,i:8–15.

See also 7857.

Styron. 8254. Bell, Bernard W. "The Confessions of Styron." *AmD* 5,i(1968):3–7.

* 8255. Core, George. "*The Confessions of Nat Turner* and the Burden of the Past." *SLJ* 2,ii:117–34.

8256. Friedman, Melvin J., and Irving Malin,eds. *William Styron's The Confessions of Nat Turner:A Critical Handbook.* Belmont, Calif.: Wadsworth. [Rptd. revs. and crit. plus Roy A. Swanson, "William Styron's Clown Show," 149–64; Karl Malkoff, "William Styron's *Divine Comedy*," 164–75; Jackson R. Bryer and Marc Newman, "William Styron:A Bibliography," 258–80.]

8257. Luttrell, William. "Tragic and Comic Modes in Twentieth Century American Literature:William Styron and Joseph Heller." *DAI* 30(1969):2537A(Bowling Green).

8258. Marres, René. "Fictie versus werkelijkheid." *Raam* 64:35–40.

8259. Morse, J. Mitchell. "Social Relevance, Literary Judgment, and the New Right:Or, The Inadvertent Confessions of William Styron." *CE* 30(1969):605–16.

8260. Ratner, Marc L. "The Rebel Purged:Styron's *The Long March*." *ArlQ* 2,ii(1969):27–42.

8261. Suyama, Shizuo. "Styron no *The Confessions of Nat*

Turner." *EigoS* 114(1968):525. [S and *The Confessions*; in Jap.]

8262. Swanson, William J. "Religious Implications in *The Confessions of Nat Turner*." *CimR* 12:57–66.

8263. Tragle, Henry I. "Styron and His Sources." *MR* 11:134–53.

8264. Wiemann, Renate. "William Styron:*Lie Down in Darkness*." *NS* 19:321–32.

See also 7368.

Tate. *8265. Davis, Robert M. "The Anthologist:Editor vs. Compiler." *PBSA* 63(1969):321–23.

8266. Smith, Mason E. "The Storyteller as Hero:Allen Tate's 'The Fathers'." [F 47]:227–40.

8267. Squires, Radcliffe. "Allen Tate's *The Fathers*." *VQR* 46:629–49.

8268. —— "Will and Vision:Allen Tate's *Terza Rima* Poems." *SR* 78:543–62.

8269. Uhlman, Thompson. "Tate's 'Death of Little Boys'." *Expl* 28:Item 58.

Teasdale. *See* 6870.

Thurber. 8270. Black, Stephen A. *James Thurber:His Masquerades.* The Hague: Mouton.

8271. Numasawa, Koji. "Everyman/Schlemiel." *EigoS* 114(1968):516–17. [From Thurber's Mr. Mitty to Friedman's Mr. Stern.]

8272. Tobias, Richard C. *The Art of James Thurber.* Athens: Ohio U.P., 1969.

Thurman, W. 8273. West, Dorothy. "Elephant's Dance:A Memoir of Wallace Thurman." *BlackW* 20,i:77–85.

Toklas. *See* 7741.

Tolson. *8274. Flasch, Joy. "Humor and Satire in the Poetry of M.B. Tolson." *SNL* 7(1969):29–36.

8275. Tolson, M.B. *Harlem Gallery.* Introd. Karl Shapiro. New York: Collier, 1969.

8276. —— *Libretto for the Republic of Liberia.* Pref. Allen Tate. New York: Collier. [Repr.]

Toomer. 8277. Ackley, Donald G. "Theme and Vision in Jean Toomer's *Cane*." *SBL* 1,i:45–65.

8278. Mason, Clifford. "Jean Toomer's Black Authenticity." *BlackW* 20,i:70–76.

8279. McKeever, Benjamin F. "*Cane* as Blues." *NALF* 4:61–63.

Torrence. *See* 7708.

Transition. 8280. McMillan, Dougald,III. "*Transition*:A Critical and Historical Account." *DAI* 30:3017A–18A(Northwestern).

Traven, B. 8281. Braybrooke, Neville. "The Hero Without a Name." *QQ* 76(1969):312–18.

8282. Irsfeld, John H. "The American as a Symbol of the Conflict Between Industry and Nature in the First Five Novels of B. Traven." *DAI* 30:3011A(Texas, Austin).

8283. Warner, John M. "Tragic Vision in B. Traven's 'The Night Visitor'." *SSF* 7:377–84.

Turner. 8284. Turner, G.K. *Hagar's Hoard.* Introd. John Duffy. Lexington: U.P. of Ky.

Updike. 8285. Hamilton, Alice and Kenneth. *The Elements of John Updike.* Grand Rapids, Mich.: William B. Eerdmans. [Crit.]

8286. —— "Theme and Technique in John Updike's *Midpoint*." *Mosaic* 4,i:79–106.

8287. Petillon, Pierre-Yves. "Le désespoir de John Updike." *Critique* 25(1969):972–77.

8288. Reising, R.W. "Updike's 'A Sense of Shelter'." *SSF* 7:651–52.

8289. Seelbach, Wilhelm. "Die antike Mythologie in John Updikes Roman *The Centaur*." *Arcadia* 5:176–94.

See also 1452, 7367, 7894.

Van Doren. 8290. Young, Marguerite. "Mark Van Doren:A Poet in an Age of Defoliation." *Voyages*(Wash., D.C.) 3,i–ii:60–62.

Van Vechten. 8291. Coleman, Leon D. "The Contribution of Carl Van Vechten to the Negro Renaissance:1920–1930." *DAI* 30:3453A(Minn.).

See also 7916, 7935.

Vonnegut. 8292. Palmer, Raymond C. "Vonnegut's Major Concerns." *IEY* 14(1969):3–10.

8293. Schatt, Stanley. "The World Picture of Kurt Vonnegut,

Jr." *DAI* 31:767A(So. Calif.).

8294. Tanner, Tony. "The Uncertain Messenger:A Study of the Novels of Kurt Vonnegut,Jr." *CritQ* 11(1969):297–315.

Wallant. *8295. Ayo, Nicholas. "The Secular Heart:The Achievement of Edward Lewis Wallant." *Crit* 12,ii:86–94.

Warren, R.P. 8296. Arnavon, Cyrille. "Robert Penn Warren: Interprète de l'histoire américaine." *Europe* 494:205–26.

8297. Burt, David J. and Annette C. "Robert Penn Warren's Debt to Ibsen in *Night Rider*." *MissQ* 22(1969):359–61.

8298. Chambers, Robert H. "Robert Penn Warren:His Growth as a Writer." *DAI* 31:381A–82A(Brown).

8299. Core, George. "In the Heart's Ambiguity:Robert Penn Warren as Poet." *MissQ* 22(1969):313–26.

8300. Dooley, Dennis M. "This Collocation of Memories:The Poetic Strategy of Robert Penn Warren." *DAI* 31:1268A–69A(Vanderbilt).

8301. Goldfarb, Russell M. "Robert P. Warren's Tollivers and George Eliot's Tullivers." *UR* 36:209–13.

8302. Meckier, Jerome. "Burden's Complaint:The Disintegrated Personality as Theme and Style in Robert Penn Warren's *All the King's Men*." *SNNTS* 2,i:7–21.

8303. Moore, L. Hugh,Jr. *Robert Penn Warren and History: "The Big Myth We Live."* (SAmL 21.) The Hague: Mouton.

8304. Shepherd, Allen. "Robert Penn Warren as a Philosophical Novelist." *WHR* 24:157–68.

8305. —— "Robert Penn Warren's 'Prime Leaf' as Prototype of *Night Rider*." *SSF* 7:469–71.

8306. Spears, Monroe K. "The Latest Poetry of Robert Penn Warren." *SR* 78:348–57. [Rev. art.]

8307. Strout, Cushing. "*All the King's Men* and the Shadow of William James." *SoR* 6:920–34.

* 8308. Sullivan, Walter. "The Historical Novelist and the Existential Peril:Robert Penn Warren's *Band of Angels*." *SLJ* 2,ii:104–16.

8309. Woods, Linda L. "The Language of Robert Penn Warren's Poetry." *DAI* 30(1969):2049A(Emory).

See also 4370, 4986.

Waters. 8310. Milton, John R. "The Land as Form in Frank Waters and William Eastlake." *KanQ* 2,ii:104–09.

Welty. 8311. Brown, Ashley. "Eudora Welty and the Mythos of Summer." *Shenandoah* 20,iii(1969):29–35.

8312. Burger, Nash K. "Eudora Welty's Jackson." *Shenandoah* 20,iii(1969):8–15.

8313. Davis, Charles E. "Eudora Welty's Art of Naming." *DAI* 30:4446A–47A(Emory).

* 8314. Gossett, Louise Y. "Eudora Welty's New Novel:The Comedy of Loss." *SLJ* 3,i:122–37. [Rev. art.]

8315. Heilman, R.B. "Salesmen's Deaths:Documentary and Myth." *Shenandoah* 20,iii(1969):20–28.

8316. Howell, Elmo. "Eudora Welty's Comedy of Manners." *SAQ* 69:[469]–79.

8317. —— "Eudora Welty's Negroes:A Note on 'A Worn Path'." *XUS* 9,i:28–32.

8318. Jones, Alun R. "A Frail Travelling Coincidence:Three Later Stories of Eudora Welty." *Shenandoah* 20,iii(1969):40–53.

8319. McDonald, W.U.,Jr. "Eudora Welty's Revisions of 'A Piece of News'." *SSF* 7:232–47.

* 8320. —— "Welty's 'Social Consciousness':Revisions of 'The Whistle'." *MFS* 16:193–98.

8321. Oates, Joyce C. "The Art of Eudora Welty." *Shenandoah* 20,iii(1969):54–57.

8322. Prenshaw, Peggy J.W. "A Study of Setting in the Fiction of Eudora Welty." *DAI* 31:1810A(Texas, Austin).

8323. Price, Reynolds. "The Onlooker, Smiling:An Early Reading of *The Optimist's Daughter*." *Shenandoah* 20,iii(1969):58–73.

8324. Russell, Diarmuid. "First Work." *Shenandoah* 20,iii(1969):16–19.

West, N. 8325. Brand, John M. "Fiction as Decreation:The Novels of Nathanael West." *DAI* 30:3449A(Texas Christian).

8326. Martin, Jay. *Nathanael West:The Art of His Life.* New York: Farrar, Straus and Giroux. [Biog.]

8327. Zlotnick, Joan C. "Nathanael West:A Study of the Paradox of Art." *DAI* 30:3482A–83A(N.Y.U.).

Wescott. 8328. Stegner, Wallace. "Rediscovery:Wescott's

Goodbye Wisconsin." *SoR* 6:674–81.

Wharton. 8329. Anderson, Hilton. "Edith Wharton as Fictional Heroine." *SAQ* 69:[118]–23.

8330. Baril, James R. "Vision as Metaphorical Perception in the Fiction of Edith Wharton." *DAI* 31:1258A(Colo.).

8331. Bretschneider, Margaret A. "Edith Wharton:Patterns of Rejection and Denial." *DAI* 30:3935A–36A(Case Western Reserve).

8332. Jones, Ann M. "Three American Responses to World War I:Wharton, Empey, and Bourne." *DAI* 31:1802A(Wis.)

* 8333. McDowell, Margaret B. "Edith Wharton's Ghost Stories." *Criticism* 12:133–52.

* 8334. Winner, Viola H. "Convention and Prediction in Edith Wharton's *Fast and Loose*." *AL* 42:[50]–69.

See also 5088.

Wheelock. 8335. Taylor, Henry. "Letting the Darkness in:The Poetic Achievement of John Hall Wheelock." *HC* 7,v:1–15

White, E.B. 8336. Sampson, Edward C. "Fiction or Friction?" *CLJ* 2(1967):78–80. [Textual problem in 'Farewell, My Lovely!']

White, W.A. 8337. White, W.A. *A Certain Rich Man.* Introd John D. Hicks. Lexington: U.P. of Ky.

Wilbur. 8338. Amabile, George N. "Homo Fecit:Four Essays on the Poetry of Richard Wilbur." *DAI* 31:1257A(Conn.).

8339. Boyers, Robert. "On Richard Wilbur." *Salmagundi* 12:76–82.

8340. Cummins, Paul. "*Walking to Sleep* by Richard Wilbur." *CP* 3,i:72–76. [Rev. art.]

8341. Mattfield, Mary S. "Some Poems of Richard Wilbur." *BSUF* 11,iii:10–24.

8342. —— "Wilbur's 'The Puritans'." *Expl* 28:Item 53.

* 8343. Miller, Stephen. "The Poetry of Richard Wilbur." *Spiri* 37,iii:30–35.

8344. Pate, Willard,ed. "Interview with Richard Wilbur." *SCR* 3,i:5–23.

Wilder. 8345. Littmann, Mark E. "Theme and Structure in Thornton Wilder's Drama." *DAI* 30:3015A(Northwestern).

8346. Mickel, Liselotte. "Thornton Wilder und der amerikanische Optimismus." *FH* 24(1969):875–82.

8347. Viswanatham, K. "The Bridge That Wilder Built." *Triveni* 38,ii(1969):9–16.

Williams, T. 8348. Blackwell, Louise. "Tennessee Williams and the Predicament of Women." *SAB* 35,ii:9–14.

* 8349. Blitgen, Sister M. Carol,B.V.M. "Tennessee Williams: Modern Idolator." *Renascence* 22:192–97.

8350. Fritscher, John J. "Some Attitudes and a Posture: Religious Metaphor and Ritual in Tennessee Williams' Query of the American God." *MD* 13:201–15.

8351. Howell, Elmo. "The Function of Gentlemen Callers:A Note on Tennessee Williams' *The Glass Menagerie*." *NMW* 2:83–90.

8352. Ishida, Akira. "Tennessee Williams' 'Slapstick Tragedy'." [F 1]:439–65. [In Jap.]

8353. Kalson, Albert E. "Tennessee Williams' *Kingdom of Earth*:A Sterile Promontory." *D&T* 8:90–93.

8354. Presley, Delma E. "The Theological Dimension of Tennessee Williams:A Study of Eight Major Plays." *DAI* 30(1969):2038A(Emory).

8355. Presley, Delma E., and Hari Singh. "Epigraphs to the Plays of Tennessee Williams." *NMW* 3:2–12.

8356. Starnes, Leland. "The Grotesque Children of *The Rose Tattoo*." *MD* 12:357–69.

8357. Steen, Mike. *A Look at Tennessee Williams.* New York: Hawthorn, 1969. [Interviews with W's friends.]

Williams, W.C. 8358. Engels, John. *Checklist of William Carlos Williams.* (Merrill Checklists.) Columbus, Ohio: Charles E Merrill, 1969.

8359. —— *Guide to William Carlos Williams.* (Merrill Guides.) Columbus, Ohio: Charles E. Merrill, 1969.

8360. Haya, Kenichi. "W.C. Williams—Hitei no Seishin." *Oberon* 22:59–68. [W—spirit of negation.]

8361. Holton, Milne. "To Hit Love Aslant:Poetry and William Carlos Williams." [F 57]:50–69.

8362. Jacobs, Willis D. "Williams' 'Between Walls'." *Expl* 28:Item 68.

8363. —— "Williams' 'Great Mullen'." *Expl* 28:Item 63

8364. —— "Williams' 'The Young Housewife'." *Expl* 28:Item 81.

* 8365. —— "Williams' 'To Waken an Old Lady'." *Expl* 29:Item 6.

* 8366. LeClair, Thomas. "The Poet as Dog in *Paterson*." *TCL* 16:97–108.

8367. Levin, Harry. "William Carlos Williams and the Old World." *YR* 59:520–31.

8368. McAlice, Edward F. "The Conflict of Romantic and Naturalistic Ideas in the Poetry of William Carlos Williams." *DAI* 31:362A–63A(Brown).

8369. Miller, J. Hillis. "Williams' *Spring and All* and the Progress of Poetry." *Dædalus* 99:405–34.

* 8370. Myers, Neil. "Williams' Imitation of Nature in 'The Desert Music'." *Criticism* 12:38–50.

8371. Otten, Terry. "William Carlos Williams' 'Red Wheelbarrow'." *HussR* 2(1969):117–18.

8372. Paul, Sherman. "A Sketchbook of the Artist in His Thirty-Fourth Year:William Carlos Williams' *Kora in Hell: Improvisations*." [F 60]:21–44.

8373. Ranta, Jerrald L. "William Carlos Williams' Prosody to 1940." *DAI* 31:400A–01A(Kent State).

8374. Riddel, Joseph N. "The Wanderer and the Dance: William Carlos Williams' Early Poetics." [F 60]:45–71.

8375. Sweeney, Richard M. " 'Editur Ez' and 'Old Hugger-Scrunch':The Influence of Ezra Pound on the Poems of William Carlos Williams." *DAI* 31:404A–05A(Brown).

8376. Thirlwall, John C. "William Carlos Williams and John C. Thirlwall:Record of a Ten-Year Relationship." *YULG* 45:15–21.

* 8377. Wagner, Linda W. "*Spring and All*:The Unity of Design." *TSL* 15:61–73.

8378. —— "Williams' Search:'To Have a Country'." *Criticism* 12:226–38.

8379. Willard, Nancy. *Testimony of the Invisible Man:William Carlos Williams, Francis Ponge, Rainer Maria Rilke, Pablo Neruda.* Columbia: U. of Mo. P.
See also 6859, 7471.

Willingham. 8380. Parr, J.L. "Calder Willingham:The Forgotten Novelist." *Crit* 11,iii(1969):57–65.

Wilson, E. 8381. Dabney, Lewis M. "Edmund Wilson:*Axel's Castle* to *Patriotic Gore*." [F 57]:70–85.

8382. Dayananda, James Y. "Marxist Contribution to Edmund Wilson's Literary Criticism." *DAI* 30(1969):2524A(Temple).

8383. Frank, Charles P. *Edmund Wilson.* (TUSAS 152.) New York: Twayne. [Crit.]

Winslow. 8384. White, Helen, and Redding S. Sugg,Jr. "Lady Into Artist:The Literary Achievement of Anne Goodwin Winslow." *MissQ* 22(1969):289–302.

Winters. *8385. Fraser, John. "Yvor Winters:The Perils of Mind." *CentR* 14:396–420.

Wister. *8386. Simms, L. Moody,Jr. "*Lady Baltimore*:Owen Wister and the Southern Race Question." *Serif* 7,ii:23–26.
See also 7788.

Wolfe, T. 8387. Boyle, Thomas E. "Frederick Jackson Turner and Thomas Wolfe:The Frontier as History and Literature." *WAL* 4:273–85.

8388. Field, Leslie A. "Thomas Wolfe and the Kicking Season Again." *SAQ* 69:[364]–72.

8389. Holman, C. Hugh. "Focus on Thomas Wolfe's *You Can't Go Home Again*:Agrarian Dream and Industrial Nightmare." [F 63]:149–57.

8390. Huntley, Reid D. "Thomas Wolfe's Idea of the Imagination:Similarities to the Views of the Nineteenth Century English Romantic Poets and Critics." *DAI* 31:390A(N.C., Chapel Hill).

8391. Johnson, Elmer D. *Thomas Wolfe:A Checklist.* (Serif Ser. of Bibliogs. and Checklists 12.) Kent, Ohio: Kent State U.P.

8392. Kennedy, Richard S., and Paschal Reeves,eds. *The Notebooks of Thomas Wolfe.* 2 vols. With Introd. Chapel Hill: U. of N.C. Press.

8393. Martelle, Gordon A. "Thomas Wolfe's Conception of the American Character." *DAI* 31:1806A(Neb.).

8394. Plunkett, James T. "The Quest for a Father-God in the Fiction of Thomas Wolfe." *DAI* 31:399A(Minn.).

8395. Reeves, Paschal. *Checklist of Thomas Wolfe.* (Merrill Checklists.) Columbus, Ohio: Charles E. Merrill.

8396. —— "The Second Homeland of His Spirit:Germany in the Fiction of Thomas Wolfe." [F 62]:53–60.

8397. Reeves. Paschal,ed. *Studies in* Look Homeward, Angel. (Merrill Studies.) With Pref. Columbus, Ohio: Charles E. Merrill. [Rptd. crit.]

8398. Ryan, Pat M.,ed. *The Mountains.* With Introd. Chapel Hill: U. of N.C. Press.

* 8399. Skipp, Francis E. "*Of Time and the River*:The Final Editing." *PBSA* 64:313–22.

8400. Wank, Martin. "Thomas Wolfe:Two More Decades of Criticism." *SAQ* 69:[244]–56.

Wouk. 8401. Hudson, William S. "Herman Wouk:A Biographical and Critical Study." *DAI* 30:4987A(Geo. Peabody Coll. for Teachers).

Wright, C. *8402. Sedlack, Robert P. "Jousting with Rats: Charles Wright's *The Wig*." *SNL* 7(1969):37–39.

Wright, J. *See* 7380.

Wright, R. 8403. Brignano, Russell C. *Richard Wright:An Introduction to the Man and His Works.* Pittsburgh: U. of Pittsburgh P.

8404. Brown, Lloyd W. "Stereotypes in Black and White:The Nature of Perception in Wright's *Native Son*." *BARev* 1,iii:35–44.

* 8405. Gibson, Donald B. "Wright's Invisible Native Son." *AQ* 21(1969):[728]–38.

8406. Goede, William. "On Lower Frequencies:The Buried Men in Wright and Ellison." *MFS* 15(1969):483–501.

8407. Meyer, Shirley. "The Identity of 'The Man Who Lived Underground'." *NALF* 4:52–55.

8408. Mitra, B.K. "The Wright-Baldwin Controversy." *IJAS* 1,i(1969):101–05.

8409. Reed, Kenneth T. "*Native Son*:An American *Crime and Punishment*." *SBL* 1,ii:33–34.

8410. Ridenour, Ronald. " 'The Man Who Lived Underground':A Critique." *Phylon* 31:54–57.

8411. Rubin, Steven J. "Richard Wright and Ralph Ellison: Black Existential Attitudes." *DAI* 30(1969):2041A(Mich.).

8412. *SBL* 1,iii. Spec. No. on Richard Wright. [James A. Emanuel, "Lines for Richard Wright," 2; Michel Fabre, "Impressions of Richard Wright:An Interview with Simone DeBeauvoir," 3–5; Michel Fabre, "A Letter from Dorothy Padmore," 5–9; Michel Fabre, "The Poetry of Richard Wright," 10–22; Raman K. Singh, "Wright's Tragic Vision in 'The Outsider'," 23–27.]

8413. Williams, John A. *The Most Native of Sons:A Biography of Richard Wright.* Garden City, N.Y.: Doubleday.
See also 1440, 7539.

Wylie, E. 8414. Gray, Thomas A. *Elinor Wylie.* (TUSAS 165.) New York: Twayne, 1969. [Crit.]

8415. Helmick, Evelyn T. "Elinor Wylie:The Woman in Her Work." *DAI* 30:3459A–60A(U. of Miami).

Zukofsky. 8416. Spann, Marcella J. "An Analytical and Descriptive Catalogue of the Manuscripts and Letters in the Louis Zukofsky Collection at the University of Texas at Austin." *DAI* 30:5459A(Texas, Austin).

MEDIEVAL AND NEO-LATIN LITERATURE†

I. GENERAL

Bibliography. 8417. Benzing, J. *Die Frühdrucke der Hofbibliothek Aschaffenburg bis zum Jahre 1550.* (Veröffentlichen d. Geschichts- und Kunstvereins Aschaffenburg 11.) Aschaffenburg: Pattlock, 1968.

8418. Dotto, A.M. "Gli incunaboli del 'Fondo Monreale' della Biblioteca nazionale di Palermo." *Bibliofilia* 71(1969): 205–21.

8419. Rodriguez, I. "Autores espirituales españoles en la edad media." *Repert. de Historia de las Ciencias ecles. en España* 1(1967):175–351.

8420. Sajo, Geza, and Erzsebry Soltesz,eds. *Catalogus incunabulorum quae in bibliothecis publicis Hungariae asservantur, I. II.* Budapest: Hung. Acad. of Sciences.

8421. Ypma, E. "Les auteurs augustins français:Liste de leurs noms et de leurs ouvrages." *Augustiniana* 19(1969):487–531. *See also* 459, 8901, 8936, 9061, 9069.

General and Miscellaneous. 8422. Alberigo, Giuseppe. *Cardinalato e collegialità:Studi sull'ecclesiologia tra l'XI e il XIV secolo.* (Ist. per le Scienze Religiose di Bologna, Testi e ricerche di Scienze Religiose 5.) Florence: Vallecchi, 1969.

8423. Baker, Dom Aelred. "Early Syriac Asceticism." *DownR* 88:393–409.

8424. Barley, M.W., and R.P.C. Hanson,eds. *Christianity in Britain, 300–700.* Leicester: Leicester U.P.; New York: Humanities, 1968.

8425. Bataillon, L.-J. "Bulletin d'histoire des doctrines médiévales:La période scolastique (XIIIᵉ-XVᵉ s.)." *RSPT* 53(1969): 707–43.

8426. Bäuml, Franz H. *Medieval Civilization in Germany, 800–1273.* (Ancient Peoples and Places 67.) New York: Praeger, 1969.

8427. Biffi, I. "Aspetti dell'imitazione di Cristo nella letteratura monastica del secolo XII." *La Scuola Cattolica* 96(1968):451–90.

8428. Bigg, C. *The Christian Platonists of Alexandria.* London: Oxford U.P., 1968.

8429. Bishop, M. *The Horizon Book of the Middle Ages.* London: Cassell, 1969.

8430. Bowers, R.H. "A Twelfth Century Battle of the Books." *AnM* 11:65–73.

8431. Brooke, Christopher. *The Twelfth Century Renaissance.* (Hist. of Eur. Civilization Lib.) New York: Harcourt, Brace and World, 1969.

8432. Cantor, Norman F., and Peter L. Klein. *Medieval Thought:Augustine and Thomas Aquinas.* (Monuments of Western Thought 2.) London: Collier-Macmillan, 1969.

8433. Catena, Claudio. *Le carmelitane, storia e spiritualità.* (Textus et Studia Historica Carmelitana 9.) Rome: Inst. Carmelitanum, 1969.

8434. Chenu, M.-D. *L'éveil de la conscience dans la civilisation médiévale.* Montréal: Inst. d'Etudes Médiévales; Paris: J. Vrin, 1969.

8435. —— "L'homme, la nature, l'esprit:Un avatar de la philosophie grecque en Occident, au XIIIᵉ siècle." *AHDLMA* 36(1969):123–30.

8436. Chydenius, Johna. *The Symbolism of Love in Medieval Thought.* (CHLSSF 44,1.) Helsinki.

8437. Congar, Y. "*Gentilis* et *Iudaeus* au moyen âge." *RTAM* 36(1969):222–25.

8438. De Rosa, Luca M. "Per una valorizzazione della via crucis." *SFran* 65(1968):365–68.

8439. Dufort, Jean-Marc. *Le Symbolisme Eucharistique aux origines de l'Eglise.* (Studia 23.) Brussels and Paris: Desclée de Brouwer, 1969.

8440. Dupille, Ch. *Les enragés du XVᵉ siècle. Les étudiants du Moyen âge.* (Chrétiens de tous les temps 31.) Paris: Eds. du Cerf, 1969.

8441. Ehrle, Franz Kardinal. *Gesammelte Aufsätze zur englischen Scholastik.* (Storia e Letteratura 50.) Introd. Franz Pelster. Rome: Ediz. di Storia e Letteratura.

8442. Ermatinger, Charles J. "Some Unstudied Sources for the History of Philosophy in the Fourteenth Century." *Manuscripta* 14:3–33.

† *Festschriften* and Other Analyzed Collections are listed in the first division of this Bibliography, and have been assigned Item numbers 1–95. "F" numbers in brackets following a title refer to these items.

8443. Fischer, Hanns. "Deutsche Literatur und lateinisches Mittelalter." [F 70]:1–19.

8444. Fontaine, Jacques. *La littérature latine Chrétienne* Paris: Presses univs.

8445. Gabriel, Astrik L. *Garlandia:Studies in the History of the Mediaeval University.* Frankfurt: Knecht; Notre Dame, Ind. Mediaeval Inst., 1969.

8446. —— *The Mediaeval Universities of Pécs and Pozsony Commemoration of the 500th and 600th Anniversary of Their Foundation:1367–1467–1967.* Notre Dame, Ind.: Mediaeval Inst. 1969; Frankfurt: J. Knecht, 1969.

8447. Gandillac, M. de, and É. Jeauneau. *Entretiens sur la renaissance du XII siècle.* (Décades du Centre Culturel Internat de Cerisy-la-Salle. 9.) Paris and La Haye: Mouton, 1968.

8448. Garin, E[ugenio]. *Moyen âge et Renaissance.* Paris Gallimard, 1969.

8449. Glockmann, Guenter. "Homer in der christlicher Apologetik des zweiten Jahrhunderts." *Orpheus* 14(1967):33–40

8450. Hillgarth, J.N. *The Conversion of Western Europe 350–750.* Englewood Cliffs, N.J.: Prentice-Hall, 1969.

8451. Hübinger, P.,ed. *Zur Frage der Periodengrenze zwischen Altertum und Mittelalter.* (Wege der Forschung 51.) Darmstadt Wissenschaftliche Buchgesellschaft, 1969.

8452. Jungmann, J.A. "Mittelalterliche Frömmigkeit:Ihr Werden unter der Nachwirkung der christologischen Kämpfe.' *Geist und Leben* 41(1968):429–43.

8453. Klinck, Roswitha. *Die lateinische Etymologie des Mittel alters.* (MÆ Philologische Studien 17.) Munich: Fink.

8454. La Roncière, Ch. M. de,et al. *L'Europe au Moyen âge, Documents expliqués, I:395–888.* (Coll. U. Sér. Hist. Médiévale. Paris: A. Colin, 1969.

8455. Le Goff, J. *La civiltà dell'Occidente medioevale.* (Le grandi civiltà.) Florence: Sansoni, 1969.

8456. Leach, A.F. *The Schools of Medieval England.* London Methuen, 1969.

8457. LeClercq, Dom Jean. "Violence and the Devotion to St Benedict in the Middle Ages." *DownR* 88:344–60. [Draws upon the *Miracles de Saint Benoît.]*

8458. Leclercq, J. "Monastic Historiography from Leo IX to Callistus II." *StM* 12:57–86.

8459. Lohse, Bernhard. *Askese und Mönchtum in der Antike und in der alten Kirche.* (Religion und Kultur der alten Mittelmeerwelt in Parallelforschungen 1.) Munich: Oldenbourg 1969.

8460. Marchi, Gian Paolo. "Sacra scrittura e tradizione classica negli scrittori latini del medioevo Veronese." *Scriptorium* 22(1968):294–300.

8461. Martins, M. "Enciclopédias medievais e divulgação filosófica." *RPFilos* 25(1969):24–37.

8462. Mehus, Lorenzo. *Historia litteraria Florentina:Ab anno 1192 usque ad annum 1439.* (Humanistische Bibliog., Reihe 2,ii. München-Allach: Fink, 1969. [Repr. of Munich ed., 1874.

8463. Miquel, P. "*Praesumere-praesumptio* dans l'ancienne littérature monastique." *RB* 79(1969):424–36.

8464. Morrison, Karl F. *Tradition and Authority in the Western Church, 300–1140.* Princeton: Princeton U.P., 1969.

8465. Nagel, D.W. *Geschichte des christlichen Gottesdienstes.* (Sammlung Göschen 1202–1202a.) Berlin: de Gruyter. [2nd. ed.]

8466. Parkes, Henry B. *The Divine Order:Western Culture in the Middle Ages and the Renaissance.* New York: Knopf, 1969.

8467. Platelle, H. "Peurs et espérance au Moyen Âge." *MSR* 26(1969):3–21.

8468. Plezia, Marian. "Quattuor stili modernorum:Ein Kapitel mittellateinischer Stillehre." [F 69]:192–210.

8469. Pretzel, Ulrich. "Beiträge zur Geschichte der mittel-lateinischen Philologie." *MitJ* 5(1968):242–69.

8470. Raasch, Juana. "The Monastic Concept of Purity of Heart and Its Sources (IV)." *StM* 11(1969):269–314; 12:7–41. [See Bibliog. for 1968, Item 11550.]

8471. Reynolds, L.D., and N.G. Wilson. *Scribes and Scholars:A Guide to the Transmission of Greek and Latin Literature.* London: Oxford U.P., 1968.

8472. Rodón, Eulalia. "Nombres de lugar en documentos latinos medievales." [F 26],I:285–91.

8473. Roth, Charles. "Du bestiaire divin au bestiaire d'amour." *EdL* Sér. 3:2(1969):199–216.

8474. Schreiner, Klaus. "Nachträge zu 'Venus' und 'Virginitas'." *MitJ* 5(1968):18–23.

8475. Sivers, P. von. *Respublica christiana. Politisches Denken des orthodoxen Christentums im Mittelalter.* (List-Hochschulreihe 1506.) Munich: List, 1969.

8476. Thouzellier, Chr. *Catharisme et valdéisme en Languedoc à la fin du XIIᵉ et au début du XIIIᵉ s. Politique pontificale. Controverses.* 2nd Ed. Louvain: Nauwelaerts; Paris: Béatrice-Nauwelaerts, 1969.

8477. Van Steenberghen, Fernand. *Filosofiá medieval.* (Biblioteca Argentina de Filosofiá.) Buenos-Aires: Club de Lectores, 1968.

8478. Vogel, Cyrille. *Le pécheur et la pénitence au Moyen âge.* (Chrétiens de tous les temps 30.) Paris: Eds. du Cerf, 1969.

8479. Volz, Carl A. *The Church of the Middle Ages:Growth and Change from 600 to 1400.* (Church in Hist. Ser.) Saint Louis, Mo., and London: Concordia.

8480. Wachinger, Burghart. "Rätsel, Frage und Allegorie im Mittelalter." [F 70]:137–60.

8481. Wippel, J.F., and A.B. Wolter. *Medieval Philosophy: From St. Augustine to Nicholas of Cusa.* London: Collier-Macmillan, 1969.

See also 1614, 1683, 8734.

Dictionaries. 8482. Bassols de Climent, M.,et al. *Glossarium mediae latinitatis Cataloniae. Voces latinas y romances documentadas en fuentes catalanas del ãno 800 al 1100. V:Clausa-confrater.* Barcelona: Escuela de filología de Barcelona, 1969.

8483. Blatt, Frans,ed. *Novum Glossarium Mediae Latinitatis ab Anno DCCC usque ad Annum MCC:Norma-Nysus.* (Union Internationale des Académies.) Copenhagen: Munksgaard, 1969.

8484. Prinz, O., and J. Schneider,eds. *Mittellateinisches Wörterbuch bis zum ausgehenden XIII. Jht.II.2* [fasc. 12]: *canicularis-casalinus.* Munich: Beck, 1969.

8485. Westerbergh, Ulla. *Glossarium till medeltidslatinet i Sverige. Glossarium mediae latinitatis Sueciae, I,2:Altineo-confinis.* (KVHAA.) Stockholm: Almqvist & Wiksell, 1969.

See also 8762.

Drama and Theater. 8486. Brennan, Malcolm M. "A Play from the Twelfth Century." *SAB* 35,ii:28–34.

8487. Stemmler, Theo. *Liturgische Feiern und geistliche Spiele:Studien zu Erscheinungsformen des Dramatischen im Mittelalter.* (Buchreihe der *Anglia* 15.) Tübingen: Niemeyer.

8488. Sticca, Sandro. *The Latin Passion Play:Its Origins and Development.* Albany: State U. of N.Y. Press.

See also 9231, 9291.

Exegesis. 8489. Affeldt, Werner. *Die weltliche Gewalt in der Paulus-Exegese. Rom.13, 1–7 in den Römerbriefkommentaren des lateinischen Kirche bis zum Ende des 13. Jahrhunderts.* (Forschungen zur Kirchen- und Dogmengeschichte 22.) Göttingen: Vandenhoeck & Ruprecht, 1969.

8490. Lohfink, N. *Exégesis bíblica y teología. La exégesis bíblica en evolución.* (Verdad e imagen 15.) Tr. J.L. Sicre. Salamanca: Ed. Sigueme, 1969.

8491. Smalley, Beryl. "An Early Twelfth-Century Commentator on the Literal Sense of Leviticus." *RTAM* 36(1969):78–99.

Hagiography. 8492. Colker, M.L. "A Gotha Codex Dealing with the Saints of Barking Abbey." *StM* 10(1968):321–74.

8493. Gaiffier, Baudouin de. "Le Culte de Sainte Lucine à Lucques." *AnBol* 88:17–21.

8494. Kunze, Karl. *Studien zur Legende der heiligen Maria Aegyptiaca im deutschen Sprachgebiet.* (PSuQ 49.) Berlin: E. Schmidt, 1969.

8495. Smith, C.I. "The Christianity of St. Patrick's Home." *DownR* 88:57–59.

8496. Straeten, Joseph van der. "Manuscrits hagiographiques de Boulogne-sur-Mer." *AnBol* 87(1969):373–86.

8497. —— "L'auteur des Vies de S. Hugues et de S. Aycadre." *AnBol* 88:63–73.

8498. Undhagen, Carl-Gustaf. "Un acrostiche en l'honneur de Sainte Brigitte de Suède." *Eranos* 67(1969):81–143.

See also 8457, 8903, 9201.

Homilies. 8499. Gatch, Milton M.,Jr. "The Eschatology of the Anglo-Saxon Homilists." *DAI* 30(1969):1133A–34A(Yale).

8500. Halkin, François. "Homélies de Bryennios dans un manuscrit de Jérusalem." *AnBol* 88:60.

8501. Saxer, V. "Un sermon médiéval sur la Madeleine: Reprise d'une homélie antique pour Pâques attribuable à Optat de Milève (✠ 392)." *RB* 80:17–50.

See also 1788, 1887, 2951.

Hymns. 8502. Kroll, J. *Die christliche Hymnodik bis zu Klemens von Alexandreia.* 2nd. Ed. Darmstadt: Wissenschaftl. Buchgesellschaft, 1968.

8503. O'Malley, Jerome F. "An Introduction to the Study of the Hymns on St. James as Literature." *Traditio* 26:255–92.

8504. Schupp, Volker. "Der Dichter des 'Modus Liebinc'." *MitJ* 5(1968):29–41.

See also 1618.

Iconography. 8505. Dobrzeniecki, T. "Le Christ affligé dans la littérature du Moyen âge." *Biuletyn Historii Sztuki* 30(1968): 279–99. [In Polish.]

8506. Hughes, R. *Heaven and Hell in Western Art.* London: Weidenfeld and Nicolson, 1968.

8507. Kirschbaum, Engelbert. *Lexikon der christlichen Ikonographie, II. F-K.* Freiburg: Herder.

8508. Onasch, K. *Die Ikonenmalerei:Grundzüge einer systematischen Darstellung.* Leipzig: Koehler & Amelang, 1968.

8509. Teisseyre, Charles. "L'iconographie médiévale des grands docteurs de l'Eglise, grecs et latins." *L'Information d'Histoire de l'Art* 14(1969):233–35.

See also 9268.

Language. 8510. Cortabarría, A. "Originalidad y significación de los *Studia linguarum* de los dominicos españoles de los siglos XIII y XIV." *Pensamiento* 25(1969):71–92.

8511. Paladini, V., and M. de Marco. *Lingua de letteratura mediolatina.* (Testi e manuali per l'insegnamento universitario del latino 7.) Bologna: Pàtron.

Liturgy. 8512. Casarsa, M. *I codici liturgici dell'abbazia di Moggio.* Undine: Ed. Arti Grafiche Friulane, 1968.

8513. Klauser, Theodor. *A Short History of the Western Liturgy.* Tr. J. Halliburton. London: Oxford U.P., 1969.

8514. Kurzeja, A. "Die Liturgie von der Karolingerzeit bis zur Tridentinischen Reform." *Archiv für Liturgiewissenschaft* 10(1968):545–65.

8515. Olivar, A. *Los manuscritos Litúrgicos de la biblioteca de Montserrat.* (Scripta et documenta 18.) Montserrat: Monastery Press, 1969.

8516. Salmon, P. *Les manuscrits liturgiques latins de la Bibliothèque Vaticane, II:Sacramentaires, épistoliers, évangéliaires, graduels, missels.* (Studi e testi 253.) Rome: Vatican Library, 1968.

See also 8543, 8792, 9114.

Manuscripts. 8517. Aubreton, Robert. "L'Archétype de la tradition planudéene de l'Anthologie Grecque." *Scriptorium* 23(1969):69–87.

8518. Becquet, Iohannes,ed. *Scriptores Ordinis Grandimontensis.* (CC Continuatio Mediaevale 8.) Turnholt: Brepols, 1968.

8519. Bischoff, Bernhard. "La miniscule caroline et le renouveau culturel sous Charlemagne." *BIIRHT* 15(1969): 333–36.

8520. Bogaert, P.-M. "Fragments de la vieille version latine du livre de Tobie." *RB* 80:166–70.

8521. Boutemy, André. "Un manuscrit rémois peu connu du British Museum:Les Evangiles d'Eller (Ms. Harley 2826)." *Scriptorium* 23(1969):24–38.

8522. Brandis, T., and H. Maehler. *Katalog der Handschriften der Staats- und Universitätsbibliothek Hamburg; Die Handschriften der Sankt-Petri-Kirche Hamburg; Die Handschriften der Sankt-Jacobi-Kirche Hamburg.* Hamburg: Hauswell, 1967.

8523. Calkins, Robert. "The Brussels Hours Re-evaluated." *Scriptorium* 24:3–26.

8524. Cresi, Domenico. "Antichi manoscritti liturgici nell'archivio della Verna." *SFran* 65(1968):425–39.

8525. D'Ancona, P., and E. Aeschlimann. *The Art of Illumination:An Anthology of Manuscripts from the 6th to the 16th Century.* London: Phaidon Press, 1969.

8527. De Poerck, Guy. "Le Ms. Paris, B.N., Lat. 1139:Etude

codicologique d'un recueil factice de pièces paraliturgiques XIᵉ–XIIIᵉ siècles." *Scriptorium* 23(1969):298–312.

8528.   Devreesse, Robert. "Les manuscrits grecs de Cervini." *Scriptorium* 22(1968):250–70.

8529.   Dhanens, E. "Le scriptorium des Hiéronymites à Gand." *Scriptorium* 23(1969):361–83.

8530.   Díaz y Díaz, Manuel C. "La circulation des manuscrits dans la Péninsule Ibérique du VIIIᵉ au XIᵉ siècle." *CCM* 12(1969):219–41.

8531.   Diez Macho, A. "Nuevos materiales para la historia de la transmisión del texto hebreo y arameo de la Biblia." *Augustinianum* 10:5–41.

8532.   Dondaine, Antoine. "Un cas majeur d'utilisation d'un argument paléographique en critique textuelle." *Scriptorium* 21(1967):261–76.

8533.   Eizenhöfer, L., and H. Knaus. *Die liturgischen Handschriften der Hessischen Landes- und Hochschulbibliothek Darmstadt.* (Die Handschriften der Hessischen Landes- u. Hochschulbibliothek Darmstadt 2.) Wiesbaden: Harrassowitz, 1968.

8534.   Etaix, R., and R. de Vregille. "Les manuscrits de Besançon, Pierre-François Chifflet et la bibliothèque Bouhier." *Scriptorium* 24:27–39.

8535.   Fornasari, M.,ed. *Collectio canonum.* (CC Continuatio Mediaevale 6.) Turnholt: Brepols, 1968.

8536.   Fransen, G. "Textes de l'école d'Orléans dans le manuscrit Urgel 2036." *Studi Senesi* 81(1969):7–26.

8537.   Gaborit-Chopin, D. *La décoration des manuscrits à Saint-Martial de Limoges et en Limousin du IXᵉ au XIIᵉ siècle.* (Mémoires et documents publiés par la Soc. de l'Ecole des Chartres 17.) Paris, Geneva: Droz, 1969.

8538.   Garand, Monique-Cécile. "Les copistes de Jean Budé (1430–1502)." *BIIRHT* 15(1969):293–332.

8539.   Gasnault, P., and J. Vezin. *Bibliothèque nationale. Catalogue général des manuscrits latins. Tables des tomes I:Nᵒˢ 1 à 1438 et II:Nᵒˢ 1439 à 2692.* Paris: Bib. Nat., 1968.

8540.   Gribomont, J. "La tradition manuscrite de S. Nil. I:La correspondance." *StM* 11(1969):231–67.

8541.   Häring, N. "Der Literaturkatalog von Affligem." *RB* 80:64–96.

8542.   Hudry-Bichelonne, Françoise. "Manuscrits de Jean Darquet à Laon et à Leyde." *Scriptorium* 22(1968):287–90.

8543.   Janini, J., and J. Serrano. *Manuscritos litúrgicos de la Biblioteca nacional. Catálogo.* Madrid: Dirección General de Archivos y Bibliotecas, 1969.

8544.   Kremer, M. *Die Handschriften der Murhardschen Bibliothek der Stadt Kassel und Landesbibliothek. II:Manuscripta iuridica.* Wiesbaden: Harrassowitz, 1969.

8545.   Krinsky, Carol H. "Seventy-Eight Vitruvius Manuscripts." *JWCI* 30(1967):36–70.

8546.   Lieftinck, G.I. "Quelques publications récentes intéressant la paléographie." *Scriptorium* 22(1968):66–73.

8547.   Lilli, Maria Clara di Franco. *La biblioteca manoscritta di Celso Cittadini.* (Studi e testi 259.) Vatican City: Biblioteca Apostolica Vaticana.

8548.   Mabille, Madeleine. "Pierre de Limoges, copiste de manuscrits." *Scriptorium* 24:45–47.

8549.   Marston, Thomas E. "A Legal Manuscript of the Ninth Century." *YULG* 44:111–13.

8550.   Masai, F., and M. Wittek. *Manuscrits datés conservés en Belgique, I:819–1400.* Brussells: E. Story-Scientia, 1968.

8551.   Moreau-Maréchal, J. "La linguistique médiévale et ses témoins manuscrits." *Scriptorium* 22(1968):300–05.

8552.   Perl, Gerhard von. "Der alte Codex der *Historiae* Sallusts." *BIIRHT* 15(1969):29–38.

8553.   Ronig, F. *Die Buchmalerei des XI. und XII. Jhts. in Verdun.* Aachen: Aachener Kunstblätter, 1969.

8554.   Samaran, Ch., and R. Marichal. *Catalogue des manuscrits en écriture latine portant des indications de date, de lieu, ou de copiste, VI:Bourgogne, Centre, Sud-Est et Sud-Ouest de la France.* (Comité international de paléographie.) 2 vols. Paris: Ed. du Centre National de la Recherche Scientifique, 1968.

8555.   Santiago-Otero, H. "Manuscritos de los teólogos medievales españoles en el 'Fondo Reginense latino' de la Biblioteca Vaticana. Siglos XII–XV." *Repert. de Historia de las Ciencias ecles. en España* 1(1967):353–76.

8556.   Scarazza, Celeste. "Dal Cod. E 60 di Sarnano ai 'Fiori dei Tre Compagni'." *Laurentianum* 9(1968):100–02.

8557.   Schneider, K. "Handschriften aus dem Bayerischen Nationalmuseum jetzt in der Bayerischen Staatsbibliothek München und in der Staatsbibliothek Bamberg." *Scriptorium* 22(1968):314–23.

8558.   Unterkircher, F. *Die datierten Handschriften der Österreichischen Nationalbibliothek bis zum Jahre 1400.* (Österreichische Akad. der Wissenschaften. Katalog der datierten Handschriften in lateinischer Schrift in Österreich 1.) Wien: Böhlau, 1969.

8559.   Verbraken, P. "Les pièces inédites du manuscrit latin 1771 de la Bibliothèque Nationale de Paris." *RB* 80:51–63.

8560.   Weisheiple, James A. "Repertorium Mertonense." *MS* 31(1969):174–224.

See also 1097, 8492, 8515, 8516, 8575, 8680, 8730, 8733, 8751, 8937, 8941, 8959, 8977, 8988, 9160, 9192, 9200.

Mysticism. 8561.   Wentzlaff-Eggebert, F.-W. *Deutsche Mystik zwischen Mittelalter und Neuzeit:Einheit und Wandlung ihrer Erscheinungsformen.* 3ʳᵈ Ed. Berlin: W. de Gruyter, 1969.

Paleography. 8562.   Kirchner, Joachim. *Scriptura Latina Libraria, a saeculo primo usque ad finem medii aevi.* Munich: R. Oldenbourg.

Patristics. 8563.   Barlow, Claude W.,ed and tr. *Iberian Fathers, 2:Braulio of Saragossa, Fructuosus of Braga.* (FC 63.) Wash., D.C.: Catholic U. of Amer. P., 1969.

8564.   Barlow, Claude W.,tr. *Iberian Fathers, I:Martin of Braga, Paschasius of Dumium, Leander of Seville.* (FC 62.) Wash., D.C.: Catholic U. of Amer. P., 1969.

8565.   Barnard, L.W. "The Antecedents of Arius." *VigC* 24:172–88.

8566.   Bettenson, H. *The Early Christian Fathers:A Selection from the Writings of the Fathers from St. Clement of Rome to St. Athanasius.* London: Oxford U.P., 1969.

8567.   ——,ed. & tr. *The Later Christian Fathers:A Selection from the Writings of the Fathers from St. Cyril of Jerusalem to St. Leo the Great.* London: Oxford U.P.

8568.   Durand, G.-M. de. "'Sa génération, qui la racontera?' Is 53.8b:l'exégèse des Pères." *RSPT* 53(1969):638–57.

8569.   Liebaert, Jacques. *Les enseignements moraux des pères apostoliques.* (Recherches et Synthèses, sect. morale 4.) Gembloux: Duculot.

8570.   Molland, E. *Opuscula patristica.* (Bibl. theologica norvegica 2.) Oslo: Universitetsforlaget.

8571.   Testa, E. *Il peccato di Adamo nella Patristica (Gen. III).* (Studii Biblici Franciscani Analecta 3.) Jerusalem: Tip. dei Patri Francescani.

8572.   Voss, Bernd R. *Der Dialog in der frühchristlichen Literatur.* (Studia et Testimonia Antiqua 9.) Munich: Fink.

Poetry. 8573.   Boggess, William F. "Hermannus Alemannus' Latin Anthology of Arabic Poetry." *JAOS* 88(1969):657–70.

8574.   Dronke, Peter. *Poetic Individuality in the Middle Ages. New Departures in Poetry, 1000–1150.* Oxford: Clarendon.

8575.   Forstner, Karl. "Das mittellateinische Alexisgedicht und die zwei folgenden Gedichte im Admonter Codex 664." *MitJ* 5(1968):42–53.

8576.   Mendell, Clarence W. *Latin Poetry:Before and After.* Hamden, Conn.: Archon.

8577.   Schaller, Dieter. "Bemerkungen zu einigen Texten der mittellateinischen Liebeslyrik in P. Dronkes neuer Edition." *MitJ* 5(1968):7–17.

8578.   Schmidt, Paul G. " 'De rebus obscuris'—Eine allegorische Dichtung um 1200." *MitJ* 5(1968):181–98.

See also 8937, 9006.

Preaching. 8579.   Schneyer, J.-B. *Repertorium der lateinischen Sermones des Mittelalters, für die Zeit von 1150–1350. I:Autoren A–D.* (BGPTM 43.1.) Münster: Aschendorff, 1969.

See also 8743, 8938.

Proverbs. 8580.   Walther, Hans. *Lateinische Sprichwörter und Sentenzen des Mittelalters in alphabetischer Anordnung.* Carmina Medii Aevi Posterioris Latina, II. 6:*Register der Namen, Sachen und Wörter.* Göttingen: Vandenhoeck and Ruprecht, 1969.

Rhetoric. 8581. Georgi, Annette. *Das lateinische und deutsche Preisgedicht des Mittelalters in der Nachfolge des genus demonstrativum.* (PSuQ 48.) Berlin: Erich Schmidt, 1969.

8582. Marechal-Moreau, J. "Recherches sur la pontuation." *Scriptorium* 22(1968):56–66.

8583. Pizzorusso, V.B. "Un trattato di *Ars dictandi* dedicato ad Alfonso X." *SMV* 15(1968):9–88.

See also 8698, 8890, 9303.

Sermons. 8584. Brounts, Albert. "Un guide des sermonnaires latins médiévaux." *Scriptorium* 21(1967):296–307.

Themes. 8585. Meyer-Baer, Kathi. *Music of the Spheres and the Dance of Death:Studies in Musical Iconology.* Princeton: Princeton U.P.

8586. Schneider, Johannes. "Zum Wandel des Androklus-Motivs in der mittellateinischen Fabel- und Erzählliteratur." [F 69]:241–52.

See also 1759, 9031, 9111.

Typology. 8587. Preus, J.S. *From Shadow to Promise:Old Testament Interpretation from Augustine to the Young Luther.* Cambridge: Harvard U.P., 1969.

II. MEDIEVAL LATIN LITERATURE

Abelard. *8588. Archambault, Paul. "The Silencing of Cornelia:Heloise, Abelard, and Their Classics." *PLL* 6:3–17.

8589. Buytaert, Eligius M.,ed. *Petri Abaelardi Opera Theologica, I:Commentaria in Epistolam Pauli ad Romanos, Apologia contra Bernardum.* (CC Continuatio Mediaevale 11.) Turnholt: Brepols, 1969.

8590. —— *Petri Abaelardi Opera Theologica, II:Theologia Christiana, Theologia Scholarium.* (CC Continuatio Mediaevale 12.) Anon. *Capitula Haeresum Petri Abaelardi.* Turnholt: Brepols, 1969.

8591. Fumagalli, Maria Teresa Beonio-Brocchieri. *The Logic of Abelard.* (Synthese Hist. Lib.) 2nd. ed. Dordrecht, Netherlands: D. Reidel; New York: Humanities.

8592. Grana, Leif. *Peter Abelard:Philosophy and Christianity in the Middle Ages.* Tr. Frederick and Christine Crowley. New York: Harcourt, Brace & World.

8593. Jolivet, Jean. *Arts du langage et théologie chez Abélard.* (EPM 57.) Paris: J. Vrin, 1969.

8594. Pézard, André. "Le sceau d'or:Dante, Abélard, Saint Augustin." *SD* 45(1968):29–93.

8595. Weingart, Richard. *The Logic of Divine Love:A Critical Analysis of the Soteriology of Peter Abailard.* Oxford: Clarendon.

8596. Weinrich, Lorenz. " 'Dolorum solatium'—Text und Musik von Abaelards Planctus." *MitJ* 5(1968):59–78.

Achard of St. Victor. 8597. Chatillon, J. *Théologie, spiritualité et métaphysique dans l'œuvre oratoire d'Achard de Saint-Victor.* (Etudes de philosophie médiévale 58.) Paris: J. Vrin, 1968.

Aelfric. *See* 1560.

Aelred of Rievaulx. 8598. Hallier, Amédée. *The Monastic Theology of Aelred of Rievaulx:An Experiential Theology.* (Cistercian Studies 2.) Tr. C. Heaney. Spencer, Mass.: Cistercian Pubs., 1969.

8599. Paolini, R. "La *spiritualis amicitia* in Aelred di Rievaulx." *Aevum* 42(1968):455–73.

8600. Smith, Constance. "Aelred's Immersion." *HTR* 62(1969):429.

8601. Squire, A. *Aelred of Rievaulx.* London: S.P.C.K., 1969.

Aeneas of Gaza. 8602. Wacht, M. *Aeneas von Gaza als Apologet:Seine Kosmologie in Verhältnis zum Platonismus.* (Theophaneia 21.) Bonn: Hanstein, 1969.

Aenigmata. 8603. Glorie, Fr.,ed. *Variae collectiones aenigmatum Merovingicae aetatis, pars altera.* (CC, Ser. lat. 133A.) Turnholt: Brepols, 1968.

See also 9152.

Agobard of Lyon. 8604. Boshof, E. *Erzbishof Agobard von Lyon:Leben und Werk.* (Kölner historische Abhandlungen 17.) Köln: Böhlau, 1969.

Alan of Lille. 8605. Bertola, Ermenegildo. "Alano di Lilla, Filippo il Cancelliere ed una inedita 'quaestio' sull'immortalità dell'anima umana." *RFNS* 62:245–71.

8606. Chamberlain, David S. "Anticlaudianus, III. 412–445 and Boethius' *De musica*." *Manuscripta* 13(1969):167–69.

8607. Wetherbee, W. "The Function of Poetry in the *De planctu naturae* of Alain de Lille." *Traditio* 25(1969):87–125.

Albert the Great. 8608. Cunningham, S.B. "Albertus Magnus and the Problem of Moral Virtue." *Vivarium* 7(1969):81–119.

8609. Lamy de la Chapelle, Marie. "L'unité ontologique du Christ selon saint Albert le Grand." *RThom* 70:181–226.

8610. Ruello, F. "Deux précurseurs de Jean Duns Scot:Albert le Grand et Ulger d'Angers." [F 68],I:271–84.

8611. —— *La notion de vérité chez S. Albert le Grand et S. Thomas d'Aquin de 1243 à 1254.* Paris: Béatrice-Nauwelaerts, 1969.

8612. Schneyer, J.B. "Alberts des Grossen Augsburger Prediktzyklus über den hl. Augustinus." *RTAM* 36(1969):100–47.

8613. Stroick, C.,ed. *Alberti Magni opera omnia; 7,i:Alberti Magni, Ordinis Fratrum Praedicatorum, "De Anima."* Münster: Aschendorff, 1968.

Albertano of Brescia. *8614. Hoffman, Richard L. "A Newly Acquired Manuscript of Albertano of Brescia." *LC* 36:105–09.

Aldhelm. 8615. Marston, Thomas E. "The Earliest Manuscript of St. Aldhelm's *De Laude Virginitatis.*" *YULG* 44:204–06.

Alexander of Hales. 8616. Jarosz, Thomas J. "Sacramental Penance in Alexander of Hales' *Glossa.*" *FranS* 69(1969):302–46.

8617. Ruiz Caracheo, R. "Comparación entre las leyes morales del Antiguo y del Nuevo Testamento en las obras de Alejandro de Hales." *VyV* 26(1968):61–89.

See also 9196.

Ambrose. 8618. Beato, L. *Teologia della malattia in S. Ambrogio.* Turin: Marietti, 1968.

8619. Charles, Sister. "The Character of St. Ambrose as Revealed in His Letters." *Orpheus* 13(1966):27–49.

8620. Johanny, R. *L'Eucharistie, centre de l'histoire du salut chez S. Ambroise de Milan.* (Coll. Theologie Historique 9.) Paris: Beauchesne, 1968.

8621. Schmitz, J. "Zum Autor der Schrift *De sacramentis.*" *Zeitschrift für Katholische Theologie* 91(1969):59–69.

See also 9041.

Amphilochius. 8622. Oberg, E.,ed. *Amphilochius (episcopus Iconiensis) Iambi ad Seleucum (De recta studiorum ac vitae ratione).* (Patristische Texte und Studien 9.) Berlin: de Gruyter, 1969.

Andrew of Fleury. 8623. Bautier, R.-H., and G. Labory,eds. and trs. André de Fleury, *Vie de Gauzin, abbé de Fleury. Vita Gauzlini, abbatis Floriacensis monasterii.* (Sources d'hist. méd. 2.) Paris: Centre national de la recherche scientifique, 1969.

Anselm. 8624. Naulin, P. "Réflexions sur la portée de la preuve ontologique chez Anselme de Cantorbéry." *RMM* 74(1969):1–20.

8625. Southern, R.W., and F.S. Schmitt,eds. *Memorials of Saint Anselm.* (Auctores Britannici Medii Aevi 1.) London and New York: Oxford U.P., 1969.

8627. Stacpoole, Dom Alberic. "St. Anselm's Memorials." *DownR* 88:160–80.

8628. Torrance, Th. F. "The Ethical Implications of Anselm's *De veritate.*" *Theologische Zeitschrift* 26(1968):309–19.

See also 8740, 8812.

Apollinaris of Laodicea. 8629. Mühlenberg, E. *Apollinaris von Laodicea.* (Forschungen zur Kirchen- und Dogmengeschichte 23.) Göttingen: Vandenhoeck & Ruprecht, 1969.

Aristotle. *8630. Boggess, William F. "Aristotle's *Poetics* in the Fourteenth Century." *SP* 67:278–94.

8631. Lohr, Charles H. "Medieval Latin Aristotle Commentaries, Authors:Jacobus-Johannes Tuff." *Traditio* 26:135–216.

8632. Otte, G. "Die Aristoteleszitate in der Glosse:Beobachtungen zur philosophischen Vorbildung der Glossatoren." *Zeitschrift der Savigny-Stiftung für Rechtsgeschichte* 85(1968): 368–93.

8633. Zimmermann, A. *Ein Kommentar zur Physik des Aristoteles aus der Pariser Artistenfakultät um 1273.* (Quellen und Studien zur Geschichte der Philosophie 11.) Berlin: de Gruyter,

1968.

See also 8770, 8771, 8848, 9159, 9276.

Asinarius. 8634. Langosch, Karl. "Neue Überlieferung des 'Asinarius'." [F 69]:123–44.

Athanagoras. 8635. Barnard, L.W. "Church and Sacraments in the Works of Athanagoras." *RB* 80:138–52.

8636. Malherbe, A.J. "The Holy Spirit in Athanagoras." *JTS* 20(1969):538–42.

8637. —— "The Structure of Athenagoras, *Supplicatio pro christianis.*" *VigC* 23(1969):1–20.

Athanasius. 8638. Kannengiesser, Charles. "La date de l'Apologie d'Athanase *Contre les Païens* et *Sur l'Incarnation du Verbe.*" *RechSR* 58:383–428.

8639. Laminski, A. *Der Heilige Geist als Geist Christi und Geist der Gläubingen:Der Beitrag des Athanasios von Alexandrien zur Formulierung des trinitarischen Dogmas im IV Jht.* (Erfurter theologische Studien 23.) Leipzig: St. Benno-Verl., 1969.

8640. Meijering, E.P. *Orthodoxy and Platonism in Athanasius: Synthesis or Antithesis?* Leyden: E.J. Brill, 1968.

Augustine. 8641. Bailleux, E. "La création et le temps selon saint Augustin." *MSR* 26(1969):65–94.

8642. Bambeck, Manfred. "Spanisch und portugiesisch *querer* und die Bibelexegese Augustins." *Archiv* 207:30–35.

8643. Bavel, T. van,tr. *Augustinus. Eenheid en liefde. Preken over de eerste brief van Johannes.* Louvain: Augustijns historische Inst., 1969.

8644. Berrouard, M.-F. "S. Augustin et l'indissolubilité du mariage:Evolution de sa pensée." *RechA* 5(1968):139–55.

8645. Blázquez, Niceto. "El concepto de substancia según san Agustín:Los libros *De Trinitate.*" *Augustinus* 14(1969):305–50.

8646. Bogan, Mary I.,tr. *The Retractions.* (FC 60.) Wash., D.C.: Catholic U. of Amer. P., 1968.

8647. Bonnefoy, J. "L'idée du chrétien dans la doctrine augustinienne de la grâce." *RechA* 5(1968):41–66.

8648. Börresen, K.E. "Augustin, interprète du dogme de la résurrection:Quelques aspects de son anthropologie dualiste." *StTh* 23(1969):141–55.

8649. Brechtken, J. "Fruitio und Agape:Der Liebesgedanke bei Augustin." *Theologie und Glaube* 59(1969):446–63.

8650. Bütler, Hans Peter. "Antikes und Mittelalterliches in Augustins Villendialogen." [F 5]:103–17.

8651. Cilleruelo, L. "El concepto de *regula* en S. Agustín." *CdD* 181(1968):816–24.

8652. Courcelle, Jean and Pierre. *Iconographie de S. Augustin. Les cycles du XVᵉ siècle.* Paris: Etudes Augustiniennes, 1969.

8653. Courcelle, Pierre. "Le visage de philosophie [A propos de *Contra Academicos* II,2,5]." *REAnc* 70(1968):110–20.

8654. —— "Jugements de Rufin et de Saint Augustin sur les empereurs du IVᵉ siècle et la défaite suprème du paganisme." *REAnc* 71(1969):100–30.

8655. —— *Recherches sur les "Confessions" de S. Augustin.* Paris: E. de Boccard, 1968.

8656. Cowdrey, H.E.J. "The Dissemination of St. Augustine's Doctrine of Holy Orders During the Later Patristic Age." *JTS* 20(1969):448–81.

8657. Dassmann, E. "Überlegungen zu Augustins Vorträgen über das Johannesevangelium." *Trierer Theologische Zeitschrift* 78(1969):257–82.

8658. De Veer, Albert C. "La date des sermons I, XII et L de saint Augustin." *REA* 15(1969):241–46.

8659. Folliet, G. "Les éditions du *Contra Gaudentium* de 1505 à 1576." *CdD* 181(1968):601–13.

8660. García Montaño, Gonzalo. "La oración y la voluntad salvífica de Dios según san Agustín." *Augustinus* 14(1969): 295–304.

8661. Gentili, Domenico,tr. *Sant'Agostino, Dialoghi, I.* Rome: Citta'Nuova Editrice.

8662. Halliburton, R.J. "Fact and Fiction in the Life of St. Augustine:An Essay in Medieval Monastic History and 17th-Century Exegesis." *RechA* 5(1968):15–40.

8663. Howie, C.G. *Educational Theory and Practice in St. Augustine.* London: Routledge & K. Paul, 1969.

8664. Huftier, M. "Les yeux de la foi chez saint Augustin (I), (II)." *MSR* 25(1968):57–66,105–14.

8665. Jay, Pierre. "Saint Augustin et la doctrine du purgatoire." *RTAM* 36(1969):17–30.

8666. Lombardi, F.V.,ed. and tr. S. Augustinus Aurelius *De Magistro.* Padua: R.A.D.A.R., 1968.

8667. Lubac, Henri de. *Augustinianism and Modern Theology.* Tr. L. Sheppard. London: G. Chapman, 1969.

8668. Manferdini, T. *L'estetica religiosa in S. Agostino.* (Studi e ricerche 16.) Bologna: Zanichelli, 1969.

8669. Manrique, A. "Interpretación y utilización de la Biblia en S. Agustín." *CdD* 183(1969):157–74.

8670. —— "Nuevas aportaciones al problema de la *Regula S. Augustini*:Datación y dos destinatarios." *CdD* 181(1968):707–46.

8671. Markus, R.A. *Saeculum:History and Society in the Theology of St. Augustine.* Cambridge and New York: Cambridge U.P.

8672. Marzullo, A.,ed. and tr. *Sant'Agostino, Le confessioni.* Bologna: Zanichelli, 1968.

8673. Mayer, C.P. *Die Zeichen in der geistigen Entwicklung und in der Theologie des jungen Augustinus.* Würzburg: Augustinus-Verl., 1969.

8674. —— "Die Zeichen und die Bekehrung Augustins in den *Confessiones.*" *Augustiniana* 19(1969):5–13.

8675. Morán, J. "San Agustín y la Escolástica." *Augustinianum* 10:118–41.

8676. Mountain, M.J., and Fr. Glorie,eds. *Sancti Aurelii Augustine Opera, XVI.2:De Trinitate (Libre XIII-XV).* (CC, Ser. lat. 50A.) Turnholt: Brepols, 1968.

8677. —— *Sancti Aurelii Augustinii Opera, XVI.1:De Trinitate (Libri I-XII).* (CC, Ser. lat. 50.) Turnholt: Brepols, 1968.

8678. Mutzenbecher, Almut,ed. *Sancti Aurelii Augustini Opera, XIII.1:De diversis quaestionibus ad Simplicianum.* (CC ser. lat. 44.) Turnholt: Brepols.

8679. Newton, John T.,Jr. "Neoplatonism and Augustine's Doctrine of the Person and Work of Christ." *DAI* 30:4536A (Emory).

8680. Oberleitner, M. *Die handschriftliche Überlieferung der Werke des hl. Augustinus, I, 1:Italien. Werkverzeichnis.* Vienna: Böhlau, 1969.

8681. O'Meara, John J. "St. Augustine's Attitude to Love in the Context of His Influence on Christian Ethics." *Arethusa* 2(1969):46–60.

8682. Orlandi, T. "Sallustio e Varrone in Agostino, *De civitate Dei* I–VII." *La Parola del Passato* 118(1968):19–44.

8683. Oroz, J. "En torno a una metáfora agustiniana:*El puerto de la filosofía.*" *CdD* 181(1968):825–44.

8684. Perler, O., and J.-L. Maier. *Les voyages de S. Augustin.* Paris: Etudes augustiniennes, 1969.

8685. Pinès, S. "S. Augustin et la théorie de l'*impetus.*" *AHDLMA* 36(1969):7–21.

8686. Pizzolato, L.F. *Le "Confessioni" di S. Agostino:Da biografia a confessio.* (Saggi e ricerche. 3ᵉ sér.:Scienze filologiche e letteratura Fasc. 7.) Milan: Vita e pensiero, 1969.

8687. Prete, S[erafino]. *La città di Dio nelle lettere di Agostino.* Bologna: R. Pátron, 1968.

8688. Ramage, Carol I. "*The Confessions of St. Augustine*:The *Aeneid* Revisited." *PCP* 5:54–60.

8689. Réveillaud, M. "Le Christ-Homme, tête de l'Eglise: Etude d'ecclésiologie selon les *Enarrationes in Psalmos* d'Augustin." *RechA* 5(1968):67–94.

8690. Riga, P.J. "The Effect of God's Love on Man According to St. Augustine." *The Thomist* 32(1968):366–86.

8691. Rist, John M. "Augustine on Free Will and Predestination." *JTS* 20(1969):420–47.

8692. Sage, A[thanase]. "L'Eucharistie dans la pensée de saint Augustin." *REA* 15(1969):209–40.

8693. Sage, Athanase,tr. and comp. *La Règle de S. Àugustin.* Paris: La Vie Augustinienne, 1969.

8694. Sagüés Remón, Javier. "El educador de la fe en las obras catequéticas de san Agustín." *Augustinus* 15:35–56.

8695. —— "La Catequesis del *De agone christiano* de san Agustín." *Augustinus* 15:169–86.

8696. Sancti Aurelii Augustini. *Opera, XIII.2:De fide rerum invisibilium, Enchiridion ad Laurentium, De fide et spe et caritate, De catechizandis rudibus, Sermo ad catechumenos de symbolo,*

Sermo de disciplina Christiana, Sermo de utilitate ieiunii, Sermo de excidio urbis Romae, De haeresibus. (CC, Ser. lat. 46.) Turnholt: Brepols, 1969.

8697. Sauser, E. "Zum Bild der unselbständigen Kirche in der Theologie des hl. Augustinus." *CdD* 181(1968):747–75.

8698. Schmidt-Dengler, Wendelin. "Der rhetorische Aufbau des achten Buches der *Konfessionen* des heiligen Augustin." *REA* 15(1969):195–208.

8699. Schöpf, Alfred. *Augustinus.* Freiburg and Munich: Karl Alber.

8700. Şebu, S. "S. Augustin, prédicateur de l'unité chrétienne." *STeol* 21(1969):232–44. [In Romanian.]

8701. TeSelle, Eugene. "Nature and Grace in Augustine's Expositions of Genesis ı, 1–5." *RechA* 5(1968):95–137.

8702. —— *Augustine, the Theologian.* New York: Herder.

8703. Turrado, A. "Nuestra imagen y semejanza divina:En torno a la evolución de esta doctrina en S. Agustín." *CdD* 181(1968):776–801.

8704. Valentin, P. "Un *protréptique* conservé de l'antiquité:Le *Contra academicos* de S. Augustin." *Revue des Sciences Religieuses de l'Université de Strasbourg* 43(1969):1–26,97–117.

8705. Verheijen, L.M.J. "Contributions à une édition critique améliorée des *Confessions* de saint Augustin." *Augustiniana* 20:54–106.

8706. Vericat Núñez, José F. "La idea de creación en san Agustín." *Augustinus* 15:151–68.

8707. —— "La idea de creación según san Agustín." *Augustinus* 15:19–34.

8708. Wohlfarth, K.A. *Der metaphysische Ansatz bei Augustinus.* (Monographien z. philosophischen Forschung 60.) Meisenheim: Hain, 1969.

8709. Young, Archibald M. "Some Aspects of St. Augustine's Literary Aesthetics, Studied Chiefly in *De Doctrina Christiana.*" *HTR* 62(1969):289–99.

8710. Zum Brunn, E. *Le dilemme de l'être et du néant chez S. Augustin:Des premiers dialogues aux* Confessions. Paris: Etudes augustiniennes, 1969.

8711. Zwinggi, Anton. "Die Perikopenordnungen der Osterwoche in Hippo und die Chronologie der Predigten des hl. Augustinus." *Augustiniana* 20:5–34.

See also 3399, 5217, 8559, 8594, 8889, 9164, 9236.

Averroes. 8712. Davidson, Herbert A.,ed. *Averroes' Middle Commentary on Porphyry's Isagoge, Translated from the Hebrew and Latin Versions, and on Aristotle's Categories, Translated from the Original Arabic and the Hebrew and Latin Versions.* (Corpus Commentariorum Averroes in Aristotelem, Versio Anglica, ı, a, 1–2. Mediaeval Acad. of Amer. 79.) Cambridge, Mass.: Med. Acad. of Amer.; Berkeley & Los Angeles: U. of Calif. P., 1969.
See also 8843.

Avicenna. 8713. d'Alverny, Marie-Thèrese. "*Avicenna latinus* ıx." *AHDLMA* 36(1969):243–80. [See Bibliog. for 1969, Vol. ı, Item 8304.]

8714. Gilson, Etienne. "Avicenne en Occident au moyen âge." *AHDLMA* 36(1969):89–121.

8715. Goichon, A.M. *The Philosophy of Avicenna and Its Influence on Medieval Europe.* Tr. M.S. Khan. Delhi: Motilal Banarsidass, 1969.

8716. Verbeke, G. "L'immortalité de l'âme dans le *De anima* d'Avicenne:Une synthèse de l'aristotélisme et du néoplatonisme." *Pensamiento* 25(1969):271–90.
See also 8843.

Bacon. 8717. Bettoni, Efrem. "La teoria ilemorfica nell'interpretazione di Ruggero Bacone." *RFNS* 61(1969):666–92.
See also 8757.

Basil of Caesarea. 8718. St. Giet[sic],ed. and tr. *Basile de Césarée:Homélies sur l'Hexaeméron.* (SCh 26 bis.) Paris: Eds. du Cerf, 1968.

Basil the Great. 8719. Knorr, U.W. "Einige Bermerkungen zu vier unechten Basilius-Briefen." *Zeitschrift für Kirchengeschichte* 80(1969):375–81.

Bede. *8720. Bolton, W.F. "*Epistola Cuthberti de Obitu Bedae:*A Caveat." *M&H* N.S. 1:127–39.

8721. Bryant, W.N. "Bede of Jarrow." *Hist. Today* 19(1969):373–81.

8722. Colgrave, Bertram, and R.A. Mynors,eds. *Bede's Ecclesiastical History of the English People.* (Oxford Medieval Texts.) Oxford: Clarendon, 1969. [Lat. text.]

8723. Heidenreich, Helmut. "Beda Venerabilis in Spain." *MLN* 85:120–37.

8724. Meyvaert, Paul. "The Registrum of Gregory the Great and Bede." *RB* 80:162–66.

8725. Ross, Alan S. "A Connection Between Bede and the Anglo-Saxon Gloss to the Lindisfarne Gospels?" *JTS* 20(1969):482–94.

8726. Weber, H. "Der hl. Kirchenlehrer Beda der Ehrwurdige als Exeget." *Theologie und Glaube* 59(1969):360–65.

Benedict. 8727. Borias, A. "*Dominus* et *Deus* dans la Règle de saint Benoît." *RB* 79(1969):414–23.

8728. Colombas, G.M.,et al. *San Benito:Su vida y su regla.* 2nd Ed. Madrid: La Edit. católica, 1968.

8729. Delatte, P.,ed. *Commentaire sur la Règle de S. Benoît.* Sablé-s.-Sarthe: Abbaye de St.-Pierre de Solesmes, 1969.

8730. Engelbert, P. "Paläographische Bemerkungen zur Faksimileaúsgabe der ältesten Handschrift der *Regula Benedicti* (Oxford Bodl. Libr. Hatton 48)." *RB* 79(1969):399–413.

8731. Hickey, Philip E. "The Theology of Community in the *Rule* of St. Benedict." *ABR* 20(1969):431–71.

8732. Masai, François, and Eugène Manning. "Les états du Ch. ıᵉʳ du Maître et la fin du Prologue de la Régle Bénédictine." *Scriptorium* 23(1969):393–433.

8733. —— "Recherches sur les manuscrits et les états de la *Regula Monasteriorum* (ııı)." *Scriptorium* 22(1968):3–19.

8735. Penco, G. "S. Benedetto nel ricordo del medio evo monastico." *Benedictina* 16(1969):173–87.

8736. Turbessi, G. "*Quaerere Deum:*Variazioni pastristiche su un tema centrale della *Regula sancti Benedictii*, ıı." *Benedictina* 15(1968):181–205.

8737. Vogüé, Adalbert de. "Prayer in the Rule of Saint Benedict." *MSt* 7(1969):113–40.
See also 8457.

Bernard of Clairvaux. 8738. Farkasfalvy, Denis. "The Role of the Bible in St. Bernard's Spirituality." *ACist* 25(1969):3–13.

8739. Pennington, M. Basil. "Three Stages of Spiritual Growth According to St. Bernard." *StM* 11(1969):315–26.

8740. Steinen, W. von den. *Vom heiligen Geist des Mittelalters:Anselm von Canterbury, Bernhard von Clairvaux.* Darmstadt: Wissenschaftl. Buchgesellschaft, 1968. [Repr. of 1926 ed.]

8741. Vallery-Radot, I. *Bernard de Fontaines, abbé de Clairvaux, T. II:Le prophète de l'Occident.* Paris: Desclée, 1969.
See also 8589, 9199.

Bernardine of Siena. 8742. McAodha, Loman. "The Holy Name of Jesus in the Preaching of St. Bernardine of Siena." *FranS* 29(1969):37–65.

Berthold of Regensburg. 8743. Richter, Dieter. *Die deutsche Überlieferung der Predigten Bertholds von Regensburg: Untersuchungen zur geistlichen Literatur des Spätmittelalters.* (MTUDLM 21.) München: C.H. Beck, 1969.

Biondo. 8744. Robathan, Dorothy M. "Flavio Biondo's *Roma Instaurata.*" *M&H* N.S. 1:203–16.

Boethius. 8745. Chamberlain, David S. "Philosophy of Music in the *Consolatio* of Boethius." *Speculum* 45:80–97.

8746. Crespo, Roberto. "Jean de Meun traduttore della *Consolatio philosophia* di Boezio." *Atti dell'Accad. delle Scienze di Torino* 103(1969):65–170.

8747. del Re, Rafaello,ed. and tr. *Boethius, Philosophiae Consolatio.* Rome: Ediz. del'Ateneo, 1968.

8748. Dwyer, Richard A. "Villon's Boethius." *AnM* 11:74–80.

8749. Gegenschatz, E., and O. Gigon. *Boethius, "Trost der Philosophie." Lateinisch und deutsch.* (Bibliotek d. Alten Welt. Antike u. Christentum.) 2nd Ed. Zürich: Artemis, 1969.

8750. Gruber, J. "Die Erscheinung der Philosophie in der *Consolatio philosophiae* des Boethius." *RMP* 112(1969):166–86.

8751. Häring, Nicholas M. "Four Commentaries on the *De Consolatione Philosophiae* in MS Heiligenkreuz 130." *MS* 31(1969):287–316.

8752. Meese, Arnold. "Zur Funktion der Carmina in der *Consolatio philosophiae* des Boethius." [F 21]:332.

8753. Reiche, Rainer. "Unbekannte Boethiusglossen der Wiener Handschrift 271." *ZDA* 99:90–95.

8754. Traenkle, H. "Textkritische Bemerkungen zur *Philosophiae consolatio* des Boethius." *VigC* 22(1968):272–86.

8755. Wes, M.A. "De dood van Boëthius." *Spiegel Historiael* 4(1969):471–78.

See also 1744, 1756, 8606.

Bonaventure. 8756. Bérubé, Camille. "De la philosophie à la sagesse dans l'itinéraire bonaventurien." *CollFran* 38(1968): 257–307.

8757. —— "Le dialogue de S. Bonaventure et de Roger Bacon." *CollFran* 39(1969):59–103.

8758. Bougerol, J. Guy. "La perfection chrétienne et la structuration des trois voies de la vie spirituelle dans la pensée de saint Bonaventure." *EFran* 19(1969):397–409.

8759. —— "S. Bonaventure et la hiérarchie dionysienne." *AHDLMA* 36(1969):131–67.

8760. —— "S. Bonaventure et le Pseudo-Denys l'Aréopagite." *EFran* 18(1968):33–123.

8761. —— "Il senso del rinnovamento bonaventureano." *SFran* 65(1968):245–52.

8762. —— *Lexique saint Bonaventure.* (BBST.) Paris: Eds. franciscaines, 1969.

8763. Guillén Preckler, F. "Algunos aspectos del prólogo del *Itinerarium mentis in Deum* de S. Bonaventura." *Estudios Franciscanos* 70(1969):69–85.

8764. Hülsbusch, W. *Elemente einer Kreuzestheologie in den Spätschriften Bonaventuras.* (Themen u. Thesen d. Theologie.) Düsseldorf: Patmos, 1968.

8765. Quinn, J.F. "Caractère historique de la philosophie de S. Bonaventure." *EFran* 18(1968):127–33.

8766. Stoevesandt, H. *Die letzten Dinge in der Theologie Bonaventuras.* (Basler Studien z. historischen u. systematischen Theologie 8.) Zurich: EVZ-Verl., 1969.

8767. Van der Laan, H. *De wijsgerige grondslag van Bonaventura's theologie.* Amsterdam: Buijten and Schipperheijn, 1968.

See also 8811, 9007.

Boniface. 8768. Eckhardt, W.A. "Das Kaufunger Fragment der Bonifatius-Grammatik." *Scriptorium* 23(1969):280–97.

Braulio of Saragossa. *See* 8563.

Bruno of Segni. 8769. Rüthing, Heinrich. "Untersuchungen zum ersten Psalmkommentar Brunos von Segni." *RTAM* 36(1969):46–77.

Burley. 8770. Daly, Lowrie. "The Conclusions of Walter Burley's Commentary on the *Politics*, Books v and vi." *Manuscripta* 13(1969):142–49.

8771. Scott, F., and H. Shapiro. "Walter Burley's Commentary on Aristotle's *De motu animalium*." *Traditio* 25(1969):171–90.

Caesarius of Arles. 8772. Daly, William M. "Caesarius of Arles, a Precursor of Medieval Christendom." *Traditio* 26:1–28.

See also 1636, 8775.

Capgrave. 8773. Lucas, Peter J. "John Capgrave and the *Nova legenda Anglie*:A Survey." *Library* 25:1–10.

Carmina Burana. 8774. Northcott, Kenneth J. "Some Functions of 'Love' in the *Carmina Burana*." *DBGÜ* 6:11–25.

Cassian. 8775. Christophe, P. *Cassien et Césaire, prédicateurs de la morale monastique.* (Recherches et Synthèses, Section de morale.) Gembloux: J. Duculot, 1969.

8776. Kar, A. van der. *Johannes Cassianus, Gesprekken I-X.* Bilthoven: Nelissen, 1968.

Cassiodorus. 8777. Milde, W. *Der Bibliothekskatalog des Klosters Murbach aus dem IX. Jht. Ausgabe und Untersuchung zu Cassiodors "Institutiones."* (Euphorion. Fasc. Supp. 4.) Heidelberg: Winter, 1968.

8778. Svennung, J. "Zu Cassiodor und Jordanes." *Eranos* 67(1969):71–80.

See also 9287.

Cesarius of Heisterbach. 8779. Huygens, R.B.C. "Deux commentaires sur la séquence *Ave praeclara maris stella*." *CCCist* 20:108–69.

Chromatius of Aquileia. 8780. Lemarié, J.,ed. *Chromace d'Aquilée, Sermons I:Sermons 1–17A.* (SCh 154.) Tr. H. Tardif. Paris: Eds. du Cerf, 1969.

Claudian. 8781. Christiansen, Peder G. *The Use of Images by Claudius Claudianus.* The Hague: Mouton, 1969.

8782. Dilke, O.A. *Claudian:Poet of Declining Empire and Morals.* Leeds: Leeds U.P., 1969.

Clement of Alexandria. 8783. Bernard, J. *Die apologetische Methode bei Klemens von Alexandrien:Apologetik als Entfaltung der Theologie.* (Erfurter Theologische Studien 21.) Leipzig: St. Benno-Verl., 1968.

8784. Horn, H.-J. "Zur Motivation der allegorischen Schriftexegese bei Clemens Alexandrinus." *Hermes* 97(1969):489–96.

8785. Mees, M. *Die Zitate aus dem Neuen Testament bei Clemens von Alexandrien.* (Quaderni di 'Vetera Christianorum' 2.) Bari: Ist. di Letteratura Cristiana Antica.

Clement VI. 8786. Wrigley, John E. "Clement VI Before His Pontificate:The Early Life of Pierre Roger, 1290/91–1342." *CHR* 56:433–73.

Constantinus Africanus. *8787. Delany, Paul. "Constantinus Africanus' *De Coitu*:A Translation." *ChauR* 4:55–65.

Cuthbert. 8788. Stoltz, Linda E. "The Development of the Legend of St. Cuthbert." *DAI* 30(1969):1995A–96A(Ariz.).

Cyprian. 8789. Matellanes, A. "*Communicatio*:El contenido de la comunión eclesial en S. Cipriano." *Communio* 1(1968): 347–401.

8790. Petitmengin, P. "Le *Codex Veronensis* de saint Cyprien:Philologie et histoire de la Philologie." *RELat* 46(1968): 330–78.

8791. Sava, M.I. "L'attitude de S. Cyprien á l'ègard du problème de l'unité de l'Église et son actualité." *STeol* 21(1969): 210–19. [In Romanian.]

8792. Saxer, V. *Vie liturgique et quotidienne à Carthage vers le milieu du iiie siècle. Le témoignage de S. Cyprien et de ses contemporains d'Afrique.* (Studi di antichità cristiana 29.) Vatican City: Pont. Ist. di archeologia cristiana, 1969.

8793. Szołdrski, W.,et al.,eds. and trs. *Św. Cyprian, Listy.* Warsaw: Akad. Teologii Katolickiej, 1969. [Letters.]

Cyril of Jerusalem. 8794. McCauley, L.P., and A.A. Stephenson. *The Works of Saint Cyril of Jerusalem,I: Procatechesis. Catecheses 1–12.* (FC 61.) Wash.,D.C.: Catholic U.P., 1969.

Dares Phrygius. 8795. Roberts, Gildas,tr. *Joseph of Exeter:The Iliad of Dares Phrygius.* With Introd., Notes, and Glossary. Cape Town: A.A. Balkema.

Denys the Little. 8796. Cranenburgh, H. van,ed. *La Vie latine de S. Pachôme traduite du grec par Denys le Petit.* (Subsidia hagiographica 46.) Brussels: Soc. des Bollandistes, 1969.

Didymus. 8797. Gronewald, M. *Didymos der Blinde (Didymus Caecus):Psalmenkommentar, II.* (Papyrologische Texte u. Abhandl. 4.) Bonn: Habelt, 1968.

8798. Gronewald, M.,et al.,eds. and trs. *Didymos der Blinde. Psalmenkommentar, III:Kommentar zu Psalm 29–34.* (Papyrologische Texte und Abhandlungen 8.) Bonn: Habelt, 1969.

8799. Hagedorn, U.,et al. *Didymos der Blinde (Didymus Caecus):Kommentar zu Hiob.,III.* (Papyrologische Texte u. Abhandl. 3.) Bonn: Habelt, 1968.

Dionysius the Areopagite. *See* 8759.

Dionysius the Carthusian. 8800. Maginot, N. *Der actus humanus moralis unter dem Einfluss des Hl. Geistes nach Dionysius Carthusianŭs.* (Münchener Theolog. Studien 2: Systemat. Abt. 35.) Munich: Hueber, 1968.

Duns Scotus. 8801. Alaimo, B. "Attualità della dottrina scotistica della carità." [F 68],iii:599–615.

8802. Alluntis, F. "Demostrabilidad y demostración de la existencia de Dios según Escoto." *VyV* 26(1968):355–90.

8803. —— "Filosofiá y la existencia de Dios según Escoto." [F 68],ii:447–60.

8804. —— *Obras del doctor sutil Juan Duns Escoto:"Cuestiones cuodlibetales."* Madrid: Biblioteca de Autores Cristianos, 1968. [Biling. ed.]

8805. Balić, C. "De methodo Ioannis Duns Scoti." [F 68],i:395–422.

8806. Barth, T. "Die Notwendigkeit Gottes und seine Begründung bei Duns Scotus." [F 68],ii:409–25.

8807. Belić, M. "Aristotelis doctrina de individuo et Joannes Duns Scotus." [F 68],i:245–56.

8808. Bérubé, Camille. "Jean Duns Scot:Critique de *l'avicennisme augustinisant*." [F 68],I:207–43.

8809. —— "*Eros* et *agape* chez Duns Scot en marge d'un livre récent." *Laurentianum* 9(1968):439–49.

8810. Bettoni, E. "Duns Scoto nella scolastica del secolo XIII." [F 68],I:101–11.

8811. Bigi, V. Ch. "Il concetto di *tempo* in S. Bonaventura e in Giovanni Duns Scoto." [F 68],II:349–59.

8812. Bonansea, B.M. "Duns Scotus and St. Anselm's Ontological Argument." [F 68],II:461–75.

8813. Borak, A. "Libertà e prudenza nel pensiero di Duns Scoto." *Laurentianum* 10(1969):105–41.

8814. Borak, H. "Aspectus fundamentales platonismi in doctrina Duns Scoti." [F 68],I:113–38.

8815. Borowsky, W. "Mensch-Sein und die Dinge nach Scotus (Die Personhaftigkeit und das Nichtpersonhafte des Menschen nach Scotus)." [F 68],II:589–604.

8816. Boublik, Vl. "S. Tommaso e la dottrina di Scoto sulla predestinazione." [F 68],III:487–99.

8817. Brampton, C.K. "Scotus and the Doctrine of the *potentia Dei absoluta*." [F 68],II:567–74.

8818. Brown, St. F. "Scotus' Univocity in the Early XIVth Century." [F 68],IV:35–41.

8819. Cacciatore, G. "L'unità dell'individuo come interiorità del concreto secondo Duns Scoto." [F 68],II:199–228.

8820. Čapkun-Delić, P. "Commissio omnibus operibus Ioannis Duns Scoti critice edendis." [F 68],I:361–73.

8821. Cardaropoli, G. "Il cristocentrismo nel pensiero di Duns Scoto e di Teilhard de Chardin." [F 68],III:259–90.

8822. Chauvet, F. "La posición del escotismo en la escolástica medieval." [F 68],I:75–99.

8823. Chrysostomus a Pampilona. *De Christologia Duns Scoti. Investigatio critico-historica.* (Bibl. Pampilonensis 1.) Barcelona: Herder, 1969.

8824. Ciappi, L. "Duns Scoto e Ambrogio Caterino, O.P., difensori dell'Immacolata alla luce del Magistero." [F 68],IV:249–58.

8825. Cranny, T. "Duns Scotus and Christian Unity." [F 68],III:727–56.

8826. Cruz Hernández, M. "El avicenismo de Duns Escoto." [F 68],I:183–205.

8827. Docherty, H. "The Brockie Mss. and Duns Scotus." [F 68],I:327–60.

8828. Doyle, E. "Duns Scotus and Ecumenism." [F 68],III:633–52.

8829. Echeverría Ruiz, B. "John Duns Scotus and the Immortality of the Soul." [F 68],II:577–87.

8830. Effler, R.R. "Duns Scotus and the Necessity of First Principles of the Knowledge." [F 68],II:3–20.

8831. Eguiluz, A. "Presupuestos metafísicos de la teología de la preservación en Juan Duns Escoto." [F 68],III:385–437.

8832. Enrique del Sdo Corazón. "Juan Duns Escoto en la doctrina de los Salmanticenses sobre el motivo de la encarnación." [F 68],IV:461–515.

8833. Franchi, A. "Il *Filoque* al concilio II di Lione (1274) e il pensiero di Giovanni Duns Scoto." [F 68],III:777–85.

8834. Franic, F. "De peccato originali secundum Duns Scotum et recentiores theorias." [F 68],III:439–48.

8835. Gavran, I. "The Idea of Freedom as a Basic Concept of Human Existence According to John Duns Scotus." [F 68],II:645–69.

8836. Giacon, C. "L'intuizione dell'essere in Duns Scoto." [F 68],II:33–45.

8837. Giamberardini, G. "Due tesi scotiste nella tradizione copta:Il primato assoluto di Cristo e l'Immacolata Concezione di Maria." [F 68],III:317–84.

8838. Guimet, F. "Conformité à la droite raison et possibilité surnaturelle de la charité:Attaches traditionnelles et structures dialectiques de la doctrine scotiste." [F 68],III:539–97.

8839. Hoeres, W. "Platonismus und Gegebenheit bei Duns Scotus." [F 68],I:139–68.

8840. Jammarrone, L. "L'io psicologico di Cristo secondo la dottrina di G. Duns Scoto." [F 68],III:291–316.

8841. La Verdière, E. "Divine Worship and the Presence of Christ in the Eucharist According to Duns Scotus." [F 68],III:473–86.

8842. Lobato, A. "La metafísica cristiana de Duns Escoto." [F 68],II:71–85.

8843. Madkour, I. "Duns Scot entre Avicenne et Averroes." [F 68],I:169–82.

8844. Masson, R. "Duns Scotus According to John of St. Thomas:An Appraisal." [F 68],IV:517–34.

8845. Mellone, A. "Esaltazione di Duns Scoto nel *Paradiso* di Dante Alighieri?" [F 68],IV:83–104.

8846. Messerich, V. "The Awareness of Causal Initiative and Existential Responsibility in the Thought of Duns Scotus." [F 68],II:629–44.

8847. Messner, R.O. "Die oekumenische Bedeutung der skotischen Trinitätslehre." [F 68],III:653–726.

8848. Mignucci, M. "Le pseudo-scotiste *Quaestiones super libros Priorum analyticorum Aristotelis* e la sillogistica dello Stagirita." [F 68],IV:57–71.

8849. Miguéns, M. "Base escriturística de la doctrina de Escoto sobre el primado de Cristo." [F 68],III:105–68.

8850. North, R. "The Scotist Cosmic Christ." [F 68],III:169–217.

8851. O'Connor, E.D. "The Scientific Character of Theology According to Scotus." [F 68],III:3–50.

8852. Palacz, R. "Un manuel scotiste de la fin du XVᵉ siècle a l'université de Cracovie." [F 68],IV:185–87.

8853. Petruzzellis, N. "L'infinito nel pensiero di S. Tommaso e di G. Duns Scoto." [F 68],II:435–45.

8854. Platzeck, E.W. "De reductione analogiae ad univocationem ope conceptus scotistici relationis univocae non universalis seu relationis uni-interpretativae." [F 68],II:127–41.

8855. Poppi, A. "Il significato storico di un *Tractatus formalitatum* attribuito a Giovanni Duns Scoto." [F 68],IV:171–83.

8856. Prentice, Robert. "The Evolution of Scotus' Doctrine on the Unity and Unicity of the Supreme Nature." [F 68],II:377–408.

8857. —— "The Fundamental Metaphysics of Scotus Presumed by the *De Primo Principio* (II)." *Antonianum* 44(1969):227–308. [See Bibliog. for 1969, Vol. I, Item 8400.]

8858. Roberts, Lawrence D. "John Duns Scotus and the Concept of Human Freedom." *DAI* 31:428A(Ind.).

8859. Rosales, E. "La visión escotista y la teología moral." [F 68],III:511–23.

8860. Sagüés Azcona, P. "Apuntes para la historia del escotismo en España en el siglo XIV." [F 68],IV:3–19.

8861. Sagüés Iturralde, J.F. "Escoto y la eficacia del concurso divino ante Suárez." [F 68],IV:339–74.

8862. Scapin, P. "Il significato fondamentale della libertà divina secondo Giovanni Duns Scoto." [F 68],II:519–66.

8863. Scapin, P.,ed. *Joannes Duns Scotus. Il primo principio degli esseri.* (Universa 34.) Rome: Ediz. Paoline, 1968.

8864. Solaguren, C. "Contingencia y creación en la filosofía de Duns Escoto." [F 68],II:297–348.

8865. Stella, P.T. "La teoria ilemorfica nel sistema scotista." [F 68],II:241–95.

8866. Szabó, T. "Ioannes Duns Scotus et evolutio dogmatis Immaculatae Conceptionis." [F 68],III:449–60.

8867. Tonna, I. "The Problem of Individuation in Scotus and Other Franciscan Thinkers of Oxford in the XIIth Century." [F 68],I:257–70.

8868. Torrance, Th. F. "Intuitive and Abstractive Knowledge:From Duns Scotus to John Calvin." [F 68],IV:291–305.

8869. Traina, M. "Il fondamento metafisico della distinzione formale *ex natura rei* in Scoto." [F 68],II:143–73.

8870. —— "Aspetti fondamentali della teodicea di Scoto." *Laurentianum* 10(1969):307–28.

8871. Trapè, A. "La nozione della teologia presso Scoto e la scuola agostiniana." [F 68],IV:73–81.

8872. Van Breda, H.L. "La preuve de l'existence de Dieu dans la *Lectura*." [F 68],II:363–75.

8873. Van Steenberghen, F. "La philosophie à la veille de l'entrée en scène de Jean Duns Scot." [F 68],I:65–74.

8874. Veuthey, L. "Duns Scot et le mystère de la transsubstantiation." [F 68],III:461–71.

8875. Wetter, F. "Die Erkenntnis der Freiheit Gottes nach

Johannes Duns Scotus." [F 68],ıı:477–517.

8876. Zavalloni, R. "Personal Freedom and Scotus' Voluntarism." [F 68],ıı:687–704.

8877. Zečević, S. "Problema actuum moraliter indifferentium." [F 68],ııı:525–38.

See also 8610, 9003, 9004, 9105, 9177, 9295.

Durand of St. Porcain. 8878. Fumagalli, M.B.B. *Durando di S. Porziano. Elementi filosofici della terza redazione del "Commento alle Sentenze."* (Pub. della Facoltà di Lettere e Filosofia dell'Università di Milano 53.) Florence: "La Nuova Italia," 1969.

Eckhart. 8879. Haas, Alois M. "Zur Frage der Selbsterkenntnis bei Meister Eckhart." *Freiburger Zeitschrift f. Philosophie u. Theologie* 15(1968):190–261.

8880. Margetts, John. *Die Satzstruktur bei Meister Eckhart.* (SPGL 8.) Stuttgart: Kohlhammer, 1969.

8881. Mieth, D. *Die Einheit von "vita activa" und "vita contemplativa" in den deutschen Predigten und Traktaten Meister Eckharts und bei Johannes Tauler:Untersuchungen zur Struktur des christlichen Lebens.* (Studien z. Geschichte d. Kathol. Moraltheologie 15.) Ratisbonne: Pustet, 1969.

8882. Quint, Josef. *Meister Eckhart. Die deutschen und lateinischen Werke. Untersuchungen. Fasc. 2:Fundbericht zur handschriftlichen Überlieferung der deutschen Werke Meister Eckarts und anderer Mystiktexte.* Stuttgart: Kohlhammer, 1969.

8883. —— "Meister Eckhart:Die deutschen und lateinischen Werke herausgegeben im Auftrage der Deutschen Forschungsgemeinschaft." *JIG* 1,i(1969):152–58.

8884. Schaller, T. "Die Meister Eckhart-Forschung von der Jahrhundertwende bis zur Gegenwart." *Freiburger Zeitschrift f. Philosophie u. Theologie* 15(1968):262–316,403–26.

8885. —— "Zur Eckhart-Deutung der letzten 30 Jahre." *Freiburger Zeitschrift f. Philosophie u. Theologie* 16(1969):22–39.

8886. Schneider, Richard. "The Functional Christology of Meister Eckhart." *RTAM* 35(1968):291–322.

Eucherius of Lyon. 8887. Pricoco, S. *Per una nuova edizione del "De contemptu mundi" di Eucherio di Lione.* Turin: Bottega d'Erasmo, 1967.

Eusebius of Caesarea. 8888. Buccola, Loris A. "Eusebius and the History of the Church." *U. of Portland Rev.* 20,i(1968):25–36.

8889. O'Meara, J.J. "Porphyry's *Philosophy from Oracles* in Eusebius's *Praeparatio evangelica* and Augustine's *Dialogues of Cassiciacum.*" *RechA* 6(1969):103–39.

Faba. 8890. Campbell, A.P. "The Perfection of *Ars dictaminis* in Guido Faba." *RUO* 39(1969):315–21.

Francis of Assisi. 8891. De Aspurz, Lázaro. *"Appropriatio* et *expropriatio* in doctrina Sancti Francisci." *Laurentianum* 11:3–35.

8892. Omaechevarria, I. "Inspiración teológica en los escritos de S. Francisco." *VyV* 26(1968):227–61.

8893. Schmucki, Octavianus. "Franciscus 'Dei laudator et cultor'." *Laurentianum* 10(1969):3–36,173–215,245–82. [See Bibliog. for 1969, Vol. ı, Item 8430.]

8894. Schmucki, O[ctavianus]. *"Secretum solitudinis.* De circumstantiis externis orandi penes S. Franciscum Assisiensem." *CollFran* 39(1969):5–58.

8895. Wingene, Hilarius a. "S. Franciscus et S. Maria de Angelis." *Laurentianum* 10(1969):329–52.

Fructuosus of Braga. *See* 8563.

Fulcher of Chartres. 8896. Ryan, Frances Rita,tr. *A History of the Expedition to Jerusalem, 1095–1127.* Knoxville: U. of Tenn. P., 1969.

Geoffrey of Auxerre. 8897. Gastaldelli, F. "Una sconosciuta redazione latina della *Chanson du chevalier au cygne* nel *Commento all'Apocalisse* di Goffredo d'Auxerre(1187–1188)." *Aevum* 42(1968):491–501.

Geoffrey of Monmouth. 8898. Sterckx, Claude. " 'Princeps militiae' dans l'*Historia Regum Britanniae* de Geoffrey de Monmouth." *AnBret* 76(1969):725–30.

Geoffrey of Vinsauf. 8899. Gallo, Ernest. "Geoffrey of Vinsauf and Erasmus' *De Copia.*" *AN&Q* 9:38–39.

8900. Kelly, Douglas. "Theory of Composition in Medieval Narrative Poetry and Geoffrey of Vinsauf's *Poetria Nova.*" *MS* 31(1969):117–48.

Gerald the Welshman. *See* 9455.

Gerard of Abbeville. 8901. Glorieux, P. "Bibliothèques de Maîtres parisiens. Gérard d'Abbeville." *RTAM* 36(1969):148–83.

Gerbert of Reims. 8902. Hoffmann, Hartmut. "Die Briefsammlung Gerberts von Reims." *QFIAB* 49(1969):395–98.

Germanus of Auxerre. 8903. Gessel, Wilhelm. "Germanus von Auxerre (um 738 bis 448)—De Vita des Konstantius von Lyon als homiletische Paränese in hagiographischer Form." *RQCAK* 65:1–14.

Gerson. *8904. Ozment, Steven E. "The University and the Church:Patterns of Reform in Jean Gerson." *M&H* N.S. 1:111–26.

8905. Schmiel, D. *"Via propria" and "via mystica" in the Theology of Jean le Charlier de Gerson.* St. Louis: Oliver Slave, 1969.

Gilbert of Nogent. 8906. Benton, J.F., and C.C. Swinton Bland,eds. and trs. *Self and Society in Medieval France. The Memoirs of Guibert of Nogent (1064?–c.1125).* New York: Harper and Row.

Gilbert of Poitiers. 8907. Häring, Nicholas M. "Epitaphs and Necrologies on Bishop Gilbert II of Poitiers." *AHDLMA* 36(1969):57–87.

Gilbert of Tournai. 8908. Amsterdam, Baudoin d'. "Un traité 'De locis mundi' attribué à Guibert de Tournai, O. Min." *Laurentianum* 9(1968):205–13.

Giles of Rome. 8909. Riesco, J. "El ser metafísico en el pensamiento de Egidio Romano." *Salmanticensis* 16(1969): 563–74.

8910. Trapé, G. "L'*esse* partecipato e distinzione reale in Egidio Romano (Ipsum esse simplex, esse partecipatum compositum)." *Aquinas* 12(1969):443–68.

Giraldus Cambrensis. 8911. Richter, Michael. "Giraldus Cambrensis." *NLWJ* 16:193–252. [Pt. 3.]

Glanville. 8912. Russell, Josiah C. "Ranulf de Glanville." *Speculum* 45:69–79.

Gonsalvus Hispanus. 8913. Gracia, Jorge T. "The Doctrine of the Possible and Agent Intellects in Gonsalvus Hispanus' Question xııı." *FranS* 29(1969):5–36.

Gratian. 8914. Vetulani, A. "Autour du Décret de Gratien." *Apollinaris* 41(1968):43–58.

Gregory Nazianzen. 8915. Galavaris, George. *The Illustrations of the Liturgical Homilies of Gregory Nazianzenus.* (Studies in Manuscript Illumination 6.) Princeton, N.J.: Princeton, U.P., 1969.

8916. Memoli, A.F. "*Eloquentia* classica e *sapientia* cristiana nell'*Oratio funebris in laudem Basilii Magni* di Gregorio Nazianzeno." *Orpheus* 15(1968):33–71.

8917. Postupalski, Igor. "Grzegorz z Nazjansu." *Meander* 22(1967):44.

8918. Sykes, D.A. "The *Poemata Arcana* of Gregory Nazianzen." *JTS* 21:32–42.

8919. Tulier, A.,ed. and tr. *Grégoire de Nazianze, La Passion du Christ. Tragédie.* (SCh 149.) Paris: Eds. du Cerf, 1969.

Gregory of Nyssa. 8920. Bouchet, J.R. "Le vocabulaire de l'union et du rapport des natures chez S. Grégoire de Nysse." *RThom* 68(1968):533–82.

8921. Daniélou, J. "Chrismation prébaptismale et divinité de l'Esprit chez Grégoire de Nysse." *RechSR* 56(1968):177–98.

8922. —— "Salbung und Taufe bei Gregor von Nyssa." *Kyrios* 10:1–7.

8923. May, G. "Die Datierung der Rede *In suam ordinationem* des Gregor von Nyssa und die Verhandlungen mit den Pneumatomachen auf dem Konzil von Konstantinopel 381." *VigC* 23(1969):38–57.

8924. Parys, M. van. "Grégoire de Nysse, moine, théologien et évêque." *Seminarium* 9(1969):292–312.

8925. Staats, R[einhart]. "Die Datierung von *In suam ordinationem* des Gregor von Nyssa." *VigC* 23(1969):58–59.

8926. Wolfson, Henry A. "The Identification of *Ex Nihilo* with Emanation in Gregory of Nyssa." *HTR* 63:53–60.

Gregory of Rimini. 8927. García Lescún, E. *La teología trinitaria de Gregorio de Rimini:Contribución a la historia de la escolástica tardía.* (Fac. Teol. del Norte de España. Sede de Burgos.) Burgos: Edic. Aldecoa.

Gregory of Tours. 8928. Brehaut, Ernest,ed. and tr. *History of the Franks, by Gregory, Bishop of Tours:Selections.* New York:

Norton, 1969.

Gregory Thaumaturgus. 8929. Crouzel, H. "L'Ecole d'Origène à Césarée:Postscriptum à une édition de Grégoire le Thaumaturge." *BLE* 71:15–27.

Gregory the Great. 8930. Cremascoli, G. *S. Gregorio Magno, Omelie sui Vangeli. Regola pastorale.* (Classici d. Religioni 4.) Turin: U.T.E.T., 1968.

8931. Dagens, Claude. "La fin des temps et l'Eglise selon saint Grégoire le Grand." *RechSR* 58:273–88.

8932. Frank, S. "*Actio* und *contemplatio* bei Gregor dem Grossen." *Trierer Theologische Zeitschrift* 78(1969):283–95.

8933. Gillet, R. "S. Grégoire le Grand, pape." *Dictionnaire de Spiritualité* 6:872–910.

8934. Wasselynck, René. "La présence des Moralia de S. Grégoire le Grand dans les ouvrages de morale du XIIᵉ siècle." *RTAM* 35(1968):197–240; 36(1969):31–45.

See also 8724, 9019.

Grosseteste. 8935. Callus, D.A. *Robert Grosseteste:Scholar and Bishop.* London: Oxford U.P., 1969. [Repr.]

8936. Gieben, Servus. "Bibliographia universa Roberti Grosseteste ab an. 1473 ad an. 1969." *CollFran* 39(1969):362–418.

* 8937. Hunt, Richard W. "Verses on the Life of Robert Grosseteste." *M&H* N.S. 1:241–50.

Guerric of Igny. 8938. Pennington, M. Basil. "Guerric of Igny and His Sermons for the Feast of the Assumption." *StM* 12:87–95.

Guido delle Colonne. 8939. Norris, Frank P. "Notes on the First Castilian Translation of Guido de Colonna's *Historia Destructionis Troiae.*" *KRQ* 14(for 1967):61–70.

Harvey of Nedellec. 8940. Mannath, Joseph T. "Harvey of Nedellec's Proofs for the Existence of God:*De cognitione Primi Principii,* QQ. III–IV." *Salesianum* 31(1969):46–112.

Henry of Ghent. 8941. Macken, R. "Le *De poenitentia* d'Henri de Gand retrouvé?" *RTAM* 36(1969):184–94.

8942. Macken, S. "L'argumentation contre une éternité possible du monde chez Henri de Gand." [F 68],I:309–23.

8943. Pegis, Anton C. "A New Way to God:Henry of Ghent (II)." *MS* 31(1969):93–116.

Henry of Huntingdon. 8944. Schirmer, W.F. "Heinrich von Huntingdons *Historia Anglorum.*" *Anglia* 88:26–41.

Henry of Langenstein. 8945. Pirzio, Paolo. "Le prospettive filosofiche del Trattato di Enrico di Langenstein (1325–1397):*De Habitudine causarum.*" *RCSF* 24(1969):363–73.

Herrade of Landsberg. 8946. Heinsius, M. *Herrad von Landsberg, "Der Paradiesgarten (Hortus deliciarum)." Ein Zeugnis mittelalterlicher Kultur- und Geistesgechichte im Elsass.* Colmar: Alsatia-Verl., 1968.

Hilary of Poitiers. 8947. Doignon, Jean. "Le prologue du *De Trinitate* d'Hilaire de Poitiers et l'histoire ecclésiastique aux 17ᵉ et 18ᵉ siècles." *REA* 15(1969):185–93.

8948. Rondeau, Marie-Josèphe. "L'arrière-plan scripturaire d'Hilaire, *Hymne* II, 13–14." *RechSR* 57(1969):438–50.

Hildemar. 8949. Vogüé, Adalbert de. "Une citation de la Règle du Maître dans le Commentaire d'Hildemar." *RAM* 46:355–56.

Hippolytus. 8950. Dix, G. *The Treatise on "The Apostolic Tradition" of St. Hippolytus of Rome.* Ed. H. Chadwick. London: S.P.C.K., 1968.

8950a. Lengeling, E.J. "Hippolyt von Rom und die Wendung *extendit manus suas cum patreretur.*" *Questions Liturgiques et Paroissiales* 50(1969):141–44.

8951. Stam, J.E. *Episcopacy in the "Apostolic Tradition" of Hippolytus.* (Theologische Dissertationen 3.) Basle: F. Reinhardt, 1969.

Hrosvitha of Gandersheim. 8953. Homeyer, H[elene]. *Hrotsvithae Opera.* München: Schöningh.

8954. Sticca, Sandro. "Hrotswitha's *Dulcitius* and Christian Symbolism." *MS* 32:108–27.

Hugh of Saint-Victor. 8955. Zinn, Grover A.,Jr. "History and Contemplation:The Dimensions of the Restoration of Man in Two Treatises on the Ark of Noah by Hugh of St. Victor." *DAI* 30:3092A(Duke).

Hugh of St. Cher. 8956. Matanic, A. "La pericope di Lc. x, 38–42, spiegata da Ugo di St-Cher, primo esegeta degli ordini mendicanti (+ 1263)." *Divinitas* 13(1969):715–24.

Ignatius of Antioch. 8957. Weijenborg, Reinoud. *Les lettres d'Ignace d'Antioche:Etude de critique littéraire et de théologie.* 2 vols. Tr. Barthelemy Héroux. Leiden: Brill, 1969.

Innocent III. 8958. Howard, Donald R.,ed. *Lothario dei Segni (Pope Innocent III),* On The Misery of the Human Condition. Tr. Margaret M. Dietz. Indianapolis: Bobbs-Merrill, 1969.

* 8959. Kuttner, Stephan. "A Collection of Decretal Letters of Innocent III in Bamberg." *M&H* N.S. 1:41–56.

Irenaeus. 8960. Brox, N. "Ein vermeintliches Irenäus-Fragment." *VigC* 24:40–44.

8960a. Clerici, A.M. "Incontro tra storia biblica e storia profana in Ireneo." *Aevum* 43(1969):1–30.

8961. Farkasfalvy, D. "Theology of Scripture in St. Ireneus." *RB* 78(1968):319–32.

8962. Jossa, G. *Regno di Dio e Chiesa. Ricerche sulla concezione escatologica ed ecclesiologica dell'Adversus haereses di Ireneo di Lione.* (Historia salutis. Serie storica 2.) Naples: M. d'Auria.

8963. Nielsen, J.T. *Adam and Christ in the Theology of Irenaeus of Lyons.* (Van Gorcum's Theologische Bibliotheek 40.) Assen: Van Gorcum, 1968.

8964. Orbe, A. "S. Ireneo y el discurso de Nazaret." *Scriptorium Victoriense* 17:5–33.

8965. O'Rourke Boyle, Marjorie. "Irenaeus' Millenial Hope: A Polemical Weapon." *RTAM* 36(1969):5–16.

8966. Rousseau, A.,et al.,eds. *Irénée de Lyon, "Contre les hérésies." Livre V. (Ed. critique d'après les versions arménienne et latine.)* (SCh 152–153.) 2 vols. Paris: Eds. du Cerf, 1969.

8967. Vives, J. "Pecado original y progreso evolutivo del hombre en Ireneo." *Estudios Eclesiasticos* 43(1968):561–89.

Isaiah. 8969. Regnault, Lucien. "Isaïe de Scété ou de Gaza? Notes critiques en marge d'une introduction au problème isaïen." *RAM* 46:33–44.

Isidore of Seville. 8970. Elorduy, E. "San Isidoro interpretado por Suárez." *Archivos Leoneses* 22(1966):7–75.

8971. Ferrari, A. "Octavio Agusto según S. Isidoro." *Boletín de la Real Academia de la Historia* 164(1969):159–87.

8972. Ford, Gordon B.,Jr., and Guido Donini, trs. *Isidore of Seville's History of the Goths, Vandals, and Suevi.* 2nd Rev. Ed. Leiden: E.J. Brill.

8973. Ford, Gordon B.,Jr.,ed. and tr. *The Letters of St. Isidore of Seville.* 2nd Rev. Ed. Amsterdam: A.M. Hakkert.

8974. Gasparotto, G. "Le citazioni poetiche nel libro XIII delle *Etymologiae* d'Isidoro di Siviglia." *CdD* 181(1968):668–81.

Itinerarium Egeriae. 8975. Milani, C. "I grecismi nell'*Itinerarium Egeriae.*" *Aevum* 43(1969):200–34.

Jacob of Viterbo. 8976. Ruello, Francis. "L'analogie de l'être selon Jacques de Viterbe, Quodlibet 1, Quaestio 1." *Augustiniana* 20:145–80.

Jerome. 8978. Brown, R.E. *The Jerome Bible Commentary, I,II.* London: G. Chapman, 1968.

8979. Duval, Yves-Marie. "Sur les insinuations de Jérôme contre Jean de Jérusalem:De l'arianisme à l'origénisme." *RHE* 65:353–74.

8980. Hamblenne, P. "La longévité de Jérôme. Prosper avait-il raison?" *Latomus* 28(1969):1081–1119.

8981. Hendrikx, E. "S. Jérôme en tant qu'hagiographe." *CdD* 181(1968):661–67.

8982. Hurst, D., and M. Adriaen,eds. *S. Hieronymi Presbyteri opera. 1ʳᵉ section:Opera exegetica. T. VII:"Commentariorum in Matheum libri IV."* (CC, Ser. Lat. 77.) Turnholt: Brepols, 1969.

8983. Kozik, I.S. *The First Desert Hero:St. Jerome's "Vita Pauli."* Mount Vernon, N.Y.: King Lithographers, 1968.

8984. Lambert, B. *Bibliotheca Hieronymiana manuscripta:La tradition manuscrite des œuvres de S. Jerome, IA, IB, II.* (Instrumenta Patristica 4.) Bruges: Abbaye St. Pierre, 1969.

8985. S. Hieronymi Presbyteri. *Opera, I.6:Commentarii in prophetas minores.* (CC, Ser. lat. 76.) Turnholt: Brepols, 1969.

8987. Schatkin, Margaret A. "The Influence of Origen upon St. Jerome's Commentary on Galatians." *VigC* 24:49–58.

8988. Silvia, D.S., and John P. Brennan,Jr. "Medieval Manuscripts of *Jerome against Jovinian.*" *Manuscripta* 13(1969): 161–66.

8989. Testard, Maurice. *Saint Jérôme:L'Apôtre savant et pauvre du patriciat romain.* (Coll. d'Etudes Ancienne.) Paris: Budé, 1969.

8990. Vega, A.C. "Algunas palabras más sobre la autenticidad del opúsculo *De adventu Enoch et Eliae et Antichristi a beato Hieronymo expositum.*" *CdD* 182(1969):619–26.

8991. —— "Un opúsculo desconocido de S. Jerónimo." *CdD* 182(1969):207–24.

8992. Waźbiński, Zygmunt. "*Vanitas Romana*:Z historii przedstawień św. Hieronima na tle ruin." *Meander* 22(1967): 45–56. [Illus.]

Joachim of Flora. 8993. Reeves, M. *The Influence of Prophecy in the Later Middle Ages:A Study in Joachimism.* London: Oxford U.P., 1969.

8994. Sendrail, Marcel. "Joachim de Flore, le messager des derniers temps." *BAGB* 44:407–24.

John Chrysostom. 8995. Leduc, F. "Le thème de la vaine gloire chez S. Jean Chrysostome." *Proche-Orient Chrétien* 19(1969):3–32.

8996. —— "L'eschatologie:Une préoccupation centrale de S. Jean Chrysostome." *Proche-Orient Chrétien* 19(1969):109–34.

8997. Malingrey, A.-M. "Un essai de classement dans la tradition manuscrite des homélies de Jean Chrysostome *De incomprehensibili.*" *Traditio* 25(1969):339–53.

8998. Micle, V. "S. Jean Chrysostome, prédicateur de l'unité chrétienne." *STeol* 21(1969):220–31. [In Romanian.]

8999. Moldovan, I.D. "L'aspect christologique et pneumatologique de l'Église selon S. Jean Chrysostome." *STeol* 20(1968):706–21. [In Romanian.]

9000. Nikolaou, T. *Der Neid bei Johannes Chrysostomus:Unter Berücksichtigung der griechischen Philosophie.* Bonn: Bouvier, 1969.

John of Damascus. 9001. Kotter, B.,ed. *Die Schriften des Johannes von Damaskos, I:"Institutio elementaris. Capita philosophia (Dialecta)." Als Anhang:Die philosophischen stücke aus Cod. Oxon. Bodl. Auc. T.I.6.* (Patristische Texte und Studien 7.) Berlin: de Gruyter, 1969.

John of Ford. 9002. A., D. "John of Ford:Commentary on the Latter Part of the Song of Songs." *CCCist* 21:105–10.

John of Reading. 9003. Gál, Gedeon. "Quaestio Ioannis de Reading De Necessitate Specierum Intelligibilium Defensio Doctrinae Scoti." *FranS* 29(1969):66–156.

John of Ripa. 9004. Vignaux, P. "Être et infini selon Duns Scot et Jean de Ripa." [F 68],IV:43–56.

John of Salisbury. 9005. Brucker, Ch. "Les néologismes de Denis Foulechat, traducteur de Charles V, d'après les trois premiers livres du *Policratique.*" *RLiR* 33(1969):317–24.

9006. Sheerin, Daniel J. "John of Salisbury's *Entheticus de dogmate philosophorum.*" *DAI* 31:329A(N.C., Chapel Hill).

John of St. Thomas. See 8844.

John Pecham. 9007. Harkins, Conrad. "The Authorship of a Commentary on the Franciscan Rule Published Among the Works of St. Bonaventure." *FranS* 29(1969):157–248.

John Scotus Erigena. 9008. Cappuyns, M. *Jean Scot Erigène: Sa vie, son oeuvre, sa pensée.* Brussels: Culture and Civilization, 1969. [Repr. of 1933 ed.]

9009. Jeauneau, Edouard,ed. and tr. *Homélie sur le Prologue de Jean.* Paris: Eds. du Cerf, 1969.

9011. Rini, Rodolfo. "Dio come *essentia omnium* nel pensiero di G. Scoto Eriugena." *RFNS* 62:101–32.

9012. Sheldon-Williams, I.P. *Iohannes Scottus Eriugena, "Periphyseon" (De divisione naturae):Bk. I.* (Scriptores Latini Hiberniae 7.) Dublin: Inst. of Advanced Studies, 1968.

John Sharpe. 9013. Kennedy, Leonard A. "The *De Anima* of John Sharpe." *FranS* 29(1969):249–70.

Jordanes. See 8778.

Joseph of Exeter. See 8795.

Kerckmeister. 9014. Kerckmeister, Johannes. Codrus:*Ein neulateinisches Drama aus dem Jahre 1485.* Hrsg. von Lothar Mundt. Berlin: de Gruyter, 1969.

Lactantius. 9015. Heck, E. "Bemerkungen zum Text von Lactanz, *De opificio Dei.*" *VigC* 23(1969):273–92.

9016. Loi, V. *Lattanzio nella storia del linguaggio e del pensiero teologico pre-niceno.* (Bibliotheca theologica salesiana 5.) Zürich:

Pas-Verlag.

9017. Speigl, Jakob. "Zum Kirchenbegriff des Laktanz." *RQCAK* 65:15–28.

Langton. 9018. Barzillay, Phyllis. "Stephanus de Lingua Tonante:Studies in the Sermons of Stephen Langton (ca 1155–1228)." *DAI* 30(1969):1488A(Columbia).

Lathcen. 9019. Adriaen, M.,ed. *Egloga quam scripsit Lathcen filius Baith de Moralibus Iob quas Gregorius fecit.* (CC ser. lat. 145.) Turnholt: Brepols, 1969.

Laurence of Brindisi. 9020. Aspurz, Lázaro de. "La vocación en San Lorenzo de Brindis." *Laurentianum* 10(1969):434–56

9022. Borak, Adriano. "Il celibato sacerdotale nel pensiero di S. Lorenzo da Brindisi." *Laurentianum* 10(1969):457–70.

9023. Cagliari, Filippo da. "Le citazioni bibliche latine nella 'Explanatio in Genesim' di S. Lorenzo da Brindisi." *Laurentianum* 10(1969):379–400.

9023a. Giordano, Antonino. "Un aspetto della Mariologia di S. Lorenzo de Brindisi Maria Madre della Chiesa." *Laurentianum* 9(1968):267–78.

9024. McCreary, Robert C. "The Glorification of Christ in the Thought of St. Lawrence." *Laurentianum* 10(1969):401–12.

9025. Wingene, Hilarius a. "Spiritualis laurentianae lineamenta fundamentalia." *Laurentianum* 10(1969):414–33.

Laurence of Durham. 9026. Kindermann, Udo. "Das Emmausgedicht des Laurentius von Durham." *MitJ* 5(1968): 79–100.

Leander of Seville. See 8564.

Leo the Great. 9027. Mariucci, T. *Omelie, lettere di S. Leone Magno.* Turin: Unione tipografica, 1969.

Liber Floridus. 9028. Derolez, Albert. "Un colloque sur le *Liber Floridus.*" *Scriptorium* 21(1967):307–12.

Liber Scintillarum. 9029. Derolez, René. "Some Notes on the *Liber Scintillarum* and Its Old English Glosses." [F 54]:142–51.

Lucas of Penna. 9030. Ullmann, Walter. *The Medieval Idea of Law as Represented by Lucas de Penna:A Study in Fourteenth-Century Legal Scholarship.* New York: Barnes & Noble; London: Methuen, 1969.

Lull. 9031. Artus, Walter W. "The Tradition of the *Ars brevis.*" *ELul* 13(1969):153–82.

9032. Bauzá y Bauzá, Rafael. "Doctrinas jurídicas internacionales de Ramón Llull." *ELul* 13(1969):37–50.

9033. Colom Ferrá, Guillermo. "Ramón Llull y los orígenes de la literatura catalana." *ELul* 13(1969):133–52.

9034. Garcías Palou, S. "La primera obra que escribió Ramón Llull." *ELul* 13(1969):67–82.

9035. Longpré, Ephrem. "La primauté du Christ selon Raymond Lulle." *ELul* 13(1969):5–36.

9036. Mercant, Trías. "La ética luliana en el *Félix de les Meravelles.*" *ELul* 13(1969):113–32.

9037. Oliver, Antonio. "El Beato Ramón Llull en sus relaciones con la Escuela Franciscana en los siglos XIII–XIV." *ELul* 13(1969):51–66. [See Bibliog. for 1969, Vol. I, Item 8567.]

Marius Victorinus. 9038. Schäfer, K.T. "Marius Victorinus und die marcionitischen Prologe zu den Paulusbriefen." *RB* 80:7–16.

Marston. 9039. Etskorn, G.F., and I.C. Brady,eds. Fr. Rogeri Marston, O.F.M., *Quodlibeta quatuor.* (Bibliotheca franciscana scholastica medii aevi 26.) Quaracchi: Collège St. Bonaventure, 1968.

Martin of Braga. See 1560, 8564.

Martin of Tours. 9040. Jacques, F. "Saint Martin titulaire d'églises et de chapelles dans l'ancien diocèse et la province de Namur." *RB* 80:97–137.

9041. Lof, L.J. van der. "Ambrosius en Martinus van Tours." *Nederlands Archief voor Kerkgeschiedenis* 50(1969):1–10.

Mathew of Aquasparta. 9042. Bonafede, G. *Matteo d'Acquasparta.* (Collana di Filosofia e Pedagogia.) 2d. ed. Trapani: A. Vento, 1968.

Meyronnes. 9043. Barbet, J. "Un témoin de la discussion entre les écoles scotiste et thomiste selon François de Meyronnes." [F 68],IV:21–33.

9044. Kunzle, P. "Petrus Thomae oder Franciscus de Maironis?" *AFH* 61(1968):462–63.

Nassyngton. 9045. Gunn, Agnes D. "Accidia and Prowess in he Vernon Version of Nassyngton's *Speculum Vitae.*" *DAI* 30:4945A(Pa.).

Niceta of Rheims. 9046. Alexe, St. C. "S. Nicétas de Remesiana et l'oecuménicité patristique aux IVe et Ve siècles." *STeol* 21(1969):453–587. [In Romanian.]

9047. Gamber, Klaus. *Niceta von Remesiana, De lapsu Susannae.* (Textus patristici et liturgici 7.) Mit einer Wortkonkordanz zu den Schriften des Niceta, by S. Rehle. Ratisbon: Pustet, 1969.

Nicholas of Cusa. 9048. Bruckner, János. "Angelus Silesius und Nikolaus von Kues:Kusanisches im *Cherubinischen Wandersmann.*" *Euphorion* 64:143–66.

9049. Dangelmayr, S. *Gotteserkenntnis und Gottesbegriff in den philosophischen Schriften des Nikolaus von Kues.* (Monographien z. philosophischen Forschung 54.) Meisenheim: Hain, 1969.

9050. —— "Vernunft und Glaube bei Nicolaus von Kues." *Tübinger Theologische Quartalschrift* 148(1968):429–62.

9051. Dupré, W. "Marginalien zu den Schriften des III. Bandes der Wiener Cusanusedition." *MFCG* 7(1969):103–19.

9052. Gandillac, M. de. "Le *De concordantia catholica* de Nicolas de Cues." *RHE* 64(1969):418–23.

9053. Gutwenger, E. "Das *Nichtandere* bei Nikolaus von Kues." *Zeitschrift für Katholische Theologie* 91(1969):488–92.

9054. Haubst, R. "Zur Datierung der frühesten Cusanus-Predigten:Ein Predigtzyklus des jungen Cusanus über tätiges und beschauliches Leben." *MFCG* 7(1969):15–46.

9055. Henke, Norbert. *Der Abbildbegriff in der Erkenntnislehre des Nikolaus von Kues.* Münster: Aschendorff, 1969.

9056. Jungandreas, W. "Zur Überlieferung und Sprache der deutschen Vaterunserauslegung des Nikolaus von Kues." *MFCG* 7(1969):67–88.

9057. Lübke, Anton. *Nikolaus von Kues:Kirchenfürst zwischen Mittelalter und Neuzeit.* München: Callwey, 1968.

9058. Piccard, G. "Zur Datierung der frühesten Cusanus-Predigten:Die Papiermarken des Cod. Cus. 220." *MFCG* 7(1969):47–66.

9059. Van de Vyver, E. "Die Handschriften aus dem Besitz des Nikolaus von Kues in der Königlichen Bibliothek zu Brüssel." *MFCG* 7(1969):129–45.

9060. Weier, R. "Anthropologische Ansätze des Cusanus als Beitrag zur Gegenwartsdiskussion um den Menschen." *MFCG* 7(1969):89–102.

See also 2884.

Nicholas of Lyra. 9061. Gosselin, Edward A. "A History of the Printed Editions of Nicolaus of Lyra." *Traditio* 26:399–426.

Nigel. 9062. Floyd, Harvey L. "Nigel's *Speculum Stultorum*:A Study in Literary Influences." *DAI* 30:4432A(Vanderbilt).

Novatian. 9063. De Simone, R. "Christ the True God and True Man by Novatian *De Trinitate.*" *Augustinianum* 10:42–117.

Ockham. 9064. Adams, Marilyn M. "Intuitive Cognition, Certainty, and Scepticism in William Ockham." *Traditio* 26:389–98.

9065. Adams, Marilyn M., and Norman Kretzmann,trs. *Predestination, God's Foreknowledge, and Future Contingents.* (Century Philosophy Sourcebooks.) New York: Appleton, Century, Crofts, 1969.

9066. Andrés, T. de. *El nominalismo de Guillermo de Ockham como filosofía del lenguaje.* (Bibl. hispánica de filosofía 60.) Madrid: Gredos, 1969.

9067. Bérubé, Camille. "Ockham sous le feu des projecteurs." *Laurentianum* 11:202–15.

9068. Brampton, C.K. "The Probable Date of William of Ockham's Noviciate." *FrSt* 51(1969):78–85.

9069. Ghisalberti, Alessandro. "Bibliografia su Guglielmo di Occam dal 1950 al 1968." *RFNS* 61(1969):545–71. [See Bibliog. for 1969, Vol. I, Item 8596.]

9070. —— "Il Dio dei filosofi secondo Guglielmo di Occam." *RFNS* 62:272–90.

9071. Junghans, H. *Ockham im Lichte der neueren Forschung.* (Arbeiten z. Geschichte u. Theologie d. Luthertums 21.) Berlin: Lutherisches Verlagshaus, 1968.

9072. Leff, Gordon. "Knowledge and Its Relation to the Status of Theology According to Ockham." *Jour. of Eccles. Hist.* 20(1969):7–17.

9073. Miethke, J. *Ockhams Weg zur Sozialphilosophie.* Berlin: de Gruyter, 1969.

9074. Pernoud, Mary A. "Tradition and Innovation in Ockham's Theory of Divine Omnipotence:A Study of Possibility and Singularity." *DAI* 30:3506A(St. Louis U.).

See also 9003.

Oderic Vitalis. 9075. Chibnall, M. *The "Ecclesiastical History" of Oderic Vitalis:Vol. II., Bks. 3 and 4.* Oxford: Clarendon, 1969.

9076. Rousset, P. "La description du monde chevaleresque chez Orderic Vital." *MA* 75(1969):427–44.

Oresme. 9077. Menut, Albert D. "A Provisional Bibliography of Oresme's Writings:A Supplementary Note." *MS* 31(1969):346–47.

Origen. 9078. Chênevert, Jacques. *L'Eglise dans le commentaire d'Origène sur le Cantique des Cantiques.* (Studia 24.) Brussels and Paris: Desclée de Brouwer, 1969.

9079. Crouzel, H. "Chronique origénienne." *BLE* 71:113–26. [Rev. art.]

9080. —— *La mariologia di Origene.* Milan: Ed. Patristiche, 1968.

9081. —— "Origène et le sens littéral dans ses 'Homélies sur l'Hexateuque'." *BLE* 70(1969):241–63.

9082. Eichinger, M. *Die Verklärung Christi bei Origenes:Die Bedeutung des Menschen Jesus in seiner Christologie.* (Wiener Beiträge zur Theologie 23.) Vienna: Herder, 1969.

9083. Garijo Guembe, M.M. "Aspectos de la pneumatología origeniana, IV:Relación del Espíritu Santo con ambos Testamentos." *Scriptorium Victoriense* 16(1969):65–93.

9084. Horn, H.-J. "*Ignis aeturnus*:Une interprétation morale du feu éternel chez Origène." *REG* 82(1969):76–88.

9085. Losada, J. "El sacrificio de Cristo en los cielos según Orígenes." *Miscelánea Comillas* 50(1969):5–19.

9086. Simonetti, Manlio. *'I Principi' di Origene.* (Classici d. Religioni.) Turin: U.T.E.T., 1968.

9087. Trevijano Etcheverría, R.M. "Notas para la historia de la edición impresa de algunas obras de Orígenes," in *Miscelánea José M. Lacarra.* Saragossa, 1968.

See also 8929, 8987.

Orosius. 9088. Karrer, S. *Der gallische Krieg bei Orosius.* (Geist u. Werk d. Zeiten Fasc. 23.) Zürich: Fretz and Wasmuth, 1969.

9089. Lippold, A. "Orosius, christlicher Apologet und römischer Bürger." *PZKA* 113(1969):92–105.

Ovid. 9090. Thiel, Erich J. "Mittellateinische Nachdichtungen von Ovids 'Ars amatoria' und 'Remedia amoris'." *MitJ* 5(1968):115–81.

Parce Continuis. 9091. Stock, Brian. "*Parce Continuis*:Some Textual and Interpretive Notes." *MS* 31(1969):164–73.

Paris. 9092. Bryant, W.N. "Matthew Paris, Chronicler of St. Albans." *Hist. Today* 19(1969):772–82.

Pascasius Radbertus. 9093. Paulus, Bedae,ed. *Pascasius Radbertus, De corpore et sanguine Domini, Epistola ad Fredugardum.* (CC Continuatio Mediaevale 16.) Turnholt: Brepols, 1969.

Paschasius of Dumium. *See* 8564.

Paulinus of Aquileja. 9094. Prinz, Otto. "Mittellateinisch 'Bibicus':Bemerkungen zum Wortschatz des Paulinus von Aquileja." [F 69]:211–22.

Paulinus of Nola. 9095. Bouma, J.A. *Het "Epithalamium" van Paulinus van Nola. "Carmen XXV," met inleiding, vertaling, en commentaar.* Assen: Van Gorcum-Prakke, 1968.

9096. Walsh, Peter G. "The Textual Notes on the *Epistulae* of Paulinus Nolanus." *Orpheus* 13(1966):153–58.

Pelagius. 9097. Brown, Peter. "The Patrons of Pelagius:The Roman Aristocracy Between East and West." *JTS* 21:56–72.

Peter Aureolus. 9098. Streuer, Severin Rudolf. *Die theologische Einleitungslehre des Petrus Aureoli. Auf Grund seines "Scriptum super primum sententiarum" und ihre theologiegeschichtliche Einordnung.* (Franziskanische Forschungen 20.) Werl: Dietrich-Coelde, 1968.

Peter Lombard. *See* 8878.

Peter of Bergamo. 9099. Tyrrell, G. "The *Tabula aurea* of Peter de Bergamo." *Heythrop Journal* 10(1969):275–79.

Peter of Falco. 9100. Gondras, A.-J. "La matière selon Pierre de Falco." [F 68],ɪ:297–308.

Peter of Spain. 9101. De Rijk, L.M. "Significatio y suppositio en Pedro Hispano." *Pensamiento* 25(1969):225–34.

9101a. —— "On the Genuine Text of Peter of Spain's *Summule logicales*." *Vivarium* 6(1968):69–101; 7(1969):8–61,120–62; 8:10–55.

9102. Kohlmeier, J. " 'Vita est actus primus.' Ein Beitrag zur Erhellung der ersten Hälfte des XIII Jhts. anhand der Lebensmetaphysik des Petrus Hispanus." *Freiburger Zeitschrift f. Philosophie u. Theologie* 16(1969):40–91.

9103. Pozzi, L. "Nota sull'edizione Bocheński delle *Summulae* di Pietro Ispano." *RCSF* 23(1968):330–42.

Peter of Trabibus. 9105. Huning, H.A. "Petrus de Trabibus, ein Vorläufer des Johannes Duns Scotus in der Lehre von Formalunterschied." [F 68],ɪ:285–95.

Peter the Chanter. 9106. Baldwin, John W. *Masters, Princes, and Merchants: The Social Views of Peter the Chanter & His Circle.* 2 vols. Princeton: Princeton U.P.

Peter the Venerable. 9107. Hoffmann, Hartmut. "Zu den Briefen des Petrus Venerabilis." *QFIAB* 49(1969):399–441.

Petrus Thomae. *See* 9044.

Philo of Alexandria. 9108. Christiansen, I. *Die Technik der allegorischen Auslegungswissenschaft bei Philon von Alexandrien.* (Beiträge d. Biblischen Hermeneutik 7.) Tübingen: Mohr, 1969.

9109. Otte, Kl. *Das Sprach verständnis bei Philo von Alexandrien: Sprache als Mittel der Hermeneutik.* (Beiträge zur Geschichte der Biblischen Exegese 7.) Tübingen: Mohr, 1968.

Pilatus Leontius. 9110. Pellegrin, Élisabeth. "Léonce Pilate et les premières traductions latines d'Homère." *Scriptorium* 21(1967):321–26.

***Planctus* of Oedipus.** *9111. Clogan, Paul M. "The *Planctus* of Oedipus: Text and Comment." *M&H* N.S. 1:233–39.

Plato. 9112. Gibson, M. "The Study of the *Timaeus* in the 11th and 12th Centuries." *Pensamiento* 25(1969):183–94.

Polenton. 9113. Polenton, Sicco. *Catinia.* Ed. crit. a cura di Giorgio Padoan. Venezia: Ist. Veneto di Scienze, Lettere, ed Arte, 1969.

Porphyry. *See* 8889.

Prepositinus Cremonensis. 9114. Corbett, James A.,ed. *Praepositini Cremonensis Tractatus de officiis.* (U. of Notre Dame Pubs. in Med. St. 21.) Notre Dame, Ind.: U. of Notre Dame P., 1969.

Primas. 9115. Latzke, Therese. "Die Mantelgedichte des Primas Hugo von Orléans und Martial." *MitJ* 5(1968):54–58.

Prosper of Aquitaine. *See* 8980.

Prudentius. 9116. Argenio, R. "Due corone di Prudenzio." *RSCl* 16(1968):257–83.

9117. Cunningham, M.P. "The Problem of Interpolation in the Textual Tradition of Prudentius." *Trans. and Proc. of the Am. Philolog. Assn.* 99(1968):119–41.

* 9118. Mickel, Emanuel J.,Jr. "Parallels in Prudentius' *Psychomachia* and *La Chanson de Roland*." *SP* 67:439–52.

9119. Witke, Charles. "Prudentius and the Tradition of Latin Poetry." *Trans. and Proc. of the Am. Philolog. Assn.* 99(1968): 509–25.

Pseudo-Cyprian. 9120. Van Damme, D. *Pseudo-Cyprian, Adversus Iudaeos, Gegen die Judenchristen, Die älteste lateinische Predigt.* (Paradosis 22.) Freiburg: Universitätsverlag, 1969.

Pseudo-Dionysius. 9121. Riggi, Calogero. "Il simbolo dionisiano dell'estetica teologica." *Salesianum* 32:47–91.

9122. Spearritt, Dom Placid. "The Soul's Participation in God According to Pseudo-Dionysius." *DownR* 88:378–92.

Pseudo-Isidore. 9123. Fontaine, J. "Quelques observations sur les *Institutionum disciplinae* pseudo-Isidoriennes." *CdD* 181(1968):617–55.

Pseudo-Ovid. 9124. Lenz, Friedrich W. "Das pseudo-ovidische Gedicht 'De sompnio'." *MitJ* 5(1968):101–14.

Rahewin. 9125. Munz, P. "Why Did Rahewin Stop Writing the *Gesta Frederici*? A Further Consideration." *EHR* 84(1969): 771–79.

Rainald of Merton. 9126. Colker, Marvin L. "The Life of Guy of Merton by Rainald of Merton." *MS* 31(1969):250–61.

Ralph of Rochester. 9127. Farmer, D.H. "Ralph's Octo Puncta of Monastic Life." *StM* 11(1969):19–29.

Rather. 9128. Reece, Benny R. *Sermones Ratherii Episcop Veronensis.* Worcester, Mass.: Holy Cross College, 1969.

Rhythmus de b[eata] Maria Virg[ine]. *9129. Rendall, Thomas " 'Quis est hic qui pulsat ad ostium?' An Explication." *PC* 49:145–51.

Roland of Cremona. 9130. Hess, C.R. "Roland of Cremona' Place in the Current of Thought." *Angelicum* 45(1968):429–77

Rudolf of Biberach. 9131. Schmidt, Margot,ed. *Rudolf voɪ Biberach: Die siben strassen zu got. Die hochalemannische Über tragung nach der Handschrift Einsiedeln 278.* (Spicilegium Bonaventurianum 6.) Hrsg. u. eingeleitet. Quaracchi, Firenze Collegio Internazionale S. Bonaventura, 1969.

Ruodlieb. 9132. Dronke, Peter. "*Ruodlieb*. Les première traces du roman courtois." *CCM* 12(1969):365–82.

Rupert of Deutz. 9133. Arancibia, J.M. "Ruperto de Deutz ɪ la crisis sacerdotal del siglo XII." *Scriptorium Victoriense* 17:34–64

9134. Haacke, Rhabanus,ed. *Ruperti Tuitiensis Commentariɔ in Evangelium Sancti Iohannis.* (CC Continuatio Mediaevale 9.' Turnholt: Brepols, 1969.

9135. Peinador, M. "La actitud negativa de Ruperto de Deutz ante la Inmaculada Concepción de la Virgen: Ambiente doctrinaɪ y motivación de la misma." *Marianum* 30(1968):192–217.

9136. —— "María y la Iglesia en la historia de la salvaciór según Ruperto de Deutz." *Ephemerides Mariologicae* 18(1968) 337–81.

Ruysbroeck. 9137. De Baere, G. "*Dat boecksen deɪ verclaringhe* van Jan van Ruusbroec: Tekstuitgave als steekproef." *Ons Geestelijk Erf* 42(1969):97–170.

Rymyngton. 9138. O'Brien, Robert. "Two Sermons at York Synod of William Rymyngton, 1372 and 1373." *CCCist* 19:40–67

Salutaris poeta. 9139. Bujnoch, Josef. "Die Spruchdichtung des Salutaris poeta." *MitJ* 5(1968):199–241.

Salutati. 9140. Witt, R.G. "Coluccio Salutati, Chancellor and Citizen of Lucca (1370–1372)." *Traditio* 25(1969):191–216.

Sedulius Scotus. 9141. Düchting, Reinhard. "Sedulius Scotus und P. Optatianus Porfyrius." *MitJ* 5(1968):24–28.

Siger of Brabant. 9142. Bukowski, Thomas P. "The Eternity of the World According to Siger of Brabant: Probable or Demonstrative?" *RTAM* 36(1969):225–29.

Simeon. 9143. Koder, J., and J. Paramelle,eds. Syméone le Nouveau Théologien, Hymnes. I: Hymnes 1–15. (SCh 156.) Paris: Eds. du Cerf, 1969.

Simon of Faversham. 9144. Yokoyama, Tetsuo. "Simon of Faversham's Sophisma: 'Universale Est Intentio'." *MS* 31(1969): 1–14.

Simon of Tournai. 9145. Masi, R. "La dottrina della transustanziazione nella teologico del XII secolo." *RCSF* 23(1968):371–90.

9146. Santiago-Otero, H. "El conocimiento humano de Cristo en el pensamiento de Simon de Tournai." *Divinitas* 13(1969): 557–67.

Solinus. 9147. Walter, Hermann. *Die Collectanea Rerum Memorabilium des Caius Iulius Solinus: Ihre Entstehung und die Echtheit ihrer Zweitfassung.* (Hermes-Einzelschriften 22.) Wiesbaden: Franz Steiner, 1969.

Speculum Virginum. 9148. Bultot, Robert. "Autour du *Speculum Virginum*." *RHE* 64(1969):808–10.

St. Patrick. 9149. Powell, D. "The Textual Integrity of St. Patrick's Confession." *AnBol* 87(1969):387–409.

Statius. 9150. Clogan, Paul M.,ed. *The Medieval Achilleid of Statius.* Leiden: Brill, 1968.

9151. Waite, Stephen V.F. "Metrical Indices to Statius' *Achilleid.*" *Hephaistos* 1,i:28–70.

Tatuinus. 9152. DeMarco, Maria,ed. *Tatuini Opera Omnia, Variae Collectiones aenigmatum Merovingicae aetatis, I.* (CC ser. lat. 133.) Turnholt: Brepols, 1968.

Tertullian. 9153. Diego, J.R. de. "Significado eclesial del tratado de Tertuliano sobre el bautismo." *Estudios Eclesiásticos* 44(1969):91–104.

9154. Klein, R. *Tertullian und das Römische Reich.* (Bibliothek d. Klassischen Altertumswissenschaften. N.S. sect. 2,22.) Heidelberg: Winter, 1968.

9155. Moingt, J. *Théologie trinitaire de Tertullien. IV: Répertoire lexicographique et tables.* Paris: Aubier, 1969.

9156. Rordorf, W. "Tertullians Beurteilung des Soldaten-standes." *VigC* 23(1969):105–41.

9157. Spanneut, M. *Tertullien et les premiers moralistes africains.* Gembloux: J. Duculot, 1969.

9158. Swift, L.J. "Forensic Rhetoric in Tertullian's *Apologeticum.*" *Latomus* 27(1968):864–77.

9159. Tibiletti, C. "Un motivo del primo Aristotele in Tertulliano." *VigC* 23(1969):21–29.

Theodore of Mopsuestia. 9160. Gibson, Margaret. "Theodore of Mopsuestia:A Fragment in the Bodleian Library." *JTS* 21:104–05.

Theophrastus. *See* 9276.

Thomas à Kempis. 9161. Valentini, Eugenio. "Nuove scoperte sul vero autore dell'*Imitazione di Cristo.*" *Salesianum* 31(1969):265–332.

Thomas Aquinas. 9162. Anderson, Thomas C. "Intelligible Matter and the Objects of Mathematics in Aquinas." *New Scholasticism* 43(1969):555–56.

9163. Bernath, Kl. *Anima forma corporis:Eine Untersuchung über die ontologischen Grundlagen der Anthropologie des Thomas von Aquin.* (Abhandlungen z. Philosophie, Psychologie u. Pädagogik 57.) Bonn: Bouvier, 1969.

9164. Borresen, K.E. *Subordination et équivalence:Nature et rôle de la femme d'après Augustin et Thomas d'Aquin.* Paris: Mame, 1968.

9165. Boublik, Vl. *L'azione divina "praeter ordinem naturae" secondo S. Tommaso d'Aquino.* (Cathedra S. Thomae 7.) Rome: Libreria ed. d. Pont. Università Lateranense, 1968.

9166. Boulogne, Ch.D. *S. Thomas d'Aquin:Essai biographique.* Paris: Nouv. Ed. Latines, 1968.

9167. Bourke, D., and A. Littledale,eds. and trs. *St. Thomas Aquinas,* Summa theologiae, *Vol. 29:The Old Law* (1ª 2ᵃᵉ, 98–105). London: Eyre and Spottiswoode, 1969.

9168. Casciaro, J.M. *El diálogo teológico de S. Tomás con musulmanes y judíos:El tema de la profecía y la revelación.* (Biblioteca hispana bíblica 2.) Madrid: Inst. Fran. Suárez, 1969.

9169. Courtès, P.-C. "Participation et contingence selon S. Thomas d'Aquin." *RThom* 69(1969):201–35.

9170. Fellermeier, J. "Wahrheit und Existenz bei Thomas von Aquin." *MTZ* 20(1969):136–45.

9171. Garceau, B. *"Judicium":Vocabulaire, sources, doctrine de S. Thomas d'Aquin.* (U. of Montréal Pub. de l'Inst. d'Etudes Médiévales 22.) Paris: J. Vrin, 1968.

9172. Gils, Pierre-M. "Deux nouveau fragments autographes de Thomas d'Aquin." *Scriptorium* 24:44–45.

9173. Keller, A. *Sein oder Existenz? Die Auslegung des Seins bei Thomas von Aquin in der heutigen Scholastik.* (Pullacher Philosophische Forschungen 7.) Munich: Hueber, 1968.

9174. Kenny, A. *The Five Ways:St. Thomas Aquinas' Proofs of God's Existence.* London: Routledge & K. Paul, 1969.

9175. ———,ed. *Aquinas:A Collection of Critical Essays.* Garden City, N.Y.: Doubleday (Anchor), 1969.

9176. Laverdière, Raymond. *Le principe de causalité:Recherches thomistes récentes.* (Bibliothèque Thomiste 39.) Paris: J. Vrin, 1969.

9177. McMorrow, Kevin F. "A Reevaluation of Christ's Special Religious Knowledge (Beata):An Historical Investigation of Thomas Aquinas and His Commentators." *DAI* 30(1969):1625A(Catholic U.).

9178. Montagnes, B. "Le deux fonctions de la sagesse: Ordonner et juger." *RSPT* 53(1969):675–86.

9179. Murphy, Th. "The Date and Purpose of the *Contra Gentiles.*" *Heythrop Journal* 10(1969):405–15.

9180. Owens, Joseph. "Aquinas—Existential Permanence and Flux." *MS* 31(1969):71–92.

9181. Pandellaro De Angelis, R. *Il problema del male nell'alta scolastica. S. Tommaso.* Rome: E. De Santis, 1968.

9182. Persson, Per Erik. *Sacra Doctrina:Reason and Revelation in Aquinas.* Tr. Ross Mackenzie. Philadelphia: Fortress.

9183. Petruzzellis, N. "S. Tommaso filosofo del concreto." *Asprenas* 16(1969):253–67.

9184. Polestra, G. *Omelie di S. Tommaso.* (Temi di predicazione 68–70.) Naples: Ediz. domenicane italiane, 1968.

9185. Raeymaeker, Le de. "L'analogie de l'être dans la perspective d'une philosophie thomiste." *RIPh* 23(1969):89–106.

9186. Thiry, L. "The Ethical Theory of Saint Thomas Aquinas:Interpretations and Misinterpretations." *JR* 50:169–85. *See also* 5356, 8611, 8816, 8853, 9122, 9233.

Thomas of Cantimpré. 9187. Boese, H. "Zur Textüberlieferung von Thomas Cantimpratensis *Liber de natura rerum.*" *AFP* 39(1969):53–68.

Thomas of Sutton. 9188. Schmaus, M., and M. González-Haba,eds. Thomas von Sutton, *Quodlibeta.* (Bayerische Akad. der Wissenschaften. Veröf. der Kommission für die Herausgabe ungedruckter Texte aus der mittelalterl. Geisteswelt 2.) Munich: C.H. Beck, 1969.

Thomas of Walden. 9189. Seibel, F.X. "Die Kirche als Lehrautorität nach dem *Doctrinale antiquitatum fidei catholicae Ecclesiae* des Thomas Waldensis (um 1372–1431)." *Carmelus* 16(1969):3–69.

Ulger of Angers. *See* 8610.

Visio Anselli. 9190. Leclercq, Jean. "Une rédaction en prose de la *Visio Anselli* dans un manuscrit de Subiaco." *Benedictina* 16(1969):188–95.

Vita Amici et Amelii. *See* 823.

Vital du Four. 9191. Lunch, John E. "The Knowledge of Singular Things According to Vital du Four." *FranS* 29(1969): 271–301.

Walter of Odington. 9192. Thomas, Phillip D. "Missing Fragments of British Museum Additional Manuscript 15549." *Scriptorium* 24:51–53.

William Euvrie. 9193. Pellegrin, Élisabeth. "Un humaniste normand du temps de Charles VI:Guillaume Euvrie." *BIIRHT* 15(1969):9–28.

William of Alnwick. 9194. Veliath, D. "The 'Scotism' of William of Alnwick in His *determinationes de anima.*" *Salesianum* 32:93–134.

William of Auvergne. 9195. Bridges, John H.,Sr. "The Philosophy of William of Auvergne with Respect to Thirteenth Century Christian Aristotelianism." *DAI* 30:4487A(Emory).

William of Auxerre. 9196. Chatillon, Jean. "L'union hypostatique chez les théologiens du début du XIIIᵉ siècle: Guillaume d'Auxerre et Alexandre de Hales." *CCM* 12(1969): 161–64.

William of St. Thierry. 9197. Guillermo de Saint Thierry. *Carta de oro:Reflexiones sobre la vida religiosa.* (Fuentes de Espiritualidad Monástica 1.) Madrid: Ed. Studium, 1968.

9198. Hart, Columba,tr. *The Works of William of St. Thierry. II:Exposition on the Song of Songs.* (Cistercian Fathers Ser. 6.) Spencer, Mass.: Cistercian Pubs.

9199. Leclercq, J. "Les lettres de Guillaume de Saint-Thierry à saint Bernard." *RB* 79(1969):375–91.

William Woodford. 9200. Doyle, Eric. "A Manuscript of William Woodford's *De dominio civili clericorum.*" *AFH* 62(1969):377–81.

Winebrand. 9201. Gaiffier, Baudouin de. "Vie de S. Illidius [Allyre] par Winebrand:Nouveaux fragments." *AnBol* 87(1969): 337–42.

Wyclif. *9202. Leff, Gordon. "Wyclif and the Augustinian Tradition:With Special Reference to His *De Trinitate.*" *M&H* N.S. 1:29–39.

9203. Tatnall, E.C. "John Wyclif and Ecclesia anglicana." *Jour. of Eccles. Hist.* 20(1969):19–43.

9204. Wilks, M.J. "The Early Oxford Wyclif:Papist or Nominalist?" *Studies in Church Hist.* 5(1969):69–98.

III. NEO-LATIN LITERATURE

Bibliography. 9205. Desgraves, L.,et al. *Répertoire bibliographique des livres imprimés en France au XVIᵉ siècle, III:Auch,* *Limoges, Montbéliard, Mulhouse, Nevers.* (Bibliographica Aureliana 29.) Baden-Baden: Heitz, 1969.

9206. IJsewijn, J. "Neo-Latin Bibliography, III." *HZM* 23(1969):123–65.

9207. Troeyer, Benjamin de. *Bio-Bibliographia franciscana neerlandica saeculi XVI.* 2 vols. Nieuwkoop: B. de Graaf, 1969–70.

General and Miscellaneous. 9208. Hoven, J., and J. Hoyoux. *Exposition:Le livre scolaire au temps d'Erasme et des humanistes.* (Centre Interuniversit. d'Histoire de l'Humanisme.) Liège: Université, 1969.

9209. Kleineidam, Erich. *Universitas Erffordensis, Überblick über die Geschichte der Universität Erfurt im Mittelalter 1392–1521. II:1460–1521.* (Erfurter Theologische Studien 22.) Leipzig: St. Benno, 1969.

9210. Leclercq, J., and M.-F. Valkhoff. *Les premiers défenseurs de la liberté religieuse:Textes choisis et présentés.* (Chrétiens de tous les temps 34 et 35.) 2 vols. Paris: Eds. du Cerf, 1969.

9211. Samaran, Charles, and M.-L. Concasty. "Christophe Auer, copiste de grec et de latin au XVIᵉ siècle." *Scriptorium* 23(1969):199–214.

9212. Seigel, J.E. *Rhetoric and Philosophy in Renaissance Humanism:The Union of Eloquence and Wisdom, Petrarch to Valla.* London: Oxford U.P., 1969.

Poetry. 9212a. Hejnic, J., and J. Martinek,eds. *Rukovet humanistického Basnictvi v Cechac a na Morave. Enchiridion renatae poesis Latinae in Bohemia et Moravia cultae.* Vol. III:*K-M.* Prague: Czech Acad. of Sciences, 1969.

9212b. Joukovsky, F. *Orphée et ses disciples dans la poésie française et néo-latine du XVIᵉ siècle.* (PRF 109.) Genève: Droz. *See also* 1487.

Alonso of Veracruz. 9221. Gutiérrez, D. "Edición de las obras inéditas de fray Alonso de la Veracruz." *Augustinianum* 9:380–87.

Baptista Mantuanus. 9222. Sullivan, A. "A Contribution to the History of Intellectual Freedom:The *Opus aureum in Thomistas* of Blessed Baptista Mantuanus, O.Carm. (1447–1516)." [F 68],IV:155–69.

Barbaro, Ermolao. 9223. Branca, Vittore,ed. *De Coelibatu —De Officio Legati.* (Nuova Collezione di Testi Umanistici o Rari 14.) Florence: Olschki, 1969.

Bebel. 9224. Hess, Günther. " 'Vulgaris cantio':Gattungs-probleme zwischen Volkssprache und Latinität um 1500." [F 70]:346–70.

Bernhard of Luxemburg. 9225. Vekene, E. van der. "Das gedruckte Schrifttum des Bernhard von Luxemburg. Ein Beitrag zur Bibliographie des XVI. Jhts.," 452–80 in *Refugium animae bibliotheca. Mélanges offerts à Albert Kolb.* Wiesbaden, 1969.

Bona. 9226. Stella, P.T. "Il *De sacrificio Missae* del card. Bona (1668). Note per una storia del testo." *Salesianum* 31(1969):629–66.

Campanella. 9227. Femiano, Salvatore. "L'antiaristotelismo essenziale di Tommaso Campanella." *Sapienza* 22(1969):137–59.

9228. Firpo, L. "Il *De conceptione Virginis* di Tommaso Campanella." *Sapienza* 22(1969):182–248.

9229. Gillon, L.B. "Tommaso Campanella et les doctrines de la grâce." *Sapienza* 22(1969):8–26.

9230. Milano, A. "Magia e teologia in Tommaso Campanella." *Sapienza* 22(1969):160–71.

Campion. 9231. Simons, Joseph,ed. *Ambrosia:A Neo-Latin Drama by Edmund Campion.* Assen: Royal, Van Gorcum.

Caterino. *See* 8824.

Celtis. 9232. Frei, Ursula. "Conradus Celtis, Od. 1, 16 Ad Sepulum disidemonem." [F 5]:118–23.

Dominic of Flanders. 9233. Dominikus von Flandern. *Quaestiones in Thomae de Aquino commentaria super libros posteriorum.* Frankfurt: Minerva. [Repr. of Venice ed., 1514.]

Erasmus. 9234. Bainton, Roland H. *Erasmus of Christendom.* New York: Scribners, 1969.

9235. Bataillon, Marcel. "Un extremo del irenismo erasmiano en el *Adagio Bellum.*" [F 34]:35–49.

9236. Béné, Ch. *Erasme et S. Augustin ou influence de S. Augustin sur l'humanisme d'Erasme.* (THR 103.) Geneva: Droz, 1969.

9237. Beumer, J. *Erasmus, der Europäer. Die Beziehungen des Rotterdamers zu den Humanisten seiner Zeit unter den verschiedenen Nationen Europas.* (Franziskanische Forschungen

22.) Werl: Dietrich-Doelde-Verl., 1969.

9238. —— "Erasmus von Rotterdam:Seine humanistischen Gegner in Italien." *Theologie und Philosophie* 44(1969):1–24.

9239. —— "Erasmus von Rotterdam und Georg Witzel:Ihr gegenseitiges Verhältnis und ihre Stellungnahme zur Reformation." *Catholica* 22(1968):41–67.

9240. —— "Erasmus von Rotterdam und seine Freunde aus dem Franziskanerorden." *FrSt* 51(1969):117–29.

9241. Boyer, Ch. "Luther et Erasme." *Doctor Communis* 22(1969):5–24.

9241a. Chantraine, Georges. "Érasme théologien?" *RHE* 64(1969):811–20.

9242. —— "Le mustérion paulinien selon les Annotations d'Erasme." *RechSR* 58:351–82.

9243. —— "Théologie et vie spirituelle:Un aspect de la méthode théologique selon Erasme." *Nouvelle Revue Théologique* 91(1969):809–33.

9244. Cherchi, Paolo. "*La sinagoga degli ignoranti* di C. Garzoni e gli *Adagia* di Erasmo." *GSLI* 146(1969):391–96.

9245. Devereux, E.J. *A Checklist of English Translations of Erasmus to 1700.* (Oxford Bibliog. Soc.) Oxford: Bodleian Lib., 1968.

9246. —— "The Publication of the English *Paraphrases* of Erasmus." *BJRL* 51(1968–69):348–67.

9246a. Gail, A.J.,ed. and tr. *Erasmus (von Rotterdam), Fürstenerziehung:Institutio principis christiani.* Paderborn: Schöningh, 1968.

9247. Gay, Peter. *The Bridge of Criticism:Dialogues Among Lucian, Erasmus, and Voltaire on the Enlightenment....* New York: Harper & Row.

9248. Gerlo, Aloïs, and Frans de Raeve. *Répertoire des lettres traduites d'Erasme.* Bruxelles: Presses univs., 1969.

9249. Halkin, L.-E. "Erasme, enfant terrible de l'Eglise romaine." *RGB* 6(1969):15–23.

9250. —— *Erasme et l'humanisme chrétien.* (CVS 107.) Paris: Eds. Univs., 1969.

9251. —— "Erasme et les langues." *RLV* 35(1969):566–79.

9252. Hirsch, Elisabeth F. "Erasmus and Portugal." *BHR* 32:539–57.

9253. Ijsevyn, Jozef. "Die *Stultitia Laus* des Erasmus und die *De Triumpho Stultitiae libri III* des Faustinus Perisauli." *Meander* 22(1967):327–39.

9254. Jakštas, Juozas. "Erazmas Roterdamietis ir Žygimantas Senasis." *Aidai* :66–70.

9255. Jarrott, C.A.L. "Erasmus' Biblical Humanism." *SRen* 17:119–52.

9256. Kaegi, W. *Erasmus ehedem und heute, 1469–1969.* (Basler Universitätsreden Fasc. 61.) Bâle: Helbing and Lichtenhahn, 1969.

9257. Koch, A.C.F. *The Year of Erasmus' Birth and Other Contributions to the Chronology of His Life.* Utrecht: Haentjes, Dekker, and Gumbert, 1969. [Pamphlet.]

9258. Kristeller, Paul O. "Erasmus from an Italian Perspective." *RenQ* 23:1–14.

9259. Lochner, G.W. "Zwingli und Erasmus." *Zwingliana* 13,i(1969):37–61.

9260. Margolin, Jean-Claude. "Du nouveau sur Erasme:Un billet inédit de l'humaniste hollandais." *BHR* 32:107–13.

9261. —— *Quatorze années de bibliographie érasmienne (1936–1949).* Paris: Vrin, 1969.

9262. —— *Recherches érasmiennes.* (THR 105.) Genève: Droz, 1969.

9263. Matheeussen, Constant. "De verhouding van de godsdienst en de cultuur in Erasmus' ideaal van de mens." *HZM* 23(1969):189–203.

9264. Mesnard, Pierre (✝). *Érasme.* (Philosophes de tous les temps 51.) Paris: Seghers, 1969.

9265. Nauwelaerts, M.A. "Erasmus." *Spiegel Historiael* 4(1969):195–202.

9266. Nugent, D. "The Erasmus Renaissance." *Month* 229:36–45.

9267. Palacios, B. "Carranza y Erasmo." *Rev. de la Univ. de Madrid* 34(1968):41–89.

9268. Panofsky, Erwin. "Erasmus and the Visual Arts."

JWCI 32(1969):200–27.

9268a. Petruzzellis, N. *Erasmo pensatore.* 2nd Ed. Naples: Lib. Scientifica Editrice, 1969.

9269. Reulos, M. *Érasme à Paris.* (La Montagne Ste. Geneviève et ses abords 121.) Paris: Soc. Histor. et Archéol. du 5ᵉ Arrondissement, 1968.

9270. Rudolph, G. "Das sozialökonomische Denken des Erasmus von Rotterdam." *Deutsche Zeitschrift für Philosophie* 17(1969):1076–92.

9271. Steinmetz, M. "Desiderius Erasmus von Rotterdam." *Zeitschrift für Geschichtswissenschaft* 17(1969):1416–26.

9272. Tobriner, Sister Marion L. "Juan Luis Vives and Erasmus." *Moreana* 24(1969):35–44.

9273. Uscatescu, G. *Erasmo.* (CEn.) Madrid: Edit. Nacional, 1969.

9274. Vloemans, Antoon. "Erasmus 1469–1969." *VlG* 53, ii(1969):3–11.

9275. Williams, Mary R. "Selections from the Letters of Erasmus (1529–1536):Translation and Commentary." *DAI* 30: 3441A(St. Louis U.).
See also 2250, 8899.

Faber Stapulensis. 9276. Faber Stapulensis. *Metphysica [sic] Aristotelis bessarione latinitate donatum, cum adiecto argyropoli interpretamento; Theophrasti metaphysicorum liberi; Metaphysica introductio Fabri Stapulensis.* Frankfurt: Minerva. [Repr. of Paris ed., 1515.]

Fludd. 9277. Ammann, Peter J. "The Musical Theory and Philosophy of Robert Fludd." *JWCI* 30(1967):198–227.

Francisco de Vitoria. 9278. Langford, M.J. "A Defence of the Theory of the Just War, with Special Reference to Francisco de Vitoria." *HAB* 21,iii:54–64.

Gager. 9279. Binns, J.W. "William Gager's *Meleager* and *Ulysses Redux.*" [F 46]:26–41.

Gemma, Cornelius. 9280. Secret, F. "Cornelius Gemma et la prophétie de la *Sibylle tiburtine.*" *RHE* 64(1969):423–31.

Giles of Viterbo. 9281. O'Malley, John W. "Fulfillment of the Christian Golden Age under Pope Julius II:Text of a Discourse of Giles of Viterbo, 1507." *Traditio* 25(1969):265–338.

Goclenius. 9281a. Rudolph Goclenius. *Apologeticus pro astromantia discursus.* Frankfurt: Minerva. [Repr. of Marburg ed., 1611.]

9281b. —— *Liber mirabilium naturae.* Frankfurt: Minerva. [Repr. of Frankfurt ed., 1625.]

9281c. —— *Psychologia, hoc est de hominis perfectione, animo et in primis ortu huius commentationes.* Frankfurt: Minerva. [Repr. of Marburg ed., 1594.]

Grotius. 9282. *De Dichtwerken van Hugo Grotius.* I:*Oorspronkelijke Dichtwerken:Sacra in quibus Adamus Exul.* Vol. A. Tekst en Vertaling, in samenwerking met G. Kuiper on L. Ph. Rank vertaald door B.L. Meulenbroek. Met gebruikmaking van onuitgegeven werk van J.M. Hoek. Assen: Van Gorcum.

Guido of Baysio. 9283. Guido de Baysio [Archidiaconus Bononiensis]. *Super decreto.* Frankfurt: Minerva. [Repr. of Lyon ed., 1558.]

Hassenstein. 9284. Martinek, J., and D. Martinková,eds. *Bohuslai Hassensteinii a Lobkowicz Epistulae.* T. I:*Epistulae de re publica scriptae.* Leipzig: Teubner, 1969.

Heimeric of Campo. 9285. Kaluza, Zénon. "Les écrits de Heimeric de Campo sur sainte Brigitte de Suède." *RTAM* 36(1969):213–21.

Jacobellus of Stříbro. 9286. De Vooght, Paul. "Le sermon *Factum est ut moreretur mendicus* de Jacobellus de Stříbro (nov. 1413)." *RTAM* 36(1969):195–212.

Jordaens. 9287. Svennung, J. "Zu Cassiodor und Jordanes." *Eranos* 67(1969):71–80.

Kircher. 9288. Fletcher, J.E. "A Brief Survey of the Unpublished Correspondence of Athanasius Kircher, S.J. (1602–1680)." *Manuscripta* 13(1969):150–60.

Loot, John. 9289. Van Peteghem, Paul. "Joannes Chrysostomus Loot (1598–1656)." *Augustiniana* 19(1969):552–82.

Muret. 9290. Ornato, E. "L'umanista Jean Muret ed il suo dialogo *De contemptu mortis.*" *Misc. di Studi e Ricerche sul Quattrocento Francese* (1967):241–353.

Perfidus Hetruscus. 9291. Wittmann, Richard G. "*Perfidus Hetruscus*:A Neo-Latin Tragedy Edited and Translated with a Commentary." *DAI* 30:3442A(St. Louis U.).

Peter the Martyr. 9292. Petrus Martyr. *De rebus oceanicis et novo orbe.* Frankfurt: Minerva. [Repr. of Köln ed., 1574.]

Piccolomini. 9293. Baca, Albert R.,tr. and ed. *Selected Letters of Aeneas Silvius Piccolomini.* (RESFV 2.) Northridge, Calif.: San Fernando Valley State Coll., 1969.

Pierre Assalhit. 9294. Alonso, C. "Pierre Assalhit O.S.A., Obispo de Alet y Sacrista pontificio (+ 1441)." *Augustiniana* 20:107–44.

Pio da Costacciaro. 9295. Heynck, V. "Der Einfluss des Skotismus auf dem Konzil von Trent (Bonaventura Pio da Costacciaro, O.F.M.Conv., der Führer der skotistischen Gruppe in der ersten Tagungsperiode, 1545–1547)." [F 68],IV:259–90.

Ramus. 9296. Dunn, Catherine M.,ed. *The Logike of the Moste Excellent Philosopher P. Ramus Martyr.* (RESFV 3.) Tr. by Roland MacIlmaine (1574). Northridge, Calif.: San Fernando Valley State Coll., 1969.

Reinking. 9297. Theodor Reinking. *Tractatus de regimine saeculari et ecclesiastico.* Frankfurt: Minerva. [Repr. of 1651 ed.]

Sabellicus. 9298. M. Antonius Coccius Sabellicus. *Opera.* 2 vols. Frankfurt: Minerva. [Repr. of Basel ed., 1538.]

Seripand. 9299. Forster, A.,ed *Girolamo Seripando, "De iustitia et libertate christiana."* (Cor. Cath. 30.) Münster: Aschendorff, 1969.

9300. Hieronymus Seripandus. *Doctrina orandi.* Frankfurt: Minerva. [Repr. of Louvain ed., 1661.]

Sigea. 9301. Sauvage, Odette,ed. *Louise Sigée. Dialogue de deux jeunes filles sur la vie de coeur et la vie de retraite.* Présenté, traduit, et annoté. Paris: Presses univs. [Crit. ed. and Fr. tr. of *Duarum virginum colloquium de vita aulica et privata* by Loysa Sigea (1522–1560).]

Simon, Richard. 9302. Richard Simon [Jerome à Costa]. *Antiquitates ecclesiae orientalis.* Frankfurt: Minerva. [Repr. of London ed., 1682.]

Trapezunt. 9303. Georg von Trapezunt. *Rhetoricorum libri Quinque.* Frankfurt: Minerva. [Repr. of Paris ed., 1538.]

William Worcestre. 9304. Harvey, John H.,ed. and tr. *William Worcestre Itineraries.* (Oxford Medieval Texts.) Oxford: Clarendon, 1969.

CELTIC LITERATURES†

I. GENERAL

General. 9305. Arnold, Matthew. *The Study of Celtic Literature.* Port Washington, N.Y.: Kennikat. [Repr. of 1905 ed.; orig. pub. 1867.]

9305a. Bowen, Emrys G. "The Irish Sea in the Age of the Saints." *StC* 4(1969):56–71.

9306. —— *Saints, Seaways, and Settlements in the Celtic Lands.* Cardiff: U. of Wales P., 1969.

9307. Boyle, Alexander. "St. Servanus and the Manuscript Tradition of the Life of St. Kentigern." *Innes Rev.* 21:37–45.

9308. Cormier, Raymond J. "Tom Peete Cross:An American Celticist (1879–1951)." *Éire* 5,iv:112–15.

9309. Dunn, Charles W. "The Present State of Celtic Studies in North America." *StC* 4(1969):112–18.

† *Festschriften* and Other Analyzed Collections are listed in the first division of this Bibliography, and have been assigned Item numbers 1–95. "F" numbers in brackets following a title refer to these items.

9310. Feachem, Richard. "Mons Craupius Duncrub?" *Antiquity* 44:120–24.

9311. Hogg, A.H.A. "A Sample of French Hill-forts." *Antiquity* 43(1969):260–73.

9312. Le Roux, Françoise. "Notes d'histoire des religions XVIII." *Celticum* 16(1967):239–56.

9313. Lengyel, Lancelot. *Le secret des Celtes.* Paris, 1969.

9314. Mac Cana, Proinsias. *Celtic Mythology.* London.

9315. MacLean, Magnus. *The Literature of the Celts.* Port Washington, N.Y.: Kennikat. [Repr. of 1902 ed.]

9316. Markale, Jean. *Les Celtes et la civilisation celtique. Mythe et histoire.* Paris, 1969. [Maps and index.]

9317. Meid, Wolfgang. *Indogermanisch und Keltisch.* Innsbruck, 1968.

9318. Nyssen, Wilhelm, and Franz-Peter Sonntag. *Der Gott der wandernden Völker.* Leipzig, 1969.

9319. Rivet, A.L.F. *The Roman Villa in Britain.* London, 1969.

9320. Ross, Anne. *Everyday Life of the Pagan Celts.* London. [Drawings by R.W. Feachem.]

9321. Serbanesco, Gérard. *Les Celtes et les Druides.* Paris, 1968. [Illus.]

9322. Travis, James. *Miscellanea Musica Celtica.* Brooklyn, N.Y.: Inst. of Mediaeval Music, 1968. [See esp. Pt. 2, "The Celtic Provenance of the Reading Rota."]

* 9323. Vesce, Thomas E. "Celtic Material in *Les Mervelles de Rigomer.*" *RomN* 11:640–46.

See also 4940, 9545.

II. BIBLIOGRAPHY

9325. *Bibliotheca Celtica:A Register of Publications Relating to Wales and the Celtic Peoples and Languages:1967.* Aberystwyth: Nat. Lib. of Wales.

9326. Davies, Alun Eirug. "Sir Ifor Williams:A Bibliography." *StC* 4(1969):1–55.

9327. Johnston, Edith M. *Irish History.* London, 1969. [A select bibliog.]

9328. Keaney, Marian. *Westmeath Authors.* Mullingar, 1969. [A bibliog. and biog. study.]

9329. Ó Dufaigh, Seosamh. "Irish Local Historical and Archaeological Journals." *Éire* 5,iii:90–99.

9330. Ó Riain, Pádraig. *Clár na Lámhscríbhinni Gaeilge sa Bhreatain Bhig.* Dublin, 1968.

9331. Watts, Garrett O., comp. "A List of Books, Articles, etc., Concerning Various Aspects of the Celtic Languages, Received at the National Library of Wales, Aberystwyth, During 1968." *StC* 4(1969):122–28.

9332. Watts, Garrett O.,comp. "A List of Books, Articles, etc., Concerning Various Aspects of the Celtic Languages, Received at the National Library of Wales, Aberystwyth, During 1967." *StC* 3(1968):141–46.

See also 459.

III. BRETON

9333. Bernier, G. "Staer-Ster-Estoer-Ester." *AnBret* 76(1969):649–58.

9334. ——. "Vieux-breton *Arrith,* Vannetais de Quiberon *Arrèheu.*" *AnBret* 76(1969):659–61.

9335. Bullock-Davies, Constance. "Lanval and Avalon." *BBCS* 23(1969):128–42.

9336. Corbes, H. "Les traductions en langues étrangères du 'Barzaz-Breis'." *Lochlann* 4(1969):160–78.

9337. Latimer, G. "L'inscription des Aulnays en Gomene." *AnBret* 76(1969):625–48.

9338. Pinault, G. "*An Novelov Ancien* ha devot (§§ 534–580)." *AnBret* 76(1969):663–703.

See also 9340.

IV. CORNISH

9339. Evans, D. Simon. "The Story of Cornish." *Studies* 58(1969):293–308.

9340. Fleuriot, L. "Breton et Cornique à la fin du moyen-âge." *AnBret* 76(1969):705–24.

V. GAULISH

9341. Carcopino, Jérôme. "Per extremos fines Lingonum." *REAnc* 71(1969):57–64. [On the location of the Sequani and the Lingones.]

9342. Rogers, Mary. "Faremoutiers:A Legacy from St. Columbanus." *Éire* 3,iv(1968):35–45.

VI. IRISH GAELIC

9343. Acton, Charles. "This Heritage to the Race of Kings." *Éire* 4,iv(1969):112–34. [On Irish harps, harpers, violinists, flutists, bagpipers, bardic poems, etc.]

9344. Arbois de Jubainville, Henry d'. *The Irish Mythological Cycle and Celtic Mythology.* Tr. from Fr. with Addit. Notes by Richard I. Best. New York: Lemma Pubs. [Repr. of 1903 ed.]

9345. Beechhold, Henry F. "*A Gaelic Lexicon for* Finnegans Wake, by Brendan Ó Hehir." *Éire* 5,i:136–38. [Rev. art.; adds items to Ó Hehir's list.]

9346. Breatnach, Pádraig A. "*Séadna:*Saothar Ealaíne." *SH* 9(1969):109–24.

9347. Bruford, Alan. *Gaelic Folk-Tales and Mediaeval Romances.* Dublin, 1969.

9348. Brún, Pádraig de. "Caoine ar Mhac Fínín Duibh." *Éigse* 13:221–24.

9349. ——. "Ranna Fáin." *Éigse* 13:104.

9350. Buday, G. "Notes upon My Wood-Engraving Illustration of the Ancient Irish Folk Saga *Oisín i dTír na nÓg.*" *AEASH* 19:91–93.

9351. Buí ab Fhómhair. *Cnuasach Próis agus Filíochta arna roghnú ag na Bráithre Críostaí.* Dublin, 1969.

9352. Calder, Grace J. *George Petrie and* The Ancient Music of Ireland. (New Dolmen Chapbooks 10.) Dublin: Dolmen Press; Chester Springs, Pa.: Dufour.

9353. Carney, James. "Gas Lossa." *Éigse* 13:99–103.

9354. ——. "The Ó Cianáin Miscellany." *Ériu* 21(1969):122–47. [From Nat. Lib. of Ireland MSS. G2 and G3; 14th cent., attrib. to Ádhamh Ó Cianáin.]

9355. ——. "The So-called 'Lament of Créidhe'." *Éigse* 13:227–42.

9356. Carney, Maura. "The Works of the Sixth Day." *Ériu* 21(1969):148–66. [From Nat. Lib. of Ireland MS. G3; 15th cent.]

9357. Cormier, Raymond J. "Early Irish Tradition and Memory of the Norsemen in 'The Wooing of Emer'." *SH* 9(1969):65–75.

9358. Cullen, L.M. "The Hidden Ireland:Re-assessment of a Concept." *SH* 9(1969):7–47.

9359. De Blacam, Aodh Sandrach. *A First Book of Irish Literature:Hiberno-Latin, Gaelic, Anglo-Irish from the Earliest Times to the Present Day.* Port Washington, N.Y.: Kennikat. [Repr. of 1934 ed.]

9360. Dillon, Myles. "An Saighead." *Éigse* 13:186–87.

9361. —— *Stories from the Acallam.* Dublin: Dublin Inst. for Advanced Studies.

9362. Fackler, Herbert V. "Nineteenth-Century Sources for the Deirdre Legend." *Éire* 4,iv(1969):56–63.

9363. Flanagan, Deirdre. "Ecclesiastical Nomenclature in Irish Texts and Place-Names:A Comparison." [F 26],I:378–88.

9364. Flood, Joseph M. *Ireland:Its Myths and Legends.* Port Washington, N.Y.: Kennikat. [Illus. C. MacDowell. Repr.]

9365. —— *Ireland:Its Saints and Scholars.* Port Washington, N.Y.: Kennikat. [Repr.]

9366. Gaechter, Paul. *Die Gedächtniskultur in Irland.* Innsbruck: Inst. für Vergleichende Sprachwissenschaft. [64-p. pamphlet.]

9367. Gillies, William. "A Poem on the Downfall of the Gaodhil." *Éigse* 13:203–10.

9368. Herity, Michael. "A Tour of John Windele's in South Kerry, 1848." *JKAHS* 3:99–115.

9369. Hoppen, K. Theodore, and Pádraig de Brún. "Samuel Molyneux's Tour of Kerry, 1709." *JKAHS* 3:59–80.

9370. Hyde, Douglas. *Love Songs of Connacht.* Shannon: Irish U.P., 1969. [Repr. of the 1893 ed.]

9371. Jones, R. Brinley. *The Old British Tongue. The Vernacular in Wales 1540–1640.* Cardiff.

9372. Kennedy, Patrick,coll. *Legendary Fictions of the Irish Celts.* New York: Blom, 1969. [Repr. of 1866 ed.]

9373. Kennelly, Brendan. *A Drinking Cup. Poems From the Irish.* Dublin.

9374. Kennelly, Brendan,ed. and introd. *The Penguin Book of Irish Verse.* Harmondsworth: Penguin.

9375. Kinsella, Thomas,ed. *The Tain.* London: Oxford U.P. [Eng. tr.]

9376. Kinsella, Thomas,tr. and introd. "Cuchulainn's Boyhood Deeds. Translated from the *Taín Bó Cuailnge* and Introduced." *MHRev* 8(1968):91–104.

9377. Lehmann, Ruth P. "The Banquet of the Fort of the Geese." *Lochlann* 4(1969):131–59.

9378. Mac Carvill, Eileen. "Jonathan Swift, Aodh Buí Mac Cruitin and Contemporary Thomond Scholars." *N. Munster Antiquarian Jour.* 11(1968):36–45.

9379. Malachy, Saint, abp. of Armagh. *Prophecies of St. Malachy & St. Columbkille.* Gerrards Cross, 1969.

9380. Martin, B.K. *Aspects of Old Irish Literature and European Antiquity.* (Austral. Acad. of the Humanities, Monog. 1.) Sydney: Sydney U.P. for the Austral. Acad. [Bound with S.T. Knight, *The Nature of Early Welsh Poetry.* 47-p. pamphlet.]

9381. Meid, Wolfgang. *Die Romanze Von Froech und Findabair:Taín Bó Froích:Altirischer Text, mit Einleitung, deutscher Übersetzung, ausführlischem philologisch-linguistischem Kommentar und Glosser kritisch herausgegeben von Wolfgang Meid.* (Innsbrucker Beiträge zur Kulturwissenschaft; hrsg. von der Innsbrucker Gesellschaft zur Pflege der Geisteswissenschaften, Sonderheft 30.) Innsbruck.

9382. —— *Táin Bó Froích.* Innsbruck. [Old Irish text, Ger. tr., and commentary.]

9383. Merriman, Brian. *Cúirt an Mhéan Oíche.* Dublin, 1969.

9384. Messenger, John C. *Inis Beag, Isle of Ireland.* New York: Holt, 1969. [Case studies in cultural anthropol.]

9385. Mhág Craith, Cuthbert. "A Note on Alliteration in Irish Bardic Poetry, c. 1200–c. 1650." *StC* 4(1969):110–11.

9386. Mooney, Canice. *The Church in Gaelic Ireland:Thirteenth to Fifteenth Centuries.* Dublin, 1969.

9387. Ní Mhuiríosa, Máirín. *Réamhchonraitheoirí.* Dublin,

1968.

9388. Ó Baoill, Colm. "Cleimhrián:Clocharán." *Éigse* 13:90–91.

9389. Ó Buachalla, Breandán. "Murchadh Mac Briain agus an Díthreachach." *Éigse* 13:85–89.

9390. Ó Buachalla, Breandán,ed. *Peadar Ó Doirnín.* Dublin, 1969.

9391. Ó Cadhain, Máirtín. *An tSraith dhá Tógáil.* Dublin.

9392. Ó Conaire, Pádhraic Óg. *Éan Cuideáin.* Dublin.

9393. Ó Corráin, Donncha. "Later Eóganacht Pedigrees." *JCHAS* 74(1969):141–46.

9394. —— "Lugaid Cál and the Callraige." *Éigse* 13:225–26.

9395. —— "Raigne, Roigne, Mag Raigni." *Éigse* 13:81–84.

9396. —— "Studies in West Munster History:IIa. A Further Note on the Alltraighe." *JKAHS* 3:19–22.

9397. Ó Cuív, Brian. "A Pilgrim's Poem." *Éigse* 13:105–09.

9398. —— "A Poem for Cathal Croibhdhearg Ó Conchubhair." *Éigse* 13:195–202.

9399. —— "A Seventeenth-Century Irish Manuscript." *Éigse* 13:143–52.

9400. Ó Daly, Máirín. "Three Poems Ascribed to Máol Cobha." *Ériu* 21(1969):103–15.

9401. Ó Fiannachta, Pádraig. "Lámhscríbhinní Gaeilge i Leabharlainn Dheoise Chiarraí." *Éigse* 13:188–94.

9402. —— "Two Love Poems." *Ériu* 21(1969):115–21. [From two 18th cent. MSS. of St. Patrick's College, Maynooth, O'Curry 59 (anon.) and O'Curry 97 (by 'Labhrás Cuimíne').]

9403. Ó Fiannachta, Pádraig,ed. *Léachtaí Cholm Cille 1970. I-Litríocht na Gaeilge.* Má Nuat.

9404. Ó Gaoithín, Mícheál. *Reatha Pheig Sayers.* Dublin.

9405. Ó Háinle, Cathal. "An Chléir agus an Fhiliocht sa 17ú Céad." *Éire* 5,ii:4–19. [With Eng. sum.]

9406. Ó Muireadhaigh, Réamonn. "Moladh ar Ailín Mac Dubhghaill." *Éigse* 13:211–20.

9407. Ó Muirgheasa, Énrí,ed. *Dánta Diadha Uladh.* Dublin, 1969.

9408. Ó Rathaille, Aogán. *Dánta.* Dublin, 1969.

9409. Ó Riain, Pádraig. "A Poem on Séafraidh Ó Donnchadha an Ghleanne." *JKAHS* 3:48–58.

9410. Ó Sé, Seán. "Pádraig Feiritéar (1856–1924):A Shaol agus a Shaothar." *JKAHS* 3:116–30.

9411. Ó Súilleabháin, Seán. "Peig Sayers." *Éire* 5,i:86–91.

9412. O'Brien, Frank. *Duanaire Nuafhilíochta.* Dublin, 1969.

9413. —— "Sliocht as Beathaisnéis:An Piarsach Óg agus Conradh na Gaeilge." *SH* 9(1969):76–85.

9414. O'Connor, Frank,tr. *Kings, Lords, & Commons. An Anthology from the Irish.* Dublin.

9415. O'Grady, Standish. *Early Bardic Literature, Ireland.* New York: Lemma Pubs. [Repr. of 1879 ed.]

9416. O'Rahilly, Cecile. "Words Descriptive of Hair in Irish." *Éigse* 13:177–80.

9417. Oskamp, H.P.A. "Mochen, Mochen, a Brénaind." *Éigse* 13:92–98.

9418. —— "Notes on the History of Lebor na hUidre." *Proc. of the Royal Irish Acad.* 65 C6(1967):117–37.

9419. —— *The Voyage of Máel Dúin:A Study in Early Irish Voyage Literature.* Groningen: Wolters-Noordhoff. [Foll. by an ed. of *Immram curaig Máele Dúin* from the Yellow Book of Lecan in Trinity Coll., Dublin.]

9420. Powell, Roger. "Further Notes on *Lebor na h-Uidre.*" *Ériu* 21(1969):99–102.

9421. Power, Patrick C. *A Literary History of Ireland.* Cork, 1969.

9422. Ridge, Seamus. *Conamara Man.* Englewood Cliffs, N.J.: Prentice-Hall, 1969.

9423. Sealy, Douglas,tr. "Five Poems by Mairtin Ó Direáin." *DM* 8,i–ii(1969):63–65.

9424. Sullivan, Daniel J. "Standish James O'Grady's *All Ireland Review.*" *SH* 9(1969):125–36.

9425. Williams, N.J.A. "Eachtra Áodh Mhic Goireachtaidh." *Éigse* 13:111–42.

See also 1595, 5307, 5308, 5804, 5986, 9911, 10442, 10622, 10780, 10841, 11101.

VII. MANX

9426. Cregeen, Archibald. *A Dictionary of the Manks Lan-* *guage.* Douglas, 1969. [Repr. of 1835 ed.]

VIII. SCOTTISH GAELIC

9427. Alger, Leclaire. *By Loch and By Lin.* New York: Holt, 1969. [Tales from Scottish ballads retold by Sorche Nic Leodhas and illus. by Vera Bock.]

9428. Barron, Hugh. "Dan na h-Iomairt, 1757." *SGS* 11(1968):192–201. [Pt. 2.]

9429. —— "Some Gaelic Verse from North Inverness-shire." *TGSI* 45(for 1967–68):370–92.

9430. Bruford, Alan. "Logaidh Longsach." *ScS* 12(1968): 190–92. [Pt. 2.]

9431. Campbell, Duncan. "Gaelic Proverbs." *TGSI* 45(for 1967–68):1–32.

9432. Campbell, John L. "Notes on the Poems Ascribed to Mary Mac Leod in D.C. Macpherson's Duanaire." *SGS* 11(1968):171–91. [Pt. 2.]

9433. Cross, Tom P. *Motif-Index of Early Irish Literature.* New York: Kraus, 1969. [Repr. of 1952 Ind. U. ed.]

9434. Dorian, Nancy C. "East Sutherland By-Naming." *ScS* 14:59–66. [Pt. 1.]

9435. Mac Lean, Fitzroy. *A Concise History of Scotland.* London. [With 231 illus., 2 maps, and an Index.]

9436. Maclean, John. "Translating Homer." *TGSI* 45(for 1967–68):354–69.

9437. Maclean, S. "Silis of Keppoch." *TGSI* 45(for 1967–68): 98–112.

9438. MacLeoid, Calum Iain M. *Sgialachdan a Albainn Nuaidh.* Glasgow, 1969.

9439. Matheson, William. "Further Gleanings from the Cornie Manuscripts." *TGSI* 45(for 1967–68):148–95.

9440. Nicolaisen, W.F.H. "Aspects of Scottish Mountain Names." [F 26],I:109–15.

9441. —— "Norse Settlement in the Northern and Western Isles." *Scottish Hist. Rev.* 48(1969):6–17.

9442. —— "The Distribution of Certain Gaelic Mountain Names." *TGSI* 45(for 1967–68):113–28.

9443. Thomson, Derick S. "Unpublished Letters by the Poet Ewen MacLachlan." *SGS* 11(1968):202–36. [Pt. 2.]
See also 10274.

IX. WELSH

9444. Bowen, D.J. "Nodiadau ar Waith y Cywyddwyr." *Llên Cymru* 10(1969):113–21.

9445. Bowen, Geraint. "Tribanu John Jones, y Resiwsant o Frycheiniog." *Llên Cymru* 10(1968):70–75.

9446. Brady, Charles A. *"The Gododdin.* The Oldest Scottish Poem, by Kenneth Hurlstone Jackson." *Éire* 5,i:153–56. [Rev. art.; see Bibliog. for 1969, Vol. I, Item 9060.]

9447. Clancy, Joseph P. *The Earliest Welsh Poetry.* London: Macmillan. [Taliesin and Aneirin through Dafydd Bach ap Madawg Wladaidd.]

9448. Clarke, Basil. "Calidon and the Caledonian Forest." *BBCS* 23(1969):191–201.

9449. Edwards, Owain Tudor. *Joseph Barry, 1841–1903.* Caerdydd (Cardiff): Gwasg Prifysgol Cymru.

9450. Ellis, Tecwyn. "Bardd y Brenin, Iolo Morganwg a Derwyddiaeth, pt. vii." *NLWJ* 15(1967):177–96. [Pt. 2; sum. in Eng.]

9451. Evans, Simon D. "A Welsh Bible:The Defeat of the Armada." *Trivium* 5:47–56.

9452. Foster, I. Ll. "Wales and North Britain." *Archaeologia Cambrensis* 118(1969):1–16.

9453. Great Britain, Central Advisory Council for Education (Wales). *Primary Education in Wales.* London, 1967.

9454. Gruffydd, R. Geraint. "Yny Lhyvyr Hwnn (1546):The Earliest Welsh Printed Book." *BBCS* 23(1969):105–16.

* 9455. Holmes, Urban T. "The *Kambriae Descriptio* of Gerald the Welshman." *M&H* N.S. 1:217–31.

9456. Humphries, Rolfe,comp. *Nine Thorny Thickets.* Selected Poems by Dafydd ap Gwilym in New Arrangements by Rolfe Humphries. With Four Trs. by Jon Roush. Kent, Ohio: Kent State U.P., 1969[1970].

9457. Huws, Daniel. "Iewan ab Iago." *NLWJ* 16(1969): 172–84. [Pt. 2.]

9458. Jones, Bedwyr L. "R. Williams Parry a Phantycelyn." *Y Traethodydd* 125(Hydref):230–33.

9459. Jones, Emyr Gwynne. "Llythyrau Lewis Morris at William Vaughan, Corsygedol." *Llên Cymru* 10(1968):3–58.

9460. Jones, Gwilym R. "Williams, Bardd y Seiat." *Y Traethodydd* 125(Gorff.):165–72.

9461. Jones, John Gwilym. "Emyn gan Pantycelyn." *Y Traethodydd* 125(Ionawr):9–12.

9462. Jones, John Gwilym,tr. *Goronwy Owen's Virginian Adventure:His Life, Poetry, and Literary Opinions, with a Translation of His Virginian Letters.* (BBSP 2.) With a Lecture. Williamsburg, Va.: The Botetourt Bibliog. Soc., 1969. [36–p. pamphlet.]

9463. Jones, John Maxwell,Jr.,ed. *Cyfarwyddiadur Awduron Cymraeg Cyfoes:Bywgraffyddol a Llyfryddol.* Philadelphia: Cyhoeddwyd gan y Golygydd.

9464. Jones, Richard. "Atgofion am Cynan." *Yr Eurgrawn* 162:74–79. [Memories of the poet Albert Evans Jones.]

9465. Jones, R.M. *Highlights in Welsh Literature. Talks with a Prince.* Swansea and Llandybie, 1969. [With portraits and select bibliog.]

9466. Knight, S.T. *The Nature of Early Welsh Poetry.* (Austral. Acad. of the Humanities, Monog. 1.) Sydney: Sydney U.P. for the Austral. Acad. [Bound with B.K. Martin, *Aspects of Old Irish Literature and European Antiquity.* 47-p. pamphlet.]

9467. Lewis, Saunders. "Ardwyre Reget Ryssed Riu." *Llên Cymru* 10(1968):110–13. [Notes on a poem in *Canu Taliesin.*]

9468. Lloyd, D. Tecwyn. "Daniel Owen ar y Llwyfran, [sic] 1909–1937." *Llên Cymru* 10(1968):59–69.

9469. Rhys, John, and David Brynmor-Jones. *The Welsh People:Chapters on Their Origin, History and Laws, Language, Literature and Characteristics.* New York: Greenwood, 1969. [Repr. of 1923 ed.]

9470. Roberts, Glyn. *Aspects of Welsh History.* Cardiff, 1969.

9471. Wakelin, Martyn F. "Welsh Influence in the West of England:Dialectal 'Tallet'." *FoL* 8:72–80.

9472. Williams, Gwyn. *An Introduction to Welsh Poetry:From the Beginnings to the Sixteenth Century.* Freeport, N.Y.: Books for Libs. [Repr. of 1953 ed.]

9473. Williams, Trevor L. *Caradoc Evans.* Cardiff: U. of Wales P.

9474. Wyn Jones, Emyr. "Ieuan Lleyn ac Ynys Enlli." *NLWJ* 15(1968):290–309. [Pt. 3; sum. in Eng.]
See also 4757, 8898, 8911, 9586, 11097.

FOLKLORE†

I. GENERAL

Bibliography and Discography

9475. Andral, Maguy P. "Discographie 1967." *ATP* 16(1968):344–51.
9476. Andral, M[aguy] P. "Discographie 1968." *ATP* 17(1969):169–75.
9477. Ferris, William R.,Jr. "Discography of Mississippi Negro Folk Music." *MissFR* 2(1968):51–54.
9478. Gibson, Gordon D.,comp. "A Bibliography of Anthropological Bibliographies:Africa." *CAnth* 10(1969):527–66.
9479. Haltsonen, Sulo. "Finnische linguistische und volkskundliche Bibliographie für die Jahre 1967–1968." *Studia Fennica* 14(1969):81–128.
9480. Haque, Abu Saeed Zahurul. "A Bibliography of Mississippi Folklore." *MissFR* 2(1968):43–50.
9481. Klymasz, Robert B. *A Bibliography of Ukranian Folklore in Canada, 1902–64.* (Anth. Papers 21.) Ottawa: National Museum of Canada, 1969.
9482. Lapadu-Hargues, Françoise. "Bibliographie d'ethnographie française 1967." *ATP* 16(1968):352–427.
9483. Mambretti, Mabel. "Bibliografía general del folklore y la etnomusica de Venezuela:Años 1968–70." *RVF* 3:129–48.
9484. Noy, Dov. "The Study of Jewish Folklore in 1968: Selective Bibliography." [F 87]:389–423. [In Hebr.; Eng. sum.]
9485. Paden, John N., and Edward W. Soja. "The African Experience:Bibliography." [F 88],IIIA:1–1103. [Incl. a number of specialized bibliogs.:"Literature and Oral Tradition," 45–51; "Contemporary African Literature," 434–44.]
9486. Pop, M[ihai]. *Bibliografia generală a etnografici și folclorului românesi:I (1800–1891).* Introd. Foehi A[drian]. București: Editura Pentru Literatură, 1968.
9487. Schmidt, Nancy J. "A Bibliography of American Doctoral Dissertations on African Literature." *RAL* 1:62–65.
9488. Sidel'nikov, V.M. *Ustnoe poètičeskoe tvorčestvo kazaxskogo naroda:Bibliografičeskij ukazatel' 1771–1966 gg.* Alma-Ata: Nauka, 1969.
9489. Skrodenis, Stasys. "Užgavėnių papročiai ir tautosaka: Medžiaga bibliografijai." *Liaudies Kūryba*(Vilnius) 1(1969): 343–54. [Sum. in Rus.]
9490. Tremaud, Hélène. "Filmographie 1967." *ATP* 16(1968):340–43.
9491. —— "Filmographie 1968." *ATP* 17(1969):166–68.
9492. Tyler, Sara. "Addendum to Gordon Wilson Bibliography." *KFR* 15(1969):91–92.
9493. Ullom, Judith C.,ed. *Folklore of the North American Indians:An Annotated Bibliography.* Wash., D.C.: Lib. of Congress, 1969.
See also 9524, 9571.

History and Study of Folklore

9498. Agblemagnon, F. N'Sougan. *Sociologie des société orales d'Afrique noire:Les Eve du Sud-Togo.* Pref. R. Bastide. La Haye: Mouton, 1969.
9499. Almeida-Topor, Hélène. "Rigueur historique et imprécision de la tradition orale." *Bull. de l'Enseignement Supérieur du Bénin*(Lomé, Togo) 11(1969):46–54.
9500. Antonijević, Dragoslav. "Folklorismus in Jugoslawien." *ZV* 65(1969):29–39.
9501. Balandin, A.I. *P.I. Jakuškin:Iz istorii russkoj fol'kloristiki.* Moscow: Nauka, 1969.
9502. Balys, Jonas. "Folklore Research in the Baltic Countries, Especially Lithuania, in the Soviet Period." *LD* 2(1969): 67–75.

† *Festschriften* and Other Analyzed Collections are listed in the first division of this Bibliography, and have been assigned Item numbers 1–95. "F" numbers in brackets following a title refer to these items.

9503. Baumanis, Fricis. "Haralds Biezais un viņa darbi." *ADz* 12(1969):83–87.
9504. Bausinger, Hermann. "Folklorismus in Europe:Eine Umfrage." *ZV* 65(1969):1–8.
9505. Berezovs'kyj, I.P. "Major Aspects of the Study of Ukrainian Folk Poetry After the October Revolution." [F 91]:380–84. [Sum. in Rus.]
9506. Bhabagrahi, Misra. "An Evaluative Study of the Work of Verrier Elwin, Folklorist." *DAI* 30:3875A–76A(Ind.).
9507. Biezais, Haralds. "Darbi folkloristikā." *JGa* 77:54–57.
9508. Bodinga-bwa-Bodinga, S. *Traditions orales de la race eviya.* Paris: T.M.T., 1969.
9509. Boggs, Edna. "Virginia Rodriguez Rivera (1894–1968)." *JAF* 82(1969):68.
9510. Burrison, John A. "Editor's Comment [on Trends in Folklore Scholarship]." *SLitI* 3,i:1–3.
9511. Burszta, Józef. "Folklorismus in Polen." *ZV* 65(1969): 9–20.
9512. Caramella, Santino. "Demopsicologia e folklore." [F 94],I:75–80.
9513. Chițimia, J.C. "Bases et conditions de la création folklorique contemporaine." [F 91]:145–48.
9513a. —— *Folcloriști și folcloristică românească.* Bucharest: Editura Academiei RSR, 1968.
9514. Cocq, Antonius P.L. de. *Andrew Lang, a Nineteenth Century Anthropologist.* Tilburg: Zwijsen, 1968.
9515. Creslaw, Hernas. "Is Folklore Dead?" *FolkloreC* 9(1968):376–80.
9516. Davidson, Harry C. "Muestras de un 'Diccionario Folclórico'." *BCB* 11,xi(1968):44–75.
9517. Dias, Jorge. "Folklorismus in Portugal." *ZV* 65(1969): 47–55.
9518. Djurić, Vojislav. "Rapports entre la littérature orale et la littérature écrite serbocroates." [F 3]:481–96.
9519. Dömötör, Tekla. "Folklorismus in Ungarn." *ZV* 65(1969):21–28.
9520. Dorson, Richard M. "The Ethnic Research Survey of Northwest Indiana." [F 79]:65–69.
9521. Eretescu, Constantin. "Noțiunea de metamorfoză în folclor." *REF* 15:121–32.
9522. Èterlej, E.N. "Neutomimyj sobiratel'." *RusRe* 4:38–41. [On V.P. Birjukov, Ural folklorist.]
9523. Evans, George E. "Folk Life Studies in East Anglia." [F 82]:35–46.
9523a. Finnegan, Ruth. *Oral Literature in Africa.* (Oxford Lib. of Afr. Lit.) London: Oxford U.P.
9524. Fojtík, Karel, and Oldřich Sirovátka. "Czech Ethnology and Folklore:A Short Outline of Their Development." [F 85]:1–12.
9525. "Folclorul:Autenticitate și impostură." *Contemporanul* 8 May [Spec. section]:6–7.
9526. Friderici, Robert. "Wer entdeckte die Märchenfrau?" *HBV* 60(1969):166–67.
9527. Galkin, I.S. *Voprosy finno-ugrovedenija. Vyp. 5. Lingvistika, fol'kloristika, ètnografija, arxeologija.* Joškar-Ola: Narknigoizdat.
9528. Granger, Byrd H. "Folklore Along the Colorado River." *WR* 6,ii(1969):3–11.
9529. Greverus, Ina-Maria. "Die Chronikerzählung:Ein Beitrag zur Erzählforschung am Beispiel von Chr. Lehmanns 'Historischem Schauplatz' (1699)." [F 81]:37–80.
9530. Gusev, V.E. "Tipizacija dejstvitel'nosti v partizanskom fol'klore." [F 91]:149–55. [Sum. in Fr.]
9531. Hand, Wayland D. "American Occupational and Industrial Folklore:The Miner." [F 79]:453–60.
9532. —— "North American Folklore Societies:Supplement II." *JAF* 82(1969):3–33. [Essays by many hands.]
9533. Hapusenko, I.M. *Dmytro Ivanovyč Javornyc'kyj.* Kyjiv: Naukova dumka, 1969. [Bibliog. incl.]

9534. Hautala, Jouko. *Finnish Folklore Research 1828–1918.* (The Hist. of Learning and Science in Finland 1828–1918.) Helsinki: Societas Scientiarum Fennica, 1969.

9535. Heilfurth, Gerhard. "Über Riehls 'Handwerksgeheimnisse des Volksstudiums'." *HBV* 60(1969):29–38.

* 9536. Hendricks, William O. "Folklore and the Structural Analysis of Literary Texts." *Lang&S* 3:83–121.

9537. Hnatjuk, V.M. *Vybrani statti pro narodnu tvorčist'.* Kyjiv: Naukova dumka, 1966.

9538. Höck, Alfred. "Notizen zur hessischen Landes- und Volkskunde im 19. Jahrhundert." *HBV* 60(1969):39–61.

9539. Hofer, Tamas. "Anthropologists and Native Ethnographers at Work in Central European Villages." *Anthropologica* 12:5–22.

9540. Hofherr, R. "La tradition orale au service de la documentation sur l'Outre-Mer." *Etudes sociales*(Paris) 75/76 (1968):30–34.

9541. Hrycaj, Myxajlo. "Fol'klor u tvorax ukrajins'kyx pys'mennykiv-polemistiv." *NTE* 45,ii(1969):92–96.

9542. Hryčenko, I.T.,et al. *Narodni muzeji Sumščyny.* Kharkiv: Prapor.

9542a. Hunt, Harriett F. "African Folklore:The Role of Copyright." *Afr. Law Studies* 1,i(1969):87–97.

9543. Jacenko, M.T. *Volodymyr Hnatjuk:Žyttja i fol'klorystyčna dijal'nist'.* Kyjiv: Naukova dumka.

9544. Jansen, W. Hugh. "Lots of Luck." *IndF* 1(1968):5–6. [Hist. of Hoosier Folklore Soc.]

9546. Jones, Eldred. "African Literature and Folklore Studies at Fourah Bay College, the University of Sierra Leone." *RAL* 1:53–56.

9547. Ki-Zerbo, Joseph. "Une source de l'histoire de l'Afrique:La tradition orale." *Diogène* 67(1969):127–40. [Fr. tr. of Bibliog. for 1969, Vol. II, Item 11324.]

9548. Kolessa, Filaret. *Fol'klorystyčni praci.* Kyjiv: Naukova dumka.

9549. Köngäs-Maranda, Elli. "Perinteen transformaatiosäänotjen tutkimisesta. (Sur la recherche des règles transformationelles des traditions.)" *Vir* 74:277–92.

9550. Levin, Isidor. "Erzählungsforschung im Parmirgebiet." [F 81]:159–63.

9551. Lindfors, Bernth. "Approaches to Folklore in African Literature." *Conch* 2,ii:102–11.

9552. Lutz, Gerhard. "Volkskunde und Ethnologie." *ZV* 65(1969):65–80.

9553. Martin, Bernhard. "Mundartforschung und Volkskunde." [F 79]:161–63.

9554. Michaelis-Jena, Ruth. *The Brothers Grimm.* New York: Praeger; London: Routledge & K. Paul.

9555. Miklós, Pál. "Les littératures orales de notre époque." [F 3]:472–79.

9556. Milius, Vacys,ed. *Lietuvininkai:Apie Vakarų Lietuvą ir jos gyventojus devynioliktajame amžiuje.* Vilnius: Vaga. [Writings of Eduard Gisevius, Otto Glagau, Carl Cappeller, and "Lietuviškos vestuvés" by anon.]

9557. Mukherjee, S.K. "Folklore Museum in India." *FolkloreC* 9(1968):309–56.

9558. Nedeljković, D. "Le problème ethnologique et esthétique de la renaissance du folklore à notre époque transitoire examiné dans le cas typique du développement du folklore yougoslave contemporain." [F 91]:156–62. [Sum. in Rus.]

9559. Newall, Venetia. "The Anglo-American Folklore Conference at Ditchley Park, Oxfordshire 9–12 September, 1969." *Folklore* 80(1969):266–71.

9560. Niculescu, Radu. "Contribuţii la certarea problematicii literare a cîntecului de leagăn." *REF* 15:99–111.

9561. Niederer, Arnold. "Zur gesellschaftlichen Verantwortung der gegenwärtigen Volksforschung." [F 79]:1–10.

9562. Novak, Vilko. "Slovenci v nemških etnoloških priročnikih." *SE* 20(1967):173–79.

9563. Ó Duilearga, Séamus. "Once Upon a Time." [F 82]:47–58.

9564. Paden, John N., and Edward W. Soja. "Literature and Oral Tradition." [F 88],ii:45–47.

9565. Paredes, Américo. "Concepts about Folklore in Latin America and the United States." *JFI* 6(1969):20–38.

9566. Paulme, Denise. "Etudes sur la littérature africaine orale à l'Ecole des Hautes Etudes, Sorbonne, Paris." *RAL* 1:56–57.

9567. Peek, Phil. "African Oral Literature in the African Studies Association Center for African Oral Data, Archives of Traditional Music, Indiana University." *RAL* 1:58–61.

9568. Peeters, Karel C. "Not an neuem und zuverlässigem Material in der Erzählforschung." [F 81]:287–95.

9569. Pentikäinen, Juha. "Perinne- ja uskontoantropologisen syväutkimuksen menetelmästä. [On the Method of Tradition and Religio-anthropological Depth Research.]" *Sananjalka* 12:72–119.

9570. Perlick, Alfons. "Das Ostdeutsche Volkskunde-Archiv in Nordrhein-Westfalen." *JOV* 11(1968):167–73.

9571. Podolák, Ján. "The Development of Ethnography and Its Present State in Slovakia." [F 85]:13–26.

9572. Rasmussen, Holger. "Some Central Points of View in European Ethnology." *Anthropologica* 12:142–48.

9573. Šapoval, Ivan. "Poet mynuvšyny našoji." *Vitčyzna* 37,xi(1969):211–14. [On D.I. Javornyc'kyj as folklorist.]

9574. Sauka, Leonardas. "Užmiršti folkloro žanrai." *Kraštotyra 1969*(Vilnius) :238–49.

9575. ——— "Zenonas Slaviūnas—folkloristas (Paminėjus 60 metų sukakti)." *Liaudies Kūryba*(Vilnius) 1(1969):320–27. [With bibliog. of his main writings. Sum. in Rus.]

9576. Schenda, Rudolf. "Statik und Dynamik der aktuellen italienischen Volkskunde." *ZV* 65(1969):251–63.

9577. Schoof, Wilhelm. "Freiligrath als Mitarbeiter Uhlands auf den Spuren Niederländischer Volksliedforschung." *Volkskunde* 69(1968):103–09.

9578. Schroubek, Georg R. "Volksforschung im nationalen Spannungsgebiet:Zur Geschichte der Volkskunde des 19. Jahrhunderts in Böhmen." *ZV* 65(1969):216–23.

9578a. Schwartz, Alfred. "La mise en place des populations guéré et wobé:Essai d'interprétation historique des données de la tradition orale." *Cahiers ORSTOM, Sciences humaines* 5,iv (1968):3–38.

9579. "Simpozium 13:Rabočij fol'klor." [F 91]:439–67. [Concl. by W. Steinitz.]

9580. Sison, Herminia A. "Folklore and the Changing World." *Solidarity* 4,ix(1969):44–47.

9581. Strömbäck, Dag. "The Institute for Dialect and Folklore Research in Uppsala." [F 82]:15–27.

9582. Syska, Henryk. *Adam Chętnik, działacz, pisarz, badacz Kurpiowszczyzny.* Warsaw: Ludz. Spółdz. Wydawn., 1969.

9583. Syvačenko, Mykola. "Na nyvi mystectvoznavstva i narodoznavstva." *Vitčyzna* 37,vi(1969):172–78.

9584. Szwed, John F. "Africa Lies Just Off Georgia." *AfricaR* 15,vii:29–31. [On the Gullah lang., tales, songs, etc.]

9585. Tabak, Fridrix. "Ukrajins'kyj fol'klor u tvorax Karla Francoza." *NTE* 45,i(1969):24–28.

9586. Thompson, G.B. "The Welsh Contribution to the Development of the Ulster Folk Museum." [F 82]:29–33.

9587. Trümpy, Hans. "Folklorismus in der Schweiz." *ZV* 65(1969):40–46.

9588. Tyxonovyč, Zinovij. "Instytut imeny M.T. Ryl's'koho v 1968 roci." *NTE* 45,ii(1969):104–08. [Survey of work in the Folklore Inst.]

9589. Varagnac, A. "Les causes de la décadence des folklores au xx siècle." [F 91]:183–86. [Sum. in Rus.]

9590. Verves, H.D.,ed. *Slovjans'ke literaturoznavstvo i fol'klorystyka.* Vols. 3 and 5. Kyjiv: Naukova dumka, 1967–70.

9591. Weber-Kellermann, Ingeborg. "Familienforschung im 19. Jahrhundert zwischen Volkskunde und Gesellschaftslehre." [F 79]:329–36. [Riehl, Morgan, Engels.]

9592. Wildhaber, Robert, and Fritz Harkort. "Kurt Rankes wissenschaftliches Werk." [F 81]:545–607.

9593. Wilson, Gordon, and Kenneth Clarke. "Folklore in Certain Professions:VII. The English Teacher and Folklore." *TFSB* 36:25–28.

9594. Wollman, Frank. "*Interna slavistica* z VI. sjezdu i odjinud." *Slavia* 38(1969):242–61.

9595. Zilyns'kyj, Orest. "Ivan Pan'kevyč jak fol'kloryst." *NZMUKS* 4,i(1969):233–48. [Sum. in Eng.]

See also 6100, 8139, 9702, 9895, 9987, 10560, 11059.

Theory and Method

9596. Abrahams, Roger [D.] "Patterns of Performance in the British West Indies." [F 95]:163–79.

9597. Bausinger, Hermann. "Kontakthorizont und Über-lieferung." [F 79]:49–56.

9598. —— "Kritik der Tradition:Anmerkungen zur Situation der Volkskunde." *ZV* 65(1969):232–50.

9599. Ben-Amos, Dan. *Em direcção a um modelo componencial de comunicação folclórica.* (Cadernos de Etnografia 8 N.S.) Tr. Carlos Silva. Introd. Jorge Dias. Barcelos: Mus. de Cerâmica Popul. Portug., 1969.

9600. —— "The Writing of African Oral Tradition:A Folkloristic Approach." *Conch* 2,ii:69–79.

9601. —— "The Writing of African Oral Tradition:A Folkloristic Approach." [F 77],III:362–65.

9602. —— "Toward a Componential Model of Folklore Communication." [F 77],II:309–11.

9603. Bogatyrev, P.G. "Tradition and Improvisation in Folk Art." [F 91]:228–33. [Sum. in Rus.]

9604. Bremond, Claude. "Combinaisons syntaxiques entre fonctions et séquences narratives." [F 24]:585–90.

9605. Burton, Michael L. "Computer Applications in Cultural Anthropology." *CHum* 5:37–45.

9606. Bynum, David E. "Thematic Sequences and Trans-formation of Character in Oral Narrative Tradition." *FP* 8,i–ii:1–21.

9607. Cammann, Alfred. "Die Forschungsstelle für Ost-deutsche Volkskunde in Bremen und Niedersachsen." *JOV* 11(1968):161–66.

9608. Carvalho-Neto, Paulo de. "Guia de folklore com-parado." *RVF* 2(1969):35–61.

9609. Ciobanu, G[heorghe]. "La structure du système de versification populaire roumaine; sa relation avec la versification latine." [F 91]:303–08. [Sum. in Rus.]

9610. Crowley, Daniel J. "A Method for Identifying Folkloric Themes in African Oral Tradition." [F 77],III:380–81.

9611. —— "The Uses of African Verbal Art." *JFI* 6(1969):118–32. [Foll. by Jerome R. Mintz, "Discussion . . . ," 133–36.]

9612. Curtin, Philip D. "Oral Traditions and African His-tory." *JFI* 6(1969):137–55. [Foll. by Leonard Thompson, "Dis-cussion . . . ," 156–63.]

9613. Denisoff, R. Serge. "The Proletarian Renascence:The Folkness of the Ideological Folk." *JAF* 82(1969):51–65.

9614. Dorson, Richard M. "The Debate Over the Trust-worthiness of Oral Traditional History." [F 81]:19–35.

9615. Dundes, Alan. "The Devolutionary Premise in Folklore Theory." *JFI* 6(1969):5–19.

9616. Fojtík, Karel. "Professional Groups in the Devel-opment of Folk Culture in Middle Europe." [F 85]:53–61.

9617. Gavazzi, Milovan. "Über die Relevanz der sprachlichen Tatsachen in der kulturkundlichen Forschung." [F 79]:155–59.

9618. Georges, Robert A. "Toward an Understanding of Storytelling Events." *JAF* 82(1969):313–28.

9619. Greimas, Algirdas J. "Apie folklorą, religiją ir istoriją." *Metmenys* 19:32–51.

9620. Greverus, Ina-Maria. "Grenzen und Kontakte:Zur Territorialität des Menschen." [F 79]:11–26.

9621. —— "Zu einer nostalgisch-retrospektiven Bezugs-richtung der Volkskunde." *HBV* 60(1969):11–28.

9622. Harkort, Fritz. "Volkserzählungsforschung und Para-psychologie:Gemeinsame Probleme." [F 81]:89–105.

9623. Hiatt, L.R. "Totemism Tomorrow:The Future of an Illusion." *Mankind* 7(1969):83–93.

9624. Hoppál, Mihály, and Vilmos Voigt. "Kultúra és kommunikáció. Beszámoló egy munkaértekezletről." *Ethno-graphia* 80(1969):579–91. [Culture and communication. Rev. of a conf. in the Hung. Acad. of Sciences.]

9625. Huckenbeck, Herbert. "Probleme ethnopsychologischer Forschung." [F 79]:35–48.

9626. Jageland, A. van. "De angst in de Volkspsychologie." *Volkskunde* 69(1968):110–15.

9627. Jech, Jaromir. "Relativitätsaspekte bei der Beurteilung der Variabilität und Stabilität." [F 81]:115–31.

9628. Kramer, Karl-S. "Die 'vergessene Ecke'." [F 79]:57–63.

9629. —— "Zur Erforschung der historischen Volkskultur: Prinzipielles und Methodisches." *RJV* 19(1969):7–41.

9630. List, George. "A Statement on Archiving." *JFI* 6(1969):222–31.

9631. Manning, Ambrose. "Collecting Folklore:One Proce-dure." *TFSB* 35(1969):117–23.

9632. Maranda, Pierre, and Elli Köngäs. "Le crâne et l'uterus:Deux théorèmes nord-Malaitains." [F 89],II:829–61.

9633. Miroglio, Abel. "Réflexions sur l'importance des frontières des états et des ethnies." [F 79]:27–34.

9634. Ortutay, Gyula. "Zakonomernosti peredači po nasledstvu ustnogo poètičeskogo tvorčestva." [F 91]:223–27. [Sum. in Fr.]

9636. Petőfi, S. János. "Az összehasonlító strukturális elemzésről. (Vázlat.)." *Ethnographia* 80(1969):349–54. [On compar. struct. anal.]

9637. Petőfi, S. János, and Éva Szöllősy. "Computers in Folklore Research." *ComputL* 8(1969):65–70.

9638. Pop, Mihai. "Die direkte Beobachtung als empirisches Verfahren in der Volkskunde." [F 79]:521–26.

9639. Rosenberg, Neil V. "The Indiana University Folklore Archives." *IndF* 1(1968):110–12.

9640. Scharfe, Martin. "Dokumentation und Feldforschung." *ZV* 65(1969):224–31.

9641. Sirovátka, Oldřich. "Influence and Reception in the Inter-Ethnic Relations of Folk Belles-Lettres." [F 85]:62–69.

9642. Skalníková, Olga. "La fonction de la tradition en tant que norme sociale de la société moderne." [F 85]:41–52.

9643. Smith, Robert J. "The Concept of Equivalence:A Polemical Analysis." *JAF* 82(1969):329–41.

9644. Stojkova, S. "Tradicija i novatorstvo v bolgarskom narodnom pesennom tvorčestve." [F 91]:252–58. [Sum. in Fr.]

9645. Strobach, H[ermann]. "Variabilität und Variation in der Volksliederüberlieferung." [F 91]:246–51. [Sum. in Rus.]

9646. Thompson, Laura. "Some Limitations of the Peasant Concept as a Tool in Investigating European Rural Communi-ties." *Anthropologica* 12:59–82.

9647. Thompson, Stith. "Hypothetical Forms in Folktale Study." [F 81]:369–72.

* 9648. Trindell, Roger T. "American Folklore Studies and Geography." *SFQ* 34:1–11.

9649. Voigt, Vilmos. "Modellálási kísérletek a folklor-isztikában." *Ethnographia* 80(1969):355–92. [Attempts at model formation in folklore; sums. in Rus. and Ger.]

9650. —— "Structural Definition of Oral (Folk) Literature." [F 3]:461–67.

9651. Vrabie, Gheorghe. *Folclorul:Obiect-Principii-Metoda-Categorii.* Bucureşti: Ed. Acad. Rupublicii Socialiste România.

9652. Weber-Kellermann, Ingeborg. *Deutsche Volkskunde zwischen Germanistik un Sozialwissenschaften.* Stuttgart: Metzler, 1969.

9653. Webster, J.B. "Research Methods in Teso." *EAJ* 7,ii:30–38. [Problems of conducting field work in segmentary societies.]

9654. Woeller, W. "Die Prägung von Elementen der volks-tümlichen Literatur in der Folklore." [F 91]:318–27. [Sum. in Rus.]

9655. Wolf-Beranek, Hertha. "Das Volkskundliche Archiv des Sudetendeutschen Wörterbuchs im Rahmen der Volkstums-forschung in Böhmen und Mähren." *JOV* 11(1968):155–60.

9656. Yoneyama, Toshinao. "A Tradition of Use of Oral Tradition in Japan and Its Application to African Studies." [F 77],III:366–67.

See also 9594, 9659, 9678, 9813, 9895, 10452, 10500, 10513, 10717, 10728, 10928, 11065.

II. PROSE NARRATIVES

General

Bibliography. 9657. Gorog, Veronika. "Toward a Method of Analysis of African Oral Literature:Introduction to a Selective Analytical Bibliography." *Conch* 2,ii:59–68. [Eng. tr. of Item 11279, Vol. ii, Bibliog. for 1969.]
General and Miscellaneous. 9658. Chiţimia, Ion Const. "Origine et diffusion des narratives populaires en Orient et en Occident." [F 77],ii:311–14.
9659. Čistov, K.V. "Zur Frage der Klassifikationsprinzipien der Prosa-Volksdichtung." [F 91]:365–71. [Sum. in Rus.]
9660. Dégh, Linda. "Two Old World Narrators in Urban Setting." [F 79]:71–86.
9661. Dobos, Ilona. "A történeti mondák rendszerezéséről." *Ethnographia* 81:97–112. [On the systematization of hist. legends; sums. in Rus. and Ger.]
9662. Đurić, Vojislav. "Odnos usmene i pismene književnosti srpskohrvatske." *FP* 5,i–iv(1967):1–14.
9663. Giancristoforo, Emiliano. "Documenti folkloristici abruzzesi inediti raccolti nel territorio di Guardiagrele." *RAbr* 21(1968):21–38.
9664. Greimas, A. Julien. "Éléments d'une grammaire narrative." *Homme* 9,iii(1969):71–92.
9665. Hoffmann, Frank A. "An Analytical Survey of Anglo-American Traditional Erotica." *DAI* 30(1969):1479A(Ind.).
9666. Jech, Jaromír. "Chain Variability in Oral Prosaic Reproduction." [F 85]:70–79.
9667. Lavondes, H. "Le Vocabulaire des Valeurs Culturelles dans la littérature orale des Iles Marquises." [F 77],ii:420–21.
9668. Lüthi, Max. "Das Bild des Menschen in der Volksliteratur." *SAV* 65(1969):75–91.
9669. Mel'nyk, V. *Istorija Zakarpattja v usnyx narodnyx perekazax ta istoryčnyx pisnjax.* L'viv: University.
9670. Nathhorst, Bertel. *Formal or Structural Studies of Traditional Tales:The Usefulness of Some Methodological Proposals Advanced by Vladimir Propp, Alan Dundes, Claude Lévi-Strauss and Edmund Leach.* (Stockholm Studies in Comp. Religion 9.) Stockholm: U. of Stockholm, 1969. [Almquist & Wiksell, Gamla Brogaton 26,S-111 20 Stockholm, Sweden.]
9671. Nsuka, Y. *La prose en littérature orale kongo.* Kinshasa: Lovanium U., 1968. [Diss.]
9672. Peacock, James L. "Society as Narrative." [F 93]:167–77.
9673. "Simpozium 12:Klassifikacija ustno-poètičeskix žanrov." [F 91]:391–436. [Introd. by K.V. Čistov, 391–94, foll. by "Diskussija," 395–428. Concl. by K.V. Čistov, 435–36.]
9674. Sirovátka, Oldřich. "Deutsch-tschechische Beziehungen in der Volksdichtung." [F 79]:87–92.
9675. Thompson, Stith. "Story-telling to Story-writing." [F 3]:433–42.
9676. Tubach, Frederic C. *Index Exemplorium:A Handbook of Medieval Religious Tales.* (FFC 204.) Helsinki: Akademia Scientiarum Fennica, 1969.
See also 9563, 9604, 9618, 10899.

Myths and Legends

General and Miscellaneous. 9677. Bastide, Roger. "Le rire et les courts-circuits de la pensée." [F 89],ii:953–63. [The trickster in myth.]
9678. Belmont, Nicole. "Les croyances populaires comme récit mythologique." *Homme* 10:94–108.
9679. Bolle, Kees W. "In Defense of Euhemerus." [F 90]:19–38.
9680. Buchler, Ira A., and Henry A. Selby. *A Formal Study of Myth.* (Center for Intercultural Stud. in Folk. and Oral Hist. Monog. Ser.1.) Austin: U. of Texas, 1968.
9681. Campbell, Joseph. *The Flight of the Wild Gander: Explorations in the Mythological Dimension.* New York: Viking, 1969.
9682. Killy, Walter. "Mythologie und Lyrik." *NRs* 80(1969): 694–721.

9683. Kirk, G.S. *Myth:Its Meaning and Function in Ancient and Other Cultures.* (Sather Classical Lectures 40.) Berkeley and Los Angeles: U. of Calif. P.; London: Cambridge U.P.
9684. Leach, Edmund. *Genesis as Myth and Other Essays.* London: Jonathan Cape, 1969.
9685. Littleton, C. Scott. "The 'Kingship in Heaven' Theme." [F 90]:83–121. [In Greek, Hurrian-Hittite, Phoenician, Iranian, Norse, and Babylonian versions.]
9686. Morazé, Charles. "Pensée sauvage et logique géometrique." [F 89],ii:964–80.
9687. Puhvel, Jaan. "Aspects of Equine Functionality." [F 90]:159–72. [Role of the horse as integral component of Indo-Eur. mythic structures.]
9688. Turner, Terence S. "Oedipus:Time and Structure in Narrative Form." [F 93]:26–67.
9689. Ward, Donald J. "The Separate Functions of the Indo-European Divine Twins." [F 90]:193–202.
See also 9831.
Africa. 9690. Ansah-Yamoah, K. "Atebubu Myths and Traditions." *Research Rev.*(Legon) Supp. 2:39–122.
9691. Beidelmann, Thomas O. "Myth, Legend and Oral History:A Kaguru Traditional Text." *Anthropos* 65:74–97.
9692. Boston, J.S. "Oral Tradition and the History of the Igala." *Jour. Afr. Hist.* 10(1969):29–43.
9693. Chevrier, Jacques. "L'Afrique noire d'expression française." *Le Monde* 21 juin(1969):iv–v. [Supp. on oral trad., negritude, fiction, etc.]
9694. Fordjuor, P.K. "Myths and Traditions of Prang." *Research Rev.*(Legon) Supp. 2:123–40.
9695. —— "Myths and Traditions of Yeji." *Research Rev.*(Legon) Supp. 2:141–201.
9696. Frimpong, G.E. "Myths and Traditions of Sekyedomase." *Research Rev.*(Legon) Supp. 2:202–09.
9697. —— "Myths and Traditions of Ejura." *Research Rev.*(Legon) Supp. 2:210–15.
9698. Holmes, Charles F. "A History of the Bakwimba of Usukuma, Tanzania, from Earliest Times to 1945." *DAI* 30(1969):1958A(Boston U.). [Based partly on oral trad.]
9699. Knappert, Jan,ed. *Myths and Legends of the Swahili.* (Afr. Writers Ser. 75.) With Introd. London: Heinemann; New York: Humanities. [All texts in Eng. only.]
9700. Langworthy, Harry W.,III. "A History of Undi's Kingdom to 1890:Aspects of Chewa History in East Central Africa." *DAI* 30(1969):1942A(Boston U.). [Based on oral trad.]
9701. Latham, C.J.K. "Dzimbadzemabgwe." *Nada* 10,ii: 24–30.
9702. Rayfield, J.R. "Truth in Liberia:Oral and Printed Versions of Tribal History." [F 77],iii:372–80.
9703. Schlosser, Katesa. "Zulu Mythology as Told and Illustrated by the Zulu Lightning Doctor Laduma Madela." [F 77],iii:76–77.
9704. Smith, Pierre. "La forge de l'intelligence." *Homme* 10:5–21. [Legitimacy of dynasty and social hierarchy in Rwanda established by myth.]
9705. —— "La lance d'une jeune fille (mythe et poésie au Rwanda)." [F 89],ii:1381–1408.
9706. Tsodzo, T. K. "Rwambiwa." *Nada* 10,ii:44–48.
9707. Young, J. "The Legendary History of the Hodi and Ngorima Chiefs." *Nada* 10,ii:49–60.
See also 9677.
Asia. 9708. Bratton, Fred G. *Myths and Legends of the Ancient Near East.* New York: Crowell.
9709. Chang, Chugŭn. "Folkloric Study on the Korean Myths." [F 77],ii:284–86.
9710. Chikovani, M.Y. "The Figure of Amirani (The Bound Hero) in Colcho-Iberian Folklore." [F 91]:194–99. [Sum. in Rus.]
9711. Djarylgasinova, R. "Ethnogenetical Myths and Legends of the Koreans." [F 77],ii:286–88.
9712. Hameed, K.P.S. "Structural Analysis and Pattern Description of a Primitive Legend of the West Coast of South India." [F 42],ii:208–23.
9713. Levy, Howard S. " 'Rainbow Skirt and Feather

Jacket'." *LE&W* 13(1969):111–40. [Poem by Po Chu-i, 8th cent.; incl. discussion of feather garment myth.]

9714. Littleton, C. Scott. "Some Possible Indo-European Themes in the *Iliad*." [F 90]:229–46.

9715. Peacock, James. "President Sukarno as Myth Maker." [F 89],II:1409–16.

9716. Riftin, B.L. "Problems of the Development of the Chinese Historical Narrative." [F 91]:357–64. [Sum. in Rus.]

9717. Robinson, Marguerite S. " 'The House of the Mighty Hero' or 'The House of the Enough Paddy'? Some Implications of a Sinhalese Myth." [F 83]:122–52.

9718. Schwarzbaum, Haim. "The Short-Sightedness of the Angel of Death." [F 87]:323–37. [In Hebr.; Eng. sum.]

9719. Sinha, Rakesh Ranjan. "The Story of Creation." *FolkloreC* 9(1968):151–54.

9720. Stein, R.A. "La légende du joyer dans le monde chinois." [F 89],II:1280–1305.

9721. Subramanian, P.R. "A Myth—Its Development and Treatment." [F 42],II:181–89.

9722. Taylor, Archer. "This Too Will Pass (Jason 910 Q)." [F 81]:345–50.

9723. Trible, Phyllis. "Existence in Times and Words." *CimR* 11:8–12. [On ancient Hebr. narrative mode, esp. in the legend of Elijah.]

9724. Utley, Francis Lee. "Rabghuzi—Fourteenth-Century Turkic Folklorist:A Contribution to Biblical-Koranic Apocrypha and to the Bible of the Folk." [F 81]:373–400.

9725. Veerasamy, V. "The Legendary Structure of *Periapuranam*." [F 42],II:190–95.

9726. Vilnay, Zev. "The Land of Israel in the Koran." [F 87]:153–62. [In Hebr.; Eng. sum.]

9727. Yamamoto, Tatsuro. "Myths Explaining the Vicissitudes of Political Power in Ancient Vietnam." *ActaA* 18:70–94. See also 9754.

Australia and Oceania. 9728. Alpers, Antony. *Legends of the South Seas:The World of the Polynesians Seen Through Their Myths and Legends, Poetry, and Art.* New York: Crowell.

9729. Berndt, Catherine H. "Monsoon and Honey Wind." [F 89],II:1306–26.

9730. —— "Myth and Mother-in-Law:A Question of Meaning and Interpretation in Myth, an Example from Aboriginal Australia." [F 77],II:295–97.

9731. Bolens, Jacqueline. "Le sel de la terre." [F 89],II:1327–30.

9732. Roberton, J.B. "A Culture Nomenclature Based on Tradition." *JPS* 78(1969):252–58. See also 9667, 10075, 10437.

Europe. 9733. Belmont, Nicole. "La coiffe et le serpent." [F 89],II:1223–28.

9734. Ben-Amos, Dan, and Jerome R. Mintz,eds. *In Praise of the Baal Shem Tov* [Shivḥei ha-Besht]:*The Earliest Collection of Legends about the Founder of Hasidism.* Bloomington: Ind. U.P.

9735. Bosnyák, Sándor. "A tenger fenekéről felhozott föld motívuma a magyar teremtésmondákban." *Ethnographia* 80(1969):462–64. [The motive of earth brought up from the sea-bottom in Hung. Creation myths.]

9736. Burde-Scheidewind, G. "Die Volkssage als historische Quelle (Dargestellt an einem Sagenbeispiel aus Nord-Deutschland)." [F 91]:341–46. [Sum. in Rus.]

9737. Christie, Janet B.T. "Reflections on the Legend of Wayland the Smith." *Folklore* 80(1969):286–94.

9738. Cohn, Norman. "The Myth of Satan and His Human Servants." [F 75]:3–16.

9739. Davies, J.C. "Mythological Influences on the First Emergence of Greek Scientific and Philosophical Thought." *Folklore* 81:25–36.

9740. Devereux, Georges. "La naissance d'Aphrodite." [F 89],II:1229–52.

9741. Dumézil, Georges. "Horwendillus et Aurvandill." [F 89],II:1171–79.

9742. Ferenczi, Imre. "A kuruc kor mondavilága." *AUS-E&L* 13(1969):31–43. [The world of legends in 18th cent. Hungary; sum. in Ger.]

9743. —— "Adatok a Mátyás-mondakörhöz." *AUS-E&L* 12(1968):11–27. [Contribs. to legends on Matthias Rex; sum. in Ger.]

9744. Gatto, Giuseppe. "La figura della 'quaresima' nel folklore calabrese e le sue remote origini miticorituali." *Acme* 22(1969):167–92.

9745. Gella Iturriaga, José. "La sirena en la literatura oral española." [F 94],I:117–28.

9746. Gerndt, Helge. "Seemannssagen auf See und an Land." *ZV* 65(1969):207–15.

9747. Groeger, Alfred C. "Berggeist Rübezahl:Entstehung, Wandlung und Verbreitung der Sage." *JSUB* 15:256–79.

9748. Harmening, Dieter. "Eine neue Legende und neue Wallfahrtsbildchen von Unserer Lieben Frau:Drei-Ähren bei Colmar (Notre-Dame des Trois-Epis)." *RJV* 19(1969):92–100.

9749. Hofinger, M. "L'Eve grecque et le mythe de Pandore," 205–17 in *Mélanges de linguistique, de philologie et de méthodologie de l'enseignement des langues anciennes offerts à M. René Fohalle, Professeur à l'Université de Liège, a l'occàsion de son soixante-dixième anniversaire.* Gembloux: Eds. J. Duculot, S.A., 1969.

9750. Ivanov, Viatcheslav, and Vladimir Toporov. "Le myth indo-européen du dieu de l'orage poursuivant les serpent: Reconstruction du schéma." [F 89],II:1180–1206.

9751. Ivanov, V.V., and B.N. Toporov. "K semiotičeskomu analizu mifa i rituala (na belorusskom materiala)." [F 24]:321–89.

9752. Kaminskij, V.I. " 'Polesskaja legenda,' 'Les šumit' i problema obščestvennoj aktual'nosti literatury v tvorčestve V.G. Korolenko 1880-x godov." *RLit* 12,i(1969):171–79.

9753. Kerbelytė, Bronislava. *Lietuvių liaudies padavimai.* Vilnius: Vaga.

9754. Klímová-Rychnová, Dagmar. "Quelques réflexions sur les motifs démonologiques en Europe et leurs sources en Proche-Orient-Ancien." [F 85]:99–119.

9755. Kulišić, Špiro. *Srpski mitološki rečnik.* Beograd: Nolit.

9756. Laurent, Donatien. "Une chante fable de Noël en Pays Pourlet:La 'tragédie'." *ATP* 16(1968):153–72.

9757. Lixfeld, Hannjost. "A Guntram-monda Paulus Diaconusnál (AT 1645 A)." *Ethnographia* 81:136–47. [Guntram-Legend in the Work of Paulus Diaconus (AT 1645 A); sums. in Rus. and Ger.]

9758. Matičetov, Milko. "Die Legende von 'Josaphat und Barlaam' in Resia:Typisches Beispiel absteigender Tradition." [F 81]:197–209.

9759. Maticki, Miodrag. "Dobričin krst i Margitina unka." *NStv* 6(1967):134–36.

9760. Matulis, Anatolijus. "Lietuvių mitologija Wiecherto, Sudermanno ir Agnes Miegel kūryboje." *Aidai* (1969):111–14.

9761. Musumarra, Carmelo. "La leggenda di Candaule." [F 94],II:191–210.

9762. Nicolaisen, Wilhelm F.H. "The Prodigious Jump:A Contribution to the Study of the Relationship Between Folklore and Place Names." [F 81]:531–42.

9763. Ortutay, Gyula. "Die Faustsage in Ungarn." [F 81]:267–74.

9764. Pfeil, Sigurd Graf von. "Die Sachsensage bei Widukind von Corvey." [F 81]:297–311.

9765. Piccitto, Giorgio. "Problemi di restauro linguistico a proposito di una leggenda popolare siciliana su S. Cristoforo." [F 94],I:235–97.

9766. Röhrich, Lutz. "Die Sage von Schlangenbann (Thompson Q 597:Snake carries into fire man who has banned snakes)." [F 81]:327–44.

9767. —— "German Devil Tales and Devil Legends." *JFI* 7:21–35.

9768. Sanderson, Stewart. "The Folklore of the Motor-car." *Folklore* 80(1969):241–52.

9769. Santangelo, Salvatore. "Screzi e favori in Paradiso (Leggende popolari)." [F 94],I:421–22.

9770. Schmaus, Alois. "Volksmythologie und Heldenepik." [F 79]:121–28.

9771. Seib, Gerhard. "Die Boyneburg-Spende." *HBV* 60(1969):135–46. [Illus.]

9772. Senti, Alois. "Die Sagen der Gemeinde Flums." *SAV* 65(1969):127–79.

9773. Top, Stefaan. "De Studie van de Duitse Schaper."

Volkskunde 69(1968):24–29.

9774. Valle, Carlos. "Tradições populares de Vila Nova de Baia—narrações lendárias." *RdEt* 13(1969):419–33.

9775. Vernant, Jean-Pierre. "Ambiguïté et renversement sur la structure énigmatique d'Oedipe-roi." [F 89],II:1253–79.

9776. Violaris, Glafkos P. "Dyo Kypriakoi mythoi gia to pepromenon." *KL* 1(1969):53–54.

9777. Weisser, Herbert. "Zur Entstehung von Sagen in der Gegenwart." [F 81]:401–14.

9778. Wolf, Herbert. "Sage und Geschichte:Eine ungarisch-deutsche Bergbausage aus dem Mittelalter." [F 79]:473–80.

9779. Zender, Matthias. "Kobold, Totengeist und Wilder Jäger." [F 81]:415–27.

See also 1592, 9314, 9344, 9362, 9364, 9372, 9710, 9714, 10120, 10248, 10284, 10451, 10775, 10780, 10824, 10842, 11034.

North America. 9780. Baker, Ronald L. "The Fall in the Wall." *IndF* 2,ii(1969):29–46.

9781. Bennett, John M. "Folk Speech and Legends of the Trade of House-Painting." *SFQ* 33(1969):313–16.

9782. Bird, Donald A. "Morgan's Raiders:'That's Sure a Good Looking Rifle You Got There'." *IndF* 2,i(1969):124–30.

9783. Boyd, Maurice. *Tarascan Myths and Legends:A Rich and Imaginative History of the Tarascans.* (Texas Christian U. Monogs. in Hist. and Culture 4.) Fort Worth: Texas Christian U., 1969.

9784. Caro, F[rank] A. de. "Finding a Lost Watch." *IndF* 1(1968):25–27.

9785. —— "Indiana Miracle Legends:A Survey." *IndF* 2,i(1969):36–53.

9786. —— "The Butter Witch." *IndF* 1(1968):17–20.

9787. —— "The Witch Cat." *IndF* 1(1968):21–24.

9788. Caro, F[rank] A. de, and C. Richard K. Lunt. "The Face on the Tombstone." *IndF* 1(1968):34–41.

9789. Clements, William M. "The Chain." *IndF* 2,i(1969):91–96.

9790. —— "The Walking Coffin." *IndF* 2,ii(1969):3–10.

9791. Cord, Xenia E. "Department Store Snakes." *IndF* 2,i(1969):110–14.

9792. —— "Further Notes on 'The Assailant in the Back Seat'." *IndF* 2,ii(1969):47–54. [See art. by Drake, below.]

9793. Danielson, Larry. "The Disappearing Treasure." *IndF* 1(1968):28–33.

9794. —— "The Revenant Plays the Organ." *IndF* 1(1968):52–54.

9795. Dégh, Linda. "The Boy Friend's Death." *IndF* 1(1968):101–06.

9796. —— "The Haunted Bridges Near Avon and Danville and Their Role in Legend Formation." *IndF* 2,i(1969):54–90.

9797. —— "The Hook." *IndF* 1(1968):92–100.

9798. —— "The House of Blue Lights Revisited." *IndF* 2,ii(1969):11–28. [See art. by Einarsson-Mullarký, below.]

9799. —— "The Negro in the Concert." *IndF* 1(1968):61–67.

9800. —— "The Roommate's Death and Related Dormitory Stories in Formation." *IndF* 2,ii(1969):55–74.

9801. —— "The Runaway Grandmother." *IndF* 1(1968):68–77.

9802. Dorson, Richard M. "Defining the American Folk Legend (Abstract)." [F 78]:163–66.

9803. Drake, Carlos. "The Killer in the Back Seat." *IndF* 1(1968):107–09.

9804. Einarsson-Mullarký, Magnus. "The Heavenly Message." *IndF* 1(1968):49–51.

9805. —— "The House of the Blue Lights." *IndF* 1(1968):82–91.

9806. —— "The Mysterious Dog." *IndF* 1(1968):55–60.

9807. —— "The Warning Light." *IndF* 1(1968):42–48.

9808. Jones, Charles C. *Negro Myths from the Georgia Coast.* Told in the Vernacular. Detroit: Singing Tree, 1969. [Repr. of Boston 1888 ed.]

9809. Lunt, C. Richard K. "The Laughing Woman." *IndF* 1(1968):78–81.

9810. Merrifield, William R. "The Souls Really Do Come Back:A Chinantec Proof Text for All Saints Day." *Tlalocan* 6:163–68.

9811. Mitchell, Carol A. "The White House." *IndF* 2,i(1969):97–109.

9812. Momaday, N. Scott. *The Way to Rainy Mountain.* Albuquerque: U. of N.M. Press, 1969. [Literary rendition.]

9813. Montell, William L. *The Saga of Coe Ridge:A Study in Oral History.* Knoxville: U. of Tenn. P.

9814. Noblett, R.A. *Stavin' Chain:(A Study in Folk-Hero).* London: The Author, 1969. [Avail. from 60 Emmanuel Rd., Balham, London, S.W. 12, Eng.]

9815. Reyes G., Luis. "Hongos Aluciantes." *Tlalocan* 6:140–45.

9816. Scott, Robert W. "The Governor Fowle Ghost at the Executive Mansion." *NCarF* 18:115–16.

9817. Snow, Edward R. *True Tales and Curious Legends:Dramatic Stories from the Yankee Past.* New York: Dodd, Mead, 1969.

9818. Snyder, Sally. "Stylistic Stratification in an Oral Tradition." *Anthropologica* 10(1968):235–59.

9819. Vaudrin, Bill. *Tanaina Tales from Alaska.* (The Civil. of the Amer. Indian Ser.) Introd. Joan B. Townsend. Norman: U. of Okla. P., 1969.

9820. Wilson, William A. "Mormon Legends of the Three Nephites Collected at Indiana University." *IndF* 2,i(1969):3–35.

* 9821. Winslow, David J. "Hawthorne's Folklore and the Folklorists' Hawthorne:A Re-Examination." *SFQ* 34:34–52.

9822. Wolf, John Q. "Aunt Caroline Dye:The Gypsy in the 'St. Louis Blues'." *SFQ* 33(1969):339–46.

See also 6256, 6322, 7512, 7539, 9986, 10849.

South America. 9823. Oliver-Smith, Anthony. "The Pishtaco:Institutionalized Fear in Highland Peru." *JAF* 82(1969):363–68.

9824. Rivière, P.G. "Myth and Material Culture:Some Symbolic Interrelations." [F 93]:151–66.

See also 10467, 10938.

Folktales

Bibliography. 9825. Sauka, Donatas. "Universiteto diplominiai darbai tautosakos tematika (1949–1968)." *Liaudies Kūryba* (Vilnius) 1(1969):354–60. [Sum. in Rus.]

General and Miscellaneous. 9826. Bagdanavičius, Vytautas. *Cultural Wellsprings of Folktales.* Tr. Jeronimas Zemkalnis. New York: Manylands Books. [84–39 90th St., Woodhaven, N.Y. 11421.]

9827. Benet, S. "The Cultural Meaning of Folklore:The Cinderella Motif." [F 91]:175–77. [Sum. in Rus.]

9828. Chikovani, M.J. "On the Problem of Typological Similarities Between Three Mediaeval Novels 'Tristram and Isolde,' 'Abesselom and Eteri' and 'Vis and Ramin'." [F 77],II:337–40.

9829. Franz, Marie-Louise von. *An Introduction to the Psychology of Fairy Tales.* New York: Spring Pubs. [Suite 306, 130 E. 39th St.]

9830. Georges, Robert A. "Structure in Folktales:A Generative-Transformational Approach." *Conch* 2,ii:4–17.

9831. Greimas, A.J. "La quête de la peur (réflexions sur un groupe de contes populaires)." [F 89],II:1207–22.

9832. Jason, H[eda], and O[tto] Schnitzler. "The Eberhard-Boratav Index of Turkish Folk Tales in the Light of the New Revision of Aarne-Thompson's *Types of the Folktale.*" [F 87]:43–71.

9833. Klotz, Volker. "Weltordnung im Märchen." *NRs* 81:73–91.

9834. Krader, B[arbara]. "Hospitality Customs as Reflected in Balkan Folk Narratives." [F 91]:336–40. [Sum. in Rus.]

9835. Laiblin, Wilhelm,ed. *Märchenforschung und Tiefenpsychologie.* (Wege der Forschung 102.) Darmstadt: Wissenschaftliche Buchgesellschaft, 1969. [Prev. pub. essays by var. hands.]

9836. Lüthi, Max. *Once Upon a Time:On the Nature of Fairy Tales.* Tr. Lee Chadeayne and Paul Gottwald. Introd. Francis L. Utley. New York: Ungar.

9837. Madsen, Peter. "Det integrerede normbrud:Narratologisk analyse." *Poetik* 3:1–20.

9838. Neumann, S[iegfried]. "Zur heutigen Erzähl überlieferung und folkloristischen Sammelarbeit in Deutschland." [F 91]:372–75. [Sum. in Rus.]

9839. Propp, Vladimir Ja. *Morfologija skazki.* (Issledovanija po fol'kloru i mifologii Vostoka.) Izd. 2-e. Moskva: Nauka, 1969.

9840. Røder, Viggo. "Om Propp's *Morphology of the Folktale*." *Poetik* 3:21–33.

9841. Schwarzbaum, Haim. *Studies in Jewish and World Folklore.* (*Fabula* Supp. Ser. B Vol.3.) Berlin: de Gruyter, 1968.

9842. Taylor, Archer. "A Tentative Comparison of Studies in Folktale and Folksong." *AEASH* 19:347–51.

9843. Ting, Nai-tung. "Introducing the Second Revised Edition of Anti Aarne and Stith Thompson's *The Types of the Folktale*." *THJCS* 7(1969):233–38. [In Chinese; sum. in Eng.]

9844. Viidalepp, R. "Das Erzählen der Volksmärchen als arbeitsfördernder magischer Ritus." [F 91]:259–65. [Sum. in Rus.]
See also 1464, 9896, 10408, 10685.

Africa. 9845. Amos, Samuel, and Bruce Onobrakpeya. "Tortoise in Legend." *AfrA* 4,i:26–35. [Ibo tales.]

9846. Andreski, Iris,ed. *Old Wives' Tales:Life-Stories from Ibibioland.* With Introd. London: Routledge & K. Paul.

9847. Anon. *Contes du Nord-Cameroun:Recueillis par les élèves du Lycée de Garoua et illustrés par le Club de Dessin Unesco du Lycée.* Yaoundé: Editions C.L.E.; New York: Africana Pub. Corp.

9848. Bamgbose, Ayo. "Yoruba Folk-Tales." *Ibadan* 27(1969):6–12.

9849. Basset, R. *Contes populaires d'Afrique.* (Coll. Les litt. pop. de toutes les nations, T. 47.) Paris: G.P. Maisonneuve et Larose, 1969. [New ed.]

9850. Bebbe, Charles-Henri. *Contes du Nord-Cameroun.* Yaounde: Centre de Littérature Evangélique.

9851. Bergsma, Harold and Ruth,eds. *Tales Tiv Tell.* Ibadan: Oxford U.P., 1969. [44 tales in Eng. tr.]

9852. Bremond, Claude. " 'The Impossible Restitution' as a Specifically African Theme." *Conch* 2,ii:54–58. [Eng. tr. of Item 11393, Vol. II, Bibliog. for 1969.]

9853. Calame-Griaule, Geneviève. "L'arbre au trésor." [F 73]:25–58.

9854. Calame-Griaule, Geneviève, and Pierre-François Lacroix. "La 'mère vendue':Essai d'analyse d'un thème de conte africain." [F 89],II:1356–80.

9855. Cardinall, A.W. *Tales Told in Togoland* [and] *The Mythical and Traditional History of Dagomba* by E.F. Tamakloe. Westport, Conn.: Negro Univs. P.; London: Oxford U.P. [Repr. of 1931 ed.]

9856. Crowley, Daniel J. "A Tale Type Index for Africa." *RAL* 1:50–52.

9857. Dathorne, O.R. "African Folktales as Literature: Animals, Humans and Gods." *Conch* 2,ii:90–101.

9858. Egberipou, O.A., and Kay Williamson. *Bọlọu izọn egberi fun:Ijọ Tales.* (Occas. Pub. 15.) Book 1. Ibadan: U. of Ibadan Inst. of Afr. Studies, 1968.

9859. Fisher, Ruth. *Twilight Tales of the Black Baganda:The Traditional History of Bunyoro-Kitara, a Former Uganda Kingdom.* London: Cass. [Repr. of 1911 ed. with new introd. by Merryck Posnansky.]

9860. Fortier, J.,ed. *Le mythe et les contes Sou en pays Mbai-Moïssala.* (Classiques africains.) Paris: Julliard, 1968.

9861. Horner, George R. "A Structural Analysis of Bulu (African) Folktales." *Conch* 2,ii:18–28.

9862. Hulstaert, G. *Fables Mongo.* Bruxelles: Acad. Royale des Sciences d'Outre-Mer.

9863. Johnson, James, and David Robinson. "Deux fonds d'histoire orale sur le Fouta Toro." *BIFAN* 31B(1969):120–37.

9864. Kitereza, Aniceti. "How Men and Women Came to Live Together:A Kerebe Tale." *Natural Hist.* 79,i:9–19. [Foll. by biog. notes on the author by Gerald and Charlotte Hartwig.]

9865. Lindfors, Bernth. "The Folktale as Paradigm in Chinua Achebe's *Arrow of God*." *SBL* 1,i:1–15.

9866. Lonfernini, Bruno. "Attorno ai fuochi." *Nigrizia* 88,iv:16–19. [Sidamo tales, Ethiopia.]

9867. Makarius, Laura. "Le mythe de 'trickster'." *Rev. Hist. Religions*(Paris) 175,ii(1969):17–46. [Incl. bibliog.]

9868. Malepe, A.T. "The Character 'Dimo' in Tswana Folk-tales." *Limi* 10(June):51–57.

9869. Mallart-Guimera, Louis. "L'arbre *OVEN*." [F 73]: 59–69.

9870. Mateene, Kahombo. "Un conte hunde chanté et dialogué." *AfrS* 29,i:1–45.

9871. McCall, Daniel F. *Wolf Courts Girl:The Equivalence of Hunting and Mating in Bushman Thought.* (PSAS 7.) Athens: Ohio U. Center for Internat. Studies. [19-p. pamphlet.]

9872. Mercier, Roger. "Les contes sénégalais de Birago Diop." [F 3]:527–36.

9873. Nassau, Robert H. *Where Animals Talk:West African Folk Lore Tales.* Westport, Conn.: Negro U.P. [Repr. of 1912 ed.]

9874. Noss, Philip A. "The Performance of the Gbaya Tale." *RAL* 1:41–49.

9875. Noy, Dov. "Family Confrontation and Conflict in Jewish Magic Folk Tales." [F 87]:201–28. [In Hebr.; Eng. sum.]

9876. Noye, D. *Humour et sagesse peuls:Contes, devinettes et proverbes Foulbé.* Lyon: Afrique et Langage, 1968. [Cf. Item 11333, Vol. II, Bibliog. for 1969.]

9877. Rattray, R.S. *Akan-Ashanti Folk-Tales Illustrated by Members of the Ashanti, Fanti and Ewe Tribes.* London: Oxford U.P., 1969. [Repr. of 1930 ed.]

9878. Retel-Laurentin, Anne. "Structure and Symbolism:An Essay in Methodology for the Study of African Tales." *Conch* 2,ii:29–53. [Eng. tr. of Item 11441, Vol. II, Bibliog. for 1969.]

9879. Scelles-Millie, J. *Contes arabes du Maghreb.* Paris: Maisonneuve et Larose.

9880. Scheub, Harold. "The Technique of the Expansible Image in Xhosa *Ntsomi*-Performances." *RAL* 1:119–46.

9881. ——— "The *Ntsomi*:A Xhosa Performing Art." *DAI* 31:323A(Wis.).

9882. Skinner, Neil,tr. and ed. *Hausa Tales and Traditions:An English Translation of* Tatsuniyoyi na Hausa *Originally Compiled by Frank Edgar.* Vol. I. Introd. G.M. Smith. London: Frank Cass, 1969; New York: Africana Pub. Corp., 1969.

9883. Sow, Alfâ Ibrahim. *Chroniques et récits du Foûta Djalon.* (CLLAN 3.) Paris: Klincksieck, 1968.

9884. Sprigge, R.G.S. "Eweland's Adangbe:An Enquiry into an Oral Tradition." *Trans. of the Hist. Soc. of Ghana*(Legon) 10(1969):87–128.

9885. Thieme, Darius L. "A Summary-Report on the Oral Traditions of Yoruba Musicians." *AfricaL* 40:359–62.

9886. Thomas, Louis-Vincent. "Un exemple d'oralité négro-africaine:Les fables djugut(Basse-Casamance)." *BIFAN* 31B (1969):167–214. [Illus.]

9887. Verdier, P. "Le phénomène de la métamorphose dans le conte togolais." *Bull. de l'Enseignement Supérieur du Bénin*(Lomé, Togo) 10(1969):29–57; 11(1969):29–45; 12:45–62.

9888. Vyas, Chiman L.,ed. *Folktales of Zambia.* Foreword S.M. Kapwepwe. Lusaka: Unity Press, 1969. [22 tales in Eng. tr.]

9889. Willis, R.G. "Kaswa:Oral Tradition of a Fipa Prophet." *AfricaL* 40:248–56.
See also 9657, 9893, 9962.

Asia. 9890. Acharya, Sautibhai. "A Bhili Tale:Tom Tom Tom." *FolkloreC* 10(1969):437–38.

9891. Avrorin, V.A. "A Nanai (Gold) Tale about the Fortieth Brother and His Wife, a Washbear (*Ursus lotor*)." [F 74]:373–86. [Nanai text.]

9892. Goswami, Praphulladatta. "Folktales of the Miris." *FolkloreC* 10(1969):390–92.

9893. Horálek, Karel. "Le conte des deux frères (Anoubis et Bata):Un coup d'oeil retrospectif et la revue des variantes orientales." [F 85]:80–98.

9894. Hrdličková, V[ena]. "The Chinese Storytellers and Singers of Ballads:Their Performances and Storytelling Techniques." *TASJ* 10(1968):97–115.

9895. Islam, Mazharul. *A History of Folktale Collections in India and Pakistan.* Dacca: Bengali Acad.

9896. Jarnevskij, I.Z. *Ustnyj rasskaz kak žanr fol'klora.* Ulan-Udè: Burjatskoe knižnoe izd-vo, 1969.

9897. Kagan, Zipora. "About the Mythical Quality of Folk Tales Among Ethnic Groups in Israel." [F 87]:165–74. [In Hebr.; Eng. sum.]

9898. Levin, Isidor. "Tiermärchen im Tadschikischen." [F

79]:93–113.

9899. Mayer, Fanny Hagin. "The Setting of the Japanese Folk Tale:The Family." [F 77],III:122–23.

9900. Mukerju, N. "Chaucer's Franklin and the Tale of Madanasena of Vetalapachisi:A Comparative Study." *FolkloreC* 9(1968):75–85.

9901. Stahl, Abraham. "The Change in the Folk Tale of Oriental Jewry Following Their Immigration to Israel." [F 87]:343–48. [In Hebr.; Eng. sum.]

9902. Steinitz, W[olfgang]. "An Ostyak Tale from M.A. Castrén's Manuscripts." [F 74]:107–11.

9903. Suryanarayanan, M. "A Note on a Few Folk-Tales of Saoras." *FolkloreC* 10(1969):423–26.

9904. Ting, Nai-tung. "AT Type 301 in China and Some Countries Adjacent to China:A Study of a Regional Group and Its Significance in World Tradition." *Fabula* 11:54–125.

9905. Upadhyaya, Hari S. "Studies in the Philippine Folktales and Their Indian Versions." *FolkloreC* 10(1969):315–31.

9906. Yen, Yuan-shu. "Hsüeh Jên-Kuei and Hsüeh Ting-shan:A Chinese Oedipal Conflict." *TkR* 1,i:223–32. [On the legendary hero Hsüeh Jên-kuei and the folktale, "Hsüeh Jên-kuei Cheng Tung."]

See also 4550, 9841, 9875, 10015.

Australia and Oceania. 9907. Schütz, Albert J. *Nguna Texts:A Collection of Traditional and Modern Narratives from the Central New Hebrides.* (Oceanic Ling. Spec. Pub. 4.) Honolulu: U. of Hawaii P., 1969.

Europe. 9908. Aleksynas, Kostas. "Vienu kitu liaudies pasakų tekstologijos klausimu." *Liaudies Kūryba*(Vilnius) 1(1969):243–50. [Sum. in Rus.]

9909. Berezovs'kyj, I.P.,comp. *Mudryj opovidač.* Kyjiv: Naukova dumka, 1969. [Fairy-tales, fables, folk anecdotes.]

9910. Briggs, Katharine M. *A Dictionary of British Folk-Tales in the English Language, Incorporating the F.J. Norton Collection. Part A:Folk Narratives.* 2 Vols. Bloomington: Ind. U.P.; London: Routledge & K. Paul.

9911. Brudford, Alan. *Gaelic Folk-Tales and Mediaeval Romances:A Study of the Early Modern Irish 'Romantic Tales' and Their Oral Derivatives.* Dublin: Folk. of Ireland Soc., 1969.

9912. Carch, Henry. "The Role of the Devil in Grimms' Tales:An Exploration of the Content and Function of Popular Tales." *SocR* 35(1968):466–99.

9913. Dickson, Keith A. "Big Bad Wolf!An Aspect of Realism in the *Märchen.*" *ML* 50(1969):155–60.

9914. Docenko, P.P. "Šče raz pro Ivasyka-Telesyka." *Mov* 4,iv:88–90.

9915. Félice, A[riane de]. "Littérature française du moyen âge et tradition orale contemporaine:Le théâtre comique médiéval et les contes populaires (Phénomènes de persistance de thèmes et de formules à travers les âges)." [F 91]:309–17. [Sum. in Rus.]

9916. Horálek, K. "Německo-české vztahy v lidové literatuře." [F 29]:358–62.

9917. —— "Zur slawischen Überlieferung des Typus AT 707 (Die neidischen Schwestern)." [F 81]:107–14.

9918. Hyrjak, M.,comp. *Ukrajins'ki narodni kazky Sxidn'oji Slovaččyny.* Prešov: Slovenské pedagogické nakladateľstvo, 1969.

9919. Imellos, Stephanos D. "Parateriseis eis demode paradosin ek Kretes." [F 10],IV:192–97.

9920. Istvánovits, Márton. "Beiträge zur belletristischen Verwendung folkloristischer Texte." *AEASH* 19:191–200.

9921. Kennedy, Patrick. *Irish Fireside Folktales.* Cork, 1969.

9922. Klerides, Nearchos. "Deka Kypriaka paramythia." *KyS* 32(1968):201–26.

9923. Künzig, Johannes, and Waltraut Werner. *Ungarndeutsche Märchenerzähler I:Die Rosibäs aus Hajós.* (Quellen zur Deutschen Volkskunde.) Freiburg im Breisgau: Rombach, 1969. [3 records.]

9924. Lo Nigro, Sebastiano. "Il tema del tempo illusorio nella narrativa tradizionale." [F 94],I:135–49.

9925. Loukatos, Dim. S. "Thalassines paradoseis stin Heptaneso." [F 4],II:58–68.

9926. Lüthi, Max. "Familie und Natur im Märchen." [F 81]:181–95.

9927. —— "Mozarts und Cervantes' Spiel mit einer

Geschichte aus dem Volksmund." [F 11]:182–201.

9928. Matičetov, Milko. "Pri treh Boganjčarjih, ki znajo 'lagati'." *SE* 18–19(1965–66):81–112.

9929. Megas, Georgios A. "Der Pflegesohn des Waldgeistes (AT 667):Eine griechische und balkanische Parallele." [F 81]:211–31.

9930. Megas, Georgios A.,ed. *Folktales of Greece.* (FW.) Tr. Helen Colaclides, Foreword Richard M. Dorson. Chicago: U. of Chicago P.

9931. Meletinsky, E. "Die Ehe im Zaubermärchen." *AEASH* 19:281–92.

9932. Nikolić, Ilija. "Narodne pripovedke iz istočne Srbije u redakciji dr. Veselina Čajkanovića." *SE* 18–19(1965–66):115–21.

9933. Nişcov, Viorica. "Variante germane din 'Kinder- und Hausmärchen' şi variante româneşti la tipurile A Th. 410, 130 şi 120." *REF* 14(1969):295–314.

9934. Petzoldt, Leander. "AT 470. Friends in Life and Death:Zur Psychologie und Geschichte einer Wundererzählung." *RJV* 19(1969):101–61.

9935. Pop, Mihai. "Die funktion der Anfangs- und Schlussformeln im rumänischen Märchen." [F 81]:321–26.

9936. Roberts, Warren E. "The Making Modesty Pay Motif:Some Folktale Analogues of a Ballad." [F 81]:469–72.

9937. Schmitt, Anneliese. "Zum Volksbuch von den vier Kaufleuten." [F 17]:149–59.

9938. Schwab, Ute. "Eine Vogelschule aus dem Jahre 1700." [F 11]:125–62.

9939. Tenèze, Marie-Louise. "Quatre récits du loup." [F 81]:351–67.

9940. Tropea, Giovanni. "Sei nuovi testi siciliani della novellina dei 'Vocaboli'." [F 94],II:299–313.

9941. Tyla, Antanas,et al.,eds. *Gaidės ir Rimšės apylinkės.* Vilnius: Vaga, 1969. [*Pasakos ir dainos*, 212–65; *Tarmė*, 267–314.]

9942. Vedernikova, N.M. "Motiv i sjužet v volšebnoj skazke." *FN* 13,ii:57–65. [Motif and theme in the fairy tale.]

9943. Viidalepp, Richard. "A mesélők és a mesemondás körülményei az észteknél." *Ethnographia* 80(1969):447–60. [Sums. in Rus. and Ger. Story-tellers and the circumstances of story-telling between Estonians.]

9944. Vöő, Gabriella. "Egy román mesemondó kétnyelvű meseváltozatai." *NIK* 14:121–32. [A Romanian story-teller's biling. tales; sum. in Rom.]

9945. Zečević, Divna. "Usmena kazivanja u okolici Daruvara." *NUm* 7:27–70.

9946. Žukas, Vladas. "Iš tautosakos rinkimo ir spausdinimo istorijos." *Liaudies Kūryba*(Vilnius) 1(1969):124–43. [Sum. in Rus.]

See also 838, 1571, 1762, 5307, 5308, 9347, 9411, 9430, 9489, 9654, 9838, 9953, 9976, 10039.

North America. 9947. Abrahams, Roger D. *Deep Down in the Jungle:Negro Narrative Folklore from the Streets of Philadelphia.* Foreword Alan Dundes. Chicago: Aldine. [Rev. ed.]

9948. Avendaño J., Lucio, and Ruth M. Alexander. "Stories of a Mixteco Town." *Tlalocan* 6:169–75.

9949. Harrison, Lowell H. "Davy Crockett:The Making of a Folk Hero." *KFR* 15(1969):87–90.

9950. Lastra, Yolanda. "El Conejo y el Coyote:Cuento chichimeco." *Tlalocan* 6:115–18.

* 9951. Lumpkin, Ben G. " 'The Fox and the Goose':Tale Type 62 from South Carolina." *NCarF* 18:90–94.

* 9952. —— "The Hawk and the Buzzard:How Tellers Vary the Story." *NCarF* 18:144–47.

9953. Musick, Ruth Ann. *Green Hills of Magic:West Virginia Folktales from Europe.* Lexington: U. of Ky. P.

* 9954. Nower, Joyce. "Foolin' Master." *SNL* 7(1969):5–10.

9955. Periman, Kenneth I. "Don Cacahuate to La Bruja: Hispanic Folklore of the Four Corners." *WR* 6,ii(1969):64–70. [In Colo. and N.M.]

9956. Rendón, Juan José M. "El Tlacuache y el Coyote en Zapoteco." *Tlalocan* 6:119–23.

9957. Roberts, Leonard. *Old Greasybeard:Tales from the Cumberland Gap.* Detroit: Folklore Associates, 1969.

9958. Schorer, C.E. "Indian Tales of C.C. Trowbridge:The Ornamented Head." *SFQ* 33(1969):317–32.

9959. Thomas, Mary A. "A Lad Who Doesn't Like Work:A Huasteca Nahuatl Tale." *Tlalocan* 6:146–58.

9960. Wilson, Charles M. *Stars Is God's Lanterns:An Offering of Ozark Tellin' Stories.* Norman: U. of Okla. P., 1969.
See also 6375, 6763, 7512, 9818, 9936.

South America. 9961. Amor, Sister Rose Teresa. "Afro-Cuban Folk Tales as Incorporated into the Literary Tradition of Cuba." *DAI* 30(1969):2517A(Columbia).

9962. Hurbon, Laënnée. "Dialectique de la vie et de la mort autour de l'arbre dans les contes haïtiens." [F 73]:71–92.

9963. Paredes, Américo,ed. *Folktales of Mexico.* (FW.) Foreword Richard M. Dorson. Chicago: U. of Chicago P.

9964. Pino-Saavedra, Yolando. *Cuentos orales chileno-argentinos.* Santiago: Editorial Universitaria.

9965. —— "Der verschlafene Stelldichein:Ein kleiner Beitrag zum Märchentyp AT 861." [F 81]:313–20.

9966. Wilbert, Johannes. *Folk Literature of the Warao Indians:Narrative Material and Motif Content.* (Latin Amer. Studies 15.) Los Angeles: U. of Calif. Latin Amer. Center.

9967. Wistrand, Lila M. "Folkloric and Linguistic Analyses of Cashibo Narrative Prose." *DAI* 30:5435A–36A(Texas, Austin).
See also 9608.

Anecdotes, Jokes and Fables

General and Miscellaneous. 9968. Byrd, James W. "Anecdotes and Tales:Traveling Anecdotes and War." *TFSB* 35(1969):50–51.

9969. Geissler, F. "Anton von Pforr, ein zu Unrecht vergessener Vermittler eines beliebten Volkserzählstoffes." [F 91]:376–79. [On tr. of *Panchatantra* pub. in 1480–82 as *Buch der Beispiele.* Sum. in Rus.]

9970. Loudon, J[oseph] B. "Teasing and Socialization on Tristan da Cunha." [F 86]:293–332.

9971. Zijderveld, Anton C. "Jokes and Their Relation to Social Reality." *SocR* 35(1968):286–311.

Asia. *9972. Qandil, Barbara. "A Comparative Study of Near Eastern Trickster Cycle." *SFQ* 34:18–33.

9973. Rist, Martin. "The Fable of the Dog in the Manger in the Gospel of Thomas." *IR* 25,iii(1968):13–25.

Europe. 9974. Bausinger, Hermann. "Zum Beispiel." [F 81]:9–18.

9975. Beekmann, Petr. *Whispered Anecdotes:Humor from Behind the Iron Curtain.* Boulder: Golem Press, 1969. [Bx.1342 Boulder, Colo. 80302.]

9976. Dietze, Walter. "Mündlicher Volksschwank und romanhafte Erzählformen im *Lalebuch*." [F 3]:511–14.

9977. Lixfeld, Hannjost. "Der dualistische Schöpfungsschwank von Gottes und des Teufels Herde (Thompson K483): Funktion und Gattung." [F 81]:165–79.

9978. Moser-Rath, Elfriede. "Anekdotenwanderungen in der deutschen Schwankliteratur." [F 81]:233–47.

9979. Stroesiu, Sabina C. *La typologie bibliographique de faceties roumaines.* 2 vols. Tr. Elena and Anton Marin. Bucureşti: Acad. Roumaini, 1969.

9980. Zelenka, Bedřich,ed. *Anekdoty pana Kohna.* Praha: Lidové nakl.
See also 9909, 9910, 9914, 10044.

North America. 9981. Attebery, Louise A. "Governor Jokes." *SFQ* 33(1969):350–51.

9982. Ben-Amos, Dan. "Jewish Humor—The Concept from a New Viewpoint." [F 87]:25–33. [In Hebr.; Eng. sum.]

9983. —— "The Americanization of 'The King and the Abbot'." *IndF* 2,i(1969):115–23.

9984. Brunvand, Jan H. "As the Saints Go Marching By:Modern Jokelore Concerning Mormons." *JAF* 83:53–60.

9985. Carey, George G. " 'Any Everyone of Them's Gone But Me':Another Look at Tangier Island's Oldest Inhabitant." *SLitI* 3,i:73–87.

9986. Emmons, Martha. *Deep Like the Rivers:Stories of My Negro Friends.* (Texas Folklore Soc. Paisano Book 4.) Austin: Encino Press, 1969.

* 9987. Walser, Richard. "Jemmy Critus:Folk Humorist of Charlotte." *NCarF* 18:95–100.

9988. Wukasch, Charles. "Anecdotes and Tales:Divine-Mortal Confusion of Roles as a Motif in Jocular Tales." *TFSB* 35(1969):51–53.
See also 6302, 10926.

South America. 9989. Boglár, Lajos. "Aspects of Story-telling Among the Piaroa Indians." *AEASH* 19:39–52.

9990. Carrera, Pilar Almoina de. "El cuento folklórico y su recolección:Distancia de una versión dictada a una grabada." *RVF* 1(1968):83–85.

III. GNOMIC FOLKLORE

General

General and Miscellaneous. 9991. Vanamamalai, N. "The Folk Motif in *Silappadikaram*." [F 42],ii:138–63.

9992. Rao, C.R. Prasad, and K. Radhakrishna Murty. "Some Aspects of Andhra Folklore and Folk Values." *Triveni* 39,i:42–46.
See also 9674.

Proverbs and Sayings

Bibliography. 9993. Hand, Wayland D. "Writings of Archer Taylor on Proverbs and Proverbial Lore." *Proverbium* 15:4–8.

General and Miscellaneous. 9994. Abrahams, Roger D. "Such Matters as Every Man Should Know, and Descant Upon." *Proverbium* 15:9–11.

9995. Grumbo, Ronald. "Adynaton Symbols in Proverbs:A Few Fragmentary Remarks." *Proverbium* 15:40–42.

9996. Hand, Wayland D. "Folk Beliefs in Proverbial Form." *Proverbium* 15:48–50.

9997. Hassell, J.W. "Proverbs in Riddles." *Proverbium* 15:51–53.

9998. Holbek, Bengt. "Proverb Style." *Proverbium* 15:54–56.

9999. Kuusi, M. "Internationale Aufgaben der Sprichwortforschung." [F 91]:385–87. [Sum. in Rus.]

10000. —— "How Can a Type-Index of International Proverbs Be Outlined:An Experiment and Five Questions." *Proverbium* 15:57–60.

10001. Lüthi, Max. "Das Sprichtwort in der Zeitung." *Proverbium* 15:79–81.

10002. Meertens, Pieter J. "Proverbs and Emblem Literature." *Proverbium* 15:82–83.

10003. Milner, George B. "De l'armature des locutions proverbiales:Essai de taxonomie sémantique." *Homme* 9,iii(1969):49–70.

10004. —— "From Proverbs to Riddles and Vice Versa." *Proverbium* 15:84–86.

10005. Paredes, Américo. "Proverbs and Ethnic Stereotypes." *Proverbium* 15:95–97.

10006. Stambaugh, Ria. "Proverbial and Human Corruption and Other Distortions of Popular Sayings." *Proverbium* 15:115–19.

10007. Taylor, Archer. "As Light as a Feather." [F 87]:95–96.
See also 5840, 10067.

Africa. 10008. Bascom, William. "Proverb Collecting in Africa." *Proverbium* 15:18–19.

10009. Ben-Ami, Issaehar. "One Thousand and One Jewish Proverbs from Morocco." [F 87]:35–148. [In Hebr.; Eng. sum.]

10010. Bergsma, Harold M. "Tiv Proverbs as a Means of Social Control." *AfricaL* 40:151–63.

10011. Kern, Luc. "Quelques proverbes afar." *Pount*(Djibuti) 4(1968):11–12.

10012. Kuusi, Matti. *Ovambo Proverbs with African Parallels.* (FFC 208.) Helsinki: Acad. Sci. Fennica.

10013. Lindfors, Bernth. "Perverted Proverbs in Nigeria Chapbooks." *Proverbium* 15:66–71.

10014. Prietze, Rudolf. *Haussa-Sprichwörter und Haussa-Lieder.* Leipzig: Zentralantiquariat der DDR. [Repr. of 1904 ed.]
See also 9876.

Asia. 10015. Bedi, Sohindger Sing. "Women in the Folk-Sayings of Panjab." *FolkloreC* 9(1968):381–89.

10016. Elçin, Şükrü. "Proverbs in the Turkish Language (Words, Concept, Examples)." *Proverbium* 15:28–34.

10017. Lehman, F.K. "On Chin and Kochin Marriage Regulations." *Man* 5:118–25.

10018. Levin, Isidor. "Parömiologische Erstlinge vom Pamir für Archer Taylor." *Proverbium* 15:61–65.

10019. Luomala, Katharine. "Four Aspects of Twelve Korean Proverbs Used in Hawaii." *Proverbium* 15:75–78.

10020. Piamenta, Moshe. "Birth Greetings in Arabic Dialects." [F 87]:239–58. [In Hebr.; Eng. sum.]

10021. Rezvanian, Mohamed-Hassan. "Quelques notes sur l'origine et la structure des proverbes anecdotiques persans." *Proverbium* 15:100–01.

10022. Subramanian, K. "Women in the Folk Sayings of Tamiland." *FolkloreC* 9(1968):155–60.

10023. Todor, Shimon. "The Camel in Animal Proverbs." [F 87]:369–88. [In Hebr.; Eng. sum.]

See also 9722, 10009, 10212, 10427.

Australia and Oceania. 10024. Kobak, Cantius J.,O.F.M. "Alzina's *Historia de las Islas é Indios de Bisayas . . . 1688*:A Translation of the Lenox Text." *LSS* 3(1969):14–36. [Incl. data on Bisayan vocab., folklore, etc.]

Europe. 10025. Baffioni, Giovanni. "Il dialetto ischiano: Raccolta di detti e proverbi." *GIF* 21(1969):29–72.

10026. Barrick, Mac E. "Rhyme and the Dating of Proverbs." *Proverbium* 15:15–17.

10027. Butovski, Jovanka. "Bitoljske zagonetke, izreke i poslovice." *NStv* 6(1967):196–99.

10028. Červenka, Matěj, and Jan Blahoslav. *Česká přislovi.* Ed. Josef Spilka. Praha: Odeon.

10029. Chaves, Luís. "Pele e osso . . . utilidades facultadas ao nomen pelos animais na sua economia." *RdEt* 13(1969):17–104.

10030. Dal, Eric. "Proverbs in Danish Prosodies and Grammars before 1700." *Proverbium* 15:20–22.

10031. Devoto, Daniel. " 'Stolen Fruit' en Español." *Proverbium* 15:25.

10032. Dopheide, Maria. "Sprichwortsammlung im Archiv für Westfälische Volkskunde." *Proverbium* 15:26–27.

10033. Gallacher, Stuart A. " 'By Hook or by Crook'." *Proverbium* 15:35–37.

10034. Golopenţia-Eretescu, Sanda. "Infinite Proverbs." *Proverbium* 15:38–39.

10035. Grigas, Kazys. "Litauische Entsprechungen zu germanisch-romanischen Sprichwörtern bei Düringsfeld." *Proverbium* 15:43–45.

10036. Hain, Mathilde. "Das Schauspiel Teutscher Sprichwörter." *Proverbium* 15:46–47.

10037. Huryn, Ivan,comp. *Obrazne slovo:Postijni narodni porivnjannja.* Kyjiv: Dnipro, 1966. [Ukr. proverbs and sayings.]

10038. Kondrat'eva, T.N. "O Titax, Titax Tityčax i Titovyx detjax." *RusRe* 1:78–81.

10039. Krzyżanowski, Julian. "Sprichwort und Märchen in der polnischen Volkserzählung." [F 81]:151–58.

10040. Krzyżanowski, Julian,et al.,eds. *Nowa księga przysłów i wyrażeń przysłowiowych polskich, T. I:A-J.* Warsaw: PIW, 1969. [New ed., based on Samuel Adalberg, *Księga przysłów polskich,* 1894.]

10041. Leino, Pentti. "Pienfolkloren dialogimuotteja." *KSVK* 49(1969):124–70.

10042. Loukatos, Démétrios. "Que Dieu nous garde de . . ." *Proverbium* 15:72–74.

10043. Meyer, M[aurits] de. "Een spreekwoordenprent van J.C. Jegher, Antwerpen 1618–1666." *Volkskunde* 69(1968):89–102. [Illus.]

10044. Neumann, Siegfried. "Sagwörter im Schwank —Schwankstoffe im Sagwort." [F 81]:249–66.

10045. Pinon, Roger. "Et cœtera, que sais-je encore? De quelques formules de l'et cœtera." *Proverbium* 15:98–99.

10046. Röhrich, Lutz. "Die Bildwelt von Sprichwort und Redensart in der [F 79]:175–207.

10047. Röhrich, Lutz, and Gertraud Meinel. "Nochmals 'Schabab'." *Proverbium* 15:102–05.

10048. Sallinen, Pirkko. "Skandinavische Entsprechungen finnischer Wellerismen." *Proverbium* 15:106–09.

10049. Sauka, Leonardas. "Zum Versbau der litauischen Sprichwörter und Redensarten." *Proverbium* 15:110–11.

10050. Scheiber, Alexander. "Er hätte sich vielleicht selbst in den Kleiner Finger scheiden lassen." *Proverbium* 15:112–13.

10051. Selig, Karl-Ludwig. "Spanish Proverbs and the Comedia de Aman y Mordochay." *Proverbium* 15:114.

10052. Ströbele, Eugen. " 'X ist die Mutter von y' (zum Lebenslauf einer Bildformel)." *Proverbium* 15:120–21.

10053. Tabarcea, C. "Valorificarea conceptelor structuraliste în cercetarea proverbelor românesti." *AUB* 17(1968):169–73.

10054. Tillhagen, Carl-Herman. "Die Sprichwörterfrequenz in einigen nordschwedischen Dörffen." *Proverbium* 15:122–24.

10055. Uccello, Antonino. "Proverbi calendariali brianzoli: Note di folklore lombardo." [F 94],I:451–58.

10056. Voigt, Vilmos. "Variantenschichten eines ungarischen Proverbiums." *Proverbium* 15:125–28.

10057. Winther, Chr. "Ordsprog fra Herfølge [Zealand]." *Folkeminder* 14(1969):76–85.

10058. Ziltener, Werner. "Parömiologie und provenzalische Philologie." *Proverbium* 15:132–34.

See also 9431, 9722, 10060, 10279, 11093.

North America. 10059. McNeil, W.K. "Proverbs Used in New York Autograph Albums 1820–1900." *SFQ* 33(1969):352–59.

See also 6674, 7571, 10019, 10060.

South America. 10060. Arora, Shirley L. " 'Coma la carabina de Ambrosio'." *Proverbium* 15:12–14.

10061. Barco, Rafael Rodríguez. "Refranes y dichos populares." *RVF* 1(1968):45–47.

10062. Câmara Cascudo, Luís da. *"O morto no Brasil."* *RdEt* 14:5–18.

10063. Monteiro, George. "Brazil, 1969:A Sampling of New World Proverbs." *Proverbium* 15:87–88.

South American. 10064. Coluccio, Marta Isabel. "El gallo." *RdEt* 14:59–81. [Role of rooster in folk art, beliefs, refrains, sayings, games, vocab. of Hispanic peoples.]

Riddles

General and Miscellaneous. 10065. Köngäs-Maranda, Elli. "Structure des énigmes." *Homme* 9,iii(1969):5–48.

See also 9997, 10004.

Europe. 10066. Boswell, George W. "Tolkien's Riddles in *Lord of the Rings*." *TFSB* 25(1969):44–49.

See also 10029.

South America. *See* 9608.

Names

General and Miscellaneous. 10067. O'Kane, Sister Eleanor. "What's in a Name?" *Proverbium* 15:92–94.

Africa. 10068. Corcos, David. "Réflexions sur l'onomastique Judéo-Nord-Africaine." [F 87]:1–27.

10069. Grant, S. "Place Names in the Kgatleng." *BN&R* 2:115–19. [Botswana.]

10070. Mafukidze, Takawira S. "The Origin and Significance of African Personal Names." *BlackW* 19,ix:4–6.

Asia. 10071. Antoun, Richard T. "On the Significance of Names in an Arab Village." *Ethnology* 7(1968):158–70.

10072. Cuisenier, Jean. "Une tente turque d'anatolie centrale." *Homme* 10:59–72.

10073. Mándoki, L. "Two Asiatic Sidereal Names." [F 74]:485–96.

10074. Panfilov, V.Z. "Remarks on Nivkhi (Gilyak) Proper Names (Anthroponyms)." [F 74]:423–31.

See also 10088, 10880.

Australia and Oceania. 10075. Walker, R.J. "Proper Names in Maori Myth and Tradition." *JPS* 78(1969):405–16.

Europe. 10076. Dorian, Nancy C. "A Substitute Name System in the Scottish Highlands." *AA* 72:303–19.

10077. Oinas, Felix. "The Foreigner as Devil, Thistle, and Gadfly." *Proverbium* 15:89–91.

10078. Richards, Melville. "The Supernatural in Welsh-

Place-Names." [F 82]:303–13.
See also 9762, 10029.
North America. 10079. Collier, George A., and Victoria R. Bricker. "Nicknames and Social Structure in Zinacantan." *AA* 72:289–302.
10080. D'Anglure, Bernard Saludin. "Nom et parenté chez les Esquimaux tarramiut du Nouveau-Québec (Canada)." [F 89],II:1013–39.
10081. Markotic, Vladimir. "North American Gypsy Terms: A Comment." *AA* 72:847–48.
10082. Tarpley, Fred. *From Blinky to Blue-John:A Word Atlas of Northeast Texas.* Wolfe City, Texas: Univ. P. [On 127 folk idioms.]
10083. Wilson, Gordon, and Russell Starr. "Folklore in Certain Professions v:The Ornithologist and Folklore." *TFSB* 35(1969):75–79.
10084. Winslow, David J. "Children's Derogatory Epithets." *AF* 82(1969):255–63.
See also 7571, 10935.

South America. 10085. Camara Cascudo, Luís da. "Notícia das chuvas e dos ventos no Brasil." *RdEt* 13(1969):243–56.
10086. Fernandez Pereiro, N.G.B. de. "Nombres de persona puestos a animales en cuentos populares argentinos." [F 26],I:259–67.
10087. Montero, Dario Novoa. "El lenguaje médico de nuestro pueblo." *RVF* 3:105–26.

Others

Asia. 10088. Befu, Harumi. "Studies in Japanese Kinship." *RUS* 56,iv:113–21.
Australia and Oceania. 10089. Cook, Edwin A. "On the Conversion of Non-Agnates into Agnates among the Manga, Jimi River, Western Highlands District, New Guinea." *SJA* 26:190–96.
Europe. 10090. Astakhova, A.M. "The Poetical Image and Elements of Philosophy in Russian Exorcisms." [F 91]:266–72. [Sum. in Rus.]

IV. FOLK POETRY

General

Bibliography. *See* 9488.
General and Miscellaneous. 10091. Acton, Charles. "A Review of Phonograph Records of Irish Interest." *Éire* 3, ii(1968):113–56. [Incl. materials on folk song, ballads, popular songs, etc.]
10092. Edmonson, Munro S. "Metáfora maya en literatura y en arte," II, 37–50 in *Verhandlungen des XXXVIII. Internationalen Amerikanistenkongresses (Stuttgart-München 12. bis 18. August 1968).* München: Klaus Renner Verl.
10093. Katona, Imre. "Die Gliederung der ungarischen Volkslyrik nach Kunstgaltungen und Thematik." *AEASH* 19:207–27.
10094. Kondakov, G.V. *Altajskij fol'klor v tvorčestve V.Ja. Šiškova.* Barnaul: Altajskoe knižnoe izd-vo, 1969.
10095. Piø, Iørn. *Produktionen af danske skillingsviser mellem 1770 og 1821 og samtidens syn på genren.* (Pub. by Inst. for Folkemindevidenskab.) Copenhagen: Copenhagen U.P., 1969. [Offset-reprod. of typed MS.]
10096. Poliščuk, F.M.,ed. *Ukrajins'ka narodna poetyčna tvorčist:Xrestomatija.* Kyjiv: Radjans'ka škola, 1968.
10097. Rosenberg, Bruce A. *The Art of the American Folk Preacher.* New York: Oxford U.P.
10098. —— "The Formulaic Quality of Spontaneous Sermons." *JAF* 83:3–20.
10099. Skrypka, V.M. *Ukrajins'ka, čes'ka ta slovac'ka narodna liryka:Istoryko-porivnjal'ne doslidžennja.* Kyjiv: Naukova dumka.
10100. Virsaladzé, Helene. "Le problème de la classification des œuvres lyriques populaires." [F 77],II:334–37.
10101. Whallon, William. "Who Wrote Down the Formulaic Poem?" [F 3]:469–72.
See also 894, 9662, 9674.

Oral Epics

General and Miscellaneous. 10102. Meletinsky, E.M. "Primitive Heritage in Archaic Epics." [F 91]:187–93. [Sum. in Rus.]
10103. Utley, Francis L. "Oral Genres as Bridge to Written Literature." *AEASH* 19:389–99.
Africa. 10104. Clark, J.P. "The Ozidi Saga." *BO* 2,ii(1968):18–24. [Prologue from 1st night of Ijaw saga.]
10105. Kisala, Piliwe. "Lubango Nkundungulu:A Kaondé Epic." Ed. and Introd. Han F.W. Bantje. *JoA* 2,iii/iv:9–16. [Kaondé text, Eng. tr. & notes.]
10106. N'sanda, J.B. *Epopée Kiguma:Essai d'étude d'un genre littéraire Lega.* Kinshasa: Lovanium U. [Diss.]
Asia. 10107. AN SSSR, IMLI. *Skazanija o nartax—èpos narodov Kavkaza:Sbornik statej.* Moscow: Nauka, 1969.
10108. Arant, Patricia. "Concurrence of Patterns in the

Russian *Bylina.*" *JFI* 7:80–88.
10109. Auèzova, L.M. *Istoričeskie osnovy èpopei* Put' Abaja. (AN KazSSR, Inst. literatury i iskusstva im. M.O. Auèzova, 1969.) Alma-Ata: Nauka, 1969.
10110. Kirejew, A.N. "Widerspiegelung mythologischer Vorstellungen in der epischen Volksdichtung der Baschkiren." [F 77],II:297–300.
10111. Radlov, Vasilii V. *South-Siberian Oral Literature: Turkic Texts.* (IUPUAS 79,2.) Bloomington: Ind. U.P., 1968. [See also Bibliog. for 1968, Item 21004.]
10112. Zhirmunsky, V.M. "The Epic Folk-Singers in Central Asia (Tradition and Artistic Improvisation)." [F 91]:234–45. [Sum. in Rus.]
See also 9488, 9714.
Europe. 10113. Abbasov, A. "Kobzari Poltavščyny." *Prapor* 13,xii(1968):90–93.
10114. Annist, August. *Kalevala ku kunstiteos.* Tallinn: Eesti Raamat, 1969.
10115. Bergman, Gun. "Miloradović, Poslanik Petra Velikoga—1711 God. Mjeseca Marta." *SSl* 15(1969):263–73. [On a Montenegrin folk epic. With facsim. In Eng.]
10116. Bîrgu-Georgescu, Ligia. "Analiza cîntecului epico-liric Ciobănaş de la miori." *REF* 14(1969):353–68.
10117. Burkhart, Dagmar. *Untersuchungen zur Stratigraphie und Chronologie der südslavischen Volksepik.* München: Slavistische Beiträge, 1968.
10118. Ćurić, Hajrudin. "Narodna pjesma o Muji Hrnjici i Kostreš harambaši." *NStv* 6(1967):109–20.
10119. Dej, Oleksij. "Perše vydannja ukrajins'kyx dum." *NTE* 45,vi(1969):7–13.
10120. Fisher, Robert L.,Jr. "Indo-European Elements in Baltic and Slavic Chronicles." [F 90]:147–58.
10121. Jaremenko, V.V.,comp. *Narodni dumy, pisni, balady.* Kyjiv: Molod'.
10122. Kirdan, B.P. *Ukrainskie narodnye dumy (XV—načalo XVII v.).* Moscow: Nauka.
10123. Kireev, A.N. "On Epical Genres in Bashkir Folk Poetry." [F 91]:200–05. [Sum. in Rus.]
10124. Kristó, Gyula. "Ősi epikánk és az Árpád-kori íráshagyomány." *Ethnographia* 81:113–35. [Proto-Finno-Ugric epic poetry and the writing tradit. from the Age of Arpad; sums. in Rus. and Ger.]
10125. Kubjas, E. "Rahvalaulude suurraamatu ilmumise puhul." *KjK* 13:118–21.
10126. Lönnrot, Elias,comp. *The Old Kalevala and Certain Antecedents.* Tr. and Ed. Francis P. Magoun,Jr. Cambridge: Harvard U.P., 1969.
10127. Markiewicz, Z. "Roman Zmorski—exemple de l'attitude romantique envers la littérature orale serbe." [F 3]:497–502.
10128. Mladenović, Ž[ivomir]. "Ustnaja poèzija kak istoriko-

ètnografičeskij istočnik dlja Vuka Stefanoviča Karadžiča." [F 91]:347–52. [Sum. in Fr.]

10129. Murko, Vladimir. "Končna usoda literarne zapuščine Matije Murka, zlasti posnetkov srbskohrvaških epičnih pesmi." *SE* 20(1967):181–84.

10130. Poliščuk, F.M. "Heroji ukrajins'kyx narodnyx dum." *UkrM* 20,ix:10–17.

10131. Putilov, B.N. "O nekotoryx strukturnyx osobennostjax slavjanskogo èposa." *AEASH* 9:325–40.

10132. Stolz, Benjamin A. Nikac and Hamza:Multiformity in the Serbo-Croatian Heroic Epic." *JFI* 7:60–79.

10133. Vargyas, L[ajos]. "O nekotoryx principial'nyx voprosax izučenija épičeskix žanrov." [F 91]:178–82. [Sum. in Fr.]
See also 9714.

Ballads

Bibliography. *See* 3280.
General and Miscellaneous. 10134. Gower, Herschel. "Jeannie Robertson:Portrait of a Traditional Singer." *ScS* 12(1968): 113–26. [Pt. 2.]

10135. Kash, Graham S. "The Poisoning in Lord Randal." *TFSB* 36:6–10.

10136. Nud'ha, H.A. *Ukrajins'ka balada:Z teoriji ta istoriji žanru.* Kyjiv: Dnipro.

10137. Smyrniw, Walter. "The Treatment of the Ballad by Shevchenko and His Contemporaries in Relation to Western Balladry." *CSP* 12,ii:142–74.

10138. Yates, Michael. "The Welcome Sailor." *EDS* 32: 103–04. [Disguised lover theme in balladry.]
See also 10198.

Africa. 10139. Lonfernini, Bruno. "Amore e morte nei canti sidamo." *Nigrizia* 87(Dec 1969):12–16.

10140. Lorelle, Yves. "Littératures pour l'oreille (2):Niger: 'Des paroles qui montent au coeur'." *FE* 212(1969):38–41.

Asia. 10141. Bhattacharya, Deben,comp. *Songs of the Bards of Bengal.* (UNESCO Coll. of Rep. Works, Ind. Ser.) Tr. from Bengali with Introd. and Notes. New York: Grove, 1969. [Also pub. as *Mirror of the Sky*. London: Allen & Unwin, 1969.]

10142. Eberhard, Wolfram. "Die Soziale Welt der südchinesischen Volksballaden." [F 81]:429–44.

10143. Koržan, V.V. *Esenin i narodnaja poèzija.* Moscow: Nauka, 1969.

10144. Sharma, N. "Women in Magahi Folklore." *FolkloreC* 9(1968):86–105.

10145. Vanamamalai, N. "A Study of the Historical Ballads of Tamiland." [F 42],i:597–620.
See also 9894.

Europe. 10147. Annist, August. *Karske Pireta, Maheda Mareta ja Mehetapja Maie lood.Perekonnaballaade vanast orjaajast / Rahvapärimustest põiminud August Annist.* Tallinn: Eesti Raamat.

10148. Armistead, S.G.,and J.H. Silverman. "*La dama de Aragón*:Its Greek and Romance Congeners." *KRQ* 14(for 1967):227–38. [Catalan *Dama de Aragón*, Castilian *Bella en Misa*, and Neo-Hellenic *Tēs koumparás poù égine núfē*.]

10149. Bošković-Stulli, Maja. "Balada o pastiru i tri vještice." *NStv* 7(1968):20–35.

10150. —— "Umirući junak oprašta se od družine:O jednoj slovačko-češkoj i hrvatsko-slovenskoj narodnoj baladi." *ForumZ* 20:516–32.

10151. Brednich, Rolk W., and Wolfgang Suppan,eds. *Gottscheer Volkslieder, Band I:Volksballaden.* Mainz: B. Schott's Söhne, 1969.

10152. Bronzini, Giovanni B. "La canzone dell'avvelenamento nella tradizione popolare italiana." [F 94],i:39–74.

10153. Buchan, David. "The Maid, the Palmer, and the Cruel Mother." *MHRev* 3(1967):98–107. [On Child 21,20,178,95.]

* 10154. Buchan, David D. "Lady Isabel and the Whipping Boy." *SFQ* 34:62–70.

10155. Burlasová, Soňa. *L'udové balady na Horehroní.* Bratislava: SAV, 1969.

10156. Chironi, Elena. "La poesia popolare nel nuorese." *Frontiera*(Roma) 2(1969):265–70,328–31,365–68.

10157. Cirese, Alberto M. "I rapporti italo-rumeni nella filologia demologica." *Veltro* 13(1969):275–72.

10158. Djordjević, Miloš. "Jacob Burckhardt und die Heldenlieder der Serben." [F 3]:737–46.

10159. Faragó, József. " 'A leány átka' lozsádi népballadája." *NIK* 13(1969):323–30. [Sum. in Rom.]

10161. Faragó, József, and János Ráduly. "A népballadák egy romániai magyar falu mai köztudatában." *Ethnographia* 80(1969):504–13. [Folk-ballads in a Hung. village in Romania; sums. in Rus. and Ger.]

10162. Friedman, Adele C. "Gérard de Nerval and the Folksong Tradition." *DAI* 30:3940A(Yale).

10163. Giankoullis, Konstantinos G. "He synecheia tis laïkis poiitikis mas paradosis." *KL* 1(1969):158–63.

10164. Gower, Herschel, and James Porter. "Jeannie Robertson:The Child Ballads." *ScS* 14:35–58. [Pt. 1.]

10165. Greene, Juris. "The Typology of Anaphorae and Polyptota in Latvian Folksongs," 142–54 in Velta Rūķe-Draviņa,ed., *Donum Balticum. To Professor Christian S. Stang on the Occasion of His Seventieth Birthday, 15 March 1970.* Stockholm: Almqvist & Wiksell.

10166. Korompay, K. "Zapadnaja ballada za Karpatami." [F 91]:219–22. [Sum. in Fr.]

10167. Kríza, Ildikó. "Balladakutatás—balladaköltészet. (Ballada a román népköltészetben.)" *Ethnographia* 80(1969): 73–90. [Ballad-research—ballad-poetry. Ballad in Rom. folk poetry; sums. in Rus. and Ger.]

10168. Kumer, Zmaga. "Skladnosti in razlike v južnoslovanskih variantah balade o razbojnikovi ženi." *NStv* 7(1968): 52–60.

10169. Lyle, E.B. "The Opening of 'Tam Lin'." *JAF* 83:33–43.

10170. Makris, Theodoros S. "Ho thanatos tou Megalou Panos (ho historikos thrylos tis nisou ton Paxon)." [F 4],ii:94–112.

10171. Malecore, Irene Maria. "I valori estetici della poesia popolare abruzzese." *Abruzzo* 7,ii–iii(1969):289–98.

10172. Mario, Alberto. "Revisione di nozioni correnti:Lo stornello." [F 94],ii:87–103.

10173. Oikonomidis, Dimitrios V. "Anonymon Kretikon stichourgima tou 16´ aionos kai scheseis autou pros tim prophorikin paradosin." [F 10],iv:335–43.

10174. Ortutay, Gyula. "Die europäischen Volksballaden: Eine Skizze." [F 79]:115–20.

10175. Papagrigorakis, Idomeneus. "Ta Kretika rizitika tragoudia." [F 10],iv:344–46.

10176. —— "Tragoudi tis machis tou Thersiou (1821)." [F 10],iv:347–52.

10177. Piø, Iørn. "Overnaturlige væsner i nordisk balladetradition ii:DgFT 38 Agnete og havmanden." *DS* 65: 24–51. [Also as *Meddelanden från Svenskt Visarkiv*, 25.]

10178. Pop, M[ihai]. "Eléments comuns et traits nationaux spécifiques de la poésie épique de la zone des Carpates." [F 91]:206–12. [Sum. in Rus.]

10179. Putilov, B.N. "Historical Roots and Genesis of Slav Ballads About Incest." [F 91]:213–18. [Sum. in Rus.]

10180. Rogers, Edith. "A New Genealogy for 'Rico Franco'." *JAF* 82(1969):369–73.

10181. Sanarov, V.J. "Trois chansons tsiganes russes." *ETs* 15,iii(1969):1–7. [Music.]

10182. Spyridakis, Georgios K. "Dimodi asmata kai laïka poiimata peri tin pyrpolisin tis Monis Arkadiou (9 Noemvriou 1866)." [F 10],iv:430–37.

10183. Stauffacher, W. "Carl Spitteler und die serbischen Heldenlieder." [F 3]:747–54.

10184. Talley, Jeannine E. "The Threefold Death in Finnish Lore." [F 90]:143–46.

10185. Zeps, Valdis. "The Meter of the Latvian Folk Dactyl." *Ceļi* 14(1969):45–47.
See also 1446, 9427, 9936, 9972, 10121, 10133, 10134, 10189, 10299, 10775.

North America. 10186. Bethke, Robert D. "Narrative Obituary Verse and Native American Balladry." *JAF* 83:61–68.

10187. Bronson, Bertrand H. *The Ballad as Song.* Berkeley and Los Angeles: U. of Calif. P., 1969. [Prev. pub. essays.]

10188. Fife, Austin E. and Alta S. *Ballads of the Great West.*

Palo Alto: Amer. West Pub. Co.

10189. Foster, Charles Wm. " 'The Butcher Boy' in New Market, Alabama." *TFSB* 35(1969):81–85.

10190. Hippensteel, Faith. " 'Sir Hugh':The Hoosier Contribution to the Ballad." *IndF* 2,ii(1969):75–140.

South America. 10191. Ramón y Rivera, Luis Felipe. "Origen de algunos corridos tachirenses." *RVF* 3:37–71.

Songs

Bibliography. 10192. Gupta, Shaligram. "A Selected Bibliography of Hindi Folksongs." *FolkloreC* 10(1969):427–33.

General and Miscellaneous. 10193. Anon. "The Miramichi Folk Song Festival." *Mysterious East*(New Brunswick, Canada) (Nov 1969):28–30.

10194. Hankiss, Elemér. "Kommunikációelméleti modellek és a népdalkutatás." *Ethnographia* 80(1969):354–55. [Models of communication-theory and research in folksongs. Abst.]

10195. Hogan, Homer. "Hermeneutics and Folk Songs." *JAAC* 28(1969):223–29.

10196. Hugill, Stan. *Shanties and Sailors' Songs.* New York: Praeger; London: Herbert Jenkins, 1969.

10197. Klusen, Ernst. *Volkslied:Fund und Erfindung.* Köln: Musikverlage Hans Gerig, 1969.

10198. Munch, Peter A. *The Song Tradition of Tristan da Cunha.* (FIMS 22.) Bloomington: Ind. U.P.; The Hague: Mouton.

10199. Steinitz, W[olfgang]. "Arbeiterlied und Volkslied." [F 91]:163–74. [Sum. in Rus.]

See also 9842.

Africa. 10200. Anyumba, H. Owuor. "Performing African Songs and Dances:The Folk-Song Versus the Festival." *EAJ* 7,iv:37–42.

10201. Bartels, Lambert. "Birth Songs of the Macha Galla." *Ethnology* 8(1969):406–22. [Ethiopia.]

10202. Boyayo, Abraham. "Berceuses du Burundi." *AfrA* 3,ii:32–37,90.

10203. Cerulli, Enrico. "Canti amarici delle corti e delle campagne." [F 13]:415–23.

10204. Coupez, A., and Th. Kamanzi. *Littérature de cour au Rwanda.* Oxford: Clarendon.

10205. Hale, Sondra. "Sudanese Cultural Renaissance." *AfricaR* 15,ix:29–31. [Lit. and songs.]

10206. Kakoma, George W. *Songs from Buganda.* London: U. of London P., 1969.

10207. Leslau, Charlotte and Wolf,eds. *African Poems and Love Songs.* Mount Vernon, N.Y.: Peter Pauper.

10208. Mensah, Atta A. "The Popular Song and Ghanaian Writer." *Okyeame* 4,i(1968):110–19.

10209. Moore, Bai T. "Categories of Traditional Liberian Songs." *LiberianSJ* 2:117–37.

10210. Santandrea, Stefano. "Praise-Songs for 'Killers' in Jur-Luo." *Africa*(Rome) 24,ii/iii(1969):182–216.

See also 9705, 10014, 10418, 10501, 10723.

Asia. 10211. Berger, Donald P. *Folk Songs of Japanese Children.* Rutland, Vt. and Tokyo: Charles E. Tuttle, 1969.

10212. Bhatnagar, Manja. "The Position of Women as Depicted in Rajastani Folklore." *FolkloreC* 9(1968):17–36.

10213. Diószegi, Vilmos. "Libation Songs of the Altaic Turks." *AEASH* 19:95–106.

10214. Gáldi, L. "On Some Problems of Versification in Samoyed Shamanistic Song." [F 74]:125–36.

10215. Goswami, Praphulladatta. "Women in Assam's Folklore." *FolkloreC* 9(1968):39–45.

10216. Gupta, Sankar Sen. "On Ethnomusicology and India." *FolkloreC* 9(1968):229–42.

10217. Malm, W[illiam] P. "A Study in the Japanese Song Narrative Tradition." [F 91]:108–10. [Sum. in Rus.]

10218. Mishra, S.D. "Importance of Women in Hindi Folksongs." *FolkloreC* 9(1968):140–47.

10219. Reinhard, Ursula and Kurt. *Auf der Fiedel Mein: Volkslieder von der Osttürkischen Schwarzmeerkunde.* Berlin: Museum für Völkerkunde, 1968.

10220. Shiloah, Amnon. "The Aliyah Songs in the Traditional Folk Literature of Israel." [F 87]:349–68. [In Hebr.; Eng. sum.]

10221. Singh, K. Jagjit. "Women in Punjabi Folksongs." *FolkloreC* 9(1968):124–31.

10222. Sinha, Purnima. "Light Classical Music." *FolkloreC* 10(1969):198–205.

10223. Uchida, Ruriko. "The Musical Character of Rice Planting Song in 'Tokunoshima' Island—Compare the Rice Planting Song in 'Chugoku' District in Mainland Japan and One in 'Tokunoshima' Island." [F 77],ii:340–42.

10224. Upadhyaya, Hari S. "Patterns of Mother-Son Behavior in the Hindu Family as Depicted in the Bhojpuri Folksongs of India." *Anthropologica* 11(1969):203–14.

10225. ——— "Wife-Husband Relationship Patterns in the Joint Hindu Family:A Study Based upon the Oral Literature of Northern India." *RVF* 2(1969):69–76.

10226. Vanamamalai, N. "Women in Tamil Folklore." *FolkloreC* 9(1968):285–301.

10227. Vasilevič, G.M. "Shamanistic Songs of the Evenki (Tungus)." [F 74]:351–72.

10228. Vértes, Edith. "On the Trail of the Ostyak (Khanty) Mythical Songs." [F 74]:113–22.

See also 10015, 10108, 10424, 10522, 10526, 10534, 10642.

Australia and Oceania. 10229. Elbert, Samuel H., and Noelani Mahoe. *Na Mele o Hawaii Nei:101 Hawaiian Songs.* Honolulu: U. of Hawaii P.

10230. Ellis, Catherine J. "Structure and Significance in Aboriginal Song." *Mankind* 7(1969):3–14.

10231. Lloyd, A.L. "Folklore and Australia." *Overland* 45:17–26.

Europe. 10232. Aavik, Johannes. *Eesti rahvalaule.* New York: Eesti Kultuurfond. [Rev. 3d Ed.]

10233. Alevizos, Susan and Ted. *Folk Songs of Greece.* New York: Oak Pubs., 1968.

10234. Anderluh, Anton. *Kärntens Volksliederschatz, Erste Abteilung:Liebeslieder, Fünfter Band.* (Buchreihe des Landesmuseums für Kärnten 26.) Klagenfurt: Landesmuseums für Kärnten, 1969.

10235. ——— *Kärntens Volksliederschatz, Erste Abteilung: Liebeslieder, Vierter Band.* (Buchreihe des Landesmuseums für Kärnten 25.) Klagenfurt: Landesmuseums für Kärnten, 1968.

10236. Antanavičius, Juozas. "Profesinės polifonijos principų ir formų analogijos liaudies sutartinėse." *Liaudies Kūryba*(Vilnius) 1(1969):27–52. [Sum. in Rus.]

10237. Arratia, J.M. de. *Cancionero popular del País Vasco.* 2 vols. San Sebastian: Aunamendi, 1968.

* 10238. Bailey, James. "Literary Usage of a Russian Folk Song Meter." *SEEJ* 14:436–52.

10239. Baud-Bovy, Samuel. "La chanson crétoise de la 'tavla'." [F 10],iv:114–20.

10240. Brťáň, Rudo. "Na okraj *Kompozície ľudovej piesne.*" *SlovP* 86,vii:117–24. [Rev. art.]

10241. Burkšaitienė, Laima. "Nebaigtas baras." *Liaudies Kūryba*(Vilnius) 1(1969):79–95. [On melodies of A. Juška's colls. of folksongs. Sum. in Rus.]

10242. Comişel, E[milia]. "Les particularités stylistiques musicales des genres folkloriques au cours de différentes périodes historiques." [F 92]:221–25. [Sum. in Rus.]

10243. Darbiniece, J. "Žanra problēma gadskārtu ieražu dziesmās salīdzinošās analīzes skatījumā." *LZAV* 8:98–107.

10244. D'Arcais, F.,ed. *Canti delle tradizioni marinare.* Rome: Edindustria, 1968.

10245. Dej, O.,et al.,eds. *Žartivlyvi pisni:Rodynno-pobutovi.* Kyjiv: Naukova dumka, 1967.

10246. ——— "Pisnja pravdoju ne postupajeť'sja." *NTE* 45,i (1969):58–68. [On a new Ukr. folk song.]

10247. ——— "Uljublena pisnja Jurija Fed'kovyča ta Ivana Franka." *NTE* 44,i(1968):53–55.

10248. Dömötör, Tekla. "Mythical Elements in Hungarian Midwinter Quête Songs." *AEASH* 19:119–46.

10249. Evseev, V.Ja. "Dva rusla vengerskoj narodnoj poèzii." *AEASH* 19:201–05. [20th cent. Hung. workers' songs.]

10250. Gensane, Bernard. "Le thème de l'enfance chez les Beatles." *LanM* 64:60–66.

10251. Giancristoforo, Emiliano. "Una canzone popolare inedite raccolta da Benedetto Croce a Raiano nel 1907." *RAbr*

21(1968):175–78.

10252. Goegginger, W. "Lettische Volkslieder in neuer Sicht." *BHe* 15(1969):251–56.

10253. Goman, N.N. "La chanson de Yozli." *ETs* 15, iv(1969):3.

10254. Gorali, Moshe, Gideon Almagor, and Moshe Bick,eds. *The Golden Peacock:Yiddish Folksongs.* Haifa: Music Museum and A.M.L.I. Library. [In Yiddish; sum. in Eng.]

10255. Hankiss, Elemér. "Kommunikációelméleti modellek és a népdalkutatás." *Ethnographia* 80(1969):354–55. [Models of communication-theory and research in folk songs. Abst.]

10256. Heilfurth, Gerhard. "Bänkelgesang, Geschichten 'aus dem Bergmannsleben' auf fliegenden Blättern." [F 81]:445–67.

10257. Hryca, Sofija,et al. "Slovo i naspiv u fol'klori." *NTE* 45,iv(1969):15–20.

10258. Hummel, Carz. "Ein mittelniederdeutsches Falkenlied." *NJ* 91(1968):68–76.

10259. Ioannides, C.P. "A Short Collection of Cyprus Folksongs." *KyS* 32(1968):265–300.

10260. Ivanenko, Volodymyr. "Šukač krasy:Klyment Kvitka." *Prapor* 15,x:95–100. [On a famous collector of Ukr. songs.]

10261. Jakelaitis, Vytautas. *Lietuvos dainų šventės.* Vilnius: Vaga.

10262. Jokimaitenė, Pranė. *Lietuvų liaudies vaikų dainos.* Vilnius: Vaga. ["Lietuvių liaudies vaikų dainų tipų katalogas," 173–247. Sum. in Rus.]

10263. Katona, I[mre]. "Die lyrischen Lieder der ungarischen landwirtschaftlichen Arbeiter (1848–1945) (Textanalyse)." [F 91]:297–302. [Sum. in Rus.]

10264. Katona, Imre. "Kísérlet egyszakaszos népdalszövegek változatképződésének mennyyiségi vizsgálatára." *Ethnographia* 80(1969):398–401. [Essay in quantitative anal. of version-formation of one-strophe folksong texts.]

10265. Kevess, Arthur. *German Folk Songs.* New York: Oak Pubs., 1968.

10266. Knabben, Pieter. "Een oud lied gevonden te Boorsem." *Volkskunde* 69(1968):30–34.

10267. Kolessa, Filaret. *Melodiji ukrajins'kyx narodnyx dum.* Kyjiv: Naukova dumka.

10268. Kras, Ivan. "Starodavni lemkivs'ki koljadky v zapysax I. Birec'koho." *NTE* 45,i(1969):69–71.

10269. Krauss, Paul G. *German Folksongs in Praise of Women.* (OPLLL A11.) Athens: Ohio U. Mod. Lang. Dept., 1969. [15-p. pamphlet, mimeo.]

10270. Kumer, Zmaga. *Das Slovenische Volkslied in Seiner Mannigfaltigkeit.* (Litterae Slovenicae 1.) Munich: R. Trodenik, 1968.

10271. —— "Rudeževa zbirka Slovenskih ljudskih pesmi." *SE* 20(1967):129–41.

10272. Lefftz, Joseph. *Das Volkslied in Elsass:Dritter Band.* Paris and Freiburg: Alsatia Colmar, 1969.

10273. Lenkauskas, Leonardas. "Adutiškio apylinkių vestuvinės dainos." *Liaudies Kūryba*(Vilnius) 1(1969):95–109. [Sum. in Rus.]

10274. MacCormick, Donald. *Hebridean Folksongs:A Collection of Waulking Songs.* Fair Lawn, N.J. and London: Oxford U.P., 1969. [Ed. J.L. Campbell.]

10275. Manga, János. "Varianten der Hochzeitlieder eines Dorfes." *AEASH* 19:247–79.

10276. Marčok, Viliam. "Kompozícia ľudovej piesne." *SlovP* 85,xii(1969):36–46; 86,i:114–23.

10277. —— "Významové zameranie pomenovania v ľudovej piesni." *SlovP* 86,ii:111–20.

10278. —— "Základy poetiky ľudovej piesne." *SlovP* 85, xi(1969):86–97.

10279. Monteiro, George. "The Portuguese Element in New England by Henry R. Lang. Notes From Another Century." *RdEt* 13(1969):339–52.

10280. Moorman, Charles. "Those Heroic Beatles." *SoQ* 8(1969):75–89. [The Beatles as folk heroes.]

10281. Nazarenko, I. *Ukrajins'ki narodni pisni z repertuaru I.S. Kozlovs'koho.* Kyjiv: Muzyčna Ukrajina.

10282. Nettel, Reginald. "Folk Elements in Nineteenth-Century Puritanism." *Folklore* 80(1969):272–85.

10283. Nud'ha, Hryhorij. "Ukrajins'ka pisnja i duma v Juhoslaviji." *NTE* 44,i(1968):30–39.

10284. Oinas, Felix J. *Studies in Finnic-Slavic Folklore Relations:Selected Papers.* (FFC 205.) Helsinki: Acad. Scientiarum Fennica, 1969. [Prev. pub. essays plus "The Goose Lost," "Some Motifs of the Balto-Finnic War Song," "The Legend of the Torture of Flax."]

10285. O'Shaughnessy, Patrick. *Twenty-One Lincolnshire Folk-Songs from the Manuscript Collection of Percy Grainger.* London: Oxford U.P., 1968.

10286. Pan'kevyč, Ivan. "Ukrajins'ka narodna pisnja." *NZMUKS* 4,i(1969):44–61. [Sum. in Eng.]

10287. Papadima, Ovidiu. *Literatura populara română; din istoria și poetica ei.* Bucharest: Editura pentru Literatură, 1968.

10288. Požar, Breda. "Anastasius Grüns unveröffentliche Übersetzungen slowenischer Volkslieder." *AN* 2(1969):65–88.

10289. Pribić, Nikola. "Goethe, Talvj und das südslawische Volkslied." [F 21]:17–27.

10290. —— "Goethe, Talvj und das südslavische Volkslied." *BalSt* 10:135–44.

10291. Purslow, Frank. *The Wanton Seed:More English Folk Songs from the Hammond and Gardiner Mss.* London: E.F.D.S. Pubs., 1969.

10292. Rihtman, Dunja. "Arhaični elementi u svatovskim pjesmama Srba i Hrvata bosansko-hercegovačkog sela." *NStv* 7(1968):70–74.

10293. Saint Erlich, Vera. "Love Sentiments and Love Relations in Rural Yugoslavia." *Anthropologica* 12:23–44.

10294. Sauermann, Dietmar. *Historische Volkslieder der 18. und 19. Jahrhunderts:Ein Beitrag zur Volksliedforschung und zum Problem der Volkstümlichen Geschichtsbetrachtung.* (Schriften der Volkskundlichen Kommission des Landschaftsverbandes Westfalen-Lippe 18.) Munich: Aschendorff, 1968.

10295. Siuts, Hinrich. *Die Ansingelieder zu den Kalenderfesten:Ein Beitrag zur Geschichte, Biologie und Funktion des Volksliedes.* Göttingen: Otto Schwartz, 1968.

10296. Slaviūnas, Zenonas. "Sutartinių daugiabalsiškumo tipai ir jų chronologijos problema." *Liaudies Kūryba*(Vilnius) 1(1969):9–27. [Sum. in Rus.]

10297. Stephan, Brigette. *Studien zur russischen Častuška und Ihrer Entwicklung.* (Slavistische Beiträge 38.) Munich: Otto Sagner, 1969.

10298. Stubbs, Ken. *The Life of a Man:English Folk Songs from the Home Counties.* London: E.F.D.S. Pubs.

10299. Suppan, Wolfgang. "Untersuchung zum Lied-Repertoire des Russlanddeutschen Georg Sänger aus Leichtling an der Wolga." *JOV* 12(1969):215–48. [Music.]

10300. Tedre, Ülo,ed. *Eesti rahvalaulud:Antoloogia.* 2 vols. in 4 parts. Tallinn: Eesti Raamat, 1969–70.

10301. Turjanycja, Ju.D. "Motyvy social'noho protestu v ukrajins'kyx narodnyx dumax pro rekrutčynu." *ULz* 8:61–67.

10302. Valtonen, Pertti. "Poèmes et chants tsiganes:Poèmes en dialecte tsigane finlandais." *ETs* 15,i–ii(1969):1–3.

10303. Vasiljević, Zorislava M. "Šest srpskih narodnih pesama iz rukopisa Miodraga Vasiljevića." *NStv* 7(1968):96–98.

10304. Virsaladzé, H.B. "La poésie des rondes printanières en Georgie." [F 91]:284–89. [Sum. in Rus.]

10305. Vlahović, Petar. "Savremene vezene tužbalice Brodareva." *NStv* 6(1967):104–08.

10306. Voigt, Vilmos. " 'A szerelem kertjében.' Szempontok lírai népdalszövegeink kialakulásának és alkotásmódjának vizsgálatához." *Ethnographia* 80(1969):235–75; 81:28–54. ['In the Garden of Love.' Aspects of the anal. of the devel. and poetic creation of lyric folksong texts. Sum. in Eng.]

10307. Vuković, Milutin. "Tužbalica za sinom jedincem." *NStv* 6(1967):189–95.

10309. Wales, Tony,ed. *Field and Furrow:Songs of Farm and Countryside.* London: Eng. Folk Dance and Song Soc., 1968.

10310. Zemcovski, Izalijj. "Prilog pitanju strofike narodnih pesama." *NStv* 7(1968):61–69.

10311. Zlatanović, Momčilo. "Lazaričke pesme u Vranju i okolini." *NStv* 6(1967):121–33.

See also 1463, 9336, 9352, 9644, 9669, 9756, 9941, 10113, 10121,

10181, 10391, 10392, 10547, 10549, 10551, 10553, 10563, 10564, 10569, 10570, 10571, 10574, 10899, 11104.

North America. 10312. Abrahams, Roger D. "Creativity, Individuality, and the Traditional Singer." *SLitI* 3,i:5–34.

10313. Bluestein, Gene. "Folk Tradition, Individual Talent:A Note on the Poetry of Rock." *MR* 11:373–84. [Refs. to B. Dylan.]

10314. Burton, Thomas G., and Ambrose M. Manning. *The East Tennessee State University Collection of Folklore:Folksongs II.* Johnson City: Research Advisory Council of East Tenn. State U., 1969.

10315. Bush, Michael E. *Folk Songs of Central West Virginia.* Ripley, W. Va.: M.E. Bush, 1969.

10316. Cansler, Loman D. "He Hewed His Own Path: William Henry Scott, Ozark Songmaker." *SLitI* 3,i:37–63.

10317. Cray, Ed. *The Erotic Muse.* New York: Oak Pubs., 1969.

10318. Denisoff, R. Serge. " 'Take It Easy, But Take It':The Almanac Singers." *JAF* 83:21–32.

10319. Fife, Austin E. and Alta S. *Cowboy and Western Songs:A Comprehensive Anthology.* New York: Clarkson N. Potter, 1969.

10320. —— *Heaven on Horseback:Revivalist Songs and Verse in the Cowboy Idiom.* (Western Texts Soc. Ser. 1:1.) Logan: Utah State U.P.

10321. Fowke, Edith. "Labor and Industrial Protest Songs in Canada." *JAF* 82(1969):34–50.

10322. —— *Lumbering Songs from the Northern Woods.* (PAFS, Memoir Ser. 55.) Tunes Transcr. Norman Cazden. Austin: U. of Texas P. for the Amer. Folklore Soc.

10323. Green, Archie. "Recorded American Coal Mining Songs." *DAI* 30:4894A–95A(Pa.).

10324. Grossman, Stefan,ed. *Rev. Gary Davis:The Holy Blues.* New York: Robbins Music Corp. and Chandon Music Co.

10325. Leadbitter, Mike. *Delta Country Blues.* Bexhill-on-Sea, Eng.: Blues Unlimited, 1968.

10326. Lingenfelter, Richard E., Richard A. Dwyer, and David Cohen. *Songs of the American West.* Berkeley and Los Angeles: U. of Calif. P., 1968.

* 10327. Lumpkin, Ben G. "Tune for 'Baldy Green'." *SFQ* 34:12–17.

10328. Manny, Louise, and James R. Wilson. *Songs of Miramichi.* Fredericton, N.B.: Brunswick P., 1968.

10329. Oliver, Paul. *Screening the Blues:Aspects of the Blues Tradition.* London: Cassell, 1968. [Pub. as *Aspects of the Blues Tradition.* New York: Oak Pubs.]

10330. —— *The Story of the Blues.* Philadelphia: Chilton, 1969.

10331. Rosenberg, Bruce A. *The Folksongs of Virginia:A Checklist of the WPA Holdings, Alderman Library, Univ. of Virginia.* Charlottesville: U.P. of Va., 1969.

10332. Russell, Tony. *Blacks, Whites and Blues.* New York: Stein and Day.

10333. Shellans, Herbert. *Folk Songs of the Blue Ridge Mountains.* New York: Oak Pubs., 1968.

10334. Twining, Mary A., and William C. Saunders. " 'One of These Days':The Function of Two Singers in the Sea Island Community." *SLitI* 3,i:65–71.

See also 6099, 6101, 9631, 9814, 10187, 10279, 10348, 10580.

South America. 10335. Barthélemy, André. "Poèmes et Chants Tsiganes:Poèmes recueillis en Amérique latine." *ETs* 15,i–ii(1969):3–7.

10336. Chapman, Anne. "La fin d'un monde." [F 89],i:61–76. [Descrip. of an old informant singer from the Ona people of Argentina.]

10337. Clastres, Pierre. "Prophètes dans la jungle." [F 89],i:535–42.

See also 9608, 10468, 10597, 10601.

Rhymes and Verses

Africa. 10338. Abimbola, Wande. "The Second Odu of Ifa." *BO* 2,ii(1968):7–12. [Yoruba Ifa verses with Eng. tr. and notes.]

10339. Armstrong, Robert G. "Onugbo mlOko:Ancestral Mask Chant in Idoma." *BO* 2,ii(1968):13–17. [Text, Eng. tr., and notes.]

10340. Beier, Ulli,ed. *Yoruba Poetry:An Anthology of Traditional Poems.* Cambridge: Cambridge U.P.

10341. Lomax, Alan, and Raoul Abdul, comps. *3000 Years of Black Poetry:An Anthology.* With Introd. New York: Dodd, Mead. [Incl. some Afr. oral poetry.]

10342. p'Bitek, Okot. "The Poet in Politics." *BO* 2,iii(1968): 29–33. [Trad. and contemp. polit. poetry in Uganda.]

10343. Tomiche, Nada. "Le *mawwāl* égyptien." [F 13]:429–38.

10344. Ziervogel, D. "A Swazi Dialogue." *Limi* 10(June): 25–29. [Nursery rhyme.]

Europe. 10345. Gerov, Boris. "Zur Lesung und Deutung des Epigramms von Čekančevo (Bez. Sofia)." *IIBE* 16(1968):97–106.

10346. Katona, Imre. "A magyar népi líra tartalmi-tematikai tagolódása." *Ethnographia* 81:288–307. [Hung. folk lyric poetry: content and theme; sums. in Rus. and Ger.]

10347. Kirnbauer, Franz. "Ein alter Bergspruch aus Kuttenberg (Kutná Hora)." [F 79]:481–85.

North America. 10348. Fowke, Edith [F.] *Sally Go Round the Sun:300 Songs, Rhymes and Games of Canadian Children.* Toronto and Montreal: McClelland and Stewart Ltd., 1969; Garden City, N.Y.: Doubleday.

See also 10186, 10926.

South America. 10349. Carrera, Pilar Almoina de. "Sobre la conservación de denominaciones tradicionales de la Decima en Curiepe." *RVF* 1(1968):79–82.

V. FOLK GAMES AND TOYS

General

General and Miscellaneous. 10350. Allardt, Erik. "Basic Approaches in Comparative Sociological Research and the Study of Sport." [F 84]:14–30.

10351. Damm, Hans. "The So-Called Sport Activities of Primitive People:A Contribution Towards the Genesis of Sport." [F 84]:52–69.

10352. Elias, Norbert, and Eric Dunning. "The Quest for Excitement in Unexciting Societies." [F 84]:31–51.

10353. Heinilä, Kalevi. "Notes on the Inter-Group Conflicts in International Sport." [F 84]:174–82.

10354. Henriot, Jacques. *Le Jeu.* Paris: Presses Univs., 1969.

10355. Lüsehen, Günther. "Sociology of Sport and the Cross-Cultural Analysis of Sport and Games." [F 84]:6–13.

10356. —— "The Interdependence of Sport and Culture." [F 84]:85–99.

10357. Robinson, John P. "Daily Participation in Sport Across Twelve Countries." [F 84]:156–73.

10358. Sutton-Smith, Brian, and John M. Roberts. "The Cross-Cultural and Psychological Study of Games." [F 84]: 100–08.

10359. Yeager, Allison. "Historic Egg Fight." *TFSB* 35(1969):41–43.

See also 10064.

Europe. *See* 11093.

Children

General and Miscellaneous. 10360. Seagoe, May V. "Children's Play as an Indicator of Cross-Cultural and Intra-Cultural Differences." [F 84]:132–55.

Africa. 10361. Mayer, Philip and Iona. "Socialization by Peers:The Youth Organization of the Red Xhosa." [F 86]:159–89.

Asia. 10362. Hama, Kazue. "Takeuma." *ActaA* 17:39–58.

10363. Vatuk, Ved Prakash. "Let's Dig up Some Dirt:The Idea of Humor in Children's Folklore in India." [F 77],ii:274–77.

Europe. 10364. Opie, Peter and Iona. *Children's Games in Street and Playground:Chasing, Catching, Seeking, Hunting, Racing, Duelling, Exerting, Daring, Guessing, Acting, Pretending.*

Oxford: Clarendon, 1969.
North America. *See* 10348.
South America. *See* 9608.

Adults

General and Miscellaneous. 10365. Perusini, Gaetano. "Amuleti ittici." [F 41]:283–306.
Australia and Oceania. 10366. Moyle, Richard. "An Account of the Game of Tāgāti'a." *JPS* 79:233–44.
Europe. 10367. Paulaharju, Ahti. "Riekonpyynti ajanvietteineen. Vetsikkojoen riekonpyyntialue." *KSVK* 50:310–23.

[On old games.]
10368. Ranta-Knuuttila, Raija. "August Reinholmista ja Toivo Okkolasta nykypäiviin." *KSVK* 49(1969):196–219. [On old folk-games.]
See also 10921.
North America. 10369. Glassford, R. Gerald. "Organization of Games and Adaptive Strategies of the Canadian Eskimo." [F 84]:70–84.
See also 10370.
South America. 10370. Zurcher, Louis A.,Jr., and Arnold Meadow. "On Bullfights and Baseball:An Example of Interaction of Social Institutions." [F 84]:109–31.

VI. DRAMATIC FOLKLORE

Folk Drama

General and Miscellaneous. 10371. Awdejeff, A.D. [Avdeev, A.D.]. "Die Maske und ihre Bedeutung im Prozess der Entstehung des Teaters." [F 91]:80–86. [Sum. in Rus.]
10372. Savushkina, N.I. "Dramatized Image in Some Genres of Russian Folklore." [F 91]:120–27. [Sum. in Rus.]
See also 10217.
Africa. 10373. Adedeji, J.A. "The Origin of the Yoruba Masque Theatre:The Use of Ifa Divination Corpus as Historical Evidence." *AfrN* 6,i:70–86.
10374. Akyea, E. Ofori. "The Atwia-Ekumfi Kodzidan—An Experimental African Theatre." *Okyeame* 4,i(1968):82–84.
10375. Clerk, S.I. "African Puppet Theater." *AfrA* 4,i:66.
10376. Graham-White, Anthony. "West African Drama: Folk, Popular, and Literary." *DAI* 30:3573A–74A(Stanford).
10377. Kedjanyi, John. "Masquerade Societies in Ghana." *Okyeame* 4,i(1968):85–90.
10378. Khaznadar, Chérif. "Les danses de possession sont-elles 'des danses sauvages'?" *JeuneA* 13 oct:56–58. [In ritual and mod. drama.]
10379. Owomoyela, Oyekan. "Yoruba-Language Theater Draws Inspiration from Tradition." *AfricaR* 15,vi:32–33.
10380. Vavilov, B. "Open-air Theatre." *Abbia* 23(1969):133–36. [Trad. and modern Afr. drama; foll. by Fr. tr., 137–40.]
See also 10104.
Asia. 10381. Jeanneret, A. "Le théâtre d'ombres en Orient." *ASEA* 23(1969):155–66.
10382. Kadyrov, M.N. "Women Folk Theatre in Uzbekistan." [F 91]:94–99. [Sum. in Rus.]
10383. Kim, Moon-hwan. "Folk Drama and Its Tradition." *KoJ* 10,v:31–41.
10384. Nurjanov, N.H. "Old Tajik Pantomimes." [F 91]:87–93. [Sum. in Rus.]
10385. Yoh, Suk-kee. "Traditional Korean Plays and Humor —With Special Reference to Sandae Mask Play." *KoJ* 10,v:19–22.
See also 9672, 10428.
Europe. 10386. Bogatyrev, P.G. "Zametki o narodnom teatre." *AEASH* 19:53–64.
10387. Čubelić, T. "Créations dramatiques populaires en Yougoslavie." [F 91]:72–79. [Sum. in Rus.]
10388. Gailey, Alan. *Christmas Rhymers and Mummers in Ireland.* Ibstock, Leisc.: Guizer Press, 1968.
10389. Gatsak, V.M. [Gaţac, V.M.]. "Voinic and Haiduc Folk Theatre in Moldavian Soviet Socialist Republic." [F 91]:100–107. [Sum. in Rus.]
10390. Hont, Ferenc. "Folklore und Theaterwissenschaft." *AEASH* 19:183–90.
10391. Karasek-Langer, Alfred. "Ein spätbarockes 'Samsonspiel' der Donauschwaben und seine geographische Verbreitung." *JOV* 12(1969):41–70. [Music.]
10392. Lanz, Josef. "Das Felizienthaler Bethlohemspiel: Ausklang und Vergehen der Böhmerwälder Weihnachtsspiellandschaft." *JOV* 12(1969):71–145. [Illus., music.]
10393. Muşlea, I. "Le 'jeu de paradis' ('Paradiesspiel') chez les Roumains." [F 91]:111–19. [Sum. in Rus.]
10394. Schubert, Karl. "Neue Forschungsergebnisse zum Krippentheater des Andreas Schubert in Eger." *JOV* 12(1969):

146–78.
10395. Spears, James E. "A Note on the Shetland Sword Dance." *SFQ* 33(1969):347–49.
10396. Veleckaja, N.N. "Dramaturgičeskie, postanovočno-ispolnitel'skie principy russkogo narodnogo teatra (Narodnaja drama *Car' Maksimilian* v poslednij period žizni zanra)." [F 91]:128–34. [Sum. in Fr.]
See also 2238, 10036, 10372, 11052.
North America. 10397. Ben-Dor, Shmuel. "The 'Naluyuks' of Northern Labrador:A Mechanism of Social Control." [F 80]:119–27.
10398. Chiaramonte, Louis J. "Mumming in 'Deep Harbour':Aspects of Social Organization in Mumming and Drinking." [F 80]:76–103.
10399. Faris, James C. "Mumming in an Outport Fishing Settlement:A Description and Suggestions on the Cognitive Complex." [F 80]:128–44.
10400. Firestone, Melvin M. "Mummers and Strangers in Northern Newfoundland." [F 80]:62–75.
10401. Halpert, Herbert. "A Typology of Mumming." [F 80]:34–61.
10402. Story, G.M. "Mummers in Newfoundland History:A Survey of the Printed Record." [F 80]:165–207.
10403. Szwed, John F. "The Mask of Friendship:Mumming as a Ritual of Social Relations." [F 80]:104–18.
10404. Widdowson, J.D.A. "Mummering and Janneying: Some Explanatory Notes." [F 80]:216–21.
10405. Widdowson, J.D.A., and Herbert Halpert. "The Disguises of Newfoundland Mummers." [F 80]:145–64.
See also 10937.

Festivals and Rituals

General and Miscellaneous. 10406. Dömötör, T[ekla]. "Festbräuche im Jahreslauf und Volksdichtung." [F 91]:273–76. [Sum. in Rus.]
10407. Turner, Victor W. "Forms of Symbolic Action: Introduction." [F 93]:3–25.
10408. Ward, Donald J. "The Threefold Death:An Indo-European Trifunctional Sacrifice?" [F 90]:123–42.
See also 9687, 9844, 10359, 10416, 10417, 10676, 10708.
Africa. 10409. Curley, Richard T. "Persistence and Change in Lango Ceremonialism." *DAI* 31:1666B(Calif., Berkeley).
10410. Deluz, Ariane. "Un dualisme africain." [F 89],II:782–800.
10411. Horton, Robin. "Types of Spirit Possession in Kalabari Religion." [F 72]:14–49.
10412. Rigby, Peter. "Some Gogo Rituals of 'Purification':An Essay on Social and Moral Categories." [F 83]:153–78.
10413. Spencer, Paul. "The Function of Ritual in the Socialization of the Samburu Moran." [F 86]:127–57.
10414. Turner, Victor W. "Symbolization and Patterning in the Circumcision Rites of Two Bantu-Speaking Societies." [F 76]:229–44.
10415. Turner, V[ictor] W. *The Drums of Affliction:A Study of Religious Processes Among the Ndembu of Zambia.* Oxford: Clarendon, 1968.
10416. Turner, Victor [W]. *The Forest of Symbols:Aspects of*

Ndembu Ritual. Ithaca, N.Y.: Cornell U.P., 1967.

10417. Turner, Victor W. *The Ritual Process:Structure and Anti-Structure.* Chicago: Aldine, 1969.

10418. Verger, Pierre. "Trance and Convention in Nago-Yoruba Spirit Mediumship." [F 72]:50–66.

See also 10200, 10605, 10718.

Asia. 10419. Bor, Kálmán. "Two Purification Rites in the Bear Cult of the Ob-Ugrians." [F 74]:85–92.

10420. Boyer, Martha, and Jikai Fujiyoshi. "Omizutori, One of Japan's Oldest Buddhist Ceremonies." *EB* 3,i:67–96.

10421. Hockings, Paul. "On Giving Salt to Buffaloes:Ritual as Communication." *Ethnology* 7(1968):411–25.

10422. Immoos, Thomas. "The Birth of the Japanese Theater." *MN* 24(1969):403–14.

10423. Kadyrov, P.K. "The Ritual Folklore of Tajiks of South Uzbekistan (Kashka-Darya River Valley)." [F 91]:290–96. [Sum. in Rus.]

10424. Kramer, Samuel N. *The Sacred Marriage Rite:Aspects of Faith, Myth and Ritual in Ancient Sumer.* Bloomington: Ind. U.P., 1969.

10425. Leach, Edmund. "A Critique of Yalman's Interpretation of Sinhalese Girls' Puberty Ceremonial." [F 89],II:819–28.

10426. Nair, P. Thankappan. "Onam—The National Festival of Kerala." *FolkloreC* 9(1968):46–55.

10427. —— "Malayalam Women:Their Past and Present." *FolkloreC* 10(1969):157–77.

10428. Obeyesekere, Gananath. "The Ritual Drama of the Sanni Demons:Collective Representations of Disease in Ceylon." *Compar. Studies in Society and Hist.* 11(1969):174–216.

10429. Parpola, Asko. *The Śrautasūtras of Lātyāyana and Drāhyāyana and Their Commentaries. An English Translation and Study.* (CHLSSF 43:a.) Vol. I:2. Helsinki: Keskuskirjapaino, 1969.

10430. —— *The Śrautasūtras of Lātyāyana and Drāhyāyana and Their Commentaries:An English Translation and Study.* (CHLSSF 42:2.) Vol. I:1. General Introduction and Appendices to Vol. I. Helsinki: Keskuskirjapaino, 1968.

10431. Rao, D.V. Rghava. "Ritual Activity in the Kubi Society." *FolkloreC* 9(1968):132–39.

10432. Srivastava, S.L. "Jiutia Festival:A Reconsideration of the Concept of 'Generalization'." *FolkloreC* 10(1969):274–78.

10433. Stutley, Margaret. "The Aśvamedha or Indian Horse Sacrifice." *Folklore* 80(1969):253–61.

10434. Wiesinger, Rita, and Josef Haekel. *Contributions to the Swinging Festival in Western Central India.* (Acta Ethnologica et Ling. 13, Ser. Indica 2.) Vienna: Inst. für Univ. Wien, 1968. [1969.]

See also 10453, 10616, 11133.

Australia and Oceania. 10435. Brown, Paula. "Chimbu Transactions." *Man* 5:99–117.

10436. Mead, S[idney] M. "Imagery, Symbolism and Social Values in Maori Chants." *JPS* 78(1969):378–404.

10437. Munn, Nancy D. "The Effectiveness of Symbols in Murngin Rite and Myth." [F 93]:178–207.

See also 10893.

Europe. 10438. Antonijevic, Dragoslav. " 'Premlaz':Ein Ritual bei Viehzüchtern auf dem Balkan." *SAV* 64(1968):68–73.

10439. Bouteiller, Marcelle. "Le pèlerinage de Notre-Dame de Bellevau (Charente)." *ATP* 16(1968):135–50.

10440. —— "Tradition folklorique et 'parentés parallèles':Le couple Parrain-Marraine et ses implications dans les lignées familiales." [F 89],I:153–61.

10441. Butovski, Jovanka. "Svetkovina žive vatre u Azanji." *NStv* 6(1967):141–43.

10442. Dalton, G.F. "The Ritual Killing of the Irish Kings." *Folklore* 81:1–22.

10443. Dürst, Hans. "Das Cliquenwesen und die Basler Fasnacht." *SAV* 65(1969):2–24.

10444. Fotino, Stanca. "Leruit—cîntec ceremonial de înmormîntare." *REF* 15:157–63.

10445. Ganter, Theo. "Die Katholiken und die Basler Fastnacht." *SAV* 65(1969):25–35.

10446. Heim, P. Walter. "Das Erntedankfest bei den Katholiken der deutschen Schweiz." *SAV* 64(1968):115–34.

10447. Jeřábek, Richard. "Masken und Maskenbrauchtum in den tschechischen Ländern." *SAV* 64(1968):1–21. [Illus.]

10448. Jula, N., and V. Mănăstireanu. *Tradiţii şi obiceiuri româneşti; anul nou în Moldova şi Bucovina.* Bucharest: Editura pentru Literatură, 1968. [New Year's customs; sum. in Fr.]

10449. Lecotté, R. "Corporations et vie populaire en France." *Volkskunde* 69(1968):116–23. [Illus.]

10450. Löber, Karl. "Kräuterholen und Bergzusammenkünfte an Christi Himmelfahrt im Kreis Eschwege." *HBV* 60(1969): 111–13.

10451. Polomé, Edgar. "The Indo-European Component in Germanic Religion." [F 90]:55–82.

10452. Sarmela, Matti. *Reciprocity Systems of the Rural Society in the Finnish-Karelian Culture Area with Special Reference to Social Intercourse of the Youth.* (FFC 207.) Tr. Matt T. Salo. Helsinki: Academia Scientiarum Fennica, 1969.

10453. Suavé, James L. "The Divine Victim:Aspects of Human Sacrifice in Viking Scandinavia and Vedic India." [F 90]:173–91.

10454. Tremaud, Hélène. "Les joutes languedociennes." *ATP* 16(1968):3–44. [Illus., music.]

10455. Vlahović, Petar. "Prilog proučavanju krsne slave." *SE* 20(1967):120–28.

10456. Weidkuhn, Peter. "Ideologiekritisches zum Streit zwischen Fasnacht und Protestantismus in Basel." *SAV* 65(1969):36–74.

See also 10261, 10292, 10295, 10311, 10545, 10662, 10771, 10777, 10896, 10897, 10909, 11125.

North America. 10457. Cazeneuve, Jean. "Spectacles, rituels et changement culturel dans le Nouveau Méxique et l'Arizona." [F 89],I:502–11.

10458. Collins, John J. "A Descriptive Introduction to the Taos Peyote Ceremony." *Ethnology* 7(1968):427–49.

10459. Graymont, Barbara. "The Tuscarora New Year Festival." *NYH* 50(1969):143–63. [Illus.]

10460. Lamphere, Louise. "Ceremonial Co-Operation and Networks:A Reanalysis of the Navajo Outfit." *Man* 5:39–59.

10461. Opler, Morris E. "Remuneration to Supernaturals and Man in Apachean Ceremonialism." *Ethnology* 7(1968):356–93.

10462. Powell, Peter J. *Sweet Medicine:The Continuing Role of the Sacred Arrows, the Sun Dance, and the Sacred Buffalo Hat in Northern Cheyenne History.* 2 Vols. Norman: U. of Okla. P., 1969.

10463. Tooker, Elisabeth. *The Iroquois Ceremonial of Midwinter.* Syracuse: Syracuse U.P.

10464. Woodward, John A. "The Anniversary:A Contemporary Diequeño Complex." *Ethnology* 7(1968):86–94.

10465. Wyman, Leland C. *Blessingway.* Tucson: U. of Ariz. P. [Navaho ceremonial.]

See also 10400, 10403, 10590, 10669.

South America. 10466. Bourguignon, Erika. "Ritual Dissociation and Possession Belief in Caribbean Negro Religion." [F 95]:87–101.

10467. Crumrine, Lynne S., and N. Ross. "Ritual Service and Blood Sacrifice as Mediating Binary Oppositions:A Structural Analysis of Several Mayo Myths and Rituals." *JAF* 83:69–76.

10468. Liscano, Juan. "Apuntes de folklore comparado." *RVF* 1(1968):65–69.

See also 10349, 10597, 10792, 10938.

VII. MUSIC AND DANCE

General

Bibliography. 10469. Anon. "Theses Presented for the M.A. in African Studies and Diploma in African Music at the Institute of African Studies, University of Ghana, Legon." *Research Rev.*(Legon) 6,ii:70–75.

10470. Elschek, Oskár, Erich Stockmann, and Ivan Mačák, eds. *Musikethnologische Jahresbibliographie Europas:Annual Bibliography of European Ethnomusicology 2, 1967.* Bratislava: Slovenské Národné Múzeum, 1968.

10471. [Gillis, Frank J.] "Special Bibliography:Willard Rhodes." *Ethnomusicology* 13(1969):305–08.

10472. Günther, Robert. "Special Bibliography:Marius Schneider." *Ethnomusicology* 13(1969):518–26.

10473. Hickerson, Joseph C., Neil V. Rosenberg, and Frank J. Gillis. "Current Bibliography and Discography." *Ethnomusicology* 14:321–52,468–98.

10474. Kealiinohomoku, Joann W., and Frank J. Gillis. "Special Bibliography:Gertrude Prokosch Kurath." *Ethnomusicology* 14:114–28.

10475. Kennedy, Peter,ed. *Films on Traditional Music and Dance:A First International Catalogue.* Paris: UNESCO.

10476. Lerma, Dominique-René de, and Michael Phillips. "Entries of Ethnomusicological Interest in *MGG*:A Preliminary Listing." *Ethnomusicology* 13(1969):129–38.

10477. Noyes, Ruth. "Northumbrian Folk Song, Music and Dance." *EDS* 32:27.

10478. Stanford, Thomas,ed. *Catálogo de Grabaciones del Laboratorio de Sonido del Museo Nacional de Antropología.* Mexico City: Inst. Nacional de Antropología e Hist., 1968.

General and Miscellaneous. 10479. Anon. "Hans R.H. Hickmann:1908-1968." *Ethnomusicology* 13(1969):316–19. [Ger. musicologist. Incl. bibliog.]

10480. Blacking, John. "Songs, Dances, Mimes and Symbolism of Venda Girls' Initiation Schools, Part 1:Vhusha; Part 2:Milayo; Part 3:Domba; Part 4:The Great Domba Song." *AfrS* 28(1969):3–36,69–118,149–200,215–66.

10481. Haney, James E. *Ethnomusicology:The World of Music Cultures.* (Research News 21:2.) Ann Arbor: U. of Mich. Office of Research Admin.

10482. Katz, Israel J. "Marius Barbeau:1883–1969." *Ethnomusicology* 14:129–42. [Canadian ethnomusicologist. Incl. bibliog.]

10483. Laade, Wolfgang. *Die Situation von Musikleben und Musikforschung in den Ländern Afrikas und Asiens und die Neuen Aufgaben der Musikethnologie.* Tutzing: Hans Schneider, 1969.

10484. Merriam, Alan P. "Ethnomusicology Revisited." *Ethnomusicology* 13(1969):213–29.

10485. Reinhard, Kurt. *Einführung in die Musikethnologie.* (Beiträge zur Schulmusik 21.) Wolfenbüttel and Zürich: Möseler Verlag, 1968.

Music

Bibliography. 10486. Weisser, Albert. *Bibliography of Publications and Other Resources on Jewish Music.* Rev. and enl. ed. New York: Jewish Music Council, Nat'l. Jewish Welfare Bd., 1969.

See also 9477, 10516.

General and Miscellaneous. 10487. Boulton, Laura. *The Music Hunter:The Autobiography of a Career.* Garden City, N.Y.: Doubleday, 1969.

10488. Gorali, M. "Stranstvujuščie melodii." [F 92]:291–92. [Sum. in Fr.]

10489. "Priloženie 1." [F 92]:455–538. [Supp., containing musical examples.]

10490. Rouget, Gilbert, and Jean Schwarz. "Transcrire ou décrire? Chant soudanais et chant fuégien." [F 89],I:677–706.

10491. Seeger, Charles. "On the Formational Apparatus of the Music Compositional Process." *Ethnomusicology* 13(1969):230–47.

See also 10198, 10546.

Africa. 10492. Afr. Bibliog. Center. *Phase Two of "The Beat Goes On":A Supplementary Guide to Resources for African Music and Dance.* Wash., D.C.: Afr. Bibliog. Center, 1969.

10493. —— *"The Beat Goes On":A Selected Guide to Resources on African Music and Dance, 1965–1967.* Wash., D.C.: Afr. Bibliog. Center, 1968.

10494. Anon. *Patterns of Progress:Music, Dance and Drama in Ethiopia.* Book IX. Addis Ababa: Ministry of Information, 1968.

10495. Bebey, Francis. *Musique de l'Afrique.* Paris: Horizon de France, 1969.

10496. Besmer, Fremont E. "An Hausa Song from Katsina." *Ethnomusicology* 14:418–38.

10497. Blacking, John. "Tonal Organization in the Music o Two Venda Initiation Schools." *Ethnomusicology* 14:1–56.

10498. Euba, Akin. "Music Adapts to a Changed World." *AfricaR* 15,viii:24–27.

10499. Kauffman, Robert. "Some Aspects of Aesthetics in the Shona Music of Rhodesia." *Ethnomusicology* 13(1969):507–11

10500. Lomax, Alan. "The Homogeneity of African-Afro American Musical Style." [F 95]:181–201.

10501. Nketia, J.H. *Funeral Dirges of the Akan People* Westport, Conn.: Negro U.P. [Repr. of 1955 ed.]

10502. —— "The Poetry of Akan Drums." *BO* 2,ii(1968):27–35.

10503. Obatala, J.K. "U.S. 'Soul' Music in Africa." *Afr Communist* 41:80–89.

10504. Oppong, C. "A Note on Dagomba Fiddlers." *Research Rev.*(Legon) 6,ii:27–33.

10505. —— "A Preliminary Account of the Role anc Recruitment of Drummers in Dagbon." *Research Rev.*(Legon 6,i(1969):38–51.

10506. Ottenheimer, H.J. "Culture Contact and Musica Style:Ethnomusicology in the Comorow Islands." *Ethno musicology* 14:458–62.

10507. Oven, Cootje van. "Music of Sierra Leone." *AfrA 3,iv:20–27,71.

10508. Paden, John N., and Edward W. Soja. "Traditiona Music." [F 88],II:56–58.

10509. Powne, Michael. *Ethiopian Music.* London: Oxforc U.P., 1968.

10510. Roberts, John S. "Music." [F 71]:41–46. [Trad. anc modern in Africa.]

10511. Tracey, Hugh T., Gerhard Kubik, and Andrew T.N Tracey. *African Music:Codification and Textbook Project:Practica Suggestions for Field Research.* Roodeport, S. Afr.: Internat. Lib of African Music, 1969.

10512. Wachsmann, Klaus. "Ethnomusicology in Africa." [F 88],I:128–51.

10513. —— "Music." *JFI* 6(1969):164–91. [Foll. by George List, "Discussion . . . ," 192–99.]

See also 10483, 10490.

Asia. 10514. Adriaansz, Willem. "Rōsai." *Ethnomusicology 13(1969):101–23. [Jap. musical form.]

10515. Alekseev, È.E. "Novoe v tradicionnyx stilja› jakutskogo muzykal'nogo fol'klora 'd'ièrètii yrya' i 'dègèrè› yrya'." [F 92]:319–24,514–17. [Sum. in Fr.]

10516. Barnett, Elise B. "Special Bibliography:Art Music o India." *Ethnomusicology* 14:278–312.

10517. Becker, Judith. "The Anatomy of a Mode. *Ethnomusicology* 13(1969):267–79. [Burma.]

10518. Beljaev, V.M. "Persidskie tesnify (K voprosu c kvantitativnom stixosloženii)." [F 92]:340–42,534–36. [Sum. ir Fr.]

10519. Bhattacharya, Sudhibhushan. "Ethnomusicology anc India." *FolkloreC* 9(1968):1–6.

10520. —— *Ethno-Musicology and India.* Calcutta: Indiar Pubs., 1968.

10521. —— "Rhythm in Indian Music." *FolkloreC* 9(1968) 113–21.

10522. —— "Scales in Indian Music." *FolkloreC* 9(1968) 189–227,251–59.

10523. —— "Uncultivated Music of India." *FolkloreC 9(1968):56–68.

10524. Ghosh, Nikhil. *Fundamentals of Rága and Tála with a New System of Notation.* Bombay: N. Ghosh, 1968.

10525. Hausman, Ruth L. *Hawaii:Music in Its History* Rutland, Vt. and Tokyo: Charles E. Tuttle, 1968.

10526. Heyman, Alan C. "The Music and Dance of the Korean Buddhist Ceremony." [F 77],II:345–47.

10527. Karomatov, F.M. "O lokal'nyx stiljax uzbeksko narodnoj muzyki." [F 92]:243–47. [Sum. in Fr.]

10528. Kaufmann, Walter. *The Ragas of North India.*

Bloomington: Ind. U.P., 1968.

10529. Lieberman, Frederic. *Chinese Music:An Annotated Bibliography.* (Asian Music Pubs., Ser. A:1.) New York: Soc. for Asian Music.

10530. Melamed, Ezra Q. "Biblical Cantillations Among Biblical Commentators." [F 87]:195–99. [In Hebr.; Eng. sum.]

10531. Moore, Sidney. "Thai Songs in 7/4 Meter." *Ethnomusicology* 13(1969):309–12.

10532. Omchery, Leela. "Ideals in Music as Seen Through Mahabharata." *IAC* 18,iii(1969):17–25.

10533. Picken, L.E.R. "T'ang Music and Musical Instruments." *TPA* 55(1969):74–122.

10534. Qureshi, Regula. "Tarannum:The Chanting of Urdu Poetry." *Ethnomusicology* 13(1969):425–68.

10535. Raman, V.P. "The Music of the Ancient Tamils." [F 42],II:389–402.

10536. Ramanathan, S. "Ancient Muscial Modes in *Cilappatikāram.*" [F 42],II:371–78.

10537. Reinhard, Kurt and Ursula. *Turquie.* (Les Traditions Musicales 4.) Paris: Buchet/Chastel, 1969.

10538. Sambamoorthy, P. *South Indian Music:Book VI.* Madras: Indian Music Pub. House, 1969.

10539. Sinha, Purnima. "The Structure of Indian Music:The Basic Concepts." *FolkloreC* 9(1968):468–79.

10540. Slobin, Mark. "Music and the Structure of Town Life in Northern Afghanistan." *Ethnomusicology* 14:450–58.

10541. Tsuge, Gen'ichi. "Rhythmic Aspects of the *Âvâz* in Persian Music." *Ethnomusicology* 14:205–27. [Vocal style.]

10542. Vellaivaranar, K. "Vārap pāṭaliṉ torṛamum valarcciyum." [F 42],II:460–69. [The orig. and devel. of Vsrappāṭal.]

See also 10216, 10217, 10483, 10643.

Europe. 10543. Atajan, R.A. "Komitas— sobiratel' armjanskoj narodnoj pesni." [F 92]:329–33,525–29. [On Komitas (1869–1935), collector of Armen. folk songs. Sum. in Fr.]

10544. Axobadze, V.V. "Gruzinskie narodnye trudovye pesni 'naduri'." [F 92]:287–90,510–12.

10545. Balašov, D.M., and Ju. E. Krasovskaja. *Russkie svadebnye pesni Terskogo berega Belogo morja.* Leningrad: "Muzyka," 1969. [Rus. Wedd. rit. and songs. White Sea. Mus. anal.]

10546. Brăilou, Constantin. "Outline of a Method of Musical Folklore." *Ethnomusicology* 14:389–417. [Orig. pub. 1931 in Rom. and Fr. Tr. Margaret Mooney. Ed. with notes by Ann Briegleb and Mariana Kahane.]

10547. Braun, Hartmut. "Zur Charakteristik des Volksliedsängers Paul Ruscheinski aus Karamurat." *JOV* 11(1968):140–51. [Music.]

10548. Browne, John Paddy. "With Bullet & Hook & Bow:The Folksongs of Hunting." *EDS* 32:89–91.

10549. Citovič, G.I. "Novye stilevye čerty tradicionnoj belorusskoj narodnoj pesni." [F 92]:253–58,486–92. [Sum. in Fr.]

10550. Čiurlonytė, Ja[dviga]. "Stilističeskie osobennosti tradicionnoj litovskoj narodnoj melodii." [F 92]:325–28,518–24. [Sum. in Fr.]

10551. Čxikvadze, G.Z. "Osnovnye tipy gruzinskogo narodnogo mnogogolos'ja." [F 92]:232–37,478–85. [Sum. in Fr.]

10552. Deutsch, Walter, and Gerlinde Hofer. *Die Volksmusiksammlung der Gesellschaft der Musikfreunde in Wien (Sonnleithner-Sammlung).* (Schriften zur Volksmusik 2.) Vienna: A. Schendl, 1969.

10553. Gordejčuk, N.M. "Sovremennaja ukrainskaja narodnaja pesnja." [F 92]:259–64,493–95. [Sum. in Fr.]

10555. Howes, Frank. *Folk Music of Britain:And Beyond.* London: Methuen, 1969.

10556. Kodály, Zoltán. "Pentatonicism in Hungarian Folk Music." *Ethnomusicology* 14:228–42. [Tr. Stephen Erdely.]

10557. Korsten, Bjarne. *77 Norwegian Lullabies According to Dr. O.M. Sandvik.* Bergen: The Author. [Solbakken 17.]

10558. —— *Tonal and Formal Structure of Norwegian Religious Folk Tunes.* Bergen: B. Korsten, 1969.

10559. Koschmieder, E. "Pohled na dějiny staré slovanské hudby." *BSl* 31:12–41.

10560. Krader, Barbara. "Bulgarian Folk Music Research."

Ethnomusicology 13(1969):248–66.

10561. Lebedinskij, L.N. "Baškirskaja protjažnaja pesnja 'Zjul'xizja'." [F 92]:309–18,513. [Sum. in Fr.]

10562. Lys'ko, Zinovij. *Ukrajins'ki narodni melokiji.* Vols. 1–5. New York: Z. Lys'ko Foundation. [5,000 Ukr. songs with mus. notes.]

10563. Morrissey, Patrick. "Dúchas:A Personal Essay." *Éire* 4,ii(1969):117–27.

10564. Muxarinskaja, L.S. "Partizanskie pesni Belorussii i ix slagateli (čerty stilja)." [F 92]:268–71,496–501. [Sum. in Fr.]

10565. Nigmedzjanov, M.N. "Stilevye osobennosti muzykal'nogo fol'klora tatar-krjašen." [F 92]:343–48,537–38. [Sum. in Fr.]

10566. Petrov, S[tojan]. "Muzykal'naja kul'tura banatskix bolgar." [F 92]:272–77,502–04. [Sum. in Fr.]

10567. Rihtman, C[vjetko]. "Les formes polyphoniques dans la musique traditionelle yougoslave." [F 92]:265–67. [Sum. in Rus.]

10568. Schmidt, Leopold. *Volksgesang und Volkslied:Proben und Probleme.* Berlin: E. Schmidt.

10569. Slaviūnas, Z[enonas Jono]. "Litovskie narodnye trudovye pesni 'sutartinės'." [F 92]:278–82,505–09. [Sum. in Fr.]

10570. Stockmann, D[oris]. "Wandlungen des deutschen Volksgesanges vom 19. Jahrhundert bis zur Gegenwart." [F 92]:238–42. [Sum. in Rus.]

10571. Stoin, E[lena]. "K voprosu o svjazi teksta s muzykoj v bolgarskoj narodnoj pesne." [F 92]:248–52. [Sum. in Fr.]

10572. Suchoff, Benjamin. "Some Problems in Computer-Oriented Bartókian Ethnomusicology." *Ethnomusicology* 13(1969):489–97.

10573. Tampere, H[erbert]. "Stilevye tipy melodiki èstonskix run." [F 92]:334–39,530–33. [Sum. in Ger.]

10574. Vitoliņš, J[ēkabs]. "Stilevye osobennosti latyšskoj narodnoj pesni godovogo zemledel 'českogo cikla." [F 92]:266–31,456–77. [Sum. in Fr.]

10575. Volynjak, Petro. "50-littja novoho kobzars'koho mystectva." *Novi dni* 20,iv(1969):5–10. [On Ukr. *bandurysty* in U.S.A.]

10576. Wales, Tony. "Folk Music by Post:The Collecting of Folk Subjects on Picture Postcards." *EDS* 32:52–53,56.

10577. Wittrock, Wolfgang. *Die Ältesten Melodietypen im Ostdeutschen Volksgesang.* (Schriftenreihe der Kommission für Ostdeutsche Volkskunde in der Deutschen Gesellschaft für Volkskunde 7.) Marburg: N.G. Elwert, 1969.

See also 9322, 10091, 10242, 10257, 10267, 10299, 10391, 10392, 10448, 10454, 10486, 10656, 10657.

North America. 10578. Baca, Cleo R. *Baca's Musical History 1860–1968:An Old Texas Czech Band and Orchestra.* LaGrange, Tex.: The LaGrange Journal, 1968.

10579. Boswell, George W. "Text-Occasioned Ornamentation in Folksinging." *SFQ* 33(1969):333–38.

* 10580. —— "Verse and Music in the Sacred Harp." *SFQ* 34:53–61.

10581. Dixon, Robert M.W., and John Godrich. *Recording the Blues.* New York: Stein and Day.

10582. Ferris, William J.,Jr. "Racial Repertoires among Blues Performers." *Ethnomusicology* 14:439–49.

10583. Gahr, David, and Robert Shelton. *The Face of Folk Music.* New York: Citadel, 1968.

10584. Godrich, John, and Robert M.W. Dixon. *Blues and Gospel Records:1902–1942.* London: Storyville Pubs., 1969. [Extensive rev. of 1963 pub.]

10585. Haralambos, Michael. "Soul Music and Blues:Their Meaning and Relevance in Northern United States Black Ghettos." [F 95]:367–84.

10586. Hofmann, Charles. *Frances Densmore and American Indian Music:A Memorial Volume.* (Contribs. of the Museum of the Amer. Indian, Heye Foundation 23.) New York, 1968.

10587. Jackson, Clyde O. *The Songs of Our Years:A Study of Negro Folk Music.* New York: Exposition, 1968.

10588. Korson, Rae, and Joseph C. Hickerson. "The Willard Rhodes Collection of American Indian Music in the Archive of Folk Song." *Ethnomusicology* 13(1969):296–304.

10589. Kurath, Gertrude P. "A Comparison of Plains and

Pueblo Songs." *Ethnomusicology* 13(1969):512–17.

10590. León Pérez, A. "El área de la fiesta de bembé en Cuba." [F 92]:283–86. [Sum. in Rus.]

10591. Malm, Krister. *Writings on Ethnic Music and Mesomusic in the Lesser Antilles Including Aruba, Bonaire, Curacao, Tobago, Trinidad, and the Virgin Islands:A Bibliography.* Uppsala: U. of Uppsala, Inst. of Musicology, 1969.

10592. Schuller, Gunther. *Early Jazz:Its Roots and Musical Development.* New York: Oxford U.P., 1968.

10593. Szwed, John F. "Afro-American Musical Adaptation." [F 95]:219–28.

10594. Ware, Naomi. "Survival and Change in Pima Indian Music." *Ethnomusicology* 14:100–13.

10595. Weinman, Janice. "The Influence of Pueblo Worldview on the Construction of Its Vocal Music." *Ethnomusicology* 14:313–15.

See also 10187, 10327, 10482, 10500.

South America. 10596. Aretz, Isabel. "Cantos araucanos de mujeres." *RVF* 3:73–104. [In Eng.]

10597. Ramón y Rivera, Luis F. "El culto religioso en el folklore musical de Venezuela." *RVF* 1(1968):70–78. [Music.]

10598. —— *La música folklórica de Venezuela.* Caracas: Monte Avila Editores, 1969.

10599. Stevenson, Robert. *Music in Aztec and Inca Territory.* Berkeley and Los Angeles: U. of Calif. P., 1968.

10600. Whitten, Norman E.,Jr. "Personal Networks and Musical Contexts in the Pacific Lowlands of Columbia and Ecuador." [F 95]:203–17.

10601. Wistrand, Lila M. "Music and Song Texts of Amazonian Indians." *Ethnomusicology* 12(1969):469–88.

Musical Instruments

General and Miscellaneous. 10602. Buchner, Alexander. *Musikinstrumente der Völker.* Hanau/Main: W. Dausien, 1968.

10603. "Simpozium:Narodnye muzykal'nye instrumenty." [F 92]:383–454,539–63. [Incl. "Priloženie 2," supp. containing folk music instrument examples.]

Africa. 10604. Dias, M[argot]. "Gruppenbildende und individuelle Musikinstrumente in Moçambique." [F 92]:293–308. [Bibliog. Sum. in Rus.]

10605. Kinney, Sylvia. "Drummers in Dagbon:The Role of the Drummer in the Damba Festival." *Ethnomusicology* 14: 258–65.

10606. Merriam, Alan P. "The Ethnographic Experience: Drum-Making among the Bala (Basongye)." *Ethnomusicology* 13(1969):74–100.

10607. Nketia, J.H. Kwabena. *Our Drums and Drummers.* Accra: Ghana Pub. House, 1968.

10608. Varnum, John P. "The Ibirongwe of the Kuria:A Cattle Herding Flute in East Africa." *Ethnomusicology* 14:462–67.

See also 10502.

Asia. 10609. Jairazbhoy, Nazir A. "A Preliminary Survey of the Oboe in India." *Ethnomusicology* 14:375–88.

10610. Kothari, K.S. *Indian Folk Musical Instruments.* New Delhi: Natl. Acad. of Dance, Drama & Music for India, 1968.

10611. Miller, Lloyd. *Eastern Drum Rhythms.* Salt Lake City: U. of Utah, Middle East Center, 1969.

10612. Rimmer, Joan. *Ancient Musical Instruments of Western Asia in the Department of Western Asiatic Antiquities, The British Museum.* London: British Museum, 1969.

10613. Sinha, Purnima. "Instrumental Music of North India." *FolkloreC* 10(1969):136–42.

10614. Slobin, Mark. *Kirgiz Instrumental Music.* (Asian Music Pubs., Ser. D,2.) New York: Soc. for Asian Music, 1969.

10615. Spector, Johanna. "Classical 'Ud Music in Egypt with Special Reference to *Maqamat.*" *Ethnomusicology* 14:243–57.

10616. Vajnštejn, S.I. "The Tuvan (Soyot) Shaman's Drum and the Ceremony of Its 'Enlivening'." [F 74]:331–38.

10617. Ventatarama Iyer, Tinniam. *The Art of Playing Mridangam:A Percussion Instrument in Karnataka Music.* Madras: Bharati Vijayam P., 1969.

Europe. 10618. Bartham, Chris. "English Country Fiddle:A Personal View." *EDS* 32:55–56.

10619. Berry, Margaret. "The Pipes of Northumberland." *EDS* 32:25–27.

10620. Cassie, Bill. "The Caisley Family." *EDS* 32:14–15. [Northumbrian pipers.]

10621. George, David. *The Flamenco Guitar.* Madrid: Soc. of Span. Studies, 1969.

10622. Mac Lochlainn, Alf. "Thomas O'Shea, a Kerry Harper." *JKAHS* 3:81–83.

10623. MacNeill, Seamus. *Piobaireachd:Classical Music of the Highland Bagpipe.* London: British Broadcasting Corp., 1968. *See also* 9343, 10241.

North America. 10624. Almstedt, Ruth. *Diegueno Deer Toe Rattles.* (Ethnic Technology Notes 2.) San Diego: San Diego Museum of Man, 1968.

10625. Evans, John. "Jean Carignan:Traditional Fiddler." *EDS* 32:125–26. [Canadian.]

10626. Grossman, Stefan. *Delta Blues Guitar.* New York: Oak Pubs., 1969.

10627. —— *The Country Blues Guitar.* New York: Oak Pubs., 1968.

10628. Traum, Happy. *Traditional and Contemporary Guitar Finger-Picking Styles.* New York: Oak Pubs., 1969.

Dance

Bibliography. *See* 10474.

General and Miscellaneous. 10629. Lange, R. "Kinetography Laban (Movement Notation) and Folk Dance Research in Poland." [F 91]:43–59. [Sum. in Rus.]

Africa. 10630. Dorsinville, Roger. "The Making of Liberian Ballet." *AfrA* 4,i:36–39,67.

10631. Hanna, Judith L. and William J. "The Dance-Plays of Biafra's Uba Kala Clan." *Anthropologica* 11(1969):243–73.

10632. Harper, Peggy. "A Festival of Nigerian Dances." *AfrA* 3,ii:48–53.

10633. —— "Dance in Nigeria." *Ethnomusicology* 13(1969): 280–95.

10634. —— "Tsough:A Tiv Dance." *AfrN* 6,i:52–59.

10635. Imperato, Pascal J. "The Dance of the Tyi Wara." *AfrA* 4,i:8–13,71–80. [Bambara and Makinke of Mali.]

10636. Ogunba, Oyin. "Ghana Through Dance." *BO* 2, ii(1968):25–26. [Ghana Dance Ensemble.]

10637. Williams, Drid, J.S. Steemers, and J.E.K. Kumah. "Sokodae:Come and Dance!" *AfrA* 3,iii:36–39,80. [Dance of Ntwumuru of Ghana.]

See also 10378, 10494, 10715, 11076.

Asia. 10638. Agpalo, Remigio E. *Pandanggo-Sa-Ilaw:The Politics of Occidental Mindoro.* (PSSEAS 9.) Athens: Ohio U. Center for Internat. Studies, 1969. [23-p. pamphlet; incl. material on the "oil-lamp folk dance."]

10639. Duchène, Albert. *Danses folkloriques d'Israel.* Mont-sur-Marchienne, Fr.: The Author [Rue de la Ronche, 6], 1969.

10640. Kaeppler, Adrienne L. "Tongan Dance:A Study in Cultural Change." *Ethnomusicology* 14:266–77.

10641. Miller, Hugh M. "Polynesian Dance Films in Color with Sound." *Ethnomusicology* 14:315–20.

10642. Nadirov, I.I. "Sovremennye igrovye i pljasovye pesni tatarskogo naroda." [F 91]:14–20. [Sum. in Fr.]

10643. Oshida, Yoshihisa. *Gagaku kanshô.* Tokyo: Bunkendô Shichisei Sha, 1969. [On tradit. music and dance.]

10644. Ramachandran, Nirmala. "Classical Dance of the Ancient Tamils." [F 42],II:379–88.

10645. Rudolph, Beth. "The Medieval *Tanzhaus*:A Checklist of Writings." *TD* 2,i–ii(1969–70):121–23.

10646. Soedarsono. "Classical Javanese Dance:History and Characterization." *Ethnomusicology* 13(1969):498–506.

10647. Zhornitskaya, M.Y. [Žornickaja, M.Ja.]. "Study of the Traditional Dances of the Peoples of Yakutia." [F 91]:7–13. [Sum. in Rus.]

See also 10526.

Europe. 10648. Arizmendi, María Elena de. "Espíritu de la danza vasca." *RdEt* 14:19–53.

10649. Armstrong, Lucile. "The Stilt Dancers of Anguiano-Logroño, North Eastern Castile, 21st July 1968." *RdEt* 14:

129–36.

10650. Binless, Grahame, and Mike Robson. "The Traditional Social Dance in Northumberland." *EDS* 32:11–12.

10651. Brown, Alan. " 'Five Sons an' Nivvor a Dowter'." *EDS* 32:13,15. [Rapper sword dancing in Northumberland.]

10652. Bucşan, A., and E. Balaci. "La méthode d'analyse de la morphologie et du style de la danse populaire Roumaine." [F 91]:60–63. [Sum. in Rus.]

10653. Czompo, Andor and Ann I. *Hungarian Dances.* Cortland, N.Y.: Quik-Print Service, 1968.

10654. Friedhaber, Zvi. "The 'Instructor' of Folk Dance." [F 87]:275–79. [In Hebr.; Eng. sum.]

10655. Garasimčuk, R.P. "Osobennosti ukrainskix narodnyx tancev Karpatskogo rajona." [F 91]:21–27. [Sum. in Fr.]

10656. Guilcher, Jean-Michel. "Les derniers branles de Béarn et Bigorre." *ATP* 16(1968):259–92. [Illus., music.]

10657. —— "Les formes basques de la danse en chaîne." *ATP* 17(1969):1–54. [Illus., music.]

10658. Gvaramadze, E.L. "Some Specific Features of Georgian Popular Dance." [F 91]:135–41. [Sum. in Rus.]

10659. Holland, Anne V. "Some Times Around Mutton Hall." *TFSB* 35(1969):11–19.

10660. Janković, Ljubica S. "Paradoxes in the Living Creative Process of Dance Tradition." *Ethnomusicology* 13(1969):124–27. [Yugoslavian kolo.]

10661. Krogsaeter, Johan. *Folk Dancing in Norway.* Oslo: Johan Grundt Tanum, 1968.

10662. Lancelot, Francine. "La danse à la fête votive du caylar." *ATP* 16(1968):63–66.

10663. Lissitzian, S.S. "Danses et théâtre folkloriques du peuple arménien." [F 91]:64–71. [Sum. in Rus.]

10664. MacDougall, John. *Scottish Country Dances:A Listing Index of 900 Dances with Reference Sources.* Boston: Boston Branch of the Royal Scottish Country Dance Soc., 1968.

10665. Milligan, Jean C. *Introducing Scottish Country Dancing.* Glasgow and London: Collins, 1968.

10666. Suna, H. "People's Choreography at Festivals of Song and Dance in Soviet Latvia." [F 91]:35–42. [Sum. in Rus.]

10667. Vladykina-Bačinskaja, N.M. "Podmoskovnye xorovody." [F 91]:28–34. [Sum. in Fr.]

See also 3338, 10304, 10452, 10629.

North America. 10668. Dempsey, Hugh A. *Blackfoot Ghost Dance.* (Glenbow Foundation Occas. Paper 3.) Calgary: Glenbow-Alberta Inst., 1968.

10669. Kurath, Gertrude P. *Dance and Song Rituals of Six Nations Reserve, Ontario.* Ottawa: Natl. Museum of Canada, 1968.

10670. Stearns, Marshall and Jean. *Jazz Dance:The Story of American Vernacular Dance.* New York: Macmillan, 1969.

See also 10462.

South America. 10671. Lange, Francisco Curt. "As danças coletivas públicas no perído colonial brasileiro e as danças das corporações de ofícios de Minas Gerais." *Barroco* 1(1969):15–62.

10672. Pollak-Eltz, Angelina. "El Baile de los diablos de Patanemo:Rito agrario africano?" *RVF* 3:29–31.

See also 10468, 10792, 10938.

VIII. FOLK CUSTOMS, BELIEFS AND SYMBOLISM

General

General and Miscellaneous. 10673. Albert, Ethel M. "Conceptual Systems in Africa." [F 88],i:99–107.

10674. Aron, Raymond. "Le paradoxe du même et de l'autre." [F 89],ii:943–52.

10675. Cortelazzo, Manlio. "Notizie popolari su alcuni animali marini." [F 41]:377–407.

10676. Douglas, Mary. *Natural Symbols:Explorations in Cosmology.* London: Barrie & Rockliff, Cresset P.

10677. Fikry, Mona. "Significance of Written and Oral Traditions in the Social Organisation of the Wala." *Research Rev.*(Legon) 3,iii(1967):87–90.

10678. Karbusický, Vladimir. "Primär-kulturelle Erscheinungen in der Industriegesellschaft." [F 79]:165–74.

10679. La Barre, Weston. *The Ghost Dance:Origins of Religion.* Garden City, N.Y.: Doubleday.

10680. Lebra, William P. "The Ryukyu Islands." *RUS* 56,iv:283–93. [Customs, relig., etc.]

10681. Paden, John N., and Edward W. Soja. "Conceptual Systems and Religion." [F 88],ii:48–52.

10682. Tremearne, A.J.N. *Hausa Superstitions and Customs: An Introduction to the Folk-lore and the Folk.* London: Cass. [Repr. of 1913 ed. with new introd. by M. Hiskett.]

See also 9623.

Medical Beliefs and Practices

General and Miscellaneous. 10683. Brewster, Paul G. "The Myth of Modernity." *TFSB* 35(1969):37–40.

10684. Fabrega, Horacio,Jr. "On the Specificity of Folk Illnesses." *SJA* 26:305–14.

10685. Hand, Wayland D. "The Curing of Blindness in Folk Tales." [F 81]:81–87.

Africa. 10686. Boston, J.S. "The Supernatural Aspect of Disease and Therapeutics Among the Igala." *AfrN* 5,iii:41–56.

10687. Lee, S.G. "Spirit Possession Among the Zulu." [F 72]:128–56.

10688. Owen, John. "The Medico-Social and Cultural Significance of *Adansonia Digitata* (Baobab) in African Communities." *AfrN* 6,i:24–36.

10689. Tanner, R.E.S. "The Theory and Practice of Sukuma Spirit Mediumship." [F 72]:273–89.

See also 10722, 10729.

Asia. *See* 10428.

Australia and Oceania. 10690. Skingle, D.C. "Some Medicinal Herbs Used by the Natives of New Guinea." *Mankind* 7:223–25.

10691. Webb, L.J. "The Use of Plant Medicines and Poisons by Australian Aborigines." *Mankind* 7(1969):137–46.

See also 10821.

Europe. 10692. Blum, Richard and Eva. *The Dangerous Hour:The Lore of Crisis and Mystery in Rural Greece.* Assist. by Anna Amera and Sophie Kallijatidou. Foreword Prince Peter of Greece. London: Chatto & Windus.

10693. Grabner, Elfriede. "Die Korallen in Volksmedizin und Volksglaube." *ZV* 65(1969):183–95.

10694. Keil, Gundolf. "Acht Parallelen zu den Blutschau-Texten des Bremer Arzneibuchs:Untersuchungen zur spätmittelalterlichen Hämatoskopie." *NdM* 25(1969):117–35.

10695. Löber, Karl. "Der Wald-Gamander (Teucrium scorodonia L.) im Volksleben des Grenzgebiets von Westerwald und Rothaar." [F 79]:425–38.

10696. Meyer, Maurits de. "De rol van de plaatsnamen en de heiligennamen in de volksgeneeskunde." *Nku* 1(1969):119–26.

10697. Möller, Helmut. "Angewandte Aufklärung und magia naturalis:Versuch über ein konfisziertes Hausbuch des ausgehenden 18. Jahrhunderts." [F 81]:491–502.

See also 10921, 11143.

North America. 10698. Anderson, John Q. *Texas Folk Medicine:1,333 Cures, Remedies, Preventives, and Health Practices.* (Texas Folklore Soc. Paisano Book 5.) Austin: Encino Press.

10699. Booker, Elsie H. and Curtis. "Patent Medicines Before the Wiley Act of 1906." *NCarF* 18:130–42.

10700. Brooks, Juanita. "Mariah Huntsman Leavitt:Midwife of the Desert Frontier." [F 78]:119–31.

10701. Brown, Marice. "Notes on Classical and Renaissance Analogues of Mississippi Negro Folklore." *MissFR* 2(1968): 37–41.

10702. Hand, Wayland D. "Folk Medical Magic and Symbolism in the West." [F 78]:103–18.

10703. Ingham, John M. "On Mexican Folk Medicine." *AA* 72:76–87.

10704. O'Neill, Carl W., and Henry A. Selby. "Sex Differences in the Incidence of Susto in the Two Zapotec Pueblos:An

Analysis of the Relationships Between Sex Role Expectations and a Folk Illness." *Ethnology* 7(1968):95–105.

10705. Wilson, Gordon, and Jesse Funk. "Folklore in Certain Professions iv:The Physician and Folklore." *TFSB* 35(1969):1–5.

10706. Wilson, Gordon, and Mr. and Mrs. Raymond Hazelip. "Folklore in Certain Professions:vi. The Pharmacist and Folklore." *TFSB* 35(1969):113–16.

10707. Wolf, John Q. "Two Folk Scientists in Action." *TFSB* 35(1969):6–10.

See also 10847, 10849.

Religious Beliefs and Symbols

General and Miscellaneous. 10708. Douglas, Mary. "Social Preconditions of Enthusiasm and Heterodoxy." [F 93]:69–80.

10709. Nordland, Odd. "Folklore and Religion Among the Northern Peoples, a Contribution to the Discussion of the Arctic Circumpolar Theory." [F 77],ii:305–09.

10710. Plessner, Martin. "New and Old Topics Relative to Left and Right." [F 87]:259–74. [In Hebr.; Eng. sum.]

10711. Sprio, Melford E. "Religious Symbolism and Social Behavior." *PAPS* 113(1969):341–39.

See also 10756.

Africa. 10712. Assimeng, Max. "Religious and Secular Messianism in Africa." *Research Rev.*(Legon) 6,i(1969):1–19.

10713. Beattie, John. "Spirit Mediumship in Bunyoro." [F 72]:159–70.

10714. Colson, Elizabeth. "Converts and Tradition:The Impact of Christianity on Valley Tonga Religion." *SJA* 26:143–56.

10715. —— "Spirit Possession Among the Tonga of Zambia." [F 72]:69–103.

10716. Davis, Ronald W. "A Note on Symbols at Grand Cess, Liberia." *LiberianSJ* 2,i(1969):65–75.

10717. Fernandez, J[ames] W. "Preying Among Priests and Prophets:Oral Data in the Study of African Religion." *JFI* 6(1969):200–17. [See art. by Messenger, below.]

10718. Field, M.J. "Spirit Possession in Ghana." [F 72]:3–13.

10719. Garbett, G. Kingsley. "Spirit Mediums as Mediators in Korekore Society." [F 72]:104–27.

10720. Gelfand, M. "The Ceremony of Mishashe (Green Vegetables) Held in Mashonaland." *Zambezia* 1,ii:9–11. [Illus.]

10721. —— "The Shona Religion." *Zambezia* 1,i(1969):37–45. [Illus.]

10722. Gray, Robert F. "The Shetani Cult Among the Segeju of Tanzania." [F 72]:171–87.

10723. Lewis, I.M. "Spirit Possession in Northern Somaliland." [F 72]:188–219.

10724. Lienhardt, Godfrey. "The Situation of Death:An Aspect of Anuak Philosophy." [F 75]:279–91.

10725. MacGaffey, Wyatt. "The Religious Commissions of the Bakongo." *Man* 5:27–38.

10726. Mbiti, John S. *African Religions and Philosophy.* New York: Praeger, 1969.

10727. —— *Concepts of God in Africa.* New York: Praeger.

10728. Messenger, John C. "Discussion of J.W. Fernandez' Paper." *JFI* 6(1969):218–21. [See art. by Fernandez, above.]

10729. Middleton, John. "Oracles and Divination among the Lugbara." [F 76]:261–77.

10730. —— "Spirit Possession Among the Lugbara." [F 72]:220–31.

10731. Onwuejeogwu, Michael. "The Cult of the *Bori* Spirits Among the Hausa." [F 76]:279–305.

10732. Opoku, K.A. "Kingdom:A Religious Community." *Research Rev.*(Legon) 6,i(1969):66–69.

10733. Rehfisch, Fornham. "Death, Dreams and the Ancestors in Mambila Culture." [F 76]:307–15.

10734. Sangree, Walter H. "Tribal Ritual, Leadership, and the Mortality Rate in Irigwe, Northern Nigeria." *SJA* 26:32–39.

10735. Southall, Aidan. "Spirit Possession and Mediumship Among the Alur." [F 72]:232–72.

10736. Swartz, Marc J. "The Cultural Dynamics of Blows and Abuse among the Bena of Southern Tanzania:A Study of Dominant Symbols in Everyday Life." [F 93]:126–33.

10737. Welbourn, F.B. "Spirit Initiation in Ankole and Christian Spirit Movement in Western Kenya." [F 72]:290–306.

10738. Williamson, Kay, and A.O. Timitimi. "A Note on Ijo Number Symbolism." *AfrN* 5,iii:9–16.

10739. Willis, Roy G. "Changes in Mystical Concepts and Practices Among the Fipa." *Ethnology* 7(1968):139–57.

See also 9853, 9869, 10411, 10412, 10415, 10418, 10687, 10689.

Asia. 10740. Babb, Lawrence A. "The Food of the Gods in Chhattisgarh:Some Structural Features of Hindu Ritual." *SJA* 26:287–304.

10741. Basu, M.N. "The Moon and the Man." *FolkloreC* 10(1969):235–42.

10742. Durbin, Mridula A. "The Transformational Model of Linguistics and Its Implications for an Ethnology of Religion:A Case Study of Jainism." *AA* 72:334–42.

10743. Ganesan, Saw. "Some Iconographic Concepts." [F 42],ii:403–16.

10744. Hajdú, P[éter]. "The Classification of Samoyed Shamans." [F 74]:147–73.

10745. Lauf, D.I. "Initiationsrituale des tibetischen Totenbuches." *ASEA* 24:10–24.

10746. Lévi-Strauss, Claude. "Les champignons dans la culture:A propos d'un livre de M.R.G. Wasson." *Homme* 10,i:5–16.

10747. Lindenbaum, Shirley. "Women and the Left Hand: Social Status and Symbolism in East Pakistan." *Mankind* 7(1968):537–44.

10748. Lot-Falck, Eveline. "Psychopathes et chamans Yakoutes." [F 89],i:115–29.

10749. Norbeck, Edward. *Religion and Society in Modern Japan:Continuity and Change.* (*RUS* 56,i.) Houston: Rice U.P.

10750. Obeyesekere, Gananath. "Theodicy, Sin and Salvation in a Sociology of Buddhism." [F 83]:7–40.

10751. Raghaviah, V. *Nomads.* New Delhi: Bharateeya Adimajati Sevak Sangh, 1968.

10752. Ratzahbi, Yehuda. "Apocalypses and Reckoning of the End of Days Among Yemenite Jewry." [F 87]:295–322. [In Hebr.; Eng. sum.]

10753. Sakurai, Tokutarō. "The Major Features and Characteristics of Japanese Folk Beliefs." *Jour. of Asian and Afr. Studies*(Leiden) 3(1963):13–24.

10754. Tambiah, S.J. "The Ideology of Merit and the Social Correlates of Buddhism in a Thai Village." [F 83]:41–121.

10755. Wimberley, Howard, and Edward Norbeck. "The Study of Religion." *RUS* 56,iv:151–59. [Japan.]

Australia and Oceania. 10756. Berndt, Ronald M. "Two in One, and More in Two." [F 89],ii:1040–68.

10757. Firth, Raymond. *Rank and Religion in Tikopia:A Study in Polynesian Paganism and Conversion to Christianity.* Boston: Beacon Press.

10758. Keesing, Roger M. "Shrines, Ancestors, and Cognatic Descent:The Kwaio and Tallensi." *AA* 72:755–75.

10759. Peterson, Nicolas. "Secular and Ritual Links:Two Basic and Opposed Principles of Australian Social Organization, as Illustrated by Walbiri Ethnography." *Mankind* 7(1969):27–35.

10760. Silverman, M.G. "Maximize Your Options:A Study in Values, Symbols, and Social Structure." [F 93]:97–115.

10761. Simmons, David, and Bruce G. Biggs. "The Sources of 'The Lore of the Whare-wānanga'." *JPS* 79:22–42.

See also 10820, 11081.

Europe. 10762. Baumer, Iso. "Christentum-Religion-Magie." *SAV* 66:28–40.

10763. Bonomi, Eugen. "Die Mirakelbücher der Wallfahrtsorte Óbuda-Kiscell/Kleinzell bei Altofen und Makkos Mária/Maria-Eichel bei Budakeszi in Ungarn." *JOV* 12(1969):271–300.

10764. —— "Máriaremete/Maria-Einsiedel." *JOV* 11(1968):113–28. [Illus.]

10765. Brückner, Wolfgang. "Sterben im Mönchsgewand: Zum Funktionswandel einer Totenkleidsitte." [F 79]:259–77.

10766. Buchholz, Peter. *Schamanistische Züge in der altisländischen Überlieferung.* Münster, 1968. [Diss., Münster.]

10767. Čurmaeva, N.V. "Naši predki byli jazyčnikami." *RusRe* 1:66–70.

10768. Fojtík, Karel. "Die Inhalts- und Funktionswandlungen der Gevatterschaft in Böhmen, Mähren und Schlesien vom xiv. bis zum xx. Jahrhundert." [F 79]:337–43.

10769. Heim, Walter. "Die 'Erneuerte Kirche' Papst Clemens XV in der Schweiz." *SAV* 66:41–96.

10770. —— "Garabandal und die Schweiz." *SAV* 65(1969): 208–33.

10771. —— "Klimawechsel in der katholischen Volksfrömmigkeit der Schweiz." *SAV* 64(1968):55–67.

10772. Hoppál, Mihály. "A magyar lidérc-hiedelemkör szemantikai modellje." *Ethnographia* 80(1969):402–14. [Semantic model of Hung. nightmare beliefs; sums. in Rus. and Ger.]

10773. Körner, Tamás. "Mutatvány a készülő magyar hiedelem-katalógusból." *Ethnographia* 81:55–96. [Examples from Hung. Belief-Catalogue in prep.; sums. in Rus. and Ger.]

10774. Kramer, Karl-S. "Protestantisches in der Volkskultur Frankens:Konfessionelle Rivalität und Nachbarschaft." *HBV* 60(1969):77–92.

10775. Kretzenbacher, Leopold. "Eschatologisches Erzählgut in Bildkunst und Dichtung:Erscheinungsformen und exemplum-Funktion eines apokryphen Höllenstrafe-Motives." [F 81]: 133–50.

10776. Laugier, E.-F. "Oratoires:Niches et chapelles d'arbres." *ATP* 17(1969):107–18. [Illus.]

10777. Meisen, Karl. "Sankt Martin im volkstümlichen Glauben und Brauch." *RJV* 19(1969):42–91.

10778. Moser-Rath, Elfriede. "Volksfrömmigkeit im Spiegel der Barockpredigt." *ZV* 65(1969):196–206.

10779. Narr, Dieter. "Zum Charakterbild protestantischer Volksfrömmigkeit." *HBV* 60(1969):63–76.

10780. Ó Súilleabháin, Seán. "The Devil in Irish Folk Narrative." [F 81]:275–86.

10781. Pinto Ferreira, J.A. "Nossa senhora de copacabana —elemento contribuinte para a humanização religiosa da região duriense." *RdEt* 13(1969):137–64.

10782. Ricard, Robert. "Vrais et faux 'Justo Juiz'." *RdEt* 14:55–57.

10783. Scharfe, Martin. "Der Heilige in der protestantischen Volksfrömmigkeit." *HBV* 60(1969):93–106.

10784. Sieber, Friedrich. "Die Tulpenkanzel zu Freiberg —Eine Darstellung der 'Berglegende' um Daniel?" [F 79]:289–98.

10785. Trümpy, Hans. "Die Reformation als volkskundliches Problem." [F 79]:249–58.

See also 9335, 10439, 10456, 10692, 10921, 11029, 11037, 11045.

North America. 10786. Frigout, Arlette. "Le repos des nuages." [F 89],i:100–14.

10787. Savard, Rémi. "La déesse sous-marine d'Eskimo." [F 89],ii:1331–55.

10788. Schnider, David M. "Kinship, Nationality and Religion in American Culture:Toward a Definition of Kinship." [F 93]:116–25.

10789. Weigle, Marta. *The Penitentes of the Southwest.* Santa Fe, N.M.: Ancient City Press. [P.O.B. 5401.]

See also 10847.

South America. 10790. Bryce-Laporte, Roy S. "Crisis, Contraculture, and Religion Among West Indians in the Panama Canal Zone." [F 95]:103–18.

10791. Crumrine, Lynne S. "Mayo Santos:A Paradigmatic Analysis of a Sacred Symbol." [F 93]:134–50.

10792. Thays, Carmen Delgado de. *Religión y Magia en Tupe (Yauyos).* Cuernavaca: Centro Intercultural de Documentación, 1968.

10793. Vogt, Evon Z. "Human Souls and Animal Spirits in Zinacantan." [F 89],ii:1148–67.

See also 10466.

Magic and Superstition

General and Miscellaneous. 10794. Beidelman, T[homas] O. "Toward More Open Theoretical Interpretations." [F 75]:351–56.

10795. Douglas, Mary. "Introduction:Thirty Years after *Witchcraft, Oracles and Magic.*" [F 75]:xiii–xxxviii.

10796. Jahoda, Gustav. *The Psychology of Superstition.* London: Allen Lane, Penguin P., 1969.

10797. Lewis, I[oan] M[yrddin]. "A Structural Approach to Witchcraft and Spirit Possession." [F 75]:293–309.

10798. Marwick, Max. *Witchcraft and Sorcery:Selected Readings.* Harmondsworth: Penguin. [Prev. pub. essays.]

10799. Ward, Donald J. "Weather Signs and Weather Magic:Some Ideas on Causality in Popular Belief." *PCP* 3(1968):67–72.

See also 9844, 9996.

Africa. 10800. Ardener, Edwin. "Witchcraft, Economics and the Continuity of Belief." [F 75]:141–60.

10801. Brain, Robert. "Child-witches." [F 75]:161–79.

10802. Goody, Esther. "Legitimate and Illegitimate Aggression in a West African State." [F 75]:207–44.

10803. Hemans, T.J. "The Exorcism of Evil Spirits or Modern Exorcism." *Nada* 10:64–66. [Illus.]

10804. Heusch, Luc de. "Pour une approache structuraliste de la pensée magico-religieuse bantoue." [F 89],ii:801–18.

10805. Jones, G.I. "A Boundary to Accusations." [F 75]: 321–32.

10806. Kaberry, Phyllis M. "Witchcraft of the Sun:Incest in Nso." [F 76]:175–95.

10807. Lonfernini, Bruno "Stregone si nasce." *Nigrizia* 87(1969):12–17.

10808. Mair, Lucy. *Witchcraft.* New York: McGraw-Hill, 1969.

10809. Okonji, M. Ogbolu. "Ogbanje (An African Conception of Predestination)." *AfrSch* 1,iv:1–2.

10810. Redmayne, Alison. "Chikanga:An African Diviner with an International Reputation." [F 75]:103–28.

10811. Ruel, Malcolm. "Were-animals and the Introverted Witch." [F 75]:333–50.

10812. Stillman, Yedida. "The Evil Eye in Morocco." [F 87]:81–94.

10813. Vansina, Jan. "The Bushong Poison Ordeal." [F 76]:245–60.

10814. Willis, R. G[eoffrey]. "Instant Millennium:The Sociology of African Witch-cleansing Cults." [F 75]:129–39.

See also 10725, 11076.

Asia. 10815. Jusupov, G.V. "Survivals of Totemism in the Ancestor Cult of the Kazan Tatars." [F 74]:193–204.

10816. Malachi, E[leasar] R[ephael]. "Dibbukim in Beirut and Jerusalem in the Nineteenth Century." [F 87]:175–93. [In Hebr.; Eng. sum.]

10817. Spooner, Brian. "The Evil Eye in the Middle East." [F 75]:311–19.

See also 10880.

Australia and Oceania. 10818. Forge, Anthony. "Prestige, Influence, and Sorcery:A New Guinea Example." [F 75]:257–75.

10819. Lessa, William A. "The Chinese Trigrams of Micronesia." *JAF* 82(1969):353–62.

10820. Strathern, A.J. "Sickness and Frustration:Variations in Two New Guinea Highlands Societies." *Mankind* 7(1968): 545–51.

10821. Strathern, Andrew and Marilyn. "Marsupials and Magic:A Study of Spell Symbolism Among the Mbowamb." [F 83]:179–202.

Europe. 10822. Balázs, J. "The Hungarian Shaman's Teaching of Trance Induction." [F 74]:53–75.

10823. Beck, Jane C. "Ghostlore of the British Isles and Ireland." *DAI* 30:4352A(Pa.).

10824. Brøndegaard, V.J. "Elfentanz und Hexenring." *RJV* 19(1969):162–210.

10825. Brown, Peter. "Sorcery, Demons, and the Rise of Christianity from Late Antiquity into the Middle Ages." [F 75]:17–45.

10826. Brown, Theo. "Charming in Devon." *Folklore* 81: 37–47.

10827. Heikkinen, Antero. *Paholaisen liittolaiset:Noita- ja magiakäsityksiä ja -oikeudenkäyntejä Suomessa 1600-luvun jälkipuoliskolla (n. 1640–1712).* (Historiallisia tutimuksia 78.) Helsinki, 1969. [*Allies of the Devil:Notions of Witchcraft and Demonic Magic and Trials for Witchcraft and Demonic Magic in Late Seventeenth-Century Finland (ea. 1640–1712).*]

10828. Huggar, Paul. "Die Darstellung soeben Verstorbener

durch Lebende:Eine vergleichende volkskundliche Studie." *SAV* 65(1969):180–207.

10829. Jaenecke-Nickel, Johanna. "Schutzzauber im Jahre 1967." *SAV* 64(1968):163–67.

10830. Lovrenčević, Zvonko. "Mitološke predaje Bilo-gore." *NUm* 7:71–100.

10831. Macfarlane, Alan. "Witchcraft in Tudor and Stuart Essex." [F 75]:81–99.

10832. Monter, William E. *European Witchcraft*. New York: Wiley, 1969.

10833. Onac'kyj, Jevhen. "Kul't xliba ta ukrajins'ki zvyčaji, z nym zvjazani." *Ovyd* 20,iv(1969):11–16. [On the cult of bread and related customs.]

10834. Pomeranceva, È. "Russkij folklor o rusalkax." *AEASH* 19:303–18.

10835. Robbins, Rossell H. "Yellow Cross and Green Fagot." *CLJ* 10:2–33. [Witchcraft in Western Europe, 14th–18th c.]

10836. Roeck, F. "Volkskundig onderzoek naar de weerwolfsage." *WT* 27(1968):145–60.

10837. Thomas, Keith. "The Relevance of Social Anthropology to the Historical Study of English Witchcraft." [F 75]:47–79.

10838. Tillhagen, Carl-Herman. "Finnen und Lappen als Zauberkundige in der skandinavischen Volksüberlieferung." [F 79]:129–43.

10839. Toura, Yoshio. "Scotland no Yojutsushia." *EigoS* 114(1968):368–69. [Witches in Scotland.]

10840. Valle, Carlos. "Tradições populares de Vila Nova de Gaia—crenças e prescrições do povo." *RdEt* 13(1969):165–84.

10841. Webb, Denzil. "Irish Charms in Northern England." *Folklore* 80(1969):262–65.

10842. Wolf-Beranek, Hertha. "Zur Geographie der Geister- und Spukwelt in den Sudetenländern." *JOV* 12(1969):301–22.
See also 9768, 9779, 10078, 10438, 10896, 10899, 10921, 11093.

North America. 10843. Clark, Joseph D. "North Carolina Popular Beliefs and Superstitions." *NCarF* 18,i:1–68.

10844. Granger, Byrd H. "Witchcraft in the Southwest." *WR* 5,i(1968):3–12.

10845. Hall, Joseph S. "Witchlore and Ghostlore in the Great Smokies. Parts I and II." *TFSB* 36:1–6,31–36.

10846. Hand, Wayland D. "North Carolina Folk Beliefs and Superstitions Collected in California." *NCarF* 18:117–23.

10847. Hyatt, Harry M. *Hoodoo-Conjuration-Witchcraft-Rootwork:Beliefs Accepted by Many Negroes and White Persons, These Being Orally Recorded Among Blacks and Whites*. Hannibal, Mo.: Western Pub., Inc. [2 vols.]

10848. Lett, Anna. "Some West Tennessee Superstitions about Conjurers, Witches, Ghosts, and the Devil." *TFSB* 36:37–45.

10849. Peterson, Tracey. "The Witch of Franklin." *SFQ* 33(1969):297–312.

* 10850. Sackett, Samuel J. "Using a Computer on a Belief Collection." *WF* 29:105–10. [Beliefs and superstitions in Kansas.]
See also 6133, 10083, 10707.

South America. 10851. Da Matta, Roberto. "Les présages Apinayé." [F 89],I:77–99.

10852. Pitt-Rivers, Julian. "Spiritual Power in Central America:The Naguals of Chiapas." [F 75]:183–206.

10853. Rivière, Peter. "Factions and Exclusions in Two South American Village Systems." [F 75]:245–55.
See also 9608, 10792.

Customs

General and Miscellaneous. 10854. Gómez Tabanera, José M. "Les rites de la vie humaine." *RdEt* 13(1969):113–35.

10855. Hobsbawm, Eric. *Bandits*. New York: Delacorte, 1969.

10856. Sahlins, Marshall. "The Spirit of the Gift:Une explication de texte." [F 89],II:998–1011.

10857. Schnitzler, Otto. "The Particularity of the Number Seven and the Origin of the Seven Days' Week." [F 87]:73–80.

10858. Tsiviane, Tatjana V. "Contributions à l'étude de certains systèmes sémiotiques simples (système de l'étiquette)." [F 24]:390–400.

Africa. 10859. Evans-Pritchard, E.E. "A Zande Funeral Custom." *Man* 5:126–29.

10860. —— "Zande Bridewealth." *AfricaL* 40:115–24.

10861. Gitywa, V.Z. "Initiation Among the Xhosa at Ncera near Alice." *FHP* 4,iv:9–24. [Illus.]

10862. Hammond-Tooke, W.D. "Urbanization and the Interpretation of Misfortune:A Quantitative Analysis." *AfricaL* 40:25–39.

10863. Horton, Robin. "Ikpataka Dogi:A Kalabari Funeral Rite." *AfrN* 5,iii:57–72.

10864. Huffman, Ray. *Nuer Customs and Folk-lore*. Introd. D. Westermann. London: Cass. [Repr. of 1931 ed.]

10865. Keesing, Hilary. "Death, Property, and the Ancestors:A Reconsideration of Goody's Concepts." *AfricaL* 40:40–49.

10866. Mends, E.H. "Some Aspects of Periodic Ritual Ceremonies of the Anomabo Fante." *Ghana Jour. of Sociol.* (Legon) 5(Feb 1969):39–48.

10867. Opoku, K.A. "Training the Priestess at the Akonnedi Shrine." *Research Rev.*(Legon) 6,ii:34–50.

10868. Yoneyama, Toshinao. "Some Basic Notions Among the Iraqw of Northern Tanzania." *Kyoto U. Afr. Studies* 5:81–100. *See also* 9704.

Asia. 10869. Alkire, William H. "Porpoises and Taro." *Ethnology* 7(1968):280–89.

10870. Barua, Dipak Kumar. "Folklife of Women as Revealed with Early Buddhist Texts." *FolkloreC* 9(1968):161–73.

10871. Coppet, Daniel de. "1,4,8;9,7. La monnaie:Présence des morts et mesure du temps." *Homme* 10,i:17–39.

10872. Gupta, Sankar Sen. "Socio-Cultural Organizations of the People of India with Special Reference to Women." *FolkloreC* 10(1969):242–71,284–304,332–45,374–89,394–422,464–85.

10873. Gupta, Sankar Sen,ed. "Some Mohammadan Customs." *FolkloreC* 10(1969):309–12.

10874. "Japanese Comic Story-Telling." *AsSt* 14 Nov:6.

10875. Kiefer, Thomas. "Institutionalized Friendship and Warfare Among the Tausug of Jolo." *Ethnology* 7(1968):225–44.

10876. Kobak, Cantius J.,O.F.M. "Alzina's *Historia de las Islas é Indios de Bisayas . . . 1668*:A Translation of the Lenox Text (Continued)." *LSS* 4:17–28. [On Chap. Four, "About the Custom of Tattooing . . . ."]

10877. Koentjaraningrat. "Javanese Data on the Unresolved Problems of the Kindred." *Ethnology* 7(1968):53–58.

10878. Kurata, Satoru. *Shokubutsu to minzoku [Plants and Folkways]*. Tokyo: Chikyû Shuppan, 1969. [Provincial Jap. botanical names and their use in Jap. folk customs.]

10879. Lanham, Betty B. "Early Socialization:Stability and Change." *RUS* 56,iv:219–30. [Child rearing in Japan.]

10880. Lemelin, P. Bernard. "Notes de recherche sur la famille et le mariage à Sémeri." *Anthropologica* 10(1968):61–80.

10881. Macdonald, Alexander W. "La hiérarchie des *jat* inférieurs dans les Muluki Ain de 1955." [F 89],I:139–52.

10882. Maithani, B.R. "Lotus in Ancient Indian Culture." *IAC* 18,iii(1969):3–10.

10883. Majmudar, M.R. "Women in Gujarati Folklore." *FolkloreC* 9(1968):267–84.

10884. Nandi, Ajoy Kumar. "Evolution of the Hindu Marriage System." *FolkloreC* 10(1969):178–86.

10885. Ranasinghe, Alex. "The Betrothal and Marriage Customs of the Hebrews During the Time of Christ." *Folklore* 81:48–62.

10886. Sankar, R.M. "Women in Tribal India Through Custom and Tradition." *FolkloreC* 9(1968):458–67.

10887. Scheans, Daniel J., and Karl Hutterer,S.V.D. "Some Oracion Tattoos from Samar." *LSS* 4:29–45. [Illus.]

10888. Shamsuddin. "Status of Women in Ancient India." *IAC* 18,i(1969):58–60.

10889. Wagatsuma, Hiroshi. "Study of Personality and Behavior in Japanese Society and Culture." *RUS* 56,iv:53–63. *See also* 10225, 10749.

Australia and Oceania. 10890. Coppet, Daniel de. "Cycles de meurtres et cycles funéraires:Esquisse de deux structures d'échange." [F 89],II:759–81.

10891. Hiatt, Betty. "Cremation in Aboriginal Australia." *Mankind* 7(1969):104–19.

10892. Jackes, Mary. "Wikmonkan Joking Relationships." *Mankind* 7(1969):128–31.

10893. Maddock, Kenneth. "Necrophagy and the Circulation of Mothers:A Problem in Mara Ritual and Social Structure." *Mankind* 7(1969):94–103.

10894. Scheffler, H.W. "Ambrym Revisited:A Preliminary Report." *SJA* 26:52–66. [Kinship and marriage.]
See also 10759, 10856, 10955.

Europe. 10895. Asplund, Anneli. "Kannakselainen kontinkanto." *KSVK* 49(1969):187–95. [On an old Karelian wooing custom.]

10896. Brekilien, Yann. *La vie quotidienne des paysans en Bretagne au XIXᵉ siècle.* Paris: Hachette, 1967.

10897. Bühler, Theodor. "Die Mandate der Basler Fürstbischöfe als Volkskundliche Quelle." *SAV* 64(1968):135–62.

10898. —— "Wüstung und Fehde." *SAV* 66:1–27.

10899. Cammann, Alfred. "Georg Sänger aus Leichtling an der Wolga als Träger der volkstümlichen Überlieferung seines Dorfes." *JOV* 12(1969):179–214.

10900. Dömötör, Tekla. "Das 'Blochziehen' in Rábatótfalu 1968—Eine ungarische Variante eines interethnische verbreiteten Faschingsbrauches." [F 79]:385–92.

10901. Égető, Melinda. "Gergelyjárási ének és János napi köszönő a XVIII. századból." *Ethnographia* 80(1969):568–72. [Gregory-Song and Johann-Greeting from the 18th cent.]

10902. Handle, Johnny. "What's So Special About Northumberland?" *EDS* 32:7–10.

10903. Heike, Otto. "Deutsche Handwerkszünfte und Innungen in Polen." *JOV* 11(1968):129–39.

10904. Holzapfel, Otto. " 'Volkskundliche Tendenzen' in der bündischen Jugend:Ein Beitrag zur Vereinsforschung." *RJV* 19(1969):211–21.

10905. Honigmann, John J. "Rationality and Fantasy in Styrian Villagers." *Anthropologica* 12:129–39.

10906. Jolas, Tina, and François Zonabend. "Cousinage, voisinage." [F 89],I:169–80.

10907. Kuret, Niko. "Drei slowenische Erntebräuche." [F 79]:361–66.

10908. Lang, Francis. "L'Adieu au Camp Tsigane (en Pologne)." *ETs* 15,iv(1969):5–14.

10909. Lehmann, Siegfried. "Einfluss der Sinne auf Brauch und Kult." *HBV* 60(1969):147–57.

10910. Morin, Edgar. *The Red and the White:Report from a French Village.* Tr. A.M. Sheridan-Smith. New York: Pantheon.

10911. Pinon, Roger. "Qu'est-ce qu'un charivari? Essai en vue d'une définition opératoire." [F 79]:393–405.

10912. Schier, Bruno. "Abendländische Gemeinsamkeiten in der deutschen und tschechischen Volkskultur." *JOV* 12(1969): 7–26.

10913. Schmidt, Leopold. "Erinnerte Jahresfeuer. 'Erlesenes' aus deutschen Lebenszeugnissen." [F 79]:407–24.

10914. Schwedt, Herbert. "Heimatvertriebene in württembergischen Landgemeinden." *JOV* 12(1969):27–40.

10915. Skalníková, Olga. "Die Nachbarschaft in Prager Mietshäusern am Ende des vorigen und am Anfang dieses Jahrhunderts." [F 79]:345–52.

10916. Szabó, T. Attila. "Sebből pirosan buzog a vér..." *NIK* 14:133–39. [Sum. in Rom.]

10917. Tcherenkov, L.N. "Brève esquisse sur les Tsiganes en U.R.S.S." *ETs* 15,iii(1969):11–25.

10918. Tolksdorf, Ulrich. "Das Schlachten in Ost- und Westpreussen." *JOV* 11(1968):86–112.

10919. Trümpy, Hans. "Fuhren die Leute von Saanen schon im 18. Jahrhundert Ski? Untersuchung zu C.V. von Bonstettens Schrift über das Saanenland." *SAV* 64(1968):29–54.

10920. Voropaj, Oleksa. *Zvyčaji našoho narodu:Etnohrafičnyj narys.* Vol. II. London: Ukrajins'ke vydavnyctvo, 1966. [Vol. I pub. 1958.]

10921. Wailly, Jacques de, and Maurice Crampon. *Le folklore de Picardie (Somme, Oise, Aisne).* Amiens: Musée de Picardie, 1968.

10922. Weber-Kellermann, I[ngeborg]. "Landarbeiterbräuche im Deutschland des 19. Jahrhunderts." [F 91]:277–83. [Sum. in Rus.]

10923. —— "Über den Brauch des Schenkens:Ein Beitrag zur Geschichte der Kinderbescherung." [F 81]:1–8.

10924. Werner, Waltraut. "Altschwäbisches aus dem ungarndeutschen Dorf Hajós." *JOV* 12(1969):249–70. [Illus., music.]

10925. Woropay, O. "Customs of Our People." *UkrR* 16,iv(1969):41–48; 17,i:43–48.
See also 9523, 9771, 10308, 10450, 10452, 10777, 10828, 10930, 11052.

North America. 10926. Abrahams, Roger D. *Positively Black.* Englewood Cliffs, N.J.: Prentice-Hall.

10927. Beals, Ralph L. "Gifting, Reciprocity, Savings, and Credit in Peasant Oaxaca." *SJA* 26:231–41.

10928. Blauner, Robert. "Black Culture:Myth or Reality?" [F 95]:347–64.

10929. Dumond, D.E. "Competition, Cooperation, and the Folk Society." *SJA* 26:261–86.

* 10930. Duncan, Gwyneth. "Irish Customs and Beliefs in North Carolina." *NCarF* 18:148–53.

10931. Evans, James L. "The Socio-Cultural Life of the Lower Rio Grande Valley to 1859 (Abstract)." [F 78]:167–71.

10932. Folan, William J., and Phil. C. Weigand. "Fictive Widowhood in Rural and Urban Mexico." *Anthropologica* 10(1968):119–27.

10933. Hostetler, John A., and Gertrude E. Huntington. "Communal Socialization Patterns in Hutterite Society." *Ethnology* 7(1968):331–55.

10934. Koch, William E. "Kansas and the Lindsborg Swedes (Abstract)." [F 78]:172–76.

10935. Tally, Frances. "American Folk Customs of Courtship and Marriage:The Bedroom." [F 78]:138–58.

10936. Thurman, Robert S. " 'Twas Only a Joke." *TFSB* 35(1969):86–94.

10937. Williams, Clyde E. "Janneying in 'Coughlin Cave'." [F 80]:209–15.
See also 10359, 10398.

South America. 10938. Boglar, L. "Nota sobre la cultura de los Piaroa." *RVF* 2(1969):63–67.

10939. Domínguez, Luís Arturo. "Costumbres funerarias del Estado Falcón." *RVF* 3:17–25.

10940. Price, Richard. "Saramaka Emigration and Marriage: A Case Study of Social Change." *SJA* 26:157–89.

IX. MATERIAL CULTURE

General

General and Miscellaneous. 10941. Bernot, Lucien. "Les inventeurs d'épreuves." [F 89],II:926–32.

10942. Edwards, Robert. "The South Australian Ethnographic Collection." *Mankind* 7(1968):673–75.

10943. Fel, Edit, and Tamás Hofer. "Das Ordnungsgefüge bäuerlicher Gegenstände am Beispiel der Aussteuer in Kalotaszentkirály (Siebenbürgen)." [F 79]:367–84.

10944. Gunda, Béla. "Kulturverbindungen zwischen des Vorraum der Ostalpen und dem ungarischen Transdanubien." [F 79]:145–54.

10945. Höck, Alfred. "Wandernde Geschirrhändler und ihre Verbindungen zum Gaunertum." [F 79]:439–51.

10946. Jones, Frank P. "The Gwerin of Wales." [F 82]:1–13.

10947. Kring, Hilda A. "The Harmonists—A Folk-Cultural Approach." *DAI* 30(1969):2439A(Pa.).

10948. Roden, David. "Changing Settlement in the Chiltern Hills before 1850." *FoL* 8:57–71.

Architecture

Africa. 10949. Bourdieu, Pierre. "La Maison Kabyle ou le monde renversé." [F 89],II:739–58.

10950. Prussin, Labelle. "Sudanese Architecture and the Manding." *AfrA* 3,iv:13–19,64–67.

10951. Vallois, H.V. "L'habitation et les campements chez les pygmées (Négrilles) Bakà du Cameroun." [F 89],i:50–60.

Asia. 10952. Aščepkov, E.A. "Osobennosti razvitija arxitektury narodnogo žilišča Sibiri." [F 92]:38–43. [Sum. in Fr.]

10953. Pezeu-Massabuau, Jacques. "La Maison Japonaise et La Neige." *BMFJ* 8,i(1966):1–229.

10954. Zakhidov, P.Sh. "Uzbekistan Folk Architects Traditions." [F 92]:57–61. [Sum. in Rus.]

See also 10072, 10743.

Australia and Oceania. 10955. Ottino, Paul. "Les fare tupana ou 'maisons de famille' en Polynésie orientale." *Homme* 10:45–58.

10956. Parsonson, G.S. "The Problem of Melanesia." *Mankind* 7(1968):571–84.

Europe. 10957. Aalen, F.H.A. "The House Types of Gola Island, Co. Donegal." *FoL* 8:32–44.

10958. Barabás, Jenő. "A lakóház füsttelenítéséről." *Ethnographia* 81:276–87. [Über das Abrauchen des Wohnhauses im ungarischen Sprachgebiet; sums. in Rus. and Ger.]

10959. Baumgarten, Karl. "Das mittelalterliche Bauernhaus Mecklenburgs—Ein ethnographisch-historischer Forschungskomplex." [F 79]:353–60.

10960. Evans, E. Estyn. "Sod and Turf Houses in Ireland." [F 82]:79–90.

10961. Filep, Antal. "A kisalföldi lakóház helye népi építészetünk rendszerében. (Tüzelőberendezések, konyhák.)" *Ethnographia* 81:327–49. [Die Bauernhäuser in der kleinen ungarischen Tiefebene und ihre Einordnung im System der ungarischen Volksbaukunst; sums. in Rus. and Ger.]

10962. Füzes, Endre. "A gerendavázas gabonás." *Ethnographia* 81:376–87. [Kornbehälter mit Balkengerüst; sums. in Rus. and Ger.]

10963. Herrmann, Hans August. "Scheunen in Schleswig-Holstein." [F 81]:479–89.

10964. Lucas, A.T. "Contributions to the History of the Irish House: A Possible Ancestry of the Bed-Outshot (*Cúilteach*)." *FoL* 8:81–98.

10965. Makoveckij, I.V. "Arxitektura russkogo narodnogo žilišča." [F 92]:179–83. [Sum. in Fr.]

10966. Maksimović, B. "Funkcional'nye osnovy estetičeskix cennostej narodnogo zodčestva v Jugoslavii." [F 92]:44–47. [Sum. in Fr.]

10967. Ó Danachair, Caoimhín. "Representations of Houses on Some Irish Maps of c.1600." [F 82]:91–103.

10968. Pavlović, D. "L'art des vieilles églises de Serbie construites en bois." [F 92]:51–56. [Sum. in Rus.]

10969. Pešić-Maksimović, N. "Sur la protection des monuments de l'architecture traditionelle et d'agglomération rurales en Yougoslavie." [F 92]:48–50. [Sum. in Rus.]

10970. Samojlovič, V.P. "Narodnoe tvorčestvo v arxitekture ukrainskogo žilišča." [F 92]:33–37. [Sum. in Fr.]

10971. Šarf, Fanči. "Domovi v Drašičih; s posebnim pogledom na stanovanjsko raven." *SE* 20(1967):6–34.

10972. Smith, J.T. "The Concept of Diffusion in Its Application to Vernacular Building." [F 82]:59–78.

10973. Stahl, Henri H. and Paul H. *Civilizaţia vechilor sate româneşti.* Bucharest: Editura Ştiinţifică, 1968. [Old Romanian villages.]

10974. Tagányi, Zoltán. "A homlokzati árkád. A paraszti kultúra értelmezési lehetőségei." *Ethnographia* 81:398–420. [Die Vorlaube; Deutungsmöglichkeiten von Tatsachen der bäuerlichen Kultur; sums. in Rus. and Ger.]

10975. Walton, James. "Megalithic Building Survivals." [F 82]:105–22.

See also 10921, 10924, 11058.

North America. 10976. Glassie, Henry H. "The Impact of the Georgian Form on American Folk Housing (Abstract)." [F 78]:23–25.

10977. Roberts, Warren E. "The Waggoner Log House Near Paragon, Indiana (Abstract)." [F 78]:28–30.

10978. Sultz, Philip W. "Architectural Values of Early Frontier Log Structures." [F 78]:31–40.

10979. Trindell, Roger T. "Building in Brick in Colonial North America: The Patterned Brick Housing of West New Jersey (Abstract)." [F 78]:26.

10980. Wacker, Peter O. "Dutch Barns and Barracks in New Jersey (Abstract)." [F 78]:27.

10981. Welsch, Roger L. *Sod Walls: The Story of the Nebraska Sod House.* Broken Bow, Neb.: Purcells, 1968.

Folk Arts

General and Miscellaneous. 10982. Cicišvili, D.N. "Narodnye tradicii v sovremennoj gruzinskoj xudožestvennoj keramike." [F 92]:204–09. [Sum. in Fr.]

10983. Koev, I. "Sostojanie izučenija problemy narodnogo iskusstva v Bolgarii." [F 92]:7–12. [Sum. in Fr.]

10984. Sachs, Ignacy. "L'art 'primitif': Le point de vue de l'économiste." [F 89],II:919–25.

10985. Schuster, C. "Pendants in the Forms of Inverted Human Figures from Paleolithic to Modern Times." [F 92]:105–17. [Sum. in Rus.]

10986. "Simpozium: Metodika sobiratel'noj raboty po narodnomu iskusstvu i posledujuščej obrabotki materialov." [F 92]:351–80. [Symposium: Methodology of collecting folk art materials and subsequent arrangement of these.]

10987. Voigt, Vilmos. "Vom Neofolklorismus in der Kunst." *AEASH* 19:401–23.

See also 10092, 11002, 11122.

Africa. 10988. Anon. "African Art in the Collection of Jacques Lipchitz." *AfrA* 3,iv:48–51. [Illus.]

10989. Armstrong, Robert P. *Forms and Processes of African Sculpture.* (OPARI 1.) Foreword Bernth Lindfors. Austin: African and Afro-Amer. Research Inst., U. of Texas. [Illus.]

10990. Atherton, John H., and Milan Kalous. "Nomoli." *Jour. Afr. Hist.* 11:303–17. [Stone sculptures of so. Sierra Leone.]

10991. Barbour, J.M. "Adire." *AfrN* 5,iii:7–8. [Yoruba cloth patterns.]

10992. Campbell, Alec C. "Notes on Some Rock Paintings at Savuti." *BN&R* 2:15–23. [Illus.]

10993. Celis, Georges. "The Decorative Arts in Rwanda and Burundi." *AfrA* 4,i:41–42.

10994. Cooke, C.K. "Rock Paintings—Botswana and Elsewhere." *BN&R* 2:24–28.

10995. Crowley, Daniel J. "The Contemporary-Traditional Art Market in Africa." *AfrA* 4,i:43–49,80.

10996. Daler, Judith von. "A New Gallery in Kampala." *AfrA* 4,i:50–52. [Illus.]

10997. Eyo, Ekpo. "*1969 Excavations at Ile-Ife.*" *AfrA* 3,ii:44–47,87. [Illus.]

10998. Fagg, William. "Art." [F 71]:55–66.

10999. Imperato, Pascal J., and Marli Shamir. "Bokolanfini: Mud Cloth of the Bamana of Mali." *AfrA* 3,iv:32–41,80.

11000. Jeanneret, Alain. "Exhibition at Basel." *AfrA* 4,i:64–65. [Illus.]

11001. Laye, Camara. "The Black Man and Art." *AfrA* 4,i:58–59.

11002. Leroi-Gourhan, André. "Observations technologiques sur le rhythme statuaire." [F 89],I:658–76.

11003. Odugbesan, Clara. "Femininity in Yoruba Religious Art." [F 76]:199–211.

11004. Paden, John N., and Edward W. Soja. "Visual Arts." [F 88],II:52–55.

11005. Rubin, Barbara. "Calabash Decoration in North East State, Nigeria." *AfrA* 4,i:20–25. [Illus.]

11006. Štrukelj, Pavla. "Afriška zbirka vzhodnosudanskih plemen Bari in Čir v Slovenskem etnografskem muzeju." *SE* 20(1967):143–71.

11007. Teel, William. *An Outline of African Art.* (Supp. to Univ. Prints, Ser. N, Sect. 1.) Cambridge, Mass.: Univ. Prints. [See art. by Wingert, below.]

11008. Thompson, Robert F. "The Sign of the Divine King: An Essay on Yoruba Bead-Embroidered Crowns with Veil and Bird Decorations." *AfrA* 3,iii:8–17,74–80.

11009. Wardwell, Allen. "New Acquisitions of African Art at the Art Institute of Chicago." *AfrA* 4,i:14–19. [Illus.]

11010. —— "The Herbert Baker Collection." *AfrA* 3,iii:30–35.

African art.]

11011. Willett, Frank. "Visual Art in Africa." [F 88],I:108–27.

11012. Wingert, Paul S.,ed. *African Art.* (Univ. Prints, Ser. N, Sect. 1.) Cambridge, Mass.: Univ. Prints. [Catalog of prints. See art. by Teel, above.]

11013. Zwernemann, Jurgen. "A Short Survey on African Art in the Linden-Museum, Stuttgart." *AfrA* 3,ii:14–23,90. [Illus.] *See also* 11075.

Asia. 11014. Hisamatsu, Shin'ichi. "The Nature of *Sadō* Culture." *EB* 3,ii:9–19.

11015. Jaquillard, Pierre. "Eventails chinois de la collection de F. Vannotti." *ASEA* 24:1–9.

11016. Khoroshikh, P.P. [Xorošix, P.P.]. "Yakut Art of Ivory Carving." [F 92]:201–03. [Sum. in Rus.]

11017. Maury, Curt. *Folk Origins of Indian Art.* New York: Columbia U.P. [Illus.]

11018. Morozova, A.S. "Local Features in the Popular Decorative Art of Uzbekistan." [F 92]:187–92. [Sum. in Rus.]

11019. Rakhimov, M.K. "Folk Traditions in Uzbekistan's Ceramic Art Today." [F 92]:144–48. [Sum. in Rus.]

11020. Savitsky, I.V. [Savickij, I.V.]. "Kara-Kalpak Folk Applied Art." [F 92]:92–97. [Sum. in Rus.]

11021. Sharma, R.K. "Gandhara:Hellenistic School of Ancient Indian Art." *IAC* 18,iii(1969):42–44. [Sculpture.]

Australia and Oceania. 11022. Abrahamson, J.A. "Style in New Guinea Highlands Shields." *Mankind* 7(1969):59–66.

11023. Forge, Anthony. "Learning to See in New Guinea." [F 86]:269–91.

11024. Lauer, Peter K. "Amphlett Islands' Pottery Trade and the Kula." *Mankind* 7(1969):165–76.

11025. Sim, I.M. "Records of the Rock Engravings of the Sydney District, Nos. 168–174:Gosford District, Part 2." *Mankind* 7(1969):52–58.

11026. Woolston, F.P., and P.J. Trezise. "Petroglyphs of Cape York Penninsula." *Mankind* 7(1969):120–27.

Europe. 11027. Amiranašvili, Š.Ja. "Xudožestvennye tradicii gruzinskogo narodnogo iskusstva." [F 92]:210–14. [Sum. in Fr.]

11028. Arbat, Ju.A. "Novoe i maloizvestnoe v izučenii russkogo iskusstva." [F 92]:175–78. [Sum. in Rus.]

11029. Armand-Calliat, Louis. "Homage à L. Armand-Calliat:I. Croix anciennes en Chalonnais." *ATP* 16(1968):96–121. [Illus.]

11030. —— "Hommage à L. Armand-Calliat:II. L'art populaire en Chalonnais." *ATP* 16(1968):122–34.

11031. Bachmann, Manfred. "Das 'Schokoladenmädchen' von J.E. Liotard als Motiv der Volkskunst." [F 79]:317–19.

11032. Baltrušaitis, Jurgis. "Eléments de l'art populaire lituanien," 1–42 in *Studies in Honor of Giacomo Devoto on the Occasion of His Seventieth Birthday.* Studi Baltici 10. Firenze: Olschki, 1969.

11033. Binjaševs'kyj, Erast. *Ukrajins'ki pysanky.* Kyjiv: Mystectvo, 1968. [On Ukr. decorated Easter eggs.]

11034. Bogouslavskaya, I.J. [Boguslavskaja, I.Ja.]. "Sur la transformation des motifs de l'ornement liés à l'ancienne mythologie dans la broderie nationale russe." [F 92]:74–83. [Sum. in Rus.]

11035. Brednich, Rolf Wilhelm. "Ein Beitrag zur volkskundlichen Interpretation ikonographischer Quellen:Der Saugbeutel." [F 79]:299–316.

11036. Butnik-Siversky, B.S. "Tradition and Innovation in Soviet Ukrainian Folk Art." [F 92]:22–26. [Sum. in Rus.]

11037. Choux, Jacques (Abbé). "La vièrge de miséricorde dans l'art populaire lorrain." *ATP* 16(1968):47–62. [Illus.]

11038. Davtian, S.S. "L'expansion de l'art de la dentelle arménienne." [F 92]:68–73. [Sum. in Rus.]

11039. Drahan, Myxajlo. *Ukrajins'ka dekoratyvna riz'ba XVI-XVII st.* Kyjiv: Naukova dumka.

11040. Faragó, József. "A Contribution to the Table Motif of the Bird Concealed in the Vessel." *AEASH* 19:147–59.

11041. Frenkel, H.G. "Découpages en papier juifs." [F 92]:84–91. [Sum. in Rus.]

11042. Höck, Alfred. "Beiträge zur hessischen Töpferei v:Zunftbrief aus 1583 für die Töpfer in der Grafschaft Ziegenhain." *HBV* 60(1969):159–66.

11043. Ivanova, G.A. "Development of Applied Art in Soviet Latvia." [F 92]:128–31. [Sum. in Rus.]

11044. Jeřábek, Richard. "Der Ursprung einer volkstümlichen Darstellung der Hl. Dreifaltigkeit:Von einem siebenbürgischen Hinterglasbild bis zu P.P. Rubens." [F 79]:279–88.

11045. Karasek-Langer, Alfred, and Josef Lanz. "Die Volkskunst der 'Mannlmalerei' im Jeschken- und Isergebirge." *JOV* 11(1968):9–61. [Illus.]

11046. Keim, J.A. "Les fixés sur verre populaires:A propos d'une exposition au Musée Cantini de Marseille." *ATP* 16(1968): 315–19.

11047. Kresz, M. "Historical Background and Character of Hungarian Popular Pottery." [F 92]:166–68.

11048. Lanhas, Fernando. "As gravuras rupestres de Montedor." *RdEt* 13(1969):367–86.

11049. Ludvik, Dušan. "Odkod fače, faček?" *SE* 18–19(1965-66):129–31.

11050. Malančuk, V.A. "Nekotorye osobennosti krest'janskoj odeždy, vyšivki i xudožestvennogo tkačestva Sokal'ščiny." [F 92]:184–86. [Sum. in Fr.]

11051. Mironescu, Al.N. "Figurines paysannes en terre cuite." [F 92]:215–18. [Sum. in Rus.]

11052. Mulkiewicz-Goldberg, Olga. "The Image of the Jew in Polish Folk Culture." [F 87]:149–52. [In Hebr.; Eng. sum.]

11053. Nicolesco, C. "La tradition romaine et byzantine de la poterie populaire Roumaine." [F 92]:132–43. [Sum. in Rus.]

11054. Orel, J. "Die volkstümliche kunstgewerbliche Erzeugung in der Tschechoslowakischen Sozialistischen Republik." [F 92]:169–74.

11055. Pardinas, F. "Presencia o imagen:Arte popular (folk) y arte urbano en algunos poblados de México." [F 92]:19–21. [Sum. in Rus.]

11056. Plicková, Ester. "Das Montanwesen von Banská Stiavnica als Quelle und Gegenstand volkskünstlerischen Schaffens." [F 79]:509–19.

11057. Razina, T.M., and E.T. Jakovleva. "Tradicii i nacional'noe svoeobrazie v iskusstve sovremennyx xudožestvennyx promyslov RSFSR." [F 92]:123–27. [Sum. in Fr.]

11058. Roure, Nicole. "Les tuiles décorées à dessins géométriques des Pyrénées Orientales." *ATP* 17(1969):119–29.

11059. Schwedt, Herbert. "Zur Geschichte des Problems 'Volkskunst'." *ZV* 65(1969):169–82.

11060. Spas'kyj, I.H. *Dukaty i dukači Ukrajiny:Istorykonumizmatyčne doslidžennja.* Kyjiv: Naukova dumka. [On folk adornments; sum. in Eng.]

11061. Taranovskaya, N.V. "Types of Northern Folk Painting on Household Ware." [F 92]:193–200. [Sum. in Rus.]

11062. Tomić, P. "Narodnaja keramika v Jugoslavii." [F 92]:149–65.

11063. Vorob'ev, N.I., and F.X. Valeev. "Narodnoe prikladnoe iskusstvo tatar Povolž'ja." [F 92]:62–67. [Sum. in Fr.]

11064. Weinhold, Rudolf. "Buttenträgerfiguren—Gebrauchsund Ziergeräte aus der Weinbauüberlieferung." [F 79]:321–27.

11065. Wildhaber, Robert. "Zur Begriffsbestimmung der Volkskunst." [F 81]:473–78.

11066. Žoltovskij, P.N. "Drevnie motivy v gucul'skoj ornamentike." [F 92]:13–18. [Sum. in Fr.]

See also 9748, 10043, 10064, 10576, 10764, 10776, 10982, 10983.

North America. 11067. Brunvand, Jan H., and John C. Abramson. "Aspen Tree Doodlings in the Wasatch Mountains:A Preliminary Survey of Traditional Tree Carvings." [F 78]:89–102.

11068. Ferris, William R.,Jr. " 'If You Ain't Got It in Your Head, You Can't Do It in Your Hand':James Thomas, Mississippi Delta Folk Sculptor." *SLitI* 3,i:89–107. [Illus.]

11069. Fife, Austin E. "Folklife and Folk Arts in the United States Exhibit:Merrill Art Gallery and Special Collections Library Utah State University, July-August, 1968." [F 78]:9–22.

11070. Haseltine, Maury. "A Progress Report on the Pictorial Documentation of Early Utah Gravestones (Abstract)." [F 78]:79–88.

11071. Rinzler, Ralph. "Cheever Meaders:North Georgia Potter (1887–1967) (Abstract)." [F 78]:76–78. *See also* 10405.

South America. *See* 9824.

Craft and Technology

General and Miscellaneous. 11072. Csilléry, Klára K. " 'Ősi hagyaték'—'felülről érkezett szálladék'? (A szék történetének kezdetei.)" *Ethnographia* 81:453–66. ['Primitives Gemeinschaftsgut' oder 'Gesunkenes Kulturgut'? Anfänge der Geschichte des Stuhls; sums. in Rus. and Ger.]

11073. Scheufler, Vladimir. "Classification System of Pottery-Making Tools." [F 85]:27–40.

Africa. 11074. Adnan, Etel. "The Weavings of the Children of Harrania." *AfrA* 3,iii:41–42.

11075. Dieterlen, Germaine. "La serrure et sa clef (Dogon, Mali)." [F 89],ɪ:7–28.

11076. Evans-Pritchard, E.E. "Zande Conversation Pieces." [F 89],ɪ:29–49.

11077. McNaughton, Pat R. "The Throwing Knife in African History." *AfrA* 3,ii:54–60,89.

11078. Micaud, Ellen. "The Craft Tradition in North Africa." *AfrA* 3,ii:38–43,90–91.

See also 10606, 10951.

Asia. 11079. Margoulan, A.Kh. "The Kazakh Yourta and Its Furniture." [F 92]:98–104. [Sum. in Rus.]

Australia and Oceania. 11080. Kay, C.A. "Pottery Manufacture in the Wanigela Area of Collingwood Bay, Papua." *Mankind* 7(1968):653–57.

11081. Kelly, James D. "Hut Sites, Rock Engravings, Stone Arrangements and Tjurunga. Mulligan River, Queensland." *Mankind* 7(1968):563–66.

11082. Peterson, Nicolas. "The Pestle and Mortar:An Ethnographic Analogy for Archaeology in Arnheim Land." *Mankind* 7(1968):567–70.

11083. Rowlands, R.J. and J.M. "An Aboriginal Dam in Northwestern New South Wales." *Mankind* 7(1968):132–36.

11084. White, Peter J. "Fabrication, Outils écaillés on Scalar Cores?" *Mankind* 7(1968):658–66.

Europe. 11085. Bachmann, M. "Die Wiederspiegelung des modernen Bergbaus in der traditionellen Volksschnitzerei des Sächsischen Erzgebirges." [F 92]:118–22. [Sum. in Rus.]

11086. Casanova, Antoine. "L'aire de diffusion en corse au xɪxᵉ siècle du type le plus ancien de pressoir (le pressoir à torsion)." *ATP* 16(1968):237–57. [Illus.]

11087. Čerevan', H.P. *Opišnjans'ka keramika.* Kharkiv: Prapor. [Sum. in Eng.]

11088. Debrie, René. "Lexique picard du chaisier." *ATP* 16(1968):293–312. [Illus.]

11089. Diver, Anthea V. "The 'Welland' Type of Thistle Tongs." *FoL* 8:99–100.

11090. Erixon, Sigurd. "Investigation of an Industry and Its Products:An Ethnological Programme." [F 82]:293–301.

11091. Fenton, Alexander. "Sheep in North Ronaldsay, Orkney." [F 82]:205–33.

11092. Gáborján, Alice. "Adatok a szűr kialakulásához." *Ethnographia* 81:467–90. [Daten zur Ausgestaltung einer Art des Bauernmantels (ung. Szűr); sums. in Rus. and Ger.]

11093. Galtier, Charles. "De la récolte au cassage des amandes en Alpilles et Crau." *ATP* 17(1969):55–93. [Illus.]

11094. Goñi, Karmele de. "Cestería en el país vasco." *RdEt* 13(1969):303–37.

11095. Helm, Alex. "Rushcarts of the Northwest of England." *FoL* 8:20–31.

11096. Hoffmann, Marta. "The 'Great Wheel' in the Scandinavian Countries." [F 82]:281–92.

11097. Jenkins, David. "The Community and the Land in South Cardiganshire at the Close of the Nineteenth Century." *FoL* 8:5–12.

11098. Kundegraber, Maria. "Vom Heutragen und Heuziehen in Gotteschee." *JOV* 11(1968):62–85. [Illus.]

11099. Lucas, A.T. "Sea Sand and Shells as Manure." [F 82]:183–203.

11100. Makarovič, Gorazd. "Križevato kolo na Slovenskem." *SE* 18–19(1965-66):21–34.

11101. O'Neill, Timothy P. "Some Irish Techniques of Collecting Seaweed." *FoL* 8:13–19.

11102. Owen, Trefor M. "Historical Aspects of Peat-Cutting in Wales." [F 82]:123–55.

11103. Parain, Charles. "Voies et formes de la différenciation dans les vignobles du Nord-Est de la France:Champagne et Lorraine." *ATP* 16(1968):201–35. [Illus.]

11104. Payne, Ffransis G. "The Welsh Plough Team to 1600." [F 82]:235–52.

11105. Percier, Albert. "Chaluts atlantiques et méditerranéens—conception et évolution." *RdEt* 14:119–28.

11106. Petrenko, M.Z. *Ukrajins'ke zolotarstvo XVI-XVIII st.* Kyjiv: Naukova dumka. [Illus.]

11107. Porter, Enid. "Fenland Peat." [F 82]:157–82.

11108. Raulin, Henri. "Note sur les Martinets." *ATP* 17(1969):95–105. [Illus.]

11109. Rivière, Georges-Henri. "Une écobue des Monts d'Arrée." [F 89],ɪ:181–87.

11110. Sanderson, Stewart F. "The Tweed Salmon Coble." [F 82]:273–80.

11111. Schenk, Georg W. "Bergmannstracht, bergmännische Aufzüge und Bergparaden im Příbramer Erzbergbaurevier in Böhmen gegen Ende des 19. Jahrhunderts." [F 79]:487–507.

11112. Takács, Lajos. "A magyarországi rövid kaszák történetéhez." *Ethnographia* 81:187–220. [Sums. in Rus. and Ger.]

11113. Theuwissen, J. "De Analyse van de landbouwkruiwagen en zijn kaartbeeld." *Volkskunde* 69(1968):3–23. [Illus.]

11114. Wildhaber, Robert. "The 'Rope-Wood' and Its European Distribution." [F 82]:253–72.

See also 9471, 10454.

North America. 11115. Boatright, Mody C. "How Will Boatright Made Bits and Spurs." *JAF* 83:77–80.

11116. Cook, Scott. "Price and Output Variability in a Peasant-Artisan Stoneworking Industry in Oaxaca, Mexico:An Analytic Essay in Economic Anthropology." *AA* 72:776–801.

11117. Hume, Ivor N. *A Guide to Artifacts of Colonial America.* New York: Knopf.

See also 9531, 11069.

South America. 11118. Griffith, James S. "Opportunities for Folklife Study in Northwest Mexico (Abstract)." [F 78]:159–62.

11119. Nardi, Ricardo L.J., and Susana Chertudi. "Instrumentos arcaicos para majar y moler en San Juan (Argentina)." *RdEt* 13(1969):387–418; 14:137–88.

11120. Reyes, Abilio. "Secuencia fotográfica de la confección de una cesta en el estado sucre." *RVF* 1(1968):87–91. [Illus.]

11121. Saignes, Miguel Acosta. "Como se hace una alcancía." *RVF* 1(1968):51–64. [Illus.]

Costumes

General and Miscellaneous. 11122. Matejko, E.I., and S.I. Sidorovič. "Ukrainskie narodnye motivy v sovremennoj odežde." [F 92]:27–32. [Sum. in Fr.]

Africa. 11123. Hale, Sjarief. "Kente Cloth of Ghana." *AfrA* 3,iii:26–29.

11124. Vansina, J. "The Bells of Kings." *Jour. Afr. Hist.* 10(1969):187–97.

See also 11076.

Europe. 11125. Horváthová, Emilia. "Maskenbrauchtum in der Slowakei." *SAV* 64(1968):22–28.

11126. Makarovič, Marija. "Glavna gibala v razvoju slovenske kmečke noše v 19. in 20. stoletju." *SE* 20(1967):92–119.

11127. —— "Moške srajce slovenske kmečke noše." *SE* 18–19(1965-66):37–54.

See also 10447, 10454, 10896, 10924, 11050.

North America. 11128. Yoder, Don. "Sectarian Costume Research in the United States." [F 78]:41–75.

See also 10398, 10405.

South America. *See* 9824.

Food

General and Miscellaneous. 11129. Anderson, E.N.,Jr. "Réflexions sur la cuisine." *Homme* 10:122–23.

11130. Bringéus, Nils-Arvid. "Man, Food and Milieu." *FoL*

8:45–56.

Africa. 11131. Fukui, Katsuyoshi. "Alcoholic Drinks of the Iraqw:Brewing Methods and Social Functions." *Kyoto U. Afr. Studies* 5:125–48.

Asia. 11132. Sharma, Janaki Nath. "Beef-Eating in Mauryan Times:A Rejoinder." *IAC* 18,i(1969):65–68.

11133. Yalman, Nur. "On the Meaning of Food Offerings in Ceylon." [F 93]:81–96.

Australia and Oceania. 11134. Roosman, Raden S. "Breadfruit and Taro in Pacific Oral Literature." *JPS* 79:219–32. *See also* 10435.

Europe. 11135. Balassa, M. Iván. "Előfás méhtartás a Kárpát-medencében." *Ethnographia* 81:531–44. [Waltbienenzucht im Karpatenbecken; sums. in Rus. and Ger.]

11136. Égető, Melinda. "A szőlő ültetése a Solt-vidéken." *Ethnographia* 81:516–30. [Weinanbau in der Gegend von Solt; sums. in Rus. and Ger.]

11137. FitzGibbon, Theodora. *A Taste of Ireland:Irish Traditional Food.* Boston: Houghton Mifflin, 1969.

11138. Gama, Eurico. "In vino veritas." *RdEt* 13(1969): 257–302.

11139. Kisbán, Eszter. "Ujítások Észak-Dunántúl újkori népi táplálkozásában." *Ethnographia* 81:305–15. [Neuerungen in der neuzeitlichen Volksnahrung im Nördlichen Transdanubien; sums. in Rus. and Ger.]

11140. Kósa, László. " 'Buza szükségben felsegéllő jegyzések'. A burgonya a magyarországi táplálkozásban a xviii. század végén és a xix. század elején." *Ethnographia* 81:363–75. [Die Kartoffeln in der Ernährung in Ungarn am Ende des 18. und Angang des 19. Jh.; sums. in Rus. and Ger.]

11141. Kovács, K. László. "Adatok tejkonzerválásunk egyik régi módjahoz." *Ethnographia* 81:617–34. [Daten zu einem alten System der Milchkonservierung bei den Ungarn; sums. in Rus. and Ger.]

11142. Marçal, Horácio. "Doçaria monástica, regional e popular da área distrital do Porto." *RdEt* 14:83–117.

11143. Riemann, Erhard. "Gründonnerstagskringel in Ost- und Westpreussen." *JOV* 12(1969):323–36. *See also* 11093.

North America. 11144. Anderson, Berniеu A. "Uses of Native Plants in Early Mormon Country (Abstract)." [F 78]:132–37.

Author Index